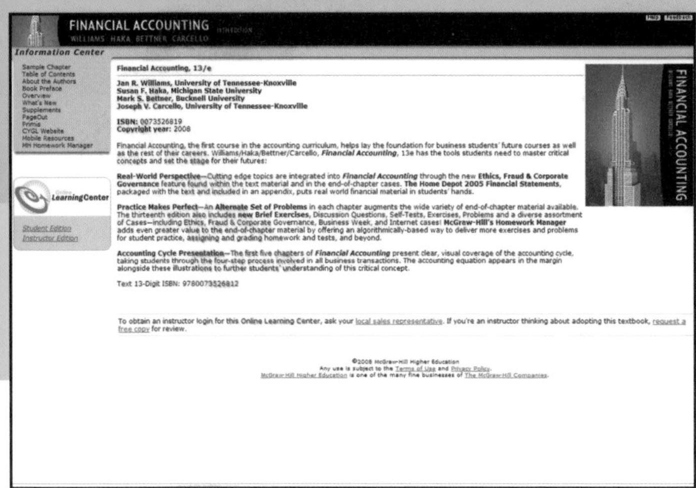
FINANCIAL ACCOUNTING
WILLIAMS HAKA BETTNER CARCELLO
Information Center
Sample Chapter
Table of Contents
About the Authors
Book Preface
Overview
What's New
Supplements
PageOut
Primis
CYGL Website
Mobile Resources
MH Homework Manager
LearningCenter
Student Edition
Instructor Edition
Financial Accounting, 13/e
Jan R. Williams, University of Tennessee-Knoxville
Susan F. Haka, Michigan State University
Mark S. Bettner, Bucknell University
Joseph V. Carcello, University of Tennessee-Knoxville
ISBN: 0073526819
Copyright year: 2008
Financial Accounting, the first course in the accounting curriculum, helps lay the foundation for business students' future courses as well as the rest of their careers. Williams/Haka/Bettner/Carcello, Financial Accounting, 13e has the tools students need to master critical concepts and set the stage for their futures:
Real-World Perspective—Cutting edge topics are integrated into Financial Accounting through the new Ethics, Fraud & Corporate Governance feature found within the text material and in the end-of-chapter cases. The Home Depot 2005 Financial Statements, packaged with the text and included in an appendix, puts real world financial material in students' hands.
Practice Makes Perfect—An Alternate Set of Problems in each chapter augments the wide variety of end-of-chapter material available. The thirteenth edition also includes new Brief Exercises, Discussion Questions, Self-Tests, Exercises, Problems and a diverse assortment of Cases—including Ethics, Fraud & Corporate Governance, Business Week, and Internet cases! McGraw-Hill's Homework Manager adds even greater value to the end-of-chapter material by offering an algorithmically-based way to deliver more exercises and problems for student practice, assigning and grading homework and tests, and beyond.
Accounting Cycle Presentation—The first five chapters of Financial Accounting present clear, visual coverage of the accounting cycle, taking students through the four-step process involved in all business transactions. The accounting equation appears in the margin alongside these illustrations to further students' understanding of this critical concept.
Text 13-Digit ISBN: 9780073526812
To obtain an instructor login for this Online Learning Center, ask your local sales representative. If you're an instructor thinking about adopting this textbook, request a free copy for review.
©2008 McGraw-Hill Higher Education
Any use is subject to the Terms of Use and Privacy Policy.
McGraw-Hill Higher Education is one of the many fine businesses of The McGraw-Hill Companies.
FINANCIAL ACCOUNTING

McGraw-Hill's HOMEWORK **MANAGER**
HELPS YOU EFFICIENTLY

McGraw-Hill's HOMEWORK MANAGER™

Problems and exercises from the book, as well as questions from the test bank, have been integrated into McGraw-Hill's Homework Manager to give you a variety of options as you deliver assignments and quizzes to students via the web. You can choose from static or algorithmic questions and have the graded results automatically stored in your grade book online.

Have you ever wished that you could assign a different set of problems to each of your students, individualizing their educational experience? The algorithmic question capabilities of McGraw-Hill's Homework Manager give you the opportunity to do so. The problem-making function inserts new numbers and data from an endless supply into the set question structure. Each student will have a different answer while learning the same principles from the text. This also enables the students to master concepts by revisiting the same questions with different data.

Assign coursework online.

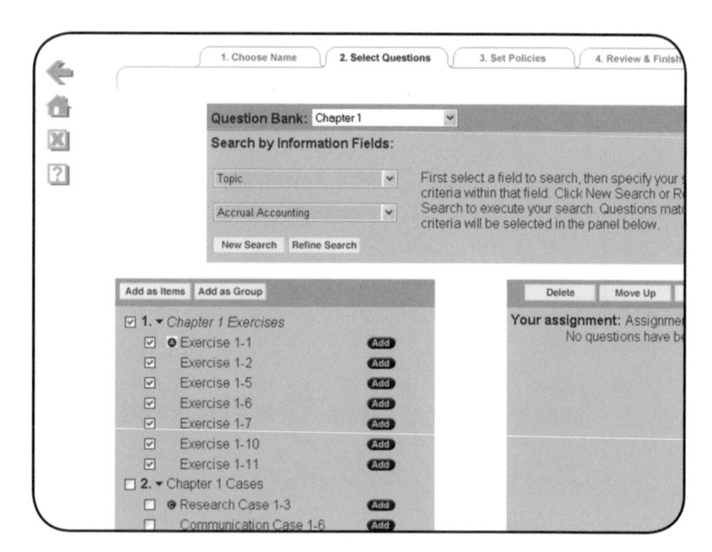

Problem 2-13: (Appendix 2A) Classification of Labor Costs [LO8]

Lynn Bjorland is employed by Southern Laboratories, Inc., and is directly involved in preparing the company's leading antib
half (i.e., $36 per hour) for any work in excess of 40 hours per week.

Required:

1. Suppose that in a given week Lynn works 45 hours. Compute Lynn's total wages for the week. How much of this co
2. Suppose in another week that Lynn works 50 hours but is idle for 4 hours during the week due to equipment break allocated to direct labor cost? To manufacturing overhead cost?
3. Southern Laboratories has an attractive package of fringe benefits that costs the company $8 for each hour of emp but is idle for 3 hours due to material shortages. Compute Lynn's total wages and fringe benefits for the week. If th Lynn's wages and fringe benefits for the week would be allocated to direct labor cost? To manufacturing overhead
4. Refer to the data in (3) above. If the company treats that part of fringe benefits relating to direct labor as added d to direct labor cost? To manufacturing overhead cost?

1. Total wages for the week:

Regular time: 40 hours × $24 per hour	$ 960
Overtime: 5 hours × $36 per hour	180
Total Wages	1140
Allocation of total wages:	
Direct labor: 45 hours × $24 per hour	$
Manufacturing overhead: 5 hours × $12 per hour	

MANAGE YOUR CLASS.

Control how content is presented.

McGraw-Hill's Homework Manager gives you a flexible and easy way to present course work to students. You determine which questions to ask and how much help students will receive as they work through assignments. You can determine the number of attempts a student can make with each problem or provide hints and feedback with each question. The questions can also be linked to an online version of the text for quick and simple reference while students complete an assignment.

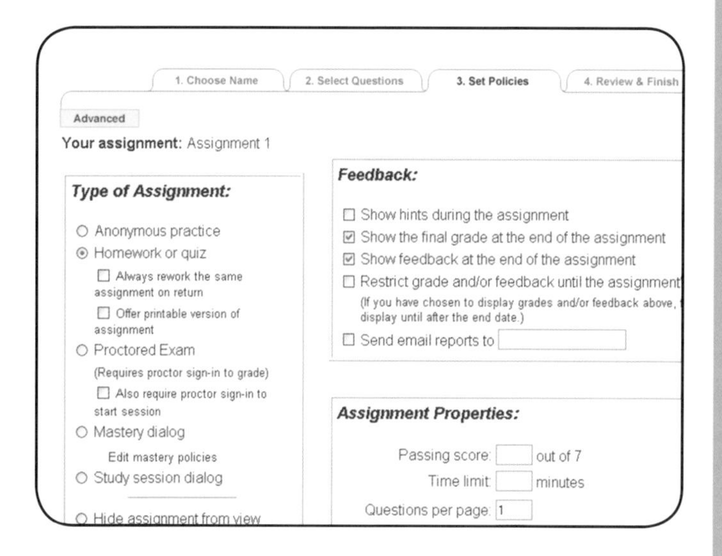

Track student progress.

Assignments are graded automatically, with the results stored in your private grade book. Detailed results let you see at a glance how each student does on an assignment or an individual problem. You can even see how many attempts it took them to solve it. You can monitor how the whole class does on each problem and even determine where individual students might need extra help.

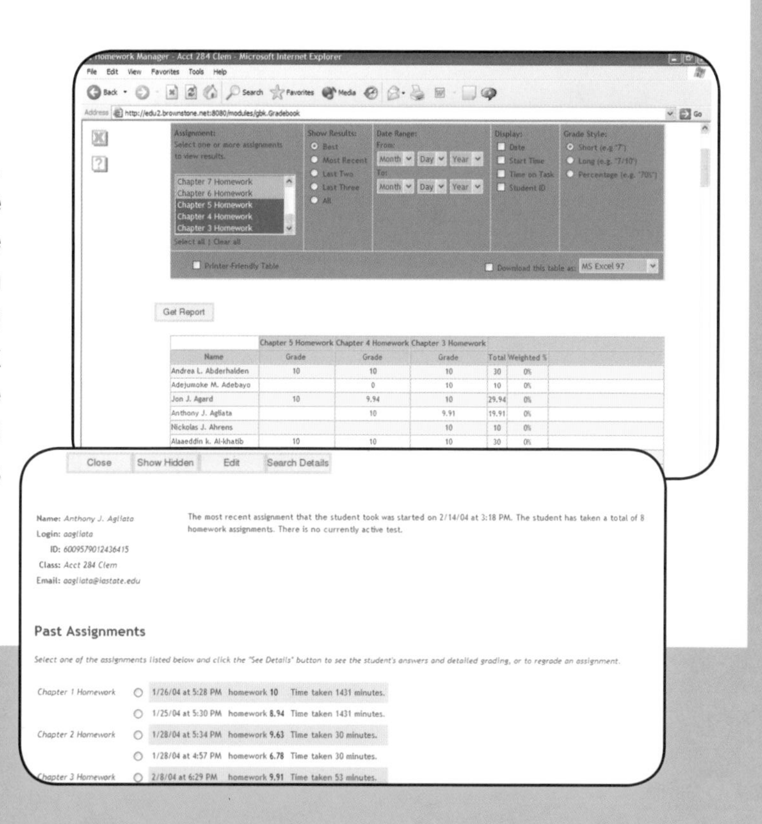

PROFESSORS CAN ALLOW McGraw-Hill's HOMEWORK **MANAGER** TO GIVE STUDENTS HELPFUL FEEDBACK

Auto-grading and feedback.

Question 1: *Score 6.5/8*

Your response	Correct response

Your response

Exercise 2-1: Using Cost Terms [LO2, LO5, LO7]

Following are a number of cost terms introduced in the chapter:

Period cost	Fixed cost
Variable cost	Prime cost
Opportunity cost	Conversion cost
Product cost	Sunk cost

Choose the cost term or terms above that most appropriately describe the costs identified in each of the following situations. A cost term can be used more than once.

1. Crestline Books, Inc., prints a small book titled *The Pocket Speller* . The paper going into the manufacture of the book would be called direct materials and classified as a `Product cost` (6%). In terms of cost behavior, the paper could also be described as a `Product cost` (0%) with respect to the number of books printed.
2. Instead of compiling the words in the book, the author hired by the company could have earned considerable fees consulting with business organizations. The consulting fees forgone by the author would be called `Opportunity cost` (6%).
3. The paper and other materials used in the manufacture of the book, combined with the direct labor cost involved, would be called `Prime cost` (6%).
4. The salary of Crestline Books' president would be classified as a `Product cost` (0%), and the salary will appear on the income statement as an expense in the time period in which it is incurred.
5. Depreciation on the equipment used to print the book would be classified by Crestline Books as a `Product cost` (6%). However, depreciation on any equipment used by the company in selling and administrative activities would be classified as a `Period cost` (6%). In terms of cost behavior, depreciation would probably be classified as a `Fixed cost` (6%) with respect to the number of books printed.
6. A `Product cost` (6%) is also known as an inventoriable cost,

Correct response

Exercise 2-1: Using Cost Terms [LO2, LO5, LO7]

Following are a number of cost terms introduced in the chapter:

Period cost	Fixed cost
Variable cost	Prime cost
Opportunity cost	Conversion cost
Product cost	Sunk cost

Choose the cost term or terms above that most appropriately describe the costs identified in each of the following situations. A cost term can be used more than once.

1. Crestline Books, Inc., prints a small book titled *The Pocket Speller* . The paper going into the manufacture of the book would be called direct materials and classified as a `Product cost`. In terms of cost behavior, the paper could also be described as a `variable cost` with respect to the number of books printed.
2. Instead of compiling the words in the book, the author hired by the company could have earned considerable fees consulting with business organizations. The consulting fees forgone by the author would be called `Opportunity cost`.
3. The paper and other materials used in the manufacture of the book, combined with the direct labor cost involved, would be called `Prime cost`.
4. The salary of Crestline Books' president would be classified as a `Period cost`, and the salary will appear on the income statement as an expense in the time period in which it is incurred.
5. Depreciation on the equipment used to print the book would be classified by Crestline Books as a `Product cost`. However, depreciation on any equipment used by the company in selling and administrative activities would be classified as a `Period cost`. In terms of cost behavior, depreciation would probably be classified as a `Fixed cost` with respect to the number of books printed.
6. A `Product cost` is also known as an inventoriable cost, since

Immediately after finishing an assignment, students can compare their answers side-by-side with the detailed solutions. Students can try again with new numbers to see if they have mastered the concept.

13th Edition

Financial Accounting

Jan R. Williams
University of Tennessee

Susan F. Haka
Michigan State University

Mark S. Bettner
Bucknell University

Joseph V. Carcello
University of Tennessee

Boston Burr Ridge, IL Dubuque, IA Madison, WI New York San Francisco St. Louis
Bangkok Bogotá Caracas Kuala Lumpur Lisbon London Madrid Mexico City
Milan Montreal New Delhi Santiago Seoul Singapore Sydney Taipei Toronto

FINANCIAL ACCOUNTING

Published by McGraw-Hill/Irwin, a business unit of The McGraw-Hill Companies, Inc., 1221 Avenue of the Americas, New York, NY, 10020.

This book is printed on acid-free paper.

1 2 3 4 5 6 7 8 9 0 WCK/WCK 0 9 8 7 6

ISBN: 978-0-07-352681-2
MHID: 0-07-352681-9

Editorial director: *Stewart Mattson*
Executive editor: *Tim Vertovec*
Developmental editor: *Daryl Horrocks*
Marketing manager: *Melissa Larmon*
Senior media producer: *Victor Chiu*
Lead project manager: *Lori Koetters*
Production supervisor: *Gina Hangos*
Senior designer: *Kami Carter*
Photo research coordinator: *Kathy Shive*
Photo researcher: *Mary Reeg*
Media project manager: *Matthew Perry*
Cover design: *George Kokkonas*
Interior design: *Kami Carter*
Cover image: © *Ed Howard, Howard Digital*/Background image: © *Getty*
Typeface: *10/12 Times Roman*
Compositor: *Techbooks*
Printer: *Quebecor World Versailles Inc.*

Library of Congress Cataloging-in-Publication Data

Financial accounting / Jan R. Williams...[et al.]. — 13/e.
p. cm.
Includes index.
ISBN-13: 978-0-07-352681-2 (alk. paper)
ISBN-10: 0-07-352681-9 (alk. paper)
1. Accounting. I. Williams, Jan R.
HF5636.F5315 2008
657—dc22

2006016862

www.mhhe.com

To Ben and Meg Wishart and Asher and Lainey Hunt, who have taught me the joys of being a grandfather.

—Jan R. Williams

For Cliff, Abi, and my mother, Fran.

—Susan F. Haka

To my parents, Fred and Marjorie.

—Mark S. Bettner

To Terri, Stephen, Karen, and Sarah, whose sacrifices enabled me to participate in writing this book. Thank you—I love you!

—Joseph V. Carcello

Jan R. Williams is Dean of the College of Business Administration and the Pilot Chair of Excellence in Leadership at the University of Tennessee, where he has been a faculty member since 1977. He received a BS degree from George Peabody College, an MBA from Baylor University, and a PhD from the University of Arkansas. He previously served on the faculties at the University of Georgia and Texas Tech University. A CPA in Tennessee and Arkansas, Dr. Williams is also the coauthor of three books and has published over 70 articles on issues of corporate financial reporting and accounting education. He served as president of the American Accounting Association in 1999–2000 and has been actively involved in Beta Alpha Psi, the Tennessee Society of CPAs, and the American Institute of CPAs. He currently serves on the Board of Directors of AACSB International—the Association to Advance Collegiate Schools of Business—the accrediting organization for business schools and accounting programs.

Susan F. Haka is the Ernst & Young Professor of Accounting in the Department of Accounting and Information Systems at Michigan State University. Dr. Haka received her PhD from the University of Kansas and a master's degree in accounting from the University of Illinois. She is an active member of the American Accounting Association and has served as vice president of finance, director of the Doctoral Consortium, and president of the Management Accounting Section. Dr. Haka is active in editorial processes and has been editor of *Behavioral Research in Accounting* and an associate editor of *Journal of Management Accounting Research, Accounting Horizons, The International Journal of Accounting,* and *Contemporary Accounting Research*. Dr. Haka has been honored by Michigan State University with several teaching and research awards, including both universitywide Teacher-Scholar and Distinguished Faculty awards.

Meet the **Authors**

Mark S. Bettner is the Christian R. Lindback Chair of Business Administration at Bucknell University. Dr. Bettner received his PhD in business administration from Texas Tech University and his MS in accounting from Virginia Tech University. He has received numerous teaching and research awards. In addition to his work on *Financial Accounting* and *Financial & Managerial Accounting*, he has written many ancillary materials, published in scholarly journals, and presented at academic and practitioner conferences. Professor Bettner is also on the editorial advisory boards of several academic journals, including the *International Journal of Accounting and Business Society* and the *Accounting Forum*, and has served as a reviewer for several journals, including *Advances in Public Interest Accounting* and *Hospital and Health Services Administration*.

Joseph V. Carcello is the Ernst & Young Professor in the Department of Accounting and Information Management at the University of Tennessee. He also is the cofounder and director of research for UT's Corporate Governance Center. Dr. Carcello received his PhD from Georgia State University, his MAcc from the University of Georgia, and his BS from the State University of New York College at Plattsburgh. Dr. Carcello is currently the author or coauthor of four books, more than 40 journal articles, and two monographs. Dr. Carcello serves on the Public Company Accounting Oversight Board's Standing Advisory Group. He also served as a member of a COSO task force that developed guidance on applying COSO's internal control framework for smaller public companies. Dr. Carcello is active in the American Accounting Association—he is the incoming vice president of finance; he serves as an associate editor of *Accounting Horizons*; and he has served as president of the Auditing Section. Dr. Carcello has consulted with three of the Big Four accounting firms, regional and local accounting firms, and the Securities and Exchange Commission.

A STRONG FOUNDATION FOR THE FUTURE

The tallest buildings rise from the strongest foundations. Each step in the process—from drawing up floor plans to pouring the footings to installing the bearing walls—is done to create a solid foundation upon which the structure will be built. The same principles apply in business, where careful planning and meticulous execution are essential to carrying out all tasks, from preparing income statements to analyzing foreign exchange rates.

The financial accounting course serves as a foundation for success in the business world. For this reason, the Williams team has focused years of teaching experience on **three key textbook components** to help students succeed. ➤

"This is the best feature of this text—I like how you've included the journal entries, T-accounts, and effect on the accounting equation."

Tara Laken, Joliet Junior College

Clear Accounting Cycle Presentation. In the first five chapters of *Financial Accounting*, the authors present the Accounting Cycle in a clear, graphically interesting four-step process. Central to this presentation is the dedication of three successive chapters to three key components of the cycle: recording entries (Chapter 3), adjusting entries (Chapter 4), and closing entries (Chapter 5). The Williams team places easy-to-read margin notes explaining each equation used in particular journal entries.

Student Motivation. The Williams team has put together a market-leading student package that will not only motivate your students, but help you see greater retention rates in your accounting courses. Vital pieces of technology supplement the core curriculum covered in the book: My Mentor provides a visual learning tool with interactive videos and self-tests; the Online Learning Center provides supplemental tools for both students and instructors; and McGraw-Hill Homework Manager uses end-of-chapter material pulled directly from the textbook to create static and algorithmic questions that can be used for homework and practice tests. The full *Financial Accounting* package encourages students to apply what they're learning and improve their grades.

"The end-of-chapter material is great. The authors have been very creative and effective."

Carol Collinsworth, University of Texas at Brownsville

"It covers topics clearly at a very accessible level, and puts tools in the students' hands that they can use to progress into the most interesting issues in accounting at their own pace."

Grace Pownall, Emory University

Problem-Solving Skills. *Financial Accounting* challenges your students to think about real-world situations and put themselves in the role of the decision maker through Case In Point, Your Turn, and Ethics, Fraud & Corporate Governance boxes. Students reference the Home Depot Financial Statements—included in the text as an appendix—to further hone problem-solving skills by evaluating real world financial data. The authors show a keen attention to detail when creating high quality end-of-chapter material, such as the Critical Thinking Cases and Problems, ensuring that all homework is tied directly back to chapter learning objectives.

Step-by-Step Process for the Accounting Cycle

Financial Accounting was the FIRST text to illustrate Balance Sheet and Income Statement transactions using the four-step process described below. This hallmark coverage has been further revised and refined in 14e.

The Williams team breaks down the Accounting Cycle into three full chapters to help students absorb and understand this material: recording entries (Chapter 3), adjusting entries (Chapter 4), and closing entries (Chapter 5). Transactions are demonstrated visually to help students conquer recording transactions by showing the four steps in the process:

1. Analysis—shows which accounts are recorded with an increase/decrease.
2. Debit/Credit Rules—helps students to remember whether the account should be debited/credited.
3. Journal Entry—shows the result of the two previous steps.
4. Ledger T-Accounts—shows students what was recorded and where.

The Williams team puts the Accounting Equation (A = L + OE) in the margin by transaction illustrations to show students the big picture!

106 **Chapter 3** The Accounting Cycle

Feb. 15 Collected $4,980 cash for repairs made to vehicles of Airport Shuttle Service.

Revenue earned and collected

Assets	= Liabilities +	Owners' Equity
+$4,980		+$4,980

ANALYSIS: The asset Cash is increased. Revenue has been earned.

DEBIT–CREDIT RULES: Increases in assets are recorded by debits; debit Cash $4,980. Revenue increases owners' equity and is recorded by a credit; credit Repair Service Revenue $4,980.

JOURNAL ENTRY:

Feb. 15	Cash	4,980	
	Repair Service Revenue		4,980

ENTRIES IN LEDGER ACCOUNTS:

Cash

1/31 Bal. 16,600	2/1 360
2/15 4,980	

Repair Service Revenue

	1/31 Bal. 2,200
	2/15 4,980

Feb. 28 Billed Harbor Cab Co. $5,400 for maintenance and repair services Overnight provided in February. The agreement with Harbor Cab calls for payment to be received by March 10.

Revenue earned but not yet collected

Assets	= Liabilities +	Owners' Equity
+$5,400		+$5,400

ANALYSIS: An asset Accounts Receivable is established. Revenue has been earned.

DEBIT–CREDIT RULES: Increases in assets are recorded by debits; debit Accounts Receivable $5,400. Revenue increases owners' equity and is recorded by a credit; credit Repair Service Revenue $5,400.

JOURNAL ENTRY:

Feb. 28	Accounts Receivable	5,400	
	Repair Service Revenue		5,400

ENTRIES IN LEDGER ACCOUNTS:

Accounts Receivable

1/31 Bal. 1,200	
2/28 5,400	

Repair Service Revenue

	1/31 Bal. 2,200
	2/15 4,980
	2/28 5,400

"This is one of the better explanations of the accounting cycle I have seen. It is succinct and logical. I normally prepare my own explanation of the accounting cycle or have to modify the explanation in the text. However, with this text, I would use the explanation verbatim."

Nicholas Marudas, Auburn University at Montgomery

More End-of-Chapter Material

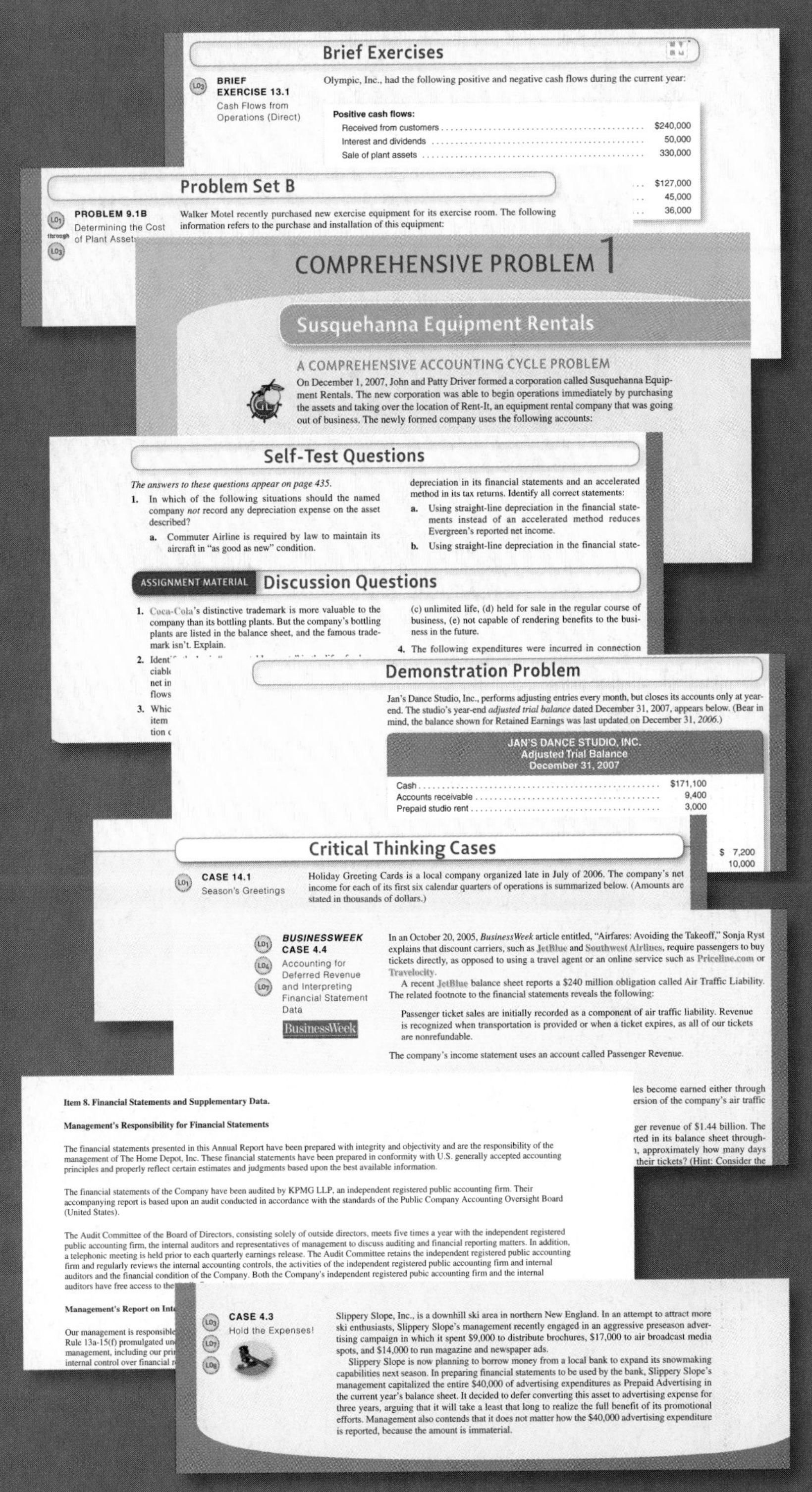

Brief Exercises

BRIEF EXERCISE 13.1
Cash Flows from Operations (Direct)

Olympic, Inc., had the following positive and negative cash flows during the current year:

Positive cash flows:	
Received from customers	$240,000
Interest and dividends	50,000
Sale of plant assets	330,000
	$127,000
	45,000
	36,000

Problem Set B

PROBLEM 9.1B
Determining the Cost of Plant Assets

Walker Motel recently purchased new exercise equipment for its exercise room. The following information refers to the purchase and installation of this equipment:

COMPREHENSIVE PROBLEM 1

Susquehanna Equipment Rentals

A COMPREHENSIVE ACCOUNTING CYCLE PROBLEM

On December 1, 2007, John and Patty Driver formed a corporation called Susquehanna Equipment Rentals. The new corporation was able to begin operations immediately by purchasing the assets and taking over the location of Rent-It, an equipment rental company that was going out of business. The newly formed company uses the following accounts:

Self-Test Questions

The answers to these questions appear on page 435.

1. In which of the following situations should the named company *not* record any depreciation expense on the asset described?
   a. Commuter Airline is required by law to maintain its aircraft in "as good as new" condition.

depreciation in its financial statements and an accelerated method in its tax returns. Identify all correct statements:
   a. Using straight-line depreciation in the financial statements instead of an accelerated method reduces Evergreen's reported net income.
   b. Using straight-line depreciation in the financial state-

ASSIGNMENT MATERIAL

Discussion Questions

1. Coca-Cola's distinctive trademark is more valuable to the company than its bottling plants. But the company's bottling plants are listed in the balance sheet, and the famous trademark isn't. Explain.
2. Ident…
3. Whic…

(c) unlimited life, (d) held for sale in the regular course of business, (e) not capable of rendering benefits to the business in the future.

4. The following expenditures were incurred in connection

Demonstration Problem

Jan's Dance Studio, Inc., performs adjusting entries every month, but closes its accounts only at year-end. The studio's year-end *adjusted trial balance* dated December 31, 2007, appears below. (Bear in mind, the balance shown for Retained Earnings was last updated on December 31, *2006*.)

JAN'S DANCE STUDIO, INC.
Adjusted Trial Balance
December 31, 2007

Cash	$171,100	
Accounts receivable	9,400	
Prepaid studio rent	3,000	
		$ 7,200
		10,000

Critical Thinking Cases

CASE 14.1
Season's Greetings

Holiday Greeting Cards is a local company organized late in July of 2006. The company's net income for each of its first six calendar quarters of operations is summarized below. (Amounts are stated in thousands of dollars.)

BUSINESSWEEK CASE 4.4
Accounting for Deferred Revenue and Interpreting Financial Statement Data

BusinessWeek

In an October 20, 2005, *BusinessWeek* article entitled, "Airfares: Avoiding the Takeoff," Sonja Ryst explains that discount carriers, such as JetBlue and Southwest Airlines, require passengers to buy tickets directly, as opposed to using a travel agent or an online service such as Priceline.com or Travelocity.

A recent JetBlue balance sheet reports a $240 million obligation called Air Traffic Liability. The related footnote to the financial statements reveals the following:

> Passenger ticket sales are initially recorded as a component of air traffic liability. Revenue is recognized when transportation is provided or when a ticket expires, as all of our tickets are nonrefundable.

The company's income statement uses an account called Passenger Revenue.

…les become earned either through …ersion of the company's air traffic … ger revenue of $1.44 billion. The …rted in its balance sheet through… …, approximately how many days … their tickets? (Hint: Consider the

Item 8. Financial Statements and Supplementary Data.

Management's Responsibility for Financial Statements

The financial statements presented in this Annual Report have been prepared with integrity and objectivity and are the responsibility of the management of The Home Depot, Inc. These financial statements have been prepared in conformity with U.S. generally accepted accounting principles and properly reflect certain estimates and judgments based upon the best available information.

The financial statements of the Company have been audited by KPMG LLP, an independent registered public accounting firm. Their accompanying report is based upon an audit conducted in accordance with the standards of the Public Company Accounting Oversight Board (United States).

The Audit Committee of the Board of Directors, consisting solely of outside directors, meets five times a year with the independent registered public accounting firm, the internal auditors and representatives of management to discuss auditing and financial reporting matters. In addition, a telephonic meeting is held prior to each quarterly earnings release. The Audit Committee retains the independent registered public accounting firm and regularly reviews the internal accounting controls, the activities of the independent registered public accounting firm and internal auditors and the financial condition of the Company. Both the Company's independent registered public accounting firm and the internal auditors have free access to the…

Management's Report on Int…

Our management is responsible… Rule 13a-15(f) promulgated un… management, including our pri… internal control over financial r…

CASE 4.3
Hold the Expenses!

Slippery Slope, Inc., is a downhill ski area in northern New England. In an attempt to attract more ski enthusiasts, Slippery Slope's management recently engaged in an aggressive preseason advertising campaign in which it spent $9,000 to distribute brochures, $17,000 to air broadcast media spots, and $14,000 to run magazine and newspaper ads.

Slippery Slope is now planning to borrow money from a local bank to expand its snowmaking capabilities next season. In preparing financial statements to be used by the bank, Slippery Slope's management capitalized the entire $40,000 of advertising expenditures as Prepaid Advertising in the current year's balance sheet. It decided to defer converting this asset to advertising expense for three years, arguing that it will take a least that long to realize the full benefit of its promotional efforts. Management also contends that it does not matter how the $40,000 advertising expenditure is reported, because the amount is immaterial.

NEW Brief Exercises supplement the exercises with shorter, single-concept exercises that test the basic concepts of each chapter. These brief exercises give instructors more flexibility in their homework assignments.

A NEW Alternate Problem Set has been added to each chapter, complementing an already robust end-of-chapter problem section.

Four Comprehensive Problems, ranging from two to five pages in length, present students with real-world scenarios and challenge them to apply what they've learned in the chapters leading up to them.

Defined Key Terms and Self-Test Questions review and reinforce chapter material.

Demonstration Problems and their solutions allow students to test their knowledge of key points in the chapters.

Critical Thinking Cases and Problems put students' analytical skills to the test by having them think critically about key concepts from the chapter and apply them to business decisions. TWO sets of Problems and a full set of Exercises in EACH chapter give *Financial Accounting* the edge in homework materials.

BusinessWeek Cases are pulled from recent headlines and require students to relate accounting concepts to current events.

The 2005 Home Depot Financial Statements are included in Appendix A. Students are referred to key aspects of the 10-K in the text material and in end-of-chapter material to illustrate actual business applications of chapter concepts.

Ethics Cases in *each* chapter challenge students to explore the ethical impact of decisions made in business.

General Ledger Application Software (GLAS)

Excel Templates

Homework Manager

Ethical

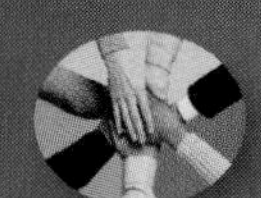

Group Activities

Writing

Internet

International

What makes the **Williams**

High-profile companies frame each chapter discussion through the use of dynamic CHAPTER OPENER vignettes. Students learn to frame the chapter's topic in a real world scenario.

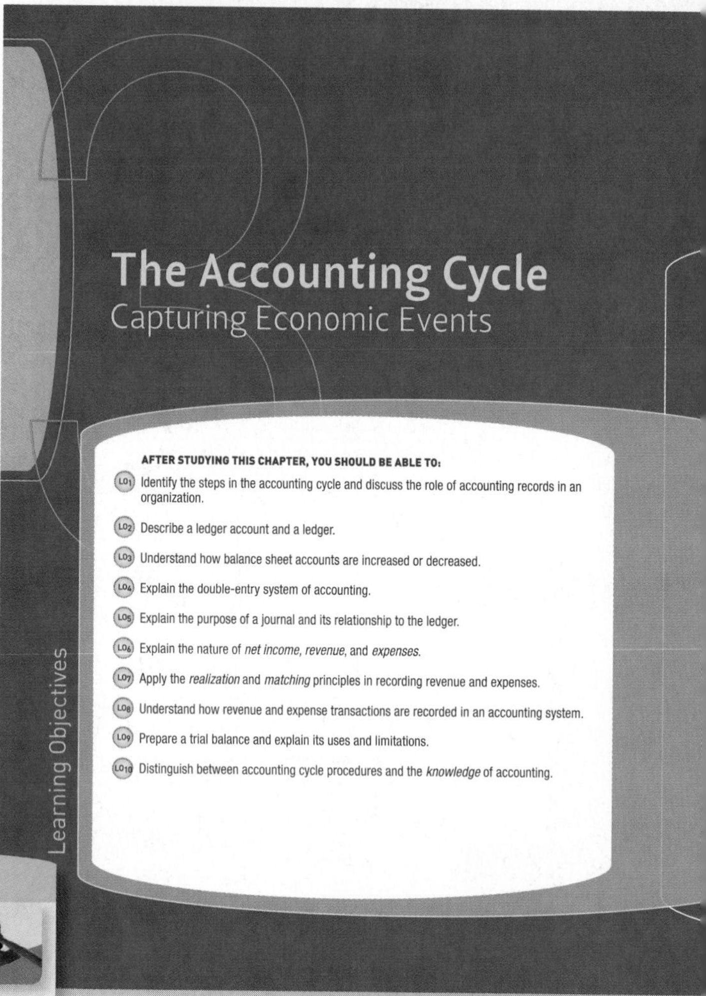

YOUR TURN boxes challenge students to interpret a situation and offer their best judgment; the authors challenge students with ethically demanding situations. They must apply what they've learned to real situations faced by investors, creditors, and managers.

YOUR TURN **You as Manager of the Credit Department**

Assume you are the manager of NTI's credit department. Nancy Conrad, the founder of NTI, has asked you to manage receivables and payables by leading and lagging. Leading receivables implies collecting cash from customers more quickly than previously. Lagging payables means delaying payment to creditors. You are concerned that what Conrad is suggesting is unethical. What should you do?

(See our comments on the Online Learning Center Web site.)

The Accounting Cycle
Capturing Economic Events

Learning Objectives

AFTER STUDYING THIS CHAPTER, YOU SHOULD BE ABLE TO:

- LO1 Identify the steps in the accounting cycle and discuss the role of accounting records in an organization.
- LO2 Describe a ledger account and a ledger.
- LO3 Understand how balance sheet accounts are increased or decreased.
- LO4 Explain the double-entry system of accounting.
- LO5 Explain the purpose of a journal and its relationship to the ledger.
- LO6 Explain the nature of *net income, revenue,* and *expenses.*
- LO7 Apply the *realization* and *matching* principles in recording revenue and expenses.
- LO8 Understand how revenue and expense transactions are recorded in an accounting system.
- LO9 Prepare a trial balance and explain its uses and limitations.
- LO10 Distinguish between accounting cycle procedures and the *knowledge* of accounting.

"Students can relate to the real world examples and companies highlighted."

Susan Logorda, Lehigh Carbon Community College

Exhibit 14–21
OPERATING CYCLE

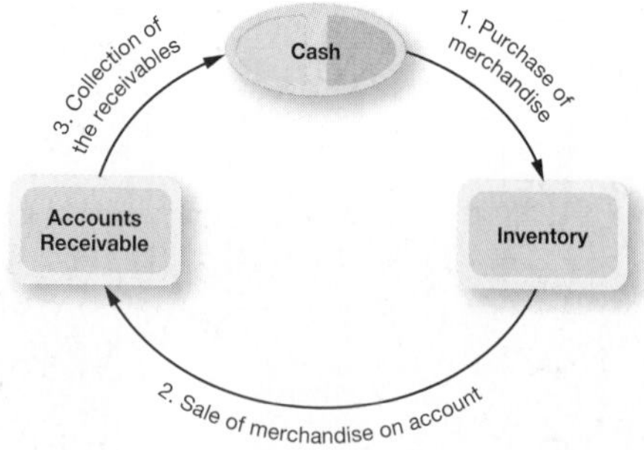

Cash
1. Purchase of merchandise
Inventory
2. Sale of merchandise on account
Accounts Receivable
3. Collection of the receivables

EXHIBITS help illustrate key concepts in the text.

pedagogy work?

PEPSICO, INC.

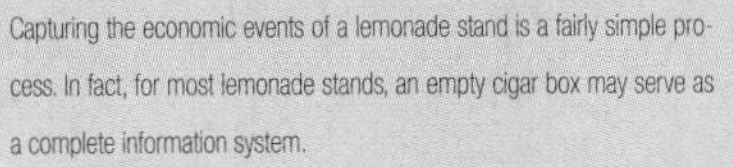

Capturing the economic events of a lemonade stand is a fairly simple process. In fact, for most lemonade stands, an empty cigar box may serve as a complete information system.

Capturing the economic events of **PepsiCo, Inc.**, however, is an entirely different matter. This giant corporation generates annual revenue of over $30 billion from sales of its beverage products, its **Frito-Lay** snack foods, and its **Quaker Oats** cereal and pasta products. Employing nearly 150,000 people, and operating hundreds of manufacturing facilities and thousands of warehouses and distribution centers, **PepsiCo, Inc.**, must somehow capture complex business transactions occurring in more than 200 countries worldwide.

From lemonade stands to multinational corporations, being able to efficiently capture the effects of economic events, such as sales orders and raw material purchases, is absolutely essential for survival. Companies like **PepsiCo, Inc.**, rely upon sophisticated computer systems to capture economic activities. Some small enterprises, however, may use paper ledgers and journals to record business transactions.

87

"This text...is accurate, well-organized, and covers the material thoroughly."

Jeff Jackson, San Jacinto College Central

CASE IN POINT

Texas Instruments's Materials and Control Group tracked its cost of quality categories over a six-year period. It discovered that after the initial adoption of TQM practices, prevention and appraisal costs increased and remained fairly constant over the six-year period. However, as the six-year period wore on, failure costs declined, causing the total cost of quality to decrease. Many of these prevention-related costs were associated with ensuring high-quality inputs through managing supplier relations.

Courtesy of Texas Instruments Incorporated

CASE IN POINT boxes link accounting concepts in the chapter to their use in the real world. These examples often present an international scenario to expose students to accounting practices around the world.

Ethics, Fraud & Corporate Governance

As discussed in this chapter, nonfinancial objectives are important to many companies in evaluating their performance. For example, many retailers closely monitor sales per square foot and same store sales. Investors and creditors are interested in nonfinancial performance measures as well, and companies often disclose key nonfinancial performance measures in press releases, interactions with stock analysts, and financial reports filed with the Securities and Exchange Commission (SEC).

In addition to the presentation of nonfinancial measures, some companies believe that their performance is best portrayed by excluding certain GAAP items from the computation of income. For example, companies in the cable, entertainment, and telecommunications industries often suggest that EBITDA (earnings before interest, taxes, depreciation, and amortization) is a better measure of periodic operating performance than is net income. Other companies may believe that excluding restructuring and impairment charges from the computation of income provides a better measure of sustainable earnings than would a GAAP-based measure. Companies that present financial results (often in press releases) that are calculated on a non-GAAP basis refer to these results as *pro forma*. The SEC believes that such pro forma reporting has often been abused. For example, the pro forma earnings number is typically higher than comparable GAAP-based earnings.

The Sarbanes-Oxley Act (SOX) attempts to reduce or eliminate the abuses associated with pro forma reporting. SOX requires public companies to provide a reconciliation of the difference between any non-GAAP financial measure provided to investors and creditors and the comparable GAAP-based result. In addition, SOX prohibits the publication of pro forma results that are misleading or that contain untrue statements. The objective of this SOX requirement is to enable investors and creditors to simultaneously compare non-GAAP pro forma measures with the comparable GAAP numbers.

ETHICS, FRAUD & CORPORATE GOVERNANCE boxes delve deep into the accounting scandals of recent years that have sparked such comprehensive legislation as Sarbanes-Oxley. The inclusion of EFCG boxes in each chapter helps bring complex accounting and ethical issues into the classroom.

What's New about the 13th Edition

The following list of revisions is a testament to the enthusiastic response of dozens of reviewers who contributed their considerable expertise. In doing so they have helped to make the 13th edition of *Financial Accounting* the best book of its kind.

In this edition, the authors focused on two key revisions: Streamlining the text and providing even more end-of-chapter material. The Williams team accomplished this goal with the following revisions for each chapter:

- Addition of new exercises and problems, PLUS new brief exercises
- Inclusion of at least 10 new brief exercises in each chapter
- Revision of graphics to match new design and improve the illustration of key concepts
- Home Depot Financial Statement featured in Appendix A and tied to end-of-chapter material
- New, vibrant design that features revised graphics in each chapter and an all-new layout
- Selected problems and exercises now available with McGraw-Hill's Homework Manager
- Incorporation of Management Strategy and Cash Effects features into the text to streamline the discussion

Chapter 1

- New coverage of the Committee of Sponsoring Organizations of the Treadway Commission (COSO)
- New coverage of COSO's *Internal Control—Integrated Framework*
- New coverage of the Public Company Accounting Oversight Board (PCAOB)
- Emphasis on why the study of accounting is important to non-accounting majors, both in their business careers and in their personal lives
- Incorporation of Management Strategy feature into the text

Chapter 2

- Redesigned graphics make accounting more lively and eye-catching
- Revised discussion of real-world companies like Wal-Mart, Walt Disney, and JCPenney demonstrates theory in action
- Addition of a new exhibit showing cash flow versus income statement recognition

of *Financial Accounting*?

Chapter 3
- Addition of many new exercises
- Revised coverage of accounting cycle procedures

Chapter 4
- Addition of many new exercises

Chapter 5
- Addition of many new exercises
- Addition of new short comprehensive problems (3 "A" and 3 "B")
- Addition of two new unstructured cases addressing Sarbanes-Oxley issues
- Addition of a new comprehensive problem that covers the full accounting cycle

Chapter 6
- Addition of new "real world" exhibits
- New Home Depot end-of-chapter exercise
- Revision of solutions to incorporate five skill areas
- Addition of regular exercises and problems to the end-of-chapter material

Chapter 7
- Addition of many new exercises

Chapter 8
- Addition of brief exercises
- Replacement of Safeway exercise with Wal-Mart exercise

Chapter 9
- Revised graphics
- Incorporation of supplemental topic (Other Depreciation Methods) into primary text
- Addition of one new exercise and four new problems

Chapter 10
- Incorporation of supplemental topic (Special Types of Liabilities) into primary text

Chapter 11
- Streamlining of chapter text
- Addition of two new exercises

Chapter 12
- Revision of Case in Point boxes
- Streamlining of chapter text
- Revised Financial Analysis and Decision Making Section
- Addition of one new exercise

Chapter 13
- Streamlining of chapter text
- Incorporation of supplemental topic (A Worksheet for Preparing a Statement of Cash Flows) into primary text
- Replacement of one exercise and addition of two new exercises

Chapter 14
- Addition of numerous illustrations
- Streamlining of chapter text
- Updating of demonstration problem

Industry Leader in Online Technology

Online Learning Center (OLC) www.mhhe.com/williamsfinancial13e

The Online Learning Center (OLC) that accompanies *Financial Accounting* provides a wealth of extra material for both instructors and students. With content specific to each chapter of the book, the Williams OLC doesn't require any building or maintenance on your part and is ready to go the moment you and your students type in the URL.

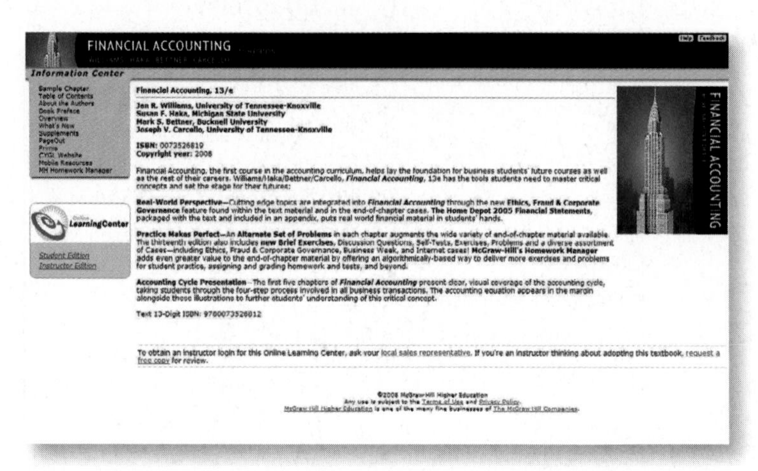

As your students study, they can refer to the OLC for such benefits as:

- Self-grading quizzes
- Electronic flashcards
- Audio-narrated PowerPoints
- ALEKS
- Excel templates
- Check figures
- Sample study guide
- Sample working papers
- Links to professional resources
- Internet assignments
- My Mentor
- Text updates

> "The text is clear and understandable. Our students will be able to read and understand the material. The companion Web site has additional information and study aids."
>
> *Marjorie Ashton,*
> *Truckee Meadows Community College*

The new **Classroom Performance System** (CPS) RF Gen2 devices enable students to provide immediate feedback to classroom questions using a touch pad. Responses can be tabulated anonymously and can be helpful in facilitating an interactive classroom experience.

eInstruction

A secure **Instructor Resource Center** stores your essential course materials to save you prep time before class. The **Instructor's Manual**, **Solutions Manual**, **PowerPoint presentations**, and **sample syllabi** are now just a couple of clicks away. You will also find useful packaging information about other available supplements. Products like **WebCT**, **Blackboard**, **eCollege**, and **Top-Class** (a product of WBT) all expand the reach of your course. McGraw-Hill/Irwin offers premium content with your course cartridge. Online discussion and message boards will now complement your office hours. Thanks to a sophisticated tracking system, you will know which students need more attention—even if they don't ask for help. That's because online testing scores are recorded and automatically placed in your grade book, and if a student is struggling with coursework, a special alert message lets you know.

The OLC Web site also serves as a doorway to McGraw-Hill's other technology solutions.

How Can Students Study on the Go Using Their iPod?

iPod Content

Harness the power of one of the most popular technology tools students use today—the Apple iPod. Our innovative approach allows students to download audio and video presentations right into their iPod and take learning materials with them wherever they go. It makes review and study time as easy as putting in headphones. Visit the Online Learning Center (**www.mhhe.com/williamsfinancial13e**) to learn more details on available iPod content—and enhance your learning experience today.

PageOut®

McGraw-Hill's Course Management System

PageOut is the easiest way to create a Web site for your accounting course.

There's no need for HTML coding, graphic design, or a thick how-to book. Just fill in a series of boxes with simple English and click on one of our professional designs. In no time, your course is online with a Web site that contains your syllabus!

Should you need assistance in preparing your Web site, we can help. Our team of product specialists is ready to take your course materials and build a custom Web site to your specifications. Simply call a McGraw-Hill/Irwin PageOut specialist to start the process. Best of all, PageOut is *free* when you adopt *Financial Accounting*! To learn more, please visit **www.pageout.net**.

ALEKS® for the Accounting Cycle

ALEKS for the Accounting Cycle uses innovative adaptive learning technology to provide individualized, guided learning to each and every student. ALEKS defines the key concepts, offers explanations and opportunities to practice, analyzes and corrects errors, and moves on to new topics when the student is ready.

What are the benefits of ALEKS for the Accounting Cycle?

- Students can use ALEKS for a review of the accounting cycle. ALEKS is self-guided, which helps reduce the amount of time needed to cover the accounting cycle.
- ALEKS can be used as the curriculum for a bridge course between financial accounting and intermediate accounting.
- MBA students can use ALEKS for a self-guided review of accounting to prepare for their MBA program. Since it is online, students can do their work from anywhere in the world.

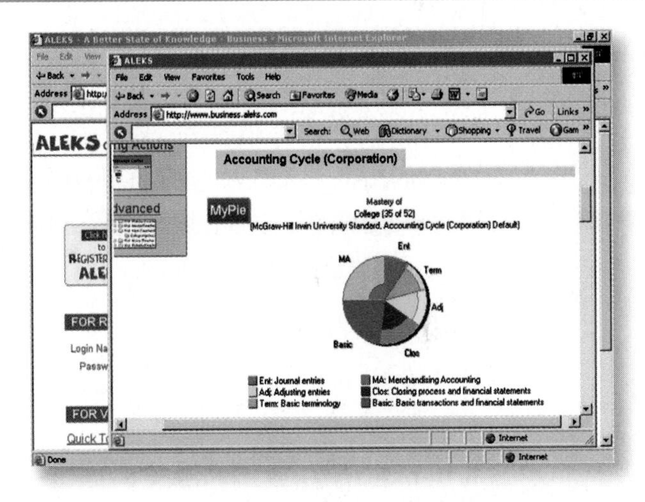

Contact your McGraw-Hill representative today to learn more about ALEKS, or e-mail aleks@mcgraw-hill.com.

> **"I found that for every 10 hours that the student put into ALEKS their final average increased by 2.2 percentage points. I have never had a semester with results this good."**
>
> *T. Sexton, SUNY Suffolk*

McGraw-Hill's
HOMEWORK
MANAGER

McGraw-Hill's Homework Manager

Ever wish you could assign one problem again and again, giving students all the practice they need to master an especially stubborn topic or function? McGraw-Hill's Homework Manager makes it possible.

This Web-based study and review tool reproduces exercises and problems from the text, allowing you to electronically assign textbook problems for homework or practice. For more flexibility, a sophisticated algorithm can generate "look-alike" problems containing different values within the same structure as the end-of-chapter material found in the book. This algorithmic engine allows students to practice and refine the exact skills they need. Say goodbye to cheating on homework assignments or tests—McGraw-Hill's Homework Manager can generate infinite variations on almost any text problem, enabling you to assign unique versions to every single student.

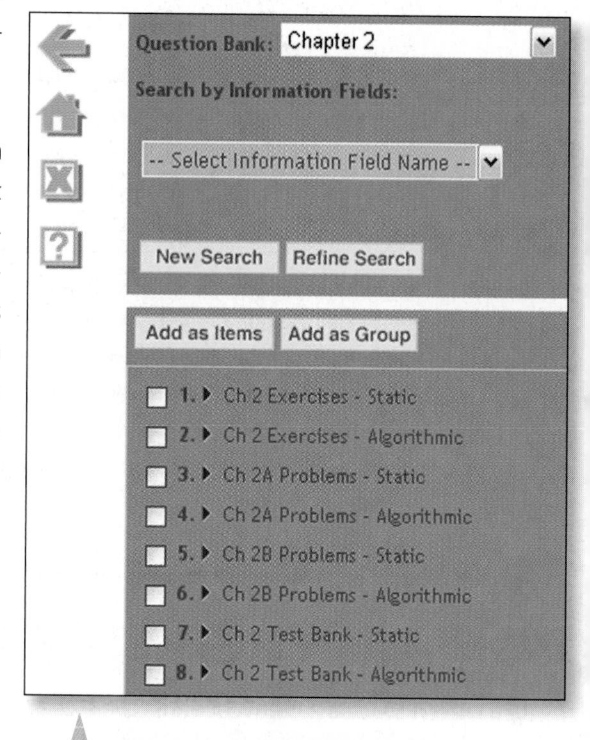

A robust selection of problems, exercises and test bank questions is available for each chapter.

Look what McGraw-Hill's Homework Manager gives you:

- Textbook-specific exercises and problems.
- Fill-in-the-blank question types.
- Immediate grading and feedback for students.
- Automatically graded assignments and analysis for instructors.
- Algorithmic exercises and problems.
- Instructor course management tools.

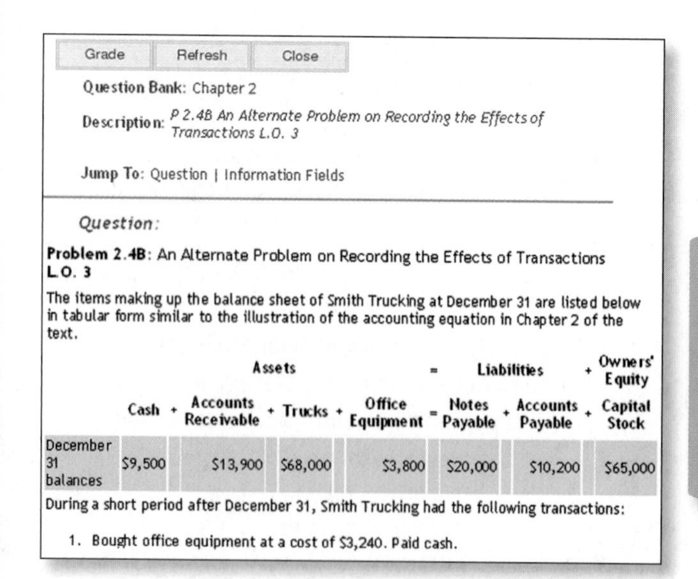

Grade Refresh Close

Question Bank: Chapter 2

Description: *P 2.4B An Alternate Problem on Recording the Effects of Transactions L.O. 3*

Jump To: Question | Information Fields

Question:

Problem 2.4B: An Alternate Problem on Recording the Effects of Transactions L.O. 3

The items making up the balance sheet of Smith Trucking at December 31 are listed below in tabular form similar to the illustration of the accounting equation in Chapter 2 of the text.

	Assets				=	Liabilities		+	Owners' Equity
	Cash	+ Accounts Receivable	+ Trucks	+ Office Equipment	=	Notes Payable	+ Accounts Payable	+	Capital Stock
December 31 balances	$9,500	$13,900	$68,000	$3,800		$20,000	$10,200		$65,000

During a short period after December 31, Smith Trucking had the following transactions:

1. Bought office equipment at a cost of $3,240. Paid cash.

McGraw-Hill's Homework Manager custom homework assignments or quizzes can be completed either online or with pencil and paper. Online assignments are graded automatically, with the results stored in a secure online gradebook.

My Mentor

The interactive accounting software My Mentor teaches students visually what's actually happening in a business transaction through flash presentations—without using numbers. Then, when a student understands the basics of the transaction, My Mentor shows them the same presentation but with numbers included. A difficult concept for each chapter is featured on the software.

The five integrated steps of My Mentor:

- **THE VIDEO:** A video begins each chapter, featuring a professional from the industry outlining the content covered in the chapter.
- **THE BASICS:** A flash presentation showing business transactions—without the numbers—comes next.
- **LINKING THE NUMBERS:** The same visual presentation of a business transaction is shown, but this time with the numbers.
- **WORKING WITH EXCEL:** Students get a chance to apply what they've learned in the first three steps in an actual Excel problem.
- **THE QUIZ:** Students are given another chance to test their knowledge of what they've learned in the program through short, five-question quizzes—complete with instant feedback!

"I would highly recommend that the students have available and use the mentor portion of their supplements to enhance the material covered in the textbook."

Jim Dougher, DeVry University

McGraw-Hill's HOMEWORK MANAGER **PLUS**™

Homework Manager Plus is an extension of McGraw-Hill's popular Homework Manager System. With Homework Manager Plus you get all of the power of Homework Manager plus an integrated online version of the text. Students simply receive one single access code which provides access to all of the resources available through Homework Manager Plus.

When students find themselves needing to reference the textbook in order to complete their homework, now they can simply click on hints and link directly to the most relevant materials associated with the problem or exercise they are working on.

Supplements for *Financial Accounting*

INSTRUCTOR SUPPLEMENTS

A strong foundation needs support.

Financial Accounting authors Williams, Haka, Bettner, and Carcello know that every component of the learning package must be integrated and supported by strong ancillaries. Instructors and students have a wealth of material at their fingertips to help make the most of a challenging course in accounting.

Instructor's CD-ROM

ISBN: 9780073281728
MHID: 0073281727

This all-in-one resource contains the Instructor's Resource Manual, Solutions Manual, Testbank Word files, Computerized TB, PowerPoint® slides, and Instructor Excel Templates.

Instructor's Resource Manual

This manual provides for each chapter: (1) a chapter summary detailing what has changed, new problems that have been added, and author suggestions on how to incorporate new material; (2) brief topical outline; (3) sample "10-minute quizzes" designed to test the basic concepts in each chapter; and (4) suggestions for group, Internet, *BusinessWeek*, and other class exercises to supplement the material in the book.

Solutions Manual

The Solutions Manual includes detailed solutions for every question, exercise, problem, and case in the text.

Testbank

Written by Carol Klinger, this comprehensive Testbank contains over 2,000 problems and true/false, multiple-choice, and essay questions. New to this edition are written explanations to the solutions—making it easier than ever for you to see where students have gone wrong in their calculations.

Computerized Testbank with Algorithmic Problem Generator

ISBN: 9780073281704
MHID: 0073281700

The computerized testbank includes an algorithmic problem generator enabling instructors to create similarly structured problems with different values, allowing every student to be assigned a unique quiz or test. The user-friendly interface allows faculty to easily create different versions of the same test, change the answer order, edit or add questions, and even conduct online testing.

Audio PowerPoint Slides

The Audio PowerPoint slides are created by Jon Booker and Charles Caldwell of Tennessee Technological University and Susan Galbreath of David Lipscomb University. The slides include an accompanying audio lecture with notes and are available on the Online Learning Center (OLC) and Instructor's CD-ROM.

STUDENT SUPPLEMENTS

Study Guide

ISBN: 9780073268156

MHID: 0073268151

The Study Guide, written by the text authors, provides chapter summaries, detailed illustrations, and a wide variety of self-study questions, exercises, and multiple-choice problems (with solutions).

Working Papers

ISBN: 9780073268170

MHID: 0073268178

Working Papers provide students with formatted templates to aid them in doing homework assignments.

> "The text offers some powerful assistance to students, like . . . the Online Learning Center. The end-of-chapter materials are excellent."
>
> *Mary Hollars, Vincennes University*

Excel Templates

Selected end-of-chapter exercises and problems, marked in the text with an Excel icon, can be solved using these Microsoft Excel templates, located on the OLC.
www.mhhe.com/williamsfinancial13e

McGraw-Hill Homework Manager

Homework Manager

ISBN: 9780073281735

MHID: 0073281735

Homework Manager Plus

ISBN: 9780073281759

MHID: 0073281751

This optional online supplement uses an intelligent algorithm to generate an infinite number of problems for students based on problem structures from the text, enabling students to practice particular types of problems repeatedly until they master key concepts.

Online Learning Center (Web site)
www.mhhe.com/williamsfinancial13e

The OLC is full of resources for students, including: Chapter Summaries, Online Quizzing, Key Term Reviews, Internet Exercises, PowerPoint Presentations, Alternate Problems, Check Figures, Excel Templates, Homework Manager, Links to Professional Resources, and Text Updates.

ALEKS for the Accounting Cycle

ALEKS uses assessments in key areas of the accounting cycle to measure student progress. This software has been proven to cut study time on the accounting cycle dramatically by offering students step-by-step progress reports—all of which is available to the instructor to review. **www.business.aleks.com**

My Mentor

This interactive accounting software is available on the OLC. It makes accounting visual and helps students learn key concepts for each chapter of this textbook!

Carol Yacht's General Ledger and Peachtree Complete 2007

ISBN: 9780073281711

MHID: 0073281719

The General Ledger and Peachtree accounting program saves time and minimizes errors because it operates as an integrated system. Amounts entered in the general journal or special journals can be posted to the general ledger with a single keystroke. The Peachtree icons show students where this tool can be used to solve end-of-chapter problems.

Zinio E-Book

Experience the speed (no bookstore lines), convenience (portability), affordability (almost 50 percent savings) and intelligence (full interactivity) of Zinio eBooks. Digital textbooks are exact replicas of the print version, but better. They are easy to navigate, allowing you to flip back and forth between pages, with continual access to the Table of Contents with a tool bar button to jump directly to a chapter, topic, or page of interest. To learn more or to download a free sample, visit **http://www.zinio.com/**.

Acknowledgments

Many of our colleagues reviewed *Financial Accounting*, as well as its many supplements. Through their time and effort, we are able to continually improve and update the book to meet the needs of students and professors. We sincerely thank each of you for your valuable time and suggestions.

Twelfth Edition Reviewers

Brad Badertscher, *University of Iowa*
Roderick Barclay, *Texas A&M University*
Cheryl Bartlett, *Albuquerque Technical Vocational Institute*
Eric Blazer, *Millersville University*
Paul Brazina, *La Salle University*
H. Francis Bush, *Virginia Military Institute*
Cal Christian, *East Carolina University*
Linda Christiansen, *Indiana University Southeast*
Catherine Collins, *Wanbonsee Community College*
Judy Cowell, *Northern Okalahoma College*
Laura Delaune, *Louisiana State University*
Gerald Doyle, *Marshall Community Technical College*
David Durkee, *Weber State University*
John Garlick, *Fayetteville University*
Lisa Gillespie, *Loyola University-Chicago*
Diane Glowacki, *Tarrant County College*
Randall Glover, *Brevard Community College*
Edward Goodhart, *Shippensburg University of Pennsylvania*
Allan Graybill, *Redlands Community College*
Rosalie Hallbauer, *Florida International University*
Cindy Harris, *Ursinus College*
Sueann Hely, *West Kentucky Community & Technical College*
Sheri Henson, *Western Kentucky University*
Michael Hetue, *Cardinal Stritch University*
Lyle Hicks, *Danville Area Community College*
Robert Holtfreter, *Central Washington University*
John Karayan, *Occidental Community College*
Cindi Khanlarian, *University of North Carolina at Greensboro*
Dennis Kovach, *Community College Of Allegheny County*
Steven Lafave, *Augsburg College*
William Link, *University of Missouri-St. Louis*
James Lukawitz, *University of Memphis*
Earnest Marquez, *Columbia College*
Florence Mcgovern, *Bergen Community College*
Noel Mckeon, *Florida Community College-Jacksonville*
Joseph Micheli, *Cardinal Stritch University*
Johnna Murray, *University of Missouri-St. Louis*
Albert Nagy, *John Carroll University*
Margaret O'Reilly-Allen, *Rider University*
Stephen Owusu-Ansah, *The University of Texas-Pan American*
Craig Pence, *Highland Community College*
Kris Portz, *St. Cloud State University*
Grace Pownall, *Emory University*
Lora Reinholz, *Cardinal Stritch University*
Maryann Reynolds, *Western Washington University*
Brandi Roberts, *Southeastern Louisiana University*
Sandy Scheuermann, *University Of Louisiana-Lafayette*
Janine Sickafuse, *Allegheny College*
Linda Tarrago, *Hillsborough Community College-Tampa*
Daniel Tschopp, *Daemen College*
Josephina Vandras, *Orange City Community College*
Jeanne Yamamura, *University of Nevada-Reno*

Previous Edition Reviewers

Sheila Ammons, *Austin Community College*
Elenito Ayuyao, *Los Angeles City College*
Walter Baggett, *Manhattan College*
Sharla Bailey, *Southwest Baptist University*
Craig Bain, *Northern Arizona University*
Jill Bale, *Doane College*
Frederic S. Bardo, *Shippensburg University*
Scott Barhight, *Northampton County Area Community College*
Glenn S. Barnette, *Gustavus Adolphus College*
William Barze, *St. Petersburg Junior College*
Peter Battelle, *University of Vermont*
Daniel Bayak, *Northampton Community College*
John Bayles, *Oakton Community College*
Janet Becker, *University of Pittsburg*
Jerard Berardino, *Community College of Allegheny*
Teri Bernstein, *Santa Monica College*
Cynthia Bolt-Lee, *The Citadel*
Nancy Boyd, *Middle Tennessee State University*
Sallie Branscom, *Virginia Western Community College*
Russell Bresslauer, *Chabot College*
R.E. Bryson, *University of Alabama*
Paul M. Buck, *Plymouth State College*
Priscilla Burnaby, *Bentley College*
Bryan Burks, *Harding University*
Scott N. Cairns, *Shippensburg University*
Loring Carlson, *Western New England College*
David Chu, *College of the Holy Cross*
Stanley Chu, *Borough Manhattan Community College*
Pamela H. Church, *Rhodes College*
Carolyn E. Clark, *St. Joseph's University*
Darlene Coarts, *University of Northern Iowa*
Lisa M. Cole, *Pima Community College*
Alice R. Cooperstein, *Central Connecticut State University*
William Cravey, *Jersey City State College*
Marcia Croteau, *University of Maryland—Baltimore County*
Brian Curtis, *Raritan Valley Community College*
Steve Czarsty, *Mary Washington College*
David L. Davis, *Tallahassee Community College*
Larry Davis, *Southwest Virginia County College*
Victoria Doby, *Villa Julie College*
Carlton Donchess, *Bridgewater State College*
Steve Driver, *Horry—Georgetown Tech*
Pamela Druger, *Augustana College*
Anita Ellzey, *Hartford Community College*
Emmanuel Emenyonu, *Sacred Heart University*
David Erlach, *CUNY—Queens College*
Paul Everson, *Northern State University*
Mary Lou Gamma, *East Tennessee State University*
Mary Feifel, *Mira Costa College*
Brother Gerald Fitzgerald, *LaSalle University*
Tom Forehand, *Marist College*
Ralph Fritsch, *Midwestern State University*
Mike Fujita, *Leeward Community College*
Joseph F. Gallo, *Cuyahoga Community College*
Don Van Gieson, *Kapiolani Community College*
Peter Gilbert, *Thomas College*
Donald Geren, *Northeastern Illinois University*
Penny Hanes, *Mercyhurst College*
Richard Hanna, *Ferris State University*
Stephen Hano, *Rockland Community College*
Joseph M. Hargadon, *Widener University*

Sara Harris, *Arapahoe Community College*
Medhat Helmi, *University of Alabama—Birmingham*
Paul J. Herz, *Western State College of Colorado*
Lyle Hicks, *Danville Area Community College*
Jeannelou Hodgens, *Florence-Darlington Technical College*
Patricia H. Holmes, *Des Moines Area Community College*
Michael Holt, *Eastern Nazarene College*
Evelyn Honaker, *Walters State Community College*
Gordon Hosch, *University of New Orleans*
Eugene A. Imhoff, *University of Michigan Business School*
Dave Jensen, *Bucknell University*
Christopher Jones, *George Washington University*
David Junnola, *Eastern Michigan University*
Leo Jubb, *Essex Community College*
Khondkar Karim, *Monmouth University*
James Kennedy, *Texas A&M University*
Rita M. Kingery, *University of Delaware*
Jane Kingston, *Piedmont Virginia Community College*
Ed Knudson, *Linn Benton Community College*
Raymond Krasniewski, *Ohio State University*
Orsay Kucukemiroglu, *Penn State University*
David Lardie, *Tunxis Community College*
Bill Lasher, *Jamestown Community College*
Lawrence Lease, *Shasta College*
Suk Jun Lee, *Chapman University*
Kenneth Leibham, *Columbia Gorge Community Center*
Annette M. Leps, *Goucher College*
Eric Lewis, *Union College*
Philip Little, *Western Carolina University*
J. Thomas Love, *Walters State Community College*
Dewey Martin, *Husson College*
John A. Marts, *The University of North Carolina at Wilmington*
Allie F. Miller, *Drexel University*
Josie Miller, *Mercer Community College*
Cheryl Mitchem, *Virginia State University*
Kevin M. Misiewicz, *Notre Dame*
Merrill Moore, *Delaware Tech & Community College*
Deborah Most, *Dutchess Community College*
Haim Mozes, *Fordham University*
Frank Olive, *Nicholas College*
Bruce Oliver, *Rochester Institute of Technology*
Ginger Parker, *Creighton University*
Wendy W. Peffley, *North Carolina Wesleyan College*
Michael Prockton, *Finger Lakes Community College*
Glenn Rechtschaffen, *York College of Pennsylvania*
Gary Reynolds, *Ozarks Technical College*
Renee Rigoni, *Monroe Community College*
Earl Roberts, *Delaware Tech & Community College*
Julie Rosenblatt, *Delaware Tech & Community College*
Bob Rothenberg, *SUNY—Oneonta*
Karen N. Russom, *North Harris College*
Victoria Rymer, *University of Maryland*
Francis A. Sakiey, *Mercer County Community College*
Linda Schain, *Hofstra University*
Mike Schoderbek, *Rutgers University–New Brunswick*
Monica Seiler, *Queensborough Community College*
E. Daniel Shim, *Sacred Heart University*
Janine Sickafuse, *Allegheny College*
Larry Sidwell, *Rend Lake College*
Stan Stanley, *Skagit Valley College*
Jim Stanton, *Mira Costa College*
Carolyn Strickler, *Ohlone College*
Robert Stilson, *City University of New York*
Barbara Sturdevant, *State University of New York*
Gene Sullivan, *Liberty University and Central Virginia Community College*
Mary Ann Swindlehurst, *Carroll Community College*
Larry Tartaglino, *Cabrillo College*
Martin Taylor, *University of Texas at Arlington*
Anne Tippett, *Tarrant County College South*
Bruce Toews, *Walla Walla College*
Cynthia Tomes, *Des Moines Area Community College*
Grace Tsao, *Colgate University*
Harold Wilson, *Middle Tennessee State University*
Steve Wilts, *Bucknell University*
Teri Yohn, *Georgetown University*
Myung Ho Yoon, *Northeastern Illinois University*

We are grateful . . .

We would like to acknowledge the following individuals for their help authoring some of the text's supplements: PowerPoint Presentations: Jon Booker and Charles W. Caldwell, both of Tennessee Technological University, and Susan C. Galbreath of David Lipscomb University; Excel Templates: Jack Terry, Comsource Associates; Carol Yacht's General Ledger and Peachtree Complete 2007: Carol Yacht and Jack Terry; Testbank: Carol Klinger, Queens College–CUNY.

Our special thanks go to Ilene Persoff for accuracy checking the text manuscript, solutions manual, and working papers, as well as Beth Woods, Accuracy Counts!, for accuracy checking the text page proof, solutions manual proofs, and working paper proofs. We appreciate the expert attention given to this project by the staff at McGraw-Hill/Irwin, especially Stewart Mattson, Editorial Director; Tim Vertovec, Executive Editor; Daryl Horrocks, Developmental Editor; Melissa Larmon, Marketing Manager; Lori Koetters, Project Manager; Matthew Perry, Media Project Manager; Kathy Shive, Photo Research Coordinator; Kami Carter, Senior Designer; Gina Hangos, Production Supervisor; and Victor Chiu, Senior Media Technology Producer.

Sincerely,

Jan R. Williams, Susan F. Haka, Mark S. Bettner, and Joseph V. Carcello

Brief Contents

Contents

1 Accounting: Information for Decision Making

2 Basic Financial Statements

3 The Accounting Cycle: Capturing Economic Events

4 The Accounting Cycle: Accruals and Deferrals

5 The Accounting Cycle: Reporting Financial Results

6 Merchandising Activities

7 Financial Assets

8 Inventories and the Cost of Goods Sold

9 Plant and Intangible Assets

10 Liabilities

11 Stockholders' Equity: Paid-In Capital

14 Financial Statement Analysis

B The Time Value of Money: Future Amounts and Present Values

Financial Accounting

THE BASIS FOR BUSINESS DECISIONS

Accounting
Information for Decision Making

Learning Objectives

AFTER STUDYING THIS CHAPTER, YOU SHOULD BE ABLE TO:

LO1 Discuss accounting as the language of business and the role of accounting information in making economic decisions.

LO2 Discuss the significance of accounting systems in generating reliable accounting information and understand the five components of internal control per COSO's *Internal Control–Integrated Framework.*

LO3 Explain the importance of financial accounting information for external parties—primarily investors and creditors—in terms of the objectives and the characteristics of that information.

LO4 Explain the importance of accounting information for internal parties—primarily management—in terms of the objectives and the characteristics of that information.

LO5 Discuss elements of the system of external and internal financial reporting that create integrity in the reported information.

LO6 Identify and discuss several professional organizations that play important roles in preparing and communicating accounting information.

LO7 Discuss the importance of personal competence, professional judgment, and ethical behavior on the part of accounting professionals.

LO8 Describe various career opportunities in accounting.

WORLDCOM, INC., AND MCI

WorldCom began in 1983 as a small company called **Long Distance Discount Services, Inc.**, in Jackson, Mississippi. Within 15 years it became one of the largest telecommunications companies in the world. In 2002, **WorldCom** filed the largest bankruptcy in U.S. history. **WorldCom** renamed itself **MCI** and is in the process of being acquired by **Verizon Communications, Inc.** With more than 20 million business and residential customers, **MCI** has a workforce that includes 55,000 employees deployed around the world. **MCI** service spans six continents and over 200 countries.

How does a company as global and large as **WorldCom (MCI)** come under the careful scrutiny of federal bankruptcy regulators and the Securities and Exchange Commission (SEC)?

Acting on a hunch and a few tips, Cynthia Cooper and two other **WorldCom** internal auditors investigated the accounting practices at **WorldCom**. What they found—that the company had artificially boosted profits—eventually led to charges by U.S. regulators that **WorldCom** committed fraud. Its management admitted it hid almost $4 billion of costs. The 2000 and 2001 **WorldCom** financial accounting statements had to be restated for adjustments to revenue, expenses, and earnings as well as write-downs of assets and adjustments to liabilities resulting in a cumulative net reduction of *$74.4 billion* to previously reported income numbers. The scandal pushed the now defunct **WorldCom** stock to an all-time low of just a few cents after being over $60 per share at one point.

SOURCE: "Special Report—The Best and Worst Managers," *BusinessWeek*, January 13, 2003. Reprinted by permission © 2003 by The McGraw-Hill Companies, Inc., and **www.mci.com**.

Understanding and using accounting information is an important ingredient of any business undertaking. Terms such as sales revenue, net income, cost, expense, operating margin, and cash flow have clearly defined meanings and are commonly used in business-related communications. Although the precise meaning of these terms may be unfamiliar to you at this point, to become an active participant in the business world, you must gain a basic understanding of these and other accounting concepts. Our objective in this book is to provide those who both use and prepare accounting information with that basic understanding.

Information that is provided to external parties who have an interest in a company is sometimes referred to as financial accounting information. Information used internally by management and others is commonly referred to as managerial accounting information. Whereas these two types of information have different purposes and serve different audiences, they have certain attributes in common. This text focuses on and introduces you to financial accounting concepts that are critical in order to understand the financial condition of a business enterprise. The situation described in the chapter opener involving **WorldCom, Inc.**, is an example of the importance of providing reliable financial accounting information to investors and creditors. Determining a company's net income by subtracting its expenses from its revenue is a particularly important part of financial reporting today. This may appear to be a simple process of keeping accounting records and preparing reports from those records, but a great deal of judgment is required. For example, when should the cost of acquiring a resource that is used for several years be recognized as an expense in the company's financial statements? How should information be packaged and presented for maximum understanding by those with a financial interest in the company? What information is particularly useful for management, but not appropriate for public distribution because of the potential competitive disadvantage that might result? These are among the many complex issues that business faces on a day-to-day basis and which have a critical impact on the company's responsibility to its owners, creditors, the government, and society in general.

As we begin the study of financial accounting, keep in mind that business does not exist solely to earn a return for its investors and creditors that supply a company's financial resources. As shown by the chapter opener, business also has a responsibility to operate in a socially responsible manner and to balance its desire for financial success within this broader social responsibility. We begin our development of these ideas in this chapter, and continue their emphasis throughout this text.

Accounting Information: A Means to an End

The primary objective of accounting is to provide information that is useful for decision-making purposes. From the very start, we emphasize that accounting is *not an end*, but rather it is *a means to an end*. The final product of accounting information is the decision that is enhanced by the use of that information, whether the decision is made by owners, management, creditors, governmental regulatory bodies, labor unions, or the many other groups that have an interest in the financial performance of an enterprise.

LO1 Discuss accounting as the language of business and the role of accounting information in making economic decisions.

Because accounting is widely used to describe all types of business activity, it is sometimes referred to as the *language of business*. Costs, prices, sales volume, profits, and return on investment are all accounting measurements. Investors, creditors, managers, and others who have a financial interest in an enterprise need a clear understanding of accounting terms and concepts if they are to understand and communicate about the enterprise. While our primary orientation in this text is the use of accounting information in business, from time to time we emphasize that accounting information is also used by governmental agencies, nonprofit organizations, and individuals in much the same manner as it is by business organizations.

ACCOUNTING FROM A USER'S PERSPECTIVE

Many people think of accounting as simply a highly technical field practiced only by professional accountants. In reality, nearly everyone uses accounting information daily.

Accounting information is the means by which we measure and communicate economic events. Whether you manage a business, make investments, or monitor how you receive and use your money, you are working with accounting concepts and accounting information.

Our primary goal in this book is to develop your ability to understand and use accounting information in making economic decisions. To do this, you need to understand the following:

- The nature of economic activities that accounting information describes.
- The assumptions and measurement techniques involved in developing accounting information.
- The information that is most relevant for making various types of decisions.

Exhibit 1–1 illustrates how economic activities flow into the accounting process. The accounting process produces accounting information used by decision makers in making economic decisions and taking specific actions. These decisions and actions result in economic activities that continue the cycle.

Exhibit 1–1
THE ACCOUNTING PROCESS

Accounting links decision makers with economic activities—and with the results of their decisions

TYPES OF ACCOUNTING INFORMATION

Just as there are many types of economic decisions, there are also many types of accounting information. The terms *financial accounting, management accounting*, and *tax accounting* often are used in describing three types of accounting information that are widely used in the business community.

Financial Accounting

Financial accounting refers to information describing the financial resources, obligations, and activities of an economic entity (either an organization or an individual). Accountants use the term *financial position* to describe an entity's financial resources and obligations at a point in time and the term *results of operations* to describe its financial activities during the year.

CASE IN POINT

In **Sony Corporation**'s 2004 financial statements to owners, financial position is presented as consisting of $88,777 million in assets (including cash, inventories, property, and equipment), with obligations against those assets of $61,951 million. This leaves $26,826 million as the owners' interest in those assets. In the same report, results of operations as measured by net income (which measures the excess of revenue over expenses) were $1,531 million for the year ending March 31, 2005.

Financial accounting information is designed primarily to assist investors and creditors in deciding where to place their scarce investment resources. Such decisions are important to society, because they determine which companies and industries will receive the financial resources necessary for growth.

Financial accounting information also is used by managers and in income tax returns. In fact, financial accounting information is used for so many different purposes that it often is called "general-purpose" accounting information.

Management Accounting

Management (or managerial) **accounting** involves the development and interpretation of accounting information intended *specifically to assist management* in operating the business. Managers use this information in setting the company's overall goals, evaluating the performance of departments and individuals, deciding whether to introduce a new line of products, and making virtually all types of managerial decisions.

A company's managers and employees constantly need information to run and control daily business operations. For example, they need to know the amount of money in the company's bank accounts; the types, quantities, and dollar amounts of merchandise in the company's warehouse; and the amounts owed to specific creditors. Much management accounting information is financial in nature but is organized in a manner relating directly to the decision at hand.

Tax Accounting

The preparation of income tax returns is a specialized field within accounting. To a great extent, tax returns are based on financial accounting information. However, the information often is adjusted or reorganized to conform with income tax reporting requirements. We introduce the idea of tax accounting information to contrast it with financial and management accounting information. Although tax information is important for a company's successful operations and is related to financial and management accounting information, it results from a different system and complies with specialized legal requirements that relate to a company's responsibility to pay an appropriate amount of taxes. Laws and regulations governing taxation are often different from those underlying the preparation of financial and management accounting information, so it should not be a surprise that the resulting figures and reports are different.

The most challenging aspect of **tax accounting** is not the preparation of an income tax return, but *tax planning*. Tax planning means anticipating the tax effects of business transactions and structuring these transactions in a manner that will minimize the income tax burden. Because the focus of this text is financial accounting, and because tax accounting is quite complex, we defer coverage of tax accounting subjects to subsequent accounting courses.

Accounting Systems

LO2 Discuss the significance of accounting systems in generating reliable accounting information and understand the five components of internal control per COSO's *Internal Control–Integrated Framework*.

An **accounting system** consists of the personnel, procedures, technology, and records used by an organization (1) to develop accounting information and (2) to communicate this information to decision makers. The design and capabilities of these systems vary greatly from one organization to another. In small businesses, accounting systems may consist of little more than a cash register, a checkbook, and an annual trip to an income tax preparer. In large businesses, accounting systems include computers, highly trained personnel, and accounting reports that affect the daily operations of every department. But in every case, the basic purpose of the accounting system remains the same: *to meet the organization's needs for information as efficiently as possible.*

Many factors affect the structure of the accounting system within a particular organization. Among the most important are (1) the company's *needs for accounting information* and (2) the *resources available* for operation of the system.

Describing accounting as an information system focuses attention on the information accounting provides, the users of the information, and the support for financial decisions that is provided by the information. These relationships are depicted in Exhibit 1–2. While some of the terms may not be familiar to you at this early point in your study of business and accounting, you will be introduced to them more completely as we proceed through this textbook and as you undertake other courses in business and accounting. Observe, however, that the information system produces the information presented in the middle of the diagram—financial position, profitability, and cash flows. This information meets the needs of users of the information—investors, creditors, managers, and so on—and supports many kinds of financial decisions—performance evaluation and resource allocation, among others. These relationships are consistent with what we have already learned—namely, that accounting information is intended to be useful for decision-making purposes.

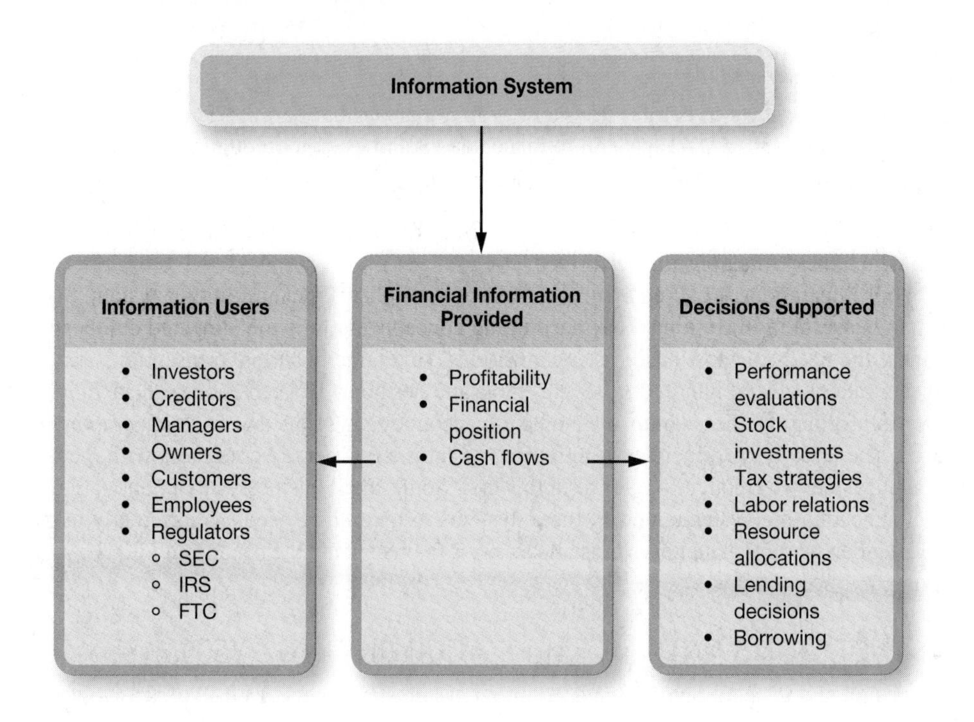

Exhibit 1–2
ACCOUNTING AS AN INFORMATION SYSTEM

DETERMINING INFORMATION NEEDS

The types of accounting information that a company develops vary with such factors as the size of the organization, whether it is publicly owned, and the information needs of management. The need for some types of accounting information may be prescribed by law. For example, income tax regulations require every business to have an accounting system that can measure the company's taxable income and explain the nature and source of every item in the company's income tax return. Federal securities laws require publicly owned companies to prepare financial statements in conformity with generally accepted accounting principles. These statements must be filed with the Securities and Exchange Commission, distributed to stockholders, and made available to the public.

Other types of accounting information are required as matters of practical necessity. For example, every business needs to know the amounts owed to it by each customer and the amounts owed by the company to each creditor, and uses generally accepted accounting principles for financial reporting.

Although much accounting information clearly is essential to business operations, management still has many choices as to the types and amount of accounting information to be developed. For example, should the accounting system of a department store measure separately the sales of each department and of different types of merchandise? The answer to such questions depends on *how useful* management considers the information to be and the *cost* of developing the information.

THE COST OF PRODUCING ACCOUNTING INFORMATION

Accounting systems must be *cost-effective*—that is, the value of the information produced should exceed the cost of producing it. Management has no choice but to produce the types of accounting reports required by law or contract. In other cases, however, management may use *cost-effectiveness* as a criterion for deciding whether or not to produce certain information.

In recent years, the development and installation of computer-based information systems have increased greatly the types and amount of accounting information that can be produced in a cost-effective manner.

BASIC FUNCTIONS OF AN ACCOUNTING SYSTEM

In developing information about the activities of a business, every accounting system performs the following basic functions:

1. *Interpret and record* the effects of business transactions.
2. *Classify* the effects of similar transactions in a manner that permits determination of the various *totals* and *subtotals* useful to management and used in accounting reports.
3. *Summarize and communicate* the information contained in the system to decision makers.

The differences in accounting systems arise primarily in the manner, frequency, and speed with which these functions are performed.

In our illustrations, we often assume the use of a simple manual accounting system. Such a system is useful in illustrating basic accounting concepts, but it is too slow and cumbersome to meet the needs of most business organizations. In a large business, transactions may occur at a rate of several hundred or several thousand per hour. To keep pace with such a rapid flow of information, these companies must use accounting systems that are largely computer-based. The underlying principles within these systems are generally consistent with the basic manual system we frequently refer to in this text. Some small businesses that continue to use manual accounting systems modify these systems to meet their needs as efficiently as possible. Understanding manual systems allows users to understand the needs that must be met in a computerized system.

WHO DESIGNS AND INSTALLS ACCOUNTING SYSTEMS?

The design and installation of large accounting systems is a specialized field. It involves not just accounting, but expertise in management, information systems, marketing, and—in many cases—computer programming. Thus accounting systems generally are designed and installed by a team of people with many specialized talents.

Large businesses have a staff of systems analysts, internal auditors, and other professionals who work full-time in designing and improving the accounting system. Medium-size companies often hire a CPA firm to design or update their systems. Small businesses with limited resources often purchase one of the many packaged accounting systems designed for small companies in their line of business. These packaged systems are available through office supply stores, computer stores, and software manufacturers.

COMPONENTS OF INTERNAL CONTROL[1]

In developing its accounting system, an organization also needs to be concerned with developing a sound system of internal control. **Internal control** is a process designed to provide reasonable assurance that the organization produces reliable financial reports, complies with applicable laws and regulations, and conducts its operations in an efficient and effective manner. A company's board of directors, its management, and other personnel are charged with developing and monitoring internal control. The five components of internal control, as discussed in *Internal Control-Integrated Framework* (Committee of Sponsoring

[1] The information in this section is taken from *Internal Control–Integrated Framework*, Committee of Sponsoring Organizations of the Treadway Commission, September 1992.

Organizations of the Treadway Commission), are the *control environment, risk assessment, control activities, information and communication*, and *monitoring*.

An organization's **control environment** is the foundation for all the other elements of internal control, setting the overall tone for the organization. Factors that affect a company's control environment are: (1) the integrity, ethical values, and competence of the company's personnel, (2) management's philosophy and operating style, (3) management's assignment of authority and responsibility, (4) procedures for the hiring and training of personnel, and (5) oversight by the board of directors. The control environment is particularly important because fraudulent financial reporting often results from an ineffective control environment.

Risk assessment involves identifying, analyzing, and managing those risks that pose a threat to the achievement of the organization's objectives. For example, a company should assess the risks that might prevent it from preparing reliable financial reports and then take steps to minimize those risks.

Control activities are the policies and procedures that management puts in place to address the risks identified during the risk assessment process. Examples of control activities include approvals, authorizations, verifications, reconciliations, reviews of operating performance, physical safeguarding of assets, and segregation of duties.

Information and communication involves developing information systems to capture and communicate operational, financial, and compliance-related information necessary to run the business. Effective information systems capture both internal and external information. In addition, an effective control system is designed to facilitate the flow of information downstream (from management to employees), upstream (from employees to management), and across the organization. Employees must receive the message that top management views internal control as important, and they must understand both their role in the internal control system and the roles of others.

All internal control systems need to be monitored. **Monitoring** enables the company to evaluate the effectiveness of its system of internal control over time. Monitoring is generally accomplished through ongoing management and supervisory activities, as well as by periodic separate evaluations of the internal control system. Most large organizations have an internal audit function, and the activities of internal audit represent separate evaluations of internal control.

As a result of the large financial frauds at **Enron** and **WorldCom** the U.S. Congress passed, and President George W. Bush signed, the **Sarbanes-Oxley Act** (SOX) of 2002. SOX has been described as the most far-reaching securities law since the 1930s. One of the SOX requirements is that public companies must issue a yearly report indicating whether they have an effective system of internal control over financial reporting. In essence, management must indicate whether the entity's internal control system provides reasonable assurance that financial statements will be prepared in accordance with laws and regulations governing financial reporting. In addition, the company's external auditor must issue its own report as to whether the auditor believes that the company's internal control system is effective. These requirements are contained in Section 404 of SOX; therefore, many businesspeople describe the above process as the 404 certification and the audit under Section 404. This certification process has been extremely expensive and time-consuming and some businesspeople believe that the costs associated with this certification requirement exceed the benefits.

Financial Accounting Information

Financial accounting is an important subject for students who need only an introduction to the field of accounting, as well as for students who will pursue accounting as a major and take many additional accounting courses. Financial accounting provides information about the financial resources, obligations, and activities of an enterprise that is intended for use primarily by external decision makers—investors and creditors.

Explain the importance of financial accounting information for external parties—primarily investors and creditors—in terms of the objectives and the characteristics of that information. LO3

EXTERNAL USERS OF ACCOUNTING INFORMATION

What do we mean by *external users* and who are they? **External users** of accounting information are individuals and other enterprises that have a current or potential financial interest in

the reporting enterprise, but that are not involved in the day-to-day operations of that enterprise. External users of financial information may include the following:

- Owners
- Creditors
- Potential investors
- Labor unions
- Governmental agencies
- Suppliers
- Customers
- Trade associations
- General public

Each of these groups of external decision makers requires unique information to be able to make decisions about the reporting enterprise. For example, customers who purchase from the enterprise need information to allow them to assess the quality of the products they buy and the faithfulness of the enterprise in fulfilling warranty obligations. Governmental agencies such as the Federal Trade Commission may have an interest in whether the enterprise meets certain governmental regulations that apply. The general public may be interested in the extent to which the reporting enterprise is socially responsible (for example, does not pollute the environment).

Providing information that meets the needs of such a large set of diverse users is difficult, if not impossible, in a single set of financial information. Therefore, external financial reporting is primarily used by two groups—investors and creditors. As you will soon see, investors are individuals and other enterprises that own the reporting enterprise. Creditors, on the other hand, are individuals and other enterprises to whom the reporting entity owes money, goods, or services. For example, a commercial bank may have loaned money to the reporting enterprise, or a supplier may have permitted the reporting enterprise to purchase goods and to pay for those goods later. Our assumption is that by meeting the financial information needs of investors and creditors, we provide information that is also useful to many other users of financial information.

For these reasons, we sometimes refer to investors and creditors as the primary external financial information users. When you see references like these, keep in mind that we are talking about both current investors and creditors and those individuals and other enterprises that may become investors and creditors in the future.

OBJECTIVES OF EXTERNAL FINANCIAL REPORTING

If you had invested in a company, or if you had loaned money to a company, what would be your primary financial interest in the company? You probably would be interested in two things, both of which make up the company's **cash flow prospects**. You would be interested in the return to you at some future date of the amount you had invested or loaned. We refer to this as the **return *of* your investment**. In addition, you would expect the company to pay you something for the use of your funds, either as an owner or a creditor. We refer to this as the **return *on* your investment**. Information that is useful to you in making judgments about the company's ability to provide you with what you expect in terms of the return *of* your funds as well as a return *on* your funds while you do not have use of them is what we mean by information about *cash flow prospects*.

Assume that you have a friend who wants to start a business and needs some help getting the money required to rent space and acquire the needed assets to operate the business (for

You as a Creditor

You are a loan officer at a bank that makes small loans to individuals to help finance purchases such as automobiles and appliances. You are considering an application from a young woman who needs to purchase a new car. She is requesting a loan of $10,000 which, when combined with the trade-in value of her old car, will allow her to meet her needs. What are your expectations with regard to repayment of the loan, and what information would help you decide whether she is a good credit risk for your bank?

(See our comments on the Online Learning Center Web site.)

example, delivery truck, display fixtures) and pay employees for their work before the doors open and customers begin paying for the products the company plans to sell. You are in a financially strong position and agree to loan your friend $100,000. Your intent is not to be a long-term investor or co-owner of the business, but rather to help your friend start his company and at the same time earn a return on the funds you have loaned him. Assume further that you agree to let your friend have the use of your $100,000 for one year and, if you had not loaned this amount to him, you could have earned an 8 percent return by placing your money in another investment.

In addition to wanting to help a friend, you are interested in knowing how much risk you are taking with regard to your $100,000. You expect your friend to pay that $100,000 back, and to also pay you an additional amount of $8,000 ($100,000 × 8%) for his use of your money. The total return of your investment ($100,000) back to you one year later, added to the amount you expect to receive for his having used your money for a year ($8,000), is shown in Exhibit 1–3.

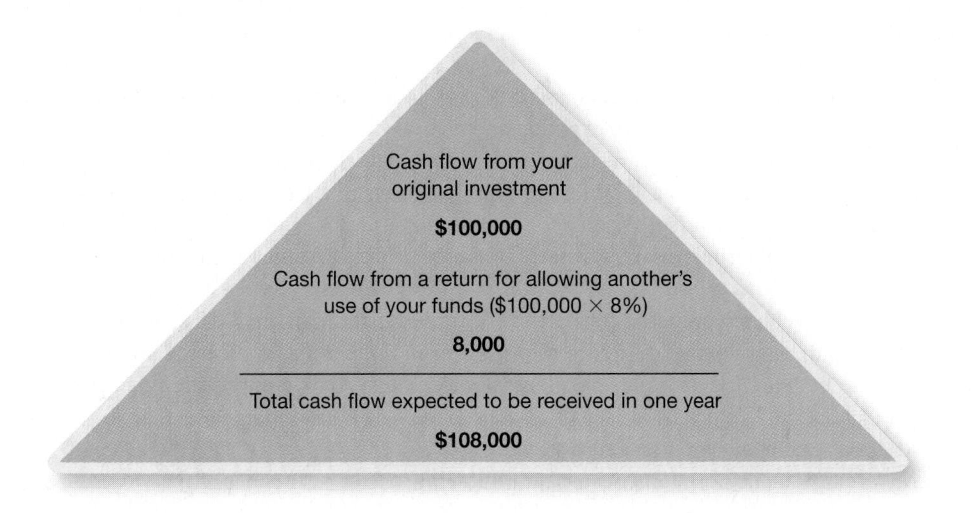

Exhibit 1–3
INVESTMENT ANALYSIS

Providing information for you to assess your friend's ability to meet his cash flow commitment to you is essentially what financial reporting is about. You need information to assess the risk you are taking and the prospects that your friend will be able to deliver $108,000 to you one year from the time you loan him the $100,000. While this is a relatively simple example, it sets the stage for your understanding of the kinds of information that will help you make this important investment decision.

The accounting profession has identified certain objectives of external financial reporting to guide its efforts to refine and improve the reporting of information to external decision makers. These general objectives are displayed in Exhibit 1–4 and are best understood if studied from the bottom up—from general to specific.[2]

The first objective is the most general and is to provide information that is useful in making investment and credit decisions. As we indicated earlier, investors and creditors are the primary focus of external financial reporting. We believe that, by meeting the information needs of investors and creditors, we provide general information that is also useful to many other important financial statement users.

The second objective, which is more specific than the first, is to provide information that is useful in assessing the amount, timing, and uncertainty of future cash flows. As we discussed earlier, investors and creditors are interested in future cash flows to them, so an important objective of financial reporting is to provide general information that permits that kind of analysis.

The most specific objective of external financial reporting is to provide information about the enterprise's resources, claims to those resources, and how both the resources and claims to

[2] FASB *Statement of Financial Accounting Concepts No. 1*, "Objectives of Financial Reporting by Business Enterprises" (Norwalk, Conn.: 1978), p. 4.

Exhibit 1–4

OBJECTIVES OF FINANCIAL REPORTING: BUILDING FROM THE GENERAL TO THE SPECIFIC

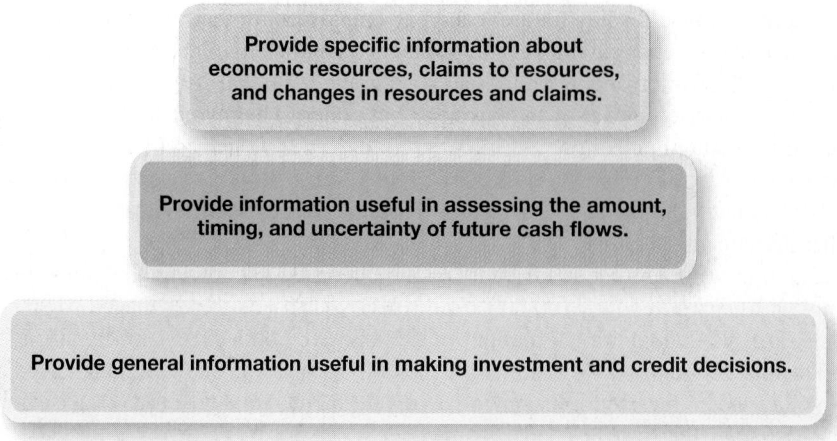

Provide specific information about economic resources, claims to resources, and changes in resources and claims.

Provide information useful in assessing the amount, timing, and uncertainty of future cash flows.

Provide general information useful in making investment and credit decisions.

resources change over time. An enterprise's resources are often referred to as *assets*, and the primary claims to those resources are the claims of creditors and owners, known as liabilities and owners equity.

One of the primary ways investors and creditors assess whether an enterprise will be able to make future cash payments is to examine and analyze the enterprise's financial statements. In the general sense of the word, a statement is simply a declaration of something believed to be true. A **financial statement**, therefore, is simply a monetary declaration of what is believed to be true about an enterprise. When accountants prepare financial statements, they are describing in financial terms certain attributes of the enterprise that they believe fairly represent its financial activities.

Financial statements prepared for periods of time shorter than one year (for example, for three months or one month) are referred to as *interim financial statements*. Throughout this text, we use both annual and interim financial statements. As you approach a company's financial statements—either as a user or as a preparer—it is important to establish the time period those statements are intended to cover.

The primary financial statements are the following:

- *Statement of financial position (balance sheet).* The **balance sheet** is a position statement that shows where the company stands in financial terms at a specific date.
- *Income statement.* The **income statement** is an activity statement that shows details and results of the company's profit-related activities for a period of time (for example, a month, quarter [three months], or year).
- *Statement of cash flows.* The **statement of cash flows** is an activity statement that shows the details of the company's activities involving cash during a period of time.

The names of the three primary financial statements are descriptive of the information you find in each. The **statement of financial position**, or balance sheet, for example, is sometimes described as a snapshot of the business in financial or dollar terms (that is, what the enterprise looks like at a specific date). An income statement is an activity statement that depicts the profitability of an enterprise for a designated period of time. The statement of cash flows is particularly important in understanding an enterprise for purposes of investment and credit decisions. As its name implies, the statement of cash flows depicts the ways cash has changed during a designated period. While the interest of investors and creditors is in cash flows to themselves rather than to the enterprise, information about cash activity of the enterprise is considered to be an important signal to investors and creditors.

At this early stage in your study of accounting, you are not expected to understand these financial statements or how they precisely help you assess the cash flow prospects of a company. The statement of financial position (balance sheet), income statement, and statement of cash flows are introduced more fully to you in the next chapter. Thereafter, you will learn a great deal about how these statements are prepared and how the information contained in them can be used to help you understand the underlying business activities they represent.

CHARACTERISTICS OF EXTERNALLY REPORTED INFORMATION

Financial information that is reported to investors, creditors, and others external to the reporting enterprise has certain qualities that must be understood for the information to have maximum usefulness. Some of these qualities are discussed in the following paragraphs.

Financial Reporting—A Means As we learned in the introduction to this chapter, financial information is a means to an end, not an end in and of itself. The ultimate outcome of providing financial information is to improve the quality of decision making by external parties. Financial statements themselves are simply a means by which that end is achieved.

Financial Reporting versus Financial Statements Financial reporting is broader than financial statements. Stated another way, financial statements are a subset of the total information encompassed by financial reporting. Investors, creditors, and other external users of financial information learn about an enterprise in a variety of ways in addition to its formal financial statements (for example, press releases sent directly to investors and creditors, articles in *The Wall Street Journal*, and more recently open communications via the Internet). Serious investors, creditors, and other external users take advantage of many sources of information that are available to support their economic decisions about an enterprise.

Historical in Nature Externally reported financial information is largely historical in nature. It looks back in time and reports the results of events and transactions that already have occurred. While historical information is very useful in assessing the future, the information itself is more about the past than it is about the future.

Inexact and Approximate Measures Externally reported financial information may have a look of great precision, but in fact much of it is based on estimates, judgments, and assumptions that must be made about both the past and the future. For example, assume a company purchases a piece of equipment for use in its business. To account for that asset and to incorporate the impact of it into the company's externally reported financial information, some assumptions must be made about how long it will be used by the company—how many years it will be used, how many machine-hours it will provide, and so on. The fact that a great deal of judgment underlies most accounting information is a limitation that is sometimes misunderstood.

General-Purpose Assumption As we have already mentioned, we assume that, by providing information that meets the needs of investors and creditors, we also meet the information needs of other external parties. We might be able to provide superior information if we were to treat each potential group of external users separately and prepare different information for each group. This approach is impractical, however, and we instead opt for preparing what is referred to as **general-purpose information** that we believe is useful to multiple user groups (that is, "one size fits all").

Usefulness Enhanced via Explanation The accounting profession believes that the value of externally reported financial information is enhanced by including explanations from management. This information is often nonquantitative and helps to interpret the financial numbers that are presented. For this reason, financial information, including financial statements, is accompanied by a number of notes and other explanations that help explain and interpret the numerical information.

Management Accounting Information

Explain the importance of accounting information for internal parties—primarily management—in terms of the objectives and the characteristics of that information. LO4

Internal decision makers employed by the enterprise, often referred to as management, create and use internal accounting information not only for exclusive use inside the organization but also to share with external decision makers. For example, in order to meet a production schedule, a producer may design an accounting information system for suppliers detailing its production plans. The producer shares this information with its supplier companies so that they can help the producer meet its objectives. Thus, although the creator and distributor of the accounting information is an internal decision maker, the recipient of the information is, in this case, an external decision maker. Other types of accounting information, however, are not made available to external decision makers. Long-range plans, research and development results, capital budget details, and competitive strategies typically are closely guarded corporate secrets.

USERS OF INTERNAL ACCOUNTING INFORMATION

Every employee of the enterprise uses internal accounting information. From basic labor categories to the chief executive officer (CEO), all employees are paid, and their paychecks are generated by the accounting information system. However, the amount of use and, in particular, the involvement in the design of accounting information systems vary considerably. Examples of **internal users** of accounting information systems are as follows:

- Board of directors
- Chief executive officer (CEO)
- Chief financial officer (CFO)
- Vice-presidents (information services, human resources, ethics, and so forth)
- Business unit managers
- Plant managers
- Store managers
- Line supervisors

Employees have different specific goals and objectives that are designed to help the enterprise achieve its overall strategies and mission. Looking at the typical, simple organization chart in Exhibit 1–5 you can see that the information created and used by various employees

Exhibit 1–5 **TYPICAL SIMPLE ORGANIZATION CHART**

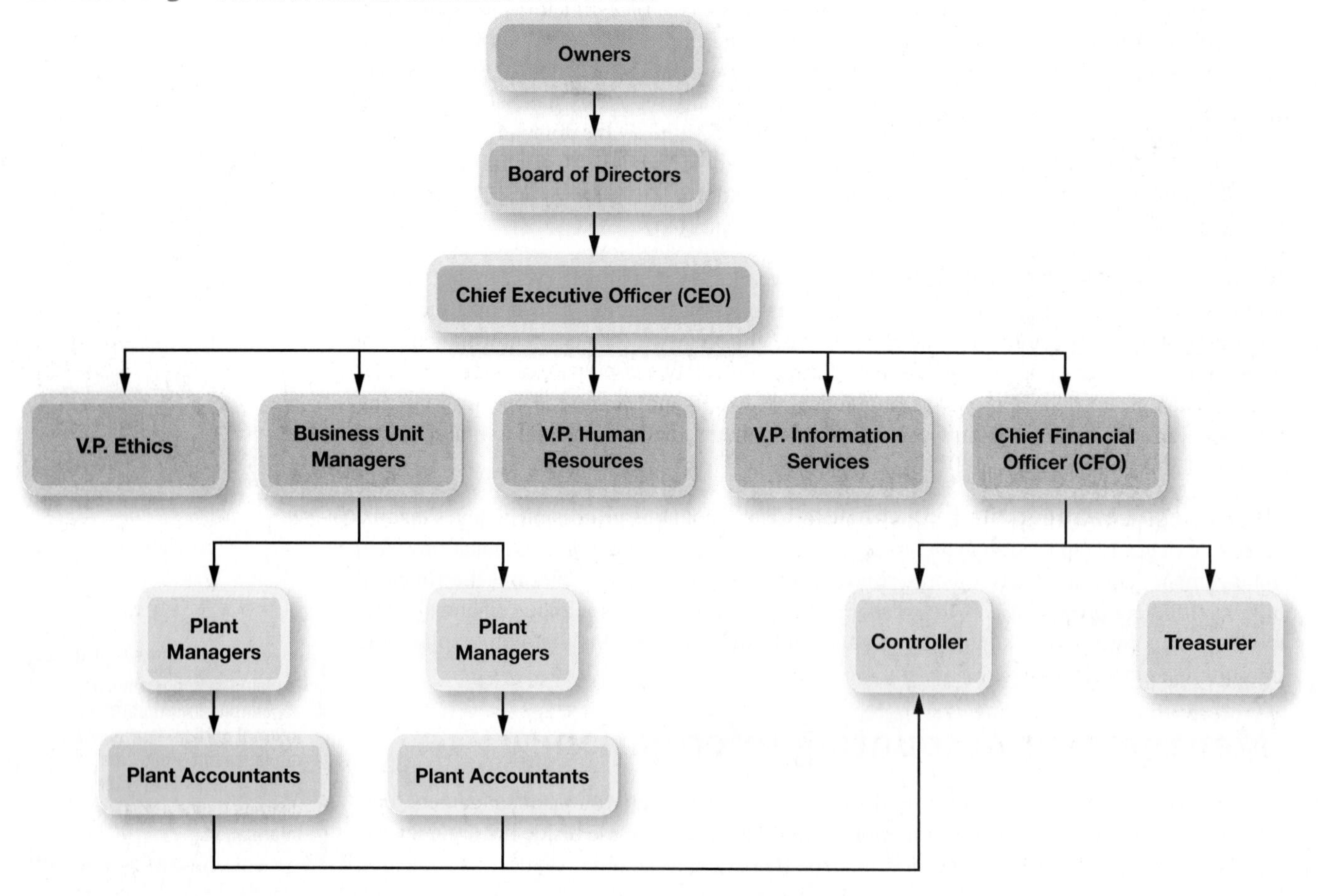

will differ widely. All enterprises follow rules about the design of their accounting information systems to ensure the integrity of accounting information and to protect the enterprise's assets. There are no rules, however, about the type of internal reports or the kind of accounting information that can be generated. A snapshot look inside a firm will demonstrate the diversity of accounting information generated and used in the decision-making processes of employees.

Many enterprises use a database warehousing approach for the creation of accounting information systems. This approach, coupled with user-friendly software, allows management and other designated employees access to information to create a variety of accounting reports, including required external financial reports. For example, detailed cost information about a production process is used by the production line supervisor to help control production costs. A process design engineer, when considering the best configuration of equipment and employees, uses the same information to reduce costs or to increase efficiency. Finally, production-related cost information appears in the external financial statements used by investors and creditors.

OBJECTIVES OF MANAGEMENT ACCOUNTING INFORMATION

Each enterprise has implicit and explicit goals and objectives. Many enterprises have a mission statement that describes their goals. These goals can vary widely among enterprises ranging from nonprofit organizations, where goals are aimed at serving specified constituents, to for-profit organizations, where goals are directed toward maximizing the owners' objectives. For example, the **American Cancer Society**, a nonprofit organization, has the following mission:

> The American Cancer Society is the nationwide community-based voluntary health organization dedicated to eliminating cancer as a major health problem by preventing cancer, saving lives, and diminishing suffering from cancer, through research, education, advocacy, and service.[3]

Procter & Gamble, a for-profit, global producer of consumer products, has the following purpose:

> We will provide branded products and services of superior quality and value that improve the lives of the world's consumers.[4]

Procter & Gamble's annual report to shareholders provides more detail on how the company will achieve its mission. The following growth strategies were identified in P&G's 2005 annual letter to its shareholders:

- Build existing core businesses into stronger global leaders.
- Grow leading brands, big countries, winning customers.
- Develop faster-growing, higher-margin, more asset-efficient businesses with global leadership potential.
- Regain growth momentum and leadership in Western Europe.
- Drive growth among lower-income consumers in developing markets.[5]

The Procter & Gamble Company

The constituents of these organizations receive external financial information that helps them assess the progress being made in achieving these goals and objectives. In the case of **Procter & Gamble**, quarterly and annual information is provided to shareholders. The **American Cancer Society** is required to report its activities and financial condition to regulators. Providing constituents evaluative information is only one objective of accounting systems.

Enterprises design and use their internal accounting information systems to help them achieve their stated goals and missions. Multiple reports, some as part of the normal reporting process and some that are specially constructed and designed, are produced and distributed regularly. To motivate managers to achieve organizational goals, the internal accounting system is also used to evaluate and reward decision-making performance. When the accounting system compares the plan or budget to the actual outcomes for a period, it creates a signal about the performance

[3] www.cancer.org

[4] www.pg.com

[5] Procter & Gamble, 2005 Annual Report, Letter to Shareholders.

of the employee responsible for that part of the budget. In many enterprises management creates a reward system linked to performance as measured by the accounting system.

Thus the objectives of accounting systems begin at the most general level with the objectives and mission of the enterprise. These general organizational goals create a need for information. The enterprise gathers historical and future information from both inside the enterprise and external sources. This information is used by the decision makers who have authority over the firm's resources and who will be evaluated and rewarded based on their decision outcomes.

CHARACTERISTICS OF MANAGEMENT ACCOUNTING INFORMATION

The accounting information created and used by management is intended primarily for planning and control decisions. Because the goal of creating and using management accounting information differs from the reasons for producing externally reported financial information, its characteristics are different.

Both the processes used to create financial accounting reports and the structure of those reports significantly impact management strategy. For example, because external financial reporting standards require companies to include pension-related obligations on their financial statements, management monitors those obligations closely. These pension-related obligations impact labor negotiations and labor-related corporate strategies.

Another example is that the processes necessary to create required external financial reports have historically determined the type of accounting information available inside of companies for internal decision making. Most plants within companies are organized as profit centers where plant-related financial statements mirror those necessary for external reporting purposes.

As you read the chapters of this book, we will remind you about how financial reporting has an impact on and is impacted by management strategies. The following paragraphs identify internal accounting information characteristics.

Importance of Timeliness In order to plan for and control ongoing business processes, accounting information needs to be timely. The competitive environment faced by many enterprises demands immediate access to information. Enterprises are responding to this demand by creating computerized databases that link to external forecasts of industry associations, to their suppliers and buyers, and to their constituents. Time lines for the development and launch of new products and services are becoming shorter and shorter, making quick access to information a priority.

In addition to needing timely information for planning purposes, enterprises are constantly monitoring and controlling ongoing activities. If a process or activity goes out of control, the enterprise can incur significant costs. For example, recalls of products can be very expensive for a company. If the company can monitor processes and prevent low-quality or defective products from reaching its customers, it can experience significant savings.

Identity of Decision Maker Information that is produced to monitor and control processes needs to be provided to those who have decision-making authority to correct problems. Reporting scrap and rework information to line workers without providing them the responsibility for fixing the process is counterproductive. However, a self-directed work team that has been assigned decision-making responsibility over equipment and work-related activities can have a significant impact on rework and scrap if team members control the process causing the problems.

Oriented toward the Future Although some accounting information, like financial accounting information, is historical in nature, the purpose in creating and generating it is to affect the future. The objective is to motivate management to make future decisions that are in the best interest of the enterprise, consistent with its goals, objectives, and mission.

Measures of Efficiency and Effectiveness Accounting information measures the efficiency and effectiveness of resource usage. By comparing the enterprise's resource inputs and outputs with measures of competitors' effectiveness and efficiency, an assessment can be made of how effective management is in achieving the organization's mission. The accounting system uses money as a common unit to achieve these types of comparisons.

Management Accounting Information—A Means As with financial accounting information, management accounting information is a means to an end, not an end in and of itself. The ultimate objective is to design and use an accounting system that helps management achieve the goals and objectives of the enterprise.

Integrity of Accounting Information

What enables investors and creditors to rely on financial accounting information without fear that the management of the reporting enterprise has altered the information to make the company's performance look better than it actually was? How can management be sure that internally generated information is free from bias that might favor one outcome over another? The word **integrity** refers to the following qualities: complete, unbroken, unimpaired, sound, honest, and sincere. Accounting information must have these qualities because of the significance of the information to individuals who rely on it in making important financial decisions.

LO5 Discuss elements of the system of external and internal financial reporting that create integrity in the reported information.

The integrity of accounting information is enhanced in three primary ways. First, certain institutional features add significantly to the integrity of accounting information. These features include standards for the preparation of accounting information, an internal control structure, and audits of financial statements. Second, several professional accounting organizations play unique roles in adding to the integrity of accounting information. Finally, and perhaps most important, is the personal competence, judgment, and ethical behavior of professional accountants. These three elements of the accounting profession come together to ensure that users of accounting information—investors, creditors, managers, and others—can rely on the information to be a fair representation of what it purports to represent.

INSTITUTIONAL FEATURES

Standards for the Preparation of Accounting Information Accounting information that is communicated externally to investors, creditors, and other users, must be prepared in accordance with standards that are understood by both the preparers and users of that information. We call these standards **generally accepted accounting principles**, often shortened to GAAP. These principles provide the general framework for determining what information is included in financial statements and how this information is to be prepared and presented. GAAP includes broad principles of measurement and presentation, as well as detailed rules that are used by professional accountants in preparing accounting information and reports.

Accounting principles are not like physical laws; they do not exist in nature waiting to be discovered. Rather, they are developed by people, in light of what we consider to be the most important objectives of financial reporting. In many ways accounting principles are similar to the rules established for an organized sport, such as baseball or basketball. For example, accounting principles, like sports rules:

- Originate from a combination of tradition, experience, and official decree.
- Require authoritative support and some means of enforcement.
- Are sometimes arbitrary.
- May change over time as shortcomings in the existing rules come to light.
- Must be clearly understood and observed by all participants in the process.

Accounting principles vary somewhat from country to country. The phrase "generally accepted accounting principles" refers to the accounting concepts in use in the United States. However, the principles in use in Canada, Great Britain, and a number of other countries are quite similar. Also, foreign companies that raise capital from American investors usually issue financial statements in conformity with generally accepted accounting principles.

The International Accounting Standards Board (IASB) is currently attempting to establish greater uniformity among the accounting principles in use around the world in order to facilitate business activity that increasingly is carried out in more than one country.

In the United States two organizations are particularly important in establishing generally accepted accounting principles—the Financial Accounting Standards Board (FASB) and the Securities and Exchange Commission (SEC).

Financial Accounting Standards Board Today, the most authoritative source of generally accepted accounting principles is the **Financial Accounting Standards Board**. The FASB is an independent rule-making body, consisting of seven members from the accounting profession, industry, government, and accounting education. Lending support to these members are an advisory council and a large research staff.

The FASB is authorized to issue *Statements of Financial Accounting Standards* (and other authoritative accounting pronouncements), which represent official expressions of generally accepted accounting principles.

In addition to issuing authoritative *Statements*, the FASB has completed a project describing a *conceptual framework* for financial reporting. This conceptual framework sets forth the FASB's views as to the:

- Objectives of financial reporting.
- Desired characteristics of accounting information (such as relevance, reliability, and understandability).
- Elements of financial statements.
- Criteria for deciding what information to include in financial statements.
- Valuation concepts relating to financial statement amounts.

The primary purpose of the conceptual framework is to provide guidance to the FASB in developing new accounting standards. By making each new standard consistent with this framework, the FASB believes that its official *Statements* resolve accounting problems in a logical and consistent manner.

The FASB is part of the private sector of the economy—*it is not a governmental agency.* The development of accounting principles in the United States traditionally has been carried out in the private sector, although the government, acting through the SEC, exercises considerable influence.

International Accounting Standards Board When an enterprise operates beyond the borders of its own country, differences in financial reporting practices between countries can pose significant problems. For example, when a company buys or sells products in another country, the lack of comparability of accounting information can create uncertainties. Similarly, cross-border financing where companies sell their securities in the capital markets of another country, is increasingly popular. Business activities that cross borders create the need for more comparable information between companies that reside in different countries.

As a result of increasing cross-border activities, efforts are under way to harmonize accounting standards around the world. The **International Accounting Standards Board (IASB)** is playing a leading role in the harmonization process. The London-based IASB is an elite panel of 14 professionals with deep knowledge of accounting methods used in the most vibrant capital markets. The objectives of the IASB as stated in its constitution are:

> (a) to develop, in the public interest, a single set of high quality, understandable and enforceable global accounting standards that require high quality, transparent and comparable information in financial statements and other financial reporting to help participants in the world's capital markets and other users make economic decisions;
> (b) to promote the use and rigorous application of those standards; and
> (c) to bring about convergence of national accounting standards and International Accounting Standards and International Financial Reporting Standards to high quality solutions.

The IASB issues *International Financial Reporting Standards (IFRSs).* Many countries' stock exchange listing requirements or national securities legislation permit foreign companies that issue securities in those countries to prepare their consolidated financial statements using IFRSs, including Australia, Germany, and the United Kingdom. However, certain countries do not permit companies to use IFRSs without a reconciliation to domestic generally accepted accounting principles. Most notable among these countries are Canada, Hong Kong, Japan, and the United States.

CASE IN POINT

The European Union (EU) has decided that for each financial year starting on or after January 1, 2005, companies governed by the law of an EU member state shall use *International Financial Reporting Standards (IFRSs)* if their securities are traded on a regulated market of any member state. As a result, the European Commission has called for the 7,000 listed companies in its 15 member states to follow IASB standards by 2005. The U.S. Congress, appalled by **Enron** and other scandals, has directed U.S. regulators to work with the IASB to improve U.S. generally accepted accounting principles (GAAP). The FASB and the IASB have agreed to work toward harmonization.

Securities and Exchange Commission The **Securities and Exchange Commission** is a governmental agency with the *legal power* to establish accounting principles and financial reporting requirements for publicly owned corporations. In the past, the SEC has generally adopted the recommendations of the FASB, rather than develop its own set of accounting principles. Thus accounting principles continue to be developed in the private sector but are given the *force of law* when they are adopted by the SEC.

To ensure widespread acceptance of new accounting standards, the FASB *needs the support* of the SEC. Therefore, the two organizations work closely together in developing new accounting standards. The SEC also reviews the financial statements of publicly owned corporations to ensure compliance with its reporting requirements. In the event that a publicly owned corporation fails to comply with these requirements, the SEC may initiate legal action against the company and the responsible individuals. Thus the SEC enforces compliance with generally accepted accounting principles that are established primarily by the FASB.

Public Company Accounting Oversight Board The **Public Company Accounting Oversight Board (PCAOB)** is a quasi-governmental body charged with oversight of the public accounting profession. The Board was created as a result of the Sarbanes-Oxley Act of 2002 and began operations in the spring of 2003.

The PCAOB has extensive powers in overseeing the accounting profession. Any accounting firm wishing to audit a public company must register with the PCAOB. The PCAOB sets auditing standards for audits of publicly traded companies, an activity that previously was performed by the accounting profession. The Board also will inspect the quality of audits performed by public accounting firms and will conduct investigations and administer penalties when substandard audit work is alleged.

The PCAOB is headquartered in Washington, D.C., and has regional offices in major cities throughout the United States. The PCAOB has five members who serve a five-year term and are eligible to be reappointed once. No more than two members of the Board can be certified public accountants. The Board also maintains a large and well-qualified staff. The PCAOB is funded by a mandatory assessment on publicly traded companies. The assessment is a function of the company's market value relative to overall stock market value in the United States.

The PCAOB has only issued a few auditing standards to date. Although it is premature to draw any firm conclusions, the auditing standards already issued by the Board are longer and more detailed than the auditing standards typically issued by the accounting profession. In the view of the authors, the public accounting profession and audits of public companies are likely to be significantly impacted as a result of the activities of the PCAOB.

Audits of Financial Statements What assurance do outsiders have that the financial statements issued by management provide a complete and reliable picture of the company's financial position and operating results? In large part, this assurance is provided by an *audit* of the company's financial statements, performed by a firm of *certified public accountants (CPAs)*. These auditors are experts in the field of financial reporting and are *independent* of the company issuing the financial statements.

An **audit** is an *investigation* of a company's financial statements, designed to determine the fairness of these statements. Accountants and auditors use the term *fair* in describing financial statements that are reliable and complete, conform to generally accepted accounting principles, and are *not misleading*.

In auditing financial statements, generally accepted accounting principles are the standard by which those statements are judged. For the auditor to reach the conclusion that the financial statements are fair representations of a company's financial position, results of operations, and cash flows, the statements must comply in all important ways with generally accepted accounting principles.

Legislation As discussed previously, Congress passed the Sarbanes-Oxley Act in 2002. Among the more important provisions of Sarbanes-Oxley is the creation of the Public Company Accounting Oversight Board described earlier in this chapter. Another important provision of the Act is to ban auditors from providing many nonaudit services for their audit clients on an assumption that those services interfere with the objectivity required of auditors in rendering opinions regarding financial statements upon which investors and creditors rely. Sarbanes-Oxley also places additional responsibilities on corporate boards of directors and audit committees with regard to their oversight of external auditors, and it places responsibility on chief executive officers and chief financial officers of companies to certify the fairness of the company's financial statements.

PROFESSIONAL ORGANIZATIONS

LO6 Identify and discuss several professional organizations that play important roles in preparing and communicating accounting information.

Several professional accounting organizations play an active role in improving the quality of accounting information that is used by investors, creditors, management, and others. In addition to the Financial Accounting Standards Board and the Securities and Exchange Commission, discussed earlier, the American Institute of CPAs, the Institute of Management Accountants, the Institute of Internal Auditors, the American Accounting Association, and the Committee of Sponsoring Organizations of the Treadway Commission are particularly important.

American Institute of CPAs (AICPA) The **American Institute of CPAs** is a professional association of certified public accountants. Its mission is to provide members with the resources, information, and leadership to enable them to provide valuable services in the highest professional manner to benefit the public, employers, and clients. The AICPA participates in many aspects of the accounting profession. The AICPA conducts accounting research and works closely with the FASB in the establishment and interpretation of generally accepted accounting principles. In fact, prior to the establishment of the FASB, the AICPA had primary responsibility for the establishment of accounting principles. The AICPA's Auditing Standards Board has developed the standards by which audits of private companies are conducted, and the PCAOB has accepted most of these standards for audits of public companies. The AICPA also issues standards for the conduct of other professional services. Finally, the AICPA is responsible for the preparation and grading of the CPA examination, which is discussed later in this chapter.

Institute of Management Accountants (IMA) The mission of the **Institute of Management Accountants** is to provide members personal and professional development opportunities through education, association with business professionals, and certification. The IMA is recognized by the financial community as a respected organization that influences the concepts and ethical practice of management accounting and financial management. The IMA sponsors a number of educational activities for its members, including national seminars and conferences, regional and local programs, self-study courses, and in-house and online programs. Two certification programs are available through the IMA—the Certificate in Management Accounting (CMA) and the Certificate in Financial Management (CFM). These designations testify to the individual's competence and expertise in management accounting and financial management.

Institute of Internal Auditors (IIA) With more than 110,000 members in 165 countries, the **Institute of Internal Auditors** is the primary international professional association dedicated to the promotion and development of the practice of internal auditing. It provides professional development through the Certified Internal Auditor® Program and leading-edge conferences and seminars; research through the IIA Research Foundation on trends, best practices, and other internal auditing issues; guidance through the *Standards for the Professional Practice of Internal Auditing*; and educational products on virtually all aspects of the profession. The IIA also provides audit specialty services and industry-specific auditing programs, as well as quality assurance reviews and benchmarking services.

American Accounting Association (AAA)

Membership in the **American Accounting Association** is made up primarily of accounting educators, although many practicing accountants are members as well. The mission of the AAA includes advancing accounting education and research, as well as influencing accounting practice. The focus of many of the AAA's activities is on improving accounting education by better preparing accounting professors and on advancing knowledge in the accounting discipline through research and publication. An important contribution of the AAA to the integrity of accounting information is its impact through accounting faculty on the many students who study accounting in college and subsequently become professional accountants.

Committee of Sponsoring Organizations of the Treadway Commission (COSO)

COSO is a voluntary private sector organization dedicated to improving the quality of financial reporting through business ethics, effective internal controls, and corporate governance. COSO was originally formed in 1985 to sponsor the National Commission on Fraudulent Financial Reporting (chaired by former SEC Commissioner James C. Treadway, Jr.). The National Commission on Fraudulent Financial Reporting studied the causal factors that lead to fraudulent financial reporting and made a series of recommendations for improving financial reporting, auditing, and accounting education. The original sponsors of the National Commission on Fraudulent Financial Reporting, and the current sponsors of COSO, are the AAA, the AICPA, Financial Executives International, the IIA, and the IMA.

COSO is best known for its work in developing the standards for evaluating internal control—particularly internal control over financial reporting. As a result of the Sarbanes-Oxley Act, public companies now need to evaluate the effectiveness of their internal control over financial reporting on a yearly basis, as well as have their auditors separately report on the auditors' evaluation of the effectiveness of internal control over financial reporting. The standard for evaluating the effectiveness of internal control over financial reporting is contained in COSO's 1992 publication, *Internal Control–Integrated Framework*. More recently, in October 2005, COSO issued an exposure draft of a document (*Guidance for Smaller Public Companies Reporting on Internal Control Over Financial Reporting*) that seeks to provide implementation guidance to smaller businesses in applying the original COSO internal control framework.

COMPETENCE, JUDGMENT, AND ETHICAL BEHAVIOR

Discuss the importance of personal competence, professional judgment, and ethical behavior on the part of accounting professionals. (LO7)

Preparing and presenting accounting information is not a mechanical task that can be performed entirely by a computer or even by well-trained clerical personnel. A characteristic common to all recognized professions, including medicine, law, and accounting, is the need for competent individual practitioners to solve problems using their professional judgment and applying strong ethical standards. The problems encountered in the practice of a profession are often complex, and the specific circumstances unique. In many cases, the well-being of others is directly affected by the work of a professional.

To illustrate the importance of competence, professional judgment, and ethical behavior in the preparation of financial statements, consider the following complex issues that must be addressed by the accountant:

- At what point have certain complex transactions actually taken place, thereby making it necessary to include them in financial statements that are sent to investors and creditors?
- At what point should an enterprise account for transactions that continue over a long period of time, such as a long-term contract to construct an interstate highway?
- What constitutes adequate disclosure of information that would be expected by a reasonably informed user of financial statements?

- At what point are a company's financial problems sufficient to question whether it will be able to remain in business for the foreseeable future, and when should that information be communicated to users of its financial statements?
- When have efforts by management to improve (that is, "window dress") its financial statements crossed a line that is inappropriate, making the financial statements actually misleading to investors and creditors?

Judgment always involves some risk of error. Some errors in judgment result from carelessness or inexperience on the part of the preparer of financial information or the decision maker who uses that information. Others occur simply because future events are uncertain and do not work out as expected when the information was prepared.

If the public is to have confidence in the judgment of professional accountants, these accountants first must demonstrate that they possess the characteristic of *competence.* Both the accounting profession and state governments have taken steps to assure the public of the technical competence of **certified public accountants** (CPAs). CPAs are licensed by the states, in much the same manner as states license physicians and attorneys. The licensing requirements vary somewhat from state to state, but in general, an individual must be of good character, have a college education with a major in accounting, pass a rigorous examination, and have accounting experience. In addition, most states require all CPAs to spend at least 40 hours per year in continuing professional education throughout their careers.

Beginning in the year 2000, the AICPA has required its new members to have completed 150 semester hours of college work. This represents about one additional year beyond a bachelor's degree, which usually requires approximately 120–125 semester hours. Most states have changed their licensing requirements to reflect this expectation of better-educated entrants into the accounting profession.

Management accountants are not required to be licensed as CPAs. However, they voluntarily may earn a **Certificate in Management Accounting** (CMA) or a **Certificate in Internal Auditing** (CIA) as evidence of their professional competence. These certificates are issued by the IMA and the IIA, and signify competence in management accounting and internal auditing, respectively. The requirements for becoming a CMA and CIA are similar to those for becoming a CPA.

Integrity in accounting requires honesty and a strong commitment to ethical conduct—doing the right thing. For a professional accountant, ethical behavior is just as important as competence. However, it is far more difficult to test or enforce.

Many professional organizations have codes of ethics or professional conduct that direct the activities of their members. The AICPA, for example, has a code of professional conduct that expresses the accounting profession's recognition of its responsibilities to the public, to clients, and to colleagues. The principles included in the code guide AICPA members in the performance of their professional responsibilities. This code expresses the basic tenets of ethical and professional behavior and is enforced in conjunction with state professional societies of CPAs, although state regulatory boards take precedence in regulating the CPA license.

YOUR TURN **You as a Professional Accountant**

You are a professional accountant working for a public accounting firm and find yourself in a difficult situation. You have discovered some irregularities in the financial records of your firm's client. You are uncertain whether these irregularities are the result of carelessness on the part of the company's employees or represent intentional steps taken to cover up questionable activities. You approach your superior about this and she indicates that you should ignore it. Her response is, "These things happen all of the time and usually are pretty minor. We are on a very tight time schedule to complete this engagement, so let's just keep our eyes on our goal of finishing our work by the end of the month." What would you do?

(See our comments on the Online Learning Center Web site.)

Exhibit 1–6 contains excerpts from the AICPA code of professional conduct. One of the principles expressed in the AICPA's code of professional conduct is the commitment of CPAs to the public interest, shown in Article II. The public interest is defined as the collective well-being of the community of people and institutions the profession serves. Other principles emphasize the importance of integrity, objectivity, independence, and due care in the performance of one's duties.

Exhibit 1–6

EXCERPTS FROM THE AICPA CODE OF PROFESSIONAL CONDUCT

Preamble

These Principles of the Code of Professional Conduct of the American Institute of Certified Public Accountants express the profession's recognition of its responsibilities to the public, to clients, and to colleagues. They guide members in the performance of their professional responsibilities and express the basic tenets of ethical and professional conduct. The Principles call for an unswerving commitment to honorable behavior, even at the sacrifice of personal advantage.

Articles

I. Responsibilities

In carrying out their responsibilities as professionals, members should exercise sensitive professional and moral judgments in all their activities.

II. The Public Interest

Members should accept the obligation to act in a way that will serve the public interest, honor the public trust, and demonstrate commitment to professionalism.

III. Integrity

To maintain and broaden public confidence, members should perform all professional responsibilities with the highest sense of integrity.

IV. Objectivity and Independence

A member should maintain objectivity and be free of conflicts of interest in discharging professional responsibilities. A member in public practice should be independent in fact and appearance when providing auditing and other attestation services.

V. Due Care

A member should observe the profession's technical and ethical standards, strive continually to improve competence and the quality of service, and discharge professional responsibility to the best of the member's ability.

VI. Scope and Nature of Services

A member in public practice should observe the Principles of the Code of Professional Conduct in determining the scope and nature of services to be provided.

Expectations of ethical conduct are also important for other accountants. The code of ethics of the IMA, for example, includes the following requirements:

- *Competence*. Management accountants should be professionally competent to perform their duties of providing relevant and reliable information in accordance with relevant laws, regulations, and technical standards.
- *Confidentiality*. Management accountants should refrain from disclosing confidential information or using confidential information to their own advantage.
- *Integrity*. Management accountants should avoid conflicts of interest by refusing compromising gifts and favors, by refusing to subvert organizational objectives, by refusing to communicate biased information, and by avoiding activities that could discredit the profession.
- *Credibility*. Management accountants should communicate information fairly and objectively and disclose all relevant information.

Users of accounting information—both external and internal—recognize that the reliability of the information is affected by the competence, professional judgment, and ethical standards of accountants. While the institutional features and professional organizations that were discussed earlier are important parts of the financial reporting system, the personal attributes of competence, professional judgment, and ethical behavior ultimately ensure the quality and reliability of accounting information.

In this text, we address the topic of ethical conduct primarily through questions, exercises, problems, and cases that emphasize the general concepts of honesty, fairness, and adequate disclosure. Most chapters include assignment material in which you are asked to make judgment calls in applying these concepts. (These assignments are identified by the scales of justice logo appearing in the margin.)

Careers in Accounting

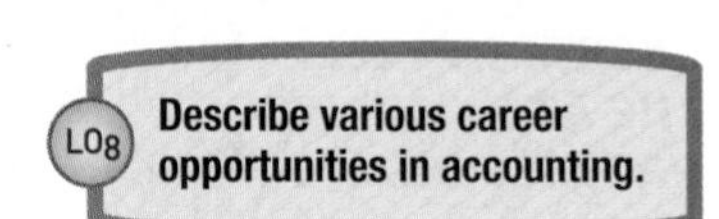

Accounting—along with such fields as architecture, engineering, law, medicine, and theology—is recognized as a profession. What distinguishes a profession from other disciplines? There is no single recognized definition of a profession, but all of these fields have several characteristics in common.

First, all professions involve a complex and evolving body of knowledge. In accounting, the complexity and the ever-changing nature of the business world, financial reporting requirements, management's demands for increasingly complex information, and income tax laws certainly meet this criterion.

Second, in all professions, practitioners must use their professional judgment to resolve problems and dilemmas. Throughout this text, we will point out situations requiring accountants to exercise professional judgment.

Of greatest importance, however, is the unique responsibility of professionals *to serve the public's best interest, even at the sacrifice of personal advantage*. This responsibility stems from the fact that the public has little technical knowledge in the professions, yet fair and competent performance by professionals is vital to the public's health, safety, or well-being. The practice of medicine, for example, directly affects public health, while engineering affects public safety. Accounting affects the public's well-being in many ways, because accounting information is used in the allocation of economic resources throughout society. Thus accountants have a basic social contract to avoid being associated with misleading information.

Accountants tend to specialize in specific fields, as do the members of other professions. Career opportunities in accounting may be divided into four broad areas: (1) public accounting, (2) management accounting, (3) governmental accounting, and (4) accounting education.

PUBLIC ACCOUNTING

Certified public accountants offer a variety of accounting services to the public. These individuals may work in a CPA firm or as sole practitioners.

The work of public accountants consists primarily of auditing financial statements, income tax work, and management advisory services (management consulting).

Management advisory services extend well beyond tax planning and accounting matters; CPAs advise management on such diverse issues as international mergers, manufacturing processes, and the introduction of new products. CPAs assist management because *financial considerations enter into almost every business decision*.

A great many CPAs move from public accounting into managerial positions with organizations. These "alumni" from public accounting often move directly into such top management positions as controller, treasurer, chief financial officer, or chief executive officer.

The CPA Examination To become a CPA, a person must meet several criteria, including an extensive university education requirement, passing the CPA examination, and meeting a practice experience requirement. CPA certificates are granted by 55 legal jurisdictions (50 U.S. states, Guam, Puerto Rico, the Virgin Islands, Washington, D.C., and the Mariana Islands). The CPA examination is a rigorous, two-day examination that covers a variety of accounting and business subjects that allow candidates to demonstrate their knowledge and skills in areas believed important for protecting the public.

Prior to 2004, the CPA examination was given in traditional paper-and-pencil form. Beginning in the spring of 2004, the examination was converted to a computer-based examination, and the content was updated to expand the breadth of coverage in both accounting and other business subjects. Candidates are no longer required to congregate in a single location twice a year, as was previously the case, but can now schedule the four-part examination at their convenience at one of the many testing centers at which the CPA exam is available. In addition to testing via computer a broader set of knowledge and skills, candidates are expected to be able to integrate their knowledge in different areas much like what is required of them in the business world. The computerization and expansion of the content of the CPA examination are important elements in protecting the public by licensing to practice only those individuals who have demonstrated a high level of knowledge and skill.

MANAGEMENT ACCOUNTING

In contrast to the public accountant who serves many clients, the management accountant works for one enterprise. Management accountants develop and interpret accounting information designed specifically to meet the various needs of management.

The chief accounting officer of an organization usually is called the *chief accounting officer (CAO)* or *controller*. The term *controller* has been used to emphasize the fact that one basic purpose of accounting data is to aid in controlling business operations. The CAO or controller is part of the top management team, which is responsible for running the business, setting its objectives, and seeing that these objectives are met.

In addition to developing information to assist managers, management accountants are responsible for operating the company's accounting system, including the recording of transactions and the preparation of financial statements, tax returns, and other accounting reports. Because the responsibilities of management accountants are so broad, many areas of specialization have developed. Among the more important are the following.

Financial Forecasting

A **financial forecast** (or budget) is a plan of financial operations for some *future* period. Actually, forecasting is much like financial reporting, except that the accountant is estimating future outcomes, rather than reporting past results. A forecast provides each department of a business with financial goals. Comparison of the results actually achieved with these forecast amounts is one widely used means of evaluating performance.

Cost Accounting

Knowing the cost of each business operation and of each manufactured product is essential to the efficient management of a business. Determining the per-unit cost of business activities and of manufactured products, and interpreting these cost data, comprise a specialized field called **cost accounting**.

Internal Auditing

Large organizations usually maintain a staff of *internal auditors*. **Internal auditing** is the study of the internal control structure and evaluation of the efficiency and effectiveness of many different aspects of the company's operations. As employees, internal auditors are not independent of the organization. Therefore, they *do not* perform independent audits of the company's financial statements.

Careers in management accounting often lead to positions in top management—just as do careers in public accounting.

GOVERNMENTAL ACCOUNTING

Governmental agencies use accounting information in allocating their resources and in controlling their operations. Therefore, the need for management accountants in governmental agencies is similar to that in business organizations.

The GAO: Who Audits the Government?

The **Government Accountability Office** (GAO) audits many agencies of the federal government, as well as some private organizations doing business with the government. The GAO reports its findings directly to Congress, which, in turn, often discloses these findings to the public.

GAO investigations may be designed either to evaluate the efficiency of an entity's operations or to determine the fairness of accounting information reported to the government.

The IRS: Audits of Income Tax Returns

Another governmental agency that performs extensive auditing work is the **Internal Revenue Service** (IRS). The IRS handles the millions of income tax returns filed annually by individuals and business organizations and frequently performs auditing functions to verify data contained in these returns.

The SEC: The "Watchdog" of Financial Reporting

The SEC works closely with the FASB in establishing generally accepted accounting principles. Most publicly owned corporations must file audited financial statements with the SEC each year. If the SEC believes that a company's financial statements are deficient in any way, it conducts an investigation. If the SEC concludes that federal securities laws have been violated, it initiates legal action against the reporting entity and responsible individuals.

Many other governmental agencies, including the FBI, the Treasury Department, and the FDIC (Federal Deposit Insurance Corporation), use accountants to audit compliance with governmental regulations and to investigate suspected criminal activity. People beginning their careers in governmental accounting often move into top administrative positions.

ACCOUNTING EDUCATION

Some accountants, including your instructor and the authors of this textbook, have chosen to pursue careers in accounting education. A position as an accounting faculty member offers opportunities for teaching, research, consulting, and an unusual degree of freedom in developing individual skills. Accounting educators contribute to the accounting profession in many ways. One, of course, lies in effective teaching; second, in publishing significant research findings; and third, in influencing top students to pursue careers in accounting.

WHAT ABOUT BOOKKEEPING?

Some people think that the work of professional accountants consists primarily of bookkeeping. Actually, it doesn't. In fact, many professional accountants do *little or no* bookkeeping.

Bookkeeping is the clerical side of accounting—the recording of routine transactions and day-to-day record keeping. Today such tasks are performed primarily by computers and skilled clerical personnel, not by accountants.

Professional accountants are involved more with the *interpretation and use* of accounting information than with its actual preparation. Their work includes evaluating the efficiency of operations, resolving complex financial reporting issues, forecasting the results of future operations, auditing, tax planning, and designing efficient accounting systems. There is very little that is "routine" about the work of a professional accountant.

A person might become a proficient bookkeeper in a few weeks or months. To become a professional accountant, however, is a far greater challenge because this requires more than understanding the bookkeeping systems. It requires years of study, experience, and an ongoing commitment to keeping current.

We will illustrate and explain a number of bookkeeping procedures in this text, particularly in the next several chapters. But teaching bookkeeping skills is *not* our goal; the primary purpose of this text is to develop your abilities to *understand and use* accounting information in today's business world.

ACCOUNTING AS A STEPPING-STONE

We have mentioned that many professional accountants leave their accounting careers for key positions in management or administration. An accounting background is invaluable in such positions, because top management works continuously with issues defined and described in accounting terms and concepts.

An especially useful stepping-stone is experience in public accounting. Public accountants have the unusual opportunity of getting an inside look at many different business organizations, which makes them particularly well suited for top management positions in other organizations.

BUT WHAT ABOUT ME? I'M NOT AN ACCOUNTING MAJOR

Most students who use this book are not accounting majors. However, the study of accounting is still important to you. You need to understand accounting concepts, both for your professional careers and for many aspects of your personal life. Finance students need to understand accounting concepts if they seek positions in investment banking, consulting, or in corporate America as a financial analyst. Approximately 50 percent of the chief financial officers of large U.S. corporations have a background in accounting. A management student seeking a career as a management trainee—with the ultimate goal of running a corporation or a corporate division—needs to understand accounting in order to be able to run, control, and evaluate the performance of a business unit. Accounting is the language of business, and trying to run a business without understanding accounting information is analogous to trying to play sports without understanding the rules. Marketing students often take positions in sales. It is imperative that marketing students understand the principles of revenue recognition, as well as the obligations of a public company under the U.S. securities laws. A lack of this understanding has led many a marketing/sales executive to become involved in improper revenue recognition schemes. Many of these executives have been subject to civil and criminal prosecution.

Ethics, Fraud & Corporate Governance

The last few years have been a time of unprecedented business failures amid allegations of fraudulent financial reporting that include corporations that have now become household names—Enron, WorldCom, HealthSouth, Adelphia Communications, Tyco, and Qwest, among others. These problems are not exclusively a problem with financial reporting in the United States, as evidenced by fraud allegations at Parmalat, a large Italian company.

Fraud typically is perpetrated by senior management; for example, a 1999 study indicates that the company's chief executive officer and/or chief financial officer is involved in 83% of the fraud-related enforcement actions brought by the Securities and Exchange Commission. Committing fraud, an illegal act, obviously suggests a serious lack of ethical awareness and ethical sensitivity on the part of the perpetrators. Another feature of many frauds is that the company where the fraud occurred had a weak corporate governance environment. **Corporate governance** entails corporate structures and processes for overseeing the company's affairs, including oversight by the board of directors of the actions of top management to ensure that the company is being managed with the best interests of shareholders in mind.

In each chapter, we will discuss common fraud-related schemes relevant to the material covered in that chapter, ethical quandaries and challenges faced by businesspeople, or efforts to improve corporate governance and by extension the quality of accounting information in the United States.

Dennis Kozlowski, the former CEO of Tyco, leaves court upon his conviction for conspiracy, securities fraud, and falsifying records. Kozlowski was sentenced to 8⅓ to 25 years in prison. A failure to understand and apply securities laws exposes management to great personal and professional risk.

Finally, accounting knowledge is helpful in many aspects of your personal lives. Accounting concepts are integral to such everyday decisions as personal budgeting, retirement and college planning, lease versus buy decisions, evaluation of loan terms, and evaluation of investment opportunities. Since accounting skills are designed to help you make better economic decisions, you will be using these skills for the rest of your life. The only question is the degree of skill with which you will apply these concepts.

Concluding Remarks

In this chapter we have established a framework for your study of accounting. You have learned how financial accounting provides information for external users, primarily investors and creditors, and how accounting provides information for internal management. We have established the importance of integrity in accounting information and have learned about several things that build integrity. Looking ahead, in Chapter 2 we begin to look in greater depth at financial accounting and, more specifically, financial statements. You will be introduced to the details of the three primary financial statements that provide information for investors and creditors. As the text progresses, you will learn more about the important information that these financial statements provide and how that information is used to make important financial decisions.

END-OF-CHAPTER REVIEW

SUMMARY OF LEARNING OBJECTIVES

LO1 **Discuss accounting as the language of business and the role of accounting information in making economic decisions.** Accounting is the means by which information about an enterprise is communicated and, thus, is sometimes called the language of business. Many different users have need for accounting information in order to make important decisions. These users include investors, creditors, management, governmental agencies, labor unions, and others. Because the primary role of accounting information is to provide useful information for decision-making purposes, it is sometimes referred to as a means to an end, with the end being the decision that is helped by the availability of accounting information.

LO2 **Discuss the significance of accounting systems in generating reliable accounting information and understand the five components of internal control per COSO's *Internal Control–Integrated Framework*.** Information systems are critical to the production of quality accounting information on a timely basis and the communication of that information to decision makers. While there are different types of information systems, they all have one characteristic in common—to meet the organization's needs for accounting information as efficiently as possible. Per the COSO framework, the five elements of internal control are: (1) control environment, (2) risk assessment, (3) control activities, (4) information and communication, and (5) monitoring.

LO3 **Explain the importance of financial accounting information for external parties—primarily investors and creditors—in terms of the objectives and the characteristics of that information.** The primary objectives of financial accounting are to provide information that is useful in making investment and credit decisions; in assessing the amount, timing, and uncertainty of future cash flows; and in learning about the enterprise's economic resources, claims to resources, and changes in claims to resources. Some of the most important characteristics of financial accounting information are: it is a means to an end, it is historical in nature, it results from inexact and approximate measures of business activity, and it is based on a general-purpose assumption.

LO4 **Explain the importance of accounting information for internal parties—primarily management—in terms of the objectives and the characteristics of that information.** Accounting information is useful to the enterprise in achieving its goals, objectives, and mission; assessing past performance and future directions; and evaluating and rewarding decision-making performance. Some of the important characteristics of internal accounting information are its timeliness, its relationship to decision-making authority, its future orientation, its relationship to measuring efficiency and effectiveness, and the fact that it is a means to an end.

LO5 **Discuss elements of the system of external and internal financial reporting that create integrity in the reported information.** Integrity of financial reporting is important because of the reliance that is placed on financial information by users both outside and inside the reporting organization. Important dimensions of financial reporting that work together to ensure integrity in information are institutional features (accounting principles, internal structure, audits, and legislation); professional organizations (the AICPA, IMA, IIA, AAA); and the competence, judgment, and ethical behavior of individual accountants.

LO6 **Identify and discuss several professional organizations that play important roles in preparing and communicating accounting information.** The FASB, PCAOB, and SEC are important organizations in terms of standard setting in the United States. The FASB is a private-sector organization that works closely with the SEC, which has legal authority to designate financial reporting standards for publicly held companies. The PCAOB sets auditing standards. Professional organizations that provide services to individual accountants in various segments of the accounting profession are the AICPA, IMA, IIA, AAA, and COSO.

LO7 **Discuss the importance of personal competence, professional judgment, and ethical behavior on the part of accounting professionals.** Personal competence and professional judgment are, perhaps, the most important factors in ensuring the integrity of financial information. Competence is demonstrated by one's education and professional certification (CPA, CMA, CIA). Professional judgment is important because accounting information is often based on inexact measurements and assumptions are required. Ethical behavior refers to the quality of accountants being motivated to "do the right thing."

LO8 **Describe various career opportunities in accounting.** Accounting opens the door to many career opportunities. Public accounting is the segment of the profession where professionals offer audit, tax, and consulting services. Management, or managerial, accounting refers to that segment of the accounting profession where professional accountants work for individual companies in a wide variety of capacities. Many accountants work for governmental agencies. Some accountants choose education as a career and work to prepare students for future careers in one of the other segments of the accounting profession. While keeping detailed records (that is, bookkeeping) is a part of accounting, it is not a distinguishing characteristic of a career in accounting; in fact, many accounting careers involve little or no bookkeeping. Accounting skills are important to nonaccounting majors and to all students in their personal lives.

Key Terms Introduced or Emphasized in Chapter 1

accounting system (p. 6) The personnel, procedures, devices, and records used by an organization to develop accounting information and communicate that information to decision makers.

American Accounting Association (p. 21) A professional accounting organization consisting primarily of accounting educators that is dedicated to improving accounting education, research, and practice.

American Institute of CPAs (p. 20) A professional accounting organization of certified public accountants that engages in a variety of professional activities, including establishing auditing standards for private companies, conducting research, and establishing industry-specific financial reporting standards.

audit (p. 20) An investigation of financial statements designed to determine their fairness in relation to generally accepted accounting principles.

balance sheet (p. 12) A position statement that shows where the company stands in financial terms at a specific date. (Also called the statement of financial position.)

bookkeeping (p. 26) The clerical dimension of accounting that includes recording the routine transactions and day-to-day record keeping of an enterprise.

cash flow prospects (p. 10) The likelihood that an enterprise will be able to provide an investor with both a return on the investor's investment and the return of that investment.

Certificate in Internal Auditing (p. 22) A professional designation issued by the Institute of Internal Auditors signifying expertise in internal auditing.

Certificate in Management Accounting (p. 22) A professional designation issued by the Institute of Management Accountants signifying expertise in management accounting.

certified public accountant (p. 22) An accountant who is licensed by a state after meeting rigorous education, experience, and examination requirements.

Committee of Sponsoring Organizations of the Treadway Commission (p. 21) A voluntary private-sector organization dedicated to improving the quality of financial reporting through business ethics, effective internal controls, and corporate governance.

control activities (p. 9) Policies and procedures that management puts in place to address the risks identified during the risk assessment process.

control environment (p. 9) The foundation for all the other elements of internal control, setting the overall tone for the organization.

corporate governance (p. 27) Includes the corporate structures and processes for overseeing a company's affairs, for example, the board of directors and the company's internal control processes.

cost accounting (p. 25) Determining the cost of certain business activities and interpreting cost information.

external users (p. 9) Individuals and other enterprises that have a financial interest in the reporting enterprise but that are not involved in the day-to-day operations of that enterprise (e.g., owners, creditors, labor unions, suppliers, customers).

financial accounting (p. 5) Providing information about the financial resources, obligations, and activities of an economic entity that is intended for use primarily by external decision makers—investors and creditors.

Financial Accounting Standards Board (FASB) (p. 18) A private-sector organization that is responsible for determining generally accepted accounting principles in the United States.

financial forecast (p. 25) A plan of financial operations for some future period.

financial statement (p. 12) A monetary declaration of what is believed to be true about an enterprise.

Government Accountability Office (p. 25) A federal government agency that audits many other agencies of the federal government and other organizations that do business with the federal government and reports its findings to Congress.

generally accepted accounting principles (p. 17) Principles that provide the framework for determining what information is to be included in financial statements and how that information is to be presented.

general-purpose information (p. 13) Information that is intended to meet the needs of multiple users that have an interest in the financial activities of an enterprise rather than tailored to the specific information needs of one user.

income statement (p. 12) An activity statement that shows details and results of the company's profit-related activities for a period of time.

information and communication (p. 9) The organization's process for capturing operational, financial, and compliance-related information necessary to run the business, and communicating that information downstream (from management to employees), upstream (from employees to management), and across the organization.

Institute of Internal Auditors (p. 20) A professional accounting organization that is dedicated to the promotion and development of the practice of internal auditing.

Institute of Management Accountants (p. 20) A professional accounting organization that intends to influence the concepts and ethical practice of management accounting and financial management.

integrity (p. 17) The qualities of being complete, unbroken, unimpaired, sound, honest, and sincere.

internal auditing (p. 25) The study of internal control structure and evaluation of the efficiency and effectiveness of many different aspects of the enterprise's operations.

internal control (p. 8) A process designed to provide reasonable assurance that the organization produces reliable financial reports, complies with applicable laws and regulations, and conducts its operations in an efficient and effective manner.

Internal Revenue Service (p. 25) A government organization that handles millions of income tax returns filed by individuals and businesses and performs audit functions to verify the data contained in those returns.

internal users (p. 14) Individuals who use accounting information from within an organization (for example, board of directors, chief financial officer, plant managers, store managers).

International Accounting Standards Board (IASB) (p. 18) The group responsible for creating and promoting *International Financial Reporting Standards (IFRSs).*

management accounting (p. 6) Providing information that is intended primarily for use by internal management in decision making required to run the business.

monitoring (p. 9) The process of evaluating the effectiveness of an organization's system of internal control over time, including both ongoing management and supervisory activities and periodic separate evaluations.

Public Company Accounting Oversight Board (PCAOB) (p. 19) A quasi-governmental body charged with oversight of the public accounting profession. The PCAOB sets auditing standards for audits of publicly traded companies.

return of investment (p. 10) The repayment to an investor of the amount originally invested in another enterprise.

return on investment (p. 10) The payment of an amount (interest, dividends) for using another's money.

risk assessment (p. 9) A process of identifying, analyzing, and managing those risks that pose a threat to the achievement of the organization's objectives.

Sarbanes-Oxley Act (p. 9) A landmark piece of securities law, designed to improve the effectiveness of corporate financial reporting through enhanced accountability of auditors, boards of directors, and management.

Securities and Exchange Commission (SEC) (p. 19) A governmental organization that has the legal power to establish accounting principles and financial reporting requirements for publicly held companies in the United States.

statement of cash flows (p. 12) An activity statement that shows the details of the company's activities involving cash during a period of time.

statement of financial position (p. 12) Also called the balance sheet.

tax accounting (p. 6) Preparation of income tax returns and anticipating the tax effects of business transactions and structuring them in such a way as to minimize the income tax burden.

Demonstration Problem

Find the **Intel Corporation** annual 10-K report from 2004 at the following Internet address (**http://download.intel.com/intel/annualreports/AR_2004.pdf**) to answer the following questions:

a. Name the titles of the financial reports in the **Intel Corp.** annual report that provide specific information about economic resources, claims to resources, and changes in resources and claims.

b. Name three other sections from **Intel**'s 2004 annual report that provide information useful in assessing the amount, timing, and uncertainty of future cash flows.

c. Which main categories of other general information are useful in making investment and credit decisions?

Solution to the Demonstration Problem

a.
- **Intel Corporation**
  Consolidated Balance Sheets
- **Intel Corporation**
  Consolidated Statements of Stockholders' Equity
- **Intel Corporation**
  Consolidated Statements of Income
- **Intel Corporation**
  Consolidated Statements of Cash Flows

b.
- Management's Discussion and Analysis of Financial Condition and Results of Operations
- Quantitative and Qualitative Disclosures about Market Risk
- Notes to the Consolidated Financial Statements

c.
- Business Discussion
- Management's Discussion and Analysis of Financial Condition and Results of Operations that contains general discussions about competitors, sales and marketing plans, seasonality, inflation, forward-looking statements, and market risk assessments
- Report of the Independent Auditors

Self-Test Questions

The answers to these questions appear on page 37.

1. Which of the following does *not* describe accounting?

a. Language of business.

b. Is an end rather than a means to an end.

c. Useful for decision making.

d. Used by business, government, nonprofit organizations, and individuals.

2. To understand and use accounting information in making economic decisions, you must understand:
   a. The nature of economic activities that accounting information describes.
   b. The assumptions and measurement techniques involved in developing accounting information.
   c. Which information is relevant for a particular type of decision that is being made.
   d. All of the above.
3. Purposes of an accounting system include all of the following *except*:
   a. Interpret and record the effects of business transactions.
   b. Classify the effects of transactions to facilitate the preparation of reports.
   c. Summarize and communicate information to decision makers.
   d. Dictate the specific types of business transactions that the enterprise may engage in.
4. External users of financial accounting information include all of the following *except*:
   a. Investors.
   b. Labor unions.
   c. Line managers.
   d. General public.
5. Objectives of financial reporting to external investors and creditors include preparing information about all of the following *except*:
   a. Information used to determine which products to produce.
   b. Information about economic resources, claims to those resources, and changes in both resources and claims.
   c. Information that is useful in assessing the amount, timing, and uncertainty of future cash flows.
   d. Information that is useful in making investment and credit decisions.
6. Financial accounting information is characterized by all of the following *except*:
   a. It is historical in nature.
   b. It sometimes results from inexact and approximate measures.
   c. It is factual, so it does not require judgment to prepare.
   d. It is enhanced by management's explanation.
7. Which of the following is *not* a user of internal accounting information?
   a. Store manager.
   b. Chief executive officer.
   c. Creditor.
   d. Chief financial officer.
8. Characteristics of internal accounting information include all of the following *except*:
   a. It is audited by a CPA.
   b. It must be timely.
   c. It is oriented toward the future.
   d. It measures efficiency and effectiveness.
9. Which of the following are important factors in ensuring the integrity of accounting information?
   a. Institutional factors, such as standards for preparing information.
   b. Professional organizations, such as the American Institute of CPAs.
   c. Competence, judgment, and ethical behavior of individual accountants.
   d. All of the above.
10. The code of conduct of the American Institute of Certified Public Accountants includes requirements in which of the following areas?
    a. The Public Interest.
    b. Objectivity.
    c. Independence.
    d. All of the above.

ASSIGNMENT MATERIAL Discussion Questions

1. What do we mean when we say that accounting is a means rather than an end?
2. Accounting is sometimes described as the language of business. What is meant by this description?
3. What kinds of organizations, in addition to businesses, use accounting information?
4. What is the primary distinction between financial accounting and other accounting?
5. Describe the relationship among the accounting process, accounting information, decision makers, and economic activities.
6. What is an accounting system, and what is the primary objective of such a system?
7. What do we mean when we say that an accounting system needs to be cost-effective?
8. What are the three basic functions of every accounting system?
9. Who designs and installs accounting systems?
10. Generally describe and give several examples of external users of accounting information.
11. What are the two primary external groups to which financial accounting information is directed?
12. What do we mean when we say that investors and creditors are interested in a company's cash flow prospects?
13. When you invest your savings in a company, what is the difference between the return *on* your investment and the return *of* your investment?
14. Going from general to specific, what are the three primary objectives of financial accounting information?

15. What are the three primary financial statements with which we communicate financial accounting information?
16. Do the terms *financial reporting* and *financial statements* mean the same thing? Explain.
17. Is externally reported financial information always precise and accurate?
18. What do we mean when we say that financial accounting information is "general-purpose"?
19. How does management's explanation enhance the usefulness of financial accounting information?
20. What are several examples of internal, management-prepared information that ordinarily would not be communicated externally?
21. What are some examples of internal users of accounting information?
22. What are the three primary ways enterprises use their internal accounting information?
23. Why does internal accounting information need to be timely?
24. Is internal accounting information primarily historical or future-oriented? How does that compare with financial accounting information?
25. How does accounting information assist management in measuring efficiency and effectiveness?
26. Why is it important for accounting information to have the quality of integrity?
27. What is meant by *generally accepted accounting principles*, and how do these principles add to the integrity of financial accounting information?
28. What is the definition of *internal control*, and what are the five components of COSO's internal control framework?
29. What is an *audit*, and how does it add to the integrity of accounting information?
30. What is meant by the professional designations *CPA, CMA*, and *CIA*, and how do these designations add to the integrity of accounting information?
31. Why was the Sarbanes-Oxley legislation passed in 2002, and what are its implications for the accounting profession?
32. What is a *code of ethics*, and how do such codes add to the integrity of accounting information?
33. What is the Financial Accounting Standards Board (FASB), and what is its role in external financial reporting?
34. What is the Securities and Exchange Commission (SEC), and what is its role in external financial reporting?
35. What is the role of the Public Company Accounting Oversight Board in the audit of financial statements?
36. What is the primary mission of the Institute of Management Accountants?
37. What is the mission of the American Institute of Certified Public Accountants, and does the organization have primarily a U.S. or an international focus?
38. Who makes up the majority of the members of the American Accounting Association, and how has this organization affected the practice of accounting?
39. What is the International Accounting Standards Board (IASB), and what are its objectives?

Brief Exercises

BRIEF EXERCISE 1.1
Users of Information

List four external users of accounting information.

BRIEF EXERCISE 1.2
Components of Internal Control

Match the terms on the left with the descriptions on the right. Each description should be used only once.

Term	Description
______ Control environment	a. Identifying, analyzing, and managing those risks that pose a threat to the achievement of the organization's objectives.
______ Risk assessment	b. A process, involving both ongoing activities and separate evaluations, that enables an organization to evaluate the effectiveness of its system of internal control over time.
______ Control activities	c. The process of capturing and communicating operational, financial, and compliance-related information.
______ Information and communication	d. The foundation for all the other elements of internal control, setting the overall tone for the organization.
______ Monitoring	e. Policies and procedures put in place by management to address the risks identified during the risk assessment process.

BRIEF EXERCISE 1.3
Inexact or Approximate Measures

Why does accounting rely on inexact or approximate measures?

BRIEF EXERCISE 1.4
Standards for the Preparation of Accounting Information

What are the two primary organizations in the U.S. that are responsible for setting standards related to the preparation of accounting information?

BRIEF EXERCISE 1.5
FASB Conceptual Framework

The FASB's conceptual framework sets forth the Board's views on which topics?

BRIEF EXERCISE 1.6
Public Company Accounting Oversight Board (PCAOB)

Use the Web to find the home page of the PCAOB. What are the four primary activities of the PCAOB?

BRIEF EXERCISE 1.7
Committee of Sponsoring Organizations (COSO)

Who are the sponsoring organizations of COSO, and what is COSO best known for doing?

BRIEF EXERCISE 1.8
Professional Certifications in Accounting

List three professional certifications offered in accounting and the organizations that offer them.

BRIEF EXERCISE 1.9
AICPA Code of Professional Conduct

Match the terms on the left with the descriptions on the right. Each description should be used only once.

Term	Description
______ Responsibilities	a. A member should observe the profession's technical and ethical standards, strive continually to improve competence and the quality of service, and discharge professional responsibility to the best of the member's ability.
______ The Public Interest	b. In carrying out their responsibilities as professionals, members should exercise sensitive professional and moral judgments in all their activities.
______ Integrity	c. A member should maintain objectivity and be free of conflicts of interest in discharging professional responsibilities. A member in public practice should be independent in fact and appearance when providing auditing and other attestation services.
______ Objectivity and Independence	d. A member in public practice should observe the Principles of the Code of Professional Conduct in determining the scope and nature of services to be provided.
______ Due Care	e. Members should accept the obligation to act in a way that will serve the public interest, honor the public trust, and demonstrate commitment to professionalism.
______ Scope and Nature of Services	f. To maintain and broaden public confidence, members should perform all professional responsibilities with the highest sense of integrity.

BRIEF EXERCISE 1.10
Personal Benefits of Accounting Skills

List three accounting-related skills that are useful to many people in their personal lives.

Exercises

EXERCISE 1.1
You as a User of Accounting Information

Identify several ways in which *you* currently use accounting information in your life as a student. Also identify several situations in which, while you are still a student, you might be required to supply financial information about yourself to others.

EXERCISE 1.2
Users of Accounting Information

Boeing Company is the largest manufacturer of commercial aircraft in the United States and is a major employer in Seattle, Washington. Explain why each of the following individuals or organizations would be interested in financial information about the company.

a. **California Public Employees Retirement System**, one of the world's largest pension funds.

b. **China Airlines**, a rapidly growing airline serving the Pacific Rim.

c. Henry James, a real estate investor considering building apartments in the Seattle area.

d. **Boeing**'s management.

e. **International Aerospace Machinists**, a labor union representing many **Boeing** employees.

EXERCISE 1.3
What Is Financial Reporting?

A major focus of this course is the process of financial reporting.

a. What is meant by the term *financial reporting*?

b. What are the principal accounting reports involved in the financial reporting process? In general terms, what is the purpose of these reports?

c. Do all business entities engage in financial reporting? Explain.

d. How does society benefit from the financial reporting process?

EXERCISE 1.4
Generally Accepted Accounting Principles

Generally accepted accounting principles play an important role in financial reporting.

a. What is meant by the phrase *generally accepted accounting principles*?

b. What are the major sources of these principles?

c. Is there a single comprehensive list of generally accepted accounting principles? Explain.

d. What types of accounting reports are prepared in conformity with generally accepted accounting principles?

EXERCISE 1.5
Accounting Organizations

Describe the roles of the following organizations in establishing generally accepted accounting principles:

a. The FASB **b.** The AICPA **c.** The SEC

From which of these organizations can you most easily obtain financial information about publicly owned companies?

EXERCISE 1.6
Investment Return

You recently invested $12,000 of your savings in a security issued by a large company. The security agreement pays you 7 percent per year and has a maturity two years from the day you purchased it. What is the total cash flow you expect to receive from this investment, separated into the return on your investment and the return of your investment?

through

EXERCISE 1.7
Accounting Terminology

Match the terms on the left with the descriptions on the right. Each description should be used only once.

Term	Description
______ Financial accounting	a. The procedural aspect of accounting that involves keeping detailed records of business transactions, much of which is done today by computers.
______ Management accounting	b. A broad term that describes all information provided to external users, including but not limited to financial statements.
______ Financial reporting	c. An important quality of accounting information that allows investors, creditors, management, and other users to rely on the information.
______ Financial statements	d. The segment of the accounting profession that relates to providing audit, tax, and consulting services to clients.
______ General-purpose assumption	e. Procedures and processes within an organization that ensure the integrity of accounting information.
______ Integrity	f. Statement of financial position (balance sheet), income statement, statement of cash flows.
______ Internal control	g. The fact that the same information is provided to various external users, including investors and creditors.
______ Public accounting	h. The area of accounting that refers to providing information to support internal management decisions.
______ Bookkeeping	i. The area of accounting that refers to providing information to support external investment and credit decisions.

EXERCISE 1.8
Accounting Organizations

Match the organizations on the left with the functions on the right. Each function should be used only once.

Organization	Function
______ Institute of Internal Auditors	a. Government agency responsible for financial reporting by publicly held companies.
______ Securities and Exchange Commission	b. International organization dedicated to the advancement of internal auditing.
______ American Institute of CPAs	c. Organization dedicated to providing members personal and professional development opportunities in the area of management accounting.
______ Institute of Management Accountants	d. The body charged with setting auditing standards for audits of public companies.
______ Financial Accounting Standards Board	e. Organization consisting primarily of accounting educators that encourages improvements in teaching and research.
______ American Accounting Association	f. The group that creates and promotes International Financial Reporting Standards (IFRSs).
______ Public Company Accounting Oversight Board	g. Professional association of Certified Public Accountants.
______ International Accounting Standards Board	h. Private-sector organization that establishes accounting standards.

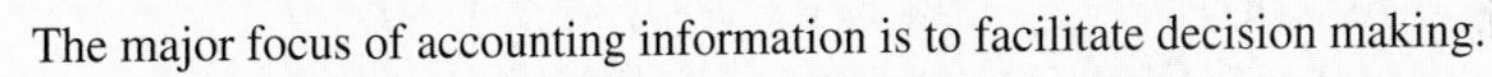

EXERCISE 1.9
Financial and Management Accounting

The major focus of accounting information is to facilitate decision making.

a. As an investor in a company, what would be your primary objective?

b. As a manager of a company, what would be your primary objective?

c. Is the same accounting information likely to be equally useful to you in these two different roles?

EXERCISE 1.10
Management Accounting Information

Internal accounting information is used primarily for internal decision making by an enterprise's management.

a. What are the three primary purposes of internal accounting information?

b. Which of these is the most general and which is the most specific?

c. Give several examples of the kinds of decisions that internal accounting information supports.

EXERCISE 1.11
Accounting Organizations

Describe which professional organization(s) would most likely be of greatest value to you if your position involved each of the following independent roles:

a. Accounting educator.

b. Management accountant.

c. Certified public accountant.

EXERCISE 1.12
Purpose of an Audit

Audits of financial statements are an important part of the accounting process to ensure integrity in financial reporting.

a. What is the purpose of an audit?

b. As an external user of accounting information, what meaning would you attach to an audit that concludes that the financial statements are fairly presented in conformity with generally accepted accounting principles?

c. Would your interest in investing in this same company be affected by an auditor's report that concluded the financial statements were *not* fairly presented? Why or why not?

EXERCISE 1.13
Audits of Financial Statements

The annual financial statements of all large, publicly owned corporations are audited.

a. What is an audit of financial statements?

b. Who performs audits?

c. What is the purpose of an audit?

EXERCISE 1.14
Ethics and Professional Judgment

Ethical conduct and professional judgment each play important roles in the accounting process.

a. In general terms, explain why it is important to society that people who prepare accounting information act in an ethical manner.

b. Identify at least three areas in which accountants must exercise *professional judgment*, rather than merely relying on written rules.

EXERCISE 1.15
Careers in Accounting

Four accounting majors, Maria Acosta, Kenzo Nakao, Helen Martin, and Anthony Mandella, recently graduated from Central University and began professional accounting careers. Acosta entered public accounting, Nakao became a management accountant, Martin joined a governmental agency, and Mandella (who had completed a graduate program) became an accounting faculty member.

Assume that each of the four graduates was successful in his or her chosen career. Identify the types of accounting *activities* in which each of these graduates might find themselves specializing several years after graduation.

EXERCISE 1.16
Home Depot, Inc.
General and Specific Information

Locate the **Home Depot, Inc.**, 2005 financial statements in Appendix A of this text. Briefly peruse the financial statements and answer the following questions:

a. Name the titles of each of **Home Depot**'s financial statements that provide specific information about economic resources, claims to resources, and changes in resources and claims.

b. Name three other sections from **Home Depot**'s 2005 financial statements that might be useful to a potential investor or creditor.

Due to the introductory nature of this chapter and the conceptual nature of its contents, no items labeled ***Problems*** *are included. In all future chapters you will find two problem sets, A and B, that generally include computations, are more complex, and generally require more time to complete than the Exercises.*

Critical Thinking Cases

CASE 1.1
Reliability of Financial Statements

In the early 1980s, **Chrysler Corporation** was in severe financial difficulty and desperately needed large loans for the company to survive. What factors prevented **Chrysler** from simply providing potential lenders with misleading financial statements to make the company look like a risk-free investment?

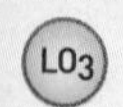

CASE 1.2
Objectives of Financial Accounting

Divide into groups as instructed by your professor and discuss the following:

a. How does the description of accounting as the "language of business" relate to accounting as being useful for investors and creditors?

b. Explain how the decisions you would make might differ if you were an external investor or a member of an enterprise's management team.

CASE 1.3
Accounting Systems

You are employed by a business consulting firm as an information systems specialist. You have just begun an assignment with a startup company and are discussing with the owner her need for an accounting system. How would you respond to the following questions from the owner?

a. What is the meaning of the term *accounting system*?

b. What is the purpose of an accounting system and what are its basic functions?

c. Who is responsible for designing and implementing an accounting system?

CASE 1.4
Codes of Ethics

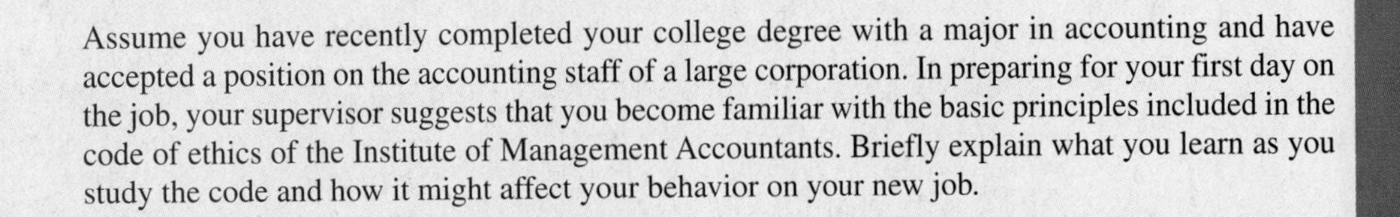

Assume you have recently completed your college degree with a major in accounting and have accepted a position on the accounting staff of a large corporation. In preparing for your first day on the job, your supervisor suggests that you become familiar with the basic principles included in the code of ethics of the Institute of Management Accountants. Briefly explain what you learn as you study the code and how it might affect your behavior on your new job.

***BUSINESSWEEK* CASE 1.5**
Accounting Reports Lack Candor

In 2001 and 2002, several accounting scandals were uncovered which resulted in very significant financial losses for investors and creditors of U.S. corporations. This led to legislation that placed the primary players in the financial reporting process, including reporting companies and their auditors, under closer government scrutiny. In a *BusinessWeek* article, "Annual Reports: Still Not Enough Candor," dated March 14, 2003, author Mike McNamee raises the question, "Did corporate America get the message?"

McNamee goes on to state that he believes the answer to this question is "no." He describes accounting practices that still result in vague information that does not meet the needs of financial statements users. He specifically cites the rules by which accountants count revenue as an example of an area where practices are inadequate, particularly in the high-tech, energy, pharmaceutical, and retail industries.

Instructions

a. Identify the objectives of external financial reporting discussed in this chapter. How would information that meets these objectives help investors make a decision concerning a potential investment in a company?

b. What institutional and other features that are part of the accounting profession are intended to enhance the integrity of financial reporting?

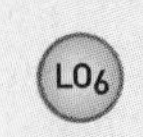

INTERNET CASE 1.6
Accessing Information on the Internet

The Internet is a good place to get information that is useful to you in your study of accounting. For example, you can find information about current events, professional accounting organizations, and specific companies that may support your study.

Instructions

a. Access the **Rutgers University** Internet site. Look under the category "Accounting Resources." Identify eight links to many other sites that provide information about accounting.

http://accounting.rutgers.edu/

b. Look under the category "Accounting Resources" and then "Big-Five." Identify the names of the largest public accounting firms.

c. Under "Accounting Resources," look under the category "Publishers" and then the subcategory of "U.S. Accounting Publishers" to locate the publisher of this textbook.

d. Find the Internet sites of the following professional accounting organizations and learn what you can about them from the information provided:
American Accounting Association (AAA)
Financial Accounting Standards Board (FASB)
Institute of Internal Auditors (IIA)
Institute of Management Accountants (IMA)

Internet sites are time and date sensitive. It is the purpose of these exercises to have you explore the Internet. You may need to use the Yahoo! search engine **http://www.yahoo.com** *(or another favorite search engine) to find a company's current Web address.*

Answers to Self-Test Questions

1. b **2.** d **3.** d **4.** c **5.** a **6.** c **7.** c **8.** a
9. d **10.** d

Basic Financial Statements

Learning Objectives

AFTER STUDYING THIS CHAPTER, YOU SHOULD BE ABLE TO:

LO1 Explain the nature and general purpose of financial statements.

LO2 Explain certain accounting principles that are important for an understanding of financial statements and how professional judgment by accountants may affect the application of those principles.

LO3 Demonstrate how certain business transactions affect the elements of the accounting equation: Assets = Liabilities + Owners' Equity.

LO4 Explain how the statement of financial position, often referred to as the balance sheet, is an expansion of the basic accounting equation.

LO5 Explain how the income statement reports an enterprise's financial performance for a period of time in terms of the relationship of revenues and expenses.

LO6 Explain how the statement of cash flows presents the change in cash for a period of time in terms of the company's operating, investing, and financing activities.

LO7 Explain important relationships among the statement of financial position, income statement, and statement of cash flows, and how these statements relate to each other.

LO8 Explain common forms of business ownership—sole proprietorship, partnership, and corporation—and demonstrate how they differ in terms of their presentation in the statement of financial position.

LO9 Discuss the importance of financial statements to a company and its investors and creditors and why management may take steps to improve the appearance of the company in its financial statements.

INTEL

Intel supplies the computing and communications industries with chips, boards, and systems building blocks that are the ingredients of computers and servers as well as networking and communications products. These industries use Intel's products to create advanced computing and communications systems. Intel states that its mission is to be the preeminent building block supplier in the worldwide Internet economy.

Technology-based companies like Intel operate in highly competitive markets and continuously introduce new products. Intel's management discusses the company's business strategy in a recent annual report by explaining the importance of meeting the needs of its customers: "Our goal is to be the preeminent building block supplier to the worldwide Internet economy. Focusing on our core competencies in the design and manufacture of integrated circuits, as well as our expertise in digital computing and communications, we believe we are well positioned to drive the convergence of computing and communications through silicon integration. We focus on developing advanced technology solutions tailored to meet user requirements in specific settings, providing the features people want in their homes, at work and at play."

Modern-day historians indicate that we are rapidly moving from the industrial age, with an emphasis on heavy manufacturing, to the information age. Companies like Intel, Microsoft, Cisco Systems, and others are major players in this transformation of business. For information-age companies the factors of success are quite different than for industrial-age companies. Information-age companies rely more heavily on intellectual capital, research and development, and other intangibles that were less important for companies whose focus was heavy manufacturing or, even earlier in our history, primarily agricultural.

If you were a person with considerable wealth who wanted to invest in a forward-looking company as we transition into the information age, how would you know whether **Intel** or any other company is a wise investment? What information would you seek out to help you decide where to place your investment dollars? A primary source of financial information is a company's financial statements. These statements, which are prepared at least once a year and in many cases more frequently, provide tremendous insight into the current financial status of the company and how successful the company has been in meeting its financial goals. In this chapter you are introduced to the three primary financial statements—the statement of financial position (often referred to as the balance sheet), the income statement, and the statement of cash flows. Combined with information presented in notes and other accompanying discussions, these financial statements provide for investors, creditors, and other interested parties a wealth of useful information. In fact, financial information is what this entire textbook is about, and in this chapter you receive your initial introduction to how financial statements come about and how they may be used to better understand a company.

Introduction to Financial Statements

In Chapter 1 we learned that investors and creditors are particularly interested in cash flows that they expect to receive in the future. Creditors, for example, are interested in the ability of the enterprise, to which they have made loans or sold merchandise on credit, to meet its payment obligations, which may include payment of interest. Similarly, investors are interested in the market value of their stock holdings, as well as dividends that the enterprise will pay while they own the stock.

One of the primary ways investors and creditors assess the probability that an enterprise will be able to make future cash payments is to study, analyze, and understand the enterprise's financial statements. As discussed in Chapter 1, a **financial statement** is simply a declaration of what is believed to be true about an enterprise, communicated in terms of a monetary unit, such as the dollar. When accountants prepare financial statements, they are describing in financial terms certain attributes of the enterprise that they believe fairly represent its financial activities.

In this chapter, we introduce three primary financial statements:

- Statement of financial position (commonly referred to as the balance sheet).
- Income statement.
- Statement of cash flows.

In introducing these statements, we use the form of business ownership referred to as a *corporation*. The corporation is a unique form of organization that allows many owners to combine their resources into a business enterprise that is larger than would be possible based on the financial resources of a single or a small number of owners. While businesses of any size may be organized as corporations, many large businesses are corporations because of their need for a large amount of capital that the corporate form of business organization makes possible. Later in this chapter we introduce two other forms of business organization—the sole proprietorship and the partnership—which are alternatives to the corporate form for some business enterprises.

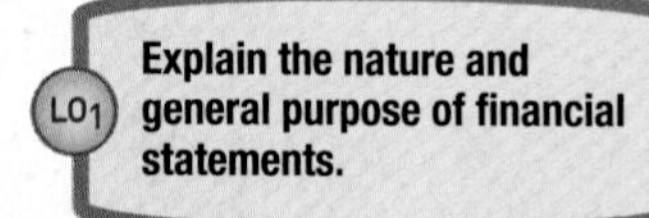

The names of the three primary financial statements describe the information you find in each. The **statement of financial position**, or **balance sheet**, is a financial statement that describes where the enterprise stands at a specific date. It is sometimes described as a snapshot of the business in financial or dollar terms (that is, what the enterprise "looks like" at a specific date).

As businesses operate, they engage in transactions that create revenues and incur expenses that are necessary to earn those revenues. An **income statement** is an activity statement that depicts the revenues and expenses for a designated period of time. Revenues are transactions of the enterprise that already have resulted in positive cash flows or that are expected to do so in the near future, meaning that cash will come *into* the enterprise as a result of the transaction. For example, a company might sell a product for $100. This revenue transaction results in an immediate positive cash flow into the enterprise if the customer pays cash at the time of the transaction. An expected future cash flow results if it is a credit transaction in which payment is to be received later. Expenses have the opposite effect in that they result in an immediate cash flow *out* of the enterprise (if a cash transaction) or an expected future flow of cash out of the enterprise (if a credit transaction). For example, if a company incurs a certain expense of $75 and pays it at that time, an immediate cash outflow takes place. If payment is delayed until some future date, the transaction represents an expected future cash outflow. Revenues result in **positive cash flows**—either past, present, or future—while expenses result in **negative cash flows**—either past, present, or future. *Positive* and *negative* indicate the directional impact on cash. The term *net income* (or *net loss*) is simply the difference between revenues and expenses for a designated period of time.

The **statement of cash flows** is particularly important in understanding an enterprise for purposes of investment and credit decisions. As its name implies, the statement of cash flows depicts the ways cash changed during a designated period—the cash received from revenues and other transactions as well as the cash paid for certain expenses and other acquisitions during the period. While the primary focus of investors and creditors is on cash flows to themselves rather than to the enterprise, information about cash activity of the enterprise is considered to be an important signal to investors and creditors about the prospects of future cash flows to them.

A Starting Point: Statement of Financial Position

All three financial statements contain important information, but each includes different information. For that reason, it is important to understand all three financial statements and how they relate to each other. The way they relate is sometimes referred to as **articulation**, a term we will say more about later in this chapter.

A logical starting point for understanding financial statements is the statement of financial position, also called the balance sheet. The purpose of this financial statement is to demonstrate where the company stands, in financial terms, at a specific point in time. As we will see later in this chapter, the other financial statements relate to the statement of financial position and show how important aspects of a company's financial position change over time. Beginning with the statement of financial position also allows us to understand certain basic accounting principles and terminologies that are important for understanding all financial statements.

Every business prepares a balance sheet at the end of the year, and many companies prepare one at the end of each month, week, or even day. It consists of a listing of the assets, the liabilities, and the owners' equity of the business. The *date* is important, as the financial position of a business may change quickly. Exhibit 2–1 shows the financial position of Vagabond Travel Agency at December 31, 2007.

Exhibit 2–1

STATEMENT OF FINANCIAL POSITION

VAGABOND TRAVEL AGENCY
Statement of Financial Position
December 31, 2007

Assets		**Liabilities & Owners' Equity**		
Cash	$ 22,500	Liabilities:		
Notes Receivable	10,000	Notes Payable.	$ 41,000	
Accounts Receivable . . .	60,500	Accounts Payable . . .	36,000	
Supplies	2,000	Salaries Payable	3,000	$ 80,000
Land	100,000	Owners' Equity:		
Building.	90,000	Capital Stock.	$150,000	
Office Equipment	15,000	Retained Earnings . .	70,000	220,000
Total	$300,000	Total		$300,000

A balance sheet shows financial position at a specific date

Let us briefly describe several features of the statement of financial position, using Exhibit 2–1 as an example. First, the heading communicates three things: (1) the name of the business, (2) the name of the financial statement, and (3) the date. The body of the balance sheet also consists of three distinct sections: *assets*, *liabilities*, and *owners' equity*.

Notice that cash is listed first among the assets, followed by notes receivable, accounts receivable, supplies, and any other assets that will *soon be converted into cash or used up in business operations*. Following these assets are the more permanent assets, such as land, buildings, and equipment.

Moving to the right side of the balance sheet, liabilities are shown before owners' equity. Each major type of liability (such as notes payable, accounts payable, and salaries payable) is listed separately, followed by a figure for total liabilities.

Owners' equity is separated into two parts—capital stock and retained earnings. Capital stock represents the amount that owners originally paid into the company to become owners. It consists of individual shares and each owner has a set number of shares. Notice in this illustration that capital stock totals $150,000. This means that the assigned value of the shares held by owners, multiplied by the number of shares, equals $150,000. For example, assuming an assigned value of $10 per share, there would be 15,000 shares ($10 × 15,000 = $150,000). Alternatively, the assigned value might be $5 per share, in which case there would be 30,000 shares ($5 × 30,000 = $150,000). The retained earnings part of owners' equity is simply the accumulated earnings of previous years that remain within the enterprise. Retained earnings is considered part of the equity of the owners and serves to enhance their investment in the business.

Finally, notice that the amount of total assets ($300,000) is *equal* to the total amount of liabilities and owners' equity (also $300,000). This relationship *always exists*—in fact, the *equality of these totals* is why this financial statement is frequently called a *balance* sheet.

LO2 **Explain certain accounting principles that are important for an understanding of financial statements and how professional judgment by accountants may affect the application of those principles.**

The Concept of the Business Entity

Generally accepted accounting principles require that a set of financial statements describes the affairs of a specific economic entity. This concept is called the *entity principle.*

A **business entity** is an economic unit that engages in identifiable business activities. For accounting purposes, the business entity is regarded as *separate from the personal activities of its owners*. For example, Vagabond is a business organization operating as a travel agency. Its owners may have personal bank accounts, homes, cars, and even other businesses. These items are not involved in the operation of the travel agency and do not appear in Vagabond's financial statements.

If the owners were to commingle their personal activities with the transactions of the business, the resulting financial statements would fail to describe clearly the financial activities of the business organization. Distinguishing business from personal activities of the owners may require judgment by the accountant.

ASSETS

Assets are economic resources that are owned by a business and are expected to benefit future operations. In most cases, the benefit to future operations comes in the form of positive future cash flows. The positive future cash flows may come directly as the asset is converted into cash (collection of a receivable) or indirectly as the asset is used in operating the business to create other assets that result in positive future cash flows (buildings and land used to manufacture a product for sale). Assets may have definite physical characteristics such as buildings, machinery, or an inventory of merchandise. On the other hand, some assets exist not in physical or tangible form, but in the form of valuable legal claims or rights; examples are amounts due from customers, investments in government bonds, and patent rights.

One of the most basic and at the same time most controversial problems in accounting is determining the dollar amount for the various assets of a business. At present, generally accepted accounting principles call for the valuation of many assets in a balance sheet at *cost*, rather than at their current value. The specific accounting principles supporting cost as the basis for asset valuation are discussed below.

The Cost Principle Assets such as land, buildings, merchandise, and equipment are typical of the many economic resources that are required in producing revenue for the business. The prevailing accounting view is that such assets should be presented at their cost. When we say that an asset is shown in the balance sheet at its *historical cost*, we mean the original amount the business entity paid to acquire the asset. This amount may be different from what it would cost to purchase the same asset today.

For example, let us assume that a business buys a tract of land for use as a building site, paying $100,000 in cash. The amount to be entered in the accounting records for the asset will be the cost of $100,000. If we assume a booming real estate market, a fair estimate of the market value of the land 10 years later might be $250,000. Although the market price or economic value of the land has risen greatly, the accounting amount as shown in the accounting records and in the balance sheet would continue unchanged at the cost of $100,000. This policy of accounting for many assets at their cost is often referred to as the **cost principle** of accounting.

Exceptions to the cost principle are found in some of the most liquid assets (that is, assets that are expected to soon become cash). Amounts receivable from customers are generally included in the balance sheet at their *net realizable value*, which is an amount that approximates the cash that will be received when the receivable is collected. Similarly, certain investments in other enterprises are included in the balance sheet at their current market value if management's plan includes conversion into cash in the near future.

In reading a balance sheet, it is important to keep in mind that the dollar amounts listed for most assets do not indicate the prices at which the assets could be sold or the prices at which they could be replaced. A frequently misunderstood feature of a balance sheet is that it *does not* show how much the business currently is worth.

The Going-Concern Assumption *Why* don't accountants change the recorded amounts of assets to correspond with changing market prices for these properties? One reason is that assets like land and buildings are being used to house the business and were acquired for *use* and not for resale; in fact, these assets usually cannot be sold without disrupting the business. The balance sheet of a business is prepared on the assumption that the business is a continuing enterprise, or a **going concern**. Consequently, the present estimated prices at which assets like land and buildings could be sold are of less importance than if these properties were intended for sale. These are frequently among the largest dollar amounts of a company's assets. Determining that an enterprise is a going concern may require judgment by the accountant.

The Objectivity Principle Another reason for using cost rather than current market values in accounting for most assets is the need for a definite, factual basis for valuation. The cost of land, buildings, and many other assets that have been purchased can be definitely determined. Accountants use the term *objective* to describe asset valuations that are factual and can be verified by independent experts. For example, if land is shown on the balance sheet at cost, any CPA who performed an audit of the business would be able to find objective evidence that the land was actually measured at the cost incurred in acquiring it. On the other hand, estimated market values for assets such as buildings and specialized machinery are not factual and objective. Market values are constantly changing, and estimates of the prices at which assets could be sold are largely a matter of judgment.

YOUR TURN **You as a Home Owner**

First, assume you have owned your home for 10 years and need to report the value of your home to the city assessor for real estate tax assessment purposes. What information would you provide? Second, assume you are planning to sell your home. What type of information would you provide to potential buyers? What ethical issues arise in these two situations that the objectivity principle helps address?

(See our comments on the Online Learning Center Web site.)

At the date an asset is acquired, the cost and market value are usually the same. With the passage of time, however, the current market value of assets is likely to differ considerably from the cost recorded in the owners' accounting records.

The Stable-Dollar Assumption

A limitation of measuring assets at historical cost is that the value of the monetary unit or dollar is not always stable. **Inflation** is a term used to describe the situation where the value of the monetary unit decreases, meaning that it will purchase less than it did previously. **Deflation**, on the other hand, is the opposite situation in which the value of the monetary unit increases, meaning that it will purchase more than it did previously. Typically, countries like the United States have experienced inflation rather than deflation. When inflation becomes severe, historical cost amounts for assets lose their relevance as a basis for making business decisions. For this reason, some consideration has been given to the use of balance sheets that would show assets at current appraised values or at replacement costs rather than at historical cost.

Accountants in the United States, by adhering to the cost basis of accounting, are implying that the dollar is a stable unit of measurement, as is the gallon, the acre, or the mile. The cost principle and the **stable-dollar assumption** work well in periods of stable prices but are less satisfactory under conditions of rapid inflation. For example, if a company bought land 20 years ago for $100,000 and purchased a second similar tract of land today for $500,000, the total cost of land shown by the accounting records would be $600,000. This treatment ignores the fact that dollars spent 20 years ago had greater purchasing power than today's dollar. Thus the $600,000 total for the cost of land is a mixture of two "sizes" of dollars with different purchasing power.

CASE IN POINT

Many countries experience prolonged and serious inflation. Inflation can undermine the stable-currency assumption. Accounting rules have been designed in some foreign countries to address the impact of inflation on a company's financial position. For example, Mexican corporate law requires Mexican companies to adjust their balance sheets to current purchasing power by using indexes provided by the government. Because inflation is significant, the indexes are used to devalue the Mexican currency (pesos) to provide a more transparent representation of the company's financial condition.

After much research into this problem, the FASB required on a trial basis that large corporations annually disclose financial data adjusted for the effects of inflation. But after several years of experimentation, the FASB concluded that the costs of developing this information exceeded its usefulness. At the present time, this disclosure is optional, as judged appropriate by the accountant who prepares the financial statements.

LIABILITIES

Liabilities are financial obligations or debts. They represent negative future cash flows for the enterprise. The person or organization to whom the debt is owed is called a **creditor**.

All businesses have liabilities; even the largest and most successful companies often purchase merchandise, supplies, and services "on account." The liabilities arising from such purchases are called *accounts payable*. Many businesses borrow money to finance expansion or the purchase of high-cost assets. When obtaining a loan, the borrower usually must sign a formal note payable. A *note payable* is a written promise to repay the amount owed by a particular date and usually calls for the payment of interest as well.

Accounts payable, in contrast to notes payable, involve no written promises and generally do not call for interest payments. In essence, a note payable is a *more formal* arrangement.

When a company has both notes payable and accounts payable, the two types of liabilities are listed separately in the balance sheet. Liabilities are usually listed in the order in which they are expected to be repaid.[1] Liabilities that are similar may be combined to avoid unnecessary detail in the financial statement. For example, if a company had several expenses payable at the end of the year (for example, wages, interest, taxes), it might combine these into a single line called *accrued expenses*. The word *accrued* is an accounting term communicating that the payment of certain expenses has been delayed or deferred.

Liabilities represent claims against the borrower's assets. As we shall see, the owners of a business *also* have claims on the company's assets. But in the eyes of the law, creditors' claims *take priority* over those of the owners. This means that creditors are entitled to be *paid in full*, even if such payment would exhaust the assets of the business and leave nothing for its owners.

OWNERS' EQUITY

Owners' equity represents the *owners' claims* on the assets of the business. Because liabilities or creditors' claims have legal priority over those of the owners, owners' equity is a *residual amount*. If you are the owner of a business, you are entitled to assets that are left after the claims of creditors have been satisfied in full. Therefore, owners' equity is always equal to *total assets minus total liabilities*. For example, using the data from the illustrated balance sheet of Vagabond Travel Agency (Exhibit 2–1):

Vagabond has total assets of	$300,000
And total liabilities of.	(80,000)
Therefore, the owners' equity must be	$220,000

Owners' equity does *not* represent a specific claim to cash or any other particular asset. Rather, it is the owners' overall financial interest in the entire company.

Increases in Owners' Equity

The owners' equity in a business comes from two sources:

1. *Investments of cash or other assets* by owners.
2. *Earnings* from profitable operation of the business.

Decreases in Owners' Equity

Decreases in owners' equity also are caused in two ways:

1. *Payments of cash or transfers of other assets* to owners.
2. *Losses* from unprofitable operation of the business.

Accounting for payments to owners and net losses are addressed in later chapters.

THE ACCOUNTING EQUATION

A fundamental characteristic of every statement of financial position is that the total for assets always equals the total of liabilities plus owners' equity. This agreement or balance of total assets with the total of liabilities and owners' equity is the reason for calling this financial statement a *balance sheet*. But *why* do total assets equal the total of liabilities and owners' equity?

The dollar totals on the two sides of the balance sheet are always equal because these two sides are *two views of the same business*. The listing of assets shows us what things the business owns; the listing of liabilities and owners' equity tells us who supplied these resources to the business and how much each group supplied. Everything that a business owns has been supplied to it either by creditors or by the owners. Therefore, the total claims of the creditors plus the claims of the owners equal the total assets of the business.

Demonstrate how certain business transactions affect the elements of the accounting equation: Assets = Liabilities + Owners' Equity.

[1] Short-term liabilities generally are those due within one year. Long-term liabilities are shown separately in the balance sheet, after the listing of all short-term liabilities. Long-term liabilities are addressed in Chapter 10.

The equality of the assets on the one hand and the claims of the creditors and the owners on the other hand is expressed in the following **accounting equation**:

The accounting equation

$$\text{Assets} = \text{Liabilities} + \text{Owners' Equity}$$
$$\$300{,}000 = \$80{,}000 + \$220{,}000$$

The amounts listed in the equation were taken from the balance sheet illustrated in Exhibit 2–1. The balance sheet is simply a detailed statement of this equation. To illustrate this relationship, compare the balance sheet of Vagabond Travel Agency with the above equation.

Every business transaction, no matter how simple or how complex, can be expressed in terms of its effect on the accounting equation. A thorough understanding of the equation and some practice in using it are essential to the student of accounting.

Regardless of whether a business grows or contracts, the equality between the assets and the claims on the assets is always maintained. Any increase in the amount of total assets is necessarily accompanied by an equal increase on the other side of the equation—that is, by an increase in either the liabilities or the owners' equity. Any decrease in total assets is necessarily accompanied by a corresponding decrease in liabilities or owners' equity. The continuing equality of the two sides of the accounting equation can best be illustrated by taking a new business as an example and observing the effects of various transactions.

THE EFFECTS OF BUSINESS TRANSACTIONS: AN ILLUSTRATION

How does a statement of financial position come about? What has occurred in the past for it to exist at any point in time? The statement of financial position is a picture of the results of past business transactions that has been captured by the company's information system and organized into a concise financial description of where the company stands at a point in time. The specific items and dollar amounts are the direct results of the transactions in which the company has engaged. The balance sheets of two separate companies would almost always be different due to the unique nature, timing, and dollar amounts of each company's business transactions.

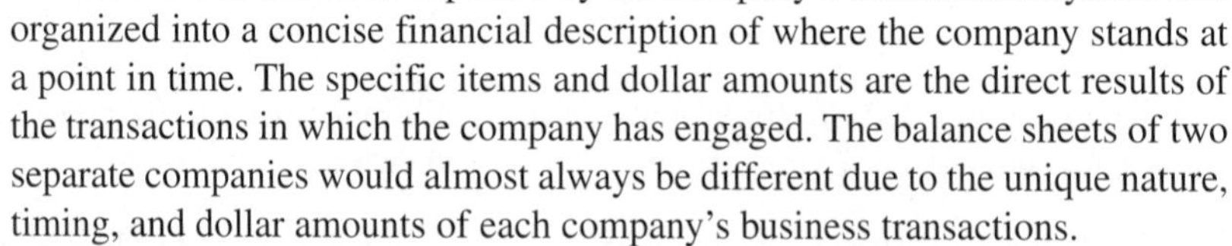

© Royalty-Free/Corbis

To illustrate how a balance sheet comes about, and later to show how the income statement and statement of cash flows relate to the balance sheet, we use an example of a small auto repair business, Overnight Auto Service.

The Business Entity

Assume that Michael McBryan, an experienced auto mechanic, opens his own automotive repair business, Overnight Auto Service. A distinctive feature of Overnight's operations is that all repair work is done at night. This strategy offers customers the convenience of dropping off their cars in the evening and picking them up the following morning.

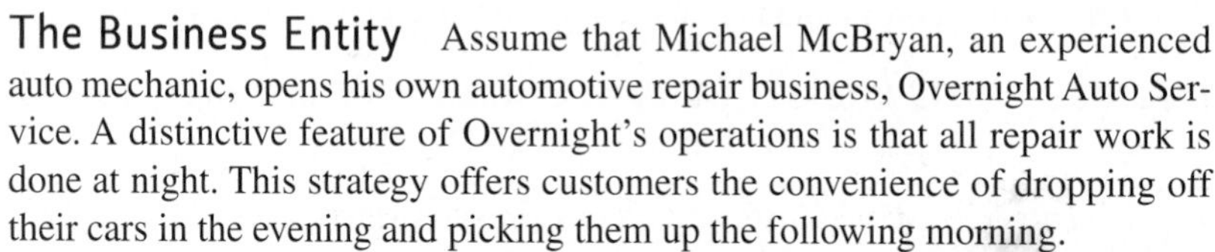

Operating at night also enables Overnight to minimize its labor costs. Instead of hiring full-time employees, Overnight offers part-time work to mechanics who already have day jobs at major automobile dealerships. This eliminates the need for costly employee training programs and for such payroll fringe benefits as group health insurance and employees' pension plans, benefits usually associated with full-time employment.

Overnight's Accounting Policies

McBryan has taken several courses in accounting and maintains Overnight's accounting records himself. He knows that small businesses such as his are not required to prepare formal financial statements, but he prepares them anyway. He believes they will be useful to him in running the business. In addition, if Overnight is successful, McBryan plans to open more locations. He anticipates needing to raise substantial amounts of capital from investors and creditors. He believes that the financial history provided by a series of monthly financial statements will be helpful in obtaining investment capital.

The Company's First Transaction

McBryan officially started Overnight on January 20, 2007. On that day he received a charter from the state to begin a small, closely held corporation whose owners consisted of himself and several family members. Capital stock issued to these investors included 8,000 shares at $10 per share. McBryan opened a bank account in the name of Overnight Auto Service, into which he deposited the $80,000 received from the issuance of the capital stock.

This transaction provided Overnight with its first asset—Cash—and also created the initial owners' equity in the business entity. See the balance sheet showing the company's financial position after this initial transaction in Exhibit 2–2.

Exhibit 2–2
BALANCE SHEET, JAN. 20

OVERNIGHT AUTO SERVICE
Balance Sheet
January 20, 2007

Assets		Owners' Equity	
Cash	$80,000	Capital Stock.	$80,000

Beginning balance sheet of a new business

Overnight's next two transactions involved the acquisition of a suitable site for its business operations.

Purchase of an Asset for Cash Representing the business, McBryan negotiated with both the City of Santa Teresa and the Metropolitan Transit Authority (MTA) to purchase an abandoned bus garage. (The MTA owned the garage, but the city owned the land.)

On January 21, Overnight purchased the land from the city for *$52,000 cash.* This transaction had two immediate effects on the company's financial position: first, Overnight's cash was reduced by $52,000; and second, the company acquired a new asset—Land. We show the company's financial position after this transaction in Exhibit 2–3.

Exhibit 2–3
BALANCE SHEET, JAN. 21

OVERNIGHT AUTO SERVICE
Balance Sheet
January 21, 2007

Assets		Owners' Equity	
Cash	$28,000	Capital Stock.	$80,000
Land	52,000		
Total	$80,000	Total	$80,000

Balance sheet totals unchanged by purchase of land for cash

Purchase of an Asset and Financing Part of the Cost On January 22, Overnight purchased the old garage building from Metropolitan Transit Authority for *$36,000.* Overnight made a cash down payment of *$6,000* and issued a 90-day non-interest-bearing note payable for the *$30,000* balance owed.

As a result of this transaction, Overnight had (1) $6,000 less cash; (2) a new asset, Building, which cost $36,000; and (3) a new liability, Notes Payable, in the amount of $30,000. This transaction is reflected in Exhibit 2–4.

Exhibit 2–4
BALANCE SHEET, JAN. 22

OVERNIGHT AUTO SERVICE
Balance Sheet
January 22, 2007

Assets		Liabilities & Owners' Equity	
Cash	$ 22,000	Liabilities:	
Land	52,000	Notes Payable	$ 30,000
Building.	36,000	Owners' equity:	
		Capital Stock.	80,000
Total	$110,000	Total	$110,000

Totals increased equally by debt incurred in acquiring assets

Purchase of an Asset on Account On January 23, Overnight purchased tools and automotive repair equipment from Snappy Tools. The purchase price was *$13,800*, due within 60 days. After this purchase, Overnight's financial position is depicted in Exhibit 2–5.

Exhibit 2–5

BALANCE SHEET, JAN. 23

Totals increased equally by debt incurred in acquiring assets

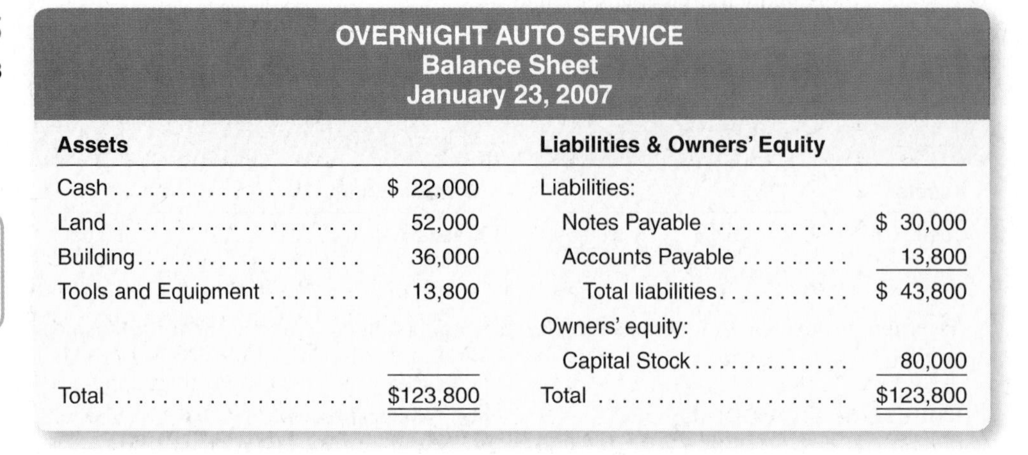

OVERNIGHT AUTO SERVICE Balance Sheet January 23, 2007			
Assets		**Liabilities & Owners' Equity**	
Cash	$ 22,000	Liabilities:	
Land	52,000	Notes Payable	$ 30,000
Building	36,000	Accounts Payable	13,800
Tools and Equipment	13,800	Total liabilities	$ 43,800
		Owners' equity:	
		Capital Stock	80,000
Total	$123,800	Total	$123,800

Sale of an Asset After taking delivery of the new tools and equipment, Overnight found that it had purchased more than it needed. Ace Towing, a neighboring business, offered to buy the excess items. On January 24, Overnight sold some of its new tools to Ace for *$1,800*, a price equal to Overnight's cost.[2] Ace made no down payment but agreed to pay the amount due within 45 days. This transaction reduced Overnight's tools and equipment by $1,800 and created a new asset, Accounts Receivable, for that same amount. A balance sheet as of January 24 appears in Exhibit 2–6.

Exhibit 2–6

BALANCE SHEET, JAN. 24

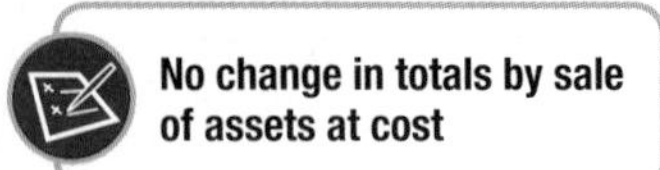

No change in totals by sale of assets at cost

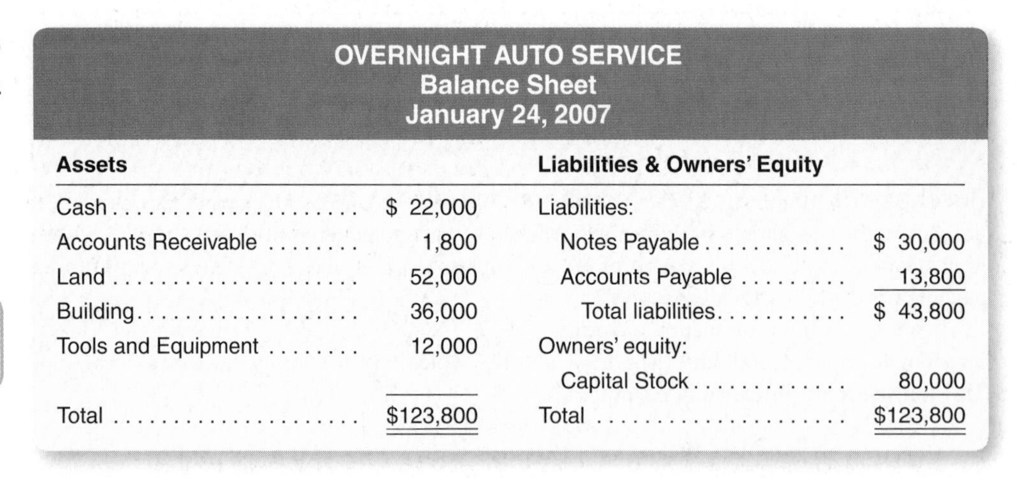

OVERNIGHT AUTO SERVICE Balance Sheet January 24, 2007			
Assets		**Liabilities & Owners' Equity**	
Cash	$ 22,000	Liabilities:	
Accounts Receivable	1,800	Notes Payable	$ 30,000
Land	52,000	Accounts Payable	13,800
Building	36,000	Total liabilities	$ 43,800
Tools and Equipment	12,000	Owners' equity:	
		Capital Stock	80,000
Total	$123,800	Total	$123,800

Collection of an Account Receivable On January 26, Overnight received $600 from Ace Towing as partial settlement of its account receivable from Ace. This transaction caused an increase in Overnight's cash but a decrease of the same amount in accounts receivable. This transaction converts one asset into another of equal value; there is no change in the

[2] Sales of assets at prices above or below cost result in gains or losses. Such transactions are discussed in later chapters.

amount of total assets. After this transaction, Overnight's financial position is summarized in Exhibit 2–7.

Exhibit 2–7

BALANCE SHEET, JAN. 26

OVERNIGHT AUTO SERVICE
Balance Sheet
January 26, 2007

Assets		Liabilities & Owners' Equity	
Cash	$ 22,600	Liabilities:	
Accounts Receivable	1,200	Notes Payable	$ 30,000
Land	52,000	Accounts Payable	13,800
Building	36,000	Total liabilities	$ 43,800
Tools and Equipment	12,000	Owners' equity:	
		Capital Stock	80,000
Total	$123,800	Total	$123,800

Totals unchanged by collection of a receivable

Payment of a Liability

On January 27, Overnight made a partial payment of $6,800 on its account payable to Snappy Tools. This transaction reduced Overnight's cash and accounts payable by the same amount, leaving total assets and the total of liabilities plus owners' equity in balance. Overnight's balance sheet at January 27 appears in Exhibit 2–8.

Exhibit 2–8

BALANCE SHEET, JAN. 27

OVERNIGHT AUTO SERVICE
Balance Sheet
January 27, 2007

Assets		Liabilities & Owners' Equity	
Cash	$ 15,800	Liabilities:	
Accounts Receivable	1,200	Notes Payable	$ 30,000
Land	52,000	Accounts Payable	7,000
Building	36,000	Total liabilities	$ 37,000
Tools and Equipment	12,000	Owners' equity:	
		Capital Stock	80,000
Total	$117,000	Total	$117,000

Both totals decreased by paying a liability

Earning of Revenue

By the last week in January, McBryan had acquired the assets Overnight needed to start operating, and he began to provide repair services for customers. Rather than recording each individual sale of repair services, he decided to accumulate them and record them at the end of the month. Sales of repair services for the last week of January were $2,200, all of which was received in cash.

Earning of revenue represents the creation of value by Overnight. It also represents an increase in the financial interest of the owners in the company. As a result, cash is increased by $2,200 and owners' equity is increased by the same amount. To distinguish owners' equity that is earned from that which was originally invested by the owners, the account *Retained Earnings* is used in the owners' equity section of the balance sheet. The balance sheet in Exhibit 2–9, as of January 31, reflects the increase in assets (cash) and owners' equity (retained earnings) from the revenue earned and received in cash during the last week of January, but before the payment of expenses (see next section).

Exhibit 2–9

BALANCE SHEET, JAN. 31

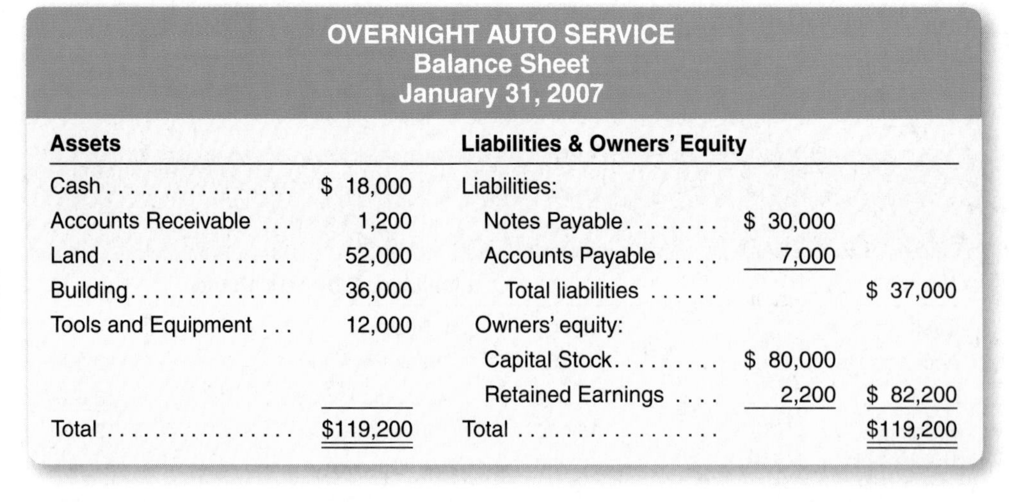

OVERNIGHT AUTO SERVICE
Balance Sheet
January 31, 2007

Assets		**Liabilities & Owners' Equity**		
Cash	$ 18,000	Liabilities:		
Accounts Receivable . . .	1,200	Notes Payable	$ 30,000	
Land	52,000	Accounts Payable	7,000	
Building	36,000	Total liabilities		$ 37,000
Tools and Equipment . . .	12,000	Owners' equity:		
		Capital Stock	$ 80,000	
		Retained Earnings	2,200	$ 82,200
Total	$119,200	Total		$119,200

Revenues increase assets and owners' equity

Explain how the statement of financial position, often referred to as the balance sheet, is an expansion of the basic accounting equation. (LO4)

Payment of Expenses In order to earn the $2,200 of revenue that we have just recorded, Overnight had to pay some operating expenses, namely utilities and wages. McBryan decided to pay all operating expenses at the end of the month. For January, he owed $200 for utilities and $1,200 for wages to his employees, a total of $1,400, which he paid on January 31. Paying expenses has an opposite effect from revenues on the owners' interest in the company—their investment is reduced. Of course, paying expenses also results in a decrease of cash. The January 31 balance sheet, after the payment of utilities and wages, is presented in Exhibit 2–10.

Exhibit 2–10

BALANCE SHEET, JAN. 31

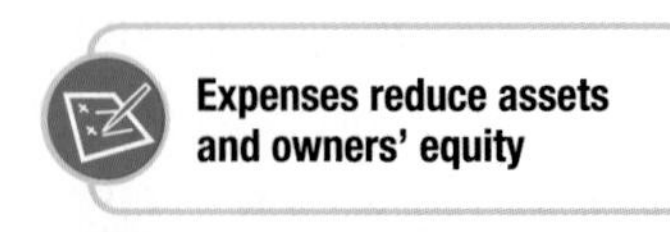

OVERNIGHT AUTO SERVICE
Balance Sheet
January 31, 2007

Assets		**Liabilities & Owners' Equity**		
Cash	$ 16,600	Liabilities:		
Accounts Receivable . . .	1,200	Notes Payable	$ 30,000	
Land	52,000	Accounts Payable	7,000	
Building	36,000	Total liabilities		$ 37,000
Tools and Equipment . . .	12,000	Owners' equity:		
		Capital Stock	$ 80,000	
		Retained Earnings . . .	800	80,800
Total	$117,800	Total		$117,800

Notice that the expenses of $1,400 ($200 for utilities and $1,200 for wages) reduce the amount of retained earnings in the balance sheet. That balance was formerly $2,200, representing the revenues for the last week of January. It is now $800, representing the difference between the revenues for the last week of January and the $1,400 of expenses that Overnight incurred during the same period of time. From this illustration we can see that revenues enhance or increase the financial interest of owners while expenses diminish or reduce the interest of owners. In a corporation, the net effect of this activity is reflected in the balance sheet as retained earnings.

EFFECTS OF THESE BUSINESS TRANSACTIONS ON THE ACCOUNTING EQUATION

As we learned earlier, the statement of financial position, or balance sheet, is a detailed expression of the accounting equation:

Assets = Liabilities + Owners' Equity

As we have progressed through a series of business transactions, we have illustrated the effects of Overnight's January transactions on the balance sheet.

To review, Overnight's transactions during January were as follows, with the resulting balance sheet indicated in parentheses:

Jan. 20 Michael McBryan started the business by depositing $80,000 received from the sale of capital stock in a company bank account (Exhibit 2–2).

Jan. 21 Purchased land for $52,000, paying cash (Exhibit 2–3).

Jan. 22 Purchased a building for $36,000, paying $6,000 in cash and issuing a note payable for the remaining $30,000 (Exhibit 2–4).

Jan. 23 Purchased tools and equipment on account, $13,800 (Exhibit 2–5).

Jan. 24 Sold some of the tools at a price equal to their cost, $1,800, collectible within 45 days (Exhibit 2–6).

Jan. 26 Received $600 in partial collection of the account receivable from the sale of tools (Exhibit 2–7).

Jan. 27 Paid $6,800 in partial payment of an account payable (Exhibit 2–8).

Jan. 31 Recorded $2,200 of sales revenue received in cash (Exhibit 2–9).

Jan. 31 Paid $1,400 of operating expenses in cash—$200 for utilities and $1,200 for wages (Exhibit 2–10).

The expanded accounting equation in Exhibit 2–11 shows the effects of these transactions on the accounting equation. The effect of each transaction is shown in red. Notice that the "balances," shown in black, are the amounts appearing in Overnight's balance sheets in Exhibits 2–2 through 2–10. Notice also that the accounting equation is in balance after each transaction.

Multiple transactions significantly change the enterprise's financial position

While this table represents the impact of Overnight's transactions on the accounting equation, and thus on its financial position as shown in its balance sheet, we can now see how the income statement and statement of cash flows enter the picture. Specifically, the income statement is a separate financial statement that shows how the statement of financial position changed as a result of its revenue and expense transactions. The statement of cash flows shows how the company's cash increased and decreased during the period. In other words, the income statement is simply a separate financial statement that shows how retained earnings changed because of revenues and expenses during the period (far right column). The statement of cash flows is a separate financial statement that details how the company's cash changed during the period (far left column).

Income Statement

Explain how the income statement reports an enterprise's financial performance for a period of time in terms of the relationship of revenues and expenses. LO5

The income statement is a summarization of the company's revenue and expense transactions for a period of time. It is particularly important for the company's owners, creditors, and other interested parties to understand the income statement. Ultimately the company will succeed or fail based on its ability to earn revenues in excess of its expenses. Once the company's assets are acquired and business commences, revenues and expenses are important dimensions of the company's operations. **Revenues** are increases in the company's assets from its profit-directed activities, and they result in positive cash flows. **Expenses** are decreases in the company's assets from its profit-directed activities, and they result in negative cash flows. *Net income* is the difference between the revenues and expenses for a specified period of time. Should a company find itself in the undesirable situation of having expenses greater than revenues, we call the difference a *net loss*.

Overnight's income statement for January 20–31 is relatively simple because the company did not have a large number of complex revenue and expense transactions.[3] Taking information

[3] In this illustration, only revenue and expense transactions change the amount of owners' equity from the original $80,000 investment of the owner. Examples of other events and transactions that affect the amount of owners' equity, but that are *not included in net income*, are the sale of additional shares of capital stock and the payment of dividends to shareholders. These subjects are covered in later chapters.

Exhibit 2–11 EXPANDED ACCOUNTING EQUATION

OVERNIGHT AUTO SERVICE
Expanded Accounting Equation
January 20–31, 2007

	Assets					=	Liabilities	+	Owners' Equity	
	Cash	+ Accounts Receivable	+ Land	+ Building	+ Tools and Equipment	=	Notes Payable	+ Accounts Payable	+ Capital Stock	+ Retained Earnings
Jan. 20	$80,000					=			$80,000	
Balances	$80,000					=			$80,000	
Jan. 21	−52,000		+$52,000			=				
Balances	$28,000		$52,000			=			$80,000	
Jan. 22	−6,000			+$36,000		=	+$30,000			
Balances	$22,000		$52,000	$36,000		=	$30,000		$80,000	
Jan. 23					+$13,800	=		+$13,800		
Balances	$22,000		$52,000	$36,000	$13,800	=	$30,000	$13,800	$80,000	
Jan. 24		+$1,800			−1,800	=				
Balances	$22,000	$1,800	$52,000	$36,000	$12,000	=	$30,000	$13,800	$80,000	
Jan. 26	+600	−600				=				
Balances	$22,600	$1,200	$52,000	$36,000	$12,000	=	$30,000	$13,800	$80,000	
Jan. 27	−6,800					=		−6,800		
Balances	$15,800	$1,200	$52,000	$36,000	$12,000	=	$30,000	$ 7,000	$80,000	
Jan. 31	+2,200					=				+$2,200
Jan. 31	−1,400					=				−1,400
Balances	$16,600	$1,200	$52,000	$36,000	$12,000	=	$30,000	$ 7,000	$80,000	$ 800

Cash → Statement of Cash Flows

Retained Earnings → Income Statement

directly from the Retained Earnings column in Exhibit 2–11, we can prepare the company's income statement as shown in Exhibit 2–12.

OVERNIGHT AUTO SERVICE
Income Statement
For the Period January 20–31, 2007

Sales Revenues		$2,200
Operating expenses:		
Wages	$1,200	
Utilities	200	1,400
Net Income		$ 800

Exhibit 2–12
INCOME STATEMENT

An income statement displays revenues and expenses for a period of time

Notice that the heading for the income statement refers to a *period* of time rather than a *point* in time, as was the case with the balance sheet. The income statement reports on the financial performance of the company in terms of earning revenue and incurring expenses *over a period of time* and explains, in part, how the company's financial position changed between the beginning and ending of that period.

Statement of Cash Flows

Explain how the statement of cash flows presents the change in cash for a period of time in terms of the company's operating, investing, and financing activities.

We already have established the importance of cash flows to investors and creditors and that the cash flows of the company are an important consideration in investors' and creditors' assessments of cash flows to them. As a result, a second set of information that is particularly important concerning how a company's financial position changed between two points in time is cash flow information.

We can use the entire Cash column of the analysis in Exhibit 2–11 to create a statement of cash flows for Overnight Auto Service. The statement classifies the various cash flows into three categories—operating, investing, and financing—and relates these categories to the beginning and ending cash balances. Cash flows from **operating activities** are the cash effects of revenue and expense transactions that are included in the income statement.[4] Cash flows from **investing activities** are the cash effects of purchasing and selling assets. Cash flows from **financing activities** are the cash effects of the owners investing in the company and creditors loaning money to the company and the repayment of either or both.

The statement of cash flows for Overnight Auto Service for the period January 20–31 is presented in Exhibit 2–13.

Notice that the operating, investing, and financing categories include both positive and negative cash flows. (The negative cash flows are in parentheses.) Also notice that the combined total of the three categories of the statement (increase of $16,600) explains the total change in cash from the beginning to the end of the period. On January 20, the beginning balance was zero because the company was started on that day. Several transactions and parts of transactions had no cash effects and, therefore, are not included in the statement of cash flows. For example, on January 22, Overnight purchased a building for $36,000, only $6,000 of which was paid in cash. The remaining $30,000 is not included in the statement of cash flows because it did not affect the amount of cash. Similarly, on January 23, Overnight purchased tools and equipment for $13,800, paying no cash at that time. That transaction has no cash effect on January 23, although

[4] In this illustration, net cash amounts provided by operating activities and net income are equal. This is because all of Overnight Auto Service's revenues and expenses were cash transactions. This will not always be the case. As we learn more about the accrual method of accounting, you will see that revenues and expenses may be recorded in a different accounting period than the period when cash is received or paid. This will cause net income and net cash from operating activities to be different amounts.

Exhibit 2–13
STATEMENT OF CASH FLOWS

OVERNIGHT AUTO SERVICE Statement of Cash Flows For the Period January 20–31, 2007		
Cash flows from operating activities:		
Cash received from revenue transactions.	$ 2,200	
Cash paid for expenses	(1,400)	
Net cash provided by operating activities		$ 800
Cash flows from investing activities:		
Purchase of land.	$(52,000)	
Purchase of building	(6,000)	
Purchase of tools	(6,800)	
Sale of tools	600	
Net cash used by investing activities		(64,200)
Cash flows from financing activities:		
Sale of capital stock		80,000
Increase in cash for the period.		$16,600
Beginning cash balance, January 20, 2007		-0-
Ending cash balance, January 31, 2007		$16,600

A statement of cash flows shows how cash changed during the period

CASE IN POINT

It is not unusual for a company to report an increase in cash from operating activities, but a decrease in the total amount of cash. This outcome results from decreases in cash from investing and/or financing activities. For example, one year **Carnival Corporation**, which owns and operates several cruise lines, reported cash provided by operating activities of almost $1.1 billion but a decrease in total cash of almost $3 million. This was due primarily to large expenditures for property and equipment, such as cruise ships, which are presented as investing activities in the company's statement of cash flows.

the cash payment of $6,800 on January 27, which is a continuation of that transaction, did affect cash and is included in the statement of cash flows. Transactions that did not affect cash are called *noncash investing and financing transactions*. In a formal statement of cash flows, these transactions are required to be noted as we explain later in this text, even though they do not affect the actual flow of cash into and out of the company.

Relationships Among Financial Statements

LO7 Explain important relationships among the statement of financial position, income statement, and statement of cash flows, and how these statements relate to each other.

As our discussion of Overnight Auto Service indicates, the statement of financial position (balance sheet), the income statement, and the statement of cash flows are all based on the same transactions, but they present different "views" of the company. They should not be thought of as alternatives to each other; rather, all are important in terms of presenting key financial information about the company.

The diagram in Exhibit 2–14 explains how the three financial statements relate to the period of time they cover. The horizontal line represents time (for example, a month or a year). At the beginning and ending points in time, the company prepares a statement of financial position (balance sheet) that gives a static look in financial terms of where the company stands. The other two financial statements—the income statement and the statement of cash flows—cover the intervening *period of time* between the two balance sheets and help explain important changes that occurred during the period.

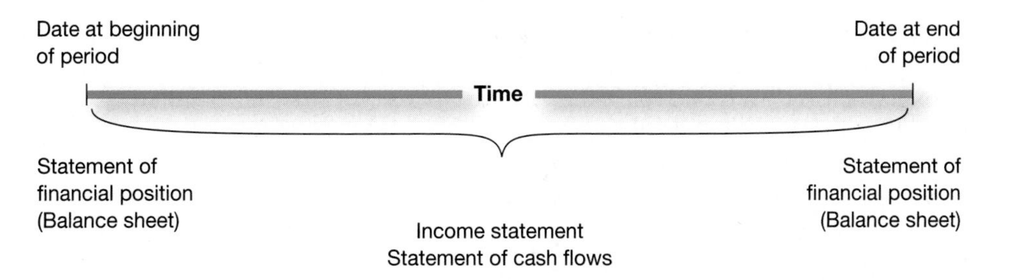

Exhibit 2–14

FINANCIAL REPORTING TIME LINE

Financial statements are closely tied to time periods

If we understand where a company stands financially at two points in time, and if we understand the changes that occurred during the intervening period in terms of the company's profit-seeking activities (income statement) and its cash activities (statement of cash flows), we know a great deal about the company that is valuable in assessing its future cash flows—information that is useful to investors, creditors, management, and others.

Because the balance sheet, income statement, and statement of cash flows are derived from the same underlying financial information, they are said to "articulate," meaning that they relate closely to each other. The diagram in Exhibit 2–15 indicates relationships that we have discussed in this chapter as we have introduced these three important financial statements. The dollar amounts are taken from the Overnight Auto Service example presented earlier in this chapter. In the balance sheet, the property, plant, and equipment amount of $100,000 represents the total of land ($52,000), building ($36,000), and tools and equipment ($12,000).

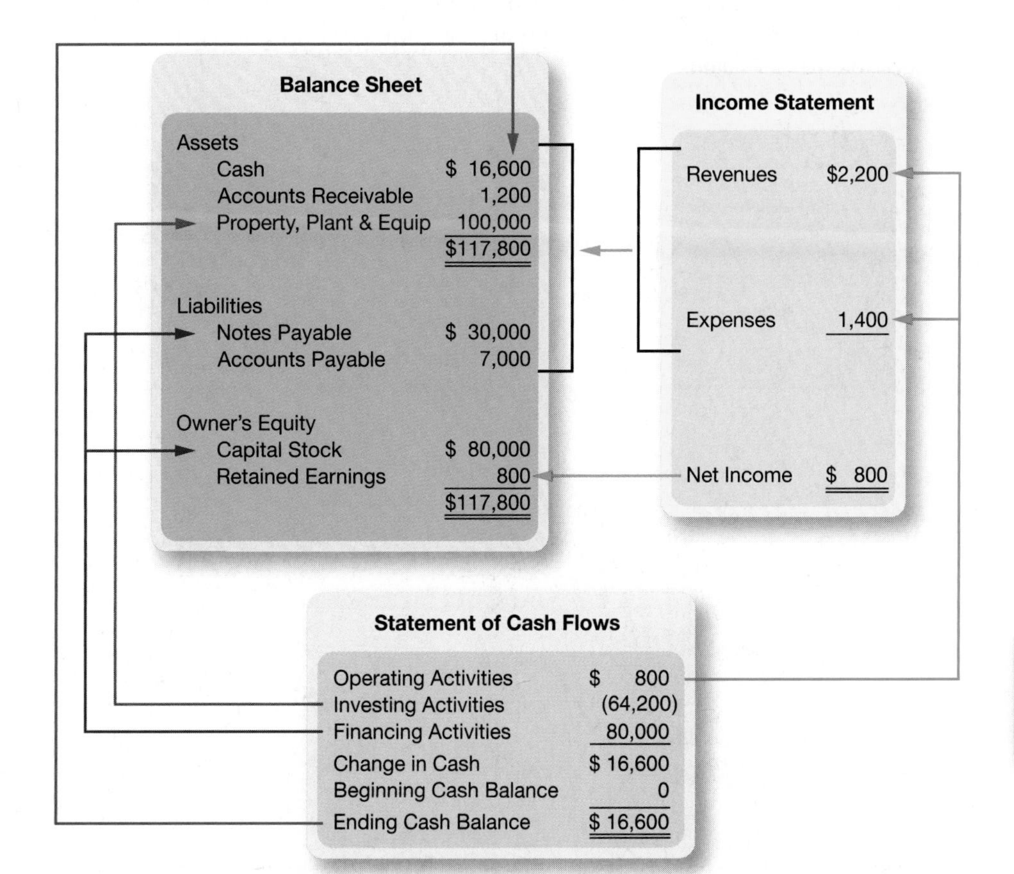

Exhibit 2–15

FINANCIAL STATEMENT ARTICULATION

Financial statements are based on the same underlying transactions

The balance sheet represents an expansion of the accounting equation and explains the various categories of assets, liabilities, and owners' equity. The income statement explains changes in financial position that result from profit-generating transactions in terms of revenue and expense transactions. The resulting number, net income, represents an addition to the owners' equity in the enterprise. The statement of cash flows explains the ways cash increased and decreased during the period in terms of the enterprise's operating, investing, and financing activities. In this illustration, the cash paid for investing activities ($64,200) represents only part of the property, plant, and equipment balance ($100,000). These relationships among the financial statements are called articulation.

While these three key financial statements present important information, they do not include all possible information that might be presented about a company. For example, look again at Overnight's activities during the latter part of January. We could have prepared a separate financial statement on how liabilities changed or how the Tools and Equipment asset account changed. There is also important nonfinancial information that underlies the statement of financial position, the income statement, and the statement of cash flows that could be presented and that would benefit users of the statements. Accountants have developed methods of dealing with these other types of information, which we will learn about later in this text. At this point, we have focused our attention on the three primary financial statements that companies most often use to describe the activities that are capable of being captured in financial terms.

Financial reporting, and financial statements in particular, can be thought of as a lens through which you can view a business. (See Exhibit 2–16.) A lens allows you to see things from a distance that you would not otherwise be able to see; it also allows you to focus in greater detail on certain aspects of what you are looking at. Financial information, and particularly financial statements, allows you to do just that—focus in on certain financial aspects of the enterprise that are of particular interest to you in making important investing and credit decisions. Because financial statements are only one source of financial accounting information, financial reporting provides a broader view of the business than that provided by financial statements. In other words, financial reporting encompasses financial statements, but it is not limited to financial statements.

Exhibit 2–16

FINANCIAL REPORTING AND FINANCIAL STATEMENTS

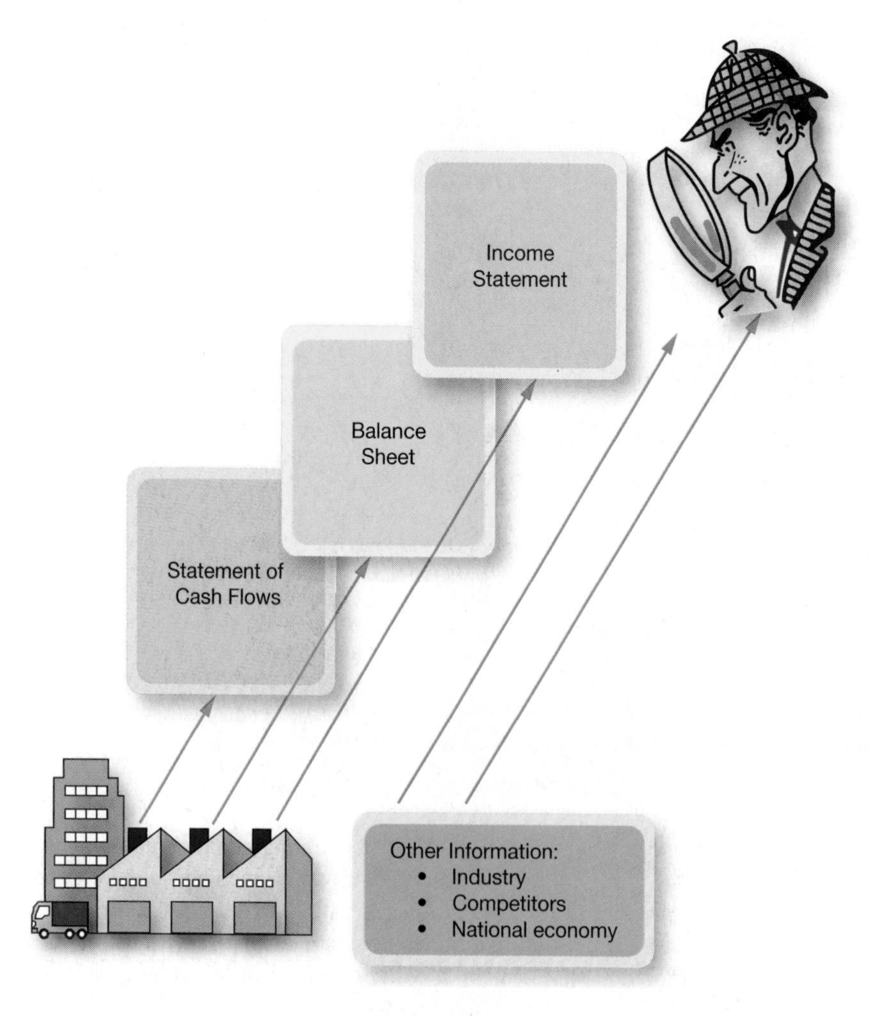

Financial Analysis and Decision Making

Relationships among the three primary financial statements provide the opportunity to learn a great deal about a company by bringing pieces of information together in a meaningful way. In fact, some people believe that relationships in the financial statements are more important than the actual dollar figures in those statements.

For example, take another look at the balance sheet in Exhibit 2–10. Notice that the company has $16,600 of cash and $1,200 of accounts receivable, a total of $17,800 in what are sometimes referred to as *current* assets, denoting that they either are cash or will soon become cash. Now look at the liabilities in the balance sheet and notice that the company has notes payable of $30,000 and accounts payable of $7,000 for a total of $37,000 of liabilities. If both types of liabilities are current liabilities, meaning that they will be due in the near future and, therefore, can be expected to require the use of current assets, Overnight Auto Service may have difficulty paying them because it does not have enough liquid assets to cover its liabilities. The relationship of current assets to current liabilities is called the *current ratio*. For Overnight Auto Service it is a low .48 ($17,800 divided by $37,000). This means that Overnight Auto Service has only 48 cents available for every $1 of liabilities that will come due in the near future. On the other hand, if the $30,000 notes payable resulting from the building purchase is not due in the near future, the company's liquidity is much stronger and the company may have sufficient time to bring in enough cash through its operations to pay the note when it is due.

While the above refers exclusively to information found in the balance sheet, key information from one financial statement often is combined with information from another financial statement. For example, we may be interested in knowing the amount of cash provided by operations (cash flow statement) relative to the amount of a company's currently maturing liabilities (balance sheet). Or we might want to compare a company's net income (income statement) with the investment in assets (balance sheet) that were used to generate that income.

Many of the chapters in this text introduce you to various types of financial analysis. We build on those introductory discussions in Chapter 14, Financial Statement Analysis, in which we provide a comprehensive treatment of how financial statements are used to inform investors and creditors.

You as a Creditor

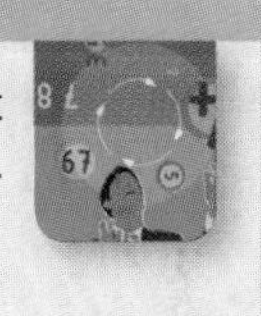

Assume that you are a financial analyst for a potential supplier to Overnight Auto Service. Overnight wants to buy goods from your firm on credit. What factors might you consider in deciding whether to extend credit to Overnight?

(See our comments on the Online Learning Center Web site.)

Forms of Business Organization

Explain common forms of business ownership—sole proprietorship, partnership, and corporation—and demonstrate how they differ in terms of their presentation in the statement of financial position. LO8

In the United States, most business enterprises are organized as a *sole proprietorship*, a *partnership*, or a *corporation*. Generally accepted accounting principles can be applied to the financial statements of all three forms of organization.

SOLE PROPRIETORSHIPS

An unincorporated business owned by one person is called a **sole proprietorship**. Often the owner also acts as the manager. This form of business organization is common for small retail stores, farms, service businesses, and professional practices in law, medicine, and accounting. In fact, the sole proprietorship is the most common form of business organization in our economy.

From an accounting viewpoint, a sole proprietorship is regarded as a business entity *separate from the other affairs of its owner*. From a legal viewpoint, however, the business and its owner are not regarded as separate entities. Thus, *the owner is personally liable* for the debts of the business. If the business encounters financial difficulties, creditors can force the owner to sell his or her personal assets to pay the business debts. While an advantage of the sole proprietorship form of organization is its simplicity, this *unlimited liability* feature is a disadvantage to the owner.

PARTNERSHIPS

An unincorporated business owned by two or more persons voluntarily acting as partners (co-owners) is called a **partnership**. Partnerships, like sole proprietorships, are widely used for small businesses. In addition, some very large professional practices, including CPA firms, are organized as partnerships. As in the case of the sole proprietorship, the owners of a partnership are personally responsible for all debts of the business. From an accounting standpoint, a partnership is viewed as a business entity separate from the personal affairs of its owners.[5] A benefit of the partnership form over the sole proprietorship form is the ability to bring together larger amounts of capital investment from multiple owners.

CORPORATIONS

A **corporation** is a type of business organization that is recognized *under the law* as an entity separate from its owners. Therefore, the owners of a corporation are *not* personally liable for the debts of the business. These owners can lose no more than the amounts they have invested in the business—a concept known as *limited liability*. This concept is the principal reason that corporations are an attractive form of business organization to many investors. Overnight Auto Service, the company used in our illustrations, is a corporation.

Ownership of a corporation is divided into transferable shares of capital stock, and the owners are called **stockholders** or shareholders. Stock certificates are issued by the corporation to each stockholder showing the number of shares that he or she owns. The stockholders are generally free to sell some or all of these shares to other investors at any time. This *transferability of ownership* adds to the attractiveness of the corporate form of organization, because investors can more easily get their money out of the business. Corporations offer an even greater opportunity than partnerships to bring together large amounts of capital from multiple owners.

There are many more sole proprietorships and partnerships than corporations, but most large businesses are organized as corporations. Thus corporations are the dominant form of business organization in terms of the *dollar volume* of business activity. Of the three types of business, corporations are most likely to distribute financial statements to investors and other outsiders.

REPORTING OWNERSHIP EQUITY IN THE STATEMENT OF FINANCIAL POSITION

Assets and liabilities are presented in the same manner in the statement of financial position of all three types of business organization. Some differences arise, however, in the presentation of the ownership equity.

Sole Proprietorships

A *sole proprietorship* is owned by only one person. Therefore, the owner's equity section of the balance sheet includes only one item—the equity of the owner. If Overnight Auto Service had been organized as a sole proprietorship with Michael McBryan the owner, owner's equity in the January 31 balance sheet would appear as follows:

Ownership equity in a sole proprietorship

Owner's equity:	
Michael McBryan, Capital	$80,800

Partnerships

A *partnership* has two or more owners. Accountants use the term *partners' equity* instead of owners' equity and usually list separately the amount of each partner's equity in the business. If, for example, Michael McBryan had been in partnership with his sister, Rebecca McBryan, in Overnight Auto Service, and if each had contributed an equal amount of cash ($40,000) and had shared equally in the net income ($400), the partners' equity section of the balance sheet would have been presented as follows:

. . . in a partnership

Partners' equity:		
Michael McBryan, Capital	$40,400	
Rebecca McBryan, Capital	40,400	
Total partners' equity		$80,800

[5] Creditors of an unincorporated business often ask to see the *personal* financial statements of the business owners, as these owners ultimately are responsible for paying the debts of the business.

Corporations In a business organized as a *corporation,* it is *not* customary to show separately the equity of each stockholder. In the case of large corporations, this clearly would be impossible, as these businesses may have *several million* individual stockholders (owners).

Returning to our original assumption that Overnight Auto Service is organized as a corporation, owners' equity (also referred to as **stockholders' equity** or shareholders' equity) is presented in two amounts—capital stock and retained earnings. This section of the balance sheet appears as follows:

Owner's equity:		
Capital Stock.	$80,000	
Retained Earnings	800	
Total stockholders' equity.		$80,800

. . . and in a corporation

Capital stock represents the amount that the stockholders originally invested in the business in exchange for shares of the company's stock. **Retained earnings**, in contrast, represents the increase in owners' equity that has accumulated over the years as a result of profitable operations.

The Use of Financial Statements by External Parties

As we learned in Chapter 1, investors and creditors use financial statements in making *financial decisions*—that is, in selecting those companies in which they will invest resources or to which they will extend credit. For this reason, financial statements are designed primarily to meet the needs of creditors and investors. Two factors of particular concern to creditors and investors are the *liquidity* and *profitability* of a business organization.

Creditors are interested in **liquidity**—the ability of the business to pay its debts as they come due. Liquidity is critical to the very survival of a business organization—a business that is not liquid may be forced into bankruptcy by its creditors. Once bankrupt, a business may be forced by the courts to stop its operations, sell its assets (for the purpose of paying its creditors), and eventually go out of existence.

Investors also are interested in the liquidity of a business organization, but often they are even more interested in its profitability. *Profitable operations increase the value of the owners' equity* in the business. A company that continually operates unprofitably will eventually exhaust its resources and be forced out of existence. Therefore, most users of financial statements study these statements carefully for clues to the company's liquidity and future profitability.

The Short Run versus the Long Run In the short run, liquidity and profitability may be independent of each other. A business may be operating profitably but nevertheless run out of cash needed to meet its obligations. On the other hand, a company may operate unprofitably during a given year yet have enough cash from previous periods to pay its bills and remain liquid.

Over a longer term, however, liquidity and profitability go hand in hand. If a business is to survive, it must remain liquid and, in the long run, must operate profitably.

Evaluating Short-Term Liquidity As discussed earlier in this chapter, one key indicator of short-term liquidity is the relationship between an entity's *liquid* assets and the liabilities requiring payment *in the near future*. By studying the nature of a company's assets, and the amounts and due dates of its liabilities, users of financial statements often may anticipate whether the company is likely to have difficulty in meeting its upcoming obligations. This simple type of analysis meets the needs of many *short-term* creditors. Evaluating long-term debt-paying ability is a more difficult matter and is discussed in later chapters.

In studying financial statements, users should *always* read the accompanying notes and the auditors' report.

THE NEED FOR ADEQUATE DISCLOSURE

The concept of adequate **disclosure** is an important generally accepted accounting principle. Adequate disclosure means that users of financial statements are informed of any facts *necessary for the proper interpretation* of the statements. Adequate disclosure is made in the body of the financial statements and in *notes* accompanying these statements. It is not unusual to find a series of notes to financial statements that are longer than the statements themselves.

Among the events that may require disclosure in notes to the financial statements are occurrences after the date of the financial statements. For example, assume that Overnight Auto Service's building is destroyed by fire on February 2, and that Michael McBryan is using the financial statements to acquire additional financing for the business after that date. Assume also that McBryan has less insurance on the building than will be needed to replace it. Users of the financial statements, such as bankers who might be considering lending money to Overnight, must be informed of this important "subsequent event." This disclosure usually would be done with a note like the following:

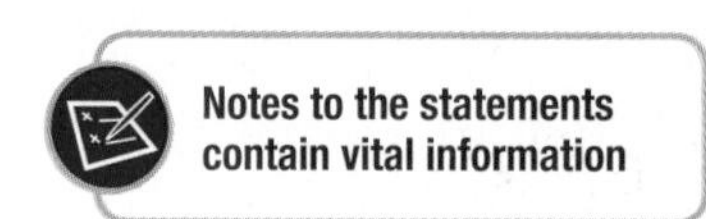
Notes to the statements contain vital information

Note 7: Events occurring after the financial statement date
On February 2, 2007, the building included in the January 31 statement of financial position at $36,000 was destroyed by fire. While the company has insurance on this facility, management expects to recover only approximately $30,000 of the loss.

In addition to important subsequent events, many other situations may require disclosure in notes to the financial statements. Examples include lawsuits against the company, due dates of major liabilities, assets pledged as collateral to secure loans, amounts receivable from officers or other "insiders," and contractual commitments requiring large future cash outlays. One note that is included with all financial statements explains the significant accounting policies applied in preparing those statements.

There is no comprehensive list of the items and events that may require disclosure. As a general rule, a company should disclose any financial facts that a reasonably informed person would consider *necessary for the proper interpretation* of the financial statements. Events that clearly are unimportant *do not* require disclosure. Determining information that should be disclosed in financial statements is another situation that requires significant judgment on the part of the accountant.

MANAGEMENT'S INTEREST IN FINANCIAL STATEMENTS

LO9 Discuss the importance of financial statements to a company and its investors and creditors and why management may take steps to improve the appearance of the company in its financial statements.

While we have emphasized the importance of financial statements to investors and creditors, the management of a business organization is vitally concerned with the financial position of the business and with its profitability and cash flows. Therefore, management is anxious to receive financial statements as frequently and as quickly as possible so that it may take action to improve areas of weak performance. Most large organizations provide managers with financial statements on at least a monthly basis. With modern technology, financial statements prepared on a weekly, daily, or even hourly basis are possible.

Managers have a special interest in the *annual* financial statements, because these statements are used by decision makers outside of the organization. For example, if creditors view the annual financial statements as strong, they will be more willing to extend credit to the business than if they regard the company's financial statements as weak. Management is concerned with its ability to obtain the funds it needs to meet its objectives, so it is particularly interested in how investors and creditors react to the company's financial statements.

A strong statement of financial position is one that shows relatively little debt and large amounts of liquid assets relative to the liabilities due in the near future. A strong income statement is one that shows large revenues relative to the expenses required to earn the revenues. A strong statement of cash flows is one that not only shows a strong cash balance but also indicates that cash is being generated by operations. Demonstrating that these positive characteristics of the company are ongoing and can be seen in a series of financial statements is particularly helpful in creating confidence in the company on the part of investors and creditors. Because of the importance of the financial statements, management may take steps that are specifically intended to improve the company's financial position and financial performance. For example, cash purchases of assets may be delayed until the beginning of the next accounting period so that large amounts of cash will be included in the statement of financial position and the statement of cash flows. On the other hand, if the company is in a particularly strong cash position, liabilities due in the near future may be paid early, replaced with longer-term liabilities, or even replaced by additional investments by owners to communicate that future negative cash flows will not be as great as they might otherwise appear.

These actions are sometimes called **window dressing**—measures taken by management to make the company appear as strong as possible in its financial statements. Users of financial statements should realize that, while the financial statements are fair representations of the financial position at the end of the period and financial performance for the period, they may not necessarily describe the typical financial situation of the business throughout the entire financial reporting period. In its annual financial statements, in particular, management tries to make the company appear as strong as is reasonably possible. As a result, many creditors regard more frequent financial statements (for example, quarterly or even monthly) as providing important additional information beyond that in the annual financial statements. The more frequently financial statements are presented, the less able management is to window dress and make a company look financially stronger than it actually is.

Ethics, Fraud & Corporate Governance

A major outgrowth from the business failures amid allegations of fraudulent financial reporting discussed in the last chapter was the passage of the Sarbanes-Oxley Act of 2002. This Act—named after its primary sponsors in the U.S. Senate and House of Representatives, Senator Paul Sarbanes and Representative Michael Oxley—was signed into law by President George W. Bush on July 30, 2002. The Sarbanes-Oxley Act (hereafter SOX or the Act) is generally viewed as the most far-reaching piece of securities legislation since the original Securities Acts were passed in the 1930s.

GARY TRAMONTINA/Bloomberg News/Landov

The Act is a lengthy and detailed piece of securities legislation, but its major provisions involve: (1) the creation of a new quasi-governmental agency to oversee the public accounting profession, the Public Company Accounting Oversight Board; (2) restrictions on the types of consulting services that accounting firms can provide to audit clients; (3) greater responsibility for audit committees in overseeing the financial reporting process; (4) requiring the chief executive officer (CEO) and the chief financial officer (CFO) to certify the accuracy of their company's financial statements; (5) requiring management to report on the effectiveness of the company's internal controls over financial reporting, which must be audited by the same accounting firm that audits the financial statements; and (6) substantial increases in civil and criminal penalties related to securities fraud, including fraudulent financial reporting.

Although all of the Act's provisions are important, we will briefly discuss the new requirement for CEOs and CFOs to certify the accuracy of their company's financial statements. The CEOs and CFOs of all public companies must now certify on an annual and quarterly basis that they (1) have reviewed their company's financial statements, (2) are not aware of any error or omission that would make the financial statements misleading, and (3) believe that the financial statements fairly present in all material respects the company's financial condition (balance sheet) and results of operations (income statement). There is already some limited evidence that this new certification requirement is affecting corporate behavior. For example, a former CFO of HealthSouth (Weston Smith, shown above) contacted federal authorities about the massive (alleged) accounting fraud at that company because he was not willing to certify that HealthSouth's financial statements were materially accurate.

Concluding Remarks

Throughout this text, we emphasize how accounting information is the basis for business decisions. In this chapter, you have been introduced to business transactions and how they are combined and presented in the form of three basic financial statements—the statement of financial position (balance sheet), the income statement, and the statement of cash flows. These financial statements constitute some of the primary products of the accountant's work, and they provide investors, creditors, and other parties with pertinent information that is useful for decision making.

As you continue your study of financial accounting, in Chapter 3 you will learn how business transactions are actually recorded, how they move through an accounting system, and how they eventually lead to the preparation of financial statements. The foundation you have received in Chapter 2 will be helpful to you as we move into a more sophisticated discussion of business transactions and how they impact a company's financial position, results of operations, and cash flows.

END-OF-CHAPTER REVIEW

SUMMARY OF LEARNING OBJECTIVES

LO1 **Explain the nature and general purpose of financial statements.** Financial statements are presentations of information in financial terms about an enterprise that are believed to be fair and accurate. They describe certain attributes of the enterprise that are important for decision makers, particularly investors (owners) and creditors.

LO2 **Explain certain accounting principles that are important for an understanding of financial statements and how professional judgment by accountants may affect the application of those principles.** Accountants prepare financial statements by applying a set of standards or rules referred to as generally accepted accounting principles. Consistent application of these standards permits comparisons between companies and between years of a single company. Generally accepted accounting principles allow for significant latitude in how certain transactions should be accounted for, meaning that professional judgment is particularly important.

LO3 **Demonstrate how certain business transactions affect the elements of the accounting equation: Assets = Liabilities + Owners' Equity.** Business transactions result in changes in the three elements of the basic accounting equation. A transaction that increases total assets must also increase total liabilities and owners' equity. Similarly, a transaction that decreases total assets must simultaneously decrease total liabilities and owners' equity. Some transactions increase one asset and reduce another. Regardless of the nature of the specific transaction, the accounting equation must stay in balance at all times.

LO4 **Explain how the statement of financial position, often referred to as the balance sheet, is an expansion of the basic accounting equation.** The statement of financial position, or balance sheet, presents in detail the elements of the basic accounting equation. Various types of assets are listed and totaled. The enterprise's liabilities are listed, totaled, and added to the owners' equity. The balancing feature of this financial statement is one of its dominant characteristics because the statement is simply an expansion of the basic accounting equation.

LO5 **Explain how the income statement reports an enterprise's financial performance for a period of time in terms of the relationship of revenues and expenses.** Revenues are created as the enterprise provides goods and services for its customers. Many expenses are required to be able to provide those goods and services. The difference between the revenues and expenses is net income or net loss.

LO6 **Explain how the statement of cash flows presents the change in cash for a period of time in terms of the company's operating, investing, and financing activities.** Cash is one of the most important assets, and the statement of cash flows shows in detail how the enterprise's cash balance changed between the beginning and end of the accounting period. Operating activities relate to ongoing revenue and expense transactions. Investing activities relate to the purchase and sale of various types of assets (for example, land, buildings, and equipment). Financing activities describe where the enterprise has received its debt and equity financing. The statement of cash flows combines information about all of these activities into a concise statement of changes in cash that reconciles the beginning and ending cash balances.

LO7 **Explain important relationships among the statement of financial position, income statement, and statement of cash flows, and how these statements relate to each other.** The three primary financial statements are based on the same underlying transactions. They are not alternatives to each other, but rather represent three different ways of looking at the financial activities of the reporting enterprise. Because they are based on the same transactions, they relate, or "articulate," closely with each other.

LO8 **Explain common forms of business ownership—sole proprietorship, partnership, and corporation—and demonstrate how they differ in terms of their presentation in the statement of financial position.** Owners' equity is one of three major elements in the basic accounting equation. Regardless of the form of organization, owners' equity represents the interest of the owners in the assets of the reporting enterprise. For a sole proprietorship, owner's equity consists of the interest of a single owner. For a partnership, the ownership interests of all partners are added together to determine the total owners' equity of the enterprise. For a corporation, which usually has many owners, the total contribution to the enterprise represents its owners' equity. In all cases, the enterprise's net income is added to owners' equity.

LO9 **Discuss the importance of financial statements to a company and its investors and creditors and why management may take steps to improve the appearance of the company in its financial statements.** Financial statements are particularly important for investors and creditors in their attempts to evaluate future cash flows from the enterprise to them. Management is interested in the enterprise looking as positive as possible in its financial statements and may take certain steps to improve the overall appearance of the enterprise. A fine line, however, exists between the steps management can take and the steps that are unethical, or even illegal.

Key Terms Introduced or Emphasized in Chapter 2

accounting equation (p. 46) Assets are equal to the sum of liabilities plus owners' equity.

articulation (p. 41) The close relationship that exists among the financial statements that are prepared on the basis of the same underlying transaction information.

assets (p. 42) Economic resources owned by an entity.

balance sheet (p. 40) The financial statement showing the financial position of an enterprise by summarizing its assets, liabilities, and owners' equity at a point in time. Also called the statement of financial position.

business entity (p. 42) An economic unit that controls resources, incurs obligations, and engages in business activities.

capital stock (p. 59) Transferable units of ownership in a corporation.

corporation (p. 58) A business organized as a separate legal entity and chartered by a state, with ownership divided into transferable shares of capital stock.

cost principle (p. 43) The widely used principle of accounting for assets at their original cost to the current owner.

creditor (p. 44) A person or organization to whom debt is owed.

deflation (p. 44) A decline in the general price level, resulting in an increase in the purchasing power of the monetary unit.

disclosure (p. 60) The accounting principle of providing with financial statements any financial and other facts that are necessary for proper interpretation of those statements.

expenses (p. 51) Past, present, or future reductions in cash required to generate revenues.

financial statement (p. 40) A declaration of information believed to be true and communicated in monetary terms.

financing activities (p. 53) A category in the statement of cash flows that reflects the results of debt and equity financing transactions.

going-concern assumption (p. 43) An assumption by accountants that a business will operate in the foreseeable future unless specific evidence suggests that this is not a reasonable assumption.

income statement (p. 40) An activity statement that subtracts from the enterprise's revenue those expenses required to generate the revenues, resulting in a net income or a net loss.

inflation (p. 44) An increase in the general price level, resulting in a decline in the purchasing power of the monetary unit.

investing activities (p. 53) A category in the statement of cash flows that reflects the results of purchases and sales of assets, such as land, buildings, and equipment.

liabilities (p. 44) Debts or obligations of an entity that resulted from past transactions. They represent the claims of creditors on the enterprise's assets.

liquidity (p. 59) Having the financial ability to pay debts as they become due.

negative cash flows (p. 41) A payment of cash that reduces the enterprise's cash balance.

operating activities (p. 53) A category in the statement of cash flows that includes the cash effects of all revenues and expenses included in the income statement.

owners' equity (p. 45) The excess of assets over liabilities. The amount of the owners' investment in the business, plus profits from successful operations that have been retained in the business.

partnership (p. 58) An unincorporated form of business organization in which two or more persons voluntarily associate for purposes of carrying out business activities.

positive cash flows (p. 41) Increases in cash that add to the enterprise's cash balance.

retained earnings (p. 59) The portion of stockholders' equity that has accumulated as a result of profitable operations.

revenues (p. 51) Increases in the enterprise's assets as a result of profit-oriented activities.

sole proprietorship (p. 57) An unincorporated business owned by a single individual.

stable-dollar assumption (p. 44) An assumption by accountants that the monetary unit used in the preparation of financial statements is stable over time or changes at a sufficiently slow rate that the resulting impact on financial statements does not distort the information.

statement of cash flows (p. 41) An activity statement that explains the enterprise's change in cash in terms of its operating, investing, and financing activities.

statement of financial position (p. 40) Same as balance sheet.

stockholders (p. 58) Owners of capital stock in a corporation.

stockholders' equity (p. 59) The owners' equity of an enterprise organized as a corporation.

window dressing (p. 61) Measures taken by management specifically intended to make a business look as strong as possible in its balance sheet, income statement, and statement of cash flows.

Demonstration Problem

Account balances for Crystal Auto Wash at September 30, 2007, are shown below. The figure for retained earnings is not given, but it can be determined when all the available information is assembled in the form of a balance sheet.

Accounts Payable	$ 14,000	Land	$68,000
Accounts Receivable	800	Machinery & Equipment	65,000
Buildings	52,000	Notes Payable (due in 30 days)	29,000
Cash	9,200	Salaries Payable	3,000
Capital Stock	100,000	Supplies	400
Retained Earnings	?		

Instructions

a. Prepare a balance sheet at September 30, 2007.

b. Does this balance sheet indicate that the company is in a strong financial position? Explain briefly.

c. How would an income statement and a statement of cash flows allow you to better respond to part **b**?

Solution to the Demonstration Problem

a.

CRYSTAL AUTO WASH
Balance Sheet
September 30, 2007

Assets		**Liabilities & Owners' Equity**	
Cash	$ 9,200	Liabilities:	
Accounts Receivable	800	Notes Payable	$ 29,000
Supplies	400	Accounts Payable	14,000
Land	68,000	Salaries Payable	3,000
Buildings	52,000	Total liabilities	$ 46,000
Machinery & Equipment	65,000	Owners' equity:	
		Capital Stock	$100,000
		*Retained Earnings	49,400
Total	$195,400	Total	$195,400

*Computed as $195,400 (total assets) − $46,000 (total liabilities) = $149,400 (owners' equity); $149,400 − $100,000 (capital stock) = $49,400.

b. The balance sheet indicates that Crystal Auto Wash is in a *weak* financial position. The only liquid assets—cash and receivables—total only $10,000, but the company has *$46,000* in liabilities due in the near future.

c. An income statement for Crystal Auto Wash would show the company's revenues and expenses for the period (month, quarter, or year) ending on the date of the balance sheet, September 30, 2007. This information would be helpful in determining whether the company is successful in selling its auto wash services at an amount that exceeds its cost of providing those services, something the company must do to remain in business and be successful. The statement of cash flows for the same period as the income statement would show where the company's cash came from and where it went in terms of its operating, investing, and financing activities. This information would be particularly helpful in assessing the strength of the company's ability to satisfy its obligations as they come due in light of the relatively weak balance sheet.

Self-Test Questions

The answers to these questions appear on page 85.

Note: In order to review as many chapter concepts as possible, some self-test questions include *more than one* correct answer. In these cases, you should indicate *all* of the correct answers.

1. A set of financial statements:

a. Is intended to assist users in evaluating the financial position, profitability, and future prospects of an entity.

b. Is intended to assist the Internal Revenue Service in determining the amount of income taxes owed by a business organization.

c. Includes notes disclosing information necessary for the proper interpretation of the statements.

d. Is intended to assist investors and creditors in making decisions involving the allocation of economic resources.

2. Which of the following statements is (are) *not* consistent with generally accepted accounting principles relating to asset valuation?

a. Many assets are originally recorded in accounting records at their cost to the business entity.

b. Subtracting total liabilities from total assets indicates what the owners' equity in the business is worth under current market conditions.

c. Accountants assume that assets such as office supplies, land, and buildings will be used in business operations rather than sold at current market prices.

d. Accountants prefer to base the valuation of assets upon objective, verifiable evidence rather than upon appraisals or personal opinion.

3. Waterworld Boat Shop purchased a truck for $12,000, making a down payment of $5,000 cash and signing a $7,000 note payable due in 60 days. As a result of this transaction:
   a. Total assets increased by $12,000.
   b. Total liabilities increased by $7,000.
   c. From the viewpoint of a short-term creditor, this transaction makes the business more liquid.
   d. This transaction had no immediate effect on the owners' equity in the business.
4. A transaction caused a $15,000 *decrease* in both total assets and total liabilities. This transaction could have been:
   a. Purchase of a delivery truck for $15,000 cash.
   b. An asset with a cost of $15,000 destroyed by fire.
   c. Repayment of a $15,000 bank loan.
   d. Collection of a $15,000 account receivable.
5. Which of the following is (are) correct about a company's balance sheet?
   a. It displays sources and uses of cash for the period.
   b. It is an expansion of the basic accounting equation: Assets = Liabilities + Owners' Equity.
   c. It is sometimes referred to as a statement of financial position.
   d. It is unnecessary if both an income statement and statement of cash flows are available.
6. Which of the following would you expect to find in a correctly prepared income statement?
   a. Cash balance at the end of the period.
   b. Revenues earned during the period.
   c. Contributions by the owner during the period.
   d. Expenses incurred during the period to earn revenues.
7. What information would you find in a statement of cash flows that you would not be able to get from the other two primary financial statements?
   a. Cash provided by or used in financing activities.
   b. Cash balance at the end of the period.
   c. Total liabilities due to creditors at the end of the period.
   d. Net income.
8. Which of the following statements relating to the role of professional judgment in the financial reporting process is (are) valid?
   a. Different accountants may evaluate similar situations differently.
   b. The determination of which items should be disclosed in notes to financial statements requires professional judgment.
   c. Once a complete list of generally accepted accounting principles is prepared, judgment by accountants will no longer enter into the financial reporting process.
   d. The possibility exists that professional judgment later may prove to have been incorrect.

ASSIGNMENT MATERIAL

Discussion Questions

1. In broad general terms, what is the purpose of accounting?
2. Why is a knowledge of accounting terms and concepts useful to persons other than professional accountants?
3. In broad terms, what is a financial statement?
4. What is the relationship between time and financial statements?
5. What is the distinction between annual and interim financial statements?
6. What is a business transaction? Give several examples of business transactions and several events that may occur that are not business transactions.
7. Explain briefly why each of the following groups might be interested in the financial statements of a business:
   a. Creditors.
   b. Potential investors.
   c. Labor unions.
8. What is the primary characteristic of the form of business organization called the sole proprietorship?
9. In general terms, what are revenues and expenses? How are they related in the determination of an enterprise's net income or net loss?
10. Why is the statement of financial position, or balance sheet, a logical place to begin a discussion of financial statements?
11. What is the basic accounting equation? Briefly define the three primary elements in the equation.
12. What is meant by the cost principle, and how is the cost principle related to accounting for assets?
13. Why is the going-concern assumption an important consideration in understanding financial statements?
14. What is meant by the terms *inflation* and *deflation*, and how do they relate to the stable monetary unit assumption underlying financial statements?
15. Can a business transaction cause one asset to increase without affecting any other asset, liability, or owners' equity?
16. Give an example of business transactions that would:
    a. Cause one asset to increase and another asset to decrease, with no effect on either liabilities or owners' equity.
    b. Cause both total assets and liabilities to increase with no effect on owners' equity.
17. What is meant by the terms *positive cash flows* and *negative cash flows*? How do they relate to revenues and expenses?
18. What are the three categories commonly found in a statement of cash flows, and what is included in each category?
19. What is meant by the statement that the financial statements *articulate*?

20. What are the major differences in the owners' equity sections of the balance sheet for a sole proprietorship, partnership, and corporation?

21. What is meant by the term *adequate disclosure*, and how do accountants fulfill this requirement in the preparation of financial statements?

22. What is meant by the term *window dressing* when referring to financial statements?

23. What are the characteristics of a strong income statement?

24. What are the characteristics of a strong statement of cash flows?

Brief Exercises

LO3 BRIEF EXERCISE 2.1

Recording Transactions

Green Company purchased a piece of machinery on credit for $10,000. Briefly state the way this transaction affects the company's basic accounting equation.

LO3 BRIEF EXERCISE 2.2

Recording Transactions

Foster, Inc., purchased a truck by paying $5,000 and borrowing the remaining $25,000 required to complete the transaction. Briefly state how this transaction affects the company's basic accounting equation.

LO4 BRIEF EXERCISE 2.3

Computing Retained Earnings

Amber Company's assets total $150,000 and its liabilities total $85,000. What is the amount of Amber's retained earnings if its capital stock amounts to $50,000?

LO4 BRIEF EXERCISE 2.4

Computing Total Liabilities

White Company's assets total $780,000 and its owners' equity consists of capital stock of $500,000 and retained earnings of $150,000. Does White Company have any outstanding liabilities and, if so, what is the total amount of its liabilities?

LO5 BRIEF EXERCISE 2.5

Computing Net Income

Wiley Company had total revenues of $300,000 for a recent month. During the month the company incurred operating expenses of $205,000 and purchased land for $45,000. Compute the amount of Wiley's net income for the month.

LO5 BRIEF EXERCISE 2.6

Computing Net Income

Wexler, Inc.'s income statement showed total expenses for the year to be $50,000. If the company's revenues for the year were $125,000 and its year-end cash balance was $35,000, what was Wexler's net income for the year?

LO6 BRIEF EXERCISE 2.7

Computing Change in Cash

Xavier Company had the following transactions during the current year:

- Had revenues of $100,000 and expenses of $56,000, all in cash.
- Purchased a truck for $20,000.
- Sold land for $10,000.
- Borrowed $15,000 from a local bank.

What was the total change in cash during the year?

LO8 BRIEF EXERCISE 2.8

Alternative Forms of Equity

Solway Company is a sole proprietorship whose owner, Joe Solway, has an equity interest of $50,000. Had Solway been a partnership rather than a sole proprietorship, and the two equal partners were Joe and his brother Tom, how would the $50,000 owners' equity be presented in the company's balance sheet?

LO8 BRIEF EXERCISE 2.9

Alternative Forms of Equity

Repeat Brief Exercise 2.8, except assume that rather than being a sole proprietorship, Solway Company is organized as a corporation with capital stock of $40,000. How would the $50,000 of owners' equity be presented in the company's balance sheet?

LO7 BRIEF EXERCISE 2.10

Articulation of Financial Statements

John Franklin, sole owner of Franklin Mattress Company, has an ownership interest in the company of $50,000 at January 1, 2007. During that year, he invests an additional $10,000 in the company and the company reports a net income of $25,000. Determine the balance of owners' equity that will appear in the balance sheet at the end of the year, and explain how the amount of net income articulates with that figure in the balance sheet.

Exercises

EXERCISE 2.1
The Nature of Assets and Liabilities

Assets and liabilities are important elements of a company's financial position.

a. Define *assets*. Give three examples of assets other than cash that might appear in the balance sheet of (1) **American Airlines** and (2) a professional sports team, such as the **Boston Celtics**.

b. Define *liabilities*. Give three examples of liabilities that might appear in the balance sheet of (1) **American Airlines** and (2) a professional sports team, such as the **Boston Celtics**.

EXERCISE 2.2
Preparing a Balance Sheet

The night manager of Dixie Transportation Service, who had no accounting background, prepared the following balance sheet for the company at February 28, 2007. The dollar amounts were taken directly from the company's accounting records and are correct. However, the balance sheet contains a number of errors in its headings, format, and the classification of assets, liabilities, and owners' equity.

DIXIE TRANSPORTATION SERVICE
Manager's Report
8 p.m. Thursday

Assets		Owners' Equity	
Capital Stock	$ 92,000	Accounts Receivable	$ 70,000
Retained Earnings	62,000	Notes Payable	288,000
Cash	69,000	Supplies	14,000
Building	80,000	Land	70,000
Automobiles	165,000	Accounts Payable	26,000
	$468,000		$468,000

Prepare a corrected balance sheet. Include a proper heading.

EXERCISE 2.3
Preparing a Balance Sheet

The balance sheet items of Mercer Company as of December 31, 2007, follow in random order. You are to prepare a balance sheet for the company, using a similar sequence for assets as illustrated in Exhibit 2–9. You must compute the amount for Retained Earnings.

Land	$90,000	Office Equipment	$ 12,400
Accounts Payable	43,800	Building	210,000
Accounts Receivable	56,700	Capital Stock	75,000
Cash	36,300	Notes Payable	207,000
		Retained Earnings	?

EXERCISE 2.4
Accounting Principles and Asset Valuation

The following cases relate to the valuation of assets. Consider each case independently.

a. World-Wide Travel Agency has office supplies costing $1,700 on hand at the balance sheet date. These supplies were purchased from a supplier that does not give cash refunds. World-Wide's management believes that the company could sell these supplies for no more than $500 if it were to advertise them for sale. However, the company expects to use these supplies and to purchase more when they are gone. In its balance sheet, the supplies were presented at $500.

b. Perez Corporation purchased land in 1955 for $20,000. In 2007, it purchased a similar parcel of land for $300,000. In its 2007 balance sheet, the company presented these two parcels of land at a combined amount of $320,000.

c. At December 30, 2007, Lenier, Inc., purchased a computer system from a mail-order supplier for $14,000. The retail value of the system—according to the mail-order supplier—was $20,000. On January 7, however, the system was stolen during a burglary. In its December 31, 2007, balance sheet, Lenier showed this computer system at $14,000 and made no reference to its retail value or to the burglary. The December balance sheet was issued in February 2008.

In each case, indicate the appropriate balance sheet amount of the asset under generally accepted accounting principles. If the amount assigned by the company is incorrect, briefly explain the accounting principles that have been violated. If the amount is correct, identify the accounting principles that justify this amount.

EXERCISE 2.5

Using the Accounting Equation

Compute the missing amounts in the following table:

	Assets	= Liabilities	+ Owners' Equity
a.	$578,000	$342,000	?
b.	?	562,500	$570,000
c.	307,500	?	187,200

EXERCISE 2.6

The Accounting Equation

A number of business transactions carried out by Smalling Manufacturing Company are as follows:

a. Borrowed money from a bank.

b. Sold land for cash at a price equal to its cost.

c. Paid a liability.

d. Returned for credit some of the office equipment previously purchased on credit but not yet paid for. (Treat this the opposite of a transaction in which you purchased office equipment on credit.)

e. Sold land for cash at a price in excess of cost. (Hint: The difference between cost and sales price represents a gain that will be in the company's income statement.)

f. Purchased a computer on credit.

g. The owner invested cash in the business.

h. Purchased office equipment for cash.

i. Collected an account receivable.

Indicate the effects of each of these transactions on the total amounts of the company's assets, liabilities, and owners' equity. Organize your answer in tabular form, using the following column headings and the code letters **I** for increase, **D** for decrease, and **NE** for no effect. The answer for transaction **a** is provided as an example:

Transaction	Assets	= Liabilities	+ Owners' Equity
(a)	I	I	NE

EXERCISE 2.7

Effects of Business Transactions

For each of the following categories, state concisely a transaction that will have the required effect on the elements of the accounting equation.

a. Increase an asset and increase a liability.

b. Decrease an asset and decrease a liability.

c. Increase one asset and decrease another asset.

d. Increase an asset and increase owners' equity.

e. Increase one asset, decrease another asset, and increase a liability.

EXERCISE 2.8

Forms of Business Organization

Fellingham Software Company has assets of $850,000 and liabilities of $460,000.

a. Prepare the owners' equity section of the company's balance sheet under each of the following *independent* assumptions:

1. The business is organized as a sole proprietorship, owned by Johanna Small.
2. The business is organized as a partnership, owned by Johanna Small and Mikki Yato. Small's equity amounts to $240,000.
3. The business is a corporation with 25 stockholders, each of whom originally invested $10,000 in exchange for shares of the company's capital stock. The remainder of the stockholders' equity has resulted from profitable operation of the business.

b. Assume that you are a loan officer at Security Bank. Fellingham has applied to your bank for a large loan to finance the development of new products. Does it matter to you whether Fellingham is organized as a sole proprietorship, a partnership, or a corporation? Explain.

EXERCISE 2.9

Factors Contributing to Solvency

Explain whether each of the following balance sheet items increases, reduces, or has no direct effect on a company's ability to pay its obligations as they come due. Explain your reasoning.

a. Cash.

b. Accounts Payable.

c. Accounts Receivable.

d. Capital Stock.

EXERCISE 2.10
Professional Judgment

Professional judgment plays a major role in the practice of accounting.

a. In general terms, explain why judgment enters into the accounting process.

b. Identify at least three situations in which accountants must rely on their professional judgment, rather than on official rules.

EXERCISE 2.11
Statement of Cash Flows

During the month of October 2007, Gardial Company had the following transactions:

1. Revenues of $10,000 were earned and received in cash.
2. Bank loans of $2,000 were paid off.
3. Equipment of $2,500 was purchased.
4. Expenses of $7,200 were paid.
5. Additional shares of capital stock were sold for $6,000.

Assuming that the cash balance at the beginning of the month was $7,450, prepare a statement of cash flows that displays operating, investing, and financing activities and that reconciles the beginning and ending cash balances.

EXERCISE 2.12
Income Statement

Hernandez, Inc., had the following transactions during the month of March 2007. Prepare an income statement based on this information, being careful to include only those items that should appear in that financial statement.

1. Cash received from bank loans was $10,000.
2. Revenues earned and received in cash were $9,500.
3. Dividends of $4,000 were paid to stockholders.
4. Expenses incurred and paid were $5,465.

EXERCISE 2.13
Income Statement

An inexperienced accountant for Yarnell Company prepared the following income statement for the month of August 2007:

YARNELL COMPANY
August 31, 2007

Revenues:		
Services provided to customers	$15,000	
Investment by stockholders	5,000	
Loan from bank	15,000	$35,000
Expenses:		
Payments to long-term creditors	$12,000	
Expenses required to provide services to customers	7,500	
Purchase of land	16,000	35,500
Net loss		$ 500

Prepare a revised income statement in accordance with generally accepted accounting principles.

EXERCISE 2.14
Statement of Cash Flows

Based on the information for Yarnell Company in Exercise 2.13, prepare a statement of cash flows in a form consistent with generally accepted accounting principles. You may assume all transactions were in cash and that the beginning cash balance was $7,200.

EXERCISE 2.15
Window Dressing Financial Statements

Prepare a two-column analysis that illustrates steps management might take to improve the appearance of its company's financial statements. In the left column, briefly identify three steps that might be taken. In the right column, briefly describe for each step the impact on the balance sheet, income statement, and statement of cash flows. If there is no impact on one or more of these financial statements, indicate that.

through

EXERCISE 2.16
Home Depot, Inc. Financial Statements

Locate the balance sheet, income statement, and statement of cash flows of **Home Depot, Inc.**, in Appendix A of your text. Review those statements and then respond to the following for the year ended January 29, 2006 (fiscal year 2005).

a. Did the company have a net income or net loss for the year? How much?

b. What were the cash balances at the beginning and end of the year? What were the most important causes of the cash decrease during the year? (Treat "cash equivalents" as if they were cash.)

c. What is the largest asset and the largest liability included in the company's balance sheet at the end of the year?

EXERCISE 2.17
Assessing Financial Results

Intel's 2005 annual report actually includes income statements for three years—2003, 2004, and 2005. Net income for these three years is presented as follows (all in millions): $5,641 (2003), $7,516 (2004), and $8,664 (2005). Further analysis of the same income statements reveals that revenues were the following amounts for these same years (all in millions): $30,141 (2003), $34,209 (2004), and $38,826 (2005). State each year's net income as a percentage of revenues and comment briefly on the trend over the three-year period.

Problem Set A

PROBLEM 2.1A
Preparing and Evaluating a Balance Sheet

Listed below in random order are the items to be included in the balance sheet of Smokey Mountain Lodge at December 31, 2007:

Equipment	$ 39,200	Buildings	$450,000
Land	425,000	Capital Stock	135,000
Accounts Payable	54,800	Cash	31,400
Accounts Receivable	10,600	Furnishings	58,700
Salaries Payable	33,500	Snowmobiles	15,400
Interest Payable	12,000	Notes Payable	620,000
		Retained Earnings	?

Instructions

a. Prepare a balance sheet at December 31, 2007. Include a proper heading and organize your balance sheet similar to Exhibit 2–9. (After "Buildings," you may list the remaining assets in any order.) You will need to compute the amount to be shown for Retained Earnings.

b. Assume that no payment is due on the notes payable until 2009. Does this balance sheet indicate that the company is in a strong financial position as of December 31, 2007? Explain briefly.

PROBLEM 2.2A
Interpreting the Effects of Business Transactions

The following six transactions of Ajax Moving Company, a corporation, are summarized in equation form, with each of the six transactions identified by a letter. For each of the transactions **(a)** through **(f)** write a separate statement explaining the nature of the transaction. For example, the explanation of transaction **(a)** could be as follows: Purchased equipment for cash at a cost of $3,200.

	Assets					=	Liabilities	+	Owners' Equity
	Cash	+ Accounts Receivable	+ Land	+ Building	+ Equipment	=	Accounts Payable	+	Capital Stock
Balances	$26,000	$39,000	$45,000	$110,000	$36,000		$42,000		$214,000
(a)	−3,200				+3,200				
Balances	$22,800	$39,000	$45,000	$110,000	$39,200		$42,000		$214,000
(b)	+900	−900							
Balances	$23,700	$38,100	$45,000	$110,000	$39,200		$42,000		$214,000
(c)	−3,500				+13,500		+10,000		
Balances	$20,200	$38,100	$45,000	$110,000	$52,700		$52,000		$214,000
(d)	−14,500						−14,500		
Balances	$ 5,700	$38,100	$45,000	$110,000	$52,700		$37,500		$214,000
(e)	+15,000								+15,000
Balances	$20,700	$38,100	$45,000	$110,000	$52,700		$37,500		$229,000
(f)					+7,500		+7,500		
Balances	$20,700	$38,100	$45,000	$110,000	$60,200		$45,000		$229,000

PROBLEM 2.3A
Recording the Effects of Transactions

Goldstar Communications was organized on December 1 of the current year and had the following account balances at December 31, listed in tabular form:

	Assets							=	Liabilities			+	Owners' Equity
	Cash	+	Land	+	Building	+	Office Equipment	=	Notes Payable	+	Accounts Payable	+	Capital Stock
Balances	$37,000		$95,000		$125,000		$51,250		$80,000		$28,250		$200,000

Early in January, the following transactions were carried out by Goldstar Communications:

1. Sold capital stock to owners for $35,000.
2. Purchased land and a small office building for a total price of $90,000, of which $35,000 was the value of the land and $55,000 was the value of the building. Paid $22,500 in cash and signed a note payable for the remaining $67,500.
3. Bought several computer systems on credit for $9,500 (30-day open account).
4. Obtained a loan from Capital Bank in the amount of $20,000. Signed a note payable.
5. Paid the $28,250 account payable due as of December 31.

Instructions

a. List the December 31 balances of assets, liabilities, and owners' equity in tabular form as shown.

b. Record the effects of each of the five transactions in the format illustrated in Exhibit 2–11. Show the totals for all columns after each transaction.

PROBLEM 2.4A
An Alternate Problem on Recording the Effects of Transactions

The items making up the balance sheet of Rankin Truck Rental at December 31 are listed below in tabular form similar to the illustration of the accounting equation in Exhibit 2–11.

	Assets							=	Liabilities			+	Owners' Equity
	Cash	+	Accounts Receivable	+	Trucks	+	Office Equipment	=	Notes Payable	+	Accounts Payable	+	Capital Stock
Balances	$9,500		$13,900		$68,000		$3,800		$20,000		$10,200		$65,000

During a short period after December 31, Rankin Truck Rental had the following transactions:

1. Bought office equipment at a cost of $2,700. Paid cash.
2. Collected $4,000 of accounts receivable.
3. Paid $3,200 of accounts payable.
4. Borrowed $10,000 from a bank. Signed a note payable for that amount.
5. Purchased two trucks for $30,500. Paid $15,000 cash and signed a note payable for the balance.
6. Sold additional stock to investors for $75,000.

Instructions

a. List the December 31 balances of assets, liabilities, and owners' equity in tabular form as shown above.

b. Record the effects of each of the six transactions in the preceding tabular arrangement. Show the totals for all columns after each transaction.

PROBLEM 2.5A
Preparing a Balance Sheet; Effects of a Change in Assets

HERE COME THE CLOWNS! is the name of a traveling circus. The ledger accounts of the business at June 30, 2007, are listed here in alphabetical order:

Accounts Payable	$ 26,100	Notes Payable	$180,000
Accounts Receivable	7,450	Notes Receivable	9,500
Animals	189,060	Props and Equipment	89,580
Cages	24,630	Retained Earnings	27,230
Capital Stock	310,000	Salaries Payable	9,750
Cash	?	Tents	63,000
Costumes	31,500	Trucks & Wagons	105,840

Instructions

a. Prepare a balance sheet by using these items and computing the amount of Cash at June 30, 2007. Organize your balance sheet similar to the one illustrated in Exhibit 2–10. (After "Accounts Receivable," you may list the remaining assets in any order.) Include a proper balance sheet heading.

b. Assume that late in the evening of June 30, after your balance sheet had been prepared, a fire destroyed one of the tents, which had cost $14,300. The tent was not insured. Explain what changes would be required in your June 30 balance sheet to reflect the loss of this asset.

PROBLEM 2.6A
Preparing a Balance Sheet—A Second Problem

The following list of balance sheet items are in random order for Wilson Farms, Inc., at September 30, 2007:

Land	$490,000	Fences and Gates	$ 33,570
Barns and Sheds	78,300	Irrigation System	20,125
Notes Payable	330,000	Cash	16,710
Accounts Receivable	22,365	Livestock	120,780
Citrus Trees	76,650	Farm Machinery	42,970
Accounts Payable	77,095	Retained Earnings	?
Property Taxes Payable	9,135	Wages Payable	5,820
Capital Stock	290,000		

Instructions

a. Prepare a balance sheet by using these items and computing the amount for Retained Earnings. Use a sequence of assets similar to that illustrated in Exhibit 2–10. (After "Barns and Sheds," you may list the remaining assets in any order.) Include a proper heading for your balance sheet.

b. Assume that on September 30, immediately after this balance sheet was prepared, a tornado completely destroyed one of the barns. This barn had a cost of $13,700 and was not insured against this type of disaster. Explain what changes would be required in your September 30 balance sheet to reflect the loss of this barn.

PROBLEM 2.7A
Preparing a Balance Sheet and Statement of Cash Flows; Effects of Business Transactions

The balance sheet items for The Oven Bakery (arranged in alphabetical order) were as follows at August 1, 2007. (You are to compute the missing figure for Retained Earnings.)

Accounts Payable	$16,200	Equipment and Fixtures	$44,500
Accounts Receivable	11,260	Land	67,000
Building	84,000	Notes Payable	74,900
Capital Stock	80,000	Salaries Payable	8,900
Cash	6,940	Supplies	7,000

During the next two days, the following transactions occurred:

Aug. 2 Additional capital stock was sold for $25,000. The accounts payable were paid in full. (No payment was made on the notes payable or income taxes payable.)

Aug. 3 Equipment was purchased at a cost of $7,200 to be paid within 10 days. Supplies were purchased for $1,250 cash from a restaurant supply center that was going out of business. These supplies would have cost $1,890 if purchased through normal channels.

Instructions

a. Prepare a balance sheet at August 1, 2007.

b. Prepare a balance sheet at August 3, 2007, and a statement of cash flows for August 1–3. Classify the payment of accounts payable and the purchase of supplies as operating activities.

c. Assume the notes payable do not come due for several years. Is The Oven Bakery in a stronger financial position on August 1 or on August 3? Explain briefly.

PROBLEM 2.8A

LO4 through LO6

Preparing Financial Statements; Effects of Business Transactions

eXcel

The balance sheet items of The Sweet Soda Shop (arranged in alphabetical order) were as follows at the close of business on September 30, 2007:

Accounts Payable	$ 8,500	Furniture and Fixtures	20,000
Accounts Receivable	1,250	Land	$55,000
Building	45,500	Notes Payable	?
Capital Stock	50,000	Retained Earnings	4,090
Cash	7,400	Supplies	3,440

The transactions occurring during the first week of October were:

Oct. 3 Additional capital stock was sold for $30,000. The accounts payable were paid in full. (No payment was made on the notes payable.)

Oct. 6 More furniture was purchased on account at a cost of $18,000, to be paid within 30 days. Supplies were purchased for $1,000 cash from a restaurant supply center that was going out of business. These supplies would have cost $1,875 if purchased under normal circumstances.

Oct. 1–6 Revenues of $5,500 were earned and paid in cash. Expenses required to earn the revenues of $4,000 were incurred and paid in cash.

Instructions

a. Prepare a balance sheet at September 30, 2007. (You will need to compute the missing figure for Notes Payable.)

b. Prepare a balance sheet at October 6, 2007. Also prepare an income statement and a statement of cash flows for the period October 1–6, 2007. In your statement of cash flows, treat the purchase of supplies and the payment of accounts payable as operating activities.

c. Assume the notes payable do not come due for several years. Is The Sweet Soda Shop in a stronger financial position on September 30 or on October 6? Explain briefly.

PROBLEM 2.9A

LO4 LO8

Preparing a Balance Sheet; Discussion of Accounting Principles

Helen Berkeley is the founder and manager of Berkeley Playhouse. The business needs to obtain a bank loan to finance the production of its next play. As part of the loan application, Berkeley was asked to prepare a balance sheet for the business. She prepared the following balance sheet, which is arranged correctly but which contains several errors with respect to such concepts as the business entity and the valuation of assets, liabilities, and owner's equity.

BERKELEY PLAYHOUSE
Balance Sheet
September 30, 2007

Assets		Liabilities & Owner's Equity	
Cash	$ 21,900	Liabilities:	
Accounts Receivable	132,200	Accounts Payable	$ 6,000
Props and Costumes	3,000	Salaries Payable	29,200
Theater Building	27,000	Total liabilities	$35,200
Lighting Equipment	9,400	Owner's equity:	
Automobile	15,000	Helen Berkeley, Capital	50,000
Total	$208,500	Total	$85,200

In discussions with Berkeley and by reviewing the accounting records of Berkeley Playhouse, you discover the following facts:

1. The amount of cash, $21,900, includes $15,000 in the company's bank account, $1,900 on hand in the company's safe, and $5,000 in Berkeley's personal savings account.
2. The accounts receivable, listed as $132,200, include $7,200 owed to the business by Artistic Tours. The remaining $125,000 is Berkeley's estimate of future ticket sales from September 30 through the end of the year (December 31).
3. Berkeley explains to you that the props and costumes were purchased several days ago for $18,000. The business paid $3,000 of this amount in cash and issued a note payable to Actors' Supply Co. for the remainder of the purchase price ($15,000). As this note is not due until January of next year, it was not included among the company's liabilities.
4. Berkeley Playhouse rents the theater building from Kievits International at a rate of $3,000 a month. The $27,000 shown in the balance sheet represents the rent paid through September 30 of the current year. Kievits International acquired the building seven years ago at a cost of $135,000.
5. The lighting equipment was purchased on September 26 at a cost of $9,400, but the stage manager says that it isn't worth a dime.
6. The automobile is Berkeley's classic 1978 Jaguar, which she purchased two years ago for $9,000. She recently saw a similar car advertised for sale at $15,000. She does not use the car in the business, but it has a personalized license plate that reads "PLAHOUS."
7. The accounts payable include business debts of $3,900 and the $2,100 balance of Berkeley's personal Visa card.
8. Salaries payable include $25,000 offered to Mario Dane to play the lead role in a new play opening next December and $4,200 still owed to stagehands for work done through September 30.
9. When Berkeley founded Berkeley Playhouse several years ago, she invested $20,000 in the business. However, Live Theatre, Inc., recently offered to buy her business for $50,000. Therefore, she listed this amount as her equity in the above balance sheet.

Instructions

a. Prepare a corrected balance sheet for Berkeley Playhouse at September 30, 2007.

b. For each of the nine numbered items above, explain your reasoning in deciding whether or not to include the items in the balance sheet and in determining the proper dollar valuation.

PROBLEM 2.10A
Preparing a Balance Sheet; Discussion of Accounting Principles

Big Screen Scripts is a service-type enterprise in the entertainment field, and its manager, William Pippin, has only a limited knowledge of accounting. Pippin prepared the following balance sheet, which, although arranged satisfactorily, contains certain errors with respect to such concepts as the business entity and asset valuation. Pippin owns all of the corporation's outstanding stock.

BIG SCREEN SCRIPTS
Balance Sheet
November 30, 2007

Assets		Liabilities & Owner's Equity	
Cash	$ 5,150	Liabilities:	
Notes Receivable	2,700	Notes Payable	$ 67,000
Accounts Receivable	2,450	Accounts Payable	35,805
Land	70,000	Total liabilities	$102,805
Building	54,320	Owner's equity:	
Office Furniture	8,850	Capital Stock	5,000
Other Assets	22,400	Retained Earnings	58,065
Total	$165,870	Total	$165,870

In discussion with Pippin and by inspection of the accounting records, you discover the following facts:

1. The amount of cash, $5,150, includes $3,400 in the company's bank account, $540 on hand in the company's safe, and $1,210 in Pippin's personal savings account.
2. One of the notes receivable in the amount of $500 is an IOU that Pippin received in a poker game several years ago. The IOU is signed by "B.K.," whom Pippin met at the game but has not heard from since.
3. Office furniture includes $2,900 for a Persian rug for the office purchased on November 20. The total cost of the rug was $9,400. The business paid $2,900 in cash and issued a note payable to Zoltan Carpet for the balance due ($6,500). As no payment on the note is due until January, this debt is not included in the liabilities above.
4. Also included in the amount for office furniture is a computer that cost $2,525 but is not on hand because Pippin donated it to a local charity.
5. The "Other Assets" of $22,400 represent the total amount of income taxes Pippin has paid the federal government over a period of years. Pippin believes the income tax law to be unconstitutional, and a friend who attends law school has promised to help Pippin recover the taxes paid as soon as he passes the bar exam.
6. The asset "Land" was acquired at a cost of $39,000 but was increased to a valuation of $70,000 when one of Pippin's friends offered to pay that much for it if Pippin would move the building off the lot.
7. The accounts payable include business debts of $32,700 and the $3,105 balance owed on Pippin's personal MasterCard.

Instructions

a. Prepare a corrected balance sheet at November 30, 2007.

b. For each of the seven numbered items above, use a separate numbered paragraph to explain whether the treatment followed by Pippin is in accordance with generally accepted accounting principles.

Problem Set B

PROBLEM 2.1B
Preparing and Evaluating a Balance Sheet

Listed below in random order are the items to be included in the balance sheet of Deep River Lodge at December 31, 2007:

Equipment	$ 9,000	Buildings	$430,000
Land	140,000	Capital Stock	?
Accounts Payable	27,400	Cash	9,100
Accounts Receivable	3,300	Furnishings	22,600
Salaries Payable	13,200	Notes Payable	217,000
Interest Payable	4,000	Retained Earnings	202,400

Instructions

a. Prepare a balance sheet at December 31, 2007. Include a proper heading and organize your balance sheet similar to the illustrations shown in Chapter 2. (After "Buildings," you may list the remaining assets in any order.) You will need to compute the amount to be shown for Capital Stock.

b. Assume that no payment is due on the notes payable until 2009. Does this balance sheet indicate that the company is in a strong financial position as of December 31, 2007? Explain briefly.

PROBLEM 2.2B
Interpreting the Effects of Business Transactions

Six transactions of Brigal Company, a corporation, are summarized below in equation form, with each of the six transactions identified by a letter. For each of the transactions **(a)** through **(f)** write a separate statement explaining the nature of the transaction. For example, the explanation of transaction **(a)** could be as follows: Purchased furniture for cash at a cost of $800.

	Cash	+	Accounts Receivable	+	Land	+	Building	+	Furniture	=	Accounts Payable	+	Capital Stock
	Assets									**=**	**Liabilities**	**+**	**Owners' Equity**
Balances	$ 9,000		$30,000		$40,000		$90,000		$10,000		$30,000		$149,000
(a)	−800								+800				
Balances	$ 8,200		$30,000		$40,000		$90,000		$10,800		$30,000		$149,000
(b)	+500		−500										
Balances	$ 8,700		$29,500		$40,000		$90,000		$10,800		$30,000		$149,000
(c)	−3,000								+5,000		+2,000		
Balances	$ 5,700		$29,500		$40,000		$90,000		$15,800		$32,000		$149,000
(d)	−2,000										−2,000		
Balances	$ 3,700		$29,500		$40,000		$90,000		$15,800		$30,000		$149,000
(e)	+10,000												+10,000
Balances	$13,700		$29,500		$40,000		$90,000		$15,800		$30,000		$159,000
(f)									+3,000		+3,000		
Balances	$13,700		$29,500		$40,000		$90,000		$18,800		$33,000		$159,000

PROBLEM 2.3B
Recording the Effects of Transactions

Delta Corporation was organized on December 1 of the current year and had the following account balances at December 31, listed in tabular form:

	Cash	+	Land	+	Building	+	Office Equipment	=	Notes Payable	+	Accounts Payable	+	Capital Stock
	Assets							**=**	**Liabilities**			**+**	**Owners' Equity**
Balances	$12,000		$80,000		$66,000		$41,300		$42,000		$7,300		$150,000

Early in January, the following transactions were carried out by Delta Corporation:

1. Sold capital stock to owners for $40,000.
2. Purchased land and a small office building for a total price of $80,000, of which $30,000 was the value of the land and $50,000 was the value of the building. Paid $10,000 in cash and signed a note payable for the remaining $70,000.
3. Bought several computer systems on credit for $8,000 (30-day open account).
4. Obtained a loan from 2nd Bank in the amount of $12,000. Signed a note payable.
5. Paid the $4,000 account payable due as of December 31.

Instructions

a. List the December 31 balances of assets, liabilities, and owners' equity in tabular form as shown above.

b. Record the effects of each of the five transactions in the format illustrated in Chapter 2 of the text. Show the totals for all columns after each transaction.

PROBLEM 2.4B
An Alternate Problem on Recording the Effects of Transactions

The items making up the balance sheet of Smith Trucking at December 31 are listed below in tabular form similar to the illustration of the accounting equation in Chapter 2 of the text.

	Cash	+	Accounts Receivable	+	Trucks	+	Office Equipment	=	Notes Payable	+	Accounts Payable	+	Capital Stock
	Assets							**=**	**Liabilities**			**+**	**Owners' Equity**
Balances	$4,700		$8,300		$72,000		$3,000		$10,000		$8,000		$70,000

During a short period after December 31, Smith Trucking had the following transactions:

1. Bought office equipment at a cost of $2,600. Paid cash.
2. Collected $2,500 of accounts receivable.
3. Paid $2,000 of accounts payable.
4. Borrowed $5,000 from a bank. Signed a note payable for that amount.
5. Purchased three trucks for $60,000. Paid $5,000 cash and signed a note payable for the balance.
6. Sold additional stock to investors for $25,000.

Instructions

a. List the December 31 balances of assets, liabilities, and owners' equity in tabular form as shown above.

b. Record the effects of each of the six transactions in the tabular arrangement illustrated above. Show the totals for all columns after each transaction.

PROBLEM 2.5B

Preparing a Balance Sheet; Effects of a Change in Assets

Circus World is the name of a traveling circus. The ledger accounts of the business at June 30, 2007, are listed here in alphabetical order:

Accounts Payable	$ 25,000	Notes Payable	$115,000
Accounts Receivable	5,600	Notes Receivable	1,200
Animals	310,000	Props and Equipment	108,000
Cages	15,000	Retained Earnings	89,000
Capital Stock	400,000	Salaries Payable	1,250
Cash	?	Tents	40,000
Costumes	16,000	Trucks & Wagons	125,300

Instructions

a. Prepare a balance sheet by using these items and computing the amount of Cash at June 30, 2007. (After "Accounts Receivable," you may list the remaining assets in any order.) Include a proper balance sheet heading.

b. Assume that late in the evening of June 30, after your balance sheet had been prepared, a fire destroyed one of the tents, which had cost $10,000. The tent was not insured. Explain what changes would be required in your June 30 balance sheet to reflect the loss of this asset.

PROBLEM 2.6B

Preparing a Balance Sheet—A Second Problem

Shown below in random order is a list of balance sheet items for Apple Valley Farms at September 30, 2007:

Land	$ 50,000	Fences and Gates	$14,100
Barns and Sheds	19,100	Irrigation System	10,200
Notes Payable	65,000	Cash	9,300
Accounts Receivable	15,000	Livestock	5,000
Apple Trees	84,000	Farm Machinery	20,000
Accounts Payable	8,100	Retained Earnings	?
Property Taxes Payable	4,700	Wages Payable	1,200
Capital Stock	100,000		

Instructions

a. Prepare a balance sheet by using these items and computing the amount for Retained Earnings. Use a sequence of assets similar to that illustrated in Chapter 2 of the text. (After "Barns and Sheds," you may list the remaining assets in any order.) Include a proper heading for your balance sheet.

b. Assume that on September 30, immediately after this balance sheet was prepared, a tornado completely destroyed one of the barns. This barn had a cost of $4,500 and was not insured against this type of disaster. Explain what changes would be required in your September 30 balance sheet to reflect the loss of this barn.

PROBLEM 2.7B
Preparing a Balance Sheet and Statement of Cash Flows; Effects of Business Transactions

LO3 LO4 LO6

The balance sheet items for The City Butcher (arranged in alphabetical order) were as follows at July 1, 2007. (You are to compute the missing figure for Retained Earnings.)

Accounts Payable	$ 7,000	Equipment and Fixtures	$25,000
Accounts Receivable	8,200	Land	50,000
Building	90,000	Notes Payable	40,000
Capital Stock	100,000	Salaries Payable	3,700
Cash	4,100	Supplies	7,000

During the next few days, the following transactions occurred:

July 4 Additional capital stock was sold for $30,000. The accounts payable were paid in full. (No payment was made on the notes payable or income taxes payable.)

July 5 Equipment was purchased at a cost of $6,000 to be paid within 10 days. Supplies were purchased for $1,000 cash from a restaurant supply center that was going out of business. These supplies would have cost $2,000 if purchased through normal channels.

Instructions

a. Prepare a balance sheet at July 1, 2007.

b. Prepare a balance sheet at July 5, 2007, and a statement of cash flows for July 1–5. Classify the payment of accounts payable and the purchase of supplies as operating activities.

c. Assume the notes payable do not come due for several years. Is The City Butcher in a stronger financial position on July 1 or on July 5? Explain briefly.

PROBLEM 2.8B
Preparing Financial Statements; Effects of Business Transactions

LO4 through LO6

The balance sheet items of The Candy Shop (arranged in alphabetical order) were as follows at the close of the business on September 30, 2007:

Accounts Payable	$ 6,800	Furniture and Fixtures	$ 9,000
Accounts Receivable	5,000	Land	72,000
Building	80,000	Notes Payable	?
Capital Stock	100,000	Retained Earnings	19,100
Cash	6,900	Supplies	3,000

The transactions occurring during the first week of October were:

Oct. 3 Additional capital stock was sold for $30,000. The accounts payable were paid in full. (No payment was made on the notes payable.)

Oct. 6 More furniture was purchased on account at a cost of $8,000, to be paid within 30 days. Supplies were purchased for $900 cash from a restaurant supply center that was going out of business. These supplies would have cost $2,000 if purchased under normal circumstances.

Oct. 1–6 Revenues of $8,000 were earned and paid in cash. Expenses required to earn the revenues of $3,200 were incurred and paid in cash.

Instructions

a. Prepare a balance sheet at September 30, 2007. (You will need to compute the missing figure for Notes Payable.)

b. Prepare a balance sheet at October 6, 2007. Also prepare an income statement and a statement of cash flows for the period October 1–6, 2007. In your statement of cash flows, treat the purchase of supplies and the payment of accounts payable as operating activities.

c. Assume the notes payable do not come due for several years. Is The Candy Shop in a stronger financial position on September 30 or on October 6? Explain briefly.

PROBLEM 2.9B
Preparing a Balance Sheet; Discussion of Accounting Principles

LO4 LO8

Howard Jaffe is the founder and manager of Old Town Playhouse. The business needs to obtain a bank loan to finance the production of its next play. As part of the loan application, Jaffe was asked to prepare a balance sheet for the business. He prepared the following balance sheet, which is arranged correctly but which contains several errors with respect to such concepts as the business entity and the valuation of assets, liabilities, and owner's equity.

OLD TOWN PLAYHOUSE
Balance Sheet
September 30, 2007

Assets		Liabilities & Owner's Equity	
Cash	$ 19,400	Liabilities:	
Accounts Receivable	150,200	Accounts Payable	$ 7,000
Props and Costumes	3,000	Salaries Payable	32,000
Theater Building	26,000	Total liabilities	$ 39,000
Lighting Equipment	10,000	Owner's equity:	
Automobile	15,000	Howard Jaffe, Capital	184,600
Total	$223,600	Total	$223,600

In discussions with Jaffe and by reviewing the accounting records of Old Town Playhouse, you discover the following facts:

1. The amount of cash, $19,400, includes $16,000 in the company's bank account, $2,400 on hand in the company's safe, and $1,000 in Jaffe's personal savings account.
2. The accounts receivable, listed as $150,200, include $10,000 owed to the business by Dell, Inc. The remaining $140,200 is Jaffe's estimate of future ticket sales from September 30 through the end of the year (December 31).
3. Jaffe explains to you that the props and costumes were purchased several days ago for $18,000. The business paid $3,000 of this amount in cash and issued a note payable to Ham's Supply Co. for the remainder of the purchase price ($15,000). As this note is not due until January of next year, it was not included among the company's liabilities.
4. Old Town Playhouse rents the theater building from Time International. The $26,000 shown in the balance sheet represents the rent paid through September 30 of the current year. Time International acquired the building seven years ago at a cost of $180,000.
5. The lighting equipment was purchased on September 26 at a cost of $10,000, but the stage manager says that it isn't worth a dime.
6. The automobile is Jaffe's classic 1935 Olds, which he purchased two years ago for $12,000. He recently saw a similar car advertised for sale at $15,000. He does not use the car in the business, but it has a personalized license plate that reads "OTPLAY."
7. The accounts payable include business debts of $6,000 and the $1,000 balance of Jaffe's personal Visa card.
8. Salaries payable include $30,000 offered to Robin Needelman to play the lead role in a new play opening next December and $2,000 still owed to stagehands for work done through September 30.
9. When Jaffe founded Old Town Playhouse several years ago, he invested $20,000 in the business. However, New Theatre, Inc., recently offered to buy his business for $184,600. Therefore, he listed this amount as his equity in the above balance sheet.

Instructions

a. Prepare a corrected balance sheet for Old Town Playhouse at September 30, 2007.

b. For each of the nine numbered items above, explain your reasoning for deciding whether or not to include the items in the balance sheet and in determining the proper dollar valuation.

PROBLEM 2.10B

Preparing a Balance Sheet; Discussion of Accounting Principles

Hit Scripts is a service-type enterprise in the entertainment field, and its manager, Joe Debit, has only a limited knowledge of accounting. Joe prepared the following balance sheet, which, although arranged satisfactorily, contains certain errors with respect to such concepts as the business entity and asset valuation. Joe owns all of the corporation's outstanding stock.

HIT SCRIPTS
Balance Sheet
November 30, 2007

Assets		Liabilities & Owner's Equity	
Cash	$ 5,000	Liabilities:	
Notes Receivable	4,000	Notes Payable	$ 65,000
Accounts Receivable	3,000	Accounts Payable	32,000
Land	60,000	Total liabilities	$ 97,000
Building	75,000	Owner's equity:	
Office Furniture	9,600	Capital Stock	10,000
Other Assets	25,000	Retained Earnings	74,600
Total	$181,600	Total	$181,600

In discussion with Joe and by inspection of the accounting records, you discover the following facts:

1. The amount of cash, $5,000, includes $2,000 in the company's bank account, $1,200 on hand in the company's safe, and $1,800 in Joe's personal savings account.
2. One of the notes receivable in the amount of $600 is an IOU that Joe received in a poker game five years ago. The IOU is signed by "G.W.," whom Joe met at the game but has not heard from since.
3. Office furniture includes $2,500 for an Indian rug for the office purchased on November 15. The total cost of the rug was $10,000. The business paid $2,500 in cash and issued a note payable to Jana Carpet for the balance due ($7,500). As no payment on the note is due until January, this debt is not included in the liabilities above.
4. Also included in the amount for office furniture is a computer that cost $800 but is not on hand because Joe donated it to a local charity.
5. The "Other Assets" of $25,000 represent the total amount of income taxes Joe has paid the federal government over a period of years. Joe believes the income tax law to be unconstitutional, and a friend who attends law school has promised to help Joe recover the taxes paid as soon as he passes the bar exam.
6. The asset "Land" was acquired at a cost of $15,000 but was increased to a valuation of $60,000 when one of Joe's friends offered to pay that much for it if Joe would move the building off the lot.
7. The accounts payable include business debts of $30,000 and the $2,000 balance owed on Joe's personal MasterCard.

Instructions

a. Prepare a corrected balance sheet at November 30, 2007.

b. For each of the seven numbered items above, use a separate numbered paragraph to explain whether the treatment followed by Joe is in accordance with generally accepted accounting principles.

Critical Thinking Cases

CASE 2.1

Content of a Balance Sheet

You are to prepare a balance sheet for a *hypothetical* business entity of your choosing (or specified by your instructor). Include in your balance sheet the types of assets and liabilities that you think the entity might have, and show these items at what you believe would be realistic dollar amounts. Make reasonable assumptions with regard to the company's capital stock and retained earnings.

Note: The purpose of this assignment is to help you consider the types of assets and liabilities required for the operations of a specific type of business. You should complete this assignment *without* referring to an actual balance sheet for this type of business.

LO4 through LO6

CASE 2.2 Using Financial Statements

Obtain from the library the *annual report* of a well-known company (or a company specified by your instructor).

Instructions

From the balance sheet, income statement, statement of cash flows, and notes to the financial statements, answer the following:

a. What are the largest assets included in the company's balance sheet? Why would a company of this type (size and industry) have a large investment in this particular type of asset?

b. In reviewing the company's statement of cash flows:

1. What are the primary sources and uses of cash from investing activities?
2. Did investing activities cause the company's cash to increase or decrease?
3. What are the primary sources and uses of cash from financing activities?
4. Did financing activities cause the company's cash to increase or decrease?

c. In reviewing the company's income statement, did the company have a net income or a net loss for the most recent year? What percentage of total revenues was that net income or net loss?

d. Select three items in the notes accompanying the financial statements and explain briefly the importance of these items to people making decisions about investing in, or extending credit to, this company.

e. Assume that you are a lender and this company has asked to borrow an amount of cash equal to 10 percent of its total assets, to be repaid in 90 days. Would you consider this company to be a good credit risk? Explain.

LO4

CASE 2.3 Using a Balance Sheet

Moon Corporation and Star Corporation are in the same line of business and both were recently organized, so it may be assumed that the recorded costs for assets are close to current market values. The balance sheets for the two companies are as follows at July 31, 2007:

MOON CORPORATION
Balance Sheet
July 31, 2007

Assets		Liabilities & Owner's Equity		
Cash	$ 18,000	Liabilities:		
Accounts Receivable	26,000	Notes Payable		
Land	37,200	(due in 60 days)		$ 12,400
Building	38,000	Accounts Payable		9,600
Office Equipment	1,200	Total liabilities		$ 22,000
		Stockholders' equity:		
		Capital Stock	$60,000	
		Retained Earnings	38,400	98,400
Total	$120,400	Total		$120,400

STAR CORPORATION
Balance Sheet
July 31, 2007

Assets		Liabilities & Owner's Equity		
Cash	$ 4,800	Liabilities:		
Accounts Receivable	9,600	Notes Payable		
Land	96,000	(due in 60 days)		$ 22,400
Building	60,000	Accounts Payable		43,200
Office Equipment	12,000	Total liabilities		$ 65,600
		Stockholders' equity:		
		Capital Stock	$72,000	
		Retained Earnings	44,800	116,800
Total	$182,400	Total		$182,400

Instructions

a. Assume that you are a banker and that each company has applied to you for a 90-day loan of $12,000. Which would you consider to be the more favorable prospect? Explain your answer fully.

b. Assume that you are an investor considering purchasing all the capital stock of one or both of the companies. For which business would you be willing to pay the higher price? Do you see any indication of a financial crisis that you might face shortly after buying either company? Explain your answer fully. (For either decision, additional information would be useful, but you are to reach your decision on the basis of the information available.)

CASE 2.4
Using Statements of Cash Flows

John Marshall is employed as a bank loan officer for First State Bank. He is comparing two companies that have applied for loans, and he wants your help in evaluating those companies. The two companies—Morris, Inc., and Walker Company—are approximately the same size and had approximately the same cash balance at the beginning of 2005. Because the total cash flows for the three-year period are virtually the same, John is inclined to evaluate the two companies as equal in terms of their desirability as loan candidates.

Abbreviated information (in thousands of dollars) from Morris, Inc., and Walker Company is as follows:

	Morris, Inc.			Walker Company		
	2005	2006	2007	2005	2006	2007
Cash flows from:						
Operating activities	$10	$13	$ 15	$ 8	$ 3	$(2)
Investing activities	(5)	(8)	(10)	(7)	(5)	8
Financing activities	8	(3)	1	12	4	-0-
Net from all activities	$13	$ 2	$ 6	$13	$ 2	$ 6

Instructions

a. Do you agree with John's preliminary assessment that the two companies are approximately equal in terms of their strength as loan candidates? Why or why not?

b. What might account for the fact that Walker Company's cash flow from financing activities is zero in 2007?

c. Generally, what would you advise John with regard to using statements of cash flows in evaluating loan candidates?

CASE 2.5
Ethics and Window Dressing

The date is November 18, 2007. You are the chief executive officer of Omega Software—a publicly owned company that is currently in financial difficulty. Omega needs new large bank loans if it is to survive.

You have been negotiating with several banks, but each has asked to see your 2007 financial statements, which will be dated December 31. These statements will, of course, be audited. You are now meeting with other corporate officers to discuss the situation, and the following suggestions have been made:

1. "We are planning to buy WordMaster Software Co. for $8 million cash in December. The owners of WordMaster are in no hurry; if we delay this acquisition until January, we'll have $8 million more cash at year-end. That should make us look a lot more solvent."
2. "At year-end, we'll owe accounts payable of about $18 million. If we were to show this liability in our balance sheet at half that amount—say, $9 million—no one would know the difference. We could report the other $9 million as stockholders' equity and our financial position would appear much stronger."
3. "We owe Delta Programming $5 million, due in 90 days. I know some people at Delta. If we were to sign a note and pay them 12 percent interest, they'd let us postpone this debt for a year or more."
4. "We own land that cost us $2 million but today is worth at least $6 million. Let's show it at $6 million in our balance sheet, and that will increase our total assets and our stockholders' equity by $4 million."

Instructions

Separately evaluate each of these four proposals to improve Omega Software's financial statements. Your evaluations should consider ethical and legal issues as well as accounting issues.

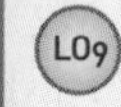

CASE 2.6
Public Company Accounting Oversight Board

The Public Company Accounting Oversight Board (PCAOB) is a direct outcome of the Sarbanes-Oxley Act of 2002. This is considered one of the most significant pieces of legislation to have been enacted in terms of financial reporting in several decades. To respond to the instructions in this case, use the methodology of your choice to locate the Web site of the PCAOB.

Instructions

a. State the mission of the PCAOB.

b. Access the category "About Us" and list the names of the members of the PCAOB.

c. Access the category "Enforcement" and describe the authority the PCAOB has been granted by the Sarbanes-Oxley Act of 2002.

d. Access the category "Standards" and describe the responsibility of the PCAOB to establish standards that impact corporate financial reporting.

through

***BUSINESSWEEK* CASE 2.7**
Evaluating Company Efficiency

Evaluating Company Efficiency

One of the ways a company's financial statement can be used is to evaluate a company's efficiency. This includes, for example, evaluating how well the company controls its costs. In the *BusinessWeek* article, "How Efficient Is That Company?" (December 23, 2002, by Susan Scherreik), the importance of how often a company turns over its receivables and inventories is explained: "In today's tough business climate, many companies succeed by running financially efficient operations. That means they keep costs down—and reduce the need to borrow—by trimming their inventories and speeding up collections of what's owed them." The article goes on to say that you can obtain the necessary information to determine these aspects of a company from the Securities and Exchange Commission's Web site, www.sec.gov.

Instructions

a. Explain how a company would benefit from collecting its receivables from customers quickly rather than allowing them to remain "outstanding" (uncollected) for a long period of time.

b. Explain how a company would benefit from selling its inventory rapidly rather than allowing it to accumulate for long periods of time before selling it.

through

INTERNET CASE 2.8
Gathering Financial Information

This assignment introduces you to EDGAR, the Securities and Exchange Commission's database of financial information about publicly owned companies. The SEC maintains EDGAR to increase the efficiency of financial reporting in the American economy and also to give the public free and easy access to information about publicly owned companies.

Instructions

Access EDGAR at the following Internet address: www.sec.gov.

Click "Search for Company Filings" and then "Companies and Other Filers." Then type Cisco Systems into the search box and click on "Find Companies." Locate the most recent 10Q (quarterly) report.

a. What is the business address of **Cisco Systems**?

b. Locate the balance sheet in Form 10Q and determine whether the amount of the company's cash (and cash equivalents) increased or decreased in the most recent quarter.

c. Locate the income statement (called the "statement of operations"). What was the company's net income for the most recent quarter? Is that amount higher or lower than in the previous quarter?

d. Analyzing the statement of cash flows, how much cash was provided by operations to date for the current year?

e. While you are in EDGAR, pick another company that interests you and learn more about it by studying that company's information. Be prepared to tell the class which company you selected and explain what you learned.

Internet sites are time and date sensitive. It is the purpose of these exercises to have you explore the Internet. You may need to use the Yahoo! search engine **http://www.yahoo.com** *(or another favorite search engine) to find a company's current Web address.*

Answers to Self-Test Questions

1. a, c, d **2.** b **3.** b, d **4.** c **5.** b, c **6.** b, d **7.** a **8.** a, b, d

The Accounting Cycle
Capturing Economic Events

Learning Objectives

AFTER STUDYING THIS CHAPTER, YOU SHOULD BE ABLE TO:

LO1 Identify the steps in the accounting cycle and discuss the role of accounting records in an organization.

LO2 Describe a ledger account and a ledger.

LO3 Understand how balance sheet accounts are increased or decreased.

LO4 Explain the double-entry system of accounting.

LO5 Explain the purpose of a journal and its relationship to the ledger.

LO6 Explain the nature of *net income, revenue*, and *expenses*.

LO7 Apply the *realization* and *matching* principles in recording revenue and expenses.

LO8 Understand how revenue and expense transactions are recorded in an accounting system.

LO9 Prepare a trial balance and explain its uses and limitations.

LO10 Distinguish between accounting cycle procedures and the *knowledge* of accounting.

© PUNIT PARANJPE/Reuters/Corbis

PEPSICO, INC.

Capturing the economic events of a lemonade stand is a fairly simple process. In fact, for most lemonade stands, an empty cigar box may serve as a complete information system.

Capturing the economic events of **PepsiCo, Inc.**, however, is an entirely different matter. This giant corporation generates annual revenue of over $30 billion from sales of its beverage products, its **Frito-Lay** snack foods, and its **Quaker Oats** cereal and pasta products. Employing nearly 150,000 people, and operating hundreds of manufacturing facilities and thousands of warehouses and distribution centers, **PepsiCo, Inc.**, must somehow capture complex business transactions occurring in more than 200 countries worldwide.

From lemonade stands to multinational corporations, being able to efficiently capture the effects of economic events, such as sales orders and raw material purchases, is absolutely essential for survival. Companies like **PepsiCo, Inc.**, rely upon sophisticated computer systems to capture economic activities. Some small enterprises, however, may use paper ledgers and journals to record business transactions.

Although Overnight Auto Service engaged in several business transactions in the previous chapter, we did not illustrate how these events were captured by Overnight for use by management and other interested parties. This chapter demonstrates how accounting systems record economic events related to a variety of business transactions.

The Accounting Cycle

LO1 **Identify the steps in the accounting cycle and discuss the role of accounting records in an organization.**

In Chapter 2, we illustrated several transactions of Overnight Auto Service that occurred during the last week in January 2007. We prepared a complete set of financial statements immediately following our discussion of these transactions. For practical purposes, businesses do not prepare new financial statements after every transaction. Rather, they accumulate the effects of individual transactions in their *accounting records*. Then, at regular intervals, the data in these records are used to prepare financial statements, income tax returns, and other types of reports.

The sequence of accounting procedures used to record, classify, and summarize accounting information in financial reports at regular intervals is often termed the **accounting cycle**. The accounting cycle begins with the initial recording of business transactions and concludes with the preparation of a complete set of formal financial statements. The term *cycle* indicates that these procedures must be repeated continuously to enable the business to prepare new, up-to-date financial statements at reasonable intervals.

The accounting cycle generally consists of eight specific steps. In this chapter, we illustrate how businesses (1) journalize (record) transactions, (2) post each journal entry to the appropriate ledger accounts, and (3) prepare a trial balance. The remaining steps of the cycle will be addressed in Chapters 4 and 5. They include (4) making end-of-period adjustments, (5) preparing an adjusted trial balance, (6) preparing financial statements, (7) journalizing and posting closing entries, and (8) preparing an after-closing trial balance.

THE ROLE OF ACCOUNTING RECORDS

The cyclical process of collecting financial information and maintaining accounting records does far more than facilitate the preparation of financial statements. Managers and employees of a business frequently use the information stored in the accounting records for such purposes as:

1. Establishing **accountability** for the assets and/or transactions under an individual's control.
2. Keeping track of routine business activities—such as the amounts of money in company bank accounts, amounts due from credit customers, or amounts owed to suppliers.
3. Obtaining detailed information about a particular transaction.
4. Evaluating the efficiency and performance of various departments within the organization.
5. Maintaining documentary evidence of the company's business activities. (For example, tax laws require companies to maintain accounting records supporting the amounts reported in tax returns.)

The Ledger

LO2 **Describe a ledger account and a ledger.**

An accounting system includes a separate record for each item that appears in the financial statements. For example, a separate record is kept for the asset cash, showing all increases and decreases in cash resulting from the many transactions in which cash is received or paid. A similar record is kept for every other asset, for every liability, for owners' equity, and for every revenue and expense account appearing in the income statement.

The record used to keep track of the increases and decreases in financial statement items is termed a "ledger account" or, simply, an **account**. The entire group of accounts is kept together in an accounting record called a **ledger**. Exhibit 3–8 on page 110 illustrates the ledger of Overnight Auto Service.

The Use of Accounts

An account is a means of accumulating in one place all the information about changes in specific financial statement items, such as a particular asset or liability. For example, the Cash account provides a company's current cash balance, a record of its cash receipts, and a record of its cash disbursements.

In its simplest form, an account has only three elements: (1) a title; (2) a left side, which is called the *debit* side; and (3) a right side, which is called the *credit* side. This form of an account, illustrated below and on the following page, is called a *T account* because of its resemblance to the letter "T." In a computerized system, of course, the elements of each account are stored and formatted electronically. More complete forms of accounts will be illustrated later.

Title of Account	
Left or Debit Side	Right or Credit Side

Debit and Credit Entries

An amount recorded on the left, or debit, side of an account is called a **debit**, or a debit entry. Likewise, any amount entered on the right, or credit, side is called a **credit**, or a credit entry. In simple terms, debits refer to the left side of an account, and credits refer to the right side of an account.

To illustrate the recording of debits and credits in an account, let us go back to the eight cash transactions of Overnight Auto Service, described in Chapter 2. When these cash transactions are recorded in the Cash account, the receipts are listed on the debit side, and the payments are listed on the credit side. The dates of the transactions may also be listed, as shown in the following illustration:

Cash transactions entered in ledger account

Cash			
1/20	80,000	1/21	52,000
1/26	600	1/22	6,000
1/31	2,200	1/27	6,800
		1/31	200
		1/31	1,200
1/31 Balance	16,600		

Each debit and credit entry in the Cash account represents a cash receipt or a cash payment. The amount of cash owned by the business at a given date is equal to the *balance* of the account on that date.

Determining the Balance of a T Account The balance of an account is the difference between the debit and credit entries in the account. If the debit total exceeds the credit total, the account has a *debit balance*; if the credit total exceeds the debit total, the account has a *credit balance*.

In our illustrated Cash account, a line has been drawn across the account following the last cash transaction recorded in January. The total cash receipts (debits) recorded in January amount to $82,800, and the total cash payments (credits) amount to $66,200. By subtracting the credit total from the debit total ($82,800 − $66,200), we determine that the Cash account has a debit balance of *$16,600* on January 31.

This debit balance is entered in the debit side of the account just below the line. In effect, the line creates a "fresh start" in the account, with the month-end balance representing the *net result* of all the previous debit and credit entries. The Cash account now shows the amount of cash owned by the business on January 31. In a balance sheet prepared at this date, Cash in the amount of $16,600 would be listed as an asset.

Debit Balances in Asset Accounts In the preceding illustration of a Cash account, increases were recorded on the left, or debit, side of the account and decreases were recorded on the right, or credit, side. The increases were greater than the decreases and the result was a debit balance in the account.

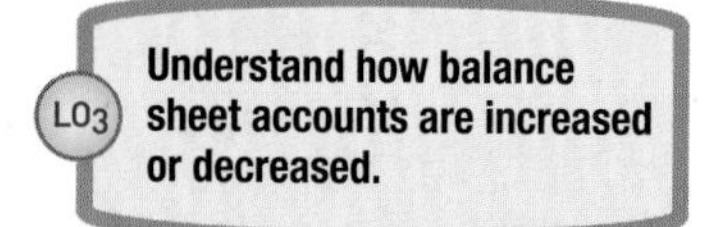

All asset accounts *normally have debit balances*. It is hard to imagine an account for an asset such as land having a credit balance, as this would indicate that the business had disposed of more land than it had ever acquired. (For some assets, such as cash, it is possible to acquire a credit balance—but such balances are only *temporary*.)

The fact that assets are located on the *left* side of the balance sheet is a convenient means of remembering the rule that an increase in an asset is recorded on the *left* (debit) side of the account and an asset account normally has a debit *(left-hand)* balance.

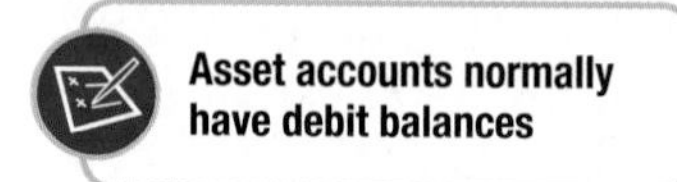

Any Asset Account	
Debit (to record an increase)	Credit (to record a decrease)

Credit Balances in Liability and Owners' Equity Accounts Increases in liability and owners' equity accounts are recorded by credit entries and decreases in these accounts are recorded by debits. The relationship between entries in these accounts and their position on the balance sheet may be summed up as follows: (1) liabilities and owners' equity belong on the *right* side of the balance sheet, (2) an increase in a liability or an owners' equity account is recorded on the *right* (credit) side of the account, and (3) liability and owners' equity accounts normally have credit *(right-hand)* balances.

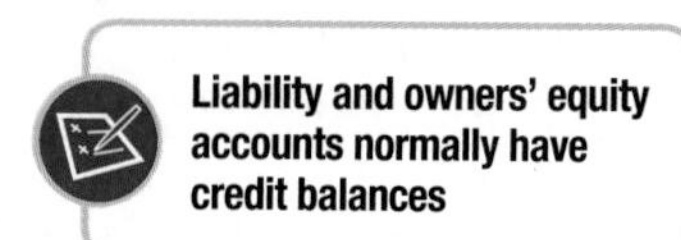

Any Liability Account or Owners' Equity Account	
Debit (to record a decrease)	Credit (to record an increase)

Concise Statement of the Debit and Credit Rules The use of debits and credits to record changes in assets, liabilities, and owners' equity may be summarized as follows:

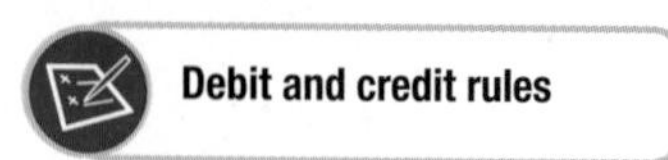

Asset Accounts	Liability & Owners' Equity Accounts
Normally have debit balances. Thus, increases are recorded by debits and decreases are recorded by credits.	Normally have credit balances. Thus, increases are recorded by credits and decreases are recorded by debits.

DOUBLE-ENTRY ACCOUNTING—THE EQUALITY OF DEBITS AND CREDITS

The rules for debits and credits are designed so that *every transaction is recorded by equal dollar amounts of debits and credits*. The reason for this equality lies in the relationship of the debit and credit rules to the accounting equation:

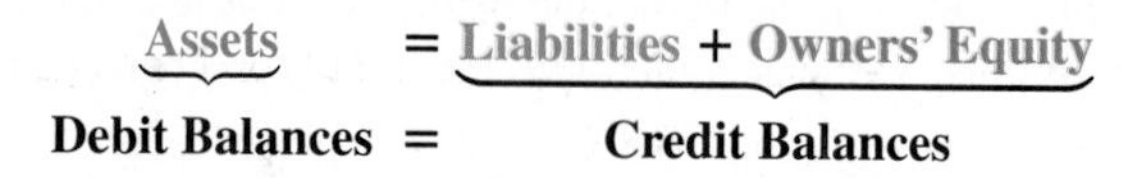

If this equation is to remain in balance, any change in the left side of the equation (assets) *must be accompanied by an equal change* in the right side (either liabilities or owners' equity). According to the debit and credit rules that we have just described, increases in the left side of the equation (assets) are recorded by *debits*, while increases in the right side (liabilities and owners' equity) are recorded by *credits*, as illustrated below:

Explain the double-entry system of accounting. LO4

Assets		=	Liabilities		+	Owners' Equity	
Debit to increase (+)	Credit to decrease (−)		Debit to decrease (−)	Credit to increase (+)		Debit to decrease (−)	Credit to increase (+)

This system is often called **double-entry accounting**. The phrase *double-entry* refers to the need for both *debit entries* and *credit entries*, equal in dollar amount, to record every transaction. Virtually every business organization uses the double-entry system regardless of whether the company's accounting records are maintained manually or by computer. In addition, the double-entry system allows us to measure net income at the same time we record the effects of transactions on the balance sheet accounts.

The Journal

Explain the purpose of a journal and its relationship to the ledger. LO5

In the preceding discussion we illustrated how the debit and credit rules of double-entry accounting are applied in the recording of economic events. Using T accounts, we stressed the effects that business transactions have on individual asset, liability, and owners' equity accounts that comprise a company's general ledger. It is important to realize, however, that transactions are rarely recorded *directly* in general ledger accounts. In an actual accounting system, the information about each business transaction is *initially* recorded in an accounting record called the **journal**. This information is *later* transferred to the appropriate accounts in the general ledger.

The journal is a chronological (day-by-day) record of business transactions. At convenient intervals, the debit and credit amounts recorded in the journal are transferred (posted) to the accounts in the ledger. The updated ledger accounts, in turn, serve as the basis for preparing the company's financial statements.

To illustrate the most basic type of journal, called a **general journal**, let us examine the very first business transaction of Overnight Auto Service. Recall that on January 20, 2007, the McBryan family invested $80,000 in exchange for capital stock. Thus, the asset Cash increased by $80,000, and the owners' equity account Capital Stock increased by the same amount.

Applying the debit and credit rules discussed previously, we know that increases in assets are recorded by debits, whereas increases in owners' equity are recorded by credits. As such, this event requires a *debit* to Cash and a *credit* to Capital Stock in the amount of $80,000. The transaction is recorded in the company's general journal as illustrated in Exhibit 3–1. Note the basic characteristics of this general journal entry:

1. The name of the account debited (Cash) is written first, and the dollar amount to be debited appears in the left-hand money column.
2. The name of the account credited (Capital Stock) appears below the account debited and is indented to the right. The dollar amount appears in the right-hand money column.
3. A brief description of the transaction appears immediately below the journal entry.

Accounting software packages automate and streamline the way in which transactions are recorded. However, recording transactions manually—without a computer—is an effective way to conceptualize the manner in which economic events are captured by accounting systems and subsequently reported in a company's financial statements.

Exhibit 3–1

RECORDING A TRANSACTION IN THE GENERAL JOURNAL

GENERAL JOURNAL			
Date	**Account Titles and Explanation**	**Debit**	**Credit**
2007			
Jan. 20	Cash	80,000	
	Capital Stock		80,000
	Owners invest cash in the business.		

A familiarity with the general journal form of describing transactions is just as essential to the study of accounting as a familiarity with plus and minus signs is to the study of mathematics. The journal entry is a *tool* for *analyzing* and *describing* the impact of various transactions on a business entity. The ability to describe a transaction in journal entry form requires an understanding of the nature of the transaction and its effect on the financial position of the business.

POSTING JOURNAL ENTRIES TO THE LEDGER ACCOUNTS (AND HOW TO "READ" A JOURNAL ENTRY)

We have made the point that transactions are recorded *first* in the journal. Ledger accounts are updated *later,* through a process called **posting**. (In a computerized system, postings often occur instantaneously, rather than later.)

Posting simply means *updating the ledger accounts* for the effects of the transactions recorded in the journal. Viewed as a mechanical task, posting basically amounts to performing the steps you describe when you "read" a journal entry aloud.

Consider the first entry appearing in Overnight's general journal. If you were to read this entry aloud, you would say: "Debit Cash, $80,000; credit Capital Stock, $80,000." That's precisely what a person posting this entry should do: Debit the Cash account for $80,000, and credit the Capital Stock account for $80,000.

The posting of Overnight's first journal entry is illustrated in Exhibit 3–2. Notice that no new information is recorded during the posting process. Posting involves copying into the ledger accounts information that *already has been recorded in the journal*. In manual accounting systems, this can be a tedious and time-consuming process, but in computer-based systems, it is done instantly and automatically. In addition, computerized posting greatly reduces the risk of errors.

Exhibit 3–2

POSTING A TRANSACTION FROM THE JOURNAL TO LEDGER ACCOUNTS

GENERAL JOURNAL			
Date	**Account Titles and Explanation**	**Debit**	**Credit**
2007			
Jan. 20	Cash	80,000	
	Capital Stock		80,000
	Owners invest cash in the business.		

GENERAL LEDGER

Cash		Capital Stock	
1/20 80,000			1/20 80,000

Recording Balance Sheet Transactions: An Illustration

To illustrate how to use debits and credits for recording transactions in accounts, we return to the January transactions of Overnight Auto Service. At this point, we discuss only those transactions related to changes in the company's financial position and reported directly in its balance sheet. The revenue and expense transactions that took place on January 31 will be addressed later in the chapter.

Each transaction from January 20 through January 27 is analyzed first in terms of increases in assets, liabilities, and owners' equity. Second, we follow the debit and credit rules for entering these increases and decreases in specific accounts. Asset ledger accounts are shown on the left side of the analysis; liability and owners' equity ledger accounts are shown on the right side. For convenience in the following transactions, both the debit and credit figures for the transaction under discussion are shown in *red*. Figures relating to earlier transactions appear in *black*.

Jan. 20 Michael McBryan and family invested $80,000 cash in exchange for capital stock.

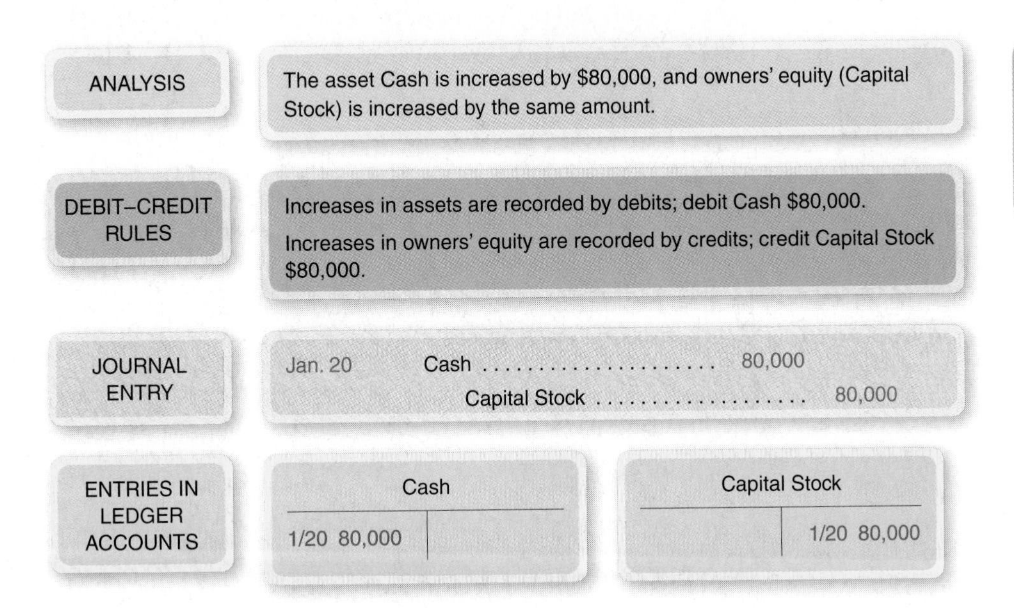

Owners invest cash in the business

Assets	= Liabilities +	Owners' Equity
+$80,000		+$80,000

Jan. 21 Representing Overnight, McBryan negotiated with both the City of Santa Teresa and Metropolitan Transit Authority (MTA) to purchase an abandoned bus garage. (The city owned the land, but the MTA owned the building.) On January 21, Overnight Auto Service purchased the land from the city for $52,000 cash.

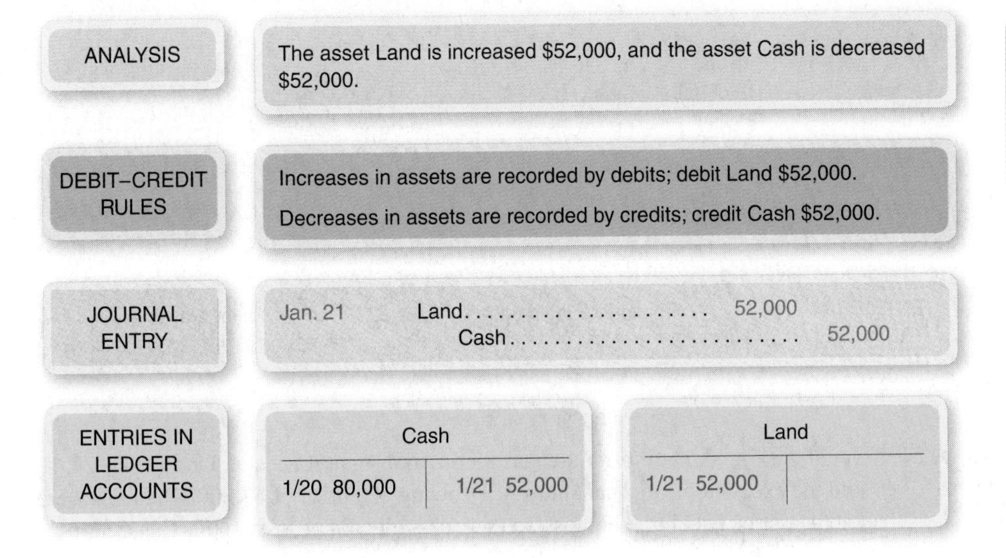

Purchase of an asset for cash

Assets	= Liabilities +	Owners' Equity
+$52,000		
−$52,000		

Jan. 22 Overnight completed the acquisition of its business location by purchasing the abandoned building from the MTA. The purchase price was $36,000; Overnight made a $6,000 cash down payment and issued a 90-day, non-interest-bearing note payable for the remaining $30,000.

Purchase of an asset, making a small down payment

Assets	= Liabilities	+ Owners' Equity
+$36,000	+$30,000	
−$ 6,000		

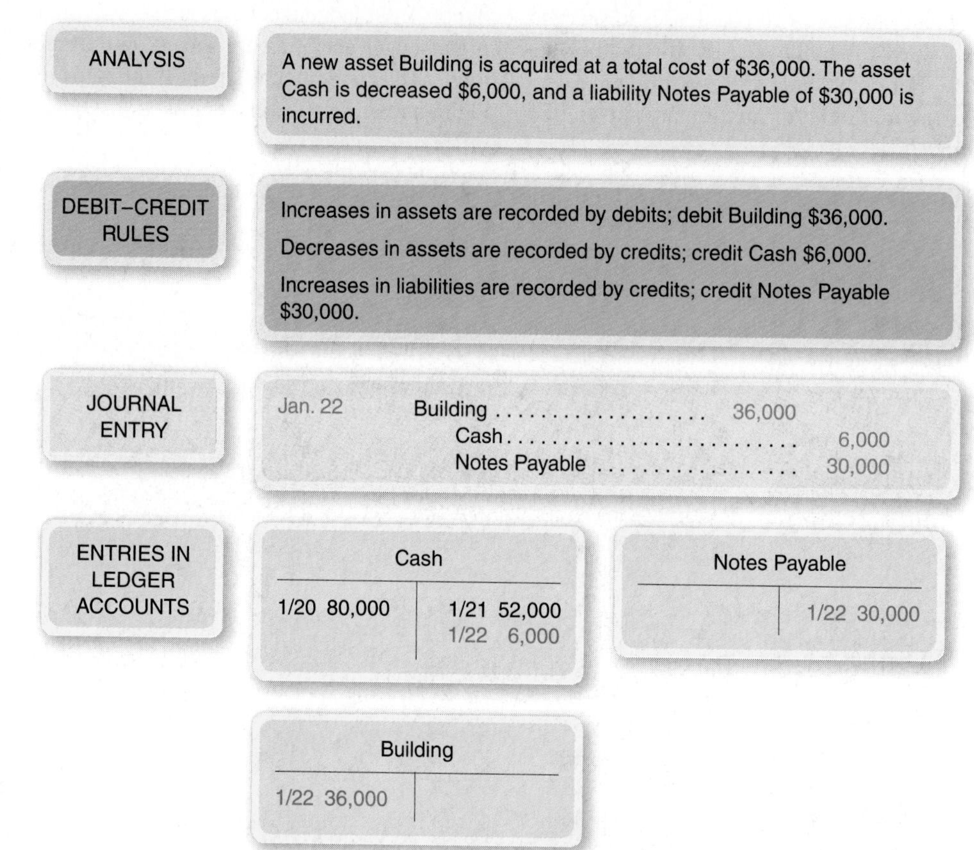

Jan. 23 Overnight purchased tools and equipment on account from Snappy Tools. The purchase price was $13,800, due in 60 days.

Credit purchase of an asset

Assets	= Liabilities	+ Owners' Equity
+$13,800	+$13,800	

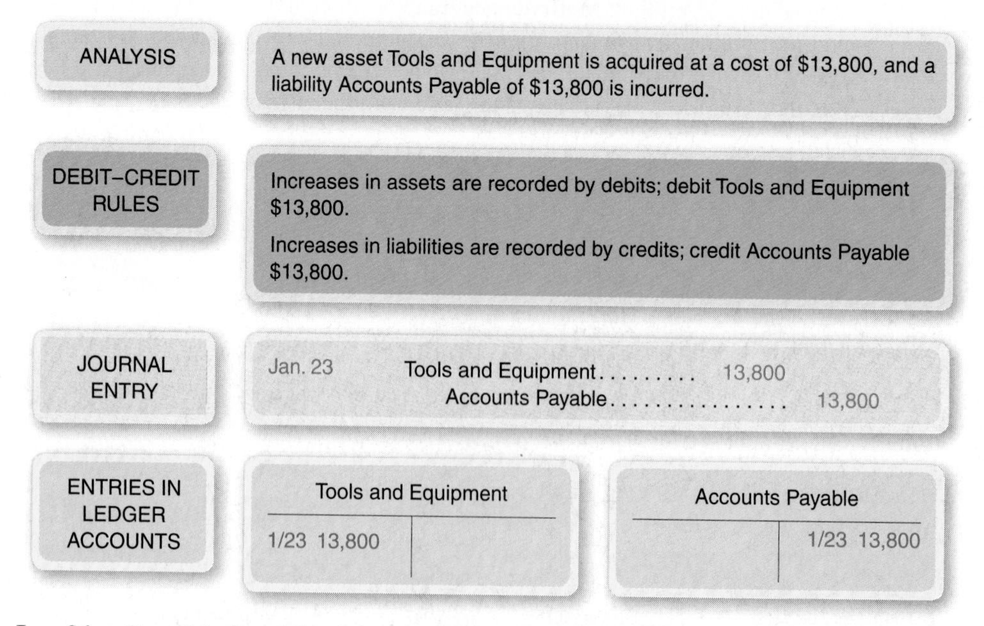

Jan. 24 Overnight found that it had purchased more tools than it needed. On January 24, it sold the excess tools on account to Ace Towing at a price of $1,800. The tools were sold at a price equal to their cost, so there was no gain or loss on this transaction.

ANALYSIS

Since the tools are sold at cost, there is no gain or loss on this transaction. An asset Accounts Receivable is acquired in the amount of $1,800; the asset Tools and Equipment is decreased $1,800.

DEBIT–CREDIT RULES

Increases in assets are recorded by debits; debit Accounts Receivable $1,800.

Decreases in assets are recorded by credits; credit Tools and Equipment $1,800.

JOURNAL ENTRY

Jan. 24	Accounts Receivable	1,800	
	Tools and Equipment		1,800

ENTRIES IN LEDGER ACCOUNTS

Accounts Receivable	
1/24 1,800	

Tools and Equipment	
1/23 13,800	1/24 1,800

Credit sale of an asset (with no gain or loss)

Assets	= Liabilities +	Owners' Equity
+$1,800		
−$1,800		

Jan. 26 Overnight received $600 in partial collection of the account receivable from Ace Towing.

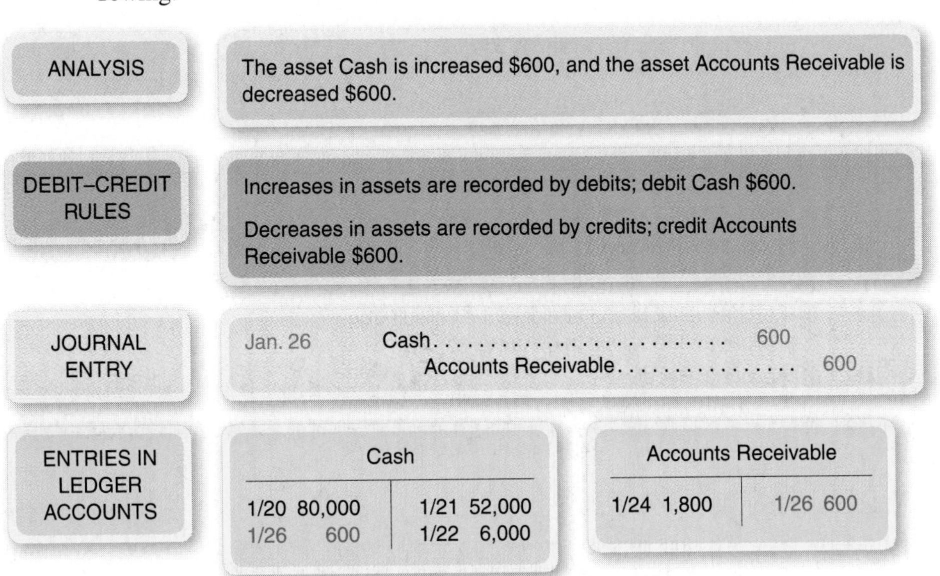

Collection of an account receivable

Assets	= Liabilities +	Owners' Equity
+$600		
−$600		

Jan. 27 Overnight made a $6,800 partial payment of its account payable to Snappy Tools.

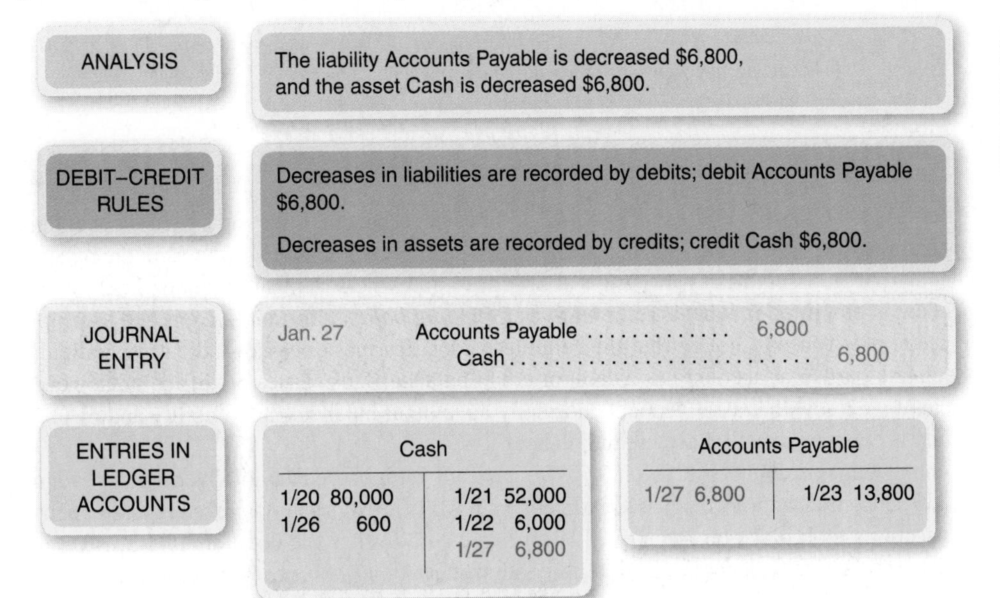

Payment of an account payable

Assets	= Liabilities +	Owners' Equity
−$6,800	−$6,800	

Ledger Accounts after Posting

The seven journal entries made by Overnight Auto Service from January 20 through January 27 are summarized in Exhibit 3–3.

Exhibit 3–3
GENERAL JOURNAL ENTRIES: JANUARY 20 THROUGH 27

OVERNIGHT AUTO SERVICE
General Journal
January 20–27, 2007

Date	Account Titles and Explanation	Debit	Credit
2007			
Jan. 20	Cash	80,000	
	Capital Stock		80,000
	Owners invest cash in the business.		
21	Land	52,000	
	Cash.		52,000
	Purchased land for business site.		
22	Building	36,000	
	Cash.		6,000
	Notes Payable		30,000
	Purchased building from the MTA. Paid part cash; balance payable within 90 days.		
23	Tools and Equipment.	13,800	
	Accounts Payable.		13,800
	Purchased tools and equipment on credit from Snappy Tools. Due in 60 days.		
24	Accounts Receivable.	1,800	
	Tools and Equipment		1,800
	Sold unused tools and equipment at cost to Ace Towing.		
26	Cash	600	
	Accounts Receivable		600
	Collected part of account receivable from Ace Towing.		
27	Accounts Payable	6,800	
	Cash.		6,800
	Made partial payment of the liability to Snappy Tools.		

After all of the journal entries in Exhibit 3–3 have been posted, Overnight's ledger accounts appear as shown in Exhibit 3–4. The accounts are arranged in the same order as in the balance sheet—that is, assets first, followed by liabilities and owners' equity accounts. Each ledger account is presented in what is referred to as a *running balance* format (as opposed to simple T accounts). You will notice that the running balance format does not indicate specifically whether a particular account has a debit or credit balance. This causes no difficulty, however, because we know that asset accounts normally have debit balances, and liability and owners' equity accounts normally have credit balances.

In the ledger accounts in Exhibit 3–4, we have not yet included any of Overnight's revenue and expense transactions discussed in Chapter 2. All of the company's revenue and expense transactions took place on January 31. Before we can discuss the debit and credit rules for revenue and expense accounts, a more in-depth discussion of *net income* is warranted.

Exhibit 3–4
LEDGER SHOWING TRANSACTIONS

CASH

Date	Debit	Credit	Balance
2007			
Jan. 20	80,000		80,000
21		52,000	28,000
22		6,000	22,000
26	600		22,600
27		6,800	15,800

ACCOUNTS RECEIVABLE

Date	Debit	Credit	Balance
2007			
Jan. 24	1,800		1,800
26		600	1,200

LAND

Date	Debit	Credit	Balance
2007			
Jan. 21	52,000		52,000

BUILDING

Date	Debit	Credit	Balance
2007			
Jan. 22	36,000		36,000

TOOLS AND EQUIPMENT

Date	Debit	Credit	Balance
2007			
Jan. 23	13,800		13,800
24		1,800	12,000

NOTES PAYABLE

Date	Debit	Credit	Balance
2007			
Jan. 22		30,000	30,000

ACCOUNTS PAYABLE

Date	Debit	Credit	Balance
2007			
Jan. 23		13,800	13,800
27	6,800		7,000

CAPITAL STOCK

Date	Debit	Credit	Balance
2007			
Jan. 20		80,000	80,000

What Is Net Income?

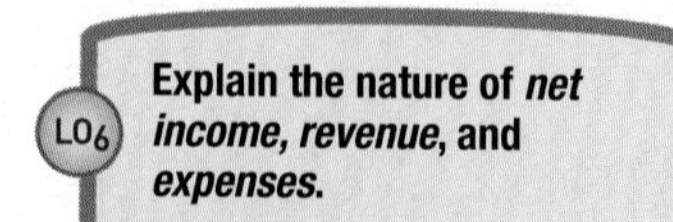

As previously noted, **net income** is *an increase in owners' equity resulting from the profitable operation of the business.* Net income does not consist of any cash or any other specific assets. Rather, net income is a *computation* of the overall effects of many business transactions on *owners' equity.* The effects of net income on the basic accounting equation are illustrated as follows:

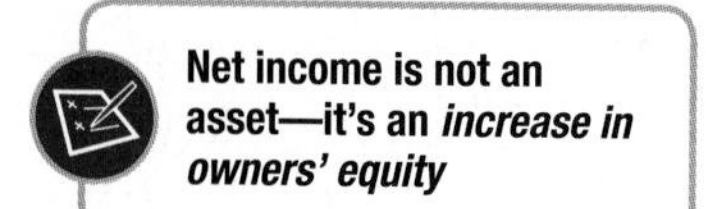

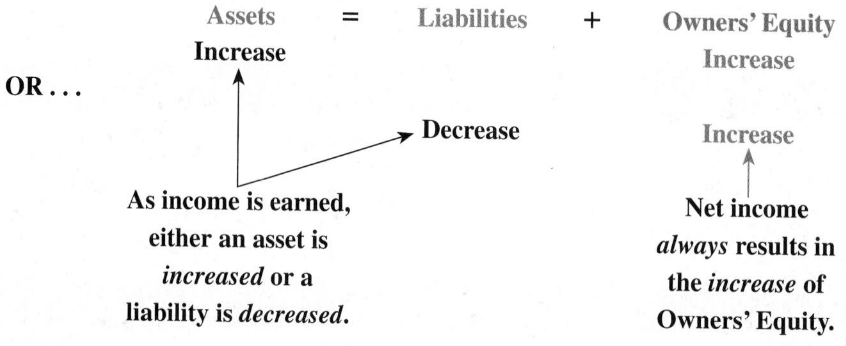

Our point is that net income represents an *increase in owners' equity* and has no direct relationship to the types or amounts of assets on hand. Even a business operating at a profit may run short of cash.

In the balance sheet, the changes in owners' equity resulting from profitable or unprofitable operations are reflected in the balance of the stockholders' equity account, *Retained Earnings.* The assets of the business organization appear in the *assets* section of the balance sheet.

RETAINED EARNINGS

As illustrated in Chapter 1, the Retained Earnings account appears in the stockholders' equity section of the balance sheet. Earning net income causes the balance in the Retained Earnings account to increase. However, many corporations follow a policy of distributing to their stockholders some of the resources generated by profitable operations. Distributions of this nature are termed **dividends**, and they reduce both total assets and stockholders' equity. The reduction in stockholders' equity is reflected by decreasing the balance of the Retained Earnings account.

The balance in the **Retained Earnings** account represents the total net income of the corporation over the *entire lifetime* of the business, less all amounts that have been distributed to the stockholders as dividends. In short, retained earnings represent the earnings that have been *retained* by the corporation to finance growth. Some of the largest corporations have become large by consistently retaining in the business most of the resources generated by profitable operations. For instance, a recent annual report of Wal-Mart Stores, Inc., shows total stockholders' equity of $47 billion. Of this amount, retained earnings of $43 billion account for over 90 percent of the company's total equity.

THE INCOME STATEMENT: A PREVIEW

An **income statement** is a financial statement that summarizes the profitability of a business entity for a specified period of time. In this statement, net income is determined by comparing *sales prices* of goods or services sold during the period with the *costs* incurred by the business in delivering these goods or services. The technical accounting terms for these components of net income are **revenue** and **expenses**. Therefore, accountants say that net income is equal to *revenue minus expenses.* Should expenses exceed revenue, a **net loss** results.

A sample income statement for Overnight Auto Service for the year ended December 31, 2007, is shown in Exhibit 3–5. In Chapter 5, we show exactly how this income statement was developed from the company's accounting records. For now, however, the illustration will assist us in discussing some of the basic concepts involved in measuring net income.

Exhibit 3–5

A PREVIEW OF OVERNIGHT'S INCOME STATEMENT

OVERNIGHT AUTO SERVICE Income Statement For the Year Ended December 31, 2007		
Revenue:		
Repair service revenue		$172,000
Rent revenue earned		3,000
Total revenue		$175,000
Expenses:		
Advertising	$ 3,900	
Salaries and wages	58,750	
Supplies	7,500	
Depreciation: building	1,650	
Depreciation: tools and equipment	2,200	
Utilities	19,400	
Insurance	15,000	
Interest	30	108,430
Income before income taxes		$ 66,570
Income taxes		26,628
Net income		$ 39,942

Income Must Be Related to a Specified Period of Time Notice that our sample income statement covers a *period of time*—namely, the year 2007. A balance sheet shows the financial position of a business at a *particular date*. We cannot evaluate net income unless it is associated with a specific time period. For example, if an executive says, "My business earns a net income of $10,000," the profitability of the business is unclear. Does it earn $10,000 per week, per month, or per year?

CASE IN POINT

The late J. Paul Getty, one of the world's first billionaires, was once interviewed by a group of business students. One of the students asked Getty to estimate the amount of his income. As the student had not specified a time period, Getty decided to have some fun with his audience and responded, "About $11,000." He paused long enough to allow the group to express surprise over this seemingly low amount, and then completed his sentence, "an hour." (Incidentally, $11,000 per hour, 24 hours per day, amounts to about $100 million per year.)

© Tom Carter/PhotoEdit

Accounting Periods The period of time covered by an income statement is termed the company's **accounting period**. To provide the users of financial statements with timely information, net income is measured for relatively short accounting periods of equal length. This concept, called the **time period principle**, is one of the underlying accounting principles that guide the interpretation of financial events and the preparation of financial statements.

The length of a company's accounting period depends on how frequently managers, investors, and other interested people require information about the company's performance.

Every business prepares annual income statements, and most businesses prepare quarterly and monthly income statements as well. (Quarterly statements cover a three-month period and are prepared by all large corporations for distribution to their stockholders.)

The 12-month accounting period used by an entity is called its **fiscal year**. The fiscal year used by most companies coincides with the calendar year and ends on December 31. Some businesses, however, elect to use a fiscal year that ends on some other date.

For example, **The Walt Disney Company** ends its fiscal year on September 30. Why? For one reason, September and October are relatively slow months at the company's theme parks. Furthermore, September financial statements provide timely information about the preceding summer, which is the company's busiest season. Most large retailers, such as **Wal-Mart** and **JCPenney**, end their fiscal years at the end of January, after the rush of the holiday season. Many choose the last Saturday of January as their cutoff, which results in an exact 52-week reporting period approximately five out of every six years.

Let us now explore the meaning of the accounting terms *revenue* and *expenses* in more detail.

REVENUE

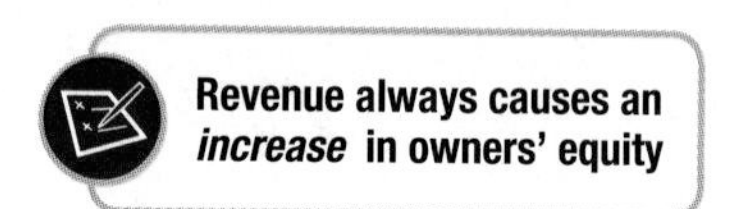

Revenue always causes an *increase* in owners' equity

Revenue is the price of goods sold and services rendered during a given accounting period. Earning revenue causes owners' equity to increase. When a business renders services or sells merchandise to its customers, it usually receives cash or acquires an account receivable from the customer. The inflow of cash and receivables from customers increases the total assets of the company; on the other side of the accounting equation, owners' equity increases to match the increase in total assets. Thus revenue is the gross *increase in owners' equity* resulting from operation of the business.

Various account titles are used to describe different types of revenue. For example, a business that sells merchandise rather than services, such as **Wal-Mart** or **General Motors**, uses the term *Sales* to describe its revenue. In the professional practices of physicians, CPAs, and attorneys, revenue usually is called *Fees Earned.* A real estate office, however, might call its revenue *Commissions Earned.*

Overnight Auto Service's income statement reveals that the company records its revenue in two separate accounts: (1) *Repair Service Revenue* and (2) *Rent Revenue Earned.* A professional sports team might also have separate revenue accounts for *Ticket Sales, Concessions Revenue*, and *Revenue from Television Contracts*. Another type of revenue common to many businesses is *Interest Revenue* (or Interest Earned), stemming from the interest earned on bank deposits, notes receivable, and interest-bearing investments.

LO7 Apply the *realization* and *matching* principles in recording revenue and expenses.

The Realization Principle: When to Record Revenue

When should revenue be recognized? In most cases, the **realization principle** indicates that revenue should be recognized *at the time goods are sold or services are rendered.* At this point, the business has essentially completed the earnings process, and the sales value of the goods or services can be measured objectively. At any time prior to the sale, the ultimate value of the goods or services sold can only be estimated. After the sale, the only step that remains is to collect from the customer, usually a relatively certain event.

To illustrate, assume that on July 25 a radio station contracts with a car dealership to air a series of one-minute advertisements during August. If all of the agreed-upon ads are aired in August, but payment for the ads is not received until September, in which month should the station recognize the advertising revenue? The answer is August, the month in which it *rendered the services* that earned the advertising revenue. In other words, revenue is recognized when it is *earned*, without regard to when a contract is signed or when cash payment for providing goods or services is received.

EXPENSES

Expenses are the costs of the goods and services used up in the process of earning revenue. Examples include the cost of employees' salaries, advertising, rent, utilities, and the depreciation of buildings, automobiles, and office equipment. All these costs are necessary to attract and serve customers and thereby earn revenue. Expenses are often called the "costs of doing business," that is, the cost of the various activities necessary to carry on a business.

An expense always causes a *decrease in owners' equity*. The related changes in the accounting equation can be either (1) a decrease in assets or (2) an increase in liabilities. An expense reduces assets if payment occurs at the time that the expense is incurred. If the expense will not be paid until later, as, for example, the purchase of advertising services on account, the recording of the expense will be accompanied by an increase in liabilities.

Expenses always cause a *decrease* in owners' equity

The Matching Principle: When to Record Expenses A significant relationship exists between revenue and expenses. Expenses are incurred for the *purpose of producing revenue*. In measuring net income for a period, revenue should be offset by *all the expenses incurred in producing that revenue*. This concept of offsetting expenses against revenue on a basis of cause and effect is called the **matching principle**.

Timing is an important factor in matching (offsetting) revenue with the related expenses. For example, in preparing monthly income statements, it is important to offset this month's expenses against this month's revenue. We should not offset this month's expenses against last month's revenue because there is no cause and effect relationship between the two.

Assume that the salaries earned by a company's marketing team for serving customers in July are not paid until early August. In which month should these salaries be regarded as expenses—July or August? The answer is July, because July is the month in which the marketing team's services *helped to produce revenue*. Just as revenue and cash receipts are not one and the same, expenses and cash payments are not identical. In fact, the cash payment of an expense may occur before, after, or in the same period that revenue is earned. In deciding when to report an expense in the income statement, the critical question is, "In what period does the cash expenditure help to produce revenue?"—*not*, "When does the payment of cash occur?"

Expenditures Benefiting More than One Accounting Period Many expenditures made by a business benefit two or more accounting periods. Fire insurance policies, for example, usually cover a period of 12 months. If a company prepares monthly income statements, a portion of the cost of such a policy should be allocated to insurance expense each month that the policy is in force. In this case, apportionment of the cost of the policy by months is an easy matter. If the 12-month policy costs $2,400, for example, the insurance expense for each month amounts to $200 ($2,400 cost ÷ 12 months).

Not all transactions can be divided so precisely by accounting periods. The purchase of a building, furniture and fixtures, machinery, a computer, or an automobile provides benefits to the business over all the years in which such an asset is used. No one can determine in advance exactly how many years of service will be received from such long-lived assets. Nevertheless, in measuring the net income of a business for a period of one year or less, accountants must *estimate* what portion of the cost of the building and other long-lived assets is applicable to the current year. Since the allocations of these costs are estimates rather than precise measurements, it follows that income statements should be regarded as useful *approximations* of net income rather than as absolutely correct measurements.

For some expenditures, such as those for advertising or employee training programs, it is not possible to estimate objectively the number of accounting periods over which revenue is likely to be produced. In such cases, generally accepted accounting principles require that the expenditure be charged *immediately to expense*. This treatment is based upon the accounting principle of **objectivity** and the concept of **conservatism**. Accountants require *objective evidence* that an expenditure will produce revenue in future periods before they will view the expenditure as creating an asset. When this objective evidence does not exist, they follow the conservative practice of recording the expenditure as an expense. *Conservatism*, in this context, means applying the accounting treatment that results in the *lowest* (most conservative) estimate of net income for the current period.

CASE IN POINT

International financial reporting standards (IFRSs) differ significantly from U.S. GAAP with respect to costs that are expensed immediately and costs that are capitalized. For example, IFRS 38 allows development costs to be capitalized if certain criteria are met, but under U.S. GAAP these same costs would need to be expensed in the period in which they occur. Alternatively, idle capacity and spoilage costs need to be expensed immediately under IFRS 2, but U.S. GAAP allows these costs to be capitalized in inventory. The FASB and the IASB have made an agreement to work toward eliminating differences between international accounting standards and GAAP over the next several years.

THE ACCRUAL BASIS OF ACCOUNTING

The policy of recognizing revenue in the accounting records when it is *earned* and recognizing expenses when the related goods or services are *used* is called the **accrual basis of accounting**. The purpose of accrual accounting is to measure the profitability of the *economic activities conducted* during the accounting period.

The most important concept involved in accrual accounting is the *matching principle*. Revenue is offset with all of the expenses incurred in generating that revenue, thus providing a measure of the overall profitability of the economic activity.

An alternative to the accrual basis is called *cash basis accounting*. Under cash basis accounting, revenue is recognized when cash is collected from the customer, rather than when the company sells goods or renders services. Expenses are recognized when payment is made, rather than when the related goods or services are used in business operations. The cash basis of accounting measures the amounts of cash received and paid out during the period, but it does *not* provide a good measure of the *profitability of activities* undertaken during the period.

Exhibit 3–6 illustrates that, under the accrual basis of accounting, cash receipts or disbursements may occur *prior to* or *after* revenue is earned or an expense is incurred.

Exhibit 3–6
CASH FLOW VERSUS INCOME STATEMENT RECOGNITION

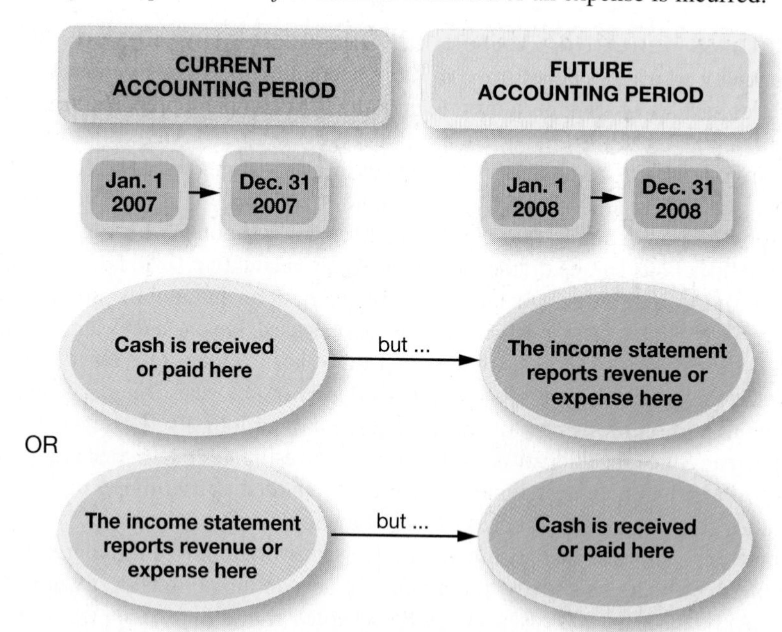

DEBIT AND CREDIT RULES FOR REVENUE AND EXPENSES

We have stressed that revenue increases owners' equity and that expenses decrease owners' equity. The debit and credit rules for recording revenue and expenses in the ledger accounts are a natural extension of the rules for recording changes in owners' equity. The rules previously stated for recording increases and decreases in owners' equity are as follows:

- *Increases* in owners' equity are recorded by *credits*.
- *Decreases* in owners' equity are recorded by *debits*.

This rule is now extended to cover revenue and expense accounts:

- *Revenue* increases owners' equity; therefore, revenue is recorded by *credits*.
- *Expenses* decrease owners' equity; therefore, expenses are recorded by *debits*.

Dividends

A dividend is a distribution of assets (usually cash) by a corporation to its stockholders. In some respects, dividends are similar to expenses—they reduce both the assets and the owners' equity in the business. However, *dividends are not an expense, and they are not deducted from revenue in the income statement*. The reason why dividends are not viewed as an expense is that these payments do not serve to generate revenue. Rather, they are a *distribution of profits* to the owners of the business.

Since the declaration of a dividend reduces stockholders' equity, the dividend could be recorded by debiting the Retained Earnings account. However, a clearer record is created if a separate Dividends account is debited for all amounts distributed as dividends to stockholders. The disposition of the Dividends account when financial statements are prepared will be illustrated in Chapter 5.

The debit–credit rules for revenue, expenses, and dividends are summarized below:

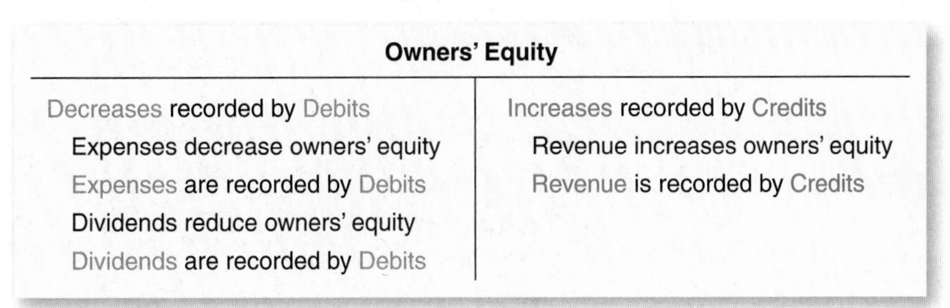

Owners' Equity	
Decreases recorded by Debits	Increases recorded by Credits
Expenses decrease owners' equity	Revenue increases owners' equity
Expenses are recorded by Debits	Revenue is recorded by Credits
Dividends reduce owners' equity	
Dividends are recorded by Debits	

Debit–credit rules related to effect on owners' equity

Recording Income Statement Transactions: An Illustration

Understand how revenue and expense transactions are recorded in an accounting system. LO8

In Chapter 2, we introduced Overnight Auto Service, a small auto repair shop formed on January 20, 2007. Early in this chapter we journalized and posted all of Overnight's balance sheet transactions through January 27. At this point we will illustrate the manner in which Overnight's January income statement transactions were handled and continue into February with additional transactions.

Three transactions involving revenue and expenses were recorded by Overnight on January 31, 2007. The following illustrations provide an analysis of each transaction.

Jan. 31 Recorded revenue of $2,200, all of which was received in cash.

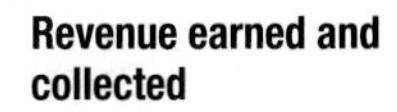

Revenue earned and collected

Assets	= Liabilities +	Owners' Equity
+$2,200		+$2,200

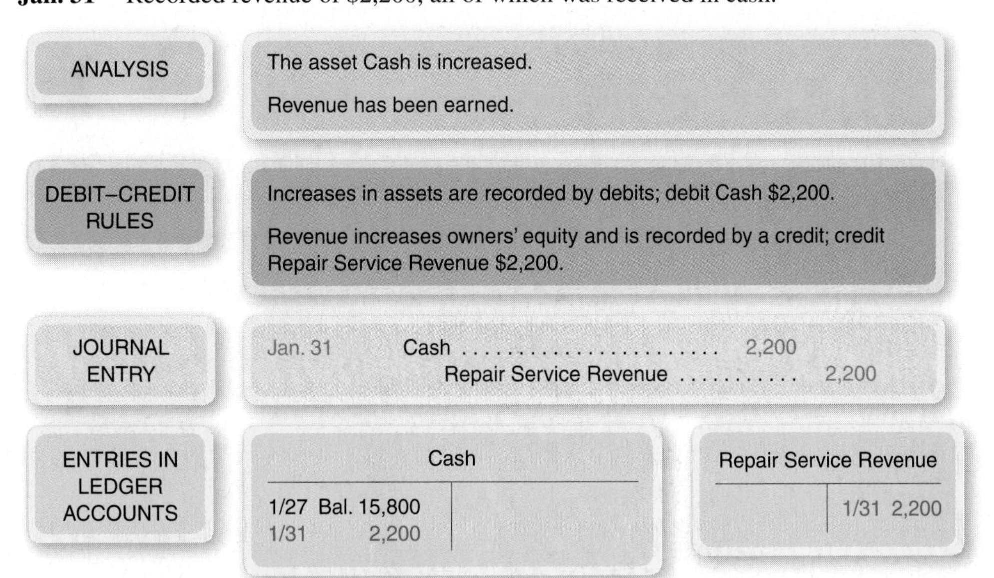

ANALYSIS

The asset Cash is increased.

Revenue has been earned.

DEBIT–CREDIT RULES

Increases in assets are recorded by debits; debit Cash $2,200.

Revenue increases owners' equity and is recorded by a credit; credit Repair Service Revenue $2,200.

JOURNAL ENTRY

		Debit	Credit
Jan. 31	Cash	2,200	
	Repair Service Revenue		2,200

ENTRIES IN LEDGER ACCOUNTS

Cash	
1/27 Bal. 15,800	
1/31 2,200	

Repair Service Revenue	
	1/31 2,200

Jan. 31 Paid employees' wages earned in January, $1,200.

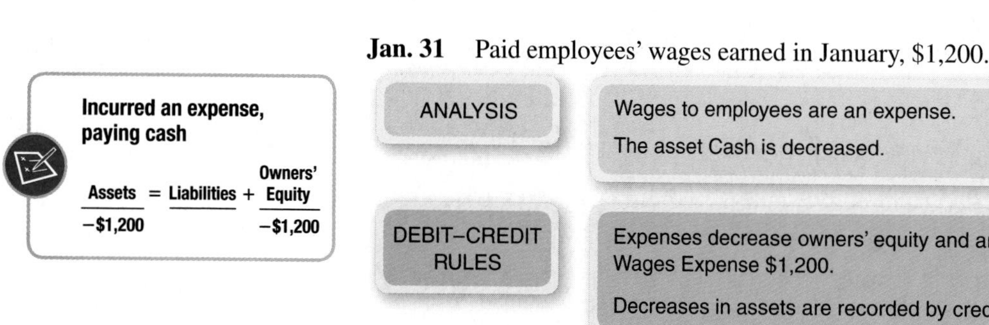

Incurred an expense, paying cash

Assets	=	Liabilities	+	Owners' Equity
−$1,200				−$1,200

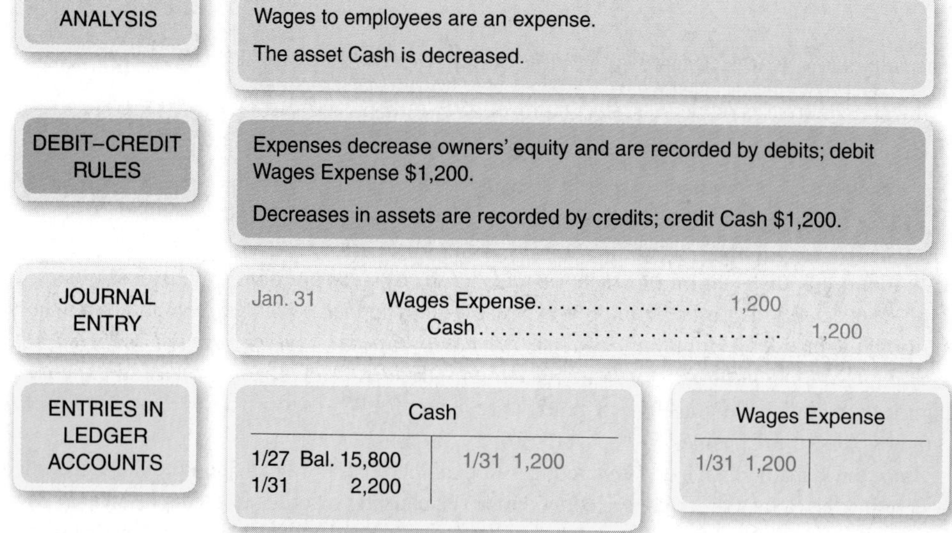

ANALYSIS

Wages to employees are an expense.

The asset Cash is decreased.

DEBIT–CREDIT RULES

Expenses decrease owners' equity and are recorded by debits; debit Wages Expense $1,200.

Decreases in assets are recorded by credits; credit Cash $1,200.

JOURNAL ENTRY

Jan. 31	Wages Expense	1,200	
	Cash		1,200

ENTRIES IN LEDGER ACCOUNTS

Cash		
1/27 Bal.	15,800	1/31 1,200
1/31	2,200	

Wages Expense	
1/31 1,200	

Jan. 31 Paid for utilities used in January, $200.

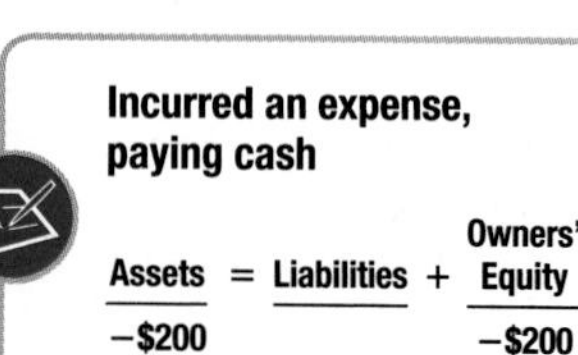

Incurred an expense, paying cash

Assets	=	Liabilities	+	Owners' Equity
−$200				−$200

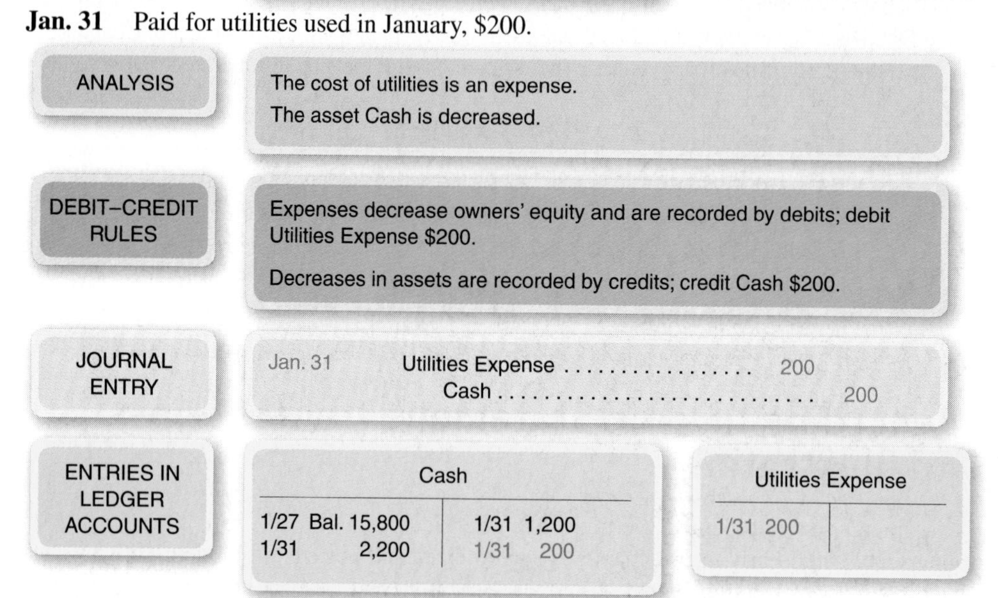

ANALYSIS

The cost of utilities is an expense.

The asset Cash is decreased.

DEBIT–CREDIT RULES

Expenses decrease owners' equity and are recorded by debits; debit Utilities Expense $200.

Decreases in assets are recorded by credits; credit Cash $200.

JOURNAL ENTRY

Jan. 31	Utilities Expense	200	
	Cash		200

ENTRIES IN LEDGER ACCOUNTS

Cash		
1/27 Bal.	15,800	1/31 1,200
1/31	2,200	1/31 200

Utilities Expense	
1/31 200	

Having analyzed and recorded all of Overnight's January transactions, next we focus upon the company's February activities. Overnight's February transactions are described, analyzed, and recorded as follows:

Feb. 1 Paid *Daily Tribune* $360 cash for newspaper advertising to be run during February.

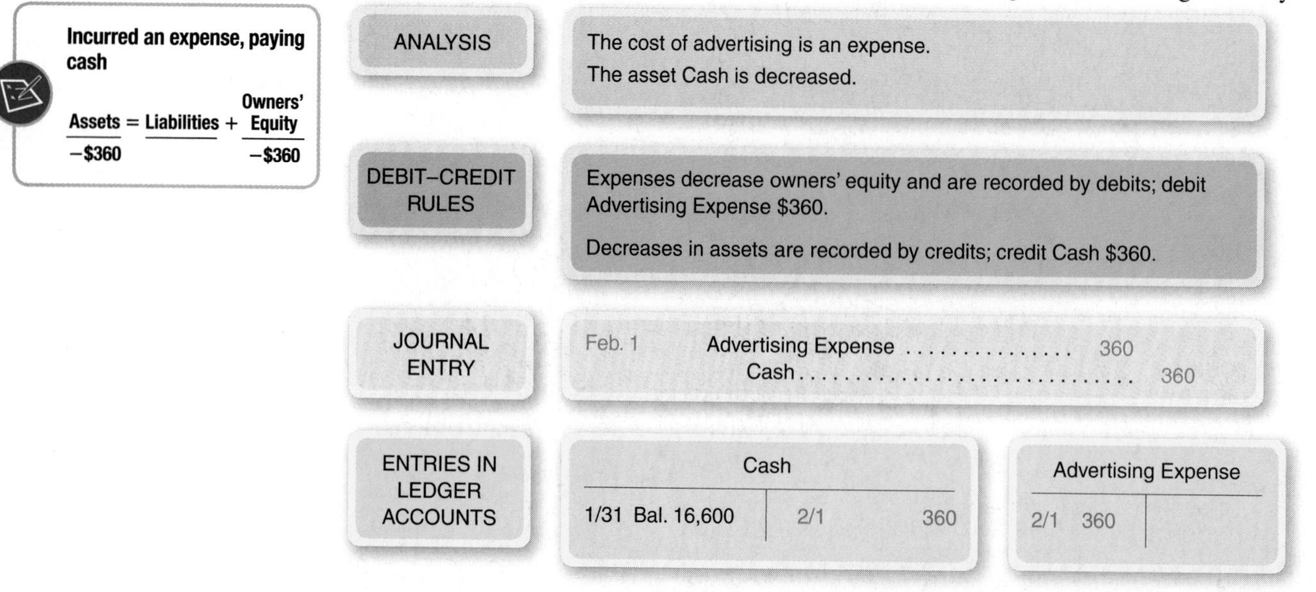

Incurred an expense, paying cash

Assets	=	Liabilities	+	Owners' Equity
−$360				−$360

ANALYSIS

The cost of advertising is an expense.

The asset Cash is decreased.

DEBIT–CREDIT RULES

Expenses decrease owners' equity and are recorded by debits; debit Advertising Expense $360.

Decreases in assets are recorded by credits; credit Cash $360.

JOURNAL ENTRY

Feb. 1	Advertising Expense	360	
	Cash		360

ENTRIES IN LEDGER ACCOUNTS

Cash		
1/31 Bal.	16,600	2/1 360

Advertising Expense	
2/1 360	

Feb. 2 Purchased radio advertising from KRAM to be aired in February. The cost was $470, payable within 30 days.

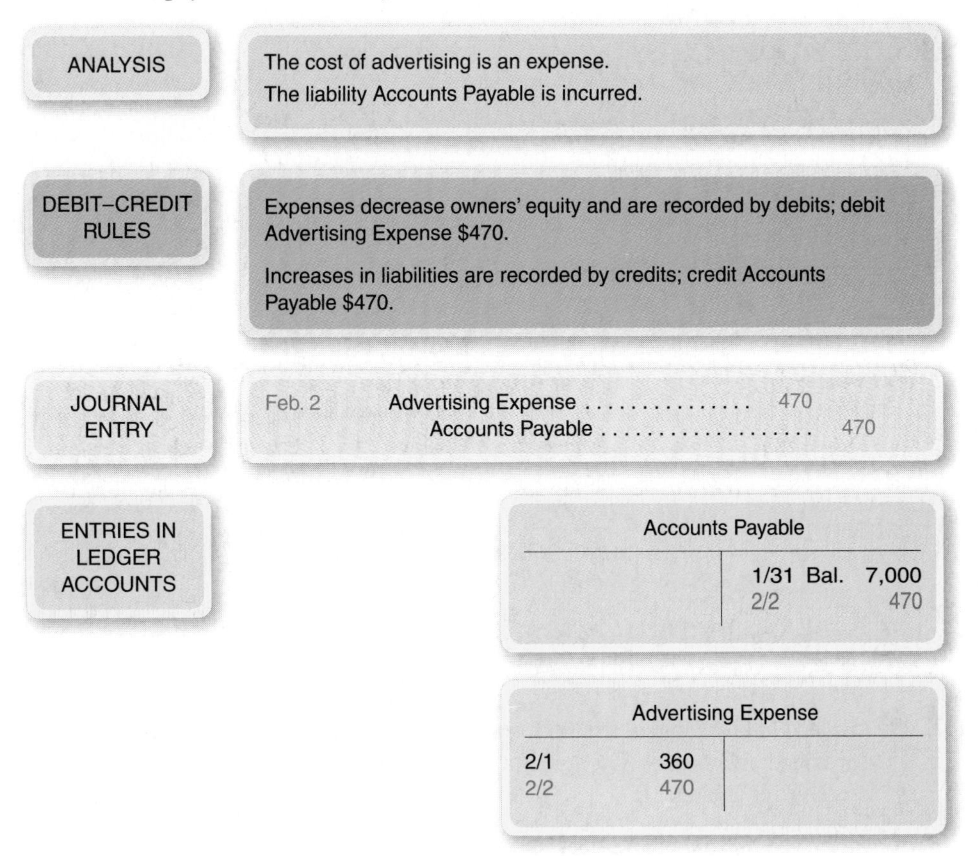

Incurred an expense to be paid later

Assets	=	Liabilities	+	Owners' Equity
		+$470		−$470

Feb. 4 Purchased various shop supplies (such as grease, solvents, nuts, and bolts) from CAPA Auto Parts; the cost was $1,400, due in 30 days. These supplies are expected to meet Overnight's needs for *three or four months*.

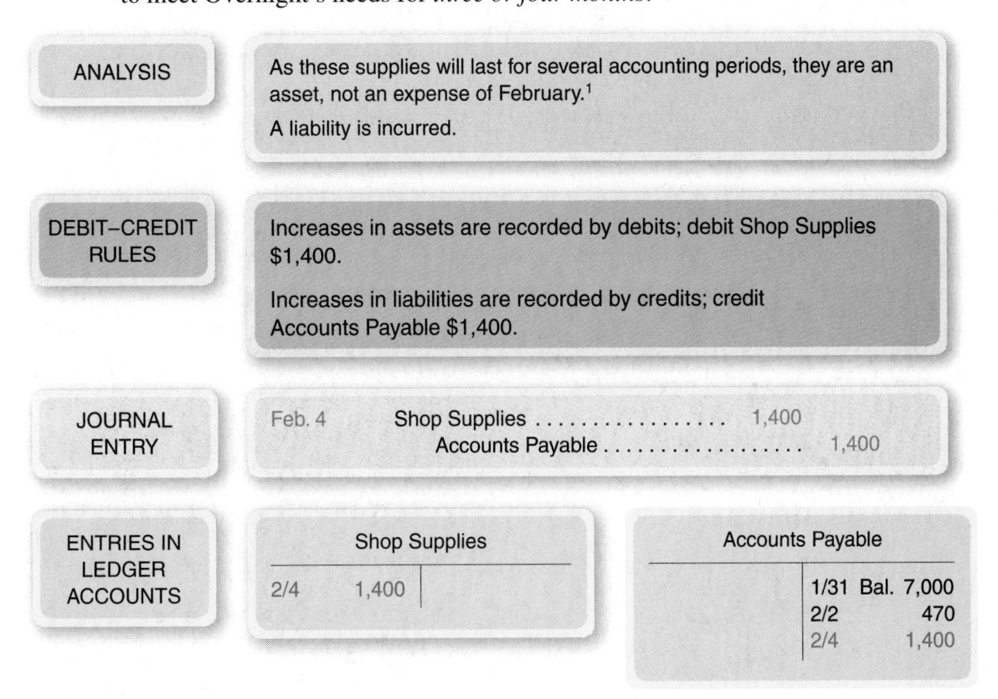

When a purchase clearly benefits future accounting periods, it's an asset, not an expense

Assets	=	Liabilities	+	Owners' Equity
+$1,400		+$1,400		

[1] If the supplies are expected to be used within the *current* accounting period, their cost may be debited directly to the Supplies Expense account, rather than to an asset account.

Feb. 15 Collected $4,980 cash for repairs made to vehicles of Airport Shuttle Service.

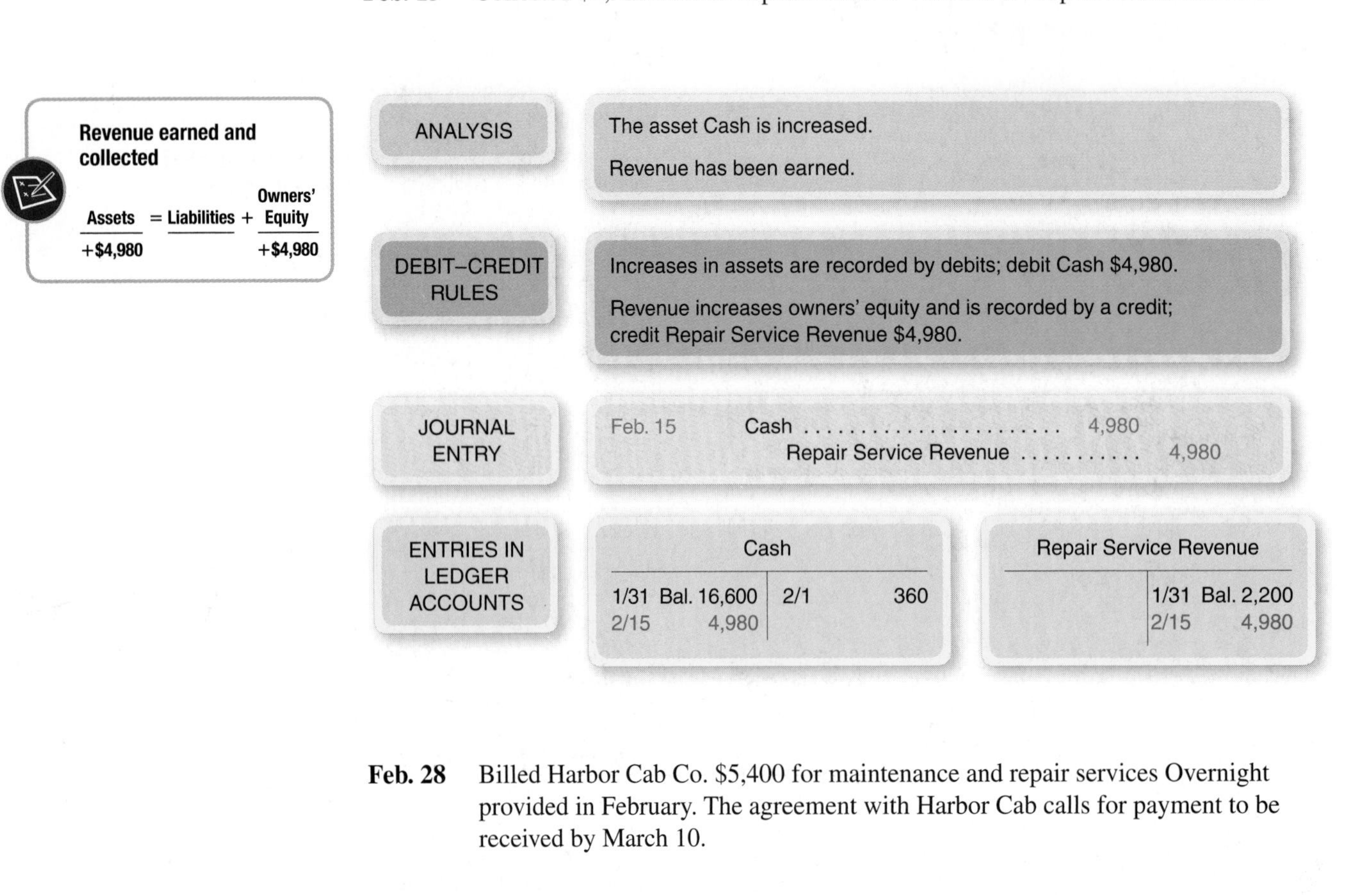

Feb. 28 Billed Harbor Cab Co. $5,400 for maintenance and repair services Overnight provided in February. The agreement with Harbor Cab calls for payment to be received by March 10.

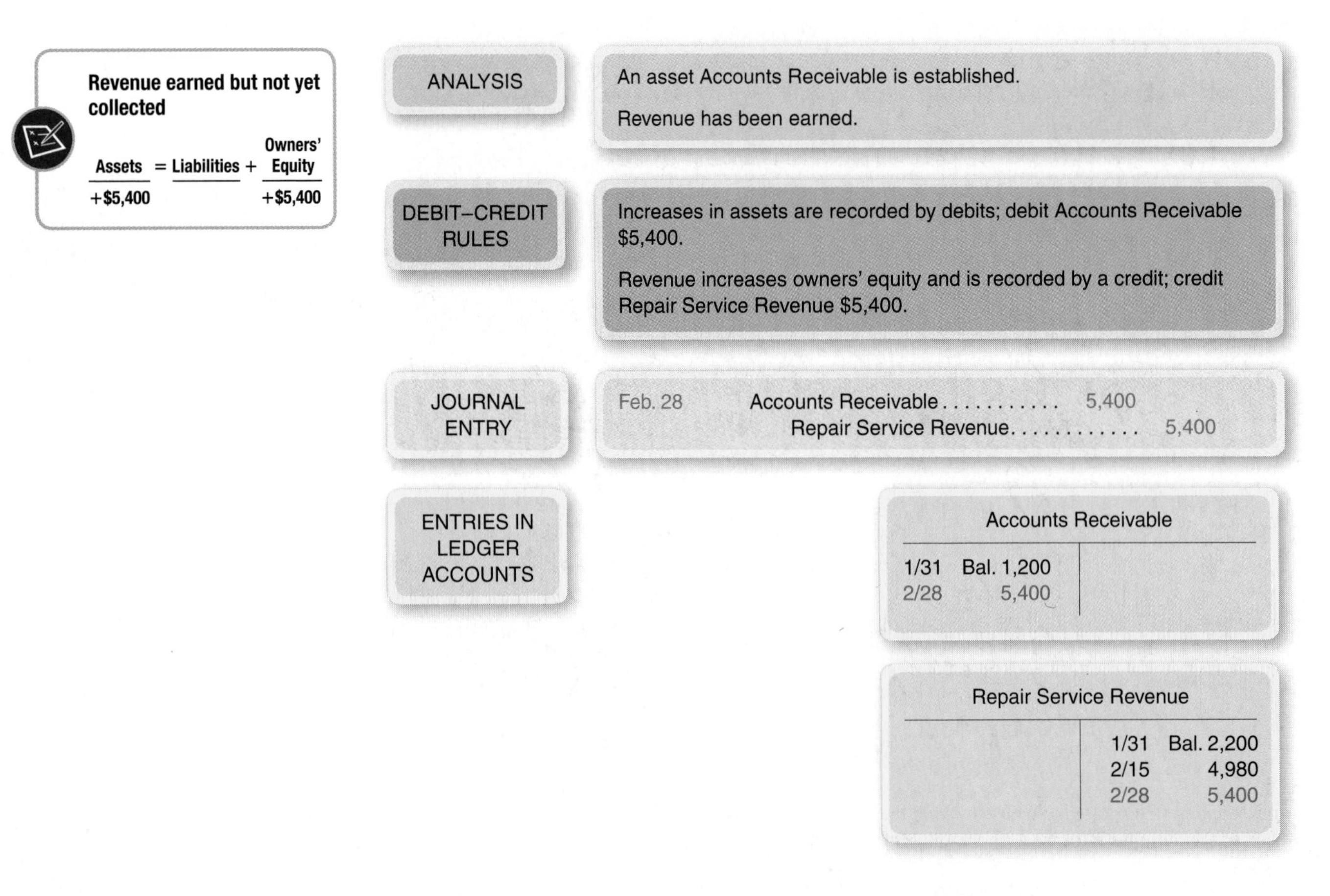

YOUR TURN **You as Overnight Auto Service's Accountant**

Your good friend, Fred Jonas, is the manager of Harbor Cab Co. Your family and Fred's family meet frequently outside of your respective workplaces for fun. At a recent barbecue, Fred asked you about the amount of repair services rendered by Overnight Auto to Airport Shuttle Services in February. Airport Shuttle Services competes with Harbor Cab Co. for fares to and from the airport. What should you say to Fred?

(See our comments on the Online Learning Center Web site.)

Feb. 28 Paid employees' wages earned in February, \$4,900.

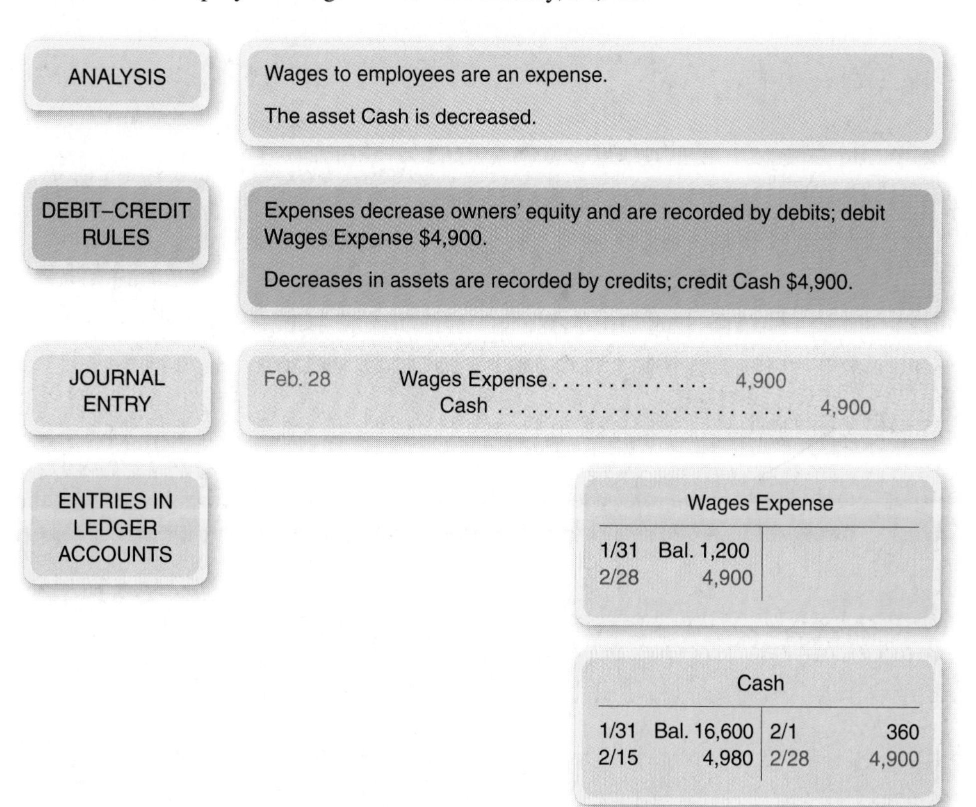

Incurred an expense, paying cash

Assets	=	Liabilities	+	Owners' Equity
−\$4,900				−\$4,900

Feb. 28 Recorded $1,600 utility bill for February. The entire amount is due March 15.

Incurred an expense to be paid later

Assets	= Liabilities	+ Owners' Equity
	+$1,600	−$1,600

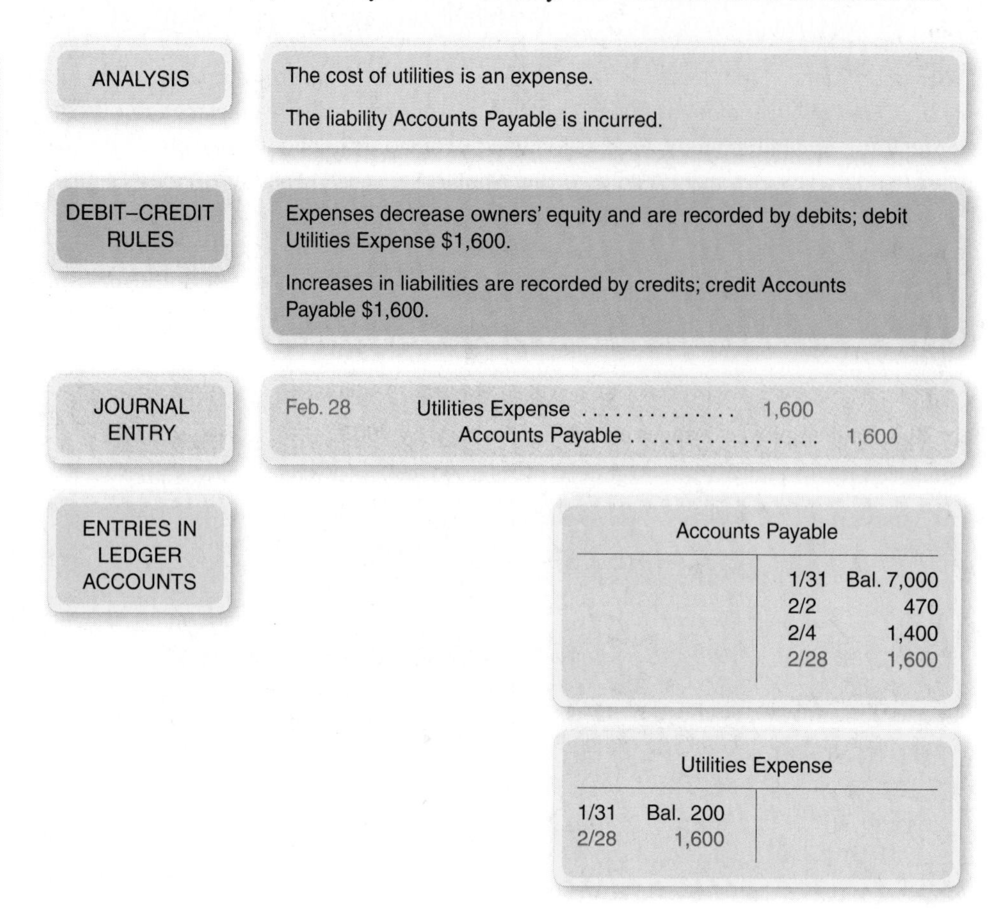

Feb. 28 Overnight Auto Services declares and pays a dividend of 40 cents per share to the owners of its 8,000 shares of capital stock—a total of $3,200.[2]

A Dividends account signifies a reduction in owners' equity—but it is not an expense

Assets	= Liabilities	+ Owners' Equity
−$3,200		−$3,200

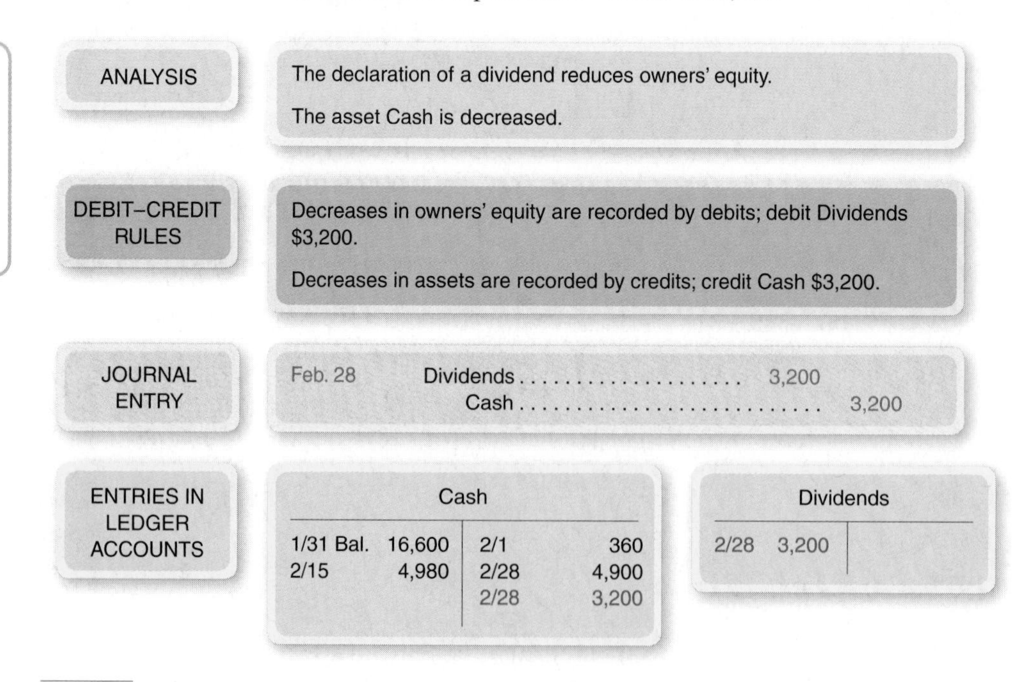

[2] As explained earlier, dividends are not an expense. In Chapter 5, we will show how the balance in the Dividends account eventually reduces the amount of Retained Earnings reported in the owners' equity section of the balance sheet.

THE JOURNAL

In our illustration, journal entries were shown in a very abbreviated form. The actual entries made in Overnight's journal appear in Exhibit 3–7. Notice that these formal journal entries include short *explanations* of the transactions, which include such details as the terms of credit transactions and the names of customers and creditors.

Exhibit 3–7

GENERAL JOURNAL ENTRIES: JANUARY 31 THROUGH FEBRUARY 28

OVERNIGHT AUTO SERVICE
General Journal
January 31–February 28, 2007

Date	Account Titles and Explanation	Debit	Credit
2007			
Jan. 31	Cash	2,200	
	Repair Service Revenue		2,200
	Repair services rendered to various customers.		
31	Wages Expense	1,200	
	Cash		1,200
	Paid all wages for January.		
31	Utilities Expense	200	
	Cash		200
	Paid all utilities for January.		
Feb. 1	Advertising Expense	360	
	Cash		360
	Purchased newspaper advertising from *Daily Tribune* to run in February.		
2	Advertising Expense	470	
	Accounts Payable		470
	Purchased radio advertising on account from KRAM; payment due in 30 days.		
4	Shop Supplies	1,400	
	Accounts Payable		1,400
	Purchased shop supplies on account from CAPA; payment due in 30 days.		
15	Cash	4,980	
	Repair Service Revenue		4,980
	Repair services rendered to Airport Shuttle Service.		
28	Accounts Receivable	5,400	
	Repair Service Revenue		5,400
	Billed Harbor Cab for services rendered in February.		
28	Wages Expense	4,900	
	Cash		4,900
	Paid all wages for February.		
28	Utilities Expense	1,600	
	Accounts Payable		1,600
	Recorded utility bill for February.		
28	Dividends	3,200	
	Cash		3,200
	Paid cash dividend of 40 cents per share on 8,000 shares of capital stock owned by the McBryan family.		

Journal entries contain more information than just dollar amounts

February's Ledger Balances

After posting all of the January and February transactions, Overnight's ledger accounts appear as shown in Exhibit 3–8. To conserve space, we have illustrated the ledger in T account form and have carried forward each account's summary balance from January 31. For convenience,

Exhibit 3–8 OVERNIGHT AUTO SERVICE'S LEDGER ACCOUNTS

OVERNIGHT AUTO SERVICE
The Ledger

Asset Accounts

Cash

Balance	Date	Debit	Date	Credit
	1/31 Bal.	16,600	2/1	360
	2/15	4,980	2/28	4,900
Bal. $13,120			2/28	3,200

Accounts Receivable

Balance	Date	Debit	Date	Credit
	1/31 Bal.	1,200		
Bal. $6,600	2/28	5,400		

Shop Supplies

Balance	Date	Debit	Date	Credit
	1/31 Bal.	0		
Bal. $1,400	2/4	1,400		

Land

Balance	Date	Debit	Date	Credit
Bal. $52,000	1/31 Bal.	52,000		

Building

Balance	Date	Debit	Date	Credit
Bal. $36,000	1/31 Bal.	36,000		

Tools and Equipment

Balance	Date	Debit	Date	Credit
Bal. $12,000	1/31 Bal.	12,000		

Liability and Owners' Equity Accounts

Notes Payable

Date	Debit	Date	Credit	Balance
		1/31 Bal.	30,000	Bal. $30,000

Accounts Payable

Date	Debit	Date	Credit	Balance
		1/31 Bal.	7,000	
		2/2	470	
		2/4	1,400	
		2/28	1,600	Bal. $10,470

Capital Stock

Date	Debit	Date	Credit	Balance
		1/31 Bal.	80,000	Bal. $80,000

Dividends

Balance	Date	Debit	Date	Credit
	1/31 Bal.	0		
Bal. $3,200	2/28	3,200		

Repair Service Revenue

Date	Debit	Date	Credit	Balance
		1/31 Bal.	2,200	
		2/15	4,980	
		2/28	5,400	Bal. $12,580

Advertising Expense

Balance	Date	Debit	Date	Credit
	2/1	360		
Bal. $830	2/2	470		

Wages Expense

Balance	Date	Debit	Date	Credit
	1/31 Bal.	1,200		
Bal. $6,100	2/28	4,900		

Utilities Expense

Balance	Date	Debit	Date	Credit
	1/31 Bal.	200		
Bal. $1,800	2/28	1,600		

we show in *red* the *February 28 balance* of each account (debit balances appear to the left of the account; credit balances appear to the right).

The accounts in this illustration appear in *financial statement order*—that is, balance sheet accounts first (assets, liabilities, and owners' equity), followed by the income statement accounts (revenue and expenses).

The Trial Balance

Prepare a trial balance and explain its uses and limitations. LO9

Since equal dollar amounts of debits and credits are entered in the accounts for every transaction recorded, the sum of all the debits in the ledger must be equal to the sum of all the credits. If the computation of account balances has been accurate, it follows that the total of the accounts with debit balances must be equal to the total of the accounts with credit balances.

Before using the account balances to prepare a balance sheet, it is desirable to *prove* that the total of accounts with debit balances is in fact equal to the total of accounts with credit balances. This proof of the equality of debit and credit balances is called a **trial balance**. A trial balance is a two-column schedule listing the names and balances of all the accounts *in the order in which they appear in the ledger*; the debit balances are listed in the left-hand column and the credit balances in the right-hand column. The totals of the two columns should agree. A trial balance taken from Overnight Auto's ledger accounts on page 110 is shown in Exhibit 3–9.

Exhibit 3–9
OVERNIGHT AUTO SERVICE'S TRIAL BALANCE

OVERNIGHT AUTO SERVICE
Trial Balance
February 28, 2007

Cash	$ 13,120	
Accounts receivable	6,600	
Shop supplies	1,400	
Land	52,000	
Building	36,000	
Tools and equipment	12,000	
Notes payable		$ 30,000
Accounts payable		10,470
Capital stock		80,000
Retained earnings		0
Dividends	3,200	
Repair service revenue		12,580
Advertising expense	830	
Wages expense	6,100	
Utilities expense	1,800	
	$133,050	$133,050

A trial balance proves the equality of debits and credits—but it also gives you a feel for how the business stands; but wait—there's more to consider

This trial balance proves the equality of the debit and credit entries in the company's accounting system. Notice that the trial balance contains both balance sheet and income statement accounts. Note also that the Retained Earnings balance is *zero*. It is zero because *no debit or credit entries were made to the Retained Earnings account in January or February*. Overnight, like most companies, updates its Retained Earnings balance only *once each year*. In Chapter 5, we will show how the Retained Earnings account is updated to its proper balance at year-end on December 31.[3]

[3] The balance of $0 in the Retained Earnings account is a highly unusual situation. Because the company is still in its first year of operations, no entries have ever been made to update the account's balance. In any trial balance prepared after the first year of business activity, the Retained Earnings account may be expected to have a balance other than $0.

USES AND LIMITATIONS OF THE TRIAL BALANCE

The trial balance provides proof that the ledger is in balance. The agreement of the debit and credit totals of the trial balance gives assurance that:

1. Equal debits and credits have been recorded for all transactions.
2. The addition of the account balances in the trial balance has been performed correctly.

Ethics, Fraud & Corporate Governance

As discussed in Chapter 2, the Sarbanes-Oxley Act (SOX) substantially increases the civil and criminal penalties associated with securities fraud, including fraudulent financial reporting. The increased penalties are intended to reduce illegal behaviors. Even prior to SOX, the penalties available to the government and the Securities and Exchange Commission for prosecuting securities fraud were substantial. For example, Andrew Fastow, Enron's former chief financial officer, and primary architect of Enron's fraudulent actions, pled guilty to a number of fraud-related criminal charges and has received a 10-year prison sentence. And the former chief executive officers of Enron, Kenneth Lay and Jeffrey Skilling, were convicted of numerous criminal charges related to their roles at Enron and are expected to receive lengthy prison sentences. As another example, Scott Sullivan, WorldCom's former chief financial officer, and the driver of the WorldCom fraud, also has pled guilty to a number of criminal charges. Sullivan has been sentenced to five years in prison. Bernard Ebbers, WorldCom's former chief executive officer, chose to stand trial related to his WorldCom related activities. He was found guilty, and has been sentenced to 25 years in federal prison.

© AP Wide World Photo

Businesspeople are sometimes told by their superiors to commit actions that are unethical and in some instances even illegal. The clear message of management is "participate in this behavior or find a job elsewhere." For instance, Buford Yates, a former WorldCom financial officer, told another WorldCom employee who was considering informing Arthur Andersen (WorldCom's former auditor) about certain transactions that were being hidden from Andersen, "Tell this to the (expletive deleted) auditor, and I'll throw you out the damn window." Management pressure and intimidation can make it difficult to resist demands to engage in unethical behavior. Employees sometimes believe that they are insulated from responsibility and liability because "they were just following orders." Like the Nazis at Nuremberg and Lieutenant Calley in Vietnam, the corporate defense of "I was just following orders" has failed to protect a number of midlevel Enron and WorldCom employees from criminal prosecution. James Comey, the U.S. Deputy Attorney General, stated that the government seeks guilty pleas from certain midlevel WorldCom executives for the express purpose of emphasizing that "I was just following orders" is not an acceptable defense.

As you encounter ethical dilemmas during your business career, remember that obeying orders from your superiors that are unethical, and certainly those that are illegal, may expose you to serious consequences, including criminal prosecution and incarceration.

Suppose that the debit and credit totals of the trial balance do not agree. This situation indicates that one or more errors have been made. Typical of such errors are (1) the posting of a debit as a credit, or vice versa; (2) arithmetic mistakes in determining account balances; (3) clerical errors in copying account balances into the trial balance; (4) listing a debit balance in the credit column of the trial balance, or vice versa; and (5) errors in addition of the trial balance.

The preparation of a trial balance does *not* prove that transactions have been correctly analyzed and recorded in the proper accounts. If, for example, a receipt of cash were erroneously recorded by debiting the Land account instead of the Cash account, the trial balance would still balance. Also, if a transaction were completely omitted from the ledger, the error would not be disclosed by the trial balance. In brief, *the trial balance proves only one aspect of the ledger, and that is the equality of debits and credits.*

Concluding Remarks

THE ACCOUNTING CYCLE IN PERSPECTIVE

In this chapter we have (1) journalized (recorded) transactions, (2) posted each journal entry to the appropriate ledger accounts, and (3) prepared a trial balance. The steps to be covered in Chapters 4 and 5 include (4) making end-of-period adjustments, (5) preparing an adjusted trial balance, (6) preparing financial statements, (7) journalizing and posting closing entries, and (8) preparing an after-closing trial balance.

We view the accounting cycle as an efficient means of introducing basic accounting terms, concepts, processes, and reports. This is why we introduce it early in the course. As we conclude the accounting cycle in Chapters 4 and 5, please don't confuse your familiarity with this sequence of procedures with a knowledge of *accounting*. The accounting cycle is but one accounting process—and a relatively simple one at that.

Distinguish between accounting cycle procedures and the *knowledge* of accounting. LO10

Computers now free accountants to focus upon the more *analytical* aspects of their discipline. These include, for example:

- Determining the information needs of decision makers.
- Designing systems to provide the information quickly and efficiently.
- Evaluating the efficiency of operations throughout the organization.
- Assisting decision makers in interpreting accounting information.
- Auditing (confirming the reliability of accounting information).
- Forecasting the probable results of future operations.
- Tax planning.

We will emphasize such topics in later chapters of this text. But let us first repeat a very basic point from Chapter 1: The need for some familiarity with accounting concepts and processes is not limited to individuals planning careers in accounting. Today, an understanding of accounting information and of the business world go hand in hand. You cannot know much about one without understanding quite a bit about the other.

END-OF-CHAPTER REVIEW

SUMMARY OF LEARNING OBJECTIVES

LO1 **Identify the steps in the accounting cycle and discuss the role of accounting records in an organization.** The accounting cycle generally consists of eight specific steps: (1) journalizing (recording) transactions, (2) posting each journal entry to the appropriate ledger accounts, (3) preparing a trial balance, (4) making end-of-period adjustments, (5) preparing an adjusted trial balance, (6) preparing financial statements, (7) journalizing and posting closing entries, and (8) preparing an after-closing trial balance.

Accounting records provide the information that is summarized in financial statements, income tax returns, and other accounting reports. In addition, these records are used by the company's management and employees for such purposes as:

- Establishing accountability for assets and transactions.
- Keeping track of routine business activities.
- Obtaining details about specific transactions.
- Evaluating the performance of units within the business.
- Maintaining a documentary record of the business's activities. (Such a record is required by tax laws and is useful for many purposes, including audits.)

LO2 **Describe a ledger account and a ledger.** A ledger account is a device for recording the increases or decreases in one financial statement item, such as a particular asset, a type of liability, or owners' equity. The general ledger is an accounting record that includes all the ledger accounts—that is, a separate account for each item included in the company's financial statements.

LO3 **Understand how balance sheet accounts are increased or decreased.** Increases in assets are recorded by debits and decreases are recorded by credits. Increases in liabilities and in owners' equity are recorded by credits and decreases are recorded by debits. Notice that the debit and credit rules are related to an account's *location in the balance sheet.* If the account appears on the *left side* of the balance sheet (asset accounts), increases in the account balance are recorded by *left-side entries* (debits). If the account appears on the *right side* of the balance sheet (liability and owners' equity accounts), increases are recorded by *right-side entries* (credits).

LO4 **Explain the double-entry system of accounting.** The double-entry system of accounting takes its name from the fact that every business transaction is recorded by *two types of entries*: (1) debit entries to one or more accounts and (2) credit entries to one or more accounts. In recording any transaction, the total dollar amount of the debit entries must equal the total dollar amount of the credit entries.

LO5 **Explain the purpose of a journal and its relationship to the ledger.** The journal is the accounting record in which business transactions are initially recorded. The entry in the journal shows which ledger accounts have increased as a result of the transaction and which have decreased. After the effects of the transaction have been recorded in the journal, the changes in the individual ledger accounts are then posted to the ledger.

LO6 **Explain the nature of *net income, revenue,* and *expenses.*** Net income is an increase in owners' equity that results from the profitable operation of a business during an accounting period. Net income also may be defined as revenue minus expenses. Revenue is the price of goods sold and services rendered to customers during the period, and expenses are the costs of the goods and services used up in the process of earning revenue.

LO7 **Apply the *realization* and *matching* principles in recording revenue and expenses.** The realization principle indicates that revenue should be recorded in the accounting records when it is *earned*—that is, when goods are sold or services are rendered to customers. The matching principle indicates that expenses should be offset against revenue on the basis of *cause and effect.* Thus, an expense should be recorded in the period in which the related good or service is consumed in the process of earning revenue.

LO8 **Understand how revenue and expense transactions are recorded in an accounting system.** The debit and credit rules for recording revenue and expenses are based on the rules for recording *changes in owners' equity.* Earning revenue *increases* owners' equity; therefore, revenue is recorded with a credit entry. Expenses *reduce* owners' equity and are recorded with debit entries.

LO9 **Prepare a trial balance and explain its uses and limitations.** In a trial balance, separate debit and credit columns are used to list the balances of the individual ledger accounts. The two columns are then totaled to prove the equality of the debit and credit balances. This process provides assurance that (1) the total of the debits posted to the ledger was equal to the total of the credits and (2) the balances of the individual ledger accounts were correctly computed. While a trial balance proves the equality of debit and credit entries in the ledger, it does *not* detect such errors as failure to record a business transaction, improper analysis of the accounts affected by the transaction, or the posting of debit or credit entries to the wrong accounts.

LO10 **Distinguish between accounting cycle procedures and the *knowledge* of accounting.** Accounting procedures involve the steps and processes necessary to *prepare* accounting information. A knowledge of the discipline enables one to *use* accounting information in evaluating performance, forecasting operations, and making complex business decisions.

Key Terms Introduced or Emphasized in Chapter 3

account (p. 88) A record used to summarize all increases and decreases in a particular asset, such as cash, or any other type of asset, liability, owners' equity, revenue, or expense.

accountability (p. 88) The condition of being held responsible for one's actions by the existence of an independent record of those actions. Establishing accountability is a major goal of accounting records and of internal control procedures.

accounting cycle (p. 88) The sequence of accounting procedures used to record, classify, and summarize accounting information. The cycle begins with the initial recording of business transactions and concludes with the preparation of formal financial statements.

accounting period (p. 99) The span of time covered by an income statement. One year is the accounting period for much financial reporting, but financial statements are also prepared by companies for each quarter of the year and for each month.

accrual basis of accounting (p. 102) Calls for recording revenue in the period in which it is earned and recording expenses in the period in which they are incurred. The effect of events on the business is recognized as services are rendered or consumed rather than when cash is received or paid.

conservatism (p. 101) The traditional accounting practice of resolving uncertainty by choosing the solution that leads to the lower (more conservative) amount of income being recognized in the current accounting period. This concept is designed to avoid overstatement of financial strength or earnings.

credit (p. 89) An amount entered on the right side of a ledger account. A credit is used to record a decrease in an asset or an increase in a liability or in owners' equity.

debit (p. 89) An amount entered on the left side of a ledger account. A debit is used to record an increase in an asset or a decrease in a liability or in owners' equity.

dividends (p. 98) A distribution of resources by a corporation to its stockholders. The resource most often distributed is cash.

double-entry accounting (p. 91) A system of recording every business transaction with equal dollar amounts of both debit and credit entries. As a result of this system, the accounting equation always remains in balance; in addition, the system makes possible the measurement of net income and also the use of error-detecting devices such as a trial balance.

expenses (p. 98) The costs of the goods and services used up in the process of obtaining revenue.

fiscal year (p. 100) Any 12-month accounting period adopted by a business.

general journal (p. 91) The simplest type of journal, it has only two money columns—one for credits and one for debits. This journal may be used for all types of transactions, which are later posted to the appropriate ledger accounts.

income statement (p. 98) A financial statement summarizing the results of operations of a business by matching its revenue and related expenses for a particular accounting period. Shows the net income or net loss.

journal (p. 91) A chronological record of transactions, showing for each transaction the debits and credits to be entered in specific ledger accounts. The simplest type of journal is called a general journal.

ledger (p. 88) An accounting system includes a separate record for each item that appears in the financial statements. Collectively, these records are referred to as a company's ledger. Individually, these records are often referred to as ledger accounts.

matching principle (p. 101) The generally accepted accounting principle that determines when expenses should be recorded in the accounting records. The revenue earned during an accounting period is matched (offset) with the expenses incurred in generating that revenue.

net income (p. 98) An increase in owners' equity resulting from profitable operations. Also, the excess of revenue earned over the related expenses for a given period.

net loss (p. 98) A decrease in owners' equity resulting from unprofitable operations.

objectivity (p. 101) Accountants' preference for using dollar amounts that are relatively factual—as opposed to merely matters of personal opinion. Objective measurements can be verified.

posting (p. 92) The process of transferring information from the journal to individual accounts in the ledger.

realization principle (p. 100) The generally accepted accounting principle that determines when revenue should be recorded in the accounting records. Revenue is realized when services are rendered to customers or when goods sold are delivered to customers.

retained earnings (p. 98) That portion of stockholders' (owners') equity resulting from profits earned and retained in the business.

revenue (p. 98) The price of goods and services charged to customers for goods and services rendered by a business.

time period principle (p. 99) To provide the users of financial statements with timely information, net income is measured for relatively short accounting periods of equal length. The period of time covered by an income statement is termed the company's accounting period.

trial balance (p. 111) A two-column schedule listing the names and the debit or credit balances of all accounts in the ledger.

Demonstration Problem

Epler Consulting Services, Inc., opened for business on January 25, 2007. The company maintains the following ledger accounts:

Cash	Capital Stock
Accounts Receivable	Retained Earnings
Office Supplies	Consulting Revenue
Office Equipment	Rent Expense
Accounts Payable	Utilities Expense

The company engaged in the following business activity in January:

Jan. 20 Issued 5,000 shares of capital stock for $50,000.

Jan. 20 Paid $400 office rent for the remainder of January.

Jan. 21 Purchased office supplies for $200. The supplies will last for several months, and payment is not due until February 15.

Jan. 22 Purchased office equipment for $15,000 cash.

Jan. 26 Performed consulting services and billed clients $2,000. The entire amount will not be collected until February.

Jan. 31 Recorded $100 utilities expense. Payment is not due until February 20.

Instructions

a. Record each of the above transactions in general journal form.

b. Post each entry to the appropriate ledger accounts.

c. Prepare a trial balance dated January 31, 2007.

d. Explain why the Retained Earnings account has a zero balance in the trial balance.

Solution to the Demonstration Problem

a.

EPLER CONSULTING SERVICES, INC.
General Journal

Date	Account Titles and Explanation	Debit	Credit
2007			
Jan. 20	Cash	50,000	
	Capital Stock		50,000
	To record the issue of 5,000 shares of capital stock at $10 per share.		
20	Rent Expense	400	
	Cash		400
	To record payment of January rent expense.		
21	Office Supplies	200	
	Accounts Payable		200
	To record purchase of office supplies on account.		
22	Office Equipment	15,000	
	Cash		15,000
	To record the purchase of office equipment.		
26	Accounts Receivable	2,000	
	Consulting Revenue		2,000
	Billed clients for consulting services rendered.		
31	Utilities Expense	100	
	Accounts Payable		100
	To record January utilities expense due in February.		

b.

EPLER CONSULTING SERVICES, INC.
The Ledger
January 20–31, 2007

Asset Accounts

Cash

Balance	Date	Debit	Date	Credit
	1/20	50,000	1/20	400
Bal. $34,600			1/22	15,000

Accounts Receivable

Balance	Date	Debit	Date	Credit
Bal. $2,000	1/26	2,000		

Office Supplies

Balance	Date	Debit	Date	Credit
Bal. $200	1/21	200		

Office Equipment

Balance	Date	Debit	Date	Credit
Bal. $15,000	1/22	15,000		

Liability and Owners' Equity Accounts

Accounts Payable

Date	Debit	Date	Credit	Balance
		1/21	200	
		1/31	100	Bal. $300

Capital Stock

Date	Debit	Date	Credit	Balance
		1/20	50,000	Bal. $50,000

Retained Earnings

Date	Debit	Date	Credit	Balance
				Bal. $0

Consulting Revenue

Date	Debit	Date	Credit	Balance
		1/26	2,000	Bal. $2,000

Rent Expense

Balance	Date	Debit	Date	Credit
Bal. $400	1/20	400		

Utilities Expense

Balance	Date	Debit	Date	Credit
Bal. $100	1/31	100		

c.

EPLER CONSULTING SERVICES, INC. Trial Balance January 31, 2007		
Cash	$34,600	
Accounts receivable	2,000	
Office supplies	200	
Office equipment	15,000	
Accounts payable		$ 300
Capital stock		50,000
Retained earnings		0
Consulting revenue		2,000
Rent expense	400	
Utilities expense	100	
	$52,300	$52,300

d. Epler's Retained Earnings account balance is zero because the company has been in business for only one week and has not yet updated the Retained Earnings account for *any* revenue or expense activities. The periodic adjustment needed to update the Retained Earnings account is discussed in Chapter 5.

Self-Test Questions

The answers to these questions appear on page 139.

1. According to the rules of debit and credit for balance sheet accounts:

- **a.** Increases in asset, liability, and owners' equity accounts are recorded by debits.
- **b.** Decreases in asset and liability accounts are recorded by credits.
- **c.** Increases in asset and owners' equity accounts are recorded by debits.
- **d.** Decreases in liability and owners' equity accounts are recorded by debits.

2. Sunset Tours has a $3,500 account receivable from the Del Mar Rotary. On January 20, the Rotary makes a partial payment of $2,100 to Sunset Tours. The journal entry made on January 20 by Sunset Tours to record this transaction includes:

- **a.** A debit to the Cash Received account of $2,100.
- **b.** A credit to the Accounts Receivable account of $2,100.
- **c.** A debit to the Cash account of $1,400.
- **d.** A debit to the Accounts Receivable account of $1,400.

3. Indicate all of the following statements that correctly describe net income. Net income:

- **a.** Is equal to revenue minus expenses.
- **b.** Is equal to revenue minus the sum of expenses and dividends.
- **c.** Increases owners' equity.
- **d.** Is reported by a company for a specific period of time.

4. Which of the following is provided by a trial balance in which total debits equal total credits?

- **a.** Proof that no transaction was completely omitted from the ledger during the posting process.
- **b.** Proof that the correct debit or credit balance has been computed for each account.
- **c.** Proof that the ledger is in balance.
- **d.** Proof that transactions have been correctly analyzed and recorded in the proper accounts.

5. Which of the following explains the debit and credit rules relating to the recording of revenue and expenses?

- **a.** Expenses appear on the left side of the balance sheet and are recorded by debits; revenue appears on the right side of the balance sheet and is recorded by credits.
- **b.** Expenses appear on the left side of the income statement and are recorded by debits; revenue appears on the right side of the income statement and is recorded by credits.
- **c.** The effects of revenue and expenses on owners' equity.
- **d.** The realization principle and the matching principle.

6. Which of the following is *not* considered an analytical aspect of the accounting profession?

- **a.** Evaluating an organization's operational efficiency.
- **b.** Forecasting the probable results of future operations.
- **c.** Designing systems that provide information to decision makers.
- **d.** Journalizing and posting business transactions.

7. Indicate all correct answers. In the accounting cycle:
   - **a.** Transactions are posted before they are journalized.
   - **b.** A trial balance is prepared after journal entries have been posted.
   - **c.** The Retained Earnings account is not shown as an up-to-date figure in the trial balance.
   - **d.** Journal entries are posted to appropriate ledger accounts.

8. Indicate all correct answers. Dividends:
   - **a.** Decrease owners' equity.
   - **b.** Decrease net income.
   - **c.** Are recorded by debiting the Dividend account.
   - **d.** Are a business expense.

ASSIGNMENT MATERIAL Discussion Questions

1. Baker Construction is a small corporation owned and managed by Tom Baker. The corporation has 21 employees, few creditors, and no investor other than Tom Baker. Thus, like many small businesses, it has no obligation to issue financial statements to creditors or investors. Under these circumstances, is there any reason for this corporation to maintain accounting records?

2. In its simplest form, an account has only three elements or basic parts. What are these three elements?

3. What relationship exists between the position of an account in the balance sheet equation and the rules for recording increases in that account?

4. State briefly the rules of debit and credit as applied to asset accounts and as applied to liability and owners' equity accounts.

5. Does the term *debit* mean increase and the term *credit* mean decrease? Explain.

6. What requirement is imposed by the double-entry system in the recording of any business transaction?

7. For each of the following transactions, indicate whether the account in parentheses should be debited or credited, and *give the reason* for your answer.
   - **a.** Purchased land for cash. (Cash)
   - **b.** Sold an old, unneeded computer on 30-day credit. (Office Equipment)
   - **c.** Obtained a loan of $30,000 from a bank. (Cash)
   - **d.** Purchased a copying machine on credit, promising to make payment in full within 30 days. (Accounts Payable)
   - **e.** Williams Word Processing, Inc., issued 10,000 shares of capital stock. (Capital Stock)

8. Explain the effect of operating profitably on the balance sheet of a business entity.

9. Does net income represent a supply of cash that could be distributed to stockholders in the form of dividends? Explain.

10. What is the meaning of the term *revenue*? Does the receipt of cash by a business indicate that revenue has been earned? Explain.

11. What is the meaning of the term *expenses*? Does the payment of cash by a business indicate that an expense has been incurred? Explain.

12. A service enterprise performs services in the amount of $500 for a customer in May and receives payment in June. In which month is the $500 of revenue recognized? What is the journal entry to be made in May and the entry to be made in June?

13. When do accountants consider revenue to be realized? What basic question about recording revenue in accounting records is answered by the *realization principle*?

14. Late in March, Classic Auto Painters purchased paint on account, with payment due in 60 days. The company used the paint to paint customers' cars during the first three weeks of April. Late in May, the company paid the paint store from which the paint had been purchased. In which month should Classic Auto Painters recognize the cost of this paint as expense? What underlying accounting principle determines the answer to this question?

15. In what accounting period does the *matching principle* indicate that an expense should be recognized?

16. Explain the rules of debit and credit with respect to transactions recorded in revenue and expense accounts.

17. What are some of the limitations of a trial balance?

18. How do dividends affect owners' equity? Are they treated as a business expense? Explain.

19. How does the accrual basis of accounting differ from the cash basis of accounting? Which gives a more accurate picture of the profitability of a business? Explain.

20. List some of the more *analytical* functions performed by professional accountants.

Brief Exercises

BRIEF EXERCISE 3.1

The Accounting Cycle

Listed below in *random order* are the eight steps comprising a complete accounting cycle:

Prepare a trial balance.
Journalize and post the closing entries.
Prepare financial statements.
Post transaction data to the ledger.
Prepare an adjusted trial balance.
Make end-of-period adjustments.

Journalize transactions.

Prepare an after-closing trial balance.

a. List these steps in the sequence in which they would normally be performed. (A detailed understanding of these eight steps is not required until Chapters 4 and 5.)

b. Describe ways in which the information produced through the accounting cycle is used by a company's management and employees.

LO3 through LO5

BRIEF EXERCISE 3.2
Recording Transactions in a Journal

Record the following selected transactions in general journal form for Sun Orthopedic Clinic, Inc. Include a brief explanation of the transaction as part of each journal entry.

Oct. 1 The clinic issued 4,000 additional shares of capital stock to Doctor Soges at $50 per share.

Oct. 4 The clinic purchased diagnostic equipment. The equipment cost $75,000, of which $25,000 was paid in cash; a note payable was issued for the balance.

Oct. 12 Issued a check for $9,000 in full payment of an account payable to Zeller Laboratories.

Oct. 19 Purchased surgical supplies for $2,600. Payment is not due until November 28.

Oct. 25 Collected a $24,000 account receivable from Health One Insurance Company.

Oct. 30 Declared and paid a $300,000 cash dividend to stockholders.

LO7 LO8

BRIEF EXERCISE 3.3
Recording Transactions

Brown Consulting Services organized as a corporation on January 18 and engaged in the following transactions during its first two weeks of operation:

Jan. 18 Issued capital stock in exchange for $30,000 cash.

Jan. 22 Borrowed $20,000 from its bank by issuing a note payable.

Jan. 23 Paid $100 for a radio advertisement aired on January 24.

Jan. 25 Provided $1,000 of services to clients for cash.

Jan. 26 Provided $2,000 of services to clients on account.

Jan. 31 Collected $800 cash from clients for the services provided on January 26.

a. Record each of these transactions.

b. Determine the balance in the Cash account on January 31. Be certain to state whether the balance is debit or credit.

LO3 LO8

BRIEF EXERCISE 3.4
Debit and Credit Rules

Five account classifications are shown as column headings in the table below. For each account classification, indicate the manner in which increases and decreases are recorded (i.e., by debits or by credits).

	Revenue	Expenses	Assets	Liabilities	Owners' Equity
Increases recorded by:					
Decreases recorded by:					

LO3 LO6

BRIEF EXERCISE 3.5
Changes in Retained Earnings

Jackson Corporation's Retained Earnings account balance was $75,000 on January 1. During January, the company recorded revenue of $100,000, expenses of $60,000, and dividends of $5,000. The company also purchased land during the period for $20,000 cash.

Determine the company's Retained Earnings account balance on January 31.

LO6 LO7

BRIEF EXERCISE 3.6
Realization and Matching Principles

On May 26, Breeze Camp Ground paid KPRM Radio $500 cash for ten 30-second advertisements. Two of the ads were aired in May, seven in June, and one in July.

a. Apply the realization principle to determine how much advertising revenue KPRM Radio earned from Breeze Camp Ground in May, June, and July.

b. Apply the matching principle to determine how much advertising expense Breeze Camp Ground incurred in May, June, and July.

BRIEF EXERCISE 3.7
When Is Revenue Realized?

The following transactions were carried out during the month of May by M. Palmer and Company, a firm of design architects. For each of the five transactions, you are to state whether the transaction represented revenue to the firm during the month of May. Give reasons for your decision in each case.

a. M. Palmer and Company received $25,000 cash by issuing additional shares of capital stock.

b. Collected cash of $2,400 from an account receivable. The receivable originated in April from services rendered to a client.

c. Borrowed $12,800 from Century Bank to be repaid in three months.

d. Earned $83 interest on a company bank account during the month of May. No withdrawals were made from this account in May.

e. Completed plans for guesthouse, pool, and spa for a client. The $5,700 fee for this project was billed to the client in May, but will not be collected until June 25.

BRIEF EXERCISE 3.8
When Are Expenses Incurred?

During March, the activities of Evergreen Landscaping included the following transactions and events, among others. Which of these items represented expenses in March? Explain.

a. Purchased a copying machine for $2,750 cash.

b. Paid $192 for gasoline purchases for a delivery truck during March.

c. Paid $2,280 salary to an employee for time worked during March.

d. Paid an attorney $560 for legal services rendered in January.

e. Declared and paid an $1,800 dividend to shareholders.

BRIEF EXERCISE 3.9
Realization Principle

Up & Away Airlines has provided the following information regarding cash received for ticket sales in September and October:

Cash received in September for October flights	$500,000
Cash received in October for October flights	300,000
Cash received in October for November flights	400,000

Apply the realization principle to determine how much revenue Up & Away Airlines should report in its October income statement.

BRIEF EXERCISE 3.10
Matching Principle

Wilson Consulting has provided the following information regarding cash payments to its employees in May and June:

Salary payments in May for work performed by employees in April	$ 8,000
Salary payments in May for work performed by employees in May	15,000
Salary payments in June for work performed by employees in May	9,000

Apply the matching principle to determine how much salary expense Wilson Consulting should report in its May income statement.

Exercises

through

EXERCISE 3.1
Accounting Terminology

Listed below are eight technical accounting terms introduced in this chapter:

Realization principle	Credit
Time period principle	Accounting period
Matching principle	Expenses
Net income	Accounting cycle

Each of the following statements may (or may not) describe one of these technical terms. For each statement, indicate the term described, or answer "None" if the statement does not correctly describe any of the terms.

a. The span of time covered by an income statement.

b. The sequence of accounting procedures used to record, classify, and summarize accounting information.

c. The traditional accounting practice of resolving uncertainty by choosing the solution that leads to the lowest amount of income being recognized.

d. An increase in owners' equity resulting from profitable operations.

e. The underlying accounting principle that determines when revenue should be recorded in the accounting records.

f. The type of entry used to decrease an asset or increase a liability or owners' equity account.

g. The underlying accounting principle of offsetting revenue earned during an accounting period with the expenses incurred in generating that revenue.

h. The costs of the goods and services used up in the process of generating revenue.

EXERCISE 3.2
The Matching Principle: You as a Driver

The purpose of this exercise is to demonstrate the *matching principle* in a familiar setting. Assume that you own a car that you drive about 15,000 miles each year.

a. List the various costs to you associated with owning and operating this car. Make an estimate of the total annual cost of owning and operating the car, as well as the average cost-per-mile that you drive.

b. Assume also that you have a part-time job. You usually do not use your car in this job, but today your employer asks you to drive 100 miles (round-trip) to deliver some important documents. Your employer offers to "reimburse you for your driving expenses."

You already have a full tank of gas, so you are able to drive the whole 100 miles without stopping and you don't actually spend any money during the trip. Does this mean that you have incurred no "expenses" for which you should be reimbursed? Explain.

EXERCISE 3.3
Relationship between Journal and Ledger Accounts

Transactions are *first* journalized and *then* posted to ledger accounts. In this exercise, however, your understanding of the relationship between the journal and the ledger is tested by asking you to study some ledger accounts and determine the journal entries that probably were made to produce these ledger entries. The following accounts show the first six transactions of Avenson Insurance Company. Prepare a journal entry (including a written explanation) for each transaction.

Cash

Nov. 1	120,000	Nov. 8	33,600
		Nov. 25	12,000
		Nov. 30	1,400

Vehicles

Nov. 30	9,400		

Land

Nov. 8	70,000		

Notes Payable

Nov. 25	12,000	Nov. 8	95,000
		Nov. 30	8,000

Building

Nov. 8	58,600		

Accounts Payable

Nov. 21	480	Nov. 15	3,200

Office Equipment

Nov. 15	3,200	Nov. 21	480

Capital Stock

		Nov. 1	120,000

EXERCISE 3.4
Preparing a Trial Balance

Using the information in the ledger accounts presented in Exercise 3.3, prepare a trial balance for Avenson Insurance Company dated November 30.

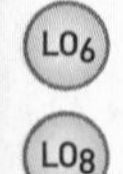

EXERCISE 3.5
Relationship between Net Income and Equity

The following information came from a recent balance sheet of **Apple Computer, Inc.**:

	End of Year	Beginning of Year
Assets	$6.3 billion	$6.0 billion
Liabilities	$2.2 billion	?
Owners' Equity	?	$3.9 billion

a. Determine the amount of total liabilities reported in Apple Computer's balance sheet at the beginning of the year.

b. Determine the amount of total owners' equity reported in Apple Computer's balance sheet at the end of the year.

c. Capital stock reported in Apple Computer's year-end balance sheet was $135 million more than the amount reported in the company's beginning balance sheet. If the company did not declare any dividends, determine its net income for the year.

LO2 through LO6

EXERCISE 3.6
Effects of Transactions on the Accounting Equation

Satka Fishing Expeditions, Inc., recorded the following transactions in July:

1. Provided an ocean fishing expedition for a credit customer; payment is due August 10.
2. Paid Marine Service Center for repairs to boats performed in June. (In June, Satka Fishing Expeditions, Inc., had received and properly recorded the invoice for these repairs.)
3. Collected the full amount due from a credit customer for a fishing expedition provided in June.
4. Received a bill from Baldy's Bait Shop for bait purchased and used in July. Payment is due August 3.
5. Purchased a new fishing boat on July 28, paying part cash and issuing a note payable for the balance. The new boat is first scheduled for use on August 5.
6. Declared and paid a cash dividend on July 31.

Indicate the effects that each of these transactions will have upon the following six *total amounts* in the company's financial statements for the month of July. Organize your answer in tabular form, using the column headings shown, and use the code letters **I** for increase, **D** for decrease, and **NE** for no effect. The answer to transaction **1** is provided as an example.

	Income Statement			Balance Sheet		
Transaction	Revenue −	Expenses =	Net Income	Assets =	Liabilities +	Owners' Equity
1	I	NE	I	I	NE	I

LO2 through LO6

EXERCISE 3.7
Effects of Transactions on the Accounting Equation

A number of transactions of Claypool Construction are described below in terms of accounts debited and credited:

1. Debit Wages Expense; credit Wages Payable.
2. Debit Accounts Receivable; credit Construction Revenue.
3. Debit Dividends; credit Cash.
4. Debit Office Supplies; credit Accounts Payable.
5. Debit Repairs Expense; credit Cash.
6. Debit Cash; credit Accounts Receivable.
7. Debit Tools and Equipment; credit Cash and Notes Payable.
8. Debit Accounts Payable; credit Cash.

a. Indicate the effects of each transaction upon the elements of the income statement and the balance sheet. Use the code letters **I** for increase, **D** for decrease, and **NE** for no effect. Organize your answer in tabular form using the column headings shown below. The answer for transaction **1** is provided as an example.

	Income Statement			Balance Sheet		
Transaction	Revenue −	Expenses =	Net Income	Assets =	Liabilities +	Owners' Equity
1	NE	I	D	NE	I	D

b. Write a one-sentence description of each transaction.

LO4 LO6 through LO8

EXERCISE 3.8
Preparing Journal Entries for Revenue, Expenses, and Dividends

Shown below are selected transactions of the architectural firm of Baxter, Claxter, and Stone, Inc.

April 5 Prepared building plans for Spangler Construction Company. Sent Spangler an invoice for $900 requesting payment within 30 days. (The appropriate revenue account is entitled Drafting Fees Earned.)

May 17 Declared a cash dividend of $5,000. The dividend will not be paid until June 25.

May 29 Received a $2,000 bill from Bob Needham, CPA, for accounting services performed during May. Payment is due by June 10. (The appropriate expense account is entitled Professional Expenses.)

June 4 Received full payment from Spangler Construction Company for the invoice sent on April 5.

June 10 Paid Bob Needham, CPA, for the bill received on May 29.

June 25 Paid the cash dividend declared on May 17.

a. Prepare journal entries to record the transactions in the firm's accounting records.

b. Identify any of the above transactions that *will not* result in a change in the company's net income.

LO3 LO6 LO7

EXERCISE 3.9
Effects of Transactions on the Financial Statements

Listed below are eight transactions the Foster Corporation made during November:

a. Issued stock in exchange for cash.

b. Purchased land. Made partial payment with cash and issued a note payable for the remaining balance.

c. Recorded utilities expense for November. Payment is due in mid-December.

d. Purchased office supplies with cash.

e. Paid outstanding salaries payable owed to employees for wages earned in October.

f. Declared a cash dividend that will not be paid until late December.

g. Sold land for cash at an amount equal to the land's historical cost.

h. Collected cash on account from customers for services provided in September and October.

Indicate the *effects of the above transactions* on each of the financial statement elements shown in the column headings below. Use the following symbols: **I** = Increase, **D** = Decrease, and **NE** = no effect.

Transaction	Net Income	Assets	Liabilities	Equity
a.				
b.				
c.				
d.				
e.				
f.				
g.				
h.				

LO3 LO5 LO8 LO9

EXERCISE 3.10
Journalizing, Posting, and Preparing a Trial Balance
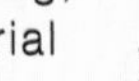

Trafflet Enterprises incorporated on May 3, 2007. The company engaged in the following transactions during its first month of operations:

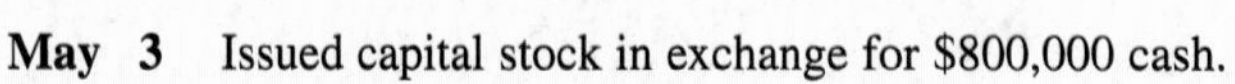
May 3 Issued capital stock in exchange for $800,000 cash.

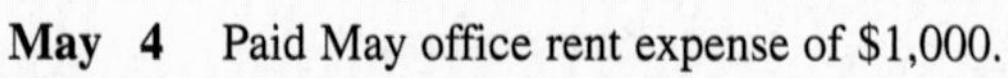
May 4 Paid May office rent expense of $1,000.

May 5 Purchased office supplies for $400 cash. The supplies will last for several months.

May 15 Purchased office equipment for $8,000 on account. The entire amount is due June 15.

May 18 Purchased a company car for $27,000. Paid $7,000 cash and issued a note payable for the remaining amount owed.

May 20 Billed clients $32,000 on account.

May 26 Declared a $5,000 dividend. The entire amount will be distributed to shareholders on June 26.

May 29 Paid May utilities of $200.

May 30 Received $30,000 from clients billed on May 20.

May 31 Recorded and paid salary expense of $14,000.

A partial list of the account titles used by the company includes:

Cash	Dividends Payable
Accounts Receivable	Dividends
Office Supplies	Capital Stock
Office Equipment	Client Revenue
Vehicles	Office Rent Expense
Notes Payable	Salary Expense
Accounts Payable	Utilities Expense

a. Prepare journal entries, including explanations, for the above transactions.

b. Post each entry to the appropriate ledger accounts (use the T account format illustrated in Exhibit 3–8 on page 110).

c. Prepare a trial balance dated May 31, 2007. Assume accounts with zero balances are not included in the trial balance.

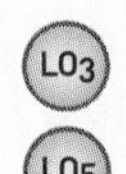

LO3 LO5 LO8 LO9

EXERCISE 3.11

Journalizing, Posting, and Preparing a Trial Balance

The McMillan Corporation incorporated on September 2, 2007. The company engaged in the following transactions during its first month of operations:

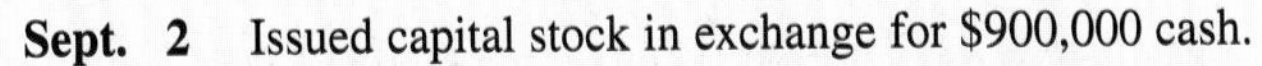

Sept. 2 Issued capital stock in exchange for $900,000 cash.

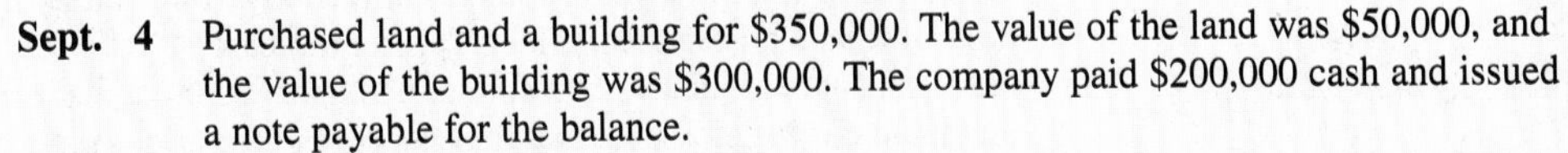

Sept. 4 Purchased land and a building for $350,000. The value of the land was $50,000, and the value of the building was $300,000. The company paid $200,000 cash and issued a note payable for the balance.

Sept. 12 Purchased office supplies for $600 on account. The supplies will last for several months.

Sept. 19 Billed clients $75,000 on account.

Sept. 29 Recorded and paid salary expense of $24,000.

Sept. 30 Received $30,000 from clients billed on September 19.

A partial list of the account titles used by the company includes:

Cash	Notes Payable
Accounts Receivable	Accounts Payable
Office Supplies	Capital Stock
Land	Client Revenue
Building	Salary Expense

a. Prepare journal entries, including explanations, for the above transactions.

b. Post each entry to the appropriate ledger accounts (use the T account format illustrated in Exhibit 3–8 on page 110).

c. Prepare a trial balance dated September 30, 2007. Assume accounts with zero balances are not included in the trial balance.

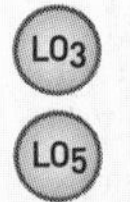

LO3 LO5 LO8 LO9

EXERCISE 3.12

Journalizing, Posting, and Preparing a Trial Balance

Herrold Consulting incorporated on February 1, 2007. The company engaged in the following transactions during its first month of operations:

Feb. 1 Issued capital stock in exchange for $750,000 cash.

Feb. 5 Borrowed $50,000 from the bank by issuing a note payable.

Feb. 8 Purchased land, building, and office equipment for $600,000. The value of the land was $100,000, the value of the building was $450,000, and the value of the office equipment was $50,000. The company paid $300,000 cash and issued a note payable for the balance.

Feb. 11 Purchased office supplies for $600 on account. The supplies will last for several months.

Feb. 14 Paid the local newspaper $400 for a full-page advertisement. The ad will appear in print on February 18.

Feb. 20 Several of the inkjet printer cartridges that Herrold purchased on February 11 were defective. The cartridges were returned and the office supply store reduced Herrold's outstanding balance by $100.

Feb. 22 Performed consulting services for $6,000 cash.

Feb. 24 Billed clients $9,000.

Feb. 25 Paid salaries of $5,000.

Feb. 28 Paid the entire outstanding balance owed for office supplies purchased on February 11.

A partial list of the account titles used by the company includes:

Cash	Notes Payable
Accounts Receivable	Accounts Payable
Office Supplies	Capital Stock
Land	Client Service Revenue
Building	Advertising Expense
Office Equipment	Salaries Expense

a. Prepare journal entries, including explanations, for the above transactions.

b. Post each entry to the appropriate ledger accounts (use the T account format as illustrated in Exhibit 3–8 on page 110).

c. Prepare a trial balance dated February 28, 2007. Assume accounts with zero balances are not included in the trial balance.

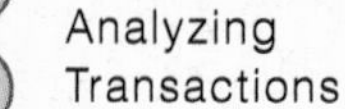

EXERCISE 3.13
Analyzing Transactions

Listed below are descriptions of six transactions, followed by a table listing six unique combinations of financial statement effects (**I** is for increase, **D** is for decrease, and **NE** is for no effect). In the blank space to the left of each transaction description, place the appropriate letter from the table that indicates the effects of that transaction on the various elements of the financial statements.

1. _____ Purchased machinery for $5,000, paying $1,000 cash and issuing a $4,000 note payable for the balance.

2. _____ Billed clients $16,000 on account.

3. _____ Recorded a $500 maintenance expense of which $100 was paid in cash and the remaining amount was due in 30 days.

4. _____ Paid an outstanding account payable of $400.

5. _____ Recorded monthly utilities costs of $300. The entire amount is due in 20 days.

6. _____ Declared a $40,000 dividend to be distributed in 60 days.

Transaction	Revenue	Expenses	Assets	Liabilities	Owners' Equity
a.	NE	NE	D	D	NE
b.	NE	I	D	I	D
c.	NE	NE	NE	I	D
d.	NE	I	NE	I	D
e.	NE	NE	I	I	N
f.	I	NE	I	NE	I

EXERCISE 3.14
Analyzing Transactions

Listed below are descriptions of six transactions, followed by a table listing six unique combinations of financial statement effects (**I** is for increase, **D** is for decrease, and **NE** is for no effect). In the blank space to the left of each transaction description, place the appropriate letter from the table that indicates the effects of that transaction on the various elements of the financial statements.

1. _____ Issued capital stock in exchange for $50,000 cash.

2. _____ Billed clients $20,000 on account.

3. _____ Placed a $300 advertisement in the local newspaper. The entire amount is due in 30 days.

4. ______ Collected $100 on account from clients.
5. ______ Recorded and paid a $12,000 dividend.
6. ______ Recorded and paid salaries of $15,000.

Transaction	Revenue	Expenses	Assets	Liabilities	Owners' Equity
a.	NE	I	NE	I	D
b.	NE	I	D	NE	D
c.	NE	NE	D	NE	D
d.	NE	NE	I	NE	I
e.	I	NE	I	NE	I
f.	NE	NE	NE	NE	NE

LO1 through LO3  LO10

EXERCISE 3.15
Using the Financial Statements of Home Depot, Inc.

Throughout this text we have many assignments based on the financial statements of **Home Depot, Inc.**, in Appendix A. Refer to the financial statements to respond to the following items:

a. Does the company's fiscal year end on December 31? How can you tell?

b. State the company's balance sheet in terms of A = L + E.

c. Did the company post more debits to the Cash account during the year than credits? How can you tell?

Problem Set A

 through 

PROBLEM 3.1A
Journalizing Transactions

Glenn Grimes is the founder and president of Heartland Construction, a real estate development venture. The business transactions during February while the company was being organized are listed below.

Feb. 1 Grimes and several others invested $500,000 cash in the business in exchange for 25,000 shares of capital stock.

Feb. 10 The company purchased office facilities for $300,000, of which $100,000 was applicable to the land and $200,000 to the building. A cash payment of $60,000 was made and a note payable was issued for the balance of the purchase price.

Feb. 16 Computer equipment was purchased from PCWorld for $12,000 cash.

Feb. 18 Office furnishings were purchased from Hi-Way Furnishings at a cost of $9,000. A $1,000 cash payment was made at the time of purchase, and an agreement was made to pay the remaining balance in two equal installments due March 1 and April 1. Hi-Way Furnishings did not require that Heartland sign a promissory note.

Feb. 22 Office supplies were purchased from Office World for $300 cash.

Feb. 23 Heartland discovered that it paid too much for a computer printer purchased on February 16. The unit should have cost only $359, but Heartland was charged $395. PCWorld promised to refund the difference within seven days.

Feb. 27 Mailed Hi-Way Furnishings the first installment due on the account payable for office furnishings purchased on February 18.

Feb. 28 Received $36 from PCWorld in full settlement of the account receivable created on February 23.

Instructions

a. Prepare journal entries to record the above transactions. Select the appropriate account titles from the following chart of accounts:

Cash	Land
Accounts Receivable	Office Building
Office Supplies	Notes Payable
Office Furnishings	Accounts Payable
Computer Systems	Capital Stock

b. Indicate the effects of each transaction on the company's assets, liabilities, and owners' equity for the month of February. Organize your analysis in tabular form as shown for the February 1 transaction:

Transaction	Assets	=	Liabilities	+	Owner's Equity
Feb. 1	+$500,000 (Cash)		$0		+$500,000 (Capital Stock)

LO3 through LO8

PROBLEM 3.2A
Analyzing and Journalizing Transactions

Environmental Services, Inc., performs various tests on wells and septic systems. A few of the company's business transactions occurring during August are described below:

1. On August 1, the company billed customers $2,500 on account for services rendered. Customers are required to make full payment within 30 days.
2. On August 3, the company purchased testing supplies costing $3,800, paying $800 cash and charging the remainder on the company's 30-day account at Penn Chemicals. The testing supplies are expected to last several months.
3. On August 5, the company returned to Penn Chemicals $100 of testing supplies that were not needed. The return of these supplies reduced by $100 the amount owed to Penn Chemicals.
4. On August 17, the company issued an additional 2,500 shares of capital stock at $8 per share. The cash raised will be used to purchase new testing equipment in September.
5. On August 22, the company received $600 cash from customers it had billed on August 1.
6. On August 29, the company paid its outstanding account payable to Penn Chemicals.
7. On August 30, a cash dividend totaling $6,800 was declared and paid to the company's stockholders.

Instructions

a. Prepare an analysis of each of the above transactions. Transaction 1 serves as an example of the form of analysis to be used.

   1. (a) The asset Accounts Receivable was increased. Increases in assets are recorded by debits. Debit Accounts Receivable $2,500.

      (b) Revenue has been earned. Revenue increases owners' equity. Increases in owners' equity are recorded by credits. Credit Testing Service Revenue $2,500.

b. Prepare journal entries, including explanations, for the above transactions.

c. How does the *realization principle* influence the manner in which the August 1 billing to customers is recorded in the accounting records?

d. How does the *matching principle* influence the manner in which the August 3 purchase of testing supplies is recorded in the accounting records?

PROBLEM 3.3A
Analyzing and Journalizing Transactions

Weida Surveying, Inc., provides land surveying services. During September, its transactions included the following:

Sept. 1 Paid rent for the month of September, $4,400.

Sept. 3 Billed Fine Line Homes $5,620 for surveying services. The entire amount is due on or before September 28. (Weida uses an account entitled Surveying Revenue when billing clients.)

Sept. 9 Provided surveying services to Sunset Ridge Developments for $2,830. The entire amount was collected on this date.

Sept. 14 Placed a newspaper advertisement in the *Daily Item* to be published in the September 20 issue. The cost of the advertisement was $165. Payment is due in 30 days.

Sept. 25 Received a check for $5,620 from Fine Line Homes for the amount billed on September 3.

Sept. 26 Provided surveying services to Thompson Excavating Company for $1,890. Weida collected $400 cash, with the balance due in 30 days.

Sept. 29 Sent a check to the *Daily Item* in full payment of the liability incurred on September 14.

Sept. 30 Declared and paid a $7,600 cash dividend to the company's stockholders.

Instructions

a. Analyze the effects that each of these transactions will have on the following six components of the company's financial statements for the month of September. Organize your answer in tabular form, using the column headings shown. Use **I** for increase, **D** for decrease, and **NE** for no effect. The September 1 transaction is provided for you:

	Income Statement			Balance Sheet		
Transaction	Revenue −	Expenses =	Net Income	Assets =	Liabilities +	Owners' Equity
Sept. 1	**NE**	**I**	**D**	**D**	**NE**	**D**

b. Prepare a journal entry (including explanation) for each of the above transactions.

c. Three of September's transactions involve cash payments, yet only one of these transactions is recorded as an expense. Describe three situations in which a cash payment would *not* involve recognition of an expense.

PROBLEM 3.4A

LO1 through LO10

The Accounting Cycle: Journalizing, Posting, and Preparing a Trial Balance

In June 2007, Wendy Winger organized a corporation to provide aerial photography services. The company, called Aerial Views, began operations immediately. Transactions during the month of June were as follows:

June 1 The corporation issued 60,000 shares of capital stock to Wendy Winger in exchange for $60,000 cash.

June 2 Purchased a plane from Utility Aircraft for $220,000. Made a $40,000 cash down payment and issued a note payable for the remaining balance.

June 4 Paid Woodrow Airport $2,500 to rent office and hangar space for the month.

June 15 Billed customers $8,320 for aerial photographs taken during the first half of June.

June 15 Paid $5,880 in salaries earned by employees during the first half of June.

June 18 Paid Hannigan's Hangar $1,890 for maintenance and repair services on the company plane.

June 25 Collected $4,910 of the amounts billed to customers on June 15.

June 30 Billed customers $16,450 for aerial photographs taken during the second half of the month.

June 30 Paid $6,000 in salaries earned by employees during the second half of the month.

June 30 Received a $2,510 bill from Peatree Petroleum for aircraft fuel purchased in June. The entire amount is due July 10.

June 30 Declared a $2,000 dividend payable on July 15.

The account titles used by Aerial Views are:

Cash	Retained Earnings
Accounts Receivable	Dividends
Aircraft	Aerial Photography Revenue
Notes Payable	Maintenance Expense
Accounts Payable	Fuel Expense
Dividends Payable	Salaries Expense
Capital Stock	Rent Expense

Instructions

a. Analyze the effects that each of these transactions will have on the following six components of the company's financial statements for the month of June. Organize your answer in tabular form, using the column headings shown. Use **I** for increase, **D** for decrease, and **NE** for no effect. The June 1 transaction is provided for you:

	Income Statement			Balance Sheet		
Transaction	Revenue −	Expenses =	Net Income	Assets =	Liabilities +	Owners' Equity
June 1	**NE**	**NE**	**NE**	**I**	**NE**	**I**

b. Prepare journal entries (including explanations) for each transaction.

c. Post each transaction to the appropriate ledger accounts (use a running balance format as illustrated in Exhibit 3–4 on page 97).

d. Prepare a trial balance dated June 30, 2007.

e. Using figures from the trial balance prepared in part **d**, compute total assets, total liabilities, and owners' equity. Are these the figures that the company will report in its June 30 balance sheet? Explain your answer briefly.

PROBLEM 3.5A

The Accounting Cycle: Journalizing, Posting, and Preparing a Trial Balance

Dr. Schekter, DVM, opened a veterinary clinic on May 1, 2007. The business transactions for May are shown below:

May 1 Dr. Schekter invested $400,000 cash in the business in exchange for 5,000 shares of capital stock.

May 4 Land and a building were purchased for $250,000. Of this amount, $70,000 applied to the land, and $180,000 to the building. A cash payment of $100,000 was made at the time of the purchase, and a note payable was issued for the remaining balance.

May 9 Medical instruments were purchased for $130,000 cash.

May 16 Office fixtures and equipment were purchased for $50,000. Dr. Schekter paid $20,000 at the time of purchase and agreed to pay the entire remaining balance in 15 days.

May 21 Office supplies expected to last several months were purchased for $5,000 cash.

May 24 Dr. Schekter billed clients $2,200 for services rendered. Of this amount, $1,900 was received in cash, and $300 was billed on account (due in 30 days).

May 27 A $400 invoice was received for several radio advertisements aired in May. The entire amount is due on June 5.

May 28 Received a $100 payment on the $300 account receivable recorded May 24.

May 31 Paid employees $2,800 for salaries earned in May.

A partial list of account titles used by Dr. Schekter includes:

Cash	Notes Payable
Accounts Receivable	Accounts Payable
Office Supplies	Capital Stock
Medical Instruments	Veterinary Service Revenue
Office Fixtures and Equipment	Advertising Expense
Land	Salary Expense
Building	

Instructions

a. Analyze the effects that each of these transactions will have on the following six components of the company's financial statements for the month of May. Organize your answer in tabular form, using the column headings shown below. Use **I** for increase, **D** for decrease, and **NE** for no effect. The May 1 transaction is provided for you:

	Income Statement			Balance Sheet		
Transaction	Revenue −	Expenses =	Net Income	Assets =	Liabilities +	Owners' Equity
May 1	**NE**	**NE**	**NE**	**I**	**NE**	**I**

b. Prepare journal entries (including explanations) for each transaction.

c. Post each transaction to the appropriate ledger accounts (use the T account format illustrated in Exhibit 3–8 on page 110).

d. Prepare a trial balance dated May 31, 2007.

e. Using figures from the trial balance prepared in part **d**, compute total assets, total liabilities, and owners' equity. Did May appear to be a profitable month?

PROBLEM 3.6A
Short Comprehensive Problem

LO3 through LO5

Donegan's Lawn Care Service began operations in July 2007. The company uses the following general ledger accounts:

Cash	Capital Stock
Accounts Receivable	Retained Earnings
Office Supplies	Mowing Revenue
Mowing Equipment	Salaries Expense
Accounts Payable	Fuel Expense
Notes Payable	

The company engaged in the following transactions during its first month of operations:

July 18 Issued 500 shares of capital stock to Patrick Donegan for $1,500.

July 22 Purchased office supplies on account for $100.

July 23 Purchased mowing equipment for $2,000, paying $400 cash and issuing a 60-day note payable for the remaining balance.

July 24 Paid $25 cash for gasoline. All of this fuel will be used in July.

July 25 Billed Lost Creek Cemetery $150 for mowing services. The entire amount is due July 30.

July 26 Billed Golf View Condominiums $200 for mowing services. The entire amount is due August 1.

July 30 Collected $150 from Lost Creek Cemetery for mowing services provided on July 25.

July 31 Paid $80 salary to employee Teddy Grimm for work performed in July.

a. Record each of the above transactions in general journal form. Include a brief explanation of the transaction as part of each journal entry.

b. Post each entry to the appropriate ledger accounts (use the T account format illustrated in Exhibit 3–8 on page 110).

c. Prepare a trial balance dated July 31, 2007.

d. Explain why the Retained Earnings account has a zero balance in the trial balance.

PROBLEM 3.7A
Short Comprehensive Problem

LO3 through LO5, LO7 through LO9

Sanlucas, Inc., provides home inspection services to its clients. The company's trial balance dated *June 1, 2007*, is shown below:

SANLUCAS, INC.
Trial Balance
June 1, 2007

Cash	$ 5,100	
Accounts receivable	2,600	
Inspection supplies	800	
Accounts payable		$ 850
Notes payable		2,000
Dividends	600	
Capital stock		3,000
Retained earnings		1,800
Inspection revenue		8,350
Salaries expense	4,900	
Advertising expense	300	
Testing expense	1,700	
	$16,000	$16,000

Sanlucas engaged in the following transactions in June:

June 4 Borrowed cash from Community Bank by issuing a $1,500 note payable.

June 9 Collected a $1,600 account receivable from Nina Lesher.

June 10 Purchased $150 of inspection supplies on account.

June 17 Billed home owners $1,650 for inspection services. The entire amount is due on July 17.

June 25 Paid WLIR Radio $200 for ads to be aired on June 27.

June 28 Recorded and paid $1,300 for testing expenses incurred in June.

June 30 Recorded and paid June salaries of $1,100.

Instructions

a. Record the company's June transactions in general journal form. Include a brief explanation of the transaction as part of each journal entry.

b. Post each entry to the appropriate ledger accounts (use the T account format illustrated in Exhibit 3–8 on page 110).

c. Prepare a trial balance dated June 30, 2007. (Hint: Retained Earnings will be reported at the same amount as on June 1. Accounting for changes in the Retained Earnings account resulting from revenue, expense, and dividend activities is discussed in Chapter 5.)

d. Has the company paid all of the dividends that it has declared? Explain.

LO3 LO8

PROBLEM 3.8A
Analyzing the Effects of Accounting Errors

Home Team Corporation recently hired Steve Willits as its bookkeeper. Mr. Willits is somewhat inexperienced and has made numerous errors recording daily business transactions.

Indicate the *effects of the errors* described below on each of the financial statement elements shown in the column headings. Use the following symbols: **O** for overstated; **U** for understated, and **NE** for no effect.

Error	Net Income	Total Assets	Total Liabilities	Owners' Equity
Recorded the issuance of capital stock by debiting Capital Stock and crediting Service Revenue.				
Recorded the declaration and payment of a dividend by debiting Capital Stock and crediting Cash.				
Recorded the payment of an account payable by debiting Cash and crediting Rent Expense.				
Recorded the collection of an outstanding account receivable by debiting Cash and crediting Service Revenue.				
Recorded client billings on account by debiting Accounts Receivable and crediting Advertising Expense.				
Recorded the cash purchase of land by debiting Supplies Expense and crediting Notes Payable.				
Recorded the purchase of a building on account by debiting Cash and crediting Dividends Payable.				

Problem Set B

through

PROBLEM 3.1B
Journalizing Transactions

Chris North is the founder and president of North Enterprises, a real estate development venture. The business transactions during April while the company was being organized are listed below.

Apr. 1 North and several others invested $650,000 cash in the business in exchange for 10,000 shares of capital stock.

Apr. 6 The company purchased office facilities for $300,000, of which $60,000 was applicable to the land and $240,000 to the building. A cash payment of $100,000 was made and a note payable was issued for the balance of the purchase price.

Apr. 10 Computer equipment was purchased from Comp Central for $6,000 cash.

Apr. 12 Office furnishings were purchased from Sam's Furniture at a cost of $12,000. A $1,000 cash payment was made at the time of purchase, and an agreement was made to pay the remaining balance in two equal installments due May 1 and June 1. Sam's Furniture did not require that North sign a promissory note.

Apr. 20 Office supplies were purchased from Office Space for $750 cash.

Apr. 25 North discovered that it paid too much for a computer printer purchased on April 10. The unit should have cost only $600, but North was charged $800. Comp Central promised to refund the difference within seven days.

Apr. 28 Mailed Sam's Furniture the first installment due on the account payable for office furnishings purchased on April 12.

Apr. 29 Received $200 from Comp Central in settlement of the account receivable created on April 25.

Instructions

a. Prepare journal entries to record the above transactions. Select the appropriate account titles from the following chart of accounts:

Cash	Land
Accounts Receivable	Office Building
Office Supplies	Notes Payable
Office Furnishings	Accounts Payable
Computer Systems	Capital Stock

b. Indicate the effects of each transaction on the company's assets, liabilities, and owners' equity for the month of April. Organize your analysis in tabular form as shown below for the April 1 transaction:

Transaction	Assets	=	Liabilities	+	Owners' Equity
Apr. 1	+$650,000 (Cash)	=	$0		+$650,000 (Capital Stock)

PROBLEM 3.2B

LO3 through LO8

Analyzing and Journalizing Transactions

Lyons, Inc., provides consulting services. A few of the company's business transactions occurring during June are described below:

1. On June 1, the company billed customers $5,000 on account for consulting services rendered. Customers are required to make full payment within 30 days.
2. On June 3, the company purchased office supplies costing $3,200, paying $800 cash and charging the remainder on the company's 30-day account at Office Warehouse. The supplies are expected to last several months.
3. On June 5, the company returned to Office Warehouse $100 of supplies that were not needed. The return of these supplies reduced by $100 the amount owed to Office Warehouse.
4. On June 17, the company issued an additional 1,000 shares of capital stock at $5 per share. The cash raised will be used to purchase new equipment in September.
5. On June 22, the company received $1,200 cash from customers it had billed on June 1.
6. On June 29, the company paid its outstanding account payable to Office Warehouse.
7. On June 30, a cash dividend totaling $1,800 was declared and paid to the company's stockholders.

Instructions

a. Prepare an analysis of each of the above transactions. Transaction 1 serves as an example of the form of analysis to be used.

1. (a) The asset Accounts Receivable was increased. Increases in assets are recorded by debits. Debit Accounts Receivable $5,000.

(b) Revenue has been earned. Revenue increases owners' equity. Increases in owners' equity are recorded by credits. Credit Consulting Revenue $5,000.

b. Prepare journal entries, including explanations, for the above transactions.

c. How does the *realization principle* influence the manner in which the June 1 billings to customers is recorded in the accounting records?

d. How does the *matching principle* influence the manner in which the June 3 purchase of supplies is recorded in the accounting records?

through

PROBLEM 3.3B
Analyzing and Journalizing Transactions

Dana, Inc., provides civil engineering services. During October, its transactions included the following:

Oct. 1 Paid rent for the month of October, $4,000.

Oct. 4 Billed Milton Hotels $8,500 for services. The entire amount is due on or before October 28. (Dana uses an account entitled Service Revenue when billing clients.)

Oct. 8 Provided services to Dirt Valley Development for $4,700. The entire amount was collected on this date.

Oct. 12 Placed a newspaper advertisement in the *Daily Reporter* to be published in the October 25 issue. The cost of the advertisement was $320. Payment is due in 30 days.

Oct. 20 Received a check for $8,500 from Milton Hotels for the amount billed on October 4.

Oct. 24 Provided services to Dudley Company for $3,600. Dana collected $300 cash, with the balance due in 30 days.

Oct. 25 Sent a check to the *Daily Reporter* in full payment of the liability incurred on October 12.

Oct. 29 Declared and paid a $2,600 cash dividend to the company's stockholders.

Instructions

a. Analyze the effects that each of these transactions will have on the following six components of the company's financial statements for the month of October. Organize your answer in tabular form, using the column headings shown below. Use **I** for increase, **D** for decrease, and **NE** for no effect. The October 1 transaction is provided for you:

	Income Statement			Balance Sheet		
Transaction	Revenue −	Expenses =	Net Income	Assets =	Liabilities +	Owners' Equity
Oct. 1	**NE**	**I**	**D**	**D**	**NE**	**D**

b. Prepare a journal entry (including explanation) for each of the above transactions.

c. Three of October's transactions involve cash payments, yet only one of these transactions is recorded as an expense. Describe three situations in which a cash payment would *not* involve recognition of an expense.

through

PROBLEM 3.4B
The Accounting Cycle: Journalizing, Posting, and Preparing a Trial Balance

In March 2007, Mary Tone organized a corporation to provide package delivery services. The company, called Tone Deliveries, Inc., began operations immediately. Transactions during the month of March were as follows:

Mar. 2 The corporation issued 40,000 shares of capital stock to Mary Tone in exchange for $80,000 cash.

Mar. 4 Purchased a truck for $45,000. Made a $15,000 cash down payment and issued a note payable for the remaining balance.

Mar. 5 Paid Sloan Properties $2,500 to rent office space for the month.

Mar. 9 Billed customers $11,300 for services for the first half of March.

Mar. 15 Paid $7,100 in salaries earned by employees during the first half of March.

Mar. 19 Paid Bill's Auto $900 for maintenance and repair services on the company truck.

Mar. 20 Collected $3,800 of the amounts billed to customers on March 9.

Mar. 28 Billed customers $14,400 for services performed during the second half of the month.

Mar. 30 Paid $7,500 in salaries earned by employees during the second half of the month.

Mar. 30 Received an $830 bill from SY Petroleum for fuel purchased in March. The entire amount is due by April 15.

Mar. 30 Declared a $1,200 dividend payable on April 30.

The account titles used by Tone Deliveries are:

Cash	Retained Earnings
Accounts Receivable	Dividends
Truck	Service Revenue
Notes Payable	Maintenance Expense
Accounts Payable	Fuel Expense
Dividends Payable	Salaries Expense
Capital Stock	Rent Expense

Instructions

a. Analyze the effects that each of these transactions will have on the following six components of the company's financial statements for the month of March. Organize your answer in tabular form, using the column headings shown below. Use **I** for increase, **D** for decrease, and **NE** for no effect. The March 2 transaction is provided for you:

	Income Statement			Balance Sheet		
Transaction	Revenue −	Expenses =	Net Income	Assets =	Liabilities +	Owners' Equity
Mar. 2	**NE**	**NE**	**NE**	**I**	**NE**	**I**

b. Prepare journal entries (including explanations) for each transaction.

c. Post each transaction to the appropriate ledger accounts (use a running balance format as shown in Exhibit 3–4, page 97).

d. Prepare a trial balance dated March 31, 2007.

e. Using figures from the trial balance prepared in part **d**, compute total assets, total liabilities, and owners' equity. Are these the figures that the company will report in its March 31 balance sheet? Explain your answer briefly.

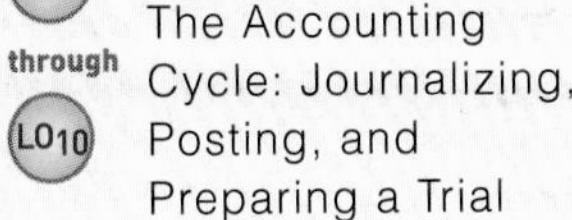

PROBLEM 3.5B
The Accounting Cycle: Journalizing, Posting, and Preparing a Trial Balance
LO1 through LO10

Dr. Cravati, DMD., opened a dental clinic on August 1, 2007. The business transactions for August are shown below:

Aug. 1 Dr. Cravati invested $280,000 cash in the business in exchange for 1,000 shares of capital stock.

Aug. 4 Land and a building were purchased for $400,000. Of this amount, $60,000 applied to the land and $340,000 to the building. A cash payment of $80,000 was made at the time of the purchase, and a note payable was issued for the remaining balance.

Aug. 9 Medical instruments were purchased for $75,000 cash.

Aug. 16 Office fixtures and equipment were purchased for $25,000. Dr. Cravati paid $10,000 at the time of purchase and agreed to pay the entire remaining balance in 15 days.

Aug. 21 Office supplies expected to last several months were purchased for $4,200 cash.

Aug. 24 Dr. Cravati billed patients $13,000 for services rendered. Of this amount, $1,000 was received in cash, and $12,000 was billed on account (due in 30 days).

Aug. 27 A $450 invoice was received for several newspaper advertisements placed in August. The entire amount is due on September 8.

Aug. 28 Received a $500 payment on the $12,000 account receivable recorded August 24.

Aug. 31 Paid employees $2,200 for salaries earned in August.

A partial list of account titles used by Dr. Cravati includes:

Cash	Office Fixtures and Equipment
Accounts Receivable	Land
Office Supplies	Building
Notes Payable	Service Revenue
Accounts Payable	Advertising Expense
Capital Stock	Salary Expense
Medical Instruments	

Instructions

a. Analyze the effects that each of these transactions will have on the following six components of the company's financial statements for the month of August. Organize your answer in tabular form, using the column headings shown below. Use **I** for increase, **D** for decrease, and **NE** for no effect. The August 1 transaction is provided for you:

	Income Statement			Balance Sheet		
Transaction	Revenue −	Expenses =	Net Income	Assets =	Liabilities +	Owners' Equity
Aug. 1	**NE**	**NE**	**NE**	**I**	**NE**	**I**

b. Prepare journal entries (including explanations) for each transaction.

c. Post each transaction to the appropriate ledger accounts (use the T account format as illustrated in Exhibit 3–8 on page 110).

d. Prepare a trial balance dated August 31, 2007.

e. Using figures from the trial balance prepared in part **d**, compute total assets, total liabilities, and owners' equity. Did August appear to be a profitable month?

through

PROBLEM 3.6B
Short Comprehensive Problem

Clown Around, Inc., provides party entertainment for children of all ages. The company's trial balance dated *February 1, 2007*, is shown below.

CLOWN AROUND, INC.
Trial Balance
February 1, 2007

Cash	$2,850	
Accounts receivable	900	
Accounts payable		$ 800
Capital stock		2,000
Retained earnings		750
Dividends	—	
Party revenue		1,350
Salaries expense	830	
Party food expense	240	
Travel expense	80	
	$4,900	$4,900

Clown Around engaged in the following transactions in February:

Feb. 2 Paid $750 in partial settlement of the outstanding account payable reported in the trial balance dated February 1.

Feb. 6 Collected $900 in full settlement of the outstanding accounts receivable reported in the trial balance dated February 1.

Feb. 18 Billed Sunflower Child Care $175 for clown services. The entire amount is due March 15.

Feb. 26 Billed and collected $480 for performing at several birthday parties.

Feb. 28 Paid clown salaries of $260 for work done in February.

Feb. 28 Recorded and paid $40 for travel expenses incurred in February.

Feb. 28 Declared and paid a $100 dividend to Ralph Jaschob, the company's only shareholder.

a. Record the company's February transactions in general journal form. Include a brief explanation of the transaction as part of each journal entry.

b. Post each entry to the appropriate ledger accounts (use the T account format as illustrated in Exhibit 3–8 on page 110).

c. Prepare a trial balance dated February 28, 2007. (Hint: Retained Earnings will be reported at the same amount as it was on February 1. Accounting for changes in the Retained Earnings account resulting from revenue, expense, and dividend activities is discussed in Chapter 5.)

d. Will the $100 dividend paid February 28 decrease the company's income? Explain.

through

through

PROBLEM 3.7B
Short Comprehensive Problem

Ahuna, Inc., provides in-home cooking lessons to its clients. The company's trial balance dated *March 1, 2007*, is shown below:

AHUNA, INC.
Trial Balance
March 1, 2007

Cash	$ 5,700	
Accounts receivable	1,800	
Cooking supplies	800	
Accounts payable		$ 300
Dividends payable		500
Dividends	500	
Capital stock		6,000
Retained earnings		1,400
Client revenue		5,800
Salaries expense	3,100	
Travel expense	1,500	
Printing expense	600	
	$14,000	$14,000

Ahuna engaged in the following transactions in March:

Mar. 3 Collected a $1,200 account receivable from Kim Mitchell.
Mar. 11 Purchased cooking supplies for $700 cash.
Mar. 15 Paid $200 of outstanding accounts payable.
Mar. 20 Issued additional shares of capital stock for $4,000 cash.
Mar. 24 Recorded $6,200 of client revenue on account.
Mar. 27 Paid March salaries of $900.
Mar. 30 Recorded and paid March travel expenses of $400.
Mar. 31 Recorded $300 in printing expenses for recipe books. Payment is due April 12.

Instructions

a. Record the company's March transactions in general journal form. Include a brief explanation of the transaction as part of each journal entry.

b. Post each entry to the appropriate ledger accounts (use the T account format illustrated in Exhibit 3–8 on page 110).

c. Prepare a trial balance dated March 31, 2007. (Hint: Retained Earnings will be reported at the same amount as it was on March 1. Accounting for changes in the Retained Earnings account resulting from revenue, expense, and dividend activities is discussed in Chapter 5.)

d. Has the company paid all of the dividends that it has declared? Explain.

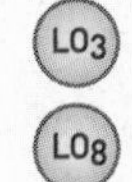

PROBLEM 3.8B
Analyzing the Effects of Accounting Errors

Blind River, Inc., recently hired Neil Young as its bookkeeper. Mr. Young is somewhat inexperienced and has made numerous errors recording daily business transactions.

Indicate the *effects of the errors* described below on each of the financial statement elements shown in the column headings. Use the following symbols: **O** for overstated; **U** for understated; and **NE** for no effect.

Error	Net Income	Total Assets	Total Liabilities	Owners' Equity
Recorded the issuance of capital stock by debiting Dividends and crediting Cash.				
Recorded the payment of an account payable by debiting Cash and crediting Accounts Receivable.				
Recorded the collection of an outstanding account receivable by debiting Service Revenue and crediting Cash.				
Recorded client billings on account by debiting Accounts Payable and crediting Cash.				
Recorded the payment of an outstanding dividend payable by debiting Dividends and crediting Cash.				
Recorded the payment of salaries payable by debiting Salaries Expense and crediting Salaries Payable.				
Recorded the purchase of office supplies on account by debiting Rent Expense and crediting Office Supplies.				

Critical Thinking Cases

CASE 3.1
Revenue Recognition

The realization principle determines when a business should recognize revenue. Listed next are three common business situations involving revenue. After each situation, we give two alternatives as to the accounting period (or periods) in which the business might recognize this revenue. Select the appropriate alternative by applying the realization principle, and explain your reasoning.

a. Airline ticket revenue: Most airlines sell tickets well before the scheduled date of the flight. (Period ticket sold; period of flight)

b. Sales on account: In June 2007, a San Diego–based furniture store had a big sale, featuring "No payments until 2008." (Period furniture sold; periods that payments are received from customers)

c. Magazine subscriptions revenue: Most magazine publishers sell subscriptions for future delivery of the magazine. (Period subscription sold; periods that magazines are mailed to customers)

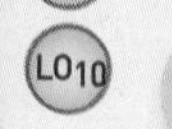

CASE 3.2
Measuring Income Fairly

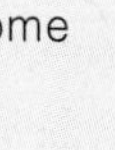

Kim Morris purchased Print Shop, Inc., a printing business, from Chris Stanley. Morris made a cash down payment and agreed to make annual payments equal to 40 percent of the company's net income in each of the next three years. (Such "earn-outs" are a common means of financing the purchase of a small business.) Stanley was disappointed, however, when Morris reported a first year's net income far below Stanley's expectations.

The agreement between Morris and Stanley did not state precisely how "net income" was to be measured. Neither Morris nor Stanley was familiar with accounting concepts. Their agreement stated only that the net income of the corporation should be measured in a "fair and reasonable manner."

In measuring net income, Morris applied the following policies:

1. Revenue was recognized when cash was received from customers. Most customers paid in cash, but a few were allowed 30-day credit terms.
2. Expenditures for ink and paper, which are purchased weekly, were charged directly to Supplies Expense, as were the Morris family's weekly grocery and dry cleaning bills.
3. Morris set her annual salary at $60,000, which Stanley had agreed was reasonable. She also paid salaries of $30,000 per year to her husband and to each of her two teenage children. These family members did not work in the business on a regular basis, but they did help out when things got busy.
4. Income taxes expense included the amount paid by the corporation (which was computed correctly), as well as the personal income taxes paid by various members of the Morris family on the salaries they earned working for the business.

5. The business had state-of-the-art printing equipment valued at $150,000 at the time Morris purchased it. The first-year income statement included a $150,000 equipment expense related to these assets.

Instructions

a. Discuss the fairness and reasonableness of these income-measurement policies. (Remember, these policies do *not* have to conform to generally accepted accounting principles. But they should be *fair* and *reasonable*.)

b. Do you think that the net *cash flow* generated by this business (cash receipts less cash outlays) is higher or lower than the net income as measured by Morris? Explain.

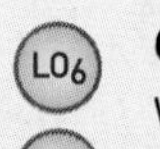

CASE 3.3
Whistle-Blowing

Happy Trails, Inc., is a popular family resort just outside Yellowstone National Park. Summer is the resort's busy season, but guests typically pay a deposit at least six months in advance to guarantee their reservations.

The resort is currently seeking new investment capital in order to expand operations. The more profitable Happy Trails appears to be, the more interest it will generate from potential investors. Ed Grimm, an accountant employed by the resort, has been asked by his boss to include $2 million of unearned guest deposits in the computation of income for the current year. Ed explained to his boss that because these deposits had not yet been earned they should be reported in the balance sheet as liabilities, not in the income statement as revenue. Ed argued that reporting guest deposits as revenue would inflate the current year's income and may mislead investors.

Ed's boss then *demanded* that he include $2 million of unearned guest deposits in the computation of income or be fired. He then told Ed in an assuring tone, "Ed, you will never be held responsible for misleading potential investors because you are just following my orders."

Instructions

Should Ed Grimm be forced to knowingly overstate the resort's income in order to retain his job? Is Ed's boss correct in saying that Ed cannot be held responsible for misleading potential investors? Discuss.

***BUSINESSWEEK* CASE 3.4**
Considering Information Needs at PepsiCo, Inc.

In a July 21, 2005, *BusinessWeek* article, "Could PepsiCo Digest Danone?" Carol Matlack discusses a move by **PepsiCo, Inc.**, to launch a takeover bid to acquire **Groupe Danone**, the French food company that sells Dannon yogurt and Evian bottled water. **PepsiCo**'s previous acquisitions of **Tropicana** and **Quaker Oats** have helped to expand its offerings beyond its traditional soft drink and snack food products.

Instructions

As a group, discuss various types of financial and nonfinancial information that might be used by **PepsiCo** in deciding whether or not to acquire **Groupe Danone**.

INTERNET CASE 3.5
Revenue from Various Sources

Visit the EDGAR database of the Security and Exchange Commission at the following Internet location: **www.sec.gov/edgar/searchedgar/companysearch.html**

Enter **PC Connection** in the company name search box and access **PC Connection**'s most recent 10-K report. (Note: This report may also be shown as a 10-K/A report.) What percent of the company's total revenue is generated by sales to public sector customers (e.g., governmental agencies, educational institutions, etc.)? Have sales to public sector customers increased or decreased during the past three years?

Internet sites are time and date sensitive. It is the purpose of these exercises to have you explore the Internet. You may need to use the Yahoo! search engine **http://www.yahoo.com** *(or another favorite search engine) to find a company's current Web address.*

Answers to Self-Test Questions

1. d **2.** b **3.** a, c, and d **4.** c **5.** c **6.** d **7.** b, c, and d
8. a and c

The Accounting Cycle
Accruals and Deferrals

Learning Objectives

AFTER STUDYING THIS CHAPTER, YOU SHOULD BE ABLE TO:

- LO1 Explain the purpose of adjusting entries.
- LO2 Describe and prepare the four basic types of adjusting entries.
- LO3 Prepare adjusting entries to convert assets to expenses.
- LO4 Prepare adjusting entries to convert liabilities to revenue.
- LO5 Prepare adjusting entries to accrue unpaid expenses.
- LO6 Prepare adjusting entries to accrue uncollected revenue.
- LO7 Explain how the principles of *realization* and *matching* relate to adjusting entries.
- LO8 Explain the concept of *materiality*.
- LO9 Prepare an adjusted trial balance and describe its purpose.

Carnival Cruise Lines

CARNIVAL CORPORATION

When is revenue actually *earned* by a company? In many cases, revenue is earned when cash is received at the point of sale. For instance, when a taxicab driver takes someone to the airport, revenue is earned when the passenger is dropped off at the appropriate terminal and the fare is collected.

Suppose the same passenger boards a **Carnival** cruise ship to the Bahamas using a ticket that was purchased six months in advance. At what point should the cruise line recognize that ticket revenue has been earned? A recent **Carnival Corporation** balance sheet provides the answer to this question.

In its balance sheet, **Carnival Corporation** reports a $2.01 billion liability account called Customer Deposits. As passengers purchase tickets in advance, **Carnival Corporation** credits the Customer Deposits account for an amount equal to the cash it receives. It is not until passengers actually *use* their tickets that the company reduces this liability account and records Passenger Revenue in its income statement.

For most companies, revenue is *not* always earned as cash is received, nor is an expense necessarily incurred as cash is disbursed. Timing differences between cash flows and the recognition of revenue and expenses are referred to as *accruals* and *deferrals.* In this chapter we examine how accounting information must be adjusted for accruals and deferrals prior to the preparation of financial statements.

The first three steps of the accounting cycle were discussed in Chapter 3. They included (1) recording transactions, (2) posting transactions, and (3) preparing a trial balance. In this chapter, we focus solely upon the fourth step of the accounting cycle: performing the end-of-period adjustments required to measure business income. The remaining steps of the cycle are covered in Chapter 5.

Adjusting Entries

There is more to the measurement of business income than merely recording simple revenue and expense transactions that affect only a single accounting period. Certain transactions affect the revenue or expenses of *two* or *more* accounting periods. The purpose of adjusting entries is to assign to each accounting period appropriate amounts of revenue and expense. For example, Overnight Auto Service purchased shop supplies that will be used for several months. Thus, an adjusting entry is required to record the expense associated with the shop supplies that Overnight *uses* each month.

THE NEED FOR ADJUSTING ENTRIES

LO1 Explain the purpose of adjusting entries.

For purposes of measuring income and preparing financial statements, the life of a business is divided into a series of *accounting periods.* This practice enables decision makers to compare the financial statements of successive periods and to identify significant trends.

But measuring net income for a relatively short accounting period—such as a month or even a year—poses a problem because, as mentioned above, some business activities affect the revenue and expenses of *multiple accounting periods.* Therefore, **adjusting entries** are needed at the end of each accounting period to make certain that appropriate amounts of revenue and expense are reported in the company's income statement.

For example, magazine publishers often sell two- or three-year subscriptions to their publications. At the end of each accounting period, these publishers make adjusting entries recognizing the portion of their advance receipts that have been earned during the current period. Most companies also purchase insurance policies that benefit more than one period. Therefore, an adjusting entry is needed to make certain that an appropriate portion of each policy's total cost is reported in the income statement as insurance expense for the period. In short, adjusting entries are needed whenever transactions affect the revenue or expenses of more than one accounting period. These entries assign revenues to the period in which they are *earned*, and expenses to the periods in which related goods or services are *used.*

In theory, a business could make adjusting entries on a daily basis. But as a practical matter, these entries are made *only at the end of each accounting period.* For most companies, adjusting entries are made on a monthly basis.

TYPES OF ADJUSTING ENTRIES

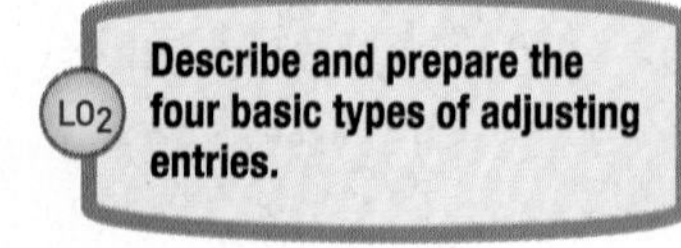

The number of adjustments needed at the end of each accounting period depends entirely upon the nature of the company's business activities. However, most adjusting entries fall into one of four general categories:[1]

1. *Converting assets to expenses.* A cash expenditure (or cost) that will benefit more than one accounting period usually is recorded by debiting an asset account (for example, Supplies,

[1]A fifth category of adjusting entries consists of adjustments related to the valuation of certain assets, such as marketable securities and accounts receivable. These valuation adjustments are explained and illustrated in Chapter 7.

Unexpired Insurance, and so on) and by crediting Cash. The asset account created actually represents the *deferral* (or the postponement) of an expense. In each future period that benefits from the use of this asset, an adjusting entry is made to allocate a portion of the asset's cost from the balance sheet to the income statement as an expense. This adjusting entry is recorded by debiting the appropriate expense account (for example, Supplies Expense or Insurance Expense) and crediting the related asset account (for example, Supplies or Unexpired Insurance).

2. *Converting liabilities to revenue.* A business may collect cash in advance for services to be rendered in future accounting periods. Transactions of this nature are usually recorded by debiting Cash and by crediting a liability account (typically called Unearned Revenue). Here, the liability account created represents the *deferral* (or the postponement) of a revenue. In the period that services are actually rendered (or that goods are sold), an adjusting entry is made to allocate a portion of the liability from the balance sheet to the income statement to recognize the revenue earned during the period. The adjusting entry is recorded by debiting the liability (Unearned Revenue) and by crediting *Revenue Earned* (or a similar account) for the value of the services.
3. *Accruing unpaid expenses.* An expense may be incurred in the current accounting period even though no cash payment will occur until a future period. These *accrued* expenses are recorded by an adjusting entry made at the end of each accounting period. The adjusting entry is recorded by debiting the appropriate expense account (for example, Interest Expense or Salary Expense) and by crediting the related liability (for example, Interest Payable or Salaries Payable).
4. *Accruing uncollected revenue.* Revenue may be earned (or *accrued*) during the current period, even though the collection of cash will not occur until a future period. Unrecorded earned revenue, for which no cash has been received, requires an adjusting entry at the end of the accounting period. The adjusting entry is recorded by debiting the appropriate asset (for example, Accounts Receivable or Interest Receivable) and by crediting the appropriate revenue account (for example, Service Revenue Earned or Interest Earned).

ADJUSTING ENTRIES AND TIMING DIFFERENCES

In an accrual accounting system, there are often *timing differences* between cash flows and the recognition of expenses or revenue. A company can pay cash in advance of incurring certain expenses or receive cash before revenue has been earned. Likewise, it can incur certain expenses before paying any cash or it can earn revenue before any cash is received. These timing differences, and the adjusting entries that result from them, are summarized below.

- Adjusting entries to convert assets to expenses result from cash being paid prior to an expense being incurred.
- Adjusting entries to convert liabilities to revenue result from cash being received prior to revenue being earned.
- Adjusting entries to accrue unpaid expenses result from expenses being incurred before cash is paid.
- Adjusting entries to accrue uncollected revenue result from revenue being earned before cash is received.

As illustrated in Exhibit 4–1, adjusting entries provide important linkages between accounting periods related to these timing differences. Specifically, they link: (1) *prior* period cash outflows to *current* period expenses, (2) *prior* period cash inflows to *current* period revenue, (3) *current* period expenses to *future* cash outflows, and (4) *current* period revenue to *future* period cash inflows.

Exhibit 4–1 **ADJUSTING ENTRIES PROVIDE LINKS BETWEEN ACCOUNTING PERIODS**

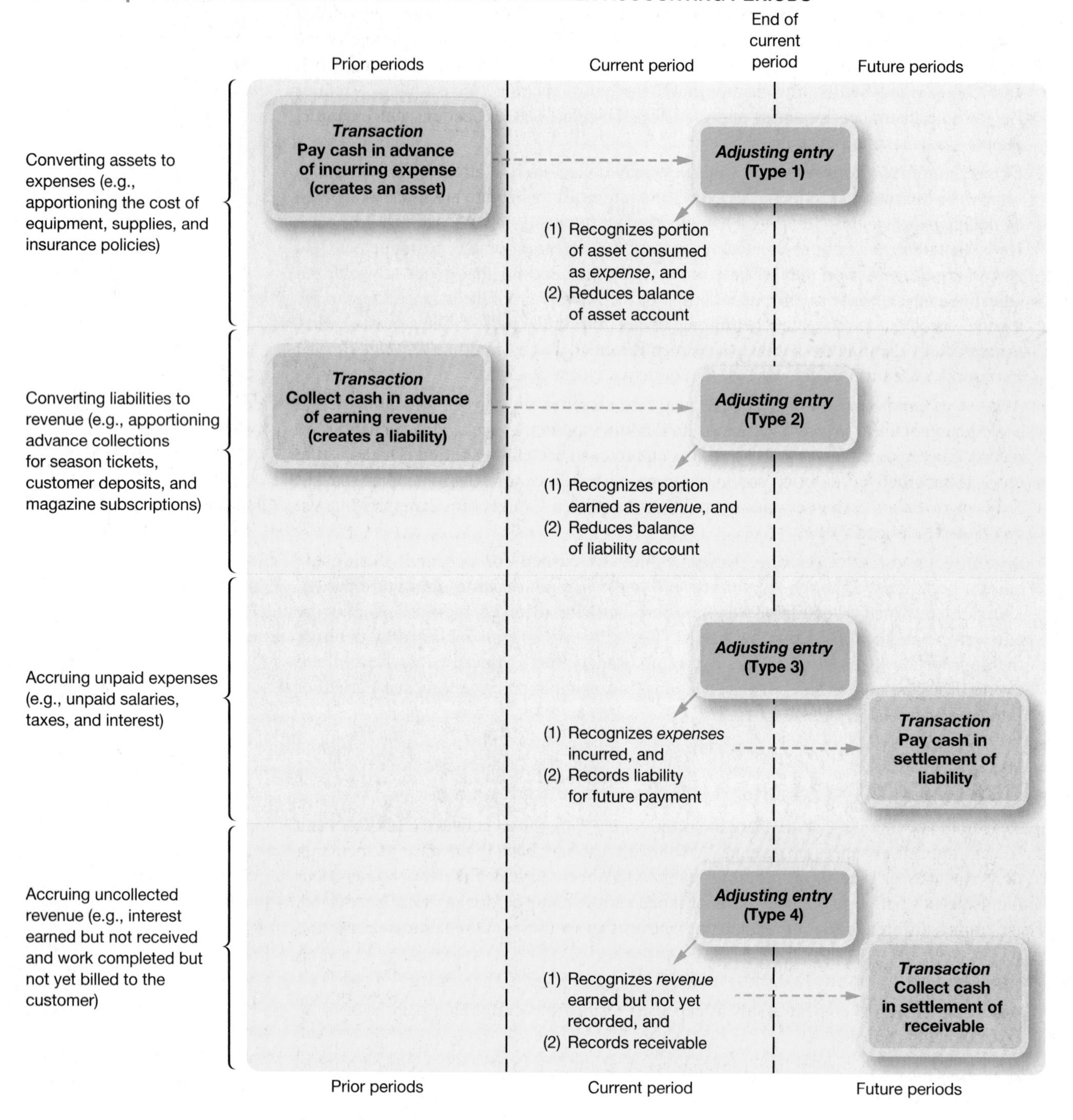

CHARACTERISTICS OF ADJUSTING ENTRIES

Keep in mind two important characteristics of all adjusting entries: First, every adjusting entry *involves the recognition of either revenue or expenses.* Revenue and expenses represent changes in owners' equity. However, owners' equity cannot change by itself; *there also must be a corresponding change in either assets or liabilities.* Thus every adjusting entry affects both an income statement account (revenue or expense) and a balance sheet account (asset or liability). Rarely do adjusting entries include an entry to Cash.

Second, adjusting entries are based on the concepts of accrual accounting, *not upon monthly bills or month-end transactions.* No one sends Overnight Auto Service a bill saying, "Shop Supply Expense for the month is $500." Yet, Overnight must be aware of the need to record the estimated cost of shop supplies consumed if it is to measure income properly for the period. Making adjusting entries requires a greater understanding of accrual accounting concepts than does the recording of routine business transactions. In many businesses, the adjusting process is performed by the controller or by a professional accountant, rather than by the regular accounting staff.

YEAR-END AT OVERNIGHT AUTO SERVICE

To illustrate the various types of adjusting entries, we will again use our example involving Overnight Auto Service. Chapter 3 concluded with Overnight's trial balance dated February 28, 2007 (the end of the company's second month of operations). We will now skip ahead to *December 31, 2007*—the end of Overnight's first *year* of operations. This will enable us to illustrate the preparation of *annual* financial statements, rather than statements that cover only a single month.

Most companies make adjusting entries every *month*. We will assume that Overnight has been following this approach throughout 2007. The company's *unadjusted* trial balance dated December 31, 2007, appears in Exhibit 4–2. It is referred to as an unadjusted trial balance because Overnight last made adjusting entries on *November 30*; therefore, it is still necessary to make adjusting entries for the month of December.

Exhibit 4–2

UNADJUSTED TRIAL BALANCE

OVERNIGHT AUTO SERVICE
Trial Balance
December 31, 2007

Account	Debit	Credit
Cash	$ 18,592	
Accounts receivable	6,500	
Shop supplies	1,800	
Unexpired insurance	4,500	
Land	52,000	
Building	36,000	
Accumulated depreciation: building		$ 1,500
Tools and equipment	12,000	
Accumulated depreciation: tools and equipment		2,000
Notes payable		4,000
Accounts payable		2,690
Income taxes payable		1,560
Unearned rent revenue		9,000
Capital stock		80,000
Retained earnings		0
Dividends	14,000	
Repair service revenue		171,250
Advertising expense	3,900	
Wages expense	56,800	
Supplies expense	6,900	
Depreciation expense: building	1,500	
Depreciation expense: tools and equipment	2,000	
Utilities expense	19,400	
Insurance expense	13,500	
Income taxes expense	22,608	
	$272,000	$272,000

In the next few pages we illustrate several transactions, as well as the related adjusting entries. Both are shown in the format of general journal entries. To help distinguish between transactions and adjusting entries, transactions are printed in *blue* and adjusting entries in *red*.

CONVERTING ASSETS TO EXPENSES

When a business makes an expenditure that will benefit more than one accounting period, the amount usually is debited to an asset account. At the end of each period benefiting from this expenditure, an adjusting entry is made to transfer an appropriate portion of the cost from the asset account to an expense account. This adjusting entry reflects the fact that part of the asset has been used up—or become an expense—during the current accounting period.

An adjusting entry to convert an asset to an expense consists of a debit to an expense account and a credit to an asset account (or contra-asset account). Examples of these adjustments include the entries to apportion the costs of **prepaid expenses** and entries to record depreciation expense.

Prepaid Expenses

Payments in advance often are made for such items as insurance, rent, and office supplies. If the advance payment (or prepayment) will benefit more than just the current accounting period, the cost *represents an asset* rather than an expense. The cost of this asset will be allocated to expense in the accounting periods in which the services or the supplies are used. In summary, *prepaid expenses are assets*; they become expenses only as the goods or services are used up.

Shop Supplies

To illustrate, consider Overnight's accounting policies for shop supplies. As supplies are purchased, their cost is debited to the asset account Shop Supplies. It is not practical to make journal entries every few minutes as supplies are used. Instead, an estimate is made of the supplies remaining on hand at the end of each month; the supplies that are "missing" are assumed to have been used.

Prior to making adjusting entries at December 31, the balance in Overnight's Shop Supplies account is $1,800. The balance of this asset account represents shop supplies on hand on November 30. The Supplies Expense account shows a balance of $6,900, which represents the cost of supplies used through November 30. Assume that approximately $1,200 of shop supplies remain on hand at December 31. This suggests that supplies costing about $600 have been *used in December*; thus, the following *adjusting entry* is made:

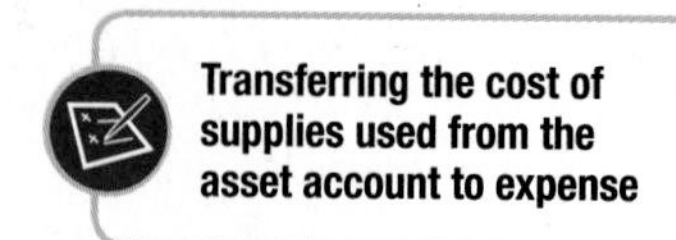

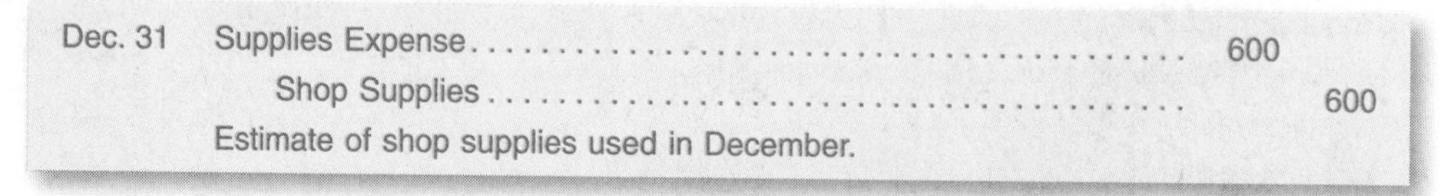

Dec. 31	Supplies Expense	600	
	Shop Supplies		600
	Estimate of shop supplies used in December.		

This adjusting entry serves two purposes: (1) it charges to expense the cost of supplies used in December, and (2) it reduces the balance of the Shop Supplies account to $1,200—the amount of supplies estimated to be on hand at December 31.

Insurance Policies

Insurance policies also are a prepaid expense. These policies provide a service, insurance protection, over a specific period of time. As the time passes, the insurance policy *expires*—that is, it is used up in business operations.

To illustrate, assume that on March 1, Overnight purchased for $18,000 a one-year insurance policy providing comprehensive liability insurance and insurance against fire and damage to customers' vehicles while in Overnight's facilities. This expenditure (a *transaction*) was debited to an asset account, as follows:

Mar. 1	Unexpired Insurance	18,000	
	Cash		18,000
	Purchased an insurance policy providing coverage for the next 12 months.		

This $18,000 expenditure provides insurance coverage for a period of one full year. Therefore, 1/12 of this cost, or $1,500, is recognized as insurance expense every month. The $13,500 insurance expense reported in Overnight's trial balance represents the portion of the insurance policy that has expired between March 1 and November 30 ($1,500/mo. × 9 months). The $4,500 amount of unexpired insurance shown in the trial balance is the remaining cost of the 12-month policy still in effect as of November 30 ($1,500/mo. × 3 months). By December 31, another full month of the policy has expired. Thus, the insurance expense for December is recorded by the following *adjusting entry* at month-end:

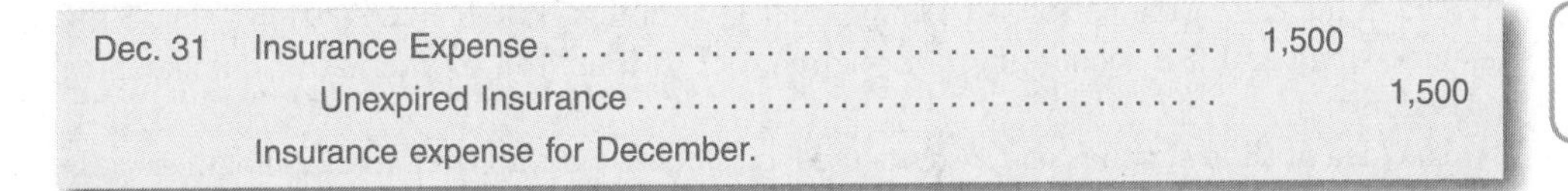

Dec. 31	Insurance Expense	1,500	
	Unexpired Insurance		1,500
	Insurance expense for December.		

Cost of insurance coverage expiring in December

Notice the similarities between the *effects* of this adjusting entry and the one that we made previously for shop supplies. In both cases, the entries transfer to expense that portion of an asset used up during the period. This flow of costs from the balance sheet to the income statement is illustrated in Exhibit 4–3.

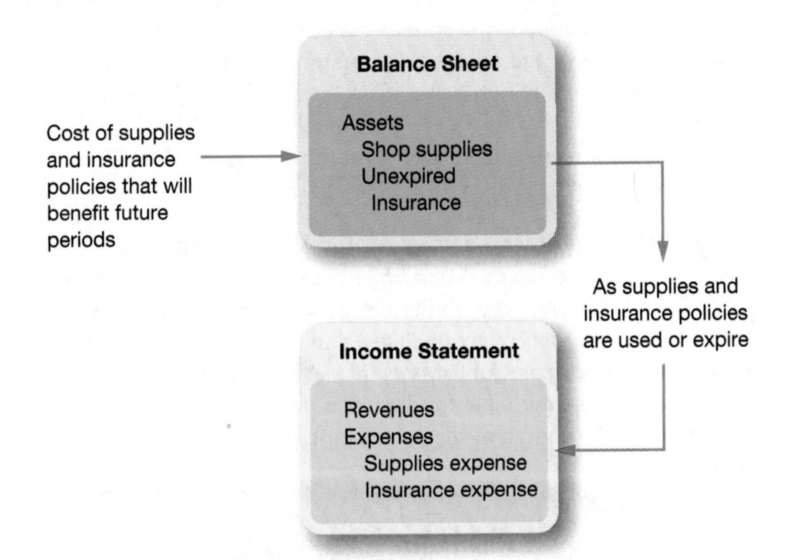

Exhibit 4–3
AN EXPIRED ASSET BECOMES AN EXPENSE

YOUR TURN **You as a Car Owner**

Car owners typically pay insurance premiums six months in advance. Assume that you recently paid your six-month premium of $600 on February 1 (for coverage through July 31). On March 31, you decide to switch insurance companies. You call your existing agent and ask that your policy be canceled. Are you entitled to a refund? If so, why, and how much will it be?

(See our comments on the Online Learning Center Web site.)

Recording Prepayments Directly in the Expense Accounts In our illustration, payments for shop supplies and for insurance covering more than one period were debited to asset accounts. However, some companies follow an alternative policy of debiting such prepayments directly to an expense account, such as Supplies Expense. At the end of the period, the adjusting entry then would be to debit Shop Supplies and credit Supplies Expense for the cost of supplies that had *not* been used.

This alternative method leads to the *same results* as does the procedure used by Overnight. Under either approach, the cost of supplies used during the current period is treated as an *expense*, and the cost of supplies still on hand is carried forward in the balance sheet as an *asset*.

In this text, we will follow Overnight's practice of recording prepayments in asset accounts and then making adjustments to transfer these costs to expense accounts as the assets expire. This approach correctly describes the *conceptual flow of costs* through the elements of financial statements. That is, a prepayment *is* an asset that later becomes an expense. The alternative approach is used widely in practice only because it is an efficient "shortcut," which standardizes the recording of transactions and may reduce the number of adjusting entries needed at the end of the period. Remember, our goal in this course is to develop your ability to understand and use accounting information, not to train you in alternative bookkeeping procedures.

The idea of shop supplies and insurance policies being used up over several months is easy to understand. But the same concept also applies to assets such as buildings and equipment. These assets are converted to expenses through the process of *depreciation*.

THE CONCEPT OF DEPRECIATION

Depreciable assets are *physical objects* that retain their size and shape but that eventually wear out or become obsolete. They are not physically consumed, as are assets such as supplies, but nonetheless their economic usefulness diminishes over time. Examples of depreciable assets include buildings and all types of equipment, fixtures, furnishings—and even railroad tracks. Land, however, is *not* viewed as a depreciable asset, as it has an *unlimited* useful life.

Each period, a portion of a depreciable asset's usefulness *expires*. Therefore, a corresponding portion of its cost is recognized as *depreciation expense*.

What Is Depreciation?

In accounting, the term **depreciation** means the *systematic allocation of the cost of a depreciable asset to expense* over the asset's useful life. This process is illustrated in Exhibit 4–4. Notice the similarities between Exhibit 4–4 and Exhibit 4–3.

Depreciation *is not* an attempt to record changes in the asset's market value. In the short run, the market value of some depreciable assets may even increase, but the process of depreciation continues anyway. The rationale for depreciation lies in the *matching principle*. Our goal is to offset a reasonable portion of the asset's cost against revenue in each period of the asset's **useful life**.

Exhibit 4–4
THE DEPRECIATION PROCESS

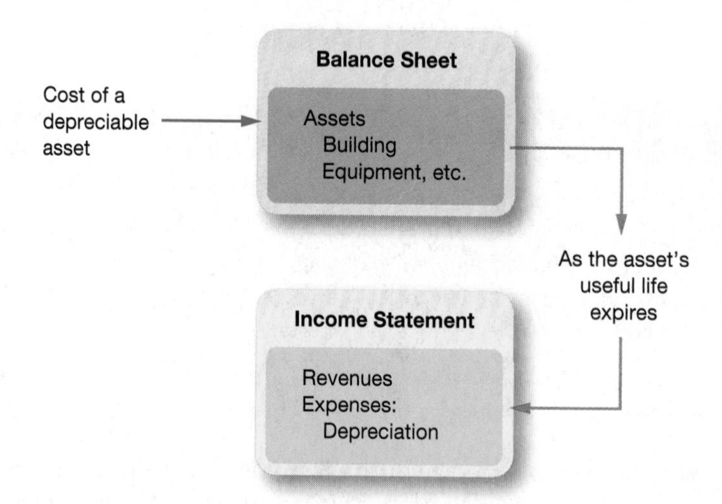

Depreciation expense occurs continuously over the life of the asset, but there are no daily "depreciation transactions." In effect, depreciation expense is paid in advance when the asset is originally purchased. Therefore, *adjusting entries* are needed at the end of each accounting period to transfer an appropriate amount of the asset's cost to depreciation expense.

Depreciation Is Only an Estimate

The appropriate amount of depreciation expense is *only an estimate*. After all, we cannot look at a building or a piece of equipment and determine precisely how much of its economic usefulness has expired during the current period.

The most widely used means of estimating periodic depreciation expense is the **straight-line method of depreciation**. Under the straight-line approach, an *equal portion* of the asset's cost is allocated to depreciation expense in every period of the asset's estimated useful life. The formula for computing depreciation expense by the straight-line method is:[2]

$$\textbf{Depreciation expense (per period)} = \frac{\textbf{Cost of the asset}}{\textbf{Estimated useful life}}$$

The use of an *estimated useful life* is the major reason that depreciation expense is *only an estimate*. In most cases, management does not know in advance exactly how long the asset will remain in use.

CASE IN POINT

© Adam Woolfitt/CORBIS

How long does a building last? For purposes of computing depreciation expense, most companies estimate about 30 or 40 years. But the Empire State Building was built in 1931, and it's not likely to be torn down anytime soon. And how about Windsor Castle? While these are not typical examples, they illustrate the difficulty in estimating in advance just how long depreciable assets may remain in use.

Depreciation of Overnight's Building Overnight purchased its building for \$36,000 on January 22. Because the building was old, its estimated remaining useful life is only 20 years. Therefore, the building's monthly depreciation expense is \$150 (\$36,000 cost ÷ 240 months). We will assume that Overnight did *not* record any depreciation expense in January because it operated for only a small part of the month. Thus, the building's \$1,500 depreciation expense reported in Overnight's trial balance illustrated in Exhibit 4–2 on page 145 represents 10 *full months* of depreciation recorded in 2007, from February 1 through November 30 (\$150/mo. × 10 months). An additional \$150 of depreciation expense is still needed on the building for December (bringing the total to be reported in the income statement for the year to \$1,650).

The adjusting entry to record depreciation expense on Overnight's building for the month of December is:

Dec. 31	Depreciation Expense: Building	150	
	Accumulated Depreciation: Building		150
	Monthly depreciation on building (\$36,000 ÷ 240 mo.).		

The adjusting entry for monthly depreciation on the building

The *Depreciation Expense: Building* account will appear in Overnight's income statement along with other expenses for the year ended December 31, 2007. The balance in the

[2] At this point in our discussion, we are ignoring any possible *residual value* that might be recovered upon disposal of the asset. Residual values are discussed in Chapter 9. We will assume that Overnight Auto Service depreciates its assets using the straight-line method computed without any residual values.

Accumulated Depreciation: Building account will be reported in the December 31 balance sheet as a *deduction* from the Building Account, as shown below.

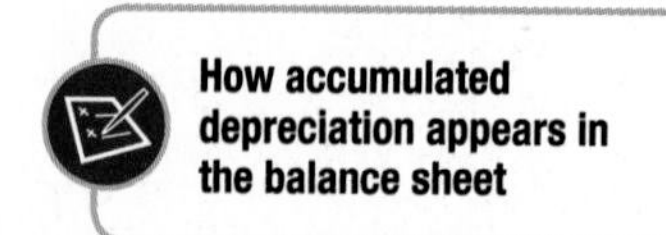
How accumulated depreciation appears in the balance sheet

Building	$36,000
Less: Accumulated Depreciation: Building	(1,650)
Book Value	$34,350

Accumulated Depreciation: Building is an example of a **contra-asset account** because (1) it has a credit balance, and (2) it is offset against an asset account (Building) to produce the book value for the asset. Accountants often use the term **book value** (or *carrying value*) to describe the net valuation of an asset in a company's accounting records. For depreciable assets, such as buildings and equipment, book value is equal to the cost of the asset, less the related amount of accumulated depreciation. The end result of crediting the Accumulated Depreciation: Building account is much the same as if the credit had been made directly to the Building account; that is, the book value reported in the balance sheet for the building is reduced from $36,000 to $34,350.

Book value is of significance primarily for accounting purposes. It represents costs that will be offset against the revenue of future periods. It also gives users of financial statements an indication of the age of a company's depreciable assets (older assets tend to have larger amounts of accumulated depreciation associated with them than newer assets). It is important to realize that the computation of book value is based upon an asset's *historical* cost. Thus, book value is *not* intended to represent an asset's current *market value*.

Depreciation of Tools and Equipment Overnight depreciates its tools and equipment over a period of five years (60 months) using the straight-line method. The December 31 trial balance shows that the company owns tools and equipment that cost $12,000. Therefore, the adjusting entry to record December's depreciation expense is:

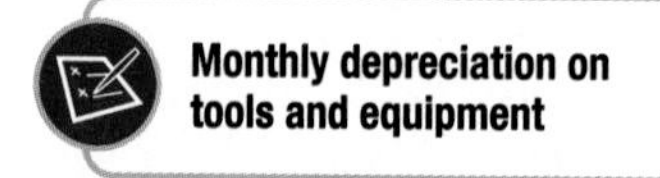
Monthly depreciation on tools and equipment

Dec. 31	Depreciation Expense: Tools and Equipment	200	
	Accumulated Depreciation: Tools and Equipment		200
	Monthly depreciation on tools and equipment ($12,000 ÷ 60 months = $200/mo.)		

Again, we assume that Overnight did *not* record depreciation expense for tools and equipment in January because it operated for only a small part of the month. Thus, the related $2,000 depreciation expense reported in Overnight's trial balance in Exhibit 4–2 on page 145 represents 10 *full months* of depreciation, from February 1 through November 30 ($200/mo. × 10 months). The tools and equipment still require an additional $200 of depreciation for December (bringing the total to be reported in the income statement for the year to $2,200).

What is the book value of Overnight's tools and equipment at December 31, 2007? If you said *$9,800*, you're right.[3]

Depreciation—A Noncash Expense Depreciation is a *noncash* expense. We have made the point that net income does not represent an inflow of cash or any other asset. Rather, it is a *computation* of the overall effect of certain business transactions on owners' equity. The recognition of depreciation expense illustrates this point. As depreciable assets expire, depreciation expense is recorded, net income is reduced, and owners' equity declines, but there is no corresponding cash outlay in the current period. For this reason, depreciation is called a noncash expense. Often it represents the largest difference between net income and the cash flow from business operations.

[3] Cost, $12,000, less accumulated depreciation, which amounts to $2,200 after the December 31 adjusting entry.

CONVERTING LIABILITIES TO REVENUE

Prepare adjusting entries to convert liabilities to revenue. LO4

In some instances, customers may *pay in advance* for services to be rendered in later accounting periods. For example, a football team collects much of its revenue in advance through the sale of season tickets. Health clubs collect in advance by selling long-term membership contracts. Airlines sell many of their tickets well in advance of scheduled flights.

For accounting purposes, amounts collected in advance *do not represent revenue*, because these amounts have *not yet been earned*. Amounts collected from customers in advance are recorded by debiting the Cash account and crediting an *unearned revenue* account. **Unearned revenue** also may be called *deferred revenue*.

When a company collects money in advance from its customers, it has an *obligation* to render services in the future. Therefore, the balance of an unearned revenue account is considered to be a liability; *it appears in the liability section of the balance sheet, not in the income statement*. Unearned revenue differs from other liabilities because it usually will be settled by rendering services, rather than by making payment in cash. In short, it will be *worked off* rather than *paid off*. Of course, if the business is unable to render the service, it must discharge this liability by refunding money to its customers.

When a company renders the services for which customers have paid in advance, it is working off its liability to these customers and is earning the revenue. At the end of the accounting period, an adjusting entry is made to transfer an appropriate amount from the unearned revenue account to a revenue account. This adjusting entry consists of a debit to a liability account (unearned revenue) and a credit to a revenue account. For instance, The New York Times Company reports a $78 million current liability in its balance sheet called Unexpired Subscriptions. This account represents unearned revenue from selling subscriptions for future newspaper deliveries. The liability is converted to Circulation Revenue and reported in the company's income statement as the actual deliveries occur.

To illustrate these concepts, assume that on December 1, Harbor Cab Co. agreed to rent space in Overnight's building to provide indoor storage for some of its cabs. The agreed-upon rent is $3,000 per month, and Harbor Cab paid for the first three months in advance. The journal entry to record this *transaction* on December 1 was:

Dec. 1	Cash	9,000	
	Unearned Rent Revenue		9,000
	Collected in advance from Harbor Cab for rental of storage space for three months.		

Remember that Unearned Rent Revenue is a *liability* account, *not a revenue account*. Overnight will earn rental revenue *gradually* over a three-month period as it provides storage facilities for Harbor Cab. At the end of each of these three months, Overnight will make an *adjusting entry*, transferring $3,000 from the Unearned Rent Revenue account to an earned revenue account, Rent Revenue Earned, which will appear in Overnight's income statement. The first in this series of monthly transfers will be made at December 31 with the following adjusting entry:

An "advance"—it's not revenue; it's a liability

Dec. 31	Unearned Rent Revenue	3,000	
	Rent Revenue Earned		3,000
	Portion of rent received in advance from Harbor Cab that was earned in December ($9,000 ÷ 3 mo.).		

An adjusting entry showing that some unearned revenue has now been earned

After this adjusting entry has been posted, the Unearned Rent Revenue account will have a $6,000 credit balance. This balance represents Overnight's obligation to render $6,000 worth of service over the next two months and will appear in the liability section of the company's balance sheet. The Rent Revenue Earned account will appear in Overnight's income statement.

The transfer of unearned revenue to earned revenue is illustrated in Exhibit 4–5.

Exhibit 4–5

UNEARNED REVENUE BECOMES EARNED REVENUE

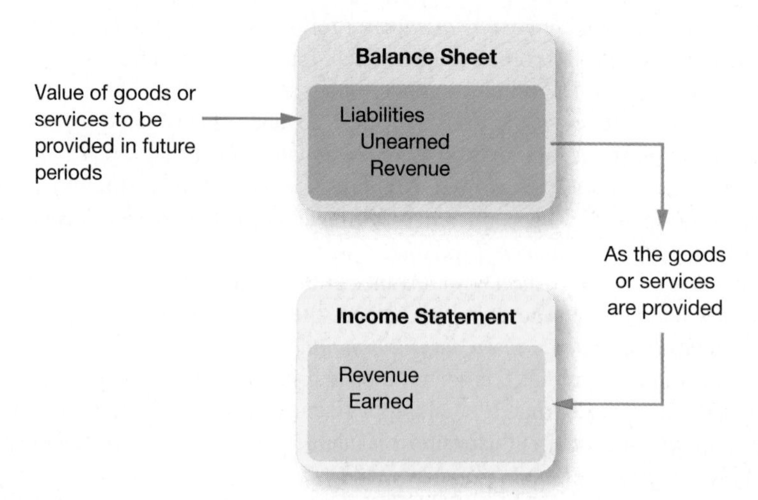

Recording Advance Collections Directly in the Revenue Accounts We have stressed that amounts collected from customers in advance represent liabilities, not revenue. However, some companies follow an accounting policy of crediting these advance collections directly to revenue accounts. The adjusting entry then should consist of a debit to the revenue account and a credit to the unearned revenue account for the portion of the advance payments *not yet earned.* This alternative accounting practice leads to the same results as does the method used in our illustration.

In this text, we will follow the originally described practice of crediting advance payments from customers to an unearned revenue account.

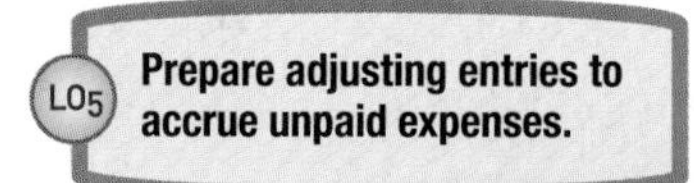

Prepare adjusting entries to accrue unpaid expenses.

ACCRUING UNPAID EXPENSES

This type of adjusting entry recognizes expenses that will be paid in *future* transactions; therefore, no cost has yet been recorded in the accounting records. Salaries of employees and interest on borrowed money are common examples of expenses that accumulate from day to day but that usually are not recorded until they are paid. These expenses are said to **accrue** over time, that is, to grow or to accumulate. At the end of the accounting period, an adjusting entry should be made to record any expenses that have accrued but that have not yet been recorded. Since these expenses will be paid at a future date, the adjusting entry consists of a debit to an expense account and a credit to a liability account. We shall now use the example of Overnight Auto Service to illustrate this type of adjusting entry.

Accrual of Wages (or Salaries) Expense Overnight, like many businesses, pays its employees every other Friday. This month, however, ends on a Tuesday—three days before the next scheduled payday. Thus Overnight's employees have worked for more than a week in December *for which they have not yet been paid.*

Time cards indicate that since the last payroll date, Overnight's employees have worked a total of 130 hours. Including payroll taxes, Overnight's wage expense averages about $15 per hour. Therefore, at December 31, the company owes its employees approximately *$1,950* for work performed in December.[4] The following adjusting entry should be made to record this amount both as wages expense of the current period and as a liability:

Wages owed as of month-end

Dec. 31	Wages Expense	1,950	
	Wages Payable		1,950
	To accrue wages owed to employees but unpaid as of month-end.		

[4] In preparing a formal payroll, wages and payroll taxes must be computed "down to the last cent." But this is not a payroll; it is an amount to be used in the company's financial statements. Therefore, a reasonable estimate will suffice. The accounting principle of *materiality* is discussed later in this chapter.

This adjusting entry increases Overnight's wages expense for 2007 and also creates a liability—wages payable—that will appear in the December 31 balance sheet.

On Friday, January 3, 2008, Overnight will pay its regular biweekly payroll. Let us assume that this payroll amounts to $2,397. In this case, the entry to record payment is as follows:[5]

2008			
Jan. 3	Wages Expense (for January)	447	
	Wages Payable (accrued in December)	1,950	
	Cash		2,397
	Biweekly payroll, $1,950 of which had been accrued at December 31.		

Payment of wages earned in two accounting periods

Accrual of Interest Expense

On January 22, 2007, Overnight purchased its building, an old bus garage, from the Metropolitan Transit Authority for $36,000. Overnight paid $6,000 cash, and issued a $30,000, 90-day note payable for the balance owed. Overnight paid the $30,000 obligation in April. There was no interest expense to accrue because this note payable was *non-interest-bearing*.

On November 30, 2007, Overnight borrowed $4,000 from American National Bank by issuing an *interest-bearing* note payable. This loan is to be repaid in three months (on February 28, 2008), along with interest computed at an annual rate of 9 percent. The entry made on November 30 to record this borrowing transaction is:

Nov. 30	Cash	4,000	
	Notes Payable		4,000
	Borrowed cash from American National Bank, issuing a 9%, $4,000 note payable, due in three months.		

On February 28, Overnight must pay the bank $4,090. This represents the $4,000 amount borrowed, *plus $90 interest* ($4,000 × .09 × 3/12). The $90 interest charge covers a period of *three months*. Although no payment will be made until February 28, 2008, interest expense is *incurred* (or accrued) at a rate of $30 per month, as shown in Exhibit 4–6.

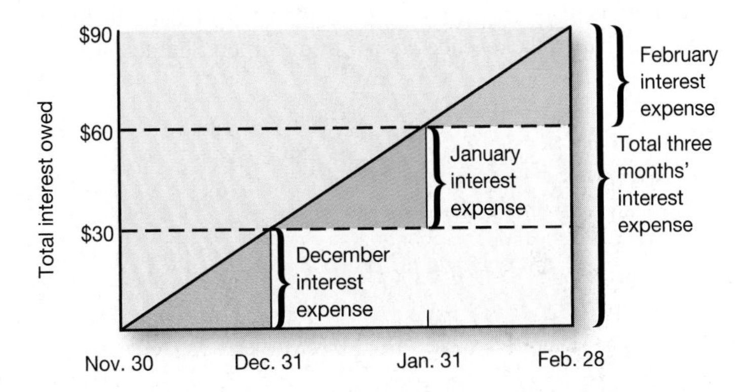

Exhibit 4–6
ACCRUAL OF INTEREST

The following adjusting entry is made at December 31 to charge December operations with one month's interest expense and to record the amount of interest owed to the bank at month-end:

Dec. 31	Interest Expense	30	
	Interest Payable		30
	Interest expense accrued during December on note payable ($4,000 × .09 × 1/12).		

Adjusting entry for interest expense accrued in December

[5] In this illustration, we do not address the details associated with payroll taxes and amounts withheld. These topics are discussed in Chapter 10.

The $30 interest expense that accrued in December will appear in Overnight's 2007 income statement. Both the $30 interest payable and the $4,000 note payable to American National Bank will appear as *liabilities* in the December 31, 2007, balance sheet.

Overnight will make a second adjusting entry recognizing another $30 in interest expense on January 31 of the coming year. The entry on February 28 to record the repayment of this loan, including $90 in interest charges, is:

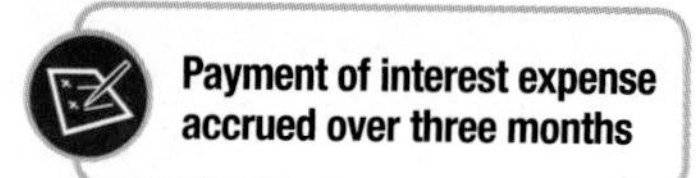

2008			
Feb. 28	Notes Payable	4,000	
	Interest Payable (from December and January)	60	
	Interest Expense (February only)	30	
	Cash		4,090
	Repaid $4,000 note payable to American National Bank, including $90 in interest charges.		

ACCRUING UNCOLLECTED REVENUE

A business may earn revenue during the current accounting period but not bill the customer until a future accounting period. This situation is likely to occur if additional services are being performed for the same customer, in which case the bill might not be prepared until all services are completed. Any revenue that has been *earned but not recorded* during the current accounting period should be recorded at the end of the period by means of an adjusting entry. This adjusting entry consists of a debit to an account receivable and a credit to the appropriate revenue account. The term *accrued revenue* often is used to describe revenue that has been earned during the period but that has not been recorded prior to the closing date.

To illustrate this type of adjusting entry, assume that in December, Overnight entered into an agreement to perform routine maintenance on several vans owned by Airport Shuttle Service. Overnight agreed to maintain these vans for a flat fee of $1,500 per month, payable on the fifteenth of each month.

No entry was made to record the signing of this agreement, because no services had yet been rendered. Overnight began rendering services on *December 15*, but the first monthly payment will not be received until January 15. Therefore, Overnight should make the following adjusting entry at December 31 to record the revenue *earned* from Airport Shuttle during the month:

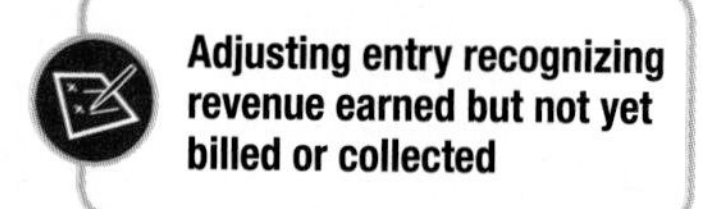

Dec. 31	Accounts Receivable	750	
	Repair Service Revenue		750
	To recognize revenue from services rendered on Airport Shuttle maintenance contract during December. Account is settled on the fifteenth of each month.		

The collection of the first monthly fee from Airport Shuttle will occur in the next accounting period (January 15, to be exact). Of this $1,500 cash receipt, half represents collection of the receivable recorded on December 31; the other half represents revenue earned in January. Thus the entry to record the receipt of $1,500 from Airport Shuttle on January 15 will be:

2008			
Jan. 15	Cash	1,500	
	Accounts Receivable		750
	Repair Service Revenue		750
	Collected from Airport Shuttle for van maintenance, Dec. 15 through Jan. 15.		

The net result of the December 31 adjusting entry has been to divide the revenue from maintenance of Airport Shuttle's vans between December and January in proportion to the services rendered during each month.

ACCRUING INCOME TAXES EXPENSE: THE FINAL ADJUSTING ENTRY

As a corporation earns taxable income, it incurs income taxes expense, and also a liability to governmental tax authorities. This liability is paid in four installments called *estimated quarterly payments*. The first three payments normally are made on April 15, June 15, and September 15. The final installment actually is due on *December 15*; but for purposes of our illustration and assignment materials, we will assume the final payment is not due until *January 15* of the following year.[6]

In its unadjusted trial balance (Exhibit 4–2 on page 145), Overnight shows income taxes expense of $22,608. This is the income taxes expense recognized from January 20, 2007, (the date Overnight opened for business) through November 30, 2007. Income taxes accrued through September 30 have already been paid. Thus, the $1,560 liability for income taxes payable represents only the income taxes accrued in *October* and *November*.

The amount of income taxes expense accrued for any given month is only an *estimate*. The actual amount of income taxes cannot be determined until the company prepares its annual income tax return. In our illustrations and assignment materials, we estimate income taxes expense at *40 percent of taxable income*. We also assume that taxable income is equal to *income before income taxes*, a subtotal often shown in an income statement. This subtotal is total revenue less all expenses *other than* income taxes.

CASE IN POINT

Corporate income tax rates vary around the world. A recent survey shows that rates range from less than 15 percent in Cyprus and Ireland, to 42 percent in Japan.* In addition to corporate income taxes, some countries also (1) withhold taxes on dividends, interest, and royalties, (2) charge value-added taxes at specified production and distribution points, and (3) impose border taxes such as customs and import duties.

*KPMG Corporate Tax Rate Survey (January 2004).

In 2007, Overnight earned income before income taxes of $66,570 (see the income statement in Exhibit 5–2, page 196, in Chapter 5). Therefore, income taxes expense *for the entire year* is estimated at $26,628 ($66,570 × 40 percent). Given that income taxes expense recognized through November 30 amounts to $22,608 (see the unadjusted trial balance in Exhibit 4–2), an additional $4,020 in income taxes expense must have accrued during *December* ($26,628 − $22,608). The adjusting entry to record this expense is:

Dec. 31	Income Taxes Expense	4,020	
	Income Taxes Payable		4,020
	Estimated income taxes applicable to taxable income earned during December.		

Adjusting entry to record income taxes for December

This entry increases the balance in the Income Taxes Expense account to the $26,628 amount required for the year ended December 31, 2007. It also increases the liability for

[6] This assumption enables us to accrue income taxes in December in the same manner as in other months. Otherwise, income taxes for this month would be recorded as a mid-month transaction, rather than in an end-of-month adjusting entry. The adjusting entry for income taxes is an example of an accrued, but unpaid, expense.

income taxes payable to $5,580 ($1,560 + $4,020). The entry to record the payment of this liability on January 15, 2008, will be:

2008			
Jan. 15	Income Taxes Payable	5,580	
	Cash		5,580
	Paid final installment on 2007 income tax liability.		

The above transaction is simply the payment of an outstanding liability; therefore, it is *not* considered an adjusting entry.

Income Taxes in Unprofitable Periods What happens to income taxes expense when *losses* are incurred? In these situations, the company recognizes a "negative amount" of income taxes expense. The adjusting entry to record income taxes at the end of an *unprofitable* accounting period consists of a *debit* to Income Taxes Payable and a *credit* to Income Taxes Expense.

"Negative" income taxes expense means that the company may be able to recover from the government some of the income taxes recognized as expense in prior periods.[7] If the Income Taxes Payable account has a *debit* balance at year-end, it is reclassified as an *asset*, called "Income Tax Refund Receivable." A credit balance in the Income Taxes Expense account is offset against the amount of the before-tax loss, as shown in Exhibit 4–7.

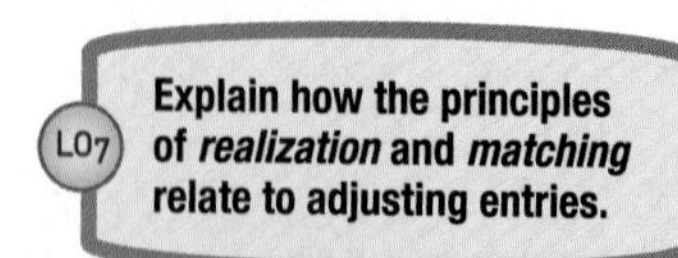

Exhibit 4–7

PARTIAL INCOME STATEMENT

Partial Income Statement—for an *Unprofitable* Period

Income (loss) before income taxes	$(20,000)
Income tax benefit (recovery of previously recorded taxes)	8,000
Net loss	$(12,000)

We have already seen that income taxes *expense* reduces the amount of before-tax *profits*. Notice now that income tax *benefits*—in the form of tax refunds—can reduce the amount of a pretax *loss*. Thus, income taxes reduce the size of *both* profits and losses. The detailed reporting of profits and losses in the income statement is illustrated in Chapter 5.

Adjusting Entries and Accounting Principles

LO7 **Explain how the principles of *realization* and *matching* relate to adjusting entries.**

Adjusting entries are *tools* by which accountants apply the **realization** and **matching** principles. Through these entries, revenues are recognized as they are *earned,* and expenses are recognized as resources are *used* or consumed in producing the related revenue.

In most cases, the realization principle indicates that revenue should be recognized *at the time goods are sold or services are rendered.* At this point the business has essentially completed the earning process and the sales value of the goods or services can be measured objectively. At any time prior to sale, the ultimate sales value of the goods or services sold can only be estimated. After the sale, the only step that remains is to collect from the customer, and this is usually a relatively certain event.

The matching principle underlies such accounting practices as depreciating plant assets, measuring the cost of supplies used, and amortizing the cost of unexpired insurance policies. All end-of-the-period adjusting entries involving recognition of expense are applications of the matching principle.

Costs are matched with revenue in one of two ways:

1. *Direct association of costs with specific revenue transactions.* The ideal method of matching revenue with expenses is to determine the amount of expense associated with the

[7] Tax refunds may be limited to tax payments in recent years. In this introductory discussion, we assume the company has paid sufficient taxes in prior years to permit a full recovery of any "negative tax expense" relating to the loss in the current period.

specific revenue transactions occurring during the period. However, this approach works only for those costs and expenses that can be directly associated with specific revenue transactions. Commissions paid to salespeople are an example of costs that can be *directly associated* with the revenue of a specific accounting period.

2. *Systematic allocation of costs over the useful life of the expenditure.* Many expenditures contribute to the earning of revenue for a number of accounting periods but cannot be directly associated with specific revenue transactions. Examples include the costs of insurance policies, depreciable assets, and intangible assets such as patents. In these cases, accountants attempt to match revenue and expenses by *systematically allocating the cost to expense* over its useful life. Straight-line depreciation is an example of a systematic technique used to match revenue with the related costs and expenses.

THE CONCEPT OF MATERIALITY

Explain the concept of *materiality*. LO8

Another underlying accounting principle also plays a major role in the making of adjusting entries—the concept of **materiality**. The term *materiality* refers to the *relative importance* of an item or an event. An item is considered material if knowledge of the item might reasonably *influence the decisions* of users of financial statements. Accountants must be sure that all material items are properly reported in financial statements.

However, the financial reporting process should be *cost-effective*—that is, the value of the information should exceed the cost of its preparation. By definition, the accounting treatment accorded to **immaterial** items is of *little or no consequence to decision makers*. Therefore, accountants do not waste time accounting for immaterial items; these items may be handled in the *easiest and most convenient manner*.

In summary, the concept of materiality allows accountants to use estimated amounts and even to ignore other accounting principles if the results of these actions do not have an important impact on the financial statements. Materiality is one of the most important accounting principles; you will encounter applications of this concept throughout the study of accounting.

Materiality and Adjusting Entries

The concept of materiality enables accountants to shorten and simplify the process of making adjusting entries in several ways. For example:

1. Businesses purchase many assets that have a very low cost or that will be consumed quickly in business operations. Examples include wastebaskets, lightbulbs, and janitorial supplies. The materiality concept permits charging such purchases *directly to expense accounts*, rather than to asset accounts. This treatment conveniently eliminates the need for an adjusting entry at the end of the period to transfer a portion of these costs from an asset account to expense. This accounting shortcut is acceptable as long as the cost of the *unused* items on hand at the end of the period is immaterial.
2. Some expenses, such as telephone bills and utility bills, may be charged to expenses as the bills are *paid*, rather than as the services are used. Technically this treatment violates the *matching principle*. However, accounting for utility bills on a cash basis is very convenient, as the monthly cost of utility service is not even known until the utility bill is received. Under this cash basis approach, one month's utility bill is charged to an expense each month. Although the bill charged to expense is actually the *prior* month's bill, the resulting "error" in the financial statements is not likely to be material.
3. Adjusting entries to accrue unrecorded expenses or unrecorded revenue may be ignored if the dollar amounts are immaterial.
4. If the amount of error is not likely to be material, adjusting entries may be based on *estimates*. For example, earlier we illustrated an adjusting entry allocating part of the $1,800 balance in the Supplies account to an expense. The amount of supplies used during the period ($600) was based on an *estimate* of the supplies still on hand ($1,200). This $1,200 estimate is an educated guess; no one actually counts all of the shop supplies on hand and looks up their cost. The adjusting entry recording accrued wages payable also was based on an estimate, not a detailed calculation.

Materiality Is a Matter of Professional Judgment Whether a specific item or event is material is a matter of *professional judgment*. In making these judgments, accountants consider several factors.

First, what constitutes a material amount varies with the size of the organization. For example, a $1,000 expenditure may be material in relation to the financial statements of a small business but not to the statements of a large corporation such as General Electric.[8] There are no official rules as to what constitutes a material amount, but most accountants would consider amounts of less than 2 percent or 3 percent of net income to be immaterial, unless there were other factors to consider. One such other factor is the *cumulative effect* of numerous immaterial events. Each of a dozen items may be immaterial when considered by itself. When viewed together, however, the combined effect of all 12 items may be material.

Finally, materiality depends on the *nature* of the item, as well as its dollar amount. Assume, for example, that several managers systematically have been stealing money from the company that they manage. Stockholders probably would consider this fact important even if the dollar amounts were small in relation to the company's total resources.

You as Overnight Auto's Service Department Manager

You just found out that Betty, one of the best mechanics that you supervise for Overnight Auto, has taken home small items from the company's supplies, such as a screwdriver and a couple of cans of oil. When you talk to Betty, she suggests that these items are immaterial to Overnight Auto because they are not recorded in the inventory and they are expensed when they are purchased. How should you respond to Betty?

(See our comments on the Online Learning Center Web site.)

Note to students: In the assignment material accompanying this textbook, you are to consider all dollar amounts to be material, unless the problem specifically raises the question of materiality.

EFFECTS OF THE ADJUSTING ENTRIES

On pages 142 and 143, we identified four types of adjusting entries, each of which involve one income statement account and one balance sheet account. The effects of these adjustment types on the income statement and balance sheet are summarized in Exhibit 4–8.

Exhibit 4–8 THE EFFECTS OF ADJUSTING ENTRIES ON THE FINANCIAL STATEMENTS

	Income Statement			Balance Sheet		
Adjustment	**Revenue**	**Expenses**	**Net Income**	**Assets**	**Liabilities**	**Owners' Equity**
Type I Converting Assets to Expenses	No effect	Increase	Decrease	Decrease	No effect	Decrease
Type II Converting Liabilities to Revenue	Increase	No effect	Increase	No effect	Decrease	Increase
Type III Accruing Unpaid Expenses	No effect	Increase	Decrease	No effect	Increase	Decrease
Type IV Accruing Uncollected Revenue	Increase	No effect	Increase	Increase	No effect	Increase

[8] This point is emphasized by the fact that General Electric rounds the dollar amounts shown in its financial statements to the nearest $1 million. This rounding of financial statement amounts is, in itself, an application of the materiality concept.

The four adjustment types were illustrated and discussed in nine separate adjusting entries made by Overnight on December 31. These adjustments appear in the format of general journal entries in Exhibit 4–9. (Overnight also recorded many transactions throughout the month of December. These transactions are not illustrated here but were accounted for in the manner described in Chapter 3.)

Exhibit 4–9
ADJUSTING ENTRIES

Adjusting entries are recorded only at the end of the period

OVERNIGHT AUTO SERVICE
General Journal
December 31, 2007

Date	Account Titles and Explanation	Debit	Credit
2007			
Dec. 31	Supplies Expense	600	
	Shop Supplies		600
	Shop supplies used during December.		
31	Insurance Expense	1,500	
	Unexpired Insurance		1,500
	Insurance expense for December.		
31	Depreciation Expense: Building	150	
	Accumulated Depreciation: Building.		150
	Monthly depreciation on building ($36,000 ÷ 240 mo.).		
31	Depreciation Expense: Tools and Equipment	200	
	Accumulated Depreciation: Tools and Equipment		200
	Monthly depreciation on tools and equipment ($12,000 ÷ 60 mo.)		
31	Unearned Rent Revenue.	3,000	
	Rent Revenue Earned		3,000
	Portion of rent received in advance from Harbor Cab that was earned in December ($9,000 ÷ 3 mo.).		
31	Wages Expense	1,950	
	Wages Payable.		1,950
	To accrue wages owed to employees but unpaid as of month-end.		
31	Interest Expense	30	
	Interest Payable		30
	Interest expense accrued during December on note payable ($4,000 × .09 × 1/12).		
31	Accounts Receivable.	750	
	Repair Service Revenue		750
	To recognize revenue from services rendered on Airport Shuttle maintenance contract during December.		
31	Income Taxes Expense	4,020	
	Income Taxes Payable		4,020
	Estimated income taxes applicable to taxable income earned in December.		

After these adjustments are posted to the ledger, Overnight's ledger accounts will be up-to-date (except for the balance in the Retained Earnings account).[9] The company's **adjusted trial balance** at December 31, 2007, appears in Exhibit 4–10. (For emphasis, those accounts affected by the month-end adjusting entries are shown in red.)

Overnight's financial statements are prepared directly from the adjusted trial balance. Note the order of the accounts: All balance sheet accounts are followed by the statement of retained earnings accounts and then the income statement accounts. In Chapter 5, we illustrate exactly how these three financial statements are prepared.

LO9 **Prepare an adjusted trial balance and describe its purpose.**

Exhibit 4–10

ADJUSTED TRIAL BALANCE

OVERNIGHT AUTO SERVICE
Adjusted Trial Balance
December 31, 2007

	Account	Debit	Credit
Balance sheet accounts	Cash	$ 18,592	
	Accounts receivable	7,250	
	Shop supplies	1,200	
	Unexpired insurance	3,000	
	Land	52,000	
	Building	36,000	
	Accumulated depreciation: building		$ 1,650
	Tools and equipment	12,000	
	Accumulated depreciation: tools and equipment		2,200
	Notes payable		4,000
	Accounts payable		2,690
	Wages payable		1,950
	Income taxes payable		5,580
	Interest payable		30
	Unearned rent revenue		6,000
	Capital stock		80,000
Statement of retained earnings accounts	Retained earnings (***Note:*** still must be updated for transactions recorded in the accounts listed below. Closing entries serve this purpose.)		0
	Dividends	14,000	
Income statement accounts	Repair service revenue		172,000
	Rent revenue earned		3,000
	Advertising expense	3,900	
	Wages expense	58,750	
	Supplies expense	7,500	
	Depreciation expense: building	1,650	
	Depreciation expense: tools and equipment	2,200	
	Utilities expense	19,400	
	Insurance expense	15,000	
	Interest expense	30	
	Income taxes expense	26,628	
		$279,100	$279,100

[9] The balance in the Retained Earnings account will be brought up-to-date during the closing process, discussed in Chapter 5.

Ethics, Fraud & Corporate Governance

Improper accounting for operating costs has often resulted in the SEC bringing action against companies for fraudulent financial reporting. Expenditures that are expected only to benefit the year in which they are made should be expensed (deducted from revenue in the determination of net income for the current period). Companies that engage in fraud will often defer these expenditures by capitalizing them (they debit an asset account reported in the balance sheet instead of an expense account reported in the income statement).

Prior to Enron and WorldCom, one of the largest financial scandals in U.S. history occurred at Waste Management. Waste Management was the world's largest waste services company. The improper accounting at Waste Management lasted for approximately five years and resulted in an overstatement of earnings during this time period of $1.7 billion. Investors lost over $6 billion when Waste Management's improper accounting was revealed.

Waste Management's scheme for overstating earnings was simple. The company deferred recognizing normal operating expenditures as expenses until future periods. These improper deferrals were accomplished in a number of different ways, many of which involved improper accounting for long-term assets. For example, Waste Management incurred costs in buying and developing land to be used as landfills (i.e., garbage dumps). Capitalizing these costs—treating them as long-term assets—was proper accounting. However, in certain cases, the company was not able to secure the necessary governmental permits and approvals to use the purchased land as intended. In these cases, the costs that had been capitalized and reported as landfills in the balance sheet should have been expensed immediately, thereby reducing net income for the year in which the company's failure to obtain government permits and approvals occurred.

Concluding Remarks

Throughout this chapter, we illustrated end-of-period adjusting entries arising from *timing differences* between cash flows and revenue or expense recognition. In short, the adjusting process helps to ensure that appropriate amounts of revenue and expense are measured and reported in a company's income statement.

In Chapter 5, we continue with our illustration of Overnight Auto Service and demonstrate how adjusting entries are reflected throughout a company's financial statements.

Later chapters explain why accurate income measurement is of critical importance to investors and creditors in estimating the timing and amounts of a company's future cash flows. We also illustrate how understanding certain timing differences enables managers to budget and to plan for future operations.

END-OF-CHAPTER REVIEW

SUMMARY OF LEARNING OBJECTIVES

LO1 **Explain the purpose of adjusting entries.** The purpose of adjusting entries is to allocate revenue and expenses among accounting periods in accordance with the realization and matching principles. These end-of-period entries are necessary because revenue may be earned and expenses may be incurred in periods other than the period in which related cash flows are recorded.

LO2 **Describe and prepare the four basic types of adjusting entries.** The four basic types of adjusting entries are made to (1) convert assets to expenses, (2) convert liabilities to revenue, (3) accrue unpaid expenses, and (4) accrue uncollected revenue. Often a transaction affects the revenue or expenses of *two or more* accounting periods. The related cash inflow or outflow does not always coincide with the period in which these revenue or expense items are recorded. Thus, the need for adjusting entries results from *timing differences* between the receipt or disbursement of cash and the recording of revenue or expenses.

LO3 **Prepare adjusting entries to convert assets to expenses.** When an expenditure is made that will benefit more than one accounting period, an asset account is debited and cash is credited. The asset account is used to *defer* (or postpone) expense recognition until a later date. At the end of each period benefiting from this expenditure, an adjusting entry is made to transfer an appropriate amount from the asset account to an *expense* account. This adjustment reflects the fact that part of the asset's cost has been *matched* against revenue in the measurement of income for the current period.

LO4 **Prepare adjusting entries to convert liabilities to revenue.** Customers sometimes pay in advance for services to be rendered in later accounting periods. For accounting purposes, the cash received does *not* represent revenue until it has been *earned*. Thus, the recognition of revenue must be *deferred* until it is earned. Advance collections from customers are recorded by debiting Cash and by crediting a *liability* account for *unearned* revenue. This liability is sometimes called Customer Deposits, Advance Sales, or Deferred Revenue. As unearned revenue becomes earned, an adjusting entry is made at the end of each period to transfer an appropriate amount from the liability account to a *revenue* account. This adjustment reflects the fact that all or part of the company's obligation to its customers has been fulfilled and that revenue has been realized.

LO5 **Prepare adjusting entries to accrue unpaid expenses.** Some expenses accumulate (or *accrue*) in the current period but are not *paid* until a future period. These accrued expenses are recorded as part of the adjusting process at the end of each period by debiting the appropriate expense (e.g., Salary Expense, Interest Expense, or Income Taxes Expense), and by crediting a liability account (e.g., Salaries Payable, Interest Payable, or Income Taxes Payable). In future periods, as cash is disbursed in settlement of these liabilities, the appropriate liability account is debited and Cash is credited. ***Note:*** Recording the accrued expense in the current period is the adjusting entry. Recording the disbursement of cash in a future period is *not* considered an adjusting entry.

LO6 **Prepare adjusting entries to accrue uncollected revenue.** Some revenues are earned (or *accrued*) in the current period but are not *collected* until a future period. These revenues are normally recorded as part of the adjusting process at the end of each period by debiting an asset account called Accounts Receivable, and by crediting the appropriate revenue account. In future periods, as cash is collected in settlement of outstanding receivables, Cash is debited and Accounts Receivable is credited. ***Note:*** Recording the accrued revenue in the current period is the adjusting entry. Recording the receipt of cash in a future period is *not* considered an adjusting entry.

LO7 **Explain how the principles of *realization* and *matching* relate to adjusting entries.** Adjusting entries are the *tools* by which accountants apply the realization and matching principles. Through these entries, revenues are recognized as they are *earned*, and expenses are recognized as resources are *used* or consumed in producing the related revenue.

LO8 **Explain the concept of *materiality*.** The concept of materiality allows accountants to use estimated amounts and to ignore certain accounting principles if these actions will not have a material effect on the financial statements. A material effect is one that might reasonably be expected to influence the decisions made by the users of financial statements. Thus, accountants may account for immaterial items and events in the easiest and most convenient manner.

LO9 **Prepare an adjusted trial balance and describe its purpose.** The adjusted trial balance reports all of the balances in the general ledger *after* the end-of-period adjusting entries have been made and posted. Generally, all of a company's balance sheet accounts are listed, followed by the statement of retained earnings accounts and, finally, the income statement accounts. The amounts shown in the adjusted trial balance are carried forward directly to the financial statements. The adjusted trial balance is *not* considered one of the four general-purpose financial statements introduced in Chapter 2. Rather, it is simply a *schedule* (or tool) used in preparing the financial statements.

Key Terms Introduced or Emphasized in Chapter 4

accrue (p. 152) To grow or accumulate over time; for example, interest expense.

Accumulated Depreciation (p. 150) A contra-asset account shown as a deduction from the related asset account in the balance sheet. Depreciation taken throughout the useful life of an asset is accumulated in this account.

adjusted trial balance (p. 160) A schedule indicating the balances in ledger accounts *after* end-of-period adjusting entries have been posted. The amounts shown in the adjusted trial balance are carried directly into financial statements.

adjusting entries (p. 142) Entries made at the end of the accounting period for the purpose of recognizing revenue and expenses that are not properly measured as a result of journalizing transactions as they occur.

book value (p. 150) The net amount at which an asset appears in financial statements. For depreciable assets, book value represents cost minus accumulated depreciation. Also called *carrying value.*

contra-asset account (p. 150) An account with a credit balance that is offset against or deducted from an asset account to produce the proper balance sheet amount for the asset.

depreciable assets (p. 148) Physical objects with a limited life. The cost of these assets is gradually recognized as depreciation expense.

depreciation (p. 148) The systematic allocation of the cost of an asset to expense during the periods of its useful life.

immaterial (p. 157) Something of little or no consequence. Immaterial items may be accounted for in the most convenient manner, without regard to other theoretical concepts.

matching (principle) (p. 156) The accounting principle of offsetting revenue with the expenses incurred in producing that revenue. Requires recognition of expenses in the periods that the goods and services are used in the effort to produce revenue.

materiality (p. 157) The relative importance of an item or amount. Items significant enough to influence decisions are said to be *material.* Items lacking this importance are considered *immaterial.* The accounting treatment accorded to immaterial items may be guided by convenience rather than by theoretical principles.

prepaid expenses (p. 146) Assets representing advance payment of the expenses of future accounting periods. As time passes, adjusting entries are made to transfer the related costs from the asset account to an expense account.

realization (principle) (p. 156) The accounting principle that governs the timing of revenue recognition. Basically, the principle indicates that revenue should be recognized in the period in which it is earned.

straight-line method of depreciation (p. 149) The widely used approach of recognizing an equal amount of depreciation expense in each period of a depreciable asset's useful life.

unearned revenue (p. 151) An obligation to deliver goods or render services in the future, stemming from the receipt of advance payment.

useful life (p. 148) The period of time that a depreciable asset is expected to be useful to the business. This is the period over which the cost of the asset is allocated to depreciation expense.

Demonstration Problem

Internet Consulting Service, Inc., adjusts its accounts every month. On the following page is the company's year-end *unadjusted* trial balance dated December 31, 2007. (Bear in mind that adjusting entries already have been made for the first 11 months of 2007, but have *not* been made for December.)

Other Data

1. On December 1, the company signed a new rental agreement and paid three months' rent in advance at a rate of $2,100 per month. This advance payment was debited to the Prepaid Office Rent account.
2. Dues and subscriptions expiring during December amounted to $50.
3. An estimate of supplies on hand was made at December 31; the estimated cost of the unused supplies was $450.
4. The useful life of the equipment has been estimated at five years (60 months) from date of acquisition.
5. Accrued interest on notes payable amounted to $100 at year-end. (Set up accounts for Interest Expense and for Interest Payable.)
6. Consulting services valued at $2,850 were rendered during December to clients who had made payment in advance.

INTERNET CONSULTING SERVICE, INC. Unadjusted Trial Balance December 31, 2007		
Cash	$ 49,100	
Consulting fees receivable	23,400	
Prepaid office rent	6,300	
Prepaid dues and subscriptions	300	
Supplies	600	
Equipment	36,000	
Accumulated depreciation: equipment		$ 10,200
Notes payable		5,000
Income taxes payable		12,000
Unearned consulting fees		5,950
Capital stock		30,000
Retained earnings		32,700
Dividends	60,000	
Consulting fees earned		257,180
Salaries expense	88,820	
Telephone expense	2,550	
Rent expense	22,000	
Income taxes expense	51,000	
Dues and subscriptions expense	560	
Supplies expense	1,600	
Depreciation expense: equipment	6,600	
Miscellaneous expenses	4,200	
	$353,030	$353,030

7. It is the custom of the firm to bill clients only when consulting work is completed or, in the case of prolonged engagements, at monthly intervals. At December 31, consulting services valued at $11,000 had been rendered to clients but not yet billed. No advance payments had been received from these clients.
8. Salaries earned by employees but not paid as of December 31 amount to $1,700.
9. Income taxes expense for the year is estimated at $56,000. Of this amount, $51,000 has been recognized as expense in prior months, and $39,000 has been paid to tax authorities. The company plans to pay the $17,000 remainder of its income tax liability on January 15.

Instructions

a. Prepare the necessary adjusting journal entries on December 31, 2007.

b. Determine the amounts to be reported in the company's year-end adjusted trial balance for each of the following accounts:

Consulting Fees Earned	Dues and Subscriptions Expense
Salaries Expense	Depreciation Expense: Equipment
Telephone Expense	Miscellaneous Expenses
Rent Expense	Interest Expense
Supplies Expense	Income Taxes Expense

c. Determine the company's net income for the year ended December 31, 2007. (Hint: Use the amounts determined in part **b** above.)

Solution to the Demonstration Problem

a.

INTERNET CONSULTING SERVICE, INC.
General Journal
December 31, 2007

Date	Account Titles and Explanation	Debit	Credit
Dec. 31 2007			
1.	Rent Expense	2,100	
	Prepaid Office Rent		2,100
	Rent expense for December.		
2.	Dues and Subscriptions Expense	50	
	Prepaid Dues and Subscriptions		50
	Dues and subscriptions expense for December.		
3.	Supplies Expense	150	
	Supplies		150
	Supplies used during December.		
4.	Depreciation Expense: Equipment	600	
	Accumulated Depreciation: Equipment		600
	Depreciation expense for December ($36,000 ÷ 60 mos.).		
5.	Interest Expense	100	
	Interest Payable		100
	Interest accrued on notes payable in December.		
6.	Unearned Consulting Fees	2,850	
	Consulting Fees Earned		2,850
	Consulting services performed for clients who paid in advance.		
7.	Consulting Fees Receivable	11,000	
	Consulting Fees Earned		11,000
	Consulting services performed in December for which billings have not been made nor payments received.		
8.	Salaries Expense	1,700	
	Salaries Payable		1,700
	Salaries accrued in December but not yet paid.		
9.	Income Taxes Expense	5,000	
	Income Taxes Payable		5,000
	Estimated income taxes accrued on income in December.		

b.

INTERNET CONSULTING SERVICE, INC.
Adjusted Trial Balance
December 31, 2007

	Unadjusted Trial Balance Amount	+	Adjustment	=	Adjusted Trial Balance Amount
Consulting Fees Earned	$257,180		(6) $ 2,850		
			(7) $11,000		$271,030
Salaries Expense	$ 88,820		(8) $ 1,700		$ 90,520
Telephone Expense	$ 2,550		None		$ 2,550
Rent Expense	$ 22,000		(1) $ 2,100		$ 24,100
Supplies Expense	$ 1,600		(3) $ 150		$ 1,750
Dues and Subscriptions Expense	$ 560		(2) $ 50		$ 610
Depreciation Expense: Equipment	$ 6,600		(4) $ 600		$ 7,200
Miscellaneous Expenses	$ 4,200		None		$ 4,200
Interest Expense	None		(5) $ 100		$ 100
Income Taxes Expense	$ 51,000		(9) $ 5,000		$ 56,000

c. Using the figures computed in part **b**, net income for the year is computed as follows:

Consulting Fees Earned		$271,030
Salaries Expense	$90,520	
Telephone Expense	2,550	
Rent Expense	24,100	
Supplies Expense	1,750	
Dues and Subscriptions Expense	610	
Depreciation Expense: Equipment	7,200	
Miscellaneous Expenses	4,200	
Interest Expense	100	
Income Taxes Expense	56,000	(187,030)
Net Income		$ 84,000

Self-Test Questions

The answers to these questions appear on page 191.

1. The purpose of adjusting entries is to:
   a. Adjust the Retained Earnings account for the revenue, expense, and dividends recorded during the accounting period.
   b. Adjust daily the balances in asset, liability, revenue, and expense accounts for the effects of business transactions.
   c. Apply the realization principle and the matching principle to transactions affecting two or more accounting periods.
   d. Prepare revenue and expense accounts for recording the transactions of the next accounting period.

2. Before month-end adjustments are made, the January 31 trial balance of Rover Excursions contains revenue of $27,900 and expenses of $17,340. Adjustments are necessary for the following items:

   Portion of prepaid rent applicable to January, $2,700
   Depreciation for January, $1,440
   Portion of fees collected in advance earned in January, $3,300
   Fees earned in January, not yet billed to customers, $1,950

Net income for January is:

a. $10,560 c. $7,770

b. $17,070 d. Some other amount

3. The CPA firm auditing Mason Street Recording Studios found that total stockholders' equity was understated and liabilities were overstated. Which of the following errors could have been the cause?
   a. Making the adjustment entry for depreciation expense twice.
   b. Failure to record interest accrued on a note payable.
   c. Failure to make the adjusting entry to record revenue that had been earned but not yet billed to clients.
   d. Failure to record the earned portion of fees received in advance.

4. Assume Fisher Corporation usually earns taxable income, but sustains a *loss* in the current period. The entry to record income taxes expense in the current period will most likely (indicate all correct answers):
   a. Increase the amount of that loss.
   b. Include a credit to the Income Taxes Expense account.
   c. Be an adjusting entry, rather than an entry to record a transaction completed during the period.
   d. Include a credit to Income Taxes Payable.

5. The concept of *materiality* (indicate all correct answers):
   a. Requires that financial statements be accurate to the nearest dollar, but need not show cents.
   b. Is based upon what users of financial statements are thought to consider important.
   c. Permits accountants to ignore generally accepted accounting principles in certain situations.
   d. Permits accountants to use the easiest and most convenient means of accounting for events that are *immaterial*.

ASSIGNMENT MATERIAL Discussion Questions

1. What is the purpose of making adjusting entries? Your answer should relate adjusting entries to the goals of accrual accounting.
2. Do all transactions involving revenue or expenses require adjusting entries at the end of the accounting period? If not, what is the distinguishing characteristic of those transactions that do require adjusting entries?
3. Do adjusting entries affect income statement accounts, balance sheet accounts, or both? Explain.
4. Why does the recording of adjusting entries require a better understanding of the concepts of accrual accounting than does the recording of routine revenue and expense transactions occurring throughout the period?
5. Why does the purchase of a one-year insurance policy four months ago give rise to insurance expense in the current month?
6. If services have been rendered to customers during the current accounting period but no revenue has been recorded and no bill has been sent to the customers, why is an adjusting entry needed? What types of accounts should be debited and credited by this entry?
7. What is meant by the term *unearned revenue*? Where should an unearned revenue account appear in the financial statements? As the work is done, what happens to the balance of an unearned revenue account?
8. The weekly payroll for employees of Ryan Company, who work a five-day week, amounts to $20,000. All employees are paid up-to-date at the close of business each Friday. If December 31 falls on Thursday, what year-end adjusting entry is needed?
9. At year-end the adjusting entry to reduce the Unexpired Insurance account by the amount of insurance premium applicable to the current period was accidentally omitted. Which items in the income statement will be in error? Will these items be overstated or understated? Which items in the balance sheet will be in error? Will they be overstated or understated?
10. Briefly explain the concept of *materiality*. If an item is not material, how is the item treated for financial reporting purposes?
11. Assets are defined as economic resources owned by a business and expected to benefit future business operations. By this definition, the gasoline in the tank of a business automobile, unused printer cartridges, and even ballpoint pens are actually assets. Why, then, are purchases of such items routinely charged directly to expense?
12. Discuss the realization principle and how it is applied in the recognition of revenue. Does the receipt of cash for customers necessarily coincide with the recognition of revenue? Explain.
13. Discuss the matching principle and how it is applied in the recognition of expenses. Does the payment of cash necessarily coincide with the recognition of an expense? Explain.
14. Would a $1,000 expenditure be considered material to all businesses? Explain.
15. What happens to the income taxes expense of an *unprofitable* company?
16. List various accounts in the balance sheet that represent *deferred expenses*.
17. How is *deferred revenue* reported in the balance sheet?
18. How do accrued but unpaid expenses affect the balance sheet?
19. How does accrued but uncollected revenue affect the balance sheet?
20. Explain how **Carnival Corporation** accounts for customer deposits as passengers purchase cruise tickets in advance.

Brief Exercises

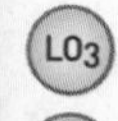

BRIEF EXERCISE 4.1
Prepaid Expenses and Unearned Revenue

On November 1, Able Corporation purchased a six-month insurance policy from The Baylor Agency for $3,000.

a. Prepare the necessary adjusting entry for Able Corporation on November 30, assuming it recorded the November 1 expenditure as Unexpired Insurance.

b. Prepare the necessary adjusting entry for The Baylor Agency on November 30, assuming it recorded Able's payment as Unearned Insurance Premiums.

BRIEF EXERCISE 4.2
Prepaid Expenses and Unearned Revenue

On February 1, Watson Storage agreed to rent Hillbourne Manufacturing warehouse space for $175 per month. Hillbourne Manufacturing paid the first three months' rent in advance.

a. Prepare the necessary adjusting entry for Hillbourne Manufacturing on February 28, assuming it recorded the expenditure on February 1 as Prepaid Rent.

b. Prepare the necessary adjusting entry for Watson Storage on February 28, assuming it recorded Hillbourne Manufacturing's payment as Unearned Rent Revenue.

BRIEF EXERCISE 4.3
Accounting for Supplies

On March 1, Dillmore Corporation had office supplies on hand of $900. During the month, Dillmore purchased additional supplies costing $600. Approximately $400 of unused office supplies remain on hand at the end of the month.

Prepare the necessary adjusting entry on March 31 to account for office supplies.

BRIEF EXERCISE 4.4
Accounting for Depreciation

On January 2, 2002, Hagen Corporation purchased equipment costing $72,000. Hagen performs adjusting entries monthly.

a. Record this equipment's depreciation expense on December 31, 2007, assuming its estimated life was eight years on January 2, 2002.

b. Determine the amount of the equipment's accumulated depreciation reported in the balance sheet dated December 31, 2007.

BRIEF EXERCISE 4.5
Accruing Uncollected Revenue

Marvin's Tax Service had earned—but not yet recorded—the following client service revenue at the end of the current accounting period:

Account Number	Billable Hours	Hourly Billing Rate
Account #4067	10	$85
Account #3940	14	$75
Account #1852	16	$90

Prepare the necessary adjusting entry to record Marvin's unbilled client service revenue.

BRIEF EXERCISE 4.6
Unearned Revenue

Jasper's unadjusted trial balance reports Unearned Client Revenue of $3,200 and Client Revenue Earned of $29,000. An examination of client records reveals that $2,800 of previously unearned revenue has now been earned.

a. Prepare the necessary adjusting entry pertaining to these accounts.

b. At what amount will Client Revenue Earned be reported in Jasper's income statement?

LO5

BRIEF EXERCISE 4.7
Accruing Unpaid Salaries

Milford Corporation pays its employees on the fifteenth of each month. Accrued, but unpaid, salaries on December 31, 2007, totaled $175,000. Salaries earned by Milford's employees from January 1 through January 15, 2008, totaled $180,000.

a. Prepare the necessary adjusting entry for salaries expense on December 31, 2007.

b. Record the company's payment of salaries on January 15, 2008.

LO5

BRIEF EXERCISE 4.8
Accruing Unpaid Interest

Norbert Corporation borrowed $24,000 on December 1, 2007, by issuing a two-month, 8 percent note payable to Service One Credit Union. The entire amount of the loan, plus interest, is due February 1, 2008.

a. Prepare the necessary adjusting entry for interest expense on December 31, 2007.

b. Record the repayment of the loan plus interest on February 1, 2008.

BRIEF EXERCISE 4.9
Accruing Unpaid Income Taxes

Normington's unadjusted trial balance dated December 31, 2007, reports Income Taxes Expense of $57,200, and Income Taxes Payable of $14,300. The company's accountant estimates that income taxes expense for the *entire year* ended December 31, 2007, is $62,800.

a. Prepare the necessary adjusting entry for income taxes expense on December 31, 2007.

b. Determine the amount of income taxes expense reported in the balance sheet dated December 31, 2007.

BRIEF EXERCISE 4.10
Concept of Materiality

The concept of materiality is an underlying principle of financial reporting.

a. Briefly explain the concept of materiality.

b. Is $2,500 a "material" dollar amount? Explain.

c. Describe two ways in which the concept of materiality may save accountants' time and effort in making adjusting entries.

Exercises

through

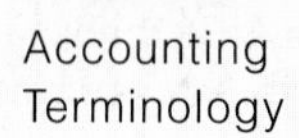

EXERCISE 4.1
Accounting Terminology

Listed below are nine technical accounting terms used in this chapter:

Unrecorded revenue	Adjusting entries	Accrued expenses
Book value	Matching principle	Accumulated depreciation
Unearned revenue	Materiality	Prepaid expenses

Each of the following statements may (or may not) describe one of these technical terms. For each statement, indicate the accounting term described, or answer "None" if the statement does not correctly describe any of the terms.

a. The net amount at which an asset is carried in the accounting records as distinguished from its market value.

b. An accounting concept that may justify departure from other accounting principles for purposes of convenience and economy.

c. The offsetting of revenue with expenses incurred in generating that revenue.

d. Revenue earned during the current accounting period but not yet recorded or billed, which requires an adjusting entry at the end of the period.

e. Entries made at the end of the period to achieve the goals of accrual accounting by recording revenue when it is earned and by recording expenses when the related goods and services are used.

f. A type of account credited when customers pay in advance for services to be rendered in the future.

g. A balance sheet category used for reporting advance payments of such items as insurance, rent, and office supplies.

h. An expense representing the systematic allocation of an asset's cost over its useful life.

through

EXERCISE 4.2
Effects of Adjusting Entries

Security Service Company adjusts its accounts at the end of the month. On November 30, adjusting entries are prepared to record:

a. Depreciation expense for November.

b. Interest expense that has accrued during November.

c. Revenue earned during November that has not yet been billed to customers.

d. Salaries, payable to company employees, that have accrued since the last payday in November.

e. The portion of the company's prepaid insurance that has expired during November.

f. Earning a portion of the amount collected in advance from a customer, Harbor Restaurant.

Indicate the effect of each of these adjusting entries on the major elements of the company's income statement and balance sheet—that is, on revenue, expenses, net income, assets, liabilities, and owners' equity. Organize your answer in tabular form, using the column headings shown and the symbols **I** for increase, **D** for decrease, and **NE** for no effect. The answer for adjusting entry **a** is provided as an example.

Adjusting Entry	Revenue	− Expenses	= Net Income	Assets	= Liabilities	+ Owners' Equity
	Income Statement			**Balance Sheet**		
a	NE	I	D	D	NE	D

EXERCISE 4.3
LO1 through LO7
Preparing Adjusting Entries to Convert an Asset to an Expense and to Convert a Liability to Revenue

The Golden Goals, a professional soccer team, prepares financial statements on a monthly basis. The soccer season begins in May, but in April the team engaged in the following transactions:

1. Paid $1,200,000 to the municipal stadium as advance rent for use of the facilities for the five-month period from May 1 through September 30. This payment was initially recorded as Prepaid Rent.
2. Collected $4,500,000 cash from the sale of season tickets for the team's home games. The entire amount was initially recorded as Unearned Ticket Revenue. During the month of May, the Golden Goals played several home games at which $148,800 of the season tickets sold in April were used by fans.

Prepare the two adjusting entries required on May 31.

EXERCISE 4.4
LO1 through LO7
Preparing Adjusting Entries to Convert an Asset to an Expense and to Convert a Liability to Revenue

Carnival Corporation is the world's largest cruise line company. Its printing costs for brochures are initially recorded as Prepaid Advertising and are later charged to Advertising Expense when they are mailed. Passenger deposits for upcoming cruises are considered unearned revenue and are recorded as Customer Deposits as cash is received. Deposited amounts are later converted to Cruise Revenue as voyages are completed.

a. Where in its financial statements does Carnival Corporation report Prepaid Advertising? Where in its financial statements does it report Customer Deposits?
b. Prepare the adjusting entry necessary when brochures costing $18 million are mailed.
c. In its most recent annual report, Carnival Corporation reported Customer Deposits in excess of $2 billion. Prepare the adjusting entry necessary in the following year as $90 million of this amount is earned.
d. Consider the entire adjusting process at Carnival Corporation. Which adjusting entry do you think results in the most significant expense reported in the company's income statement?

EXERCISE 4.5
LO1 through LO7
Preparing Adjusting Entries to Accrue Revenue and Expenses for Which No Cash Has Been Received

The geological consulting firm of Gilbert, Marsh, & Kester prepares adjusting entries on a monthly basis. Among the items requiring adjustment on December 31, 2007, are the following:

1. The company has outstanding a $50,000, 9 percent, two-year note payable issued on July 1, 2006. Payment of the $50,000 note, *plus* all accrued interest for the two-year loan period, is due in full on June 30, 2008.
2. The firm is providing consulting services to Texas Oil Company at an agreed-upon rate of $1,000 per day. At December 31, 10 days of unbilled consulting services have been provided.

a. Prepare the two adjusting entries required on December 31 to record the accrued interest expense and the accrued consulting revenue earned.
b. Assume that the $50,000 note payable plus all accrued interest are paid in full on June 30, 2008. What portion of the total interest expense associated with this note will be reported in the firm's *2008* income statement?
c. Assume that on January 30, 2008, Gilbert, Marsh, & Kester receive $25,000 from Texas Oil Company in full payment of the consulting services provided in December and January. What portion of this amount constitutes revenue earned in *January*?

EXERCISE 4.6
LO1 LO2 LO4
Deferred Revenue

When American Airlines sells tickets for future flights, it debits Cash and credits an account entitled Air Traffic Liability (as opposed to crediting Passenger Revenue Earned). This account, reported recently at $3 billion, is among the largest liabilities appearing in the company's balance sheet.

a. Explain why this liability is often referred to as a deferred revenue account.
b. What activity normally *reduces* this liability? Can you think of any *other* transaction that would also reduce this account?
c. Assume that, in a recent flight, passengers of the airline used tickets that they had purchased in advance for $200,000. Record the entry American Airlines would make upon completion of this flight.

through

EXERCISE 4.7
Preparing Various Adjusting Entries

Sweeney & Associates, a large marketing firm, adjusts its accounts at the end of each month. The following information is available: -

1. A bank loan had been obtained on December 1. Accrued interest on the loan at December 31 amounts to $1,200. No interest expense has yet been recorded.
2. Depreciation of the firm's office building is based on an estimated life of 25 years. The building was purchased in 2003 for $330,000.
3. Accrued, but unbilled, revenue during December amounts to $64,000.
4. On March 1, the firm paid $1,800 to renew a 12-month insurance policy. The entire amount was recorded as Prepaid Insurance.
5. The firm received $14,000 from King Biscuit Company in advance of developing a six-month marketing campaign. The entire amount was initially recorded as Unearned Revenue. At December 31, $3,500 had actually been *earned* by the firm.
6. The company's policy is to pay its employees every Friday. Since December 31 fell on a Wednesday, there was an accrued liability for salaries amounting to $2,400.

a. Record the necessary adjusting journal entries on December 31, 2007.

b. By how much did Sweeney & Associates's net income increase or decrease as a result of the adjusting entries performed in part **a**? (Ignore income taxes.)

LO5

EXERCISE 4.8
Notes Payable and Interest

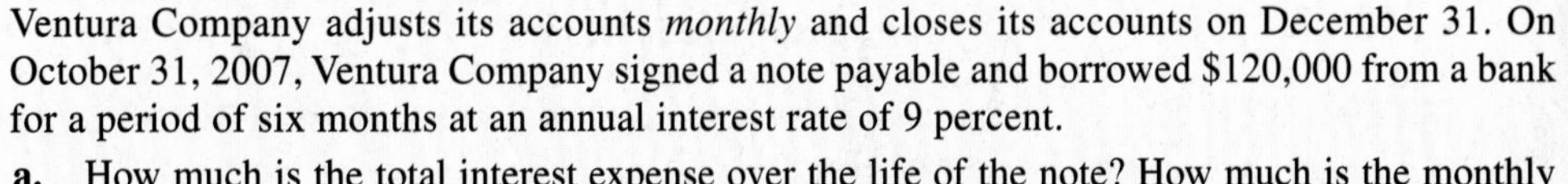

Ventura Company adjusts its accounts *monthly* and closes its accounts on December 31. On October 31, 2007, Ventura Company signed a note payable and borrowed $120,000 from a bank for a period of six months at an annual interest rate of 9 percent.

a. How much is the total interest expense over the life of the note? How much is the monthly interest expense? (Assume equal amounts of interest expense each month.)

b. In the company's annual balance sheet at December 31, 2007, what is the amount of the liability to the bank?

c. Prepare the journal entry to record issuance of the note payable on October 31, 2007.

d. Prepare the adjusting entry to accrue interest on the note at December 31, 2007.

e. Assume the company prepared a balance sheet at March 31, 2008. State the amount of the liability to the bank at this date.

through
LO7
LO9

EXERCISE 4.9
Relationship of Adjusting Entries to Business Transactions

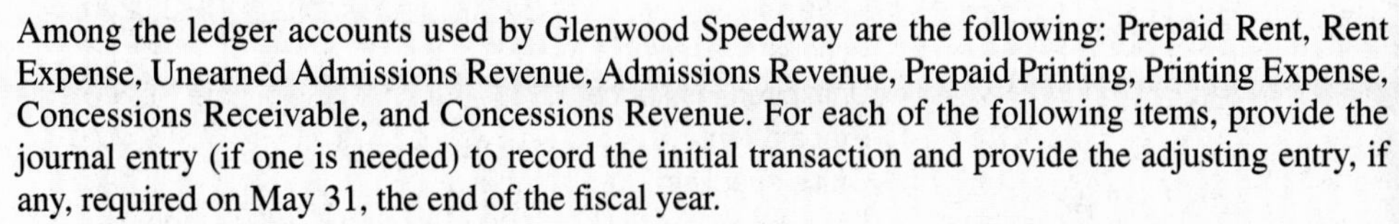

Among the ledger accounts used by Glenwood Speedway are the following: Prepaid Rent, Rent Expense, Unearned Admissions Revenue, Admissions Revenue, Prepaid Printing, Printing Expense, Concessions Receivable, and Concessions Revenue. For each of the following items, provide the journal entry (if one is needed) to record the initial transaction and provide the adjusting entry, if any, required on May 31, the end of the fiscal year.

a. On May 1, borrowed $300,000 cash from National Bank by issuing a 12 percent note payable due in three months.

b. On May 1, paid rent for six months beginning May 1 at $30,000 per month.

c. On May 2, sold season tickets for a total of $910,000 cash. The season includes 70 racing days: 20 in May, 25 in June, and 25 in July.

d. On May 4, an agreement was reached with Snack-Bars, Inc., allowing that company to sell refreshments at the track in return for 10 percent of the gross receipts from refreshment sales.

LO7

EXERCISE 4.10
Adjusting Entries and the Balance Sheet

The following information was reported in a recent balance sheet issued by Microsoft Corporation:

1. The book value of property and equipment is listed at $2.326 billion (net of depreciation). Related notes to the financial statements reveal that accumulated depreciation on property and equipment totals $4.029 billion.
2. Accrued compensation of $1.339 billion is listed as a liability.
3. Short-term unearned revenue is reported at $6.514 billion, whereas long-term unearned revenue is reported at $1.663 billion. The short-term figure will be converted to revenue within a year. The long-term figure will be converted to revenue over several years. Related notes to the financial statements reveal that the company engages in multiyear leasing of its software products.

a. Determine the original historical cost of the property and equipment reported in Microsoft Corporation's balance sheet.

b. Four types of adjusting entries are illustrated in Exhibit 4–1 (page 144). Explain which type of adjusting entry resulted in the company's accrued compensation figure.

c. Explain why Microsoft Corporation reports unearned revenue in its balance sheet. Why might the company report short-term unearned revenue separately from long-term unearned revenue?

EXERCISE 4.11
Reporting of Unearned Revenue

LO1, LO4, LO7

Listed below are seven corporations that receive cash from customers prior to earning revenue:

America West Corporation (airline)
The New York Times Company (newspaper)
Carnival Corporation (cruise company)
Devry, Inc. (for-profit technical college)
Clear Channel Communications, Inc. (radio broadcasting)
AFLAC Incorporated (health insurance)
Bally Total Fitness Corporation (fitness club)

a. Listed below are the accounts used by these corporations to report unearned revenue:

Deferred Advertising Income	Unearned Premiums
Air Traffic Liability	Unexpired Subscriptions
Deferred Member Revenues	Deferred Tuition Revenue
Customer Deposits	

Match each corporation with the account title it uses to report unearned revenue.

b. Apply the *realization* principle to explain when each of these corporations converts unearned revenue to earned revenue.

EXERCISE 4.12
Preparing Adjusting Entries from a Trial Balance

LO1 through LO7, LO9

The *unadjusted* and *adjusted* trial balances for Tinker Corporation on December 31, 2007, are shown below:

TINKER CORPORATION
Trial Balances
December 31, 2007

	Unadjusted		Adjusted	
	Debit	**Credit**	**Debit**	**Credit**
Cash	$ 35,200		$ 35,200	
Accounts receivable	29,120		34,120	
Unexpired insurance	1,200		600	
Prepaid rent	5,400		3,600	
Office supplies	680		380	
Equipment	60,000		60,000	
Accumulated depreciation: equipment		$ 49,000		$ 50,000
Accounts payable		900		900
Notes payable		5,000		5,000
Interest payable		200		250
Salaries payable		—		2,100
Income taxes payable		1,570		2,170
Unearned revenue		6,800		3,800
Capital stock		25,000		25,000
Retained earnings		30,000		30,000
Fees earned		91,530		99,530
Advertising expense	1,500		1,500	
Insurance expense	6,600		7,200	
Rent expense	19,800		21,600	
Office supplies expense	1,200		1,500	
Repairs expense	4,800		4,800	
Depreciation expense: equipment	11,000		12,000	
Salaries expense	26,300		28,400	
Interest expense	200		250	
Income taxes expense	7,000		7,600	
	$210,000	$210,000	$218,750	$218,750

Journalize the nine adjusting entries that the company made on December 31, 2007.

through

EXERCISE 4.13
Effects of Adjusting Entries

Four types of adjusting entries were identified in this chapter:

Type I Converting Assets to Expenses
Type II Converting Liabilities to Revenue
Type III Accruing Unpaid Expenses
Type IV Accruing Uncollected Revenue

Complete the following table by indicating the effect of each adjusting entry type on the major elements of the income statement and balance sheet. Use the symbols **I** for increase, **D** for decrease, and **NE** for no effect.

	Income Statement			Balance Sheet		
Adjustment Type	**Revenue**	**Expenses**	**Net Income**	**Assets**	**Liabilities**	**Owners' Equity**
Type I						
Type II						
Type III						
Type IV						

through

EXERCISE 4.14
Accounting Principles

For each of the situations described below, indicate the underlying accounting principle that is being *violated*. Choose from the following principles:

Matching
Materiality
Cost
Realization
Objectivity

If you do not believe that the practice violates any of these principles, answer "None" and explain.

a. The bookkeeper of a large metropolitan auto dealership depreciates the $7.20 cost of metal wastebaskets over a period of 10 years.

b. A small commuter airline recognizes no depreciation expense on its aircraft because the planes are maintained in "as good as new" condition.

c. Palm Beach Hotel recognizes room rental revenue on the date that a reservation is received. For the winter season, many guests make reservations as much as a year in advance.

EXERCISE 4.15
Using the Financial Statements of Home Depot, Inc.

The financial statements of Home Depot, Inc., appear in Appendix A at the end of this textbook. Examine the company's consolidated balance sheet and identify specific accounts that may have required adjusting entries at the end of the year.

Problem Set A

through

PROBLEM 4.1A
Preparing Adjusting Entries

Florida Palms Country Club adjusts its accounts *monthly*. Club members pay their annual dues in advance by January 4. The entire amount is initially credited to Unearned Membership Dues. At the end of each month, an appropriate portion of this amount is credited to Membership Dues Earned. Guests of the club normally pay green fees before being allowed on the course. The amounts collected are credited to Green Fee Revenue at the time of receipt. Certain guests, however, are billed for green fees at the end of the month. The following information is available as a source for preparing adjusting entries at December 31:

1. Salaries earned by golf course employees that have not yet been recorded or paid amount to $9,600.

2. The Tampa University golf team used Florida Palms for a tournament played on December 30 of the current year. At December 31, the $1,800 owed by the team for green fees had not yet been recorded or billed.

3. Membership dues earned in December, for collections received in January, amount to $106,000.
4. Depreciation of the country club's golf carts is based on an estimated life of 15 years. The carts had originally been purchased for $180,000. The straight-line method is used.

   (*Note:* The clubhouse building was constructed in 1925 and is fully depreciated.)
5. A 12-month bank loan in the amount of $45,000 had been obtained by the country club on November 1. Interest is computed at an annual rate of 8 percent. The entire $45,000, plus all of the interest accrued over the 12-month life of the loan, is due in full on October 31 of the upcoming year. The necessary adjusting entry was made on November 30 to record the first month of accrued interest expense. However, no adjustment has been made to record interest expense accrued in December.
6. A one-year property insurance policy had been purchased on March 1. The entire premium of $7,800 was initially recorded as Unexpired Insurance.
7. In December, Florida Palms Country Club entered into an agreement to host the annual tournament of the Florida Seniors Golf Association. The country club expects to generate green fees of $4,500 from this event.
8. Unrecorded Income Taxes Expense accrued in December amounts to $19,000. This amount will not be paid until January 15.

Instructions

a. For each of the above numbered paragraphs, prepare the necessary adjusting entry (including an explanation). If no adjusting entry is required, explain why.

b. Four types of adjusting entries are described at the beginning of the chapter. Using these descriptions, identify the type of each adjusting entry prepared in part **a** above.

c. Although Florida Palms's clubhouse building is fully depreciated, it is in excellent physical condition. Explain how this can be.

PROBLEM 4.2A
Preparing and Analyzing the Effects of Adjusting Entries

Enchanted Forest, a large campground in South Carolina, adjusts its accounts *monthly*. Most guests of the campground pay at the time they check out, and the amounts collected are credited to Camper Revenue. The following information is available as a source for preparing the adjusting entries at December 31:

1. Enchanted Forest invests some of its excess cash in certificates of deposit (CDs) with its local bank. Accrued interest revenue on its CDs at December 31 is $400. None of the interest has yet been received. (Debit Interest Receivable.)
2. A six-month bank loan in the amount of $12,000 had been obtained on September 1. Interest is to be computed at an annual rate of 8.5 percent and is payable when the loan becomes due.
3. Depreciation on buildings owned by the campground is based on a 25-year life. The original cost of the buildings was $600,000. The Accumulated Depreciation: Buildings account has a credit balance of $310,000 at December 31, prior to the adjusting entry process. The straight-line method of depreciation is used.
4. Management signed an agreement to let Boy Scout Troop 538 of Lewisburg, Pennsylvania, use the campground in June of next year. The agreement specifies that the Boy Scouts will pay a daily rate of $15 per campsite, with a clause providing a minimum total charge of $1,475.
5. Salaries earned by campground employees that have not yet been paid amount to $1,250.
6. As of December 31, Enchanted Forest has earned $2,400 of revenue from current campers who will not be billed until they check out. (Debit Camper Revenue Receivable.)
7. Several lakefront campsites are currently being leased on a long-term basis by a group of senior citizens. Six months' rent of $5,400 was collected in advance and credited to Unearned Camper Revenue on October 1 of the current year.
8. A bus to carry campers to and from town and the airport had been rented the first week of December at a daily rate of $40. At December 31, no rental payment has been made, although the campground has had use of the bus for 25 days.
9. Unrecorded Income Taxes Expense accrued in December amounts to $8,400. This amount will not be paid until January 15.

Instructions

a. For each of the above numbered paragraphs, prepare the necessary adjusting entry (including an explanation). If no adjusting entry is required, explain why.

b. Four types of adjusting entries are described at the beginning of the chapter. Using these descriptions, identify the type of each adjusting entry prepared in part **a** above.

c. Indicate the effects that each of the adjustments in part **a** will have on the following six *total amounts* in the campground's financial statements for the month of *December*. Organize your answer in tabular form, using the column headings shown below. Use the letters **I** for increase, **D** for decrease, and **NE** for no effect. Adjusting entry **1** is provided as an example.

	Income Statement			Balance Sheet		
Adjusting	Revenue −	Expenses =	Net Income	Assets =	Liabilities +	Owners' Equity
1	I	NE	I	I	NE	I

d. What is the amount of interest expense recognized for the *entire current year* on the $12,000 bank loan obtained September 1?

e. Compute the *book value* of the campground's buildings to be reported in the current year's December 31 balance sheet. (Refer to paragraph **3**.)

LO1 through LO7 LO9

PROBLEM 4.3A
Analysis of Adjusted Data

Gunflint Adventures operates an airplane service that takes fishing parties to a remote lake resort in northern Manitoba, Canada. Individuals *must* purchase their tickets at least one month in advance during the busy summer season. The company adjusts its accounts only once each month. Selected balances appearing in the company's June 30 *adjusted* trial balance appear as follows:

	Debit	Credit
Prepaid airport rent	$ 7,200	
Unexpired insurance	3,500	
Airplane	240,000	
Accumulated depreciation: airplane		$36,000
Unearned passenger revenue		90,000

Other Information

1. The airplane is being depreciated over a 20-year life with no residual value.
2. Unearned passenger revenue represents advance ticket sales for bookings in July and August at $300 per ticket.
3. Six months' airport rent had been prepaid on May 1.
4. The unexpired insurance is what remains of a 12-month policy purchased on February 1.
5. Passenger revenue earned in June totaled $75,000.

Instructions

a. Determine the following:
   1. The age of the airplane in months.
   2. The monthly airport rent expense.
   3. The amount paid for the 12-month insurance policy on February 1.

b. Prepare the adjusting entries made on June 30 involving the following accounts:
   1. Depreciation Expense: Airplane
   2. Airport Rent Expense
   3. Insurance Expense
   4. Passenger Revenue Earned

through
LO7

PROBLEM 4.4A
Preparing Adjusting Entries from a Trial Balance

Campus Theater adjusts its accounts every *month*. Below is the company's *unadjusted* trial balance dated August 31, 2007. Additional information is provided for use in preparing the company's adjusting entries for the month of August. (Bear in mind that adjusting entries *have* already been made for the first seven months of 2007, but *not* for August.)

CAMPUS THEATER Unadjusted Trial Balance August 31, 2007		
Cash	$ 20,000	
Prepaid film rental	31,200	
Land	120,000	
Building	168,000	
Accumulated depreciation: building		$ 14,000
Fixtures and equipment	36,000	
Accumulated depreciation: fixtures and equipment		12,000
Notes payable		180,000
Accounts payable		4,400
Unearned admissions revenue (YMCA)		1,000
Income taxes payable		4,740
Capital stock		40,000
Retained earnings		46,610
Dividends	15,000	
Admissions revenue		305,200
Concessions revenue		14,350
Salaries expense	68,500	
Film rental expense	94,500	
Utilities expense	9,500	
Depreciation expense: building	4,900	
Depreciation expense: fixtures and equipment	4,200	
Interest expense	10,500	
Income taxes expense	40,000	
	$622,300	$622,300

Other Data

1. Film rental expense for the month is $15,200. However, the film rental expense for several months has been paid in advance.
2. The building is being depreciated over a period of 20 years (240 months).
3. The fixtures and equipment are being depreciated over a period of five years (60 months).
4. On the first of each month, the theater pays the interest that accrued in the prior month on its note payable. At August 31, accrued interest payable on this note amounts to $1,500.
5. The theater allows the local YMCA to bring children attending summer camp to the movies on any weekday afternoon for a fixed fee of $500 per month. On June 28, the YMCA made a $1,500 advance payment covering the months of July, August, and September.
6. The theater receives a percentage of the revenue earned by Tastie Corporation, the concessionaire operating the snack bar. For snack bar sales in August, Tastie owes Campus Theater $2,250, payable on September 10. No entry has yet been made to record this revenue. (Credit Concessions Revenue.)
7. Salaries earned by employees, but not recorded or paid as of August 31, amount to $1,700. No entry has yet been made to record this liability and expense.
8. Income taxes expense for August is estimated at $4,200. This amount will be paid in the September 15 installment payment.

9. Utilities expense is recorded as monthly bills are received. No adjusting entries for utilities expense are made at month-end.

Instructions

a. For each of the numbered paragraphs, prepare the necessary adjusting entry (including an explanation).

b. Refer to the balances shown in the *unadjusted* trial balance at August 31. How many *months* of expense are included in each of the following account balances? (Remember, Campus Theater adjusts its accounts *monthly*. Thus, the accounts shown were last adjusted on July 31, 2007.)
   1. Utilities Expense
   2. Depreciation Expense
   3. Accumulated Depreciation: Building

c. Assume the theater has been operating profitably all year. Although the August 31 trial balance shows substantial income taxes *expense*, income taxes *payable* is a much smaller amount. This relationship is quite normal throughout much of the year. Explain.

LO1 through LO7 LO9

PROBLEM 4.5A
Preparing Adjusting Entries and Determining Account Balances

Terrific Temps fills temporary employment positions for local businesses. Some businesses pay in advance for services; others are billed after services have been performed. Advanced payments are credited to an account entitled Unearned Fees. Adjusting entries are performed on a *monthly* basis. An unadjusted trial balance dated December 31, 2007, follows. (Bear in mind that adjusting entries have already been made for the first 11 months of 2007, but *not* for December.)

TERRIFIC TEMPS
Unadjusted Trial Balance
December 31, 2007

Cash	$ 27,020	
Accounts receivable	59,200	
Unexpired insurance	900	
Prepaid rent	3,000	
Office supplies	600	
Equipment	60,000	
Accumulated depreciation: equipment		$ 29,500
Accounts payable		4,180
Notes payable		12,000
Interest payable		320
Unearned fees		6,000
Income taxes payable		4,000
Unearned revenue		20,000
Retained earnings		49,000
Capital stock		25,000
Dividends	3,000	
Fees earned		75,000
Travel expense	5,000	
Insurance expense	2,980	
Rent expense	9,900	
Office supplies expense	780	
Utilities expense	4,800	
Depreciation expense: equipment	5,500	
Salaries expense	30,000	
Interest expense	320	
Income taxes expense	12,000	
	$225,000	$225,000

Other Data

1. Accrued but unrecorded fees earned as of December 31, 2007, amount to $1,500.
2. Records show that $2,500 of cash receipts originally recorded as unearned fees had been earned as of December 31.
3. The company purchased a six-month insurance policy on September 1, 2007, for $1,800.
4. On December 1, 2007, the company paid its rent through February 28, 2008.
5. Office supplies on hand at December 31 amount to $400.
6. All equipment was purchased when the business first formed. The estimated life of the equipment at that time was 10 years (or 120 months).
7. On August 1, 2007, the company borrowed $12,000 by signing a six-month, 8 percent note payable. The entire note, plus six months' accrued interest, is due on February 1, 2008.
8. Accrued but unrecorded salaries at December 31 amount to $2,700.
9. Estimated income taxes expense for the *entire year* totals $15,000. Taxes are due in the first quarter of 2008.

Instructions

a. For each of the numbered paragraphs, prepare the necessary adjusting entry (including an explanation).

b. Determine that amount at which each of the following accounts will be reported in the company's 2007 income statement:

   1. Fees Earned
   2. Travel Expense
   3. Insurance Expense
   4. Rent Expense
   5. Office Supplies Expense
   6. Utilities Expense
   7. Depreciation Expense: Equipment
   8. Interest Expense
   9. Salaries Expense
   10. Income Taxes Expense

c. The unadjusted trial balance reports dividends of $3,000. As of December 31, 2007, have these dividends been paid? Explain.

through

LO9

PROBLEM 4.6A
Preparing Adjusting Entries and Determining Account Balances

Alpine Expeditions operates a mountain climbing school in Colorado. Some clients pay in advance for services; others are billed after services have been performed. Advance payments are credited to an account entitled Unearned Client Revenue. Adjusting entries are performed on a *monthly* basis. An unadjusted trial balance dated December 31, 2007, follows. (Bear in mind that adjusting entries have already been made for the first 11 months of 2007, but *not* for December.)

ALPINE EXPEDITIONS Unadjusted Trial Balance December 31, 2007		
Cash	$ 13,900	
Accounts receivable	78,000	
Unexpired insurance	18,000	
Prepaid advertising	2,200	
Climbing supplies	4,900	
Climbing equipment	57,600	
Accumulated depreciation: climbing equipment		$ 38,400
Accounts payable		1,250
Notes payable		10,000
Interest payable		150
Income taxes payable		1,200
Unearned client revenue		9,600
Capital stock		17,000
Retained earnings		62,400
Client revenue earned		188,000
Advertising expense	7,400	
Insurance expense	33,000	
Rent expense	16,500	
Climbing supplies expense	8,400	
Repairs expense	4,800	
Depreciation expense: climbing equipment	13,200	
Salaries expense	57,200	
Interest expense	150	
Income taxes expense	12,750	
	$328,000	$328,000

Other Data

1. Accrued but unrecorded fees earned as of December 31 amount to $6,400.
2. Records show that $6,600 of cash receipts originally recorded as unearned client revenue had been earned as of December 31.
3. The company purchased a 12-month insurance policy on June 1, 2007, for $36,000.
4. On December 1, 2007, the company paid $2,200 for numerous advertisements in several climbing magazines. Half of these advertisements have appeared in print as of December 31.
5. Climbing supplies on hand at December 31 amount to $2,000.
6. All climbing equipment was purchased when the business first formed. The estimated life of the equipment at that time was four years (or 48 months).
7. On October 1, 2007, the company borrowed $10,000 by signing an eight-month, 9 percent note payable. The entire note, plus eight months' accrued interest, is due on June 1, 2008.
8. Accrued but unrecorded salaries at December 31 amount to $3,100.
9. Estimated income taxes expense for the *entire year* totals $14,000. Taxes are due in the first quarter of 2008.

Instructions

a. For each of the numbered paragraphs, prepare the necessary adjusting entry (including an explanation).

b. Determine that amount at which each of the following accounts will be reported in the company's balance sheet dated December 31, 2007:

1. Cash
2. Accounts Receivable
3. Unexpired Insurance
4. Prepaid Advertising
5. Climbing Supplies
6. Climbing Equipment
7. Accumulated Depreciation: Climbing Equipment
8. Salaries Payable
9. Notes Payable
10. Interest Payable
11. Income Taxes Payable
12. Unearned Client Revenue

c. Which of the accounts listed in part **b** represent *deferred expenses*? Explain.

through

LO9

PROBLEM 4.7A
Preparing Adjusting Entries from a Trial Balance

Ken Hensley Enterprises, Inc., is a small recording studio in St. Louis. Rock bands use the studio to mix high-quality demo recordings distributed to talent agents. New clients are required to pay in advance for studio services. Bands with established credit are billed for studio services at the end of each month. Adjusting entries are performed on a *monthly* basis. An *unadjusted* trial balance dated December 31, 2007, follows. (Bear in mind that adjusting entries already have been made for the first eleven months of 2007, but *not* for December.)

KEN HENSLEY ENTERPRISES, INC.
Unadjusted Trial Balance
December 31, 2007

Cash	$ 43,170	
Accounts receivable	81,400	
Studio supplies	7,600	
Unexpired insurance	500	
Prepaid studio rent	4,000	
Recording equipment	90,000	
Accumulated depreciation: recording equipment		$ 52,500
Notes payable		16,000
Interest payable		840
Income taxes payable		3,200
Unearned studio revenue		9,600
Capital stock		80,000
Retained earnings		38,000
Studio revenue earned		107,000
Salaries expense	18,000	
Supplies expense	1,200	
Insurance expense	2,680	
Depreciation expense: recording equipment	16,500	
Studio rent expense	21,000	
Interest expense	840	
Utilities expense	2,350	
Income taxes expense	17,900	
	$307,140	$307,140

Other Data

1. Records show that $4,400 in studio revenue had not yet been billed or recorded as of December 31.
2. Studio supplies on hand at December 31 amount to $6,900.
3. On August 1, 2007, the studio purchased a six-month insurance policy for $1,500. The entire premium was initially debited to Unexpired Insurance.
4. The studio is located in a rented building. On November 1, 2007, the studio paid $6,000 rent in advance for November, December, and January. The entire amount was debited to Prepaid Studio Rent.
5. The useful life of the studio's recording equipment is estimated to be five years (or 60 months). The straight-line method of depreciation is used.
6. On May 1, 2007, the studio borrowed $16,000 by signing a 12-month, 9 percent note payable to First Federal Bank of St. Louis. The entire $16,000 plus 12 months' interest is due in full on April 30, 2008.
7. Records show that $3,600 of cash receipts originally recorded as Unearned Studio Revenue had been earned as of December 31.
8. Salaries earned by recording technicians that remain unpaid at December 31 amount to $540.
9. The studio's accountant estimates that income taxes expense for the *entire year* ended December 31, 2007, is $19,600. (Note that $17,900 of this amount has already been recorded.)

Instructions

a. For each of the above numbered paragraphs, prepare the necessary adjusting entry (including an explanation).

b. Using figures from the company's unadjusted trial balance in conjunction with the adjusting entries made in part **a**, compute net income for the year ended December 31, 2007.

c. Was the studio's monthly rent for the last 2 months of 2007 more or less than during the first 10 months of the year? Explain your answer.

d. Was the studio's monthly insurance expense for the last five months of 2007 more or less than the average monthly expense for the first seven months of the year? Explain your answer.

e. If the studio purchased all of its equipment when it first began operations, for how many months has it been in business? Explain your answer.

f. Indicate the effect of each adjusting entry prepared in part **a** on the major elements of the company's income statement and balance sheet. Organize your answer in tabular form using the column headings shown. Use the symbols **I** for increase, **D** for decrease, and **NE** for no effect. The answer for the adjusting entry number **1** is provided as an example.

	Income Statement			Balance Sheet		
Adjusting Entry	Revenue −	Expenses =	Net Income	Assets =	Liabilities +	Owners' Equity
1	I	NE	I	I	NE	I

LO1 through LO7 LO9

PROBLEM 4.8A
Understanding the Effects of Various Errors

Coyne Corporation recently hired Elaine Herrold as its new bookkeeper. Herrold was not very experienced and made six recording errors during the last accounting period. The nature of each error is described in the following table.

Instructions

Indicate the effect of the following errors on each of the financial statement elements described in the column headings in the table. Use the following symbols: **O** = overstated, **U** = understated, and **NE** = no effect.

Error	Total Revenue	Total Expenses	Net Income	Total Assets	Total Liabilities	Owners' Equity
a. Recorded a dividend as an expense reported in the income statement.						
b. Recorded the payment of an account payable as a debit to accounts payable and a credit to an expense account.						
c. Failed to record depreciation expense.						
d. Recorded the sale of capital stock as a debit to cash and a credit to retained earnings.						
e. Recorded the receipt of a customer deposit as a debit to cash and a credit to fees earned.						
f. Failed to record expired portion of an insurance policy.						
g. Failed to record accrued interest earned on an outstanding note receivable.						

Problem Set B

LO1 through LO7

PROBLEM 4.1B
Preparing Adjusting Entries

The Georgia Gun Club adjusts its accounts *monthly* and closes its accounts annually. Club members pay their annual dues in advance by January 4. The entire amount is initially credited to Unearned Membership Dues. At the end of each month, an appropriate portion of this amount is credited to Membership Dues Earned. Guests of the club normally pay their fees before being allowed to use the facilities. The amounts collected are credited to Guest Fee Revenue at the time of receipt. Certain guests, however, are billed at the end of the month. The following information is available as a source for preparing adjusting entries at December 31:

1. Salaries earned by the club's employees that have not yet been recorded or paid amount to $13,600.
2. The Georgia State Police used the club's facilities for target practice on December 30 of the current year. At December 31, the $3,200 owed by the state police for guest fees had not yet been recorded or billed.
3. Membership dues earned in December, for collections received at the beginning of the year, amount to $140,000.
4. Depreciation of the furniture and fixtures in the clubhouse is based on an estimated life of eight years. These items had originally been purchased for $120,000. The straight-line method is used. (*Note:* The clubhouse building was constructed in 1776 and is fully depreciated.)
5. A 12-month bank loan in the amount of $60,000 had been obtained by the club on October 4. Interest is computed at an annual rate of 8 percent. The entire $60,000, plus all of the interest accrued over the 12-month life of the loan, is due in full on September 30 of the upcoming year. The necessary adjusting entry was made on November 30 to record the first two months of accrued interest expense. However, no adjustment has been made to record interest expense accrued in December.
6. A one-year property insurance policy had been purchased on April 30. The entire premium of $10,800 was initially recorded as Unexpired Insurance.
7. In December, the club entered into an agreement to host the annual tournament of the Georgia Junior Rifle Association. The club expects to generate guest fees of $7,200 from this event.
8. Unrecorded Income Taxes Expense accrued in December amounts to $12,600. This amount will not be paid until January 22.

Instructions

a. For each of the above numbered paragraphs, prepare the necessary adjusting entry (including an explanation). If no adjusting entry is required, explain why.

b. Four types of adjusting entries are described at the beginning of the chapter. Using these descriptions, identify the type of each adjusting entry prepared in part **a** above.

c. Although the clubhouse building is fully depreciated, it is in excellent physical condition. Explain how this can be.

LO1 through LO6 LO9

PROBLEM 4.2B

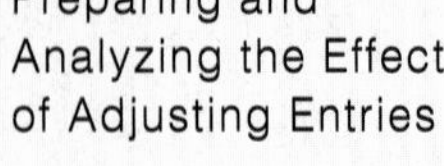

Preparing and Analyzing the Effects of Adjusting Entries

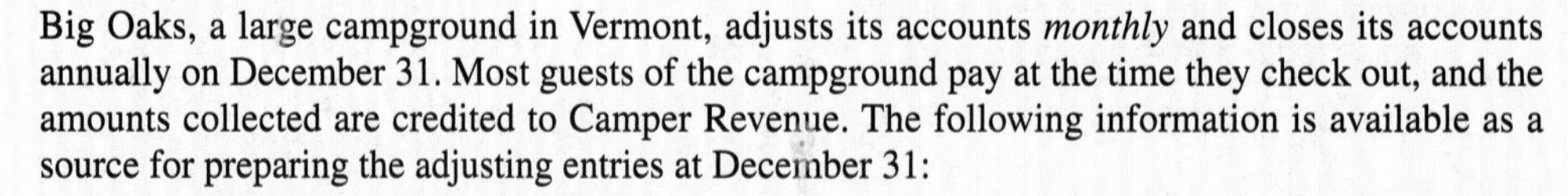

Big Oaks, a large campground in Vermont, adjusts its accounts *monthly* and closes its accounts annually on December 31. Most guests of the campground pay at the time they check out, and the amounts collected are credited to Camper Revenue. The following information is available as a source for preparing the adjusting entries at December 31:

1. Big Oaks invests some of its excess cash in certificates of deposit (CDs) with its local bank. Accrued interest revenue on its CDs at December 31 is $425. None of the interest has yet been received. (Debit Interest Receivable.)
2. An eight-month bank loan in the amount of $12,000 had been obtained on October 1. Interest is to be computed at an annual rate of 8 percent and is payable when the loan becomes due.
3. Depreciation on buildings owned by the campground is based on a 20-year life. The original cost of the buildings was $720,000. The Accumulated Depreciation: Buildings account has a credit balance of $160,000 at December 31, prior to the adjusting entry process. The straight-line method of depreciation is used.
4. Management signed an agreement to let Girl Scouts from Easton, Connecticut, use the campground in June of next year. The agreement specifies that the Girl Scouts will pay a daily rate of $15 per campsite, with a clause providing a minimum total charge of $1,200.
5. Salaries earned by campground employees that have not yet been paid amount to $1,515.

6. As of December 31, Big Oaks has earned $2,700 of revenue from current campers who will not be billed until they check out. (Debit Camper Revenue Receivable.)
7. Several lakefront campsites are currently being leased on a long-term basis by a group of senior citizens. Five months' rent of $7,500 was collected in advance and credited to Unearned Camper Revenue on November 1 of the current year.
8. A bus to carry campers to and from town and the airport had been rented the first week of December at a daily rate of $45. At December 31, no rental payment has been made, although the campground has had use of the bus for 18 days.
9. Unrecorded Income Taxes Expense accrued in December amounts to $6,600. This amount will not be paid until January 15.

Instructions

a. For each of the above numbered paragraphs, prepare the necessary adjusting entry (including an explanation). If no adjusting entry is required, explain why.

b. Four types of adjusting entries are described at the beginning of the chapter. Using these descriptions, identify the type of each adjusting entry prepared in part **a** above.

c. Indicate the effects that each of the adjustments in part **a** will have on the following six *total amounts* in the campground's financial statements for the month of *December.* Organize your answer in tabular form, using the column headings shown below. Use the letters **I** for increase, **D** for decrease, and **NE** for no effect. Adjusting entry **1** is provided as an example.

	Income Statement			Balance Sheet		
Adjusting Entry	Revenue −	Expenses =	Net Income	Assets =	Liabilities +	Owners' Equity
1	I	NE	I	I	NE	I

d. What is the amount of interest expense recognized for the *entire current year* on the $12,000 bank loan obtained October 1?

e. Compute the *book value* of the campground's buildings to be reported in the current year's December 31 balance sheet. (Refer to paragraph **3**.)

through

LO9

PROBLEM 4.3B
Analysis of Adjusted Data

River Rat, Inc., operates a ferry that takes travelers across the Wild River. The company adjusts its accounts at the end of each month. Selected account balances appearing in the April 30 *adjusted* trial balance are as follows:

	Debit	Credit
Prepaid rent	$12,000	
Unexpired insurance	2,400	
Ferry	96,000	
Accumulated depreciation: ferry		$20,000
Unearned passenger revenue		1,040

Other Data

1. The ferry is being depreciated over an eight-year estimated useful life.
2. The unearned passenger revenue represents tickets good for future rides sold to a resort hotel for $2 per ticket on April 1. During April, 160 of the tickets were used.
3. Five months' rent had been prepaid on April 1.
4. The unexpired insurance is a 12-month fire insurance policy purchased on March 1.

Instructions

a. Determine the following:
   1. The age of the ferry in months.
   2. How many $2 tickets for future rides were sold to the resort hotel on April 1.
   3. The monthly rent expense.
   4. The original cost of the 12-month fire insurance policy.

b. Prepare the adjusting entries that were made on April 30.

LO1 through LO7 LO9

PROBLEM 4.4B
Preparing Adjusting Entries from a Trial Balance

The Off-Campus Playhouse adjusts its accounts every *month.* Below is the company's *unadjusted* trial balance dated September 30, 2007. Additional information is provided for use in preparing the company's adjusting entries for the month of September. (Bear in mind that adjusting entries *have already* been made for the first eight months of 2007, but *not* for September.)

OFF-CAMPUS PLAYHOUSE
Unadjusted Trial Balance
September 30, 2007

Account	Debit	Credit
Cash	$ 8,200	
Prepaid costume rental	1,800	
Land	80,000	
Building	150,000	
Accumulated depreciation: building		$ 18,500
Fixtures and equipment	18,000	
Accumulated depreciation: fixtures and equipment		4,500
Notes payable		100,000
Accounts payable		4,700
Unearned admissions revenue (nursing homes)		600
Income taxes payable		4,700
Capital stock		10,000
Retained earnings		27,300
Dividends	9,000	
Admissions revenue		180,200
Concessions revenue		19,600
Salaries expense	57,400	
Costume rental expense	2,700	
Utilities expense	7,100	
Depreciation expense: building	4,000	
Depreciation expense: fixtures and equipment	2,400	
Interest expense	8,500	
Income taxes expense	21,000	
	$370,100	$370,100

Other Data

1. Costume rental expense for the month is $600. However, the costume rental expense for several months has been paid in advance.
2. The building is being depreciated over a period of 25 years (300 months).
3. The fixtures and equipment are being depreciated over a period of five years (60 months).
4. On the first of each month, the theater pays the interest which accrued in the prior month on its note payable. At September 30, accrued interest payable on this note amounts to $1,062.
5. The playhouse allows local nursing homes to bring seniors to the plays on any weekday performance for a fixed price of $500 per month. On August 31, the nursing home made a $1,500 advance payment covering the months of September, October, and November.
6. The theater receives a percentage of the revenue earned by Sweet Corporation, the concessionaire operating the snack bar. For snack bar sales in September, Sweet owes Off-Campus Playhouse $4,600, payable on October 14. No entry has yet been made to record this revenue. (Credit Concessions Revenue.)
7. Salaries earned by employees, but not recorded or paid as of September 30, amount to $2,200. No entry has yet been made to record this liability and expense.
8. Income taxes expense for September is estimated at $3,600. This amount will be paid in the October 15 installment payment.
9. Utilities expense is recorded as monthly bills are received. No adjusting entries for utilities expense are made at month-end.

Instructions

a. For each of the numbered paragraphs, prepare the necessary adjusting entry (including an explanation).

b. Refer to the balances shown in the *unadjusted* trial balance at September 30. How many *months* of expense are included in each of the following balances? (Remember, Off-Campus Playhouse adjusts its accounts *monthly*. Thus, the accounts shown were last adjusted on August 31, 2007.)

1. Utilities expense
2. Depreciation expense
3. Accumulated depreciation: building

c. Assume the playhouse has been operating profitably all year. Although the September 30 trial balance shows substantial income taxes *expense*, income taxes *payable* is a much smaller amount. This relationship is quite normal throughout much of the year. Explain.

LO1 through LO7 LO9

PROBLEM 4.5B
Preparing Adjusting Entries and Determining Account Balances

Marvelous Music provides music lessons to student musicians. Some students pay in advance for lessons; others are billed after lessons have been provided. Advance payments are credited to an account entitled Unearned Lesson Revenue. Adjusting entries are performed on a *monthly* basis. An unadjusted trial balance dated December 31, 2007, follows. (Bear in mind that adjusting entries have already been made for the first 11 months of 2007, but *not* for December.)

MARVELOUS MUSIC
Unadjusted Trial Balance
Decemebr 31, 2007

Cash	$ 15,800	
Accounts receivable	2,100	
Unexpired insurance	3,200	
Prepaid rent	6,000	
Sheet music supplies	450	
Music equipment	180,000	
Accumulated depreciation: music equipment		$ 72,000
Accounts payable		3,500
Notes payable		5,000
Dividends payable		1,000
Interest payable		25
Income taxes payable		3,400
Unearned lesson revenue		1,100
Capital stock		20,000
Retained earnings		56,600
Dividends	1,000	
Lesson revenue earned		154,375
Advertising expense	7,400	
Insurance expense	4,400	
Rent expense	16,500	
Sheet music supplies expense	780	
Utilities expense	5,000	
Depreciation expense: music equipment	33,000	
Salaries expense	27,500	
Interest expense	25	
Income taxes expense	13,845	
	$317,000	$317,000

Other Data

1. Accrued but unrecorded lesson revenue earned as of December 31, 2007, amounts to $3,200.
2. Records show that $800 of cash receipts originally recorded as unearned lesson revenue had been earned as of December 31.
3. The company purchased a 12-month insurance policy on August 1, 2007, for $4,800.
4. On October 1, 2007, the company paid $9,000 for rent through March 31, 2008.
5. Sheet music supplies on hand at December 31 amount to $200.
6. All music equipment was purchased when the business was first formed. Its estimated life at that time was five years (or 60 months).
7. On November 1, 2007, the company borrowed $5,000 by signing a three-month, 6 percent note payable. The entire note, plus three months' accrued interest, is due on February 1, 2008.
8. Accrued but unrecorded salaries at December 31 amount to $3,500.
9. Estimated income taxes expense for the *entire year* totals $22,000. Taxes are due in the first quarter of 2008.

Instructions

a. For each of the numbered paragraphs, prepare the necessary adjusting entry (including an explanation).

b. Determine that amount at which each of the following accounts will be reported in the company's 2007 income statement:

1. Lesson Revenue Earned
2. Advertising Expense
3. Insurance Expense
4. Rent Expense
5. Sheet Music Supplies Expense
6. Utilities Expense
7. Depreciation Expense: Music Equipment
8. Interest Expense
9. Salaries Expense
10. Income Taxes Expense

c. The unadjusted trial balance reports dividends of $1,000. As of December 31, 2007, have these dividends been paid? Explain.

LO1 through LO7 LO9

PROBLEM 4.6B

Preparing Adjusting Entries and Determining Account Balances

Mate Ease is an Internet dating service. All members pay in advance to be listed in the database. Advance payments are credited to an account entitled Unearned Member Dues. Adjusting entries are performed on a *monthly* basis. An unadjusted trial balance dated December 31, 2007, follows. (Bear in mind that adjusting entries have already been made for the first 11 months of 2007, but *not* for December.)

MATE EASE Unadjusted Trial Balance December 31, 2007		
Cash	$169,500	
Unexpired insurance	12,800	
Prepaid rent	14,600	
Office supplies	2,160	
Computer equipment	108,000	
Accumulated depreciation: computer equipment		$ 54,000
Accounts payable		4,300
Notes payable		90,000
Interest payable		6,750
Income taxes payable		7,500
Unearned member dues		36,000
Capital stock		40,000
Retained earnings		28,000
Client fees earned		508,450
Advertising expense	17,290	
Insurance expense	35,200	
Rent expense	80,300	
Office supplies expense	18,400	
Internet connection expense	24,000	
Depreciation expense: computer equipment	33,000	
Salaries expense	239,000	
Interest expense	6,750	
Income taxes expense	14,000	
	$775,000	$775,000

Other Data

1. Records show that $21,000 of cash receipts originally recorded as unearned member dues had been earned as of December 31, 2007.
2. The company purchased a six-month insurance policy on October 1, 2007, for $19,200.
3. On November 1, 2007, the company paid $21,900 for rent through January 31, 2008.
4. Office supplies on hand at December 31 amount to $440.
5. All computer equipment was purchased when the business first formed. The estimated life of the equipment at that time was three years (or 36 months).
6. On March 1, 2007, the company borrowed $90,000 by signing a 12-month, 10 percent note payable. The entire note, plus 12 months' accrued interest, is due on March 1, 2008.
7. Accrued but unrecorded salaries at December 31 amount to $10,500.
8. Estimated income taxes expense for the *entire year* totals $16,000. Taxes are due in the first quarter of 2008.

Instructions

a. For each of the numbered paragraphs, prepare the necessary adjusting entry (including an explanation).

b. Determine that amount at which each of the following accounts will be reported in the company's balance sheet dated December 31, 2007:

1. Cash
2. Unexpired Insurance
3. Prepaid Rent
4. Office Supplies
5. Computer Equipment
6. Accumulated Depreciation: Computer Equipment
7. Accounts Payable
8. Notes Payable
9. Salaries Payable
10. Interest Payable
11. Income Taxes Payable
12. Unearned Member Dues

c. Why doesn't the company immediately record advance payments from customers as *revenue*?

through

LO9

PROBLEM 4.7B
Preparing Adjusting Entries from a Trial Balance

Clint Stillmore operates a private investigating agency called Stillmore Investigations. Some clients pay in advance for services; others are billed after services have been performed. Advance payments are credited to an account entitled Unearned Retainer Fees. Adjusting entries are performed on a *monthly* basis. An *unadjusted* trial balance dated December 31, 2007, follows. (Bear in mind that adjusting entries have already been made for the first 11 months of 2007, but *not* for December.)

Other Data

1. Accrued but unrecorded client fees earned at December 31 amount to $1,500.
2. Records show that $2,500 of cash receipts originally recorded as Unearned Retainer Fees had been earned as of December 31.
3. Office supplies on hand at December 31 amount to $110.
4. The company purchased all of its office equipment when it first began business. At that time, the equipment's estimated useful life was six years (or 72 months).
5. On October 1, 2007, the company renewed its rental agreement paying $1,800 cash for six months' rent in advance.
6. On March 1 of the current year, the company paid $1,080 cash to renew its 12-month insurance policy.
7. Accrued but unrecorded salaries at December 31 amount to $1,900.
8. On June 1, 2007, the company borrowed money from the bank by signing a $9,000, 8 percent, 12-month note payable. The entire note, plus 12 months' accrued interest, is due on May 31, 2008.
9. The company's CPA estimates that income taxes expense for the *entire year* is $7,500.

STILLMORE INVESTIGATIONS
Unadjusted Trial Balance
December 31, 2007

Cash	$ 40,585	
Accounts receivable	2,000	
Office supplies	205	
Prepaid rent	1,200	
Unexpired insurance	270	
Office equipment	54,000	
Accumulated depreciation: office equipment		$ 35,250
Accounts payable		1,400
Interest payable		360
Income taxes payable		1,750
Note payable		9,000
Unearned retainer fees		3,500
Capital stock		30,000
Retained earnings		8,000
Dividends	1,000	
Client fees earned		60,000
Office supplies expense	605	
Depreciation expense: office equipment	8,250	
Rent expense	5,775	
Insurance expense	1,010	
Salaries expense	27,100	
Interest expense	360	
Income taxes expense	6,900	
Totals	$149,260	$149,260

Instructions

a. For each of the above numbered paragraphs, prepare the necessary adjusting entry (including an explanation).

b. Prepare the company's adjusted trial balance dated December 31, 2007.

c. Using figures from the adjusted trial balance prepared in **b**, compute net income for the year ended December 31, 2007.

d. How much was the company's average monthly rent expense in January through September of 2007? Explain your answer.

e. How much was the company's average monthly insurance expense in January and February of 2007? Explain your answer.

f. If the company purchased all of its office equipment when it first began operations, for how many months has it been in business? Explain your answer.

g. Indicate the effect of each adjusting entry prepared in part **a** on the major elements of the company's income statement and balance sheet. Organize your answer in tabular form using the column headings shown. Use the symbols **I** for increase, **D** for decrease, and **NE** for no effect. The answer for adjusting entry number **1** is provided as an example.

	Income Statement			Balance Sheet		
Adjusting Entry	Revenue −	Expenses =	Net Income	Assets =	Liabilities +	Owners' Equity
1	I	NE	I	I	NE	I

PROBLEM 4.8B
Understanding the Effects of Various Errors

LO1 through LO7, LO9

Stephen Corporation recently hired Tom Waters as its new bookkeeper. Waters is very inexperienced and has made six recording errors during the last accounting period. The nature of each error is described in the following table.

Instructions

Indicate the effect of the following errors on each of the financial statement elements described in the column headings in the table. Use the following symbols: **O** = overstated, **U** = understated, and **NE** = no effect.

Error	Total Revenue	Total Expenses	Net Income	Total Assets	Total Liabilities	Owners' Equity
a. Recorded a declared but unpaid dividend by debiting dividends and crediting cash.						
b. Recorded a receipt of an account receivable as a debit to cash and a credit to fees earned.						
c. Recorded depreciation expense twice.						
d. Recorded the sale of capital stock as a debit to cash and a credit to revenue.						
e. Purchased equipment and debited supplies expense and credited cash.						
f. Failed to record expired portion of prepaid advertising.						
g. Failed to record accrued and unpaid interest expense.						

Critical Thinking Cases

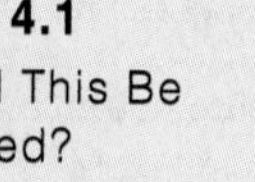

CASE 4.1
Should This Be Adjusted?

Property Management Professionals provides building management services to owners of office buildings and shopping centers. The company closes its accounts at the *end of the calendar year.* The manner in which the company has recorded several transactions occurring during 2007 is described as follows:

a. On September 1, received advance payment from a shopping center for property management services to be performed over the three-month period beginning September 1. The entire amount received was credited directly to a *revenue* account.

b. On December 1, received advance payment from the same customer described in part **a** for services to be rendered over the three-month period beginning December 1. This time, the entire amount received was credited to an *unearned* revenue account.

c. Rendered management services for many customers in December. Normal procedure is to record revenue on the date the customer is billed, which is early in the month after the services have been rendered.

d. On December 15, made full payment for a one-year insurance policy that goes into effect on January 2, 2008. The cost of the policy was debited to Unexpired Insurance.

e. Numerous purchases of equipment were debited to asset accounts, rather than to expense accounts.

f. Payroll expense is recorded when employees are paid. Payday for the last two weeks of December falls on January 2, 2008.

Instructions

For each item above, explain whether an adjusting entry is needed at *December 31, 2007*, and state the reasons for your answer. If you recommend an adjusting entry, explain the effects this entry would have on assets, liabilities, owners' equity, revenue, and expenses in the 2007 financial statements.

CASE 4.2
The Concept of Materiality

The concept of materiality is one of the most basic principles underlying financial accounting.

a. Answer the following questions:

1. Why is the materiality of a transaction or an event a matter of professional judgment?
2. What criteria should accountants consider in determining whether a transaction or an event is material?
3. Does the concept of materiality mean that financial statements are not precise, down to the last dollar? Does this concept make financial statements less useful to most users?

b. Avis Rent-a-Car purchases a large number of cars each year for its rental fleet. The cost of any individual automobile is immaterial to Avis, which is a very large corporation. Would it be acceptable for Avis to charge the purchase of automobiles for its rental fleet directly to expense, rather than to an asset account? Explain.

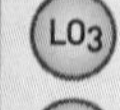

LO8

CASE 4.3
Hold the Expenses!

Slippery Slope, Inc., is a downhill ski area in northern New England. In an attempt to attract more ski enthusiasts, Slippery Slope's management recently engaged in an aggressive preseason advertising campaign in which it spent $9,000 to distribute brochures, $17,000 to air broadcast media spots, and $14,000 to run magazine and newspaper ads.

Slippery Slope is now planning to borrow money from a local bank to expand its snowmaking capabilities next season. In preparing financial statements to be used by the bank, Slippery Slope's management capitalized the entire $40,000 of advertising expenditures as Prepaid Advertising in the current year's balance sheet. It decided to defer converting this asset to advertising expense for three years, arguing that it will take a least that long to realize the full benefit of its promotional efforts. Management also contends that it does not matter how the $40,000 advertising expenditure is reported, because the amount is immaterial.

Instructions

a. Does management's decision to defer converting this $40,000 prepayment to advertising expense comply with generally accepted accounting principles? Defend your answer.

b. Could management's decision to defer reporting this expenditure as an expense for three years have any ethical implications? Explain.

LO7

***BUSINESSWEEK* CASE 4.4**

Accounting for Deferred Revenue and Interpreting Financial Statement Data

In an October 20, 2005, *BusinessWeek* article entitled, "Airfares: Avoiding the Takeoff," Sonja Ryst explains that discount carriers, such as **JetBlue** and **Southwest Airlines**, require passengers to buy tickets directly, as opposed to using a travel agent or an online service such as **Priceline.com** or **Travelocity**.

A recent **JetBlue** balance sheet reports a $240 million obligation called Air Traffic Liability. The related footnote to the financial statements reveals the following:

> Passenger ticket sales are initially recorded as a component of air traffic liability. Revenue is recognized when transportation is provided or when a ticket expires, as all of our tickets are nonrefundable.

The company's income statement uses an account called Passenger Revenue.

Instructions

a. Assume that $180 million of **JetBlue**'s advance ticket sales become earned either through use or by expiration in the current period. Record the conversion of the company's air traffic liability to passenger revenue.

b. A recent **JetBlue** income statement reports annual passenger revenue of $1.44 billion. The average balance of the Air Traffic Liability account reported in its balance sheet throughout the year was $240 million. Based on this information, approximately how many days in advance, on average, do **JetBlue**'s passengers purchase their tickets? (Hint: Consider the relationship between Passenger Revenue reported in the income statement and Air Traffic Liability reported in the balance sheet.)

through

INTERNET CASE 4.5

Identifying Accounts Requiring Adjusting Entries

Visit **Hershey's** home page at:

www.hersheys.com

From **Hershey's** home page, access its most recent annual report (see the "Investor Relations" link). Examine the company's balance sheet and identify the accounts most likely to have been involved in the end-of-year adjusting entry process.

Internet sites are time and date sensitive. It is the purpose of these exercises to have you explore the Internet. You may need to use the Yahoo! search engine **http://www.yahoo.com** *(or another favorite search engine) to find a company's current Web address.*

Answers to Self-Test Questions

1. c **2.** d, $11,670 ($27,900 − $17,340 − $2,700 − $1,440 + $3,300 + $1,950)

3. d **4.** b, c **5.** b, c, d

The Accounting Cycle

Reporting Financial Results

Learning Objectives

AFTER STUDYING THIS CHAPTER, YOU SHOULD BE ABLE TO:

LO1 Prepare an income statement, a statement of retained earnings, and a balance sheet.

LO2 Explain how the income statement and the statement of retained earnings relate to the balance sheet.

LO3 Explain the concept of *adequate disclosure*.

LO4 Explain the purposes of *closing entries*; prepare these entries.

LO5 Prepare an after-closing trial balance.

LO6 Use financial statement information to evaluate profitability and liquidity.

LO7 Explain how *interim* financial statements are prepared in a business that closes its accounts only at year-end.

*LO8 Prepare a worksheet and explain its uses.

**Supplemental Topic*, "The Worksheet."

© Rick Friedman/CORBIS

CIRCUIT CITY

Circuit City is a national retailer of televisions, video equipment, stereo systems, personal computers, cellular phones, and an array of other consumer electronic devices. The company reported net income of nearly $62 million in a recent income statement. Certain disclosures provide important information about this income figure. For example, the notes to the financial statements disclose that **Circuit City** had "spun off" its bankcard financing operation by selling it to **FleetBoston Financial**. **Circuit City**'s income statement reports a $90 million after-tax loss related to this transaction.

The numerous disclosures provided by **Circuit City** are absolutely essential for the proper interpretation of the company's financial statements. The notes to the company's financial statements also include information about store closings, outstanding receivables, executive compensation, sources of credit, and many other important issues.

In this chapter, we examine how companies prepare general-purpose financial statements used by investors, creditors, and managers. In addition, we discuss how certain events, such as Circuit City's decision to sell its bankcard financing operation to FleetBoston Financial, are disclosed in the notes that accompany financial statements. We also illustrate several methods of evaluating liquidity and profitability using financial statement information.

In Chapter 3, we introduced the first of the eight steps in the accounting cycle by illustrating how Overnight Auto Service (1) captured (journalized) economic events, (2) posted these transactions to its general ledger, and (3) prepared an *unadjusted* trial balance from its general ledger account balances. We continued our illustration of the accounting cycle in Chapter 4 by (4) performing the adjusting entries made by Overnight and (5) presenting the company's *adjusted* trial balance at year-end.

In this chapter, we complete the accounting cycle by (6) preparing Overnight's financial statements, (7) performing year-end closing entries, and (8) presenting the company's *after-closing* trial balance.

Preparing Financial Statements

LO1 Prepare an income statement, a statement of retained earnings, and a balance sheet.

Publicly owned companies—those with shares listed on a stock exchange—have obligations to release annual and quarterly information to their stockholders and to the public. These companies don't simply prepare financial statements—they publish *annual reports.*

An annual report *includes* comparative financial statements for several years and a wealth of other information about the company's financial position, business operations, and future prospects. (For illustrative purposes, the financial statements of Home Depot, Inc. appear in Appendix A.) Before an annual report is issued, the financial statements must be *audited* by a firm of certified public accountants (CPAs). Publicly owned companies must file their audited financial statements and detailed supporting schedules with the Securities and Exchange Commission (SEC).

The activities surrounding the preparation of an annual report become very intense as the new year approaches. Once the fiscal year has ended, it often takes several *months* before the annual report is available for distribution. Thus, many accountants refer to the months of December through March as the "busy season."[1] We cannot adequately discuss all of the activities associated with the preparation of an annual report in a single chapter. Thus, here we focus on the *preparation of financial statements.*

The adjusted trial balance prepared in Chapter 4 is reprinted in Exhibit 5–1. The income statement, statement of retained earnings, and balance sheet can be prepared *directly from the amounts shown in this adjusted trial balance.* For illustrative purposes, we have made marginal notes indicating which accounts appear in which financial statements. Overnight's financial statements for the year ended December 31, 2007, are illustrated in Exhibit 5–2 (page 196).

The income statement is prepared first because it determines the amount of net income to be reported in the statement of retained earnings. The statement of retained earnings is prepared second because it determines the amount of retained earnings to be reported in the balance sheet. Note that we have not included Overnight's statement of cash flows with the other three reports. An in-depth discussion of the statement of cash flows is the primary focus of Chapter 13.

THE INCOME STATEMENT

LO2 Explain how the income statement and the statement of retained earnings relate to the balance sheet.

Alternative titles for the income statement include *earnings statement, statement of operations,* and *profit and loss statement.* However, *income statement* is the most popular term for this important financial statement. The income statement is used to summarize the *operating* results of a business by matching the revenue earned during a given period of time with the expenses incurred in generating that revenue.

[1] Some companies elect to end their fiscal year after a seasonal high point in business activity. However, most companies *do* end their fiscal year on December 31.

Exhibit 5–1

ADJUSTED TRIAL BALANCE

OVERNIGHT AUTO SERVICE Adjusted Trial Balance December 31, 2007			
Cash	$ 18,592		Balance sheet accounts
Accounts receivable	7,250		
Shop supplies	1,200		
Unexpired insurance	3,000		
Land	52,000		
Building	36,000		
Accumulated depreciation: building		$ 1,650	
Tools and equipment	12,000		
Accumulated depreciation: tools and equipment		2,200	
Notes payable		4,000	
Accounts payable		2,690	
Wages payable		1,950	
Income taxes payable		5,580	
Interest payable		30	
Unearned rent revenue		6,000	
Capital stock		80,000	
Retained earnings (***Note:*** **still must be updated for transactions recorded in the accounts listed below. Closing entries serve this purpose.**)		0	Statement of retained earnings accounts
Dividends	14,000		
Repair service revenue		172,000	Income statement accounts
Rent revenue earned		3,000	
Advertising expense	3,900		
Wages expense	58,750		
Supplies expense	7,500		
Depreciation expense: building	1,650		
Depreciation expense: tools and equipment	2,200		
Utilities expense	19,400		
Insurance expense	15,000		
Interest expense	30		
Income taxes expense	26,628		
	$279,100	$279,100	

The revenue and expenses shown in Overnight's income statement are taken directly from the company's adjusted trial balance. Overnight's 2007 income statement shows that revenue exceeded expenses for the year, thus producing a net income of $39,942. Bear in mind, however, that this measurement of net income is not absolutely accurate or precise due to the *assumptions and estimates* in the accounting process.

An income statement has certain limitations. For instance, the amounts shown for depreciation expense are based upon estimates of the useful lives of the company's building and equipment. Also, the income statement includes only those events that have been evidenced by actual business transactions. Perhaps during the year Overnight's advertising has caught the attention of many potential customers. A good "customer base" is certainly an important step toward profitable operations; however, the development of a customer base is not reflected in the income statement because its value cannot be measured *objectively* until actual transactions take place. Despite these limitations, the income statement is of vital importance to the users of a company's financial statements.

Exhibit 5–2

OVERNIGHT AUTO SERVICE'S FINANCIAL STATEMENTS

Amounts are taken directly from the adjusted trial balance

Net income also appears in the statement of retained earnings

The ending balance in the Retained Earnings account also appears in the balance sheet

OVERNIGHT AUTO SERVICE
Income Statement
For the Year Ended December 31, 2007

Revenue:		
Repair service revenue		$172,000
Rent revenue earned		3,000
Total revenue		$175,000
Expenses:		
Advertising	$ 3,900	
Wages expense	58,750	
Supplies expense	7,500	
Depreciation: building	1,650	
Depreciation: tools and equipment	2,200	
Utilities expense	19,400	
Insurance	15,000	
Interest	30	108,430
Income before income taxes		$ 66,570
Income taxes		26,628
Net income		$ 39,942

OVERNIGHT AUTO SERVICE
Statement of Retained Earnings
For the Year Ended December 31, 2007

Retained earnings, Jan. 20, 2007	$ 0
Add: Net income	39,942
Subtotal	$39,942
Less: Dividends	14,000
Retained earnings, Dec. 31, 2007	$25,942

OVERNIGHT AUTO SERVICE
Balance Sheet
December 31, 2007

Assets

Cash		$ 18,592
Accounts receivable		7,250
Shop supplies		1,200
Unexpired insurance		3,000
Land		52,000
Building	$36,000	
Less: Accumulated depreciation	1,650	34,350
Tools and equipment	$12,000	
Less: Accumulated depreciation	2,200	9,800
Total assets		$126,192

Liabilities & Stockholders' Equity

Liabilities:	
Notes payable	$ 4,000
Accounts payable	2,690
Wages payable	1,950
Income taxes payable	5,580
Interest payable	30
Unearned rent revenue	6,000
Total liabilities	$ 20,250
Stockholders' equity:	
Capital stock	80,000
Retained earnings	25,942
Total stockholders' equity	$105,942
Total liabilities and stockholders' equity	$126,192

THE STATEMENT OF RETAINED EARNINGS

Retained earnings is that portion of stockholders' (owners') equity created by earning net income and retaining the related resources in the business. The resources retained from being profitable may include, but are certainly not limited to, *cash*. The statement of retained earnings summarizes the increases and decreases in retained earnings resulting from business operations during the period. Increases in retained earnings result from earning net income; decreases result from net losses and from the declaration of dividends.

The format of this financial statement is based upon the following relationships:

Statement of retained earnings

Retained Earnings at the beginning of the period	+	Net Income	−	Dividends	=	Retained Earnings at the end of the period

The amount of retained earnings at the *beginning* of the period is shown at the top of the statement. Next, the net income for the period is added (or net loss subtracted), and any dividends declared during the period are deducted. This short computation determines the amount of retained earnings at the *end* of the accounting period. The ending retained earnings ($25,942 in our example) appears at the bottom of the statement and also in the company's year-end balance sheet.

Our illustration of the statement of retained earnings for Overnight is unusual in that the beginning balance of retained earnings at the date of the company's formation (January 20, 2007) was *$0*. This occurred only because 2007 was the *first year* of Overnight's business operations. The ending retained earnings ($25,942) becomes the beginning retained earnings for the following year.

A Word about Dividends

In Chapter 3, the declaration and payment of a cash dividend were treated as a single event recorded by one journal entry. A small corporation with only a few stockholders may choose to declare and pay a dividend on the same day. In large corporations, an interval of a month or more will separate the date of declaration from the later date of payment. A liability account, Dividends Payable, comes into existence when the dividend is declared and is discharged when the dividend is paid. Because Overnight reports no dividends payable in its adjusted trial balance, we may assume that it declared and paid the entire $14,000 at December 31, 2007.[2]

Finally, it is important to realize that dividends paid to stockholders are *not* reported in the income statement as an expense. In short, dividends represent a decision by a corporation to distribute a portion of its income to stockholders. Thus, the amount of the dividend is not included in the computation of income.

THE BALANCE SHEET

The balance sheet lists the amounts of the company's assets, liabilities, and owners' equity at the *end* of the accounting period. The balances of Overnight's asset and liability accounts are taken directly from the adjusted trial balance in Exhibit 5–1. The amount of retained earnings at the end of the period, $25,942, was determined in the *statement of retained earnings*.

Balance sheets can be presented with asset accounts appearing on the left and liabilities and owners' equity accounts appearing on the right. They may also be presented in *report form*, with liabilities and owners' equity listed *below* (rather than to the right of) the asset section. It is also common for corporations to refer to owners' equity as *stockholders'* equity.

Separate Balance Sheet Subtotals

Many companies group together as separate balance sheet subtotals those assets and liabilities that are considered *current*. To be classified as a **current asset**, an asset must already be cash or must be capable of *being*

[2] Details related to the declaration and payment of dividends are discussed in Chapter 12.

Bob Pardue Photography

converted into cash within a relatively short period of time. For most companies, this period of time is usually one year or less. Those assets that get used up quickly (e.g., insurance policies and office supplies) are also classified as current assets. Of Overnight's $126,192 in total assets shown in Exhibit 5–2, the current assets include Cash, Accounts Receivable, Shop Supplies, and Unexpired Insurance. Thus, $30,042 of Overnight's total assets is considered *current.*

A **current liability** is an existing debt or obligation that a company expects to satisfy relatively soon using its current assets. Once again, this period of time is typically one year or less. While not a *debt,* unearned revenue is often considered a current liability also. *All* of Overnight's $20,250 in total liabilities shown in Exhibit 5–2 are considered current liabilities.

Computing separate subtotals for current assets and current liabilities is very useful when evaluating a company's ability to pay its debts as they come due (see this chapter's Financial Analysis discussion). The financial statements of Home Depot, Inc., in Appendix A at the end of this textbook illustrate how subtotals for current assets and current liabilities are presented in the balance sheet. Coverage of several other balance sheet subtotals appears in Chapter 14.

CASE IN POINT

International Financial Reporting Standard (IFRS) 1 identifies the international reporting requirements for the presentation of the income statement, balance sheet, cash flow statement, and statement showing changes in equity. One very significant difference between the financial reporting requirements under U.S. GAAP and IFRS requirements is that, under the latter, management and auditors are required to depart from compliance with standards when it is necessary to achieve a fair presentation. This "true and fair" override is required if, in the judgment of the management and auditors, compliance is misleading.

Relationships among the Financial Statements

A set of financial statements becomes easier to understand if we recognize that the income statement, statement of retained earnings, and balance sheet all are *related to one another.* These relationships are emphasized by the arrows in the right-hand margin of Exhibit 5–2.

The balance sheet prepared at the end of the preceding period and the one prepared at the end of the current period both include the amount of retained earnings at the respective balance sheet dates. The statement of retained earnings summarizes the factors (net income and dividends) that have caused the amount of retained earnings to change between these two balance sheet dates. The income statement explains in greater detail the change in retained earnings resulting from profitable (or unprofitable) operation of the business. Thus, the income statement and the retained earnings statement provide informative links between successive balance sheets.

DRAFTING THE NOTES THAT ACCOMPANY FINANCIAL STATEMENTS

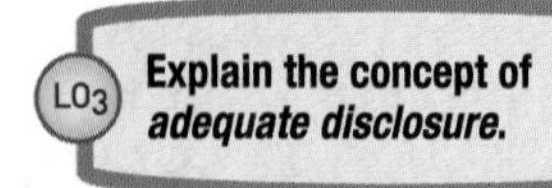

To the users of financial statements, **adequate disclosure** is perhaps the most important accounting principle. This principle simply means that financial statements should be accompanied by any information necessary for the statements to be *interpreted properly.*

Most disclosures appear within the several pages of **notes** that accompany the financial statements. Drafting these notes can be one of the most challenging tasks confronting accountants at the end of the period. The content of these notes often cannot be drawn directly from the accounting records. Rather, drafting these notes requires an *in-depth understanding* of the company and its operations, of accounting principles, and of how decision makers interpret and use accounting information.

Two items always disclosed in the notes to financial statements are the accounting methods in use and the due dates of major liabilities. Thus Overnight's 2007 financial statements should at least include the following notes:

Note 1: Depreciation policies

Depreciation expense in the financial statements is computed by the straight-line method. Estimated useful lives are 20 years for the building and 5 years for tools and equipment.

Note 2: Maturity dates of liabilities

The Company's notes payable consist of a single obligation that matures on February 28 of the coming year. The maturity value of this note, including interest charges, will amount to $4,090.

Note 1 above can be used to help ascertain whether the company may need to replace its depreciable assets in the near future. For instance, given that the estimated useful life of Overnight's building is 20 years, and only $1,650 of its $36,000 initial cost has been depreciated, it is reasonable for one to assume that it will not need to be replaced in the foreseeable future.

The maturity dates reported in Note 2 above should be of particular importance to American National Bank. Specifically, the bank will want to know if Overnight will have enough cash to pay this $4,090 liability in just two months. The company's balance sheet currently reports cash of $18,592; however, several other liabilities will require an outlay of cash in excess of $10,000 in the near future. Furthermore, the company has an $18,000 insurance policy to renew on March 1. Thus, even though Overnight's income statement reports net income of $39,942, the company's balance sheet suggests that the company may not have adequate liquid assets to satisfy all of its upcoming obligations.

WHAT TYPES OF INFORMATION MUST BE DISCLOSED?

There is no comprehensive list of all information that should be disclosed in financial statements. The adequacy of disclosure is based on a combination of official rules, tradition, and accountants' professional judgment.

As a general rule, a company should disclose any facts that an intelligent person would consider necessary for the statements to be *interpreted properly*. In addition to accounting methods in use and the due dates of major liabilities, businesses may need to disclose such matters as the following:

- Lawsuits pending against the business.
- Scheduled plant closings.
- Governmental investigations into the safety of the company's products or the legality of its pricing policies.
- Significant events occurring *after* the balance sheet date but before the financial statements are actually issued.
- Customers that account for 10 percent or more of the company's revenues.
- Unusual transactions or conflicts of interest between the company and its key officers.

Let us stress again that *there is no comprehensive list of items that must be disclosed.* Throughout this course, we will identify and discuss many items that may require disclosure in financial statements.

In some cases, companies must even disclose information that could have a *damaging effect* on the business. For example, a manufacturer may need to disclose that it is being sued by customers who have been injured by its products. The fact that a disclosure might prove embarrassing—or even damaging to the business—is *not* a valid reason for not disclosing the information. The concept of adequate disclosure demands a *good faith effort* by management to keep the users of financial statements informed about the company's operations.

Companies are *not* required to disclose information that is immaterial or that does not have a direct *financial* impact on the business. For example, a company is not required by generally accepted accounting principles to disclose the resignation, firing, or death of a key executive. Of course, companies often *do* disclose such nonfinancial events on a voluntary basis.

Disclosures that accompany financial statements should be limited to *facts* and *reasonable estimates*. They should not include *optimistic speculation* that cannot be substantiated.

For a look at the types of disclosure made by publicly owned corporations, see the **Home Depot, Inc.**, financial statements, which appear in Appendix A.

You as Overnight Auto's Independent Auditor

Assume that Overnight Auto Service is being sued by a former employee injured while on the job. The person claims that Overnight has been negligent in providing a safe work environment. If the plaintiff prevails, Overnight may have to pay damages well in excess of what is covered by its insurance policies. As Overnight's independent auditor, you have asked that the company disclose information about this lawsuit in the notes that accompany the financial statements. Overnight's management disagrees with your suggestion because in its opinion, the likelihood of the plaintiff prevailing is extremely remote. How should you respond?

(See our comments on the Online Learning Center Web site.)

Closing the Temporary Accounts

Explain the purposes of *closing entries*; prepare these entries.

As previously stated, revenue increases retained earnings, and expenses and dividends decrease retained earnings. If the only financial statement that we needed was a balance sheet, these changes in retained earnings could be recorded directly in the Retained Earnings account. However, owners, managers, investors, and others need to know amounts of specific revenues and expenses and the amount of net income earned in the period. Therefore, we maintain *separate ledger accounts* to measure each type of revenue and expense and the dividends distributed.

These revenue, expense, and dividends accounts are called *temporary*, or *nominal*, accounts, because they accumulate the transactions of *only one accounting period*. At the end of this accounting period, the changes in retained earnings accumulated in these temporary accounts are transferred into the Retained Earnings account. This process serves two purposes. First, it *updates the balance of the Retained Earnings account* for changes in retained earnings occurring during the accounting period. Second, it *returns the balances of the temporary accounts to zero*, so that they are ready for measuring the revenue, expenses, and dividends of the next accounting period.

The Retained Earnings account and other balance sheet accounts are called *permanent*, or *real*, accounts, because their balances continue to exist beyond the current accounting period. The process of transferring the balances of the temporary accounts into the Retained Earnings account is called *closing* the accounts. The journal entries made for the purpose of closing the temporary accounts are called **closing entries**.

Revenue and expense accounts are closed at the end of each accounting period by *transferring their balances* to a summary account called **Income Summary**. When the credit balances of the revenue accounts and the debit balances of the expense accounts have been transferred into one summary account, the balance of the Income Summary account will be the *net income* or *net loss* for the period. If revenues (credit balances) exceed expenses (debit balances), the Income Summary account will have a credit balance representing net income. Conversely, if expenses exceed revenues, the Income Summary account will have a debit balance representing net loss. This is consistent with the rule that increases in owners' equity are recorded by credits and decreases are recorded by debits.

While adjusting entries are usually made on a monthly basis, it is common practice to close accounts only *once each year*. Thus, we will demonstrate the closing of the temporary accounts of Overnight Auto Service at December 31, 2007, the end of its first year of operations.

On the following pages, Overnight's temporary accounts are illustrated in T account form. We have eliminated the detail of every transaction posted to each account throughout the year. Therefore, each account shows only its December 31, 2007, balance as reported in the adjusted trial balance in Exhibit 5–1.

CLOSING ENTRIES FOR REVENUE ACCOUNTS

Revenue accounts have credit balances. Therefore, closing a revenue account means transferring its credit balance to the Income Summary account. This transfer is accomplished by a journal entry debiting the revenue account in an amount equal to its credit balance, with an offsetting credit to the Income Summary account. The debit portion of this closing entry returns the balance of the revenue account to zero; the credit portion transfers the former balance of the revenue account into the Income Summary account.

Overnight uses two revenue accounts: (1) Repair Service Revenue, which had a credit balance of $172,000 at December 31, 2007, and (2) Rent Revenue Earned, which had a credit balance of $3,000 at December 31, 2007. Two separate journal entries could be made to close these accounts, but the use of one *compound journal entry* is an easier, time-saving method of closing more than one account. A compound journal entry is an entry that includes debits or credits to more than one account. The compound closing entry for Overnight's revenue accounts is displayed in Exhibit 5–3.

Exhibit 5–3
CLOSING OF REVENUE ACCOUNTS

OVERNIGHT AUTO SERVICE
General Journal
December 31, 2007

Date	Account Titles and Explanation	Debit	Credit
2007			
Dec. 31	Repair Service Revenue	172,000	
	Rent Revenue Earned.	3,000	
	Income Summary.		175,000
	To close the Repair Service Revenue and Rent Revenue Earned accounts.		

After this closing entry has been posted, the two revenue accounts each have *zero* balances, whereas Income Summary has a credit balance of $175,000, as illustrated in Exhibit 5–4.

Exhibit 5–4
TRANSFERRING REVENUE ACCOUNT BALANCES TO THE INCOME SUMMARY

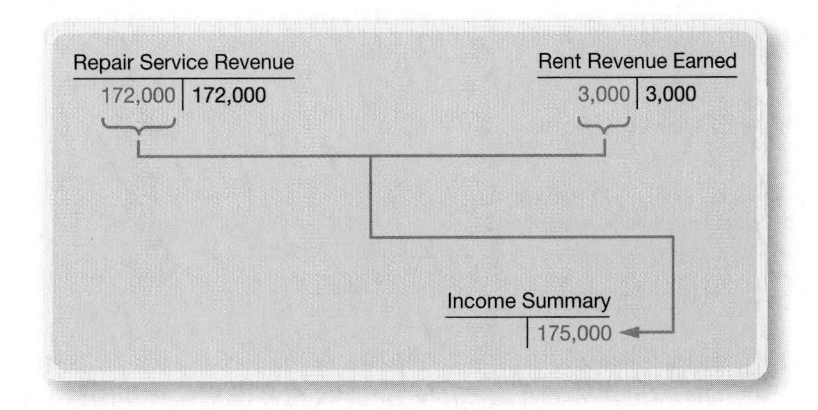

CLOSING ENTRIES FOR EXPENSE ACCOUNTS

Expense accounts have debit balances. Closing an expense account means transferring its debit balance to the Income Summary account. The journal entry to close an expense, therefore, consists of a credit to the expense account in an amount equal to its debit balance, with an offsetting debit to the Income Summary account.

There are nine expense accounts in Overnight's ledger (see the adjusted trial balance in Exhibit 5–1). Again, a compound journal entry is used to close each of these accounts. The required closing entry is displayed in Exhibit 5–5.

Exhibit 5–5

CLOSING OF EXPENSE ACCOUNTS

OVERNIGHT AUTO SERVICE
General Journal
December 31, 2007

Date	Account Titles and Explanation	Debit	Credit
2007			
Dec. 31	Income Summary	135,058	
	Advertising Expense		3,900
	Wages Expense		58,750
	Supplies Expense		7,500
	Depreciation Expense: Building		1,650
	Depreciation Expense: Tools and Equipment		2,200
	Utilities Expense		19,400
	Insurance Expense		15,000
	Interest Expense		30
	Income Taxes Expense		26,628
	To close the expense accounts.		

After this closing entry has been posted, the Income Summary account has a credit balance of *$39,942* ($175,000 credit posted − $135,058 debit posted), and the nine expense accounts each have zero balances as shown in Exhibit 5–6. This $39,942 credit balance equals the net income reported in Overnight's income statement. Had the company's income statement reported a *net loss* for the year, the Income Summary account would have a *debit balance* equal to the amount of the loss reported.

Exhibit 5–6

TRANSFERRING EXPENSE ACCOUNT BALANCES TO THE INCOME SUMMARY

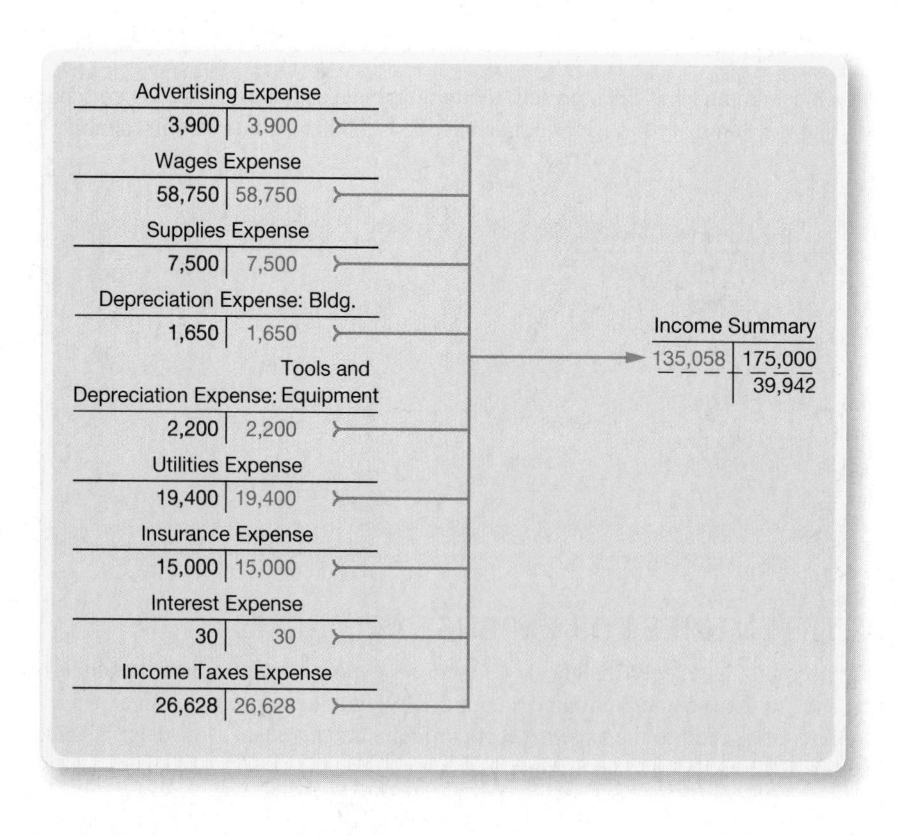

CLOSING THE INCOME SUMMARY ACCOUNT

The nine expense accounts have now been closed, and the total amount of $135,058 formerly contained in these accounts appears in the debit column of the Income Summary account. The revenue of $175,000 earned during 2007 appears in the credit column of the Income Summary account. Since the credit entry representing revenue of $175,000 is larger than the debit entry representing total expenses of $135,058, the Income Summary has a credit balance of $39,942.

The net income of $39,942 earned during the year causes an increase in Overnight's owners' equity. Thus, the $39,942 credit balance of the Income Summary account is transferred to the Retained Earnings account by the closing entry in Exhibit 5–7.

Exhibit 5–7
CLOSING THE INCOME SUMMARY ACCOUNT

OVERNIGHT AUTO SERVICE
General Journal
December 31, 2007

Date	Account Titles and Explanation	Debit	Credit
2007			
Dec. 31	Income Summary	39,942	
	Retained Earnings		39,942
	Transferring net income earned in 2007 to the Retained Earnings account.		

After this closing entry has been posted, the Income Summary account has a zero balance, and the net income for the year ended December 31, 2007, appears as an increase (or credit entry) in the Retained Earnings account as shown in Exhibit 5–8.

Exhibit 5–8 **INCOME INCREASES RETAINED EARNINGS**

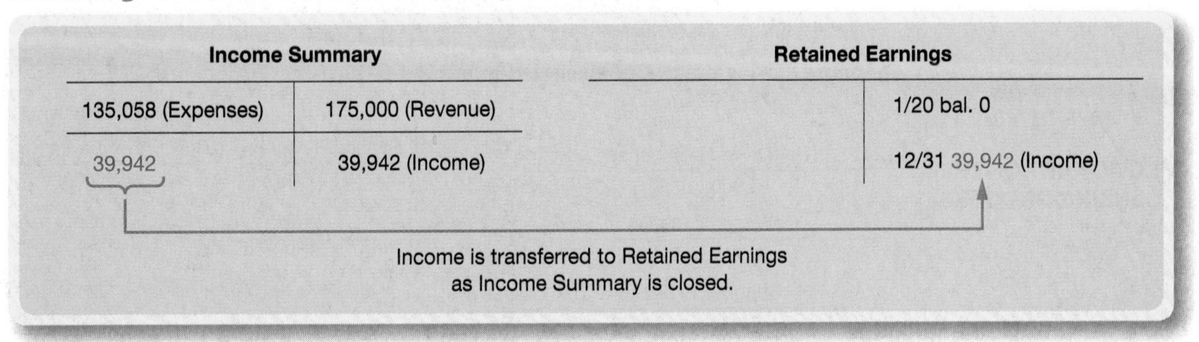

CLOSING THE DIVIDENDS ACCOUNT

As explained earlier in the chapter, dividends paid to stockholders are *not* considered an expense of the business and, therefore, are *not* taken into account in determining net income for the period. Since dividends are not an expense, the Dividends account is *not* closed to the Income Summary account. Instead, it is closed directly to the Retained Earnings account, as shown in Exhibit 5–9.

Exhibit 5–9
CLOSING THE DIVIDENDS ACCOUNT

OVERNIGHT AUTO SERVICE
General Journal
December 31, 2007

Date	Account Titles and Explanation	Debit	Credit
2007			
Dec. 31	Retained Earnings.	14,000	
	Dividends		14,000
	To transfer dividends declared in 2007 to the Retained Earnings account.		

After this closing entry has been posted, the Dividends account will have a zero balance, and the Retained Earnings account will have an ending credit balance of $25,942, as shown in Exhibit 5–10.

Exhibit 5–10 DIVIDENDS DECREASE RETAINED EARNINGS

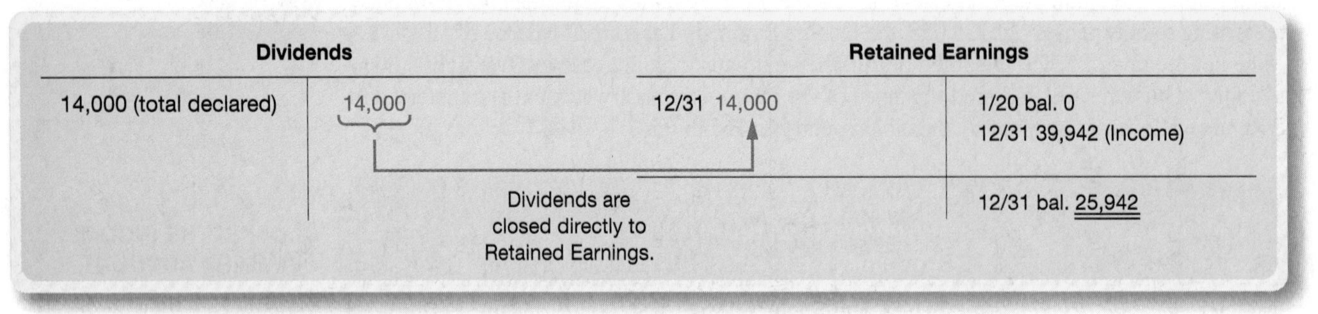

Summary of the Closing Process

Let us now summarize the process of closing the accounts.

1. Close the various *revenue* accounts by transferring their balances into the Income Summary account.
2. Close the various *expense* accounts by transferring their balances into the Income Summary account.
3. Close the *Income Summary* account by transferring its balance into the Retained Earnings account.
4. Close the *Dividends* account by transferring its balance into the Retained Earnings account.

The entire closing process is illustrated in Exhibit 5–11 using T accounts.

Exhibit 5–11

FLOWCHART OF THE CLOSING PROCESS

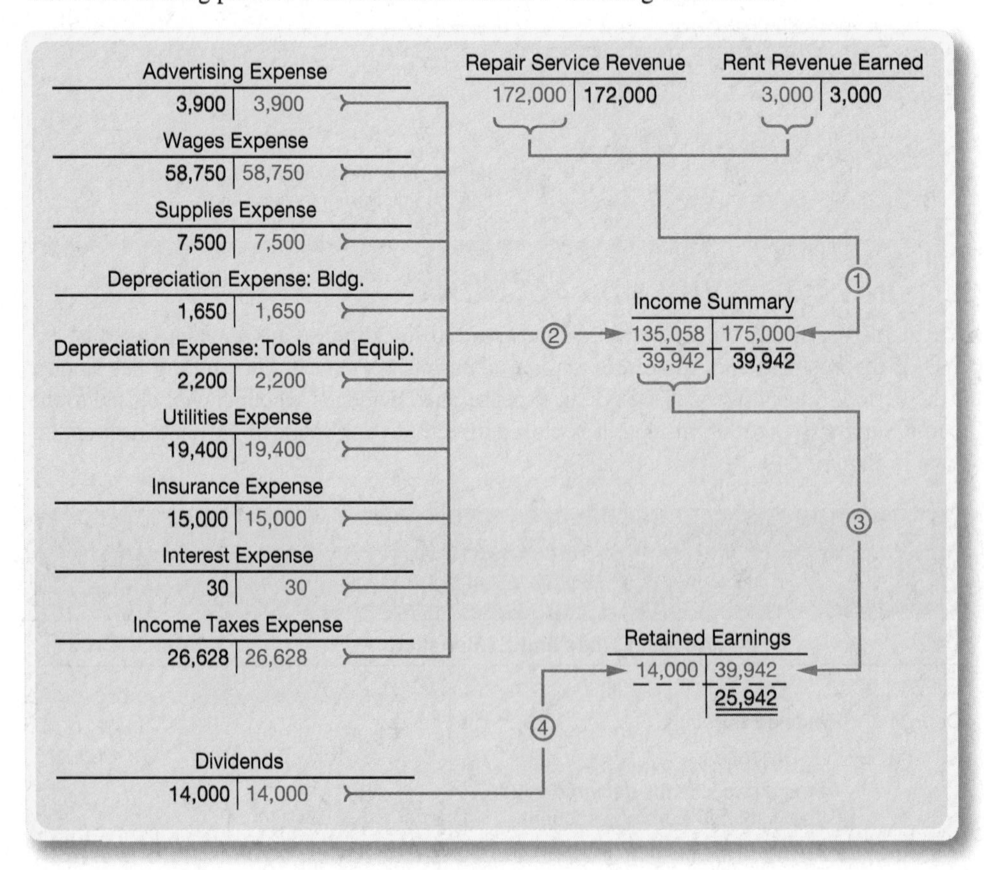

After-Closing Trial Balance

Prepare an after-closing trial balance. LO5

After the revenue and expense accounts have been closed, it is desirable to prepare an **after-closing trial balance** that consists solely of balance sheet accounts. There is always the possibility that an error in posting the closing entries may have upset the equality of debits and credits in the ledger. The after-closing trial balance, or *post-closing trial balance* as it is often called, is prepared from the ledger. It gives assurance that the accounts are in balance and ready for recording transactions in the new accounting period. The after-closing trial balance of Overnight Auto Service is shown in Exhibit 5–12.

Exhibit 5–12
AFTER-CLOSING TRIAL BALANCE

OVERNIGHT AUTO SERVICE After-Closing Trial Balance December 31, 2007		
Cash	$ 18,592	
Accounts receivable	7,250	
Shop supplies	1,200	
Unexpired insurance	3,000	
Land	52,000	
Building	36,000	
Accumulated depreciation: building		$ 1,650
Tools and equipment	12,000	
Accumulated depreciation: tools and equipment		2,200
Notes payable		4,000
Accounts payable		2,690
Wages payable		1,950
Income taxes payable		5,580
Interest payable		30
Unearned rent revenue		6,000
Capital stock		80,000
Retained earnings, Dec. 31		25,942
	$130,042	$130,042

In comparison with the adjusted trial balance in Exhibit 5–1, an after-closing trial balance contains only *balance sheet* accounts. Also, the Retained Earnings account no longer has a zero balance. Through the closing of the revenue, expense, and dividends accounts, the Retained Earnings account has been brought up-to-date.

A LAST LOOK AT OVERNIGHT: WAS 2007 A GOOD YEAR?

Use financial statement information to evaluate profitability and liquidity.

Let us now consider the financial results of Overnight's first fiscal year.

Evaluating Profitability In 2007, Overnight earned a net income of nearly *$40,000*. Thus, net income for the first year of operations amounts to 50 percent of the stockholders' $80,000 investment. This is a very impressive rate of return for the first year of operations. Of course, Overnight's stockholders (members of the McBryan family) have taken a certain amount of risk by investing their financial resources in this business. Does a 50 percent *return on investment* adequately compensate the stockholders for their risk? Stated differently, could they invest their $80,000 in a less risky venture and still generate a 50 percent rate of return? Probably not.

Brand X Pictures/Getty Images/DIL

But in evaluating profitability, the real question is not how the business *did*, but how it is *likely to do in the future*. To generate a substantial return on investment in the first year of operations indicates good profit potential. Overnight's rental contract with Harbor Cab Company is also promising. In 2007, only $3,000 in revenue was earned by renting storage space to the company for its cabs (December's rent). In 2008, Overnight will earn 12 full months of rent revenue from Harbor Cab ($33,000 more than it earned in 2007). In addition, if Harbor Cab stores its cabs in Overnight's garage, Overnight becomes the likely candidate to perform any necessary maintenance and repairs.

Evaluating Liquidity *Liquidity* refers to a company's ability to meet its cash obligations as they become due. Liquidity, at least in the short term, may be independent of profitability. And in the short term, Overnight appears to have *potential* cash flow problems. In the very near future, Overnight must make cash expenditures for the following items:

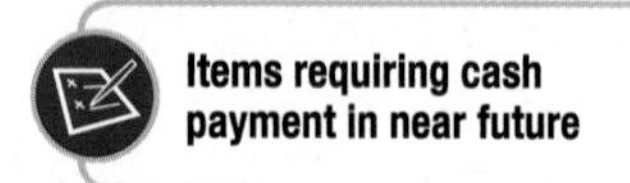
Items requiring cash payment in near future

Note and interest payable	$ 4,030
Accounts payable	2,690
Wages payable	1,950
Income taxes payable	5,580
Insurance policy renewal	18,000
Total expenditures coming due	$32,250

These outlays exceed the company's liquid assets (cash and accounts receivable) reported in its December 31, 2007, balance sheet.

It is important to note that the cash and accounts receivable amounts reported in Overnight's balance sheet represent the balances of those accounts at a *point in time*. Thus, while these liquid assets are currently insufficient to cover the cash expenditures coming due, this may not be the case for long. Based on its past performance, Overnight is likely to generate revenue in excess of $40,000 during the next several months. If a substantial amount of this revenue is received in cash, and expenses are kept under control, the company may actually become more liquid than it appears to be now.

Financial Analysis and Decision Making

Overnight's income statement reports net income of nearly $40,000 for 2007. This figure becomes more meaningful when examined in the context of management's ability to control costs or when measured relative to the average shareholders' equity throughout the year.

Two commonly used measures of *profitability* that address these issues are the *net income percentage* and *return on equity*. Using data from Overnight's financial statements, these measures are computed as follows:

$$\textbf{Net Income Percentage} = \frac{\textbf{Net Income}}{\textbf{Total Revenue}} = \frac{\$39{,}942}{\$175{,}000} = \underline{\underline{22.8\%}}$$

(continued)

Significance All companies must consume resources (incur costs) in order to generate revenue. The net income percentage is simply a measure of management's ability to control these costs. In 2007, Overnight incurred costs equal to approximately 77.2 percent of its total revenue. Thus, the company was able to convert 22.8 percent of its revenue into net income.

Significance of net income percentage

$$\textbf{Return on Equity} = \frac{\textbf{Net Income}}{\textbf{Average Stockholders' Equity*}} = \frac{\$39,942}{\$92,971} = \underline{\underline{43.0\%}}$$

Significance Return on equity is a measure of net income relative to the company's average stockholder's equity throughout the year. In 2007, Overnight's stockholders' equity averaged $92,971. Thus, for every dollar of equity capital, the company earned income of approximately $0.43.

Significance of return on equity

Overnight's balance sheet reports liabilities of $20,250, many of which require payment in the very near future. However, at December 31, the company reports cash of only $18,592, which may be an indication of potential liquidity problems.

Two common measures used to evaluate *liquidity* are *working capital* and the *current ratio*. Using data from Overnight's financial statements, these measures are computed as follows:

$$\textbf{Working Capital} = \textbf{Current Assets} - \textbf{Current Liabilities} = \$30,042 - \$20,250 = \underline{\underline{\$9,792}}$$

Significance Working capital is a measure of short-term debt-paying ability expressed in dollars. Current assets are those assets expected to leave the balance sheet in the near future. Cash and accounts receivable are Overnight's most liquid current assets. Its current assets also include shop supplies and unexpired insurance. Current liabilities are those liabilities expected to leave the balance sheet in the near future, most of which must be settled in cash. All of Overnight's liabilities are considered current liabilities. Overnight's current assets exceed its current liabilities by $9,792. Of course, this figure does not take into account that: (1) shop supplies and unexpired insurance policies are not truly liquid assets, and (2) unearned rent revenue will not require a future outlay of cash.

Significance of working capital

$$\textbf{Current Ratio} = \frac{\textbf{Current Assets}}{\textbf{Current Liabilities}} = \frac{\$30,042}{\$20,250} = \underline{\underline{1.48:1}}$$

Significance The current ratio is simply working capital expressed as a ratio. Thus, Overnight has approximately $1.48 of current assets for every dollar of current liabilities. Again, this figure does not take into account that shop supplies and unexpired insurance policies will not convert into cash, or that unearned rent revenue will not require an outlay of cash.

Significance of current ratio

Throughout this textbook additional measures of profitability will be introduced. Chapter 14 is devoted entirely to financial analysis.

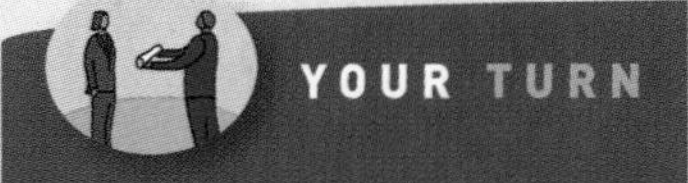

YOUR TURN **You as a Financial Analyst Evaluating Overnight Auto Service**

Assume that you are a financial analyst working for an investment firm. The owner of Overnight Auto Service has asked you to evaluate the company's net income percentage, return on equity, working capital, and current ratio. What would you tell Overnight's owner?

(See our comments on the Online Learning Center Web site.)

---

* Average stockholders' equity of $92,971 is simply the average of Overnight's beginning stockholders' equity of $80,000 and its ending stockholders' equity of $105,942.

PREPARING FINANCIAL STATEMENTS COVERING DIFFERENT PERIODS OF TIME

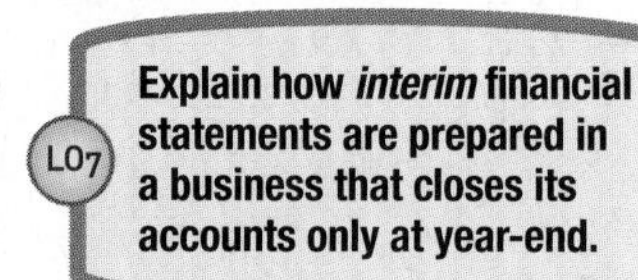

Many businesses prepare financial statements every quarter, as well as at year-end. In addition, they may prepare financial statements covering other time periods, such as one month or the year-to-date.

When a business closes its accounts only at year-end, the revenue, expense, and dividends accounts have balances representing the activities of the *year-to-date*. Thus, at *June 30*, these account balances represent the activities recorded over the past six months. Year-to-date financial statements can be prepared directly from an adjusted trial balance. But how might this business prepare **interim financial statements** covering only the month of June? Or the quarter (three months) ended June 30?

The answer is by doing a little *subtraction*. As an example, assume that the adjusted balance in Overnight's Repair Service Revenue account at the ends of the following months was as shown:

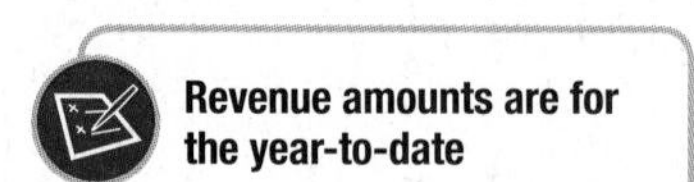

March 31 (end of the first quarter)	$38,000
May 31	67,000
June 30	80,000

At each date, the account balance represents the revenue earned since January 1. Thus the March 31 balance represents three months' revenue; the May 31 balance, five months' revenue; and the June 30 balance, the revenue earned over a period of six months.

To prepare an income statement for the *six months* ended June 30, we simply use the June 30 balance in the revenue account—*$80,000*. But to prepare an income statement for the *month* ended June 30, we would have to subtract from the June 30 balance of this account its balance as of May 31. The remainder, *$13,000*, represents the amount of revenue recorded in the account during June ($80,000 − $67,000 = $13,000).

To prepare an income statement for the *quarter* ended June 30, we would subtract from the June 30 balance in this revenue account its balance as of March 31. Thus the revenue earned during the second quarter (April 1 through June 30) amounts to *$42,000* ($80,000 − $38,000 = $42,000).

This process of subtracting prior balances from the current balance is repeated for each revenue and expense account, as well as for the dividends account.

This sounds like a bigger job than it really is. There are only about 10 or 15 accounts involved, and in a computerized system, the entire process is done automatically. Even in a manual system, a person using a spreadsheet can complete this process in a few minutes.

Computations like these are not required for the balance sheet accounts. A balance sheet always is based on the account balances *at the balance sheet date*. Therefore, a June 30 balance sheet looks exactly the same *regardless* of the time period covered by the other financial statements.

Ethics, Fraud & Corporate Governance

As stated previously in this chapter, a company should disclose any facts that an intelligent person would consider necessary for the statements to be *interpreted properly*. Public companies are required to file annual reports with the Securities and Exchange Commission (SEC). These annual reports include a section labeled, "Management Discussion and Analysis" (MD&A). The SEC requires that companies include an MD&A in their annual reports because the financial statements and related notes may be inadequate for assessing the quality and sustainability of a company's earnings.

In the late 1990s, the SEC brought an enforcement action against Sony Corporation alleging inadequate disclosure in its MD&A. Although a Japanese corporation, Sony lists its stock on the New York Stock Exchange and is therefore subject to SEC oversight. Sony had reported only two industry segments in its annual report (electronics and entertainment). The entertainment segment included two separate units, Sony Music Entertainment and Sony Pictures Entertainment. The music group was profitable, whereas the pictures group was losing significant amounts of money. By combining its music and picture units as a single entertainment segment, Sony was able to conceal significant losses incurred by Sony Pictures. This decision was at odds with both Sony's external auditor and with its U.S.–based financial staff.

Although Sony chose to report only two segments, it could have elaborated on the entertainment segment's performance in its MD&A by separately discussing the results of Sony Music and Sony Pictures. Sony did discuss Sony Pictures separately, but not in a manner necessary for an intelligent person to properly interpret the results of Sony Pictures. Sony's MD&A did not discuss the nature and extent of the losses incurred by Sony Pictures. Conversely, Sony's MD&A highlighted certain positive developments at Sony Pictures, including box office receipts, box office market share, and Academy Award nominations.

The SEC concluded that Sony's MD&A disclosures were inadequate. Sony consented to an SEC cease-and-desist order without either admitting or denying guilt. In essence, Sony did not agree that it did anything wrong, but it promised to never do what it did again. As part of its settlement, Sony also agreed to have its external auditor examine the MD&A for the following year and to publicly report the findings. This penalty was meaningful because an examination of the MD&A normally does not fall within the scope of an external audit.

Concluding Remarks

We have now completed the *entire accounting cycle*—from the initial recording of transactions in Chapter 3, through an after-closing trial balance in this chapter. The steps comprising this cycle are listed below and illustrated in a flowchart diagram in Exhibit 5–13.

Exhibit 5–13 **THE ACCOUNTING CYCLE**

1. *Journalize (record) transactions.* Enter all transactions in the journal, thus creating a chronological record of events.
2. *Post to ledger accounts.* Post debits and credits from the journal to the proper ledger accounts, thus creating a record classified by accounts.
3. *Prepare a trial balance.* Prove the equality of debits and credits in the ledger.
4. *Make end-of-period adjustments.* Make adjusting entries in the general journal and post to ledger accounts.
5. *Prepare an adjusted trial balance.* Prove again the equality of debits and credits in the ledger. (***Note:*** These are the amounts used in the preparation of financial statements.)
6. *Prepare financial statements and appropriate disclosures.* An income statement shows the results of operation for the period. A statement of retained earnings shows changes in retained earnings during the period. A balance sheet shows the financial position of the business at the end of the period. Financial statements should be accompanied by *notes* disclosing facts necessary for the proper interpretation of those statements.
7. *Journalize and post the closing entries.* The closing entries "zero" the revenue, expense, and dividends accounts, making them ready for recording the events of the next accounting period. These entries also bring the balance in the Retained Earnings account up-to-date.
8. *Prepare an after-closing trial balance.* This step ensures that the ledger remains in balance after the posting of the closing entries.

SUPPLEMENTAL TOPIC

The Worksheet

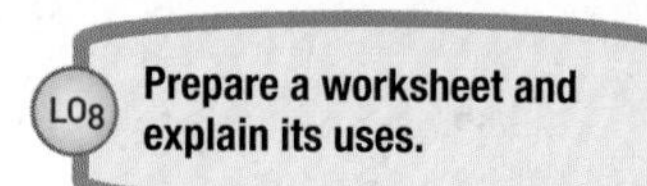

A **worksheet** illustrates in one place the relationships among the unadjusted trial balance, proposed adjusting entries, and financial statements. A worksheet is prepared at the end of the period, but *before* the adjusting entries are formally recorded in the accounting records. It is not a formal step in the accounting cycle. Rather, it is a *tool* used by accountants to work out the details of the proposed end-of-period adjustments. It also provides them with a preview of how the financial statements will look.

You can see a worksheet for Overnight Auto Service at December 31, 2007, in Exhibit 5–14 on page 212.

ISN'T THIS REALLY A SPREADSHEET?

Yes. The term *worksheet* is a holdover from the days when these schedules were prepared manually on large sheets of columnar paper. Today, most worksheets are prepared on a computer using spreadsheet software, such as *Excel*™, or with **general ledger software** such as *Peachtree*™ or *Dac-Easy*™.

Since the worksheet is simply a tool used by accountants, it often isn't printed out in hard copy—it may exist only on a computer screen. But the concept remains the same; the worksheet displays *in one place* the unadjusted account balances, proposed adjusting entries, and financial statements as they will appear if the proposed adjustments are made.

HOW IS A WORKSHEET USED?

A worksheet serves several purposes. It allows accountants to *see the effects* of adjusting entries without actually entering these adjustments in the accounting records. This makes it relatively easy for them to correct errors or make changes in estimated amounts. It also enables accountants and management to preview the financial statements before the final drafts are developed. Once the worksheet is complete, it serves as the source for recording adjusting and closing entries in the accounting records and for preparing financial statements.

Another important use of the worksheet is in the preparation of *interim financial statements*. Interim statements are financial statements developed at various points *during* the fiscal year. Most companies close their accounts only once each year. Yet they often need to develop quarterly or monthly financial statements. Through the use of a worksheet, they can develop these interim statements *without* having to formally adjust and close their accounts.

THE MECHANICS: HOW IT'S DONE

Whether done manually or on a computer, the preparation of a worksheet involves five basic steps. We begin by describing these steps as if the worksheet were being prepared manually. Afterward, we explain how virtually all of the mechanical steps can be performed automatically by a computer.

1. *Enter the ledger account balances in the Trial Balance columns.* The worksheet begins with an unadjusted trial balance—that is, a listing of the ledger account balances at the end of the period *prior* to making any adjusting entries. In our illustration, the unadjusted trial balance appears in *blue*.

   Notice our inclusion of the captions "Balance sheet accounts" and "Income statement accounts." These captions are optional, but they help clarify the relationships between the ledger accounts and the financial statements. (Hint: A few lines should be left blank immediately below the last balance sheet account. It is often necessary to add a few more accounts during the adjusting process. Additional income statement accounts also may be necessary.)

2. *Enter the adjustments in the Adjustments columns.* The next step is the most important: Enter the appropriate end-of-period adjustments in the Adjustments columns. In our illustration, these adjustments appear in *red*.

   Notice that each adjustment includes both debit and credit entries, which are linked together by the small key letters appearing to the left of the dollar amount. Thus, adjusting entry *a* consists of a $600 debit to Supplies Expense and a $600 credit to Shop Supplies. Because the individual adjusting entries include equal debit and credit amounts, the totals of the debit and credit Adjustments columns should be equal.

   Sometimes the adjustments require adding accounts to the original trial balance. (The four ledger account titles printed in *red* were added during the adjusting process.)

3. *Prepare an adjusted trial balance.* Next, an adjusted trial balance is prepared. The balances in the original trial balance (*blue*) are adjusted for the debit or credit amounts in the Adjustments columns (*red*). This process of horizontal addition or subtraction is called *cross-footing*. The adjusted trial balance is totaled to determine that the accounts remain in balance.

   At this point, the worksheet is almost complete. We have emphasized that financial statements are prepared *directly from the adjusted trial balance*. Thus we have only to arrange these accounts into the format of financial statements. For this reason, we show the adjusted trial balance amounts in *blue*—both in the Adjusted Trial Balance columns and when these amounts are *extended* (carried forward) into the financial statement columns.

4. *Extend the adjusted trial balance amounts into the appropriate financial statement columns.* The balance sheet accounts—assets, liabilities, and owners' equity—are extended into the Balance Sheet columns; income statement amounts, into the Income Statement columns. (The "Balance Sheet" and "Income Statement" captions in the original trial balance should simplify this procedure. Notice each amount is extended to only one column. Also, the account retains the same debit or credit balance as shown in the adjusted trial balance.)

5. *Total the financial statement columns; determine and record net income or net loss.* The final step in preparing the worksheet consists of totaling the Income Statement and Balance Sheet columns and then bringing each set of columns into balance. These tasks are performed on the bottom three lines of the worksheet. In our illustration, the amounts involved in this final step are shown in *black*.

When the Income Statement and Balance Sheet columns are first totaled, the debit and credit columns will not agree. But each set of columns should be out of balance by the *same amount*—and that amount should be the amount of net income or net loss for the period.

Exhibit 5–14 **THE WORKSHEET**

OVERNIGHT AUTO SERVICE
Worksheet
For the Year Ended December 31, 2007

	Trial Balance		Adjustments*		Adjusted Trial Balance		Income Statement		Balance Sheet	
	Dr	Cr	Dr	Cr	Dr	Cr	Dr	Cr	Dr	Cr
Balance sheet accounts:										
Cash	18,592				18,592				18,592	
Accounts Receivable	6,500		(h) 750		7,250				7,250	
Shop Supplies	1,800			(a) 600	1,200				1,200	
Unexpired Insurance	4,500			(b) 1,500	3,000				3,000	
Land	52,000				52,000				52,000	
Building	36,000				36,000				36,000	
Accumulated Depreciation: Building		1,500		(c) 150		1,650				1,650
Tools and Equipment	12,000				12,000				12,000	
Accumulated Depreciation: Tools and Equipment		2,000		(d) 200		2,200				2,200
Notes Payable		4,000				4,000				4,000
Accounts Payable		2,690				2,690				2,690
Income Taxes Payable		1,560		(i) 4,020		5,580				5,580
Unearned Rent Revenue		9,000	(e) 3,000			6,000				6,000
Capital Stock		80,000				80,000				80,000
Retained Earnings		0				0				0
Dividends	14,000				14,000				14,000	
Wages Payable				(f) 1,950		1,950				1,950
Interest Payable				(g) 30		30				30
Income statement accounts:										
Repair Service Revenue		171,250		(h) 750		172,000		172,000		
Advertising Expense	3,900				3,900		3,900			
Wages Expense	56,800		(f) 1,950		58,750		58,750			
Supplies Expense	6,900		(a) 600		7,500		7,500			
Depreciation Expense: Building	1,500		(c) 150		1,650		1,650			
Depreciation Expense: Tools and Equipment	2,000		(d) 200		2,200		2,200			
Utilities Expense	19,400				19,400		19,400			
Insurance Expense	13,500		(b) 1,500		15,000		15,000			
Income Taxes Expense	22,608		(i) 4,020		26,628		26,628			
Rent Revenue Earned				(e) 3,000		3,000		3,000		
Interest Expense			(g) 30		30		30			
	272,000	272,000	12,200	12,200	279,100	279,100	135,058	175,000	144,042	104,100
Net income							39,942			39,942
Totals							175,000	175,000	144,042	144,042

*Adjustments:

(a) Shop supplies used in December.
(b) Portion of insurance cost expiring in December.
(c) Depreciation on building for December.
(d) Depreciation of tools and equipment for December.
(e) Earned one-third of rent revenue collected in advance from Harbor Cab.
(f) Unpaid wages owed to employees at December 31.
(g) Interest payable accrued during December.
(h) Repair service revenue earned in December but not yet billed.
(i) Income taxes expense for December.

Let us briefly explain *why* both sets of columns initially are out of balance by this amount. First consider the Income Statement columns. The Credit column contains the revenue accounts, and the Debit column, the expense accounts. The difference, therefore, represents the net income (net loss) for the period.

Now consider the Balance Sheet columns. All of the balance sheet amounts are shown at up-to-date amounts *except* for the Retained Earnings account, which still contains the balance from the *beginning* of the period. To bring the Retained Earnings account up-to-date, we must add net income and subtract any dividends. The dividends already appear in the Balance Sheet Debit column. So what's the only thing missing? The net income (or net loss) for the period.

To bring both sets of columns into balance, we enter the net income (or net loss) on the next line. The same amount will appear in both the Income Statement columns and the Balance Sheet columns. But in one set of columns it appears as a debit, and in the other, it appears as a credit.[3] After this amount is entered, each set of columns should balance.

Computers Do the Pencil-Pushing When a worksheet is prepared by computer, accountants perform only *one* of the steps listed above—*entering the adjustments*. The computer automatically lists the ledger accounts in the form of a trial balance. After the accountant has entered the adjustments, it automatically computes the adjusted account balances and completes the worksheet. (Once the adjusted balances are determined, completing the worksheet involves nothing more than putting these amounts in the appropriate column and determining the column totals.)

WHAT IF: A SPECIAL APPLICATION OF WORKSHEET SOFTWARE

We have discussed a relatively simple application of the worksheet concept—illustrating the effects of proposed *adjusting entries* on account balances. But the same concept can be applied to proposed *future transactions*. The effects of the proposed transactions simply are entered in the "Adjustments" columns. Thus, without disrupting the accounting records, accountants can prepare schedules showing how the company's financial statements might be affected by such events as a merger with another company, a 15 percent increase in sales volume, or the closure of a plant.

There is a tendency to view worksheets as mechanical and old-fashioned. This is not at all the case. Today, the mechanical aspects are handled entirely by computer. The real purpose of a worksheet is to show quickly and efficiently how specific events or transactions will affect the financial statements. This isn't bookkeeping—it's *planning*.

[3] To bring the Income Statement columns into balance, net *income* is entered in the *Debit column*. This is because the Credit column (revenue) exceeds the Debit column (expenses). But in the balance sheet, net income is an element of owners' equity, which is represented by a credit. In the event of a net *loss*, this situation reverses.

END-OF-CHAPTER REVIEW

SUMMARY OF LEARNING OBJECTIVES

LO1 Prepare an income statement, a statement of retained earnings, and a balance sheet. The financial statements are prepared directly from the adjusted trial balance. The income statement is prepared by reporting all revenue earned during the period, less all expenses incurred in generating the related revenue. The statement of retained earnings reconciles the *beginning* Retained Earnings account balance with its *ending* balance. The retained earnings statement reports any increase to Retained Earnings resulting from net income earned for the period, as well as any decreases to Retained Earnings resulting from dividends declared or a net loss incurred for the period. The balance sheet reveals the company's financial position by reporting its economic resources (assets) and the claims against those resources (liabilities and owners' equity).

LO2 Explain how the income statement and the statement of retained earnings relate to the balance sheet. An income statement shows the revenue and expenses of a business for a specified accounting period. In the statement of retained earnings, the net income figure from the income statement is added to the beginning Retained Earnings balance, while dividends declared during the period are subtracted, in arriving at the ending Retained Earnings balance. The ending Retained Earnings balance is then reported in the balance sheet as a component of owners' equity.

LO3 Explain the concept of *adequate disclosure*. Adequate disclosure is the generally accepted accounting principle that financial statements should include any information that an informed user needs to interpret the statements properly. The appropriate disclosures usually are contained in several pages of notes that accompany the statements.

LO4 Explain the purposes of *closing entries*; prepare these entries. Closing entries serve two basic purposes. The first is to return the balances of the temporary owners' equity accounts (revenue, expense, and dividends accounts) to zero so that these accounts may be used to measure the activities of the next reporting period. The second purpose of closing entries is to update the balance of the Retained Earnings account. Four closing entries generally are needed: (1) close the revenue accounts to the Income Summary account, (2) close the expense accounts to the Income Summary account, (3) close the balance of the Income Summary account to the Retained Earnings account, and (4) close the Dividends account to the Retained Earnings account.

LO5 Prepare an after-closing trial balance. After the revenue and expense accounts have been closed, it is desirable to prepare an after-closing trial balance consisting solely of balance sheet accounts. The after-closing trial balance, or post-closing trial balance, gives assurance that the accounts of the general ledger are in balance and ready for recording transactions for the new accounting period.

LO6 Use financial statement information to evaluate profitability and liquidity. Profitability is an increase in stockholders' equity resulting from revenue exceeding expenses, whereas liquidity refers to a company's ability to meet its cash obligations as they come due. Liquidity, at least in the short term, may be *independent* of profitability. Financial statements are useful tools for evaluating both profitability and liquidity. Used separately, or in combination, the income statement and balance sheet help interested parties to measure a company's current financial performance and to forecast its profit and cash flow potential. In the Financial Analysis feature, we illustrated several measures of profitability and liquidity computed using financial statement information. Throughout the remainder of this text we introduce and discuss many additional measures.

LO7 Explain how *interim* financial statements are prepared in a business that closes its accounts only at year-end. When a business closes its accounts only at year-end, the revenue, expense, and dividends accounts have balances representing the activities of the year-to-date. To prepare an income statement for any period shorter than the year-to-date, we subtract from the current balance in the revenue or expense account the balance in the account as of the beginning of the desired period. This process of subtracting prior balances from the current balance is repeated for each revenue and expense account and for the dividends account. No computations of this type are required for the balance sheet accounts, as a balance sheet is based on the account balances at the balance sheet date.

***LO8 Prepare a worksheet and explain its uses.** A worksheet is a "testing ground" on which the ledger accounts are adjusted, balanced, and arranged in the format of financial statements. A worksheet consists of a trial balance, the end-of-period adjusting entries, an adjusted trial balance, and columns showing the ledger accounts arranged as an income statement and as a balance sheet. The completed worksheet is used as the basis for preparing financial statements and for recording adjusting and closing entries in the formal accounting records.

**Supplemental Topic*, "The Worksheet."

Key Terms Introduced or Emphasized in Chapter 5

adequate disclosure (p. 198) The generally accepted accounting principle of providing with financial statements any information that users need to interpret those statements properly.

after-closing trial balance (p. 205) A trial balance prepared after all closing entries have been made. Consists only of accounts for assets, liabilities, and owners' equity.

closing entries (p. 200) Journal entries made at the end of the period for the purpose of closing temporary accounts (revenue, expense, and dividends accounts) and transferring balances to the Retained Earnings account.

current assets (p. 197) Cash and other assets that can be converted into cash or used up within a relatively short period of time without interfering with normal business operations.

current liabilities (p. 198) Existing obligations that are expected to be satisfied with a company's current assets within a relatively short period of time.

general ledger software (p. 210) Computer software used for recording transactions, maintaining journals and ledgers, and preparing financial statements. Also includes spreadsheet capabilities for showing the effects of proposed adjusting entries or transactions on the financial statements without actually recording these entries in the accounting records.

Income Summary (p. 200) The summary account in the ledger to which revenue and expense accounts are closed at the end of the period. The balance (credit balance for a net income, debit balance for a net loss) is transferred to the Retained Earnings account.

interim financial statements (p. 208) Financial statements prepared for periods of less than one year (includes monthly and quarterly statements).

notes (accompanying financial statements) (p. 198) Supplemental disclosures that accompany financial statements. These notes provide users with various types of information considered necessary for the proper interpretation of the statements.

worksheet (p. 210) A multicolumn schedule showing the relationships among the current account balances (a trial balance), proposed or actual adjusting entries or transactions, and the financial statements that would result if these adjusting entries or transactions were recorded. Used both at the end of the accounting period as an aid to preparing financial statements and for planning purposes.

Demonstration Problem

Jan's Dance Studio, Inc., performs adjusting entries every month, but closes its accounts only at year-end. The studio's year-end *adjusted trial balance* dated December 31, 2007, appears below. (Bear in mind, the balance shown for Retained Earnings was last updated on December 31, *2006*.)

JAN'S DANCE STUDIO, INC.
Adjusted Trial Balance
December 31, 2007

Cash	$171,100	
Accounts receivable	9,400	
Prepaid studio rent	3,000	
Unexpired insurance	7,200	
Supplies	500	
Equipment	18,000	
Accumulated depreciation: equipment		$ 7,200
Notes payable		10,000
Accounts payable		3,200
Salaries payable		4,000
Income taxes payable		6,000
Unearned studio revenue		8,800
Capital stock		100,000
Retained earnings		40,000
Dividends	6,000	
Studio revenue earned		165,000
Salary expense	85,000	
Supply expense	3,900	
Rent expense	12,000	
Insurance expense	1,900	
Advertising expense	500	
Depreciation expense: equipment	1,800	
Interest expense	900	
Income taxes expense	23,000	
	$344,200	$344,200

Instructions

a. Prepare an income statement and statement of retained earnings for the year ended December 31, 2007. Also prepare the studio's balance sheet dated December 31, 2007.

b. Prepare the necessary closing entries at December 31, 2007.

c. Prepare an after-closing trial balance dated December 31, 2007.

Solution to the Demonstration Problem

a.

JAN'S DANCE STUDIO, INC.
Income Statement
For the Year Ended December 31, 2007

Revenue:		
Studio revenue earned		$165,000
Expenses:		
Salary expense	$85,000	
Supply expense	3,900	
Rent expense	12,000	
Insurance expense	1,900	
Advertising expense	500	
Depreciation expense: equipment	1,800	
Interest expense	900	106,000
Income before income taxes		$ 59,000
Income taxes expense		23,000
Net income		$ 36,000

JAN'S DANCE STUDIO, INC.
Statement of Retained Earnings
For the Year Ended December 31, 2007

Retained earnings, January 1, 2007	$40,000
Add: Net income earned in 2007	36,000
Subtotal	$76,000
Less: Dividends declared in 2007	6,000
Retained earnings, December 31, 2007	$70,000

JAN'S DANCE STUDIO, INC.
Balance Sheet
December 31, 2007

Assets		
Cash		$171,100
Accounts receivable		9,400
Prepaid studio rent		3,000
Unexpired insurance		7,200
Supplies		500
Equipment	$18,000	
Less: Accumulated depreciation: equipment	7,200	10,800
Total assets		$202,000
Liabilities & Stockholders' Equity		
Liabilities:		
Notes payable		$ 10,000
Accounts payable		3,200
Salaries payable		4,000
Income taxes payable		6,000
Unearned studio revenue		8,800
Total liabilities		$ 32,000
Stockholders' equity:		
Capital stock		$100,000
Retained earnings		70,000
Total stockholders' equity		$170,000
Total liabilities and stockholders' equity		$202,000

b.

JAN'S DANCE STUDIO, INC.
General Journal
December 31, 2007

Date	Account Titles and Explanations	Debit	Credit
Dec. 31 2007			
1.	Studio Revenue Earned	165,000	
	Income Summary		165,000
	To close Studio Revenue Earned.		
2.	Income Summary	129,000	
	Salary Expense		85,000
	Supply Expense		3,900
	Rent Expense		12,000
	Insurance Expense		1,900
	Advertising Expense		500
	Depreciation Expense: Equipment		1,800
	Interest Expense		900
	Income Taxes Expense		23,000
	To close all expense accounts.		
3.	Income Summary	36,000	
	Retained Earnings		36,000
	To transfer net income earned in 2007 to the Retained Earnings account ($165,000 − $129,000 = $36,000).		
4.	Retained Earnings	6,000	
	Dividends		6,000
	To transfer dividends declared in 2007 to the Retained Earnings account.		

c.

JAN'S DANCE STUDIO, INC.
After-Closing Trial Balance
December 31, 2007

	Debit	Credit
Cash	$171,100	
Accounts receivable	9,400	
Prepaid studio rent	3,000	
Unexpired insurance	7,200	
Supplies	500	
Equipment	18,000	
Accumulated depreciation: equipment		$ 7,200
Notes payable		10,000
Accounts payable		3,200
Salaries payable		4,000
Income taxes payable		6,000
Unearned studio revenue		8,800
Capital stock		100,000
Retained earnings, December 31		70,000
	$209,200	$209,200

Self-Test Questions

The answers to these questions appear on page 243.

1. For a publicly owned company, indicate which of the following accounting activities are likely to occur at or shortly after year-end. (More than one answer may be correct.)
   - **a.** Preparation of income tax returns.
   - **b.** Adjusting and closing of the accounts.
   - **c.** Drafting of disclosures that accompany the financial statements.
   - **d.** An audit of the financial statements by a firm of CPAs.
2. Which of the following financial statements is generally prepared first?
   - **a.** Income statement.
   - **b.** Balance sheet.
   - **c.** Statement of retained earnings.
   - **d.** Statement of cash flows.
3. Which of the following accounts would *never* be reported in the income statement as an expense?
   - **a.** Depreciation expense.
   - **b.** Income taxes expense.
   - **c.** Interest expense.
   - **d.** Dividends expense.
4. Which of the following accounts would *never* appear in the after-closing trial balance? (More than one answer may be correct.)
   - **a.** Unearned revenue.
   - **b.** Dividends.
   - **c.** Accumulated depreciation.
   - **d.** Income taxes expense.
5. Which of the following journal entries is required to close the Income Summary account of a profitable company?
   - **a.** Debit Income Summary, credit Retained Earnings.
   - **b.** Credit Income Summary, debit Retained Earnings.
   - **c.** Debit Income Summary, credit Capital Stock.
   - **d.** Credit Income Summary, debit Capital Stock.
6. Indicate those items for which generally accepted accounting principles *require* disclosure in notes accompanying the financial statements. (More than one answer may be correct.)
   - **a.** A large lawsuit was filed against the company two days *after* the balance sheet date.
   - **b.** The depreciation method in use, given that several different methods are acceptable under generally accepted accounting principles.
   - **c.** Whether small but long-lived items—such as electric pencil sharpeners and handheld calculators—are charged to asset accounts or to expense accounts.
   - **d.** As of year-end, the chief executive officer had been hospitalized because of chest pains.
7. Ski West adjusts its accounts at the end of each month but closes them only at the end of the calendar year (December 31). The ending balances in the Equipment Rental Revenue account and the Cash account in February and March appear below.

	Feb. 28	Mar. 31
Cash	$14,200	$26,500
Equipment rental revenue	12,100	18,400

   Ski West prepares financial statements showing separately the operating results of each month. In the financial statements prepared for the *month* ended March 31, Equipment Rental Revenue and Cash should appear as follows:
   - **a.** Equipment Rental Revenue, $18,400; Cash, $26,500.
   - **b.** Equipment Rental Revenue, $18,400; Cash, $12,300.
   - **c.** Equipment Rental Revenue, $6,300; Cash, $26,500.
   - **d.** Equipment Rental Revenue, $6,300; Cash, $12,300.
8. Which of the following accounts is *not* closed to the Income Summary account at the end of the accounting period? (More than one answer may be correct.)
   - **a.** Rent Expense.
   - **b.** Accumulated Depreciation.
   - **c.** Unearned Revenue.
   - **d.** Supplies Expense.

ASSIGNMENT MATERIAL Discussion Questions

1. Explain briefly the items generally included in a company's annual report. (You may use the financial statements appearing in Appendix A to support your answer.)
2. Discuss several limitations of the income statement.
3. Some people think that a company's retained earnings represent *cash* reserved for the payment of dividends. Are they correct? Explain.
4. Are dividends paid to stockholders ever reported in the income statement as an expense? Explain.
5. Discuss the relationship among the income statement, the statement of retained earnings, and the balance sheet.
6. Identify several items that may require disclosure in the notes that accompany financial statements.
7. What type of accounts are referred to as *temporary* or *nominal* accounts? What is meant by these terms?
8. What type of accounts are referred to as *permanent* or *real* accounts? What is meant by these terms?
9. Explain *why* the Dividends account is closed directly to the Retained Earnings account.

10. Which accounts appear in a company's after-closing trial balance? How do these accounts differ from those reported in an adjusted trial balance?
11. Can a company be profitable but not liquid? Explain.
12. What are interim financial statements? Do accounts that appear in a company's interim balance sheet require any special computations to be reported correctly? Explain.
13. Explain the accounting principle of *adequate disclosure*.
14. Briefly describe the content of the *notes* that accompany financial statements.
15. How does depreciation expense differ from other operating expenses?
16. Explain the need for closing entries and describe the process by which temporary owners' equity accounts are closed at year-end.
17. Assume that you are a developer of business software applications. How might you design an accounting software package that would enable a company to perform its year-end closing process *without* having to make all of the general journal entries illustrated on pages 201–203?
18. When preparing interim financial statements, why is it that the balance sheet accounts are not restated to correspond to the time period being covered?
19. Explain the significance of measuring a company's *return on equity*.

*20. Explain several purposes that may be served by preparing a worksheet (or using computer software that achieves the goals of a worksheet).

**Supplemental Topic*, "The Worksheet."

Brief Exercises

BRIEF EXERCISE 5.1

Balancing the Accounting Equation

During 2007, the total assets of Mifflinburg Corporation decreased by $60,000 and total liabilities decreased by $300,000. The company issued $100,000 of new stock in 2007, and its net income for the year was $250,000. No other changes to stockholders' equity occurred during the year. Determine the dollar amount of dividends declared by the company in 2007.

BRIEF EXERCISE 5.2

Income Statement and Balance Sheet Relationships

On December 1, 2007, Millstone Corporation invested $45,000 in a new delivery truck. The truck is being depreciated at a monthly rate of $500. During 2007, the company issued stock for $60,000 and declared dividends of $5,000. Its net income in 2007 was $70,000. Millstone's *ending* Retained Earnings balance as reported in its December 31, 2007, balance sheet was $90,000. Its beginning Capital Stock balance on January 1, 2007, was $200,000. Given this information, determine the total stockholders' equity reported in the company's balance sheet dated December 31, 2007.

BRIEF EXERCISE 5.3

Classifying Balance Sheet Accounts

Indicate in which section of the balance sheet each of the following accounts is *classified.* Use the symbols **CA** for current assets, **NCA** for noncurrent assets, **CL** for current liabilities, **LTL** for long-term liabilities, and **SHE** for stockholders' equity.

a. Prepaid Rent
b. Dividends Payable
c. Salaries Payable
d. Accumulated Depreciation: Equipment
e. Retained Earnings
f. Mortgage Payable (due in 15 years)
g. Unearned Service Revenue
h. Accounts Receivable
i. Land
j. Office Supplies

BRIEF EXERCISE 5.4

Identifying and Closing Temporary Accounts

Indicate whether a debit or credit is required to *close* each of the following accounts. Use the symbols **D** if a debit is required, **C** if a credit is required, and **N** if the account is *not* closed at the end of the period.

a. Salary Expense
b. Unexpired Insurance
c. Consulting Fees Earned
d. Depreciation Expense
e. Dividends
f. Retained Earnings
g. Interest Revenue
h. Accumulated Depreciation
i. Income Taxes Expense
j. Unearned Revenue
k. Income Summary (of a *profitable* company)
l. Income Summary (of an *unprofitable* company)

BRIEF EXERCISE 5.5

Closing Entries of a Profitable Company

The following account balances were taken from Cal Tour Corporation's year-end *adjusted* trial balance (assume these are the company's only *temporary* accounts):

Dividends	$ 600
Service revenue	19,800
Supplies expense	525
Rent expense	3,660
Depreciation expense: equipment	1,200
Salaries expense	12,700
Income taxes expense	615

Prepare the company's necessary closing entries.

BRIEF EXERCISE 5.6

Closing Entries of an Unprofitable Company

The following account balances were taken from Cal Tour Corporation's year-end *adjusted* trial balance (assume these are the company's only *temporary* accounts):

Consulting fees earned	$26,000
Interest revenue	300
Insurance expense	1,900
Rent expense	10,800
Depreciation expense: office equipment	5,600
Salaries expense	16,400
Dividends	400

Prepare the company's necessary closing entries.

BRIEF EXERCISE 5.7

After-Closing Trial Balance

Indicate whether each of the following accounts appears in the debit column or in the credit column of an *after-closing* trial balance. Use the symbols **D** for debit column, **C** for credit column, and **N** if the account does *not* appear in an after-closing trial balance.

a. Unearned Service Revenue
b. Accumulated Depreciation: Office Equipment
c. Land
d. Consulting Fees Earned
e. Capital Stock
f. Income Summary (of a *profitable* company)
g. Depreciation Expense: Office Equipment
h. Income Taxes Payable
i. Unexpired Insurance
j. Dividends
k. Retained Earnings
l. Dividends Payable

BRIEF EXERCISE 5.8

Profitability and Liquidity Measures

Dog Daze, Inc., has provided the following information from its most current financial statements:

Total revenue	$60,000
Total expenses	45,000
Total current assets	16,000
Total current liabilities	4,000
Total stockholders' equity, January 1, 2007	37,000
Total stockholders' equity, December 31, 2007	38,000

a. Compute the company's net income percentage in 2007.

b. Compute the company's return on equity in 2007.

c. Compute the company's current ratio at December 31, 2007.

BRIEF EXERCISE 5.9

Measuring Interim Revenue

The following revenue figures were taken from Rosemont Corporation's adjusted trial balance at the end of the following months (adjusting entries are performed *monthly* whereas closing entries are performed *annually*, on December 31):

March 31 (end of the first quarter)	$140,000
September 30 (end of the third quarter)	450,000
December 31 (end of the fourth quarter)	680,000

Compute how much revenue the company earned from:

a. April 1 through September 30.

b. October 1 through December 31 (the fourth quarter).

c. April 1 through December 31.

***BRIEF EXERCISE 5.10**

The Worksheet

Accountants at Warner Co. use worksheets similar to the one shown in Exhibit 5–14, on page 212. In the company's most current year-end worksheet, the amounts transferred *from* the adjusted trial balance columns *to* the balance sheet and income statement columns are as follows:

Total amount transferred to the credit column of the balance sheet	$410,000
Total amount transferred to the debit column of the balance sheet	540,000
Total amount transferred to the credit column of the income statement	380,000

a. What was the company's net income for the year?

b. What was the total amount transferred from the adjusted trial balance columns to the debit column of the income statement?

Exercises

through

EXERCISE 5.1

Accounting Terminology

Listed below are nine technical terms used in this chapter:

Liquidity	Nominal accounts	Real accounts
Adequate disclosure	After-closing trial balance	Closing entries
Income summary	Interim financial statements	Dividends

Each of the following statements may (or may not) describe one of these technical terms. For each statement, indicate the accounting term described, or answer "None" if the statement does not describe any of the items.

a. The accounting principle intended to assist users in *interpreting* financial statements.

b. A term used to describe a company's ability to pay its obligations as they come due.

c. A term used in reference to accounts that are closed at year-end.

d. A term used in reference to accounts that are not closed at year-end.

e. A document prepared to assist management in detecting whether any errors occurred in posting the closing entries.

f. A policy decision by a corporation to distribute a portion of its income to stockholders.

g. The process by which the Retained Earnings account is updated at year-end.

h. Entries made during the accounting period to correct errors in the original recording of complex transactions.

**Supplemental Topic*, "The Worksheet."

EXERCISE 5.2
Financial Statement Preparation

Tutors for Rent, Inc., performs adjusting entries every month, but closes its accounts *only at year-end.* The company's year-end *adjusted trial balance* dated December 31, 2007, was:

TUTORS FOR RENT, INC.
Adjusted Trial Balance
December 31, 2007

Cash	$ 91,100	
Accounts receivable	4,500	
Supplies	300	
Equipment	12,000	
Accumulated depreciation: equipment		$ 5,000
Accounts payable		1,500
Income taxes payable		3,500
Capital stock		25,000
Retained earnings		45,000
Dividends	2,000	
Tutoring revenue earned		96,000
Salary expense	52,000	
Supply expense	1,200	
Advertising expense	300	
Depreciation expense: equipment	1,000	
Income taxes expense	11,600	
	$176,000	$176,000

a. Prepare an income statement and statement of retained earnings for the year ended December 31, 2007. Also prepare the company's balance sheet dated December 31, 2007.

b. Does the company appear to be liquid? Defend your answer.

c. Has the company been profitable in the past? Explain.

LO6

EXERCISE 5.3
Financial Statement Preparation

Wilderness Guide Services, Inc., performs adjusting entries every month, but closes its accounts *only at year-end.* The company's year-end *adjusted trial balance* dated December 31, 2007, follows:

WILDERNESS GUIDE SERVICES, INC.
Adjusted Trial Balance
December 31, 2007

Cash	$ 12,200	
Accounts receivable	31,000	
Camping supplies	7,900	
Unexpired insurance policies	2,400	
Equipment	70,000	
Accumulated depreciation: equipment		$ 60,000
Notes payable (due 4/1/08)		18,000
Accounts payable		9,500
Capital stock		25,000
Retained earnings		15,000
Dividends	1,000	
Guide revenue earned		102,000
Salary expense	87,500	
Camping supply expense	1,200	
Insurance expense	9,600	
Depreciation expense: equipment	5,000	
Interest expense	1,700	
	$229,500	$229,500

a. Prepare an income statement and statement of retained earnings for the year ended December 31, 2007. Also prepare the company's balance sheet dated December 31, 2007. (Hint: Unprofitable companies have no income taxes expense.)

b. Does the company appear to be liquid? Defend your answer.

c. Has the company been profitable in the past? Explain.

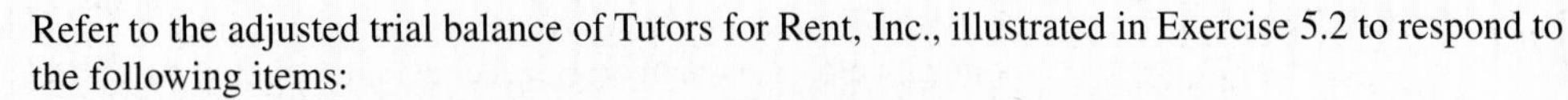
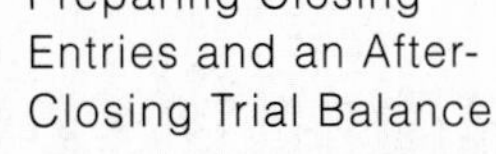

EXERCISE 5.4
Preparing Closing Entries and an After-Closing Trial Balance

Refer to the adjusted trial balance of Tutors for Rent, Inc., illustrated in Exercise 5.2 to respond to the following items:

a. Prepare all necessary closing entries at December 31, 2007.

b. Prepare an after-closing trial balance dated December 31, 2007.

c. Compare the Retained Earnings balance reported in the after-closing trial balance prepared in part **b** to the balance reported in the adjusted trial balance. Explain *why* the two balances are different. (Include in your explanation why the balance reported in the after-closing trial balance has increased or decreased subsequent to the closing process.)

EXERCISE 5.5
Preparing Closing Entries and an After-Closing Trial Balance

Refer to the adjusted trial balance of Wilderness Guide Services, Inc., illustrated in Exercise 5.3 to respond to the following items:

a. Prepare all necessary closing entries at December 31, 2007.

b. Prepare an after-closing trial balance dated December 31, 2007.

c. Compare the Retained Earnings balance reported in the after-closing trial balance prepared in part **b** to the balance reported in the adjusted trial balance. Explain *why* the two balances are different. (Include in your explanation why the balance reported in the after-closing trial balance has increased or decreased subsequent to the closing process.)

EXERCISE 5.6
Adequate Disclosure

The following information was taken directly from the footnotes to the financial statements of Circuit City:

1. "The company recognizes revenue when the earnings process is complete."

2. "The company sells gift cards and records related deferred revenue at the time of sale."

3. "Advertising costs are expensed as incurred."

4. "Property and equipment is stated at cost less accumulated depreciation. Depreciation is calculated using the straight-line method over the assets' estimated useful lives."

a. Discuss what is meant by each of the above footnote items.

b. As noted, Circuit City uses a Deferred Revenue account to record the sale of gift cards. Assume that you purchased a $500 gift card from Circuit City as a birthday present for a friend. Prepare the journal entries made by Circuit City to record (1) your purchase of the $500 gift card and (2) the *use* of the gift card by your friend to purchase a $500 television.

c. Discuss how the *matching principle* relates to Circuit City's treatment of advertising expenditures.

EXERCISE 5.7
Closing Entries of a Profitable Company

Gerdes Psychological Services, Inc., closes its temporary accounts once each year on December 31. The company recently issued the following income statement as part of its annual report:

GERDES PSYCHOLOGICAL SERVICES, INC.
Income Statement
For the Year Ended December 31, 2007

Revenue:		
Counseling revenue		$225,000
Expenses:		
Advertising expense	$ 1,800	
Salaries expense	94,000	
Office supplies expense	1,200	
Utilities expense	850	
Malpractice insurance expense	6,000	
Office rent expense	24,000	
Continuing education expense	2,650	
Depreciation expense: fixtures	4,500	
Miscellaneous expense	6,000	
Income taxes expense	29,400	170,400
Net income		$ 54,600

The firm's statement of retained earnings indicates that a $6,000 cash dividend was declared and paid during 2007.

a. Prepare the necessary closing entries on December 31, 2007.

b. If the firm's Retained Earnings account had a $92,000 balance on January 1, 2007, at what amount should Retained Earnings be reported in the firm's balance sheet dated December 31, 2007?

EXERCISE 5.8
Closing Entries of an Unprofitable Company

LO4

Ferraro Consulting provides risk management services to individuals and to corporate clients. The company closes its temporary accounts once each year on December 31. The company recently issued the following income statement as part of its annual report:

FERRARO CONSULTING
Income Statement
For the Year Ended December 31, 2007

Revenue:		
Consulting revenue—individual clients		$ 40,000
Consulting revenue—corporate clients		160,000
		$200,000
Expenses:		
Advertising expense	$ 16,000	
Depreciation expense: computers	24,000	
Rent expense	9,600	
Office supplies expense	4,400	
Travel expense	57,800	
Utilities expense	3,300	
Telephone and Internet expense	1,900	
Salaries expense	155,500	
Interest expense	2,500	275,000
Net loss		$ (75,000)

The firm's statement of retained earnings indicates that a $25,000 cash dividend was declared and paid in 2007.

a. Prepare the necessary closing entries on December 31, 2007.

b. If the firm's Retained Earnings account had a $300,000 balance on January 1, 2007, at what amount should Retained Earnings be reported in the firm's balance sheet dated December 31, 2007?

EXERCISE 5.9
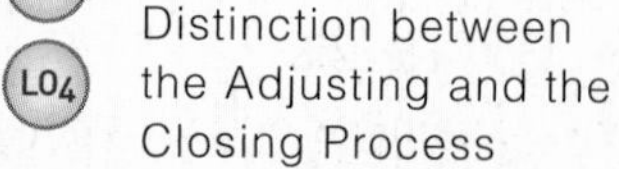

Distinction between the Adjusting and the Closing Process

When Torretti Company began business on August 1, it purchased a one-year fire insurance policy and debited the entire cost of $7,200 to Unexpired Insurance. Torretti *adjusts* its accounts at the end of each month and *closes* its books at the end of the year.

a. Give the *adjusting entry* required at December 31 with respect to this insurance policy.

b. Give the *closing entry* required at December 31 with respect to insurance expense. Assume that this policy is the only insurance policy Torretti had during the year.

c. Compare the dollar amount appearing in the December 31 adjusting entry (part **a**) with that in the closing entry (part **b**). Are the dollar amounts the same? Why or why not? Explain.

EXERCISE 5.10
Measuring and Evaluating Profitability and Liquidity

A recent balance sheet of Oregon Foods is provided below:

OREGON FOODS
Balance Sheet
December 31, 2007

Assets		
Cash		$ 6,800
Accounts receivable		7,200
Office supplies		300
Prepaid rent		1,700
Equipment	$12,000	
Accumulated depreciation: equipment	(4,800)	$ 7,200
Total assets		$23,200
Liabilities		
Accounts payable		$ 2,200
Income taxes payable		1,800
Total liabilities		$ 4,000
Stockholders' Equity		
Capital stock		$10,000
Retained earnings		9,200
Total stockholders' equity		$19,200
Total liabilities and stockholders' equity		$23,200

Other information provided by the company is as follows:

Total revenue for the year ended December 31, 2007	$25,500
Total expenses for the year ended December 31, 2007	20,400
Total stockholders' equity, January 1, 2007	14,800

Compute and discuss briefly the significance of the following measures as they relate to Oregon Foods:

a. Net income percentage in 2007.

b. Return on equity in 2007.

c. Working capital on December 31, 2007.

d. Current ratio on December 31, 2007.

EXERCISE 5.11

Measuring and Evaluating Profitability and Liquidity

A recent balance sheet of Denver Tours is provided below:

DENVER TOURS Balance Sheet December 31, 2007		
Assets		
Cash		$ 75,100
Accounts receivable		14,000
Office supplies		1,500
Prepaid rent		3,400
Buses	$ 240,000	
Accumulated depreciation: buses	(18,000)	$222,000
Total assets		$316,000
Liabilities		
Accounts payable		$140,200
Unearned revenue		94,800
Total liabilities		$235,000
Stockholders' Equity		
Capital stock		$ 80,000
Retained earnings		1,000
Total stockholders' equity		$ 81,000
Total liabilities and stockholders' equity		$316,000

Other information provided by the company is as follows:

Total revenue for the year ended December 31, 2007	$152,000
Total expenses for the year ended December 31, 2007	148,960
Total stockholders' equity, January 1, 2007	79,000

Compute and discuss briefly the significance of the following measures as they relate to Denver Tours:

a. Net income percentage in 2007.

b. Return on equity in 2007.

c. Working capital on December 31, 2007.

d. Current ratio on December 31, 2007.

EXERCISE 5.12
Interim Results

Ski Powder Resort ends its fiscal year on April 30. The business adjusts its accounts monthly, but *closes them only at year-end* (April 30). The resort's busy season is from December 1 through March 31.

Adrian Pride, the resort's chief financial officer, keeps a close watch on Lift Ticket Revenue and Cash. The balances of these accounts at the end of each of the last five months are as follows:

	Lift Ticket Revenue	Cash
November 30	$ 30,000	$ 9,000
December 31	200,000	59,000
January 31	640,000	94,000
February 28	850,000	116,000
March 31	990,000	138,000

Mr. Pride prepares income statements and balance sheets for the resort. Indicate what amounts will be shown in these statements for (1) Lift Ticket Revenue and (2) Cash, assuming they are prepared for:

a. The *month* ended February 28.

b. The entire "busy season to date"—that is, December 1 through March 31.

c. In terms of Lift Ticket Revenue and increases in Cash, which has been the resort's best month? (Indicate the dollar amounts.)

EXERCISE 5.13

Interim Results

Custodian Commandos, Inc., provides janitorial services to public school systems. The business adjusts its accounts monthly, but *closes them only at year-end.* Its fiscal year ends on December 31.

A summary of the company's total revenue and expenses at the end of five selected months is as follows:

	Total Revenue	Total Expenses
March 31	$ 69,000	$ 48,000
June 30	129,000	90,000
August 31	134,000	115,000
September 30	159,000	130,000
December 31	249,000	175,000

a. Rank the company's fiscal quarters from most profitable to least profitable.

b. Compute the company's income for the month of September.

c. Compute the company's net income (or loss) for the first two months of the *third quarter.* Provide a possible explanation why profitability for the first two months of the third quarter differs significantly from profitability achieved in the third month of the quarter (as computed in part **b**).

EXERCISE 5.14
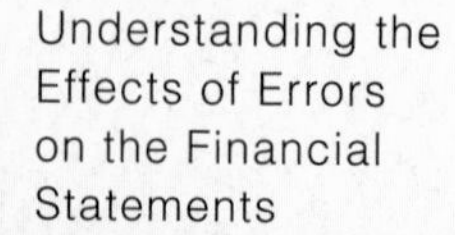
Understanding the Effects of Errors on the Financial Statements

Indicate the effect of the following errors on each of the financial statement elements described in the column headings in the table below. Use the following symbols: **O** = overstated, **U** = understated, and **NE** = no effect.

	Error	Net Income	Total Assets	Total Liabilities	Retained Earnings
a.	Recorded a dividend as an *expense* in the income statement.				
b.	Recorded unearned revenue as *earned* revenue in the income statement.				
c.	Failed to record accrued wages payable at the end of the accounting period.				
d.	Recorded a declared but unpaid dividend by debiting Dividends and crediting Cash.				
e.	Failed to disclose a pending lawsuit in the notes accompanying the financial statements.				

LO6

EXERCISE 5.15
Examining **Home Depot, Inc.**, Financial Statements

The **Home Depot, Inc.**, financial statements appear in Appendix A at the end of this textbook.

a. Does the company use straight-line depreciation? How can you tell?

b. At what point does the company recognize and record revenue from its customers?

c. Using information from the consolidated financial statements, evaluate briefly the company's profitability and liquidity.

Problem Set A

LO2

PROBLEM 5.1A
Correcting Classification Errors

Party Wagon, Inc., provides musical entertainment at weddings, dances, and various other functions. The company performs adjusting entries *monthly*, but prepares closing entries *annually* on December 31. The company recently hired Jack Armstrong as its new accountant. Jack's first assignment was to prepare an income statement, a statement of retained earnings, and a balance sheet using an *adjusted* trial balance given to him by his predecessor, dated December 31, 2007.

From the adjusted trial balance, Jack prepared the following set of financial statements:

PARTY WAGON, INC.
Income Statement
For the Year Ended December 31, 2007

Revenue:		
Party revenue earned		$130,000
Unearned party revenue		1,800
Accounts receivable		9,000
Total revenue		$140,800
Expenses:		
Insurance expense	$ 1,800	
Office rent expense	12,000	
Supplies expense	1,200	
Dividends	1,000	
Salary expense	75,000	
Accumulated depreciation: van	16,000	
Accumulated depreciation: equipment and music	14,000	
Repair and maintenance expense	2,000	
Travel expense	6,000	
Miscellaneous expense	3,600	
Interest expense	4,400	137,000
Income before income taxes		$ 3,800
Income taxes payable		400
Net income		$ 3,400

PARTY WAGON, INC.
Statement of Retained Earnings
For the Year Ended December 31, 2007

Retained earnings (per adjusted trial balance)	$15,000
Add: Income	3,400
Less: Income taxes expense	2,000
Retained earnings Dec. 31, 2007	$16,400

PARTY WAGON, INC.
Balance Sheet
December 31, 2007

Assets		
Cash		$15,000
Supplies		500
Van	$40,000	
Less: Depreciation expense: van	8,000	32,000
Equipment and music	$35,000	
Less: Depreciation expense: music and equipment	7,000	28,000
Total assets		$75,500
Liabilities & Stockholders' Equity		
Liabilities:		
Accounts payable		$ 7,000
Notes payable		39,000
Salaries payable		1,600
Prepaid rent		2,000
Unexpired insurance		4,500
Total liabilities		$54,100
Stockholders' Equity:		
Capital stock		5,000
Retained earnings		16,400
Total stockholders' equity		$21,400
Total liabilities and stockholders' equity		$75,500

Instructions

a. Prepare a corrected set of financial statements dated December 31, 2007. (You may assume that all of the figures in the company's adjusted trial balance were reported correctly except for Interest Payable of $200, which was mistakenly omitted in the financial statements prepared by Jack.)

b. Prepare the necessary year-end closing entries.

c. Using the financial statements prepared in part **a**, briefly evaluate the company's profitability and liquidity.

PROBLEM 5.2A
Preparing Financial Statements and Closing Entries of a Profitable Company

LO1 LO2 LO4 through LO6

Lawn Pride, Inc., provides lawn-mowing services to both commercial and residential customers. The company performs adjusting entries on a *monthly* basis, whereas closing entries are prepared *annually* at December 31. An *adjusted* trial balance dated December 31, 2007, follows.

LAWN PRIDE, INC.
Adjusted Trial Balance
December 31, 2007

	Debits	Credits
Cash	$ 58,525	
Accounts receivable	4,800	
Unexpired insurance	8,000	
Prepaid rent	3,000	
Supplies	1,075	
Trucks	150,000	
Accumulated depreciation: trucks		$120,000
Mowing equipment	20,000	
Accumulated depreciation: mowing equipment		12,000
Accounts payable		1,500
Notes payable		50,000
Salaries payable		900
Interest payable		150
Income taxes payable		1,050
Unearned mowing revenue		900
Capital stock		20,000
Retained earnings		30,000
Dividends	5,000	
Mowing revenue earned		170,000
Insurance expense	2,400	
Office rent expense	36,000	
Supplies expense	5,200	
Salary expense	60,000	
Depreciation expense: trucks	30,000	
Depreciation expense: mowing equipment	4,000	
Repair and maintenance expense	3,000	
Fuel expense	1,500	
Miscellaneous expense	5,000	
Interest expense	3,000	
Income taxes expense	6,000	
	$406,500	$406,500

Instructions

a. Prepare an income statement and statement of retained earnings for the year ended December 31, 2007. Also prepare the company's balance sheet dated December 31, 2007.

b. Prepare the necessary year-end closing entries.

c. Prepare an after-closing trial balance.

d. Using the financial statements prepared in part **a**, briefly evaluate the company's profitability and liquidity.

LO1 through LO4 LO6

PROBLEM 5.3A
Preparing Financial Statements and Closing Entries of an Unprofitable Company

Mystic Masters, Inc., provides fortune-telling services over the Internet. In recent years the company has experienced severe financial difficulty. Its accountant prepares adjusting entries on a *monthly* basis, and closing entries on an *annual* basis, at December 31. An *adjusted* trial balance dated December 31, 2007, follows.

MYSTIC MASTERS, INC.
Adjusted Trial Balance
December 31, 2007

	Debits	Credits
Cash	$ 960	
Accounts receivable	300	
Unexpired insurance	2,000	
Prepaid rent	1,500	
Supplies	200	
Furniture and fixtures	8,400	
Accumulated depreciation: furniture and fixtures		$ 5,200
Accounts payable		6,540
Notes payable		24,000
Salaries payable		1,700
Interest payable		360
Unearned client revenue		200
Capital stock		4,000
Retained earnings		2,600
Client revenue earned		52,000
Insurance expense	6,000	
Office rent expense	9,000	
Supplies expense	440	
Salary expense	48,000	
Depreciation expense: furniture and fixtures	1,400	
Office and telephone expense	3,000	
Internet service expense	4,900	
Legal expense	1,500	
Interest expense	4,000	
Miscellaneous expense	5,000	
	$96,600	$96,600

Instructions

a. Prepare an income statement and statement of retained earnings for the year ended December 31, 2007. Also prepare the company's balance sheet dated December 31, 2007. (Hint: The company incurred no income taxes expense in 2007.)

b. Prepare the necessary year-end closing entries.

c. Prepare an after-closing trial balance.

d. Using the financial statements prepared in part **a**, briefly evaluate the company's performance.

e. Identify information that the company is apt to disclose in the notes that accompany the financial statements prepared in part **a**.

PROBLEM 5.4A
Interim Financial Statements

Guardian Insurance Agency adjusts its accounts monthly but closes them only at the end of the calendar year. Below are the adjusted balances of the revenue and expense accounts at September 30 of the current year and at the ends of two earlier months:

	Sept. 30	Aug. 31	June 30
Commissions earned	$144,000	$128,000	$90,000
Advertising expense	28,000	23,000	15,000
Salaries expense	36,000	32,000	24,000
Rent expense	22,500	20,000	15,000
Depreciation expense	2,700	2,400	1,800

Instructions

a. Prepare a three-column income statement, showing net income for three separate time periods, all of which end on September 30. Use the format illustrated below. Show supporting computations for the amounts of revenue reported in the first two columns.

GUARDIAN INSURANCE AGENCY
Income Statement
For the Following Time Periods in 2007

	Month Ended Sept. 30	Quarter Ended Sept. 30	9 Months Ended Sept. 30
Revenue:			
Commissions earned	$	$	$
Expenses:			

b. Briefly explain how you determined the dollar amounts for each of the three time periods. Would you apply the same process to the balances in Guardian's balance sheet accounts? Explain.

c. Assume that Guardian adjusts *and closes* its accounts at the end of *each month*. Briefly explain how you then would determine the revenue and expenses that would appear in each of the three columns of the income statement prepared in part **a**.

through
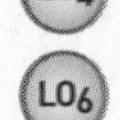

PROBLEM 5.5A
Short Comprehensive Problem Including Both Adjusting and Closing Entries

Silver Lining, Inc., provides investment advisory services. The company adjusts its accounts *monthly*, but performs closing entries *annually* on December 31. The firm's *unadjusted* trial balance dated December 31, 2007, is shown on the following page.

SILVER LINING, INC.
Unadjusted Trial Balance
December 31, 2007

	Debit	Credit
Cash	$ 42,835	
Accounts receivable	2,000	
Office supplies	205	
Prepaid rent	1,200	
Unexpired insurance	270	
Office equipment	54,000	
Accumulated depreciation: office equipment		$ 35,250
Accounts payable		1,400
Interest payable		360
Income taxes payable		1,750
Notes payable		9,000
Unearned consulting services revenue		3,500
Capital stock		30,000
Retained earnings		8,000
Dividends	1,000	
Consulting services revenue		60,000
Office supplies expense	605	
Depreciation expense: office equipment	8,250	
Rent expense	3,525	
Insurance expense	1,010	
Salaries expense	27,100	
Interest expense	360	
Income taxes expense	6,900	
Totals	$149,260	$149,260

Other Data

1. Accrued but *unrecorded* and uncollected consulting services revenue totals $1,500 at December 31, 2007.
2. The company determined that $2,500 of previously unearned consulting services revenue had been earned at December 31, 2007.
3. Office supplies on hand at December 31 total $110.
4. The company purchased all of its equipment when it first began business. At that time, the estimated useful life of the equipment was six years (72 months).
5. The company prepaid its six-month rent agreement on October 1, 2007.
6. The company prepaid its 12-month insurance policy on March 1, 2007.
7. Accrued but *unpaid* salaries total $1,900 at December 31, 2007.
8. On June 1, 2007, the company borrowed $9,000 by signing a nine-month, 8 percent note payable. The entire amount, plus interest, is due on March 1, 2008.
9. The company's CPA estimates that income taxes expense for the *entire year* is $7,500. The unpaid portion of this amount is due early in 2008.

Instructions

a. Prepare the necessary adjusting journal entries on December 31, 2007. Prepare also an *adjusted trial balance* dated December 31, 2007.

b. From the adjusted trial balance prepared in part **a**, prepare an income statement and statement of retained earnings for the year ended December 31, 2007. Also prepare the company's balance sheet dated December 31, 2007.

c. Prepare the necessary year-end closing entries.

d. Prepare an after-closing trial balance.

e. Compute the company's average *monthly* insurance expense for January and February of 2007.

f. Compute the company's average *monthly* rent expense for January through September of 2007.

g. If the company purchased all of its office equipment when it first incorporated, for how long has it been in business as of December 31, 2007?

h. Does the company appear to be liquid? Defend your answer.

LO1 through LO4 LO6

PROBLEM 5.6A

Short Comprehensive Problem Including Both Adjusting and Closing Entries

Brushstroke Art Studio, Inc., provides quality instruction to aspiring artists. The business adjusts its accounts *monthly*, but performs closing entries *annually* on December 31. This is the studio's *unadjusted* trial balance dated December 31, 2007.

BRUSHSTROKE ART STUDIO, INC.
Unadjusted Trial Balance
December 31, 2007

	Debits	Credits
Cash	$ 22,380	
Client fees receivable	71,250	
Supplies	6,000	
Prepaid studio rent	2,500	
Studio equipment	96,000	
Accumulated depreciation: studio equipment		$ 52,000
Accounts payable		6,420
Note payable		24,000
Interest payable		480
Unearned client fees		8,000
Income taxes payable		5,000
Capital stock		50,000
Retained earnings		20,000
Client fees earned		82,310
Supplies expense	4,000	
Salary expense	17,250	
Interest expense	480	
Studio rent expense	11,250	
Utilities expense	3,300	
Depreciation expense: studio equipment	8,800	
Income taxes expense	5,000	
	$248,210	$248,210

Other Data

1. Supplies on hand at December 31, 2007, total $1,000.
2. The studio pays rent quarterly (every three months). The last payment was made November 1, 2007. The next payment will be made early in February 2008.
3. Studio equipment is being depreciated over 120 months (10 years).

4. On October 1, 2007, the studio borrowed $24,000 by signing a 12-month, 12 percent note payable. The entire amount, plus interest, is due on September 30, 2008.
5. At December 31, 2007, $3,000 of previously unearned client fees had been *earned*.
6. Accrued, but *unrecorded* and uncollected client fees earned total $690 at December 31, 2007.
7. Accrued, but *unrecorded* and unpaid salary expense totals $750 at December 31, 2007.
8. Accrued income taxes expense for the *entire year* ending December 31, 2007, *total* $7,000. The full amount is due early in 2008.

Instructions

a. Prepare the necessary adjusting journal entries on December 31, 2007. Prepare also an *adjusted trial balance* dated December 31, 2007.

b. From the adjusted trial balance prepared in part **a**, prepare an income statement and statement of retained earnings for the year ended December 31, 2007. Also prepare the company's balance sheet dated December 31, 2007.

c. Prepare the necessary year-end closing entries.

d. Prepare an after-closing trial balance.

e. Has the studio's monthly rent remained the same throughout the year? If not, has it gone up or down? Explain.

*PROBLEM 5.7A

Short Comprehensive Problem Including Adjusting Entries, Closing Entries, and Worksheet Preparation

Refer to the Demonstration Problem illustrated in the previous chapter on pages 163–166. Prepare a 10-column worksheet for Internet Consulting Service, Inc., dated December 31, 2007. At the bottom of your worksheet, prepare a brief explanation keyed to each adjusting entry.

PROBLEM 5.8A

Evaluating Profitability and Liquidity

A recent annual report issued by Circuit City revealed the following data:

	End of Year	Beginning of Year
Current assets	$3.08 billion	$2.85 billion
Current liabilities	$1.42 billion	$1.29 billion
Stockholders' equity	$2.56 billion	$2.36 billion

The company's income statement reported total annual revenue of $13.4 billion and net income for the year of $191 million.

Instructions

a. Evaluate Circuit City's profitability by computing its net income percentage and its return on equity for the year.

b. Evaluate Circuit City's liquidity by computing its working capital and its current ratio at the beginning of the year and at the end of the year.

c. Does Circuit City appear to be both profitable and liquid? Explain.

Supplemental Topic, "The Worksheet."

Problem Set B

PROBLEM 5.1B
Correcting Classification Errors

LO1 LO2 LO4 LO6

Strong Knot, Inc., a service company, performs adjusting entries *monthly*, but prepares closing entries *annually* on December 31. The company recently hired Sally Addsup as its new accountant. Sally's first assignment was to prepare an income statement, a statement of retained earnings, and a balance sheet using an *adjusted* trial balance given to her by her predecessor, dated December 31, 2007. The statements Sally prepared are as follows:

STRONG KNOT, INC.
Income Statement
For the Year Ended December 31, 2007

Revenue:		
Service revenue earned		$160,000
Unearned revenue		3,500
Accounts receivable		8,200
Total revenue		$171,700
Expenses:		
Insurance expense	$ 1,800	
Office rent expense	18,000	
Supplies expense	1,200	
Dividends	3,000	
Salary expense	96,000	
Accumulated depreciation: auto	12,000	
Accumulated depreciation: equipment	13,000	
Repair and maintenance expense	1,700	
Travel expense	6,600	
Miscellaneous expense	2,100	
Interest expense	2,800	158,200
Income before income taxes		$ 13,500
Income taxes payable		400
Net income		$ 13,100

STRONG KNOT, INC.
Statement of Retained Earnings
For the Year Ended December 31, 2007

Retained earnings (per adjusted trial balance)	$17,500
Add: Income	13,100
Less: Income taxes expense	4,000
Retained earnings, Dec. 31, 2007	$26,600

STRONG KNOT, INC.
Balance Sheet
December 31, 2007

Assets		
Cash		$15,400
Supplies		900
Automobile	$37,000	
Less: Depreciation expense: automobile	4,000	33,000
Equipment and music	$39,000	
Less: Depreciation expense: equipment	3,000	36,000
Total assets		$85,300
Liabilities & Stockholders' Equity		
Liabilities:		
Accounts payable		$ 5,200
Notes payable		45,800
Salaries payable		900
Prepaid rent		800
Unexpired insurance		3,000
Total liabilities		$55,700
Stockholders' Equity:		
Capital stock		3,000
Retained earnings		26,600
Total stockholders' equity		$29,600
Total liabilities and stockholders' equity		$85,300

Instructions

a. Prepare a corrected set of financial statements dated December 31, 2007. (You may assume that all of the figures in the company's adjusted trial balance were reported correctly except for Notes Payable, which is some amount other than $45,800.)

b. Prepare the necessary year-end closing entries.

c. Using the financial statements prepared in part **a**, briefly evaluate the company's profitability and liquidity.

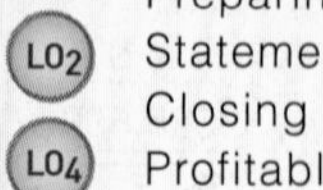
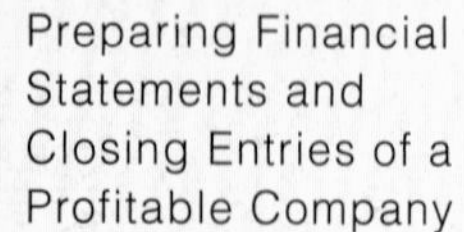
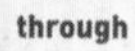

PROBLEM 5.2B
Preparing Financial Statements and Closing Entries of a Profitable Company

Garden Wizards provides gardening services to both commercial and residential customers. The company performs adjusting entries on a *monthly* basis, whereas closing entries are prepared *annually* at December 31. An adjusted trial balance dated December 31, 2007, follows.

GARDEN WIZARDS
Adjusted Trial Balance
December 31, 2007

	Debits	Credits
Cash	$ 27,800	
Accounts receivable	4,300	
Unexpired insurance	8,700	
Prepaid rent	3,200	
Supplies	1,400	
Trucks	140,000	
Accumulated depreciation: trucks		$ 75,000
Equipment	28,000	
Accumulated depreciation: equipment		14,000
Accounts payable		2,200
Notes payable		38,000
Salaries payable		900
Interest payable		300
Income taxes payable		1,700
Unearned service revenue		2,000
Capital stock		18,000
Retained earnings		21,000
Dividends	3,300	
Service revenue earned		194,000
Insurance expense	1,800	
Office rent expense	28,000	
Supplies expense	5,600	
Salary expense	72,000	
Depreciation expense: trucks	16,000	
Depreciation expense: equipment	4,000	
Repair and maintenance expense	5,300	
Fuel expense	2,200	
Miscellaneous expense	2,700	
Interest expense	3,800	
Income taxes expense	9,000	
	$367,100	$367,100

Instructions

a. Prepare an income statement and statement of retained earnings for the year ended December 31, 2007. Also prepare the company's balance sheet dated December 31, 2007.

b. Prepare the necessary year-end closing entries.

c. Prepare an after-closing trial balance.

d. Using the financial statements prepared in part **a**, briefly evaluate the company's profitability and liquidity.

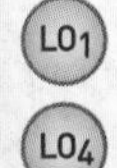

PROBLEM 5.3B
Preparing Financial Statements and Closing Entries of an Unprofitable Company

LO1, LO4 through LO6

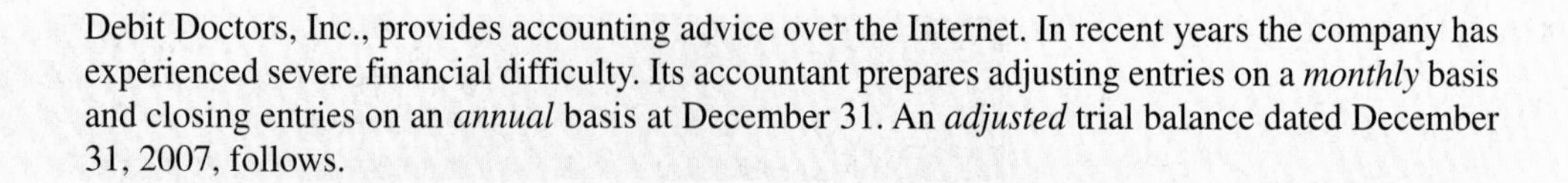

Debit Doctors, Inc., provides accounting advice over the Internet. In recent years the company has experienced severe financial difficulty. Its accountant prepares adjusting entries on a *monthly* basis and closing entries on an *annual* basis at December 31. An *adjusted* trial balance dated December 31, 2007, follows.

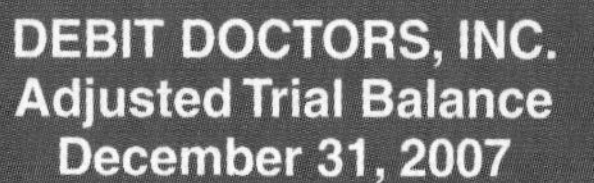

DEBIT DOCTORS, INC.
Adjusted Trial Balance
December 31, 2007

	Debits	Credits
Cash	$ 450	
Accounts receivable	220	
Unexpired insurance	1,600	
Prepaid rent	1,800	
Supplies	900	
Furniture and fixtures	10,000	
Accumulated depreciation: furniture and fixtures		$ 6,600
Accounts payable		7,100
Notes payable		24,000
Salaries payable		2,100
Interest payable		170
Unearned client revenue		600
Capital stock		4,000
Retained earnings		2,000
Client revenue earned		56,700
Insurance expense	6,200	
Office rent expense	12,000	
Supplies expense	300	
Salary expense	48,000	
Depreciation expense: furniture and fixtures	1,200	
Office and telephone expense	4,600	
Internet service expense	7,200	
Legal expense	1,800	
Interest expense	2,700	
Miscellaneous expense	4,300	
	$103,270	$103,270

Instructions

a. Prepare an income statement and statement of retained earnings for the year ended December 31, 2007. Also prepare the company's balance sheet dated December 31, 2007. (Hint: The company incurred no income taxes expense in 2007.)

b. Prepare the necessary year-end closing entries.

c. Prepare an after-closing trial balance.

d. Using the financial statements prepared in part **a**, briefly evaluate the company's performance.

e. Identify information that the company is apt to disclose in the notes that accompany the financial statements prepared in part **a**.

LO2

PROBLEM 5.4B
Interim Financial Statements

Silver Real Estate adjusts its accounts monthly but closes them only at the end of the calendar year. Below are the adjusted balances of the revenue and expense accounts at September 30 of the current year and at the ends of two earlier months:

	Sept. 30	Aug. 31	June 30
Commissions earned	$160,000	$145,000	$100,000
Advertising expense	33,000	28,000	18,000
Salaries expense	38,000	35,000	28,000
Rent expense	20,000	18,000	14,000
Depreciation expense	2,200	2,100	1,500

Instructions

a. Prepare a three-column income statement, showing net income for three separate time periods, all of which end on September 30. Use the format illustrated below. Show supporting computations for the amounts of revenue in the first two columns.

SILVER REAL ESTATE
Income Statement
For the Following Time Periods in 2007

	Month Ended Sept. 30	Quarter Ended Sept. 30	Nine Months Ended Sept. 30
Revenue:			
Commissions earned	$	$	$
Expenses:			

b. Briefly explain how you determined the dollar amounts for each of the three time periods. Would you apply the same process to the balances in Silver's balance sheet accounts? Explain.

c. Assume that Silver adjusts *and closes* its accounts at the end of *each month*. Briefly explain how you then would determine the revenue and expenses that would appear in each of the three columns of the income statement prepared in part **a**.

through LO4 LO6

PROBLEM 5.5B
Short Comprehensive Problem Including Both Adjusting and Closing Entries

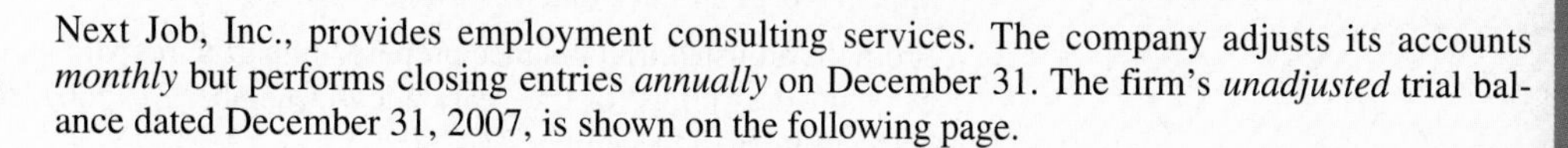
Next Job, Inc., provides employment consulting services. The company adjusts its accounts *monthly* but performs closing entries *annually* on December 31. The firm's *unadjusted* trial balance dated December 31, 2007, is shown on the following page.

Other Data

1. Accrued but *unrecorded* and uncollected consulting fees earned total $25,000 at December 31, 2007.
2. The company determined that $15,000 of previously unearned consulting services fees had been earned at December 31, 2007.
3. Office supplies on hand at December 31 total $300.
4. The company purchased all of its equipment when it first began business. At that time, the estimated useful life of the equipment was six years (72 months).
5. The company prepaid its nine-month rent agreement on June 1, 2007.
6. The company prepaid its six-month insurance policy on December 1, 2007.
7. Accrued but *unpaid* salaries total $12,000 at December 31, 2007.
8. On September 1, 2007, the company borrowed $60,000 by signing an eight-month, 4 percent note payable. The entire amount, plus interest, is due on March 1, 2008.
9. The company's accounting firm estimates that income taxes expense for the *entire year* is $50,000. The unpaid portion of this amount is due early in 2008.

NEXT JOB, INC. Unadjusted Trial Balance December 31, 2007		
Cash	$276,500	
Accounts receivable	90,000	
Office supplies	800	
Prepaid rent	3,600	
Unexpired insurance	1,500	
Office equipment	72,000	
Accumulated depreciation: office equipment		$ 24,000
Accounts payable		4,000
Notes payable (due 3/1/08)		60,000
Interest payable		600
Income taxes payable		9,000
Dividends payable		3,000
Unearned consulting fees		22,000
Capital stock		200,000
Retained earnings		40,000
Dividends	3,000	
Consulting fees earned		500,000
Rent expense	14,700	
Insurance expense	2,200	
Office supplies expense	4,500	
Depreciation expense: office equipment	11,000	
Salaries expense	330,000	
Utilities expense	4,800	
Interest expense	3,000	
Income taxes expense	45,000	
Totals	$862,600	$862,600

Instructions

a. Prepare the necessary adjusting journal entries on December 31, 2007. Also prepare an *adjusted trial balance* dated December 31, 2007.

b. From the adjusted trial balance prepared in part **a**, prepare an income statement and statement of retained earnings for the year ended December 31, 2007. Also prepare the company's balance sheet dated December 31, 2007.

c. Prepare the necessary year-end closing entries.

d. Prepare an after-closing trial balance.

e. Compute the company's average *monthly* insurance expense for January through November of 2007.

f. Compute the company's average *monthly* rent expense for January through May of 2007.

g. If the company purchased all of its office equipment when it first incorporated, for how long has it been in business as of December 31, 2007?

h. Assume that the company had a note payable outstanding on January 1, 2007, that it paid off on April 1, 2007. How much interest expense accrued on this note in 2007?

through

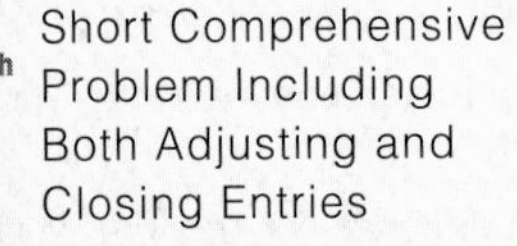

PROBLEM 5.6B

Short Comprehensive Problem Including Both Adjusting and Closing Entries

Tammy Touchtone operates a talent agency called Touchtone Talent Agency. Some clients pay in advance for services; others are billed after services have been performed. Advance payments are credited to an account entitled Unearned Agency Fees. Adjusting entries are performed on a *monthly* basis. Closing entries are performed *annually* on December 31. An *unadjusted* trial balance dated December 31, 2007, follows. (Bear in mind that adjusting entries have already been made for the first 11 months of 2007, but *not* for December.)

TOUCHTONE TALENT AGENCY
Unadjusted Trial Balance
December 31, 2007

Cash	$ 14,950	
Fees receivable	35,300	
Prepaid rent	1,200	
Unexpired insurance policies	375	
Office supplies	900	
Office equipment	15,000	
Accumulated depreciation: office equipment		$ 12,000
Accounts payable		1,500
Note payable (due 3/1/08)		6,000
Income taxes payable		3,200
Unearned agency fees		8,000
Capital stock		20,000
Retained earnings		10,800
Dividends	800	
Agency fees earned		46,500
Telephone expense	480	
Office supply expense	1,130	
Depreciation expense: office equipment	2,750	
Rent expense	6,100	
Insurance expense	1,175	
Salaries expense	24,640	
Income taxes expense	3,200	
	$108,000	$108,000

Other Data

1. Office equipment is being depreciated over 60 months (5 years).
2. At December 31, 2007, $2,500 of previously unearned agency fees had been earned.
3. Accrued but *unrecorded* and unpaid salary expense totals $1,360 at December 31, 2007.
4. The agency pays rent quarterly (every three months). The most recent advance payment of $1,800 was made November 1, 2007. The next payment of $1,800 will be made on February 1, 2008.
5. Accrued but *unrecorded* and uncollected agency fees earned total $3,000 at December 31, 2007.
6. Office supplies on hand at December 31, 2007, total $530.
7. On September 1, 2007, the agency purchased a six-month insurance policy for $750.
8. On December 1, 2007, the agency borrowed $6,000 by signing a three-month, 9 percent note payable. The entire amount borrowed, plus interest, is due March 1, 2008.
9. Accrued income taxes payable for the *entire year* ending December 31, 2007, *total* $3,900. The full amount is due early in 2008.

Instructions

a. Prepare the necessary adjusting journal entries on December 31, 2007. Also prepare an *adjusted trial balance* dated December 31, 2007.

b. From the adjusted trial balance prepared in part **a**, prepare an income statement and statement of retained earnings for the year ended December 31, 2007. Also prepare the company's balance sheet dated December 31, 2007.

c. Prepare the necessary year-end closing entries.

d. Prepare an after-closing trial balance.

e. Assume that the agency purchased all of its office equipment when it first began business activities. For how many months has the agency been in operation?

f. Has the agency's monthly office rent remained the same throughout the year? If not, has it gone up or down? Explain.

g. Has the agency's monthly insurance expense remained the same throughout the year? If not, has it gone up or down? Explain.

LO8

***PROBLEM 5.7B**
Short Comprehensive Problem Including Adjusting Entries, Closing Entries, and Worksheet Preparation

Refer to Problem 4.4A on pages 176–177 in the previous chapter. Prepare a 10-column worksheet for Campus Theater dated August 31, 2007. At the bottom of your worksheet, prepare a brief explanation keyed to each adjusting entry.

LO6

PROBLEM 5.8B
Evaluating Profitability and Liquidity

A recent annual report issued by **The Gap, Inc.**, revealed the following data:

	End of Year	Beginning of Year
Current assets	$6.69 billion	$5.74 billion
Current liabilities	$2.50 billion	$2.73 billion
Stockholders' equity	$4.78 billion	$3.66 billion

The company's income statement reported total annual revenue of $15.85 billion and net income for the year of $1.03 billion.

Instructions

a. Evaluate **The Gap**'s profitability by computing its net income percentage and its return on equity for the year.

b. Evaluate **The Gap**'s liquidity by computing its working capital and its current ratio at the beginning of the year and at the end of the year.

c. Does **The Gap, Inc.**, appear to be both profitable and liquid? Explain.

**Supplemental Topic*, "The Worksheet."

Critical Thinking Cases

LO3

CASE 5.1
Adequate Disclosure

Listed below are five items that may—or may not—require disclosure in the notes that accompany financial statements.

a. Mandella Construction Co. uses the percentage-of-completion method to recognize revenue on long-term construction contracts. This is one of two acceptable methods of accounting for such projects. Over the life of the project, both methods produce the same overall results, but the annual results may differ substantially.

b. One of the most popular artists at Spectacular Comics is leaving the company and going to work for a competitor.

c. Shortly after the balance sheet date, but before the financial statements are issued, one of Coast Foods's two processing plants was damaged by a tornado. The plant will be out of service for at least three months.

d. The management of Soft Systems believes that the company has developed systems software that will make Windows® virtually obsolete. If they are correct, the company's profits could increase by 10-fold or more.

e. College Property Management (CPM) withheld a $500 security deposit from students who, in violation of their lease, kept a dog in their apartment. The students have sued CPM for this amount in small claims court.

Instructions

For each case, explain what, if any, disclosure is required under generally accepted accounting principles. Explain your reasoning.

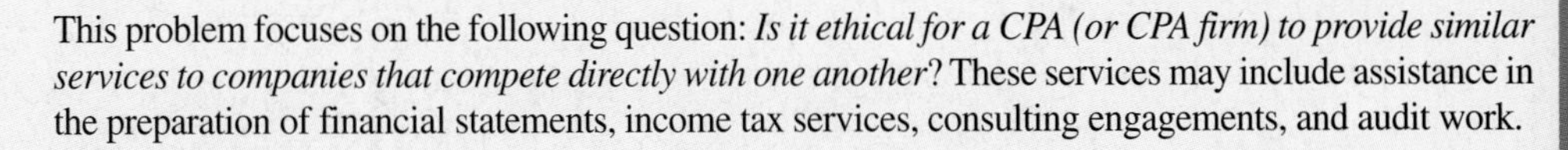

CASE 5.2
Working for the Competition

This problem focuses on the following question: *Is it ethical for a CPA (or CPA firm) to provide similar services to companies that compete directly with one another*? These services may include assistance in the preparation of financial statements, income tax services, consulting engagements, and audit work.

Instructions

a. *Before* doing any research, discuss this question as a group. Identify potential arguments on *each side* of the issue.

b. Arrange an interview with a practicing (or retired) public accountant. Learn the accounting profession's position on this issue, and discuss the various arguments developed in part **a**.

c. Develop your group's position on this issue and be prepared to explain it in class. Explain why you have chosen to overlook the conflicting arguments developed in part **a**. (If your group is not in agreement, dissenting members may draft a dissenting opinion.)

CASE 5.3
Certifications by CEOs and CFOs

The Sarbanes-Oxley Act requires that a corporation's CEO (chief executive officer) and CFO (chief financial officer) include statements of *personal certification* in the disclosures accompanying the financial reports that they file with the SEC. In essence, these statements hold the CEO and CFO personally liable for their company's annual report content. The personal certifications must be signed by both the CEO and the CFO. Each certification requires that the CEO and CFO commit to the following statements:

1. I have reviewed this annual report.
2. Based on my knowledge, this report does not contain any untrue statements of material facts or omissions of material facts.
3. Based on my knowledge, the financial statements, and other financial information included in this report, fairly present in all material respects the financial condition, results of operations, and cash flows of the business.
4. I am responsible for establishing and maintaining disclosure controls and procedures.
5. I have disclosed any fraud, whether or not material, and have disclosed all significant control deficiencies and material weaknesses involving the company's financial reporting.

Instructions

As a group, discuss the meaning and purpose of the personal certification requirement. How might this requirement contribute to improved investor confidence?

***BUSINESSWEEK* CASE 5.4**
The Aftermath of the Sarbanes-Oxley Act

In an August 1, 2005, *BusinessWeek* article entitled, "SOX: Not So Bad After All?" author Amey Stone discusses how CEOs (chief executive officers) and CFOs (chief financial officers) have adjusted to the Sarbanes-Oxley Act (SOX) since its passage in 2002.

SOX, and other new regulations imposed by the SEC, has made CEOs and CFOs personally responsible for the integrity of the annual reports issued by their companies. If high-ranking officers are aware of false disclosures in filings to the SEC, they face millions of dollars in fines and possible prison sentences of up to 20 years.

Instructions

Fear of being held individually liable for corporate reporting irregularities has prompted some CFOs and CEOs to transfer 100 percent ownership of their personal assets to spouses and other family members. By so doing, their personal assets are protected in the event of a SOX-related lawsuit.

As a group, discuss whether this practice is ethical.

INTERNET CASE 5.5
Annual Report Disclosures

Visit the home page of the **Ford Motor Company** at:

www.ford.com

From **Ford**'s home page, access the company's most recent annual report. Locate the notes to the financial statements and identify the information topics disclosed in these footnotes.

Internet sites are time and date sensitive. It is the purpose of these exercises to have you explore the Internet. You may need to use the Yahoo! search engine **http://www.yahoo.com** *(or another favorite search engine) to find a company's current Web address.*

Answers to Self-Test Questions

1. a, b, c, d **2.** a **3.** d **4.** b, d **5.** a **6.** a, b **7.** c **8.** b, c

COMPREHENSIVE PROBLEM 1

Susquehanna Equipment Rentals

A COMPREHENSIVE ACCOUNTING CYCLE PROBLEM

On December 1, 2007, John and Patty Driver formed a corporation called Susquehanna Equipment Rentals. The new corporation was able to begin operations immediately by purchasing the assets and taking over the location of Rent-It, an equipment rental company that was going out of business. The newly formed company uses the following accounts:

Cash	**Income Taxes Payable**
Accounts Receivable	**Capital Stock**
Prepaid Rent	**Retained Earnings**
Unexpired Insurance	**Dividends**
Office Supplies	**Income Summary**
Rental Equipment	**Rental Fees Earned**
Accumulated Depreciation:	**Salaries Expense**
Rental Equipment	**Maintenance Expense**
Notes Payable	**Utilities Expense**
Accounts Payable	**Rent Expense**
Interest Payable	**Office Supplies Expense**
Salaries Payable	**Depreciation Expense**
Dividends Payable	**Interest Expense**
Unearned Rental Fees	**Income Taxes Expense**

The corporation performs adjusting entries monthly. Closing entries are performed annually on December 31. During December, the corporation entered into the following transactions:

Dec. 1 Issued to John and Patty Driver 20,000 shares of capital stock in exchange for a total of $200,000 cash.

Dec. 1 Purchased for $240,000 all of the equipment formerly owned by Rent-It. Paid $140,000 cash and issued a one-year note payable for $100,000.

Dec. 1 Paid $12,000 to Shapiro Realty as three months' advance rent on the rental yard and office formerly occupied by Rent-It.

Dec. 4 Purchased office supplies on account from Modern Office Co., $1,000. Payment due in 30 days. (These supplies are expected to last for several months; debit the Office Supplies asset account.)

Dec. 8 Received $8,000 cash as advance payment on equipment rental from McNamer Construction Company. (Credit Unearned Rental Fees.)

Dec. 12 Paid salaries for the first two weeks in December, $5,200.

Dec. 15 Excluding the McNamer advance, equipment rental fees earned during the first 15 days of December amounted to $18,000, of which $12,000 was received in cash.

Dec. 17 Purchased on account from Earth Movers, Inc., $600 in parts needed to repair a rental tractor. (Debit an expense account.) Payment is due in 10 days.

Dec. 23 Collected $2,000 of the accounts receivable recorded on December 15.

Dec. 23 Rented a backhoe to Mission Landscaping at a price of $250 per day, to be paid when the backhoe is returned. Mission Landscaping expects to keep the backhoe for about two or three weeks.

Dec. 26 Paid biweekly salaries, $5,200.

Dec. 27 Paid the account payable to Earth Movers, Inc., $600.

Dec. 28 Declared a dividend of 10 cents per share, payable on January 15, 2008.

Dec. 29 Susquehanna Equipment Rentals was named, along with Mission Landscaping and Collier Construction, as a co-defendant in a $25,000 lawsuit filed on behalf of Kevin Davenport. Mission Landscaping had left the rented backhoe in a fenced construction site owned by Collier Construction. After working hours on December 26, Davenport had climbed the fence to play on parked construction equipment. While playing on the backhoe, he fell and broke his arm. The extent of the company's legal and financial responsibility for this accident, if any, cannot be determined at this time. (***Note:*** This event does not require a journal entry at this time, but may require disclosure in notes accompanying the statements.)

Dec. 29 Purchased a 12-month public-liability insurance policy for $9,600. This policy protects the company against liability for injuries and property damage caused by its equipment. However, the policy goes into effect on January 1, 2008, and affords no coverage for the injuries sustained by Kevin Davenport on December 26.

Dec. 31 Received a bill from Universal Utilities for the month of December, $700. Payment is due in 30 days.

Dec. 31 Equipment rental fees earned during the second half of December amounted to $20,000, of which $15,600 was received in cash.

Data for Adjusting Entries

a. The advance payment of rent on December 1 covered a period of three months.

b. The annual interest rate on the note payable to Rent-It is 6 percent.

c. The rental equipment is being depreciated by the straight-line method over a period of eight years.

d. Office supplies on hand at December 31 are estimated at $600.

e. During December, the company earned $3,700 of the rental fees paid in advance by McNamer Construction Co. on December 8.

f. As of December 31, six days' rent on the backhoe rented to Mission Landscaping on December 23 has been earned.

g. Salaries earned by employees since the last payroll date (December 26) amounted to $1,400 at month-end.

h. It is estimated that the company is subject to a combined federal and state income tax rate of 40 percent of income before income taxes (total revenue minus all expenses *other than* income taxes). These taxes will be payable in 2008.

Instructions

a. Journalize the December transactions.

b. Prepare the necessary adjusting entries.

c. Post the December transactions and adjusting entries to ledger accounts.

d. Prepare a 10-column worksheet for the year ended December 31.

e. Prepare an income statement and statement of retained earnings for the year ended December 31, and a balance sheet (in report form) as of December 31.

f. Prepare required disclosures to accompany the December 31 financial statements. Your solution should include a separate note addressing each of the following areas: (1) depreciation policy, (2) maturity dates of major liabilities, and (3) potential liability due to pending litigation.

g. Prepare closing entries and post to ledger accounts.

h. Prepare an after-closing trial balance as of December 31.

i. During December, this company's cash balance has fallen from $200,000 to $65,000. Does it appear headed for insolvency in the near future? Explain your reasoning.

j. Would it be ethical for Patty Driver to maintain the accounting records for this company, or must they be maintained by someone who is *independent* of the organization?

6 Merchandising Activities

Learning Objectives

AFTER STUDYING THIS CHAPTER, YOU SHOULD BE ABLE TO:

LO1 Describe the *operating cycle* of a merchandising company.

LO2 Understand the components of a merchandising company's income statement.

LO3 Account for purchases and sales of merchandise in a *perpetual* inventory system.

LO4 Explain how a *periodic* inventory system operates.

LO5 Discuss the factors to be considered in selecting an inventory system.

LO6 Account for additional merchandising transactions related to purchases and sales.

LO7 Define *special journals* and explain their usefulness.

LO8 Measure the performance of a merchandising business.

CVS CORPORATION

CVS Corporation is the largest retail pharmacy chain in the United States based on store count and the second largest based on sales. The company operates more than 5,400 stores in 36 states, and it holds either the no. 1 or the no. 2 market-share position in 70 percent of the country's top 100 markets in which its stores operate.

CVS Corporation fills over 366 million prescriptions each year and generates annual revenue in excess of $30 billion. Approximately 30 percent of its revenue comes from the sale of nonprescription medications, health and beauty aids, convenience foods, greeting cards, and other household products. The company has invested heavily in information systems used to warn customers of potential drug interactions, to automate prescription refills, and to track detailed sales and inventory data from each of its stores.

CVS Corporation's financial statements are similar to those of the service organizations illustrated in previous chapters. They differ, however, because in addition to providing the services of registered pharmacists **CVS** also sells *merchandise* to its customers. Companies that sell merchandise must report information about inventory costs in their financial statements.

In this chapter we examine accounting issues related to merchandising businesses, such as retail pharmacies and grocery stores. In addition to discussing the unique features of a merchandising company's financial statements, we illustrate ways to use financial information to evaluate the performance of these companies.

CVS Corporation's retail pharmacies are good examples of merchandising outlets. Managing **inventory** (goods that are purchased for the purpose of resale to customers) is of utmost importance to merchandising businesses. For a large chain like **CVS** to be successful, its stores must acquire thousands of inventory items and sell them quickly at competitive prices.

In most merchandising companies, inventory is a relatively liquid asset—that is, it usually is sold within a few days or weeks. For this reason, inventory appears near the top of the balance sheet, immediately below accounts receivable.

Merchandising Companies

THE OPERATING CYCLE OF A MERCHANDISING COMPANY

LO1 **Describe the *operating cycle* of a merchandising company.**

The series of transactions through which a business generates its revenue and its cash receipts from customers is called the **operating cycle**. The operating cycle of a merchandising company consists of the following basic transactions: (1) purchases of merchandise; (2) sales of the merchandise, often on account; and (3) collection of the accounts receivable from customers. As the word *cycle* suggests, this sequence of transactions repeats continuously. Some of the cash collected from the customers is used to purchase more merchandise, and the cycle begins anew. This continuous sequence of merchandising transactions is illustrated in Exhibit 6–1.

Exhibit 6–1

THE OPERATING CYCLE

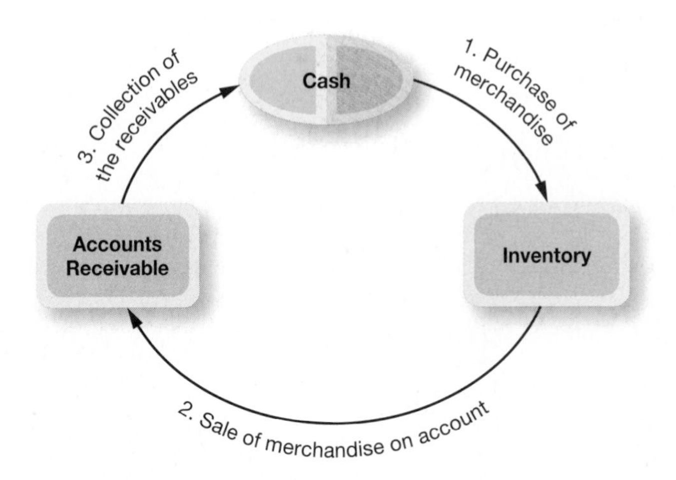

Comparing Merchandising Activities with Manufacturing Activities

Most merchandising companies purchase their inventories from other business organizations in a *ready-to-sell* condition. Companies that manufacture their inventories, such as **General Motors**, **IBM**, and **Boeing Aircraft**, are called *manufacturers*, rather than merchandisers. The operating cycle of a manufacturing company is longer and more complex than that of a merchandising company, because the first transaction—purchasing merchandise—is replaced by the many activities involved in manufacturing the merchandise.

Our examples and illustrations in this chapter are limited to companies that purchase their inventory in a ready-to-sell condition. The basic concepts, however, also apply to manufacturers.

Retailers and Wholesalers

Merchandising companies include both retailers and wholesalers. A *retailer* is a business that sells merchandise directly to the public. Retailers may be large or small; they vary in size from giant department store chains, such as **CVS**,

Sears, Roebuck & Co., and **Wal-Mart**, to small neighborhood businesses, such as gas stations and convenience stores. In fact, more businesses engage in retail sales than in any other type of business activity.

The other major type of merchandising company is the *wholesaler*. Wholesalers buy large quantities of merchandise from several different manufacturers and then resell this merchandise to many different retailers. Because wholesalers do not sell directly to the public, even the largest wholesalers are not well known to most consumers. Nonetheless, wholesaling is a major type of merchandising activity.

The concepts discussed in the remainder of this chapter apply equally to retailers and to wholesalers.

INCOME STATEMENT OF A MERCHANDISING COMPANY

Understand the components of a merchandising company's income statement. LO2

The income statements of merchandising companies differ somewhat from those of service organizations illustrated in previous chapters. Exhibit 6–2 compares the income statement structure of a service company to that of a merchandising company.

Exhibit 6–2

A COMPARISON OF INCOME STATEMENTS USED BY SERVICE COMPANIES AND MERCHANDISING COMPANIES

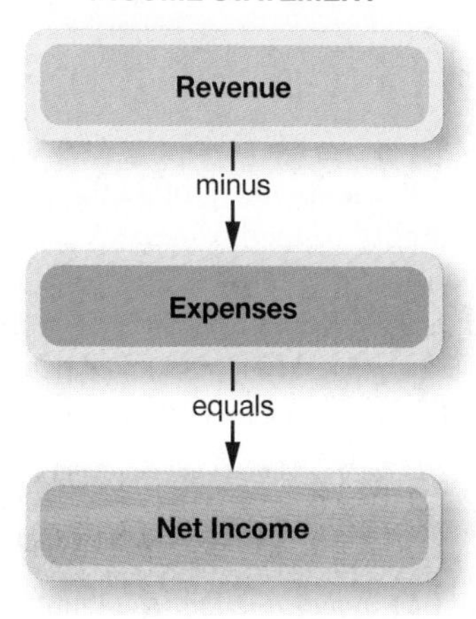

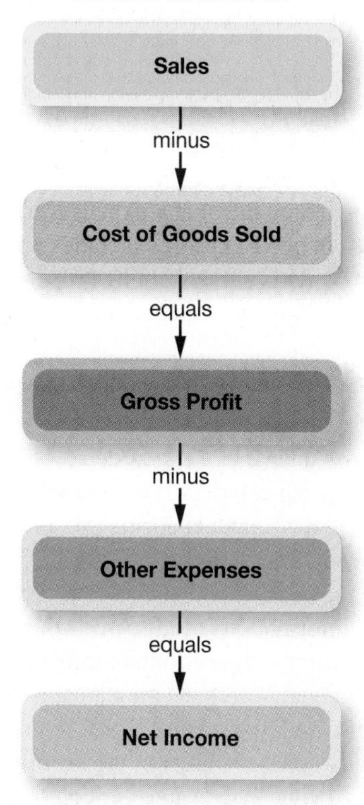

The income statement of Computer City is shown in Exhibit 6–3. The following discussion of its structure and components will illustrate the unique characteristics of income statements prepared by merchandising companies.

Computer City's $900,000 in sales represents the *selling price* of merchandise it sold to customers during the period. Selling merchandise introduces a new and major cost of doing business: the *cost* incurred by Computer City *to acquire* the inventory it sold to customers. As items are sold from inventory, their costs must be removed from the balance sheet and transferred to the income statement to offset sales revenue. This $540,000 cost subtracted from sales revenue in Computer City's income statement is referred to as the **cost of goods sold**. In essence, the cost of goods sold is an *expense*; however, this item is of such importance to a merchandising company that it is shown separately from other expenses in the company's income statement.

Exhibit 6–3

A MERCHANDISING COMPANY'S INCOME STATEMENT

COMPUTER CITY Income Statement For the Year Ended December 31, 2007		
Sales		$900,000
Less: Cost of goods sold		540,000
Gross profit		$360,000
Operating expenses:		
Wages expense	$150,900	
Advertising expense	6,800	
Insurance expense	9,600	
Utilities expense	6,400	
Office supplies expense	1,700	
Depreciation expense	58,600	234,000
Income before taxes		$126,000
Income taxes expense		36,000
Net income		$ 90,000

The $360,000 difference between sales and the cost of goods sold is Computer City's **gross profit** (or gross margin). Gross profit is a useful means of measuring the profitability of sales transactions, but it does *not* represent the overall profitability of the business. A merchandising company has many expenses in addition to the cost of goods sold. Computer City's $270,000 in other expenses includes wages expense, advertising expense, insurance expense, utilities expense, office supplies expense, depreciation expense, and income taxes expense.[1] A company earns net income only if its gross profit exceeds the sum of its other expenses.

ACCOUNTING SYSTEM REQUIREMENTS FOR MERCHANDISING COMPANIES

In previous chapters, we recorded economic events using only *general ledger* accounts. These accounts, often referred to as **control accounts**, are used to prepare financial statements that *summarize* the financial position of a business and the results of its operations. Although general ledger accounts provide a useful *overview* of a company's financial activities, they do not provide the *detailed information* needed to effectively manage most business enterprises. This detailed information is found in accounting records called *subsidiary ledgers.*

Subsidiary ledgers contain information about specific control accounts in the company's general ledger. Merchandising companies always maintain accounts receivable and accounts payable subsidiary ledgers. Thus, if a company has 500 credit customers, there are 500 individual customer accounts in the *accounts receivable subsidiary ledger* that, in total, add up to the Accounts Receivable general ledger balance reported in the balance sheet. Likewise, if a company has 20 creditors, there are 20 individual records in the *accounts payable subsidiary ledger* that contain detailed information about the amount owed to each creditor. The individual balances of these accounts add up to the Accounts Payable control balance in the general ledger.

Many merchandising companies also maintain an *inventory subsidiary ledger* by creating a separate inventory account for each item that they sell. The inventory subsidiary ledger for a large department store contains thousands of accounts. Each of these accounts tracks information for *one type of product*, showing the quantities and costs of all units purchased, sold, and currently in stock.

[1] The income statement presented in Exhibit 6–3 is somewhat condensed. For instance, it is a common practice for companies to subdivide operating expenses into *selling expenses and general and administrative expenses.* A more detailed income statement presentation is developed in Chapter 12.

It may seem that maintaining records for thousands of separate accounts would involve an incredible amount of work. And it would, in a *manual* accounting system. However, in a *computerized* accounting system, subsidiary ledger accounts and general ledger control accounts are posted *automatically* as transactions are recorded. Thus, no significant amount of effort is required.

Throughout the remainder of this chapter we will record various merchandise transactions directly in the general ledger control accounts. To avoid excessive detail, we will *assume* that the specific account information underlying these transactions has been posted to the necessary subsidiary accounts.

TWO APPROACHES USED IN ACCOUNTING FOR MERCHANDISE INVENTORIES

Either of two approaches may be used in accounting for merchandise inventories: (1) a *perpetual inventory system*, or (2) a *periodic inventory system.* In the past, both systems were in widespread use. Today, however, the growing use of computerized accounting systems has made the perpetual approach easy and cost-effective to implement. Thus, the periodic approach is used primarily by very small businesses with manual accounting systems.

Before we examine perpetual and periodic inventory systems, it is important to realize that accounting for inventory is similar to accounting for the *prepaid expenses* we discussed in Chapter 4 (for example, office supplies, unexpired insurance policies, prepaid rent, etc.). As inventory is purchased, it is initially reported as an *asset* in the balance sheet. As it is sold to customers, this asset is converted to an *expense*, specifically, the cost of goods sold.

Both perpetual and periodic inventory systems account for the flow of inventory costs from the balance sheet to the income statement as illustrated in Exhibit 6–4.

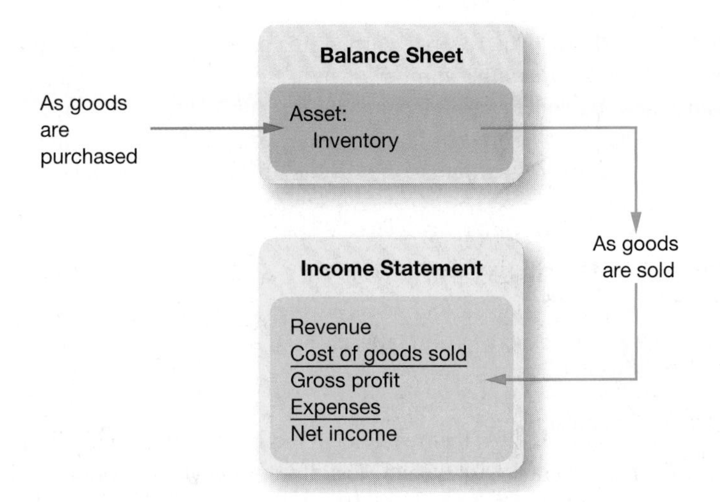

Exhibit 6–4

THE FLOW OF INVENTORY COSTS

Perpetual Inventory Systems

Account for purchases and sales of merchandise in a *perpetual* inventory system. (LO3)

In a **perpetual inventory system**, all transactions involving costs of merchandise are recorded immediately *as they occur*. The system draws its name from the fact that the accounting records are kept perpetually up-to-date. Purchases of merchandise are recorded by debiting an asset account entitled Inventory. When merchandise is sold, two entries are necessary: one to recognize the *revenue earned* and the second to recognize the related *cost of goods sold*. This second entry also reduces the balance of the Inventory account to reflect the sale of some of the company's inventory.

A perpetual inventory system uses an *inventory subsidiary ledger*. This ledger provides company personnel with up-to-date information about each type of product that the company buys and sells, including the per-unit cost and the number of units purchased, sold, and currently on hand.

To illustrate the perpetual inventory system, we follow specific items of merchandise through the operating cycle of Computer City, a retail store. The transactions comprising this illustration are as follows:

Sept. 1 Purchased 10 Regent 21-inch computer monitors on account from Okawa Wholesale Co. The monitors cost $600 each, for a total of $6,000; payment is due in 30 days.

Sept. 7 Sold two monitors on account to RJ Travel Agency at a retail sales price of $1,000 each, for a total of $2,000. Payment is due in 30 days.

Oct. 1 Paid the $6,000 account payable to Okawa Wholesale Co.

Oct. 7 Collected the $2,000 account receivable from RJ Travel Agency.

Purchases of Merchandise Purchases of inventory are recorded at cost. Thus Computer City records its purchase of the 10 computer monitors on September 1 as follows:

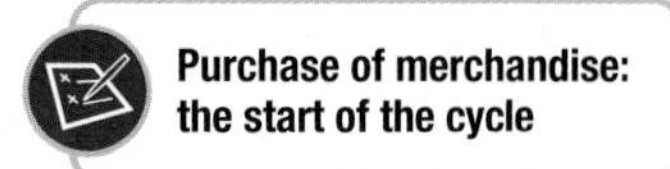
Purchase of merchandise: the start of the cycle

Inventory	6,000	
Accounts Payable (Okawa Wholesale Co.)		6,000
Purchased 10 Regent 21-inch computer monitors for $600 each; payment due in 30 days.		

This entry is posted both to the general ledger control accounts and to the *subsidiary ledgers.* Thus, the debit to Inventory is also posted to the Regent 21-Inch Monitors account in the inventory subsidiary ledger. Information regarding the quantity of monitors purchased and their unit cost is also recorded in this subsidiary ledger. Likewise, the credit to Accounts Payable is posted to the account for Okawa Wholesale Co. in Computer City's accounts payable subsidiary ledger.

Sales of Merchandise The revenue earned in a sales transaction is equal to the *sales price* of the merchandise times the number of units sold, and is credited to a revenue account entitled Sales. Except in rare circumstances, sales revenue is considered realized when the merchandise is *delivered to the customer*, even if the sale is made on account. Therefore, Computer City will recognize the revenue from the sale to RJ Travel Agency on September 7, as follows:

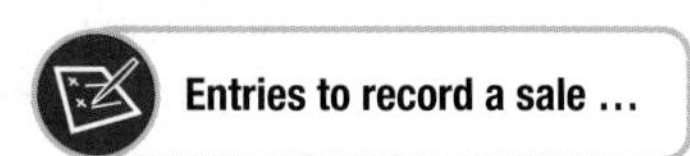
Entries to record a sale . . .

Accounts Receivable (RJ Travel Agency)	2,000	
Sales		2,000
Sold two Regent 21-inch monitors for $1,000 each; payment due in 30 days.		

The *matching principle* requires that revenue be matched (offset) with all of the costs and expenses incurred in producing that revenue. Therefore, a *second journal entry* is required at the date of sale to record the cost of goods sold.

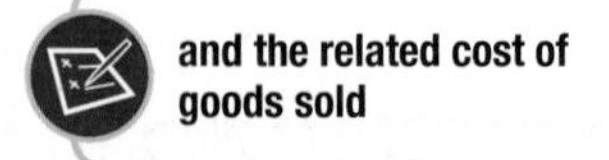
and the related cost of goods sold

Cost of Goods Sold	1,200	
Inventory		1,200
To transfer the cost of two Regent 21-inch monitors ($600 each) from Inventory to the Cost of Goods Sold account.		

Notice that this second entry is based on the *cost* of the merchandise to Computer City, not on its retail sales price.[2]

Both of the journal entries relating to this sales transaction are posted to Computer City's general ledger. In addition, the $2,000 debit to Accounts Receivable (first entry) is posted to the

[2] In our illustration, all of the Regent monitors were purchased on the same date and have the same unit cost. Often a company's inventory of a given product includes units acquired at several *different* per-unit costs. This situation is addressed in Chapter 8.

account for RJ Travel Agency in the accounts receivable ledger. The credit to Inventory (second entry) also is posted to the Regent 21-Inch Monitors account in the inventory subsidiary ledger.

Payment of Accounts Payable to Suppliers

The payment to Okawa Wholesale Co. on October 1 is recorded as follows:

Accounts Payable (Okawa Wholesale Co.)	6,000	
Cash		6,000
Paid account payable.		

Payment of an account payable

Both portions of this entry are posted to the general ledger. In addition, payment of the account payable is entered in the Okawa Wholesale Co. account in Computer City's accounts payable subsidiary ledger.

Collection of Accounts Receivable from Customers

On October 7, collection of the account receivable from RJ Travel Agency is recorded as follows:

Cash	2,000	
Accounts Receivable (RJ Travel Agency)		2,000
Collected an account receivable from a credit customer.		

Collection of an account receivable

Both portions of this entry are posted to the general ledger; the credit to Accounts Receivable also is posted to the RJ Travel Agency account in the accounts receivable ledger.

Collection of the cash from RJ Travel Agency completes Computer City's operating cycle with respect to these two units of merchandise.

TAKING A PHYSICAL INVENTORY

The basic characteristic of the perpetual inventory system is that the Inventory account is *continuously updated* for all purchases and sales of merchandise. When a *physical inventory* is taken, management uses the inventory ledger to determine on a product-by-product basis whether a physical count of the inventory on hand corresponds to the amount indicated in the inventory subsidiary ledger. Over time normal inventory shrinkage may cause some discrepancies between the quantities of merchandise shown in the inventory records and the quantities actually on hand. **Inventory shrinkage** refers to unrecorded decreases in inventory resulting from such factors as breakage, spoilage, employee theft, and shoplifting.

In order to ensure the accuracy of their perpetual inventory records, most corporations are required to take a *complete physical count* of the merchandise on hand at least once a year. This procedure is called **taking a physical inventory**, and it usually is performed near year-end.

Once the quantity of merchandise on hand has been determined by a physical count, the per-unit costs in the inventory ledger accounts are used to determine the total cost of the inventory. The Inventory control account and the accounts in the inventory subsidiary ledger then are *adjusted* to the quantities and dollar amounts indicated by the physical inventory.

To illustrate, assume that at year-end both the Inventory control account and inventory subsidiary ledger of Computer City show an inventory with a cost of $72,200. A physical count, however, reveals that some of the merchandise listed in the accounting records is missing; the items actually on hand have a total cost of $70,000. Computer City would make the following adjusting entry to correct its Inventory control account:

Cost of Goods Sold	2,200	
Inventory		2,200
To adjust the perpetual inventory records to reflect the results of the year-end physical count.		

Adjusting for inventory shrinkage

Computer City also will adjust the appropriate accounts in its inventory subsidiary ledger to reflect the quantities indicated by the physical count.

Reasonable amounts of inventory shrinkage are viewed as a normal cost of doing business and simply are debited to the Cost of Goods Sold account, as illustrated above.[3]

CASE IN POINT

International Financial Reporting Standards (IFRSs) for valuing inventory differ in some respects from U.S. GAAP rules. For example, U.S. GAAP does not allow reversals of inventory write-downs, but international standards allow such reversals if certain criteria are met. Thus, the inventory values on the balance sheet and the cost of goods sold on the income statement of a firm could differ depending on whether their financial statements are prepared under GAAP or under IFRSs.

CLOSING ENTRIES IN A PERPETUAL INVENTORY SYSTEM

As explained and illustrated in the previous chapters, revenue and expense accounts are *closed* at the end of each accounting period. A merchandising business with a perpetual inventory system makes closing entries that parallel those of a service-type business. The Sales account is a revenue account and is closed into the Income Summary account along with other revenue accounts. The Cost of Goods Sold account is closed into the Income Summary account in the same manner as the other expense accounts.

You as the Inventory Manager for Computer City

Assume you are the inventory manager for the largest store owned by Computer City. You are very busy one day when Fran Mally, an auditor from the accounting firm employed by Computer City, arrives and asks for assistance in determining the store's physical inventory on hand. You are overwhelmed with work and tell Fran that you do not have the time or the personnel needed to assist her in this task. You are also annoyed because you were not told that she was coming today to complete the physical inventory count. What should you do?

(See our comments on the Online Learning Center Web site.)

Periodic Inventory Systems

A **periodic inventory system** is an *alternative* to a perpetual inventory system. In a periodic inventory system, no effort is made to keep up-to-date records of either the inventory or the cost of goods sold. Instead, these amounts are determined only periodically—usually at the end of each year.

OPERATION OF A PERIODIC INVENTORY SYSTEM

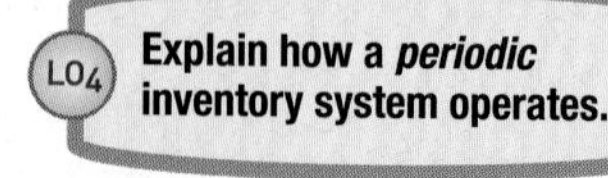

A traditional periodic inventory system operates as follows. When merchandise is purchased, its cost is debited to an account entitled *Purchases*, rather than to the Inventory account. When merchandise is sold, an entry is made to recognize the sales revenue, but *no entry* is made to record the cost of goods sold or to reduce the balance of the Inventory account. As the inventory records are not updated as transactions occur, there is no inventory subsidiary ledger.

The foundation of the periodic inventory system is the taking of a *complete physical inventory* at year-end. This physical count determines the amount of inventory appearing in the balance sheet. The cost of goods sold for the entire year then is determined by a short computation.

[3] If a large inventory shortage is caused by an event such as a fire or theft, the cost of the missing or damaged merchandise may be debited to a special loss account, such as Fire Loss. In the income statement, a loss is deducted from revenue in the same manner as an expense.

Data for an Illustration To illustrate, assume that one of Computer City's suppliers, Wagner Office Products, has a periodic inventory system. At December 31, 2007, the following information is available:

1. The inventory on hand at the end of *2006* cost $14,000.
2. During *2007*, purchases of merchandise for resale to customers totaled $130,000.
3. Inventory on hand at the end of *2007* cost $12,000.

The inventories at the end of 2006 and at the end of 2007 were determined by taking a complete physical inventory at (or very near) each year-end. (Because the Inventory account was not updated as transactions occurred during 2007, it still shows a balance of $14,000—the inventory on hand at the *beginning* of the year.)

The $130,000 cost of merchandise purchased during 2007 was recorded in the Purchases account.

Recording Purchases of Merchandise Wagner Office Products made many purchases of merchandise totaling $130,000 during 2007. The entry to record the first of these purchases is as follows:

Jan. 6	Purchases	2,000	
	Accounts Payable (Ink Jet Solutions)		2,000
	Purchased inventory on account; payment due in 30 days.		

This entry was posted to the Purchases and Accounts Payable accounts in the general ledger. The credit portion also was posted to the account for Ink Jet Solutions in Wagner's accounts payable subsidiary ledger. The debit to Purchases was *not* "double-posted," as there is *no inventory subsidiary ledger* in a periodic system.

Computing the Cost of Goods Sold The year-end inventory is determined by taking a complete physical count of the merchandise on hand. Once the ending inventory is known, the cost of goods sold for the entire year can be determined by a short computation. The following computation uses the three information items for Wagner Office Products just presented:

Inventory (beginning of the year) (1)	$ 14,000
Add: Purchases (2)	130,000
Cost of goods available for sale	$144,000
Less: Inventory (end of the year) (3)	12,000
Cost of goods sold	$132,000

Computation of the cost of goods sold

The $132,000 cost of goods sold is made up of two elements: the $130,000 cost of merchandise purchased during the year and the *decrease* in inventory of $2,000 ($14,000 beginning inventory − $12,000 ending inventory).

Recording Inventory and the Cost of Goods Sold Wagner has now determined its inventory at the end of 2007 and its cost of goods sold for the year. But neither of these amounts has yet been recorded in the company's accounting records.

In a periodic system, the ending inventory and the cost of goods sold are recorded during the company's year-end *closing procedures*. (The term *closing procedures* refers to the end-of-period adjusting and closing entries.)

CLOSING PROCESS IN A PERIODIC INVENTORY SYSTEM

There are several different ways of recording the ending inventory and cost of goods sold in a periodic system, but they all produce the same results. One approach is to *create* a Cost of Goods Sold account with the proper balance as part of the closing process. Once this account has been created, the company can complete its closing procedures in the same manner as if a perpetual inventory system had been in use.

Creating a Cost of Goods Sold Account A Cost of Goods Sold account is created with two special closing entries. The first entry creates the new account by bringing together the costs contributing toward the cost of goods sold. The second entry adjusts the Cost of Goods Sold account to its proper balance and records the ending inventory in the Inventory account.

The costs contributing to the cost of goods sold include (1) beginning inventory and (2) purchases made during the year. These costs are brought together by closing both the Inventory account (which contains its beginning-of-the-year balance) and the Purchases account into a new account entitled Cost of Goods Sold. This year-end closing entry is:

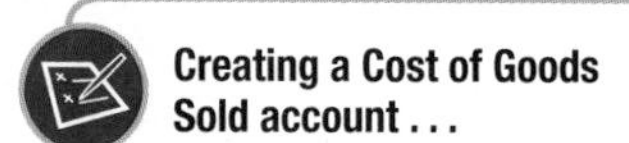

Dec. 31	Cost of Goods Sold	144,000	
	Inventory (beginning balance)		14,000
	Purchases		130,000
	To close the accounts contributing to the cost of goods sold for the year.		

Wagner's Cost of Goods Sold account now includes the cost of all goods *available for sale* during the year. Of course, not all of these goods were sold; the physical inventory taken at the end of 2007 shows that merchandise costing $12,000 is still on hand. Therefore, a second closing entry is made transferring the cost of merchandise still on hand *out* of the Cost of Goods Sold account and *into* the Inventory account. For Wagner, this second closing entry is:

Dec. 31	Inventory (year-end balance)	12,000	
	Cost of Goods Sold		12,000
	To reduce the balance of the Cost of Goods Sold account by the cost of merchandise still on hand at year-end.		

With these two entries, Wagner has created a Cost of Goods Sold account with a balance of $132,000 ($144,000 − $12,000) and has brought its Inventory account up-to-date. Exhibit 6–5 provides a T account presentation of these entries.

Exhibit 6–5

CREATING THE COST OF GOODS SOLD ACCOUNT

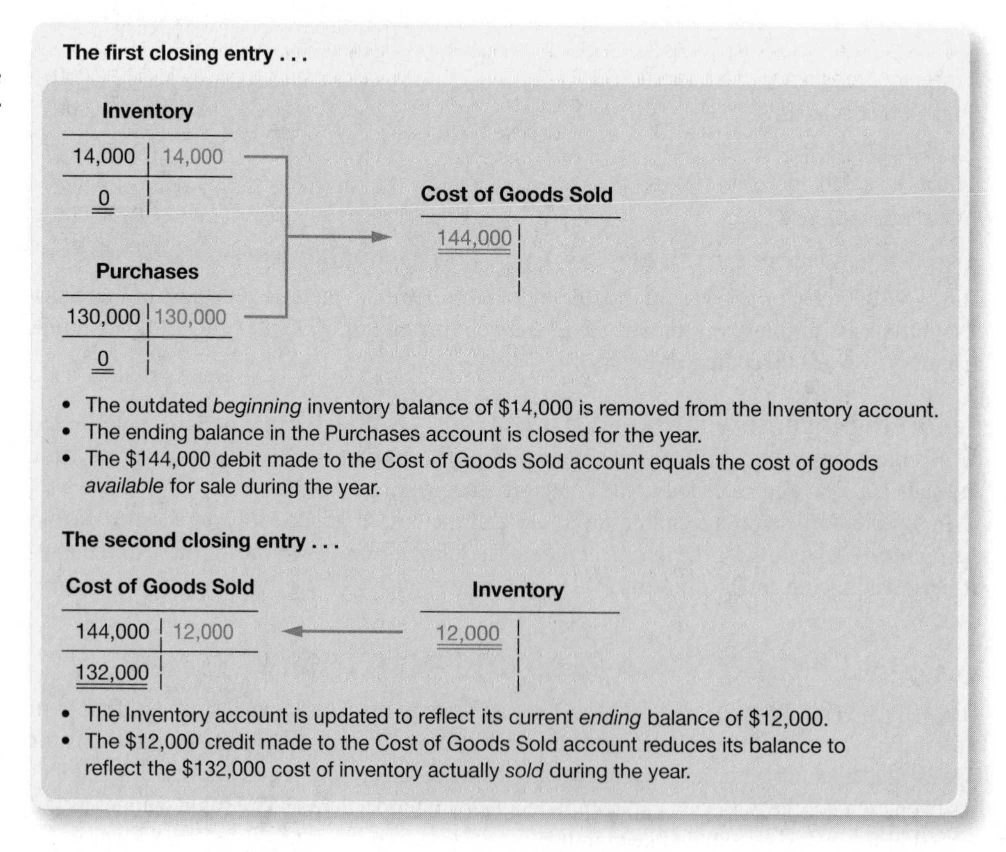

Completing the Closing Process Wagner may now complete its closing process in the same manner as a company using a perpetual inventory system. The company will make the usual four closing entries, closing the (1) revenue accounts, (2) expense accounts (including Cost of Goods Sold), (3) Income Summary account, and (4) Dividends account.

COMPARISON OF PERPETUAL AND PERIODIC INVENTORY SYSTEMS

Exhibit 6–6 provides a comparison of the way in which various events are recorded in perpetual and periodic systems. Perpetual systems are used when management needs information throughout the year about inventory levels and gross profit. Periodic systems are used when the primary goals are to develop annual data and to minimize record-keeping requirements. A single business may use *different inventory systems* to account for *different types of merchandise.*

Who Uses Perpetual Systems? When management or employees *need up-to-date information about inventory levels*, there is no substitute for a perpetual inventory system.

Exhibit 6–6 SUMMARY OF THE JOURNAL ENTRIES MADE IN PERPETUAL AND PERIODIC INVENTORY SYSTEMS

Event	Perpetual System			Periodic System		
Acquiring merchandise inventory	Inventory	xxx		Purchases	xxx	
	Accounts Payable (or Cash)		xxx	Accounts Payable (or Cash)		xxx
	To record the purchase of merchandise inventory.			To record the purchase of merchandise inventory.		
Sale of merchandise inventory	Accounts Receivable (or Cash)	xxx		Accounts Receivable (or Cash)	xxx	
	Sales		xxx	Sales		xxx
	To record the sale of merchandise inventory.			To record the sale of merchandise inventory.		
	Cost of Goods Sold	xxx		In a periodic system, no entry at the time of sale is made to update the Cost of Goods Sold and Inventory accounts.		
	Inventory		xxx			
	To update the Cost of Goods Sold and Inventory accounts.					
Settlement of Accounts Payable to suppliers	Accounts Payable	xxx		Accounts Payable	xxx	
	Cash		xxx	Cash		xxx
	To record payment for merchandise inventory purchased on account.			To record payment for merchandise inventory purchased on account.		
Collections from credit customers	Cash	xxx		Cash	xxx	
	Accounts Receivable		xxx	Accounts Receivable		xxx
	To record cash collections from credit customers.			To record cash collections from credit customers.		
Creating year-end balances for Cost of Goods Sold and Inventory accounts	No entry necessary. Cost of Goods Sold and Inventory accounts should both reflect year-end balances in a perpetual system. If a year-end physical count reveals less inventory on hand than reported in the Inventory account, the following entry is needed to record inventory shrinkage:			Cost of Goods Sold	xxx	
				Inventory (beginning bal.)		xxx
				Purchases		xxx
				To close the Purchases and Inventory balances to the Cost of Goods Sold account.		
	Cost of Goods Sold	xxx		Inventory (ending balance)	xxx	
	Inventory (shrinkage amount)		xxx	Cost of Goods Sold		xxx
	To reduce year-end inventory balance for shrinkage.			To create the year-end balance in the Inventory account.		

Note: In a periodic inventory system, the Cost of Goods Sold account is both debited and credited to create its year-end balance.

Almost all manufacturing companies use perpetual systems. These businesses need current information to coordinate their inventories of raw materials with their production schedules. Most large merchandising companies—and many small ones—also use perpetual systems.

In the days when all accounting records were maintained by hand, businesses that sold many types of low-cost products had no choice but to use periodic inventory systems. A Wal-Mart store, for example, may sell several thousand items *per hour*. Imagine the difficulty of keeping a perpetual inventory system up-to-date if the records were maintained by hand. But with today's *computerized terminals* and *bar-coded merchandise*, many high-volume retailers now use perpetual inventory systems. In fact, Wal-Mart has been a leader among retailers in developing perpetual inventory systems.

CASE IN POINT

Wal-Mart, referred to as the company Sam Walton built, is the world's largest retailer. By diversifying from its original discount stores to include Sam's Club and its super stores, Wal-Mart has fueled its retail engine. International expansion includes 262 stores in Canada, 679 in Mexico, 282 in the United Kingdom, 91 German stores, 149 stores in Brazil, 43 Chinese stores, 11 stores in Argentina, 16 South Korean stores, and 54 stores in Puerto Rico. According to a recent annual report, 20 percent of total sales came from international locations, and international sales grew at 18 percent. Wal-Mart employs nearly 1,300,000 associates in the United States and nearly 400,000 internationally.

Perpetual inventory systems are not limited to businesses with computerized inventory systems. Many small businesses with manual systems also use perpetual inventory systems. However, these businesses may update their inventory records on a weekly or a monthly basis, rather than at the time of each sales transaction.

Whether accounting records are maintained manually or by computer, most businesses use perpetual inventory systems in accounting for products with a *high per-unit cost*. Examples include automobiles, heavy machinery, electronic equipment, home appliances, and jewelry. Management has a greater interest in keeping track of inventory when the merchandise is expensive. Also, sales volume usually is low enough that a perpetual system can be used, even if accounting records are maintained by hand.

Who Uses Periodic Systems?

Periodic systems are used when the need for current information about inventories and sales *does not justify the cost* of maintaining a perpetual system. In a small retail store, for example, the owner may be so familiar with the inventory that formal perpetual inventory records are unnecessary. Most businesses—large and small—use periodic systems for inventories that are *immaterial* in dollar amount, or when management has little interest in the quantities on hand. As stated previously, businesses that sell many low-cost items and have manual accounting systems sometimes have no choice but to use the periodic method.

SELECTING AN INVENTORY SYSTEM

LO5 Discuss the factors to be considered in selecting an inventory system.

Accountants—and business managers—often must select an inventory system appropriate for a particular situation. Some of the factors usually considered in these decisions are listed in Exhibit 6–7.

The Trend in Today's Business World

Advances in technology are quickly extending the use of perpetual inventory systems to more businesses and more types of inventory. This trend is certain to continue. Throughout this textbook, you may assume that a *perpetual inventory system* is in use unless we specifically state otherwise.

Exhibit 6–7

FACTORS INFLUENCING CHOICE OF INVENTORY SYSTEM

Factors Suggesting a Perpetual Inventory System	Factors Suggesting a Periodic Inventory System
Large company with professional management.	Small company, run by owner.
Management and employees wanting information about items in inventory and the quantities of specific products that are selling.	Accounting records of inventories and specific product sales not needed in daily operations; such information developed primarily for use in annual income tax returns.
Items in inventory with a high per-unit cost.	Inventory with many different kinds of low-cost items.
Low volume of sales transactions or a computerized accounting system.	High volume of sales transactions and a manual accounting system.
Merchandise stored at multiple locations or in warehouses separate from the sales sites.	All merchandise stored at the sales site (for example, in the store).

YOUR TURN **You as a Buyer for a Retail Business**

Assume you are in charge of purchasing merchandise for **Ace Hardware Stores**. You are currently making a decision about the purchase of barbecue grills for sale during the upcoming summer season. You must decide how many of each brand and type of grill to order. Describe the types of accounting information that would be useful in making this decision and where this information might be found.

(See our comments on the Online Learning Center Web site.)

Transactions Relating to Purchases

Account for additional merchandising transactions related to purchases and sales. LO6

In addition to the basic transactions illustrated and explained in this chapter, merchandising companies must account for a variety of additional transactions relating to purchases of merchandise. Examples include discounts offered for prompt payment, merchandise returns, and transportation costs. In our discussion of these transactions, we continue to assume the use of a *perpetual* inventory system.

CREDIT TERMS AND CASH DISCOUNTS

Manufacturers and wholesalers normally sell their products to merchandisers *on account*. The credit terms are stated in the seller's bill, or *invoice*. One common example of credit terms is "net 30 days," or "n/30," meaning full payment is due in 30 days. Another common form of credit terms is "10 eom," meaning payment is due 10 days after the end of the month in which the purchase occurred.

Manufacturers and wholesalers usually allow their customers 30 or 60 days in which to pay for credit purchases. Frequently, however, sellers offer their customers a small discount to encourage earlier payment.

Perhaps the most common credit terms offered by manufacturers and wholesalers are *2/10, n/30*. This expression is read "2, 10, net 30," and means that full payment is due in 30 days, but that the buyer may take a *2 percent discount* if payment is made within 10 days. The period during which the discount is available is termed the *discount period*. Because the discount provides an incentive for the customer to make an early cash payment, it is called a *cash discount*. Buyers, however, often refer to these discounts as *purchase discounts*, while sellers frequently call them *sales discounts*.

Most well-managed companies have a policy of taking advantage of all cash discounts available on purchases of merchandise.[4] These companies initially record purchases of merchandise at the *net cost*—that is, the invoice price *minus* any available discount. After all, this is the amount that the company expects to pay.

To illustrate, assume that on November 3 Computer City purchases 100 spreadsheet programs from PC Products. The cost of these programs is $100 each, for a total of $10,000. However, PC Products offers credit terms of 2/10, n/30. If Computer City pays for this purchase within the discount period, it will have to pay only *$9,800*, or 98 percent of the full invoice price. Therefore, Computer City will record this purchase as follows:

Purchase recorded at net cost

Inventory	9,800	
Accounts Payable (PC Products)		9,800
To record purchase of 100 spreadsheet programs at net cost ($100 × 98% × 100 units).		

If the invoice is paid within the discount period, Computer City simply records payment of a $9,800 account payable.

Through oversight or carelessness, Computer City might fail to make payment within the discount period. In this event, Computer City must pay PC Products the entire invoice price of *$10,000*, rather than the recorded liability of $9,800. The journal entry to record payment *after the discount period*—on, say, December 3—is:

Recording the loss of a cash discount

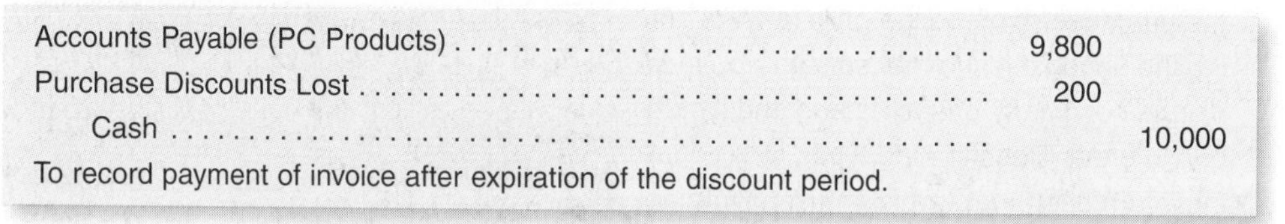

Accounts Payable (PC Products)	9,800	
Purchase Discounts Lost	200	
Cash		10,000
To record payment of invoice after expiration of the discount period.		

Notice that the $200 paid above the $9,800 recorded amount is debited to an account entitled Purchase Discounts Lost. Purchase Discounts Lost is an *expense account*. The only benefit to Computer City from this $200 expenditure was a *20-day delay* in paying an account payable. Thus the lost purchase discount is basically a *finance charge*, similar to interest expense. In an income statement, finance charges usually are classified as nonoperating expenses.

The fact that purchase discounts *not taken* are recorded in a separate expense account is the primary reason why a company should record purchases of merchandise at *net cost*. The use of a Purchase Discounts Lost account immediately brings to management's attention any failure to take advantage of the cash discounts offered by suppliers.

Recording Purchases at Gross Invoice Price As an alternative to recording purchases at net cost, some companies record merchandise purchases at the gross (total) invoice price. If payment is made within the discount period, these companies must record the amount of the purchase discount *taken*.

To illustrate, assume that Computer City followed a policy of recording purchases at gross invoice price. The entry on November 3 to record the purchase from PC Products would have been:

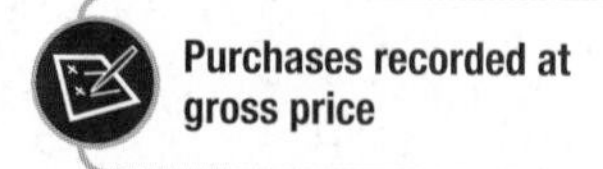

Purchases recorded at gross price

Inventory	10,000	
Accounts Payable (PC Products)		10,000
To record purchase of 100 spreadsheet programs at gross invoice price ($100 × 100 units).		

[4] The terms 2/10, n/30 offer the buyer a 2 percent discount for paying 20 days prior to when the full amount is due. Saving 2 percent over only 20 days is equivalent to earning an annual rate of return of more than 36 percent (2% × 365/20 = 36.5%). Thus, taking cash discounts represents an excellent investment opportunity. Most companies take advantage of all cash discounts, even if they must borrow the necessary cash from a bank to make payment within the discount period.

If payment is made within the discount period, Computer City will discharge this $10,000 account payable by paying only $9,800. The entry will be:

Accounts Payable (PC Products)	10,000	
Cash		9,800
Purchase Discounts Taken		200
To record payment of $10,000 invoice within the discount period; 2% purchase discount taken.		

Buyer records discounts taken

Purchase Discounts Taken is treated as a reduction in the cost of goods sold.

Both the net cost and gross price methods are widely used and produce substantially the same results in financial statements.[5] A shortcoming of the gross price method as compared to the net cost method for valuing inventory is that it does not direct management's attention to discounts lost. Instead, these discounts are buried in the costs assigned to inventory. Management can use financial reporting policies to motivate the purchasing staff to take advantage of purchase discounts when possible. By recording inventory with the net cost method, management can highlight the success of their purchasing efforts to obtain the lowest possible costs for purchased inventory. Because of the advantage of the net cost method, it is the approach recommended by the authors of this textbook.

RETURNS OF UNSATISFACTORY MERCHANDISE

On occasion, a buyer may find the purchased merchandise unsatisfactory and want to return it to the seller for a refund. Most sellers permit such returns.

To illustrate, assume that on November 9 Computer City returns to PC Products five of the spreadsheet programs purchased on November 3, because these programs were not properly labeled. As Computer City has not yet paid for this merchandise, the return will reduce the amount that Computer City owes PC Products. The gross invoice price of the returned merchandise was $500 ($100 per program). Assume that Computer City records purchases at *net cost*. Therefore, these spreadsheet programs are carried in Computer City's inventory subsidiary ledger at a per-unit cost of *$98*, or $490 for the five programs being returned. The entry to record this purchase return is:

Accounts Payable (PC Products)	490	
Inventory		490
Returned five mislabeled spreadsheet programs to supplier. Net cost of the returned items, $490 ($100 × 98% × 5 units).		

Return is based on recorded acquisition cost

The reduction in inventory must also be recorded in the subsidiary ledger accounts.

TRANSPORTATION COSTS ON PURCHASES

The purchaser sometimes may pay the costs of having the purchased merchandise delivered to its premises. Transportation costs relating to the *acquisition* of inventory, or any other asset, are *not expenses* of the current period; rather, these charges are *part of the cost of the asset* being acquired. If the purchaser is able to associate transportation costs with specific products, these costs should be debited directly to the Inventory account as part of the cost of the merchandise.

Often, many different products arrive in a single shipment. In such cases, it may be impractical for the purchaser to determine the amount of the total transportation cost applicable to each product. For this reason, many companies follow the convenient policy of debiting all transportation costs on inbound shipments of merchandise to an account entitled *Transportation-in*. The dollar amount of transportation-in usually is too small to show separately in the financial statements. Therefore, it is often simply added to the amount reported in the income statement as cost of goods sold.

[5] The net cost method values the ending inventory at net cost, whereas the gross cost method shows this inventory at gross invoice price. This difference, however, is usually *immaterial*.

This treatment of transportation costs is not entirely consistent with the *matching principle*. Some of the transportation costs apply to merchandise still in inventory rather than to goods sold during the current period. We have mentioned, however, that transportation costs are relatively small in dollar amount. The accounting principle of *materiality*, therefore, usually justifies accounting for these costs in the most convenient manner.

Transactions Relating to Sales

Credit terms and merchandise returns also affect the amount of sales revenue earned by the seller. To the extent that credit customers take advantage of cash discounts or return merchandise for a refund, the seller's revenue is reduced. Thus revenue shown in the income statement of a merchandising concern is often called *net sales*.

The term **net sales** means total sales revenue *minus* sales returns and allowances and *minus* sales discounts. The partial income statement in Exhibit 6–8 illustrates this relationship.

Exhibit 6–8

PARTIAL INCOME STATEMENT

COMPUTER CITY
Partial Income Statement
For the Year Ended December 31, 2007

Revenue:		
Sales		$912,000
Less: Sales returns and allowances	$8,000	
Sales discounts	4,000	12,000
Net sales		$900,000

The details of this computation seldom are shown in an actual income statement. The normal practice is to begin the income statement with the amount of net sales.

SALES RETURNS AND ALLOWANCES

Most merchandising companies allow customers to obtain a refund by returning any merchandise considered to be unsatisfactory. If the merchandise has only minor defects, customers sometimes agree to keep the merchandise if an *allowance* (reduction) is made in the sales price.

Under the perpetual inventory system, two entries are needed to record the sale of merchandise: one to recognize the revenue earned and the other to transfer the cost of the merchandise from the Inventory account to Cost of Goods Sold. If some of the merchandise is returned, both of these entries are partially reversed.

First, let us consider the effects on revenue of granting either a refund or an allowance. Both refunds and allowances have the effect of nullifying previously recorded sales and reducing the amount of revenue earned by the business. This journal entry reduces sales revenue as the result of a sales return (or allowance):

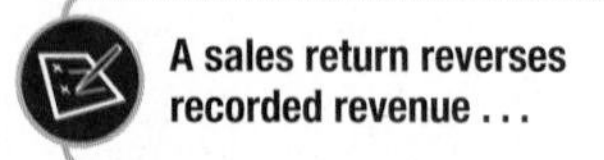

A sales return reverses recorded revenue . . .

Sales Returns and Allowances	200	
Accounts Receivable (or Cash)		200
Customer returned merchandise purchased on account for $200. Allowed customer full credit for returned merchandise.		

Sales Returns and Allowances is a **contra-revenue account**—that is, it is deducted from gross sales revenue as a step in determining net sales.

Why use a separate Sales Returns and Allowances account rather than merely debiting the Sales account? The answer is that using a separate contra-revenue account enables management to see both the total amount of sales *and* the amount of sales returns. The relationship between these amounts gives management an indication of *customer satisfaction* with the merchandise.

If merchandise is returned by the customer, a second entry is made to remove the cost of this merchandise from the Cost of Goods Sold account and restore it to the inventory records. This entry is:

Inventory	160	
Cost of Goods Sold		160
To restore in the Inventory account the cost of merchandise returned by a customer.		

and the recorded cost of goods sold

Notice that this entry is based on the *cost* of the returned merchandise to the seller, *not on its sales price*. (This entry is not necessary when a sales *allowance* is granted to a customer who keeps the merchandise.)

SALES DISCOUNTS

We have explained that sellers frequently offer cash discounts, such as 2/10, n/30, to encourage customers to make early payments for purchases on account.

Sellers and buyers account for cash discounts quite differently. To the seller, the cost associated with cash discounts is not the discounts *lost* when payments are delayed, but rather the discounts *taken* by customers who do pay within the discount period. Therefore, sellers design their accounting systems to measure the sales discounts *taken* by their customers. To achieve this goal, the seller records the sale and the related account receivable at the *gross* (full) invoice price.

To illustrate, assume that Computer City sells merchandise to the Highlander Pub for $1,000, offering terms of 2/10, n/30. The sales revenue is recorded at the full invoice price, as follows:

Accounts Receivable (Highlander Pub)	1,000	
Sales		1,000
Sold merchandise on account. Invoice price, $1,000; terms, 2/10, n/30.		

Sales are recorded at the gross sales price

If the Highlander Pub makes payment after the discount period has expired, Computer City records the receipt of $1,000 cash in full payment of this account receivable. If it pays *within* the discount period, however, the pub will pay only *$980* to settle its account. In this case, Computer City will record the receipt of the pub's payment as follows:

Cash	980	
Sales Discounts	20	
Accounts Receivable (Highlander Pub).		1,000
Collected a $1,000 account receivable from a customer who took a 2% discount for early payment.		

Seller records discounts taken by customers

Sales Discounts is another contra-revenue account. In computing net sales, sales discounts are deducted from gross sales along with any sales returns and allowances. (If the customer has returned part of the merchandise, a discount may be taken only on the gross amount owed *after* the return.)

Contra-revenue accounts have much in common with expense accounts; both are deducted from gross revenue in determining net income, and both have debit balances. Thus contra-revenue accounts (Sales Returns and Allowances and Sales Discounts) are closed to the Income Summary account *in the same manner as expense accounts*.

DELIVERY EXPENSES

If the seller incurs any costs in delivering merchandise to the customer, these costs are debited to an expense account entitled Delivery Expense. In an income statement, delivery expense is classified as a regular operating expense, not as part of the cost of goods sold.

ACCOUNTING FOR SALES TAXES

Sales taxes are levied by many states and cities on retail sales.[6] Sales taxes actually are imposed on the consumer, not on the seller. However, the seller must collect the tax, file tax returns at times specified by law, and remit to governmental agencies the taxes collected.

For cash sales, sales tax is collected from the customer at the time of the sales transaction. For credit sales, the sales tax is included in the amount charged to the customer's account. In a computerized accounting system, the liability to the governmental unit for sales taxes is recorded automatically at the time the sale is made, as shown in the following journal entry:

Cash (or Accounts Receivable)	1,070	
Sales Tax Payable		70
Sales		1,000
To record sales of $1,000, subject to 7% sales tax.		

Modifying an Accounting System

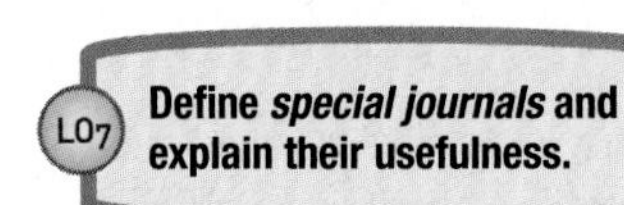

Throughout this textbook we illustrate the effects of many transactions using the format of a two-column *general journal*. This format is ideal for textbook illustrations, as it allows us to concisely show the effects of *any type* of business transaction.

But while general journal entries are useful for our purposes, they are not the most efficient way for a business to record routine transactions. A supermarket, for example, may sell 10,000 to 15,000 items *per hour*. Clearly, it would not be practical to make a general journal entry to record each of these sales transactions. Therefore, most businesses use *special journals*, rather than a general journal, to record *routine transactions that occur frequently*.

SPECIAL JOURNALS PROVIDE SPEED AND EFFICIENCY

A **special journal** is an accounting record or device designed to record *a specific type of routine transaction quickly and efficiently*.

Some special journals are maintained by hand. An example is the *check register* in your personal checkbook. If properly maintained, this special journal provides an efficient record of all cash disbursements made by check.

But many special journals are highly automated. Consider the **point-of-sale (POS) terminals** that you see in supermarkets and large retail stores. These devices record sales transactions and the related cost of goods sold as quickly as the bar-coded merchandise can be passed over the scanner.

Relative to the general journal, special journals offer the following advantages:

- Transactions are recorded faster and more efficiently.
- Many special journals may be in operation at one time, further increasing the company's ability to handle a large volume of transactions.
- Automation may reduce the risk of errors.
- Employees maintaining special journals generally do not need expertise in accounting.
- The recording of transactions may be an automatic side effect of other basic business activities, such as collecting cash from customers.

Most businesses use separate special journals to record repetitive transactions such as sales of merchandise, cash receipts, cash payments, purchases of merchandise on account, and payrolls. There are no rules for the design or content of special journals. Rather, they are tailored to suit the needs, activities, and resources of the particular business organization.

Let us stress that the *accounting principles* used in special journals are the *same* as those used for transactions recorded in a general journal. The differences lie in the *recording techniques*, not in the information that is recorded.

[6] Sales taxes are applicable only when merchandise is sold to the *final consumer*; thus no sales taxes are normally levied when manufacturers or wholesalers sell merchandise to retailers.

Remember also that special journals are *highly specialized* in terms of the transactions they can record. Thus every business still needs a general journal to record transactions that do not fit into any of its special journals, including, for example, adjusting entries, closing entries, and unusual events such as a loss sustained from a fire.

Management uses information about departments and products for many purposes. These include setting prices, deciding which products to carry and to advertise, and evaluating the performance of departmental managers. By concentrating sales efforts on the products and departments with the *highest margins*, management usually can increase the company's overall gross profit rate.

Financial Analysis and Decision Making

In evaluating the performance of a merchandising business, managers and investors look at more than just net income. Two key measures of past performance and future prospects are trends in the company's *net sales* and *gross profit.*

Net Sales

Measure the performance of a merchandising business. LO8

Most investors and business managers consider the *trend* in net sales to be a key indicator of both past performance and future prospects. Increasing sales suggest the probability of larger profits in future periods. Declining sales, on the other hand, may provide advance warning of financial difficulties.

As a measure of performance, the trend in net sales has some limitations, especially when the company is adding new stores. For these companies, an increase in overall net sales in comparison to the prior year may have resulted solely from sales at the new stores. Sales at existing stores may even be declining. Business managers and investors often focus on measures that adjust for changes in the number of stores from period to period, and on measures of space utilization. These measures include:

1. **Comparable store sales.** Net sales at established stores, excluding new stores opened during the period. Indicates whether customer demand is rising or falling at established locations. (Also called *same-store sales.*)
2. **Sales per square foot of selling space.** A measure of how effectively the company is using its physical facilities (such as floor space or, in supermarkets, shelf space).

Gross Profit Margins

Increasing net sales is *not enough* to ensure increasing profitability. Some products are more profitable than others. In evaluating the profitability of sales transactions, managers and investors keep a close eye on the company's **gross profit margin** (also called *gross profit rate*).

Gross profit margin is the dollar amount of gross profit, expressed as a *percentage* of net sales revenue. Gross profit margins can be computed for the business as a whole, for specific sales departments, and for individual products.

To illustrate the computation of gross profit margin, consider selected income statement data for **Home Depot**, **Saks**, and **Wal-Mart**. The sales, cost of sales, and gross profit for these companies are as follows (in thousands of dollars):

	Home Depot	Saks	Wal-Mart
Net sales	$73,094,000	$6,437,277	$285,222,000
Cost of sales	48,664,000	3,995,460	219,793,000
Gross profit	$24,430,000	$2,441,817	$ 65,429,000

(continued)

The Overall Gross Profit Margin The average gross profit margin (gross profit rate) is a measure of relative profitability. The gross profit rate is calculated by dividing gross profit (in dollars) by net sales. The gross profit rates for **Home Depot**, **Saks**, and **Wal-Mart** are:

- **Home Depot**: 33.42 percent ($24,430,000/$73,094,000)
- **Saks**: 37.93 percent ($2,441,817/$6,437,277)
- **Wal-Mart**: 22.94 percent ($65,429,000/$285,222,000)

In addition, gross profit rates can be computed for different segments within the company, for different departments within a store, and for individual products.

Segment Gross Profit Margins **Wal-Mart** reports three operating segments in its annual report: **Wal-Mart Stores**, **Sam's Club**, and International. The sales revenue for **Wal-Mart Stores**, **Sam's Club**, and International is $191.8 billion, $37.1 billion, and $56.3 billion, respectively. Since generally accepted accounting principles (GAAP) do not require the disclosure of segmental cost of goods sold, we cannot compute gross profit or the gross profit rate at the segment level. However, GAAP does require the disclosure of operating income. Operating income is a measure of profitability after all expenses incurred in operating the business, including cost of sales, are deducted from net sales. Operating income for **Wal-Mart Stores**, **Sam's Club**, and International is $14.2 billion, $1.3 billion, and $3.0 billion, respectively. The operating income margin (Operating Income/Net Sales) is 7.4 percent for **Wal-Mart Stores**, 3.5 percent for **Sam's Club**, and 5.3 percent for International.

Using Information about Gross Profit Margins Investors usually compute companies' overall gross profit rates from one period to the next. High—or increasing—margins generally indicate popular products and successful marketing strategies. A substandard or declining profit margin, on the other hand, often indicates weak customer demand or intense price competition.[7]

[7] We discuss the interpretation of gross profit in greater depth in Chapter 14.

Ethics, Fraud & Corporate Governance

As discussed previously in this chapter, sales discounts and allowances are contra-revenue accounts. Sales discounts and allowances reduce gross sales. As such, net income will be incorrect if discounts and allowances are not properly recorded. In 1998, the Securities and Exchange Commission (SEC) brought an enforcement action against Pepsi-Cola Puerto Rico (Pepsi PR) alleging that Pepsi PR understated its sales discounts and allowances. Pepsi PR produces, distributes, and markets PepsiCo beverages throughout Puerto Rico. Pepsi PR is a separate company and its stock was listed on the New York Stock Exchange at the time of the SEC enforcement action.

In 1995 the Coca-Cola franchise was purchased by a new bottler. The new Coke bottler attempted to gain market share by cutting prices. Pepsi PR responded by offering more generous sales discounts and allowances. However, offering these additional discounts and allowances would have reduced Pepsi PR's net income. The Pepsi PR general manager instructed the company's finance staff not to record some of the sales discounts and allowances given to customers. Pepsi PR's failure to record discounts and allowances resulted in net income for the first quarter of fiscal 1996 being overstated by $3.3 million and net income for the second quarter being overstated by $5.7 million. Pepsi PR consented to an SEC cease-and-desist order without either admitting or denying guilt.

Although Pepsi PR's general manager initiated the scheme that led to the misstatement of Pepsi PR's financial statements, the failure to record sales discounts and allowances was carried out by the company's director of finance and other finance department staffers. The individuals who carried out this scheme knew that Pepsi PR's financial results would be misstated if sales discounts and allowances were not recorded correctly. However, these individuals were unwilling to defy their superior, even when their superior was asking them to engage in unethical and illegal behavior. In cases of fraudulent financial reporting, subordinates being pressured by superiors to implement the fraud scheme is relatively common.

© AP Wide World Photo

The pressure brought to bear on subordinates to implement fraudulent schemes developed by top management can often be intense. Top management can threaten employees with termination if they fail to participate in the fraud. Unfortunately, employees who acquiesce to such pressure face tremendous legal risks. Unlike their superiors, the fingerprints of lower-level employees who actually implement the fraudulent scheme are all over the incriminating documents. For example, a midlevel tax manager who was convicted of participating in a scheme to misstate Dynergy's financial statements was sentenced to 24 years in federal prison. This individual's bosses, who were equally complicit in the scheme, pled guilty and testified against their former employee. They are expected to receive less than five years in prison.

The Sarbanes-Oxley Act provides some protection for lower-level employees who are pressured to participate in an accounting fraud. Public company audit committees must establish procedures (typically company "hotlines") that can be used by employees for reporting concerns relating to questionable accounting or auditing matters. In addition, Sarbanes-Oxley includes certain "whistle-blower" protections. No public company may discharge, demote, suspend, threaten, harass, or in any other manner discriminate against an employee if the employee provides information or assistance in an investigation involving securities fraud.

Concluding Remarks

The Overnight Auto Service illustration presented in Chapter 2 through Chapter 5 addressed measurement and reporting issues pertaining to a service-type business. Throughout this chapter, we have had an opportunity to see how merchandising companies measure and report the results for their operations. Many of the illustrations and assignments throughout the remainder of this textbook are based upon merchandising enterprises.

In Chapter 7, we examine accounts receivable and other liquid assets common to merchandisers. In Chapter 8, we focus upon issues related to merchandise inventories. Measurement and reporting issues that pertain primarily to manufacturing companies are generally covered in a subsequent course.

END-OF-CHAPTER REVIEW

SUMMARY OF LEARNING OBJECTIVES

LO1 **Describe the *operating cycle* of a merchandising company.** The operating cycle is the repeating sequence of transactions by which a company generates revenue and cash receipts from customers. In a merchandising company, the operating cycle consists of the following transactions: (1) purchases of merchandise, (2) sale of the merchandise—often on account—and (3) collection of accounts receivable from customers.

LO2 **Understand the components of a merchandising company's income statement.** In a merchandising company's income statement, *sales* (or *net sales*) represent the total revenue generated by selling merchandise to its customers. As items are sold from inventory, their costs are transferred from the balance sheet to the income statement, where they appear as the *cost of goods sold.* The cost of goods sold is subtracted from sales to determine the company's *gross profit. Other expenses* (such as wages, advertising, utilities, and depreciation) are subtracted from gross profit in the determination of *net income.* Only if a company's gross profit exceeds the sum of its other expenses will it be profitable.

LO3 **Account for purchases and sales of merchandise in a *perpetual* inventory system.** In a perpetual inventory system, purchases of merchandise are recorded by debiting the Inventory account. Two entries are required to record each sale: one to recognize sales revenue and the second to record the cost of goods sold. This second entry consists of a debit to Cost of Goods Sold and a credit to Inventory.

LO4 **Explain how a *periodic* inventory system operates.** In a periodic system, up-to-date records are *not* maintained for inventory or the cost of goods sold. Thus less record keeping is required than in a perpetual system.

The beginning and ending inventories are determined by taking a complete physical count at each year-end. Purchases are recorded in a Purchases account, and no entries are made to record the cost of individual sales transactions. Instead, the cost of goods sold is determined at year-end by a computation such as the following (dollar amounts are provided only for purposes of example):

Beginning inventory	$ 30,000
Add: Purchases	180,000
Cost of goods available for sale	$210,000
Less: Ending inventory	40,000
Cost of goods sold	$170,000

The amounts of inventory and the cost of goods sold are recorded in the accounting records during the year-end closing procedures.

LO5 **Discuss the factors to be considered in selecting an inventory system.** In general terms, a perpetual system should be used when (1) management and employees need timely information about inventory levels and product sales, and (2) the company has the resources to develop this information at a reasonable cost. A periodic system should be used when the usefulness of current information about inventories does not justify the cost of maintaining a perpetual system.

Perpetual systems are most widely used in companies with computerized accounting systems and in businesses that sell high-cost merchandise. Periodic systems are most often used in small businesses that have manual accounting systems and that sell many types of low-cost merchandise.

LO6 **Account for additional merchandising transactions related to purchases and sales.** Buyers should record purchases at the net cost and record any cash discounts lost in an expense account. Sellers record sales at the gross sales price and record in a contra-revenue account all cash discounts taken by customers.

Assuming a perpetual inventory system, the buyer records a purchase return by crediting the Inventory account for the net cost of the returned merchandise. In recording a sales return, the seller makes two entries: one to record Sales Returns and Allowances (a contra-revenue account) for the amount of the refund and the other to transfer the cost of the returned merchandise from the Cost of Goods Sold account back into the Inventory account.

Buyers record transportation charges on purchased merchandise either as part of the cost of the merchandise or directly as part of the cost of goods sold. Sellers view the cost of delivering merchandise to customers as an operating expense.

Sales taxes are collected by retailers from their customers and paid to state and city governments. Thus collecting sales taxes increases the retailer's assets and liabilities. Paying the sales tax to the government is payment of the liability, not an expense.

LO7 **Define *special journals* and explain their usefulness.** Special journals are accounting records or devices designed to record a specific type of transaction in a highly efficient manner. Because a special journal is used only to record a specific type of transaction, the journal may be located at the transaction site and maintained by employees other than accounting personnel. Thus special journals reduce the time, effort, and cost of recording routine business transactions.

(LO8) **Measure the performance of a merchandising business.** There are numerous measures used to evaluate the performance of merchandising businesses. In this chapter, we introduced three of these measures: (1) comparable store sales, which helps determine whether customer demand is rising or falling at established locations, (2) sales per square foot of selling space, which is a measure of how effectively a merchandising business is using its facilities to generate revenue, and (3) gross profit percentages, which help users of financial statements gain insight about a company's pricing policies and the demand for its products.

Key Terms Introduced or Emphasized in Chapter 6

comparable store sales (p. 265) A comparison of sales figures at established stores with existing "track records." (Also called *same-store sales.*)

contra-revenue account (p. 262) A debit balance account that is offset against revenue in the income statement. Examples include Sales Discounts and Sales Returns and Allowances.

control account (p. 250) A general ledger account that summarizes the content of a specific subsidiary ledger.

cost of goods sold (p. 249) The cost to a merchandising company of the goods it has sold to its customers during the period.

gross profit (p. 250) Net sales revenue minus the cost of goods sold.

gross profit margin (p. 265) Gross profit expressed as a percentage of net sales. Also called *gross profit rate.*

inventory (p. 248) Merchandise intended for resale to customers.

inventory shrinkage (p. 253) The loss of merchandise through such causes as shoplifting, breakage, and spoilage.

net sales (p. 262) Gross sales revenue less sales returns and allowances and sales discounts. The most widely used measure of dollar sales volume; usually the first figure shown in an income statement.

operating cycle (p. 248) The repeating sequence of transactions by which a business generates its revenue and cash receipts from customers.

periodic inventory system (p. 254) An alternative to the perpetual inventory system. It eliminates the need for recording the cost of goods sold as sales occur. However, the amounts of inventory and the cost of goods sold are not known until a complete physical inventory is taken at year-end.

perpetual inventory system (p. 251) A system of accounting for merchandising transactions in which the Inventory and Cost of Goods Sold accounts are kept perpetually up-to-date.

point-of-sale (POS) terminals (p. 264) Electronic cash registers used for computer-based processing of sales transactions. The POS terminal identifies each item of merchandise from its bar code and then automatically records the sale and updates the computer-based inventory records. These terminals permit the use of perpetual inventory systems in many businesses that sell a high volume of low-cost merchandise.

sales per square foot of selling space (p. 265) A measure of efficient use of available space.

special journal (p. 264) An accounting record or device designed for recording large numbers of a particular type of transaction quickly and efficiently. A business may use many different kinds of special journals.

subsidiary ledger (p. 250) A ledger containing separate accounts for each of the items making up the balance of a control account in the general ledger. The total of the account balances in a subsidiary ledger are equal to the balance in the general ledger control account.

taking a physical inventory (p. 253) The procedure of counting all merchandise on hand and determining its cost.

Demonstration Problem

STAR-TRACK sells satellite tracking systems for receiving television broadcasts from communications satellites in space. At December 31, 2007, the company's inventory amounted to $44,000. During the first week in January 2008, STAR-TRACK made only one purchase and one sale. These transactions were as follows:

Jan. 3 Sold a tracking system to Mystery Mountain Resort for $20,000 cash. The system consisted of seven different devices, which had a total cost to STAR-TRACK of $11,200.

Jan. 7 Purchased two Model 400 and four Model 800 satellite dishes from Yamaha Corp. The total cost of this purchase amounted to $10,000; terms 2/10, n/30.

STAR-TRACK records purchases of merchandise at net cost. The company has full-time accounting personnel and uses a manual accounting system.

Instructions

a. Briefly describe the operating cycle of a merchandising company.

b. Prepare journal entries to record these transactions, assuming that STAR-TRACK uses a perpetual inventory system.

c. Explain what information in part **b** should be posted to subsidiary ledger accounts.

d. Compute the balance in the Inventory control account at January 7.

e. Prepare journal entries to record the two transactions, assuming that STAR-TRACK uses a *periodic* inventory system.

f. Compute the cost of goods sold for the first week of January, assuming use of the periodic system. As the amount of ending inventory, use your answer to part **d**.

g. Which type of inventory system do you think STAR-TRACK should use? Explain your reasoning.

h. Determine the gross profit margin on the January 3 sales transaction.

Solution to the Demonstration Problem

a. The operating cycle of a merchandising company consists of purchasing merchandise, selling that merchandise to customers (often on account), and collecting the sales proceeds from these customers. In the process, the business converts cash into inventory, the inventory into accounts receivable, and the accounts receivable into cash.

b. Journal entries assuming use of a *perpetual* inventory system:

GENERAL JOURNAL

Date	Account Titles and Explanation	Debit	Credit
2008			
Jan. 3	Cash	20,000	
	Sales		20,000
	Sold tracking system to Mystery Mountain Resort.		
3	Cost of Goods Sold	11,200	
	Inventory		11,200
	To record cost of merchandise sold.		
7	Inventory	9,800	
	Accounts Payable (Yamaha Corp.)		9,800
	Purchased merchandise. Terms, 2/10, n/30; net cost, $9,800 ($10,000, less 2%).		

c. The debits and credits to the Inventory account should be posted to the appropriate accounts in the inventory subsidiary ledger. The information posted would be the costs and quantities of the types of merchandise purchased or sold. The account payable to Yamaha also should be posted to the Yamaha account in STAR-TRACK's accounts payable ledger. No postings are required to the accounts receivable ledger, as this was a cash sale. If STAR-TRACK maintains more than one bank account, however, the debit to cash should be posted to the proper account in the cash subsidiary ledger.

d. $42,600 ($44,000 beginning balance, less $11,200, plus $9,800).

e. Journal entries assuming use of a *periodic* inventory system:

GENERAL JOURNAL

Date	Account Titles and Explanation	Debit	Credit
2008			
Jan. 3	Cash	20,000	
	Sales		20,000
	Sold tracking system to Mystery Mountain Resort.		
7	Purchases	9,800	
	Accounts Payable (Yamaha Corp.)		9,800
	Purchased merchandise. Terms, 2/10, n/30; net cost, $9,800 ($10,000, less 2%).		

f. Computation of the cost of goods sold:

Inventory, January 1	$44,000
Add: Purchases	9,800
Cost of goods available for sale	$53,800
Less: Inventory, January 7 (per part **d**)	42,600
Cost of goods sold	$11,200

g. STAR-TRACK should use a *perpetual* inventory system. The items in its inventory have a high per-unit cost. Therefore, management will want to know the costs of the individual products included in specific sales transactions and will want to keep track of the items in stock. Although the company has a manual accounting system, its volume of sales transactions is low enough that maintaining a perpetual inventory record will not be difficult.

h. Gross profit = Sales revenue − Cost of goods sold
= $20,000 − $11,200
= $8,800

Gross profit margin = Gross profit ÷ Sales revenue
= $8,800 ÷ $20,000
= 44%

Self-Test Questions

The answers to these questions appear on page 289.

1. Mark and Amanda Carter own an appliance store and a restaurant. The appliance store sells merchandise on a 12-month installment plan; the restaurant sells only for cash. Which of the following statements are true? (More than one answer may be correct.)

a. The appliance store has a longer operating cycle than the restaurant.

b. The appliance store probably uses a perpetual inventory system, whereas the restaurant probably uses a periodic system.

c. Both businesses require subsidiary ledgers for accounts receivable and inventory.

d. Both businesses probably have subsidiary ledgers for accounts payable.

2. Which of the following statements about merchandising activities is true? (More than one answer may be correct.)

a. As inventory is purchased, the Inventory Expense account is debited and Cash (or Accounts Payable) is credited.

b. Inventory is recorded as an asset when it is first purchased.

c. As inventory is sold, its cost is transferred from the balance sheet to the income statement.

d. As inventory is sold, its cost is transferred from the income statement to the balance sheet.

3. Marietta Corporation uses a *perpetual* inventory system. All of its sales are made on account. The company sells merchandise costing $3,000 at a sales price of $4,300. In recording this transaction, Marietta will make all of the following entries *except*:

a. Credit Sales, $4,300.

b. Credit Inventory, $4,300.

c. Debit Cost of Goods Sold, $3,000.

d. Debit Accounts Receivable, $4,300.

4. Fashion House uses a *perpetual* inventory system. At the beginning of the year, inventory amounted to $50,000. During the year, the company purchased merchandise for $230,000 and sold merchandise costing $245,000. A physical inventory taken at year-end indicated shrinkage losses of $4,000. *Prior* to recording these shrinkage losses, the year-end balance in the company's Inventory account was:

a. $31,000.

b. $35,000.

c. $50,000.

d. Some other amount.

5. Best Hardware uses a *periodic* inventory system. Its inventory was $38,000 at the beginning of the year and $40,000 at the end. During the year, Best made purchases of merchandise totaling $107,000. Identify all of the correct answers:

a. To use this system, Best must take a complete physical inventory twice each year.

b. Prior to making adjusting and closing entries at year-end, the balance in Best's Inventory account is $38,000.

c. The cost of goods sold for the year is $109,000.

d. As sales transactions occur, Best makes no entries to update its inventory records or to record the cost of goods sold.

6. The two basic approaches to accounting for inventory and the cost of goods sold are the *perpetual* inventory system and the *periodic* inventory system. Indicate which of the following statements are correct. (More than one answer may be correct.)
   a. Most large merchandising companies and manufacturing businesses use periodic inventory systems.
   b. As a practical matter, a grocery store or a large department store could not maintain a perpetual inventory system without the use of point-of-sale terminals.
   c. In a periodic inventory system, the cost of goods sold is not determined until a complete physical inventory is taken.
   d. In a perpetual inventory system, the Cost of Goods Sold account is debited promptly for the cost of merchandise sold.

7. Big Brother, a retail store, purchased 100 television sets from Krueger Electronics on account at a cost of $200 each. Krueger offers credit terms of 2/10, n/30. Big Brother uses a perpetual inventory system and records purchases at *net cost*. Big Brother determines that 10 of these television sets are defective and returns them to Krueger for full credit. In recording this return, Big Brother will:
   a. Debit Sales Returns and Allowances, $1,960.
   b. Debit Accounts Payable, $1,960.
   c. Debit Cost of Goods Sold, $1,960.
   d. Credit Inventory, $2,000.

8. Two of the lawn mowers sold by Garden Products Co. are the LawnMaster and the Mark 5. LawnMasters sell for $250 apiece, which results in a 35 percent gross profit margin. Each Mark 5 costs Garden Products $300 and sells for $400. Indicate all correct answers.
   a. The dollar amount of gross profit is greater on the sale of a Mark 5 than a LawnMaster.
   b. The gross profit margin is higher on Mark 5s than on LawnMasters.
   c. Garden profits relatively more by selling one Mark 5 than by selling one LawnMaster.
   d. Garden profits more by selling $2,000 worth of Mark 5s than $2,000 worth of LawnMasters.

ASSIGNMENT MATERIAL Discussion Questions

1. Describe the operating cycle of a merchandising company.
2. Compare and contrast the merchandising activities of a wholesaler and a retailer.
3. The income statement of a merchandising company includes a major type of cost that does not appear in the income statement of a service-type business. Identify this cost and explain what it represents.
4. During the current year, Green Bay Company earned a gross profit of $350,000, whereas New England Company earned a gross profit of only $280,000. Both companies had net sales of $900,000. Does this mean that Green Bay is more profitable than New England? Explain.
5. Thornhill Company's income statement shows gross profit of $432,000, cost of goods sold of $638,000, and other expenses totaling $390,000. Compute the amounts of **(a)** revenue from sales (net sales) and **(b)** net income.
6. Explain the need for subsidiary ledgers in accounting for merchandising activities.
7. Define the term *inventory shrinkage*. How is the amount of inventory shrinkage determined in a business using a perpetual inventory system, and how is this shrinkage recorded in the accounting records?
8. Briefly contrast the accounting procedures in *perpetual* and *periodic* inventory systems.
9. Miracle Home Cleanser uses a *periodic* inventory system. During the current year the company purchased merchandise with a cost of $55,000. State the cost of goods sold for the year under each of the following alternative assumptions:
   a. No beginning inventory; ending inventory $3,500.
   b. Beginning inventory $10,000; no ending inventory.
   c. Beginning inventory $2,000; ending inventory $7,200.
   d. Beginning inventory $8,000; ending inventory $1,400.
10. Evaluate the following statement: "Without electronic point-of-sale terminals, it simply would not be possible to use perpetual inventory systems in businesses that sell large quantities of many different products."
11. Explain the distinguishing characteristics of **(a)** a general journal and **(b)** a special journal.
12. How does a balance arise in the Purchase Discounts Lost account? Why does management pay careful attention to the balance (if any) in this account?
13. European Imports pays substantial freight charges to obtain inbound shipments of purchased merchandise. Should these freight charges be debited to the company's Delivery Expense account? Explain.
14. Outback Sporting Goods purchases merchandise on terms of 4/10, n/60. The company has a line of credit that enables it to borrow money as needed from Northern Bank at an annual interest rate of 13 percent. Should Outback pay its suppliers within the 10-day discount period if it must draw on its line of credit (borrow from Northern Bank) to make these early payments? Explain.
15. TireCo is a retail store in a state that imposes a 6 percent sales tax. Would you expect to find sales tax expense and sales tax payable in TireCo's financial statements? Explain.
16. A seller generally records sales at the full invoice price, but the buyer often records purchases at *net cost*. Explain the logic of the buyer and seller recording the transaction at different amounts.

17. Western Stores, a chain of hardware stores, had an increase in net sales of 8 percent for this year in relation to the prior year. Does this mean that the company's marketing strategies, such as advertising, pricing, and product mix, are succeeding?

18. Define the term *gross profit margin*. Explain several ways in which management might improve a company's overall profit margin.

19. Under a perpetual inventory system, a company should know the quantity and price of its inventory at any moment in time. Given this, why do companies that use a perpetual inventory system still take a physical count of their merchandise inventory at least once a year?

20. Under which type of inventory system is an inventory subsidiary ledger maintained?

Brief Exercises

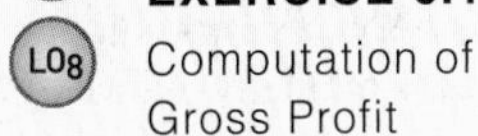

BRIEF EXERCISE 6.1
LO2 LO8
Computation of Gross Profit

Office Today is an office supply store. Office Today's revenue in the current year is $800 million and its cost of goods sold is $640 million. Compute Office Today's gross profit and its gross profit percentage.

BRIEF EXERCISE 6.2
LO7
Accounts Receivable Subsidiary Ledger

The accounts receivable subsidiary ledger for Ranalli's Lawn Care has the following customer accounts and balances at the end of the current year. What should be the Accounts Receivable balance in the general ledger? [Hint: Customer accounts with a credit balance are not considered in determining the total balance in the Accounts Receivable account; rather these amounts are reclassified as Accounts Payable.]

Customer Name	Balance	Debit or Credit
Peter Gurney	$200	Dr
Robert King	150	Dr
Bruce Landis	50	Cr
Robert McNeil	100	Dr
Mark Noakes	50	Dr
Frank Rimshaw	300	Dr
Michael Sangster	50	Dr
Lawrence Williams	100	Cr

BRIEF EXERCISE 6.3
LO2 LO3 LO8
Perpetual Inventory System—Computation of Income

Alberto & Sons, Inc., a retailer of antique figurines, engages in the following transactions during October of the current year:

Oct. 1 Purchases 100 Hummels at $50 each.
Oct. 5 Sells 50 of the Hummels at $80 each.

Compute Alberto & Sons's gross profit for October.

BRIEF EXERCISE 6.4
LO2 LO4 LO8
Periodic Inventory System—Inventory Balance During Year

Neel & Neal Inc. is a retailer of fine leather goods. The company's inventory balance at the beginning of the year was $300,000; Neel & Neal purchased $250,000 of goods during January, and sales during January were $400,000. What is the balance that would appear in Neel & Neal's inventory account on February 1 assuming use of a periodic inventory system?

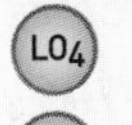

BRIEF EXERCISE 6.5
LO2 LO4 LO8
Periodic Inventory System—Determine Cost of Goods Sold

Murphy Co. is a high-end retailer of fine fashions for men. Murphy's inventory balance at the beginning of the year is $300,000, and Murphy purchases $600,000 of goods during the year. Its inventory balance at the end of the year is $250,000. What is the cost of goods sold for the year?

BRIEF EXERCISE 6.6
LO2 LO4 LO8
Periodic Inventory System—Working Backward through the COGS Section

Yang & Min Inc. is a retailer of contemporary furniture. You are told that Yang & Min's ending inventory is $200,000 and its cost of goods sold is $500,000. Yang & Min had $100,000 of inventory at the beginning of the year. What was the dollar amount of goods purchased by Yang & Min during the year?

BRIEF EXERCISE 6.7

Periodic Inventory System—Closing Process

Bronson Inc. is a retailer of sporting goods. Bronson's beginning inventory is $80,000 and its purchases during the year are $250,000. Its ending inventory is $30,000. Make the closing entries necessary given that Bronson uses a periodic inventory system.

BRIEF EXERCISE 6.8

Benefit of Taking a Purchase Discount

Pag Inc. is a clothing retailer and it has terms from one of its vendors of *1/10, n/30*. Compute the equivalent annual rate of return that Pag earns by always paying its bills within the discount period.

BRIEF EXERCISE 6.9

Sales Returns and Allowances

Inamra Inc. is a clothing manufacturer. The firm uses a periodic inventory system. Inamra shipped $20,000 of defective goods to a retailer. The retailer and Inamra agreed that the retailer would keep the goods in exchange for a $2,000 allowance. The cost of the goods was $1,000. What journal entry (or entries) would Inamra record?

BRIEF EXERCISE 6.10

Special Journals

List three special journals often used in accounting to facilitate the recording of repetitive transactions.

BRIEF EXERCISE 6.11

Ethics, Fraud, and Corporate Governance

You are the assistant controller for a public company. Wall Street stock analysts are projecting an earnings per share figure of $0.25 for your company. On December 29, a large customer returns a very large shipment of your goods that were defective. You tell the controller about the customer return and that the debit to sales returns and allowances will have the effect of reducing earnings per share from $0.25 to $0.24. The controller indicates that failing to meet the consensus earnings expectations of the analyst community will result in a large stock price decline. The controller suggests waiting until January 2 (your company operates on a calendar year-end basis) to record the customer return. What should you do?

Exercises

EXERCISE 6.1

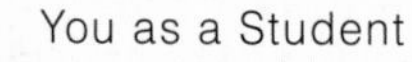

You as a Student

LO6

As a fund-raiser, the pep band at Melrose University sells T-shirts fans can wear when attending the school's 12 home basketball games. As the band's business manager, you must choose among several options for ordering and selling the T-shirts.

1. Place a single order in October large enough to last the entire season. The band must pay for the shirts in full when the order is placed. A 5 percent quantity discount applies to this option.
2. Place a series of small orders, as needed, throughout the season. Again, payment in full is due when the order is submitted. No discount applies to this option.
3. Have band members sell shirts directly to members of the student body. Cash is collected immediately as sales are made.
4. Sell all of the T-shirts through the university bookstore. The bookstore would receive a 6 percent commission on total sales and would remit to the band its share of the proceeds in a lump-sum payment at the end of the season.

a. Describe which combination of options would give the pep band the shortest operating cycle.

b. Describe which combination of options would give the pep band the longest operating cycle.

c. Discuss briefly the advantages and disadvantages of each option.

EXERCISE 6.2

Effects of Basic Merchandising Transactions

Shown below are selected transactions of Konshock's, a retail store that uses a perpetual inventory system.

a. Purchased merchandise on account.

b. Recognized the revenue from a sale of merchandise on account. (Ignore the related cost of goods sold.)

c. Recognized the cost of goods sold relating to the sale in transaction **b.**

d. Collected in cash the account receivable from the customer in transaction **b.**

e. Following the taking of a physical inventory at year-end, made an adjusting entry to record a normal amount of inventory shrinkage.

Indicate the effects of each of these transactions on the elements of the company's financial statements shown below. Organize your answer in tabular form, using the column headings shown below. (Notice that the cost of goods sold is shown separately from all other expenses.) Use the code letters **I** for increase, **D** for decrease, and **NE** for no effect.

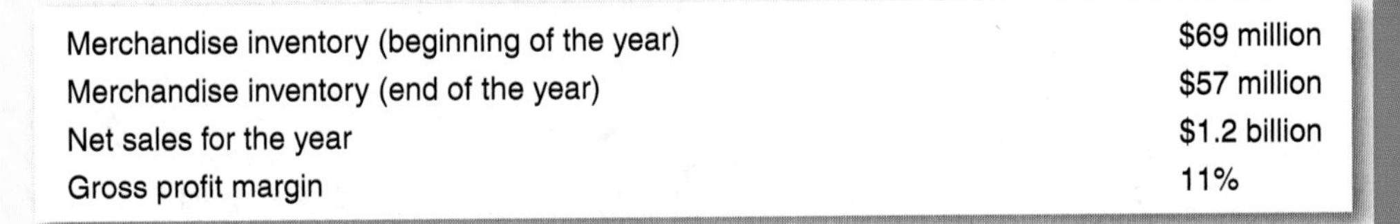

	Income Statement				Balance Sheet		
Transaction	Net Sales −	Cost of Goods Sold −	All Other Expenses =	Net Income	Assets =	Liabilities +	Owners' Equity
a	____	____	____	____	____	____	____

EXERCISE 6.3
Understanding Inventory Cost Flows

PC Connection is a leading mail order retailer of personal computers. A recent financial report issued by the company revealed the following information:

Merchandise inventory (beginning of the year)	$69 million
Merchandise inventory (end of the year)	$57 million
Net sales for the year	$1.2 billion
Gross profit margin	11%

a. Compute the company's cost of goods sold for the year.

b. Approximately how much inventory did PC Connection *purchase* during the year?

c. What factors might contribute to the company's low gross profit margin?

d. Discuss reasons why PC Connection uses a perpetual inventory system.

EXERCISE 6.4
Perpetual Inventory Systems

Ranns Supply uses a perpetual inventory system. On January 1, its inventory account had a beginning balance of $6,450,000. Ranns engaged in the following transactions during the year:

1. Purchased merchandise inventory for $9,500,000.

2. Generated net sales of $26,000,000.

3. Recorded inventory shrinkage of $10,000 after taking a physical inventory at year-end.

4. Reported gross profit for the year of $15,000,000 in its income statement.

a. At what amount was Cost of Goods Sold reported in the company's year-end income statement?

b. At what amount was Merchandise Inventory reported in the company's year-end balance sheet?

c. Immediately prior to recording inventory shrinkage at the end of the year, what was the balance of the Cost of Goods Sold account? What was the balance of the Merchandise Inventory account?

EXERCISE 6.5
Evaluating Performance

These selected statistics are from recent annual reports of two well-known retailers (the Kmart figures were generated subsequent to its filing for bankruptcy):

	Wal-Mart	Kmart
Percentage increase (decrease) in net sales	14%	3%
Percentage increase (decrease) in gross profit rate	0	<10>
Percentage increase (decrease) in comparable store net sales	3	<0.1>

a. Explain the significance of each of these three measures.

b. Evaluate briefly the performance of each company based upon these three measures.

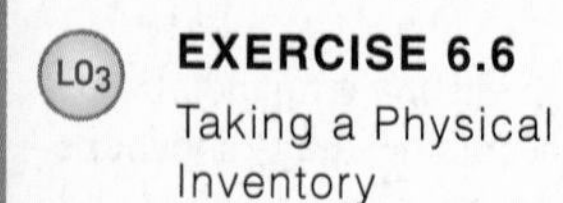

EXERCISE 6.6
Taking a Physical Inventory

Frisbee Hardware uses a perpetual inventory system. At year-end, the Inventory account has a balance of $250,000, but a physical count shows that the merchandise on hand has a cost of only $246,000.

a. Explain the probable reason(s) for this discrepancy.

b. Prepare the journal entry required in this situation.

c. Indicate all the accounting records to which your journal entry in part **b** should be posted.

LO4

EXERCISE 6.7
Periodic Inventory Systems

Boston Bait Shop uses a periodic inventory system. At December 31, Year 2, the accounting records include the following information:

Inventory (as of December 31, Year 1)	$ 2,800
Net sales	79,600
Purchases	30,200

A complete physical inventory taken at December 31, Year 2, indicates merchandise costing $3,000 remains in stock.

a. How were the amounts of beginning and ending inventory determined?

b. Compute the amount of the cost of goods sold in Year 2.

c. Prepare two closing entries at December 31, Year 2: the first to create a Cost of Goods Sold account with the appropriate balance and the second to bring the Inventory account up-to-date.

d. Prepare a partial income statement showing the shop's gross profit for the year.

e. Describe why a company such as Boston Bait Shop would use a periodic inventory system rather than a perpetual inventory system.

EXERCISE 6.8
Relationships within Periodic Inventory Systems

This exercise stresses the relationships between the information recorded in a periodic inventory system and the basic elements of an income statement. Each of the five lines represents a separate set of information. You are to fill in the missing amounts. A net loss in the right-hand column is to be indicated by placing brackets around the amount, as for example in line **e** <15,000>.

	Net Sales	Beginning Inventory	Net Purchases	Ending Inventory	Cost of Goods Sold	Gross Profit	Expenses	Net Income or (Loss)
a.	240,000	76,000	104,000	35,200	?	95,200	72,000	?
b.	480,000	72,000	272,000	?	264,000	?	?	20,000
c.	630,000	207,000	?	166,500	441,000	189,000	148,500	?
d.	810,000	?	450,000	135,000	?	234,000	270,000	?
e.	?	156,000	?	153,000	396,000	135,000	?	<15,000>

EXERCISE 6.9
Selecting an Inventory System

Year after year two huge supermarket chains—Albertsons, Inc., and Safeway, Inc.—consistently report gross profit rates between 28 percent and 31 percent. Each uses a sophisticated perpetual inventory system to account for billions of dollars in inventory transactions.

a. Discuss reasons why these firms consistently report such similar and stable gross profit rates.

b. What technologies make it possible for these retailing giants to use perpetual inventory systems?

EXERCISE 6.10
Cash Discounts

Golf World sold merchandise to Mulligans for $10,000, offering terms of 1/15, n/30. Mulligans paid for the merchandise within the discount period. Both companies use perpetual inventory systems.

a. Prepare journal entries in the accounting records of Golf World to account for this sale and the subsequent collection. Assume the original cost of the merchandise to Golf World had been $6,500.

b. Prepare journal entries in the accounting records of Mulligans to account for the purchase and subsequent payment. Mulligans records purchases of merchandise at *net cost*.

c. Assume that, because of a change in personnel, Mulligans failed to pay for this merchandise within the discount period. Prepare the journal entry in the accounting records of Mulligans to record payment *after* the discount period.

EXERCISE 6.11
Evaluating Performance

This selected information is from recent annual reports of the three largest retail pharmaceutical companies in the United States. (Dollar amounts are stated in billions.)

	CVS Corporation	Walgreen Company	Rite Aid Corporation
Net sales	$?	$42.2	$16.8
Cost of goods sold	22.6	?	12.6
Gross profit	8.0	?	?
Gross profit margin (or rate)	?%	28.0%	?%
Total square feet of selling space	43.5 million	55.4 million	37.2 million
Sales per square foot of selling space	?	?	?

a. Fill in the missing amounts and percentages. (Round all amounts to one decimal place.)

b. A significant portion of any retail pharmacy's revenue is from third-party sales. A third-party sale occurs when an insurance company is responsible for paying for a customer's prescription medicine. Insurance companies rarely reimburse retail pharmacies the full price for medications purchased by customers covered under prescription drug plans.

One of the three retail pharmacy chains listed above reported recently that its percentage of total prescription drug revenue from third-party sales had risen from 85 percent to over 90 percent, making its percentage of total prescription revenue from third-party sales one of the highest in the industry. Identify this retailer based on the information provided and from the figures computed in part **a**. Defend your answer.

EXERCISE 6.12
Comparison of Inventory Systems

Sky Probe sells state-of-the-art telescopes to individuals and organizations interested in studying the solar system. At December 31 last year, the company's inventory amounted to $250,000. During the first week of January this year, the company made only one purchase and one sale. These transactions were as follows:

Jan. 2 Sold one telescope costing $90,000 to Central State University for cash, $117,000.

Jan. 5 Purchased merchandise on account from Lunar Optics, $50,000. Terms, net 30 days.

a. Prepare journal entries to record these transactions assuming that Sky Probe uses the perpetual inventory system. Use separate entries to record the sales revenue and the cost of goods sold for the sale on January 2.

b. Compute the balance of the Inventory account on January 7.

c. Prepare journal entries to record the two transactions, assuming that Sky Probe uses the periodic inventory system.

d. Compute the cost of goods sold for the first week of January assuming use of a periodic inventory system. Use your answer to part **b** as the ending inventory.

e. Which inventory system do you believe that a company such as Sky Probe would probably use? Explain your reasoning.

EXERCISE 6.13
The Periodic Inventory System

Mountain Mabel's is a small general store located just outside of Yellowstone National Park. The store uses a periodic inventory system. Every January 1, Mabel and her husband close the store and take a complete physical inventory while watching the Rose Bowl Parade on television. The inventory balance on January 1 of the prior year was $6,240, and the inventory balance on December 31 was $4,560. Sales were $150,000 during the prior year, and purchases were $74,400.

a. Compute the cost of goods sold for the prior year.

b. Explain why a small business such as this might use the periodic inventory system.

c. Explain some of the *disadvantages* of the periodic system to a larger business, such as a Sears store.

LO8

EXERCISE 6.14
Difference between Income and Cash Flow

State College Technology Store (SCTS) is a retail computer store in the university center of a large midwestern university. SCTS engaged in the following transactions during November of the current year:

Nov. 1 Purchased 20 Nopxe laptop computers on account from Led Inc. The laptop computers cost $800 each, for a total of $16,000. Payment is due in 30 days.

Nov. 6 Sold four Nopxe laptop computers on account to the Department of Microbiology at State College at a retail sales price of $1,200 each, for a total of $4,800. Payment is due in 30 days.

Dec. 1 Paid the $16,000 account payable to Led Inc.

Dec. 6 Collected the $4,800 account receivable from State College's Department of Microbiology.

Assume that the other expenses incurred by SCTS during November and December were $1,000, and assume that all of these expenses were paid in cash. SCTS is not subject to income tax because it is a wholly-owned unit of a nonprofit organization. Compute the net income of SCTS during November and December using accrual accounting principles. Also, compute what SCTS's net income would have been had it used the cash basis of accounting. Explain the difference.

EXERCISE 6.15
Using Home Depot, Inc., Financial Statements

The Home Depot, Inc., financial statements appear in Appendix A at the end of this textbook. Use the statements to complete the following requirements:

a. Calculate the gross profit percentage of Home Depot, Inc., for each of the years shown in the company's income statements.

b. Evaluate the company's trend in sales and gross profit.

Problem Set A

LO1

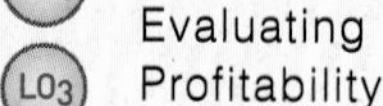

LO8

PROBLEM 6.1A
Evaluating Profitability

Claypool Hardware is the only hardware store in a remote area of northern Minnesota. Some of Claypool's transactions during the current year are as follows:

Nov. 5 Sold lumber on account to Bemidji Construction, $13,390. The inventory subsidiary ledger shows the cost of this merchandise was $9,105.

Nov. 9 Purchased tools on account from Owatonna Tool Company, $3,800.

Dec. 5 Collected in cash the $13,390 account receivable from Bemidji Construction.

Dec. 9 Paid the $3,800 owed to Owatonna Tool Company.

Dec. 31 Claypool's personnel counted the inventory on hand and determined its cost to be $182,080. The accounting records, however, indicate inventory of $183,790 and a cost of goods sold of $695,222. The physical count of the inventory was observed by the company's auditors and is considered correct.

Instructions

a. Prepare journal entries to record these transactions and events in the accounting records of Claypool Hardware. (The company uses a perpetual inventory system.)

b. Prepare a partial income statement showing the company's gross profit for the year. (Net sales for the year amount to $1,024,900.)

c. Claypool purchases merchandise inventory at the same wholesale prices as other hardware stores. Due to its remote location, however, the company must pay between $18,000 and $20,000 per year in extra transportation charges to receive delivery of merchandise. (These additional charges are included in the amount shown as cost of goods sold.)

Assume that an index of key business ratios in your library shows hardware stores of Claypool's approximate size (in total assets) average net sales of $1 million per year and a gross profit margin of 25 percent.

Is Claypool able to pass its extra transportation costs on to its customers? Does the business appear to suffer or benefit financially from its remote location? Explain your reasoning and support your conclusions with specific accounting data comparing the operations of Claypool Hardware with the industry averages.

LO1 through LO3 LO6 LO8

PROBLEM 6.2A
Preparation and Interpretation of a Merchandising Company's Income Statement

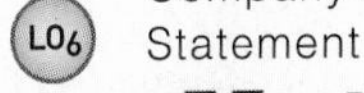

Hendry's Boutique is a retail clothing store for women. The store operates out of a rented building in Storm Lake, Iowa. Shown below is the store's *adjusted* year-end trial balance dated December 31, 2007.

HENDRY'S BOUTIQUE
Adjusted Trial Balance
December 31, 2007

Cash	$ 15,200	
Accounts receivable	2,600	
Merchandise inventory	17,500	
Prepaid rent	1,800	
Office supplies	900	
Office equipment	41,000	
Accumulated depreciation: office equipment		$ 12,000
Accounts payable		12,750
Sales taxes payable		3,200
Capital stock		18,000
Retained earnings		21,050
Sales		226,000
Sales returns and allowances	2,500	
Cost of goods sold	100,575	
Purchase discounts lost	250	
Utilities expense	4,120	
Office supply expense	520	
Depreciation expense: office equipment	2,750	
Rent expense	6,100	
Insurance expense	900	
Salaries expense	88,095	
Income taxes expense	8,190	
	$293,000	$293,000

Instructions

a. Prepare an income statement for Hendry's Boutique dated December 31, 2007.

b. Compute the store's gross profit margin as a percentage of *net sales*.

c. Do the store's customers seem to be satisfied with their purchases? Defend your answer.

d. Explain how you can tell that the business records inventory purchases *net* of any purchase discounts.

e. The store reports sales taxes payable of $3,200 in its adjusted trial balance. Explain why it does not report any *sales taxes expense*.

f. Which accounts appearing in the store's adjusted trial balance comprise its *operating cycle*?

PROBLEM 6.3A
Trend Analysis

Shown below is information from the financial reports of Knauss Supermarkets for the past few years.

	2007	2006	2005
Net sales (in millions)	$5,495	$5,184	$4,800
Number of stores	448	445	430
Square feet of selling space (in millions)	11.9	11.1	10.0
Average net sales of comparable stores (in millions)	$ 10.8	$ 11.0	$ 11.4

Instructions

a. Calculate the following statistics for Knauss Supermarkets (round your answers to one decimal place):

1. The percentage change in net sales from 2005 to 2006 and 2006 to 2007. Hint: The percentage change is computed by dividing the dollar amount of the change between years by the amount of the base year. For example, the percentage change in net sales from 2005 to 2006 is computed by dividing the difference between 2005 and 2006 net sales by the amount of 2005 net sales, or ($5,184 − $4,800) ÷ $4,800 = 8% increase.
2. The percentage change in net sales per square foot of selling space from 2005 to 2006 and 2006 to 2007.
3. The percentage change in comparable store sales from 2005 to 2006 and 2006 to 2007.

b. Evaluate the sales performance of Knauss Supermarkets.

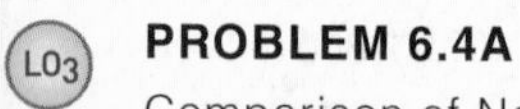

PROBLEM 6.4A
LO3 LO6
Comparison of Net Cost and Gross Price Methods

Lamprino Appliance uses a perpetual inventory system. The following are three recent merchandising transactions:

June 10 Purchased 10 televisions from Mitsu Industries on account. Invoice price, $300 per unit, for a total of $3,000. The terms of purchase were 2/10, n/30.

June 15 Sold one of these televisions for $450 cash.

June 20 Paid the account payable to Mitsu Industries within the discount period.

Instructions

a. Prepare journal entries to record these transactions assuming that Lamprino records purchases of merchandise at:

1. Net cost
2. Gross invoice price

b. Assume that Lamprino did *not* pay Mitsu Industries within the discount period but instead paid the full invoice price on July 10. Prepare journal entries to record this payment assuming that the original liability had been recorded at:

1. Net cost
2. Gross invoice price

c. Assume that you are evaluating the efficiency of Lamprino's bill-paying procedures. Which accounting method—net cost or gross invoice price—provides you with the most *useful* information? Explain.

PROBLEM 6.5A
Merchandising Transactions
eXcel

The following is a series of related transactions between Siogo Shoes, a shoe wholesaler, and Sole Mates, a chain of retail shoe stores:

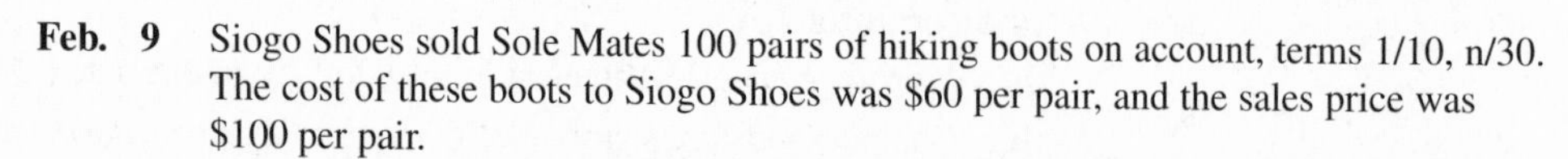

Feb. 9 Siogo Shoes sold Sole Mates 100 pairs of hiking boots on account, terms 1/10, n/30. The cost of these boots to Siogo Shoes was $60 per pair, and the sales price was $100 per pair.

Feb. 12 United Express charged $80 for delivering this merchandise to Sole Mates. These charges were split evenly between the buyer and seller and were paid immediately in cash.

Feb. 13 Sole Mates returned 10 pairs of boots to Siogo Shoes because they were the wrong size. Siogo Shoes allowed Sole Mates full credit for this return.

Feb. 19 Sole Mates paid the remaining balance due to Siogo Shoes within the discount period.

Both companies use a perpetual inventory system.

Instructions

a. Record this series of transactions in the general journal of Siogo Shoes. (The company records sales at gross sales price.)

b. Record this series of transactions in the general journal of Sole Mates. (The company records purchases of merchandise at *net cost* and uses a Transportation-in account to record transportation charges on inbound shipments.)

c. Sole Mates does not always have enough cash on hand to pay for purchases within the discount period. However, it has a line of credit with its bank, which enables Sole Mates to easily borrow money for short periods of time at an annual interest rate of 11 percent. (The bank charges interest only for the number of days until Sole Mates repays the loan.) As a matter of general policy, should Sole Mates take advantage of 1/10, n/30 cash discounts even if it must borrow the money to do so at an annual rate of 11 percent? Explain fully—and illustrate any supporting computations.

PROBLEM 6.6A

Correcting Errors—Recording of Merchandising Transactions

King Enterprises is a book wholesaler. King hired a new accounting clerk on January 1 of the current year. The new clerk does not understand accrual accounting and recorded the transactions below based on when cash receipts and disbursements changed hands rather than when the transaction occurred. King uses a perpetual inventory system, and its accounting policy calls for inventory purchases to be recorded net of any discounts offered.

Jan. 10 Paid Aztec Enterprises $9,800 for books that it received on December 15. (This purchase was recorded as a debit to Inventory and a credit to Accounts Payable on December 15 of last year, but the accounting clerk ignores that fact.)

Dec. 27 Received books from McSaw Inc. for $20,000; terms 2/10, n/30.

Dec. 30 Sold books to Booksellers Unlimited for $30,000; terms 1/10, n/30. The cost of these books to King was $24,500.

Instructions

a. As a result of the accounting clerk's errors, compute the amount by which the following accounts are overstated or understated.

1. Accounts Receivable
2. Inventory
3. Accounts Payable
4. Sales
5. Cost of Goods Sold

b. Compute the amount by which net income is overstated or understated.

c. Prepare a single journal entry to correct the errors that the accounting clerk has made. (Assume that King has yet to close its books for the current year.)

d. Assume that King has already closed its books for the current year. Make a single journal entry to correct the errors that the accounting clerk has made.

e. Assume that the ending inventory balance is correctly stated based on adjustments resulting from a physical inventory count. (Cost of Goods Sold was debited or credited based on the inventory adjustment.) Assume that King has already closed its books for the current year, and make a single journal entry to correct the errors that the accounting clerk has made.

PROBLEM 6.7A

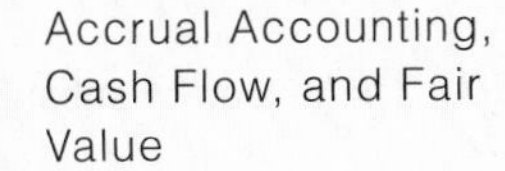

Accrual Accounting, Cash Flow, and Fair Value

Genuine Accessories Inc. is a wholesaler of automobile and truck accessories. Genuine Accessories began operations in November of the current year and engaged in the following transactions during November and December of this year. Genuine Accessories uses a perpetual inventory system.

Nov. 3 Purchased $400,000 of automotive accessories, terms n/30.

Nov. 15 Sold $300,000 of automotive accessories, terms n/60. The cost of the accessories sold is $200,000.

Nov. 28 Purchased $600,000 of automotive accessories, terms n/45.

Dec. 3 Settled the $400,000 purchase of November 3.

Dec. 15 Sold $750,000 of automotive accessories, terms n/60. The cost of the accessories sold is $500,000.

Dec. 27 Purchased $900,000 of automotive accessories, terms n/30.

Instructions

a. Compute the gross profit on Genuine Accessories's transactions during November and December.

b. Compute the gross profit on Genuine Accessories's transactions during November and December if a cash-basis accounting system was used.

c. Explain the difference between the results in **a** and **b**.

d. Assume that the fair value of Genuine Accessories's inventory at December 31 is $1,500,000. A potential lender asks Genuine Accessories to prepare a fair-value–based balance sheet. Prepare the journal entry to reflect inventory at fair value. Comment on how a wholesaler might determine fair value for inventory items. [Hint: Increase the Inventory account by the difference between fair value and book value with the offset to an account titled Revaluation of Inventory to Market Value.]

PROBLEM 6.8A
A Comprehensive Problem

CPI sells computer peripherals. At December 31, 2007, CPI's inventory amounted to $500,000. During the first week in January 2008, the company made only one purchase and one sale. These transactions were as follows:

Jan. 2 Purchased 20 modems and 80 printers from Sharp. The total cost of these machines was $25,000, terms 3/10, n/60.

Jan. 6 Sold 30 different types of products on account to Pace Corporation. The total sales price was $10,000, terms 5/10, n/90. The total cost of these 30 units to CPI was $6,100 (net of the purchase discount).

CPI has a full-time accountant and a computer-based accounting system. It records sales at the gross sales price and purchases at net cost and maintains subsidiary ledgers for accounts receivable, inventory, and accounts payable.

Instructions

a. Briefly describe the operating cycle of a merchandising company. Identify the assets and liabilities directly affected by this cycle.

b. Prepare journal entries to record these transactions, assuming that CPI uses a *perpetual* inventory system.

c. Compute the balance in the Inventory account at the close of business on January 6.

d. Prepare journal entries to record the two transactions, assuming that CPI uses a *periodic* inventory system.

e. Compute the cost of goods sold for the first week of January assuming use of the periodic system. (Use your answer to part **c** as the ending inventory.)

f. Which type of inventory system do you think CPI most likely would use? Explain your reasoning.

g. Compute the gross profit margin on the January 6 sales transaction.

Problem Set B

PROBLEM 6.1B
Evaluating Profitability

Big Oak Lumber is a lumber yard on Angel Island. Some of Big Oak's transactions during the current year are as follows:

Apr. 15 Sold lumber on account to Hard Hat Construction, $19,700. The inventory subsidiary ledger shows the cost of this merchandise was $10,300.

Apr. 19 Purchased lumber on account from LHP Company, $3,700.

May 10 Collected in cash the $19,700 account receivable from Hard Hat Construction.

May 19 Paid the $3,700 owed to LHP Company.

Dec. 31 Big Oak's personnel counted the inventory on hand and determined its cost to be $114,000. The accounting records, however, indicate inventory of $116,500 and a cost of goods sold of $721,000. The physical count of the inventory was observed by the company's auditors and is considered correct.

Instructions

a. Prepare journal entries to record these transactions and events in the accounting records of Big Oak Lumber. (The company uses a perpetual inventory system.)

b. Prepare a partial income statement showing the company's gross profit for the year. (Net sales for the year amount to $1,422,000.)

c. Big Oak purchases merchandise inventory at the same wholesale prices as other lumber yards. Because of its remote location the company must pay between $8,000 and $18,000 per year in extra transportation charges to receive delivery of merchandise. (These additional charges are included in the amount shown as cost of goods sold.)

Assume that an index of key business ratios in your library shows lumber yards of Big Oak's approximate size (in total assets) average net sales of $1 million per year and a gross profit rate of 22 percent.

Is Big Oak able to pass its extra transportation costs on to its customers? Does the business appear to suffer or benefit financially from its remote location? Explain your reasoning and support your conclusions with specific accounting data comparing the operations of Big Oak Lumber with the industry averages.

LO1 through LO3 LO6 LO8

PROBLEM 6.2B
Preparation and Interpretation of a Merchandising Company's Income Statement

Harry's Haberdashery is a retail clothing store for men. The store operates out of a rented building in Albertsville, Virginia. Shown below is the store's *adjusted* year-end trial balance dated December 31, 2007.

HARRY'S HABERDASHERY
Adjusted Trial Balance
December 31, 2007

Cash	$ 39,270	
Accounts receivable	4,400	
Merchandise inventory	29,700	
Prepaid rent	3,100	
Office supplies	1,500	
Office equipment	70,000	
Accumulated depreciation: office equipment		$ 20,000
Accounts payable		22,000
Sales taxes payable		5,000
Capital stock		31,000
Retained earnings		36,000
Sales		384,000
Sales returns and allowances	4,000	
Cost of goods sold	157,630	
Purchase discounts lost	400	
Utilities expense	7,000	
Office supply expense	900	
Depreciation expense: office equipment	4,700	
Rent expense	10,000	
Insurance expense	1,500	
Salaries expense	150,000	
Income tax expense	13,900	
	$498,000	$498,000

Instructions

a. Prepare an income statement for Harry's Haberdashery dated December 31, 2007.

b. Compute the store's gross profit margin as a percentage of *net sales*.

c. Do the store's customers seem to be satisfied with their purchases? Defend your answer.

d. Explain how you can tell that the business records inventory purchases *net* of any purchase discounts.

e. The store reports sales taxes payable of $5,000 in its adjusted trial balance. Explain why it does not report any *sales taxes expense.*

f. What is meant by the term "operating cycle" and which accounts in the trial balance comprise Harry's Haberdashery's operating cycle?

PROBLEM 6.3B
Trend Analysis

Shown below is information from the financial reports of Jill's Department Stores for the past few years.

	2007	2006	2005
Net sales (in millions)	$9,240	$8,810	$8,140
Number of stores	133	122	115
Square feet of selling space (in millions)	6.0	5.7	5.1
Average net sales of comparable stores (in millions)	$ 70.2	$ 72.3	$ 75.0

Instructions

a. Calculate the following statistics for Jill's Department Stores (round all computations to one decimal place):

1. The percentage change in net sales from 2005 to 2006 and 2006 to 2007. Hint: The percentage change is computed by dividing the dollar amount of the change between years by the amount of the base year. For example, the percentage change in net sales from 2005 to 2006 is computed by dividing the difference between 2006 and 2005 net sales by the amount of 2005 net sales, or ($8,810 − $8,140) ÷ $8,140 = 8.2% increase.

2. The percentage change in net sales per square foot of selling space from 2005 to 2006 and 2006 to 2007.

3. The percentage change in comparable store sales from 2005 to 2006 and 2006 to 2007.

b. Evaluate the sales performance of Jill's Department Stores.

PROBLEM 6.4B
Comparison of Net Cost and Gross Price Methods

Mary's TV uses a perpetual inventory system. The following are three recent merchandising transactions:

Mar. 6 Purchased eight TVs from Whosa Industries on account. Invoice price, $350 per unit, for a total of $2,800. The terms of purchase were 2/10, n/30.

Mar. 11 Sold two of these televisions for $600 cash.

Mar. 16 Paid the account payable to Whosa Industries within the discount period.

Instructions

a. Prepare journal entries to record these transactions assuming that Mary's records purchases of merchandise at:

1. Net cost.

2. Gross invoice price.

b. Assume that Mary's did *not* pay Whosa Industries within the discount period but instead paid the full invoice price on April 6. Prepare journal entries to record this payment assuming that the original liability had been recorded at:

1. Net cost.

2. Gross invoice price.

c. Assume that you are evaluating the efficiency of Mary's bill-paying procedures. Which accounting method—net cost or gross invoice price—provides you with the most *useful* information? Explain.

PROBLEM 6.5B
Merchandising Transactions

The following is a series of related transactions between Hip Pants and Sleek, a chain of retail clothing stores:

Oct. 12 Hip Pants sold Sleek 300 pairs of pants on account, terms 1/10, n/30. The cost of these pants to Hip Pants was $20 per pair, and the sales price was $60 per pair.

Oct. 15 Wings Express charged $50 for delivering this merchandise to Sleek. These charges were split evenly between the buyer and the seller and were paid immediately in cash.

Oct. 16 Sleek returned four pairs of pants to Hip Pants because they were the wrong size. Hip Pants allowed Sleek full credit for this return.

Oct. 22 Sleek paid the remaining balance due to Hip Pants within the discount period.

Both companies use a perpetual inventory system.

Instructions

a. Record this series of transactions in the general journal of Hip Pants. (The company records sales at gross sales price.)

b. Record this series of transactions in the general journal of Sleek. (The company records purchases of merchandise at *net cost* and uses a Transportation-in account to record transportation charges on inbound shipments.)

c. Sleek does not always have enough cash on hand to pay for purchases within the discount period. However, it has a line of credit with its bank, which enables Sleek to easily borrow money for short periods of time at an annual interest rate of 12 percent. (The bank charges interest only for the number of days until Sleek repays the loan.) As a matter of general policy, should Sleek take advantage of 1/10, n/30 cash discounts even if it must borrow the money to do so at an annual rate of 12 percent? Explain fully—and illustrate any supporting computations.

PROBLEM 6.6B

Correcting Errors—Recording of Merchandising Transactions

LO2 LO3 LO6

Queen Enterprises is a furniture wholesaler. Queen hired a new accounting clerk on January 1 of the current year. The new clerk does not understand accrual accounting and recorded the transactions below based on when cash receipts and disbursements changed hands rather than when the transaction occurred. Queen uses a perpetual inventory system, and its accounting policy calls for inventory purchases to be recorded net of any discounts offered.

Jan. 7 Paid Hardwoods Forever Inc. $4,900 for furniture that it received on December 20. (This purchase was recorded as a debit to Inventory and a credit to Accounts Payable on December 20 of last year, but the accounting clerk ignores that fact.)

Dec. 23 Received furniture from Koos Hoffwan Co. for $10,000; terms 2/10, n/30.

Dec. 26 Sold furniture to Beige Chipmunk Inc. for $15,000; terms 1/10, n/30. The cost of the furniture to Queen was $12,250.

Instructions

a. As a result of the accounting clerk's errors, compute the amount by which the following accounts are overstated or understated:

1. Accounts Receivable
2. Inventory
3. Accounts Payable
4. Sales
5. Cost of Goods Sold

b. Compute the amount by which net income is overstated or understated.

c. Prepare a single journal entry to correct the errors that the accounting clerk has made. (Assume that Queen has yet to close its books for the current year.)

d. Assume that Queen has already closed its books for the current year. Make a single journal entry to correct the errors that the accounting clerk has made.

e. Assume that the ending inventory balance is correctly stated based on adjustments resulting from a physical inventory count. (Cost of Goods Sold was debited or credited based on the inventory adjustment.) Assume that Queen has already closed its books for the current year, and make a single journal entry to correct the errors that the accounting clerk has made.

PROBLEM 6.7B

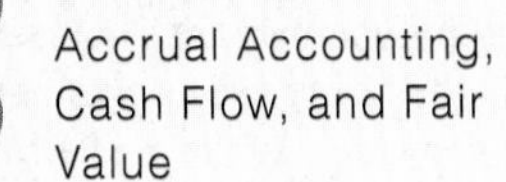

Accrual Accounting, Cash Flow, and Fair Value

LO1 LO3 LO6

Computer Resources Inc. is a computer retailer. Computer Resources began operations in December of the current year and engaged in the following transactions during that month. Computer Resources uses a perpetual inventory system.

Dec. 5 Purchased $100,000 of computer equipment, terms n/30.

Dec. 12 Sold $100,000 of computer equipment, terms n/30. The cost of the equipment sold is $50,000.

Dec. 26 Purchased $200,000 of computer equipment, terms n/30.

Instructions

a. Compute the gross profit on Computer Resources's transactions during December.

b. Compute the gross profit on Computer Resources's transactions during December if a cash-basis accounting system was used.

c. Explain the difference between the results in **a** and **b**.

d. Assume that the fair value of Computer Resources's inventory at December 31 is $375,000. A potential lender asks Computer Resources to prepare a fair-value–based balance sheet. Prepare the journal entry to reflect inventory at fair value. Comment on how a retailer might determine fair value for inventory items. [Hint: Increase the Inventory account by the difference between fair value and book value with the offset to an account titled Revaluation of Inventory to Market Value.]

through

PROBLEM 6.8B
A Comprehensive Problem

SUI sells presses. At December 31, 2007, SUI's inventory amounted to $500,000. During the first week of January 2008, the company made only one purchase and one sale. These transactions were as follows:

Jan. 5 Purchased 60 machines from Double, Inc. The total cost of these machines was $40,000, terms 3/10, n/60.

Jan. 10 Sold 30 different types of products on account to Air Corporation. The total sales price was $28,000, terms 5/10, n/90. The total cost of these 30 units to SUI was $10,000 (net of the purchase discount).

SUI has a full-time accountant and a computer-based accounting system. It records sales at the gross sales price and purchases at net cost and maintains subsidiary ledgers for accounts receivable, inventory, and accounts payable.

Instructions

a. Briefly describe the operating cycle of a merchandising company. Identify the assets and liabilities directly affected by this cycle.

b. Prepare journal entries to record these transactions, assuming SUI uses a *perpetual* inventory system.

c. Explain the information in part **b** that should be posted to subsidiary ledger accounts.

d. Compute the balance in the Inventory control account at the close of business on January 10.

e. Prepare journal entries to record the two transactions, assuming that SUI uses a *periodic* inventory system.

f. Compute the cost of goods sold for the two weeks of January assuming use of the periodic system. (Use your answer to part **d** as the ending inventory.)

g. Which type of inventory system do you think SUI most likely would use? Explain your reasoning.

h. Compute the gross profit margin on the January 10 sales transaction. [Round your answer to one decimal place.]

Critical Thinking Cases

CASE 6.1
Selecting an Inventory System

In each of the following situations, indicate whether you would expect the business to use a periodic inventory system or a perpetual inventory system. Explain the reasons for your answer.

a. The Frontier Shop is a small retail store that sells boots and Western clothing. The store is operated by the owner, who works full-time in the business, and by one part-time salesclerk. Sales transactions are recorded on an antique cash register. The business uses a manual accounting system, which is maintained by ACE Bookkeeping Service. At the end of each month, an employee of ACE visits The Frontier Shop to update its accounting records, prepare sales tax returns, and perform other necessary accounting services.

b. Allister's Corner is an art gallery in the Soho district of New York. All accounting records are maintained manually by the owner, who works in the store on a full-time basis. The store sells three or four paintings each week, at sales prices ranging from about $5,000 to $50,000 per painting.

c. A publicly owned corporation publishes about 200 titles of college-level textbooks. The books are sold to college bookstores throughout the country. Books are distributed to these bookstores from four central warehouses located in California, Texas, Ohio, and Virginia.

d. Toys-4-You operates a national chain of 86 retail toy stores. The company has a state-of-the-art computerized accounting system. All sales transactions are recorded on electronic point-of-sale terminals. These terminals are tied into a central computer system that provides the national headquarters with information about the profitability of each store on a weekly basis.

e. Mr. Jingles is an independently owned and operated ice cream truck.

f. TransComm is a small company that sells very large quantities of a single product. The product is a low-cost spindle of recordable compact disks (CDRs) manufactured by a large Japanese company. Sales are made only in large quantities, primarily to chains of computer stores and large discount stores. This year, the average sales transaction amounted to $14,206 of merchandise. All accounting records are maintained by a full-time employee using commercial accounting software and a personal computer.

LO4 LO8

CASE 6.2
A Cost-Benefit Analysis

Village Hardware is a retail store selling hardware, small appliances, and sporting goods. The business follows a policy of selling all merchandise at exactly twice the amount of its cost to the store and uses a *periodic* inventory system.

At year-end, the following information is taken from the accounting records:

Net sales	$580,000
Inventory, January 1	58,000
Purchases	$297,250

A physical count indicates merchandise costing $49,300 is on hand at December 31.

Instructions

a. Prepare a partial income statement showing computation of the gross profit for the year.

b. On seeing your income statement, the owner of the store makes the following comment: "Inventory shrinkage losses are really costing me. If it weren't for shrinkage losses, the store's gross profit would be 50 percent of net sales. I'm going to hire a security guard and put an end to shoplifting once and for all."

Determine the amount of loss from inventory shrinkage stated (1) at cost and (2) at retail sales value. (Hint: Without any shrinkage losses, the cost of goods sold and the amount of gross profit would each amount to 50 percent of net sales.)

c. Assume that Village Hardware could virtually eliminate shoplifting by hiring a security guard at a cost of $1,800 per month. Would this strategy be profitable? Explain your reasoning.

LO3 through

LO5

LO7

CASE 6.3
Group Assignment with Business Community Involvement

Identify one local business that uses a perpetual inventory system and another that uses a periodic system. Interview an individual in each organization who is familiar with the inventory system and the recording of sales transactions.

Instructions

Separately for each business organization:

a. Describe the procedures used in accounting for sales transactions, keeping track of inventory levels, and determining the cost of goods sold.

b. Explain the reasons offered by the person interviewed as to *why* the business uses this type of system.

c. Indicate whether your group considers the system in use appropriate under the circumstances. If not, recommend specific changes. *Explain your reasoning.*

CASE 6.4
Manipulating Income

You have recently taken a position with Albers, Inc., a wholesale company that relies heavily on sales outside the United States. In order to facilitate sales worldwide, the company has warehouses at several non–U.S. locations from which it services important markets in different parts of the world.

You are in the midst of year-end closings, and your supervisor approaches you about what can be done to improve the appearance of the company's performance for the current year. His idea is to intentionally overstate year-end inventory at locations outside the United States, thereby reducing cost of goods sold and improving gross profit and net income. Because of the remote locations where much of the inventory is housed, he reasons that it is unlikely that the overstatement will be discovered. You are aware that his compensation includes a bonus based, in part, on reported income. He has also indicated that he will "take care of you" in the future if you are supportive in taking steps to improve the company's reported financial performance, such as the inventory overstatement he currently proposes.

Instructions

a. Once you get over the shock of being asked to engage in this activity, how will you deal with this situation? What are the implications to you of going along with your supervisor's plan? If you are not inclined to cooperate, how will you deal with this situation?

b. Besides being unethical, what other implications does your supervisor's plan have for your company's reported peformance in future years?

BUSINESSWEEK **CASE 6.5**
CVS Is Riding High for Now

In a *BusinessWeek* article, "CVS's Potent Growth Potion," Joseph Agnese points out that the retail pharmacy sector has remained relatively strong throughout an extended period of general economic downturn. Pharmacy sales of over $200 billion reflect this sector's recent double-digit percentages in annual revenue growth. Of this nation's leading retail pharmacy chains, **CVS Corporation** has emerged as being one of the most successful and progressive. The company currently holds either the no. 1 or the no. 2 market-share position in 70 percent of the country's top 100 markets.

Instructions

Prospects for **CVS Corporation** appear to be very strong. However, some analysts believe that a shift in **CVS Corporation**'s sales mix to increased pharmacy revenue from third-party insurers could put pressure on the company's gross profit margins.

Explain what is meant by these analysts. (Hint: Refer to Exercise 6.11.)

INTERNET CASE 6.6
Exploring the Annual Report of **Gap, Inc.**

You can find a large amount of information on the Internet to evaluate the performance of companies. Many firms provide links to this information on their home pages.

Access the home page of **The Gap, Inc.**, at the following Internet location:

www.gapinc.com

Instructions

a. What links to financial information are available on the company's home page?

b. Download the company's most recent annual report and use it to answer the following questions:

1. By what percentage amounts did net sales increase or decrease in each of the three years reported?
2. What was the company's gross profit rate for each of the three years reported?
3. What were the company's sales per square foot of selling space for each of the three years reported?
4. For the most recent year reported, how many new stores were opened? How many existing stores, if any, were closed?

5. By what percentage amounts did comparable store sales increase or decrease in each of the three years reported?
6. What dollar amount of inventory does the company report in its most recent balance sheet?

Internet sites are time and date sensitive. It is the purpose of these exercises to have you explore the Internet. You may need to use the Yahoo! search engine **http://www.yahoo.com** *(or another favorite search engine) to find a company's current Web address.*

Answers to Self-Test Questions

1. a, b, d **2.** b, c **3.** b **4.** b **5.** b, d **6.** b, c, d **7.** b **8.** a, c

Financial Assets

Learning Objectives

AFTER STUDYING THIS CHAPTER, YOU SHOULD BE ABLE TO:

LO1 Define financial assets and explain their valuation in the balance sheet.

LO2 Describe the objectives of cash management and internal controls over cash.

LO3 Prepare a bank reconciliation and explain its purpose.

LO4 Describe how short-term investments are reported in the balance sheet and account for transactions involving marketable securities.

LO5 Account for uncollectible receivables using the allowance and direct write-off methods.

LO6 Explain, compute, and account for notes receivable and interest revenue.

LO7 Evaluate the liquidity of a company's accounts receivable.

© Reuters/CORBIS

MICROSOFT CORPORATION

Microsoft Corporation is a multibillion-dollar company that develops, manufactures, licenses, and supports a wide range of software products. The company operates facilities in Ireland, Singapore, and the Greater Seattle area.

You might think that **Microsoft** would have most of its resources tied up in plant assets. In fact, the company's balance sheet recently reported property and equipment of $2.4 billion. The same balance sheet, however, shows total assets of nearly $72 billion. Thus, property and equipment comprise only 3.3 percent of **Microsoft**'s total assets.

Financial assets of $46 billion account for 64 percent of **Microsoft**'s total assets. Financial assets are a company's most liquid resources. They include cash, cash equivalents, certain investments in marketable securities, accounts receivable, and notes receivable.

Financial assets are a company's most liquid (or cashlike) resources. The ability of a company to service its debt, purchase inventory, pay taxes, and cover payroll obligations hinges on the availability of these highly liquid assets. In this chapter, we will examine how companies determine and report the *current values* of financial assets, and how effective companies quickly convert certain financial assets into cash.

HOW MUCH CASH SHOULD A BUSINESS HAVE?

In response to this question, most businesspeople would say, "As little as necessary." In a well-managed company, daily cash receipts are deposited promptly in the bank. Often, a principal source of these daily receipts is the collection of accounts receivable. If the daily receipts exceed routine cash outlays, the company can meet its obligations while maintaining relatively low balances in its bank accounts.

Cash that will not be needed in the immediate future often is invested in highly liquid, short-term securities. These investments are more productive than cash because they earn revenue in the forms of interest and dividends. If the business should need more cash than it has in its bank accounts, it can easily convert some of its investments back into cash.

LO1 **Define financial assets and explain their valuation in the balance sheet.**

The term **financial assets** describes not just cash but also those assets easily and directly *convertible into known amounts of cash*. These assets include cash, short-term investments (also called **marketable securities**), and receivables. We address these three types of financial assets in a single chapter because they are so closely related. All of these assets represent *forms of money*; financial resources flow quickly among these asset categories.

In summary, businesses "store" money in three basic forms: cash, short-term investments, and receivables. The flow of cash among these types of financial assets is illustrated in Exhibit 7–1.

Exhibit 7–1

MONEY FLOWS AMONG THE FINANCIAL ASSETS

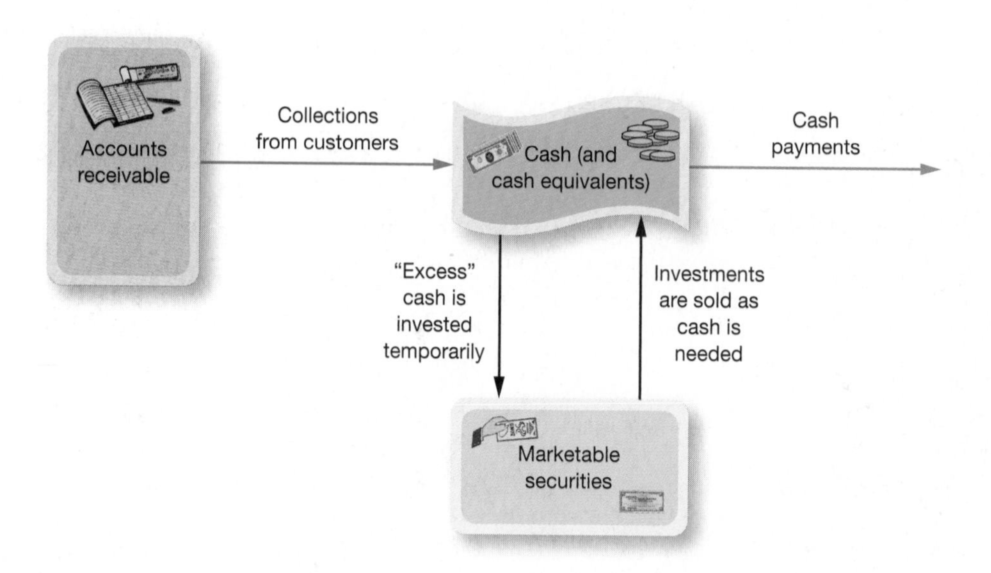

THE VALUATION OF FINANCIAL ASSETS

In the balance sheet, financial assets are shown at their *current values*, meaning the amounts of cash that these assets represent. Interestingly, current value is measured differently for each type of financial asset.

The current value of cash is simply its face amount. But the current value of marketable securities may change daily, based on fluctuations in stock prices, interest rates, and other factors. Therefore, most short-term investments appear in the balance sheet at their current *market values*. (Notice that the valuation of these investments represents an exception to the cost principle.)

Accounts receivable, like cash, have stated face amounts. But large companies usually do not expect to collect every dollar of their accounts receivable. Some customers simply will be unable to make full payment. Therefore, receivables appear in the balance sheet at the estimated *collectible* amount—called **net realizable value**.

The three methods of measuring the current value of financial assets are summarized in Exhibit 7–2.

Exhibit 7–2
METHODS OF MEASURING THE CURRENT VALUE OF FINANCIAL ASSETS

Type of Financial Asset	Basis for Valuation in the Balance Sheet
Cash (and cash equivalents)	Face amount
Short-term investments (marketable securities)	Current market value
Receivables	Net realizable value

Cash

Accountants define *cash* as money on deposit in banks and any items that banks will accept for deposit. These items include not only coins and paper money, but also checks, money orders, and travelers' checks. Banks also accept drafts signed by customers using bank credit cards, such as Visa and MasterCard. Thus sales to customers using bank cards are considered *cash sales*, not credit sales, to the enterprise that makes the sale.

Most companies maintain several bank accounts as well as keep a small amount of cash on hand. Therefore, the Cash account in the general ledger is often a *control account*. A cash subsidiary ledger includes separate accounts corresponding to each bank account and each supply of cash on hand within the organization.

REPORTING CASH IN THE BALANCE SHEET

Cash is listed first in the balance sheet because it is the most liquid of all assets. For purposes of balance sheet presentation, the balance in the Cash control account is combined with that of the control account for **cash equivalents**.

Cash Equivalents

Some short-term investments are so liquid that they are termed *cash equivalents*. Examples include money market funds, U.S. Treasury bills, and high-grade commercial paper (very short-term notes payable that are issued by large, creditworthy corporations). These assets are considered so similar to cash that they are combined with the amount of cash in the balance sheet. Therefore, the first asset listed in the balance sheet often is called Cash and Cash Equivalents.

To qualify as a cash equivalent, an investment must be very safe, have a very stable market value, and mature within 90 days of the date of acquisition. Investments in even the highest quality stocks and bonds of large corporations are *not* viewed as meeting these criteria. Short-term investments that do not qualify as cash equivalents are listed in the balance sheet as Marketable Securities.

Restricted Cash

Some bank accounts are restricted as to their use, so they are not available to meet the normal operating needs of the company. For example, a bank account may contain cash specifically earmarked for the repayment of a noncurrent liability, such as a bond payable. Restricted cash should be presented in the balance sheet as part of the section entitled "Investments and Restricted Funds."

As a condition for granting a loan, banks often require the borrower to maintain a **compensating balance** (minimum average balance) on deposit in a non-interest-bearing checking account. This agreement does not actually prevent the borrower from using the cash, but it does mean the company must quickly replenish this bank account. Compensating balances are included in the amount of cash listed in the balance sheet, but these balances should be disclosed in the notes accompanying the financial statements.

Lines of Credit

Many businesses arrange **lines of credit** with their banks. A line of credit means that the bank has agreed *in advance* to lend the company any amount of money up to a specified limit. The company can borrow this money at any time simply by drawing checks on a special bank account. A liability to the bank arises as soon as any money is borrowed—that is, as soon as a portion of the credit line is used.

The *unused* portion of a line of credit is neither an asset nor a liability; it represents only the *ability* to borrow money quickly and easily. Although an unused line of credit does not appear as an asset or a liability in the balance sheet, it increases the company's liquidity. Thus unused lines of credit usually are *disclosed* in notes accompanying the financial statements. For example, **Deb Shops, Inc.**, recently included the following information in the footnotes accompanying its financial statements:

> We have available lines of credit in the amount of $20,000,000. Of this amount, $1,007,000 has been used for the purchase of inventory.

THE STATEMENT OF CASH FLOWS

A balance sheet shows the cash owned at the end of the accounting period. As we learned in Chapter 2, cash *transactions* of the accounting period are summarized in the statement of cash flows.

In both the balance sheet and the statement of cash flows, the term *cash* includes cash equivalents. Transfers of money between bank accounts and cash equivalents do *not* appear in a statement of cash flows, because these transactions do not change the amount of cash owned. However, any *interest* received from owning cash equivalents is included in the statement of cash flows as cash receipts from operating activities.

CASH MANAGEMENT

LO2 **Describe the objectives of cash management and internal controls over cash.**

The term **cash management** refers to planning, controlling, and accounting for cash transactions and cash balances. Because cash moves so readily between bank accounts and other financial assets, cash management really means the management of *all financial resources*. Efficient management of these resources is essential to the success—even to the survival—of every business organization. The basic objectives of cash management are as follows:

- *Provide accurate accounting for cash receipts, cash disbursements, and cash balances.* Many business transactions involve the receipt or disbursement of cash. Also, cash transactions affect every classification within the financial statements—assets, liabilities, owners' equity, revenue, and expenses. If financial statements are to be reliable, it is *absolutely essential* that cash transactions be recorded correctly.
- *Prevent or minimize losses from theft or fraud.* Cash is more susceptible to theft than any other asset and, therefore, requires physical protection.
- *Anticipate the need for borrowing and assure the availability of adequate amounts of cash for conducting business operations.* Every business organization must have sufficient cash to meet its financial obligations as they come due. Otherwise, its creditors may force the business into bankruptcy.
- *Prevent unnecessarily large amounts of cash from sitting idle in bank accounts that produce no revenue.* Well-managed companies frequently review their bank balances for the purpose of transferring any excess cash into cash equivalents or other investments that generate revenue.

Using Excess Cash Balances Efficiently Cash equivalents are safe, liquid investments, but they generate only a modest rate of return. These investments are useful for investing *temporary* surpluses of cash, which soon will be needed for other purposes. If a business has large amounts of cash that can be invested on a long-term basis, however, it should expect to earn a higher rate of return than is available from cash equivalents. Cash that is available for long-term investment may be used to finance growth and expansion of the business or to repay debt. If the cash is not needed for business purposes, it may be distributed to the company's stockholders.

INTERNAL CONTROL OVER CASH

Internal control over cash is sometimes regarded merely as a means of preventing fraud and theft. A good system of internal control, however, will also aid in achieving the other objectives of efficient cash management, including accurate accounting for cash transactions, anticipating the need for borrowing, and the maintenance of adequate but not excessive cash balances.

The major steps in achieving internal control over cash transactions and cash balances include the following:

- Separate the function of handling cash from the maintenance of accounting records. Employees who handle cash *should not have access to the accounting records*, and accounting personnel should not have access to cash.
- For each department within the organization, prepare a *cash budget* (or forecast) of planned cash receipts, cash payments, and cash balances, scheduled month-by-month for the coming year.
- Prepare a *control listing* of cash receipts at the time and place the money is received. For cash sales, this listing may be a cash register tape, created by ringing up each sale on a cash register. For checks received through the mail, a control listing of incoming checks should be prepared by the employee assigned to open the mail.
- Require that all cash receipts be *deposited daily* in the bank.
- Make all payments *by check*. The only exception should be for small payments to be made in cash from a *petty cash fund*. (Petty cash funds are discussed later in this chapter.)
- Require that the validity and amount of every expenditure be verified *before* a check is issued in payment. Separate the function of approving expenditures from the function of signing checks.
- Promptly reconcile bank statements with the accounting records.

A company may supplement its system of internal control by obtaining a fidelity bond from an insurance company. Under a fidelity bond, the insurance company agrees to reimburse an employer for *proven* losses resulting from fraud or embezzlement by bonded employees.

Cash Over and Short In handling over-the-counter cash receipts, a few errors in making change inevitably will occur. These errors may cause a cash shortage or overage at the end of the day when the cash is counted and compared with the reading on the cash register.

For example, assume that total cash sales recorded on the point-of-sale terminals during the day amount to $4,500.00. However, the cash receipts in the register drawers total only $4,487.30. The following entry would be made to adjust the accounting records for this $12.70 shortage in the cash receipts:

Cash Over and Short	12.70	
Cash		12.70
To record a $12.70 shortage in cash receipts for the day ($4,500.00 − $4,487.30).		

The account entitled Cash Over and Short is debited for shortages and credited with overages. If the account has a debit balance, it appears in the income statement as a miscellaneous expense; if it has a credit balance, it is shown as a miscellaneous revenue.

BANK STATEMENTS

Each month the bank provides the depositor with a statement of the depositor's account.[1] As illustrated in Exhibit 7–3, a bank statement shows the account balance at the beginning of the month, the deposits, the checks paid, any other additions and subtractions

[1] Large businesses may receive bank statements on a weekly basis.

Exhibit 7–3

A BANK STATEMENT

Western National Bank
100 Olympic Boulevard
Los Angeles, CA

Customer Account No. 501390
Parkview Company
109 Parkview Road
Los Angeles, CA

Bank Statement for the Month Ended July 31, 2007

Date				Amount
June 30	Previous statement balance			$ 5,029.30
	Deposits and Other Increases (Credits)			
July 1		300.00		
July 2		1,250.00		
July 8		993.60		
July 12		1,023.77		
July 18		1,300.00		
July 22		500.00	CM	
July 24		1,083.25		
July 30		711.55		
July 31		24.74	INT	
	Total deposits and other increases (credits)			7,186.91
	Checks Written and Other Decreases (Debits)			
July 2	Ck. 882	1,100.00		
July 3	Ck. 883	415.20		
July 3	Ck. 884	10.00		
July 10	Ck. 885	96.00		
July 10	Ck. 886	400.00		
July 12	Ck. 887	1,376.57		
July 15	Ck. 889	425.00		
July 18	Ck. 892	2,095.75		
July 22	Ck. 893	85.00		
July 22		5.00	DM	
July 24	Ck. 894	1,145.27		
July 30		50.25	NSF	
July 31		12.00	SC	
	Total checks written and other decreases (debits)			(7,216.04)
July 31	Balance this statement			$5,000.17

Explanation of Symbols

CM	Credit Memoranda
DM	Debit Memoranda
INT	Interest Earned on Average Balance
NSF	Not Sufficient Funds
SC	Service Charge

during the month, and the new balance at the end of the month. (To keep the illustration short, we have shown a limited number of deposits rather than one for each business day in the month.)

RECONCILING THE BANK STATEMENT

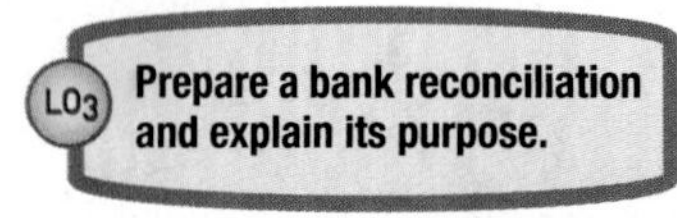

A **bank reconciliation** is a schedule *explaining any differences* between the balance shown in the bank statement and the balance shown in the depositor's accounting records. Remember that both the bank and the depositor are maintaining independent records of the deposits, the checks, and the current balance of the bank account. Each month, the depositor should prepare a bank reconciliation to verify that these independent sets of records are in agreement. This reconciliation may disclose internal control failures, such as unauthorized cash disbursements or failures to deposit cash receipts, as well as errors in either the bank statement or the depositor's accounting records. In addition, the reconciliation identifies certain transactions that must be recorded in the depositor's accounting records and helps to determine the actual amount of cash on deposit.

For strong internal control, the employee who reconciles the bank statement should not have any other responsibilities for physically handling cash.

Normal Differences between Bank Records and Accounting Records

The balance shown in a monthly bank statement seldom equals the balance appearing in the depositor's accounting records. Certain transactions recorded by the depositor may not have been recorded by the bank. The most common examples are:

- *Outstanding checks.* Checks issued and recorded by the company but not yet presented to the bank for payment.
- *Deposits in transit.* Cash receipts recorded by the depositor that reached the bank too late to be included in the bank statement for the current month.

In addition, certain transactions appearing in the bank statement may not have been recorded by the depositor. For example:

- *Service charges.* Banks often charge a fee for handling small accounts. The amount of this charge usually depends on both the average balance of the account and the number of checks paid during the month.
- *Charges for depositing NSF checks.* **NSF** stands for "Not Sufficient Funds." When checks from customers are deposited, the bank generally gives the depositor immediate credit. On occasion, one of these checks may prove to be uncollectible, because the customer who wrote the check did not have sufficient funds in his or her account. In such cases, the bank will reduce the depositor's account by the amount of this uncollectible item and return the check to the depositor marked "NSF." The depositor should view an NSF check as an account receivable from the customer, not as cash.
- *Credits for interest earned.* The checking accounts of *unincorporated* businesses often earn interest. At month-end, this interest is credited to the depositor's account and reported in the bank statement. (Current law prohibits interest on corporate checking accounts.)
- *Miscellaneous bank charges and credits.* Banks charge for services—such as printing checks, handling collections of notes receivable, and processing NSF checks. The bank *deducts* these charges from the depositor's account and notifies the depositor by including a debit memorandum in the monthly bank statement. If the bank collects a note receivable on behalf of the depositor, it credits the depositor's account and issues a credit memorandum.[2]

In a bank reconciliation, the balances shown in the bank statement and in the accounting records are both *adjusted for any unrecorded transactions.* Additional adjustments may be required to correct any errors discovered in the bank statement or in the accounting records.

Steps in Preparing a Bank Reconciliation

The specific steps in preparing a bank reconciliation are as follows:

1. Compare deposits listed in the bank statement with the deposits shown in the accounting records. Any deposits not yet recorded by the bank are deposits in transit and should be added to the balance shown in the bank statement.
2. Compare checks paid by the bank with the corresponding entries in the accounting records. Any checks issued but not yet paid by the bank should be listed as outstanding checks to be deducted from the balance reported in the bank statement.
3. Add to the balance per the depositor's accounting records any credit memoranda issued by the bank that have not been recorded by the depositor.
4. Deduct from the balance per the depositor's records any debit memoranda issued by the bank that have not been recorded by the depositor.

[2] Banks view each depositor's account as a *liability*. Debit memoranda are issued for transactions that reduce this liability, such as bank service charges. Credit memoranda are issued to recognize an increase in this liability, as results, for example, from interest earned by the depositor.

5. Make appropriate adjustments to correct any errors in either the bank statement or the depositor's accounting records.
6. Determine that the adjusted balance of the bank statement is equal to the adjusted balance in the depositor's records.
7. Prepare journal entries to record any items in the bank reconciliation listed as adjustments to the balance per the depositor's records.

Illustration of a Bank Reconciliation The July bank statement sent by the bank to Parkview Company was illustrated in Exhibit 7–3. This statement shows a balance of cash on deposit at July 31 of *$5,000.17*. Assume that on July 31, Parkview's ledger shows a bank balance of *$4,262.83*. The employee preparing the bank reconciliation has identified the following reconciling items:

1. A deposit of $410.90 made after banking hours on July 31 does not appear in the bank statement.
2. Four checks issued in July have not yet cleared the bank. These checks are:

Check No.	Date	Amount
881	July 1	$100.00
888	July 14	10.25
890	July 16	402.50
891	July 17	205.00

3. Two credit memoranda were included in the bank statement:

Date	Amount	Explanation
July 22	$500.00	Proceeds from collection of a non-interest-bearing note receivable from J. David. The bank's collection department collected this note for Parkview Company.
July 31	24.74	Interest earned on average account balance during July.

4. Three debit memoranda accompanied the bank statement:

Date	Amount	Explanation
July 22	$ 5.00	Fee charged by bank for handling collection of note receivable.
July 30	50.25	Check from customer J. B. Ball deposited by Parkview Company charged back as NSF.
July 31	12.00	Service charge by bank for the month of July.

5. Check no. 893 was issued to the telephone company in the amount of $85 but was erroneously recorded in the cash payments journal as $58. The check, in payment of telephone expense, was paid by the bank and correctly listed at $85 in the bank statement. In Parkview's ledger, the Cash account is *overstated* by $27 because of this error ($85 − $58 = $27).

The July 31 bank reconciliation for Parkview Company is shown in Exhibit 7–4. (The numbered arrows coincide both with the steps in preparing a bank reconciliation and with the reconciling items just listed.)

Updating the Accounting Records The last step in reconciling a bank statement is to update the depositor's accounting records for any unrecorded cash transactions brought to

Exhibit 7–4

THE BANK RECONCILIATION

PARKVIEW COMPANY Bank Reconciliation July 31, 2007		
Balance per bank statement, July 31, 2007		$5,000.17
① Add: Deposit of July 31 not recorded by bank		410.90
		$5,411.07
② Deduct: Outstanding checks:		
No. 881	$100.00	
No. 888	10.25	
No. 890	402.50	
No. 891	205.00	717.75
Adjusted cash balance		$4,693.32
Balance per depositor's records, July 31, 2007		$4,262.83
③ Add: Note receivable collected for us by bank	$500.00	
Interest earned during July	24.74	524.74
		$4,787.57
④ Deduct: Collection fee	$ 5.00	
NSF check of J. B. Ball	50.25	
Service charge	12.00	
⑤ Error on check stub no. 893	27.00	94.25
Adjusted cash balance (as above) ⑥		$4,693.32

light. In the bank reconciliation, every adjustment to the *balance per depositor's records* is a cash receipt or a cash payment that has not been recorded in the depositor's accounts. Therefore, *each of these items should be recorded.*

In this illustration and in our assignment material, we follow a policy of making one journal entry to record the unrecorded cash receipts and another to record the unrecorded cash reductions. (Acceptable alternatives would be to make separate journal entries for each item or to make one compound entry for all items.) Based on our recording policy, the entries to update the accounting records of Parkview Company are:

Per bank credit memoranda

Cash	524.74	
Notes Receivable		500.00
Interest Revenue		24.74
To record collection of note receivable from J. David collected by bank and interest earned on bank account in July.		
Bank Service Charges	17.00	
Accounts Receivable (J. B. Ball)	50.25	
Telephone Expense	27.00	
Cash		94.25
To record bank charges (service charge, $12; collection fee, $5); to reclassify NSF check from customer J. B. Ball as an account receivable; and to correct understatement of cash payment for telephone expense.		

Per bank debit memoranda (and correction of an error)

PETTY CASH FUNDS

We have emphasized the importance of making all significant cash disbursements by check. However, every business finds it convenient to have a small amount of cash on hand with which to make some minor expenditures. Examples of these expenditures include such things as small purchases of office supplies, taxi fares, and doughnuts for an office meeting.

To create a petty cash fund, a check is drawn payable to "Petty Cash" for a round amount, such as $200, which will cover these small expenditures for a period of two or three weeks. This check is cashed and the money is kept on hand in a petty cash box. One employee is designated as the *custodian* of the fund.

The custodian makes all payments from this fund and obtains a receipt or prepares a "petty cash voucher" explaining the nature and amount of each expenditure. At the end of the period (or when the fund runs low), a check is drawn payable to Petty Cash reimbursing the fund for the expenditures made during the period. The issuance of this check is recorded by debiting the appropriate expense accounts and crediting Cash. As a practical matter, because of the small amount of petty cash expenditures, the entire debit portion of this entry often is charged to the Miscellaneous Expense account.

Digital Vision/Getty Images/DIL

THE CASH BUDGET AS A CONTROL DEVICE

Many businesses prepare detailed *cash budgets* that include forecasts of the monthly cash receipts and expenditures of each department within the organization. Management (or the internal auditors) will investigate any cash flows that differ significantly from the budgeted amounts. Thus each department manager is held accountable for the monthly cash transactions occurring within his or her department.

Short-Term Investments

LO4 Describe how short-term investments are reported in the balance sheet and account for transactions involving marketable securities.

Companies with large amounts of liquid resources often hold most of these resources in the form of marketable securities rather than cash.

CASE IN POINT

It is common for enterprises to invest a portion of their excess cash in marketable securities in anticipation of earning higher returns than they would by keeping these funds in the form of cash and cash equivalents. The following sample taken from recently issued balance sheets illustrates the willingness of companies to invest millions, even billions, of dollars in marketable securities:

	Amount Invested
The Boston Beer Company	$ 24 million
Dell Computer Corporation	2.7 billion
General Motors Corporation	16.4 billion
Pfizer, Inc.	12.4 billion
Microsoft Corporation	37 billion

Marketable securities consist primarily of investments in bonds and in the capital stocks of publicly owned corporations. These marketable securities are traded (bought and sold) daily on organized securities exchanges, such as the New York Stock Exchange, the Tokyo Stock Exchange, and Mexico's Bolsa. A basic characteristic of all marketable securities is that they are *readily marketable*—meaning that they can be purchased or sold quickly and easily *at quoted market prices*.

Investments in marketable securities earn a return for the investor in the form of interest, dividends, and—if all goes well—an increase in market value. Meanwhile, these investments are *almost as liquid as cash itself*. They can be sold immediately over the telephone, simply by placing a "sell order" with a brokerage firm such as Merrill Lynch or Salomon Smith Barney, or on the Internet, by using an online brokerage firm such as E*TRADE Financial.

Due to their liquidity, investments in marketable securities usually are listed immediately after Cash in the balance sheet and are most often classified as *available for sale* securities.[3]

Accounting for Marketable Securities

There are four basic events relating to investments in marketable securities: (1) the purchase of investments, (2) the receipt of dividends or interest revenue, (3) the sale of investments, and (4) end-of-period adjustments.

PURCHASE OF MARKETABLE SECURITIES

Investments in marketable securities are originally recorded at cost, which includes any brokerage commissions. To illustrate, assume that Foster Corporation purchases as a short-term investment 4,000 shares of The Coca-Cola Company on December 1. Foster paid *$43.98 per share*, plus a brokerage commission of $80. The entry to record the purchase of these shares is:

Marketable Securities	176,000	
Cash		176,000
Purchased 4,000 shares of Coca-Cola capital stock. Total cost $176,000 ($43.98 × 4,000 shares + $80); cost per share, $44 ($176,000 ÷ 4,000 shares).		

Marketable Securities is a control account used to report *all* of a company's short-term investments. If Foster Corporation invests in other companies it will make an entry similar to the one shown above; however, it will also create a marketable securities *subsidiary ledger* to maintain a separate record of each security owned.

Notice that the $44 cost per share computed in the explanation of the above journal entry includes a portion of the total brokerage commission. The $44 per share *cost basis* will be used in computing any gains or losses when Foster Corporation sells these securities.

RECOGNITION OF INVESTMENT REVENUE

Entries to recognize interest and dividend revenue typically involve a debit to Cash and a credit to either Interest Revenue or Dividend Revenue. To illustrate, assume that on December 15, Foster Corporation receives a $0.30 per share dividend on its 4,000 shares of Coca-Cola. The entry to record this receipt is:

Cash	1,200	
Dividend Revenue		1,200
Received a quarterly dividend on shares of Coca-Cola capital stock ($0.30 per share × 4,000 shares).		

Dividend and interest revenue is reported in the income statement as a component of a company's net income. It most often appears near the bottom of the income statement in the computation of income before taxes. The reporting of investment revenue is discussed further in Chapter 11.

SALE OF INVESTMENTS

When an investment is sold, a gain or a loss often results. If an investment is sold for more than its cost basis a **gain** is recorded, whereas selling an investment for an amount less than its cost basis results in a **loss**. These items appear in the "Other Income/Expense" section of the income statement.

Investments Sold at a Gain

To illustrate, assume that Foster Corporation sells 500 shares of its Coca-Cola stock on December 18 for $46.04 per share, less a $20 brokerage

[3] To be classified as available for sale securities, these investments must be held for short-term resale. Other investment classifications include *trading* securities and *held-to-maturity* securities. These classifications are discussed in more advanced courses.

commission. Recall that Foster's cost basis, as computed on December 1, is $44 per share. Thus, the entry to record the sale and the $1,000 gain is as follows:

Cash	23,000	
Marketable Securities		22,000
Gain on Sale of Investments		1,000
Sold 500 shares of Coca-Cola stock at a gain:		
Sale proceeds ($46.04 × 500 shares − $20 commission)	$23,000	
Cost basis ($44 × 500 shares)	22,000	
Gain on sale	$ 1,000	

This transaction results in a gain because Foster Corporation sold the shares at an amount above their cost basis. The gain on the sale increases the company's net income for the period and is reported in the income statement in similar fashion to interest and dividend revenue. At the end of the period, the credit balance in the Gain on Sale of Investments account is closed to the Income Summary account, along with the credit balances of the other revenue accounts.

Investments Sold at a Loss Assume that Foster Corporation sells an additional 2,500 shares of its Coca-Cola stock on December 27 for $40.01 per share, less a $25 brokerage commission. The entry to record the sale and the $10,000 loss is recorded as follows:

Cash	100,000	
Loss on Sale of Investments	10,000	
Marketable Securities		110,000
Sold 2,500 shares of Coca-Cola stock at a loss:		
Cost basis ($44 × 2,500 shares)	$110,000	
Sale proceeds ($40.01 × 2,500 shares − $25 commission)	100,000	
Loss on sale	$ 10,000	

This loss reduces Foster Corporation's net income and is reported near the bottom of the income statement. The debit balance in the Loss on Sale of Investments account is closed to the Income Summary account at the end of the period, along with the debit balances of the other expense accounts.

ADJUSTING MARKETABLE SECURITIES TO MARKET VALUE

Securities classified as available for sale are presented in the balance sheet at their *current market value* as of the balance sheet date. Hence, this valuation principle is often called **mark-to-market**. The adjustment of marketable securities to their current market value requires the use of an account entitled **Unrealized Holding Gain (or Loss) on Investments**. This account appears as a stockholders' equity item in the balance sheet.[4]

To illustrate, let us assume that Foster Corporation's 1,000 remaining shares of Coca-Cola capital stock have a current market value of $42,000 on December 31 (1,000 shares at a market price of $42 per share). Prior to any adjustment, the company's Marketable Securities account has a balance of $44,000 (1,000 shares at $44 per share). Thus, Foster Corporation must make the following mark-to-market adjustment on December 31:

Unrealized Holding Loss on Investments	2,000	
Marketable Securities		2,000
To adjust the balance sheet valuation of marketable securities from $44,000 (1,000 shares × $44) to the December 31 market value of $42,000 (1,000 shares × $42).		

[4] Unrealized holding gains and losses are often combined with other activities and reported in a stockholders' equity account entitled Accumulated Other Comprehensive Income. Comprehensive income is discussed in Chapter 12.

Exhibit 7–5 illustrates Foster Corporation's condensed balance sheet following its marketable securities valuation adjustment.

Exhibit 7–5
PRESENTATION OF MARKETABLE SECURITIES IN THE BALANCE SHEET

FOSTER CORPORATION
Balance Sheet
As of December 31 of the Current Year

Assets		**Liabilities & Stockholders' Equity**	
Current assets:		**Liabilities:**	
Cash	$ 50,000	(Detail not shown)...........	$350,000
Marketable securities (cost, $44,000; market value, $42,000).....................	42,000	**Stockholders' equity:**	
Accounts receivable	28,000	Capital stock	$400,000
Total current assets	$120,000	Retained earnings	152,000
Other assets:		Unrealized holding loss on investments	(2,000)
		Total stockholders' equity	$550,000
(Detail not shown)	$780,000		
Total..........................	$900,000	Total	$900,000

Although the $44,000 cost of Foster Corporation's marketable securities is *disclosed* in the balance sheet, the $42,000 market value is used in the computation of total assets. The difference between the cost and market value also appears as an *element of stockholders' equity*, entitled Unrealized Holding Loss on Investments. When the market value of investment falls *below* cost, as in the case just presented, this special equity account is a *subtraction* from equity, representing a holding *loss*. But if the market value is *above* cost, this account is an *addition* to equity, representing a holding *gain*. Thus, if Foster's 1,000 shares of Coca-Cola had a market value on December 31 of $46 per share, the investment would have been reported in the asset section of the balance sheet at $46,000, and the stockholders' equity section of the balance sheet would have included the addition of a $2,000 unrealized holding *gain* on investments.

Unrealized holding gains and losses are *not* subject to income taxes. Income taxes are levied only upon *realized* gains and losses recognized when investments are sold. Nonetheless, unrealized holding gains and losses are actually reported in the balance sheet net of expected *future* income tax effects. The computation of future tax effects is beyond the scope of our introductory discussion and is addressed in more advanced accounting courses. In the assignment material at the end of this chapter, unrealized holding gains and losses simply represent the difference between the cost and the current market value of the securities owned.

CASE IN POINT

Mark-to-market is not always used internationally for valuing short-term investments. Germany and Japan continue to use the lower of cost or market valuation techniques because their accounting standards setters (Ministry of Finance for Japan and the German government) believe the techniques are more conservative.

Accounts Receivable

One of the key factors underlying the growth of the American economy is the trend toward selling goods and services on credit. Accounts receivable comprise the largest financial asset of many merchandising companies.

Accounts receivable are relatively liquid assets, usually converting into cash within a period of 30 to 60 days. Therefore, accounts receivable from customers usually appear in the balance sheet immediately after cash and short-term investments in marketable securities.

In Chapter 5, we explained that assets capable of being converted quickly into cash are classified in the balance sheet as current assets. The period used to define current assets is typically one year or the company's operating cycle, whichever is longer. The operating cycle was defined in Chapter 6 as the normal period of time required to convert cash into inventory, inventory into accounts receivable, and accounts receivable back into cash. Some companies sell merchandise on long-term installment plans that require accounts receivable be outstanding for 12, 24, or even 48 months before being collected. These receivables are part of the company's normal operating cycle. Therefore, *all* accounts receivable arising from normal sales activity are generally classified as current assets, even if the credit terms extend beyond one year.

UNCOLLECTIBLE ACCOUNTS

LO5 Account for uncollectible receivables using the allowance and direct write-off methods.

We have stated that accounts receivable are shown in the balance sheet at the estimated collectible amount—called *net realizable value*. No business wants to sell merchandise on account to customers who will be unable to pay. Many companies maintain their own credit departments that investigate the creditworthiness of each prospective customer. Nonetheless, if a company makes credit sales to hundreds—perhaps thousands—of customers, some accounts inevitably will turn out to be uncollectible.

A limited amount of uncollectible accounts is not only expected—it is evidence of a sound credit policy. If the credit department is overly cautious, the business may lose many sales opportunities by rejecting customers who should have been considered acceptable credit risks.

Reflecting Uncollectible Accounts in the Financial Statements

An account receivable that has been determined to be uncollectible is no longer an asset. The loss of this asset represents an *expense*, termed Uncollectible Accounts Expense.

In measuring business income, one of the most fundamental principles of accounting is that revenue should be *matched* with (offset by) the expenses incurred in generating that revenue. Uncollectible accounts expense is *caused by selling goods on credit* to customers who fail to pay their bills. Therefore, this expense is estimated and recorded in the time period in which the *related sales* are made, even though specific accounts receivable may not be determined to be uncollectible until a later accounting period. Thus an account receivable that originates from a credit sale in January and is determined to be uncollectible in June represents an expense in *January*. Exhibit 7–6 illustrates how uncollectible accounts expense is matched to revenue in the period in which the credit sale is made.

Exhibit 7–6
MATCHING UNCOLLECTIBLE ACCOUNTS EXPENSE TO THE PERIOD IN WHICH THE CREDIT SALE IS MADE

To illustrate the matching process, assume that World Famous Toy Co. begins business on January 1, 2007, and makes most of its sales on account. At January 31, accounts receivable amount to $250,000. On this date, the credit manager reviews the accounts receivable and *estimates* that approximately $10,000 of these accounts will prove to be uncollectible. The following adjusting entry should be made at January 31:

Uncollectible Accounts Expense	10,000	
Allowance for Doubtful Accounts		10,000
To record the portion of total accounts receivable estimated to be uncollectible.		

Provision for uncollectible accounts

The Uncollectible Accounts Expense account created by the debit part of this entry is closed into the Income Summary account in the same manner as any other expense account. The Allowance for Doubtful Accounts that was credited in the above journal entry appears in the balance sheet as a deduction from the face amount of the accounts receivable. It reduces the accounts receivable to their *net realizable value* in the balance sheet, as shown in Exhibit 7–7.

WORLD FAMOUS TOY CO.
Partial Balance Sheet
January 31, 2007

Current assets:		
Cash and cash equivalents		$ 75,000
Marketable securities		25,000
Accounts receivable	$250,000	
Less: Allowance for doubtful accounts	10,000	240,000
Inventory		300,000
Total current assets		$640,000

Exhibit 7–7

REPORTING ACCOUNTS RECEIVABLE AT ESTIMATED NET REALIZABLE VALUE

THE ALLOWANCE FOR DOUBTFUL ACCOUNTS

There is no way of telling in advance *which* accounts receivable will prove to be uncollectible. It is therefore not possible to credit the accounts of specific customers for our estimate of probable uncollectible accounts. Neither should we credit the Accounts Receivable control account in the general ledger. If the Accounts Receivable control account were to be credited with the estimated amount of doubtful accounts, this control account would no longer be in balance with the total of the numerous customers' accounts in the subsidiary ledger. A practical alternative, therefore, is to credit a separate account called **Allowance for Doubtful Accounts** with the amount estimated to be uncollectible.

The Allowance for Doubtful Accounts often is described as a *contra-asset* account or a *valuation* account. Both of these terms indicate that the Allowance for Doubtful Accounts has a credit balance, which is offset against the asset Accounts Receivable to produce a more useful and reliable measure of a company's liquidity. Because the Allowance for Doubtful Accounts is merely an estimate and not a precise calculation, *professional judgment* plays a considerable role in determining the size of this valuation account.

Monthly Adjustments of the Allowance Account

In the adjusting entry made by World Famous Toy Co. at January 31, the amount of the adjustment ($10,000) was equal to the estimated amount of uncollectible accounts. This is true only because January was the first month of operations and this was the company's first estimate of its uncollectible accounts. In future months, the amount of the adjusting entry will depend on two factors: (1) the *estimate* of uncollectible accounts and (2) the *current balance* in the Allowance for Doubtful Accounts. Before we illustrate the adjusting entry for a future month, let us see why the balance in the allowance account may change during the accounting period.

WRITING OFF AN UNCOLLECTIBLE ACCOUNT RECEIVABLE

Whenever an account receivable from a specific customer is determined to be uncollectible, it no longer qualifies as an asset and should be written off. To *write off* an account receivable is to reduce the balance of the customer's account to zero. The journal entry to accomplish this consists of a credit to the Accounts Receivable control account in the general ledger (and to the customer's account in the subsidiary ledger) and an offsetting debit to the Allowance for Doubtful Accounts.

To illustrate, assume that, early in February, World Famous Toy Co. learns that Discount Stores has gone out of business and that the $4,000 account receivable from this customer is now worthless. The entry to write off this uncollectible account receivable is:

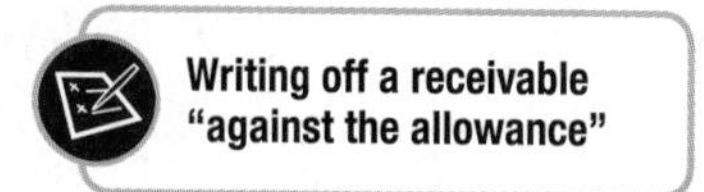

Allowance for Doubtful Accounts	4,000	
Accounts Receivable (Discount Stores)		4,000
To write off the account receivable from Discount Stores as uncollectible.		

The important thing to note in this entry is that the debit is made to the Allowance for Doubtful Accounts and *not* to the Uncollectible Accounts Expense account. The estimated expense of credit losses is charged to the Uncollectible Accounts Expense account at the end of each accounting period. When a specific account receivable is later determined to be worthless and is written off, this action does not represent an additional expense but merely confirms our previous estimate of the expense. If the Uncollectible Accounts Expense account was first charged with *estimated* credit losses and then later charged with *proven* credit losses, we would be double-counting the actual uncollectible accounts expense.

Notice also that the entry to write off an uncollectible account receivable reduces both the asset account and the contra-asset account by the same amount. Thus writing off an uncollectible account *does not change* the net realizable value of accounts receivable in the balance sheet. The net realizable value of World Famous Toy Co.'s accounts receivable before and after the write-off of the account receivable from Discount Stores is:

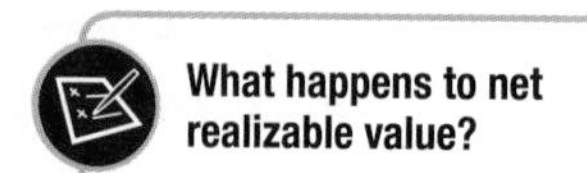

Before the Write-off		After the Write-off	
Accounts receivable	$250,000	Accounts receivable	$246,000
Less: Allowance for doubtful accounts	10,000	Less: Allowance for doubtful accounts	6,000
Net realizable value	$240,000	Net realizable value	$240,000

Let us repeat the point that underlies the allowance approach. Credit losses are recognized as an expense in the period in which the *sale occurs*, not the period in which the account is determined to be uncollectible. The reasoning for this position is based on the *matching principle*.

Write-offs Seldom Agree with Previous Estimates The total amount of accounts receivable actually written off will seldom, if ever, be exactly equal to the estimated amount previously credited to the Allowance for Doubtful Accounts.

If the amounts written off as uncollectible turn out to be less than the estimated amount, the Allowance for Doubtful Accounts will continue to show a credit balance. If the amounts written off as uncollectible are greater than the estimated amount, the Allowance for Doubtful Accounts will acquire a *temporary debit balance*, which will be eliminated by the adjustment at the end of the period.

MONTHLY ESTIMATES OF CREDIT LOSSES

At the end of each month, management should again estimate the probable amount of uncollectible accounts and adjust the Allowance for Doubtful Accounts to this new estimate.

To illustrate, assume that at the end of February the credit manager of World Famous Toy Co. analyzes the accounts receivable and estimates that approximately *$11,000* of these accounts will prove uncollectible. Currently, the Allowance for Doubtful Accounts has a credit balance of only *$6,000*, determined as follows:

Balance at January 31 (credit) . . .	$10,000
Less: Write-off of account considered worthless (Discount Stores) . . .	4,000
Credit balance at February 28 (prior to adjustment) . . .	$ 6,000

Current balance in the allowance account

To increase the balance in the allowance account to $11,000 at February 28, the month-end adjusting entry must add $5,000 to the allowance. The entry will be:

Uncollectible Accounts Expense . . .		5,000	
Allowance for Doubtful Accounts . . .			5,000
To increase the Allowance for Doubtful Accounts to $11,000, computed as follows:			
Required allowance at Feb. 28 . . .	$11,000		
Credit balance prior to adjustment . . .	6,000		
Required adjustment . . .	$ 5,000		

Increasing the allowance for doubtful accounts

In the World Famous Toy illustration, estimates of the required allowance for doubtful accounts at January 31 and February 28 were simply given. There are actually two general approaches to estimating credit losses: (1) a *balance sheet approach*, and (2) an *income statement approach.*

Estimating Credit Losses—The Balance Sheet Approach The most widely used method of estimating the probable amount of uncollectible accounts is based on **aging the accounts receivable**. This method is sometimes called the *balance sheet* approach because the method emphasizes the proper balance sheet valuation of accounts receivable.

"Aging" accounts receivable means classifying each receivable according to its age. An aging schedule for the accounts receivable of Valley Ranch Supply is illustrated in Exhibit 7–8.

Exhibit 7–8

ACCOUNTS RECEIVABLE AGING SCHEDULE

VALLEY RANCH SUPPLY
Analysis of Accounts Receivable by Age
December 31, 2007

	Total	Not Yet Due	1–30 Days Past Due	31–60 Days Past Due	61–90 Days Past Due	Over 90 Days Past Due
Animal Care Center	$ 9,000	$ 9,000				
Butterfield, John D.	2,400			$ 2,400		
Citrus Groves, Inc.	4,000	3,000	$ 1,000			
Dairy Fresh Farms	1,600				$ 600	$1,000
Eastlake Stables	13,000	7,000	6,000			
(Other customers)	70,000	32,000	22,000	9,600	2,400	4,000
Totals	$100,000	$51,000	$29,000	$12,000	$3,000	$5,000

An aging schedule is useful to management in reviewing the status of individual accounts receivable and in evaluating the overall effectiveness of credit and collection policies. In addition, the schedule is used as the basis for estimating the amount of uncollectible accounts.

The longer an account is past due, the greater the likelihood that it will not be collected in full. Based on past experience, the credit manager estimates the percentage of credit losses likely to occur in each age group of accounts receivable. This percentage, when applied to the total dollar amount in the age group, gives the estimated uncollectible portion for that group. By adding together the estimated uncollectible portions for all age groups, the *required balance* in the Allowance for Doubtful Accounts is determined. Exhibit 7–9 provides a schedule listing the group totals from the aging schedule and shows how the estimated total amount of uncollectible accounts is computed.

Exhibit 7–9

ESTIMATED DOLLAR AMOUNT OF UNCOLLECTIBLE ACCOUNTS

VALLEY RANCH SUPPLY
Estimated Uncollectible Accounts Receivable
December 31, 2007

	Age Group Total		Percentage Considered Uncollectible*		Estimated Uncollectible Accounts
Not yet due	$ 51,000	×	1%	=	$ 510
1–30 days past due	29,000	×	3	=	870
31–60 days past due	12,000	×	10	=	1,200
61–90 days past due	3,000	×	20	=	600
Over 90 days past due	5,000	×	50	=	2,500
Totals	$100,000				$5,680

*These percentages are estimated each month by the credit manager, based on recent experience and current economic conditions.

At December 31, Valley Ranch Supply has total accounts receivable of $100,000, of which $5,680 are estimated to be uncollectible. Thus an adjusting entry is needed to increase the Allowance for Doubtful Accounts from its present level to $5,680. If the allowance account currently has a credit balance of, say, $4,000, the month-end adjusting entry should be in the amount of *$1,680*, determined as follows:[5]

Determine the difference between the current balance and the required balance

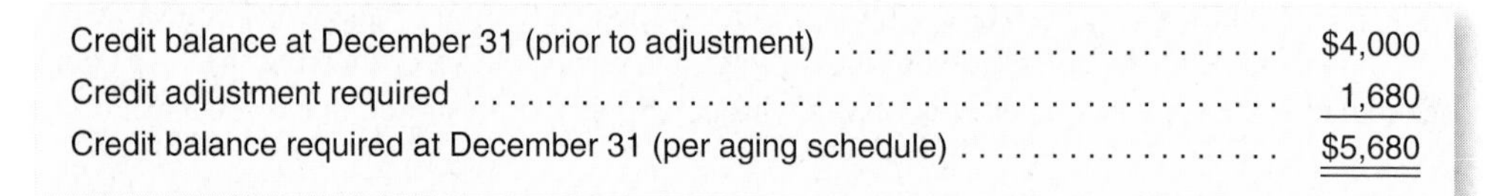

Credit balance at December 31 (prior to adjustment)	$4,000
Credit adjustment required	1,680
Credit balance required at December 31 (per aging schedule)	$5,680

Thus, the following adjusting entry is made at December 31:

The difference between the current balance and the required balance is the Uncollectible Accounts Expense matched to the period

Uncollectible Accounts Expense	1,680	
Allowance for Doubtful Accounts		1,680
To increase the Allowance for Doubtful Accounts to its required balance of $5,680.		

[5] If accounts receivable written off during the period *exceed* the Allowance for Doubtful Accounts at the last adjustment date, the allowance account temporarily acquires a *debit balance*. This situation seldom occurs if the allowance is adjusted each month but often occurs if adjusting entries are made only at year-end.

If Valley Ranch Supply makes only an annual adjustment for uncollectible accounts, the allowance account might have a debit balance of, say, $10,000. In this case, the year-end adjusting entry should be for *$15,680* in order to bring the allowance to the required credit balance of $5,680.

Regardless of how often adjusting entries are made, the balance in the allowance account of Valley Ranch Supply should be *$5,680 at year-end*. Uncollectible Accounts Expense will be the same for the year, regardless of whether adjusting entries are made annually or monthly. The only difference is in whether this expense is recognized in one annual adjusting entry or in 12 monthly adjusting entries, each for a smaller amount.

Estimating Credit Losses—The Income Statement Approach The procedures just discussed describe the *balance sheet* approach to estimating and recording credit losses. That approach is based on an aging schedule, and the Allowance for Doubtful Accounts is *adjusted to a required balance*. An alternative method, called the *income statement* approach, focuses on estimating the uncollectible accounts *expense* for the period. Based on past experience, the uncollectible accounts expense is estimated at some percentage of net credit sales. The adjusting entry is made in the *full amount of the estimated expense*, without regard for the current balance in the Allowance for Doubtful Accounts.

To illustrate, assume that a company's past experience indicates that about 2 percent of its credit sales will prove to be uncollectible. If credit sales for September amount to $150,000, the month-end adjusting entry to record uncollectible accounts expense is:

Uncollectible Accounts Expense	3,000	
Allowance for Doubtful Accounts		3,000
To record uncollectible accounts expense, estimated at 2% of credit sales ($150,000 × 2% = $3,000).		

The income statement approach

This approach is fast and simple—no aging schedule is required and no consideration is given to the existing balance in the Allowance for Doubtful Accounts. The aging of accounts receivable, however, provides a more reliable estimate of uncollectible accounts because of the consideration given to the age and collectibility of specific accounts receivable at the balance sheet date.

In past years, many small companies used the income statement approach in preparing monthly financial statements but used the balance sheet method in annual financial statements. Today, however, most businesses have computer software that quickly and easily prepares monthly aging schedules of accounts receivable. Thus most businesses today use the *balance sheet approach* in their monthly as well as annual financial statements.

Conservatism in the Valuation of Accounts Receivable We previously have made reference to the accounting concept of **conservatism**. In accounting, conservatism means resolving uncertainty in a manner that minimizes the risk of overstating the company's current financial position. With respect to the valuation of accounts receivable, conservatism suggests that the allowance for doubtful accounts should be *at least adequate*. That is, it is better to err on the side of the allowance being a little too large, rather than a little too small.

Notice that conservatism in the valuation of assets also leads to a conservative measurement of net income in the current period. The larger the valuation allowance, the larger the current charge to uncollectible accounts expense.

CONCENTRATIONS OF CREDIT RISK

Assume that a business operates a single retail store in a town in which the major employer is a steel mill. What would happen to the collectibility of the store's accounts receivable if the steel mill were to close, leaving most of the store's customers unemployed? This situation illustrates what accountants call a *concentration of credit risk*, because many of the store's credit customers can be affected *in a similar manner* by certain changes in economic conditions. Concentrations of credit risk occur if a significant portion of a company's receivables are due from a few major customers or from customers operating in the same industry or geographic region.

The Financial Accounting Standards Board (FASB) requires companies to disclose all significant concentrations of credit risk in the notes accompanying their financial statements. The basic purpose of these disclosures is to assist users of the financial statements in evaluating the extent of the company's vulnerability to credit losses stemming from changes in specific economic conditions.

RECOVERY OF AN ACCOUNT RECEIVABLE PREVIOUSLY WRITTEN OFF

Occasionally a receivable that has been written off as worthless will later be collected in full or in part. Such collections are often referred to as *recoveries* of bad debts. Collection of an account receivable previously written off is evidence that the write-off was an error; the receivable should therefore be reinstated as an asset.

Let us assume, for example, that a company wrote off a $500 account receivable from Brad Wilson on February 16. The write-off of this account was recorded as follows:

Allowance for Doubtful Accounts	500	
Accounts Receivable (Brad Wilson)		500
To write off the account receivable from Brad Wilson as uncollectible.		

If the customer, Brad Wilson, pays the account in full on February 27, the entry to reverse the previous write-off is as follows:

Accounts Receivable (Brad Wilson)	500	
Allowance for Doubtful Accounts		500
To reinstate as an asset an account receivable previously written off.		

Notice that this entry is *exactly the opposite* of the entry made when the account was written off as uncollectible. A separate entry will be made to record the cash collected from Brad Wilson and to remove his reinstated account from the system.

Cash	500	
Accounts Receivable (Brad Wilson)		500
To record the collection of account receivable from Brad Wilson.		

DIRECT WRITE-OFF METHOD

Some companies do not use any valuation allowance for accounts receivable. Instead of making end-of-period adjusting entries to record uncollectible accounts expense on the basis of estimates, these companies recognize no uncollectible accounts expense until specific receivables are determined to be worthless. This method makes no attempt to match revenue with the expense of uncollectible accounts.

When a particular customer's account is determined to be uncollectible, it is written off directly to Uncollectible Accounts Expense, as follows:

Uncollectible Accounts Expense	250	
Accounts Receivable (Bell Products)		250
To write off the account receivable from Bell Products as uncollectible.		

When the **direct write-off method** is used, the accounts receivable will be listed in the balance sheet at their gross amount, and *no valuation allowance* will be used. The receivables, therefore, are not stated at estimated net realizable value.

The allowance method is preferable to the direct write-off method because the allowance method does a better job of matching revenues and expenses. In some situations, however, use of the direct write-off method is acceptable. If a company makes most of its sales for cash, the amount of its accounts receivable will be small in relation to other assets. The expense from uncollectible accounts should also be small. Consequently, the direct write-off method is acceptable because its use does not have a *material* effect on the reported net income. Another situation in which the direct write-off method works satisfactorily is in a company that sells all or most of its output to a few large companies that are financially strong. In this setting there may be no basis for making advance estimates of any credit losses.

It is important to note that current income tax regulations *require* taxpayers to use the direct write-off method in determining the uncollectible accounts expense used in computing *taxable income*. From the standpoint of accounting theory, the allowance method is better because it enables expenses to be *matched* with the related revenue and thus provides a more logical measurement of net income. Therefore, most companies use the allowance method in their financial statements.[6]

INTERNAL CONTROLS FOR RECEIVABLES

One of the most important principles of internal control is that employees who have custody of cash or other negotiable assets must not maintain accounting records. In a small business, one employee often is responsible for handling cash receipts, maintaining accounts receivable records, issuing credit memoranda, and writing off uncollectible accounts. Such a combination of duties is an invitation to fraud. The employee in this situation is able to remove the cash collected from a customer without making any record of the collection. The next step is to dispose of the balance in the customer's account. This can be done by issuing a credit memo indicating that the customer has returned merchandise, or by writing off the customer's account as uncollectible. Thus the employee has the cash, the customer's account shows a zero balance due, and the books are in balance.

In summary, employees who maintain the accounts receivable subsidiary ledger should *not have access* to cash receipts. The employees who maintain accounts receivable or handle cash receipts should *not* have authority to issue credit memoranda or to authorize the write-off of receivables as uncollectible. These are classic examples of incompatible duties.

MANAGEMENT OF ACCOUNTS RECEIVABLE

Management has two conflicting objectives with respect to the accounts receivable. On the one hand, management wants to generate as much sales revenue as possible. Offering customers lengthy credit terms, with little or no interest, has proven to be an effective means of generating sales revenue.

Every business, however, would rather sell for cash than on account. Unless receivables earn interest, which usually is not the case, they are nonproductive assets that produce no revenue as they await collection. Therefore, another objective of cash management is to minimize the amount of money tied up in the form of accounts receivable.

Several tools are available to a management that must offer credit terms to its customers yet wants to minimize the company's investment in accounts receivable. We have already discussed offering credit customers cash discounts (such as 2/10, n/30) to encourage early payment. Other tools include *factoring* accounts receivable and selling to customers who use national credit cards.

FACTORING ACCOUNTS RECEIVABLE

The term **factoring** describes transactions in which a business either sells its accounts receivable to a financial institution (often called a *factor*) or borrows money by pledging its accounts receivable as collateral (security) for a loan. In either case, the business obtains cash immediately instead of having to wait until the receivables can be collected.

Factoring accounts receivable is a practice limited primarily to small business organizations that do not have well-established credit. Large and liquid organizations usually are able to borrow money using unsecured lines of credit, so they need not factor their accounts receivable.

[6] An annual survey of the accounting practices of 600 publicly owned corporations consistently shows more than 500 of these companies use the allowance method in their financial statements. All of these companies, however, use the direct write-off method in their income tax returns.

You as a Used Car Purchaser

Assume you purchased a car from John's Used Cars for $500 down and 24 payments of $150 per month. After making three months of payments to John's Used Cars, you are notified that John's plans to factor your account receivable to the Barb Smith Collection Agency. You are concerned about owing money to this particular collection agency because you have heard it uses very aggressive tactics to collect overdue payments. You call the car lot and speak directly with John. You question the legality and ethics of factoring accounts receivable. You state that you entered into a contract with him and not a collection agency. You state that you did not give permission to sell your receivable and that selling the receivable to another organization eliminates your obligation to pay it. John says factoring accounts receivable is legal and suggests that you consult the Uniform Commercial Code. What would you do?

Photodisc Green/Getty Images/DIL

(See our comments on the Online Learning Center Web site.)

CREDIT CARD SALES

Many retailing businesses minimize their investment in receivables by encouraging customers to use credit cards such as **American Express**, **Visa**, and **MasterCard**. A customer who makes a purchase using one of these cards signs a multiple-copy form, which includes a *credit card draft*. A credit card draft is similar to a check that is drawn on the funds of the credit card company rather than on the personal bank account of the customer. The credit card company promptly pays a discounted amount of cash to the merchant to redeem these drafts. At the end of each month, the credit card company bills the credit card holder for all the drafts it has redeemed during the month. If the credit card holder fails to pay the amount owed, the credit card company sustains the loss.

By making sales through credit card companies, merchants receive cash more quickly from credit sales and avoid uncollectible accounts expense. Also, the merchant avoids the expenses of investigating customers' credit, maintaining an accounts receivable subsidiary ledger, and making collections from customers.

Bank Credit Cards Some widely used credit cards (such as **Visa** and **MasterCard**) are issued by banks. When the credit card company is a bank, the retailing business may deposit the signed credit card drafts directly in its bank account. Because banks accept these credit card drafts for immediate deposit, sales to customers using bank credit cards are recorded as *cash sales*.

In exchange for handling the credit card drafts, the bank makes a monthly service charge that usually runs between 1¼ percent and 3½ percent of the amount of the drafts. This monthly service charge is deducted from the merchant's bank account and appears with other bank service charges in the merchant's monthly bank statement.

Other Credit Cards When customers use nonbank credit cards (such as **American Express**), the retailing business cannot deposit the credit card drafts directly in its bank account. Instead of debiting Cash, the merchant records an account receivable from the credit card company. Periodically, the credit card drafts are mailed (or transmitted electronically) to the credit card company, which then sends a check to the merchant. Credit card companies, however, do not redeem the drafts at the full sales price. The agreement between the credit card company and the merchant usually allows the credit card company to take a discount of between 3½ percent and 5 percent when redeeming the drafts.

To illustrate, assume that Bradshaw Camera Shop sells a camera for $1,200 to a customer who uses a Quick Charge credit card. The entry would be:

Accounts Receivable (Quick Charge Co.)	1,200	
Sales		1,200
To record sale to customer using Quick Charge credit card.		

This receivable is from the credit card company

At the end of the week, Bradshaw Camera Shop mails the $1,200 credit card draft to Quick Charge Company, which redeems the draft after deducting a 5 percent discount. When payment is received by Bradshaw, the entry is:

Cash	1,140	
Credit Card Discount Expense	60	
Accounts Receivable (Quick Charge Co.)		1,200
To record collection of account receivable from Quick Charge Co., less 5% discount.		

The expense account, Credit Card Discount Expense, is included among the selling expenses in the income statement of Bradshaw Camera Shop.

Notes Receivable and Interest Revenue

Explain, compute, and account for notes receivable and interest revenue. LO6

Accounts receivable usually do not bear interest. When interest will be charged, creditors usually require the debtor to sign a formal promissory note. A promissory note is an unconditional promise in writing to pay on demand or at a future date a definite sum of money.

The person who signs the note and thereby promises to pay is called the *maker* of the note. The person to whom payment is to be made is called the *payee* of the note. In Exhibit 7–10, Pacific Rim Corp. is the maker of the note and First National Bank is the payee.

Exhibit 7–10

SIMPLIFIED FORM OF PROMISSORY NOTE

$200,000 Los Angeles, California July 10, 2007

One year AFTER DATE Pacific Rim Corp. PROMISES TO PAY

TO THE ORDER OF First National Bank

---Two hundred thousand and no/100--- DOLLARS

PLUS INTEREST COMPUTED AT THE RATE OF 6% per annum

SIGNED *G. L. Smith*

TITLE Treasurer

From the viewpoint of the maker, Pacific Rim, the illustrated note is a liability and is recorded by crediting the Notes Payable account. However, from the viewpoint of the payee, First National Bank, this same note is an asset and is recorded by debiting the Notes Receivable account. The maker of a note expects to pay cash at the *maturity date* (or due date); the payee expects to receive cash at that date.

NATURE OF INTEREST

Interest is a charge made for the use of money. A borrower incurs interest expense. A lender earns interest revenue. When you encounter notes payable in a company's financial statements, you know that the company is borrowing and you should expect to find interest expense. When you encounter notes receivable, you should expect interest revenue.

Computing Interest A formula used in computing interest is as follows:

Interest = Principal × Rate of Interest × Time

(This formula is often expressed as $I = P \times R \times T$.)

Interest rates usually are stated on an *annual basis*. For example, the total interest charge on a $200,000, one-year, 6 percent note receivable is computed as follows:

$$P \times R \times T = \$200{,}000 \times .06 \times 1 = \$12{,}000$$

If the term of the note were only *four months* instead of one year, the total interest revenue earned in the life of the note would be $4,000, computed as follows:

$$P \times R \times T = \$200{,}000 \times .06 \times 4/12 = \$4{,}000$$

In making interest computations, it is convenient to assume that each month has *30* days. Thus a year has *360* days and each month represents 1/12 of the year. As these assumptions greatly simplify the computation of interest and assist students in focusing on the underlying concepts, we will use them in our illustrations and assignment material.[7]

If the term of a note is expressed in days, the exact number of days in each month must be considered in determining the maturity date of the note. The day on which a note is dated is not counted, but the date on which it matures is. Thus a two-day note dated today matures the day *after* tomorrow.

To illustrate these concepts, assume that a 60-day, 6 percent note for $200,000 is drawn on June 10. The *total* interest charge on this note will be $2,000, computed as follows:

$$P \times R \times T = \$200{,}000 \times .06 \times 60/360 = \$2{,}000$$

The $202,000 **maturity value** of the note ($200,000 principal, plus $2,000 interest) will be payable on *August 9*. The **maturity date** is determined as follows:

Days remaining in June (30 − 10)	20
Days in July	31
Subtotal	51
Days in August needed to complete the term of the note (including maturity date)	9
Specified term of note (in days)	60

ACCOUNTING FOR NOTES RECEIVABLE

In most fields of business, notes receivable are seldom encountered; in some fields they occur frequently and may constitute an important part of total assets. In banks and financial institutions, for example, notes receivable often represent the company's largest asset category and generate most of the company's revenue. Some retailers that sell on installment plans, such as **Sears, Roebuck & Co.**, also own large amounts of notes receivable from customers.

All notes receivable are usually posted to a single account in the general ledger. A subsidiary ledger is not essential because the notes themselves, when filed by due dates, are the equivalent of a subsidiary ledger and provide any necessary information as to maturity, interest rates, collateral pledged, and other details. The amount debited to Notes Receivable is always the *face amount* of the note, regardless of whether the note bears interest. When an interest-bearing note is collected, the amount of cash received may be larger than the face amount of the note. The interest collected is credited to an Interest Revenue account, and only the face amount of the note is credited to the Notes Receivable account.

[7] Prior to the widespread use of computers, these assumptions were widely used in the business community. Today, however, most financial institutions compute interest using a 365-day year and the actual number of days in each month. The differences between these assumptions usually are *not material* in dollar amount.

Illustrative Entries Assume that on December 1 a 90-day, 6 percent note receivable is acquired from a customer, Marvin White, in settlement of an existing account receivable of $60,000. The entry for acquisition of the note is as follows:

Notes Receivable	60,000	
Accounts Receivable (Marvin White)		60,000
Accepted 90-day, 6% note in settlement of account receivable.		

Note received to replace account receivable

At December 31, the end of the company's fiscal year, the interest earned to date on notes receivable should be accrued by an adjusting entry as follows:

Interest Receivable	300	
Interest Revenue		300
To accrue interest for the month of December on Marvin White note ($60,000 × 6% × 1⁄12 = $300).		

Adjusting entry for interest revenue earned in December

To simplify this illustration, we will assume our company makes adjusting entries *only at year-end*. Therefore, no entries are made to recognize the interest revenue accruing during January and February.

On March 1 (90 days after the date of the note), the note matures. The entry to record collection of the note will be:

Cash	60,900	
Notes Receivable		60,000
Interest Receivable		300
Interest Revenue		600
Collected 90-day, 6% note from Marvin White ($60,000 × 6% × 3⁄12 = $900 interest, of which $600 was earned in current year).		

Collection of principal and interest

The preceding three entries show that interest is being earned throughout the term of the note and that the interest should be apportioned between years on a time basis. The revenue of each year will then include the interest actually earned in that year.

If the Maker of a Note Defaults A note receivable that cannot be collected at maturity is said to have been **defaulted** by the maker. Immediately after the default of a note, an entry should be made by the holder to transfer the amount due from the Notes Receivable account to an account receivable from the debtor.

To illustrate, assume that on March 1 our customer, Marvin White, had defaulted on the note used in the preceding example. In this case, the entry on March 1 would have been:

Accounts Receivable (Marvin White)	60,900	
Notes Receivable		60,000
Interest Receivable		300
Interest Revenue		600
To record default by Marvin White on 90-day, 6% note.		

Notice that the interest earned on the note is recorded through the maturity date and is included in the account receivable from the maker. The interest receivable on a defaulted note is just as valid a claim against the maker as is the principal amount of the note.

If the account receivable from White cannot be collected, it ultimately will be written off against the Allowance for Doubtful Accounts. Therefore, the balance in the Allowance for

Doubtful Accounts should provide for estimated uncollectible *notes* receivable as well as uncollectible *accounts* receivable.

Discounting Notes Receivable In past years some companies sold their notes receivable to banks in order to obtain cash prior to the maturity dates of these notes. As the banks purchased these notes at a "discount" from their maturity values, this practice became known as *discounting* notes receivable.

Discounting notes receivable is not a widespread practice today because most banks no longer purchase notes receivable from their customers. Interestingly, the practice of discounting notes receivable is most widespread among banks themselves. Many banks sell large packages of their notes receivable (loans) to agencies of the federal government or to other financial institutions. From a conceptual point of view, discounting notes receivable is essentially the same as selling accounts receivable to a factor.

THE DECISION OF WHETHER TO ACCRUE INTEREST

The concept of interest accruing from day to day applies not only to notes receivable but to all interest-bearing investments (such as cash equivalents and bonds) and to interest-bearing debt. But in our discussions of cash equivalents and marketable securities, we stated that investors generally recognize interest revenue as it is received. In accounting for notes receivable, why did we accrue the interest earned, instead of recognizing revenue as cash was received?

The answer lies in the concept of *materiality*. Interest does, in fact, accrue from day to day. But the interest revenue earned from cash equivalents and investments in marketable securities usually represents only a small part of the investor's total revenue. In short, it usually is *not material* in relation to other financial statement amounts. Thus the principle of materiality often justifies investors' accounting for this revenue in the most convenient manner.

Most notes receivable, however, are owned by *financial institutions*. For these businesses, interest revenue *is* material. In fact, it generally is the company's primary source of revenue. In these circumstances, greater care must be taken to assign interest revenue to the period in which it actually is *earned*.

Financial Analysis and Decision Making

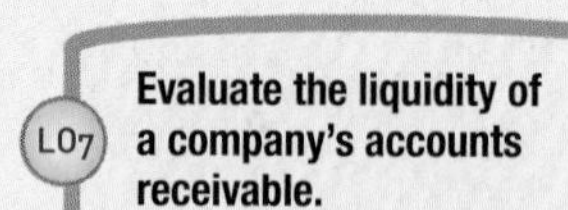

LO7 **Evaluate the liquidity of a company's accounts receivable.**

Collecting accounts receivable *on time* is important; it spells the success or failure of a company's credit and collection policies. A past-due receivable is a candidate for write-off as a credit loss. To help us judge how good a job a company is doing in granting credit and collecting its receivables, we compute the ratio of net sales to average receivables. This **accounts receivable turnover rate** tells us how many times the company's average investment in receivables was converted into cash during the year. The ratio is computed by dividing annual net sales by average accounts receivable.[8] The higher the turnover rate, the more liquid the company's receivables. Dividing 365 days by the turnover rate provides an estimate of the average number of *days* an account receivable remains outstanding before it is collected. High turnover rates result in shorter collection periods than low turnover rates.

In some companies, such as restaurants, hotels, and public utilities, turnover rates are relatively high. For other enterprises, such as large manufacturing firms, turnover rates are relatively low, making the average time it takes to collect an outstanding receivable much longer.

[8] From a conceptual point of view, net *credit* sales should be used in computing the accounts receivable turnover rate. It is common practice, however, to use the net sales figure, as the portion of net sales made on account usually is not disclosed in financial statements.

To illustrate, Exhibit 7–11 contains information taken from recent financial statements issued by Minnesota Power, Inc., and 3M (Minnesota Mining and Manufacturing Company).

Exhibit 7–11

ACCOUNTS RECEIVABLE COLLECTION PERFORMANCE

	Minnesota Power, Inc.	3M
a. Net sales	$ 1.1 billion	$16.7 billion
Accounts receivable (beginning of year)	$111 million	$ 2.9 billion
Accounts receivable (end of year)	113 million	2.7 billion
	$224 million	$ 5.6 billion
	÷ 2	÷ 2
b. Average accounts receivable	$112 million	$ 2.8 billion
c. Accounts receivable turnover rate **(a ÷ b)**	9.8 times	6.0 times
Average days outstanding **(365 days ÷ c)**	37 days	61 days

As shown in Exhibit 7–11, Minnesota Power's accounts receivable turnover rate is *9.8 times* ($1.1 billion net sales ÷ $112 million average accounts receivable), compared to 3M's turnover rate of only *6 times* ($16.7 billion net sales ÷ $2.8 billion average accounts receivable). Thus, Minnesota Power's accounts receivable remain outstanding an average of *37 days* before being collected (365 days ÷ 9.8 turnover rate), whereas 3M's accounts receivable remain outstanding an average of *61 days* prior to collection (365 days ÷ 6.0 turnover rate).

Management closely monitors these performance measures in evaluating the company's policies for extending credit to customers and the effectiveness of its collection procedures. Short-term creditors, such as factors, banks, and merchandise suppliers, also use these ratios to evaluate a company's ability to generate the cash necessary to pay its short-term liabilities.

In the annual audit of a company by a CPA firm, the independent auditors will verify receivables by communicating directly with the people who owe the money. This *confirmation* process is designed to provide evidence that the customers and other debtors actually exist and that they acknowledge their indebtedness. The CPA firm also may verify the credit rating of major debtors.

YOUR TURN **You as a Credit Manager**

Assume that you were hired by Regis Department Stores in 2004 to develop and implement a new credit policy. At the time of your hire, the average collection period for an outstanding receivable was in excess of 90 days (far greater than the industry average). Thus the primary purpose of the new policy was to better screen credit applicants in an attempt to improve the quality of the company's accounts receivable.

Shown below are sales and accounts receivable data for the past four years (in thousands):

	2007	2006	2005	2004
Sales	$17,000	$14,580	$9,600	$9,000
Average accounts receivable	1,700	1,620	1,600	1,800

Based on the above data, was the credit policy you developed successful? Explain.

(See our comments on the Online Learning Center Web site.)

Ethics, Fraud & Corporate Governance

As discussed previously in this chapter, accounts receivable is a significant account for many companies. Accounts receivable is particularly prone to misrepresentation because revenue often increases when accounts receivable increase. Manipulating accounts receivable can result in the overstatement of both revenue and income, which is the objective of many fraudulent financial reporting schemes. Management often has an incentive to overstate income because bonus plans may be tied to this figure, and the values of the stock and stock options that managers hold in the company are sensitive to reported earnings. A late 1990 study sponsored by COSO (a joint undertaking of the AICPA, IIA, IMA, FEI, and AAA—see Chapter 1 for a discussion of these groups), found that improper revenue recognition was the most common scheme in fraud-related SEC enforcement actions.[9]

In 1999, the Securities and Exchange Commission (SEC) brought an enforcement action against Sunrise Medical Inc. alleging that Bio Clinic Corporation, an operating division of Sunrise, understated expenses by improperly reporting them as assets. Many of the company's expenses were actually reported as accounts receivable. This scheme resulted in pretax earnings being overstated by as much as 40 percent.

Changes in market conditions had adversely affected Bio Clinic's earnings. In order to achieve its budgeted profitability targets, the company began capitalizing operating expenses (i.e., instead of debiting an expense account, asset accounts were debited). The asset accounts used were accounts receivable and property and equipment. This practice created discrepancies between the general ledger balances of these accounts and their respective subsidiary ledger balances. To avoid detection, management artificially increased the total on the last page of the accounts receivable subsidiary ledger to match the balance in the general ledger (note that if the individual customer account balances in the subsidiary ledger had been totaled, this fraud might have been detected).

Bio Clinic continued this scheme in the following year by creating a fictitious customer and by transferring $8.8 million (the total of operating expenses improperly added to the accounts receivable balance) into this bogus customer's account. Although this amount was included in totaling the accounts receivable subsidiary ledger, the fictitious customer's name and account balance were suppressed from the detailed listing of the ledger. When an internal auditor added the balances for each customer on the subsidiary ledger, the total was $8.8 million less than the balance in the subsidiary ledger (and in the general ledger). Management justified this discrepancy by stating that Bio Clinic was in the process of installing new software (which was true) and that the subsidiary ledger printouts reflected a test batch of data (which was not true). The internal auditor asked for a correct printout of the subsidiary ledger.

Bio Clinic's management then reallocated the $8.8 million from the fictitious customer to legitimate customers using invoice numbers and amounts that had previously been paid. The internal auditor was planning to confirm selected customer account balances—which presumably would have revealed the fraud—but the internal auditor inappropriately allowed Bio Clinic's management to send the confirmation requests. By giving control of the confirmation process to the management team engaged in the fraudulent scheme to overstate accounts receivable, the opportunity to immediately detect the fraud was lost.

[9] M. S. Beasley, J. V. Carcello, and D. R. Hermanson, 1999. *Fraudulent Financial Reporting: 1987–1997. An Analysis of U.S. Public Companies* (Committee of Sponsoring Organizations).

Concluding Remarks

This is the first of three chapters in which we explore the issues involved in accounting for assets. The central theme in these chapters is the *valuation* of assets. In Exhibit 7–2 (page 293), we have summarized how a company's financial assets are reported in the balance sheet.

We have illustrated numerous transactions involving the financial assets throughout this chapter. In addition to addressing balance sheet valuation issues, we have also determined whether these transactions are reported in the income statement and the statement of cash flows.

In the next two chapters, we explore the valuation of inventories and of plant assets. For each of these assets, you will see that several *alternative* valuation methods are acceptable. These different methods, however, may produce *significantly different results*. An understanding of these alternative accounting methods is essential to the proper use and interpretation of financial statements and in the preparation of income tax returns.

END-OF-CHAPTER REVIEW

SUMMARY OF LEARNING OBJECTIVES

LO1 Define financial assets and explain their valuation in the balance sheet. Financial assets are cash and other assets that convert directly into *known amounts* of cash. The three basic categories are cash, marketable securities, and receivables. In the balance sheet, financial assets are listed at their *current value*. For cash, this means the face amount; for marketable securities, current market value; and for receivables, net realizable value.

LO2 Describe the objectives of cash management and internal controls over cash. The objectives of cash management are accurate accounting for cash transactions, the prevention of losses through theft or fraud, and maintaining adequate—but not excessive—cash balances. The major steps in achieving internal control over cash transactions are as follows: (1) separate cash handling from the accounting function, (2) prepare departmental cash budgets, (3) prepare a control listing of all cash received through the mail and from over-the-counter cash sales, (4) deposit all cash receipts in the bank daily, (5) make all payments by check, (6) verify every expenditure before issuing a check in payment, and (7) promptly reconcile bank statements.

LO3 Prepare a bank reconciliation and explain its purpose. The cash balance shown in the month-end bank statement usually will differ from the amount of cash shown in the depositor's ledger. The difference is caused by items that have been recorded by either the depositor or the bank, but not recorded by both. Examples are outstanding checks and deposits in transit. The bank reconciliation adjusts the cash balance per the books and the cash balance per the bank statement for any unrecorded items and thus produces the correct amount of cash to be included in the balance sheet at the end of the month.

The purpose of a bank reconciliation is to achieve the control inherent in the maintenance of two independent records of cash transactions: one record maintained by the depositor and the other by the bank. When these two records are reconciled (brought into agreement), we gain assurance of a correct accounting for cash transactions.

LO4 Describe how short-term investments are reported in the balance sheet and account for transactions involving marketable securities. Short-term investments (marketable securities) are adjusted to their *market value* at each balance sheet date (a valuation principle often referred to as *mark-to-market*). If the value of a company's marketable securities has increased above their original cost, an *unrealized holding gain* is reported as a component of stockholders' equity. If the value of its marketable securities has fallen below their original cost, an *unrealized holding loss* is reported as a component of stockholders' equity.

Interest and dividends generally are recognized as revenue when they are received. When securities are sold, the cost is compared to the sales price, and the difference is recorded as a gain or a loss in the income statement.

LO5 Account for uncollectible receivables using the allowance and direct write-off methods. Under the allowance method, the portion of each period's credit sales expected to prove uncollectible is *estimated*. This estimated amount is recorded by a debit to the Uncollectible Accounts Expense account and a credit to the contra-asset account Allowance for Doubtful Accounts. When specific accounts are determined to be uncollectible, they are written off by debiting Allowance for Doubtful Accounts and crediting Accounts Receivable.

Under the direct write-off method, uncollectible accounts are charged to expense in the period that they are determined to be worthless.

The allowance method is theoretically preferable because it is based on the matching principle. However, only the direct write-off method may be used in income tax returns.

LO6 Explain, compute, and account for notes receivable and interest revenue. Accounts receivable usually do not bear interest. When interest will be charged, creditors usually require the debtor to sign a formal, legally binding promissory note. Promissory notes appear in the balance sheet as assets designated as notes receivable.

Interest on a note receivable is a contractual amount that accumulates (accrues) day by day. The amount of interest accruing over a time period may be computed by the formula **Principal × Rate × Time**.

Whether interest revenue is recognized as it *accrues* or as it *is received* depends on the *materiality* of the amounts involved.

LO7 Evaluate the liquidity of a company's accounts receivable. The most liquid financial asset is cash, followed by cash equivalents, marketable securities, and receivables. The liquidity of receivables varies depending on their collectibility and maturity dates.

The Allowance for Doubtful Accounts should provide for those receivables that may prove to be uncollectible. However, users of financial statements may also want to evaluate the concentrations-of-credit-risk disclosure and, perhaps, the credit ratings of major debtors. The accounts receivable turnover rate provides insight as to how quickly receivables are being collected.

Key Terms Introduced or Emphasized in Chapter 7

accounts receivable turnover rate (p. 316) A ratio used to measure the liquidity of accounts receivable and the reasonableness of the accounts receivable balance. Computed by dividing net sales by average receivables.

aging the accounts receivable (p. 307) The process of classifying accounts receivable by age groups such as current, 1–30 days past due, 31–60 days past due, etc. A step in estimating the uncollectible portion of the accounts receivable.

Allowance for Doubtful Accounts (p. 305) A valuation account or contra-asset account relating to accounts receivable and showing the portion of the receivables estimated to be uncollectible.

bank reconciliation (p. 296) An analysis that explains the difference between the balance of cash shown in the bank statement and the balance of cash shown in the depositor's records.

cash equivalents (p. 293) Very short-term investments that are so liquid that they are considered equivalent to cash. Examples include money market funds, U.S. Treasury bills, certificates of deposit, and commercial paper. These investments must mature within 90 days of acquisition.

cash management (p. 294) Planning, controlling, and accounting for cash transactions and cash balances.

compensating balance (p. 293) A minimum average balance that a bank may require a borrower to leave on deposit in a non-interest-bearing account.

conservatism (p. 309) A traditional practice of resolving uncertainties by choosing an asset valuation at the lower end of the range of reasonableness. Also refers to the policy of postponing recognition of revenue to a later date when a range of reasonable choices exists. Designed to avoid overstatement of financial strength and earnings.

default (p. 315) Failure to pay interest or principal of a promissory note at the due date.

direct write-off method (p. 310) A method of accounting for uncollectible receivables in which no expense is recognized until individual accounts are determined to be worthless. At that point the account receivable is written off, with an offsetting debit to uncollectible accounts expense. Fails to match revenue and related expenses.

factoring (p. 311) Transactions in which a business either sells its accounts receivable to a financial institution (often called a *factor*) or borrows money by pledging its accounts receivable as collateral.

financial assets (p. 292) Cash and assets convertible directly into known amounts of cash (such as marketable securities and receivables).

gain (p. 301) An increase in owners' equity resulting from a transaction other than earning revenue or investment by the owners. The most common example is the sale of an asset at a price above book value.

line of credit (p. 293) A prearranged borrowing agreement in which a bank stands ready to advance the borrower without delay any amount up to a specified credit limit. Once used, a line of credit becomes a liability. The unused portion of the line represents the ability to borrow cash without delay.

loss (p. 301) A decrease in owners' equity resulting from any transaction other than an expense or a distribution to the owners. The most common example is the sale of an asset at a price below book value.

marketable securities (p. 292) Highly liquid investments, primarily in stocks and bonds, that can be sold at quoted market prices in organized securities exchanges.

mark-to-market (p. 302) The balance sheet valuation standard applied to investments in marketable securities. Involves adjusting the control account for securities owned to its total market value at each balance sheet date. (Represents an exception to the cost principle.)

maturity date (p. 314) The date on which a note becomes due and payable.

maturity value (p. 314) The value of a note at its maturity date, consisting of principal plus interest.

net realizable value (p. 292) The balance sheet valuation standard applied to receivables. Equal to the gross amount of accounts and notes receivable, less an estimate of the portion that may prove to be uncollectible.

NSF check (p. 297) A customer's check that was deposited but returned because of a lack of funds (Not Sufficient Funds) in the account on which the check was drawn.

Unrealized Holding Gain (or Loss) on Investments (p. 302) A stockholders' equity account representing the difference between the cost of investments owned and their market value at the balance sheet date. In short, gains or losses on these investments that have not been "realized" through the sale of the securities.

Demonstration Problem

Shown below are selected transactions of Gulf Corp. during the month of December 2007.

Dec. 1 Accepted a one-year, 8 percent note receivable from a customer, Glenn Holler. The note is in settlement of an existing $1,500 account receivable. The note, plus interest, is due in full on November 30, 2008.

Dec. 8 An account receivable from S. Willis in the amount of $700 is determined to be uncollectible and is written off against the Allowance for Doubtful Accounts.

Dec. 15 Unexpectedly received $200 from F. Hill in full payment of her account. The $200 account receivable from Hill previously had been written off as uncollectible.

Dec. 31 Replenished the petty cash fund. Petty cash vouchers indicated office supplies expense, $44; miscellaneous expense, $32.

Dec. 31 The month-end bank reconciliation includes the following items: outstanding checks, $12,320; deposit in transit, $3,150; check from customer T. Jones returned "NSF," $358; bank service charges, $10; bank collected $20,000 in maturing U.S. Treasury bills (a cash equivalent) on the company's behalf. (These Treasury bills had cost $19,670, so the amount collected includes $330 interest revenue.)

Data for Adjusting Entries

1. An aging of accounts receivable indicates probable uncollectible accounts totaling $9,000. Prior to the month-end adjustment, the Allowance for Doubtful Accounts had a credit balance of $5,210.
2. Prior to any year-end adjustment, the balance in the Marketable Securities account was $213,800. At year-end, marketable securities owned had a cost of $198,000 and a market value of $210,000.
3. Accrued interest revenue on the note receivable from Glenn Holler dated December 1.

Instructions

a. Prepare entries in general journal entry form for the December transactions. In adjusting the accounting records from the bank reconciliation, make one entry to record any increases in the Cash account and a separate entry to record any decreases.

b. Prepare the month-end adjustments indicated by the data for adjusting entries given above.

c. What is the adjusted balance in the Unrealized Holding Gain (or Loss) on Investments account at December 31? Where in the financial statements does this account appear?

Solution to the Demonstration Problem

a.

GENERAL JOURNAL

Date		Account Titles and Explanation	Debit	Credit
Dec.	1	Notes Receivable	1,500	
		Accounts Receivable (Glenn Holler)		1,500
		Accepted a one-year, 8% note in settlement of a $1,500 account receivable.		
	8	Allowance for Doubtful Accounts	700	
		Accounts Receivable (S. Willis)		700
		To write off receivable from S. Willis as uncollectible.		
	15	Accounts Receivable (F. Hill)	200	
		Allowance for Doubtful Accounts		200
		To reinstate account receivable previously written off as uncollectible.		
	15	Cash	200	
		Accounts Receivable (F. Hill)		200
		To record collection of account receivable.		
	31	Office Supplies Expense	44	
		Miscellaneous Expense	32	
		Cash		76
		To replenish petty cash fund.		
	31	Cash	20,000	
		Cash Equivalents		19,670
		Interest Revenue		330
		To record collection of maturing T-bills by bank.		
	31	Accounts Receivable (T. Jones)	358	
		Bank Service Charges	10	
		Cash		368
		To record bank service charge and to reclassify NSF check from T. Jones as an account receivable.		

GENERAL JOURNAL (Continued)

b. **Adjusting Entries**

Dec. 31	Uncollectible Accounts Expense	3,790	
	Allowance for Doubtful Accounts		3,790
	To increase Allowance for Doubtful Accounts to $9,000 ($9,000 − $5,210 = $3,790).		
31	Unrealized Holding Gain (or Loss) on Investments.	3,800	
	Marketable Securities		3,800
	To reduce the balance in the Marketable Securities account to a market value of $210,000.		
31	Interest Receivable	10	
	Interest Revenue		10
	Accrued one-month interest revenue on note receivable: $1,500 × 8% × 1/12 = $10.		

c. The Unrealized Holding Gain (or Loss) on Investments account has a *$12,000 credit balance*, representing the unrealized gain on securities owned as of December 31. (The unrealized gain is equal to the $210,000 market value of these securities, less their $198,000 cost.) The account appears in the stockholders' equity section of Gulf Corp.'s balance sheet.

Self-Test Questions

The answers to these questions appear on page 345.

1. In general terms, financial assets appear in the balance sheet at:

a. Face value.
b. Current value.
c. Cost.
d. Estimated future sales value.

2. Which of the following practices contributes to efficient cash management?

a. Never borrow money—maintain a cash balance sufficient to make all necessary payments.
b. Record all cash receipts and cash payments at the end of the month when reconciling the bank statements.
c. Prepare monthly forecasts of planned cash receipts, payments, and anticipated cash balances up to a year in advance.
d. Pay each bill as soon as the invoice arrives.

3. Each of the following measures strengthens internal control over cash receipts *except*:

a. The use of a petty cash fund.
b. Preparation of a daily listing of all checks received through the mail.
c. The deposit of cash receipts in the bank on a daily basis.
d. The use of cash registers.

Use the following data for questions 4 and 5:
Quinn Company's bank statement at January 31 shows a balance of $13,360, while the ledger account for Cash in Quinn's ledger shows a balance of $12,890 at the same date. The only reconciling items are the following:

- Deposit in transit, $890.
- Bank service charge, $24.
- NSF check from customer Greg Denton in the amount of $426.
- Error in recording check no. 389 for rent: check was written in the amount of $1,320, but was recorded improperly in the accounting records as $1,230.
- Outstanding checks, $?????

4. What is the total amount of outstanding checks at January 31?

a. $1,048. **b.** $868. **c.** $1,900. **d.** $1,720.

5. Assuming a single journal entry is made to adjust Quinn Company's accounting records at January 31, the journal entry includes:

a. A debit to Rent Expense for $90.
b. A credit to Accounts Receivable, G. Denton, for $426.
c. A credit to Cash for $450.
d. A credit to Cash for $1,720.

6. Which of the following best describes the application of generally accepted accounting principles to the valuation of accounts receivable?

a. Realization principle—Accounts receivable are shown at their net realizable value in the balance sheet.
b. Matching principle—The loss due to an uncollectible account is recognized in the period in which the sale is made, not in the period in which the account receivable is determined to be worthless.
c. Cost principle—Accounts receivable are shown at the initial cost of the merchandise to customers, less the cost the seller must pay to cover uncollectible accounts.
d. Principle of conservatism—Accountants favor using the lowest reasonable estimate for the amount of uncollectible accounts.

7. On January 1, Dillon Company had a $3,100 credit balance in the Allowance for Doubtful Accounts. During the year, sales totaled $780,000, and $6,900 of accounts receivable were written off as uncollectible. A December 31 aging of accounts receivable indicated the amount probably uncollectible to be $5,300. (No recoveries of accounts previously written off were made during the year.) Dillon's financial statements for the current year should include:
   a. Uncollectible accounts expense of $9,100.
   b. Uncollectible accounts expense of $5,300.
   c. Allowance for Doubtful Accounts with a credit balance of $1,500.
   d. Allowance for Doubtful Accounts with a credit balance of $8,400.
8. Under the *direct write-off* method of accounting for uncollectible accounts:
   a. The current year uncollectible accounts expense is less than the expense would be under the allowance approach.
   b. The relationship between the current period net sales and current period uncollectible accounts expense illustrates the matching principle.
   c. The Allowance for Doubtful Accounts is debited when specific accounts receivable are determined to be worthless.
   d. Accounts receivable are not stated in the balance sheet at net realizable value, but at the balance of the Accounts Receivable control account.
9. Which of the following actions is *least* likely to increase a company's accounts receivable turnover?
   a. Encouraging customers to use bank credit cards, such as Visa and MasterCard, rather than other national credit cards, such as American Express.
   b. Offer customers larger cash discounts for making early payments.
   c. Reduce the interest rate charged to credit customers.
   d. Sell accounts receivable to a factor.
10. On October 1, *2007*, Coast Financial loaned Barr Corporation $300,000, receiving in exchange a nine-month, 12 percent note receivable. Coast ends its fiscal year on December 31 and makes adjusting entries to accrue interest earned on all notes receivable. The interest earned on the note receivable from Barr Corporation during *2008* will amount to:
    a. $9,000. c. $27,000.
    b. $18,000. d. $36,000.
11. Puget Sound Co. sold marketable securities costing $80,000 for $92,000 cash. In the company's income statement and statement of cash flows, respectively, this will appear as:
    a. A $12,000 gain and a $92,000 cash receipt.
    b. A $92,000 gain and an $8,000 cash receipt.
    c. A $12,000 gain and an $80,000 cash receipt.
    d. A $92,000 sale and a $92,000 cash receipt.

ASSIGNMENT MATERIAL Discussion Questions

1. Briefly describe the flow of cash among receivables, cash, and marketable securities.
2. Different categories of financial assets are valued differently in the balance sheet. These different valuation methods have one common goal. Explain.
3. What are *cash equivalents*? Provide two examples. Why are these items often combined with cash for the purpose of balance sheet presentation?
4. What are lines of credit? From the viewpoint of a short-term creditor, why do lines of credit increase a company's liquidity? How are the unused portions of these lines presented in financial statements?
5. Does the expression "efficient management of cash" mean anything more than procedures to prevent losses from fraud or theft? Explain.
6. Why are cash balances in *excess* of those needed to finance business operations viewed as relatively nonproductive assets? Suggest several ways in which these excess cash balances may be utilized effectively.
7. List several principles to be observed by a business in establishing strong internal control over cash receipts.
8. List two items often encountered in reconciling a bank statement that may cause cash per the bank statement to be *larger* than the balance of cash shown in the depositor's accounting records.
9. Describe the nature and usefulness of a *cash budget*.
10. Why are investments in marketable securities shown separately from cash equivalents in the balance sheet?
11. Why must an investor who owns numerous marketable securities maintain a marketable securities subsidiary ledger?
12. Explain the valuation procedure termed *mark-to-market* for short-term investments classified as available-for-sale securities.
13. What does the account Unrealized Holding Gain (or Loss) on Investment represent? How is this account presented in the financial statements for short-term investments classified as available-for-sale securities?
14. Explain the relationship between the *matching principle* and the need to estimate uncollectible accounts receivable.
15. In making the annual adjusting entry for uncollectible accounts, a company may utilize a *balance sheet approach* to make the estimate, or it may use an *income statement approach*. Explain these two alternative approaches.
16. What is the direct write-off method of handling credit losses as opposed to the allowance method? What is its principal shortcoming?
17. Must companies use the same method of accounting for uncollectible accounts receivable in their financial statements and in their income tax returns? Explain.

18. What are the advantages to a retailer of making credit sales only to customers who use nationally recognized credit cards?
19. Alta Mine Company, a restaurant that had always made cash sales only, adopted a new policy of honoring several nationally known credit cards. Sales did not increase, but many of Alta Mine's regular customers began charging dinner bills on the credit cards. Has the new policy been beneficial to Alta Mine Company? Explain.
20. How is the accounts receivable turnover rate computed? Why is this rate significant to short-term creditors?
21. How does an annual audit by a CPA firm provide assurance that a company's accounts receivable and notes receivable are fairly presented in the company's financial statements?
22. Explain how each of the following is presented in (1) a multiple-step income statement and (2) a statement of cash flows.
    a. Sale of marketable securities at a loss.
    b. Adjusting entry to create (or increase) the allowance for doubtful accounts.
    c. Entry to write off an uncollectible account against the allowance.
    d. Adjusting entry to increase the balance in the Marketable Securities account to a higher market value (assume these investments are classified as available-for-sale securities).
23. The market values of some marketable securities may change from day to day. How do these changes in market value affect the investor's *taxable income*?
24. Determine the maturity date and maturity value of each of the following notes. (Assume a 360-day year in computing interest and maturity values, but count actual days to the maturity dates.)
    a. A $10,000, 9 percent, one-year note dated July 1, 2007.
    b. A $20,000, 8 percent, 90-day note dated March 11.

Brief Exercises

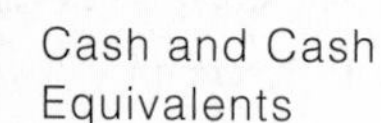

BRIEF EXERCISE 7.1

Cash and Cash Equivalents

The following footnote appeared in a recent financial statement of Westinghouse Electric:

> The Corporation considers all investment securities with a maturity of three months or less when acquired to be cash equivalents. All cash and temporary investments are placed with high-credit-quality financial institutions, and the amount of credit exposure to any one financial institution is limited. At December 31, cash and cash equivalents include restricted funds of $42 million.

a. Are the company's cash equivalents debt or equity securities? How do you know?
b. Explain what is meant by the statement that "the credit exposure to any one financial institution is limited."
c. Explain what is meant by the term *restricted funds* used in the footnote.

BRIEF EXERCISE 7.2

Bank Reconciliation and Cash Equivalents

The Cash account in the general ledger of Lyco Corporation showed a balance of $21,749 at December 31 (but prior to performing a bank reconciliation). The company's bank statement showed a balance of $22,000 at the same date. The only reconciling items consisted of: (1) a $5,000 deposit in transit, (2) a bank service charge of $200, (3) outstanding checks totaling $9,000, (4) a $3,000 check marked "NSF" from Susque Company, one of Lyco's customers, and (5) a check written for office supplies in the amount of $1,832, recorded by the company's bookkeeper as a debit to Office Supplies of $1,283, and a credit to Cash of $1,283.

In addition to the above information, Lyco owned the following financial assets at December 31: (1) a money market account of $60,000, (2) $3,000 of high-grade, 120-day commercial paper, and (3) $5,000 of highly liquid stock investments.

a. Prepare the company's December 31 bank reconciliation.
b. Determine the amount at which cash and cash equivalents will be reported in the company's balance sheet dated December 31.
c. Prepare the necessary journal entry to update the accounting records.

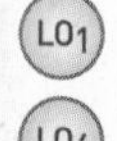

BRIEF EXERCISE 7.3

Mark-to-Market

Weis Markets accumulates large amounts of excess cash throughout the year. It typically invests these funds in marketable securities until they are needed. The company's most recent financial statements revealed a nearly $14 million unrealized gain on short-term investments. Footnotes to the financial statements disclosed that Weis classifies its short-term investments as available-for-sale securities.

a. Explain the meaning of the company's unrealized gain on short-term investments.
b. How does the unrealized gain impact the company's financial statements?
c. Is the unrealized gain included in the computation of the company's taxable income? Explain.
d. Evaluate the mark-to-market concept from the perspective of the company's creditors.

BRIEF EXERCISE 7.4

Accounting for Marketable Securities

Mumford Corporation invested $30,000 in marketable securities on December 4. On December 9, it sold some of these investments for $10,000, and on December 18, it sold more of these investments for $5,000. The securities sold on December 9 had cost the company $7,000, whereas the securities sold on December 18 had cost the company $6,000.

a. Record the purchase of marketable securities on December 4.

b. Record the sale of marketable securities on December 9.

c. Record the sale of marketable securities on December 18.

d. Record the necessary mark-to-market adjustment on December 31, assuming that the market value of the company's remaining unsold securities was $20,000.

BRIEF EXERCISE 7.5

Accounting for Uncollectible Accounts: A Balance Sheet Approach

Pachel Corporation reports the following information pertaining to its accounts receivable:

	Days Past Due			
Current	**1–30**	**31–60**	**61–90**	**Over 90**
$60,000	$40,000	$25,000	$12,000	$2,000

The company's credit department provided the following estimates regarding the percent of accounts expected to eventually be written off from each category listed above:

Current receivables outstanding	2%
Receivables 1–30 days past due	4
Receivables 31–60 days past due	16
Receivables 61–90 days past due	40
Receivables over 90 days past due	90

The company uses a *balance sheet* approach to estimate credit losses.

a. Record the company's uncollectible accounts expense, assuming it has a *$1,400 credit balance* in its Allowance for Doubtful Accounts *prior* to making the necessary adjustment.

b. Record the company's uncollectible accounts expense, assuming it has a *$1,600 debit balance* in its Allowance for Doubtful Accounts *prior* to making the necessary adjustment.

BRIEF EXERCISE 7.6

Accounting for Uncollectible Accounts: An Income Statement Approach

Wilson Corporation uses an *income statement* approach to estimate credit losses. Its *gross* Accounts Receivable of $5,000,000 at the *beginning* of the period had a *net realizable value* of $4,925,000. During the period, the company *wrote off* actual accounts receivable of $100,000 and collected $7,835,000 from credit customers. Credit sales for the year amounted to $9,000,000. Of its credit sales, 1 percent was estimated to eventually be uncollectible.

Determine the *net realizable value* of the company's accounts receivable at the *end* of the period.

BRIEF EXERCISE 7.7

Analyzing Accounts Receivable

Following are the average accounts receivable and net sales reported recently by two large beverage companies (dollar amounts are stated in millions):

	Average Accounts Receivable	Net Sales
Adolph Coors Company	$114	$ 2,842
Anheuser-Busch Companies, Inc.	615	12,262

a. Compute the accounts receivable turnover rate for each company (round your results to the nearest whole number).

b. Compute the average number of days that it takes for each company to collect its accounts receivable (round your results to the nearest whole day).

c. Based upon your computations in **a** and **b**, which company's accounts receivable appear to be most liquid? Defend your answer.

BRIEF EXERCISE 7.8

Notes Receivable and Interest

On September 1, 2007, Health Wise International acquired a 12 percent, nine-month note receivable from Herbal Innovations, a credit customer, in settlement of a $22,000 account receivable. Prepare journal entries to record the following:

a. The receipt of the note on September 1, 2007, in settlement of the account receivable.

b. The adjustment to record accrued interest revenue on December 31, 2007.

c. The collection of the principal and interest on May 31, 2008.

BRIEF EXERCISE 7.9

Industry Characteristics and Allowances for Doubtful Accounts

The following percentages were computed using figures from recent annual reports of Albertsons Inc., a large grocery store chain, and Sprint Corporation, a provider of telecommunication services:

	Albertsons	Sprint
Allowance for doubtful accounts as a percentage of net sales	0.09%	1.5%
Accounts receivable as a percentage of net sales	1.4	14.2

Explain why Sprint's percentages are so much larger than Albertsons's percentages.

BRIEF EXERCISE 7.10

Analyzing Accounts Receivable

Cromley Corporation reports annual sales of $1,500,000. Its accounts receivable throughout the year averaged $125,000.

a. Compute the company's accounts receivable turnover rate.

b. Compute the average days outstanding of the company's accounts receivable.

Exercises

EXERCISE 7.1

You as a Student

Assume that the following information relates to your most recent bank statement dated September 30:

Balance per bank statement at September 30	$3,400

Checks written that had not cleared the bank as of September 30:

#203	University tuition	$1,500
#205	University bookstore	350
#208	Rocco's Pizza	25
#210	Stereo purchase	425
#211	October apartment rent	500

Interest amounting to $4 was credited to your account by the bank in September. The bank's service charge for the month was $5. In addition to your bank statement, you received a letter from your parents informing you that they had made a $2,400 electronic funds transfer directly into your account on October 2. After reading your parents' letter, you looked in your checkbook and discovered its balance was $601. Adding your parents' deposit brought that total to $3,001.

Prepare a bank reconciliation to determine your correct checking account balance. Explain why neither your bank statement nor your checkbook shows this amount.

EXERCISE 7.2

Financial Assets

The following financial assets appeared in a recent balance sheet of Apple Computer, Inc. (dollar amounts are stated in millions):

Cash and cash equivalents	$1,191
Marketable securities (short-term investments)	2,836
Accounts receivable (net of allowance for doubtful accounts of $64)	953

a. Define *financial assets.*

b. A different approach is used in determining the balance sheet value for each category of Apple Computer's financial assets, although each approach serves a common goal. Explain.

c. Why do companies like Apple Computer hold so much of their financial assets in the form of marketable securities and receivables?

d. What types of investments might Apple Computer own that are considered cash equivalents?

e. Explain what is meant by the balance sheet presentation of Apple Computer's Accounts Receivable as shown in the table.

LO2

EXERCISE 7.3
Grandmother's Secret

The former bookkeeper of White Electric Supply is serving time in prison for embezzling nearly $416,000 in less than five years. She describes herself as "an ordinary mother of three kids and a proud grandmother of four." Like so many other "ordinary" employees, she started out by taking only small amounts. By the time she was caught, she was stealing lump sums of $5,000 and $10,000.

Her method was crude and simple. She would write a check for the correct amount payable to a supplier for, say, $15,000. However, she would record in the company's check register an amount significantly greater, say, $20,000. She would then write a check payable to herself for the $5,000 difference. In the check register, next to the number of each check she had deposited in her personal bank account, she would write the word "void," making it appear as though the check had been destroyed. This process went undetected for nearly five years.

a. What controls must have been lacking at White Electric Supply to enable the bookkeeper to steal nearly $416,000 before being caught?

b. What the bookkeeper did was definitely unethical. But *what if* one of her grandchildren had been ill and needed an expensive operation? If this had been the case, would it have been ethical for her to take company funds to pay for the operation if she intended to pay the company back in full? Defend your answer.

LO2

EXERCISE 7.4
Embezzlement Issues

D. J. Fletcher, a trusted employee of Bluestem Products, found himself in personal financial difficulties and decided to "borrow" $3,000 from the company and to conceal his theft.

As a first step, Fletcher removed $3,000 in currency from the cash register. This amount represented the bulk of the cash received in over-the-counter sales during the three business days since the last bank deposit. Fletcher then removed a $3,000 check from the day's incoming mail; this check had been mailed in by a customer, Michael Adams, in full payment of his account. Fletcher made no journal entry to record the $3,000 collection from Adams, but deposited the check in Bluestem Products's bank account in place of the $3,000 over-the-counter cash receipts he had stolen.

In order to keep Adams from protesting when his month-end statement reached him, Fletcher made a journal entry debiting Sales Returns and Allowances and crediting Accounts Receivable—Michael Adams. Fletcher posted this entry to the two general ledger accounts affected and to Adams's account in the subsidiary ledger for accounts receivable.

a. Did these actions by Fletcher cause the general ledger to be out of balance or the subsidiary ledger to disagree with the control account? Explain.

b. Assume that Bluestem Products prepares financial statements at the end of the month without discovering the theft. Would any items in the balance sheet or the income statement be in error? Explain.

c. Several weaknesses in internal control apparently exist in Bluestem Products. Indicate three specific changes needed to strengthen internal control over cash receipts.

LO3

EXERCISE 7.5
Bank Reconciliation

Shown below is the information needed to prepare a bank reconciliation for Warren Electric at December 31:

1. At December 31, cash per the bank statement was $15,200; cash per the company's records was $17,500.
2. Two debit memoranda accompanied the bank statement: service charges for December of $25, and a $775 check drawn by Jane Jones marked "NSF."
3. Cash receipts of $10,000 on December 31 were not deposited until January 4.
4. The following checks had been issued in December but were not included among the paid checks returned by the bank: no. 620 for $1,000, no. 630 for $3,000, and no. 641 for $4,500.

a. Prepare a bank reconciliation at December 31.

b. Prepare the necessary journal entry or entries to update the accounting records.

c. Assume that the company normally is *not* required to pay a bank service charge if it maintains a minimum average daily balance of $1,000 throughout the month. If the company's average daily balance for December had been $8,000, why did it have to pay a $25 service charge?

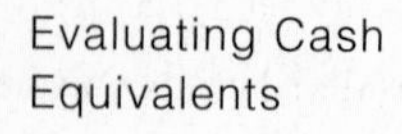

EXERCISE 7.6
Evaluating Cash Equivalents

Tyson Furniture has $100,000 in excess cash that it wants to invest in one or more cash equivalents. The treasurer has researched two money market accounts and two certificates of deposit (CDs) offered by four major banks. This is the information she gathered:

Investment Institution	Investment Type	Minimum Investment	Interest Rate	Penalty for Early Withdrawal?	Financial Risk
Nexity Bank	Money market account	$ 1,000	1.5%	No	Very low
Bank of America	Money market account	50,000	2.0	No	Very low
IndyMac Bank	90-day CD	5,000	2.1	Yes	Very low
Commerce Bank	90-day CD	100,000	2.3	Yes	Very low

The two 90-day certificates of deposit are FDIC insured for up to $100,000. The money market accounts are not FDIC insured.

Suggest how Tyson Furniture might allocate its $100,000 cash among these four opportunities. Discuss the trade-offs that management must consider.

EXERCISE 7.7
The Nature of Marketable Securities

Many companies hold a significant portion of their financial assets in the form of marketable securities. For example, **Microsoft Corporation** recently reported investments in marketable securities totaling $37 billion, an amount equal to 80 percent of its total financial assets. In contrast, only 11 percent of its financial assets were in the form of accounts receivable.

a. Define *marketable securities* (also referred to as short-term investments). What characteristics of these securities justify classifying them as financial assets?

b. What is the basic advantage of **Microsoft Corporation** keeping financial assets in the form of marketable securities instead of cash? Is there any disadvantage?

c. Explain how **Microsoft Corporation** values these investments in its balance sheet.

d. Discuss whether the valuation of marketable securities represents a departure from (1) the cost principle and (2) the objectivity principle.

e. Explain how *mark-to-market* benefits the *users* of **Microsoft Corporation**'s financial statements.

EXERCISE 7.8
Reporting Uncollectible Accounts

The credit manager of Montour Fuel has gathered the following information about the company's accounts receivable and credit losses during the current year:

Net credit sales for the year		$8,000,000
Accounts receivable at year-end		1,750,000
Uncollectible accounts receivable:		
Actually written off during the year	$96,000	
Estimated portion of year-end receivables expected to prove uncollectible (per aging schedule)	84,000	180,000

Prepare one journal entry summarizing the recognition of uncollectible accounts expense for the entire year under each of the following independent assumptions:

a. Uncollectible accounts expense is estimated at an amount equal to 2.5 percent of net credit sales.

b. Uncollectible accounts expense is recognized by adjusting the balance in the Allowance for Doubtful Accounts to the amount indicated in the year-end aging schedule. The balance in the allowance account at the *beginning* of the current year was $25,000. (Consider the effect of the write-offs during the year on the balance in the Allowance for Doubtful Accounts.)

c. The company uses the direct write-off method of accounting for uncollectible accounts.

d. Which of the three methods gives investors and creditors the most accurate assessment of a company's liquidity? Defend your answer.

EXERCISE 7.9

Industry Characteristics and Collection Performance

The following information was taken from recent annual reports of Huffy Corporation, a manufacturer of bicycles sold primarily by large retail chains, and Pennsylvania Power Company, a public utility (dollar amounts are stated in thousands):

	Huffy	PPC
Net sales.	$372,896	$7,078,000
Average accounts receivable	70,892	296,548

a. Compute for each company the accounts receivable turnover rate for the year.

b. Compute for each company the average number of days required to collect outstanding receivables (round answers to nearest whole day).

c. Explain why the figures computed for Huffy Corporation in parts **a** and **b** are so different from those computed for Pennsylvania Power Company.

EXERCISE 7.10

Analyzing the Effects of Transactions

Six events pertaining to financial assets are described as follows:

a. Invested idle cash in marketable securities and classified them as available for sale.

b. Collected an account receivable.

c. Sold marketable securities at a loss (proceeds from the sale were equal to the market value reflected in the last balance sheet).

d. Determined a particular account receivable to be uncollectible and wrote it off against the Allowance for Doubtful Accounts.

e. Received interest earned on an investment in marketable securities (company policy is to recognize interest as revenue *when received*).

f. Made a mark-to-market adjustment increasing the balance in the Marketable Securities account to reflect a rise in the market value of securities owned.

Indicate the effects of each transaction or adjusting entry upon the financial measurements in the four column headings listed below. Use the code letters **I** for increase, **D** for decrease, and **NE** for no effect.

Transaction	Total Assets	Net Income	Net Cash Flow from Operating Activities	Net Cash Flow (from any source)
a				

EXERCISE 7.11

Reporting Financial Assets

Explain how each of the following items is reported in a complete set of financial statements, including the accompanying notes. (In one or more cases, the item may not appear in the financial statements.) The answer to the first item is provided as an example.

a. Cash equivalents.

b. Cash in a special fund being accumulated as legally required for the purpose of retiring a specific long-term liability.

c. Compensating balances.

d. The amount by which the current market value of securities classified as available for sale exceeds their cost.

e. The Allowance for Doubtful Accounts.

f. The accounts receivable turnover rate.

g. Realized gains and losses on investments sold during the period.

h. Proceeds from converting cash equivalents into cash.

i. Proceeds from converting investments in marketable securities into cash.

Example: **a.** Cash equivalents normally are *not* shown separately in financial statements. Rather, they are combined with other types of cash and reported under the caption "Cash and Cash Equivalents." A note to the statements often shows the breakdown of this asset category.

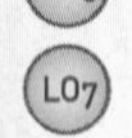

EXERCISE 7.12
Accounting for Uncollectible Accounts: An Income Statement Approach

Indicate the effects of *the following errors* on each of the items listed in the column headings below. Use the following symbols: **O** = overstated, **U** = understated, and **NE** = no effect. Assume that the company does *not* use the direct write-off method to account for uncollectible accounts.

Transaction	Gross Profit	Current Ratio	Receivables Turnover Rate	Net Income	Retained Earnings	Working Capital
a. Recorded uncollectible accounts expense by debiting Sales and crediting Accounts Receivable.						
b. Wrote off an account receivable deemed uncollectible by debiting Uncollectible Accounts Expense and crediting Accounts Receivable.						
c. Collected cash from credit customers in settlement of outstanding accounts receivable by debiting Cash and crediting Sales.						

- Gross Profit = Sales − Cost of Goods Sold
- Current Ratio = Current Assets ÷ Current Liabilities
- Receivables Turnover Rate = Sales ÷ Average Accounts Receivable (net)
- Working Capital = Current Assets − Current Liabilities

EXERCISE 7.13
Accounting for Marketable Securities

McGoun Industries pays income taxes on capital gains at a rate of 30 percent. At December 31, 2007, the company owns marketable securities that cost $90,000 but have a current market value of $260,000.

a. How will users of McGoun's financial statements be made aware of this substantial increase in the market value of the company's investments?

b. As of December 31, 2007, what income taxes has McGoun paid on the increase in value of these investments? Explain.

c. Prepare a journal entry at January 4, 2008, to record the cash sale of these investments at $260,000.

d. What effect will the sale recorded in part **c** have on McGoun's tax obligation for 2008?

EXERCISE 7.14
Notes and Interest

On August 1, 2007, Hampton Construction received a 9 percent, six-month note receivable from Dusty Roads, one of Hampton Construction's problem credit customers. Roads had owed $36,000 on an outstanding account receivable. The note receivable was taken in settlement of this amount. Assume that Hampton Construction makes adjusting entries for accrued interest revenue once each year on December 31.

a. Journalize the following three events on the books of Hampton Construction.

1. Record the receipt of the note on August 1 in settlement of the account receivable.
2. Record accrued interest at December 31, 2007.
3. Assume that Dusty Roads pays the note plus accrued interest in full. Record the collection of the principal and interest on January 31, 2008.
4. Assume that Dusty Roads did *not* make the necessary principal and interest payment on January 31, 2008. Rather, assume that he defaulted on his obligation. Record the default on January 31, 2008.

b. Indicate the effects of each of the four transactions journalized in part **a** on the elements of the financial statement shown below. Use the code letters **I** for increase, **D** for decrease, and **NE** for no effect.

Transaction	Revenue − Expenses = Net Income	Assets = Liabilities + Equity
1		

EXERCISE 7.15

Using the Financial Statements of **Home Depot, Inc.**

The **Home Depot, Inc.**, financial statements appear in Appendix A at the end of this textbook. Use these statements to answer the following questions:

a. What is the total dollar value of the company's financial assets for the most current year reported?

b. Does the company report any investments in marketable securities? If so, how does it report unrealized gains and losses?

c. What is the company's allowance for uncollectible accounts for the most current year reported? (Hint: Examine the footnotes to the financial statements.)

d. On average, for how many days do the company's accounts receivable remain outstanding before collection?

Problem Set A

PROBLEM 7.1A

Bank Reconciliation

The cash transactions and cash balances of Banner, Inc., for July were as follows:

1. The ledger account for Cash showed a balance at July 31 of $125,568.
2. The July bank statement showed a closing balance of $114,828.
3. The cash received on July 31 amounted to $16,000. It was left at the bank in the night depository chute after banking hours on July 31 and therefore was not recorded by the bank on the July statement.
4. Also included with the July bank statement was a debit memorandum from the bank for $50 representing service charges for July.
5. A credit memorandum enclosed with the July bank statement indicated that a non-interest-bearing note receivable for $4,000 from Rene Manes, left with the bank for collection, had been collected and the proceeds credited to the account of Banner, Inc.
6. Comparison of the paid checks returned by the bank with the entries in the accounting records revealed that check no. 821 for $519, issued July 15 in payment for office equipment, had been erroneously entered in Banner's records as $915.
7. Examination of the paid checks also revealed that three checks, all issued in July, had not yet been paid by the bank: no. 811 for $314; no. 814 for $625; no. 823 for $175.
8. Included with the July bank statement was a $200 check drawn by Howard Williams, a customer of Banner, Inc. This check was marked "NSF." It had been included in the deposit of July 27 but had been charged back against the company's account on July 31.

Instructions

a. Prepare a bank reconciliation for Banner, Inc., at July 31.

b. Prepare journal entries (in general journal form) to adjust the accounts at July 31. Assume that the accounts have not been closed.

c. State the amount of cash that should be included in the balance sheet at July 31.

d. Explain why the balance per the company's bank statement is often larger than the balance shown in its accounting records.

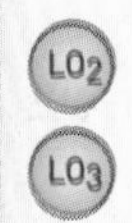

PROBLEM 7.2A
Protecting Cash

Osage Farm Supply had poor internal control over its cash transactions. Facts about the company's cash position at November 30 are described below.

The accounting records showed a cash balance of $35,400, which included a deposit in transit of $1,245. The balance indicated in the bank statement was $20,600. Included in the bank statement were the following debit and credit memoranda:

Debit Memoranda:	
Check from customer G. Davis, deposited by Osage Farm Supply, but charged back as NSF	$ 130
Bank service charges for November	15
Credit Memorandum:	
Proceeds from collection of a note receivable from Regal Farms, which Osage Farm Supply had left with the bank's collection department	$6,255

Outstanding checks were as follows:

Check No.	Amount
8231	$ 400
8263	524
8288	176
8294	5,000

Bev Escola, the company's cashier, has been taking portions of the company's cash receipts for several months. Each month, Escola prepares the company's bank reconciliation in a manner that conceals her thefts. Her bank reconciliation for November was as follows:

Balance per bank statement, Nov. 30		$20,600
Add: Deposits in transit	$2,145	
Collection of note from Regal Farms	6,255	8,400
Subtotal		$30,000
Less: Outstanding checks:		
No. 8231	$ 400	
8263	524	
8288	176	1,000
Adjusted cash balance per bank statement		$29,000
Balance per accounting records, Nov. 30		$35,400
Add: Credit memorandum from bank		6,255
Subtotal		$29,145
Less: Debit memoranda from bank:		
NSF check of G. Davis	$ 130	
Bank service charges	15	145
Adjusted cash balance per accounting records		$29,000

Instructions

a. Determine the amount of the cash shortage that has been concealed by Escola in her bank reconciliation. (As a format, we suggest that you prepare the bank reconciliation correctly. The amount of the shortage then will be the difference between the adjusted balances per the bank statement and per the accounting records. You can then list this unrecorded cash shortage as the final adjustment necessary to complete your reconciliation.)

b. Carefully review Escola's bank reconciliation and explain in detail how she concealed the amount of the shortage. Include a listing of the dollar amounts that were concealed in various ways. This listing should total the amount of the shortage determined in part **a**.

c. Suggest some specific internal control measures that appear to be necessary for Osage Farm Supply.

PROBLEM 7.3A
Aging Accounts Receivable; Write-offs

Super Star, a Hollywood publicity firm, uses the balance sheet approach to estimate uncollectible accounts expense. At year-end, an aging of the accounts receivable produced the following five groupings:

a. Not yet due	$500,000
b. 1–30 days past due	210,000
c. 31–60 days past due	80,000
d. 61–90 days past due	15,000
e. Over 90 days past due	30,000
Total	$835,000

On the basis of past experience, the company estimated the percentages probably uncollectible for the above five age groups to be as follows: Group a, 1 percent; Group b, 3 percent; Group c, 10 percent; Group d, 20 percent; and Group e, 50 percent.

The Allowance for Doubtful Accounts before adjustment at December 31 showed a credit balance of $11,800.

Instructions

a. Compute the estimated amount of uncollectible accounts based on the above classification by age groups.

b. Prepare the adjusting entry needed to bring the Allowance for Doubtful Accounts to the proper amount.

c. Assume that on January 10 of the following year, Super Star learned that an account receivable that had originated on September 1 in the amount of $8,250 was worthless because of the bankruptcy of the client, April Showers. Prepare the journal entry required on January 10 to write off this account.

d. The firm is considering the adoption of a policy whereby clients whose outstanding accounts become more than 60 days past due will be required to sign an interest-bearing note for the full amount of their outstanding balance. What advantages would such a policy offer?

PROBLEM 7.4A
Accounting for Uncollectible Accounts

Wilcox Mills is a manufacturer that makes all sales on 30-day credit terms. Annual sales are approximately $30 million. At the end of 2006, accounts receivable were presented in the company's balance sheet as follows:

Accounts receivable from clients	$3,100,000
Less: Allowance for doubtful accounts	80,000

During 2007, $165,000 of specific accounts receivable were written off as uncollectible. Of these accounts written off, receivables totaling $15,000 were subsequently collected. At the end of 2007, an aging of accounts receivable indicated a need for a $90,000 allowance to cover possible failure to collect the accounts currently outstanding.

Wilcox Mills makes adjusting entries in its accounting records *only at year-end*. Monthly and quarterly financial statements are prepared from worksheets, without any adjusting or closing entries actually being entered in the accounting records. (In short, you may assume the company adjusts its accounts only at year-end.)

Instructions

a. Prepare the following general journal entries:

   1. One entry to summarize all accounts written off against the Allowance for Doubtful Accounts during 2007.
   2. Entries to record the $15,000 in accounts receivable that were subsequently collected.
   3. The adjusting entry required at December 31, 2007, to increase the Allowance for Doubtful Accounts to $90,000.

b. Notice that the Allowance for Doubtful Accounts was only $80,000 at the end of 2006, but uncollectible accounts during 2007 totaled $150,000 ($165,000 less the $15,000 reinstated). Do these relationships appear reasonable, or was the Allowance for Doubtful Accounts greatly understated at the end of 2006? Explain.

PROBLEM 7.5A
Accounting for Marketable Securities

At December 31, *2006*, Weston Manufacturing Co. owned the following investments in capital stock of publicly traded companies (classified as available-for-sale securities):

	Cost	Current Market Value
Footlocker, Inc. (5,000 shares: cost, $17 per share; market value, $20)	$ 85,000	$100,000
The Gap, Inc. (4,000 shares: cost, $17 per share; market value, $15)	68,000	60,000
	$153,000	$160,000

In *2007*, Weston engaged in the following two transactions:

Apr. 10 Sold 1,000 shares of its investment in Footlocker, Inc., at a price of $21 per share, less a brokerage commission of $50.

Aug. 7 Sold 2,000 shares of its investment in The Gap, Inc., at a price of $14 per share, less a brokerage commission of $60.

At December 31, 2007, the market values of these stocks were: Footlocker, Inc., $18 per share; and The Gap, Inc., $16 per share.

Instructions

a. Illustrate the presentation of marketable securities and the unrealized holding gain or loss in Weston's balance sheet at December 31, *2006*. Include a caption indicating the section of the balance sheet in which each of these accounts appears.

b. Prepare journal entries to record the transactions on April 10 and August 7.

c. Prior to making a mark-to-market adjustment at the end of 2007, determine the unadjusted balance in the Marketable Securities control account and the Unrealized Holding Gain (or Loss) on Investments account. (Assume that no unrealized gains or losses have been recognized since last year.)

d. Prepare a schedule showing the cost and the market values of securities owned at the end of 2007. (Use the same format as the schedule illustrated above.)

e. Prepare the mark-to-market adjusting entry required at December 31, 2007.

f. Illustrate the presentation of the marketable securities and unrealized holding gain (or loss) in the balance sheet at December 31, *2007*. (Follow the same format as in part **a**.)

g. Illustrate the presentation of the net *realized* gains (or losses) in the 2007 income statement. Assume a multiple-step income statement and show the caption identifying the section in which this amount would appear.

h. Explain how both the realized and unrealized gains and losses will affect the company's 2007 income tax return.

PROBLEM 7.6A
Notes Receivable

Eastern Supply sells a variety of merchandise to retail stores on open account, but it insists that any customer who fails to pay an invoice when due must replace it with an interest-bearing note. The company adjusts and closes its accounts at December 31. Among the transactions relating to notes receivable were the following:

Sept. 1 Received from a customer (Party Plus) a nine-month, 10 percent note for $75,000 in settlement of an account receivable due today.

June 1 Collected in full the nine-month, 10 percent note receivable from Party Plus, including interest.

Instructions

a. Prepare journal entries (in general journal form) to record: (1) the receipt of the note on September 1; (2) the adjustment for interest on December 31; and (3) collection of principal and interest on June 1. (To better illustrate the allocation of interest revenue between accounting periods, we will assume Eastern Supply makes adjusting entries *only at year-end.*)

b. Assume that instead of paying the note on June 1, the customer (Party Plus) had defaulted. Give the journal entry by Eastern Supply to record the default. Assume that Party Plus has sufficient resources that the note eventually will be collected.

c. Explain why the company insists that any customer who fails to pay an invoice when due must replace it with an interest-bearing note.

through

PROBLEM 7.7A
Short Comprehensive Problem

The Scooter Warehouse provided the following information at December 31, 2007:

Bank Reconciliation

General ledger cash balance, 12/31/07	$17,566	Bank statement balance, 12/31/07..................	$16,306
Bank service charge..........	(25)	Deposits in transit	2,450
Returned customer checks marked NSF	(375)	Outstanding checks..........	(1,356)
Error in recording of office supplies	234		
Adjusted cash balance, 12/31/07	$17,400	Adjusted cash balance, 12/31/07.................	$17,400

Marketable Securities

The company invested $26,000 in a portfolio of marketable securities on December 22, 2007. The portfolio's market value on December 31, 2007, had increased in value to $28,500.

Notes Receivable

On November 1, 2007, The Scooter Warehouse sold 25 scooters to Bermuda Fantasy Resort for $65,000. The resort paid $5,000 at the point of sale and issued a one-year, $60,000, 5 percent note for the remaining balance. The note, plus accrued interest, is due in full on October 31, 2008. The Scooter Warehouse adjusts for accrued interest revenue monthly.

Accounts Receivable

The Scooter Warehouse uses a *balance sheet* approach to account for uncollectible accounts expense. Outstanding accounts receivable on December 31, 2007, total $450,000. After aging these accounts, the company estimates that their *net realizable value* is $435,000. Prior to making any adjustment to record uncollectible accounts expense, The Scooter Warehouse's Allowance for Doubtful Accounts has a *credit balance* of $4,000.

Instructions

a. Prepare the journal entry necessary to update the company's accounts immediately after performing its bank reconciliation on December 31, 2007.

b. Prepare the journal entry necessary to adjust the company's marketable securities to market value at December 31, 2007.

c. Prepare the journal entry necessary to accrue interest in December 2007.

d. Prepare the journal entry necessary to report the company's accounts receivable at their net realizable value at December 31, 2007.

e. Discuss briefly how the entry performed in part **d** affects the accounts receivable turnover rate. Does the *write-off* of an account receivable affect the accounts receivable turnover rate differently than the entry performed in part **d**? Explain.

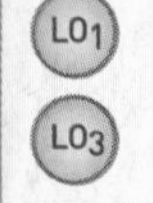
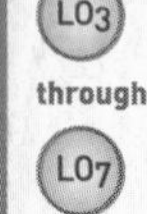

LO1 LO3 through LO7

PROBLEM 7.8A
Short Comprehensive Problem

The Cash account in the general ledger of Hendry Corporation shows a balance of $96,990 at December 31, 2007 (prior to performing a bank reconciliation). The company's bank statement shows a balance of $100,560 at the same date. An examination of the bank statement reveals the following:

1. Deposits in transit amount to $24,600.
2. Bank service charges total $200.
3. Outstanding checks total $31,700.
4. A $3,600 check marked "NSF" from Kent Company (one of Hendry Corporation's customers) was returned to Hendry Corporation by the bank. This was the only NSF check that Hendry Corporation received during 2007.
5. A canceled check (no. 244) written by Hendry Corporation in the amount of $1,250 for office equipment was incorrectly recorded in the general ledger as a debit to Office Equipment of $1,520, and a credit to Cash of $1,520.

In addition to the above information, Hendry Corporation owns the following assets at December 31, 2007: (1) money market accounts totaling $75,000, (2) $3,000 of high-grade, 90-day, commercial paper, and (3) highly liquid stock investments valued at $86,000 at December 31, 2007 (these investments originally cost Hendry Corporation $116,000).

On December 1, 2007, Hendry Corporation sold an unused warehouse to Moran Industries for $100,000. Hendry accepted a six-month, $100,000, 6 percent note receivable from Moran. The note, plus accrued interest, is due in full on May 31, 2008. Hendry Corporation adjusts for accrued interest revenue monthly.

Hendry Corporation uses the *income statement approach* to compute its uncollectible accounts expense. The general ledger had reported Accounts Receivable of $2,150,000 at *January 1, 2007*. At that time, the Allowance for Doubtful Accounts had a credit balance of $40,000. Throughout 2007, the company *wrote off* actual accounts receivable of $140,000 and collected $21,213,600 on account from credit customers (this amount includes the $3,600 NSF check received from Kent Company). Credit sales for the year ended December 31, 2007, totaled $20,000,000. Of these credit sales, 2 percent were estimated to eventually become uncollectible.

Instructions

a. Prepare Hendry Corporation's bank reconciliation dated December 31, 2007, and provide the journal entry necessary to update the company's general ledger balances.

b. Compute cash and cash equivalents to be reported in Hendry Corporation's balance sheet dated December 31, 2007.

c. Prepare the adjusting entry necessary to account for the note receivable from Moran Industries at December 31, 2007.

d. Determine the net realizable value of Hendry Corporation's accounts receivable at December 31, 2007.

e. Determine the total dollar amount of financial assets to be reported in Hendry Corporation's balance sheet dated December 31, 2007.

f. Assume that it is normal for firms similar to Hendry Corporation to take an average of 45 days to collect an outstanding receivable. Is Hendry Corporation's collection performance above or below this average?

Problem Set B

PROBLEM 7.1B
Bank Reconciliation

The cash transactions and cash balances of Dodge, Inc., for November were as follows:

1. The ledger account for Cash showed a balance at November 30 of $6,750.
2. The November bank statement showed a closing balance of $4,710.
3. The cash received on November 30 amounted to $3,850. It was left at the bank in the night depository chute after banking hours on November 30 and therefore was not recorded by the bank on the November statement.
4. Also included with the November bank statement was a debit memorandum from the bank for $15 representing service charges for November.
5. A credit memorandum enclosed with the November bank statement indicated that a non-interest-bearing note receivable for $4,000 from Wright Sisters, left with the bank for collection, had been collected and the proceeds credited to the account of Dodge, Inc.
6. Comparison of the paid checks returned by the bank with the entries in the accounting records revealed that check no. 810 for $430, issued November 15 in payment for computer equipment, had been erroneously entered in Dodge's records as $340.
7. Examination of the paid checks also revealed that three checks, all issued in November, had not yet been paid by the bank: no. 814 for $115; no. 816 for $170; no. 830 for $530.
8. Included with the November bank statement was a $2,900 check drawn by Steve Dial, a customer of Dodge, Inc. This check was marked "NSF." It had been included in the deposit of November 27 but had been charged back against the company's account on November 30.

Instructions

a. Prepare a bank reconciliation for Dodge, Inc., at November 30.
b. Prepare journal entries (in general journal form) to adjust the accounts at November 30. Assume that the accounts have not been closed.
c. State the amount of cash that should be included in the balance sheet at November 30.

PROBLEM 7.2B
Protecting Cash

Jason Chain Saws, Inc., had poor internal control over its cash transactions. Facts about the company's cash position at April 30 are described below.

The accounting records showed a cash balance of $20,325, which included a deposit in transit of $5,000. The balance indicated in the bank statement was $14,300. Included in the bank statement were the following debit and credit memoranda:

Debit Memoranda:	
Check from customer, deposited but charged back as NSF	$ 125
Bank service charges for April	50
Credit Memorandum:	
Proceeds from collection of a note receivable on company's behalf	$6,200

Outstanding checks as of April 30 were as follows:

Check No.	Amount
836	$ 500
842	440
855	330
859	1,300

Tom Crook, the company's cashier, has been taking portions of the company's cash receipts for several months. Each month, Crook prepares the company's bank reconciliation in a manner that conceals his thefts. His bank reconciliation for April is illustrated as follows:

Balance per bank statement, April 30		$14,300
Add: Deposits in transit	$7,120	
Collection of note	6,200	13,320
Subtotal		$27,620
Less: Outstanding checks:		
No. 836	$ 500	
No. 842	440	
No. 855	330	1,270
Adjusted cash balance per bank statement		$26,350
Balance per accounting records, April 30		20,325
Add: Credit memorandum from bank		6,200
Subtotal		$26,525
Less: Debit memoranda from bank:		
NSF check	$ 125	
Bank service charges	50	175
Adjusted cash balance per accounting records		$26,350

Instructions

a. Determine the amount of cash shortage that has been concealed by Crook in his bank reconciliation. (As a format, we suggest that you prepare the bank reconciliation correctly. The amount of the shortage then will be the difference between the adjusted balances per the bank statement and per the accounting records. You can then list this unrecorded cash shortage as the final adjustment necessary to complete your reconciliation.)

b. Carefully review Crook's bank reconciliation and explain in detail how he concealed the amount of the shortage. Include a listing of the dollar amounts that were concealed in various ways. This listing should total the amount of shortage determined in part **a.**

c. Suggest some specific internal control measures that appear to be necessary for Jason Chain Saws, Inc.

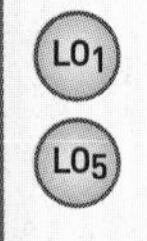

PROBLEM 7.3B
Aging Accounts Receivable; Write-offs

Starlight, a Broadway media firm, uses the balance sheet approach to estimate uncollectible accounts expense. At year-end an aging of the accounts receivable produced the following five groupings:

a. Not yet due	$500,000
b. 1–30 days past due	110,000
c. 31–60 days past due	50,000
d. 61–90 days past due	30,000
e. Over 90 days past due	60,000
Total	$750,000

On the basis of past experience, the company estimated the percentages probably uncollectible for the above five age groups to be as follows: Group a, 1 percent; Group b, 3 percent; Group c, 10 percent; Group d, 20 percent; and Group e, 50 percent.

The Allowance for Doubtful Accounts before adjustments at December 31 showed a credit balance of $4,700.

Instructions

a. Compute the estimated amount of uncollectible accounts based on the above classification by age groups.

b. Prepare the adjusting entry needed to bring the Allowance for Doubtful Accounts to the proper amount.

c. Assume that on January 18 of the following year, Starlight learned that an account receivable that had originated on August 1 in the amount of $1,600 was worthless because of the bankruptcy of the client, May Flowers. Prepare the journal entry required on January 18 to write off this account.

d. The firm is considering the adoption of a policy whereby clients whose outstanding accounts become more than 60 days past due will be required to sign an interest-bearing note for the full amount of their outstanding balance. What advantages would such a policy offer?

PROBLEM 7.4B
Accounting for Uncollectible Accounts

Walc Factory is a manufacturer that makes all sales on 30-day credit terms. Annual sales are approximately $20 million. At the end of 2006, accounts receivable were presented in the company's balance sheet as follows:

Accounts receivable from clients	$1,800,000
Less: Allowance for doubtful accounts	40,000

During 2007, $115,000 of specific accounts receivable were written off as uncollectible. Of these accounts written off, receivables totaling $9,000 were subsequently collected. At the end of 2007, an aging of accounts receivable indicated a need for a $75,000 allowance to cover possible failure to collect the accounts currently outstanding.

Walc Factory makes adjusting entries in its accounting records *only at year-end*. Monthly and quarterly financial statements are prepared from worksheets, without any adjusting or closing entries actually being entered in the accounting records. (In short, you may assume the company adjusts its accounts only at year-end.)

Instructions

a. Prepare the following general journal entries:

1. One entry to summarize all accounts written off against the Allowance for Doubtful Accounts during 2007.

2. Entries to record the $9,000 in accounts receivable that were subsequently collected.

3. The adjusting entry required at December 31, 2007, to increase the Allowance for Doubtful Accounts to $75,000.

b. Notice that the Allowance for Doubtful Accounts was only $40,000 at the end of 2006, but uncollectible accounts during 2007 totaled $106,000 ($115,000 less the $9,000 reinstated). Do these relationships appear reasonable, or was the Allowance for Doubtful Accounts greatly understated at the end of 2006? Explain.

PROBLEM 7.5B
Accounting for Marketable Securities

At December 31, *2006*, Westport Manufacturing Co. owned the following investments in the capital stock of publicly owned companies (all classified as available-for-sale securities):

	Cost	Current Market Value
Lamb Computer, Inc. (1,000 shares: cost, $30 per share; market value, $50)	$30,000	$50,000
Dry Foods (5,000 shares: cost, $9 per share; market value, $8)	45,000	40,000
Totals	$75,000	$90,000

In *2007*, Westport engaged in the following two transactions:

Apr. 6 Sold 100 shares of its investment in Lamb Computer at a price of $55 per share, less a brokerage commission of $20.

Apr. 20 Sold 2,500 shares of its Dry Foods stock at a price of $7 per share, less a brokerage commission of $20.

At December 31, 2007, the market values of these stocks were: Lamb Computer, $40 per share; Dry Foods, $7.

Instructions

a. Illustrate the presentation of marketable securities and the unrealized holding gain or loss in Westport's balance sheet at December 31, *2006*. Include a caption indicating the section of the balance sheet in which each of these accounts appears.

b. Prepare journal entries to record the transactions on April 6 and April 20.

c. Prior to making a mark-to-market adjustment at the end of 2007, determine the unadjusted balance in the Marketable Securities controlling account and the Unrealized Holding Gain (or Loss) on Investments account. (Assume that no unrealized gains or losses have been recognized since last year.)

d. Prepare a schedule showing the cost and market values of securities owned at the end of 2007. (Use the same format as the schedule illustrated above.)

e. Prepare the mark-to-market adjusting entry required at December 31, 2007.

f. Illustrate the presentation of the marketable securities and unrealized holding gain (or loss) in the balance sheet at December 31, *2007*. (Follow the same format as in part **a.**)

g. Illustrate the presentation of the net *realized* gains (or losses) in the 2007 income statement. Assume a multiple-step income statement and show the caption identifying the section in which this amount would appear.

h. Explain how both the realized and the unrealized gains and losses will affect the company's 2007 income tax return.

PROBLEM 7.6B
Notes Receivable

Southern Supply sells a variety of merchandise to retail stores on open account, but it insists that any customer who fails to pay an invoice when due must replace it with an interest-bearing note. The company adjusts and closes its accounts at December 31. Among the transactions relating to notes receivable were the following:

Nov. 1 Received from a customer (LCC) a nine-month, 12 percent note for $60,000 in settlement of an account receivable due today.

Aug. 1 Collected in full the nine-month, 12 percent note receivable from LCC, including interest.

Instructions

a. Prepare journal entries (in general journal form) to record: (1) the receipt of the note on November 1; (2) the adjustment for interest on December 31; and (3) the collection of principal and interest on August 1. (To better illustrate the allocation of interest revenue between accounting periods, we will assume Southern Supply makes adjusting entries *only at year-end*.)

b. Assume that instead of paying the note on August 1, the customer (LCC) had defaulted. Give the journal entry by Southern Supply to record the default. Assume that LCC has sufficient resources that the note eventually will be collected.

c. Explain why the company insists that any customer who fails to pay an invoice when due must replace it with an interest-bearing note.

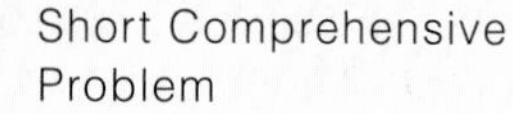
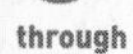

PROBLEM 7.7B
Short Comprehensive Problem

Data Management, Inc., provided the following information at December 31, 2007:

Bank Reconciliation

General ledger cash balance, 12/31/07	$44,637	Bank statement balance, 12/31/07	$37,960
Bank service charge	(125)	Deposits in transit	18,800
Returned customer checks marked NSF	(2,350)	Outstanding checks	(15,560)
Error in recording of office supplies	(962)		
Adjusted cash balance, 12/31/07	$41,200	Adjusted cash balance, 12/31/07	$41,200

Marketable Securities

The company invested $75,000 in a portfolio of marketable securities on December 9, 2007. The portfolio's market value on December 31, 2007, had decreased in value to $68,000.

Notes Receivable

On October 1, 2007, Data Management sold 50 laptop computers to the Mifflinburg School District for $74,500. The school district paid $2,500 at the point of sale and issued a one-year, $72,000, 6 percent note for the remaining balance. The note, plus accrued interest, is due in full on September 30, 2008. Data Management adjusts for accrued interest revenue monthly.

Accounts Receivable

Data Management uses a *balance sheet* approach to account for uncollectible accounts expense. Outstanding accounts receivable on December 31, 2007, total $900,000. After aging these accounts, the company estimates that their *net realizable value* is $860,000. Prior to making any adjustment to record uncollectible accounts expense, Data Management's Allowance for Doubtful Accounts has a *debit balance* of $9,000.

Instructions

a. Prepare the journal entry necessary to update the company's accounts immediately after performing its bank reconciliation on December 31, 2007.

b. Prepare the journal entry necessary to adjust the company's marketable securities to market value at December 31, 2007.

c. Prepare the journal entry necessary to accrue interest revenue in December 2007.

d. Prepare the journal entry necessary to report the company's accounts receivable at their net realizable value at December 31, 2007.

e. Discuss briefly why the company's Allowance for Doubtful Accounts had a *debit balance* prior to the adjustment made in part **d.** How might the company change the percentages it applies to the accounts receivable aging categories to avoid future debit balances in its Allowance for Doubtful Accounts?

through

PROBLEM 7.8B
Short Comprehensive Problem

The Cash account in the general ledger of Ciavarella Corporation shows a balance of $112,000 at December 31, 2007 (prior to performing a bank reconciliation). The company's bank statement shows a balance of $104,100 at the same date. An examination of the bank statement reveals the following:

1. Deposits in transit amount to $16,800.
2. Bank service charges total $100.
3. Outstanding checks total $12,400.
4. A $2,500 check marked "NSF" from Needham Company (one of Ciavarella's customers) was returned to Ciavarella Corporation by the bank. This was the only NSF check that Ciavarella received during 2007.
5. Check no. 550 was actually written by Ciavarella in the amount of $3,200 for computer equipment but was incorrectly recorded in the general ledger as a debit to Computer Equipment of $2,300, and a credit to Cash of $2,300.

In addition to the above information, Ciavarella owns the following assets at December 31, 2007: (1) money market accounts totaling $150,000, (2) $5,000 of high-grade, 60-day commercial paper, and (3) highly liquid stock investments valued at $245,000 at December 31, 2007 (these investments originally cost Ciavarella $225,000).

On December 1, 2007, Ciavarella sold a used truck to Ritter Industries for $18,000. Ciavarella accepted a three-month, $18,000, 9 percent note receivable from Ritter. The note, plus accrued interest, is due in full on March 1, 2008. Ciavarella adjusts for accrued interest revenue monthly.

Ciavarella uses the *income statement approach* to compute uncollectible accounts expense. The general ledger had reported Accounts Receivable of $540,000 at *January 1, 2007*. At that time, the Allowance for Doubtful Accounts had a credit balance of $12,000. Throughout 2007, the company *wrote off* actual accounts receivable of $14,000 and collected $5,252,500 on account from credit customers (this amount includes the $2,500 NSF check received from Needham Company). Credit sales for the year ended December 31, 2007, totaled $6,480,000. Of these credit sales, 1 percent were estimated to eventually become uncollectible.

Instructions

a. Prepare Ciavarella's bank reconciliation dated December 31, 2007, and provide the journal entry necessary to update the company's general ledger balances.

b. Compute cash and cash equivalents to be reported in Ciavarella's balance sheet dated December 31, 2007.

c. Prepare the adjusting entry necessary to account for the note receivable from Ritter Industries at December 31, 2007.

d. Determine the net realizable value of Ciavarella's accounts receivable at December 31, 2007.

e. Determine the total dollar amount of financial assets to be reported in Ciavarella's balance sheet dated December 31, 2007.

f. Assume that it is normal for firms similar to Ciavarella to take an average of 60 days to collect an outstanding receivable. Is Ciavarella Corporation's collection performance above or below this average?

Critical Thinking Cases

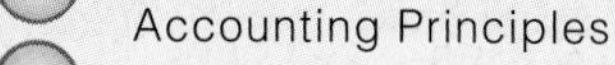

CASE 7.1
Accounting Principles

LO1 LO5 LO6

In each of the situations described below, indicate the accounting principles or concepts, if any, that have been violated and explain briefly the nature of the violation. If you believe the practice is *in accord* with generally accepted accounting principles, state this as your position and defend it.

a. A small business in which credit sales fluctuate greatly from year to year uses the direct write-off method both for income tax purposes and in its financial statements.

b. A manufacturing company charges all of its petty cash expenditures to Miscellaneous Expense, rather than to the various expense accounts that reflect the nature of each expenditure.

c. Computer Systems often sells merchandise in exchange for interest-bearing notes receivable, maturing in 6, 12, or 24 months. The company records these sales transactions by debiting Notes Receivable for the maturity value of the notes, crediting Sales for the sales price of the merchandise, and crediting Interest Revenue for the balance of the maturity value of the note. The cost of goods sold also is recorded.

d. A company has $400,000 in unrestricted cash, $1 million in a bank account specifically earmarked for the construction of a new factory, and $2 million in cash equivalents. In the balance sheet, these amounts are combined and shown as "Cash and cash equivalents . . . $3.4 million."

CASE 7.2
If Things Get Any Better, We'll Be Broke

LO2 LO5 LO7

Rock, Inc., sells stereo equipment. Traditionally, the company's sales have been in the following categories: cash sales, 25 percent; customers using national credit cards, 35 percent; sales on account (due in 30 days), 40 percent. With these policies, the company earned a modest profit, and monthly cash receipts exceeded monthly cash payments by a comfortable margin. Uncollectible accounts expense was approximately 1 percent of net sales. (The company uses the direct write-off method in accounting for uncollectible accounts receivable.)

Two months ago, the company initiated a new credit policy, which it calls "Double Zero." Customers may purchase merchandise on account, with no down payment and no interest charges. The accounts are collected in 12 monthly installments of equal amounts.

The plan has proven quite popular with customers, and monthly sales have increased dramatically. Despite the increase in sales, however, Rock is experiencing cash flow problems—it hasn't been generating enough cash to pay its suppliers, most of which require payment within 30 days.

The company's bookkeeper has prepared the following analysis of monthly operating results:

Sales	Before Double Zero	Last Month
Cash	$12,500	$ 5,000
National credit card	17,500	10,000
30-day accounts	20,000	-0-
Double Zero accounts	-0-	75,000
Total monthly sales	$50,000	$ 90,000
Cost of goods sold and expenses	40,000	65,000
Net income	$10,000	$ 25,000
Cash receipts		
Cash sales	$12,500	$ 5,000
National credit card companies	17,500	10,000
30-day accounts	19,500	-0-
Double Zero accounts	-0-	11,250
Total monthly cash receipts	$49,500	$ 26,250
Accounts written off as uncollectible	$ 500	$ -0-
Accounts receivable at month-end	$20,000	$135,000

The bookkeeper offered the following assessment: "Double Zero is killing us. Since we started that plan, our accounts receivable have increased nearly sevenfold, and they're still growing. We can't afford to carry such a large nonproductive asset on our books. Our cash receipts are down to nearly half of what they used to be. If we don't go back to more cash sales and receivables that can be collected more quickly, we'll become insolvent."

In reply Maxwell "Rock" Swartz, founder and chief executive officer, shouted out: "Why do you say that our accounts receivable are nonproductive? They're the most productive asset we have! Since we started Double Zero, our sales have nearly doubled, our profits have more than doubled, and our bad debt expense has dropped to nothing!"

Instructions

a. Is it logical that the Double Zero plan is causing sales and profits to increase while also causing a decline in cash receipts? Explain.

b. Why has the uncollectible accounts expense dropped to zero? What would you expect to happen to the company's uncollectible accounts expense in the future—say, next year? Why?

c. Do you think that the reduction in monthly cash receipts is permanent or temporary? Explain.

d. In what sense are the company's accounts receivable a "nonproductive" asset?

e. Suggest several ways that Rock may be able to generate the cash it needs to pay its bills without terminating the Double Zero plan.

f. Would you recommend that the company continue offering Double Zero financing, or should it return to the use of 30-day accounts? Explain the reasons for your answer, and identify any unresolved factors that might cause you to change this opinion in the future.

LO1 through  LO5  LO7

CASE 7.3
"Improving" the Balance Sheet

Affections manufactures candy and sells only to retailers. It is not a publicly owned company and its financial statements are not audited. But the company frequently must borrow money. Its creditors insist that the company provide them with unaudited financial statements at the end of each quarter.

In October, management met to discuss the fiscal year ending next December 31. Due to a sluggish economy, Affections was having difficulty collecting its accounts receivable, and its cash position was unusually low. Management knew that if the December 31 balance sheet did not look good, the company would have difficulty borrowing the money it would need to boost production for Valentine's Day.

Thus the purpose of the meeting was to explore ways in which Affections might improve its December 31 balance sheet. Some of the ideas discussed are as follows:

1. Offer customers purchasing Christmas candy a 10 percent discount if they make payment within 30 days.
2. Allow a 30-day grace period on all accounts receivable overdue at the end of the year. As these accounts will no longer be overdue, the company will not need an allowance for overdue accounts.
3. For purposes of balance sheet presentation, combine all forms of cash, including cash equivalents, compensating balances, and unused lines of credit.
4. Require officers who have borrowed money from the company to repay the amounts owed at December 31. This would convert into cash the "notes receivable from officers," which now appear in the balance sheet as noncurrent assets. The loans could be renewed immediately after year-end.
5. Present investments in marketable securities at their market value, rather than at cost.
6. Treat inventory as a financial asset and show it at current sales value.
7. On December 31, draw a large check against one of the company's bank accounts and deposit it in another of the company's accounts in a different bank. The check won't clear the first bank until after year-end. This will substantially increase the amount of cash in bank accounts at year-end.

Instructions

a. Separately evaluate each of these proposals. Consider ethical issues as well as accounting issues.

b. Do you consider it ethical for management to hold this meeting in the first place? That is, should management plan in advance how to improve financial statements that will be distributed to creditors and investors?

BUSINESSWEEK CASE 7.4

Cash Management

In her June 28, 2005, *BusinessWeek* article, "Cell Phones vs. Credit Cards: The Battle Begins," author Olga Kharif explains that cell phones may soon turn into our virtual wallets. Consumers will simply need to push a few buttons on their phones to pay for purchases and to consolidate all of their bills. If that happens, banks and credit card companies will lose out on the hefty fees they currently charge merchants for facilitating credit card sales. In fact, cell phone companies could eventually replace banks.

Discuss the pros and cons of using a cell phone instead of a credit card to make purchases and consolidate debts.

INTERNET CASE 7.5

Returns on Idle Cash from Various Cash Equivalents

Prudent cash management is an important function in any business. Large amounts of cash sitting idle in non-interest-bearing checking accounts can cost a company thousands—even millions—of dollars annually in foregone revenue. Thus, many businesses invest large amounts of idle cash in Treasury bills, certificates of deposit (CDs), and money market accounts.

Visit the **Bankrate.com** home page at the following address:

www.bankrate.com

Search the site for information on CDs, money market accounts, and other interest-bearing products. Look for links under the "Compare Rates" menu.

Instructions

a. Prepare a table showing the current interest rates on Treasury bills, various CDs, and money market accounts.

b. If you were in charge of investing $1 million among the cash equivalents identified in part **a**, how would you make your allocation? Defend your answer.

Internet sites are time and date sensitive. It is the purpose of these exercises to have you explore the Internet. You may need to use the Yahoo! search engine **http://www.yahoo.com** *(or another favorite search engine) to find a company's current Web address.*

Answers to Self-Test. Questions

1. b **2.** c **3.** a **4.** c **5.** a **6.** b **7.** a **8.** d **9.** c
10. b ($300,000 × 12% × 6/12) **11.** a

Inventories and the Cost of Goods Sold

Learning Objectives

AFTER STUDYING THIS CHAPTER, YOU SHOULD BE ABLE TO:

LO1 In a perpetual inventory system, determine the cost of goods sold using (a) specific identification, (b) average cost, (c) FIFO, and (d) LIFO. Discuss the advantages and shortcomings of each method.

LO2 Explain the need for taking a physical inventory.

LO3 Record shrinkage losses and other year-end adjustments to inventory.

LO4 In a periodic inventory system, determine the ending inventory and the cost of goods sold using (a) specific identification, (b) average cost, (c) FIFO, and (d) LIFO.

LO5 Explain the effects on the income statement of errors in inventory valuation.

LO6 Estimate the cost of goods sold and ending inventory by the gross profit method and by the retail method.

LO7 Compute the inventory turnover rate and explain its uses.

SAFEWAY, INC.

Having the right merchandise available at the right time and in the right place is critically important to all companies that sell products to their customers. These businesses include chain stores such as grocery stores, drugstores, and department stores.

Consider **Safeway, Inc.**—a giant grocery chain with nearly 1,700 stores nationwide. When customers shop at **Safeway**, they expect to find the items they want in stock and ready to purchase. If not, they most likely will find another place to shop. To meet the needs of every customer, each **Safeway** store must stock more than 10,000 products. Controlling such a diverse selection of inventory is a major challenge in the highly competitive environment of food retailing.

Accounting for merchandise inventory presents one of the greatest challenges for merchandising companies. These companies must maintain not only a record of inventory items for sale but also the prices at which these items are purchased and sold, both of which change over time. This adds a significant complication to accounting for inventory and the expense included in the income statement when inventory is sold to customers. You learn how to account for inventory and its cost in this chapter.

INVENTORY DEFINED

In a merchandising company, inventory consists of all goods owned and held for sale to customers. Inventory is expected to be converted into cash within the company's *operating cycle*.[1] In the balance sheet, inventory is listed immediately after accounts receivable, because it is just one step farther removed from conversion into cash than customer receivables.

The Flow of Inventory Costs

Inventory is a nonfinancial asset and usually is shown in the balance sheet at its cost.[2] As items are sold from inventory, their costs are removed from the balance sheet and transferred to the cost of goods sold, which is offset against sales revenue in the income statement. This flow of costs is illustrated in Exhibit 8–1.

Exhibit 8–1 **THE FLOW OF COSTS THROUGH FINANCIAL STATEMENTS**

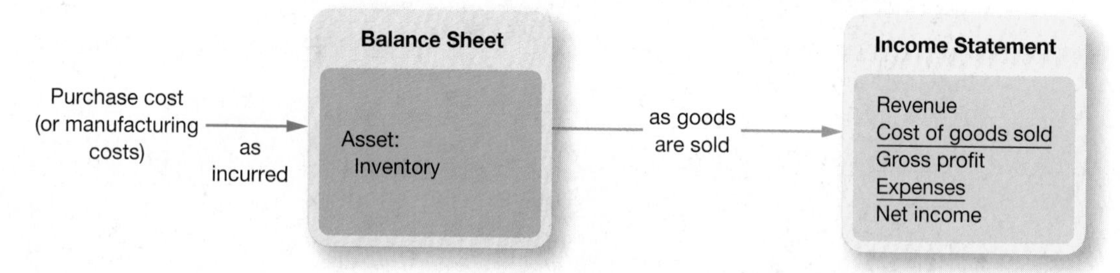

In a perpetual inventory system, entries in the accounting records parallel this flow of costs. When merchandise is purchased, its cost (net of allowable cash discounts) is added to the asset account Inventory. As the merchandise is sold, its cost is removed from the Inventory account and transferred to the Cost of Goods Sold account.

The valuation of inventory and of the cost of goods sold is of critical importance to managers and to external users of financial statements. In many cases, inventory is a company's largest asset, and the cost of goods sold is its largest expense. These two accounts have a significant effect on the financial statement subtotals and ratios used in evaluating the liquidity and profitability of the business.

Several different methods of pricing inventory and of measuring the cost of goods sold are acceptable under generally accepted accounting principles. These different methods may

[1] As explained in Chapter 6, the *operating cycle* of a merchandising business is the period of time required to convert cash into inventory, inventory into accounts receivable, and accounts receivable into cash. Assets expected to be converted into cash within one year or the operating cycle, whichever is longer, are regarded as current assets.

[2] Some companies deal in inventories that can be sold in a worldwide market at quoted market prices. Examples include mutual funds, stock brokerages, and companies that deal in commodities such as agricultural crops or precious metals. Often these companies value their inventories at market price rather than at cost. Our discussions in this chapter are directed to the far more common situation in which inventories are valued at cost.

produce significantly different results, both in a company's financial statements and in its income tax returns. Therefore, managers and investors should understand the effects of the different inventory valuation methods.

WHICH UNIT DID WE SELL?

Purchases of merchandise are recorded in the same manner under all of the inventory valuation methods. The differences in these methods lie in determining *which costs* should be removed from the Inventory account when merchandise is sold.

We illustrated the basic entries relating to purchases and sales of merchandise in Chapter 6. In that introductory discussion, however, we made a simplifying assumption: All of the units in inventory had been acquired at the same unit cost. In practice, a company often has in its inventory identical units of a given product that were acquired at *different costs*. Acquisition costs may vary because the units were purchased at different dates, from different suppliers, or in different quantities.

When identical units of inventory have different unit costs, a question arises as to *which of these costs* should be used in measuring the cost of goods sold.

DATA FOR AN ILLUSTRATION

To illustrate the alternative methods of measuring the cost of goods sold, assume that Mead Electric Company sells electrical equipment and supplies. Included in the company's inventory are five Elco AC-40 generators. These generators are identical; however, two were purchased on January 5 at a per-unit cost of *$1,000*, and the other three were purchased a month later, shortly after Elco had announced a price increase, at a per-unit cost of *$1,200*. These purchases are reflected in Mead's inventory subsidiary ledger in Exhibit 8–2.

Exhibit 8–2

INVENTORY SUBSIDIARY LEDGER

Item Elco AC-40 **Primary supplier** Elco Manufacturing

Description Portable generator **Secondary supplier** Vegas Wholesale Co.

Location Daily St. warehouse **Inventory level: Min:** 2 **Max:** 5

	Purchased			Sold			Balance		
Date	**Units**	**Unit Cost**	**Total**	**Units**	**Unit Cost**	**Cost of Goods Sold**	**Units**	**Unit Cost**	**Total**
Jan. 5	2	$1,000	$2,000				2	$1,000	$2,000
Feb. 5	3	1,200	3,600				2	1,000	
							3	1,200	5,600

Notice that, on February 5, the Balance columns contain two "layers" of unit cost information, representing the units purchased at the two different unit costs. A new **cost layer** is created whenever units are acquired at a different per-unit cost. (As all units comprising a cost layer are sold, the layer is eliminated from the inventory. Therefore, a business is unlikely to have more than three or four cost layers in its inventory at any given time.)

Now assume that, on March 1, Mead sells one of these Elco generators to Boulder Construction Company for $1,800 cash. What cost should be removed from the Inventory account and recognized as the cost of goods sold—$1,000 or $1,200?

In answering such questions, accountants may use an approach called **specific identification**, or they may adopt a **cost flow assumption**. Either of these approaches is acceptable. Once an approach has been selected, however, it should be *applied consistently* in accounting for all sales of this particular type of merchandise.

SPECIFIC IDENTIFICATION

LO1 **In a perpetual inventory system, determine the cost of goods sold using (a) specific identification, (b) average cost, (c) FIFO, and (d) LIFO. Discuss the advantages and shortcomings of each method.**

The specific identification method can be used only when the actual costs of individual units of merchandise can be determined from the accounting records. For example, each of the generators in Mead's inventory may have an identification number, and these numbers may appear on the purchase invoices. With this identification number, Mead's accounting department can determine whether the generator sold to Boulder Construction cost $1,000 or $1,200. The *actual cost* of this particular unit then is used in recording the cost of goods sold.

COST FLOW ASSUMPTIONS

If the items in inventory are *homogeneous* in nature (identical, except for insignificant differences), it is *not necessary* for the seller to use the specific identification method. Rather, the seller may follow the more convenient practice of using a *cost flow assumption.* Using a cost flow assumption, often referred to as simply a flow assumption, is particularly common where the company has a large number of virtually identical inventory items.

When a cost flow assumption is in use, the seller simply makes an *assumption* as to the sequence in which units are withdrawn from inventory. For example, the seller might assume that the oldest merchandise always is sold first or that the most recently purchased items are the first to be sold.

Three cost flow assumptions are in widespread use:

1. *Average cost.* This assumption values all merchandise—units sold and units remaining in inventory—at the *average* per-unit cost. (In effect, the average-cost method assumes that units are withdrawn from the inventory in random order.)
2. *First-in, first-out (FIFO).* As the name implies, FIFO involves the assumption that goods sold are the *first* units that were purchased—that is, the *oldest* goods on hand. Thus the remaining inventory is comprised of the most recent purchases.
3. *Last-in, first-out (LIFO).* Under LIFO, the units sold are assumed to be those *most recently* acquired. The remaining inventory, therefore, is assumed to consist of the earliest purchases.

The cost flow assumption selected by a company *need not* correspond to the actual physical movement of the company's merchandise. When the units of merchandise are identical (or nearly identical), it *does not matter* which units are delivered to the customer in a particular sales transaction. Therefore, in measuring the income of a business that sells units of identical merchandise, accountants consider the flow of *costs* to be more important than the physical flow of the merchandise.

The use of a cost flow assumption *eliminates the need for separately identifying each unit sold and looking up its actual cost.* Experience has shown that these cost flow assumptions provide useful and reliable measurements of the cost of goods sold, as long as they are applied consistently to all sales of the particular type of merchandise.

AVERAGE-COST METHOD

When the **average-cost method** is in use, the *average cost* of all units in inventory is computed after every purchase. This average cost is computed by dividing the total cost of goods available for sale by the number of units in inventory. Because the average cost may change following each purchase, this method also is called the **moving average method** when a perpetual inventory system is used.

As of January 5, Mead had only two Elco generators in its inventory, each acquired at a purchase cost of $1,000. Therefore, the average cost is $1,000 per unit. After the purchase on February 5, Mead had five Elco generators in inventory, acquired at a total cost of $5,600 (2 units @ $1,000, plus 3 units @ $1,200 = $5,600). Therefore, the *average* per-unit cost now is *$1,120* ($5,600 ÷ 5 units = $1,120).

On March 1, two entries are made to record the sale of one of these generators to Boulder Construction Company. The first recognizes the revenue from this sale, and the second recognizes the cost of the goods sold. These entries follow, with the cost of goods sold measured by the average-cost method:

Cash	1,800	
Sales		1,800
To record the sale of one Elco AC-40 generator.		
Cost of Goods Sold	1,120	
Inventory		1,120
To record the cost of one Elco AC-40 generator sold to Boulder Construction Co. Cost determined by the average-cost method.		

(The entry to recognize the $1,800 in sales revenue is the same, regardless of the inventory method in use. Therefore, we will not repeat this entry in our illustrations of the other cost flow assumptions.)

When the average-cost method is in use, the inventory subsidiary ledger is modified slightly from the format in Exhibit 8–2. Following the sale on March 1, Mead's subsidiary ledger for Elco generators would be modified to show the average unit cost as in Exhibit 8–3.

Exhibit 8–3

INVENTORY SUBSIDIARY LEDGER—AVERAGE-COST BASIS

	Purchased			Sold			Balance		
Date	Units	Unit Cost	Total	Units	Unit Cost	Cost of Goods Sold	Units	Unit Cost	Total
Jan. 5	2	$1,000	$2,000				2	$1,000*	$2,000
Feb. 5	3	1,200	3,600				5	$1,120**	5,600
Mar. 1				1	$1,120	$1,120	4	$1,120	4,480

*$2,000 total cost ÷ 2 units = $1,000.
**$5,600 total cost ÷ 5 units = $1,120.

Notice that the Unit Cost column for purchases still shows actual unit costs—$1,000 and $1,200. The Unit Cost columns relating to sales and to the remaining inventory, however, show the *average unit cost* ($5,600 total ÷ 5 units = $1,120). As all units are valued at this same average cost, the inventory has only one cost layer.

Under the average-cost assumption, all items in inventory are assigned the *same* per-unit cost (the average cost). Hence, it does not matter which units are sold; the cost of goods sold always is based on the current average unit cost. When one generator is sold on March 1, the cost of goods sold is $1,120; if three generators had been sold on this date, the cost of goods sold would have been $3,360 (3 units × $1,120 per unit).

FIRST-IN, FIRST-OUT METHOD

The **first-in, first-out method**, often called *FIFO*, is based on the assumption that the *first merchandise purchased is the first merchandise sold.* Thus the accountant for Mead Electric would assume that the generator sold on March 1 was one of those purchased on *January 5*. The entry to record the cost of goods sold would be:

Cost of Goods Sold	1,000	
Inventory		1,000
To record the cost of one Elco AC-40 generator sold to Boulder Construction Co. Cost determined by the FIFO flow assumption.		

Following this sale, Mead's inventory ledger would appear as shown in Exhibit 8–4.

Exhibit 8–4

INVENTORY SUBSIDIARY LEDGER—FIFO BASIS

	Purchased			Sold			Balance		
Date	**Units**	**Unit Cost**	**Total**	**Units**	**Unit Cost**	**Cost of Goods Sold**	**Units**	**Unit Cost**	**Total**
Jan. 5	2	$1,000	$2,000				2	$1,000	$2,000
Feb. 5	3	1,200	3,600				2	1,000	
							3	1,200	5,600
Mar. 1				1	$1,000	$1,000	1	1,000	
							3	1,200	4,600

Notice that FIFO uses actual purchase costs, rather than an average cost. Thus, if merchandise has been purchased at several different costs, the inventory will include several different cost layers. The cost of goods sold for a given sales transaction also may involve several different cost layers. To illustrate, assume that Mead had sold *four* generators to Boulder Construction, instead of only one. Under the FIFO flow assumption, Mead would assume that it first sold the two generators purchased on January 5 and then two of those purchased on February 5. Thus the total cost of goods sold ($4,400) would include items at *two different unit costs*, as shown here:

2 generators from Jan. 5 purchase @ $1,000	$2,000
2 generators from Feb. 5 purchase @ $1,200	$2,400
Total cost of goods sold (4 units)	$4,400

As the cost of goods sold always is recorded at the oldest available purchase costs, the units remaining in inventory are valued at the more recent acquisition costs.

LAST-IN, FIRST-OUT METHOD

The **last-in, first-out method**, commonly known as *LIFO*, is among the most widely used methods of determining the cost of goods sold and valuing inventory. As the name suggests, the *most recently* purchased merchandise (the last in) is assumed to be sold first. If Mead were using the LIFO method, it would assume that the generator sold on March 1 was one of those acquired on *February 5*, the most recent purchase date. Thus, the cost transferred from inventory to the cost of goods sold would be *$1,200*.

The journal entry to record the cost of goods sold is shown below. The inventory subsidiary ledger record after this entry has been posted is shown in Exhibit 8–5.

Cost of Goods Sold	1,200	
Inventory		1,200
To record the cost of one Elco AC-40 generator sold to Boulder Construction Co. Cost determined by the LIFO flow assumption.		

Exhibit 8–5

INVENTORY SUBSIDIARY LEDGER—LIFO BASIS

	Purchased			Sold			Balance		
Date	Units	Unit Cost	Total	Units	Unit Cost	Cost of Goods Sold	Units	Unit Cost	Total
Jan. 5	2	$1,000	$2,000				2	$1,000	$2,000
Feb. 5	3	1,200	3,600				2	1,000	
							3	1,200	5,600
Mar. 1				1	$1,200	$1,200	2	1,000	
							2	1,200	4,400

Like FIFO, the LIFO method uses actual purchase costs, rather than an average cost. Thus the inventory may have several different cost layers. If a sale includes more units than are included in the most recent cost layer, some of the goods sold are assumed to come from the next most recent layer. For example, if Mead had sold four generators (instead of one) on March 1, the cost of goods sold determined under the LIFO assumption would be $4,600:

3 generators from Feb. 5 purchase @ $1,200	$3,600
1 generator from Jan. 5 purchase @ $1,000	$1,000
Total cost of goods sold (4 units)	$4,600

As LIFO transfers the most recent purchase costs to the cost of goods sold, the goods remaining in inventory are valued at the oldest acquisition costs.

EVALUATION OF THE METHODS

All three of the cost flow assumptions just described are acceptable for use in financial statements and in income tax returns. As we have explained, it is not necessary that the physical flow of merchandise correspond to the cost flow assumption. Different flow assumptions may be used for different types of inventory or for inventories in different geographical locations.

The only requirement for using a flow assumption is that the units to which the assumption is applied should be *homogeneous* in nature—that is, virtually identical to one another. If each unit is unique, such as the sale of portraits by an art studio, only the specific identification method can properly match sales revenue with the cost of goods sold.

Each inventory valuation method has certain advantages and shortcomings. In the final analysis, the selection of inventory valuation methods is a managerial decision. However, the method (or methods) used in financial statements always should be disclosed in notes accompanying the statements.

Specific Identification The specific identification method is best suited to inventories of high-priced, low-volume items. This is the only method that exactly parallels the physical flow of the merchandise. If each item in the inventory is unique, as in the case of valuable paintings, custom jewelry, and most real estate, specific identification is clearly the logical choice.

The specific identification method has an intuitive appeal, because it assigns actual purchase costs to the specific units of merchandise sold or in inventory. However, when the units in inventory are identical (or nearly identical), the specific identification method may produce *misleading results* by implying differences in value that—under current market conditions—do not exist.

As an example, assume that a coal dealer has purchased 100 tons of coal at a cost of $60 per ton. A short time later, the company purchases another 100 tons of the *same grade* of coal—but this time, the cost is $80 per ton. The two purchases are in separate piles; thus it would be possible for the company to use the specific identification method in accounting for sales.

Assume now that the company has an opportunity to sell 10 tons of coal at a retail price of $120 per ton. Does it really matter from which pile this coal is removed? The answer is *no*; the coal is a homogeneous product. Under current market conditions, the coal in each pile is equally valuable. To imply that it is more profitable to sell coal from one pile rather than the other is an argument of questionable logic.

Let us try to make this point in a more personal way: Would you be willing to shovel the more recently purchased coal out of the way so that the customer could get its truck back to the lower-cost coal pile?

Average Cost Identical items will have the same accounting values only under the average-cost method. Assume, for example, that a hardware store sells a given size nail for 65 cents per pound. The hardware store buys the nails in 100-pound quantities at different times at prices ranging from 40 to 50 cents per pound. Several hundred pounds of nails are always on hand, stored in a large bin. The average-cost method properly recognizes that when a customer buys a pound of nails it is not necessary to know exactly which nails the customer selected from the bin in order to measure the cost of goods sold. Therefore, the average-cost method avoids the shortcomings of the specific identification method. It is not necessary to keep track of the specific items sold and of those still in inventory. Also, it is not possible to manipulate income merely by selecting the specific items to be delivered to customers.

A shortcoming of the average-cost method is that changes in current replacement costs of inventory are concealed because these costs are averaged with older costs. Thus neither the valuation of ending inventory nor the cost of goods sold will quickly reflect changes in the current replacement cost of merchandise.

First-In, First-Out The distinguishing characteristic of the FIFO method is that the oldest purchase costs are transferred to the cost of goods sold, while the most recent costs remain in inventory.

Over the past 50 years, we have lived in an inflationary economy, which means that most prices tend to rise over time. When purchase costs are rising, the FIFO method assigns *lower* (older) costs to the cost of goods sold and the higher (more recent) costs to the goods remaining in inventory.

By assigning lower costs to the cost of goods sold, FIFO usually causes a business to report somewhat *higher profits* than would be reported under the other inventory valuation methods. Some companies favor the FIFO method for financial reporting purposes, because their goal is to report the highest net income possible. For income tax purposes, however, reporting more income than necessary results in paying more income taxes than necessary.

Some accountants and decision makers believe that FIFO tends to *overstate* a company's profitability. Revenue is based on current market conditions. By offsetting this revenue with a cost of goods sold based on older (and lower) prices, gross profits may be overstated consistently.

A conceptual advantage of the FIFO method is that in the balance sheet inventory is valued at recent purchase costs. Therefore, this asset appears in the balance sheet at an amount closely approximating its current replacement cost.

Last-In, First-Out The LIFO method is one of the most interesting and controversial flow assumptions. The basic assumption in the LIFO method is that the most recently purchased units are sold first and that the older units remain in inventory. This assumption is *not* in accord with the physical flow of merchandise in most businesses. Yet there are strong logical arguments in support of the LIFO method, in addition to income tax considerations.

For the purpose of measuring income, most accountants consider the *flow of costs* more important than the physical flow of merchandise. Supporters of the LIFO method contend that the measurement of income should be based on *current market conditions*. Therefore, current sales revenue should be offset by the *current* cost of the merchandise sold. By the LIFO method, the costs assigned to the cost of goods sold are relatively current because they reflect the most recent purchases. By the FIFO method, on the other hand, the cost of goods sold is based on older costs.

There is one significant shortcoming to the LIFO method. The valuation of the asset inventory is based on the company's oldest inventory acquisition costs. After the company has been in business for many years, these oldest costs may greatly understate the current replacement cost of the inventory. Thus, when an inventory is valued by the LIFO method, the company also should disclose the current replacement cost of the inventory in a note to the financial statements.

During periods of rising inventory replacement costs, the LIFO method results in the lowest valuation of inventory and measurement of net income. Therefore, LIFO is regarded as the most *conservative* of the inventory pricing methods. FIFO, on the other hand, is the least conservative method.[3]

Income tax considerations are the principal strategic reason for the popularity of the LIFO method. Remember that the LIFO method assigns the most recent inventory purchase costs to the cost of goods sold. In the common situation of rising prices, these most recent costs are also the highest costs. By reporting a higher cost of goods sold than results from other inventory valuation methods, the LIFO method usually results in *lower taxable income.* In short, if inventory costs are rising, a company can reduce the amount of its income tax obligation by using the LIFO method in its income tax return.

It may seem reasonable that a company would use the LIFO method in its tax return to reduce taxable income and use the FIFO method in its financial statements to increase the amount of net income reported to investors and creditors. However, income tax regulations allow a corporation to use LIFO in its income tax return *only* if the company also uses LIFO in its financial statements. Thus income tax considerations often provide the overriding strategic reason for selecting the LIFO method.

DO INVENTORY METHODS REALLY AFFECT PERFORMANCE?

Except for their effects on income taxes, the answer to this question is *no*.

During a period of rising prices, a company might *report* higher profits by using FIFO instead of LIFO. But the company would not really *be* any more profitable. An inventory valuation method affects only the *allocation of costs* between the Inventory account and the Cost of Goods Sold account. It has *no effect* on the total costs actually *incurred* in purchasing or manufacturing inventory. Except for income taxes, differences in the profitability reported under different inventory methods exist "only on paper."

The inventory method in use *does* affect the amount of income taxes owed. To the extent that an inventory method reduces these taxes, it *does* increase profitability. In Exhibit 8–6 we summarize characteristics of the basic inventory valuation methods.

THE PRINCIPLE OF CONSISTENCY

The principle of **consistency** is one of the basic concepts underlying reliable financial statements. This principle means that, once a company has adopted a particular accounting method, it should *follow that method consistently*, rather than switch methods from one year to the next. Thus, once a company has adopted a particular inventory flow assumption (or the specific identification method), it should continue to apply that assumption to all sales of that type of merchandise.

The principle of consistency does *not* prohibit a company from *ever* changing its accounting methods. If a change is made, however, the reasons for the change must be explained, and the effects of the change on the company's net income must be fully disclosed.[4]

JUST-IN-TIME (JIT) INVENTORY SYSTEMS

In recent years, much attention has been paid to the **just-in-time (JIT) inventory system** in manufacturing operations. The phrase "just-in-time" usually means that purchases of raw materials

[3] During a prolonged period of *declining* inventory replacement costs, this situation reverses: FIFO becomes the most conservative method, and LIFO the least conservative.

[4] Disclosure of the effects of such "accounting changes" is discussed in Chapter 11. A change in the method of pricing inventory for tax purposes requires the approval of the Internal Revenue Service.

Exhibit 8–6 SUMMARY OF INVENTORY VALUATION METHODS

	Costs Allocated to:		
Valuation Method	**Cost of Goods Sold**	**Inventory**	**Comments**
Specific identification	Actual costs of the units sold	Actual cost of units remaining	• Parallels physical flow • Logical method when units are unique • May be misleading when the units are identical
Flow assumptions (acceptable only for an inventory of *homogeneous units*):			
Average cost	Number of units sold times the *average unit cost*	Number of units on hand times the *average unit cost*	• Assigns all units the same *average unit cost* • Current costs are averaged in with older costs
First-in, first-out (FIFO)	Costs of *earliest purchases* on hand at the time of the sale (first-in, first-out)	Cost of *most recently* purchased units	• Cost of goods sold is based on older costs • Inventory valued at most recent costs • May overstate income during periods of rising prices; may increase income taxes due
Last-in, first-out (LIFO)	Cost of *most recently purchased* units (last-in, first-out)	Costs of *earliest* purchases (assumed *still* to be in inventory)	• Cost of goods sold shown at most recent prices • Inventory shown at old (and perhaps out-of-date) costs • Most conservative method during periods of rising prices; often results in lower income taxes due

and component parts arrive just in time for use in the manufacturing process—often within a few hours of the time they are scheduled for use. A second application of the just-in-time concept is completing the manufacturing process just in time to ship the finished goods to customers.

Although a just-in-time system reduces the size of a company's inventories, it does not eliminate them entirely. The February 3, 2006, balance sheet of **Dell Computer Corporation**, for example, shows inventories of *$576 million* (**Dell** reports its inventories by the FIFO method).

CASE IN POINT

Courtesy of Dell Inc.

Dell Computer Corporation generates millions in revenue each day by selling computers on the Internet. The company has long been a model of just-in-time manufacturing. **Dell** doesn't start ordering components or assembling computers until an order has been booked. Most of its suppliers keep components warehoused just minutes from **Dell**'s factories. The JIT philosophy applies to suppliers, assemblers, and distributors. A customer order placed Monday morning can be on a delivery truck by Tuesday evening.

The concept of minimizing inventories applies more to manufacturing operations than to retailers. Ideally, manufacturers have buyers "lined up" for their merchandise even before the goods are produced. Many retailers, in contrast, want to offer their customers a large selection of in-stock merchandise—which means a big inventory.

The just-in-time concept actually involves much more than minimizing the size of inventories. It has been described as the philosophy of constantly working to increase efficiency throughout the organization. One basic goal of an accounting system is to provide management with useful information about the efficiency—or inefficiency—of operations.

Taking a Physical Inventory

Explain the need for taking a physical inventory. LO2

In Chapter 6 we explained the need for businesses to make a complete physical count of the merchandise on hand at least once a year. The primary reason for this procedure of "taking inventory" is to adjust the perpetual inventory records for unrecorded **shrinkage losses**, such as theft, spoilage, or breakage.

The **physical inventory** usually is taken at (or near) the end of the company's fiscal year.[5] Often a business selects a fiscal year ending after a period of high activity. For example, many large retailers use a fiscal year that starts February 1 and ends January 31.

RECORDING SHRINKAGE LOSSES

Record shrinkage losses and other year-end adjustments to inventory. 

In most cases, the year-end physical count of the inventory reveals some shortages or damaged merchandise. The costs of missing or damaged units are removed from the inventory records using the same flow assumption as is used in recording the costs of goods sold.

To illustrate, assume that a company's inventory subsidiary ledger shows the following 158 units of a particular product in inventory at year-end:

8 units purchased Nov. 2 @ $100	$ 800
150 units purchased Dec. 10 @ $115	17,250
Total (158 units)	$18,050

A year-end physical count, however, discloses that only *148* of these units actually are on hand. Based on this physical count, the company should adjust its inventory records to reflect the loss of 10 units.

The inventory flow assumption in use affects the measurement of shrinkage losses in the same way it affects the cost of goods sold. If the company uses *FIFO*, for example, the missing units will be valued at the oldest purchase costs shown in the inventory records. Thus 8 of the missing units will be assumed to have cost $100 per unit and the other 2, $115 per unit. Under FIFO, the shrinkage loss amounts to *$1,030* (8 units @ $100 + 2 units @ $115). But if this company uses *LIFO*, the missing units all will be assumed to have come from the most recent purchase (on December 10). Therefore, the shrinkage loss amounts to *$1,150* (10 units @ $115).

If shrinkage losses are small, the costs removed from inventory may be charged (debited) directly to the Cost of Goods Sold account. If these losses are *material* in amount, the offsetting debit should be entered in a special loss account, such as Inventory Shrinkage Losses. In the income statement, a loss account is deducted from revenue in the same manner as an expense account.

LCM AND OTHER WRITE-DOWNS OF INVENTORY

In addition to shrinkage losses, the value of inventory may decline because the merchandise has become obsolete or is unsalable for other reasons. If inventory has become obsolete or is otherwise unsalable, its carrying value in the accounting records should be *written down*

[5] The reason for taking a physical inventory near year-end is to ensure that any shrinkage losses are reflected in the annual financial statements. The stronger the company's system of internal control over inventories, the farther away this procedure may be moved from the balance sheet date. Obviously, no one wants to spend New Year's Eve counting inventory.

to zero (or to its "scrap value," if any). A **write-down** of inventory reduces both the carrying amount of the inventory in the balance sheet and the net income of the current period. The reduction in income is handled in the same manner as a shrinkage loss. If the write-down is relatively small, the loss is debited directly to the Cost of Goods Sold account. If the write-down is *material in amount*, however, it is charged to a special loss account, perhaps entitled Loss from Write-Down of Inventory.

The Lower-of-Cost-or-Market (LCM) Rule An asset is an economic resource. It may be argued that no economic resource is worth more than it would cost to *replace* that resource in the open market. For this reason, accountants traditionally have valued inventory in the balance sheet at the lower of its (1) cost or (2) market value. In this context, "market value" means *current replacement cost.* Thus the inventory is valued at the lower of its historical cost or its current replacement cost. This accounting convention is referred to as the **lower-of-cost-or-market (LCM) rule**.

The LCM rule can be used in conjunction with any cost flow assumption. It may also be applied on the basis of individual inventory items, major inventory categories, or the entire inventory. To illustrate, assume that Joel's Ski Shop uses the FIFO cost flow assumption. The store sells various lines of merchandise with costs and market values shown in Exhibit 8–7.

Exhibit 8–7

APPLYING THE LCM RULE BY INDIVIDUAL ITEM, BY CATEGORY, AND BY TOTAL INVENTORY

			LCM Applied on the Basis of . . .		
	FIFO Cost	Market Value	Individual Items	Inventory Category	Total Inventory
Ski equipment					
Downhill skis	$16,000	$18,000	$16,000		
Cross-country skis	4,000	3,000	3,000		
Total ski equipment	$20,000	$21,000		$20,000	
Ski accessories					
Ski boots	$ 2,400	$ 1,500	1,500		
Ski jackets	6,600	6,000	6,000		
Total ski accessories	$ 9,000	$ 7,500		7,500	
Total inventory	$29,000	$28,500	**$26,500**	**$27,500**	**$28,500**

Measured at its FIFO cost, the inventory of Joel's Ski Shop is currently recorded at $29,000 in the general ledger. If management applies the LCM rule on the basis of *individual items*, the inventory must be written down to its market value of $26,500. This is accomplished by crediting the Merchandise Inventory account for $2,500 ($29,000 − $26,500). The offsetting debit is charged to either the Cost of Goods Sold or to the Loss from Write-Down of Inventory account, depending on the materiality of the dollar amount.

If management applies the LCM rule on the basis of *inventory category*, it would write down the $29,000 FIFO cost by $1,500 ($29,000 − $27,500). Likewise, if the LCM rule is applied on the basis of *total inventory*, a write-down of only $500 is required ($29,000 − $28,500).

In their financial statements, most companies state that inventory is valued at the lower-of-cost-or-market. In an inflationary economy, however, the lower of these two amounts is usually cost, especially for companies using LIFO.[6]

THE YEAR-END CUTOFF OF TRANSACTIONS

Making a proper *cutoff* of transactions is an essential step in the preparation of reliable financial statements. A proper cutoff simply means that the transactions occurring near year-end are *recorded in the correct accounting period.*

[6] A notable exception is the petroleum industry, in which the replacement cost of inventory can fluctuate very quickly and in either direction. Large oil companies occasionally report LCM adjustments of several hundred million dollars in a single year.

One aspect of a proper cutoff is determining that all purchases of merchandise through the end of the period are recorded in the inventory records and included in the physical count of merchandise on hand at year-end. Of equal importance is determining that the cost of all merchandise sold through the end of the period has been removed from the inventory accounts and charged to the Cost of Goods Sold. This merchandise should *not* be included in the year-end physical count.

If some sales transactions have not been recorded as of year-end, the quantities of merchandise shown in the inventory records will exceed the quantities actually on hand. When the results of the physical count are compared with the inventory records, these unrecorded sales easily could be mistaken for inventory shortages.

Making a proper cutoff may be difficult if sales transactions are occurring while the merchandise is being counted. For this reason, many businesses count their physical inventory during nonbusiness hours, even if they must shut down their sales operations for a day.

Matching Revenue and the Cost of Goods Sold Accountants must determine that both the sales revenue and the cost of goods sold relating to sales transactions occurring near year-end are recorded in the *same* accounting period. Otherwise, the revenues and expenses from these transactions will not be properly matched in the company's income statements.

Goods in Transit A sale should be recorded *when title to the merchandise passes to the buyer.* In making a year-end cutoff of transactions, questions may arise when goods are in transit between the seller and the buyer as to which company owns the merchandise. The answer to such questions lies in the terms of shipment. If these terms are **F.O.B.** (free on board) **shipping point**, title passes at the point of shipment and the goods are the property of the buyer while in transit. If the terms of the shipment are **F.O.B. destination**, title does not pass until the shipment reaches its destination and the goods belong to the seller while in transit.

Many companies ignore these distinctions, because goods in transit usually arrive within a day or two. In such cases, the amount of merchandise in transit usually is *not material* in dollar amount, and the company may follow the *most convenient* accounting procedures. It usually is most convenient to record all purchases when the inbound shipments arrive and all sales when the merchandise is shipped to the customer.

In some industries, however, goods in transit may be very material. Oil companies, for example, often have millions of dollars of inventory in transit in pipelines and supertankers. In these situations, the company must consider the terms of each shipment in recording its purchases and sales.

YOUR TURN **You as a Sales Manager**

As sales manager for Tempto Co., a producer of fine home furnishings, you have responsibility for the northeast region of the country. Assume you have just returned from the company's annual sales managers' conference in New Orleans. At the conference, while strolling with some of the regional managers in the French Quarter, you became aware that several managers report sales that are scheduled for shipment in early January as if they were shipped in late December. What should you do?

(See our comments on the Online Learning Center Web site.)

PERIODIC INVENTORY SYSTEMS

In a periodic inventory system, determine the ending inventory and the cost of goods sold using (a) specific identification, (b) average cost, (c) FIFO, and (d) LIFO.

In our preceding discussions, we have emphasized the perpetual inventory system—that is, inventory records that are kept continuously up-to-date. Virtually all large business organizations use perpetual inventory systems.

Some small businesses, however, use *periodic* inventory systems. In a periodic inventory system, the cost of merchandise purchased during the year is debited to a *Purchases* account, rather than to the Inventory account. When merchandise is sold to a customer, an entry is made recognizing the sales revenue, but no entry is made to reduce the inventory account or to recognize the cost of goods sold.

The inventory on hand and the cost of goods sold for the year are not determined until year-end. At the end of the year, all goods on hand are counted and priced at cost. The cost assigned to this ending inventory is then used to compute the cost of goods sold. (The dollar amounts are assumed for the purpose of completing this illustration.)

Inventory at the beginning of the year	$10,000
Add: Purchases during the year	80,000
Cost of goods available for sale during the year	$90,000
Less: Inventory at the end of the year	7,000
Cost of goods sold	$83,000

The only item in this computation that is kept continuously up-to-date in the accounting records is the Purchases account. The amounts of inventory at the beginning and end of the year are determined by annual physical observation.

Determining the cost of the year-end inventory involves two distinct steps: counting the merchandise and pricing the inventory—that is, determining the cost of the units on hand. Together, these procedures determine the proper valuation of inventory and the cost of goods sold.

Applying Flow Assumptions in a Periodic System

In our discussion of perpetual inventory systems, we have emphasized the costs that are transferred from inventory *to the cost of goods sold* as the sales occur. In a periodic system, the emphasis shifts to determining the costs that should be assigned *to inventory* at the end of the period.

To illustrate, assume that The Kitchen Counter, a retail store, uses a periodic inventory system. The year-end physical inventory indicates that 12 units of a particular model food processor are on hand. Purchases of these food processors during the year are listed in Exhibit 8–8.

Exhibit 8–8
SUMMARY OF INVENTORY PURCHASES

	Number of Units	Cost per Unit	Total Cost
Beginning inventory	10	$ 80	$ 800
First purchase (Mar. 1)	5	90	450
Second purchase (July 1)	5	100	500
Third purchase (Oct. 1)	5	120	600
Fourth purchase (Dec. 1)	5	130	650
Available for sale	30		$3,000
Units in ending inventory	12		
Units sold	18		

In Exhibit 8–8, note that of the 30 food processors available for sale in the course of the year, 12 are still on hand. Thus 18 of these food processors apparently were sold.[7] We will now use these data to determine the cost of the year-end inventory and the cost of goods sold using the specific identification method and the average-cost, FIFO, and LIFO flow assumptions.

Specific Identification

If specific identification is used, the company must identify the 12 food processors on hand at year-end and determine their actual costs from purchase invoices. Assume that these 12 units have an actual total cost of $1,240. The cost of goods

[7] The periodic inventory method does not distinguish between merchandise sold and shrinkage losses. Shrinkage losses are included automatically in the cost of goods sold.

sold then is determined by subtracting this ending inventory from the cost of goods available for sale as shown below:

Cost of goods available for sale	$3,000
Less: Ending inventory (specific identification)	1,240
Cost of goods sold	$1,760

Average Cost The average cost is determined by dividing the total cost of goods available for sale during the year by the total number of units available for sale. Thus the average per-unit cost is *$100* ($3,000 ÷ 30 units). Under the average-cost method, the ending inventory would be priced at $1,200 (12 units × $100 per unit), and the cost of goods sold would be *$1,800* ($3,000 cost of goods available for sale, less $1,200 in costs assigned to the ending inventory).

FIFO Under the FIFO flow assumption, the oldest units are assumed to be the first sold. The ending inventory, therefore, is assumed to consist of the *most recently* acquired goods. (Remember, we are now talking about the goods *remaining in inventory*, not the goods sold.) Thus the inventory of 12 food processors would be valued at the following costs:
The cost of goods sold would be *$1,550* ($3,000 − $1,450).

5 units from the Dec. 1 purchase @ $130	$ 650
5 units from the Oct. 1 purchase @ $120	600
2 units from the July 1 purchase @ $100	200
Ending inventory, 12 units at FIFO cost	$1,450

Notice that the FIFO method results in an inventory valued at relatively recent purchase costs. The cost of goods sold, however, is based on the older acquisition costs.

LIFO Under LIFO, the last units purchased are considered to be the first goods sold. Therefore, the ending inventory is assumed to contain the *earliest* purchases. The 12 food processors in inventory would be valued as:
The cost of goods sold under the LIFO method is *$2,020* ($3,000 − $980).

10 units from the beginning inventory @ $80	$800
2 units from the Mar. 1 purchase @ $90	180
Ending inventory, 12 units at LIFO cost	$980

Notice that the cost of goods sold under LIFO is *higher* than that determined by the FIFO method ($2,020 under LIFO, as compared with $1,550 under FIFO). LIFO always results in a higher cost of goods sold when purchase costs are rising. Thus LIFO tends to minimize reported net income and income taxes during periods of rising prices in both perpetual and periodic systems.

Notice also that the LIFO method may result in an ending inventory that is priced *well below* its current replacement cost. In this illustration, ending inventory is determined at $80 and $90 per unit, but the most recent purchase price is $130 per unit.

CASE IN POINT

Although FIFO techniques are allowed for financial reporting in nearly all countries, LIFO is more controversial in international settings. In 2003, International Accounting Standard no. 2 was revised to prohibit LIFO because it leads to outdated inventory numbers in the balance sheet. Thus, to make inventory amounts between U.S. companies using LIFO and non–U.S. companies using FIFO (or weighted-average methods) comparable, a financial analyst must revalue inventory numbers.

Receiving the Maximum Tax Benefit from the LIFO Method Many companies that use LIFO in a perpetual inventory system *restate* their year-end inventory at the costs indicated by the *periodic* LIFO costing procedures illustrated above. This restatement is accomplished by either debiting or crediting the Inventory account and making an offsetting entry to the Cost of Goods Sold account.

Often, restating ending inventory using periodic costing procedures results in older (and lower) unit costs than those shown in the perpetual inventory records. By assigning less cost to the ending inventory, it follows that more of these costs will be assigned to the cost of goods sold. A higher cost of goods sold, in turn, means less taxable income.

Let us briefly explain why applying LIFO on a periodic basis at year-end may result in a lower valuation of inventory than does applying LIFO on a perpetual basis. Consider the last purchase in our example. This purchase of five food processors was made on December 1, at the relatively high unit cost of $130. Assuming that no additional units were sold in December, they would be included in the year-end inventory in perpetual inventory records, even if these records were maintained on a LIFO basis. When the ending inventory is priced using "periodic LIFO," however, a last-minute purchase is *not* included in inventory, but rather is transferred to the income statement as part of cost of goods sold.

Both the LIFO and average-cost methods produce different valuations of inventory under perpetual and periodic costing procedures. Only companies using LIFO, however, usually adjust their perpetual records to indicate the unit costs determined by periodic costing procedures. When FIFO is in use, the perpetual and periodic costing procedures result in exactly the same valuation of inventory.

Pricing the Year-End Inventory by Computer If purchase records are maintained by computer, as is now the case for most companies, the value of the ending inventory can be computed automatically using any of the flow assumptions that have been discussed. Only the number of units must be entered at year-end. A computer also can apply the specific identification method, but the system requires an identification number for each unit in the ending inventory. This is one reason why the specific identification method usually is not used for inventories consisting of a large number of low-cost items.

IMPORTANCE OF AN ACCURATE VALUATION OF INVENTORY

The most important liquid assets in the balance sheets of most companies are cash, accounts receivable, and inventory. Of these assets, inventory often is the largest. It also is the only one of these assets for which alternative valuation methods are considered acceptable.

Because of the relatively large size of inventory, and because many different products may be stored in different locations, an error in inventory valuation may not be readily apparent. Even a small error in the valuation of inventory may have a material effect on net income. Therefore, care must be taken in counting and pricing the inventory at year-end.

An error in the valuation of inventory will affect several balance sheet measurements, including assets and total owners' equity. It also will affect key figures in the *income statement*, including the cost of goods sold, gross profit, and net income. And remember that the ending inventory of one year is the beginning inventory of the next. Thus an error in inventory valuation will *carry over* into the financial statements of the following year.

Effects of an Error in Valuing Ending Inventory To illustrate, assume that some items of merchandise in a company's inventory are overlooked during the year-end physical count. As a result of this error, the ending inventory will be *understated.* The costs of the uncounted merchandise erroneously will be transferred out of the Inventory account and included in the cost of goods sold. This overstatement of the cost of goods sold, in turn, results in an understatement of gross profit and net income.[8]

[8] If income tax effects are ignored, the amount of the error is exactly the same in inventory, gross profit, and net income. If tax effects are considered, the amount of the error may be lessened in the net income figure.

Inventory Errors Affect Two Years An error in the valuation of ending inventory affects not only the financial statements of the current year but also the income statement for the *following* year.

Explain the effects on the income statement of errors in inventory valuation. LO5

Assume that the ending inventory in 2006 is *understated* by $10,000. As we have described above, the cost of goods sold in 2006 is also overstated by this amount, and both gross profit and net income are *understated.*

The ending inventory in 2006, however, becomes the *beginning inventory* in 2007. An understatement of the beginning inventory results in an understatement of the cost of goods sold and, therefore, an *overstatement* of gross profit and net income in 2007.

Notice that the original error has exactly the *opposite effects* on the net incomes of the two successive years. Net income was *understated* by the amount of the error in 2006 and *overstated* by the same amount in 2007. For this reason, inventory errors are said to be "counterbalancing" or "self-correcting" over a two-year period.

The fact that offsetting errors occur in the financial statements of two successive years does not lessen the consequences of errors in inventory valuation. Rather, it *exaggerates* the misleading effects of the error on *trends* in the company's performance from one year to the next.

Effects of Errors in Inventory Valuation: A Summary In Exhibit 8–9 we summarize the effects of an error in the valuation of ending inventory over two successive years. In this table we indicate the effects of the error on various financial statement measurements using the code letters **U** (understated), **O** (overstated), and **NE** (no effect). The effects of errors in the valuation of inventory are the same regardless of whether the company uses a perpetual or a periodic inventory system. The **NE** for owners' equity at year-end in the Following Year column results from the offsetting of the first-year error in the second year.

Exhibit 8–9

EFFECTS OF INVENTORY ERRORS

Original Error: Ending Inventory Understated	Year of the Error	Following Year
Beginning inventory	NE	U
Cost of goods available for sale	NE	U
Ending inventory	U	NE
Cost of goods sold	O	U
Gross profit	U	O
Net income	U	O
Owners' equity at year-end	U	NE

Original Error: Ending Inventory Overstated	Year of the Error	Following Year
Beginning inventory	NE	O
Cost of goods available for sale	NE	O
Ending inventory	O	NE
Cost of goods sold	U	O
Gross profit	O	U
Net income	O	U
Owners' equity at year-end	O	NE

TECHNIQUES FOR ESTIMATING THE COST OF GOODS SOLD AND THE ENDING INVENTORY

Taking a physical inventory every month would be very expensive and time-consuming. Therefore, if a business using a periodic inventory system prepares monthly or quarterly financial statements, it usually *estimates* the amounts of its inventory and cost of goods sold.

One approach to making these estimates is called the gross profit method; another—used primarily by retail stores—is the retail method.

THE GROSS PROFIT METHOD

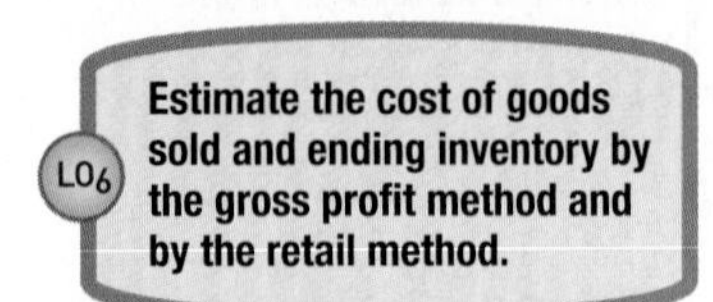

The **gross profit method** is a quick and simple technique for estimating the cost of goods sold and the amount of inventory on hand. In using this method, it is assumed that the rate of gross profit earned in the preceding year (or several years) will remain the same for the current year. When we know the rate of gross profit, we can divide the dollar amount of net sales into two elements: (1) the gross profit and (2) the cost of goods sold. We view net sales as 100 percent. If the gross profit rate, for example, is 40 percent of net sales, the cost of goods sold must be 60 percent. In other words, the cost of goods sold percentage (or **cost ratio**) is determined by deducting the gross profit rate from 100 percent.

When the gross profit rate is known, the ending inventory can be estimated by the following procedures:

1. Determine the *cost of goods available for sale* from the general ledger records of beginning inventory and net purchases.
2. Estimate the *cost of goods sold* by multiplying the net sales by the cost ratio.
3. Deduct the estimated *cost of goods sold* from the *cost of goods available for sale* to find the estimated ending inventory.

To illustrate, assume that Metro Hardware has a beginning inventory of $50,000 on January 1. During the month of January, net purchases amount to $20,000 and net sales total $30,000. Assume that the company's normal gross profit rate is 40 percent of net sales; it follows that the cost ratio is *60 percent.* Using these facts, the inventory on January 31 may be estimated as:

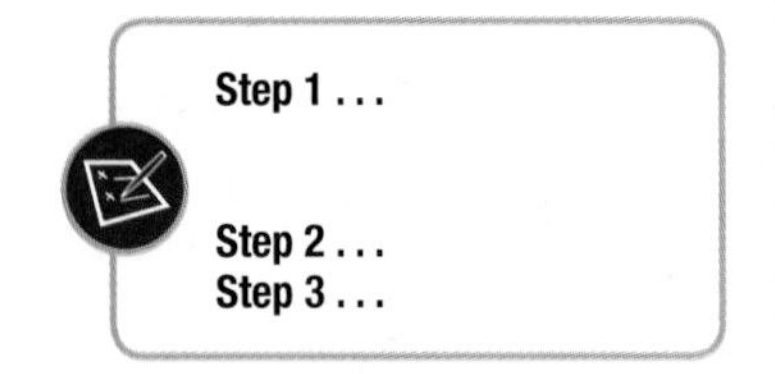

Goods available for sale:		
Beginning inventory, Jan. 1		$50,000
Purchases		20,000
Cost of goods available for sale		$70,000
Deduct: Estimated cost of goods sold:		
Net sales	$30,000	
Cost ratio (100% − 40%)	60%	
Estimated cost of goods sold ($30,000 × 60%)		18,000
Estimated ending inventory, Jan. 31		$52,000

The gross profit method of estimating inventory has several uses apart from the preparation of monthly financial statements. For example, if an inventory is destroyed by fire, the company must estimate the amount of the inventory on hand at the date of the fire to file an insurance claim. The most convenient way to determine this inventory amount may be the gross profit method.

The gross profit method is also used at year-end after the taking of a physical inventory to confirm the overall reasonableness of the amount determined by the counting and pricing process. The gross profit method is not, however, a satisfactory substitute for periodically taking an actual physical inventory.

THE RETAIL METHOD

The **retail method** of estimating inventory and the cost of goods sold is similar to the gross profit method. The basic difference is that the retail method requires that management determine the value of ending inventory at *retail* prices. The retail value of ending inventory is then converted to its approximate cost using a cost ratio.

To determine the cost ratio, a business must keep track of goods available for sale at both cost and at retail prices. To illustrate, assume that Ski Valley had merchandise available for sale costing $450,000 for the year, and that management had offered this merchandise for sale to customers at *retail* prices totaling $1,000,000. Thus Ski Valley's cost ratio for the year was 45 percent ($450,000 ÷ $1,000,000). Ski Valley will use this ratio to convert the retail value of its ending merchandise inventory to its estimated *cost.*

Assume that Ski Valley's employees determined that inventory on hand at the end of the year had a total *retail* value of $300,000. This amount is converted easily to *cost* using the 45 percent cost ratio as follows:

a	Goods available for sale at *cost*	$ 450,000
b	Goods available for sale at *retail*	1,000,000
c	Cost ratio [**a** ÷ **b**]	45%
d	Physical count of ending inventory priced at *retail*	300,000
e	Estimated ending inventory at cost [**c** × **d**]	$ 135,000

This application of the retail method approximates a valuation of ending inventory at its average cost. A widely used variation of this method enables management to estimate a LIFO valuation of ending inventory.

"TEXTBOOK" INVENTORY SYSTEMS CAN BE MODIFIED . . . AND THEY OFTEN ARE

In this chapter we have described the basic characteristics of the most common inventory systems. In practice, businesses often modify these systems to suit their particular needs. Some businesses also use *different inventory systems for different purposes.*

We described one modification in Chapter 6—a company that maintains very little inventory may simply charge (debit) all purchases directly to the cost of goods sold. Another common modification is to maintain perpetual inventory records showing only the *quantities* of merchandise bought and sold, with no dollar amounts. Such systems require less record keeping than a full-blown perpetual system, and they still provide management with useful information about sales and inventories. To generate the dollar amounts needed in financial statements and tax returns, these companies might use the gross profit method, the retail method, or a periodic inventory system.

Businesses such as restaurants often update their inventory records by physically counting products on a daily or weekly basis. In effect, they use frequent periodic counts as the basis for maintaining a perpetual inventory system.

In summary, real-world inventory systems often differ from the illustrations in a textbook. But the underlying principles remain much the same.

Financial Analysis and Decision Making

Inventory often is the largest of a company's current assets. But how liquid is this asset? How quickly will it be converted into cash? As a step toward answering these questions, short-term creditors often compute the **inventory turnover rate**.

Inventory Turnover Rate

LO7 Compute the inventory turnover rate and explain its uses.

The inventory turnover rate is equal to the cost of goods sold divided by the average amount of inventory (beginning inventory plus ending inventory, divided by 2). This ratio indicates how many *times* in the course of a year the company is able to sell the amount of its average inventory. The higher this rate, the more quickly the company sells its inventory.

To illustrate, a recent annual report of **JCPenney** shows a cost of goods sold of $11.17 billion and average inventory of $3.06 billion. The inventory turnover rate for **JCPenney**, therefore, is 3.65 ($11.17 billion ÷ $3.06 billion). We may compute the number of *days* required for the company to sell its inventory by dividing 365 days by the turnover rate. Thus **JCPenney** requires *100 days* to turn over (sell) the amount of its average inventory (365 days ÷ 3.65). The computation of **JCPenney**'s inventory turnover rate and the average number of days required to sell its inventory is summarized as follows:

© McGraw-Hill Companies/Jill Braaten, Photographer/DIL

Inventory Turnover Rate

$$\frac{\text{Cost of Goods Sold}}{\text{Average Inventory*}} = \frac{\$11.17 \text{ billion}}{\$3.06 \text{ billion}} = \underline{\underline{3.65 \text{ times}}}$$

Average Number of Days to Sell Inventory

$$\frac{\text{Days in the Year}}{\text{Inventory Turnover}} = \frac{365 \text{ days}}{3.65 \text{ times}} = \underline{\underline{100 \text{ days}}}$$

*Average Inventory = (Beginning Inventory + Ending Inventory) ÷ 2

Users of financial statements find the inventory turnover rate useful in evaluating the liquidity of the company's inventory. In addition, managers and independent auditors use this computation to help identify inventory that is not selling well and that may have become obsolete. A declining turnover rate indicates that merchandise is not selling as quickly as it used to. Comparing a company's inventory turnover with that of competitors is particularly useful in evaluating how effective a company is at managing its inventory, often one of its largest assets.

YOUR TURN **You as a Credit Analyst**

Assume that you are employed by **GE Capital** as a credit analyst, and that **JCPenney** is seeking to borrow money using its merchandise inventory as collateral. You have determined that the company's inventory turnover rate is 3.65 times, and that the average time to sell its inventory is 100 days (see previous computations). Assume that **JCPenney**'s inventory reported at *cost* is currently $3.2 billion, and that its gross profit as a percentage of sales is approximately 37 percent. Estimate the *market value* of the company's inventory for use as collateral.

(See our comments on the Online Learning Center Web site.)

(*continued*)

Receivables Turnover Rate

Most businesses sell merchandise on account. Therefore, the sale of inventory often does not provide an immediate source of cash. To determine how quickly inventory is converted into cash, the number of days required to *sell the inventory* must be combined with the number of days required to *collect the accounts receivable.*

The number of days required to collect accounts receivable depends on a company's *accounts receivable turnover rate.* This figure is computed by dividing net sales by the average accounts receivable. The number of days required to collect these receivables then is determined by dividing 365 days by the turnover rate. Data for the JCPenney annual report indicate that the company needed approximately *5 days* (on average) for receivables to convert to cash.

Length of the Operating Cycle The *operating cycle* of a merchandising company is the average time period between the purchase of merchandise and the conversion of this merchandise back into cash. In other words, the merchandise acquired as inventory gradually is converted into accounts receivable by sale of the goods on account, and these receivables are converted into cash through the process of collection.

The operating cycle of JCPenney was approximately *105 days*, computed by adding the average *100 days* required to sell its inventory and the *5 days* required to collect cash from customers. From the viewpoint of short-term creditors, the shorter the operating cycle, the higher the quality of the company's liquid assets because they will be converted into cash more quickly.

Accounting Methods Can Affect Financial Ratios

The accounting methods selected by a company may affect the ratios and financial statement subtotals used in evaluating the company's financial position and the results of its operations. To illustrate, let us consider the effects of inventory valuation methods on inventory turnover rates.

Assume that during a period of rising prices Alpha Company uses LIFO, whereas Beta Company uses FIFO. In all other respects, the two companies *are identical*; they have the same size inventories, and they purchase and sell the same quantities of merchandise at the same prices and on the same dates. Thus each company *physically* turns over its inventory at *exactly the same rate.*

Because Alpha uses the LIFO method, however, its inventory is valued at older (and lower) costs than is the inventory of Beta Company. Also, Alpha's cost of goods sold includes more recent (and higher) costs than does Beta's. When these amounts are used in computing the inventory turnover rate (cost of goods sold divided by average inventory), Alpha's rate *appears* to be higher than Beta's.

We already have stated that the physical inventories of these two companies are turning over at exactly the same rate. Therefore, the differences in the turnover rates computed from the companies' financial statements are caused *solely by the different accounting methods used in the valuation of the companies' inventories.*

Inventory turnover is not the only ratio that will be affected. Alpha will report less gross profit and lower net income than Beta.

Users of financial statements must understand the effects of using different accounting methods. Also, a financial analyst should be able to restate on a *comparable basis* the financial statements of companies that use different accounting methods. Notes accompanying the financial statements sometimes provide the information necessary for comparing the operating results of companies using LIFO with those of companies using the FIFO method.

Ethics, Fraud & Corporate Governance

As discussed previously in this chapter, the valuation of inventory and the cost of goods sold is of critical importance to managers and to users of the company's financial statements. Inventory is often a company's largest asset, whereas the cost of goods sold is often a company's largest expense. The two primary issues with regard to inventory valuation are existence and valuation. Existence refers to whether the inventory physically exists. Valuation refers to whether inventory that physically exists is valued (priced) correctly.

In a well-known case of inventory fraud, the Securities and Exchange Commission (SEC) brought an enforcement action against an officer of MiniScribe Corporation related to his involvement in overstating inventory reported in the company's balance sheet. The overstatement of inventory resulted in an understatement of cost of goods sold and an overstatement of profits reported in the company's income statement (MiniScribe's net income was actually inflated by $22 million, or *244 percent*).

Prior to being acquired by Maxtor Corporation, MiniScribe manufactured computer disk drives and its stock was quoted on NASDAQ. The company had discovered a material shortfall in its inventory balance. Reporting this shortfall would have increased the cost of goods sold and reduced the company's net income significantly. So MiniScribe concealed the shortfall from its independent auditors by taking a number of actions to inappropriately overstate its actual inventory balance. First, it recorded a fictitious transfer of nonexistent inventory from its headquarters to an overseas subsidiary. Second, it repackaged scrap items and obsolete inventory as if they were "good" inventory items. Third, in what has got to be one of the most brazen inventory frauds of all time, it packed *bricks* into computer disk drive boxes and shipped them to its distributors (these shipments were still counted as inventory by MiniScribe until the distributors sold the boxes). One can only imagine the surprised look on its customers' faces when they opened a box expecting to find a disk drive and found a brick instead.

Concluding Remarks

Throughout this chapter we have learned about different inventory valuation methods. Each method is based upon a particular assumption about cost flows and does not necessarily parallel the physical movement of merchandise. Moreover, the choice of valuation by management can have significant effects on a company's income statement, balance sheet, and tax returns.

In the following chapter, we will see that a similar situation exists with respect to alternative methods used to account for plant and equipment.

END-OF-CHAPTER REVIEW

SUMMARY OF LEARNING OBJECTIVES

LO1 **In a perpetual inventory system, determine the cost of goods sold using (a) specific identification, (b) average cost, (c) FIFO, and (d) LIFO. Discuss the advantages and shortcomings of each method.** By the *specific identification method*, the actual costs of the specific units sold are transferred from inventory to the cost of goods sold. (Debit Cost of Goods Sold: credit Inventory.) This method achieves the proper matching of sales revenue and cost of goods sold when the individual units in the inventory are unique. However, the method becomes cumbersome and may produce misleading results if the inventory consists of homogeneous items.

The remaining three methods are flow assumptions, which should be applied only to an inventory of homogeneous items.

By the *average-cost method*, the average cost of all units in the inventory is computed and used in recording the cost of goods sold. This is the only method in which all units are assigned the same (average) per-unit cost.

FIFO (first-in, first-out) is the assumption that the first units purchased are the first units sold. Thus inventory is assumed to consist of the most recently purchased units. FIFO assigns current costs to inventory but older (and often lower) costs to the cost of goods sold.

LIFO (last-in, first-out) is the assumption that the most recently acquired goods are sold first. This method matches sales revenue with relatively current costs. In a period of inflation, LIFO usually results in lower reported profits and lower income taxes than the other methods. However, the oldest purchase costs are assigned to inventory, which may result in inventory becoming grossly understated in terms of current replacement costs.

LO2 **Explain the need for taking a physical inventory.** In a perpetual inventory system, a physical inventory is taken to adjust the inventory records for shrinkage losses. In a periodic inventory system, the physical inventory is the basis for determining the cost of the ending inventory and for computing the cost of goods sold.

LO3 **Record shrinkage losses and other year-end adjustments to inventory.** Shrinkage losses are recorded by removing from the Inventory account the cost of the missing or damaged units. The offsetting debit may be to Cost of Goods Sold, if the shrinkage is normal in amount, or to a special loss account. If inventory is found to be obsolete and unlikely to be sold, it is written down to zero (or its scrap value, if any). If inventory is valued at the lower-of-cost-or-market, it is written down to its current replacement cost, if at year-end this amount is substantially below the cost shown in the inventory records.

LO4 **In a periodic inventory system, determine the ending inventory and the cost of goods sold using (a) specific identification, (b) average cost, (c) FIFO, and (d) LIFO.** The cost of goods sold is determined by combining the beginning inventory with the purchases during the period and subtracting the cost of the ending inventory. Thus the cost assigned to ending inventory also determines the cost of goods sold.

By the specific identification method, the ending inventory is determined by the specific costs associated with the units on hand. By the average-cost method, the ending inventory is determined by multiplying the number of units on hand by the average cost of the units available for sale during the year. By FIFO, the units in inventory are priced using the unit costs from the most recent cost layers. By the LIFO method, inventory is priced using the unit costs in the oldest cost layers.

LO5 **Explain the effects on the income statement of errors in inventory valuation.** In the current year, an error in the costs assigned to ending inventory will cause an opposite error in the cost of goods sold and, therefore, a repetition of the original error in the amount of gross profit. For example, understating ending inventory results in an overstatement of the cost of goods sold and an understatement of gross profit.

The error has exactly the opposite effect on the cost of goods sold and the gross profit of the following year, because the error is now in the cost assigned to *beginning* inventory.

LO6 **Estimate the cost of goods sold and ending inventory by the gross profit method and by the retail method.** Both the gross profit and retail methods use a cost ratio to estimate the cost of goods sold and ending inventory. The cost of goods sold is estimated by multiplying net sales by this cost ratio; ending inventory then is estimated by subtracting this cost of goods sold from the cost of goods available for sale.

In the gross profit method, the cost ratio is 100 percent minus the company's historical gross profit rate. In the retail method, the cost ratio is the percentage of cost to the retail prices of merchandise available for sale.

LO7 **Compute the inventory turnover rate and explain its uses.** The inventory turnover rate is equal to the cost of goods sold divided by the average inventory. Users of financial statements find the inventory turnover rate useful in evaluating the liquidity of the company's inventory. In addition, managers and independent auditors use this computation to help identify inventory that is not selling well and that may have become obsolete.

Key Terms Introduced or Emphasized in Chapter 8

average-cost method (p. 350) A method of valuing all units in inventory at the same average per-unit cost, which is recomputed after every purchase.

consistency (in inventory valuation) (p. 355) An accounting principle that calls for the use of the same method of inventory pricing from year to year, with full disclosure of the effects of any change in method. Intended to make financial statements comparable.

cost flow assumption (p. 350) Assumption as to the sequence in which units are removed from inventory for the purpose of sale. Is not required to parallel the physical movement of merchandise if the units are homogeneous.

cost layer (p. 349) Units of merchandise acquired at the same unit cost. An inventory comprised of several cost layers is characteristic of all inventory valuation methods except *average cost.*

cost ratio (p. 364) The cost of merchandise expressed as a percentage of its retail selling price. Used in inventory estimating techniques, such as the gross profit method and the retail method.

first-in, first-out (FIFO) method (p. 351) A method of computing the cost of inventory and the cost of goods sold based on the assumption that the first merchandise acquired is the first merchandise sold and that the ending inventory consists of the most recently acquired goods.

F.O.B. destination (p. 359) A term meaning the seller bears the cost of shipping goods to the buyer's location. Title to the goods remains with the seller while the goods are in transit.

F.O.B. shipping point (p. 359) The buyer of goods bears the cost of transportation from the seller's location to the buyer's location. Title to the goods passes at the point of shipment, and the goods are the property of the buyer while in transit.

gross profit method (p. 364) A method of estimating the cost of the ending inventory based on the assumption that the rate of gross profit remains approximately the same from year to year. Used for interim valuations and for estimating losses.

inventory turnover rate (p. 366) The cost of goods sold divided by the average amount of inventory. Indicates how many times the average inventory is sold during the course of the year.

just-in-time (JIT) inventory system (p. 355) A technique designed to minimize a company's investment in inventory. In a manufacturing company, this means receiving purchases of raw materials just in time for use in the manufacturing process and completing the manufacture of finished goods just in time to fill sales orders. Just-in-time also may be described as the philosophy of constantly striving to become more efficient by purchasing and storing less inventory.

last-in, first-out (LIFO) method (p. 352) A method of computing the cost of goods sold by use of the prices paid for the most recently acquired units. Ending inventory is valued on the basis of prices paid for the units first acquired.

lower-of-cost-or-market (LCM) rule (p. 358) A method of inventory pricing in which goods are valued at original cost or replacement cost (market), whichever is lower.

moving average method (p. 350) A method of valuing all units of inventory at the same average per-unit cost, recalculating this cost after each purchase. This method is used in a perpetual inventory system.

physical inventory (p. 357) A systematic count of all goods on hand, followed by the application of unit prices to the quantities counted and development of a dollar valuation of the ending inventory.

retail method (p. 364) A method of estimating the cost of goods sold and ending inventory. Similar to the gross profit method, except that the cost ratio is based on current cost-to-retail price relationships rather than on those of the prior year.

shrinkage losses (p. 357) Losses of inventory resulting from theft, spoilage, or breakage.

specific identification (p. 350) Recording as the cost of goods sold the actual costs of the specific units sold. Necessary if each unit in inventory is unique, but not if the inventory consists of homogeneous products.

write-down (of an asset) (p. 358) A reduction in the carrying amount of an asset because it has become obsolete or its usefulness has otherwise been impaired. Involves a credit to the appropriate asset account, with an offsetting debit to a loss account.

Demonstration Problem

The Audiophile sells high-performance stereo equipment. Massachusetts Acoustic recently introduced the Carnegie-440, a state-of-the-art speaker system. During the current year, The Audiophile purchased nine of these speaker systems at the following dates and acquisition costs:

Date	Units Purchased	Unit Cost	Total Cost
Oct. 1	2	$3,000	$ 6,000
Nov. 17	3	3,200	9,600
Dec. 1	4	3,250	13,000
Available for sale during the year	9		$28,600

On *November 21*, The Audiophile sold four of these speaker systems to the Boston Symphony. The other five Carnegie-440s remained in inventory at December 31.

Instructions

Assume that The Audiophile uses a *perpetual inventory system*. Compute (1) the cost of goods sold relating to the sale of Carnegie-440 speakers to the Boston Symphony and (2) the ending inventory of these speakers at December 31, using each of the following flow assumptions:

a. Average cost.

b. First-in, first-out (FIFO).

c. Last-in, first-out (LIFO).

Show the number of units and the unit costs of the cost layers comprising the cost of goods sold and the ending inventory.

Solution to the Demonstration Problem

a.	**1.**	Cost of goods sold (at average cost):		
		Average unit cost at Nov. 21 [($6,000 + $9,600) ÷ 5 units]	$ 3,120	
		Cost of goods sold (4 units × $3,120 per unit)		$12,480
	2.	Inventory at Dec. 31 (at average cost):		
		Units remaining after sale of Nov. 21 (1 unit @ $3,120)	$ 3,120	
		Units purchased on Dec. 1 (4 units @ $3,250).	13,000	
		Total cost of 5 units in inventory.	$16,120	
		Average unit cost at Dec. 31 ($16,120 ÷ 5 units)	$ 3,224	
		Inventory at Dec. 31 (5 units × $3,224 per unit)		$16,120
b.	**1.**	Cost of goods sold (FIFO basis):		
		(2 units @ $3,000 + 2 units @ $3,200)		$12,400
	2.	Inventory at Dec. 31 (4 units @ $3,250 + 1 unit @ $3,200)		$16,200
c.	**1.**	Cost of goods sold (LIFO basis):		
		(3 units @ $3,200 + 1 unit @ $3,000).		$12,600
	2.	Inventory at Dec. 31 (4 units @ $3,250 + 1 unit @ $3,000)		$16,000

Self-Test Questions

The answers to these questions appear on page 389.

1. The primary purpose for using an inventory cost flow *assumption* is to:

a. Parallel the physical flow of units of merchandise.

b. Offset against revenue an appropriate cost of goods sold.

c. Minimize income taxes.

d. Maximize the reported amount of net income.

2. Ace Auto Supply uses a perpetual inventory system. On March 10, the company sells two Shelby four-barrel carburetors. Immediately prior to this sale, the perpetual inventory records indicate three of these carburetors on hand, as follows:

Date	Quantity Purchased	Unit Cost	Units on Hand	Total Cost
Feb. 4	1	$220	1	$220
Mar. 2	2	235	3	690

With respect to the sale on March 10: (More than one of the following answers may be correct.)

a. If the average-cost method is used, the cost of goods sold is $460.

b. If these carburetors have identification numbers, Ace must use the specific identification method to determine the cost of goods sold.

c. If the company uses LIFO, the cost of goods sold will be $15 higher than if it were using FIFO.

d. If the company uses LIFO, the carburetor *remaining* in inventory after the sales will be assumed to have cost $220.

3. T-Shirt City uses a *periodic* inventory system. During the first year of operations, the company made four purchases of a particular product. Each purchase was for 500 units and the prices paid were $9 per unit in the first purchase, $10 per unit in the second purchase, $12 per unit in the third purchase, and $13 per unit in the fourth purchase. At year-end, 650 of these units remained unsold. Compute the cost of goods sold under the FIFO method and LIFO method, respectively.

a. $13,700 (FIFO) and $16,000 (LIFO).

b. $8,300 (FIFO) and $6,000 (LIFO).

c. $16,000 (FIFO) and $13,700 (LIFO).

d. $6,000 (FIFO) and $8,300 (LIFO).

4. Trent Department Store uses a perpetual inventory system but adjusts its inventory records at year-end to reflect the results of a complete physical inventory. In the physical inventory taken at the ends of 2006 and 2007, Trent's employees failed to count the merchandise in the store's window displays. The cost of this merchandise amounted to $13,000 at the end of 2006 and $19,000 at the end of 2007. As a result of these errors, the cost of goods sold for 2007 will be:
   a. Understated by $19,000.
   b. Overstated by $6,000.
   c. Understated by $6,000.
   d. None of the above.
5. In July 2007, the accountant for LBJ Imports is in the process of preparing financial statements for the quarter ended June 30, 2007. The physical inventory, however, was last taken on June 5, and the accountant must establish the approximate cost at June 30 from the following data:

Physical inventory, June 5, 2007	$900,000
Transactions for the period June 5–June 30:	
Sales	700,000
Purchases	400,000

   The gross profit on sales has consistently averaged 40 percent of sales. Using the gross profit method, compute the approximate inventory cost at June 30, 2007.
   a. $420,000.
   b. $880,000.
   c. $480,000.
   d. $1,360,000.
6. Allied Products maintains a large inventory. The company has used the LIFO inventory method for many years, during which the purchase costs of its products have risen substantially. (More than one of the following answers may be correct.)
   a. Allied would have reported a *higher* net income in past years if it had been using the average-cost method.
   b. Allied's financial statements imply a *lower* inventory turnover rate than they would if the company were using FIFO.
   c. If Allied were to let its inventory fall far below normal levels, the company's gross profit rate would *decline*.
   d. Allied would have paid more income taxes in past years if it had been using the FIFO method.

ASSIGNMENT MATERIAL Discussion Questions

1. Is the cost of merchandise acquired during the period classified as an asset or an expense? Explain.
2. Briefly describe the advantages of using a cost flow assumption, rather than the specific identification method, to value an inventory.
3. Under what circumstances do generally accepted accounting principles permit the use of an inventory cost flow assumption? Must a cost flow assumption closely parallel the physical movement of the company's merchandise?
4. Assume that a company has in its inventory units of a particular product that were purchased at several different per-unit costs. When some of these units are sold, explain how the cost of goods sold is measured under each of the following cost flow assumptions in a perpetual inventory system:
   a. Average cost
   b. FIFO
   c. LIFO
5. A large art gallery has in inventory more than 100 paintings. No two are alike. The least expensive is priced at more than $1,000 and the higher-priced items carry prices of $100,000 and more. Which of the four methods of inventory valuation discussed in this chapter would you consider to be most appropriate for this business? Give reasons for your answer.
6. During a period of steadily increasing purchase costs, which inventory flow assumption results in the highest reported profits? The lowest taxable income? The valuation of inventory that is closest to current replacement cost? Briefly explain your answers.
7. Assume that during the first year of Hatton Corporation's operation there were numerous purchases of identical items of merchandise. However, there was no change during the year in the prices paid for this merchandise. Under these special circumstances, how would the financial statements be affected by the choice between the FIFO and LIFO methods of inventory valuation?
8. Apex Corporation operates in two locations: New York and Oregon. The LIFO method is used in accounting for inventories at the New York facility and the specific identification method is used for inventories at the Oregon location. Does this concurrent use of two inventory methods indicate that Apex is violating the accounting principle of consistency? Explain.
9. What are the characteristics of a *just-in-time* inventory system? Briefly explain some advantages and risks of this type of system.
10. Why do companies that use perpetual inventory systems also take an annual *physical inventory*? When is this physical inventory usually taken? Why?
11. Under what circumstances might a company write down its inventory to carrying value below cost?
12. What is meant by the year-end *cutoff* of transactions? If merchandise in transit at year-end is material in dollar amount, what determines whether these goods should be included in the inventory of the buyer or the seller? Explain.
13. Briefly explain the operation of a *periodic* inventory system. Include an explanation of how the cost of goods sold is determined.

14. Assume that a *periodic* inventory system is in use. Explain which per-unit acquisition costs are assigned to the year-end inventory under each of the following inventory costing procedures:
    a. The average-cost method.
    b. FIFO.
    c. LIFO.
15. Why do companies using LIFO in a perpetual inventory system often restate their ending inventory at the per-unit costs that result from applying *periodic* LIFO costing procedures?
16. Explain why errors in the valuation of inventory at the end of the year are sometimes called "counterbalancing" or "self-correcting."
17. Briefly explain the *gross profit method* of estimating inventories. In what types of situations is this technique likely to be useful?
18. Estimate the ending inventory by the gross profit method, given the following data: beginning inventory, $40,000; net purchases, $100,000; net sales, $112,000; average gross profit rate, 25 percent of net sales.
19. A store using the *retail inventory method* takes its physical inventory by applying current retail prices as marked on the merchandise to the quantities counted. Does this procedure mean that the inventory will appear in the financial statements at retail selling price? Explain.
20. How is the *inventory turnover rate* computed? Why is this measurement of interest to short-term creditors?
21. Baxter Corporation has been using FIFO during a period of rising costs. Explain whether you would expect each of the following measurements to be higher or lower if the company had been using LIFO.
    a. Net income.
    b. Inventory turnover rate.
    c. Income taxes expense.
22. In anticipation of *declining* inventory replacement costs, the management of Computer Products Co. elects to use the *FIFO* inventory method rather than LIFO. Explain how this decision should affect the company's future:
    a. Rate of gross profit.
    b. Net cash flow from operating activities.
23. Notes to the financial statements of two well-known clothing manufacturers follow:

    J. P. Stevens & Co., Inc.

    Inventories: The inventories are stated at the lower of cost, determined principally by the LIFO method, or market.

    Bobbie Brooks, Incorporated

    Inventories: Inventories are stated at the lower of cost (first-in, first-out method) or market value, assuming a period of rising prices.

    a. Which company is using the more conservative method of pricing its inventories? Explain.
    b. Based on the inventory methods in use in their financial statements, which company is in the better position to minimize the amount of income taxes that it must pay? Explain.
    c. Could either company increase its cash collections from customers or reduce its cash payments to suppliers of merchandise by switching from FIFO to LIFO, or from LIFO to FIFO? Explain.

Brief Exercises

LO1 LO4 **BRIEF EXERCISE 8.1** FIFO Inventory

Smalley, Inc., purchased items of inventory as follows:

Jan. 4 100 units @ $2.00
Jan. 23 120 units @ $2.25

Smalley sold 50 units on January 28. Compute the cost of goods sold for the month under the FIFO inventory method.

LO1 LO4 **BRIEF EXERCISE 8.2** LIFO Inventory

Wasson Company purchased items of inventory as follows:

Dec. 2 50 units @ $20
Dec. 12 12 units @ $21

Wasson sold 15 units on December 20. Determine the cost of goods sold for the month under the LIFO inventory method.

LO4 **BRIEF EXERCISE 8.3** Average-Cost Inventory

Fox Company purchased items of inventory as follows:

May 3 100 units @ $3.05
May 10 150 units @ $3.10
May 15 120 units @ $3.15

By the end of the month of May, Fox had sold 125 units. If the company uses the average-cost method of accounting for inventory, what is the amount of the ending inventory?

BRIEF EXERCISE 8.4
FIFO and LIFO Inventory

Murray, Inc., purchased a new inventory item two times during the month of April, as follows:

Apr. 5 100 units @ $5.00
Apr. 15 100 units @ $5.05

a. What is the amount of the ending inventory of this item on April 30 if the company has sold 75 units and uses the LIFO inventory method?

b. How would this amount differ if the company used the FIFO inventory method?

BRIEF EXERCISE 8.5
FIFO and Average-Cost Inventory

United Co. had 10 units of an inventory item on hand at the beginning of the current year, each of which had a per-unit cost of $10. During the year, 20 additional units were purchased at $11, and 25 units were sold. What is the amount of the ending inventory under the LIFO and the average-cost methods of accounting for inventory?

BRIEF EXERCISE 8.6
Inventory Shrinkage

Wexler Company's inventory is subject to shrinkage via evaporation. At the end of the current financial reporting period, the company's inventory had a cost of $100,000. Management estimates that evaporation has resulted in a 5 percent inventory loss. Assuming that loss is recorded in a separate inventory loss account, prepare the general journal entry to record the inventory shrinkage for the year.

BRIEF EXERCISE 8.7
Inventory Error

Black and Blue, Inc., overlooked $100,000 of inventory at the end of the current year because it was stored temporarily in a warehouse owned by another company. Before discovering this error, the company's income statement showed the following:

Sales	$990,000
Cost of goods sold	(560,000)
Gross profit	$430,000

Restate these figures to reflect the inclusion of the overlooked inventory.

BRIEF EXERCISE 8.8
Inventory Error

Due to ineffective controls while counting its inventory, Walker & Comer, Inc., double-counted $50,000 of inventory at the end of the current year. Before discovering this error, the company's ending inventory was $670,000. How will correction of this error affect the company's inventory and cost of goods sold figures?

BRIEF EXERCISE 8.9
Inventory Turnover

Miller & Miller Company recorded sales, cost of goods sold, and ending inventory for the current year in the following amounts: $650,000, $500,000, and $128,000, respectively. Calculate the amount of the company's inventory turnover for the year. What is the company's average number of days to sell inventory?

BRIEF EXERCISE 8.10
Inventory Turnover

Rouse Incorporated reported sales, cost of sales, and inventory figures for 2006 and 2007 as follows (all dollars in thousands):

	Sales	Cost of Goods Sold	Inventory
2006	$100	$85	$27
2007	110	90	35

What is the amount of inventory turnover for each year, and in which year did Rouse manage its inventory most efficiently?

Exercises

EXERCISE 8.1
Accounting Terminology

LO1 through LO8

Listed below are eight technical accounting terms introduced in this chapter.

Retail method	FIFO method	Lower-of-cost-or-market
Gross profit method	LIFO method	Specific identification
Flow assumption	Average-cost method	

Each of the following statements may (or may not) describe one of these technical terms. For each statement, indicate the term described, or answer "None" if the statement does not correctly describe any of the terms.

a. A pattern of transferring unit costs from the Inventory account to the Cost of Goods Sold that may (or may not) parallel the physical flow of merchandise.

b. The only flow assumption in which all units of merchandise are assigned the same per-unit cost.

c. The method used to record the cost of goods sold when each unit in the inventory is unique.

d. The most conservative of the flow assumptions during a period of sustained inflation.

e. The flow assumption that provides the most current valuation of inventory in the balance sheet.

f. A technique for estimating the cost of goods sold and the ending inventory that is based on the relationship between cost and sales price during the *current* accounting period.

EXERCISE 8.2
Cost Flow Assumptions

On May 10, Hudson Computing sold 90 Millennium laptop computers to Apex Publishers. At the date of this sale, Hudson's perpetual inventory records included the following cost layers for the Millennium laptops:

Purchase Date	Quantity	Unit Cost	Total Cost
Apr. 9	70	$1,500	$105,000
May 1	30	$1,600	48,000
Total on hand	100		$153,000

Prepare journal entries to record the cost of the 90 Millennium laptops sold on May 10, assuming that Hudson Computing uses the:

a. Specific identification method (62 of the units sold were purchased on April 9, and the remaining units were purchased on May 1).

b. Average-cost method.

c. FIFO method.

d. LIFO method.

e. Discuss briefly the financial reporting differences that may arise from choosing the FIFO method over the LIFO method.

EXERCISE 8.3
Physical Flow versus Cost Flow

The Warm-Up Shop sells heating oil, coal, and kerosene fuel to residential customers. Heating oil is kept in large storage tanks that supply the company's fleet of delivery trucks. Coal is kept in huge bins that are loaded and emptied from the top by giant scooping machines. Kerosene is sold "off the shelf" in five-gallon containers at the company's retail outlet. Separate inventory records are maintained for each fuel type.

a. Which of the cost flow assumptions (average-cost, FIFO, or LIFO) best describes the *physical flow* of:

  1. The heating oil inventory? Explain.

  2. The coal inventory? Explain.

  3. The kerosene inventory? Explain.

b. Which of these cost flow assumptions is likely to result in the *lowest* income tax liability for the company? Explain.

c. Explain why management keeps separate inventory records for its heating oil, coal, and kerosene inventories.

EXERCISE 8.4
Effects of Different Flow Assumptions

La-Z-Boy, Inc., is a giant provider of home furnishings. The company uses the FIFO inventory method. The following information was taken from the company's recent financial statements (dollar amounts are in thousands):

Cost of goods sold	$1,753,000
Income before taxes	112,044
Income taxes expense (and payments)	44,818
Net income	67,226
Net cash provided by operating activities	116,009

The financial statements also revealed that had La-Z-Boy been using *LIFO*, its cost of goods sold would have been $1,763,384. The company's income taxes and payments amount to approximately 40 percent of income before taxes.

a. Explain how LIFO can result in a higher cost of goods sold. Would you expect LIFO to result in a greater or lesser valuation of the company's ending inventories? Defend your answer.

b. Assuming that La-Z-Boy had been using *LIFO*, compute the following amounts for the current year. Show your supporting computations, with dollar amounts in thousands.

1. Income before taxes
2. Income taxes expense (which are assumed equal to income taxes actually paid)
3. Net income
4. Net cash provided by operating activities

EXERCISE 8.5
Transfer of Title

Jensen Tire had two large shipments in transit at December 31. One was a $125,000 inbound shipment of merchandise (shipped December 28, F.O.B. shipping point), which arrived at Jensen's receiving dock on January 2. The other shipment was a $95,000 outbound shipment of merchandise to a customer, which was shipped and billed by Jensen on December 30 (terms F.O.B. shipping point) and reached the customer on January 3.

In taking a physical inventory on December 31, Jensen counted all goods on hand and priced the inventory on the basis of average cost. The total amount was $600,000. No goods in transit were included in this figure.

What amount should appear as inventory on the company's balance sheet at December 31? Explain. If you indicate an amount other than $600,000, state which asset or liability other than inventory also would be changed in amount.

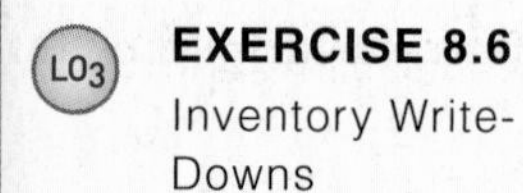

EXERCISE 8.6
Inventory Write-Downs

Late in the year, Software City began carrying WordCrafter, a new word processing software program. At December 31, Software City's perpetual inventory records included the following cost layers in its inventory of WordCrafter programs:

Purchase Date	Quantity	Unit Cost	Total Cost
Nov. 14	8	$400	$3,200
Dec. 12	20	310	6,200
Total available for sale at Dec. 31	28		$9,400

a. At December 31, Software City takes a physical inventory and finds that all 28 units of WordCrafter are on hand. However, the current replacement cost (wholesale price) of this product is only $250 per unit. Prepare the entries to record:

1. This write-down of the inventory to the lower-of-cost-or-market at December 31. (Company policy is to charge LCM adjustments of less than $2,000 to Cost of Goods Sold and larger amounts to a separate loss account.)
2. The cash sale of 15 WordCrafter programs on January 9, at a retail price of $350 each. Assume that Software City uses the FIFO flow assumption.

b. Now assume that the current replacement cost of the WordCrafter programs is $405 each. A physical inventory finds only 25 of these programs on hand at December 31. (For this part, return to the original information and ignore what you did in part **a.**)

1. Prepare the journal entry to record the shrinkage loss assuming that Software City uses the FIFO flow assumption.
2. Prepare the journal entry to record the shrinkage loss assuming that Software City uses the LIFO flow assumption.
3. Which cost flow assumption (FIFO or LIFO) results in the lowest net income for the period? Would using this assumption really mean that the company's operations are less efficient? Explain.

EXERCISE 8.7

Costing Inventory in a Periodic System

Pemberton Products uses a *periodic* inventory system. The company's records show the beginning inventory of PH4 oil filters on January 1 and the purchases of this item during the current year to be as follows:

Jan. 1	Beginning inventory	9 units @ $3.00	$ 27.00
Feb. 23	Purchase	12 units @ $3.50	42.00
Apr. 20	Purchase	30 units @ $3.80	114.00
May 4	Purchase	40 units @ $4.00	160.00
Nov. 30	Purchase	19 units @ $5.00	95.00
	Totals	110 units	$438.00

A physical count indicates 20 units in inventory at year-end.

Determine the cost of the ending inventory, based on each of the following methods of inventory valuation. (Remember to use *periodic* inventory costing procedures.)

a. Average cost

b. FIFO

c. LIFO

d. Which of the above methods (if any) results in the same ending inventory valuation under *both* periodic and perpetual costing procedures? Explain.

EXERCISE 8.8

Effects of Errors in Inventory Valuation

Boswell Electric prepared the following condensed income statements for two successive years:

	2007	2006
Sales	$2,000,000	$1,500,000
Cost of goods sold	1,250,000	900,000
Gross profit on sales	$ 750,000	$ 600,000
Operating expenses	400,000	350,000
Net income	$ 350,000	$ 250,000

At the end of 2006 (right-hand column above), the inventory was understated by $40,000, but the error was not discovered until after the accounts had been closed and financial statements prepared at the end of 2007. The balance sheets for the two years showed owner's equity of $500,000 at the end of 2006 and $580,000 at the end of 2007. (Boswell is organized as a sole proprietorship and does not incur income taxes expense.)

a. Compute the corrected net income figures for 2006 and 2007.

b. Compute the gross profit amounts and the gross profit percentages for each year based on corrected data.

c. What correction, if any, should be made in the amounts of the company's owner's equity at the end of 2006 and at the end of 2007?

EXERCISE 8.9
Estimating Inventory by the Gross Profit Method

When Laura Rapp arrived at her store on the morning of January 29, she found empty shelves and display racks; thieves had broken in during the night and stolen the entire inventory. Rapp's accounting records showed that she had inventory costing $50,000 on January 1. From January 1 to January 29, she had made net sales of $70,000 and net purchases of $80,000. The gross profit during the past several years had consistently averaged 45 percent of net sales. Rapp wishes to file an insurance claim for the theft loss.

a. Using the gross profit method, estimate the cost of Rapp's inventory at the time of the theft.

b. Does Rapp use the periodic inventory method or does she account for inventory using the perpetual method? Defend your answer.

EXERCISE 8.10
Estimating Inventory by the Retail Method

Phillips Supply uses a periodic inventory system but needs to determine the approximate amount of inventory at the end of each month without taking a physical inventory. Phillips has provided the following inventory data:

	Cost Price	Retail Selling Price
Inventory of merchandise, June 30	$300,000	$500,000
Purchases during July	222,000	400,000
Goods available for sale during July	$522,000	$900,000
Net sales during July		$600,000

a. Estimate the cost of goods sold and the cost of the July 31 ending inventory using the retail method of evaluation.

b. Was the cost of Phillips's inventory, as a percentage of retail selling prices, higher or lower in July than it was in June? Explain.

EXERCISE 8.11
Evaluating Cost Flow Assumptions

A note to a recent annual report issued by **General Motors Corporation** includes the following information:

> Inventories are valued using various cost methods. The percentage of year-end inventories valued using each of these methods is:
>
> | | |
> |---|---|
> | LIFO | 84% |
> | FIFO and Average Cost | 16% |
>
> If the LIFO method of valuation had not been used, total inventories would have been $1.8 billion *more* than reported.

a. Does the company's use of three different inventory methods violate the accounting principle of consistency? Defend your answer.

b. Had the LIFO assumption *not* been used, would the company's gross profit reported in its income statement have been higher or lower? Explain.

c. Based on the information from the company's annual report, do its inventory replacement costs appear to be rising or falling? Explain.

EXERCISE 8.12
FIFO versus LIFO: A Challenging Analysis

Ford Motor Company uses LIFO to account for all of its domestic inventories. A note to the company's recent financial statements reads in part:

> If the FIFO method had been used instead of the LIFO method, inventories would have been higher by $1.1 billion.

a. Indicate whether each of the following financial measurements would have been *higher, lower*, or *unaffected* had Ford Motor Company used FIFO instead of LIFO. Explain the reasoning behind your answers.

1. Gross profit rate.
2. Reported net income.
3. Current ratio (Ford's current ratio is greater than 1 to 1).
4. Inventory turnover rate.
5. Accounts receivable turnover rate.
6. Cash payments made to suppliers.
7. Net cash flow from operations (Ford's operating cash flows are positive).

b. Provide *your own* assessment of whether using LIFO has made Ford Motor Company more or less (1) liquid and (2) well-off. Defend your answers.

EXERCISE 8.13
Inventory Turnover Rate

A recent annual report of Gateway, Inc., reveals the following information (dollar amounts are stated in millions):

Cost of goods sold	$7,542
Inventory (beginning of year)	193
Inventory (end of year)	315
Average time required to collect accounts receivable	22 days

a. Compute Gateway's inventory turnover rate for the year (round to nearest tenth).

b. Compute the number of days required by Gateway to sell its average inventory (round to the nearest day).

c. What is the length of Gateway's *operating cycle*?

d. Gateway's inventory turnover rate is much higher than the inventory turnover of a retail computer business such as CompUSA. Explain why.

EXERCISE 8.14
Inventory Analysis

A recent balance sheet of Wal-Mart reports sales of $285,222 million and cost of goods sold of $219,793 million for the year ended January 31, 2005. The comparable sales and cost of goods sold figures for the year ended one year earlier were $256,329 million and $198,747 million, respectively. As you would expect, to be able to achieve this high level of sales, a great deal of inventory must be maintained so that customers will find what they want to buy when they shop in Wal-Mart stores. In fact, in the January 31, 2005, balance sheet, inventory is presented at $29,447 million and the comparable figure for a year earlier is $26,612 million.

a. Compute the inventory turnover rate for Wal-Mart for both 2004 and 2005.

b. Compute the average number of days required by Wal-Mart to sell its inventory for the same years.

c. In which year was the company more efficient in its management of inventory? Explain your answer.

EXERCISE 8.15
Using the Financial Statements of **Home Depot, Inc.**

The Home Depot, Inc., financial statements appear in Appendix A at the end of this textbook. Using figures from the income statement and balance sheet, answer the following questions:

a. What was the company's inventory turnover rate for the most recent year reported?

b. Using your answer from part **a**, what was the average number of days that merchandise remained in inventory before it was sold?

c. Is the company's operating cycle influenced significantly by its accounts receivable turnover rate? Explain.

Problem Set A

PROBLEM 8.1A
Four Methods of Inventory Valuation

On January 15, 2007, BassTrack sold 1,000 Ace-5 fishing reels to Angler's Warehouse. Immediately prior to this sale, BassTrack's perpetual inventory records for Ace-5 reels included the following cost layers:

Purchase Date	Quantity	Unit Cost	Total Cost
Dec. 12, 2006	600	$29	$17,400
Jan. 9, 2007	900	32	28,800
Total on hand	1,500		$46,200

Instructions

Note: We present this problem in the normal sequence of the accounting cycle—that is, journal entries before ledger entries. However, you may find it helpful to work part **b** first.

a. Prepare a separate journal entry to record the cost of goods sold relating to the January 15 sale of 1,000 Ace-5 reels, assuming that BassTrack uses:

1. Specific identification (500 of the units sold were purchased on December 12, and the remaining 500 were purchased on January 9).
2. Average cost.
3. FIFO.
4. LIFO.

b. Complete a subsidiary ledger record for Ace-5 reels using each of the four inventory valuation methods listed above. Your inventory records should show both purchases of this product, the sale on January 15, and the balance on hand at December 12, January 9, and January 15. Use the formats for inventory subsidiary records illustrated on pages 349–353 of this chapter.

c. Refer to the cost of goods sold figures computed in part **a**. For financial reporting purposes, can the company use the valuation method that resulted in the *lowest* cost of goods sold if, for tax purposes, it used the method that resulted in the *highest* cost of goods sold? Explain.

Problems 8.2A and 8.3A are based on the following data:

Speed World Cycles sells high-performance motorcycles and motocross racers. One of Speed World's most popular models is the Kazomma 900 dirt bike. During the current year, Speed World purchased eight of these cycles at the following costs:

Purchase Date	Units Purchased	Unit Cost	Total Cost
July 1.	2	$4,950	$ 9,900
July 22	3	5,000	15,000
Aug. 3	3	5,100	15,300
	8		$40,200

On *July 28*, Speed World sold four Kazomma 900 dirt bikes to the Vince Wilson racing team. The remaining four bikes remained in inventory at September 30, the end of Speed World's fiscal year.

PROBLEM 8.2A
Alternative Cost Flow Assumptions in a Perpetual System

Assume that Speed World uses a *perpetual inventory system*. (See the data given above.)

Instructions

a. Compute the cost of goods sold relating to the sale on July 28 and the ending inventory of Kazomma 900 dirt bikes at September 30, using the following cost flow assumptions:

1. Average cost.
2. FIFO.
3. LIFO.

Show the number of units and the unit costs of each layer comprising the cost of goods sold and ending inventory.

b. Using the cost figures computed in part **a**, answer the following questions:

1. Which of the three cost flow assumptions will result in Speed World Cycles reporting the *highest net income* for the current year? Would this always be the case? Explain.
2. Which of the three cost flow assumptions will *minimize the income taxes owed* by Speed World Cycles for the year? Would you expect this usually to be the case? Explain.
3. May Speed World Cycles use the cost flow assumption that results in the highest net income for the current year in its financial statements, but use the cost flow assumption that minimizes taxable income for the current year in its income tax return? Explain.

PROBLEM 8.3A
Alternative Cost Flow Assumptions in a Periodic System

Assume that Speed World uses a *periodic inventory system.* (See the data given before Problem 8.2A.)

Instructions

a. Compute the cost of goods sold relating to the sale on July 28 and the ending inventory of Kazomma 900 dirt bikes at September 30, using the following cost flow assumptions:

1. Average cost.
2. FIFO.
3. LIFO.

Show the number of units and unit costs in each cost layer of the *ending inventory*. You may determine the cost of goods sold by deducting ending inventory from the cost of goods available for sale.

b. If Speed World Cycles uses the LIFO cost flow assumption for financial reporting purposes, can it use the FIFO method for income tax purposes? Explain.

PROBLEM 8.4A
Year-End Adjustments; Shrinkage Losses and LCM

Mario's Nursery uses a perpetual inventory system. At December 31, the perpetual inventory records indicate the following quantities of a particular blue spruce tree:

	Quantity	Unit Cost	Total Cost
First purchase (oldest)	130	$25.00	$ 3,250
Second purchase	120	28.50	3,420
Third purchase	100	39.00	3,900
Total	350		$10,570

A year-end physical inventory, however, shows only 310 of these trees on hand.

In its financial statements, Mario's values its inventories at the lower-of-cost-or-market. At year-end, the per-unit replacement cost of this tree is $40. (Use $3,500 as the "level of materiality" in deciding whether to debit losses to Cost of Goods Sold or to a separate loss account.)

Instructions

Prepare the journal entries required to adjust the inventory records at year-end, assuming that:

a. Mario's uses:

1. Average cost.
2. Last-in, first-out.

b. Mario's uses the first-in, first-out method. However, the replacement cost of the trees at year-end is $20 apiece, rather than the $40 stated originally. [Make separate journal entries to record (1) the shrinkage losses and (2) the restatement of the inventory at a market value lower than cost. Record the shrinkage losses first.]

c. Assume that the company had been experiencing monthly inventory shrinkage of 30 to 60 trees for several months. In response, management placed several hidden security cameras throughout the premises. Within days, an employee was caught on film loading potted trees into his pickup truck. The employee's attorney asked that the case be dropped because the company had "unethically used a hidden camera to entrap his client." Do you agree with the attorney? Defend your answer.

PROBLEM 8.5A
Periodic Inventory Costing Procedures
eXcel

Mach IV Audio uses a periodic inventory system. One of the store's most popular products is an MP3 car stereo system. The inventory quantities, purchases, and sales of this product for the most recent year are as follows:

	Number of Units	Cost per Unit	Total Cost
Inventory, Jan. 1	10	$299	$ 2,990
First purchase (May 12)	15	306	4,590
Second purchase (July 9)	20	308	6,160
Third purchase (Oct. 4)	8	315	2,520
Fourth purchase (Dec. 18)	19	320	6,080
Goods available for sale	72		$22,340
Units sold during the year	51		
Inventory, Dec. 31	21		

Instructions

a. Using *periodic* costing procedures, compute the cost of the December 31 inventory and the cost of goods sold for the MP3 systems during the year under each of the following cost flow assumptions:

1. First-in, first-out.

2. Last-in, first-out.

3. Average cost (round to nearest dollar, except unit cost).

b. Which of the three inventory pricing methods provides the most realistic balance sheet valuation of inventory in light of the current replacement cost of the MP3 units? Does this same method also produce the most realistic measure of income in light of the costs being incurred by Mach IV Audio to replace the MP3 systems when they are sold? Explain.

PROBLEM 8.6A
Effects of Inventory Errors on Earnings

The owners of Hexagon Health Foods are offering the business for sale. The partial income statements of the business for the three years of its existence are summarized below.

	2007	2006	2005
Net sales	$875,000	$840,000	$820,000
Cost of goods sold	481,250	487,200	480,000
Gross profit on sales	$393,750	$352,800	$340,000
Gross profit percentage	45%	42%	41%

In negotiations with prospective buyers of the business, the owners of Hexagon are calling attention to the rising trends of the gross profit and the gross profit percentage as very favorable elements.

Assume that you are retained by a prospective purchaser of the business to make an investigation of the fairness and reliability of the enterprise's accounting records and financial statements. You find everything in order except for the following: (1) An arithmetic error in the computation of inventory at the end of 2005 had caused a $40,000 understatement in that inventory, and (2) a duplication of figures in the computation of inventory at the end of 2007 had caused an overstatement of $81,750 in that inventory. The company uses the periodic inventory system, and these errors had not been brought to light prior to your investigation.

Instructions

a. Prepare a revised three-year partial income statement summary.

b. Comment on the trends of gross profit and gross profit percentage before and after the revision.

PROBLEM 8.7A
Retail Method

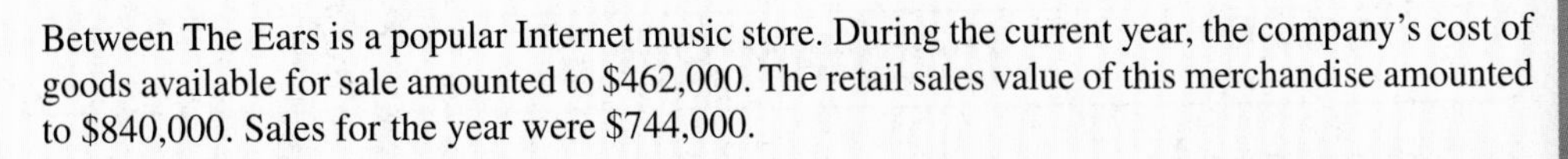

Between The Ears is a popular Internet music store. During the current year, the company's cost of goods available for sale amounted to $462,000. The retail sales value of this merchandise amounted to $840,000. Sales for the year were $744,000.

Instructions

a. Using the retail method, estimate (1) the cost of goods sold during the year and (2) the inventory at the end of the year.

b. At year-end, BTE.com takes a physical inventory. The general manager walks through the warehouse counting each type of product and reading its retail price into a tape recorder. From the recorded information, another employee prepares a schedule listing the entire ending inventory at retail sales prices. The schedule prepared for the current year reports ending inventory at $84,480 at retail sales prices.

   1. Use the cost ratio computed in part **a** to reduce the inventory counted by the general manager from its retail value to an estimate of its cost.

   2. Determine the estimated shrinkage losses (measured at cost) incurred by BTE.com during the year.

   3. Compute BTE.com's gross profit for the year. (Include inventory shrinkage losses in the cost of goods sold.)

c. What controls might BTE.com implement to reduce inventory shrinkage?

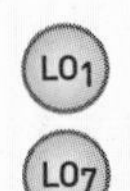

PROBLEM 8.8A
FIFO versus LIFO Comparisons

Wal-Mart uses LIFO to account for its inventories. Recent financial statements were used to compile the following information (dollar figures are in billions):

Average inventory (throughout the year)	$ 20.618
Current assets (at year-end)	26.555
Current liabilities (at year-end)	28.949
Net sales	191.329
Cost of goods sold	150.255
Gross profit	41.074
Average time required to collect outstanding receivables	3 days

Had Wal-Mart used the *FIFO* inventory method, the following differences would have occurred:

1. Average inventory would have been $20.908 billion ($290 million *higher* than the LIFO amount).

2. Ending inventory would have been $21.644 billion ($202 million *higher* than the LIFO amount).

3. The cost of goods sold would have been $150.053 billion ($202 million *lower* than the LIFO amount).

Instructions

a. Using the information provided, compute the following measures based upon the *LIFO* method:

   1. Inventory turnover rate.

   2. Current ratio (see Chapter 5 for a discussion of this ratio).

   3. Gross profit rate (see Chapter 6 for a discussion of this statistic).

b. *Recompute* your results from part **a** using the *FIFO* method.

c. Notice that the cost of goods sold is *lower* under FIFO than LIFO. What circumstances must the company have encountered to cause this situation? (Were replacement costs, on average, rising or falling?)

d. Explain why the average number of days required by Wal-Mart to collect its accounts receivable is so low. (See Chapter 7 for a discussion of the accounts receivable turnover rate.)

Problem Set B

PROBLEM 8.1B
Four Methods of Inventory Valuation

On January 22, 2007, Dome, Inc., sold 700 toner cartridges to Maxine Supplies. Immediately prior to this sale, Dome's perpetual inventory records for these units included the following cost layers:

Purchase Date	Quantity	Unit Cost	Total Cost
Dec. 12, 2006	400	$20	$ 8,000
Jan. 16, 2007	1,200	22	26,400
Total on hand	1,600		$34,400

Instructions

Note: We present this problem in the normal sequence of the accounting cycle—that is, journal entries before ledger entries. However, you may find it helpful to work part **b** first.

a. Prepare a separate journal entry to record the cost of goods sold relating to the January 22 sale of 700 toner cartridges, assuming that Dome uses:

1. Specific identification (300 of the units sold had been purchased on December 12, and the remaining 400 had been purchased on January 16).
2. Average cost.
3. FIFO.
4. LIFO.

b. Complete a subsidiary ledger record for the toner cartridges using each of the four inventory valuation methods listed above. Your inventory records should show both purchases of this product, the sale on January 22, and the balance on hand at December 12, January 16, and January 22. Use the formats for inventory subsidiary records illustrated on pages 349–353 of this chapter.

c. Refer to the cost of goods sold figures computed in part **a**. For financial reporting purposes, can the company use the valuation method that resulted in the *highest* cost of goods sold if, for tax purposes, it used the method that resulted in the *lowest* cost of goods sold? Explain.

Problems 8.2B and 8.3B are based on the following data:

Sea Travel sells motor boats. One of Sea Travel's most popular models is the Wing. During the current year, Sea Travel purchased 12 of these boats at the following costs:

Purchase Date	Units Purchased	Unit Cost	Total Cost
Apr. 1	4	$8,000	$32,000
Apr. 19	5	8,200	41,000
May 8	3	8,500	25,500
	12		$98,500

On *April 28*, Sea Travel sold five Wings to the Jack Sport racing team. The remaining seven boats remained in inventory at June 30, the end of Sea Travel's fiscal year.

PROBLEM 8.2B
Alternative Cost Flow Assumptions in a Perpetual System

Assume that Sea Travel uses a *perpetual inventory system.* (See the data given above.)

Instructions

a. Compute (a) the cost of goods sold relating to the sale on April 28 and (b) the ending inventory of Wing boats at June 30, using the following cost flow assumptions:

1. Average cost (round cost to nearest whole dollar).
2. FIFO.
3. LIFO.

Show the number of units and the unit costs of each layer comprising the cost of goods sold and ending inventory.

b. Using the cost figures computed in part **a**, answer the following questions:

1. Which of the three cost flow assumptions will result in Sea Travel reporting the *lowest net income* for the current year? Would this always be the case? Explain.
2. Which of the three cost flow assumptions will result in the *highest* income tax expense for the year? Would you expect this usually to be the case? Explain.
3. May Sea Travel use the cost flow assumption that results in the *lowest* net income for the current year in its financial statements, but use the cost flow assumption that *maximizes* taxable income for the current year in its income tax return? Explain.

PROBLEM 8.3B
Alternative Cost Flow Assumptions in a Periodic System

Assume that Sea Travel uses a *periodic inventory system.* (Refer to the data that precede Problem 8.2B.)

Instructions

a. Compute the cost of goods sold relating to the sale on April 28 and the ending inventory of Wing boats at June 30, using the following cost flow assumptions:

1. Average cost (round cost to nearest whole dollar).
2. FIFO.
3. LIFO.

Show the number of units and the unit costs of each layer comprising the *ending inventory.* You may determine the cost of goods sold by deducting ending inventory from the cost of goods available for sale.

b. If Sea Travel uses the LIFO cost flow assumption for income tax purposes, can it use the FIFO method for financial reporting purposes? Explain.

PROBLEM 8.4B
Year-End Adjustments; Shrinkage Losses and LCM

Sam's Lawn Mowers uses a perpetual inventory system. At December 31, the perpetual inventory records indicate the following quantities of a particular mower.

	Quantity	Unit Cost	Total Cost
First purchase (oldest)	80	$100	$ 8,000
Second purchase	100	110	11,000
Third purchase	20	120	2,400
Total	200		$21,400

A year-end physical inventory, however, shows only 199 of these lawn mowers on hand.

In its financial statements, Sam's values its inventories at the lower-of-cost-or-market. At year-end, the per-unit replacement cost of this particular model is $125.

Instructions

Prepare the journal entries required to adjust the inventory records at year-end assuming that:

a. Sam's uses:

1. Average cost.
2. Last-in, first-out.

b. Sam's uses the first-in, first-out method. However, the replacement cost of the lawn mowers at year-end is $90 apiece, rather than the $125 stated originally. Make separate journal entries to record (1) the shrinkage loss and (2) the restatement of the inventory at a market value lower than cost. Record the shrinkage loss first.

c. Assume that the company had been experiencing monthly inventory shrinkage of one to four lawn mowers for several months. In response, management placed several hidden security cameras throughout the premises. Within days, an employee was caught on film loading lawn mowers into his pickup truck. The employee's attorney asked that the case be dropped because the company had "unethically used a hidden camera to entrap his client." Do you agree with the attorney? Defend your answer.

PROBLEM 8.5B
Periodic Inventory Costing Procedures

Roman Sound uses a periodic inventory system. One of the store's products is a wireless headphone. The inventory quantities, purchases, and sales of this product for the most recent year are as follows:

	Number of Units	Cost per Unit	Total Cost
Inventory, Jan. 1	10	$100	$ 1,000
First purchase	30	101	3,030
Second purchase	40	104	4,160
Third purchase	5	106	530
Fourth purchase	15	110	1,650
Goods available for sale	100		$10,370
Units sold during the year	80		
Inventory, Dec. 31	20		

Instructions

a. Using *periodic* costing procedures, compute the cost of the December 31 inventory and the cost of goods sold for the year under each of the following cost assumptions:

1. First-in, first-out.
2. Last-in, first-out.
3. Average cost (round to the nearest dollar, except unit cost).

b. Which of the three inventory pricing methods provides the most realistic balance sheet valuation of inventory in light of the current replacement cost of these headphones? Does this same method also produce the most realistic measure of income in light of the costs being incurred by Roman Sound to replace these units when they are sold? Explain.

PROBLEM 8.6B
Effects of Inventory Errors on Earnings

The owners of City Software are offering the business for sale. The income statements of the business for the three years of its existence are summarized below.

	2007	2006	2005
Net sales	$1,000,000	$920,000	$840,000
Cost of goods sold	600,000	570,400	546,000
Gross profit on sales	$ 400,000	$349,600	$294,000
Gross profit percentage	40%	38%	35%

In negotiations with prospective buyers of the business, the owners are calling attention to the rising trends of the gross profit and the gross profit percentage as very favorable elements.

Assume that you are retained by a prospective purchaser of the business to make an investigation of the fairness and reliability of the enterprise's accounting records and financial statements. You find everything in order except for the following: (1) An arithmetic error in the computation of inventory at the end of 2005 has caused a $20,000 understatement in that inventory, and (2) an error in the computation of inventory at the end of 2007 has caused an overstatement of $80,000 in that inventory. The company uses the periodic inventory system, and these errors have not been brought to light prior to your investigation.

Instructions

a. Prepare a revised three-year partial income statement summary.

b. Comment on the trends of gross profit and gross profit percentage before and after the revision.

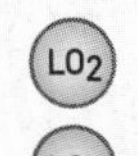

PROBLEM 8.7B
Retail Method

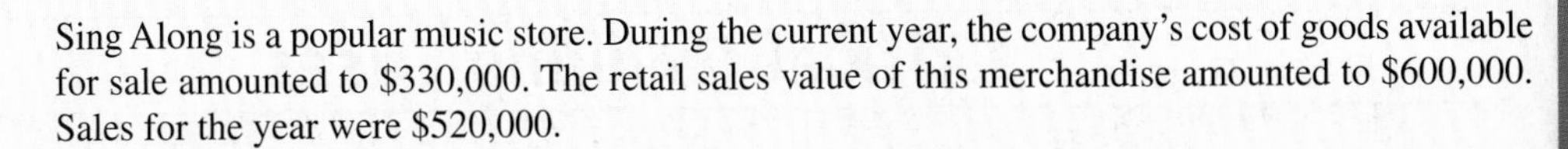

Sing Along is a popular music store. During the current year, the company's cost of goods available for sale amounted to $330,000. The retail sales value of this merchandise amounted to $600,000. Sales for the year were $520,000.

Instructions

a. Using the retail method, estimate (1) the cost of goods sold during the year and (2) the inventory at the end of the year.

b. At year-end, Sing Along takes a physical inventory. The general manager walks through the store counting each type of product and reading its retail price into a tape recorder. From the recorded information, another employee prepares a schedule listing the entire ending inventory at retail sales prices. The schedule prepared for the current year reports ending inventory of $75,000 at retail sales prices.

1. Use the cost ratio computed in part **a** to reduce the inventory counted by the general manager from its retail value to an estimate of its cost.
2. Determine the estimated shrinkage losses (measured at cost) incurred by Sing Along during the year.
3. Compute Sing Along's gross profit for the year. (Include inventory shrinkage losses in the cost of goods sold.)

c. What controls might Sing Along implement to reduce inventory shrinkage?

PROBLEM 8.8B
FIFO versus LIFO Comparisons

Toys "R" Us uses LIFO to account for its inventories. Recent financial statements were used to compile the following information (dollar figures are in billions):

Average inventory (throughout the year)	$ 2.2
Current assets (at year-end)	4.7
Current liabilities (at year-end)	2.8
Net sales	11.5
Cost of goods sold	7.8
Gross profit	3.7
Average time required to collect outstanding receivables	6 days

Had Toys "R" Us used the *FIFO* inventory method, the following differences would have occurred:

1. Average inventory would have been $2.8 billion ($600 million *higher* than the LIFO amount).
2. Ending inventory would have been $2.7 billion ($500 million *higher* than the LIFO amount).
3. The cost of goods sold would have been $7.3 billion ($500 million *lower* than the LIFO amount).

Instructions

a. Using the information provided, compute the following measures based upon the *LIFO* method:

1. Inventory turnover rate.
2. Current ratio (see Chapter 5 for a discussion of this ratio).
3. Gross profit rate (see Chapter 6 for a discussion of this statistic).

b. *Recompute* your results from part **a** using the *FIFO* method.

c. Notice that the cost of goods sold is *lower* under FIFO than LIFO. What circumstances must the company have encountered to cause this situation? (Were replacement costs, on average, rising or falling?)

d. Explain why the average number of days required by Toys "R" Us to collect its accounts receivable is so low. (See Chapter 7 for a discussion of the accounts receivable turnover rate.)

Critical Thinking Cases

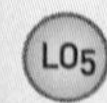

CASE 8.1
It's Not Right, but at Least It's Consistent

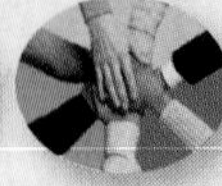

Our Little Secret is a small manufacturer of swimsuits and other beach apparel. The company is closely held and has no external reporting obligations, other than payroll reports and income tax returns. The company's accounting system is grossly inadequate. Accounting records are maintained by clerical employees with little knowledge of accounting and with many other job responsibilities. Management has decided that the company must hire a competent controller, who can establish and oversee an adequate accounting system.

Amy Lee, CPA, has applied for this position. During a recent interview, Dean Frost, the company's director of personnel, said, "Amy, the job is yours. But you should know that we have a big inventory problem here.

"For some time now, it appears that we have been understating our ending inventory in income tax returns. No one knows when this all got started, or who was responsible. We never even counted our inventory until a few months ago. But the problem is pretty big. In our latest tax return—that's for 2006—we listed inventory at only about half its actual cost. That's an understatement of, maybe, $400,000.

"We don't know what to do. We sure don't want a big scandal—tax evasion, and all that. Maybe the best thing is to continue understating inventory by the same amount as we did in 2006. That way, taxable income will be correctly stated in future years. Anyway, this is just something I thought you should know about."

Instructions

a. Briefly identify the ethical issues raised for Lee by Frost's disclosure.

b. From Lee's perspective, evaluate the possible solution proposed by Frost.

c. Identify and discuss the alternative ethical courses of action that are open to Lee.

CASE 8.2
LIFO Liquidation

Jackson Specialties has been in business for more than 50 years. The company maintains a perpetual inventory system, uses a LIFO flow assumption, and ends its fiscal year at December 31. At year-end, the cost of goods sold and inventory are adjusted to reflect periodic LIFO costing procedures.

A railroad strike has delayed the arrival of purchases ordered during the past several months of 2007, and Jackson Specialties has not been able to replenish its inventories as merchandise is sold. At December 22, one product appears in the company's perpetual inventory records at the following unit costs:

Purchase Date	Quantity	Unit Cost	Total Cost
Nov. 14, 1954	3,000	$6	$18,000
Apr. 12, 1955	2,000	8	16,000
Available for sale at Dec. 22, 2007	5,000		$34,000

Jackson Specialties has another 8,000 units of this product on order at the current wholesale cost of $30 per unit. Because of the railroad strike, however, these units have not yet arrived (the terms of purchase are F.O.B. destination). Jackson Specialties also has an order from a customer who wants to purchase 4,000 units of this product at the retail sales price of $47 per unit. Jackson Specialties intends to make this sale on December 30, regardless of whether the 8,000 units on order arrive by this date. (The 4,000-unit sale will be shipped by truck, F.O.B. shipping point.)

Instructions

a. Are the units in inventory really more than 50 years old? Explain.

b. Prepare a schedule showing the sales revenue, cost of goods sold, and gross profit that will result from this sale on December 30, assuming that the 8,000 units currently on order (1) arrive before year-end and (2) do not arrive until some time in the following year. (In each computation, show the number of units comprising the cost of goods sold and their related per-unit costs.)

c. Comment on these results.

d. Might management be wise to delay this sale by a few days? Explain.

CASE 8.3
Dealing with the Bank

Avery Frozen Foods owes the bank $50,000 on a line of credit. Terms of the agreement specify that Avery must maintain a minimum current ratio of 1.2 to 1, or the entire outstanding balance becomes immediately due in full. To date, the company has complied with the minimum requirement. However, management has just learned that a failed warehouse freezer has ruined thousands of dollars of frozen foods inventory. If the company records this loss, its current ratio will drop to approximately 0.8 to 1.

Whether any or all of this loss may be covered by insurance currently is in dispute and will not be known for at least 90 days—perhaps much longer. There are several reasons why the insurance company may have no liability.

In trying to decide how to deal with the bank, management is considering the following options: (1) postpone recording the inventory loss until the dispute with the insurance company is resolved, (2) increase the current ratio to 1.2 to 1 by making a large purchase of inventory on account, (3) explain to the bank what has happened, and request that it be flexible until things get back to normal.

Instructions

a. Given that the company hopes for at least partial reimbursement from the insurance company, is it really unethical for management to postpone recording the inventory loss in the financial statements it submits to the bank?

b. Is it possible to increase the company's current ratio from 0.8 to 1 to 1.2 to 1 by purchasing more inventory on account? Explain.

c. What approach do you think the company should follow in dealing with the bank?

BUSINESSWEEK CASE 8.4
Inventory Turnover

In most situations, the higher the inventory turnover rate, the better. In her March 3, 2003, *BusinessWeek* article, "Q&A: Putting a Tech Giant Back on Its Feet," Faith Keenan wrote:

> Data storage company EMC Corporation had plenty of fat in its operations before the tech downturn hit. Inventory turned over just four times a year, while competitors moved goods several times faster.

EMC's inventory turnover statistic was low because company policy was to test its data storage devices for 28 days before selling them to customers. Most of the firm's competitors tested their products for only 7 days before selling them. When EMC made a decision to shorten its testing period, its inventory turnover statistic improved.

Instructions

Discuss the trade-offs EMC's management had to consider in making its decision to shorten the company's product testing period.

INTERNET CASE 8.5
Inventory Turnover

A company's inventory turnover rate is one measure of its potential to convert inventory into cash. But what is considered a good inventory turnover rate? The answer to that question depends on a variety of industry and company characteristics.

Access the EDGAR database at the following Internet address:

www.sec.gov

Locate the most recent 10-K reports of **Safeway, Inc.**, and **Staples, Inc.** Compute the inventory turnover rates of each company. Does the higher turnover rate computed for **Safeway** mean that the company manages its inventory more effectively than **Staples**? Explain.

Internet sites are time and date sensitive. It is the purpose of these exercises to have you explore the Internet. You may need to use the Yahoo! search engine **http://www.yahoo.com** *(or another favorite search engine) to find a company's current Web address.*

Answers to Self-Test Questions

1. b **2.** a, c, d **3.** a **4.** b **5.** b **6.** a, d

COMPREHENSIVE PROBLEM 2

Guitar Universe, Inc.

Guitar Universe, Inc., is a popular source of musical instruments for professional and amateur musicians. The company's accountants make necessary adjusting entries *monthly*, and they make all closing entries *annually*. Guitar Universe is growing rapidly and prides itself on having no long-term liabilities.

The company has provided the following *trial balance* dated *December 31, 2007:*

GUITAR UNIVERSE, INC.
Trial Balance
December 31, 2007

Cash	$ 45,000	
Marketable securities	25,000	
Accounts receivable	125,000	
Allowance for doubtful accounts		$ 5,000
Merchandise inventory	250,000	
Office supplies	1,200	
Prepaid insurance	6,600	
Building and fixtures	1,791,000	
Accumulated depreciation		800,000
Land	64,800	
Accounts payable		70,000
Unearned customer deposits		8,000
Income taxes payable		75,000
Capital stock		1,000,000
Retained earnings		240,200
Unrealized holding gain on investments		6,000
Sales		1,600,000
Cost of goods sold	958,000	
Bank service charges	200	
Uncollectible accounts expense	9,000	
Salary and wages expense	395,000	
Office supplies expense	400	
Insurance expense	6,400	
Utilities expense	3,600	
Depreciation expense	48,000	
Income tax expense	75,000	
	$3,804,200	$3,804,200

Other information pertaining to Guitar Universe's trial balance is shown below:

1. The company's most recent bank statement reports a balance of $46,975. Included with the bank statement was a $2,500 check from Iggy Bates, a professional musician, charged back to Guitar Universe as NSF. The bank's monthly service charge was $25. Three checks written by Guitar Universe to suppliers of merchandise inventory had not yet cleared the bank for payment as of the statement date. These checks included: no. 507, $4,000; no. 511, $9,000; and no. 521, $8,000. Deposits made by Guitar Universe of $16,500 had reached the bank too late for inclusion in the current statement. The company prepares a bank reconciliation at the end of each month.
2. Guitar Universe has a portfolio of marketable securities. The initial investment in the portfolio was $19,000. As of December 31, the market value of these securities was $27,500. Management classifies all short-term investments as "available for sale."
3. During December, $6,400 of accounts receivable were written off as uncollectible. A recent aging of the company's accounts receivable helped management to conclude that an allowance for doubtful accounts of $8,500 was needed at December 31, 2007.

4. The company uses a perpetual inventory system. A year-end physical count revealed that several guitars reported in the inventory records were missing. The cost of the missing units amounted to $1,350. This amount is not considered significant relative to the total cost of inventory on hand.
5. At December 31, approximately $900 in office supplies remained on hand.
6. The company pays for its insurance policies 12 months in advance. Its most recent payment was made on November 1, 2007. The cost of this policy was slightly higher than the cost of coverage for the previous 12 months.
7. Depreciation expense related to the company's building and fixtures is $5,000 for the month ending December 31, 2007.
8. Although Guitar Universe carries an extensive inventory, it is not uncommon for musicians to order custom guitars made to their exact specifications. Manufacturers do not allow any sales returns of custom-made guitars. Thus, all customers must pay in advance for these special orders. The entire sales amount is collected at the time a custom order is placed, and it is credited to an account entitled "Unearned Customer Deposits." As of December 31, $4,800 of these deposits remained unearned. Assume that the cost of goods sold and the reduction in inventory associated with all custom orders is recorded when the custom merchandise is delivered to customers. Thus, the adjusting entry requires only a decrease to unearned customer deposits and an increase to sales.
9. Accrued income taxes payable for the *entire year ending* December 31, 2007, total $81,000. No income tax payments are due until early in 2008.

Instructions

a. Prepare a bank reconciliation and make the necessary journal entries to update the accounting records of Guitar Universe as of December 31, 2007.

b. Prepare the necessary adjusting entry to update the company's marketable securities portfolio to its mark-to-market value.

c. Prepare the adjusting entry at December 31, 2007, to report the company's accounts receivable at their net realizable value.

d. Prepare the entry to account for the guitars missing from the company's inventory at the end of the year.

e. Prepare the adjusting entry to account for the office supplies used during December.

f. Prepare the adjusting entry to account for the expiration of the company's insurance policies during December.

g. Prepare the adjusting entry to account for the depreciation of the company's building and fixtures during December.

h. Prepare the adjusting entry to report the portion of unearned customer deposits that were earned during December.

i. Prepare the adjusting entry to account for income tax expense that accrued during December.

j. Based upon the adjustments made to the accounting records in parts **a** through **i** above, prepare the company's adjusted trial balance at December 31, 2007.

k. Using the adjusted trial balance prepared in part **j** above, prepare an *annual* income statement, statement of retained earnings, and a balance sheet dated December 31, 2007.

l. Using the financial statements prepared in part **k** above, determine approximately how many days an account receivable remains outstanding before it is collected. You may assume that the company's ending accounts receivable balance on December 31 is a close approximation of its average accounts receivable balance throughout the year.

m. Using the financial statements prepared in part **k**, determine approximately how many days an item of merchandise remains in stock before it is sold. You may assume that the company's ending merchandise inventory balance on December 31 is a close approximation of its average merchandise inventory balance throughout the year.

n. Using the financial statements prepared in part **k**, determine approximately how many days it takes to convert the company's inventory into cash. Stated differently, what is the length of the company's operating cycle?

o. Comment briefly upon the company's financial condition from the perspective of a short-term creditor.

Plant and Intangible Assets

Learning Objectives

AFTER STUDYING THIS CHAPTER, YOU SHOULD BE ABLE TO:

LO1 Determine the cost of plant assets.

LO2 Distinguish between capital expenditures and revenue expenditures.

LO3 Compute depreciation by the straight-line and declining-balance methods.

LO4 Account for depreciation using methods other than straight-line or declining-balance.

LO5 Account for the disposal of plant assets.

LO6 Explain the nature of intangible assets, including goodwill.

LO7 Account for the depletion of natural resources.

LO8 Explain the cash effects of transactions involving plant assets.

UNITED PARCEL SERVICE

What kind of plant and intangible assets would you expect United Parcel Service to have? Probably the first thing you would think of is vehicles, primarily trucks, because you are used to seeing UPS trucks on the streets and highways virtually every day. In addition, UPS has a very large investment in aircraft. In fact, property, plant, and equipment make up over 43 percent of UPS's total assets ($15,289 of $35,222 million), according to the company's 2005 consolidated balance sheet. Of the $15,289 million, aircraft is the largest single type of asset and another large category is vehicles.

Plant assets are important for a company such as United Parcel Service to be successful in its daily operations. The exact types and amount of plant assets used by a particular company depend on the nature of the company and its operations. Virtually all companies need some type of plant assets to operate efficiently and be successful. In addition, some companies require certain intangible assets to do business. Intangibles are rights and privileges that have been developed or acquired, such as trade names and patents; these may be as important to a business as its equipment, buildings, and land.

In earlier chapters, we introduced the idea of plant assets and depreciation and stressed the importance of such assets to the successful functioning of businesses. In this chapter, we explore in greater depth the accounting issues surrounding plant assets and discuss intangible assets. Together, plant and intangible assets make up a significant part of corporate balance sheets because they represent major investments of resources. The future of many business enterprises depends heavily on their investment in plant and intangible assets.

PLANT ASSETS AS A "STREAM OF FUTURE SERVICES"

Plant assets represent a bundle of future services and, thus, can be thought of as long-term prepaid expenses. Ownership of a delivery truck, for example, may provide about 100,000 miles of transportation. The cost of the truck is entered in an asset account, which in essence represents the *advance purchase* of these transportation services. Similarly, a building represents the advance purchase of many years of housing services. As the years go by, these services are utilized by the business, and the cost of the plant asset gradually is transferred to depreciation expense to reflect the cost of using the asset to generate revenue.

MAJOR CATEGORIES OF PLANT ASSETS

Plant and equipment items are often classified into the following groups:

1. **Tangible plant assets**. The term *tangible* denotes physical substance, as exemplified by land, a building, or a machine. This category may be further separated into two distinct classifications:
   a. *Property subject to depreciation*. Included are plant assets of limited useful life such as buildings and office equipment.
   b. *Land*. The only plant asset not subject to depreciation is land, which has an unlimited term of existence and whose usefulness does not decline over time.
2. **Intangible assets**. The term *intangible assets* is used to describe assets that are used in the operation of the business but have no physical characteristics and are noncurrent. Examples include patents, copyrights, trademarks, franchises, and goodwill. Current assets such as accounts receivable or prepaid rent are not included in the intangible classification, even though they also are lacking in physical substance.
3. **Natural resources**. A site acquired for the purpose of extracting or removing some valuable resource such as oil, minerals, or timber is classified as a *natural resource*, not as land. This type of plant asset is gradually converted into *inventory* as the natural resource is extracted from the site.

ACCOUNTABLE EVENTS IN THE LIVES OF PLANT ASSETS

For all categories of plant assets, there are three basic *accountable events:* (1) acquisition, (2) allocation of the acquisition cost to expense over the asset's useful life (depreciation), and (3) sale or disposal.

Acquisitions of Plant Assets

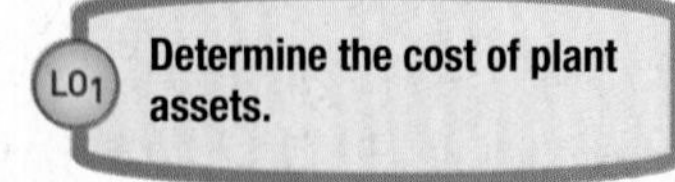

The cost of a **plant asset** includes all expenditures that are *reasonable* and *necessary* for getting the asset to the desired location and *ready for use*. Thus many incidental costs may be included in the cost assigned to a plant asset. These include, for example, sales taxes on the purchase price, delivery costs, and installation costs.

Only reasonable and necessary costs should be included. Assume, for example, that a machine is dropped and damaged while it is being unloaded. The cost of repairing this damage should be recognized as an expense of the current period, *not* added to the cost of the machine. Although it is necessary to repair the machine, it was not necessary to drop it—and that's what brought about the need for the repairs.

Companies often purchase plant assets on an installment plan or by issuing a note payable. Interest charges after the asset is ready for use are recorded as interest expense, not as part of the cost of the asset. But if a company constructs a plant asset for its own use, the interest charges *during the construction period* are viewed as part of the asset's cost.[1]

DETERMINING COST: AN EXAMPLE

The concept of including in the cost of a plant asset all of the incidental charges necessary to put the asset in use is illustrated by the following example. A factory in Mississippi orders a machine from a Colorado tool manufacturer at a list price of $10,000. Payment will be made in 48 monthly installments of $250, which include $2,000 in interest charges. Sales taxes of $600 must be paid, as well as freight charges of $1,350. Installation and other set-up costs amount to $500. The cost of this machine to be established in the Machinery account is computed as follows:

List price*	$10,000
Sales taxes	600
Transportation charges	1,350
Cost of installation and set-up	500
Total	$12,450

*The $2,000 in interest charges on the installment purchase will be recognized as interest expense over the next 48 months. (Accounting for installment notes payable is discussed in the next chapter.)

All reasonable and necessary costs are capitalized

SOME SPECIAL CONSIDERATIONS

Land

When land is purchased, various incidental costs are often incurred in addition to the purchase price. These additional costs may include commissions to real estate brokers, escrow fees, legal fees for examining and insuring the title, delinquent taxes paid by the purchaser, and fees for surveying, draining, clearing, and grading the property. All these expenditures become part of the cost of the land.

Sometimes land purchased as a building site has on it an old building that is not suitable for the buyer's use. In this case, the only useful asset being acquired is the land. Therefore, the entire purchase price is charged to the Land account, along with the costs of tearing down and removing the unusable building.

Land Improvements

Improvements to real estate such as driveways, fences, parking lots, landscaping, and sprinkler systems have a limited life and are therefore subject to depreciation. For this reason, they should be recorded in a separate account entitled Land Improvements.

Buildings

Old buildings are sometimes purchased with the intention of repairing them prior to placing them in use. Repairs made under these circumstances are charged to the Buildings account. After the building has been placed in use, however, ordinary repairs are considered to be maintenance expense when incurred.

Equipment

When equipment is purchased, all of the sales taxes, delivery costs, and costs of getting the equipment in good running order are treated as part of the cost of the asset. Once the equipment has been placed in operation, maintenance costs (including interest, insurance, and property taxes) are treated as expenses of the current period.

Allocation of a Lump-Sum Purchase

Several different types of plant assets may be purchased at one time. Separate control accounts are maintained for each type of plant asset, such as land, buildings, and equipment.[2]

When land and buildings (and perhaps other assets) are purchased for a lump sum, the purchase price must be *allocated* among the types of assets acquired. An appraisal may be needed

[1] FASB Statement No. 34, "Capitalization of Interest Costs" (Norwalk, Conn.: 1979).

[2] Each control account is supported by a subsidiary ledger providing information about the cost, annual depreciation, and book value of each asset (or group of similar assets).

for this purpose. Assume, for example, that Exercise-for-Health, Inc., purchases a complete fitness center from Golden Health Spas. Exercise-for-Health purchases the entire facility at a bargain price of $800,000. The allocation of this cost on the basis of an appraisal is illustrated as follows:

Total cost is allocated in proportion to appraised values

	Value per Appraisal	Percentage of Total Appraised Value	Allocation of $800,000 Cost
Land	$ 250,000	25%	$200,000
Land improvements	50,000	5	40,000
Building	300,000	30	240,000
Equipment	400,000	40	320,000
Total	$1,000,000	100%	$800,000

Assuming that Exercise-for-Health purchased this facility for cash, the journal entry to record this acquisition would be:

The journal entry allocating the total cost

Land	200,000	
Land Improvements	40,000	
Building	240,000	
Equipment	320,000	
Cash		800,000
To record purchase of fitness center from Golden Health Spas for cash.		

YOUR TURN **You as the New Facility Manager for Exercise-for-Health**

Assume you have been hired as manager of the new Golden Health Spas facility that was recently purchased by Exercise-for-Health. One of your responsibilities as manager is to show that the facility is profitable. In fact, your contract specifies a bonus if the profits are at least 10 percent above the budgeted amount each year. In a recent conversation with the appraiser, it becomes clear to you that some of the items classified as land in the appraisal were really building improvements. No one at Exercise-for-Health is aware of this misclassification. As a result, the appraised value for the building asset account should be $350,000 instead of $300,000. When budgeted profits for the Golden Health Spas facility are computed each year, a charge for depreciation on the building is deducted from the profits. What impact does the improper appraisal have on your ability to achieve the bonus? What should you do?

(See our comments on the Online Learning Center Web site.)

CAPITAL EXPENDITURES AND REVENUE EXPENDITURES

LO2 **Distinguish between capital expenditures and revenue expenditures.**

Expenditures for the purchase or expansion of plant assets are called **capital expenditures** and are recorded in asset accounts. Accountants often use the verb **capitalize** to mean charging an expenditure to an asset account rather than to an expense account. Expenditures for ordinary repairs, maintenance, fuel, and other items necessary to the ownership and use of plant and equipment are called **revenue expenditures** and are recorded by debiting expense accounts. The charge to an expense account is based on the assumption that the benefits from the expenditure will be used up in the current period, and therefore the cost should be deducted from the revenue of the period in determining the net income. Charging an expenditure directly to an expense account is often called "expensing" the item.

A business may purchase many small items that will benefit several accounting periods but that have a relatively low cost. Examples of such items include auto batteries, wastebaskets, and pencil sharpeners. Such items are theoretically capital expenditures, but if they are recorded as assets in the accounting records, it will be necessary to compute and record the related depreciation expense in future periods. We have previously mentioned the idea that the extra work involved in developing more precise accounting information should be weighed against the benefits that result. Thus, for reasons of convenience and economy, expenditures that are *not material* in dollar amount are treated in the accounting records as expenses of the current period.

In brief, any material expenditure that will benefit several accounting periods is considered a *capital expenditure*. Any expenditure that will benefit only the current period or that is not material in amount is treated as a *revenue expenditure*.

Many companies develop formal policy statements defining capital and revenue expenditures as a guide toward consistent accounting practice from year to year. These policy statements often set a minimum dollar amount (such as $500) for expenditures that are to be capitalized.

Depreciation

We first introduced the concept of depreciation in Chapter 4. Now we expand that discussion to address such topics as residual values and alternative depreciation methods.

ALLOCATING THE COST OF PLANT AND EQUIPMENT OVER THE YEARS OF USE

Tangible plant assets, with the exception of land, are of use to a company for only a limited number of years. **Depreciation**, as the term is used in accounting, is the *allocation of the cost of a tangible plant asset to expense in the periods in which services are received from the asset.* The basic purpose of depreciation is to offset the revenue of an accounting period with the costs of the goods and services being consumed in the effort to generate that revenue. (See Exhibit 9–1.)

Earlier in this chapter, we described a delivery truck as a stream of transportation services to be received over the years that the truck is owned and used. The cost of the truck initially is added to an asset account, because the purchase of these transportation services will benefit several future accounting periods. As these services are received, however, the cost of the truck gradually is removed from the balance sheet and allocated to expense, through the process of depreciation.

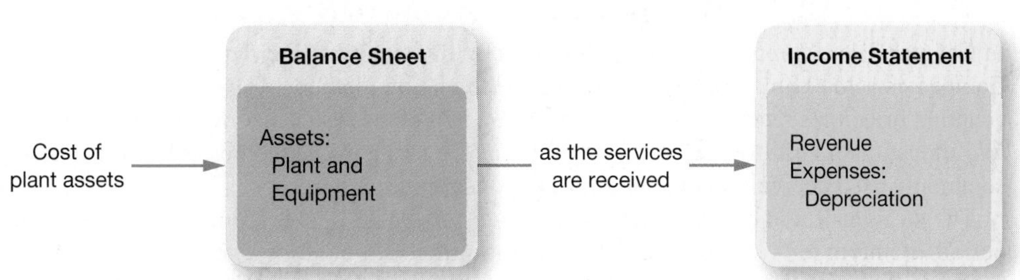

Exhibit 9–1
THE DEPRECIATION PROCESS

Depreciation: a process of allocating the cost of an asset to expense over the asset's useful life

The journal entry to record depreciation expense consists of a debit to Depreciation Expense and a credit to Accumulated Depreciation. The credit portion of the entry removes from the balance sheet that portion of the asset's cost estimated to have been used up during the current period. The debit portion of the entry allocates this expired cost to expense.

Separate Depreciation Expense and Accumulated Depreciation accounts are maintained for different types of depreciable assets, such as factory buildings, delivery equipment, and office equipment. These separate accounts help accountants to measure separately the costs of different business activities, such as manufacturing, sales, and administration.

Depreciation Is Not a Process of Valuation Depreciation is a process of *cost allocation*, not a process of asset valuation. Accounting records do not attempt to show the current market values of plant assets. The market value of a building, for example, may increase during some accounting periods within the building's useful life. The recognition of depreciation expense continues, however, without regard to such temporary increases in market value. Accountants recognize that the building will render useful services only for a limited number of years and that the full cost of the building should be *systematically allocated to expense* during these years.

Depreciation differs from most other expenses in that it does not depend on cash payments at or near the time the expense is recorded. For this reason, depreciation often is called a "noncash" expense. Bear in mind, however, that large cash payments usually are required at the time depreciable assets are purchased.

Book Value Plant assets are shown in the balance sheet at their book values (or *carrying values*). The **book value** of a plant asset is its *cost minus the related accumulated depreciation*. Accumulated depreciation is a contra-asset account, representing that portion of the asset's cost that has *already* been allocated to expense. Thus book value represents the portion of the asset's cost that remains to be allocated to expense in future periods.

CAUSES OF DEPRECIATION

The need to systematically allocate plant asset costs over multiple accounting periods arises from two major causes: (1) physical deterioration and (2) obsolescence.

Physical Deterioration Physical deterioration of a plant asset results from use, as well as from exposure to sun, wind, and other climatic factors. When a plant asset has been carefully maintained, it is not uncommon for the owner to claim that the asset is as "good as new." Such statements are not literally true. Although a good repair policy may greatly lengthen the useful life of a machine, every machine eventually reaches the point at which it must be discarded. Making repairs does not eliminate the need for recognition of depreciation.

Obsolescence The term *obsolescence* means the process of becoming out of date or obsolete. An airplane, for example, may become obsolete even though it is in excellent physical condition; it becomes obsolete because better planes of superior design and performance have become available.

METHODS OF COMPUTING DEPRECIATION

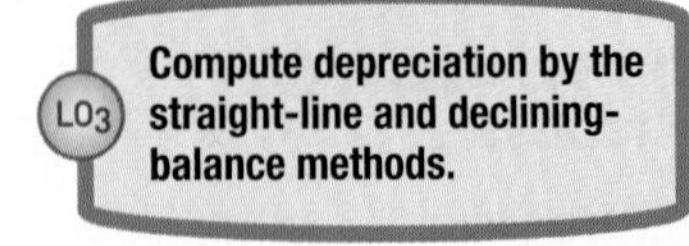

In Chapter 4, we computed depreciation only by the **straight-line depreciation** method. Companies actually may use any of several depreciation methods. Generally accepted accounting principles require only that a depreciation method result in a *rational and systematic* allocation of cost over the asset's useful life. The straight-line method is by far the most commonly used depreciation method for financial reporting purposes.

The straight-line method allocates an *equal portion* of depreciation expense to each period of the asset's useful life. Most of the other depreciation methods are various forms of accelerated depreciation. The term **accelerated depreciation** means that larger amounts of depreciation are recognized in the early years of the asset's life, and smaller amounts are recognized in the later years. Over the entire life of the asset, however, both the straight-line method and accelerated methods recognize the same *total* amount of depreciation.

The differences between the straight-line method and accelerated methods are illustrated in Exhibit 9–2.

STRAIGHT-LINE METHOD

Annual depreciation expense

1 2 3 4 5
Years

AN ACCELERATED METHOD

Annual depreciation expense

1 2 3 4 5
Years

Exhibit 9–2

STRAIGHT-LINE AND ACCELERATED DEPRECIATION METHODS

Both methods recognize the same total depreciation

There is only one straight-line method. But there are several accelerated methods, each producing slightly different results. Different depreciation methods may be used for different assets. The depreciation methods in use should be disclosed in notes accompanying the financial statements.

In this section, we illustrate and explain straight-line depreciation and one variation of the most widely used accelerated method, which is called *fixed-percentage-of-declining-balance*, or simply the *declining-balance* method. Other depreciation methods are discussed briefly in the section that follows.

© David Young-Wolff/PhotoEdit

Data for Our Illustrations Our illustrations of depreciation methods are based on the following data: On January 2, S&G Wholesale Grocery acquires a new delivery truck. The data and estimates needed for the computation of the annual depreciation expense are:

Cost	$17,000
Estimated residual value	$2,000
Estimated useful life	5 years

THE STRAIGHT-LINE METHOD

Under the straight-line method, an *equal portion* of the asset's cost is recognized as depreciation expense in each period of the asset's useful life. Annual depreciation expense is computed by deducting the estimated **residual value** (or **salvage value**) from the cost of the asset and dividing the remaining *depreciable cost* by the years of estimated useful life. Using the data in our example, the annual straight-line depreciation is computed as follows:

$$\frac{\textbf{Cost} - \textbf{Residual Value}}{\textbf{Years of Useful Life}} = \frac{\$17{,}000 - \$2{,}000}{5 \text{ years}} = \$3{,}000 \text{ per year}$$

This same depreciation computation is shown in tabular form as follows:

Cost of the depreciable asset	$17,000
Less: Estimated residual value (amount to be realized by sale of asset when it is retired from use)	2,000
Total amount to be depreciated (depreciable cost)	$15,000
Estimated useful life	5 years
Depreciation expense each year ($15,000 ÷ 5)	$ 3,000

Computing depreciation by the straight-line method

In Exhibit 9–3, the schedule summarizes the effects of straight-line depreciation over the entire life of the asset.

Exhibit 9–3

STRAIGHT-LINE DEPRECIATION SCHEDULE

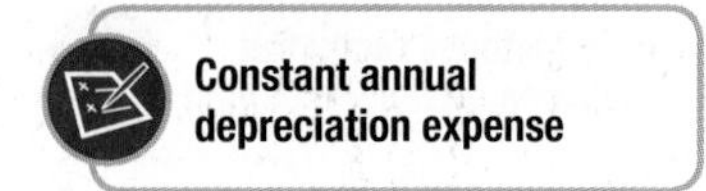

Depreciation Schedule: Straight-Line Method

Year	Computation	Depreciation Expense	Accumulated Depreciation	Book Value
				$17,000
First	$15,000 × ⅕	$ 3,000	$ 3,000	14,000
Second	15,000 × ⅕	3,000	6,000	11,000
Third	15,000 × ⅕	3,000	9,000	8,000
Fourth	15,000 × ⅕	3,000	12,000	5,000
Fifth	15,000 × ⅕	3,000	15,000	2,000
Total		$15,000		

(We present several depreciation schedules in this chapter. In each schedule we highlight in red those features that we want to emphasize.)

The term "book value" in Exhibit 9–3 is the amount of the depreciable cost of the asset that has not yet been recognized as depreciation expense at a point in time. For example, book value at the end of the third year after depreciation for that year has been recognized is $8,000, computed as follows:

Cost	$17,000
Accumulated depreciation at end of third year	(9,000)
Book value	$ 8,000

Notice that the depreciation expense over the life of the truck totals *$15,000*—the cost of the truck *minus the estimated residual value*. The residual value is *not* part of the cost "used up" in business operations. Instead, the residual value is expected to be recovered in cash upon disposal of the asset.

In practice, residual values may be ignored if they are not expected to be *material* in amount. Office equipment, furniture, fixtures, and special-purpose equipment seldom are considered to have significant residual values. Assets such as vehicles, aircraft, and construction equipment, in contrast, often do have residual values that are material in amount.

It often is convenient to state the portion of an asset's depreciable cost that will be written off during the year as a percentage, called the *depreciation rate*. When straight-line depreciation is in use, the depreciation rate is simply *1* divided by the *life* (in years) of the asset. The delivery truck in our example has an estimated life of 5 years, so the depreciation expense each year is ⅕, or *20 percent*, of the depreciable amount. Similarly, an asset with a 10-year life has a depreciation rate of ⅒, or *10 percent*; and an asset with an 8-year life, a depreciation rate of ⅛, or *12 ½ percent*.

Depreciation for Fractional Periods When an asset is acquired in the middle of an accounting period, it is not necessary to compute depreciation expense to the nearest day or week. In fact, such a computation would give a misleading impression of great precision. Since depreciation is based on an estimated useful life of many years, the depreciation applicable to any one year is *only an approximation*.

One widely used method of computing depreciation for part of a year is to round the calculation to the nearest whole month. In our example, S&G acquired the delivery truck on January 2. Therefore, we computed a full year's depreciation for the year of acquisition. Assume, however, that the truck had been acquired later in the year on *October 1*. Thus the truck would have been in use for only 3 months (or 3⁄12) of the first year. In this case, depreciation expense for the first year would be limited to only *$750*, or 3⁄12 of a full year's depreciation ($3,000 × 3⁄12 = $750).

Another widely used approach, called the **half-year convention**, is to record one-half year's depreciation on all assets acquired during the year. This approach is based on the assumption that the actual purchase dates will average out to approximately midyear. The half-year convention is widely used for assets such as office equipment, automobiles, and machinery. To complete the depreciation process for an asset by the half-year convention, a one-half-year's depreciation is also taken in the last year of the asset's life.

Assume that S&G Wholesale Grocery uses straight-line depreciation with the half-year convention. In Exhibit 9–4, we summarize depreciation on the $17,000 delivery truck with the 5-year life.

Exhibit 9–4

STRAIGHT-LINE DEPRECIATION SCHEDULE

Depreciation Schedule
Straight-Line Method with Half-Year Convention

Year	Computation	Depreciation Expense	Accumulated Depreciation	Book Value
				$17,000
First	$15,000 × 1⁄5 × 1⁄2	$ 1,500	$ 1,500	15,500
Second	15,000 × 1⁄5	3,000	4,500	12,500
Third	15,000 × 1⁄5	3,000	7,500	9,500
Fourth	15,000 × 1⁄5	3,000	10,500	6,500
Fifth	15,000 × 1⁄5	3,000	13,500	3,500
Sixth	15,000 × 1⁄5 × 1⁄2	1,500	15,000	2,000
Total		$15,000		

When the half-year convention is in use, we ignore the date on which the asset was actually purchased. We simply recognize *one-half year's depreciation* in both the first year and the last year of the depreciation schedule. Notice that our depreciation schedule now includes depreciation expense in the sixth year. Taking only a partial year's depreciation in the first year always extends the recognition of depreciation into one additional year.

The half-year convention enables us to treat similar assets acquired at different dates during the year as a single group. For example, assume that an insurance company purchases hundreds of desktop computers throughout the current year at a total cost of $600,000. The company depreciates these computers by the straight-line method, assuming a 5-year life and no residual value. Using the half-year convention, the depreciation expense on all of the computers purchased during the year may be computed as follows: $600,000 ÷ 5 years × 6⁄12 = $60,000. If we did not use the half-year convention, depreciation would have to be computed separately for computers purchased in different months.

THE DECLINING-BALANCE METHOD

The most widely used accelerated depreciation method is called **fixed-percentage-of-declining-balance depreciation**. However, the method is used primarily in *income tax returns*, rather than financial statements.[3]

Under the declining-balance method, an accelerated *depreciation rate* is computed as a specified percentage of the straight-line depreciation rate. Annual depreciation expense then

[3] In 1986, Congress adopted an accelerated method of depreciation called the *Modified Accelerated Cost Recovery System* (or MACRS). Companies may use straight-line depreciation for federal income tax purposes, but most prefer to use MACRS because of its favorable income tax consequences. MACRS is the *only* accelerated depreciation method that may be used in federal income tax returns.

is computed by applying this accelerated depreciation rate to the undepreciated cost (current book value) of the asset. This computation may be summarized as follows:

$$\textbf{Depreciation Expense} = \textbf{Remaining Book Value} \times \textbf{Accelerated Depreciation Rate}$$

The accelerated depreciation rate *remains constant* throughout the life of the asset. Hence, the rate represents the "fixed-percentage" described in the name of this depreciation method. The book value (cost minus accumulated depreciation) *decreases every year* and represents the "declining-balance."

Thus far, we have described the accelerated depreciation rate as a "specified percentage" of the straight-line rate. Most often, this specified percentage is 200 percent, meaning that the accelerated rate is exactly twice the straight-line rate. As a result, the declining-balance method of depreciation often is called *double-declining-balance* (or 200 percent declining-balance). Tax rules, however, often specify a *lower* percentage, such as 150 percent of the straight-line rate. This version of the declining-balance method may be described as "150 percent declining-balance."[4]

Double-Declining-Balance To illustrate the double-declining-balance method, consider our example of the $17,000 delivery truck. The estimated useful life is 5 years; therefore, the straight-line depreciation rate is 20 percent (1 ÷ 5 years). Doubling this straight-line rate indicates an accelerated depreciation rate of 40 percent. Each year, we will recognize as depreciation expense 40 percent of the truck's current book value, as we show in Exhibit 9–5.

Exhibit 9–5

200% DECLINING-BALANCE DEPRECIATION SCHEDULE

Depreciation Schedule: 200% Declining-Balance Method

Year	Computation	Depreciation Expense	Accumulated Depreciation	Book Value
				$17,000
First	$17,000 × 40%	$ 6,800	$ 6,800	10,200
Second	10,200 × 40%	4,080	10,880	6,120
Third	6,120 × 40%	2,448	13,328	3,672
Fourth	3,672 × 40%	1,469	14,797	2,203
Fifth	2,203 − $2,000	203	15,000	2,000
Total		$15,000		

As with the straight-line method illustrated earlier, the asset's book value is computed by subtracting depreciation recognized to date from the asset's cost. For example, from Exhibit 9–5, the book value of the asset at the end of the third year is computed as follows:

Cost	$17,000
Accumulated depreciation at end of third year	(13,328)
Book value	$ 3,672

Recall that book value at the end of the third year by the straight-line method was $8,000. The difference between that figure and the $3,672 computed above is due to the more rapid depreciation recognized by the declining-balance method compared to the straight-line method.

[4] The higher the specified percentage of the straight-line rate, the more accelerated this depreciation becomes. Experience and tradition have established 200 percent of the straight-line rate as the maximum level. For federal income tax purposes, MACRS (see footnote 3) is based upon a 200 percent declining-balance for some assets, and a 150 percent declining-balance for others. The 150 percent declining-balance slows down the rates at which taxpayers may depreciate specific types of assets in their income tax returns.

Notice that the estimated residual value of the delivery truck *does not* enter into the computation of depreciation expense until the end. This is because the declining-balance method provides an "*automatic*" residual value. As long as each year's depreciation expense is equal to only a portion of the undepreciated cost of the asset, the asset *will never be entirely written off*. However, if the asset has a significant residual value, depreciation should *stop at this point*. Since our delivery truck has an estimated residual value of *$2,000*, the depreciation expense for the fifth year is *limited to $203*, rather than the $881 indicated by taking 40 percent of the remaining book value (40% × $2,203 = $881). By limiting the last year's depreciation expense in this manner, the book value of the truck at the end of the fifth year is equal to its $2,000 estimated residual value.

In Exhibit 9–5 we computed a full year's depreciation in the first year because the asset was acquired on January 2. But if the half-year convention were in use, depreciation in the first year would be *reduced by half*, to $3,400. The depreciation in the second year would be ($17,000 − $3,400) × 40%, or *$5,440*.

150 Percent Declining-Balance Now assume that we wanted to depreciate this truck using 150 percent of the straight-line rate. In this case, the depreciation rate will be 30 percent, instead of 40 percent (a 20% straight-line rate × 150% = 30%). This depreciation schedule is in Exhibit 9–6.

Exhibit 9–6

150% DECLINING-BALANCE DEPRECIATION SCHEDULE

Depreciation Schedule: 150% Declining-Balance Method

Year	Computation	Depreciation Expense	Accumulated Depreciation	Book Value
				$17,000
First	$17,000 × 30%	$ 5,100	$ 5,100	11,900
Second	11,900 × 30%	3,570	8,670	8,330
Third	8,330 × 30%	2,499	11,169	5,831
Fourth	(5,831 − 2,000) ÷ 2	1,916*	13,085	3,915
Fifth	3,915 − 2,000	1,915*	15,000	2,000
Total		$15,000		

*Switched to the straight-line method for Years 4 and 5.

Notice that we switched to straight-line depreciation in the last two years. The undepreciated cost of the truck at the end of Year 3 was *$5,831*. To depreciate the truck to an estimated residual value of $2,000 at the end of Year 5, $3,831 in depreciation expense must be recognized over the next two years. At this point, *larger depreciation charges* can be recognized if we simply allocate this $3,831 by the straight-line method, rather than continuing to compute 30 percent of the remaining book value. (In our table, we round the allocation of this amount to the nearest dollar.)

Allocating the remaining book value over the remaining life by the straight-line method does *not* represent a change in depreciation methods. Rather, a switch to straight-line when this will result in larger depreciation is *part of the declining-balance method*. This is the way in which we arrive at the desired residual value.

WHICH DEPRECIATION METHODS DO MOST BUSINESSES USE?

Many businesses use the straight-line method of depreciation in their financial statements and accelerated methods in their income tax returns. The reasons for these choices are easy to understand.

Accelerated depreciation methods result in higher charges to depreciation expense early in the asset's life and, therefore, lower reported net income than straight-line depreciation. Most publicly owned companies want to appear as profitable as possible—certainly as profitable as their competitors. Therefore, the majority of publicly owned companies use straight-line depreciation in their financial statements.

For income tax purposes, it's a different story. Management usually wants to report the *lowest* possible taxable income in the company's income tax returns. Accelerated depreciation methods can substantially reduce both taxable income and tax payments for a period of years.[5]

Accounting principles and income tax laws both permit companies to use *different depreciation methods* in their financial statements and their income tax returns. Therefore, many companies use straight-line depreciation in their financial statements and accelerated methods (variations of the declining-balance method) in their income tax returns.

The Differences in Depreciation Methods: Are They "Real"?

Using the straight-line depreciation method will cause a company to *report* higher profits than would be reported if an accelerated method were in use. But *is* the company better off than if it had used an accelerated method? The answer is *no!* Depreciation—no matter how it is computed—*is only an estimate*. The amount of this estimate has *no effect* on the actual financial strength of the business. Thus a business that uses an accelerated depreciation method in its financial statements is simply measuring its net income *more conservatively* than a business that uses straight-line. However, the benefits of using an accelerated method for income tax purposes *are* real because the amount of depreciation claimed affects the amount of taxes owed. Lower income taxes translate directly into increased cash availability.

In the preceding chapter, we made the point that, if a company wants to use LIFO in its income tax return, it *must* use LIFO in its financial statements. *No similar requirement exists for depreciation methods*. A company may use an accelerated method in its income tax returns and the straight-line method in its financial statements—and most companies do.

FINANCIAL STATEMENT DISCLOSURES

A company must *disclose* in notes to its financial statements the methods used to depreciate plant assets. This disclosure is located in a note describing various accounting policies and methods used in preparing the financial statements. Readers of the statements should recognize that accelerated depreciation methods transfer the costs of plant assets to expense more quickly than the straight-line method. Thus accelerated methods result in more *conservative* (lower) balance sheet amounts of plant assets and measurements of net income.

Estimates of Useful Life and Residual Value

Estimating the useful lives and residual values of plant assets is the *responsibility of management*. These estimates usually are based on the company's past experience with similar assets, but they also reflect the company's current circumstances and management's future plans. Thus the estimated lives of similar assets may vary from one company to another.

The estimated lives of plant assets affect the amount of net income reported each period. The longer the estimated useful life, the smaller the amount of cost transferred each period to depreciation expense and the larger the amount of reported net income. Bear in mind, however, that all large corporations are *audited* annually by a firm of independent public accountants. One of the responsibilities of these auditors is to determine that management's estimates of the useful lives of plant assets are reasonable under the circumstances.

Automobiles typically are depreciated over relatively short estimated lives—say, from 3 to 5 years. Other types of equipment are generally depreciated over a period of 5 to 15 years. Buildings are depreciated over much longer lives—perhaps 30 to 50 years for a new building and 15 years or more for a building acquired used.

The Principle of Consistency

The *consistent* application of accounting methods is a fundamental concept underlying generally accepted accounting principles. With respect to depreciation methods, this means that a company should *not change* from year to year the method used in computing the depreciation expense for a given plant asset. However, management *may* use different methods in computing depreciation for different assets. Also, as we have stressed

[5] For a *growing* business, the use of accelerated depreciation in income tax returns may reduce taxable income *every* year. This is because a growing business may always have more assets in the early years of their recovery periods than in the later years.

repeatedly, a company may—and often *must*—use different depreciation methods in its financial statements and income tax returns.

Revision of Estimated Useful Lives What should be done if, after a few years of using a plant asset, management decides that the asset actually is going to last for a considerably longer or shorter period than was originally estimated? When this situation arises, a *revised estimate* of useful life should be made and the periodic depreciation expense decreased or increased accordingly.

The procedure for changing the depreciation schedule is to spread the remaining undepreciated cost of the asset *over the years of remaining useful life*. This change affects only the amount of depreciation expense that will be recorded in the current and future periods. The financial statements of past periods are *not* revised to reflect changes in the estimated useful lives of depreciable assets.

To illustrate, assume that a company acquires a $10,000 asset estimated to have a 5-year useful life and no residual value. Under the straight-line method, the annual depreciation expense is $2,000. At the end of the third year, accumulated depreciation amounts to $6,000, and the asset has an undepreciated cost (or book value) of $4,000.

At the beginning of the fourth year, management decides that the asset will last for 5 *more* years. The revised estimate of useful life is, therefore, a total of 8 years. The depreciation expense to be recognized for the fourth year and for each of the remaining years is $800, computed as follows:

Undepreciated cost at end of third year ($10,000 − $6,000)	$4,000
Revised estimate of remaining years of useful life	5 years
Revised amount of annual depreciation expense ($4,000 ÷ 5)	$ 800

THE IMPAIRMENT OF PLANT ASSETS

Sometimes, it becomes apparent that a company cannot reasonably expect to recover the carrying amount of certain plant assets, either through use or through sale. For example, a computer manufacturer may have paid a high price to acquire specialized production equipment. If new technology soon renders the equipment obsolete, however, it may become apparent that it is worth less than the amount at which the equipment is carried in the accounting records.

If the carrying amount of an asset cannot be recovered through future use or sale, the asset should be *written down* to its fair value. The offsetting debit is to an **impairment loss** account.

CASE IN POINT

In 2004, **Newmont Mining Corporation** recorded a write-down of long-lived assets of $39.3 million, following similar write-downs in 2003 of $35.3 million and in 2002 of $3.7 million. A note accompanying the 2004 financial statements explains that these write-downs included $16.3 million related to the long-lived assets of the Ovacik mine in Turkey. In August 2004, the Ovacik mine suspended operations as a result of a court decision ordering the suspension of operating permits pending completion of certain requirements and the submission of an updated environmental impact assessment. On March 1, 2005, the Ovacik mine was sold to a subsidiary of Koza Davetiye, a Turkish conglomerate.

Other Depreciation Methods

Account for depreciation using methods other than straight-line or declining-balance. LO4

Most companies that prepare financial statements in conformity with generally accepted accounting principles use the straight-line method of depreciation. However, any rational and systematic method is acceptable, as long as costs are allocated to expense in a reasonable manner. Several such methods are discussed here.

THE UNITS-OF-OUTPUT METHOD

Under the **units-of-output** method, depreciation is based on some measure of output *rather than* on the passage of time. When depreciation is based on units of output, more depreciation is recognized in the periods in which the assets are most heavily used.

To illustrate this method, consider S&G's delivery truck, which cost $17,000 and has an estimated salvage value of $2,000. Assume that S&G plans to retire this truck after it has been driven 100,000 miles. The depreciation rate *per mile of operation is 15 cents*, computed as follows:

$$\frac{\textbf{Cost} - \textbf{Residual Value}}{\textbf{Estimated Units of Output (Miles)}} = \textbf{Cost per Unit of Output (Mile)}$$

$$\frac{\$17{,}000 - \$2{,}000}{100{,}000 \text{ miles}} = \$0.15 \text{ Depreciation per Mile}$$

At the end of each year, the amount of depreciation to be recorded is determined by multiplying the 15-cent rate by the number of miles the truck has been driven during the year. After the truck has gone 100,000 miles, it is fully depreciated, and the depreciation process is stopped.

This method provides an excellent matching of expense with revenue. However, the method should be used only when the total units of output can be estimated with reasonable accuracy. Also, this method is used only for assets such as vehicles and certain types of machinery. Assets such as buildings, computers, and furniture do not have well-defined "units of output."

In many cases, units-of-output is an *accelerated method.* Often assets are used more extensively in the earlier years of their useful lives than in the later years.

MACRS

Most businesses use a depreciation method called **MACRS** (Modified Accelerated Cost Recovery System) in their federal income tax returns. Some small businesses also use this method in their financial statements, so they do not have to compute depreciation in several different ways. MACRS is based on the declining-balance method, but should be considered for use in financial statements only if the *designated "recovery periods"* and the *assumption of no salvage value* are reasonable. For publicly traded companies, the use of MACRS in financial statements is usually not considered to be in conformity with generally accepted accounting principles.

SUM-OF-THE-YEARS' DIGITS

Sum-of-the-years' digits, or **SYD**, is a form of accelerated depreciation. It generally produces results that lie between the double-declining-balance and 150 percent-declining-balance methods.

SYD is a traditional topic that is included in many accounting textbooks. But it is the most complex of the accelerated methods—especially when partial years are involved. SYD is rarely used in today's business world. As shown in Exhibit 9–7, only 6 of the 600 corporations surveyed—less than 1 percent—make any use of this method. Because of its complexity, it is even less frequently used in small businesses. SYD is seldom used for income tax purposes, because tax laws usually define allowable depreciation rates in terms of the declining-balance method. For these reasons, we defer coverage of the mechanics of this method to later accounting courses.

DECELERATED DEPRECIATION METHODS

Depreciation methods do exist that recognize *less* depreciation expense in the early years of an asset's useful life and *more in the later years*. Such methods may achieve a reasonable matching of depreciation expense and revenue when the plant asset is expected to become *increasingly productive* over time. Utility companies, for example, may use these methods for new power plants that will be more fully utilized as the population of the area increases.

These depreciation methods are rarely used; thus we defer coverage to later accounting courses.

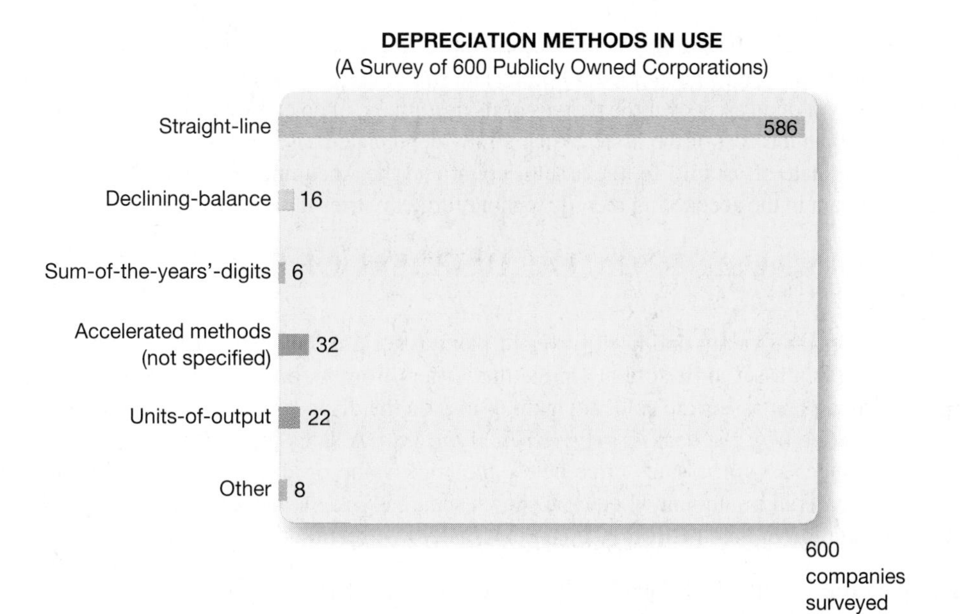

Source: AICPA, *Accounting Trends & Techniques*, New York, 2003, p. 422. Data reported for 2005.

Exhibit 9–7

COMPARATIVE USE OF DEPRECIATION METHODS

Straight-line is clearly the method most widely used in financial statements

DEPRECIATION METHODS IN USE: A SURVEY

Every year, the American Institute of Certified Public Accountants (AICPA) conducts a survey of 600 publicly owned companies to determine the accounting methods most widely used in financial statements. The various depreciation methods in use during a recent year are summarized in Exhibit 9–7. Notice that the number of methods in use exceeds 600. This is because some companies use different depreciation methods for different types of assets.

Bear in mind this survey indicates only the depreciation methods used in financial statements. In income tax returns, most companies use accelerated depreciation methods such as MACRS.

Disposal of Plant and Equipment

Account for the disposal of plant assets. LO5

When depreciable assets are disposed of at any date other than the end of the year, an entry should be made to record depreciation for the *fraction of the year* ending with the date of disposal. If the half-year convention is in use, six months' depreciation should be recorded on all assets disposed of during the year. In the following illustrations of the disposal of items of plant and equipment, it is assumed that any necessary entries for fractional-period depreciation already have been recorded.

As units of plant and equipment wear out or become obsolete, they must be scrapped, sold, or traded in on new equipment. Upon the disposal or retirement of a depreciable asset, the cost of the property is removed from the asset account, and the accumulated depreciation is removed from the related contra-asset account. Assume, for example, that office equipment purchased 10 years ago at a cost of $20,000 has been fully depreciated and is no longer useful. The entry to record the scrapping of the worthless equipment is as follows:

Accumulated Depreciation: Office Equipment	20,000	
Office Equipment		20,000
To remove from the accounts the cost and the accumulated depreciation on fully depreciated office equipment now being scrapped. No salvage value.		

Scrapping a fully depreciated asset

Once an asset has been fully depreciated, no more depreciation should be recorded on it, even though the property may be in good condition and still in use. The objective of depreciation is to spread the *cost* of an asset over the periods of its usefulness; in no case can depreciation expense be greater than the cost of the asset. When a fully depreciated asset remains in use beyond the original estimate of useful life, the asset account and the Accumulated Depreciation account should remain in the accounting records without further entries until the asset is retired.

GAINS AND LOSSES ON THE DISPOSAL OF PLANT AND EQUIPMENT

Since the residual values and useful lives of plant assets are only estimates, it is not uncommon for a plant asset to be sold at a price that differs from its book value at the date of disposal. When plant assets are sold, any gain or loss on the disposal is computed by comparing the *book value with the amount received from the sale.* A sales price in excess of the book value produces a gain; a sales price below the book value produces a loss. These gains or losses, if material in amount, should be shown separately in the income statement following the computation of income from operations, usually in a section titled "other income."

Disposal at a Price above Book Value

Assume that a machine costing $10,000 had accumulated depreciation of $8,000 and a book value of $2,000 at the time it was sold for $3,000 cash. The journal entry to record this disposal is as follows:

Cash	3,000	
Accumulated Depreciation: Machinery	8,000	
Machinery		10,000
Gain on Disposal of Plant Assets		1,000
To record sale of machinery at a price above book value.		

In this situation, the gain on the disposal is calculated as follows:

Cost	$10,000
Accumulated depreciation at time of disposal	(8,000)
Book value at time of disposal	$ 2,000
Cash received	3,000
Gain on disposal	$ 1,000

Disposal at a Price below Book Value

Now assume instead that the same machine is sold for $500. The journal entry in this case would be as follows:

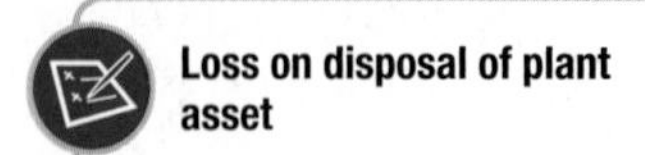

Cash	500	
Accumulated Depreciation: Machinery	8,000	
Loss on Disposal of Plant Assets	1,500	
Machinery		10,000
To record sale of machinery at a price below book value.		

In this situation, the loss on the disposal is calculated as follows:

Cost	$10,000
Accumulated depreciation at time of disposal	(8,000)
Book value at time of disposal	$ 2,000
Cash received	500
Loss on disposal	$ 1,500

The disposal of a depreciable asset at a price *equal to* book value results in neither a gain nor a loss. The entry for such a transaction consists of a debit to Cash for the amount received, a debit to Accumulated Depreciation for the balance accumulated, and a credit to the asset account for the original cost.

TRADING IN USED ASSETS FOR NEW ONES

Certain types of depreciable assets, such as automobiles and trucks, sometimes are traded in for new assets of the same kind. In most instances, a trade-in is viewed as both a *sale* of the old asset and a purchase of a new one. Transactions of this type are usually considered to have "commercial substance," and give rise to the recognition of a gain or loss.

To illustrate, assume that Rancho Landscape has an old pickup truck that originally cost $10,000 but that now has a book value (and tax basis) of $2,000. Rancho trades in this old truck for a new one with a fair market value of $15,000. The truck dealership grants Rancho a trade-in allowance of $3,500 for the old truck, and Rancho pays the remaining $11,500 cost of the new truck in cash. Rancho Landscape should record this transaction as follows:

Vehicles (new truck)	15,000	
Accumulated Depreciation: Trucks (old truck)	8,000	
Vehicles (old truck)		10,000
Cash		11,500
Gain on Disposal of Plant Assets		1,500
Traded in old truck for a new one costing $15,000. Received $3,500 trade-in allowance on the old truck, which had a book value of $2,000.		

Entry to record a typical trade-in

Notice that Rancho treats the $3,500 trade-in allowance granted by the truck dealership as the *sales price* of the old truck. Thus Rancho recognizes a *$1,500 gain* on the disposal (trade-in) of this asset ($3,500 trade-in allowance − $2,000 book value = $1,500 gain).

For financial reporting purposes, gains and losses on routine trade-ins are recorded in the accounting records whenever the transaction also involves the payment of a significant amount of cash (or the creation of debt). Income tax rules do *not* permit recognition of gains or losses on exchanges of assets that are used for similar purposes. Thus the $1,500 gain recorded in our example is not regarded as taxable income.[6]

Intangible Assets

CHARACTERISTICS

Explain the nature of intangible assets, including goodwill. LO6

As the word *intangible* suggests, assets in this classification have no physical substance. Common examples are patents, trademarks, and goodwill. Intangible assets are classified in the balance sheet as a subgroup of plant assets. However, not all assets that lack physical substance are regarded as intangible assets. An account receivable, for example, has no physical attributes but is classified as a current asset and is not regarded as an intangible. In brief, *intangible assets are assets that are used in the operation of the business but that have no physical substance and are noncurrent.*

The basis of valuation for intangible assets is cost. In some companies, however, certain intangible assets such as trademarks may be of great importance but may have been acquired without incurring any significant cost. These intangible assets appear in the balance sheet at their *cost*, regardless of their value to the company. Intangible assets are listed only if significant costs are incurred in their acquisition or development. If these costs are *insignificant*, they are treated as revenue expenditures (ordinary expenses).

[6] Had the trade-in allowance been less than book value, the resulting loss would *not be deductible* in the determination of taxable income.

OPERATING EXPENSES VERSUS INTANGIBLE ASSETS

For an expenditure to qualify as an intangible asset, there must be reasonable evidence of future benefits. Many expenditures offer some prospects of yielding benefits in subsequent years, but the existence and life span of these benefits are so uncertain that most companies treat these expenditures as operating expenses. Examples are the expenditures required to reorganize a business and the expense of training employees to work with new types of machinery or office equipment. There is little doubt that some benefits from these outlays continue beyond the current period, but because of the uncertain duration of the benefits, it is almost universal practice to treat expenditures of this nature as an expense of the current period.

AMORTIZATION

The term **amortization** describes the systematic write-off to expense of the cost of an intangible asset over its useful life. Amortization of an intangible asset is essentially the same as depreciation for a tangible asset. The usual accounting entry for amortization consists of a debit to Amortization Expense and a credit to the intangible asset account. There is no theoretical objection to crediting an accumulated amortization account rather than the intangible asset account, but this method is seldom encountered in practice.

Although it is difficult to estimate the useful life of an intangible such as a trademark, it is probable that such an asset will not contribute to future earnings on a permanent basis. The cost of the intangible asset should, therefore, be deducted from revenue during the years in which it may be expected to aid in producing revenue. The straight-line method normally is used for amortizing intangible assets.

GOODWILL

The intangible asset **goodwill** is often found in corporate balance sheets. While this word has a variety of meanings in our general vocabulary, it has a specific and specialized meaning in financial reporting. Goodwill represents an amount that a company has paid to acquire certain favorable intangible attributes as part of an acquisition of another company. For example, assume a company purchases another company that has a favorable reputation for high-quality customer service. The purchasing company might be willing to pay a price to acquire this favorable attribute because of its expectations about the positive impact this customer service will have on future profitability. Even though an intangible asset such as having a favorable reputation for customer service lacks the physical qualities of land, buildings, and equipment, such service may be just as important for the future success of a company. Goodwill is a general term that encompasses a wide variety of favorable attributes expected to permit the acquiring company to operate at a greater-than-normal level of profitability. Positive attributes often included in goodwill are:

- Favorable reputation.
- Positive market share.
- Positive advertising image.
- Reputation for high quality and loyal employees.
- Superior management.
- Manufacturing and other operating efficiency.

All of these attributes can be expected to contribute to positive future cash flows of the acquiring company. The **present value** of future cash flows is the amount that a knowledgeable investor would pay today for the right to receive those future cash flows. (The present value concept is discussed further in later chapters and in Appendix B.)

Goodwill is sometimes described and measured as the price paid to receive an *above-normal return* on the purchase of another company's net identifiable assets. This requires that we explain the phrase *normal return on the net identifiable assets. Net assets* refers to assets minus liabilities, or owners' equity. Goodwill is not a separately identifiable asset, however, and the existence of goodwill is implied by the ability of a business to earn an above-average return. The term, **net identifiable assets**, is used to mean all assets except goodwill, minus liabilities.

A *normal return* on net identifiable assets is the rate of return that investors demand in a particular industry to justify their buying a business at the fair value of its net identifiable assets. A business has goodwill when investors will pay a *higher* price because the business earns *more* than the normal rate of return.

Assume that two similar restaurants are offered for sale and that the normal return on the fair market value of the net identifiable assets of restaurants of this type is 15 percent a year. The relative earning power of the two restaurants during the past five years is as follows:

	Mandarin Coast	Golden Dragon
Fair market value of net identifiable assets	$1,000,000	$1,000,000
Normal rate of return on net assets	15%	15%
Normal earnings, computed as 15% of net identifiable assets	150,000	150,000
Average actual net income for past five years	$ 150,000	$ 200,000
Earnings in excess of normal	$ -0-	$ 50,000

Which business is worth more?

An investor presumably would be willing to pay $1,000,000 to buy Mandarin Coast, because this restaurant earns the normal 15 percent return that justifies the fair market value of its net identifiable assets. Although Golden Dragon has the same amount of net identifiable assets, an investor should be willing to pay *more* for Golden Dragon than for Mandarin Coast, because Golden Dragon has a record of superior earnings. The *extra amount* that a buyer pays to purchase Golden Dragon represents the value of this business's *goodwill.*

Estimating Goodwill How much will an investor pay for goodwill? Above-average earnings in past years are of significance to prospective purchasers only if they believe that these earnings *will continue* after they acquire the business. Investors' appraisals of goodwill, therefore, will vary with their estimates of the *future earning power* of the business. Few businesses, however, are able to maintain above-average earnings indefinitely. Consequently, the purchaser of a business will usually limit any amount paid for goodwill to not more than four or five times the amount by which annual earnings exceed normal earnings.

Estimating an amount for goodwill in the purchase of a business is a difficult and speculative process. In attempting to make such an estimate, you are essentially trying to look into the future and predict the extent to which purchasing another business will add so much value to your current business that you are willing to pay a price greater than the value of the identifiable net assets of the business you are acquiring. For example, in the previous example, how much more than $1,000,000 would you be willing to pay for Golden Dragon in comparison with Mandarin Coast? History indicates that Golden Dragon is more profitable, and thus worth more, than Mandarin Coast, but whether that extra profitability will continue in the future requires considerable judgment.

Several methods exist for placing a monetary value on the amount of goodwill in the purchase of a business. A widely used method that is consistent with this description of goodwill is to value the business as a whole and then subtract the current market value of the net identifiable assets to estimate the amount of goodwill. For example, assume that successful restaurants sell at about 6½ times annual earnings.[7] This suggests that Golden Dragon is worth about $1,300,000, which is the company's $200,000 average net income times 6.5. Because the company's net identifiable assets have a fair value of only $1,000,000, a reasonable estimate of the positive attributes of Golden Dragon, such as positive reputation or market share, is $300,000, determined as follows:

Estimated value of the business as a whole ($200,000 × 6.5)	$1,300,000
Fair market value of net identifiable assets	1,000,000
Estimated value of goodwill	$ 300,000

[7] Investments in small businesses involve more risk and less liquidity than investments in publicly owned companies. For these reasons, the price-earnings ratios of small businesses tend to be substantially lower than those of publicly owned corporations.

If a buyer of Golden Dragon pays $1,300,000 to purchase the business, $300,000 of goodwill would be recorded. On the other hand, if the buyer is able to purchase Golden Dragon for less than $1,300,000, say $1,250,000, only $250,000 of goodwill would be recorded ($1,250,000 − $1,000,000 = $250,000), even though the estimated value of goodwill is more than the amount paid.

Recording Goodwill in the Accounts Because of the difficulties in objectively estimating the value of goodwill, this asset is recorded only when it is purchased. Goodwill is purchased when one company buys another. The purchaser records the identifiable assets it has purchased at their fair values and then establishes any additional amount paid to an asset account entitled Goodwill.

Many businesses never purchase goodwill but develop goodwill attributes like good customer relations, superior management, or other factors that result in above-average earnings. Because there is no objective way of determining the value of these qualities unless the business is sold, internally generated goodwill is *not recorded* in the accounting records. The absence of internally generated goodwill is one of the principal reasons why a balance sheet does not indicate a company's current market value.

For many years, generally accepted accounting principles required that purchased goodwill be amortized over a period not exceeding 40 years. The Financial Accounting Standards Board (FASB) has now changed accounting for goodwill so that goodwill is no longer required to be amortized. The amortization of goodwill was similar to depreciation of equipment and other long-lived assets in that a portion of the cost was removed from the asset account and transferred to an expense in each accounting period. As a general rule, the straight-line method was used for amortizing goodwill and is still commonly used for other intangible assets that are subject to amortization. As part of the changes that resulted in goodwill no longer being amortized, goodwill is now subject to assessment for impairment in value, similar to that for plant assets as explained earlier in this chapter. When the recorded amount of goodwill is no longer recoverable, an impairment loss must be recorded by reducing the asset amount and including a loss in the income statement of the same accounting period.

CASE IN POINT

Goodwill was identified as a topic for harmonization efforts when the FASB and the International Accounting Standards Board (IASB) agreed to work toward convergence of reporting requirements in 2002. U.S. GAAP requires capitalization of goodwill but no amortization. Instead, goodwill is reviewed annually and its value is adjusted if subject to impairment. Until March 2004, international standards required goodwill to be capitalized and amortized over its estimated useful life (20 years or less). In 2004, the IASB issued International Financial Reporting Standard (IFRS) no. 3. IFRS no. 3 changed goodwill reporting requirements to be consistent with the U.S. GAAP approach by requiring an impairment test rather than amortization for goodwill.

PATENTS

A patent is an exclusive right granted by the federal government for manufacture, use, and sale of a particular product. The purpose of this exclusive grant is to encourage the invention of new products and processes. When a company acquires a patent by purchase from the inventor or other holder, the purchase price should be recorded by debiting the intangible asset account Patents.

Patents are granted for 20 years, and the period of amortization should not exceed that period. However, if the patent is likely to lose its usefulness in less than 20 years, amortization should be based on the shorter estimated useful life. Assume that a patent is purchased from the inventor at a cost of $100,000 after five years of the legal life have expired. The remaining *legal* life is, therefore, 15 years. But if the estimated *useful* life is only four years, amortization should be based on this shorter period. The entry to record the annual amortization expense would be:

Amortization Expense: Patents	25,000	
Patents		25,000
To amortize cost of patent on a straight-line basis over an estimated useful life of 4 years.		

Entry for amortization of patent

TRADEMARKS AND TRADE NAMES

Coca-Cola's famous name, usually printed in a distinctive typeface, is a classic example of a trademark known around the world. A trademark is a name, symbol, or design that identifies a product or group of products. A permanent exclusive right to the use of a trademark, brand name, or commercial symbol may be obtained by registering it with the federal government.

The costs of developing a trademark or brand name often consist of advertising campaigns, which should be treated as expenses when incurred. If a trademark or brand name is *purchased*, however, the cost may be substantial. Such cost should be capitalized and amortized to expense over the time period the trademark or brand name is expected to be used. If the use of the trademark is discontinued or its contribution to earnings becomes doubtful, any unamortized cost should be written off immediately.

FRANCHISES

A franchise is a right granted by a company or a governmental unit to conduct a certain type of business in a specific geographical area. An example of a franchise is the right to operate a McDonald's restaurant in a specific neighborhood. The cost of franchises varies greatly and often is quite substantial. When the cost of a franchise is small, it may be charged immediately to expense or amortized over a short period such as five years. When the cost is material, amortization should be based on the life of the franchise (if defined by the franchise agreement); the amortization period, however, should not exceed the period the franchise is expected to generate revenue.

The Image Works

COPYRIGHTS

A copyright is an exclusive right granted by the federal government to protect the production and sale of literary or artistic materials for the life of the creator plus 70 years. The cost of obtaining a copyright may be minor and therefore is chargeable to expense when paid. Only when a copyright is *purchased* from an existing owner will the expenditure be *material enough* to warrant its being capitalized and spread over the useful life. The revenue from copyrights is usually limited to only a few years, and the purchase cost should, of course, be amortized over the years in which the revenue is expected.

OTHER INTANGIBLES AND DEFERRED CHARGES

Among the other intangibles found in the published balance sheets of large corporations are moving costs, plant rearrangement costs, formulas, processes, name lists, and film rights. Some companies group items of this type under the title of Deferred Charges, meaning expenditures that will provide benefits beyond the current year and that will be written off to expense over their useful economic lives. It is also common practice to combine these items under the heading of Other Assets, which is listed at the bottom of the balance sheet.

RESEARCH AND DEVELOPMENT (R&D) COSTS

Billions of dollars are spent each year on research and development of new products. In fact, expenditures for R&D are a striking characteristic of U.S. industry. The annual research and development expenditures of some companies often exceed $1 billion and account for a substantial percentage of their total costs and expenses.

In the past, some companies treated all research and development costs as expenses in the year incurred; other companies in the same industry recorded these costs as intangible assets to be amortized over future years. This diversity of practice prevented financial statements of different companies from being comparable.

The Financial Accounting Standards Board standardized accounting for R&D when it ruled that as a general rule research and development expenditures should be charged to expense *when incurred*. This action by the FASB had the beneficial effect of reducing the number of alternative accounting practices and helping to make financial statements of different companies more comparable.

Financial Analysis and Decision Making

The success of many businesses depends on research and development activities (R&D). To better understand a company's commitment to funding R&D, users of financial statements often examine the level of, and trends in, a company's R&D expenditures as a percentage of net sales:

R&D to Sales = R&D Costs ÷ Net Sales

R&D expenditures as a percentage of net sales are naturally higher in some industries than in others. To illustrate this point, see the R&D figures for a recent year for well-known companies from five industries in Exhibit 9–8.

Exhibit 9–8
COMPARATIVE R&D EXPENDITURES

	R&D Costs (in millions)	Net Sales (in millions)	R&D (%)
Chemical Products			
DuPont	1,349	26,996	5.00
Dow Chemical	981	32,632	3.01
Computer Hardware			
Sun Microsystems	1,837	11,434	16.07
Silicon Graphics	177	1,341	13.20
Pharmaceuticals			
Eli Lilly & Co.	2,350	12,583	18.68
Pfizer	7,131	45,188	15.78
Computer Software			
Oracle	1,180	9,475	12.45
Microsoft	4,379	25,296	17.31

YOUR TURN **You as a Financial Analyst**

You are working as an equity analyst on Wall Street and a college intern asks you to explain why companies can differ greatly in the R&D expense to net sales ratio. How do you respond?

(See our comments on the Online Learning Center Web site.)

Natural Resources

ACCOUNTING FOR NATURAL RESOURCES

Account for the depletion of natural resources. LO7

Mining properties, oil and gas reserves, and tracts of standing timber are leading examples of natural resources. The distinguishing characteristic of these assets is that they are physically removed from their natural environment and are converted into inventory. Theoretically, a coal mine might be regarded as an underground inventory of coal; however, such an inventory is certainly not a current asset. In the balance sheet, mining property and other natural resources are classified as property, plant, and equipment. Once the coal is removed from the ground, however, this coal *does* represent inventory.

We have explained that plant assets such as buildings and equipment depreciate because of physical deterioration or obsolescence. A mine or an oil reserve does not depreciate for these reasons, but it is gradually *depleted* as the natural resource is removed from the ground. Once all of the coal has been removed from a coal mine, for example, the mine is "fully depleted" and will be abandoned or sold for its residual value.

To illustrate the **depletion** of a natural resource, assume that Rainbow Minerals pays $45 million to acquire the Red Valley Mine, which is believed to contain 10 million tons of coal. The residual value of the mine after all of the coal is removed is estimated to be $5 million. The depletion that will occur over the life of the mine is the original cost minus the residual value, or $40 million. This depletion will occur at the rate of *$4 per ton* ($40 million ÷ 10 million tons) as the coal is removed from the mine. If we assume that 2 million tons are mined during the first year of operations, the entry to record the depletion of the mine would be as follows:

Recording depletion

Inventory	8,000,000	
Accumulated Depletion: Red Valley Mine		8,000,000
To record depletion of the Red Valley Mine for the year; 2,000,000 tons mined @ $4 per ton.		

Once removed from the mine, coal becomes available for sale. Therefore, the estimated cost of this coal is debited to the Inventory account. As the coal is sold, this cost is transferred from the Inventory account to the Cost of Goods Sold account.

Accumulated Depletion is a *contra-asset account* similar to the Accumulated Depreciation account; it represents the portion of the mine that has been used up (depleted) to date. In Rainbow Minerals's balance sheet, the Red Valley Mine now appears as follows:

The mine gradually is turned into inventory

Property, Plant, & Equipment:		
Mining properties: Red Valley Mine	$45,000,000	
Less: Accumulated depletion	8,000,000	$37,000,000

Depreciation of Buildings and Equipment Closely Related to Natural Resources Buildings and equipment installed at a mine or drilling site may be useful only at that particular location. Consequently, such assets should be depreciated over their normal useful lives or over the life of the natural resource, *whichever is shorter*. Often depreciation on such assets is computed using the units-of-output method, which was discussed earlier in the chapter.

DEPRECIATION, AMORTIZATION, AND DEPLETION—A COMMON GOAL

The processes of depreciation, amortization, and depletion discussed in this chapter all have a common goal. That goal is to *allocate the acquisition cost of a long-lived asset to expense over the years in which the asset contributes to revenue*. Allocating the acquisition cost of long-lived assets over the years that benefit from the use of these assets is an important application of the *matching principle*. The determination of income requires matching revenue with the expenses incurred to produce that revenue.

Plant Transactions and the Statement of Cash Flows

LO8 Explain the cash effects of transactions involving plant assets.

The cash effects of plant and equipment transactions are different from the effects reported in the income statement. Cash payments for plant assets occur when those assets are *purchased*—or, more precisely, when payment is made. Cash receipts often occur when assets are sold. (These receipts are equal to the *total proceeds* received from the sale, not just the amount of any gain.) Cash flows relating to acquisitions and disposals of plant assets appear in the statement of cash flows, classified as *investing activities*.

Depreciation and amortization expense both *reduce net income*, but they have *no effect on cash flows*. As a result, both tend to make net income *less* than the net cash flows from operating activities. Likewise, the write-down of impaired assets is another example of a **noncash charge or expense** against income having no immediate effect on cash flows.

Noncash Investing Activities Not all purchases and sales of plant assets result in cash payments or cash receipts during the current accounting period. For example, a company may finance the purchase of plant assets by issuing notes payable, or it may sell plant assets in exchange for notes receivable. The noncash aspects of investing and financing activities are summarized in a special schedule that accompanies a statement of cash flows. This schedule will be illustrated and explained in Chapter 13.

Ethics, Fraud & Corporate Governance

A learning objective for this chapter is to distinguish between capital expenditures and revenue expenditures (a revenue expenditure is an operating expense). A capital expenditure is charged to an asset account rather than to an expense account. The largest instance of fraudulent financial reporting in U.S. history was largely due to improper capitalization of operating expenditures. WorldCom Inc. (WorldCom) from as early as 1999 through the first quarter of 2002 overstated its reported income by approximately $11 billion, including approximately $7 billion of ordinary operating expenses that were improperly capitalized. The revelation of the fraud led to WorldCom's filing for protection from its creditors under the provisions of the U.S. Bankruptcy Code. Although the fraud at Enron had prompted congressional interest in auditing, financial reporting, and corporate governance, by the spring of 2002 congressional efforts to draft a law in response to the Enron fraud had stalled due to disagreements between the two houses of Congress. The fraud at WorldCom broke this congressional logjam and resulted in the passage of the Sarbanes-Oxley Act less than two months after the revelation of the WorldCom fraud.

Almost immediately after the revelation of the WorldCom fraud—in June 2002—the Securities and Exchange Commission (SEC) brought an enforcement action against WorldCom. WorldCom is a major global telecommunications provider, providing services in more than 65 countries. At the time of the fraud, WorldCom was traded on NASDAQ.

As the economy began to cool in 1999, demand for WorldCom's telecommunications services was reduced, leading to a decline in profits. The slowing economy made it difficult for WorldCom to continue to meet the expectations of Wall Street analysts for reported profitability. Failing to meet the earnings expectations of Wall Street analysts often can lead to a precipitous stock price decline, particularly for companies viewed as rapid growers as was WorldCom. A decline in WorldCom's stock price was particularly distasteful to the company's senior management for at least three reasons. First, much of management's personal wealth was tied to WorldCom's stock price. Second, at least some members of management had substantial margin-related borrowings that were secured by WorldCom's stock. A decline in the value of the stock would lead to a "margin call." A margin call would result in the members of WorldCom's senior management having to provide additional collateral or having to pay off a portion of their outstanding debt. Third, WorldCom's business strategy was growth through acquisition, using the company's own stock as the "currency" for buying other companies. A decline in WorldCom's stock price would make it more expensive to buy other companies, potentially retarding WorldCom's growth strategy.

For the above reasons, WorldCom's senior management directed subordinates to take steps to hide the deterioration in WorldCom's profitability from analysts and other external parties. A primary means of carrying out the fraud was to transfer ordinary operating expenses, line costs, to a capital asset account, fixed assets. This accounting treatment resulted in the understatement of operating expenses and an increase in income. Line costs represent fees paid by telecommunications companies to other such companies for the right to access their networks. For example, WorldCom is a primary supplier of long-distance services and it owns an extensive nationwide distribution network, but it does not own the lines connecting from the main telephone switches into individual homes, referred to as "the last copper mile." This last copper mile, or connections into individual homes, is owned by the regional Bell operating companies (e.g., BellSouth, Verizon, etc.). Under GAAP, line costs must be expensed as incurred and cannot be capitalized.

The fraud at WorldCom has numerous ethical and corporate governance implications. Although the fraud at WorldCom was directed by top management, much of the implementation was carried out by midlevel finance and accounting personnel. In one particularly egregious instance, a WorldCom employee threatened to tell the company's external auditor about a questionable accounting treatment (this employee had stumbled across part of the fraud without realizing it). WorldCom's director of general accounting told this employee, "If you talk to the auditors, I'll throw you out the [expletive deleted] window." The employee backed down and never approached WorldCom's auditor with his accounting concerns. A lesson to be drawn is that in instances of fraudulent financial reporting intense pressure may be placed on you to participate, or at least to look the other way. Failing to cooperate may in some instances lead to a loss of your job. It is much easier to take a principled stand when facing such pressures if you lead a financially prudent personal life (e.g., build an emergency fund of at least six months of living expenses, avoid debt [other than mortgage debt]—particularly credit card debt—live on one income if part of a two-wage-earner family, etc.).

From a corporate governance perspective, WorldCom did not have a code of ethics. Attempts to develop such a code were met by the CEO's derisive description of a code of ethics as a "colossal waste of time." The Sarbanes-Oxley Act and related SEC interpretations require public companies to disclose whether they have a code of ethics that applies to the CEO, CFO, and chief accounting officer and, if not, why not. Moreover, the NYSE and NASDAQ now require companies listed on these exchanges to have a code of ethics. Although these requirements are a step in the right direction, they will fail to have their intended effect if senior management doesn't fully embrace the written code. In a nutshell, a code of ethics must be accepted and enforced if the code is going to be effective.

Concluding Remarks

This chapter completes our discussion of accounting for various types of assets. To briefly review, we have seen that cash is reported in the financial statements at its face value, marketable securities at their market value, accounts receivable at their net realizable value (i.e., net amount of cash expected to be collected), inventories at the lower-of-cost-or-market, and plant assets at cost less accumulated depreciation.

Two ideas that have been consistently reflected in each of these valuation bases are the matching principle and conservatism. A major determinant of the amount at which assets are accounted for in the balance sheet is the future amount to be released as an expense into the income statement. Closely related to this is the objective of not overstating the current and future expectations of a company's financial activities by overstating assets and understating current expenses.

In the next chapter we turn our attention to the measurement and presentation of liabilities.

END-OF-CHAPTER REVIEW

SUMMARY OF LEARNING OBJECTIVES

LO1 **Determine the cost of plant assets.** Plant assets are long-lived assets acquired for use in the business and not for resale to customers. The matching principle requires that we include in the plant and equipment accounts those costs that will provide services over a period of years. During these years, the use of the plant assets contributes to the earning of revenue. The cost of a plant asset includes all expenditures reasonable and necessary in acquiring the asset and placing it in a position and condition for use in the operations of the business.

LO2 **Distinguish between capital expenditures and revenue expenditures.** Capital expenditures include any material expenditure that will benefit several accounting periods. Therefore, these expenditures are charged to asset accounts (capitalized) and are recognized as expense in future periods.

Revenue expenditures are charged directly to expense accounts because either (1) there is no objective evidence of future benefits or (2) the amounts are immaterial.

LO3 **Compute depreciation by the straight-line and declining-balance methods.** Straight-line depreciation assigns an equal portion of an asset's cost to expense in each period of the asset's life. Declining-balance depreciation is an accelerated method. Each year, a fixed (and relatively high) depreciation rate is applied to the remaining book value of the asset. There are several variations of declining-balance depreciation.

LO4 **Account for depreciation using methods other than straight-line or declining-balance.** Most companies that prepare financial statements in conformity with generally accepted accounting principles use the straight-line method of depreciation (see survey results in Exhibit 9–7). Other accepted methods include the units-of-output method, sum-of-the-years' digits, and, in rare circumstances, decelerated depreciation methods.

LO5 **Account for the disposal of plant assets.** When plant assets are disposed of, depreciation should be recorded to the date of disposal. The cost is then removed from the asset account and the total recorded depreciation is removed from the Accumulated Depreciation account. The sale of a plant asset at a price above or below book value results in a gain or loss to be reported in the income statement.

Because different depreciation methods are used for income tax purposes, the gain or loss reported in income tax returns may differ from that shown in the income statement. The gain or loss shown in the financial statement is recorded in the company's general ledger accounts.

LO6 **Explain the nature of intangible assets, including goodwill.** Intangible assets are assets owned by the business that have no physical substance, are noncurrent, and are used in business operations. Examples include trademarks and patents.

Among the most interesting intangible assets is goodwill. Goodwill is the present value of future earnings in excess of a normal return on net identifiable assets. It stems from such factors as a good reputation, loyal customers, and superior management. Any business that earns significantly more than a normal rate of return actually has goodwill. But goodwill is recorded in the accounts only if it is *purchased* by acquiring another business at a price higher than the fair market value of its net identifiable assets.

LO7 **Account for the depletion of natural resources.** Natural resources (or wasting assets) include mines, oil fields, and standing timber. Their cost is converted into inventory as the resource is mined, pumped, or cut. This allocation of the cost of a natural resource to inventories is called depletion. The depletion rate per unit extracted equals the cost of the resource (less residual value) divided by the estimated number of units it contains.

LO8 **Explain the cash effects of transactions involving plant assets.** Depreciation is a noncash expense; cash expenditures for the acquisition of plant assets are independent of the amount of depreciation for the period. Cash payments to acquire plant assets (and cash receipts from disposals) appear in the statement of cash flows, classified as investing activities.

Write-downs of plant assets also are noncash charges, which do not involve cash payments.

Key Terms Introduced or Emphasized in Chapter 9

accelerated depreciation (p. 398) Methods of depreciation that call for recognition of relatively large amounts of depreciation in the early years of an asset's useful life and relatively small amounts in the later years.

amortization (p. 410) The systematic write-off to expense of the cost of an intangible asset over the periods of its economic usefulness.

book value (p. 398) The cost of a plant asset minus the total recorded depreciation, as shown by the Accumulated Depreciation account. The remaining undepreciated cost is also known as *carrying value*.

capital expenditures (p. 396) Costs incurred to acquire a long-lived asset. Expenditures that will benefit several accounting periods.

capitalize (p. 396) A verb with two different meanings in accounting. The first is to debit an expenditure to an asset account, rather than directly to expense. The second is to estimate the value of an investment by dividing the annual return by the investor's required rate of return.

depletion (p. 415) Allocating the cost of a natural resource to the units removed as the resource is mined, pumped, cut, or otherwise consumed.

depreciation (p. 397) The systematic allocation of the cost of an asset to expense over the years of its estimated useful life.

fixed-percentage-of-declining-balance depreciation (p. 401) An accelerated method of depreciation in which the rate is a multiple of the straight-line rate and is applied each year to the undepreciated cost of the asset. The most commonly used rate is double the straight-line rate.

goodwill (p. 410) The present value of expected future earnings of a business in excess of the earnings normally realized in the industry. Recorded when a business entity is purchased at a price in excess of the fair value of its net identifiable assets less liabilities.

half-year convention (p. 401) The practice of taking six months' depreciation in the year of acquisition and in the year of disposition, rather than computing depreciation for partial periods to the nearest month. This method is widely used and is acceptable for both income tax reporting and financial reports, as long as it is applied to all assets of a particular type acquired during the year. The half-year convention generally is not used for buildings.

impairment loss (p. 405) Writing down a long-lived asset for the difference between its carrying amount less its fair value.

intangible assets (p. 394) Those assets that are used in the operation of a business but that have no physical substance and are noncurrent.

MACRS (p. 406) The Modified Accelerated Cost Recovery System. The accelerated depreciation method permitted in federal income tax returns for assets acquired after December 31, 1986. Depreciation is based on prescribed recovery periods and depreciation rates.

natural resources (p. 394) Mines, oil fields, standing timber, and similar assets that are physically consumed and converted into inventory.

net identifiable assets (p. 410) The total of all assets minus liabilities.

noncash charge or expense (p. 416) A charge against earnings —either an expense or a loss—that does not require a cash expenditure at or near the time of recognition. Thus, the charge reduces net income but does not affect cash flows (except, perhaps, for income tax payments). Examples are depreciation and the write-off of asset values because an asset has become impaired.

plant assets (p. 394) Long-lived assets that are acquired for use in business operations rather than for resale to customers.

present value (p. 410) The amount that a knowledgeable investor would pay today for the right to receive future cash flows. The present value is always less than the sum of the future cash flows because the investor requires a return on the investment.

residual (salvage) value (p. 399) The portion of an asset's cost expected to be recovered through sale or trade-in of the asset at the end of its useful life.

revenue expenditures (p. 396) Expenditures that will benefit only the current accounting period.

straight-line depreciation (p. 398) A method of depreciation that allocates the cost of an asset (minus any residual value) equally to each year of its useful life.

sum-of-the-years' digits (SYD) depreciation (p. 406) A long-established but seldom-used method of accelerated depreciation. Usually produces results that lie in between the 200 percent- and 150 percent-declining-balance methods.

tangible plant assets (p. 394) Plant assets that have physical substance but that are not natural resources. Examples include land, buildings, and all types of equipment.

units-of-output (p. 406) A depreciation method in which cost (minus residual value) is divided by the estimated units of lifetime output. The unit depreciation cost is multiplied by the actual units of output each year to compute the annual depreciation expense.

Demonstration Problem

On April 1, 2007, Mattson Industries purchased new equipment at a cost of $325,000. The useful life of this equipment was estimated at five years, with a residual value of $25,000.

Instructions

Compute the annual depreciation expense for each year until this equipment becomes fully depreciated under each depreciation method listed below. Because you will record depreciation for only a fraction of a year in 2007, depreciation will extend through 2012 for both methods. Show supporting computations.

a. Straight-line, with depreciation for fractional years rounded to the nearest whole month.

b. 200 percent declining-balance, with the half-year convention. Limit depreciation in 2012 to an amount that reduces the undepreciated cost to the estimated residual value.

c. Assume that the equipment is sold at the end of December 2009 for $176,250 cash. Record the necessary gain or loss resulting from the sale under the straight-line method.

Solution to the Demonstration Problem

Expense under Each Method of Depreciation

Year	a. Straight-Line	b. 200% Declining-Balance
2007	$ 45,000	$ 65,000
2008	60,000	104,000
2009	60,000	62,400
2010	60,000	37,440
2011	60,000	22,464
2012	15,000	8,696
Totals	$300,000	$300,000

c. Entry to record sale of equipment in 2009:

Account	Debit	Credit
Cash	176,250	
Accumulated Depreciation: Equipment	165,000	
Equipment		325,000
Gain on Sale of Equipment		16,250

Supporting computations:

a. 2007: ($325,000 − $25,000) × $\frac{1}{5}$ × $\frac{9}{12}$ = $45,000

2008–2011: $300,000 × $\frac{1}{5}$ = $60,000

2012: $300,000 × $\frac{1}{5}$ × $\frac{3}{12}$ = $15,000

b.

	Undepreciated Cost		Rate		Depreciation Expense
2007	$325,000	×	40% × ½	=	$ 65,000
2008	260,000	×	40%	=	104,000
2009	156,000	×	40%	=	62,400
2010	93,600	×	40%	=	37,440
2011	56,160	×	40%	=	22,464
2012	33,696	−	$25,000	=	8,696

c. Accumulated depreciation at the end of 2009:

Depreciation expense, 2007	$ 45,000
Depreciation expense, 2008	60,000
Depreciation expense, 2009	60,000
Accumulated depreciation at the end of 2009	$165,000
Original cost of equipment in 2007	$325,000
Less: Accumulated depreciation at the end of 2009	(165,000)
Book value of equipment at time of disposal	$160,000
Cash proceeds from sale	$176,250
Less: Book value of equipment at time of disposal	(160,000)
Gain on sale of disposal	$ 16,250

Self-Test Questions

The answers to these questions appear on page 435.

1. In which of the following situations should the named company *not* record any depreciation expense on the asset described?
   a. Commuter Airline is required by law to maintain its aircraft in "as good as new" condition.
   b. Metro Advertising owns an office building that has been increasing in value each year since it was purchased.
   c. Computer Sales Company has in inventory a new type of computer, designed "never to become obsolete."
   d. None of the above answers is correct—in each case, the named company should record depreciation on the asset described.
2. Which of the following statements is (are) correct?
   a. Accumulated depreciation represents a cash fund being accumulated for the replacement of plant assets.
   b. The cost of a machine includes the cost of repairing damage to the machine during the installation process.
   c. A company may use different depreciation methods in its financial statements and its income tax return.
   d. The use of an accelerated depreciation method causes an asset to wear out more quickly than does use of the straight-line method.
3. On April 1, 2006, Sanders Construction paid $10,000 for equipment with an estimated useful life of 10 years and a residual value of $2,000. The company uses the double-declining-balance method of depreciation and applies the half-year convention to fractional periods. In 2007, the amount of depreciation expense to be recognized on this equipment is:
   a. $1,600.
   b. $1,440.
   c. $1,280.
   d. Some other amount.
4. Evergreen Mfg. is a rapidly growing company that acquires equipment every year. Evergreen uses straight-line depreciation in its financial statements and an accelerated method in its tax returns. Identify all correct statements:
   a. Using straight-line depreciation in the financial statements instead of an accelerated method reduces Evergreen's reported net income.
   b. Using straight-line depreciation in the financial statements instead of an accelerated method increases Evergreen's annual net cash flow.
   c. Using an accelerated method instead of straight-line depreciation in income tax returns increases Evergreen's cash flow from operating activities.
   d. As long as Evergreen keeps growing, it will probably report more depreciation in its income tax returns *each year* than it does in its financial statements.
5. Ladd Company sold a plant asset that originally cost $50,000 for $22,000 cash. If Ladd correctly reports a $5,000 gain on this sale, the *accumulated depreciation* on the asset at the date of sale must have been:
   a. $33,000.
   b. $28,000.
   c. $23,000.
   d. Some other amount.
6. In which of the following situations would Martinez Industries include goodwill in its balance sheet?
   a. The fair market value of Martinez's net identifiable assets amounts to $2,000,000. Normal earnings for this industry are 15 percent of net identifiable assets. Net income for the past five years has averaged $390,000.
   b. Martinez spent $800,000 during the current year for research and development for a new product that promises to generate substantial revenue for at least 10 years.
   c. Martinez acquired Baxter Electronics at a price in excess of the fair market value of Baxter's net identifiable assets.
   d. A buyer wishing to purchase Martinez's entire operation has offered a price in excess of the fair market value of the company's net identifiable assets.

ASSIGNMENT MATERIAL Discussion Questions

1. Coca-Cola's distinctive trademark is more valuable to the company than its bottling plants. But the company's bottling plants are listed in the balance sheet, and the famous trademark isn't. Explain.
2. Identify the basic "accountable events" in the life of a depreciable plant asset. Which of these events directly affect the net income of the current period? Which directly affect cash flows (other than income tax payments)?
3. Which of the following characteristics would prevent an item from being included in the balance sheet classification of plant and equipment? (a) Intangible, (b) limited life, (c) unlimited life, (d) held for sale in the regular course of business, (e) not capable of rendering benefits to the business in the future.
4. The following expenditures were incurred in connection with a new machine acquired by a metals manufacturing company. Identify those that should be included in the cost of the asset. (a) Freight charges, (b) sales tax on the machine, (c) payment to a passing motorist whose car was damaged by the equipment used in unloading the machine, (d) wages of employees for time spent in installing and testing the machine before it was placed in service, (e) wages of

employees assigned to lubricate and make minor adjustments to the machine one year after it was placed in service.

5. What is the distinction between a *capital expenditure* and a *revenue expenditure*?
6. If a capital expenditure is erroneously treated as a revenue expenditure, will the net income of the current year be overstated or understated? Will this error have any effect on the net income reported in future years? Explain.
7. Shoppers' Market purchased for $245,000 a site on which it planned to build a new store. The site consisted of three acres of land and included an old house and two barns. County property tax records showed the following appraised values for this property: land, $160,000; buildings, $40,000. Indicate what Shoppers' should do with this $245,000 cost in its financial statements, and explain your reasoning.
8. Which of the following statements best describes the nature of depreciation?
   a. Regular reduction of asset value to correspond to the decline in market value as the asset ages.
   b. A process of correlating the book value of an asset with its gradual decline in physical efficiency.
   c. Allocation of cost in a manner that will ensure that plant and equipment items are not carried on the balance sheet at amounts in excess of net realizable value.
   d. Allocation of the cost of a plant asset to the periods in which benefits are received.
9. Should depreciation continue to be recorded on a building when ample evidence exists that the current market value is greater than original cost and that the rising trend of market values is continuing? Explain.
10. Explain what is meant by an *accelerated* depreciation method. Are accelerated methods more widely used in financial statements or in income tax returns? Explain.
11. One accelerated depreciation method is called *fixed-percentage-of-declining-balance*. Explain what is meant by the terms "fixed-percentage" and "declining-balance." For what purpose is this method most widely used?
12. An accountant for a corporation said the company computes depreciation on its plant assets by using different methods for different purposes. But a note to the company's financial statements says all depreciation is computed by the straight-line method. Explain.
13. Criticize the following quotation: "We shall have no difficulty in paying for new plant assets needed during the coming year because our estimated outlays for new equipment amount to only $80,000, and we have more than twice that amount in our accumulated depreciation account at present."
14. Explain two approaches to computing depreciation for a fractional period in the year in which an asset is purchased. (Neither of your approaches should require the computation of depreciation to the nearest day or week.)
15. a. Does the accounting principle of consistency require a company to use the same method of depreciation for all of its plant assets?
    b. Is it acceptable for a corporation to use different depreciation methods in its financial statements and its income tax returns?
16. After four years of using a machine acquired at a cost of $15,000, Miller Construction Company determined that the original estimated life of 10 years had been too short and that a total useful life of 12 years was a more reasonable estimate. Explain briefly the method that should be used to revise the depreciation program, assuming that straight-line depreciation has been used and the machine has no residual value. Assume that the revision is made after recording depreciation and closing the accounts at the end of four years of use.
17. Define *intangible assets*. Would an account receivable arising from a sale of merchandise under terms of 2/10, n/30 qualify as an intangible asset under your definition?
18. Over what period of time should the cost of various types of intangible assets be amortized by regular charges against revenue? (Your answer should be in the form of a principle or guideline rather than a specific number of years.) What method of amortization is generally used?
19. Under what circumstances should *goodwill* be recorded in the accounts?
20. Mineral World recognizes $20 depletion for each ton of ore mined. During the current year the company mined 600,000 tons but sold only 500,000 tons, as it was attempting to build up inventories in anticipation of a possible strike by employees. How much depletion should be deducted from revenue of the current year?
21. Explain the meaning of an *impairment* of an asset. Provide several examples. What accounting event should occur when an asset has become substantially impaired?
22. Several years ago Walker Security purchased for $120,000 a well-known trademark for padlocks and other security products. After using the trademark for three years, Walker Security discontinued it altogether when the company withdrew from the lock business and concentrated on the manufacture of aircraft parts. Amortization of the trademark at the rate of $3,000 a year is being continued on the basis of a 20-year life, which the owner says is consistent with accounting standards. Do you agree? Explain.

Brief Exercises

LO1 LO2

BRIEF EXERCISE 9.1

Cost of Plant Asset

Padre, Inc., purchased a used piece of heavy equipment for $25,000. Delivery of the equipment to Padre's business site cost $750. Expenditures to recondition the equipment and prepare it for use totaled $2,230. The maintenance for the first year Padre owned the equipment was $1,200. Determine the cost that is the basis for calculating annual depreciation on the equipment.

LO3

BRIEF EXERCISE 9.2

Straight-Line Depreciation

Twin-Cities, Inc., purchased a building for $400,000. Straight-line depreciation was used for each of the first two years using the following assumptions: 25-year estimated useful life, with a residual value of $100,000.

a. Calculate the annual depreciation for the first two years that Twin-Cities owned the building.

b. Calculate the book value of the building at the end of the second year.

LO3

BRIEF EXERCISE 9.3

Straight-Line and Declining-Balance Depreciation

Waller Company purchased equipment for $24,000. The company is considering whether to determine annual depreciation using the straight-line method or the declining-balance method at 150 percent of the straight-line rate. Waller expects to use the equipment for 10 years, at the end of which it will have an estimated salvage value of $4,000. Prepare a comparison of these two alternatives for the first two years Waller will own the equipment.

LO3

BRIEF EXERCISE 9.4

Declining-Balance Depreciation

Equipment costing $76,000 was purchased by Spence, Inc., at the beginning of the current year. The company will depreciate the equipment by the declining-balance method, but it has not determined whether the rate will be at 150 percent or 200 percent of the straight-line rate. The estimated useful life of the equipment is eight years. Prepare a comparison of the two alternative rates for management for the first two years Spence owns the equipment.

LO3 LO4

BRIEF EXERCISE 9.5

Straight-Line and Units-of-Output Depreciation

Finx, Inc., purchased a truck for $35,000. The truck is expected to be driven 15,000 miles per year over a five-year period and then sold for approximately $5,000. Determine depreciation for the first year of the truck's useful life by the straight-line and units-of-output methods if the truck is actually driven 16,000 miles.

LO3 LO5

BRIEF EXERCISE 9.6

Disposal of Plant Asset

Alexander Company purchased a piece of equipment for $12,000 and depreciated it for three years over a five-year estimated life with an expected residual value at the end of five years of $2,000. At the end of the third year, Alex decided to upgrade to equipment with increased capacity and sold the original piece of equipment for $7,200. Calculate the gain or loss on the disposal at the end of the third year.

LO3 LO5

BRIEF EXERCISE 9.7

Disposal of Plant Asset

Tullahoma Company purchased equipment for $27,500. It depreciated the equipment over a five-year life by the double-declining-balance method until the end of the second year, at which time the asset was sold for $8,500. Calculate the gain or loss on the sale at the end of the second year.

LO6

BRIEF EXERCISE 9.8

Goodwill

Hunt Company is considering purchasing a competing company in order to expand its market share. Estimates of the excess of the value of the individual assets, less liabilities to be assumed, range from $50,000–$60,000, depending on the manner in which that excess is calculated. Hunt believes it can purchase the competitor for a direct cash outlay of $700,000, which is only $25,000 more than the value of the individual assets less the liabilities that Hunt will assume. Assuming Hunt makes the purchase for $700,000, at what amount should goodwill be recorded? Briefly explain your answer.

LO7

BRIEF EXERCISE 9.9

Natural Resources

Miller Mining acquired rights to a tract of land with the intent of extracting from the land a valuable mineral. The cost of the rights was $2,500,000 and an estimated 10,000 tons of the mineral are expected to be extracted. Assuming that 1,600 tons of the mineral are actually extracted in the first year, determine the amount of depletion expense that should be recognized for that year.

LO4

BRIEF EXERCISE 9.10

Alternative Depreciation Methods

R. C. Smith purchased a truck for $30,500 to be used in his business. He is considering depreciating the truck by two methods: units-of-output (assuming total miles driven of 80,000) and double-declining balance (assuming a five-year useful life). The truck is expected to be sold for approximately $6,500 at the end of its useful life. Prepare a comparison of the first year's depreciation expense that will be recognized under these methods, assuming the truck was actually driven 10,000 miles in the first year. Briefly state why the difference between the two is so great.

Exercises

EXERCISE 9.1
You as a Student

Assume that you recently applied for a student loan to go to graduate school. As part of the application process, your bank requested a list of your assets. Aside from an extensive CD collection, your only other asset is a pickup truck. You purchased the truck six years ago for $15,000. Its current fair value is approximately $5,000.

a. What factors caused your pickup truck to depreciate $10,000 in value?

b. Assume that the bank is willing to lend you money for graduate school. Even with the loan, however, you still need to raise an additional $5,000. Do you think that the bank will lend you $5,000 more for graduate school if you agree to use your truck as collateral? Explain.

c. Assume that the truck has been used solely in a delivery service business that you operated while in college. Would your balance sheet necessarily show $10,000 in accumulated depreciation related to the truck? Explain.

EXERCISE 9.2
Distinguishing Capital Expenditures from Revenue Expenditures

Identify the following expenditures as capital expenditures or revenue expenditures:

a. Immediately after acquiring a new delivery truck, paid $195 to have the name of the store and other advertising material painted on the vehicle.

b. Painted delivery truck at a cost of $450 after two years of use.

c. Purchased new battery at a cost of $40 for two-year-old delivery truck.

d. Installed an escalator at a cost of $17,500 in a three-story building that had been used for some years without elevators or escalators.

e. Purchased a pencil sharpener at a cost of $15.00.

f. Original life of the delivery truck had been estimated at four years, and straight-line depreciation of 25 percent yearly had been recognized. After three years' use, however, it was decided to recondition the truck thoroughly, including adding a new engine.

EXERCISE 9.3
Depreciation for Fractional Years

On August 3, Srini Construction purchased special-purpose equipment at a cost of $1,000,000. The useful life of the equipment was estimated to be eight years, with a residual value of $50,000.

a. Compute the depreciation expense to be recognized each calendar year for financial reporting purposes under the straight-line depreciation method (half-year convention).

b. Compute the depreciation expense to be recognized each calendar year for financial reporting purposes under the 200 percent declining-balance method (half-year convention) with a switch to straight-line when it will maximize depreciation expense.

c. Which of these two depreciation methods (straight-line or double-declining-balance) results in the highest net income for financial reporting purposes during the first two years of the equipment's use? Explain.

EXERCISE 9.4
Depreciation Methods

On January 2, 2007, Jansing Corporation acquired a new machine with an estimated useful life of five years. The cost of the equipment was $40,000 with a residual value of $5,000.

a. Prepare a complete depreciation table under the three depreciation methods listed below. Use a format similar to the illustrations in Exhibits 9–4, 9–5, and 9–6. In each case, assume that a full year of depreciation was taken in 2007.

1. Straight-line.
2. 200 percent declining-balance.
3. 150 percent declining-balance with a switch to straight-line when it will maximize depreciation expense.

b. Comment on significant differences or similarities that you observe among the patterns of depreciation expense recognized under each of these methods.

EXERCISE 9.5
Evaluation of Disclosures in Annual Reports

A recent annual report of H. J. Heinz Company includes the following note:

Depreciation: For financial reporting purposes, depreciation is provided on the straight-line method over the estimated useful lives of the assets. Accelerated depreciation methods generally are used for income tax purposes.

a. Is the company violating the accounting principle of consistency by using different depreciation methods in its financial statements than in its income tax returns? Explain.

b. *Why* do you think that the company uses accelerated depreciation methods in its income tax returns?

c. Would the use of accelerated depreciation in the financial statements be more conservative or less conservative than the current practice of using the straight-line method? Explain.

EXERCISE 9.6
Revision of Depreciation Estimates

Swindall Industries uses straight-line depreciation on all of its depreciable assets. The company records annual depreciation expense at the end of each calendar year. On January 11, 2004, the company purchased a machine costing $90,000. The machine's useful life was estimated to be 12 years with a residual value of $18,000. Depreciation for partial years is recorded to the nearest full month.

In 2008, after almost five years of experience with the machine, management decided to revise its estimated life from 12 years to 20 years. No change was made in the estimated residual value. The revised estimate of the useful life was decided *prior* to recording annual depreciation expense for the year ended December 31, 2008.

a. Prepare journal entries in chronological order for the above events, beginning with the purchase of the machinery on January 11, 2004. Show separately the recording of depreciation expense in 2004 through 2008.

b. What factors may have caused the company to revise its estimate of the machine's useful life?

EXERCISE 9.7
Accounting for Trade-ins

Mathews Bus Service traded in a used bus for a new one. The original cost of the old bus was $52,000. Accumulated depreciation at the time of the trade-in amounted to $34,000. The new bus cost $65,000, but Mathews was given a trade-in allowance of $10,000.

a. What amount of cash did Mathews have to pay to acquire the new bus?

b. Compute the gain or loss on the disposal for financial reporting purposes.

c. Explain how the gain or loss would be reported in the company's income statement.

EXERCISE 9.8
Estimating Goodwill

During the past several years the annual net income of Avery Company has averaged $540,000. At the present time the company is being offered for sale. Its accounting records show the book value of net assets (total assets minus all liabilities) to be $2,800,000. The fair value of Avery's net identifiable assets, however, is $3,000,000.

An investor negotiating to buy the company offers to pay an amount equal to the fair value for the net identifiable assets and to assume all liabilities. In addition, the investor is willing to pay for goodwill an amount equal to the above-average earnings for five years.

On the basis of this agreement, what price should the investor offer? A normal return on the fair value of net assets in this industry is 15 percent.

EXERCISE 9.9
The Write-Down of Impaired Assets

For several years, a number of Food Lion, Inc., grocery stores were unprofitable. The company closed, and continues to close, some of these locations. It is apparent that the company will not be able to recover the cost of the assets associated with the closed stores. Thus, the current value of these impaired assets must be written down.

A recent Food Lion income statement reports a $9.5 million charge against income pertaining to the write-down of impaired assets.

a. Explain why Food Lion must write down the current carrying value of its unprofitable stores.

b. Explain why the recent $9.5 million charge to write down these impaired assets is considered a noncash expense.

EXERCISE 9.10
Ethics: "Let the Buyer Beware"

Bill Gladstone has owned and operated Gladstone's Service Station for over 30 years. The business, which is currently the town's only service station, has always been extremely profitable. Gladstone recently decided that he wanted to sell the business and retire. His asking price exceeds the fair market value of its net identifiable assets by nearly $50,000. Gladstone attributes this premium to the above-normal returns that the service station has always generated.

Gladstone recently found out about two issues that could have a profound effect upon the future of the business: (1) A well-known service station franchise will be built across the street from his station in approximately 18 months, and (2) one of his underground fuel tanks *may* have developed a very slow leak.

a. How might these issues affect the $50,000 in goodwill that Gladstone included in his selling price?

b. Assume that Gladstone is *not* disclosing this information to potential buyers. Does he have an ethical obligation to do so? Defend your answer.

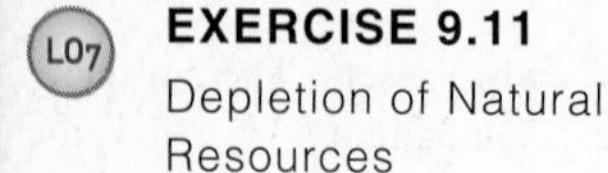

EXERCISE 9.11
Depletion of Natural Resources

Salter Mining Company purchased the Northern Tier Mine for $21 million cash. The mine was estimated to contain 2.5 million tons of ore and to have a residual value of $1 million.

During the first year of mining operations at the Northern Tier Mine, 50,000 tons of ore were mined, of which 40,000 tons were sold.

a. Prepare a journal entry to record depletion during the year.

b. Show how the Northern Tier Mine, and its accumulated depletion, would appear in Salter Mining Company's balance sheet after the first year of operations.

c. Will the entire amount of depletion computed in part **a** be deducted from revenue in the determination of income for the year? Explain.

d. Indicate how the journal entry in part **a** affects the company's current ratio (its current assets divided by its current liabilities). Do you believe that the activities summarized in this entry do, in fact, make the company any more or less liquid? Explain.

LO8

EXERCISE 9.12
Researching a Real Company

Locate an annual report in your library (or some other source) that includes a large gain or loss on the disposal of fixed assets. Report to the class the amount of the gain or loss and where in the company's income statement it is reported. Describe how the gain or loss is reported in the company's statement of cash flows. Summarize any discussion in the footnotes concerning the cause of the disposal.

EXERCISE 9.13
Units-of-Output Method

During the current year, Airport Auto Rentals purchased 60 new automobiles at a cost of $14,000 per car. The cars will be sold to a wholesaler at an estimated $5,000 each as soon as they have been driven 50,000 miles. Airport Auto Rentals computes depreciation expense on its automobiles by the units-of-output method, based on mileage.

a. Compute the amount of depreciation to be recognized for each mile that a rental automobile is driven.

b. Assuming that the 60 rental cars are driven a total of 1,770,000 miles during the current year, compute the total amount of depreciation expense that Airport Auto Rentals should recognize on this fleet of cars for the year.

c. In this particular situation, do you believe the units-of-output depreciation method achieves a better matching of expenses with revenue than would the straight-line method? Explain.

EXERCISE 9.14
Units-of-Production Depreciation Method

Dasher Company acquired a truck for use in its business for $25,500 in a cash transaction. The truck is expected to be used over a five-year period, will be driven approximately 18,000 miles per year, and is expected to have a value at the end of the five years of $4,500.

a. Compute the amount of depreciation that will be taken in the first two years of the truck's useful life if the actual miles driven are 16,000 and 18,200, respectively. Round the depreciation per mile to the nearest full cent.

b. How does the amount of accumulated depreciation at the end of the second year compare with what it would have been had the company chosen the straight-line depreciation method?

LO3

EXERCISE 9.15
Using the **Home Depot, Inc.**, Financial Statements to Determine Depreciation Methods Used

The **Home Depot** financial statements appear in Appendix A at the end of this textbook. Use these statements to answer the following questions and indicate where in the financial statements you found the information.

a. What depreciation method does **Home Depot** use for buildings, furniture, fixtures, and equipment? What are the useful lives over which these assets are depreciated?

b. From the notes to **Home Depot**'s financial statements, what can you learn about the company's policy regarding impairment of plant assets?

c. Locate **Home Depot**'s balance sheet and find the section entitled "Property and Equipment, at cost." As of January 29, 2006, determine the amount of the company's investment in property and equipment and the amount of depreciation taken to date on those assets. Are these assets, taken as a whole, near the beginning or end of their estimated useful lives? Explain your answer.

Problem Set A

PROBLEM 9.1A
Determining the Cost of Plant Assets
LO1 through LO3

Wilmet College recently purchased new computing equipment for its library. The following information refers to the purchase and installation of this equipment:

1. The list price of the equipment was $275,000; however, Wilmet College qualified for an "education discount" of $25,000. It paid $50,000 cash for the equipment, and issued a three-month, 9 percent note payable for the remaining balance. The note, plus accrued interest charges of $4,500, was paid promptly at the maturity date.
2. In addition to the amounts described in **1**, Wilmet paid sales taxes of $15,000 at the date of purchase.
3. Freight charges for delivery of the equipment totaled $1,000.
4. Installation costs related to the equipment amounted to $5,000.
5. During installation, one of the computer terminals was accidentally damaged by a library employee. It cost the college $500 to repair this damage.
6. As soon as the computers were installed, the college paid $4,000 to print admissions brochures featuring the library's new, state-of-the-art computing facilities.

Instructions

a. In one sentence, make a general statement summarizing the nature of expenditures that qualify for inclusion in the cost of plant assets such as computing equipment.

b. For each of the six numbered paragraphs, indicate which items should be included by Wilmet College in the total cost debited to its Computing Equipment account. Also briefly indicate the proper accounting treatment of those items that *are not* included in the cost of the equipment.

c. Compute the total cost debited to the college's Computing Equipment account.

d. Prepare a journal entry at the end of the current year to record depreciation on the computing equipment. Wilmet College will depreciate this equipment by the straight-line method (half-year convention) over an estimated useful life of five years. Assume a zero residual value.

PROBLEM 9.2A
Comparison of Straight-Line and Accelerated Methods
LO3 LO5

Swanson & Hiller, Inc., purchased a new machine on September 1, 2006, at a cost of $108,000. The machine's estimated useful life at the time of the purchase was five years, and its residual value was $8,000.

Instructions

a. Prepare a complete depreciation schedule, beginning with calendar year 2006, under each of the methods listed below (assume that the half-year convention is used):
   1. Straight-line.
   2. 200 percent declining-balance.
   3. 150 percent declining-balance, switching to straight-line when that maximizes the expense.

b. Which of the three methods computed in part **a** is most common for financial reporting purposes? Explain.

c. Assume that Swanson & Hiller sells the machine on December 31, 2009, for $28,000 cash. Compute the resulting gain or loss from this sale under each of the depreciation methods used in part **a**. Does the gain or loss reported in the company's income statement have any direct cash effects? Explain.

PROBLEM 9.3A
Issues Involving Alternative Depreciation Methods
LO1 through LO3 LO5

Smart Hardware purchased new shelving for its store on April 1, 2007. The shelving is expected to have a 20-year life and no residual value. The following expenditures were associated with the purchase:

Cost of the shelving	$12,000
Freight charges	520
Sales taxes	780
Installation of shelving	2,700
Cost to repair shelf damaged during installation	400

Instructions

a. Compute depreciation expense for the years 2007 through 2010 under each depreciation method listed below:
   1. Straight-line, with fractional years rounded to the nearest whole month.
   2. 200 percent declining-balance, using the half-year convention.
   3. 150 percent declining-balance, using the half-year convention.

b. Smart Hardware has two conflicting objectives. Management wants to report the highest possible earnings in its financial statements, yet it also wants to minimize its taxable income reported to the IRS. Explain how both of these objectives can be met.

c. Which of the depreciation methods applied in part **a** resulted in the lowest reported book value at the end of 2010? Is book value an estimate of an asset's fair value? Explain.

d. Assume that Smart Hardware sold the old shelving that was being replaced. The old shelving had originally cost $9,000. Its book value at the time of the sale was $400. Record the sale of the old shelving under the following conditions:
   1. The shelving was sold for $1,200 cash.
   2. The shelving was sold for $200 cash.

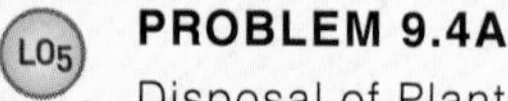

PROBLEM 9.4A
Disposal of Plant Assets

During the current year, Ramirez Developers disposed of plant assets in the following transactions:

Feb. 10 Office equipment costing $26,000 was given to a scrap dealer at no charge. At the date of disposal, accumulated depreciation on the office equipment amounted to $25,800.

Apr. 1 Ramirez sold land and a building to Claypool Associates for $900,000, receiving $100,000 cash and a five-year, 9 percent note receivable for the remaining balance. Ramirez's records showed the following amounts: Land, $50,000; Building, $550,000; Accumulated Depreciation: Building (at the date of disposal), $250,000.

Aug. 15 Ramirez traded in an old truck for a new one. The old truck had cost $26,000, and its accumulated depreciation amounted to $18,000. The list price of the new truck was $39,000, but Ramirez received a $10,000 trade-in allowance for the old truck and paid only $29,000 in cash. Ramirez includes trucks in its Vehicles account.

Oct. 1 Ramirez traded in its old computer system as part of the purchase of a new system. The old system had cost $15,000, and its accumulated depreciation amounted to $11,000. The new computer's list price was $8,000. Ramirez accepted a trade-in allowance of $500 for the old computer system, paying $1,500 down in cash and issuing a one-year, 8 percent note payable for the $6,000 balance owed.

Instructions

a. Prepare journal entries to record each of the disposal transactions. Assume that depreciation expense on each asset has been recorded up to the date of disposal. Thus you need not update the accumulated depreciation figures stated in the problem.

b. Will the gains and losses recorded in part **a** above affect the *gross profit* reported in Ramirez's income statement? Explain.

c. Explain how the financial reporting of gains and losses on plant assets differs from the financial reporting of *unrealized* gains and losses on marketable securities discussed in Chapter 7.

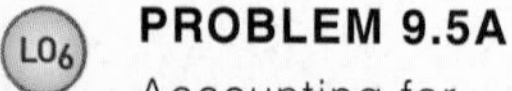

PROBLEM 9.5A
Accounting for Intangible Assets under GAAP

LO6

During the current year, Black Corporation incurred the following expenditures which should be recorded either as operating expenses or as intangible assets:

a. Expenditures were made for the training of new employees. The average employee remains with the company for five years, but is trained for a new position every two years.

b. Black purchased a controlling interest in a vinyl flooring company. The expenditure resulted in the recording of a significant amount of goodwill. Black expects to earn above-average returns on this investment indefinitely.

c. Black incurred large amounts of research and development costs in developing a dirt-resistant carpet fiber. The company expects that the fiber will be patented and that sales of the resulting products will contribute to revenue for at least 25 years. The legal life of the patent, however, will be only 20 years.

d. Black made an expenditure to acquire the patent on a popular carpet cleaner. The patent had a remaining legal life of 14 years, but Black expects to produce and sell the product for only six more years.

e. Black spent a large amount to sponsor the televising of the Olympic Games. Black's intent was to make television viewers more aware of the company's name and its product lines.

Instructions

Explain whether each of the above expenditures should be recorded as an operating expense or an intangible asset. If you view the expenditure as an intangible asset, indicate the number of years over which the asset should be amortized, if any. Explain your reasoning.

PROBLEM 9.6A
Accounting for Goodwill

Kivi Service Stations is considering expanding its operations to include the greater Dubuque area. Rather than build new service stations in the Dubuque area, management plans to acquire existing service stations and convert them into Kivi outlets.

Kivi is evaluating two similar acquisition opportunities. Information relating to each of these service stations is presented below:

	Joe's Garage	Gas N' Go
Estimated normal rate of return on net assets	20%	20%
Fair value of net identifiable assets	$950,000	$980,000
Actual average net income for past five years	220,000	275,000

Instructions

a. Compute an estimated fair value for any goodwill associated with Kivi purchasing Joe's Garage. Base your computation upon an assumption that successful service stations typically sell at about 9.25 times their annual earnings.

b. Compute an estimated fair value for any goodwill associated with Kivi purchasing Gas N' Go. Base your computation upon an assumption that Kivi's management expects excess earnings to continue for four years.

c. Many of Kivi's existing service stations are extremely profitable. If Kivi acquires Joe's Garage or Gas N' Go, should it also record the goodwill associated with its existing locations? Explain.

PROBLEM 9.7A
Alternative Depreciation Methods

Millar, Inc., purchased a truck to use for deliveries and is attempting to determine how much depreciation expense would be recognized under three different methods. The truck cost $20,000 and is expected to have a value of $4,000 at the end of its five-year life. The truck is expected to be used at the rate of 10,000 miles in the first year, 20,000 miles in the second and third years, and 15,000 miles in the fourth and fifth years.

Instructions

a. Determine the amount of depreciation expense that will be recognized under each of the following depreciation methods in the first and second years of the truck's useful life. A full year's depreciation will be recognized in the first year the truck is used.

1. Straight-line.
2. Double-declining-balance.
3. Units-of-output (based on miles).

b. Prepare the plant assets section of the balance sheet at the end of the second year of the asset's useful life under the double-declining-balance method, assuming the truck is the only plant asset owned by Millar, Inc.

c. By which of the three methods is it *not* possible to determine the actual amount of depreciation expense prior to the end of each year? What uncertainty causes this to be true?

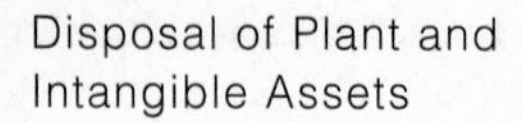
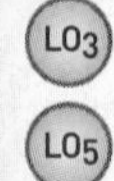

PROBLEM 9.8A
Disposal of Plant and Intangible Assets

LO2 LO3 LO5

During the current year, Rothchild, Inc., purchased two assets that are described as follows:

Heavy Equipment
Purchase price, $275,000.
Expected to be used for 10 years, with a residual value at the end of that time of $50,000.
Expenditures required to recondition the equipment and prepare it for use, $75,000.
Patent
Purchase price, $75,000.
Expected to be used for five years, with no value at the end of that time.

Rothchild depreciates heavy equipment by the declining-balance method at 150 percent of the straight-line rate. It amortizes intangible assets by the straight-line method. At the end of two years, because of changes in Rothchild's core business, it sold the patent to a competitor for $35,000.

Instructions

a. Compute the amount of depreciation expense on the heavy equipment for each of the first three years of the asset's life.

b. Compute the amount of amortization on the patent for each of the two years it was owned by Rothchild.

c. Prepare the plant and intangible assets section of Rothchild's balance sheet at the end of the first and second years. Also, calculate the amount of the gain or loss on the patent that would be included in the second year's income statement.

Problem Set B

PROBLEM 9.1B
Determining the Cost of Plant Assets

LO1 through LO3

Walker Motel recently purchased new exercise equipment for its exercise room. The following information refers to the purchase and installation of this equipment:

1. The list price of the equipment was $40,000; however, Walker qualified for a "special discount" of $5,000. It paid $10,000 cash for the equipment, and issued a three-month, 12 percent note payable for the remaining balance. The note, plus accrued interest charges of $750, was paid promptly at the maturity date.
2. In addition to the amounts described in **1**, Walker paid sales taxes of $2,100 at the date of purchase.
3. Freight charges for delivery of the equipment totaled $600.
4. Installation and training costs related to the equipment amounted to $900.
5. During installation, one of the pieces of equipment was accidentally damaged by an employee. It cost the motel $400 to repair this damage.
6. As soon as the equipment was installed, the motel paid $3,200 to print brochures featuring the exercise room's new, state-of-the-art exercise facilities.

Instructions

a. In one sentence, make a general statement summarizing the nature of expenditures that qualify for inclusion in the cost of plant assets such as exercise equipment.

b. For each of the six numbered paragraphs, indicate which items should be included by Walker in the total cost debited to its Equipment account. Also briefly indicate the proper accounting treatment of those items that *are not* included in the cost of the equipment.

c. Compute the total cost debited to the motel's Equipment account.

d. Prepare a journal entry at the end of the current year to record depreciation on the exercise equipment. Walker Motel will depreciate this equipment by the straight-line method (half-year convention) over an estimated useful life of five years. Assume a zero residual value.

PROBLEM 9.2B
Comparison of Straight-Line and Accelerated Methods

R&R, Inc., purchased a new machine on September 1, 2007, at a cost of $180,000. The machine's estimated useful life at the time of the purchase was five years, and its residual value was $10,000.

Instructions

a. Prepare a complete depreciation schedule, beginning with calendar year 2007, under each of the methods listed below (assume that the half-year convention is used):

1. Straight-line.
2. 200 percent declining-balance.
3. 150 percent declining-balance (not switching to straight-line).

b. Which of the three methods computed in part **a** is most common for financial reporting purposes? Explain.

c. Assume that R&R sells the machine on December 31, 2010, for $55,000 cash. Compute the resulting gain or loss from this sale under each of the depreciation methods used in part **a**. Does the gain or loss reported in the company's income statement have any direct cash effects? Explain.

through
LO3

PROBLEM 9.3B
Issues Involving Alternative Depreciation Methods

Davidson, DDS, purchased new furniture for its store on May 1, 2007. The furniture is expected to have a 10-year life and no residual value. The following expenditures were associated with the purchase:

Cost of the furniture	$11,000
Freight charges	375
Sales taxes	550
Installation of furniture	75
Cost to repair furniture damaged during installation	400

Instructions

a. Compute depreciation expense for the years 2007 through 2010 under each depreciation method listed below:

1. Straight-line, with fractional years rounded to the nearest whole month.
2. 200 percent declining-balance, using the half-year convention.
3. 150 percent declining-balance, using the half-year convention.

b. Davidson, DDS, has two conflicting objectives. Management wants to report the highest possible earnings in its financial statements, yet it also wants to minimize its taxable income reported to the IRS. Explain how both of these objectives can be met.

c. Which of the depreciation methods applied in part **a** resulted in the lowest reported book value at the end of 2010? Is book value an estimate of an asset's fair value? Explain.

d. Assume that Davidson, DDS, sold the old furniture that was being replaced. The old furniture had originally cost $3,000. Its book value at the time of the sale was $400. Record the sale of the old furniture under the following conditions:

1. The furniture was sold for $600 cash.
2. The furniture was sold for $300 cash.

PROBLEM 9.4B
Disposal of Plant Assets

During the current year, Blake Construction disposed of plant assets in the following transactions:

Jan. 6 Equipment costing $18,000 was given to a scrap dealer at no charge. At the date of disposal, accumulated depreciation on the office equipment amounted to $16,800.

Mar. 3 Blake sold land and a building for $800,000, receiving $100,000 cash and a five-year, 12 percent note receivable for the remaining balance. Blake's records showed the following amounts: Land, $50,000; Buildings, $680,000; Accumulated Depreciation: Building (at the date of disposal), $250,000.

Jul. 10 Blake traded in an old truck for a new one. The old truck had cost $26,000, and its accumulated depreciation amounted to $22,000. The list price of the new truck was $37,000, but Blake received a $12,000 trade-in allowance for the old truck and paid only $25,000 in cash. Blake includes trucks in its Vehicles account.

Sept. 3 Blake traded in its old computer system as part of the purchase of a new system. The old system had cost $12,000, and its accumulated depreciation amounted to $9,000. The new computer's list price was $10,000. Blake accepted a trade-in allowance of

$400 for the old computer system, paying $1,000 down in cash and issuing a one-year, 10 percent note payable for the $8,600 balance owed.

Instructions

a. Prepare journal entries to record each of the disposal transactions. Assume that depreciation expense on each asset has been recorded up to the date of disposal. Thus you need not update the accumulated depreciation figures stated in the problem.

b. Will the gains and losses recorded in part **a** above affect the *gross profit* reported in Blake's income statement? Explain.

c. Explain how the financial reporting of gains and losses on plant assets differs from the financial reporting of *unrealized* gains and losses on marketable securities discussed in Chapter 7.

PROBLEM 9.5B
Accounting for Intangible Assets under GAAP

During the current year, Omega Products Corporation incurred the following expenditures which should be recorded either as operating expenses or as intangible assets:

a. Expenditures were made for the training of new employees. The average employee remains with the company for five years, but is trained for a new position every two years.

b. Omega purchased a controlling interest in a wallpaper company. The expenditure resulted in recording a significant amount of goodwill. Omega expects to earn above-average returns on this investment indefinitely.

c. Omega incurred large amounts of research and development costs in developing a superior product. The company expects that it will be patented and that sales of the resulting products will contribute to revenue for at least 40 years. The legal life of the patent, however, will be only 20 years.

d. Omega made an expenditure to acquire the patent on a whatsa. The patent had a remaining legal life of 10 years, but Omega expects to produce and sell the product for only four more years.

e. Omega spent a large amount to sponsor the televising of the World Series. Omega's intent was to make television viewers more aware of the company's name and product lines.

Instructions

Explain whether each of the above expenditures should be recorded as an operating expense or an intangible asset. If you view the expenditure as an intangible asset, indicate the number of years over which the asset should be amortized. Explain your reasoning.

PROBLEM 9.6B
Accounting for Goodwill

Jell Stores is considering expanding its operations to include the greater Boston area. Rather than build new stores in the Boston area, management plans to acquire existing stores and convert them into Jell outlets.

Jell is evaluating two similar acquisition opportunities. Information relating to each of these stores is presented below:

	Carnie's	Mell's
Estimated normal rate of return on net assets	20%	20%
Fair market value of net identifiable assets	$900,000	$980,000
Actual average net income for past five years	250,000	280,000

Instructions

a. Compute an estimated fair value for any goodwill associated with Jell purchasing Carnie's. Base your computation upon an assumption that successful stores of this type typically sell at about 10 times their annual earnings.

b. Compute an estimated fair value for any goodwill associated with Jell purchasing Mell's. Base your computation upon an assumption that Jell's management wants to generate a target return on investment of 35 percent.

c. Many of Jell's existing stores are extremely profitable. If Jell acquires Carnie's or Mell's, should it also record the goodwill associated with its existing locations? Explain.

PROBLEM 9.7B
Alternative Depreciation Methods

Wilson, Inc., purchased a truck to use for deliveries and is attempting to determine how much depreciation expense would be recognized under three different methods. The truck cost $24,000 and is expected to have a value of $6,000 at the end of its six-year life. The truck is expected to be used at the rate of 15,000 miles in the first year, 20,000 miles in the second and third years, and 12,000 miles in the fourth, fifth, and sixth years.

Instructions

a. Determine the amount of depreciation expense that will be recognized under each of the following depreciation methods in the first and second years of the truck's useful life. A full year's depreciation will be recognized in the first year the truck is used.
   1. Straight-line.
   2. Double-declining-balance.
   3. Units-of-output (based on miles).

b. Prepare the plant assets section of the balance sheet at the end of the second year in the asset's useful life under the units-of-output method, assuming the truck is the only plant asset owned by Wilson, Inc.

c. By which of the three methods is it *not* possible to determine the actual amount of depreciation expense prior to the end of each year? What uncertainty causes this to be true?

PROBLEM 9.8B
Disposal of Plant and Intangible Assets

During the current year, Rodgers Company purchased two assets that are described as follows:

Heavy Equipment

Purchase price, $550,000.

Expected to be used for 10 years, with a residual value at the end of that time of $70,000.

Expenditures required to recondition the equipment and prepare it for use, $120,000.

Patent

Purchase price, $80,000.

Expected to be used for six years, with no value at the end of that time.

Rodgers depreciates heavy equipment by the declining-balance method at 200 percent of the straight-line rate. It amortizes intangible assets by the straight-line method. At the end of two years, because of changes in Rodgers's core business, it sold the patent to a competitor for $40,000.

Instructions

a. Compute the amount of depreciation expense on the heavy equipment for each of the first three years of the asset's life.

b. Compute the amount of amortization on the patent for each of the two years it was owned by Rodgers.

c. Prepare the plant and intangible assets section of Rodgers's balance sheet at the end of the first and second years. Also, calculate the amount of the gain or loss on the patent that would be included in the second year's income statement.

Critical Thinking Cases

CASE 9.1
Are Useful Lives "Flexible"?

Mickey Gillespie is the controller of Print Technologies, a publicly owned company. The company is experiencing financial difficulties and is aggressively looking for ways to cut costs.

Suzanne Bedell, the CEO, instructs Gillespie to lengthen from 5 to 10 years the useful life used in computing depreciation on certain special-purpose machinery. Bedell believes that this change represents a substantial cost savings, as it will reduce the depreciation expense on these assets by nearly one-half.

Note: The proposed change affects only the depreciation expense recognized in financial statements. Depreciation deductions in income tax returns will not be affected.

Instructions

a. Discuss the extent to which Bedell's idea will, in fact, achieve a cost savings. Consider the effects on both net income and cash flows.

b. Who is responsible for estimating the useful lives of plant assets?

c. Discuss any ethical issues that Gillespie should consider with respect to Bedell's instructions.

CASE 9.2
Departures from GAAP—Are They Ethical?

Martin Myers owns Myers Construction Co. The company maintains accounting records for the purposes of exercising control over its construction activities and meeting its reporting obligations regarding payrolls and income tax returns. As it has no other financial reporting obligations, Myers does not prepare formal financial statements.

The company owns land and several other assets with current market values well in excess of their historical costs. Martin Myers directs the company's accountant, Maureen O'Shaughnessey, to prepare a balance sheet in which assets are shown at estimated market values. Myers says this type of balance sheet will give him a better understanding of where the business stands. He also thinks it will be useful in obtaining bank loans, as loan applications always ask for the estimated market values of real estate owned.

Instructions

a. Would the financial statements requested by Martin Myers be in conformity with generally accepted accounting principles?

b. Is Myers Construction under any legal or ethical obligation to prepare financial statements that *do* conform to generally accepted accounting principles?

c. Discuss any ethical issues that O'Shaughnessey should consider with respect to Myers's request.

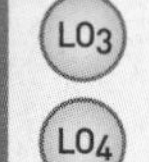

CASE 9.3
Depreciation Policies in Annual Reports

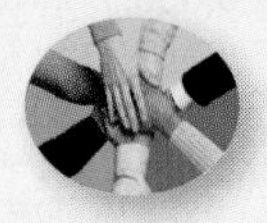

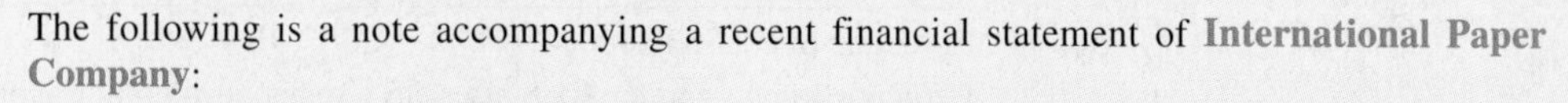

The following is a note accompanying a recent financial statement of **International Paper Company**:

Plant, Properties, and Equipment

Plant, properties, and equipment are stated at cost less accumulated depreciation.

For financial reporting purposes, the company uses the units-of-production method of depreciating its major pulp and paper mills and certain wood products facilities, and the straight-line method for other plant and equipment.

Annual straight-line depreciation rates for financial reporting purposes are as follows: buildings 2½ percent to 8 percent; machinery and equipment 5 percent to 33 percent; woods equipment 10 percent to 16 percent. For tax purposes, depreciation is computed utilizing accelerated methods.

Instructions

a. Are the depreciation methods used in the company's financial statements determined by current income tax laws? If not, who is responsible for selecting these methods? Explain.

b. Does the company violate the consistency principle by using different depreciation methods for its paper mills and wood products facilities than it uses for its other plant and equipment? If not, what does the principle of consistency mean? Explain.

c. What is the estimated useful life of the machinery and equipment being depreciated with a straight-line depreciation rate of:

1. 5 percent.
2. 33 percent (round to the nearest year).

Who determines the useful lives over which specific assets are to be depreciated?

d. Why do you think the company uses accelerated depreciation methods for income tax purposes, rather than using the straight-line method?

CASE 9.4
Capitalization vs. Expense

One of your responsibilities as division manager of an important component of Roxby Industries is to oversee accounting for the division. One of the issues you grapple with on an almost continuous basis is whether particular costs should be expensed immediately or whether they should be capitalized. The company has an accounting policy manual that includes a section on this topic, but it is rather vague in this regard. It simply says that if a cost benefits multiple accounting periods, the cost should be capitalized; otherwise, that cost should be expensed immediately. It also makes a brief reference to *materiality* by stating that, if a cost is sufficiently small, it should be immediately expensed despite the fact that it may benefit multiple accounting periods. No additional guidance is provided with regard to how these general concepts should be applied.

Over several years you have noticed a tendency of your staff to capitalize rather than expense more costs. While you and your coworkers in the division do not receive a bonus or other direct compensation that is tied to your division's performance, you know that upper management monitors carefully the financial performance of divisions. From time to time in various meetings and in written correspondence, comments are made praising individuals and divisions of the company for their positive financial performance. In fact, within your division you have done the same when you meet with your employees and either compliment them for strong financial performance or express concern about weak financial performance.

Roxby Industries has a code of professional conduct that is shown to employees when they are hired. Within that code are references to personal integrity and the responsibility of employees to carry out company policy and not engage in activities that benefit themselves at the expense of the company. Like the accounting policies referred to above, there is no guidance on how this general principle might be carried out.

Instructions

a. What behavior may your comments in meetings with your employees, or the comments made to you from upper management, be motivating in terms of the continuous decisions that are being made about capitalizing and expensing costs?

b. What steps might you take to ensure that you and the employees in your division are not taking actions that they should not take in light of the company's accounting policies and code of professional conduct?

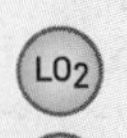

BUSINESSWEEK CASE 9.5

Accounting for Intangibles

BusinessWeek

Neil Gross claims that the value of companies has been shifting from tangible assets—the bricks and mortar—to intangible assets, such as patents, customer lists, and brands. His article, "Valuing 'Intangibles' Is a Tough Job, but It Has to Be Done," in the August 6, 2001, issue of *BusinessWeek*, claims that intangibles are the keys to shareholder value in today's economy, where so much value is placed on knowledge. However, Gross notes, accounting systems do little to acknowledge them. Gross complains that these intangibles don't appear on the balance sheet except in rare cases.

In response to concerns about the lack of information about intangibles in financial statements, the FASB has taken the issue under consideration. FASB research director Timothy S. Lucas is quoted in Gross's article as saying, "there are very significant measurement and definition problems."

Instructions

Choose two other students to form a group of three (or let the instructor assign you) and prepare a one-page paper that argues in favor of (or against) valuing brands (or internally generated goodwill) and classifying either as an asset on the balance sheet.

INTERNET CASE 9.6

R&D in the Pharmaceutical Industry

The pharmaceutical industry spends billions of dollars each year on research and development. Rather than capitalize these R&D expenditures as intangible assets, companies are required to charge them to expense in the year incurred.

Perform a keyword search of Pharmaceutical Companies using the following search engine:

www.yahoo.com

Your search will result in a list of companies that research and develop pharmaceutical products. Select five of these companies and obtain their 10-K reports (using EDGAR) at the following Internet address:

www.sec.gov

Instructions

a. For each of the companies you selected, determine:

1. Total R&D expense for the most current year.
2. Total R&D expense as a percentage of total operating costs and expenses.
3. Total R&D expense as a percentage of net sales.
4. The percentage by which operating income would have increased had the entire R&D expenditure been recorded as an intangible asset instead of being charged to expense.

b. Using information from the 10-K reports, summarize briefly the kinds of drugs being researched and developed by each of these companies. To a potential investor, which company appears to be the most innovative and promising? Explain.

Internet sites are time and date sensitive. It is the purpose of these exercises to have you explore the Internet. You may need to use the Yahoo! search engine http://www.yahoo.com *(or another favorite search engine) to find a company's current Web address.*

Answers to Self-Test Questions

1. c (Depreciation is not recorded on inventory.) **2.** c **3.** d, \$1,800 [2006 depreciation = \$10,000 × 20% × ½ = \$1,000; 2007 depreciation = (\$10,000 − \$1,000) × 20% = \$1,800] **4.** c, d **5.** a (\$22,000 selling price − \$17,000 book value = \$5,000 gain; \$50,000 cost − \$17,000 book value = \$33,000 accumulated depreciation) **6.** c

10 Liabilities

Learning Objectives

AFTER STUDYING THIS CHAPTER, YOU SHOULD BE ABLE TO:

LO1 Define *liabilities* and distinguish between current and long-term liabilities.

LO2 Account for notes payable and interest expense.

LO3 Describe the costs and the basic accounting activities relating to payrolls.

LO4 Prepare an amortization table allocating payments between interest and principal.

LO5 Describe corporate bonds and explain the tax advantage of debt financing.

LO6 Account for bonds issued at a discount or premium.

LO7 Explain the concept of present value as it relates to bond prices.

LO8 Explain how estimated liabilities, loss contingencies, and commitments are disclosed in financial statements.

LO9 Evaluate the safety of creditors' claims.

LO10 Describe reporting issues related to leases, postretirement benefits, and deferred taxes.

TRBfoto/Getty Images/DIL

DuPont

Buying items on credit has never been easier. Each day, large retailers and credit card companies seem to encourage consumers to go deeper and deeper into debt. Add to credit card debt other long-term obligations—such as home mortgages and automobile loans—and it's no wonder that payments on total household debt consume nearly 98 percent of total disposable income in the United States.

Large corporations also have jumped on the bandwagon in recent years by issuing more debt than ever to finance expansion and acquisitions. The tremendous debt service costs associated with corporate borrowing can siphon away a significant portion of a company's operating cash flows.

Consider, for example, **DuPont**. In the 2005 balance sheet, **DuPont** reports total liabilities of almost $24 billion in comparison to total stockholders' equity of only approximately $9 billion. The company's heavy reliance on debt financing burdens the company with billions of dollars in debt service costs annually. Notes accompanying **DuPont**'s recent financial statements reveal management's intent to reduce current debt levels to improve the company's overall financial flexibility. Other major corporations are likely to do the same.

Creditors and investors evaluate carefully the liabilities appearing in financial reports. Thoroughly understanding short-term versus long-term debt is important for managers choosing how to finance their businesses. This chapter provides a basic understanding of concepts related to liabilities and describes how liabilities are recorded and later presented in the financial statements. In addition, the impact of debt on various financial ratios is illustrated.

THE NATURE OF LIABILITIES

LO1 **Define *liabilities* and distinguish between current and long-term liabilities.**

Liabilities may be defined as *debts or obligations arising from past transactions or events* that require settlement at a future date. All liabilities have certain characteristics in common; however, the specific terms of different liabilities, and the rights of the creditors, vary greatly.

Distinction between Debt and Equity

Businesses have two basic sources of financing: liabilities and owners' equity. Liabilities differ from owners' equity in several respects. The feature that most clearly distinguishes the claims of creditors from owners' equity is that all liabilities eventually *mature*—that is, they come due. Owners' equity does not mature. The date on which a liability comes due is called the **maturity date**.[1]

Although all liabilities mature, their maturity dates vary. Some liabilities are so short in term that they are paid before the financial statements are prepared. Long-term liabilities, in contrast, may not mature for many years. The maturity dates of key liabilities may be a critical factor in the solvency of a business.

The providers of borrowed capital are *creditors* of the business, not owners. As creditors, they have financial claims against the business but usually do *not* have the right to control business operations. The traditional roles of owners, managers, and creditors may be modified, however, in an *indenture contract*. Creditors sometimes insist on being granted some control over business operations as a condition of making a loan, particularly if the business is in poor financial condition. Indenture contracts may impose such restrictions as limits on management salaries and on dividends, and may require the creditor's approval for additional borrowing or for large capital expenditures.

The claims of creditors have *legal priority* over the claims of owners. If a business ceases operations and liquidates, creditors must be *paid in full* before any distributions are made to the owners. The relative security of creditors' claims, however, can vary among the creditors. Sometimes the borrower pledges title to specific assets as **collateral** for a loan. If the borrower defaults on a secured loan, the creditor may foreclose on the pledged assets. Assets that have been pledged as security for loans should be identified in notes accompanying the borrower's financial statements.

Liabilities that are not secured by specific assets are termed *general credit obligations*. The priorities of general credit obligations vary with the nature of the liability and the terms of indenture contracts.

Many Liabilities Bear Interest

Many long-term liabilities, and some short-term ones, require the borrower to pay interest. Only interest accrued *as of the balance sheet date* appears as a liability in the borrower's balance sheet. The borrower's obligation to pay interest in *future* periods sometimes is disclosed in the notes to the financial statements, but it is not shown as an existing liability.

Estimated Liabilities

Most liabilities are for a definite dollar amount, clearly stated by contract. Examples include notes payable, accounts payable, and accrued expenses, such as

[1] Some liabilities are *due on demand*, which means that the liability is payable upon the creditor's request. From a bank's point of view, customers' checking accounts are "demand liabilities." Liabilities due on demand may come due at any time and are classified as current liabilities.

interest payable and salaries payable. In some cases, however, the dollar amount of a liability must be *estimated* at the balance sheet date.

Estimated liabilities have two basic characteristics: The liability is *known to exist*, and the precise dollar amount cannot be determined until a later date. For instance, the automobiles sold by most automakers are accompanied by a warranty obligating the automaker to replace defective parts for a period of several years. As each car is sold, the automaker *incurs a liability* to perform any work that may be required under the warranty. The dollar amount of this liability, however, can only be estimated.

Current Liabilities

Current liabilities are obligations that must be paid within one year or within the operating cycle, whichever is longer. Another requirement for classification as a current liability is the expectation that the debt will be paid from current assets (or through the rendering of services). Liabilities that do not meet these conditions are classified as long-term liabilities.

The time period used in defining current liabilities parallels that used in defining current assets. The amount of *working capital* (current assets less current liabilities) and the *current ratio* (current assets divided by current liabilities) are valuable indicators of a company's ability to pay its debts in the near future.

Among the most common examples of current liabilities are accounts payable, short-term notes payable, the current portion of long-term debt, accrued liabilities (such as interest payable, income taxes payable, and payroll liabilities), and unearned revenue.

ACCOUNTS PAYABLE

Accounts payable often are subdivided into the categories of *trade* accounts payable and *other* accounts payable. Trade accounts payable are short-term obligations to suppliers for purchases of merchandise. Other accounts payable include liabilities for any goods and services other than merchandise.

Technically, the date at which a trade account payable comes into existence depends on whether goods are purchased F.O.B. (free on board) shipping point or F.O.B. destination. Under F.O.B. shipping point, a liability arises and title to the goods transfers when the merchandise is *shipped* by the supplier. Under F.O.B. destination, a liability does not arise and title of ownership does not transfer until the goods are actually *received* by the buyer. However, unless *material* amounts of merchandise are purchased on terms F.O.B. shipping point, most companies follow the convenient practice of recording trade accounts payable when merchandise is received.

NOTES PAYABLE

Account for notes payable and interest expense. LO2

Notes payable are issued whenever bank loans are obtained. Other transactions that may give rise to notes payable include the purchase of real estate or costly equipment, the purchase of merchandise, and the substitution of a note for a past-due account payable.

Notes payable usually require the borrower to pay an interest charge. Normally, the interest rate is stated separately from the **principal amount** of the note.[2]

To illustrate, assume that on November 1, Porter Company borrows $10,000 from its bank for a period of six months at an annual interest rate of 12 percent. Six months later on May 1, Porter Company will have to pay the bank the principal amount of $10,000, plus $600 interest ($\$10{,}000 \times .12 \times 6/12$). As evidence of this loan, the bank will require Porter Company to issue a note payable similar to the one in Exhibit 10–1.

[2] An alternative is to include the interest charges in the face amount of the note. This form of note is seldom used today, largely because of the disclosure requirements under "truth-in-lending" laws.

Exhibit 10–1
A NOTE PAYABLE

Miami, Florida		November 1, 20__
Six months	AFTER THIS DATE	Porter Company

PROMISES TO PAY TO SECURITY NATIONAL BANK THE SUM OF $ $10,000

WITH INTEREST AT THE RATE OF 12% PER ANNUM.

SIGNED *John Caldwell*

TITLE Treasurer

The journal entry in Porter Company's accounting records for this November 1 borrowing is:

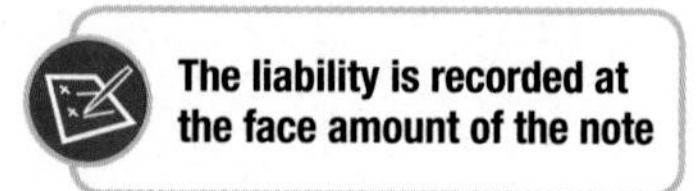
The liability is recorded at the face amount of the note

	Debit	Credit
Cash	10,000	
Notes Payable		10,000
Borrowed $10,000 for 6 months at 12% interest per year.		

Notice that no liability is recorded for the interest charges when the note is issued. At the date that money is borrowed, the borrower has a liability *only for the principal amount of the loan*; the liability for interest accrues day by day over the life of the loan. At December 31, two months' interest expense has accrued, and the following year-end adjusting entry is made:

A liability for interest accrues day by day

	Debit	Credit
Interest Expense	200	
Interest Payable		200
To record interest expense incurred through year-end on 12%, 6-month note dated Nov. 1 ($10,000 × 12% × 2⁄12 = $200).		

For simplicity, we will assume that Porter Company makes adjusting entries *only at year-end*. Thus the entry on May 1 to record payment of the note will be:

Payment of principal and interest

	Debit	Credit
Notes Payable	10,000	
Interest Payable	200	
Interest Expense	400	
Cash		10,600
To record payment of 12%, 6-month note on maturity date and to recognize interest expense incurred since Jan. 1 ($10,000 × 12% × 4⁄12 = $400).		

If Porter Company paid this note *prior* to May 1, interest charges usually would be computed only through the date of early payment.[3]

THE CURRENT PORTION OF LONG-TERM DEBT

Some long-term debts, such as mortgage loans, are payable in a series of monthly or quarterly installments. In these cases, the *principal* amount due within one year (or the operating cycle)

[3] Computing interest charges only through the date of payment is the normal business practice. However, some notes are written in a manner requiring the borrower to pay interest for the full term of the note even if payment is made early. Borrowers should look carefully at these terms.

is regarded as a current liability, and the remainder of the obligation is classified as a long-term liability.

As the maturity date of a long-term liability approaches, the obligation eventually becomes due within the current period. Long-term liabilities that become payable within one year of the balance sheet date are *reclassified* in the balance sheet as current liabilities.[4] Changing the classification of a liability does not require a journal entry; the obligation is simply shown in a different section of the balance sheet.

ACCRUED LIABILITIES

Accrued liabilities arise from the recognition of expenses for which payment will be made in a future period. Thus accrued liabilities also are called *accrued expenses*. Examples of accrued liabilities include interest payable, income taxes payable, and a number of liabilities relating to payrolls. As accrued liabilities stem from the recording of expenses, the *matching* principle governs the timing of their recognition.

All companies incur accrued liabilities. In most cases, however, these liabilities are paid at frequent intervals. Therefore, they usually do not accumulate to large amounts. In a balance sheet, accrued liabilities frequently are included in the amount shown as accounts payable.

PAYROLL LIABILITIES

Describe the costs and the basic accounting activities relating to payrolls. LO3

The preparation of a payroll is a specialized accounting function beyond the scope of this text. But we believe that every student should have some understanding of the various costs associated with payrolls. Employers must compute, record, and pay a number of costs in addition to the wages and salaries owed to employees. In fact, one might say that the total wages and salaries expense (or gross pay) represents only the starting point of payroll computations.

To illustrate, assume that Fulbright Medical Lab employs 20 highly skilled employees. If monthly wages for this workforce in January were $100,000, the *total* payroll costs incurred by this employer would actually be much higher, as shown in Exhibit 10–2.

Exhibit 10–2
THE COMPUTATION OF TOTAL PAYROLL COSTS

Gross pay (wages expense)	$100,000
Social Security and Medicare taxes	7,650
Federal and state unemployment taxes	6,200
Workers' Compensation Insurance	4,000
Group health and life insurance benefits	6,000
Employee pension plan benefits	9,500
Total payroll costs for January	$133,350

The amounts in Exhibit 10–2 shown in red are **payroll taxes** and insurance premiums required by law. Costs shown in green currently are not required by law but often are included in the total compensation package provided to employees.

In our example, total payroll-related costs exceed wages expense *by more than 30 percent*. This relationship will vary from one employer to another, but our illustration is typical of many payrolls.

Payroll Taxes and Mandated Costs

All employers must pay Social Security and Medicare taxes on the wages or salary paid to each employee. These taxes currently amount to 7.65 percent of the employee's earnings. Federal unemployment taxes apply only to the *first $7,000* earned by each employee during the year (state unemployment taxes may vary). Thus these taxes tend to drop off dramatically as the year progresses.

[4] Exceptions are made to this rule if the liability will be *refinanced* (that is, extended or renewed) on a long-term basis or if a special *sinking fund* has been accumulated for the purpose of repaying this obligation. In these cases, the debt remains classified as a long-term liability, even though it will mature within the current period.

Workers' compensation is a state-mandated program that provides insurance to employees against job-related injury. Like most other insurance policies, the premiums are generally paid *in advance* by debiting a current asset account, Prepaid Workers' Compensation Insurance, and by crediting Cash. The premiums vary greatly by state and by occupational classification. In some high-risk industries (for example, roofers), workers' compensation premiums may exceed 50 percent of the employees' wages.

Other Payroll-Related Costs Many employers pay some or all of the costs of health and life insurance for their employees as well as make contributions to employee pension plans. Annual health insurance premiums, which are generally paid *in advance*, may cost between $1,800 and $3,600 per employee (including family members). Contributions to employee pension plans, if any, vary greatly among employers.

Amounts Withheld from Employees' Pay Thus far, our illustration has specified only those taxes and other mandated costs levied on the *employer*. Employees, too, incur taxes on their earnings. In addition to federal and state income taxes, employees share in paying Social Security and Medicare taxes.[5] Employers must withhold these amounts from their employees' pay and forward them directly to the appropriate tax authorities.[6] (The net amount of cash actually paid to employees after all required withholdings have been made is often referred to as the employees' *take-home pay*.)

In our illustration, Fulbright Medical Lab's 20 employees earned gross wages of $100,000 in January. Their take-home pay will be significantly less than the gross amount, as shown in Exhibit 10–3.

Exhibit 10–3
COMPUTATION OF EMPLOYEE TAKE-HOME PAY

Gross pay (wages expense)	$100,000
Less:	
State income tax withholdings	(2,350)
Federal income tax withholdings	(22,500)
Social Security and Medicare tax withholdings	(7,650)
Employee take-home pay for January	$ 67,500

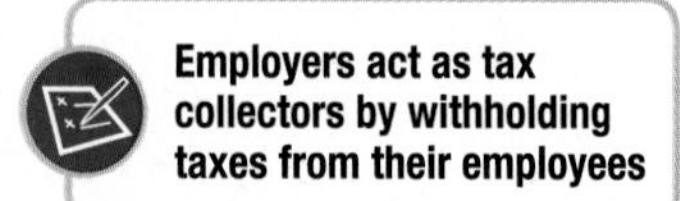
Employers act as tax collectors by withholding taxes from their employees

It is important to realize that amounts withheld from employees' pay do *not* represent taxes on the *employer*. The amounts withheld are simply a portion of the gross wages and salaries expense that must be sent directly to the tax authorities, rather than paid to the employees. In essence, the employer is required by law to act as the tax *collector*. In the employer's balance sheet, these withholdings represent current liabilities until they are forwarded to the proper tax authorities.

Recording Payroll Activities Let us conclude our illustration of Fulbright Medical Lab by making the necessary entries to record its payroll activities. In Exhibit 10–2, the lab's *total* payroll costs for January were computed as $133,350. Of this amount, $100,000 represented gross wages earned by employees, $17,850 represented employer payroll taxes and other mandated costs (shown in red), and $15,500 represented employee benefits paid for by the employer (shown in green). The accounting for these three amounts by Fulbright Medical Lab is summarized in Exhibit 10–4.

[5] Social Security and Medicare taxes are levied on *employees* at the same 7.65 percent rate as levied upon *employers*. Thus, total Social Security and Medicare taxes amount to more than 15 percent of gross wages and salaries. There is a cap on the portion of an employee's earnings that is subject to Social Security taxes. The current limit is approximately $90,000. There is no cap on employee wages or salaries subject to Medicare taxes.

[6] In many companies, employers make additional withholdings when their employees share in paying for the cost of health insurance, life insurance, retirement contributions, and other fringe benefits.

Exhibit 10–4

PAYROLL ACTIVITIES RECORDED BY THE EMPLOYER

A. Record gross wages, employee withholdings, and employee take-home pay (withholdings and take-home pay figures taken from Exhibit 10–3).

	Debit	Credit
Wages Expense	100,000	
State Income Tax Payable		2,350
Federal Income Tax Payable		22,500
Social Security and Medicare Taxes Payable		7,650
Cash (or Wages Payable)		67,500

To record gross wages, employee withholdings, and employee take-home pay.

B. Record employer's payroll tax expense (red figures taken from Exhibit 10–2).

	Debit	Credit
Payroll Tax Expense	17,850	
Social Security and Medicare Taxes Payable		7,650
Federal and State Unemployment Taxes Payable		6,200
Prepaid Workers' Compensation Insurance		4,000

To record employer payroll tax expense, $4,000 of which is the expiration of prepaid workers' compensation insurance premiums.

C. Record employee benefit expenses (green figures taken from Exhibit 10–2).

	Debit	Credit
Employee Health and Life Insurance Expense	6,000	
Pension Fund Expense	9,500	
Prepaid Employee Health and Life Insurance		6,000
Cash (or Pension Benefits Payable)		9,500

To record employee benefit expenses, $6,000 of which is the expiration of prepaid employee health and life insurance premium.

UNEARNED REVENUE

A liability for unearned revenue arises when a customer pays in advance. Upon receipt of an advance payment from a customer, the company debits Cash and credits a liability account such as Unearned Revenue or Customers' Deposits. As the services are rendered to the customer, an entry is made debiting the liability account and crediting a revenue account. Notice that the liability for unearned revenue normally is satisfied by rendering services to the creditor, rather than by making cash payments.

Unearned revenue ordinarily is classified as a current liability because activities involved in earning revenue are part of the business's normal operating cycle.

Long-Term Liabilities

Long-term obligations usually arise from major expenditures, such as acquisitions of plant assets, the purchase of another company, or refinancing an existing long-term obligation that is about to mature. Thus transactions involving long-term liabilities are relatively few in number but often involve large dollar amounts. In contrast, current liabilities usually arise from routine operating transactions.

Many businesses regard long-term liabilities as an alternative to owners' equity as a source of permanent financing. Although long-term liabilities eventually mature, they often are *refinanced*—that is, the maturing obligation simply is replaced with a new long-term liability.

MATURING OBLIGATIONS INTENDED TO BE REFINANCED

One special type of long-term liability is an obligation that will mature in the current period but that is expected to be refinanced on a long-term basis. For example, a company may have a bank loan that comes due each year but is routinely extended for the following year. Both the company and the bank may intend for this arrangement to continue on a long-term basis.

If management has both the *intent* and the *ability* to refinance soon-to-mature obligations on a long-term basis, these obligations are classified as long-term liabilities. In this situation, the accountant looks to the *economic substance* of the situation rather than to its legal form.

When the economic substance of a transaction differs from its legal form or its outward appearance, financial statements should reflect the *economic substance*. Accountants summarize this concept with the phrase *"Substance takes precedence over form."* Today's business world is characterized by transactions of ever-increasing complexity. Recognizing those situations in which the substance of a transaction differs from its form is one of the greatest challenges confronting the accounting profession.

CASE IN POINT

It is typical in Japan for short-term debt to have lower interest rates than long-term debt. Thus, Japanese managers find short-term debt more attractive than long-term debt. In addition, banks are happy to renew these loans because this allows them to adjust the interest rates to changing market conditions. Thus, short-term debt in Japan works like long-term debt elsewhere. In fact, the use of short-term debt to finance long-term assets appears to be the rule, not the exception, in Japan.

INSTALLMENT NOTES PAYABLE

My Mentor

Purchases of real estate and certain types of equipment often are financed by the issuance of long-term notes that call for a series of installment payments. These payments (often called **debt service**) may be due monthly, quarterly, semiannually, or at any other interval. If these installments continue until the debt is completely repaid, the loan is said to be "fully amortizing." Often, however, installment notes contain a due date at which the remaining unpaid balance is to be repaid in a single "balloon" payment.

Some installment notes call for installment payments equal to the periodic interest charges (an "interest only" note). Under these terms, the principal amount of the loan is payable at a specified maturity date. More often, however, the installment payments are *greater* than the amount of interest accruing during the period. Thus only a portion of each installment payment represents interest expense, and the remainder of the payment reduces the principal amount of the liability. As the amount owed is reduced by each payment, the portion of each successive payment representing interest expense will *decrease*, and the portion going toward repayment of principal will *increase*.

Allocating Installment Payments between Interest and Principal In accounting for an installment note, the accountant must determine the portion of each payment that represents interest expense and the portion that reduces the principal amount of the liability. This distinction is made in advance by preparing an **amortization table**.

LO4 **Prepare an amortization table allocating payments between interest and principal.**

To illustrate, assume that on October 15, Year 1, King's Inn purchases furnishings at a total cost of $16,398. In payment, the company issues an installment note payable for this amount, plus interest at 12 percent per annum (or 1 percent per month). This note will be paid in 18 monthly installments of $1,000 each, beginning on November 15. An amortization table for this installment note payable is shown in Exhibit 10–5 (amounts of interest expense are *rounded to the nearest dollar*).

Preparing an Amortization Table Let us explore the content of Exhibit 10–5. First, notice that the payments are made on a *monthly* basis. Therefore, the amounts of the payments (column A), interest expense (column B), and reduction in the unpaid balance (column C) are all *monthly amounts*.

Exhibit 10–5

AMORTIZATION TABLE FOR A NOTE PAYABLE

AMORTIZATION TABLE
(12% Note Payable for $16,398; Payable in 18 Monthly Installments of $1,000)

Interest Period	Payment Date	(A) Monthly Payment	(B) Interest Expense (1% of the Last Unpaid Balance)	(C) Reduction in Unpaid Balance (A) − (B)	(D) Unpaid Balance
Issue date	Oct. 15, Year 1	—	—	—	$16,398
1	Nov. 15	$1,000	$164	$836	15,562
2	Dec. 15	1,000	156	844	14,718
3	Jan. 15, Year 2	1,000	147	853	13,865
4	Feb. 15	1,000	139	861	13,004
5	Mar. 15	1,000	130	870	12,134
6	Apr. 15	1,000	121	879	11,255
7	May 15	1,000	113	887	10,368
8	June 15	1,000	104	896	9,472
9	July 15	1,000	95	905	8,567
10	Aug. 15	1,000	86	914	7,653
11	Sept. 15	1,000	77	923	6,730
12	Oct. 15	1,000	67	933	5,797
13	Nov. 15	1,000	58	942	4,855
14	Dec. 15	1,000	49	951	3,904
15	Jan. 15, Year 3	1,000	39	961	2,943
16	Feb. 15	1,000	29	971	1,972
17	Mar. 15	1,000	20	980	992
18	Apr. 15	1,000	8*	992	-0-

*In the last period, interest expense is equal to the amount of the final payment minus the remaining unpaid balance. This compensates for the cumulative effect of rounding interest amounts to the nearest dollar.

The interest rate used in the table is of special importance; this rate must coincide with the period of time *between payment dates*—in this case, one month. Thus, if payments are made monthly, column B must be based on the *monthly* rate of interest. If payments were made quarterly, this column would use the quarterly rate of interest.

An amortization table begins with the original amount of the liability ($16,398) listed at the top of the Unpaid Balance column. The amounts of the monthly payments, shown in column A, are specified by the installment contract. The monthly interest expense, shown in column B, is computed for each month by applying the monthly interest rate to the unpaid balance at the *beginning of that month*. The portion of each payment that reduces the amount of the liability (column C) is simply the remainder of the payment (column A minus column B). Finally, the unpaid balance of the liability (column D) is reduced each month by the amount indicated in column C.

Rather than continuing to make monthly payments, King's Inn could settle this liability at any time by paying the amount currently shown as the unpaid balance.

Notice that the amount of interest expense listed in column B *changes every month*. In our illustration, the interest expense is *decreasing* each month, because the unpaid balance is continually decreasing.[7]

Preparing each horizontal line in an amortization table involves making the same computations, based on a new unpaid balance. Thus an amortization table of any length can be easily

[7] If the monthly payments were *less* than the amount of the monthly interest expense, the unpaid balance of the note would *increase* each month. This, in turn, would cause the interest expense to increase each month. This pattern, termed *negative amortization*, occurs temporarily in some "adjustable-rate" home mortgages.

and quickly prepared by computer software. (Most "money management" software includes a program for preparing amortization tables.) Only three items of data need to be entered into such a program: (1) the original amount of the liability, (2) the amount of periodic payments, and (3) the interest rate (per payment period).

Using an Amortization Table Once an amortization table has been prepared, the entries to record each payment are taken directly from the amounts shown in the table. For example, the entry to record the first monthly payment (November 15, Year 1) is:

Payment is allocated between interest and principal

Interest Expense	164	
Installment Note Payable	836	
Cash		1,000
Made Nov. payment on installment note payable.		

Similarly, the entry to record the *second* payment, made on *December 15, Year 1*, is:

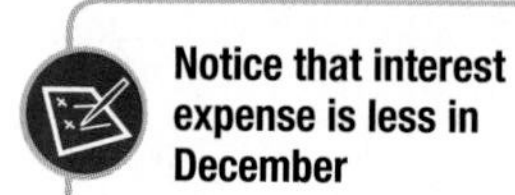

Notice that interest expense is less in December

Interest Expense	156	
Installment Note Payable	844	
Cash		1,000
Made Dec. payment on installment note payable.		

At December 31, Year 1, King's Inn should make an adjusting entry to record one-half month's accrued interest on this liability. The amount of this adjusting entry is based on the unpaid balance shown in the amortization table as of the last payment (December 15). This entry is:

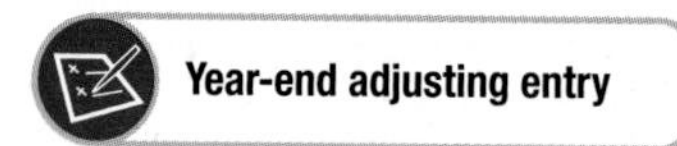

Year-end adjusting entry

Interest Expense	74	
Interest Payable		74
Adjusting entry to record interest expense on installment note for the last half of Dec.: $14,718 × 1% × ½ = $74.		

The Current Portion of Long-Term Debt Notice that as of December 31, Year 1, the unpaid balance of this note is $14,718. As of December 31, *Year 2*, however, the unpaid balance will be only $3,904. Thus the principal amount of this note will be reduced by *$10,814* during Year 2 ($14,718 − $3,904 = $10,814). In the balance sheet prepared at December 31, Year 1, the $10,814 portion of this debt that is scheduled for repayment within the *next 12 months* should be classified as a *current liability*. The remaining $3,904 should be classified as a long-term liability.

BONDS PAYABLE

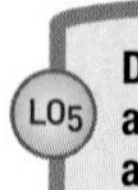

LO5 Describe corporate bonds and explain the tax advantage of debt financing.

Financially sound corporations may arrange limited amounts of long-term financing by issuing notes payable to banks or to insurance companies. But to finance a large project, such as developing an oil field or purchasing a controlling interest in the capital stock of another company, a corporation may need more capital than any single lender can supply. When a corporation needs to raise large amounts of long-term capital—perhaps 50, 100, or 500 million dollars (or more)—it generally sells additional shares of capital stock or issues **bonds payable**.

WHAT ARE BONDS?

The issuance of bonds payable is a technique for splitting a very large loan into many transferable units, called bonds. Each bond represents a *long-term, interest-bearing note payable*, usually in the face amount (or par value) of $1,000 or some multiple of $1,000. The bonds are sold to the investing public, enabling many different investors (bondholders) to participate in the loan.

Bonds usually are very long-term notes, maturing in perhaps 15 or 30 years. The bonds are transferable, however, so individual bondholders may sell their bonds to other investors at any time. Most bonds call for semiannual interest payments to the bondholders, with interest computed at a specified *contract rate* throughout the life of the bond. Thus investors often describe bonds as "fixed income" investments.

An example of a corporate bond issue is the 8½ percent bonds of Pacific Bell (a Pacific Telesis company, known as PacBell), due August 15, 2031. Interest on these bonds is payable semiannually on February 15 and August 15. With this bond issue, PacBell borrowed $225 million by issuing 225,000 bonds of $1,000 each.

PacBell did not actually print and issue 225,000 separate notes payable. Each bondholder is issued a single *bond certificate* indicating the number of bonds purchased. Each certificate is in the face amount of $25,000 and, therefore, represents ownership of 25 bonds. Investors such as mutual funds, banks, and insurance companies often buy thousands of bonds at one time.

The Issuance of Bonds Payable When bonds are issued, the corporation usually utilizes the services of an investment banking firm, called an **underwriter**. The underwriter guarantees the issuing corporation a specific price for the entire bond issue and makes a profit by selling the bonds to the investing public at a higher price. The corporation records the issuance of the bonds at the net amount received from the underwriter. The use of an underwriter assures the corporation that the entire bond issue will be sold without delay and that the entire amount of the proceeds will be available at a specific date.

Transferability of Bonds Corporate bonds, like capital stocks, are traded daily on organized securities exchanges, such as the *New York Bond Exchange*. The holders of a 25-year bond issue need not wait 25 years to convert their investments into cash. By placing a telephone call to a broker, an investor may sell bonds within a matter of minutes at the going market price. This quality of *liquidity* is one of the most attractive features of an investment in corporate bonds.

Getty Images

Quoted Market Prices Bond prices are quoted as a *percentage* of their face value or *maturity* value, which is usually $1,000. The maturity value is the amount the issuing company must pay to redeem the bond at the date it matures (becomes due). A $1,000 bond quoted at *102* would therefore have a market price of $1,020 (102 percent of $1,000). Bond prices are quoted at the nearest one-eighth of a percentage point. The following line from the financial page of a daily newspaper summarizes the previous day's trading in bonds of Sears, Roebuck & Company:

Bonds	Sales	High	Low	Close	Net Change
Sears R 7⅞ 07	245	97½	95½	97	+1

This line of condensed information indicates that 245 of Sears's 7⅞ percent, $1,000 bonds maturing in 2007 were traded during the day. The highest price is reported as 97½, or $975 for a bond of $1,000 face value. The lowest price was 95½, or $955 for a $1,000 bond. The closing price (last sale of the day) was 97, or $970. This was one point above the closing price of the previous day, an increase of $10 in the price of a $1,000 bond.

Types of Bonds Bonds secured by the pledge of specific assets are called *mortgage bonds*. An unsecured bond is called a *debenture bond*; its value rests on the general credit of the corporation. A debenture bond issued by a very large and strong corporation may have a higher investment rating than a secured bond issued by a corporation in less satisfactory financial condition.

Bond interest is paid semiannually by mailing to each bondholder a check for six months' interest on the bonds he or she owns.[8] Many bonds are *callable*, which means that the corporation has the right to redeem the bonds *in advance* of the maturity date by paying a specified *call price*. To compensate bondholders for being forced to give up their investments, the call price usually is somewhat higher than the face value of the bonds.

Traditionally, bonds have appealed to conservative investors, interested primarily in a reliable income stream from their investments. To make a bond issue more attractive to these investors, some corporations create a bond **sinking fund**, designated for repaying the bonds at maturity. At regular intervals, the corporation deposits cash into this sinking fund. A bond sinking fund is not classified as a current asset, because it is not available for the payment of current liabilities. Such funds are shown in the balance sheet under the caption "Long-Term Investments," which appears just below the current asset section.

As an additional attraction to investors, corporations sometimes include a conversion privilege in the bond indenture. A **convertible bond** is one that may be exchanged at the option of the bondholder for a specified number of shares of capital stock. Thus the market value of a convertible bond tends to fluctuate with the market value of an equivalent number of shares of capital stock.

Junk Bonds In recent years, some corporations have issued securities that have come to be known as **junk bonds**. This term describes a bond issue that involves a substantially greater risk of default than normal. A company issuing junk bonds usually has so much long-term debt that its ability to meet interest and principal repayment obligations has become questionable. To compensate bondholders for this unusual level of risk, junk bonds promise a substantially higher rate of interest than do "investment quality" bonds.

TAX ADVANTAGE OF BOND FINANCING

A principal advantage of raising money by issuing bonds instead of stock is that interest payments are *deductible* in determining income subject to corporate income taxes. Dividends paid to stockholders, however, are *not deductible* in computing taxable income.

To illustrate, assume that a corporation pays income taxes at a rate of *30 percent* on its taxable income. If this corporation issues $10 million of 10 percent bonds payable, it will incur interest expense of $1 million per year. This interest expense, however, will reduce taxable income by $1 million, thus reducing the corporation's annual income taxes by $300,000. As a result, the *after-tax* cost of borrowing the $10 million is only *$700,000*:

Interest expense ($10,000,000 × 10%)	$1,000,000
Less: Income tax savings ($1,000,000 deduction × 30%)	300,000
After-tax cost of borrowing	$ 700,000

A shortcut approach to computing the after-tax cost of borrowing is simply multiplying the interest expense by *1 minus the company's tax rate*, as follows: $1,000,000 × (1 − .30) = $700,000.

ACCOUNTING FOR BONDS PAYABLE

Accounting for bonds payable closely parallels accounting for notes payable. The accountable events for a bond issue usually are (1) issuance of the bonds, (2) semiannual interest

[8] In recent years, corporations have issued only *registered* bonds, for which interest is paid by mailing a check to the registered owners of the bonds. In past decades, some companies issued *coupon bonds* or *bearer bonds*, which had a series of redeemable coupons attached. At each interest date, the bondholder had to "clip" the coupon and present it to a bank to collect the interest. These bonds posed a considerable hazard to investors—if the investor lost the coupon, or forgot about an interest date, he or she received no interest. In many states, issuing coupon bonds now is illegal.

payments, (3) accrual of interest payable at the end of each accounting period, and (4) retirement of the bonds at maturity.[9]

To illustrate these events, assume that on March 1, 2005, Wells Corporation issues $1 million of 12 percent, 20-year bonds payable.[10] These bonds are dated March 1, 2005, and interest is computed from this date. Interest on the bonds is payable semiannually, each September 1 and March 1. If all of the bonds are sold at par value (also referred to as face value), the issuance of the bonds on March 1 will be recorded by the following entry:

Cash	1,000,000	
Bonds Payable		1,000,000
Issued 12%, 20-year bonds payable at a price of 100.		

Entry at the issuance date

Every September 1 during the term of the bond issue, Wells Corporation must pay $60,000 to the bondholders ($1,000,000 × .12 × ½ = $60,000). This semiannual interest payment will be recorded as shown below:

Bond Interest Expense	60,000	
Cash		60,000
Semiannual payment of bond interest.		

Entry to record semiannual interest payments

Every December 31, Wells Corporation must make an adjusting entry to record the four months' interest that has accrued since September 1:

Bond Interest Expense	40,000	
Bond Interest Payable		40,000
To accrue bond interest payable for four months ended Dec. 31 ($1,000,000 × .12 × 4⁄12 = $40,000).		

Adjusting entry at year-end

The accrued liability for bond interest payable will be paid within a few months and, therefore, is classified as a current liability.

Two months later, on March 1, a semiannual interest payment is made to bondholders. This transaction represents payment of the four months' interest accrued at December 31 and the two months' interest that has accrued since year-end. Thus the entry to record the semiannual interest payments every March 1 will be:

Bond Interest Expense	20,000	
Bond Interest Payable	40,000	
Cash		60,000
To record semiannual interest payment to bondholders, and to recognize two months' interest expense accrued since year-end ($1,000,000 × .12 × 2⁄12 = $20,000).		

Interest payment following the year-end adjusting entry

[9] To simplify our illustrations, we assume in all of our examples and assignment material that adjusting entries for accrued bond interest payable are made *only at year-end*. In practice, these adjustments usually are made on a monthly basis.

[10] The amount of $1 million is used only for purposes of illustration. As explained earlier, actual bond issues are for many millions of dollars.

When the bonds mature 20 years later on March 1, 2025, two entries are required: one to record the regular semiannual interest payment and a second to record the retirement of the bonds. The entry to record the retirement of the bond issue is:

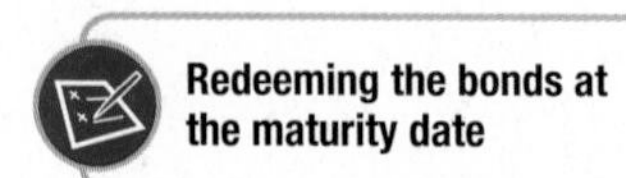

Bonds Payable	1,000,000	
Cash		1,000,000
Paid face amount of bonds at maturity.		

Bonds Issued between Interest Dates The semiannual interest dates (such as January 1 and July 1, or April 1 and October 1) are printed on the bond certificates. However, bonds are often issued between the specified interest dates. The *investor* is then required to pay the interest accrued to the date of issuance *in addition* to the stated price of the bond. This practice enables the corporation to pay a full six months' interest on all bonds outstanding at the semiannual interest payment date. The accrued interest collected from investors who purchase bonds between interest payment dates is thus returned to them on the next interest payment date.

To illustrate, let us modify our illustration to assume that Wells Corporation issues $1 million of 12 percent bonds at par value on *May 1*—two months *after* the March interest date printed on the bonds. The amount received from the bond purchasers now will include two months' accrued interest, as follows:

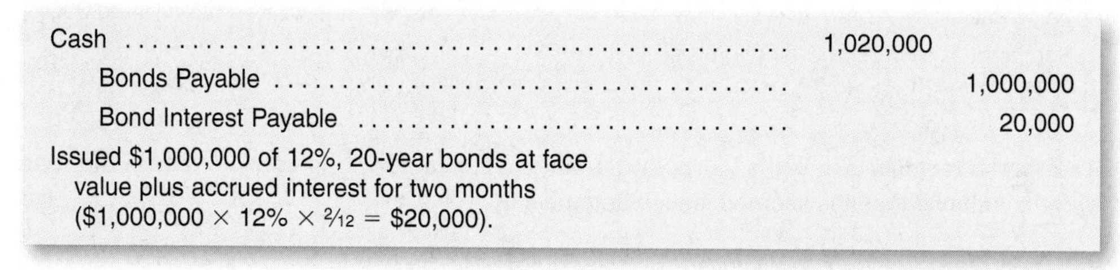

Cash	1,020,000	
Bonds Payable		1,000,000
Bond Interest Payable		20,000
Issued $1,000,000 of 12%, 20-year bonds at face value plus accrued interest for two months ($1,000,000 × 12% × 2⁄12 = $20,000).		

Four months later on the regular September 1 semiannual interest payment date, a full six months' interest ($60 per $1,000 bond) will be paid to all bondholders, *regardless of when they purchased their bonds*. The entry for the semiannual interest payment is illustrated below:

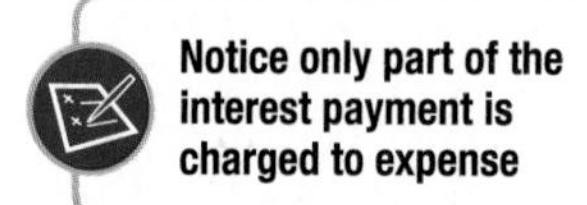

Bond Interest Payable	20,000	
Bond Interest Expense	40,000	
Cash		60,000
Paid semiannual interest on $1,000,000 face value of 12% bonds.		

Now consider these interest transactions from the standpoint of the *investors*. They paid for two months' accrued interest at the time of purchasing the bonds and then received checks for six months' interest after holding the bonds for only four months. They have, therefore, been reimbursed properly for the use of their money for four months.

When bonds are subsequently sold by one investor to another, they sell at the quoted market price *plus accrued interest* since the last interest payment date. This practice enables the issuing corporation to pay all the interest for an interest period to the investor owning the bond at the interest date. Otherwise, the corporation would have to make partial payments to every investor who bought or sold the bond during the interest period.

The amount that investors will pay for bonds is the *present value* of the principal and interest payments they will receive. The concept of present value is discussed on pages 456–457. A more in-depth coverage of present value appears in Appendix B at the end of this textbook.

BONDS ISSUED AT A DISCOUNT OR A PREMIUM

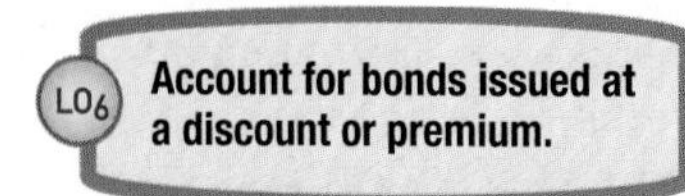

Underwriters normally sell corporate bonds to investors either at face value or at a price very close to face value. Therefore, the underwriter usually purchases these bonds from the issuing corporation at a discount—that is, at a price below face value. The discount generally is quite small—perhaps 1 percent or 2 percent of the face amount of the bonds.

When bonds are issued, the borrower records a liability equal to the *amount received.* If the bonds are issued at a small discount—which is the normal case—this liability is slightly smaller than the face value of the bond issue. At the maturity date, of course, the issuing corporation must redeem the bonds at full face value. Thus, over the term of the bond issue, the borrower's liability gradually *increases* from the original issue price to the maturity value.

ACCOUNTING FOR A BOND DISCOUNT: AN ILLUSTRATION

To illustrate, assume that on March 1, 2005, Wells Corporation sells $1 million of 12 percent, 20-year bonds payable to an underwriter at a price of *97* (meaning that the bonds were sold to the underwriter at 97 percent of their face value). On March 1, 2005, Wells Corporation receives $970,000 cash from the underwriter and records a *net* liability of this amount. When these bonds mature in 20 years, however, Wells will owe its bondholders the *full* $1 million face value of the bond issue. Thus, the company's liability must somehow be *increased* by $30,000 over the 20 years that the bonds are outstanding.

The gradual growth in the company's liability is illustrated in Exhibit 10–6. Notice that the liability increases at an average rate of $1,500 per year ($30,000 total increase ÷ 20-year life of the bond issue).

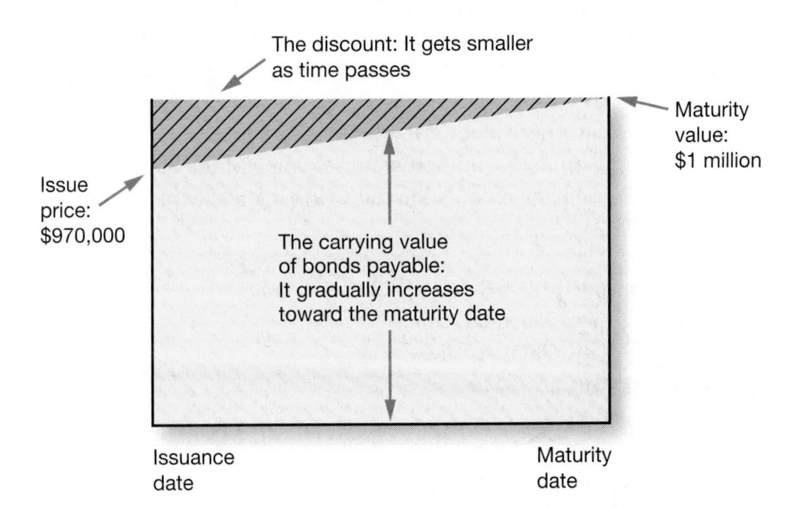

Exhibit 10–6
THE CARRYING VALUE OF A BOND DISCOUNT

Bond Discount: Part of the Cost of Borrowing When bonds are issued at a discount, the borrower must repay more than the amount originally borrowed. Thus any discount in the issuance price becomes an additional cost of the overall borrowing transaction.

In terms of cash outlays, the additional cost represented by the discount is not paid until the bonds mature. But the *matching principle* may require the borrower to recognize this cost gradually over the life of the bond issue.[11] After all, the borrower does benefit from the use of the borrowed funds throughout this entire period.

When the bonds are issued, the amount of any discount is debited to an account entitled *Discount on Bonds Payable.* Thus, Wells Corporation will record the March 1 issuance as follows:

Cash	970,000	
Discount on Bonds Payable	30,000	
Bonds Payable		1,000,000
Issued 20-year bonds with $1,000,000 face value to an underwriter at a price of 97.		

[11] If the amount of the discount is immaterial, it may be charged directly to expense as a matter of convenience. In this text, the straight-line method of amortizing bond discounts and premiums is used. The effective interest method is more common and conceptually correct and is covered in more advanced accounting textbooks.

Wells Corporation's liability at the date of issuance will appear in the balance sheet as follows:

Long-Term Liabilities	
Bonds payable	$1,000,000
Less: Discount on bonds payable	30,000
Net carrying value of bonds payable	$ 970,000

The Discount on Bonds Payable account has a debit balance and is treated as a *contra-liability account.* As illustrated, it is shown in the balance sheet as a *reduction* in the face or par value of bonds payable. Thus, the net carrying value of the bonds payable on the date of issuance is equal to the *amount borrowed.*

Amortization of the Discount On March 1, 2005, Wells Corporation received $970,000 from the underwriter. When the bonds mature 20 years later on March 1, 2025, the company must pay its bondholders the *full* $1 million face value of the bond issue. This additional $30,000 represents *interest expense* that must be amortized over the 20-year life of the bond. At each interest payment date, an adjusting entry is made to transfer a portion of the balance in the Discount on Bonds Payable account into interest expense. Thus, over time, the discount declines and the carrying value of the bonds—the face amount less the remaining discount balance—rises toward the $1 million maturity value of the bond issue.

Each September 1, the company records the following interest expense of *$60,750*:

Semiannual interest *payment* ($1,000,000 × 12% × ½)	$60,000
Add: Semiannual amortization of bond discount [($30,000 discount ÷ 20 years) × ½]	750
Semiannual interest expense	$60,750

The entry to record interest expense on September 1 throughout the life of the bond issue is:

Bond Interest Expense	60,750	
Cash		60,000
Discount on Bonds Payable		750
To record semiannual interest expense and to recognize six months' amortization of the $30,000 discount on 20-year bonds payable.		

Notice that the amortization of the discount increases Wells Corporation's semiannual interest expense by $750. It does not, however, require any immediate cash outlay. The $30,000 interest expense represented by the *entire* amortized discount will not be paid until the bonds mature on March 1, 2025.

Every December 31, Wells Corporation must make an adjusting entry to record four months' interest expense that has accrued since September 1. The computation of this $40,500 accrual is computed as follows:

Four months' accrued interest *payable* ($1,000,000 × 12% × 4⁄12)	$40,000
Add: Four months' amortization of bond discount [($30,000 discount ÷ 20 years) × 4⁄12]	500
Interest accrued from September 1 through December 31	$40,500

Thus, the adjusting entry required on December 31 throughout the life of the bond issue is as follows:

Bond Interest Expense	40,500	
Bond Interest Payable		40,000
Discount on Bonds Payable		500
To record four months' interest expense and to recognize four months' amortization of the discount on 20-year bonds payable.		

Two months later, on every March 1, a *full* semiannual interest payment is made to the company's bondholders, and an additional two months' amortization of the discount is recognized. The $20,250 interest expense recorded on this date is computed as:

Two months' accrued interest *payable* ($1,000,000 × 12% × 2⁄12)	$20,000
Add: Two months' amortization of bond discount [($30,000 discount ÷ 20 years) × 2⁄12]	250
Interest accrued from January 1 through March 1	$20,250

The semiannual interest payment recorded on March 1 throughout the life of the bond issue is:

Bond Interest Expense	20,250	
Bond Interest Payable	40,000	
Cash		60,000
Discount on Bonds Payable		250
To record two months' interest expense, to recognize two months' amortization of the discount on 20-year bonds payable, and to record semiannual interest payment to bondholders.		

When the bonds mature 20 years later on March 1, 2025, two entries are required: one to record the regular semiannual interest payment, and a second to record the retirement of the bonds. At this date, the original $30,000 discount will be *fully amortized* (that is, the Discount on Bonds Payable account will have a zero balance). Thus the carrying value of the bond issue will be $1 million, and the entry required to record the retirement of the bond issue will be:

Bonds Payable	1,000,000	
Cash		1,000,000
Paid the face amount of bonds at maturity.		

It is important to realize that over the life of this bond issue, Wells Corporation recognized *total* interest expense of $2,430,000 (40 semiannual interest payments of $60,000, plus the $30,000 discount amortized).

ACCOUNTING FOR A BOND PREMIUM: AN ILLUSTRATION

As noted previously, underwriters normally purchase bonds from the issuing corporation at a slight discount. Under some circumstances, however, an underwriter may actually pay a slight premium to the issuer—that is, a price above par.

To illustrate, assume that on March 1, 2005, Wells Corporation sells $1 million of 12 percent, 20-year bonds payable to an underwriter at a price of *103* (meaning that the bonds were sold to the underwriter at 103 percent of their face value). On March 1, 2005, Wells Corporation receives $1,030,000 cash from the underwriter and records a liability equal to this amount. When these bonds mature in 20 years, however, Wells will owe its bondholders only the $1 million *face value* of the bond issue. Thus, the company's initial liability must somehow be *reduced* by $30,000 over the 20 years that the bonds are outstanding.

The gradual decrease in the company's liability is illustrated in Exhibit 10–7. Notice that the liability decreases at an average rate of $1,500 per year ($30,000 total increase ÷ 20-year life of the bond issue).

Exhibit 10–7

THE CARRYING VALUE OF A BOND PREMIUM

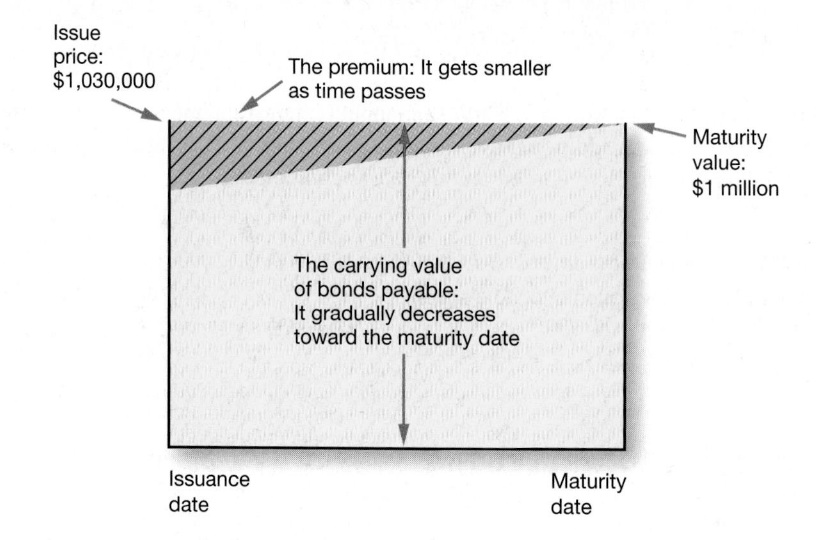

Bond Premium: A Reduction in the Cost of Borrowing When bonds are issued at a premium, the borrower repays less than the amount originally received at the date of issuance. Thus, any premium actually represents a reduction in the overall cost of borrowing. Unlike bonds issued at a discount, the interest expense associated with bonds issued at a premium will be *less* than the semiannual cash payment made to bondholders.

When the bonds are issued, the amount of any premium is credited to an account entitled *Premium on Bonds Payable*. Thus, Wells Corporation will record the March 1 issuance as follows:

Cash	1,030,000	
Premium on Bonds Payable		30,000
Bonds Payable		1,000,000
Issued 20-year bonds with $1,000,000 face value to an underwriter at a price of 103.		

Wells Corporation's liability at the date of issuance will appear in the balance sheet as follows:

Long-Term Liabilities	
Bonds payable	$1,000,000
Add: Premium on bonds payable	30,000
Carrying value of bonds payable	$1,030,000

Note that, because the Premium on Bonds Payable account has a credit balance, it is shown in the balance sheet as an *increase* in the face or par value of bonds payable.

Amortization of the Premium On March 1, 2005, Wells Corporation received $1,030,000 from the underwriter. When the bonds mature 20 years later on March 1, 2025, the company must pay back its bondholders only the $1 million *face value* of the bond issue. This $30,000 reduction in the amount owed represents *interest savings* that must be amortized over the 20-year life of the bond. Thus, over time, the premium declines, and the carrying value of the bonds—the face amount plus the remaining premium balance—also declines toward the $1 million maturity value of the bond issue.

Each September 1, the company records interest expense of *$59,250*, computed as:

Semiannual interest *payment* ($1,000,000 × 12% × ½)	$60,000
Less: Semiannual amortization of bond premium [($30,000 premium ÷ 20 years) × ½]	750
Semiannual interest expense	$59,250

The entry to record interest expense on September 1 throughout the life of the bond issue is:

Bond Interest Expense	59,250	
Premium on Bonds Payable	750	
Cash		60,000
To record semiannual interest expense and to recognize six months' amortization of the $30,000 premium on 20-year bonds payable.		

Notice that the $60,000 semiannual interest payment is the same regardless of whether the bonds are issued at face value, at a discount, or at a premium. The amortization of the premium does, however, reduce the amount of interest expense recognized by the company over the life of the bond issue.

Every December 31, Wells Corporation must make an adjusting entry to record four months' interest expense that has accrued since September 1. The $39,500 accrual is computed as follows:

Four months' accrued interest *payable* ($1,000,000 × 12% × 4/12)	$40,000
Less: Four months' amortization of bond premium [($30,000 premium ÷ 20 years) × 4/12]	500
Interest accrued from September 1 through December 31	$39,500

Thus, the following adjusting entry is required on December 31 throughout the life of the bond issue:

Bond Interest Expense	39,500	
Premium on Bonds Payable	500	
Bond Interest Payable		40,000
To record four months' interest expense and to recognize four months' amortization of the premium on 20-year bonds payable.		

Two months later, on every March 1, a *full* semiannual interest payment is made to the company's bondholders, and an additional two months' amortization of the premium is recognized. The $19,750 interest expense recorded on this date is computed as:

Two months' accrued interest *payable* ($1,000,000 × 12% × 2/12)	$20,000
Less: Two months' amortization of bond premium [($30,000 premium ÷ 20 years) × 2/12]	250
Interest accrued from January 1 through March 1	$19,750

The semiannual interest payment recorded on March 1 throughout the life of the bond issue is:

Bond Interest Expense	19,750	
Bond Interest Payable	40,000	
Premium on Bonds Payable	250	
Cash		60,000
To record two months' interest expense, to recognize two months' amortization of the premium on 20-year bonds payable, and to record semiannual interest payment to bondholders.		

When the bonds mature 20 years later on March 1, 2025, two entries are required: one to record the regular semiannual interest payment, and a second to record the retirement of the bonds. At this date, the original $30,000 premium will be *fully amortized* (that is, the Premium on Bonds Payable account will have a zero balance). Thus the carrying value of the bond issue will be $1 million, and the entry required to record the retirement of the bond issue will be as follows:

Bonds Payable	1,000,000	
Cash		1,000,000
Paid the face amount of bonds at maturity.		

In the previous illustration involving a bond discount, Wells Corporation recognized total interest expense of $2,430,000 over the life of the bonds. Had these same bonds been issued at a premium of 103, however, we see that the company would have incurred total interest expense of $2,370,000 (40 semiannual interest payments of $60,000, less the $30,000 premium amortized).

BOND DISCOUNT AND PREMIUM IN PERSPECTIVE

From a conceptual point of view, investors might pay a premium price to purchase bonds that pay an *above-market* rate of interest. If the bonds pay a *below-market* rate, investors will buy them only at a discount.

But these concepts seldom come into play when bonds are first issued. Most bonds are issued *at* the market rate of interest. Corporate bonds *almost never* are issued at a premium. Bonds often are issued at a small discount, but this discount represents only the underwriter's profit margin, not investors' response to a below-market interest rate.[12] The annual effects of amortizing bond discounts or premiums are diluted further because these amounts are amortized over the entire life of the bond issue—usually 20 years or more.

In summary, bond discounts and premiums *seldom have a material effect* on a company's annual interest expense or its financial position. For this reason, we defer further discussion of this topic to more advanced accounting courses.[13]

THE CONCEPT OF PRESENT VALUE

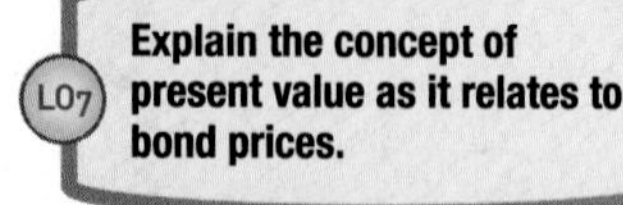

The concept of present value is based on the time value of money—the idea that receiving money today is preferable to receiving money at some later date. Assume, for example, that an investment promises to pay $1,000 five years from today and will pay no interest in the meantime. Investors would not pay $1,000 for this opportunity today, because they would receive no return on their investment over the next five years. There are prices less than $1,000, however, at which investors would be interested. For example, if the investment could be purchased for $600, the investor could expect a return (interest) of $400 over the five-year period.

[12] Professor Bill Schwartz of Virginia Commonwealth University conducted a study of 685 bond issues in a given year. *None* of these bonds were issued at a premium, and *over* 95 percent were issued either at par or at a discount of less than 2 percent of face value.

[13] Some companies issue *zero-coupon* bonds, which pay *no* interest but are issued at huge discounts. In these situations, amortization of the discount *is* material and may comprise much of the company's total interest expense. Zero-coupon bonds are a specialized form of financing that will be discussed in later accounting courses and courses in corporate finance.

The **present value** of a future cash receipt is the amount that a knowledgeable investor will pay *today* for the right to receive that future payment. The exact amount of the present value depends on (1) the amount of the future payment, (2) the length of time until the payment will be received, and (3) the rate of return required by the investor. However, the present value will always be *less* than the future amount. This is because money received today can be invested to earn interest and grow to a larger amount in the future.

The rate of interest that will cause a given present value to grow to a given future amount is called the *discount rate* or *effective rate*. The effective interest rate required by investors at any given time is regarded as the going *market rate* of interest. (The procedures for computing the present value of a future amount are illustrated in Appendix B at the end of this textbook. The concept of present value is very useful in managing your personal financial affairs. We suggest that you read Appendix B—even if it has not been assigned.)

The Present Value Concept and Bond Prices The price at which bonds sell is the present value to investors of the future principal and interest payments. If the bonds sell at face value, the market rate is equal to the *contract interest rate* (also referred to as the stated or nominal rate) printed on the bonds. The *higher* the effective interest rate that investors require, the *less* they will pay underwriters for bonds with a given contract rate of interest. For example, if investors insist on a 10 percent return, they will pay less than $1,000 for a 9 percent, $1,000 bond. Thus, if investors require an effective interest rate *greater* than the contract rate of interest, the bonds will be sold by underwriters at a *discount* (a price less than their face value). On the other hand, if market conditions support an effective interest rate of *less* than the contract rate, the bonds will sell at a *premium* (a price above their face value).

A corporation wishing to borrow money by issuing bonds must pay the going market rate of interest. Since market rates of interest fluctuate constantly, it must be expected that the contract rate of interest may vary somewhat from the market rate at the date the bonds are issued.

BOND PRICES AFTER ISSUANCE

As stated earlier, many corporate bonds are traded daily on organized securities exchanges at quoted market prices. After bonds are issued, their market prices vary *inversely* with changes in market interest rates. As interest rates rise, investors will be willing to pay less money to own a bond that pays a given contract rate of interest. Conversely, as interest rates decline, the market prices of bonds rise.

Bond prices move inversely with market interest rates

CASE IN POINT

IBM sold to underwriters $500 million of 9⅜ percent, 25-year debenture bonds. The underwriters planned to sell the bonds to the public at a price of 99⅝. Just as the bonds were offered for sale, however, a change in Federal Reserve credit policy started an upward surge in interest rates. The underwriters encountered great difficulty selling the bonds. Within one week, the market price of the bonds had fallen to 94½. The underwriters dumped their unsold inventory at this price and sustained one of the largest underwriting losses in Wall Street history.

During the months that followed, interest rates soared to record levels. Within five months, the price of the bonds had fallen to 76⅜. Thus nearly one-fourth of the market value of these bonds evaporated in less than half a year. At this time, the financial strength of IBM was never in question; this dramatic loss in market value was caused entirely by rising interest rates.

Changes in the current level of interest rates are not the only factors influencing the market prices of bonds. The length of time remaining until the bonds mature is another major force. As a bond nears its maturity date, its market price normally moves closer and closer to the maturity value. This trend is dependable because the bonds are redeemed at face value on the maturity date.

Volatility of Short-Term and Long-Term Bond Prices When interest rates fluctuate, the market prices of long-term bonds are affected to a far greater extent than are the market prices of bonds due to mature in the near future. To illustrate, assume that market interest rates suddenly soar from 9 percent to 12 percent. A 9 percent bond scheduled to mature in a few days will still have a market value of approximately $1,000—the amount to be collected in a few days from the issuing corporation. However, the market price of a 9 percent bond maturing in 10 years will drop significantly. Investors who must accept these below-market interest payments for many years will buy the bonds only at a discounted price.

In summary, fluctuations in interest rates have a far greater effect on the market prices of long-term bonds than on the prices of short-term bonds.

Remember that, after bonds have been issued, they belong to the bondholder, *not to the issuing corporation*. Therefore, changes in the market price of bonds subsequent to their issuance *do not* affect the amounts shown in the financial statements of the issuing corporation, and these changes are not recorded in the company's accounting records.

You as a Financial Advisor

Assume that you are the financial advisor for a recently retired couple. Your clients want to invest their savings in such a way as to receive a stable stream of cash flow every year throughout their retirement. They have expressed their concerns to you regarding the volatility of long-term bond prices when interest rates fluctuate.

If your clients invest their savings in a variety of long-term bonds and hold these bonds until maturity, will interest rate fluctuations affect their annual cash flow during their retirement years?

(See our comments on the Online Learning Center Web site.)

EARLY RETIREMENT OF BONDS PAYABLE

Bonds are sometimes retired before the maturity date. The principal reason for retiring bonds early is to relieve the issuing corporation of the obligation to make future interest payments. If interest rates decline to the point that a corporation can borrow at an interest rate below that being paid on a particular bond issue, the corporation may benefit from retiring those bonds and issuing new bonds at a lower interest rate.

Most bond issues contain a call provision, permitting the corporation to redeem the bonds by paying a specified price, usually a few points above face value. Even without a call provision, the corporation may retire its bonds before maturity by purchasing them in the open market. If the bonds can be purchased by the issuing corporation at less than their carrying value, a *gain* is realized on the retirement of the debt. If the bonds are reacquired by the issuing corporation at a price in excess of their carrying value, a *loss* must be recognized.[14]

For example, assume that Briggs Corporation has outstanding a 13 percent, $10 million bond issue, callable on any interest date at a price of 104. Assume also that the bonds were issued at par and will not mature for nine years. Recently, however, market interest rates have declined to less than 10 percent, and the market price of Briggs's bonds has increased to 106.[15]

Regardless of the market price, Briggs can call these bonds at 104. If the company exercises this call provision for 10 percent of the bonds ($1,000,000 face value), the entry will be:

Bonds Payable	1,000,000	
Loss on Early Retirement of Bonds	40,000	
Cash		1,040,000
To record the call of $1 million in bonds payable at a call price of 104.		

[14] The FASB has ruled that the gains and losses from early retirements of debt be classified in the income statement in the same manner as other gains and losses.

[15] Falling interest rates cause bond prices to rise. On the other hand, falling interest rates also provide the issuing company with an incentive to call the bonds and, perhaps, replace them with bonds bearing a lower rate of interest. For this reason, call prices often serve as an approximate "ceiling" on market prices.

Notice that Briggs *called* these bonds, rather than repurchasing them at market prices. Therefore, Briggs is able to retire these bonds at their call price of 104. (Had the market price of the bonds been *below* 104, Briggs might have been able to retire the bonds at less cost by purchasing them in the open market.)

Estimated Liabilities, Loss Contingencies, and Commitments

ESTIMATED LIABILITIES

Explain how estimated liabilities, loss contingencies, and commitments are disclosed in financial statements. (LO8)

The term *estimated liabilities* refers to *liabilities that appear in financial statements at estimated dollar amounts*. Let us consider the example of the automaker's liability to honor its new car warranties. A manufacturer's liability for warranty work is recorded by an entry debiting Warranty Expense and crediting Liability for Warranty Claims. The *matching principle* requires that the expense of performing warranty work be recognized in the period in which the products are *sold*, in order to offset this expense against the related sales revenue. As the warranty may extend several years into the future, the dollar amount of this liability (and expense) must be estimated. Because of the uncertainty regarding when warranty work will be performed, accountants traditionally have classified the liability for warranty claims as a current liability.

By definition, estimated liabilities involve some degree of uncertainty. However, (1) the liabilities are known to exist, and (2) the uncertainty as to dollar amount is *not so great* as to prevent the company from making a reasonable estimate and recording the liability.

LOSS CONTINGENCIES

Loss contingencies are similar to estimated liabilities but may involve much more uncertainty. A loss contingency is a *possible loss* (or expense), stemming from *past events*, that is expected to be resolved in the future.

Central to the definition of a loss contingency is the element of *uncertainty*—uncertainty as to the amount of loss and, in some cases, uncertainty as to *whether or not any loss actually has been incurred*. A common example of a loss contingency is a lawsuit pending against a company. The lawsuit is based on past events, but until the suit is resolved, uncertainty exists as to the amount (if any) of the company's liability.

Loss contingencies differ from estimated liabilities in two ways. First, a loss contingency may involve a *greater degree of uncertainty*. Often the uncertainty extends to whether any loss or expense actually has been incurred. In contrast, the loss or expense relating to an estimated liability is *known to exist*.

Second, the concept of a loss contingency extends not only to possible liabilities, but also to possible *impairments of assets*. Assume, for example, that a bank has made large loans to a foreign country now experiencing political instability. Uncertainty exists as to the amount of loss, if any, associated with this loan. From the bank's point of view, this loan is an asset that may be impaired, not a liability.

Loss Contingencies in Financial Statements

The manner in which loss contingencies are presented in financial statements depends on the *degree of uncertainty involved*.

Loss contingencies are *recorded* in the accounting records only when both of the following criteria are met: (1) It is *probable* that a loss has been incurred, and (2) the amount of loss can be *reasonably estimated*. An example of a loss contingency that usually meets these criteria and is recorded in the accounts is the obligation a company has for product warranties and defects.

When these criteria are *not* met, loss contingencies are *disclosed* in notes to the financial statements if there is a *reasonable possibility* that a material loss has been incurred. Pending lawsuits, for example, usually are disclosed in notes accompanying the financial statements, but the loss, if any, is not recorded in the accounting records until the lawsuit is settled. Companies need *not* disclose loss contingencies if the risk of a material loss having occurred is considered *remote*.

Notice the *judgmental nature* of the criteria used in accounting for loss contingencies. These criteria involve assessments as to whether the risk of material loss is "probable," "reasonably possible," or "remote." Thus the collective *professional judgment* of the company's management, accountants, legal counsel, and auditors is the deciding factor in accounting for loss contingencies.

When loss contingencies are disclosed in notes to the financial statements, the note should describe the nature of the contingency and, if possible, provide an estimate of the amount of possible loss. If a reasonable estimate of the amount of possible loss cannot be made, the disclosure should include the range of possible loss or a statement that an estimate cannot be made. The following note is typical of the disclosure of the loss contingency arising from pending litigation:

Note disclosure of a loss contingency

Note 8: Contingencies

In October of 2005, the Company was named as defendant in a $408 million patent infringement lawsuit. The Company denies all charges and is preparing its defense against them. It is not possible at this time to determine the ultimate legal or financial responsibility that may arise as a result of this litigation.

Sometimes a *portion* of a loss contingency qualifies for immediate recognition, whereas the remainder only meets the criteria for disclosure. Assume, for example, that a company is required by the Superfund Act to clean up an environmental hazard over a 10-year period. The company cannot predict the total cost of the project but considers it probable that it will lose at least $1 million. The company should recognize a $1 million expected loss and record it as a liability. In addition, it should disclose in the notes to the financial statements that the actual cost ultimately may exceed the recorded amount.

Notice that loss contingencies relate only to possible losses from *past events*. For **DuPont**, these past events were related to the improper disposal of hazardous wastes. The risk that losses may result from *future* events is *not* a loss contingency. The risk of future losses generally is *not* disclosed in financial statements for several reasons.[16] For one, any disclosure of future losses would be sheer speculation. For another, no one can foresee all of the events that might give rise to future losses.

COMMITMENTS

Contracts for future transactions are called **commitments**. They are not liabilities, but, if material, they are disclosed in notes to the financial statements. For example, a professional baseball club may issue a three-year contract to a player at an annual salary of, say, $5 million. This is a commitment to pay for services to be rendered in the future. There is no obligation to make payment until the services are received. As liabilities stem only from *past transactions*, this commitment has not yet created a liability.

Other examples of commitments include a corporation's long-term employment contract with a key officer, a contract for construction of a new plant, and a contract to buy or sell inventory at future dates. The common quality of all these commitments is an intent to enter into transactions *in the future*. Commitments that are material in amount should be disclosed in notes to the financial statements.

Evaluating the Safety of Creditors' Claims

Evaluate the safety of creditors' claims.

Creditors, of course, want to be sure that their claims are safe—that is, that they will be paid on time. Actually, *everyone* associated with a business—management, owners, employees—should be concerned with the company's ability to pay its debts. If a business becomes *illiquid* (unable to pay its obligations), it may be forced into **bankruptcy**.[17]

Not only does management want the business to remain liquid, but it also wants the company to maintain a high *credit rating* with agencies such as **Moody's** and **Standard & Poor's**. A high credit rating helps a company borrow money more easily and at lower interest rates.

[16] The risk of future losses *is* disclosed if this risk stems from *existing contracts*, such as a written guarantee of another company's indebtedness (called a loan guarantee, or an accommodation endorsement). Some guarantees require that a liability be recorded. Discussion of this topic is beyond the scope of this textbook.

[17] Bankruptcy is a legal status under which the company's fate is determined largely by the U.S. Bankruptcy Court. Sometimes the company is reorganized and allowed to continue its operations. In other cases, the business is closed and its assets are sold. Often managers and other employees lose their jobs. In almost all bankruptcies, the company's creditors and owners incur legal costs and sustain financial losses.

In evaluating debt-paying ability, short-term creditors and long-term creditors look at different relationships. Short-term creditors are interested in the company's *immediate* liquidity. Long-term creditors, in contrast, are interested in the company's ability to meet its interest obligations over a *period of years*, as well as its ability to repay or refinance large obligations as they come due.

In previous chapters we introduced several measures of short-term liquidity and long-term credit risk. These measures are summarized in Exhibit 10–8—along with the *interest coverage ratio*, which is discussed below.

METHODS OF DETERMINING CREDITWORTHINESS

Interest Coverage Ratio Creditors, investors, and managers all feel more comfortable when a company has enough income to cover its interest payments by a wide margin. One widely used measure of the relationship between earnings and interest expense is the **interest coverage ratio.**

The interest coverage ratio is computed by dividing *operating income* by the annual interest expense. From a creditor's point of view, the higher this ratio, the better. In past years, most companies with good credit ratings had interest coverage ratios of, perhaps, 4 to 1 or more.

Less Formal Means of Determining Creditworthiness Not all decisions to extend credit involve formal analysis of the borrower's financial statements. Most suppliers of goods or services, for example, will sell on account to almost any long-established business—unless they know the customer is in severe financial difficulty. If the customer is not a well-established business, these suppliers may investigate the customer's credit history by contacting a credit-rating agency.

In lending to small businesses organized as corporations, lenders may require key stockholders to *personally guarantee* repayment of the loan.

HOW MUCH DEBT SHOULD A BUSINESS HAVE?

All businesses incur some debts as a result of normal business operations. These include, for example, accounts payable and accrued liabilities. But many businesses aggressively use long-term debt, such as mortgages and bonds payable, to finance growth and expansion. Is this wise? Does it benefit the stockholders? The answer hinges on another question: *Can the borrowed funds be invested to earn a return higher than the rate of interest paid to creditors?*

Using borrowed money to finance business operations is called applying **leverage**. Extensive use of leverage—that is, a great deal of debt—sometimes benefits a business dramatically. But if things don't work out, it can "wipe out" the borrower.

If borrowed money can be invested to earn a rate of return *higher* than the interest rates paid to the lenders, net income and the return on stockholders' equity will *increase*.[18] For example, if you borrow money at an interest rate of 9 percent and invest it to earn 15 percent, you will benefit from "the spread."

But leverage is a double-edged sword—the effects may be favorable *or unfavorable*. If the rate of return earned on the borrowed money falls *below* the rate of interest being paid, the use of borrowed money *reduces* net income and the return on equity. Companies with large amounts of debt sometimes become victims of their own debt-service requirements.

The effects of leverage may be summarized as follows:

Relationship of Return on Assets to Interest Rate on Borrowed Funds	Effect on Net Income and Return on Equity
Return on Assets > Interest Rates Being Paid	Increase
Return on Assets < Interest Rates Being Paid	Decrease

Bear in mind that over time, both the return on assets and the interest rates that the company must pay may *change*.

The more leverage a company applies, the greater the effects on net income and the return on equity. Using more leverage simply means having more debt. Therefore, the *debt ratio* is a basic measure of the amount of leverage being applied.

[18] The rate of return earned on invested capital usually is viewed as the overall *return on assets*—that is, operating income divided by average total assets. *Return on equity* is net income expressed as a percentage of average stockholders' equity. Both of these return on investment measures are discussed in Chapter 14.

Financial Analysis and Decision Making

Exhibit 10–8 provides a summary of common measures used by creditors and investors to evaluate a company's *short-term and long-term debt-paying ability.*

Exhibit 10–8
MEASURES OF DEBT-PAYING ABILITY

Short-Term	Long-Term
Quick ratio—Most liquid assets divided by current liabilities; a stringent measure of liquidity.	Debt ratio—Total liabilities divided by total assets. Measures percentage of capital structure financed by creditors.
Current ratio—Current assets divided by current liabilities; the most common measure of liquidity, but less stringent than the quick ratio.	Interest coverage ratio—Operating income divided by interest expense. Shows how many times the company earns its annual interest obligations.
Working capital—Current assets less current liabilities; the "uncommitted" liquid resources.	Trend in net cash flows from operating activities—Indicates trend in cash-generating ability. Determined from comparative statements of cash flow.
Turnover rates—Measures of how quickly receivables are collected or inventory is sold. (Computed separately for receivables and inventory.)	Trend in net income—Less related to debt-paying ability than cash flow, but still an excellent measure of long-term financial health.
Operating cycle—The period of time required to convert inventory into cash.	
Net cash flows from operating activities—Measures a company's ability to generate cash. (Shown in the statement of cash flows.)	
Lines of credit—Indicates ready access to additional cash should the need arise.	

YOUR TURN **You as a Credit Analyst**

Assume that you are a credit analyst at a bank. **Dell Inc.** wants to borrow from your bank on a short-term basis. You assign the task of reviewing **Dell**'s short-term creditworthiness to a college intern working for your bank. The intern remembers that working capital (current assets minus current liabilities) and the current ratio (current assets divided by current liabilities) are useful tools for evaluating short-term liquidity. Selected financial information for **Dell** is as follows (all items are in millions):

	Current Year	Prior Year
Cash and cash equivalents	$ 4,317	$4,232
Short-term investments	835	406
Accounts receivable (net)	3,635	2,586
Inventories	327	306
Other	1,519	1,394
Total current liabilities	10,896	8,933
Cash provided by operations	3,670	3,538
Net income	2,645	2,122

The intern is concerned about lending **Dell** money because working capital is negative by $263. As a result, **Dell**'s current ratio is slightly less than 1:1. Do you agree with the intern's assessment?

(See our comments on the Online Learning Center Web site.)

Ethics, Fraud & Corporate Governance

A learning objective for this chapter is to understand how creditors evaluate the safety of their claims. Creditors are concerned with a company's ability to repay its debts. Credit rating agencies exist to help creditors evaluate the ability of a company to repay debts as they become due. The major U.S. credit rating agencies are Moody's and Standard & Poor's. A primary means used by credit rating agencies to assess a company's debt-paying ability is to compare the amount of a company's debt to the company's total assets or to its stockholders' equity. Companies with large amounts of debt on their balance sheets are perceived as more risky and are likely to have lower credit ratings. Therefore, companies have an incentive to understate liabilities, particularly interest-bearing liabilities (i.e., debt).

The most infamous financial fraud in U.S. history occurred at Enron and was revealed in the fall of 2001. A major part of the Enron fraud involved the understatement of debt. Enron understated its debt by at least $550 million each year from 1997 to 2000. Enron's management was motivated to understate debt in order to maintain a high credit rating from Moody's and Standard & Poor's. A high credit rating, referred to as an investment credit rating, was essential for Enron in being able to finance its operations.

Enron was engaged in the energy business and was also a trader of contracts to buy and sell commodities. At the time of the fraud, Enron was traded on the New York Stock Exchange. The revelation of the financial improprieties at Enron in October 2001 ultimately led to a collapse in Enron's credit rating. Without access to ongoing financing, Enron was forced to file for bankruptcy in December 2001. At the time of Enron's bankruptcy filing, it was the seventh largest corporation in the United States.

Enron understated its liabilities by transferring debt to **special purpose entities (SPEs)**. SPEs are separate entities established by corporations to accomplish specific purposes. Often, the economic objective of an SPE is to borrow money and then transfer it to the sponsoring corporation without the sponsoring corporation having to report the SPE's debt in its balance sheet. At the time of the Enron fraud, outside equity investors were required to provide at least 3 percent of an SPE's total financing, and these funds had to be "at risk" (i.e., outside equity investors were to have no guarantees regarding the performance or safety of their investments). The remaining financing could be in the form of debt. Had Enron's SPEs failed to meet the 3 percent at-risk equity financing requirement, the SPEs' debt should have been included in Enron's balance sheet.

Although the fraud at Enron was extremely complex, a major issue was that many of its SPEs did not meet the equity financing requirement. These SPEs were organized as partnerships, and Enron's chief financial officer, Andrew Fastow, was the managing general partner of a number of them. Fastow and other Enron employees were among the parties providing equity capital to the SPEs. Enron guaranteed these investors that they would not only get back what they had invested, but that they would also receive substantial returns. For instance, Fastow received over $30 million as an investor in the SPEs related to Enron. The guaranteed returns violated the 3 percent at-risk equity financing requirement. Therefore, the SPEs' debt should have been included on Enron's balance sheet.

As was the case at WorldCom (discussed in the previous chapter), the fraud at Enron has numerous ethical and corporate governance implications. Given the complexity of Enron's fraudulent activity, it could not have been accomplished without the cooperation of outside professionals (e.g., attorneys, auditors, credit rating agencies, and investment bankers). Enron needed outside legal help to create the various SPEs. These attorneys helped create the SPEs without ascertaining whether at least 3 percent of their outside equity capital was at risk. The external auditor, Arthur Andersen, issued unqualified audit opinions on Enron's financial statements despite severe doubt that Enron's filings conformed with GAAP. Credit rating agencies maintained investment grade credit ratings on Enron's debt throughout the entire period of the fraud and did not downgrade Enron's debt until a few weeks before the bankruptcy filing. Finally, major Wall Street investment banks created the SPE structures, including numerous transactions that resulted in debt being transferred from Enron's books to the SPEs. All of these outside professionals failed to act in an ethical manner.

The unethical conduct of Enron's outside professionals has not been without severe consequences. Arthur Andersen was convicted of a felony for its role in shredding its working papers related to the Enron audit. The felony indictment and conviction led to the dissolution of this former Big Five accounting firm. A number of major Wall Street investment banks have paid the U.S. government multimillion-dollar settlements stemming from their Enron involvement. Private litigation related to the Enron debacle is ongoing and is likely to remain active for a number of years.

From a corporate governance perspective, the Sarbanes-Oxley Act (which was a direct result of fraudulent activities by Enron and WorldCom) has substantially increased the criminal penalties associated with securities fraud and fraudulent financial reporting. Individuals convicted of securities fraud in the future are likely to receive lengthy prison sentences. For example, a midlevel tax manager involved in a financial fraud at Dynergy (a Houston-based energy competitor of Enron's) was sentenced to over 20 years in federal prison (and, unlike the state prison system, prisoners in the federal system must serve at least 85 percent of their sentences). As you prepare to enter the business world, it is important that you understand the severe consequences often associated with securities fraud and fraudulent financial reporting.

Special Types of Liabilities

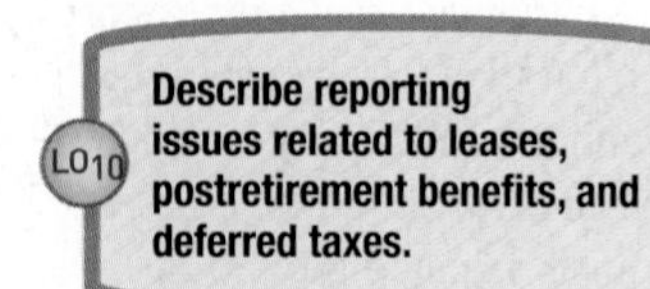

The types of liabilities discussed up to this point have been those short-term and long-term obligations encountered by most organizations. Here we examine three special types of liabilities most common to very large organizations: (1) leases, (2) postretirement benefits, and (3) deferred taxes.

LEASE PAYMENT OBLIGATIONS

A company may purchase the assets needed in its business operations or, as an alternative, it may lease them. A *lease* is a contract in which the lessor gives the lessee the right to use an asset for a specified period of time in exchange for periodic rental payments. The **lessor** is the owner of the property; the **lessee** is a tenant or renter. Examples of assets frequently acquired by lease include automobiles, building space, computers, and equipment.

OPERATING LEASES

When the lessor gives the lessee the right to use leased property for a limited period of time but retains the usual risks and rewards of ownership, the contract is known as an **operating lease**. An example of an operating lease is a contract leasing office space in an office building. If the building increases in value, the *lessor* can receive the benefits of this increase by either selling the building or increasing the rental rate once the lease term has expired. Likewise, if the building declines in value, it is the lessor who bears the loss.

In accounting for an operating lease, the lessor views the monthly lease payments received as rental revenue, and the lessee regards these payments as rental expense. No asset or liability (other than a short-term liability for accrued rent payable) relating to the lease appears in the lessee's balance sheet. Thus operating leases are sometimes termed **off-balance sheet financing** and disclosure is required of the amounts due in each of the next five years, plus the balance thereafter.

CAPITAL LEASES

Some lease contracts are intended to provide financing to the lessee for the eventual purchase of the property or to provide the lessee with use of the property over most of its useful life. These lease contracts are called **capital leases** (or financing leases). In contrast to an operating lease, a capital lease transfers most of the risks and rewards of ownership from the lessor to the *lessee*.

From an accounting viewpoint, capital leases are regarded as *essentially equivalent to a sale* of the property by the lessor to the lessee, even though title to the leased property has not been transferred. Thus a capital lease should be recorded by the *lessor as a sale* of property and by the *lessee as a purchase*.

When equipment is acquired through a capital lease, the lessee *debits an asset account*, Leased Equipment, and *credits a liability account*, Lease Payment Obligation, for the present value of the future lease payments. Lease payments made by the lessee are allocated between Interest Expense and a reduction in the liability Lease Payment Obligation. The portion of the lease payment obligation that will be repaid within the next year is classified as a current liability, and the remainder is classified as long-term.

No rent expense is recorded by the lessee in a capital lease. The asset account Leased Equipment is usually depreciated by the lessee over the life of the equipment rather than the term of the lease. Disclosure of future payments on the lease is also required. Accounting for capital leases is illustrated in Appendix B at the end of this textbook.

Distinguishing between Capital Leases and Operating Leases

The Financial Accounting Standards Board (FASB) has taken the position that the risks and returns of ownership transfer to the lessee under any of the following circumstances:

- The lease transfers ownership of the property to the lessee at the end of the lease term.
- The lease contains a bargain purchase option.

- The lease term is equal to 75 percent or more of the estimated economic life of the leased property.
- The present value of the minimum lease payments amounts to 90 percent or more of the fair value of the leased property.

Thus, if a lease contains any of these provisions, it is viewed as a capital lease. Otherwise, it is accounted for as an operating lease.

LIABILITIES FOR PENSIONS AND OTHER POSTRETIREMENT BENEFITS

Many employers agree to pay their employees a pension; that is, monthly cash payments for life, beginning at retirement. Pensions are not an expense of the years in which cash payments are made to retired workers. Employees earn the right to receive the pension *while they are working for their employer*. Therefore, the employer's cost of future pension payments *accrues* over the years that each employee is on the payroll.

The amounts of the retirement benefits that will be paid to today's workers after they retire are not known with certainty. Among other things, these amounts depend on how long retired employees live. Therefore, the employer's obligation for future pension payments arising during the current year *can only be estimated.*

Employers do not usually pay retirement pensions directly to retired employees. Most employers meet their pension obligations by making periodic deposits in a **pension fund** (or pension plan) throughout the years of each worker's employment.

A pension fund is *not an asset* of the employer. Rather, it is an *independent entity* managed by a trustee (usually a bank or an insurance company). As the employer makes deposits in the pension fund, the trustee invests the money in securities such as stocks and bonds. Over time, the pension fund earns investment income and normally accumulates to a balance far in excess of the employer's deposits. The *pension fund*—not the employer—disburses monthly pension benefits to retired workers.

If the employer meets *all* of its estimated pension obligations by promptly depositing cash in a pension fund, the pension fund is said to be *fully funded*. If a pension plan is fully funded, *no liability* for pension payments appears in the employer's balance sheet. The employer's obligation is discharged in the *current period* through the payments made to the pension fund. The employer records each payment to this fund by debiting Pension Expense and crediting Cash.

Determining Pension Expense

From a conceptual point of view, the pension expense of a given period is the *present value* of the future pension rights granted to employees as a result of their services during the period. The computation of annual pension expense is complex and involves many assumptions. The amount of this expense is computed not by accountants, but rather by an **actuary**, who considers these factors:

- Average age, retirement age, and life expectancy of employees.
- Employee turnover rates.
- Compensation levels and estimated rate of pay increases.
- Expected rate of return to be earned on pension fund assets.

For example, assume that the actuarial firm of Gibson & Holt computes a pension expense for Cramer Cable Company of $400,000 for 2007. This amount represents the present value of pension rights granted to Cramer's employees for the work they performed during the year. To fully fund this obligation, Cramer transfers $400,000 to National Trust Co., the trustee of the company's pension plan.

The following entry summarizes Cramer's fully funded pension expense for 2007:

Pension Expense	400,000	
Cash		400,000
Pension expense for the year as determined by actuarial firm of Gibson & Holt; fully funded by payments to National Trust Co.		

Postretirement Benefits Other than Pensions In addition to pension plans, many companies have promised their employees other types of **postretirement benefits**, such as continuing health insurance. In most respects, these nonpension postretirement benefits are accounted for in the same manner as are pension benefits. Most companies, however, do not fully fund their obligations for nonpension postretirement benefits. Thus recognition of the annual expense often includes a credit to an unfunded liability for part of the cost.

Continuing with our illustration of Cramer Cable Company, assume that Gibson & Holt computes for the company a $250,000 nonpension postretirement benefits expense for 2007. Unlike its pension expense, however, Cramer does *not* fully fund its nonpension obligations.

For 2007, only $140,000 of the total amount was paid in cash. The entry to summarize this expense for the year is:

Postretirement Benefits Expense	250,000	
Cash		140,000
Unfunded Liability for Postretirement Benefits		110,000
To record nonpension postretirement benefits expense per report of Gibson & Holt, actuaries; expense funded to the extent of $140,000.		

Any portion of the unfunded liability that the company intends to fund during the next year is classified as a *current liability*; the remainder is classified as a *long-term liability*.

Unfunded Postretirement Costs Are Noncash Expenses Postretirement costs are recognized as expenses as workers earn the right to receive these benefits. If these costs are fully funded, the company makes cash payments to a trustee within the current period equal to this expense. But if these benefits are *not* funded, the cash payments are not made until after the employees retire. Thus an unfunded retirement plan involves a long lag between the recognition of expense and the related cash payments.

Unfunded retirement benefits often are called a noncash expense. That is, the expense is charged against current earnings, but there are no corresponding cash payments in the period. In the journal entry above, notice that the expense exceeds the cash outlays by $110,000 ($250,000 − $140,000 = $110,000). This amount corresponds to the growth in the unfunded liability.

Unfunded Liabilities for Postretirement Costs: Can They Really Be Paid? Many of America's largest and best-known corporations have obligations for unfunded postretirement benefits that can only be described as enormous. For many companies, this liability is equal to, or *greater than*, the total amount of stockholders' equity. For example, **Ford Motor Company** recently reported an unfunded liability for postretirement benefits of approximately *$17.4 billion*. That compares with total stockholders' equity of a little more than $16 billion. One might say that **Ford**'s employees have a greater financial stake in the company's long-term prospects than do its stockholders. Many users of financial statements wonder whether **Ford**, **General Motors**, and other large corporations can really pay liabilities this large. Interesting question.

Let us suggest some things to consider in evaluating a company's ability to pay its unfunded liability for postretirement costs. First, remember that this liability represents only the *present value* of the estimated future payments. The future payments are expected to be *substantially more* than the amount shown in the balance sheet. Next, this liability may *continue to grow*, especially if the company has more employees today than in the past. On the other hand, this liability does *not* have to be paid all at once. It will be paid over a *great many years*—the life span of today's workforce.

In evaluating a company's ability to meet its postretirement obligations, we suggest looking to the *statement of cash flows*, rather than the balance sheet or income statement. In the statement of cash flows, payments of postretirement costs are classified as operating activities. Thus, if a company has a steadily increasing net cash flow from operating activities, it is more likely to be able to handle these costs—at least *at present*. But if the net cash flow from operating activities starts to decline, the company may have no choice but to reduce the benefits it provides to retired employees. Often these benefits are *not* contractual and can be reduced at management's discretion.

DEFERRED INCOME TAXES

We have seen in earlier chapters that differences sometimes exist between the way certain types of revenue or expense are recognized in financial statements and the way these same items are reported in income tax returns. For example, most companies use the straight-line method of depreciation in their financial reports but use an accelerated method in their income tax returns. Because of such differences between accounting principles and tax rules, income appearing in the income statement today may not be subject to income taxes until future years. However, the *matching principle* requires that the income shown in an income statement be offset by all related income taxes expense, regardless of when these taxes will be paid. Thus the entry to record a corporation's income tax expense might appear as follows:

Income Tax Expense	1,000,000	
Income Tax Payable		800,000
Deferred Income Taxes		200,000
To record corporate income taxes applicable to the income of the current year.		

Payment of income taxes expense often can be deferred

Income Tax Payable is a current liability representing the portion of the income taxes expense that must be paid when the company files its income tax return for the current year. The portion of income taxes expense that is deferred to future tax returns is credited to a liability account entitled **Deferred Income Taxes**.

Deferred Income Taxes in Financial Statements How deferred income taxes are classified in the balance sheet depends on the classification of the assets and liabilities that *caused* the tax deferrals. Although deferred taxes often appear as liabilities, certain conditions may require that they be classified as assets. Accounting for deferred taxes involves a number of complex issues that are addressed in more advanced accounting courses.

Concluding Remarks

Businesses have two basic sources of financing their assets: liabilities and owners' equity. Throughout this chapter, we have studied current liabilities, long-term liabilities, and estimated liabilities common to most large businesses. We have learned that liabilities differ from owners' equity in several respects. The feature that most clearly distinguishes the claims of creditors from those of owners is that virtually all liabilities eventually mature and become due. We have also learned that the claims of creditors have legal priority over the claims of owners.

In the next two chapters, we turn our attention to owners' equity. We will examine many important topics including treasury stock transactions, cash dividends, stock dividends, stock splits, and the differences between common and preferred stockholders.

END-OF-CHAPTER REVIEW

SUMMARY OF LEARNING OBJECTIVES

LO1 Define *liabilities* and distinguish between current and long-term liabilities. Liabilities are debts arising from past transactions or events that require payment (or the rendering of services) at some future date. Current liabilities are those maturing within one year or the company's operating cycle (whichever is longer) and that are expected to be paid from current assets. Liabilities classified as long-term include obligations maturing more than one year in the future and shorter-term obligations that will be refinanced or paid from noncurrent assets.

LO2 Account for notes payable and interest expense. Initially, a liability is recorded only for the principal amount of a note—that is, the amount owed *before* including any interest charges. Interest expense accrues over time. Any accrued interest expense is recognized at the end of an accounting period by an adjusting entry that records both the expense and a short-term liability for accrued interest payable.

LO3 Describe the costs and the basic accounting activities relating to payrolls. The basic cost of payrolls is, of course, the salaries and wages earned by employees. However, all employers also incur costs for various payroll taxes, such as the employer's share of Social Security and Medicare, workers' compensation premiums, and unemployment insurance. Many employers also incur costs for various employee benefits, such as health insurance and postretirement benefits. (These additional payroll-related costs often amount to 30 percent to 40 percent of the basic wages and salaries expense.)

LO4 Prepare an amortization table allocating payments between interest and principal. An amortization table includes four money columns, showing (1) the amount of each payment, (2) the portion of the payment representing interest expense, (3) the portion of the payment that reduces the principal amount of the loan, and (4) the remaining unpaid balance (or principal amount). The table begins with the original amount of the loan listed in the unpaid balance column. A separate line then is completed showing the allocation of each payment between interest and principal reduction and indicating the new unpaid balance subsequent to the payment.

LO5 Describe corporate bonds and explain the tax advantage of debt financing. Corporate bonds are transferable long-term notes payable. Each bond usually has a face value of $1,000 (or a multiple of $1,000), calls for interest payments at a contractual rate, and has a stated maturity date. By issuing thousands of bonds to the investing public at one time, the corporation divides a very large and long-term loan into many transferable units.

The principal advantage of issuing bonds instead of capital stock is that interest payments to bondholders are deductible in determining taxable income, whereas dividend payments to stockholders are not.

LO6 Account for bonds issued at a discount or premium. When bonds are issued at a discount, the borrower must repay more than the amount originally borrowed. Thus any discount in the issuance price represents additional cost in the overall borrowing transaction. The matching principle requires that the borrower recognize this cost gradually over the life of the bond issue as interest expense.

If bonds are issued at a premium, the borrower will repay an amount less than the amount originally borrowed. Thus the premium serves to reduce the overall cost of the borrowing transaction. Again, the matching principle requires that this reduction in interest expense be recognized gradually over the life of the bond issue.

LO7 Explain the concept of present value as it relates to bond prices. The basic concept of present value is that an amount of money that will not be paid or received until some future date is equivalent to a smaller amount of money today. This is because the smaller amount available today could be invested to earn interest and thereby accumulate over time to the larger future amount. The amount today considered equivalent to the future amount is termed the present value of that future amount.

The concept of present value is used in the valuation of most long-term liabilities. It also is widely used in investment decisions. Readers who are not familiar with this concept are encouraged to read Appendix B at the end of this textbook.

LO8 Explain how estimated liabilities, loss contingencies, and commitments are disclosed in financial statements. Estimated liabilities, such as an automobile manufacturer's responsibility to honor new car warranties, appear in the financial statements at their estimated dollar amounts. Loss contingencies appear as liabilities *only* when it is probable that a loss has been incurred *and* the amount can be reasonably estimated. Unless both these conditions are met, loss contingencies are simply disclosed in the notes to the financial statements. Commitments are contracts for future transactions; they are *not* liabilities. However, if considered material, they are often disclosed in the notes to the financial statements.

LO9 Evaluate the safety of creditors' claims. Short-term creditors may evaluate the safety of their claims using such measures of liquidity as the current ratio, the quick ratio, the available lines of credit, and the debtor's credit rating. Long-term creditors look more to signs of stability and long-term financial health, including the debt ratio, interest coverage ratio, and trends in net income and net cash flow from operating activities.

LO10 Describe reporting issues related to leases, postretirement benefits, and deferred taxes. Leases that are essentially equivalent to a sale of property by the lessor to the lessee are regarded as capital leases. Under a capital lease arrangement, the lessee reports in its balance sheet the present values of both an asset (for example, leased equipment) and a liability (lease payment obligations). Lease arrangements that do not qualify as capital leases are treated as operating leases, requiring that lease payments be treated as expenses when paid.

Unfunded postretirement costs are reported in the balance sheet at their discounted present values as long-term liabilities. Unfunded postretirement benefits are often called a noncash expense. That is, the expense is charged against current earnings without a corresponding outlay of cash.

Deferred income taxes result because timing differences exist between financial accounting principles and tax rules. Thus, income appearing in the income statement today may not be subject to income taxes until future years. Likewise, income subject to income taxes today may not appear in the company's income statement until future periods. Depending on the circumstances, deferred taxes may appear in the balance sheet as liabilities and/or assets (both current and long-term).

Key Terms Introduced or Emphasized in Chapter 10

accrued liabilities (p. 441) The liability to pay an expense that has accrued during the period. Also called *accrued expenses*.

actuary (p. 465) A statistician who performs computations involving assumptions as to human life spans. One function is computing companies' liabilities for pensions and postretirement benefits.

amortization table (p. 444) A schedule that indicates how installment payments are allocated between interest expense and repayments of principal.

bankruptcy (p. 460) A legal status in which the financial affairs of an illiquid business (or individual) are managed, in large part, by the U.S. Bankruptcy Court.

bonds payable (p. 446) Long-term debt securities that subdivide a very large and long-term corporate debt into transferable increments of $1,000 or multiples thereof.

capital lease (p. 464) A lease contract that finances the eventual purchase by the lessee of leased property. The lessor accounts for a capital lease as a sale of property; the lessee records an asset and a liability equal to the present value of the future lease payments. Also called a *financing lease*.

collateral (p. 438) Assets that have been pledged to secure specific liabilities. Creditors with secured claims can foreclose on (seize title to) these assets if the borrower defaults.

commitments (p. 460) Agreements to carry out future transactions. Although they are not a liability (because the transaction has not yet been performed), they may be disclosed in notes to the financial statements.

convertible bond (p. 448) A bond that may be exchanged (at the bondholder's option) for a specified number of shares of the company's capital stock.

debt service (p. 444) The combined cash outlays required for repayment of principal amounts borrowed and for payments of interest expense during the period.

Deferred Income Taxes (p. 467) A liability account to pay income taxes that have been postponed to a future year's income tax return. In some cases, this account can also be an asset account representing income taxes to be saved in a future year's income tax return.

estimated liabilities (p. 439) Liabilities known to exist, but that must be recorded in the accounting records at estimated dollar amounts.

interest coverage ratio (p. 461) Operating income divided by interest expense. Indicates the number of times that the company was able to earn the amount of its interest charges.

junk bonds (p. 448) Bonds payable that involve a greater than normal risk of default and, therefore, must pay higher than normal rates of interest in order to be attractive to investors.

lessee (p. 464) The tenant, user, or renter of leased property.

lessor (p. 464) The owner of property leased to a lessee.

leverage (p. 461) The use of borrowed money to finance business operations.

loss contingencies (p. 459) Situations involving uncertainty as to whether a loss has occurred. The uncertainty will be resolved by a future event. An example of a loss contingency is the possible loss relating to a lawsuit pending against a company. Although loss contingencies are sometimes recorded in the accounts, they are more frequently disclosed only in notes to the financial statements.

maturity date (p. 438) The date on which a liability becomes due.

off-balance sheet financing (p. 464) An arrangement in which the use of resources is financed without the obligation for future payments appearing as a liability in the balance sheet. An operating lease is a common example of off-balance sheet financing.

operating lease (p. 464) A lease contract which is in essence a rental agreement. The lessee has the use of the leased property, but the lessor retains the usual risks and rewards of ownership. The periodic lease payments are accounted for as rent expense by the lessee and as rental revenue by the lessor.

payroll taxes (p. 441) Taxes levied on an employer based on the amount of wages and salaries being paid to employees during the period. They include the employer's share of Social Security and Medicare taxes, unemployment taxes, and (though not called a "tax") workers' compensation premiums.

pension fund (p. 465) A fund managed by an independent trustee into which an employer-company makes periodic payments. The fund is used to make pension payments to retired employees.

postretirement benefits (p. 466) Benefits that will be paid to retired workers. The present value of the future benefits earned by workers during the current period is an expense of the period. If not fully funded, this expense results in a liability for unfunded postretirement benefits. (For many companies, these liabilities have become very large.)

present value (of a future amount) (p. 457) The amount of money that an informed investor would pay today for the right to receive the future amount, based on a specific rate of return required by the investor.

principal amount (p. 439) The unpaid balance of an obligation, exclusive of any interest charges for the current period.

sinking fund (p. 448) Cash set aside by a corporation at regular intervals (usually with a trustee) for the purpose of repaying a bond issue at its maturity date.

special purpose entities (p. 463) SPEs are separate entities established by corporations to accomplish specific purposes. SPEs are often used to borrow money and then transfer it to the sponsoring corporation as an off-balance sheet financing arrangement.

underwriter (p. 447) An investment banking firm that handles the sale of a corporation's stocks or bonds to the public.

workers' compensation (p. 442) A state-mandated insurance program insuring workers against job-related injuries. Premiums are charged to employers as a percentage of the employees' wages and salaries. The amounts vary by state and by the employees' occupations but, in some cases, can be very substantial.

Demonstration Problem

Listed below are selected items from the financial statements of G & H Pump Mfg. Co. for the year ended December 31, 2007.

Item	Amount
Note payable to Porterville Bank	99,000
Income taxes payable	63,000
Loss contingency relating to lawsuit	200,000
Accounts payable and accrued expenses	163,230
Mortgage note payable	240,864
Bonds payable	2,200,000
Premium on bonds payable	1,406
Accrued bond interest payable	110,000
Pension expense	61,400
Unearned revenue	25,300

Other Information

1. The note payable owed to Porterville Bank is due in 30 days. G & H has arranged with this bank to renew the note for an additional two years.
2. G & H has been sued for $200,000 by someone claiming the company's pumps are excessively noisy. It is reasonably possible, but not probable, that a loss has been sustained.
3. The mortgage note is payable at $8,000 per month over the next three years. During the next 12 months, the principal amount of this note will be reduced to $169,994.
4. The bonds payable mature in seven months. A sinking fund has been accumulated to repay the full maturity of this bond issue.

Instructions

a. Using this information, prepare the current liabilities and long-term liabilities sections of a classified balance sheet at December 31, 2007.

b. Explain briefly how the information in each of the four numbered paragraphs affected your presentation of the company's liabilities.

Solution to the Demonstration Problem

a.

G & H PUMP MFG. CO. Partial Balance Sheet December 31, 2007		
Liabilities:		
Current liabilities:		
Accounts payable and accrued expenses		$ 163,230
Income taxes payable		63,000
Accrued bond interest payable		110,000
Unearned revenue		25,300
Current portion of long-term debt		70,870
Total current liabilities		$ 432,400
Long-term liabilities:		
Note payable to Porterville Bank		$ 99,000
Mortgage note payable		169,994
Bonds payable	$2,200,000	
Add: Premium on bonds payable	1,406	2,201,406
Total long-term liabilities		$2,470,400
Total liabilities		$2,902,800

b.
1. Although the note payable to Porterville Bank is due in 30 days, it is classified as a long-term liability as it will be refinanced on a long-term basis.
2. The pending lawsuit is a loss contingency requiring disclosure, but it is not listed in the liability section of the balance sheet.
3. The $70,870 of the mortgage note that will be repaid within the next 12 months ($240,864 − $169,994) is a current liability; the remaining balance, due after December 31, 2008, is long-term debt.
4. Although the bonds payable mature in seven months, they will be repaid from a sinking fund, rather than from current assets. Therefore, these bonds retain their long-term classification.

Self-Test Questions

The answers to these questions appear on page 489.

1. Which of the following is characteristic of liabilities rather than of equity? (More than one answer may be correct.)
   - **a.** The obligation matures.
   - **b.** Interest paid to the provider of the capital is deductible in the determination of taxable income.
   - **c.** The capital providers' claims are *residual* in the event of liquidation of the business.
   - **d.** The capital providers normally have the right to exercise control over business operations.
2. On October 1, Dalton Corp. borrows $100,000 from National Bank, signing a six-month note payable for that amount, plus interest to be computed at a rate of 9 percent per annum. Indicate all correct answers.
   - **a.** Dalton's liability at October 1 is only $100,000.
   - **b.** The maturity value of this note is $104,500.
   - **c.** At December 31, Dalton will have a liability for accrued interest payable in the amount of $4,500.
   - **d.** Dalton's total liability for this loan at November 30 is $101,500.
3. Identify all correct statements concerning payrolls and related payroll costs.
   - **a.** Both employers and employees pay Social Security and Medicare taxes.
   - **b.** Workers' compensation premiums are withheld from employees' wages.
   - **c.** An employer's total payroll costs usually exceed total wages expense by about 7½ percent.
   - **d.** Under current law, employers are required to pay Social Security taxes on employees' earnings, but they are not required to pay for health insurance.

4. Identify the types of information that can readily be determined from an amortization table for an installment loan. (More than one answer may be correct.)
   a. Interest expense on this liability for the current year.
   b. The present value of the future payments under changing market conditions.
   c. The unpaid balance remaining after each payment.
   d. The portion of the unpaid balance that is a current liability.
5. Which of the following statements is (are) correct? (More than one statement may be correct.)
   a. A bond issue is a technique for subdividing a very large loan into many small, transferable units.
   b. Bond interest payments are contractual obligations, whereas the board of directors determines whether or not dividends will be paid.
   c. As interest rates rise, the market prices of bonds fall; as interest rates fall, bond prices tend to rise.
   d. Bond interest payments are deductible in determining income subject to income taxes, whereas dividends paid to stockholders are not deductible.
6. Identify all statements that are *consistent* with the concept of present value. (More than one answer may be correct.)
   a. The present value of a future amount always is *less* than that future amount.
   b. An amount of money available today is considered *more* valuable than the *same sum* that will not become available until a future date.
   c. A bond's issue price is equal to the present value of its future cash flows.
   d. The liability for an installment note payable is recorded at only the *principal* amount, rather than the sum of the scheduled future payments.
7. Identify those trends that are *unfavorable* from the viewpoint of a bondholder. (More than one answer may be correct.)
   a. Market interest rates are steadily rising.
   b. The issuing company's interest coverage ratio is steadily rising.
   c. The issuing company's net cash flow from operating activities is steadily declining.
   d. The issuing company's debt ratio is steadily declining.
8. A basic difference between *loss contingencies* and "real" liabilities is:
   a. Liabilities stem from past transactions; loss contingencies stem from future events.
   b. Liabilities always are recorded in the accounting records, whereas loss contingencies never are.
   c. The extent of uncertainty involved.
   d. Liabilities can be large in amount, whereas loss contingencies are immaterial.
9. Which of the following situations require recording a liability in 2007? (More than one answer may be correct.)
   a. In 2007, a company manufactures and sells stereo equipment that carries a three-year warranty.
   b. In 2007, a theater group receives payments in advance from season ticket holders for productions to be performed in 2008.
   c. A company is a defendant in a legal action. At the end of 2007, the company's attorney feels it is possible the company will lose and that the amount of the loss might be material.
   d. During 2007, a Midwest agricultural cooperative is concerned about the risk of loss if inclement weather destroys the crops.
10. Silverado maintains a fully funded pension plan. During 2007, $1 million was paid to retired workers, and workers currently employed by the company earned a portion of the right to receive pension payments expected to total $6 million *over their lifetimes*. Silverado's pension *expense* for 2007 amounts to:
    a. $1 million.
    b. $6 million.
    c. $7 million.
    d. Some other amount.
11. Deferred income taxes result from:
    a. The fact that bond interest is deductible in the computation of taxable income.
    b. Depositing income taxes due in future years in a special fund managed by an independent trustee.
    c. Differences between certain revenue and expense items recognized in financial statements but not in income tax returns.
    d. The inability of a bankrupt company to pay its income tax liability on schedule.

ASSIGNMENT MATERIAL Discussion Questions

1. Define *liabilities*. Identify several characteristics that distinguish liabilities from owners' equity.
2. Explain the relative priority of the claims of owners and of creditors to the assets of a business. Do all creditors have equal priority? Explain.
3. Define *current liabilities* and *long-term liabilities*. Under what circumstances might a 10-year bond issue be classified as a current liability? Under what circumstances might a note payable maturing 30 days after the balance sheet date be classified as a long-term liability?
4. Jonas Company issues a 90-day, 12 percent note payable to replace an account payable to Smith Supply Company in the amount of $8,000. Draft the journal entries (in general journal form) to record the issuance of the note payable and the payment of the note at the maturity date.

5. Explain why an employer's "total cost" of a payroll may exceed by a substantial amount the total wages and salaries earned by employees.
6. What are workers' compensation premiums? Who pays them? Who pays Social Security and Medicare taxes?
7. Ace Garage has an unpaid mortgage loan of $63,210, payable at $1,200 per month. An amortization table indicates that $527 of the current monthly payment represents interest expense. What will be the amount of this mortgage obligation immediately *after* Ace makes this current payment?
8. A friend of yours has just purchased a house and has taken out a $50,000, 11 percent mortgage, payable at $476.17 per month. After making the first monthly payment, he received a receipt from the bank stating that only $17.84 of the $476.17 had been applied to reducing the principal amount of the loan. Your friend computes that, at the rate of $17.84 per month, it will take over 233 years to pay off the $50,000 mortgage. Do you agree with your friend's analysis? Explain.
9. Briefly explain the income tax advantage of raising capital by issuing bonds rather than by selling capital stock.
10. Tampa Boat Company pays federal income taxes at a rate of 30 percent on taxable income. Compute the company's annual *after-tax* cost of borrowing on a 10 percent, $5 million bond issue. Express this after-tax cost as a percentage of the borrowed $5 million.
11. Why is the *present value* of a future amount always *less* than the future amount?
12. Why do bond prices vary inversely with interest rates?
13. Some bonds now being bought and sold by investors on organized securities exchanges were issued when interest rates were much higher than they are today. Would you expect these bonds to be trading at prices above or below their face values? Explain.
14. *The Wall Street Journal* recently quoted a market price of *102* for an issue of 8 percent Nabisco bonds. What would be the market price for $25,000 face value of these bonds (ignoring accrued interest)? Is the market rate of interest for bonds of this quality higher or lower than 8 percent? Explain.
15. The 6 percent bonds of Central Gas & Electric are selling at a market price of 72, whereas the 6 percent bonds of Interstate Power are selling at a price of 97. Does this mean that Interstate Power has a better credit rating than Central Gas & Electric? Explain. (Assume current long-term interest rates are in the 11 percent to 13 percent range.)
16. Does issuing bonds at a discount increase or decrease the issuing company's cost of borrowing? Explain.
17. A $200 million bond issue of NDP Corp. (a liquid company) recently matured. The entire maturity value was paid from a bond sinking fund. What effect did this transaction have on the company's current ratio? On its debt ratio? Explain.
18. As a result of issuing 20-year bonds payable, Low-Cal Foods now has an interest coverage ratio of .75 to 1. Should this ratio be of greater concern to short-term creditors or to stockholders? Explain.
19. There is an old business saying that "You shouldn't *be* in business if your company doesn't earn higher than bank rates." This means that if a company is to succeed, its return on assets should be *significantly higher* than its cost of borrowing. Why is this so important?
20. Identify two characteristics of *estimated liabilities*. Provide at least two examples of estimated liabilities.
21. What is the meaning of the term *loss contingency*? Give several examples. How are loss contingencies presented in financial statements? Explain.
22. What is the meaning of the term *commitment*? Give several examples. How are commitments usually presented in financial statements? Explain.
23. Explain how the lessee accounts for an operating lease and a capital lease. Why is an operating lease sometimes called *off-balance sheet financing*?
24. Ortega Industries has a fully funded pension plan. Each year, pension expense runs in excess of $10 million. At the present time, employees are entitled to receive pension benefits with a present value of $125 million. Explain what liability, if any, Ortega Industries should include in its balance sheet as a result of this pension plan.
25. Why do large corporations often show no liability for pensions owed to retired employees, but huge liabilities for "nonpension postretirement benefits"?
26. When are the costs of postretirement benefits recognized as an expense? When are the related cash payments made?
27. What are *deferred income tax liabilities*? How are these items presented in financial statements?

Brief Exercises

BRIEF EXERCISE 10.1

Cash Effects of Borrowing

Jacobs Company borrowed $10,000 on a one-year, 8 percent note payable from the local bank on April 1. Interest was paid quarterly, and the note was repaid one year from the time the money was borrowed. Calculate the amount of cash payments Jacobs was required to make in each of the two calendar years that were affected by the note payable.

BRIEF EXERCISE 10.2

Effective Interest Rate

One of the advantages of borrowing is that interest is deductible for income tax purposes.

a. If a company pays 8 percent interest to borrow $500,000, but is in an income tax bracket that requires it to pay 40 percent income tax, what is the actual net-of-tax interest cost that the company incurs?

b. What is the effective interest rate that is paid by the company?

LO6 **BRIEF EXERCISE 10.3**

Bonds Issued at a Discount

Cronan, Inc., sells $1,000,000 general obligation bonds for 98. The interest rate on the bonds, paid quarterly, is 6 percent. Calculate (**a**) the amount that the company will actually receive from the sale of the bonds, and (**b**) the amount of both the quarterly and the total annual cash interest that the company will be required to pay.

LO6 **BRIEF EXERCISE 10.4**

Bonds Issued at a Premium

Pearl Company sells $1,000,000 general obligation bonds for 101. The interest rate on the bonds, paid quarterly, is 5 percent. Calculate (**a**) the amount that the company will actually receive from the sale of the bonds, and (**b**) the amount of both the quarterly and the total annual cash interest that the company will be required to pay.

LO6 **BRIEF EXERCISE 10.5**

Recording Bonds Issued at a Discount

Red & Blue Company sold bonds at 97 on an interest payment date for $500,000. Assuming the bonds will be retired in 10 years and interest is paid annually, calculate the amount of cash that will be received and paid by Red & Blue in the first year, as well as the interest expense that will be recognized in that year. The bonds carry a stated interest rate of 5 percent.

LO6 **BRIEF EXERCISE 10.6**

Recording Bonds Issued at a Premium

Purple & Orange, Inc., sold bonds at 102 on an interest payment date for $700,000. Assuming the bonds will be retired in 10 years and interest is paid annually, calculate the amount of cash that will be received and paid by Purple & Orange in the first full year, as well as the amount of interest expense that will be recognized in that year. The bonds carry a stated interest rate of 6.5 percent.

LO9 **BRIEF EXERCISE 10.7**

Debt Ratio

Company One has debt totaling $2,000,000 and total stockholders' equity of $4,000,000. Company Two has debt totaling $3,000,000 and stockholders' equity of $5,000,000.

a. Calculate the debt ratio for each company. (Hint: You will find an explanation of the debt ratio and how it is computed in Exhibit 10–8.)

b. Briefly explain the meaning of the debt ratio.

LO6 **BRIEF EXERCISE 10.8**

Early Retirement of Bonds

Joseph Max, Inc., sold 10-year, 7 percent bonds for $1,000,000 at 98. On the interest payment date at the end of the 5th year the bonds were outstanding, 50 percent of the bonds were retired by Max at 101 under an early retirement option that was written into the bond agreement. Determine the gain or loss that Max will incur as a result of retiring the bonds.

LO10 **BRIEF EXERCISE 10.9**

Deferred Income Taxes

Gosling Company determines its annual income tax expense to be $459,000. Of that amount, $300,000 has already been paid during the year (on a quarterly basis) and charged to the Income Taxes Expense account. The company has determined that, of the amount that has not yet been paid or recorded, $75,000 will be deferred into future years under certain favorable income tax provisions available to the company. Prepare the end-of-year general journal entry to recognize income taxes accrued.

LO10 **BRIEF EXERCISE 10.10**

Pension and Other Postretirement Benefit Costs

Grammar, Inc., offers its full-time employees pension and other postretirement benefits, primarily health insurance. During the current year, pension benefits for the employees totaled $250,000. Other postretirement benefits totaled $140,000. The pension benefits are fully funded by the company by transferring cash to a trustee that administers the plan. The other postretirement benefits are similarly funded, but only at the 50 percent level. Determine the total amount that Grammar will need to transfer to its trustee for both benefit plans during the current year.

Exercises

LO4 **EXERCISE 10.1**

You as a Student

Assume that you will have a 10-year, $10,000 loan to repay to your parents when you graduate from college next month. The loan, plus 8 percent annual interest on the unpaid balance, is to be repaid in 10 annual installments of $1,490 each, beginning one year after you graduate. You have accepted a well-paying job and are considering an early settlement of the entire unpaid balance in just three years (immediately after making the third annual payment of $1,490).

Prepare an amortization schedule showing how much money you will need to save to pay your parents the entire unpaid balance of your loan three years after your graduation. (Round amounts to the nearest dollar.)

LO1 through LO6 **EXERCISE 10.2**

Effects of Transactions on the Accounting Equation

Listed below are eight events or transactions of GemStar Corporation.

a. Made an adjusting entry to record interest on a short-term note payable.

b. Made a monthly installment payment of a fully amortizing, six-month, interest-bearing installment note payable.

c. Recorded a regular biweekly payroll, including the amounts withheld from employees, the issuance of paychecks, and payroll taxes on the employer.

d. Came within 12 months of the maturity date of a note payable originally issued for a period of 18 months.

e. Deposited employee tax withholdings with proper tax authorities.

f. Issued bonds payable at face value.

g. Recognized semiannual interest expense on bonds payable described in part **f** and paid bondholders the full interest amount.

h. Recorded the necessary adjusting entry on December 31, 2007, to accrue three months' interest on bonds payable that had been issued at a discount several years prior. The next semiannual interest payment will occur March 31, 2008.

Indicate the effects of each of these transactions on the following financial statement categories. Organize your answer in tabular form, using the illustrated column headings. Use the following code letters to indicate the effects of each transaction on the accounting element listed in the column heading: **I** for increase, **D** for decrease, and **NE** for no effect.

	Income Statement			Balance Sheet			
Transaction	Revenue –	Expenses =	Net Income	Assets =	Current Liab. +	Long-Term Liab. +	Owners' Equity
a							

EXERCISE 10.3

Effects of Transactions on Various Financial Measurements

LO1 LO2 LO4 through LO6 LO8

Six events relating to liabilities follow:

a. Paid the liability for interest payable accrued at the end of the last accounting period.

b. Made the current monthly payment on a 12-month installment note payable, including interest and a partial repayment of principal.

c. Issued bonds payable at 98 on March 1, 2007. The bonds pay interest March 1 and September 1.

d. Recorded September 1, 2007, interest expense and made semiannual interest payment on bonds referred to in part **c**.

e. Recorded necessary adjusting entry on December 31, 2007, for bonds referred to in part **c**.

f. Recorded estimated six-month warranty expense on December 31, 2007.

Indicate the effects of each transaction or adjusting entry on the financial measurements in the five column headings listed below. Use the code letters **I** for increase, **D** for decrease, and **NE** for no effect.

Transaction	Current Liabilities	Long-Term Liabilities	Net Income	Net Cash Flow from Operating Activities	Net Cash Flow (from All Sources)
a					

EXERCISE 10.4

Employees—What Do They Really Cost?

LO3

Magnum Plus, Inc., is a manufacturer of hunting supplies. The following is a summary of the company's annual payroll-related costs:

Wages and salaries expense (of which $2,200,000 was withheld from employees' pay and forwarded directly to tax authorities)	$7,200,000
Payroll taxes	580,000
Workers' compensation premiums	250,000
Group health insurance premiums	725,000
Contributions to employees' pension plan	450,000

a. Compute Magnum's total payroll-related costs for the year.

b. Compute the net amount of cash actually paid to employees (their take-home pay).

c. Express total payroll-related costs as a percentage of (1) total wages and salaries expense, and (2) employees' take-home pay. (Round computations to the nearest 1 percent.)

EXERCISE 10.5
Accounting for Payroll Activities

Gruver Corporation reported the following payroll-related costs for the month of February:

Gross pay (wages expense)	$250,000
Social Security and Medicare taxes	19,125
Federal and state unemployment taxes	15,500
Workers' compensation insurance	8,500
Group health and life insurance benefits	10,000
Employee pension plan benefits	22,875
Total payroll costs for February	$326,000

Gruver's insurance premiums for workers' compensation and group health and life insurance were paid for in a prior period and recorded initially as prepaid insurance expense. Withholdings from employee wages in February were as follows:

State income tax withholdings	$ 5,875
Federal income tax withholdings	56,000
Social Security and Medicare tax withholdings	19,125

a. Record Gruver's gross wages, employee withholdings, and employee take-home pay for February.

b. Record Gruver's payroll tax expense for February.

c. Record Gruver's employee benefit expenses for February.

d. Do the amounts withheld from Gruver's employees represent taxes levied on Gruver Corporation? Explain.

EXERCISE 10.6
Use of an Amortization Table

Glen Pool Club, Inc., has a $150,000 mortgage liability. The mortgage is payable in monthly installments of $1,543, which include interest computed at an annual rate of 12 percent (1 percent monthly).

a. Prepare a partial amortization table showing (**1**) the original balance of this loan, and (**2**) the allocation of the first two monthly payments between interest expense and the reduction in the mortgage's unpaid balance. (Round to the nearest dollar.)

b. Prepare the journal entry to record the second monthly payment.

c. Will monthly interest increase, decrease, or stay the same over the life of the loan? Explain your answer.

EXERCISE 10.7
After-Tax Cost of Borrowing

DuPont reports in its balance sheet $340 million of 6.2 percent bonds payable at face value. The company's average income tax rate is approximately 40 percent.

a. Compute the company's after-tax cost of borrowing on this bond issue stated as a total dollar amount.

b. Compute the company's after-tax cost of borrowing on this bond issue stated as a percentage of the amount borrowed.

c. Describe briefly the advantage of raising funds by issuing bonds as opposed to stocks.

EXERCISE 10.8
Bond Interest on Bonds Issued at Face Value

On March 31, 2007, Gardner Corporation received authorization to issue $50,000 of 9 percent, 30-year bonds payable. The bonds pay interest on March 31 and September 30. The entire issue was dated March 31, 2007, but the bonds were not issued until April 30, 2007. They were issued at face value.

a. Prepare the journal entry at April 30, 2007, to record the sale of the bonds.

b. Prepare the journal entry at September 30, 2007, to record the semiannual bond interest payment.

c. Prepare the adjusting entry at December 31, 2007, to record bond interest expense accrued since September 30, 2007. (Assume that no monthly adjusting entries to accrue interest expense had been made prior to December 31, 2007.)

d. Explain why the issuing corporation charged its bond investors for interest accrued in April 2007, prior to the issuance date (see part **b** above).

EXERCISE 10.9
Accounting for Bonds Issued at a Premium: Issuance, Interest Payments, and Retirement

Swanson Corporation issued $8 million of 20-year, 8 percent bonds on April 1, 2007, at 102. Interest is due on March 31 and September 30 of each year, and all of the bonds in the issue mature on March 31, 2027. Swanson's fiscal year ends on December 31. Prepare the following journal entries:

a. April 1, 2007, to record the issuance of the bonds.

b. September 30, 2007, to pay interest and to amortize the bond premium.

c. March 31, 2027, to pay interest, amortize the bond premium, and retire the bonds at maturity (make two separate entries).

d. Briefly explain the effect of amortizing the bond premium upon (1) annual net income and (2) annual net cash flow from operating activities. (Ignore possible income tax effects.)

EXERCISE 10.10
Accounting for Bonds Issued at a Discount: Issuance, Interest Payments, and Retirement

Mellilo Corporation issued $5 million of 20-year, 9.5 percent bonds on July 1, 2007, at 98. Interest is due on June 30 and December 31 of each year, and all of the bonds in the issue mature on June 30, 2027. Mellilo's fiscal year ends on December 31. Prepare the following journal entries:

a. July 1, 2007, to record the issuance of the bonds.

b. December 31, 2007, to pay interest and amortize the bond discount.

c. June 30, 2027, to pay interest, amortize the bond discount, and retire the bonds at maturity (make two separate entries).

d. Briefly explain the effect of amortizing the bond discount upon (1) annual net income and (2) annual net cash flow from operating activities. (Ignore possible income tax effects.)

EXERCISE 10.11
Safety of Creditors' Claims

Shown below are data from recent reports of two publicly owned toy makers. Dollar amounts are stated in thousands.

	Tyco Toys, Inc.	Hasbro, Inc.
Total assets	$615,132	$2,616,388
Total liabilities	349,792	1,090,776
Interest expense	28,026	37,588
Operating income	13,028	304,672

a. Compute for each company (1) the debt ratio and (2) the interest coverage ratio. (Round the debt ratio to the nearest percent and the interest coverage ratio to two decimal places.)

b. In your opinion, which of these companies would a long-term creditor probably view as the safer investment? Explain.

EXERCISE 10.12
Accounting for Leases

On July 1, Pine Region Dairy leased equipment from Farm America for a period of three years. The lease calls for monthly payments of $2,500 payable in advance on the first day of each month, beginning July 1.

Prepare the journal entry needed to record this lease in the accounting records of Pine Region Dairy on July 1 under each of the following independent assumptions:

a. The lease represents a simple rental arrangement.

b. At the end of three years, title to this equipment will be transferred to Pine Region Dairy at no additional cost. The present value of the 36 monthly lease payments is $76,021, of which $2,500 is paid in cash on July 1. None of the initial $2,500 is allocated to interest expense.

c. Why is situation **a**, the operating lease, sometimes called off-balance sheet financing?

d. Would it be acceptable for a company to account for a capital lease as an operating lease to report rent expense rather than a long-term liability?

EXERCISE 10.13
Pension Plans

At the end of the current year, Western Electric received the following information from its actuarial firm:

Pension expense	$2,500,000
Postretirement benefits expense	750,000

The pension plan is fully funded. Western Electric has funded only $50,000 of the nonpension postretirement benefits this year.

a. Prepare the journal entry to summarize pension expense for the entire year.

b. Prepare the journal entry to summarize the nonpension postretirement benefits expense for the entire year.

c. If the company becomes illiquid in future years, what prospects, if any, do today's employees have of receiving the pension benefits that they have earned to date?

d. Does the company have an ethical responsibility to fully fund its nonpension postretirement benefits?

EXERCISE 10.14
Deferred Income Taxes

The following journal entry summarizes for the current year the income tax expense of Wilson's Software Warehouse:

Income Tax Expense	1,500,000	
Cash		960,000
Income Tax Payable		340,000
Deferred Income Tax		200,000
To record income tax expense for the current year.		

Of the deferred income taxes, only $30,000 is classified as a current liability.

a. Define the term *deferred income tax.*

b. What is the amount of income tax that the company has paid or expects to pay in conjunction with its income tax return for the current year?

c. Illustrate the allocation of the liabilities shown in the above journal entry between the classifications of current liabilities and long-term liabilities.

EXERCISE 10.15
Examining Home Depot's Capital Structure

To answer the following questions use the financial statements for Home Depot, Inc., in Appendix A at the end of the textbook:

a. Compute the company's current ratio and quick ratio for the most recent year reported. Do these ratios provide support that Home Depot is able to repay its current liabilities as they come due? Explain.

b. Compute the company's debt ratio. Does Home Depot appear to have excessive debt? Explain.

c. Examine the company's statement of cash flows. Does Home Depot's cash flow from operating activities appear adequate to cover its current liabilities as they come due? Explain.

Problem Set A

PROBLEM 10.1A
Effects of Transactions on Financial Statements

LO1 through LO6, LO8

Fifteen transactions or events affecting Computer Specialists, Inc., are as follows:

a. Made a year-end adjusting entry to accrue interest on a note payable.

b. A liability classified for several years as long-term becomes due within the next 12 months.

c. Recorded the regular biweekly payroll, including payroll taxes, amounts withheld from employees, and the issuance of paychecks.

d. Earned an amount previously recorded as unearned revenue.

e. Made arrangements to extend a bank loan due in 60 days for another 18 months.

f. Made a monthly payment on a fully amortizing installment note payable. (Assume this note is classified as a current liability.)

g. Called bonds payable due in seven years at a price above the carrying value of the liability in the accounting records.

h. Issued bonds payable at 97 on May 1, 2007. The bonds pay interest May 1 and November 1.

i. Recorded November 1, 2007, interest expense and made semiannual interest payment on bonds referred to in part **h**.

j. Recorded necessary adjusting entry on December 31, 2007, for bonds referred to in part **h**.

k. Issued bonds payable at 102 on July 31, 2007. The bonds pay interest July 31 and January 31.

l. Recorded necessary adjusting entry on December 31, 2007, for bonds referred to in part **k**.

m. Recorded an estimated liability for warranty claims.

n. Entered into a two-year commitment to buy all hard drives from a particular supplier at a price 10 percent below market.

o. Received notice that a lawsuit has been filed against the company for $7 million. The amount of the company's liability, if any, cannot be reasonably estimated at this time.

Instructions

Indicate the effects of each of these transactions upon the following elements of the company's financial statements. Organize your answer in tabular form, using the column headings shown below. Use the following code letters to indicate the effects of each transaction on the accounting element listed in the column headings: **I** for increase, **D** for decrease, and **NE** for no effect.

	Income Statement			Balance Sheet			
Transaction	Revenue −	Expenses =	Net Income	Assets =	Current Liab. +	Long-Term Liab. +	Owners' Equity
a							

PROBLEM 10.2A

Balance Sheet Presentation of Liabilities

The following are selected items from the accounting records of Seattle Chocolates for the year ended December 31, 2007:

Item	Amount
Note payable to Northwest Bank	$500,000
Income taxes payable	40,000
Accrued expenses and payroll taxes	60,000
Mortgage note payable	750,000
Accrued interest on mortgage note payable	5,000
Trade accounts payable	250,000
Unearned revenue	15,000
Potential liability in pending lawsuit	100,000

Other Information

1. The note payable to Northwest Bank is due in 60 days. Arrangements have been made to renew this note for an additional 12 months.
2. The mortgage requires payments of $6,000 per month. An amortization table shows that its balance will be paid down to $739,000 by December 31, 2008.
3. Accrued interest on the mortgage note payable is paid monthly. The next payment is due near the end of the first week in January 2008.
4. Seattle Chocolates has been sued for $100,000 in a contract dispute. It is not possible at this time, however, to make a reasonable estimate of the possible loss, if any, that the company may have sustained.

Instructions

a. Using the information provided, prepare the current and long-term liability sections of the company's balance sheet dated December 31, 2007. (Within each classification, items may be listed in any order.)

b. Explain briefly how the information in each of the four numbered paragraphs above influenced your presentation of the company's liabilities.

PROBLEM 10.3A
Notes Payable: Accruing Interest

During the fiscal year ended December 31, Swanson Corporation engaged in the following transactions involving notes payable:

Aug. 6 Borrowed $12,000 from Maple Grove Bank, signing a 45-day, 12 percent note payable.

Sept. 16 Purchased office equipment from Seawald Equipment. The invoice amount was $18,000, and Seawald agreed to accept, as full payment, a 10 percent, three-month note for the invoice amount.

Sept. 20 Paid Maple Grove Bank the note plus accrued interest.

Nov. 1 Borrowed $250,000 from Mike Swanson, a major corporate stockholder. The corporation issued Swanson a $250,000, 15 percent, 90-day note payable.

Dec. 1 Purchased merchandise inventory in the amount of $5,000 from Gathman Corporation. Gathman accepted a 90-day, 14 percent note as full settlement of the purchase. Swanson Corporation uses a perpetual inventory system.

Dec. 16 The $18,000 note payable to Seawald Equipment matured today. Swanson paid the accrued interest on this note and issued a new 30-day, 16 percent note payable in the amount of $18,000 to replace the note that matured.

Instructions

a. Prepare journal entries (in general journal form) to record the above transactions. Use a 360-day year in making the interest calculations.

b. Prepare the adjusting entry needed at December 31, prior to closing the accounts. Use one entry for all three notes (round to the nearest dollar).

c. Provide a possible explanation why the new 30-day note payable to Seawald Equipment pays 16 percent interest instead of the 10 percent rate charged on the September 16 note.

LO4

PROBLEM 10.4A
Preparation and Use of an Amortization Table

On September 1, 2007, Quick Lube signed a 30-year, $1,080,000 mortgage note payable to Mifflinburg Bank and Trust in conjunction with the purchase of a building and land. The mortgage note calls for interest at an annual rate of 12 percent (1 percent per month). The note is fully amortizing over a period of 360 months.

The bank sent Quick Lube an amortization table showing the allocation of monthly payments between interest and principal over the life of the loan. A small part of this amortization table is illustrated below. (For convenience, amounts have been rounded to the nearest dollar.)

AMORTIZATION TABLE
(12%, 30-Year Mortgage Note Payable for $1,080,000; Payable in 360 Monthly Installments of $11,110)

Interest Period	Payment Date	Monthly Payment	Interest Expense	Principal Reduction	Unpaid Balance
Issue date	Sept. 1, 2007	—	—	—	$1,080,000
1	Oct. 1	$11,110	$10,800	$310	1,079,690
2	Nov. 1	11,110	10,797	313	1,079,377

Instructions

a. Explain whether the amounts of interest expense and the reductions in the unpaid principal are likely to change in any predictable pattern from month to month.

b. Prepare journal entries to record the first two monthly payments on this mortgage.

c. Complete this amortization table for two more monthly installments—those due on December 1, 2007, and January 1, 2008. (Round amounts to the nearest dollar.)

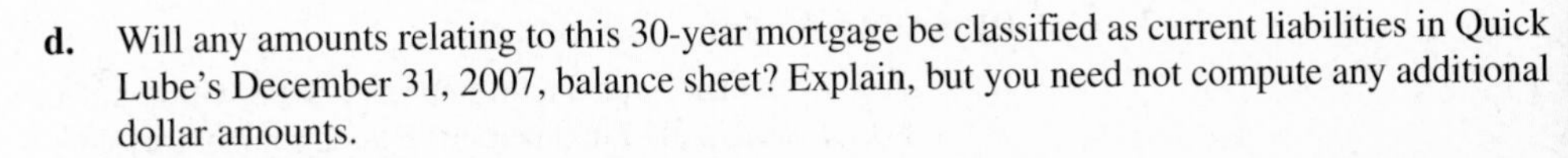

d. Will any amounts relating to this 30-year mortgage be classified as current liabilities in Quick Lube's December 31, 2007, balance sheet? Explain, but you need not compute any additional dollar amounts.

PROBLEM 10.5A
Bond Interest (Bonds Issued at Face Value)

Blue Mountain Power Company obtained authorization to issue 20-year bonds with a face value of \$10 million. The bonds are dated May 1, 2007, and have a contract rate of interest of 10 percent. They pay interest on November 1 and May 1. The bonds were issued on August 1, 2007, at 100 plus three months' accrued interest.

Instructions
Prepare the necessary journal entries in general journal form on:

a. August 1, 2007, to record the issuance of the bonds.

b. November 1, 2007, to record the first semiannual interest payment on the bond issue.

c. December 31, 2007, to record interest expense accrued through year-end. (Round to the nearest dollar.)

d. May 1, 2008, to record the second semiannual interest payment. (Round to the nearest dollar.)

e. What was the prevailing market rate of interest on the date that the bonds were issued? Explain.

PROBLEM 10.6A
Amortization of a Bond Discount and Premium

On September 1, 2007, Park Rapids Lumber Company issued \$80 million in 20-year, 10 percent bonds payable. Interest is payable semiannually on March 1 and September 1. Bond discounts and premiums are amortized at each interest payment date and at year-end. The company's fiscal year ends at December 31.

Instructions
a. Make the necessary adjusting entries at December 31, 2007, and the journal entry to record the payment of bond interest on March 1, 2008, under each of the following assumptions:

1. The bonds were issued at 98. (Round to the nearest dollar.)
2. The bonds were issued at 101. (Round to the nearest dollar.)

b. Compute the net bond liability at December 31, 2008, under assumptions **1** and **2** above. (Round to the nearest dollar.)

c. Under which of the above assumptions, **1** or **2**, would the investor's effective rate of interest be higher? Explain.

PROBLEM 10.7A
Reporting Liabilities in a Balance Sheet

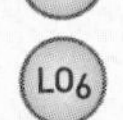

The following items were taken from the accounting records of Minnesota Satellite Telephone Corporation (MinnSat) for the year ended December 31, 2007 (dollar amounts are in thousands):

Item	Amount
Accounts payable	\$ 65,600
Accrued expenses payable (other than interest)	11,347
6¾% Bonds payable, due Feb. 1, 2008	100,000
8½% Bonds payable, due June 1, 2008	250,000
Discount on bonds payable (8½% bonds of 2008)	260
11% Bonds payable, due June 1, 2017	300,000
Premium on bonds payable (11% bonds of 2017)	1,700
Accrued interest payable	7,333
Bond interest expense	61,000
Other interest expense	17,000
Notes payable (short-term)	110,000
Lease obligations—capital leases	23,600
Pension obligation	410,000
Unfunded obligations for postretirement benefits other than pensions	72,000
Deferred income taxes	130,000
Income tax expense	66,900
Income tax payable	17,300
Operating income	280,800
Net income	134,700
Total assets	2,093,500

Other Information

1. The 6¾ percent bonds due in February 2008 will be refinanced in January 2008 through the issuance of $150,000 in 9 percent, 20-year bonds payable.
2. The 8½ percent bonds due June 1, 2008, will be repaid entirely from a bond sinking fund.
3. MinnSat is committed to total lease payments of $14,400 in 2008. Of this amount, $7,479 is applicable to operating leases, and $6,921 to capital leases. Payments on capital leases will be applied as follows: $2,300 to interest expense and $4,621 to reduction in the capitalized lease payment obligation.
4. MinnSat's pension plan is fully funded with an independent trustee.
5. The obligation for postretirement benefits other than pensions consists of a commitment to maintain health insurance for retired workers. During 2008, MinnSat will fund $18,000 of this obligation.
6. The $17,300 in income tax payable relates to income taxes levied in 2007 and must be paid on or before March 15, 2008. No portion of the deferred tax liability is regarded as a current liability.

Instructions

a. Using this information, prepare the current liabilities and long-term liabilities sections of a classified balance sheet as of December 31, 2007. (Within each classification, items may be listed in any order.)

b. Explain briefly how the information in each of the six numbered paragraphs affected your presentation of the company's liabilities.

c. Compute as of December 31, 2007, the company's **(1)** debt ratio and **(2)** interest coverage ratio.

d. Based solely on information stated in this problem, indicate whether this company appears to be an outstanding, medium, or poor long-term credit risk. State specific reasons for your conclusion.

LO5

PROBLEM 10.8A

Financial Statement Presentation of Liabilities

As of December 31 of the current year, Chernin Corporation has prepared the following information regarding its liabilities and other obligations:

Notes payable, of which $10,000 will be repaid within the next 12 months	$ 80,000
Interest expense that will result from existing liabilities over the next 12 months	125,000
Lawsuit pending against the company, in which $500,000 is claimed in damages. Legal counsel can make no reasonable estimate of the company's ultimate liability at this time	500,000
20-year bond issue that matures in two years. The entire amount will be repaid from a bond sinking fund	900,000
Accrued interest on the 20-year bond issue as of the balance sheet date	36,000
Three-year commitment to John Higgins as chief financial officer at a salary of $250,000 per year	750,000
Note payable due within 90 days (but that is expected to be extended for an additional 18 months)	75,000
Cash deposits from customers for goods and services to be delivered over the next nine months	300,000
Income taxes, of which $100,000 are currently payable and the remainder deferred indefinitely	185,000

Instructions

a. Prepare a listing of the company's current and long-term liabilities as they should be presented in the company's December 31 balance sheet.

b. Briefly explain why you have excluded any of the listed items in your listing of current and long-term liabilities.

Problem Set B

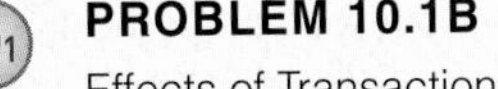

PROBLEM 10.1B

Effects of Transactions on Financial Statements

LO1 through LO6 LO8

Fifteen transactions or events affecting Westmar, Inc., are as follows:

a. Made a year-end adjusting entry to accrue interest on a note payable that has the interest rate stated separately from the principal amount.

b. A liability classified for several years as long-term becomes due within the next 12 months.

c. Recorded the regular weekly payroll, including payroll taxes, amounts withheld from employees, and the issuance of paychecks.

d. Earned an amount previously recorded as unearned revenue.

e. Made arrangements to extend a bank loan due in 60 days for another 36 months.

f. Made a monthly payment on a fully amortizing installment note payable. (Assume this note is classified as a current liability.)

g. Called bonds payable due in 10 years at a price below the carrying value of the liability in the accounting records.

h. Issued bonds payable at 101 on January 31, 2007. The bonds pay interest on January 31 and July 31.

i. Recorded July 31, 2007, interest expense and made semiannual interest payment on bonds referred to in part **h**.

j. Recorded necessary adjusting entry on December 31, 2007, for bonds referred to in part **h**.

k. Issued bonds payable at 98 on August 31, 2007. The bonds pay interest August 31 and February 28.

l. Recorded the necessary adjusting entry on December 31, 2007, for bonds referred to in part **k**.

m. Recorded an estimated liability for warranty claims.

n. Entered into a five-year commitment to buy all supplies from a particular supplier at a price 20 percent below market.

o. Received notice that a lawsuit has been filed against the company for $8 million. The amount of the company's liability, if any, cannot be reasonably estimated at this time.

Instructions

Indicate the effects of each of these transactions upon the following elements of the company's financial statements. Organize your answer in tabular form, using the column headings shown below. Use the following code letters to indicate the effects of each transaction on the accounting elements listed in the column headings: **I** for increase, **D** for decrease, and **NE** for no effect.

	Income Statement			Balance Sheet			
Transaction	Revenue −	Expenses =	Net Income	Assets =	Current Liabilities +	Long-Term Liabilities +	Owners' Equity
a							

PROBLEM 10.2B

Balance Sheet Presentation of Liabilities

LO1 LO2 LO4 LO8

The following are selected items from the accounting records of Atlanta Peach for the year ended December 31, 2007:

Note payable to Southern Bank	$ 250,000
Income taxes payable	15,000
Accrued expenses and payroll taxes	26,000
Mortgage note payable	750,000
Accrued interest on mortgage note payable	15,000
Trade accounts payable	275,000
Unearned revenue	33,000
Potential liability in pending lawsuit	2,000,000

Other Information

1. The note payable to Southern Bank is due in 60 days. Arrangements have been made to renew this note for an additional 24 months.
2. The mortgage requires payments of $10,000 per month. An amortization table shows that its balance will be paid down to $733,000 by December 31, 2008.
3. Accrued interest on the mortgage note payable is paid monthly. The next payment is due near the end of the first week in January 2008.
4. Atlanta Peach has been sued for $2,000,000 in a product damage case. It is not possible at this time, however, to make a reasonable estimate of the possible loss, if any, that the company may have sustained.

Instructions

a. Using the information provided, prepare the current and long-term liability sections of the company's balance sheet dated December 31, 2007. (Within each classification, items may be listed in any order.)

b. Explain briefly how the information in each of the four numbered paragraphs above influenced your presentation of the company's liabilities.

PROBLEM 10.3B
Notes Payable: Accruing Interest

During the fiscal year ended December 31, Swanlee Corporation engaged in the following transactions involving notes payable:

July 1	Borrowed $20,000 from Weston Bank, signing a 90-day, 12 percent note payable.
Sept. 16	Purchased office equipment from Moontime Equipment. The invoice amount was $30,000, and Moontime agreed to accept, as full payment, a 10 percent, three-month note for the invoice amount.
Oct. 1	Paid Weston Bank the note plus accrued interest.
Dec. 1	Borrowed $100,000 from Jean Will, a major corporate stockholder. The corporation issued Will a $100,000, 9 percent, 120-day note payable.
Dec. 1	Purchased merchandise inventory in the amount of $10,000 from Listen Corporation. Listen accepted a 90-day, 12 percent note as a full settlement of the purchase. Swanlee Corporation uses a perpetual inventory system.
Dec. 16	The $30,000 note payable to Moontime Equipment matured today. Swanlee paid the accrued interest on this note and issued a new 60-day, 16 percent note payable in the amount of $30,000 to replace the note that matured.

Instructions

a. Prepare journal entries (in general journal form) to record the above transactions. Use a 360-day year in making the interest calculations.

b. Prepare the adjusting entry needed at December 31, prior to closing the accounts. Use one entry for all three notes (round to the nearest dollar).

c. Provide a possible explanation why the new 60-day note payable to Moontime Equipment pays 16 percent interest instead of the 10 percent rate charged on the September 16 note.

PROBLEM 10.4B
Preparation and Use of an Amortization Table

On October 1, 2007, Walla signed a 4-year, $100,000 note payable to Vicksburg National Bank in conjunction with the purchase of equipment. The note calls for interest at an annual rate of 12 percent (1 percent per month). The note is fully amortizing over a period of 48 months.

The bank sent Walla an amortization table showing the allocation of monthly payments between interest and principal over the life of the loan. A small part of this amortization table is illustrated below. (For convenience, amounts have been rounded to the nearest dollar.)

AMORTIZATION TABLE (12%, 4-Year Note Payable for $100,000; Payable in 48 Monthly Installments of $2,633)					
Interest Period	**Payment Date**	**Monthly Payment**	**Interest Expense**	**Principal Reduction**	**Unpaid Balance**
Issue date	Oct. 1, 2007	—	—	—	$100,000
1	Nov. 1	$2,633	$1,000	$1,633	98,367
2	Dec. 1	2,633	984	1,649	96,718

Instructions

a. Explain whether the amounts of interest expense and the reductions in the unpaid principal are likely to change in any predictable pattern from month to month.

b. Prepare journal entries to record the first two monthly payments on this note.

c. Complete this amortization table for two more monthly installments.

d. Will any amounts relating to this 4-year note be classified as current liabilities in Walla's December 31, 2007, balance sheet? Explain, but you need not compute any additional dollar amounts.

PROBLEM 10.5B

Bond Interest (Bonds Issued at Face Value)

Lake Company obtained authorization to issue 10-year bonds with a face value of $5 million. The bonds are dated June 1, 2007, and have a contract rate of interest of 6 percent. They pay interest on December 1 and June 1. The bonds are issued on September 1, 2007, at 100 plus three months' accrued interest.

Instructions

Prepare the necessary journal entries in general journal form on:

a. September 1, 2007, to record the issuance of the bonds.

b. December 1, 2007, to record the first semiannual interest payment on the bond issue.

c. December 31, 2007, to record interest expense accrued through year-end.

d. June 1, 2008, to record the second semiannual interest payment.

e. What was the prevailing market rate of interest on the date that the bonds were issued? Explain.

PROBLEM 10.6B

Amortization of a Bond Discount and Premium

On September 1, 2007, Bella Company issued $5 million in 10-year, 12 percent bonds payable. Interest is payable semiannually on March 1 and September 1. Bond discounts and premiums are amortized at each interest payment date and at year-end. The company's fiscal year ends at December 31.

Instructions

a. Make the necessary adjusting entries at December 31, 2007, and the journal entry to record the payment of bond interest on March 1, 2008, under each of the following assumptions:

  1. The bonds were issued at 98. (Round to the nearest dollar.)

  2. The bonds were issued at 104. (Round to the nearest dollar.)

b. Compute the net bond liability at December 31, 2008, under assumptions **1** and **2** above. (Round to the nearest dollar.)

c. Under which of the above assumptions, **1** or **2**, would the investor's effective rate of interest be higher? Explain.

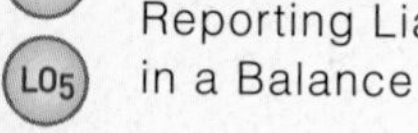

PROBLEM 10.7B
Reporting Liabilities in a Balance Sheet

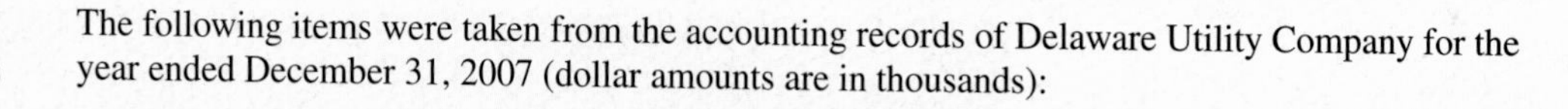

The following items were taken from the accounting records of Delaware Utility Company for the year ended December 31, 2007 (dollar amounts are in thousands):

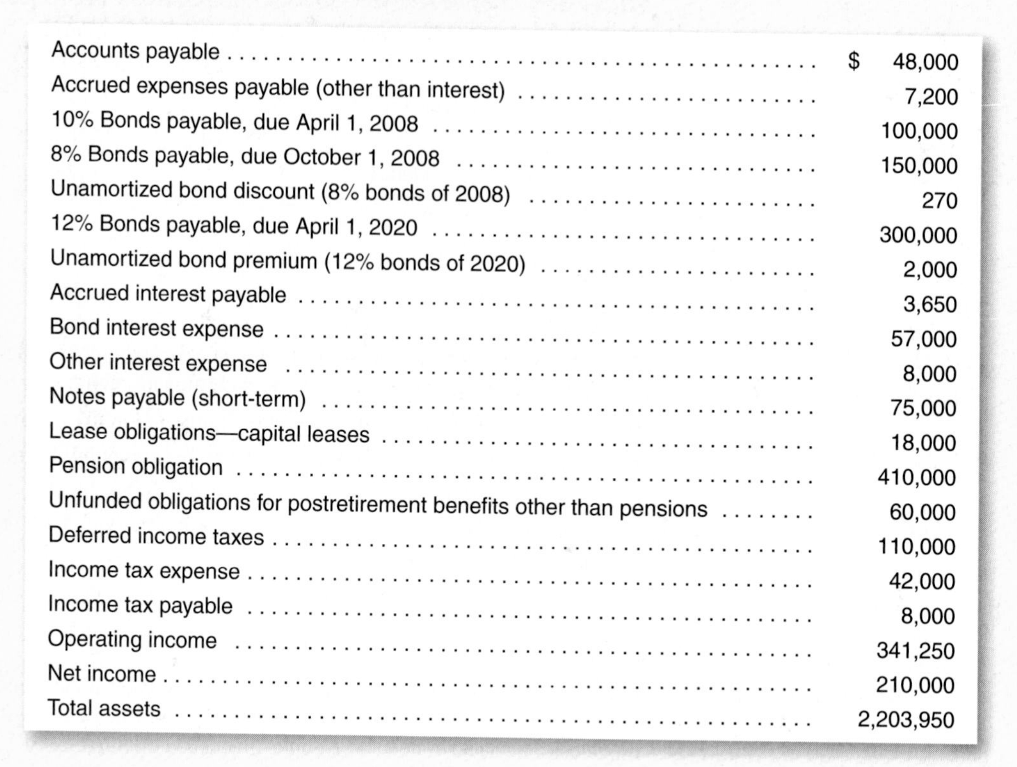

Item	Amount
Accounts payable	$ 48,000
Accrued expenses payable (other than interest)	7,200
10% Bonds payable, due April 1, 2008	100,000
8% Bonds payable, due October 1, 2008	150,000
Unamortized bond discount (8% bonds of 2008)	270
12% Bonds payable, due April 1, 2020	300,000
Unamortized bond premium (12% bonds of 2020)	2,000
Accrued interest payable	3,650
Bond interest expense	57,000
Other interest expense	8,000
Notes payable (short-term)	75,000
Lease obligations—capital leases	18,000
Pension obligation	410,000
Unfunded obligations for postretirement benefits other than pensions	60,000
Deferred income taxes	110,000
Income tax expense	42,000
Income tax payable	8,000
Operating income	341,250
Net income	210,000
Total assets	2,203,950

Other Information

1. The 10 percent bonds due in April 2008 will be refinanced in March 2008 through the issuance of $125,000 in 9 percent, 20-year bonds payable.
2. The 8 percent bonds due October 1, 2008, will be repaid entirely from a bond sinking fund.
3. Delaware Utility is committed to total lease payments of $11,000 in 2008. Of this amount, $6,000 is applicable to operating leases, and $5,000 to capital leases. Payments on capital leases will be applied as follows: $2,000 to interest expense and $3,000 to reduction in the capitalized lease payment obligation.
4. Delaware Utility's pension plan is fully funded with an independent trustee.
5. The obligation for postretirement benefits other than pensions consists commitment to maintain health insurance for retired workers. During 2008, Delaware Utility will fund $16,000 of this obligation.
6. The $8,000 in income taxes payable relates to income taxes levied in 2007 and must be paid on or before March 15, 2008. No portion of the deferred tax liability is regarded as a current liability.

Instructions

a. Using this information, prepare the current liabilities and long-term liabilities sections of a classified balance sheet as of December 31, 2007. (Within each classification, items may be listed in any order.)

b. Explain briefly how the information in each of the six numbered paragraphs affected your presentation of the company's liabilities.

c. Compute as of December 31, 2007, the company's (**1**) debt ratio and (**2**) interest coverage ratio.

d. Based solely on information stated in this problem, indicate whether this company appears to be an outstanding, medium, or poor long-term credit risk. State specific reasons for your conclusion.

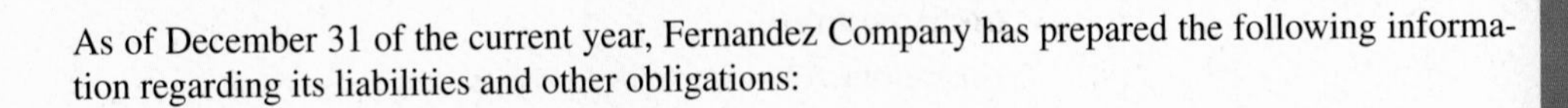

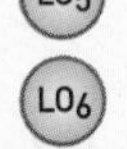

PROBLEM 10.8B

Financial Statement Presentation of Liabilities

LO1, LO5, LO6, LO8, LO10

As of December 31 of the current year, Fernandez Company has prepared the following information regarding its liabilities and other obligations:

Notes payable, of which $20,000 will be repaid within the next 12 months	$150,000
Interest expense that will result from existing liabilities over the next 12 months	175,000
Lawsuit pending against the company, in which $500,000 is claimed in damages. Legal counsel can make no reasonable estimate of the company's ultimate liability at this time	400,000
20-year bond issue that matures in two years. The entire amount will be repaid from a bond sinking fund	750,000
Accrued interest on the 20-year bond issue as of the balance sheet date	22,500
Three-year commitment to John Higgins as chief financial officer at a salary of $170,000 per year	510,000
Note payable due within 90 days (but that is expected to be extended for an additional 18 months)	90,000
Cash deposits from customers for goods and services to be delivered over the next nine months	268,000
Income taxes, of which $145,000 are currently payable and the remainder deferred indefinitely	260,000

Instructions

a. Prepare a listing of the company's current and long-term liabilities as they should be presented in the company's December 31 balance sheet.

b. Briefly explain why you have excluded any of the listed items in your listing of current and long-term liabilities.

Critical Thinking Cases

CASE 10.1

The Nature of Liabilities

LO1, LO10

Listed below are eight publicly owned corporations and a liability that regularly appears in each corporation's balance sheet:

a. **Wells Fargo & Company** (banking): Deposits: interest bearing

b. **The New York Times Company**: Unexpired subscriptions

c. **The Hollywood Park Companies** (horse racing): Outstanding mutuel tickets

d. **American Greetings** (greeting cards and gift wrap products manufacturer): Sales returns

e. **Wausau Paper Mills Company**: Current maturities of long-term debt

f. **Club Med., Inc.** (resorts): Amounts received for future vacations

g. **Apple Computer, Inc.**: Accrued marketing and distribution

h. **General Motors Corporation**: Postretirement costs other than pensions

Instructions

Briefly explain what you believe to be the nature of each of these liabilities, including how the liability arose and the manner in which it is likely to be discharged.

CASE 10.2

Factors Affecting Bond Prices

LO5 through LO7

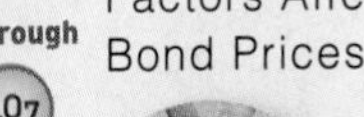

Abbott Labs has two bond issues outstanding with the following characteristics:

Issue	Interest Rate	Maturity	Current Price
A	6%	2008	115
B	6%	2012	118

Instructions

Answer the following questions regarding these bond issues:

a. Which issue, A or B, has the higher effective rate of interest? How can you tell?

b. Assume that the bonds of both issues have face values of $1,000 each. How much total interest does each bond from *issue A* provide investors in *12 months*? How much total interest does each bond from *issue B* provide investors in *12 months*?

c. Note that both issues are by the same company, have the same contract rate of interest, and have identical credit ratings. In view of these facts, explain the current price difference of each issue.

CASE 10.3
Loss Contingencies

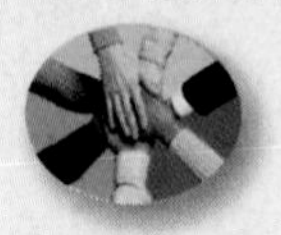

Discuss each of the following situations, indicating whether the situation is a loss contingency that should be recorded or disclosed in the financial statements of Aztec Airlines. If the situation is not a loss contingency, explain how (if at all) it should be reported in the company's financial statements. (Assume that all dollar amounts are material.)

Instructions

a. Aztec estimates that $700,000 of its accounts receivable will prove to be uncollectible.

b. The company's president is in poor health and has previously suffered two heart attacks.

c. As with any airline, Aztec faces the risk that a future airplane crash could cause considerable loss.

d. Aztec is being sued for $10 million for failing to adequately provide for passengers whose reservations were canceled as a result of the airline overbooking certain flights. This suit will not be resolved for a year or more.

CASE 10.4
Off-Balance Sheet Financing

Delta Airlines leases most of its commercial aircraft and is currently committed to pay approximately $10 billion in future lease obligations. However, **Delta** reports only $390 million of these commitments as long-term capital lease obligations in the liability section of its balance sheet. The remaining commitments are structured as operating leases. Obligations to pay future operating lease obligations are not reported in the balance sheet as liabilities. Instead, cash outlays for operating leases appear only in the income statement as expenses as the obligations come due.

Delta's recent balance sheet reports assets totaling $21.8 billion. The company's long-term liabilities, including its capital lease obligations, total approximately $21 billion, and the stockholders' equity section of its balance sheet reveals a $5.8 billion deficit balance.

Instructions

a. If **Delta** had structured its aircraft commitments as capital leases instead of operating leases, how would the appearance and potential interpretation of its balance sheet have changed?

b. Is it ethical for **Delta** to structure only $390 million of its aircraft commitments as capital leases and the remaining approximately $9.6 billion as off-balance sheet financing? Defend your answer.

c. With regard to **Delta**'s lease obligations, why is it important for investors and creditors to read and understand the footnotes accompanying the airline's financial statements?

through
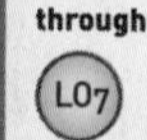

BUSINESSWEEK CASE 10.5
Bond Prices and Interest Rate

In her April 21, 2003, *BusinessWeek* article, "The Risks of Rising Rates," Susan Scherreik writes:

> For the past three years, bond investors have profited mightily from the decline in interest rates. Falling rates lifted the prices of fixed-income securities, and adding that capital gain to the interest payments provided a neat total return. But now, with yields so low, the big fear in the bond market is that interest rates will soon reverse course and start rising.

Instructions

Explain why rising interest rates would have a negative impact on the bond market. Which bond investments would suffer the most, those maturing in three years or less, or those maturing in 30 years or more? Defend your answer.

INTERNET CASE 10.6

Credit Ratings on Bonds

The Internet provides a wealth of information concerning long-term liabilities, bond ratings, and credit markets. Visit the home page of **Bonds-Online** at the following Internet address:

www.bonds-online.com

Instructions

a. Go to the "Educated Investor Center" section of the Web site and click on "Bond Basics." Define in your own words the following terms: convertible bonds, junk bonds, zero coupon bonds.

b. Return to the home page. On the left side of the screen, locate the heading that provides current market information. Summarize two things you learned about the current financial markets by studying this information.

c. Again return to the home page. Select the option "Financial Career Center" and select the job classification that interests you the most. Browse the jobs listed under that classification and select a specific job you would apply for were you currently qualified. Write a brief description why this job interests you.

Internet sites are time and date sensitive. It is the purpose of these exercises to have you explore the Internet. You may need to use the Yahoo! search engine **http://www.yahoo.com** *(or another favorite search engine) to find a company's current Web address.*

Answers to Self-Test Questions

1. a, b **2.** a, b, d **3.** a, d **4.** a, c, d **5.** a, b, c, d **6.** a, b, c, d
7. a, c **8.** c **9.** a, b **10.** d **11.** c

Stockholders' Equity: Paid-In Capital

Learning Objectives

AFTER STUDYING THIS CHAPTER, YOU SHOULD BE ABLE TO:

LO1 Discuss the advantages and disadvantages of organizing a business as a corporation.

LO2 Distinguish between publicly owned and closely held corporations.

LO3 Explain the rights of stockholders and the roles of corporate directors and officers.

LO4 Account for paid-in capital and prepare the equity section of a corporate balance sheet.

LO5 Contrast the features of common stock with those of preferred stock.

LO6 Discuss the factors affecting the market price of preferred stock and common stock.

LO7 Explain the significance of book value and market value of capital stock.

LO8 Explain the purpose and effects of a stock split.

LO9 Account for treasury stock transactions.

SEARS, ROEBUCK & COMPANY

Companies frequently invest large amounts of cash in the securities of other companies. These investments often earn returns in the form of interest, dividends, and capital appreciation. While it is common for businesses to purchase shares of stock in other companies, would a company ever purchase shares of its own stock on the open market?

The answer is a definite yes. Each year, for example, **Sears, Roebuck & Company** spends billions of dollars to repurchase shares of its own stock. Referred to as treasury shares, these shares of stock have been repurchased by the company, which intends to resell them in the future. One of the reasons companies such as **Sears** purchase their own shares of stock is to satisfy the requirements of stock option plans. Stock option plans allow employees to purchase stock in the company they work for, often at a favorable price. Because these plans are an important part of employees' compensation, the company is required to have shares available to meet its commitment under these plans. **Sears** is not unique in this regard. In fact, it is difficult to find a major corporation that does not engage in treasury stock transactions on a regular basis, and in many cases the primary motivation is for stock option plans.

In this chapter we explore numerous issues related to stockholders' equity, including treasury stock transactions, preferred stock, and stock splits. We also discuss why businesses incorporate and describe the factors that influence the price of their stock in the open market.

Corporations

The corporate form is the organization of choice for many businesses—large and small. The owners of a corporation are called **stockholders**. In many small corporations, there are only one or two stockholders. But in large corporations, such as IBM and AT&T, there are literally millions of stockholders.

A **corporation** is the only form of business organization recognized under the law as a *separate legal entity*, with rights and responsibilities *apart from those of its owners*. The assets of a corporation belong to the corporation *itself*, not to the stockholders. The corporation is responsible for its own debts and must pay income taxes on its earnings. As a separate legal entity, a corporation has status in court; it may enter into contracts, and it may sue and be sued as if it were a person. The major advantages and disadvantages of this form of business organization are summarized in Exhibit 11–1.

Exhibit 11–1

ADVANTAGES AND DISADVANTAGES OF THE CORPORATE FORM

LO1 **Discuss the advantages and disadvantages of organizing a business as a corporation.**

Advantages	Disadvantages
1. *Stockholders are not personally liable for the debts of a corporation.* This concept is called *limited personal liability* and often is cited as the greatest advantage of the corporate form of organization.	1. *Heavy taxation.* Corporate earnings are subject to **double taxation**. First, the corporation must pay *corporate income taxes* on its earnings. Second, stockholders must pay *personal income taxes* on any portion of these earnings that they receive as *dividends*.
2. *Transferability of ownership.* Ownership of a corporation is evidenced by *transferable shares of stock*, which may be sold by one investor to another.	2. *Greater regulation.* Corporations are affected by state and federal laws to a far greater extent than are unincorporated businesses.
3. *Professional management.* The stockholders own a corporation, but they do not manage it on a daily basis. To administer the affairs of the corporation, the stockholders elect a *board of directors*. The directors, in turn, hire professional managers to run the business.	3. *Cost of formation.* An unincorporated business can be formed at little or no cost. Forming a corporation, however, normally requires the services of an attorney.
4. *Continuity of existence.* Changes in the names and identities of stockholders do not directly affect the corporation. Therefore, the corporation may continue its operations *without disruption*, despite the retirement or death of individual stockholders.	4. *Separation of ownership and management.* If stockholders do not approve of the manner in which management runs the business, they may find it difficult to take the united action necessary to remove that management group.

What types of businesses choose the corporate form of organization? The answer, basically, is *all kinds*. When we think of corporations, we often think of large, well-known companies such as ExxonMobil, General Motors, and Procter & Gamble. Indeed, almost all large businesses are organized as corporations. Limited shareholder liability, transferability of ownership, professional management, and continuity of existence make the corporation the best form of organization for pooling the resources of a great many equity investors. Not all corporations, however, are large and publicly owned. Many small businesses are organized as corporations.

WHY BUSINESSES INCORPORATE

Businesses incorporate for many reasons, but the two of greatest importance are (1) limited shareholder liability and (2) transferability of ownership.

We have previously discussed the concept of **limited personal liability**. This simply means that shareholders are not personally responsible for the debts of the corporation. Thus, if the corporation becomes illiquid, the most that a stockholder usually can lose is the amount of his or her equity investment.

Another special feature of the corporation is the *transferability of ownership*—the idea that ownership is represented by transferable shares of **capital stock**. For a small, family-owned business, this provides a convenient means of gradually transferring ownership and control of the business from one generation to the next. For a large company, it makes ownership of the business a *highly liquid investment*, which can be purchased and sold in organized securities exchanges.[1]

YOUR TURN **You as a Loan Officer**

GOTCHA! is a small business that manufactures board games. It is one of the many business ventures of Gayle Woods, who is very wealthy and one of your bank's most valued customers. She has done business with your bank for more than 20 years, and the balance in her personal checking, savings, and money market accounts normally exceeds $500,000. GOTCHA! is organized as a corporation, and Woods is the only stockholder.

GOTCHA! has applied for a $200,000 line of credit, which it intends to use to purchase copyrights to additional board games. Although the company is profitable, its most recent balance sheet shows total assets of only $52,000, including $47,000 in copyrights. The corporation has just under $3,000 in liabilities and over $49,000 in stockholders' equity.

Do you consider GOTCHA! a good credit risk? Would you make the loan? Under what conditions?

(See our comments on the Online Learning Center Web site.)

PUBLICLY OWNED CORPORATIONS

The capital stock of most large corporations can be bought and sold (traded) through organized securities exchanges. As these shares are available for purchase by the general public, these large corporations are said to be **publicly owned**.

Distinguish between publicly owned and closely held corporations. LO2

Far more people have a financial interest in the shares of publicly owned companies than one might expect. If you purchase the stock of such a corporation, you become a stockholder with a *direct* ownership interest—that is, *you* are a stockholder. But mutual funds and pension funds invest heavily in the stocks of many publicly owned corporations. Thus, if you invest in a mutual fund or you are covered by a pension plan, you probably have an *indirect* financial interest in the stocks of many publicly owned corporations.

Corporations whose shares are *not* traded on any organized stock exchanges are said to be **closely held**. Because there is no organized market for buying and selling their shares, these corporations usually have relatively few stockholders. Often, a closely held corporation is owned by one individual or by the members of one family.

Publicly Owned Corporations Face Different Rules

The government seeks to protect the interests of the public. Therefore, publicly owned corporations are subject to more regulation than those that are closely held. For example, publicly owned corporations are *required by law* to:

- Prepare and issue quarterly and annual financial statements in conformity with generally accepted accounting principles. (These statements are **public information**.)
- Have their annual financial statements audited by an independent firm of certified public accountants.
- Comply with federal securities laws, which include both criminal penalties and civil liability for deliberately or carelessly distributing misleading information to the public.
- Submit much of their financial information to the Securities and Exchange Commission for review.

[1] These securities exchanges include, among others, the New York Stock Exchange, the National Association of Securities Dealers' Automated Quotations (NASDAQ), the Tokyo Stock Exchange, and Mexico's Bolsa. Collectively, stock exchanges often are described simply as *the stock market*.

Closely held corporations normally are exempt from these requirements. Our discussions will focus primarily on the accounting and reporting issues confronting *publicly owned companies.*

Formation of a Corporation

In the United States, a corporation is brought into existence under the laws of a particular state. The state in which the corporation is formed is called the **state of incorporation**.

The state of incorporation is not necessarily where the corporation does business. Rather, a state often is selected because of the leniency of its laws regulating corporate activities. Indeed, many corporations conduct most—sometimes all—of their business activities *outside* the state in which they are incorporated.

The first step in forming a corporation is to obtain a *corporate charter* from the state of incorporation. To obtain this charter, the organizers of the corporation submit an application called the *articles of incorporation.* Once the charter is obtained, the stockholders in the new corporation hold a meeting to elect a *board of directors* and to pass *bylaws* that will govern the corporation's activities. The directors in turn hold a meeting at which the top corporate officers and managers are appointed.

Organization Costs Forming a corporation is more costly than starting a sole proprietorship. The costs may include, for example, attorneys' fees, incorporation fees paid to the state, and other outlays necessary to bring the corporation into existence. Conceptually, organization costs are an *intangible asset* that will benefit the corporation over its entire life. As a practical matter, however, most corporations expense those costs immediately, even though they are often spread over a five-year period for income tax purposes.

Thus you will seldom see organization costs in the balance sheet of a publicly owned corporation. They have long since been recognized as an expense.

LO3 Explain the rights of stockholders and the roles of corporate directors and officers.

Rights of Stockholders A corporation is owned collectively by its stockholders. Each stockholder's ownership interest is determined by the number of *shares* that he or she owns. Assume that a corporation issues 10,000 shares of capital stock. If you own 1,000 of these shares, you own *10 percent* of the corporation. If you acquire another 500 shares from another stockholder, you will own *15 percent.*

Each stockholder, or the stockholder's brokerage firm, receives from the corporation a **stock certificate** indicating the number of shares he or she owns.

The ownership of capital stock in a corporation usually carries the following basic rights:

1. *To vote for directors and on certain other key issues.* A stockholder has one vote for each share owned. The issues on which stockholders may vote are specified in the corporation's bylaws. Any stockholder—or group of stockholders—that owns *more than 50 percent* of the capital stock has the power to elect the board of directors and to set basic corporate policies. Therefore, these stockholders control the corporation.
2. *To participate in any dividends declared by the board of directors.* Stockholders in a corporation *may not* make withdrawals of company assets, as may the owners of unincorporated businesses. However, the directors may elect to distribute some or all of the earnings of a profitable corporation to its stockholders in the form of cash *dividends.* Dividends can be distributed only after they have been formally *declared* (authorized) by the board of directors. Dividends are paid to all shareholders in proportion to the number of shares owned.
3. *To share in the distribution of assets if the corporation is liquidated.* When a corporation ends its existence, the creditors must first be paid in full. The shareholders have a residual interest, and any remaining assets are divided among the shareholders in proportion to the number of shares owned.

Stockholders' meetings usually are held once each year. At these meetings, stockholders may ask questions of management and vote on certain issues. In large corporations, these meetings usually are attended by relatively few people—often less than 1 percent of the company's stockholders. Prior to these meetings, however, the management group requests that stockholders who do not plan to attend send in *proxy statements*, granting management the voting rights associated with their shares.

Functions of the Board of Directors The primary functions of the **board of directors** are to set corporate policies and to protect the interests of the stockholders. Specific duties of the directors include hiring corporate officers and setting those officers' salaries, declaring dividends, and reviewing the findings of both internal auditors and independent auditors.

The board of a large corporation always includes several members of top management. In recent years, increasing importance has been attached to the inclusion of "outside" directors. The term *outside directors* refers to individuals who are *not* officers of the corporation and, therefore, bring an *independent perspective* to the board.

Functions of the Corporate Officers The top management of a corporation is appointed (hired) by the board of directors. These individuals are called the *corporate officers.* Individual stockholders *do not* have the right to transact corporate business *unless they have been properly appointed to a managerial post.*

The top level of management usually includes a chief executive officer (CEO) or president, a chief financial officer (CFO) or controller, a treasurer, and a secretary. In addition, a vice president usually oversees each functional area, such as sales, personnel, and production.

The responsibilities of the CFO (controller), treasurer, and secretary are most directly related to the accounting phase of business operation. The CFO is responsible for the maintenance of adequate internal control and for the preparation of accounting records and financial statements. Such specialized activities as budgeting, tax planning, and preparation of tax returns are usually placed under the CFO's jurisdiction. The *treasurer* has custody of the company's funds and is generally responsible for planning and controlling the company's cash position. The treasurer's department also has responsibility for relations with the company's financial institutions and major creditors.

The *secretary* represents the corporation in many contractual and legal matters and maintains minutes of the meetings of directors and stockholders. Other responsibilities of the secretary are to coordinate the preparation of the annual report and to manage the investor relations department. In small corporations, one officer frequently acts as both secretary and treasurer.

The organization chart in Exhibit 11–2 indicates lines of authority extending from stockholders to the directors to the CEO and other officers.

Exhibit 11–2 CORPORATE ORGANIZATION CHART

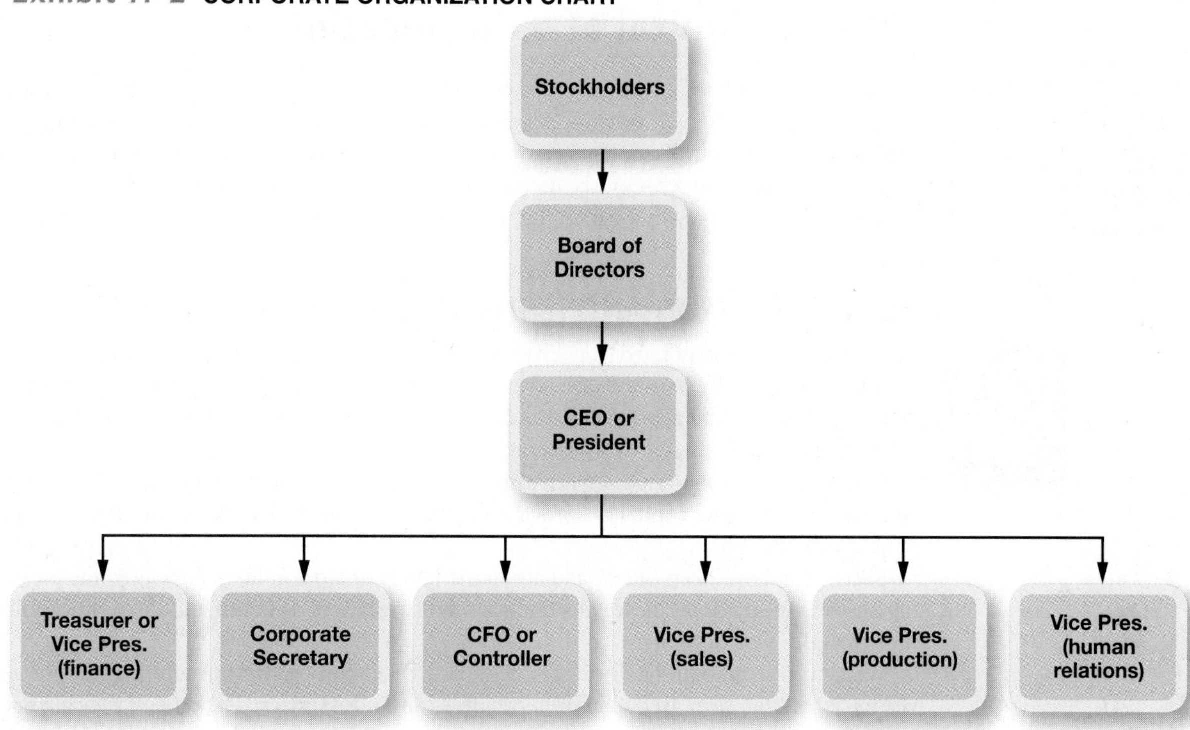

STOCKHOLDER RECORDS IN A CORPORATION

A large corporation with shares listed on the New York Stock Exchange usually has millions of shares outstanding and hundreds of thousands of stockholders. Each day many stockholders sell their shares; the buyers of these shares become new members of the company's family of stockholders.

A corporation must have an up-to-date record of the names and addresses of this constantly changing group of stockholders so that it can send dividend checks, financial statements, and voting forms to the right people.

Stockholders Subsidiary Ledger When there are numerous stockholders, it is not practical to include a separate account for each stockholder in the general ledger. Instead, a single controlling account entitled Capital Stock appears in the general ledger, and a **stockholders subsidiary ledger** is maintained. This ledger contains an account for each individual stockholder. Entries in the stockholders subsidiary ledger are made in *number of shares*, rather than in dollars. Thus each stockholder's account shows the number of shares owned and the dates of acquisitions and sales. This record enables the corporation to send each stockholder a single dividend check, even though the stockholder may have acquired shares on different dates.

Stock Transfer Agent and Stock Registrar Many large, publicly owned corporations use an independent **stock transfer agent** and a **stock registrar** to maintain their stockholder records and to establish strong internal control over the issuance of stock certificates. These transfer agents and registrars are usually banks or trust companies. When stock certificates are transferred from one owner to another, the old certificates are sent to the transfer agent, who cancels them, makes the necessary entries in the stockholders subsidiary ledger, and prepares a new certificate for the new owner of the shares. This new certificate then must be registered with the stock registrar before it represents valid and transferable ownership of stock in the corporation.

Small, closely held corporations generally do not use the services of independent registrars and transfer agents. In these companies, the stockholder records usually are maintained by a corporate officer. To prevent the accidental or fraudulent issuance of an excessive number of stock certificates, the corporation should require that each certificate be signed by at least two designated corporate officers.

Paid-In Capital of a Corporation

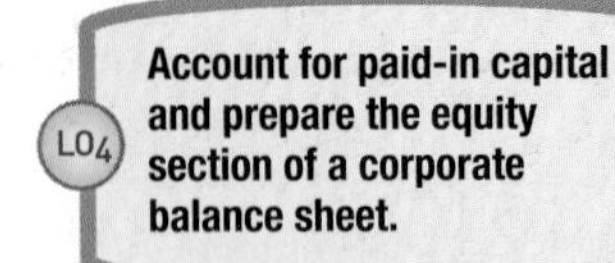

Stockholders' equity of a corporation is normally increased in one of two ways: (1) from contributions by investors in exchange for capital stock—called **paid-in capital** or **contributed capital**—and (2) from the retention of profits earned by the corporation over time—called **retained earnings**. As previously noted, our focus in this chapter is primarily on issues related to paid-in capital. In Chapter 12, we shift our attention to issues concerning retained earnings.

AUTHORIZATION AND ISSUANCE OF CAPITAL STOCK

The articles of incorporation specify the number of shares that a corporation has been *authorized* to issue by the state of incorporation. Issues of capital stock that will be sold to the general public must be approved by the federal Securities and Exchange Commission, as well as by state officials.

Corporations normally obtain authorization for more shares than they initially plan to issue. This way, if more capital is needed later, the corporation already has the authorization to issue additional shares.

Shares that have been *issued* and are in the hands of stockholders are called the *outstanding* shares. At any time, these outstanding shares represent 100 percent of the stockholders' investment in the corporation.

When a large amount of stock is to be issued, most corporations use the services of an investment banking firm, frequently referred to as an **underwriter**. The underwriter guarantees the issuing corporation a specific price for the stock and makes a profit by selling the shares to the investing public at a slightly higher price. The corporation records the issuance of the stock at the net amount received from the underwriter. The use of an underwriter assures the corporation that the entire stock issue will be sold without delay and that the entire amount of funds to be raised will be available on a specific date.

The price that a corporation will seek for a new issue of stock is based on such factors as (1) expected future earnings and dividends, (2) the financial strength of the company, and (3) the current state of the investment markets. If the corporation asks too high a price, it simply will not find an underwriter or other buyers willing to purchase the shares.

State Laws Affect the Balance Sheet Presentation of Stockholders' Equity The number of different accounts that a corporation must use in the stockholders' equity section of its balance sheet is determined largely by state laws. We have seen that corporations use separate stockholders' equity accounts to represent (1) contributed capital, or paid-in capital, and (2) earned capital, or retained earnings. Up to this point we have assumed that all paid-in capital is presented in a single account entitled Capital Stock. But this often is not the case.

Some corporations issue several *different types* (or classes) of capital stock. In these situations, a separate account is used to indicate each type of stock outstanding. A legal concept called *par value* also affects the balance sheet presentation of paid-in capital.

Par Value **Par value** (or **stated value**) represents the **legal capital** per share—the amount below which stockholders' equity cannot be reduced, except by losses from business operations (or by special legal action). Par value, therefore, may be regarded as a minimum cushion of equity capital existing for the protection of creditors.

Because of the legal restrictions associated with par value, state laws require corporations to show separately in the stockholders' equity section of the balance sheet the par value of shares issued. This special balance sheet presentation has led some people to believe that par value has some special significance. In many corporations, however, the par value of the shares issued is a small portion of total stockholders' equity.

A corporation may set the par value of its stock at $1 per share, $5 per share, or any other amount that it chooses. Most large corporations set the par value of their common stocks at nominal amounts, such as 1 cent per share or $1 per share. The par value of the stock is *not an indication of its market value*; the par value merely indicates the amount per share to be entered in the Capital Stock account. The stocks of Ford and AT&T have par values of $1, and Microsoft's stock has a par value of only one-tenth of a cent. The market value of each of these securities is far above its par value.

Issuance of Par Value Stock Authorization of a stock issue does not bring an asset into existence, nor does it give the corporation any capital. The obtaining of authorization from the state for a stock issue merely affords a legal opportunity to obtain assets through the sale of stock. Additional capital is created for the company only when that stock is sold to stockholders.

When par value stock is *issued*, the Capital Stock account is credited with the par value of the shares issued, regardless of whether the issuance price is more or less than par. Assuming that 50,000 shares of $2 par value stock have been authorized and that 10,000 of these authorized shares are sold at a price of $2 each, Cash would be debited and Capital Stock would be credited for $20,000. When stock is sold for more than par value, the Capital Stock account is credited with the par value of the shares issued, and a separate account, **Additional Paid-in Capital**, is credited for the excess of selling price over par. If, for example, our 10,000 shares were issued at a price of $10 per share, the entry would be:

Cash	100,000	
Capital Stock		20,000
Additional Paid-in Capital		80,000
Issued 10,000 shares of $2 par value stock at a price of $10 a share.		

Stockholders' investment in excess of par value

The additional paid-in capital does not represent a profit to the corporation. It is part of the *invested capital*, and it is added to the capital stock in the balance sheet to show the total paid-in capital. The stockholders' equity section of the balance sheet follows. (The $150,000 in retained earnings is assumed in order to have a complete illustration.)

Stockholders' equity:	
Capital stock, $2 par value; authorized, 50,000 shares; issued and outstanding, 10,000 shares	$ 20,000
Additional paid-in capital	80,000
Total paid-in capital	$100,000
Retained earnings	150,000
Total stockholders' equity	$250,000

If stock is issued by a corporation for *less* than par, the account Discount on Capital Stock should be debited for the difference between the issuance price and the par value. A discount on capital stock reduces, rather than increases, the amount of stockholders' equity in the balance sheet. The issuance of stock at a discount is seldom encountered because it is illegal in many states.

In some cases, stock is issued in exchange for assets other than cash. When this occurs, the appropriate asset account is debited (for example, Inventory or Land) and the stock accounts are credited as if the stock had been sold for cash. Establishing a value for recording a transaction of this type is sometimes difficult, but should be based on either the fair value of the assets received or the stock issued, whichever can be more objectively determined.

No-Par Stock Some states allow corporations to issue stock without designating a par or stated value. When this "no-par" stock is issued, the *entire issue price* is credited to the Capital Stock account and is viewed as legal capital not subject to withdrawal.

COMMON STOCK AND PREFERRED STOCK

The account title Capital Stock is widely used when a corporation has issued only *one type* of stock. In order to appeal to as many investors as possible, however, some corporations issue several types (or classes) of capital stock, each providing investors with different rights and opportunities.

LO5 **Contrast the features of common stock with those of preferred stock.**

The basic type of capital stock issued by every corporation often is called **common stock**. Common stock possesses the traditional rights of ownership—voting rights, participation in dividends, and a residual claim to assets in the event of liquidation. When the rights of stockholders are modified, the term **preferred stock** is normally used to describe the resulting type of capital stock. A few corporations issue two or more classes of preferred stock, with each class having distinctive features designed to appeal to a particular type of investor.

The following stockholders' equity section illustrates the balance sheet presentation for a corporation having both preferred and common stock. As before, a retained earnings amount is assumed so we can provide a complete example.

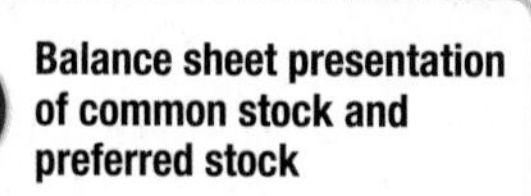

Balance sheet presentation of common stock and preferred stock

Stockholders' equity:	
9% cumulative preferred stock, $100 par value, authorized 100,000 shares, issued and outstanding 50,000 shares	$ 5,000,000
Common stock, $5 par value, authorized 3 million shares, issued and outstanding 2 million shares	10,000,000
Additional paid-in capital:	
Preferred stock	500,000
Common stock	20,000,000
Total paid-in capital	$35,500,000
Retained earnings	14,000,000
Total stockholders' equity	$49,500,000

CHARACTERISTICS OF PREFERRED STOCK

Most preferred stocks have the following distinctive features:

1. Preference over common stock as to dividends.
2. Cumulative dividend rights.
3. Preference over common stock as to assets in event of the liquidation of the company.
4. Callable at the option of the corporation.
5. No voting power.

Another important but less common feature of some preferred stocks is a clause permitting the *conversion* of preferred stock into common stock at the option of the holder. Preferred stocks vary widely with respect to the special rights and privileges granted. Careful study of the terms of the individual preferred stock contract is a necessary step in the evaluation of any preferred stock.

CASE IN POINT

Specific preferred stock characteristics can affect the reporting location on the balance sheet. For example, preferred stock that is mandatorily redeemable by the issuing company is required by international accounting standards to be classified as a liability (rather than an equity) on the balance sheet. In 2003, the FASB passed Statement of Financial Accounting Standard No. 150, thus changing U.S. GAAP reporting requirements from allowing redeemable preferred stock to be reported in the equity section to requiring it to be reported in the liability section, consistent with international standards.

Stock Preferred as to Dividends

Corporations often make periodic cash payments, called **dividends**, to stockholders.[2] Dividends normally represent a distribution of accumulated profit and therefore cannot exceed the amount of a corporation's retained earnings.

Preferred stock is said to have dividend preference because preferred stock investors are entitled to receive a specified amount each year before any dividend is paid to common stock investors. The specified dividend may be stated as a dollar amount, such as $5 per share. Some preferred stocks, however, state the specified dividend as a *percentage of par value.* For example, a share of preferred stock with a par value of $100 and a dividend preference of *9 percent* must provide a $9 dividend each year to each share of preferred stock before any dividends can be paid on the common shares.

The holders of preferred stock have no guarantee that they will always receive the indicated dividend. A corporation is obligated to pay dividends to stockholders only when the board of directors declares a dividend. Dividends must be paid on preferred stock before anything is paid to the common stockholders, but if the corporation is not prospering, it may decide not to pay any dividends at all. For a corporation to pay dividends, profits must be earned and cash must be available.

Cumulative Preferred Stock

The dividend preference carried by most preferred stocks is a *cumulative* one. If all or any part of the regular dividend on the preferred stock is omitted in a given year, the amount omitted is said to be *in arrears* and must be paid in a subsequent year before any dividend can be paid on the common stock.

Assume that a corporation is organized on January 1, 2005, with 10,000 shares of $8 preferred stock and 50,000 shares of common stock. If the preferred stock is *noncumulative*, the $8 per share dividend does not carry forward if it is not paid each year. On the other hand, if the preferred stock is *cumulative*, the $8 per share dividend carries forward to future years if it

[2] In Chapter 12, we will discuss specific accounting issues related to cash dividends and other forms of distributions to stockholders. For the purposes of this chapter, dividends may be viewed simply as the distribution to stockholders of accumulated profits that reduce both cash and retained earnings.

is not paid and the accumulated amount must be paid before any dividend can be paid on common stock. Assume that the $8 preferred dividend is paid in 2005, a partial dividend of $2 per share is paid on preferred stock in 2006, and no preferred dividend is paid in 2007. Following is an analysis of the status of the preferred dividend at the end of 2007.

	2005	2006	2007
If preferred stock is noncumulative			
Dividend paid	$80,000	$20,000	—
Dividend in arrears		Not applicable	
If preferred stock is cumulative			
Dividend paid	$80,000	$20,000	—
Dividends in arrears	—	$60,000	$140,000

In the case of noncumulative preferred stock, the unpaid dividend does not carry forward to future years and has no effect on the company's ability to pay dividends on common stock in the future. In the case of cumulative preferred stock, however, any unpaid dividend on preferred stock carries forward and must be paid before dividends can be paid on common stock. In 2006, the partial unpaid dividend of $60,000 would have to have been paid before any dividend could have been paid on common stock. At the end of 2007, this amount has grown to $140,000 (the $60,000 carried forward from 2006, plus the $80,000 that was not paid in 2007). Before a dividend could have been paid on common stock in 2007, the $60,000 preferred dividend *in arrears* from 2006 and the current preferred dividend of $80,000 for 2007 would have to have been paid. Before a dividend could be paid on common stock in 2008, the $140,000 in arrears from 2006 and 2007 *and* the $80,000 dividend on preferred for 2008 would have to be paid (total of $220,000). From this illustration, you can see why the label "cumulative" is used—the dividend accumulates from year to year and must be paid before any dividend can be paid on common stock.

Dividends in arrears are not included among the liabilities of a corporation, because no liability exists until a dividend is declared by the board of directors. The amount of any dividends in arrears on preferred stock is an important factor to investors and should always be *disclosed.* This disclosure is usually made by a note accompanying the balance sheet such as the following:

Note 6: Dividends in arrears

As of December 31, 2007, dividends on the $8 cumulative preferred stock were in arrears to the extent of $14 per share and amounted in total to $140,000.

In 2008, we shall assume that the company earned large profits, has available cash, and wished to pay dividends on both the preferred and common stocks. Before paying a dividend on the common, the corporation must pay the $140,000 in arrears on the cumulative preferred stock *plus* the regular $8 per share applicable to the current year. The preferred stockholders would, therefore, receive a total of $220,000 in dividends in 2008 ($22 per share); the board of directors would then be free to declare dividends on the common stock.

Other Features of Preferred Stock To add to the attractiveness of preferred stock as an investment, corporations sometimes offer a *conversion privilege* that entitles the preferred stockholders to exchange their shares for common stock at a stipulated ratio. If the corporation prospers, its common stock will probably rise in market value, and dividends on the common stock will probably increase. The investor who buys a convertible preferred stock rather than common stock has greater assurance of regular dividends. In addition, through the conversion privilege, the investor is assured of an opportunity to share in any substantial increase in value of the company's common stock.

The three primary elements of stockholders' equity for most companies are common stock, preferred stock, and retained earnings. While important, other elements that we learn about later in this chapter, as well as in Chapter 12, are typically smaller in amount than these three primary elements. The relationship of common stock, preferred stock, and retained earnings is depicted in Exhibit 11–3.

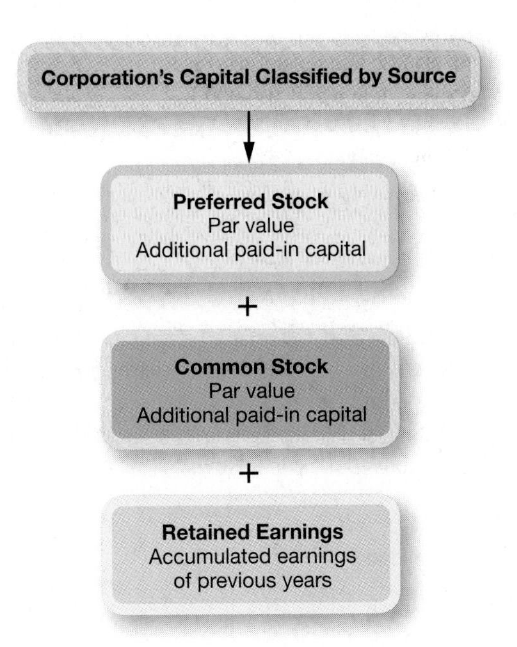

Exhibit 11–3
PRIMARY SOURCES OF CORPORATE EQUITY

BOOK VALUE PER SHARE OF COMMON STOCK

Because the equity of each stockholder in a corporation is determined by the number of shares he or she owns, an accounting measurement of interest to some stockholders is book value per share of common stock. **Book value per share** is the amount of net assets represented by each share of stock. The term *net assets* means total assets minus total liabilities; in other words, net assets are equal to *total stockholders' equity.* Thus, in a corporation that has issued common stock only, the book value per share is computed by dividing total stockholders' equity by the number of shares outstanding.

For example, assume that a corporation has 4,000 shares of common stock outstanding and the stockholders' equity section of the balance sheet is as follows:

Stockholders' equity:	
Common stock, $1 par value (4,000 shares issued and outstanding)	$ 4,000
Additional paid-in capital	40,000
Retained earnings	76,000
Total stockholders' equity	$120,000

The book value per share is *$30*; it is computed by dividing the stockholders' equity of $120,000 by the 4,000 shares of outstanding stock.

Book Value When a Company Has Both Preferred and Common Stock

Book value is usually computed only for common stock. If a company has both preferred and common stock outstanding, the computation of book value per share of common stock requires two steps. First, the amount assigned to preferred stock and any *dividends in arrears* are deducted from total stockholders' equity. Second, the remaining amount of stockholders' equity is divided by the number of common shares outstanding to determine book value per common share. This procedure reflects the fact that the common stockholders are the *residual owners* of the corporate entity.

How much is book value per share?

To illustrate the computation of book value per share when preferred stock is outstanding, assume that the stockholders' equity of Hart Company at December 31 is as follows:

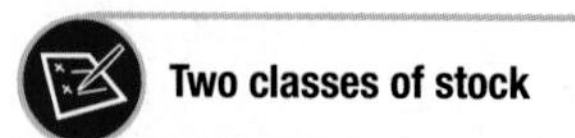

Stockholders' equity:	
8% preferred stock, $100 par value, 10,000 shares authorized, issued, and outstanding	$1,000,000
Common stock, $10 stated value, authorized 100,000 shares, issued and outstanding 50,000 shares	500,000
Additional paid-in capital: common stock	750,000
Total paid-in capital	$2,250,000
Retained earnings	130,000
Total stockholders' equity	$2,380,000

Because of a weak cash position, Hart Company has paid no dividends during the current year. As of December 31, dividends in arrears on the cumulative preferred stock total *$80,000.*

All the equity belongs to the common stockholders, except the $1,000,000 applicable to the preferred stock and the $80,000 of dividends in arrears on preferred stock. The calculation of book value per share of common stock is as follows:

Total stockholders' equity		$2,380,000
Less: Equity of preferred stockholders:		
Par value of preferred stock	$1,000,000	
Dividends in arrears	80,000	1,080,000
Equity of common stockholders		$1,300,000
Number of common shares outstanding		50,000
Book value per share of common stock ($1,300,000 ÷ 50,000 shares)		$26

In a statement of cash flows, transactions with the stockholders of a corporation are classified as *financing activities.* Thus the issuance of capital stock for cash represents a *receipt* from financing activities. Distributions of cash to stockholders—including the payment of cash dividends—represent a cash *outlay*, which is also classified under financing activities.

Transactions with owners do not always have an immediate effect on cash flows. Consider an exchange of the corporation's capital stock for a noncash asset, such as land. Cash is not increased or decreased by this event. These types of noncash transactions are described in a special schedule that accompanies the statement of cash flows.

Market Value

After shares of stock have been issued, they may be sold by one investor to another. The price at which these shares change hands represents the *current market price* of the stock. This market price may differ substantially from such amounts as par value, the original issue price, and the current book value. Which is the most relevant amount? That depends on your point of view.

After shares are issued, they belong to the stockholder, not to the issuing corporation. Thus changes in the market price of these shares directly affect the financial position of the stockholder, but not that of the issuing company. This concept explains why the issuing company and stockholders apply different accounting principles to the same outstanding shares.

Accounting by the Issuer From the viewpoint of the issuing company, outstanding stock represents an amount invested in the company by its owners at a particular date. While the market value of the stockholders' investment may change, the amount of resources that they originally invested does not change.

Thus the company issuing stock records the issue price—that is, the proceeds received from issuing the stock—in its paid-in capital accounts. The balances in these accounts remain unchanged unless (1) more shares are issued or (2) outstanding shares are permanently retired (for example, preferred stock is called or stock is purchased on the open market and then retired).

Accounting by the Investor From the investor's point of view, shares owned in a publicly owned company are an asset, usually called Marketable Securities.

To the investor, the current market value of securities owned is more relevant than the original issue price—or than the securities' par values or book values. The market value indicates what the securities are worth today. Changes in market value directly affect the investor's liquidity, financial position, and net worth. For these reasons, investors show investments in marketable securities at current market value in their balance sheets.

CASE IN POINT

In a single day, the market price of IBM's capital stock dropped over $31 per share, falling from $135 to $103.25. Of course, this was not a typical day. The date, October 19, 1987, will long be remembered as "Black Monday." On this day, stock prices around the world suffered the greatest one-day decline in history.

Royalty-Free/CORBIS/DIL

Stocks listed on the New York Stock Exchange lost about 20 percent of their value in less than six hours. Given that the annual dividends on these stocks averaged about 2 percent of their market value, this one-day market loss was approximately equal to the loss by investors of all dividend revenue for about 10 years.

How did this disastrous decline in IBM's stock price affect the balance sheet of IBM? Actually, it didn't. IBM's stock isn't owned by IBM—it is owned by the company's stockholders.

Because market prices are of such importance to investors, we will briefly discuss the factors that most affect the market prices of preferred and common stocks.

MARKET PRICE OF PREFERRED STOCK

Discuss the factors affecting the market price of preferred stock and common stock. LO6

Investors buy preferred stocks primarily to receive the dividends that these shares pay. Thus dividend rate is one important factor in determining the market price of a preferred stock. A second important factor is *risk.* In the long run, a company must be profitable enough to pay dividends. If there is a distinct possibility that the company will *not* operate profitably and pay dividends, the price of its preferred stock will probably decline.

A third factor greatly affecting the value of preferred stocks is the level of *interest rates.* What happens to the market price of an 8 percent preferred stock, originally issued at a par value of $100, if government policies and other factors cause long-term interest rates to rise to, say, 15 percent or 16 percent? If investments offering a return of 16 percent with the same level of risk are readily available, investors will no longer pay $100 for a share of preferred stock that provides a dividend of only $8 per year. Thus the market price of the preferred stock will fall to about half of its original issue price, or about $50 per share. At this market price, the stock offers a 16 percent return (called the **dividend yield**) to an investor purchasing the stock.

However, if the prevailing long-term interest rates should again decline to the 8 percent range, the market price of an 8 percent preferred stock should rise to approximately par value. In summary, the market price of preferred stock *varies inversely with interest rates.* As interest rates rise, preferred stock prices decline; as interest rates fall, preferred stock prices rise.

MARKET PRICE OF COMMON STOCK

Prevailing interest rates also affect the market price of common stock. However, dividends paid to common stockholders are not fixed in amount. Both the amount of the dividend and the market price of the stock may increase dramatically if the corporation is successful.

Alternatively, if the company is unsuccessful, the common stockholders may not even recover their original investment. Therefore, the most important factors in the market price of common stock are *investors' expectations* as to the future profitability of the business and the *risk* that this level of profitability may not be achieved.

Shares that have been issued belong to the stockholders, not to the issuing corporation. Therefore, changes in the market price of the shares do not affect the financial statements of the corporation, and these changes are not recorded in the corporation's accounting records.

BOOK VALUE AND MARKET PRICE

To some extent, *book value* is used in evaluating the reasonableness of the market price of a stock. However, it must be used with caution; the fact that a stock is selling at less than book value does not necessarily indicate a bargain.

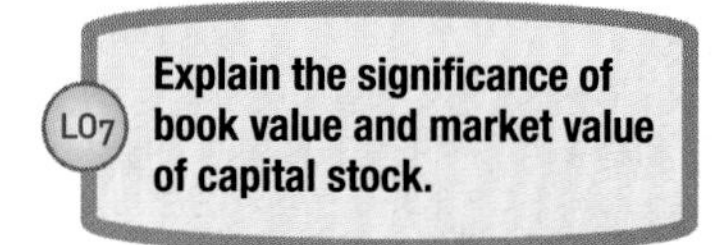

Book value is a historical concept, representing the amounts invested by stockholders plus the amounts earned and retained by the corporation. If a stock is selling at a price *above* book value, investors believe that management has created a business worth more than the historical cost of the resources entrusted to its care. This, in essence, is the sign of a successful corporation.

On the other hand, if the market price of a stock is *less than* book value, investors believe that the company's resources are worth less than their cost while under the control of current management. Thus the relationship between book value and market price is one measure of investors' *confidence in a company's management.*

STOCK SPLITS

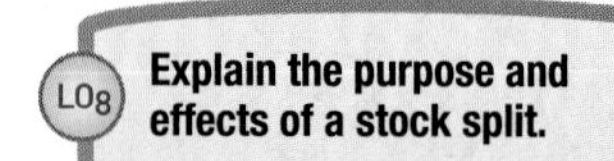

Over time, the market price of a corporation's common stock may increase in value so much that it becomes too expensive for many investors. When this happens, a corporation may *split* its stock by increasing the number of its common shares outstanding. The purpose of a **stock split** is to reduce substantially the market price of the company's common stock, with the intent of making it more affordable to investors.

Don Farrall/Getty Images/DIL

For example, assume that Felix Corporation has outstanding 1 million shares of $10 par value common stock. The market price is currently $90 per share. To make the stock more affordable, the corporation decides to increase the number of outstanding shares from 1 million to 2 million. This action is called a *2-for-1 stock split.* A stockholder who owned 100 shares of the stock before the split will own 200 shares after the split. Since the number of outstanding shares has been doubled without any change in total assets or total stockholders' equity, the market price of the stock should drop immediately from $90 to approximately $45 per share. In splitting its stock, a corporation is required to reduce the par value per share in proportion to the size of the split. As this was a 2-for-1 split, the company must reduce the par value of the stock from $10 to $5 per share. Had it been a 4-for-1 split, the par value would have been reduced from $10 to $2.50 per share and the stock price would have declined to approximately 25 percent of its former amount.

A stock split does not change the balance of any accounts in the balance sheet; consequently, the transaction is recorded merely by a *memorandum entry.* For Felix Corporation, this memorandum entry might read as follows:

Sept. 30 Memorandum: Issued additional 1 million shares of common stock in a 2-for-1 stock split. Par value reduced from $10 per share to $5 per share.

The description of common stock also is changed in the balance sheet to reflect the lower par value and the greater number of shares outstanding.

Another form of stock distribution to current stockholders is a stock dividend. While stock dividends are similar to stock splits in some respects, they are much smaller in size and have a different intent. Because they are important considerations in a company's dividend policy, we defer the detailed coverage of stock dividends to Chapter 12.

Treasury Stock

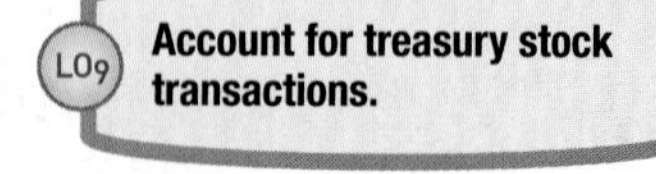

Treasury stock is defined as shares of a corporation's own capital stock that have been issued and later *reacquired by the issuing company* but that have not been canceled or permanently retired. Treasury shares may be held indefinitely or may be issued again at any time. Shares of capital stock held in the treasury are not entitled to receive dividends, to vote, or to share in assets upon dissolution of the company. In the computation of earnings per share, shares held in the treasury are not regarded as outstanding shares.

Stock option plans are an important part of employee compensation for many companies. They permit employees to purchase stock in the company, often at advantageous prices, and are a means of creating employee loyalty to the company. Treasury stock purchases are one means by which the company can have available the shares of stock needed to satisfy the requirement of stock option plans to issue shares of stock to employees. Rather than increasing the total number of outstanding shares, thereby reducing or diluting the ownership of each share, the company purchases shares of stock from the current owners and then sells the same shares a second time to its employees. Stock option plans are an important purpose for treasury stock purchases for many companies. Buying back a company's own stock also reduces the supply of shares available and may increase the market value of the stock.

RECORDING PURCHASES OF TREASURY STOCK

Purchases of treasury stock are usually recorded by debiting the Treasury Stock account with the cost of the stock. For example, if Riley Corporation reacquires 1,600 shares of its own $5 par stock at a price of $90 per share, the entry is as follows:

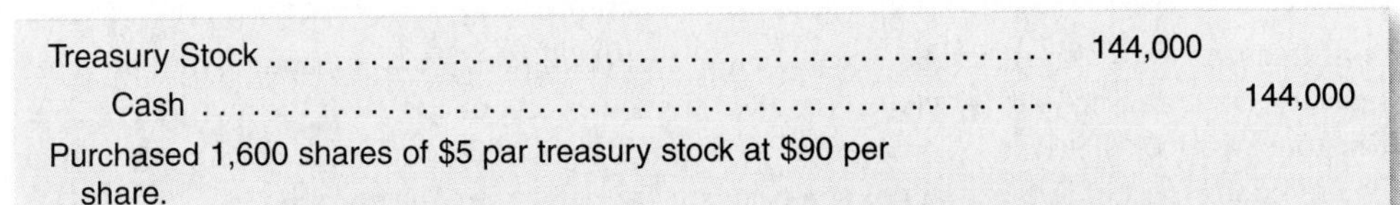

Treasury Stock	144,000	
Cash		144,000
Purchased 1,600 shares of $5 par treasury stock at $90 per share.		

Note that the Treasury Stock account is debited for the *cost* of the shares purchased, not their par value. Treasury stock is a *contra-equity* account. When treasury stock is purchased, the corporation is eliminating part of its stockholders' equity by a payment to one or more stockholders. The purchase of treasury stock should be regarded as a *reduction of stockholders' equity*, not as the acquisition of an asset. For this reason, the Treasury Stock account appears in the balance sheet as a deduction in the stockholders' equity section. Treasury shares are both authorized and issued, but while they are held by the issuing company, they are *not* outstanding.

The presentation of treasury stock in Riley Corporation's balance sheet appears as follows, based on assumed numbers (except for treasury stock):

Stockholders' equity:	
Common stock, $5 par value, authorized 250,000 shares, issued 100,000 shares (of which 1,600 are held in treasury)	$ 500,000
Additional paid-in capital: common stock	900,000
Total paid-in capital	$1,400,000
Retained earnings	600,000
Subtotal	$2,000,000
Less: Treasury stock (1,600 shares of common, at $90 cost)	144,000
Total stockholders' equity	$1,856,000

REISSUANCE OF TREASURY STOCK

When treasury shares are reissued, the Treasury Stock account is credited for the cost of the shares reissued and Additional Paid-in Capital from Treasury Stock Transactions is debited or credited for any *difference* between cost and the reissue price. To illustrate, assume that 1,000 of the treasury shares acquired by Riley Corporation at a cost of $90 per share are now reissued at a price of $115 per share. The entry to record the reissuance of these shares at a price above cost is:

Cash	115,000	
Treasury Stock		90,000
Additional Paid-in Capital: Treasury Stock		25,000
Sold 1,000 shares of treasury stock, which cost $90,000, at a price of $115 per share.		

Treasury stock reissued at a price above cost

The $25,000 of additional paid-in capital resulting from the reissuance of Riley's treasury stock is reported in the stockholders' equity section of the company's balance sheet. It appears immediately after additional paid-in capital from common stock, as shown here:

Stockholders' equity:	
Common stock, $5 par value, authorized 250,000 shares, issued 100,000 shares (of which 600 are held in treasury)	$ 500,000
Additional paid-in capital:	
Common stock	900,000
Treasury stock	25,000
Total paid-in capital	$1,425,000
Retained earnings	600,000
Subtotal	$2,025,000
Less: Treasury stock (600 shares of common, at $90 cost)	54,000
Total stockholders' equity	$1,971,000

If treasury stock is reissued at a price below cost, additional paid-in capital from previous treasury stock transactions is reduced (debited) by the excess of cost over the reissue price. To illustrate, assume that Riley Corporation reissues its remaining 600 shares of treasury stock (acquired at a cost of $90 per share) at a price of $75 per share. The entry is:

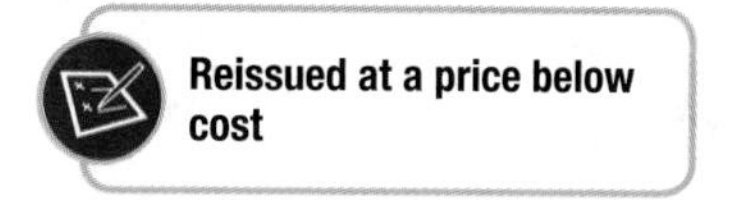

Cash	45,000	
Additional Paid-in Capital: Treasury Stock	9,000	
Treasury Stock		54,000
Sold 600 shares of treasury stock, which cost $54,000, at a price of $75 each.		

If there is no additional paid-in capital from previous treasury stock transactions, the excess of the cost of the treasury shares over the reissue price is recorded as a debit to the Additional Paid-in Capital: Common Stock account. If that account is not sufficient, Retained Earnings is debited.

Notice that *no gain or loss is recognized on treasury stock transactions*, even when the shares are reissued at a price above or below cost. A corporation earns profits by selling goods and services to outsiders, not by issuing or reissuing shares of its own capital stock. When treasury shares are reissued at a price above cost, the corporation receives from the new stockholder an amount of paid-in capital that is larger than the reduction in stockholders' equity that occurred when the corporation acquired the treasury shares. Conversely, if treasury shares are reissued at a price below cost, the corporation has less paid-in capital as a result of the purchase and reissuance of the shares.

Restriction of Retained Earnings for Treasury Stock Owned Purchases of treasury stock, like cash dividends, are distributions of assets to the stockholders in the corporation. Some states have a legal requirement that purchases of treasury stock cannot exceed the balance in the Retained Earnings account. Therefore, retained earnings usually are restricted for dividends by an amount equal to the excess over the *cost* of any shares held in the treasury.

STOCK BUYBACK PROGRAMS

Historically, most treasury stock transactions involved relatively small dollar amounts. Hence, the topic was not of much importance to investors or other users of financial statements. Some corporations have buyback programs, in which they repurchase large amounts of their own common stock. As a result of these programs, treasury stock has become a material item in the balance sheets of many corporations.

Stock buyback programs serve several purposes. By creating demand for the company's stock in the marketplace, these programs tend to increase the market value of the shares. Also, reducing the number of shares outstanding usually increases earnings per share. When stock prices are low, some companies find that they can increase earnings per share by a greater amount through repurchasing shares than through expanding business operations.

Transactions between the corporation and its stockholders are classified in the statement of cash flows as *financing activities.* When treasury stock is purchased, a financing cash *outflow* is reported in the statement of cash flows. When treasury stock is reissued, the amount of cash received is reported as a financing cash *inflow* in the statement of cash flows.

Because treasury stock transactions do not give rise to gains or losses, they have no effect on the corporation's net income. Any difference between the purchase price of the treasury stock and the cash received when it is reissued is reported as an increase or decrease in the corporation's paid-in capital.

Financial Analysis and Decision Making

The following information was taken from an annual report of **PepsiCo, Inc.** (in millions):

Net income	$ 3,568
Preferred stock dividends	$3
Average number of common shares outstanding	1,718
Average common stockholders' equity	$10,713
Average total stockholders' equity	$10,699

Several frequently used measures of profitability that are based, in part, on capital stock concepts covered in this chapter can be derived from the above figures:

Profitability Measure	Computation	Significance
Earnings per share	$\frac{\text{Net Income} - \text{Preferred Dividends}}{\text{Average Number of Common Shares Outstanding}}$	Net income applicable to each share of common stock
Return on common stockholders' equity	$\frac{\text{Net Income} - \text{Preferred Dividends}}{\text{Average Common Stockholders' Equity}}$	The appropriate rate of return earned on the common stockholders' equity when the company has both common and preferred stock
Return on equity	$\frac{\text{Net Income}}{\text{Average Total Equity}}$	The rate of return earned on the stockholders' equity in the business

Using the figures provided, **PepsiCo**'s three profitability measures would be:

Earnings per share:	($3,568 − $3) ÷ 1,718 shares = $2.07
Return on common shareholders' equity:	($3,568 − $3) ÷ $10,713 = 33%
Return on equity:	$3,568 ÷ $10,699 = 33%

You as a Financial Analyst

You are working for a stock market research firm and your boss has asked you to assess **PepsiCo**'s return on common shareholders' equity. How might you proceed?

(See our comments on the Online Learning Center Web site.)

Ethics, Fraud & Corporate Governance

A learning objective for this chapter is to understand the advantages of organizing a business as a corporation. Due to limited shareholder liability, transferability of ownership, professional management, and continuity of existence, virtually all large businesses are organized as corporations. Corporations often choose to go public in order to raise equity capital from many investors.

Unfortunately, the process of going public can be abused for the purpose of defrauding investors. A common scheme is the use of "shell companies" in a "pump-and-dump scheme." The Securities and Exchange Commission (SEC) proposes to define a shell company as a company with little or no operating activities, little or no assets, or assets consisting solely of cash and cash equivalents. Most commonly, a private operating business is combined with the public shell company in a reverse merger. In a reverse merger, the public shell company is the surviving entity but it is controlled by the shareholders of the previously private business. The rest of the "pump-and-dump scheme" works as follows: (1) the owners (promoters) of the company claim that the previously private business has high growth potential, (2) limited financial and other information on the combined company is filed with the SEC, (3) the owners (promoters) "pump" the stock through unduly positive press releases and other manipulative devices, (4) high-pressure sales tactics are often employed to get individuals to buy the stock, and (5) the owners (promoters) "dump" their stock at artificially high prices.

An example of a stock manipulation scheme using a shell company occurred in the case of **2DoTrade, Inc. 2DoTrade** was a public shell company when a group of promoters—including three individuals with previous securities law violations—secretly acquired over 99 percent of its shares. The promoters merged **2DoTrade** with a private company controlled by a convicted felon. The promoters "pumped" the stock by claiming that the company had import/export contracts worth more than $300 million and that the company was developing an antianthrax compound. In reality, the contracts were worthless because no antianthrax compound was in development, and one was never seriously contemplated. At one point during the "pump" campaign the market value of the company exceeded $46 million, yet the company had no assets and no revenue. The promoters then "dumped" their shares, reaping almost $2 million in profits.

The SEC has brought civil enforcement actions against the promoters of **2DoTrade**, and the FBI has arrested a number of the promoters as criminal charges have also been filed by the U.S. Justice Department. In order to stem the use of public shell companies in defrauding investors, the SEC has issued a rule proposal that would require much greater financial disclosures, including audited financial statements, when a previously private company acquires a public shell company in a reverse merger.

Concluding Remarks

In this chapter, we covered the aspects of stockholders' equity that result primarily from various transactions between the company and its stockholders, including the sale and repurchase of capital stock. We explored different characteristics of stock, including the unique features of preferred stock.

Another major source of stockholders' equity is the accumulated earnings of previous years that have been retained for purposes of expansion and meeting other business objectives. This is the subject of Chapter 12, which follows. While paid-in capital and retained earnings are two distinct aspects of stockholders' equity, they are closely related and, therefore, are virtually impossible to discuss totally independently of each other. For that reason, in this chapter there were occasional references to retained earnings. Similarly, in Chapter 12 you will find references to common and preferred stock, additional paid-in capital, treasury stock, and other aspects of stockholders' equity that we covered primarily in this chapter. Combining the content of Chapters 11 and 12, you will have a good working knowledge of stockholders' equity and how it fits together with assets and liabilities to form the basis for a company's balance sheet.

SUMMARY OF LEARNING OBJECTIVES

LO1 **Discuss the advantages and disadvantages of organizing a business as a corporation.** The primary advantages are no personal liability of stockholders for the debts of the business, the transferability of ownership shares, continuity of existence, the ability to hire professional management, and the relative ease of accumulating large amounts of capital. The primary disadvantages are double taxation of earnings and greater governmental regulation.

LO2 **Distinguish between publicly owned and closely held corporations.** The stock of publicly owned corporations is available for purchase by the general public, usually on an organized stock exchange. Stock in a closely held corporation, in contrast, is not available to the public.

Publicly owned corporations tend to be so large that individual stockholders seldom control the corporation; in essence, most stockholders in publicly owned companies are investors, rather than owners in the traditional sense. Closely held corporations usually are quite small, and one or two stockholders often do exercise control. Publicly owned corporations are subject to more government regulation than are closely held companies, and they must disclose to the public much information about their business operations.

LO3 **Explain the rights of stockholders and the roles of corporate directors and officers.** Stockholders in a corporation normally have the right to elect the board of directors, to share in dividends declared by the directors, and to share in the distribution of assets if the corporation is liquidated.

The directors formulate company policies, review the actions of the corporate officers, and protect the interests of the company's stockholders. Corporate officers are professional managers appointed by the board of directors to manage the business on a daily basis.

LO4 **Account for paid-in capital and prepare the equity section of a corporate balance sheet.** When capital stock is issued, appropriate asset accounts are debited for cash or the market value of the goods or services received in exchange for the stock. A capital stock account (which indicates the type of stock issued) is credited for the par value of the issued shares. Any excess of the market value received over the par value of the issued shares is credited to an Additional Paid-in Capital account.

The equity section of a corporate balance sheet shows for each class of capital stock outstanding (1) the total par value (legal capital) and (2) any additional paid-in capital. Together, these amounts represent the corporation's total paid-in capital. In addition, the equity section shows separately any earned capital—that is, retained earnings.

LO5 **Contrast the features of common stock with those of preferred stock.** Common stock represents the residual ownership of a corporation. These shares have voting rights and cannot be called. Also, the common stock dividend is not fixed in dollar amount—thus it may increase or decrease based on the company's performance.

Preferred stock has preference over common stock with respect to dividends and to distributions in the event of liquidation. This preference means that preferred stockholders must be paid in full before any payments are made to holders of common stock. The dividends on preferred stock usually are fixed in amount. In addition, the stock often has no voting rights. Preferred stocks sometimes have special features, such as being convertible into shares of common stock.

LO6 **Discuss the factors affecting the market price of preferred stock and common stock.** The market price of preferred stock varies inversely with interest rates. As interest rates rise, preferred stock prices decline; as interest rates fall, preferred stock prices rise. If a company's ability to continue the preferred dividend is in doubt, this may affect preferred stock prices.

Interest rates also affect the market price of common stock. However, common stock dividends are not fixed in amount. Both the amount of the dividend and the market value of the stock may fluctuate, based on the prosperity of the company. Therefore, the principal factor in the market price of common stock is investors' expectations as to the future profitability of the company.

LO7 **Explain the significance of book value and market value of capital stock.** Par value has the least significance. It is a legal concept, representing the amount by which stockholders' equity cannot be reduced except by losses. Intended as a buffer for the protection of creditors, it usually is so low as to be of little significance.

Book value per share is the net assets per share of common stock. This value is based on amounts invested by stockholders, plus retained earnings. It often provides insight into the reasonableness of market price.

To investors, market price is the most relevant of the three values. This is the price at which they can buy or sell the stock today. Changes in market price directly affect the financial position of the stockholder, but not of the issuing company. Therefore, market values do not appear in the equity section of the issuing company's balance sheet—but they are readily available in the daily newspaper and on the Internet.

LO8 **Explain the purpose and effects of a stock split.** When the market price of a corporation's common stock appreciates in value significantly, it may become too expensive for many investors. When this happens, the corporation may split its stock by increasing the number of its common shares outstanding. The purpose of a stock split is to reduce the market price of the company's common stock, with the intent of making it more affordable to investors. A stock split does not change the balance of any ledger account; consequently, the transaction is recorded merely by a memorandum entry.

LO9 **Account for treasury stock transactions.** Purchases of treasury stock are recorded by establishing a contra-equity account, Treasury Stock. No profit or loss is recorded when the treasury shares are reissued at a price above or below cost. Rather, any difference between the reissuance price and the cost of the shares is debited or credited to a paid-in capital account. While treasury stock transactions may affect cash flow, they have no effect on the net income of the corporation.

Key Terms Introduced or Emphasized in Chapter 11

Additional Paid-in Capital (p. 497) An account showing the amounts invested in a corporation by stockholders in excess of par value or stated value. In short, this account shows paid-in capital in excess of legal capital.

board of directors (p. 495) Persons elected by common stockholders to direct the affairs of a corporation.

book value per share (p. 501) The stockholders' equity represented by each share of common stock, computed by dividing common stockholders' equity by the number of common shares outstanding.

capital stock (p. 493) Transferable units of ownership in a corporation. A broad term that can refer to common stock, preferred stock, or both.

closely held corporation (p. 493) A corporation owned by a small group of stockholders. Not publicly owned.

common stock (p. 498) A type of capital stock that possesses the basic rights of ownership, including the right to vote. Represents the residual element of ownership in a corporation.

contributed capital (p. 496) The stockholders' equity that results from capital contributions by investors in exchange for shares of common or preferred stock. Also referred to as paid-in capital.

corporation (p. 492) A business organized as a legal entity separate from its owners. Chartered by the state with ownership divided into shares of transferable stock. Stockholders are not liable for debts of the corporation.

dividend yield (p. 503) The annual dividend paid to a share of stock, expressed as a percentage of the stock's market value. Indicates the rate of return represented by the dividend.

dividends (p. 499) Distribution of assets (usually cash) by a corporation to its stockholders. Normally viewed as a distribution of profits, dividends cannot exceed the amount of retained earnings. Must be formally declared by the board of directors and distributed on a per-share basis. ***Note:*** Stockholders *cannot* simply withdraw assets from a corporation at will.

double taxation (p. 492) The fact that corporate income is taxed to the corporation when earned and then again taxed to the stockholders when distributed as dividends.

legal capital (p. 497) Equal to the par value or stated value of capital stock issued. This amount represents a permanent commitment of capital by the owners of a corporation and cannot be removed without special legal action. Of course, it may be eroded by losses.

limited personal liability (p. 492) The concept that the owners of a corporation are not personally liable for the debts of the business. Thus stockholders' potential financial losses are limited to the amount of their equity investment.

paid-in capital (p. 496) The amounts invested in a corporation by its stockholders.

par value (or stated value) (p. 497) The legal capital of a corporation. Represents the minimum amount per share invested in the corporation by its owners and cannot be withdrawn except by special legal action.

preferred stock (p. 498) A class of capital stock usually having preferences as to dividends and in the distribution of assets in the event of liquidation.

public information (p. 493) Information that, by law, must be made available to the general public. Includes the quarterly and annual financial statements—and other financial information—about publicly owned corporations.

publicly owned corporation (p. 493) Any corporation whose shares are offered for sale to the general public.

retained earnings (p. 496) The element of owners' equity in a corporation that has accumulated through profitable business operations. Net income increases retained earnings; net losses and dividends reduce retained earnings.

state of incorporation (p. 494) The state in which the corporation is legally formed. This may or may not be the state in which the corporation conducts most or any of its business.

stock certificate (p. 494) A document issued by a corporation (or its transfer agent) as evidence of the ownership of the number of shares stated on the certificate.

stock registrar (p. 496) An independent fiscal agent, such as a bank, retained by a corporation to provide assurance against overissuance of stock certificates.

stock split (p. 504) An increase in the number of shares outstanding with a corresponding decrease in par value per share. The additional shares are distributed proportionately to all common shareholders. The purpose of a stock split is to reduce market price per share and encourage wider public ownership of the company's stock. A 2-for-1 stock split will give each stockholder twice as many shares as previously owned.

stock transfer agent (p. 496) A bank or trust company retained by a corporation to maintain its records of capital stock ownership and make transfers from one investor to another.

stockholders (p. 492) The owners of a corporation. The name reflects the fact that their ownership is evidenced by transferable shares of capital stock.

stockholders subsidiary ledger (p. 496) A record showing the number of shares owned by each stockholder.

treasury stock (p. 504) Shares of a corporation's stock that have been issued and then reacquired, but not canceled.

underwriter (p. 496) An investment banking firm that handles the sale of a corporation's stock to the public.

Demonstration Problem

The stockholders' equity section of Elmwood Corporation's balance sheet appears as follows:

Stockholders' equity:		
8% preferred stock, $100 par value, 200,000 shares authorized		$12,000,000
Common stock, $5 par value, 5,000,000 shares authorized		14,000,000
Additional paid-in capital:		
Preferred stock	$ 360,000	
Common stock	30,800,000	31,160,000
Retained earnings		2,680,000
Total stockholders' equity		$59,840,000

Instructions

On the basis of this information, answer the following questions and show any necessary supporting computations:

a. How many shares of preferred stock have been issued?
b. What is the total annual dividend requirement on the outstanding preferred stock?
c. How many shares of common stock have been issued?
d. What was the average price per share received by the corporation for its common stock?
e. What is the total amount of legal capital?
f. What is the total paid-in capital?
g. What is the book value per share of common stock? (Assume no dividends in arrears.)

Solution to the Demonstration Problem

a. 120,000 shares ($12,000,000 total par value, divided by $100 par value per share)
b. $960,000 (120,000 shares outstanding × $8 per share)
c. 2,800,000 shares ($14,000,000 total par value, divided by $5 par value per share)
d.

Par value of common shares issued	$14,000,000
Additional paid-in capital on common shares	30,800,000
Total issue price of common shares	$44,800,000
Number of common shares issued (part **c**)	2,800,000
Average issue price per share ($44,800,000 ÷ 2,800,000 shares)	$16

e. $26,000,000 ($12,000,000 preferred, $14,000,000 common)
f. $57,160,000 ($26,000,000 legal capital, plus $31,160,000 additional paid-in capital)
g.

Total stockholders' equity	$59,840,000
Less: Claims of preferred stockholders (120,000 shares × $100)	12,000,000
Equity of common stockholders	$47,840,000
Number of common shares outstanding (part **c**)	2,800,000
Book value per share ($47,840,000 ÷ 2,800,000 shares)	$17.09

Self-Test Questions

The answers to these questions appear on page 526.

1. When a business is organized as a corporation, which of the following statements is true?
   - **a.** Stockholders are liable for the debts of the business in proportion to their percentage ownership of capital stock.
   - **b.** Stockholders do *not* have to pay personal income taxes on dividends received, because the corporation is subject to income taxes on its earnings.
   - **c.** Fluctuations in the market value of outstanding shares of capital stock do *not* affect the amount of stockholders' equity shown in the balance sheet.
   - **d.** Each stockholder has the right to bind the corporation to contracts and to make other managerial decisions.
2. Western Moving Corporation was organized with authorization to issue 100,000 shares of $1 par value common stock. Forty thousand shares were issued to Tom Morgan, the company's founder, at a price of $5 per share. No other shares have yet been issued. Which of the following statements is true?
   - **a.** Morgan owns *40 percent* of the stockholders' equity of the corporation.
   - **b.** The corporation should recognize a $160,000 gain on the issuance of these shares.
   - **c.** If the balance sheet includes retained earnings of $50,000, total *paid-in* capital amounts to $250,000.
   - **d.** In the balance sheet, the Additional Paid-in Capital account will have a $160,000 balance, regardless of the profits earned or losses incurred since the corporation was organized.
3. Which of the following is *not* a characteristic of the *common stock* of a large, publicly owned corporation?
   - **a.** The shares may be transferred from one investor to another without disrupting the continuity of business operations.
   - **b.** Voting rights in the election of the board of directors.
   - **c.** A cumulative right to receive dividends.
   - **d.** After issuance, the market value of the stock is unrelated to its par value.
4. Tri-State Electric is a profitable utility company that has increased its dividend to *common* stockholders every year for 42 consecutive years. Which of the following is *least* likely to affect the market price of the company's *preferred* stock by a significant amount?
   - **a.** A decrease in long-term interest rates.
   - **b.** An increase in long-term interest rates.
   - **c.** The board of directors announces its intention to increase common stock dividends in the current year.
   - **d.** Whether or not the preferred stock carries a conversion privilege.
5. The following information is taken from the balance sheet and related disclosures of Maxwell, Inc.:

Total paid-in capital	$5,400,000
Outstanding shares:	
Common stock, $5 par value	100,000 shares
6% preferred stock, $100 par value	10,000 shares
Preferred dividends in arrears	2 years
Total stockholders' equity	$4,700,000

   Which of the following statements is (are) true? (For this question, more than one answer may be correct.)
   - **a.** The preferred dividends in arrears amount to $120,000 and should appear as a liability in the corporate balance sheet.
   - **b.** The book value per share of common stock is $35.
   - **c.** The stockholders' equity section of the balance sheet should indicate a deficit (negative amount in retained earnings) of $700,000.
   - **d.** The company has paid no dividend on its *common* stock during the past two years.
6. On December 10, 2006, Smitty Corporation reacquired 2,000 shares of its own $5 par value stock at a price of $60 per share. In 2007, 500 of the treasury shares are reissued at a price of $70 per share. Which of the following statements is correct?
   - **a.** The treasury stock purchased is recorded at cost and is shown in Smitty's December 31, 2006, balance sheet as an asset.
   - **b.** The two treasury stock transactions result in an overall net reduction in Smitty's stockholders' equity of $85,000.
   - **c.** Smitty recognizes a gain of $10 per share on the reissuance of the 500 treasury shares in 2007.
   - **d.** Smitty's stockholders' equity was increased by $110,000 when the treasury stock was acquired.

ASSIGNMENT MATERIAL

Discussion Questions

1. Why are large corporations often said to be *publicly owned*?
2. Distinguish between corporations and sole proprietorships in terms of the following characteristics:
   - **a.** Owners' liability for debts of the business.
   - **b.** Transferability of ownership interest.
   - **c.** Continuity of existence.
   - **d.** Federal taxation on income.
3. What are the basic rights of the owner of a share of corporate stock? In what way are these basic rights commonly modified with respect to the owner of a share of preferred stock?

4. Explain the meaning of the term *double taxation* as it applies to corporate profits.
5. Distinguish between *paid-in capital* and *retained earnings* of a corporation. Why is such a distinction useful?
6. Explain the significance of *par value*. Does par value indicate the reasonable market price for a share of stock? Explain.
7. Describe the usual nature of the following features as they apply to a share of preferred stock: (a) cumulative, and (b) convertible.
8. Why is noncumulative preferred stock often considered an unattractive form of investment?
9. State the balance sheet or income statement classification (asset, liability, stockholders' equity, revenue, or expense) of each of the following accounts:
   a. Cash (received from the issuance of capital stock).
   b. Organization Costs.
   c. Preferred Stock.
   d. Retained Earnings.
   e. Additional Paid-in Capital.
   f. Income Taxes Payable.
10. Explain the following terms:
    a. Stock transfer agent.
    b. Stockholders subsidiary ledger.
    c. Underwriter.
    d. Stock registrar.
11. What does *book value per share* of common stock represent? Does it represent the amount common stockholders would receive in the event of liquidation of the corporation? Explain briefly.
12. How is book value per share of common stock computed when a company has both preferred and common stock outstanding?
13. What would be the effect, if any, on book value per share of common stock as a result of each of the following independent events: (**a**) a corporation obtains a bank loan; (**b**) a dividend is declared (to be paid in the next accounting period)?
14. In the stock market crash of October 19, 1987, the market price of IBM's capital stock fell by over $31 per share. Explain the effects, if any, of this decline in share price on IBM's balance sheet.
15. Assume that you asked your stockbroker to purchase 100 shares of ExxonMobil Corporation stock. How would this transaction affect the financial statements of ExxonMobil? Explain.
16. What is the purpose of a *stock split*?
17. What is *treasury stock*? Why do corporations purchase their own shares? Is treasury stock an asset? How should it be reported in the balance sheet?
18. In many states, corporation law requires that retained earnings be restricted for dividend purposes to the extent of the cost of treasury shares. What is the reason for this legal rule?
19. The basic accounting equation for a corporation is **Assets = Liabilities + Stockholders' Equity**. Stockholders' equity is further divided into two categories: paid-in capital and retained earnings. What are the major transactions and other financial activities that impact the amount of paid-in capital of a corporation? Identify for each major type of transaction or activity whether it increases or decreases the amount of paid-in capital.
20. If you were going to start a corporation and expected to need to raise capital from several investors, would you include preferred stock in your capital structure? Why or why not? If your answer is that you would include preferred stock, what features would you incorporate into this class of stock?

Brief Exercises

BRIEF EXERCISE 11.1

Stockholders' Equity

Alpha Co. sold 10,000 shares of common stock, which has a par value of $10, for $13 per share. The company's balance in retained earnings is $75,000. Prepare the stockholders' equity section of the company's balance sheet.

BRIEF EXERCISE 11.2

Stockholders' Equity

Beta Co. sold 10,000 shares of common stock, which has a par value of $25, for $27 per share. The company also sold 1,000 shares of $100 par value preferred stock for $110. Assume the balance in retained earnings is $100,000. Prepare the stockholders' equity section of Beta's balance sheet.

BRIEF EXERCISE 11.3

Dividends on Preferred Stock

Zeta Co. has outstanding 100,000 shares of $100 par value cumulative preferred stock which has a dividend rate of 6 percent. The company has not declared any cash dividends on the preferred stock for the last three years. Calculate the amount of dividends in arrears on Zeta's preferred stock and briefly explain how this amount will be known to investors and creditors who may use the company's financial statements.

BRIEF EXERCISE 11.4

Dividends on Common and Preferred Stock

Mega, Inc., has common and 6 percent preferred stock outstanding as follows:

Preferred stock: 10,000 shares, $100 par value, cumulative

Common stock: 50,000 shares, $50 par value

The company declares a total dividend of $200,000. If the dividends on preferred stock are one year in arrears (in addition to the current year), how will the total dividend be divided between the common and preferred stock?

BRIEF EXERCISE 11.5

Dividends on Common and Preferred Stock

Walla Company has common and preferred stock outstanding as follows:

Common stock: 100,000 shares, $30 par value

8 percent preferred stock: 10,000 shares, $100 par value

Dividends on preferred stock have not been paid for the last three years (in addition to the current year). If the company pays a total of $120,000 in dividends, how much will the common stockholders receive per share if the preferred stock is not cumulative? How will your answer differ if the preferred stock is cumulative?

BRIEF EXERCISE 11.6

Book Value

Menza Company has stockholders' equity accounts as follows:

Common stock (100,000 shares @ $10 par value)	$1,000,000
Additional paid-in capital on common stock	750,000
Retained earnings	600,000

Calculate the amount of book value per share for common stock and summarize briefly what that figure means in relation to the current market value of the stock.

BRIEF EXERCISE 11.7

Book Value

Smalley, Inc., has preferred and common stock outstanding as follows:

$5 preferred stock, 40,000 shares @ $100 par value	$4,000,000
Common stock, 500,000 shares at $10 par value	5,000,000
Additional paid-in capital on common stock	800,000
Retained earnings	1,750,000

Calculate the book value on common stock, assuming preferred dividends are cumulative and are currently one year in arrears.

BRIEF EXERCISE 11.8

Stock Split

Smelling Company declared a 2-for-1 stock split on its common stock in order to intentionally reduce the market value of its stock so that it would be an attractive investment for a larger set of investors. The company's common stock is described as follows:

Common stock: 100,000 shares outstanding, $10 par value, originally sold at $12.50, current market price $50.

Describe the likely impact, if any, that the 2-for-1 stock split will have on **(a)** the number of shares outstanding, **(b)** the market price of the stock, and **(c)** the total stockholders' equity attributable to common stock.

BRIEF EXERCISE 11.9

Treasury Stock

Melcher, Inc., originally sold 100,000 shares of its $10 par value common stock at $25 per share. Several years later the company repurchased 10,000 of these shares at $55 per share. Melcher currently holds those shares in treasury. Prepare the company's stockholders' equity section of the balance sheet to reflect this information.

BRIEF EXERCISE 11.10

Treasury Stock

Reeves, Inc., sold 1,000,000 shares of $25 par value common stock at $30. It subsequently repurchased 100,000 of those shares at $50 per share and then sold 70,000 of those shares at $55. Calculate the total amount of stockholders' equity given the above transactions.

Exercises

EXERCISE 11.1

Form of Organization

LO1 through LO3

Assume that you have recently obtained your scuba instructor's certification and have decided to start a scuba diving school.

a. Describe the advantages and disadvantages of organizing your scuba diving school as a:

1. Sole proprietorship
2. Corporation

b. State your opinion about which form of organization would be best and explain the basis for your opinion.

EXERCISE 11.2

LO1 through LO9

Accounting Terminology

Listed below are 12 technical accounting terms discussed in this chapter:

Par value	Board of directors	Double taxation
Book value	Paid-in capital	Dividends in arrears
Market value	Preferred stock	Closely held corporation
Retained earnings	Common stock	Publicly owned corporation

Each of the following statements may (or may not) describe one of these technical terms. For each statement, indicate the term described, or answer "None" if the statement does not correctly describe any of the terms.

a. A major *disadvantage* of the corporate form of organization.

b. From investors' point of view, the most important value associated with capital stock.

c. Cash available for distribution to the stockholders.

d. The class of capital stock that normally has the most voting power.

e. A distribution of assets that may be made in future years to the holders of common stock.

f. A corporation whose shares are traded on an organized stock exchange.

g. Equity arising from investments by owners.

h. The element of stockholders' equity that is increased by net income.

i. Total assets divided by the number of common shares outstanding.

j. The class of stock for which market price normally rises as interest rates increase.

EXERCISE 11.3

LO4 LO5

Stockholders' Equity Section of a Balance Sheet

When Resisto Systems, Inc., was formed, the company was authorized to issue 5,000 shares of $100 par value, 8 percent cumulative preferred stock, and 100,000 shares of $2 stated value common stock.

Half of the preferred stock was issued at a price of $103 per share, and 70,000 shares of the common stock were sold for $13 per share. At the end of the current year, Resisto has retained earnings of $382,000.

a. Prepare the stockholders' equity section of the company's balance sheet at the end of the current year.

b. Assume Resisto Systems's common stock is trading at $24 per share and its preferred stock is trading at $107 per share at the end of the current year. Would the stockholders' equity section prepared in part **a** be affected by this additional information?

EXERCISE 11.4

LO4 LO5

Dividends: Preferred and Common

A portion of the stockholders' equity section from the balance sheet of Walland Corporation appears as follows:

Stockholders' equity:	
Preferred stock, 9% cumulative, $50 par, 40,000 shares authorized, issued, and outstanding	$2,000,000
Preferred stock, 12% noncumulative, $100 par, 8,000 shares authorized, issued, and outstanding	800,000
Common stock, $5 par, 400,000 shares authorized, issued, and outstanding	2,000,000
Total paid-in capital	$4,800,000

Assume that all the stock was issued on January 1 and that no dividends were paid during the first two years of operation. During the third year, Walland Corporation paid total cash dividends of $736,000.

a. Compute the amount of cash dividends paid during the third year to each of the three classes of stock.

b. Compute the dividends paid *per share* during the third year for each of the three classes of stock.

c. What was the average issue price of each type of preferred stock?

EXERCISE 11.5 Analyzing Stockholders' Equity

LO4 through LO7

The year-end balance sheet of Jackson Products, Inc., includes the following stockholders' equity section (with certain details omitted):

Stockholders' equity:	
Capital stock:	
7% cumulative preferred stock, $100 par value	$ 15,000,000
Common stock, $5 par value, 5,000,000 shares authorized, 4,000,000 shares issued and outstanding	20,000,000
Additional paid-in capital:	
Common stock	44,000,000
Retained earnings	64,450,000
Total stockholders' equity	$143,450,000

From this information, compute answers to the following questions:

a. How many shares of preferred stock have been issued?

b. What is the total amount of the annual dividends to which preferred stockholders are entitled?

c. What was the average issuance price per share of common stock?

d. What is the amount of legal capital and the amount of total paid-in capital?

e. What is the book value per share of common stock?

f. Is it possible to determine the fair market value per share of common stock from the stockholders' equity section above? Explain.

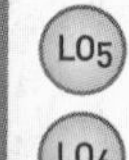

EXERCISE 11.6 Preferred Stock Alternatives

LO5 LO6

Walker, Inc., has the following capital structure:

Preferred stock—$25 par value, 10,000 shares authorized, 7,000 shares issued and outstanding	$175,000
Common stock—$10 par value, 100,000 shares authorized, 80,000 shares issued and outstanding	800,000
Total paid-in capital	$975,000
Retained earnings	550,000
Total stockholders' equity	$1,525,000

The number of issued and outstanding shares of both preferred and common stock have been the same for the last two years. Dividends on preferred stock are 8 percent of par value and have been paid each year the stock was outstanding except for the immediate past year. In the current year, management declares a total dividend of $50,000. Indicate the amount that will be paid to both preferred and common stockholders assuming (**a**) the preferred stock is not cumulative and (**b**) the preferred stock is cumulative.

EXERCISE 11.7 Reporting the Effects of Transactions

LO4 LO7

Three events pertaining to Lean Manufacturing Co. are described below.

a. Issued common stock for cash.

b. The market value of the corporation's stock increased.

c. Declared and paid a cash dividend to stockholders.

Indicate the immediate effects of the events on the financial measurements in the four columnar headings listed below. Use the code letters **I** for increase, **D** for decrease, and **NE** for no effect.

Event	Current Assets	Stockholders' Equity	Net Income	Net Cash Flow (from any source)
a				

EXERCISE 11.8 Computing Book Value (LO4 through LO7)

The following information is necessary to compute the net assets (stockholders' equity) and book value per share of common stock for Rothchild Corporation:

8% cumulative preferred stock, $100 par	$200,000
Common stock, $5 par, authorized 100,000 shares, issued 60,000 shares	300,000
Additional paid-in capital	452,800
Deficit (negative amount in retained earnings)	146,800
Dividends in arrears on preferred stock, 1 full year	16,000

a. Compute the amount of net assets (stockholders' equity).

b. Compute the book value per share of common stock.

c. Is book value per share (answer to part **b**) the amount common stockholders should expect to receive if Rothchild Corporation were to cease operations and liquidate? Explain.

EXERCISE 11.9 Recording Treasury Stock Transactions (LO9)

Johnston, Inc., engaged in the following transactions involving treasury stock:

Feb. 10 Purchased for cash 17,000 shares of treasury stock at a price of $25 per share.

June 4 Reissued 6,000 shares of treasury stock at a price of $33 per share.

Dec. 22 Reissued 4,000 shares of treasury stock at a price of $22 per share.

a. Prepare general journal entries to record these transactions.

b. Compute the amount of retained earnings that should be restricted because of the treasury stock still owned at December 31.

c. Does a restriction on retained earnings affect the dollar amount of retained earnings reported in the balance sheet? Explain briefly.

EXERCISE 11.10 Effects of a Stock Split (LO8)

The common stock of Fido Corporation was trading at $45 per share on October 15, 2006. A year later, on October 15, 2007, it was trading at $80 per share. On this date, Fido's board of directors decided to split the company's common stock.

a. If the company decides on a 2-for-1 split, at what price would you expect the stock to trade immediately after the split goes into effect?

b. If the company decides on a 4-for-1 split, at what price would you expect the stock to trade immediately after the split goes into effect?

c. Why do you think Fido's board of directors decided to split the company's stock?

EXERCISE 11.11 Treasury Stock Presentation (LO9)

Albert Company was experiencing financial difficulty late in the current year. The company's income was sluggish, and the market price of its common stock was tumbling. On December 21, the company began to buy back shares of its own stock in an attempt to boost its market price per share and to improve its earnings per share.

a. Is it unethical for a company to purchase shares of its own stock to improve measures of financial performance? Defend your answer.

b. Assume that the company classified the shares of treasury stock as short-term investments in the current asset section of its balance sheet. Is this appropriate? Explain.

EXERCISE 11.12 Authorized Stock (LO4)

The 2005 balance sheet for **Carnival Corporation** indicates that the company has 1,960 million shares of common stock authorized, of which approximately 640 million are outstanding.

a. How many additional shares of common stock could **Carnival Corporation** sell?

b. How are the shares that have not yet been issued included in the company's balance sheet? Do they represent an asset of the company?

EXERCISE 11.13 Common Stock and Treasury Stock (LO4, LO9)

Smiley, Inc., is authorized to sell 1,000,000 shares of $10 par value common stock and 50,000 shares of $100 par value 6 percent preferred stock. As of the end of the current year, the company has actually sold 550,000 shares of common stock at $12 per share and 40,000 shares of preferred stock at $110 per share. In addition, of the 550,000 shares of common that have been sold, 40,000 shares have been repurchased at $60 per share and are currently being held in treasury to be used to meet the future requirements of a stock option plan that the company intends to implement.

a. Prepare the general journal entries required to record all of the above transactions.

b. Prepare the stockholders' equity section of Smiley's balance sheet to reflect the transactions you have recorded.

LO9

EXERCISE 11.14
Treasury Stock and Stock Split

Twin Towns, Inc., was authorized to issue 200,000 shares of common stock and originally issued 100,000 shares of $10 par value stock at $18 per share. Subsequently, 25,000 shares were repurchased at $20, of which 10,000 were subsequently resold at $23.

Assume the company's retained earnings balance is $120,000.

a. Prepare the stockholders' equity section of Twin Towns's balance sheet, including all appropriate disclosures.

b. Briefly explain how the declaration and distribution of a 2-for-1 stock split subsequent to the above transactions would affect the stockholders' equity section you have prepared.

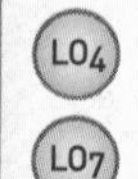

EXERCISE 11.15
Using the **Home Depot, Inc.**, Financial Statements

The financial statements of **Home Depot, Inc.**, appear in Appendix A of this text. These statements contain information describing the details of the company's stockholders' equity.

a. What is the par value of the company's common stock? Did the common stock originally sell at, above, or below par value? How do you know this?

b. For the most current year shown, how many shares of common stock are authorized? What is the meaning of "authorized shares"?

c. What is the total stockholders' equity amount for **Home Depot** for the most recent year reported? Does this figure mean that the total outstanding stock is actually worth this amount? Explain your answer.

Problem Set A

PROBLEM 11.1A
Stockholders' Equity in a Balance Sheet

Early in 2004, Robbinsville Press was organized with authorization to issue 100,000 shares of $100 par value preferred stock and 500,000 shares of $1 par value common stock. Ten thousand shares of the preferred stock were issued at par, and 170,000 shares of common stock were sold for $15 per share. The preferred stock pays an 8 percent cumulative dividend.

During the first four years of operations (2004 through 2007), the corporation earned a total of $1,085,000 and paid dividends of 75 cents per share in each year on its outstanding common stock.

Instructions

a. Prepare the stockholders' equity section of the balance sheet at December 31, 2007. Include a supporting schedule showing your computation of the amount of retained earnings reported. (Hint: Income increases retained earnings, whereas dividends decrease retained earnings.)

b. Are there any dividends in arrears on the company's preferred stock at December 31, 2007? Explain your answer.

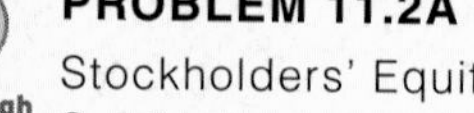

PROBLEM 11.2A
Stockholders' Equity Section

Waller Publications was organized early in 2002 with authorization to issue 20,000 shares of $100 par value preferred stock and 1 million shares of $1 par value common stock. All of the preferred stock was issued at par, and 300,000 shares of common stock were sold for $20 per share. The preferred stock pays a 10 percent cumulative dividend.

During the first five years of operations (2002 through 2006) the corporation earned a total of $4,460,000 and paid dividends of $1 per share each year on the common stock. In 2007, however, the corporation reported a net loss of $1,750,000 and paid no dividends.

Instructions

a. Prepare the stockholders' equity section of the balance sheet at December 31, 2007. Include a supporting schedule showing your computation of retained earnings at the balance sheet date. (Hint: Income increases retained earnings, whereas dividends and net losses decrease retained earnings.)

b. Draft a note to accompany the financial statements disclosing any dividends in arrears at the end of 2007.

c. Do the dividends in arrears appear as a liability of the corporation as of the end of 2007? Explain.

through

PROBLEM 11.3A
Stockholders' Equity in a Balance Sheet

Maria Martinez organized Manhattan Transport Company in January 2004. The corporation immediately issued at $8 per share one-half of its 200,000 authorized shares of $2 par value common stock. On January 2, 2005, the corporation sold at par value the entire 5,000 authorized shares of 8 percent, $100 par value cumulative preferred stock. On January 2, 2006, the company again needed money and issued 5,000 shares of an authorized 10,000 shares of no-par cumulative preferred stock for a total of $512,000. The no-par shares have a stated dividend of $9 per share.

The company declared no dividends in 2004 and 2005. At the end of 2005, its retained earnings were $170,000. During 2006 and 2007 combined, the company earned a total of $890,000. Dividends of 50 cents per share in 2006 and $1.60 per share in 2007 were paid on the common stock.

Instructions

a. Prepare the stockholders' equity section of the balance sheet at December 31, 2007. Include a supporting schedule showing your computation of retained earnings at the balance sheet date. (Hint: Income increases retained earnings, whereas dividends decrease retained earnings.)

b. Assume that on January 2, 2005, the corporation could have borrowed $500,000 at 8 percent interest on a long-term basis instead of issuing the 5,000 shares of the $100 par value cumulative preferred stock. Identify two reasons a corporation may choose to issue cumulative preferred stock rather than finance operations with long-term debt.

LO5

PROBLEM 11.4A
Stockholders' Equity: A Short Comprehensive Problem

Early in the year Bill Barnes and several friends organized a corporation called Barnes Communications, Inc. The corporation was authorized to issue 50,000 shares of $100 par value, 10 percent cumulative preferred stock and 400,000 shares of $2 par value common stock. The following transactions (among others) occurred during the year:

Jan. 6 Issued for cash 20,000 shares of common stock at $14 per share. The shares were issued to Barnes and 10 other investors.

Jan. 7 Issued an additional 500 shares of common stock to Barnes in exchange for his services in organizing the corporation. The stockholders agreed that these services were worth $7,000.

Jan. 12 Issued 2,500 shares of preferred stock for cash of $250,000.

June 4 Acquired land as a building site in exchange for 15,000 shares of common stock. In view of the appraised value of the land and the progress of the company, the directors agreed that the common stock was to be valued for purposes of this transaction at $15 per share.

Nov. 15 The first annual dividend of $10 per share was declared on the preferred stock to be paid December 20. (Hint: Record the dividend by debiting Dividends and crediting Dividends Payable.)

Dec. 20 Paid the cash dividend declared on November 15.

Dec. 31 After the revenue and expenses were closed into the Income Summary account, that account indicated a net income of $147,200.

Instructions

a. Prepare journal entries in general journal form to record the above transactions. Include entries at December 31 to close the Income Summary account and the Dividends account.

b. Prepare the stockholders' equity section of the Barnes Communications, Inc., balance sheet at December 31.

LO5

PROBLEM 11.5A
Analysis of an Equity Section of a Balance Sheet

The year-end balance sheet of Smithfield Products includes the following stockholders' equity section (with certain details omitted):

Stockholders' equity:	
7½% cumulative preferred stock, $100 par value, 100,000 shares authorized	$ 2,400,000
Common stock, $2 par value, 900,000 shares authorized	900,000
Additional paid-in capital: common stock	8,325,000
Retained earnings	2,595,000
Total stockholders' equity	$14,220,000

Instructions

From this information, compute answers to the following questions:

a. How many shares of preferred stock have been issued?

b. What is the total amount of the annual dividends paid to preferred stockholders?

c. How many shares of common stock are outstanding?

d. What was the average issuance price per share of common stock?

e. What is the amount of legal capital?

f. What is the total amount of paid-in capital?

g. What is the book value per share of common stock? (There are no dividends in arrears.)

h. Assume that retained earnings at the beginning of the year amounted to $717,500 and that net income for the year was $3,970,000. What was the dividend declared during the year on *each share* of common stock? (Hint: Net income increases retained earnings, whereas dividends decrease retained earnings.)

PROBLEM 11.6A
Analysis of an Equity Section—More Comprehensive

Quanex Corporation is a publicly owned company. The following information is excerpted from a recent balance sheet. Dollar amounts (except for per share amounts) are stated in thousands.

Stockholders' equity:	
Convertible $17.20 preferred stock, $250 par value, 1,000,000 shares authorized; 345,000 shares issued and outstanding	$ 86,250
Common stock, par value $0.50; 25,000,000 shares authorized	6,819
Additional paid-in capital	87,260
Retained earnings	57,263
Total stockholders' equity	$237,592

Instructions

From this information, answer the following questions:

a. How many shares of common stock have been issued?

b. What is the total amount of the annual dividends paid to preferred stockholders?

c. What is the total amount of paid-in capital?

d. What is the book value per share of common stock?

e. Briefly explain the advantages and disadvantages to Quanex of being publicly owned rather than operating as a closely held corporation.

f. What is meant by the term *convertible* used in the caption of the preferred stock? Is there any more information that investors need to know to evaluate this conversion feature?

g. Assume that the preferred stock currently is selling at *$248* per share. Does this provide a higher or lower dividend yield than an 8 percent, $50 par value preferred with a market price of $57 per share? Show computations (round to the nearest tenth of 1 percent). Explain why one preferred stock might yield less than another.

PROBLEM 11.7A
Par, Book, and Market Values

Techno Corporation is the producer of popular business software. Recently, an investment service published the following per-share amounts relating to the company's only class of stock:

Par value	$ 0.001
Book value (estimated)	6.50
Market value	$65.00

Instructions

a. Without reference to dollar amounts, explain the nature and significance of *par value, book value*, and *market value*.

b. Comment on the *relationships*, if any, among the per-share amounts shown for the company. What do these amounts imply about Techno Corporation and its operations? Comment on what these amounts imply about the security of *creditors'* claims against the company.

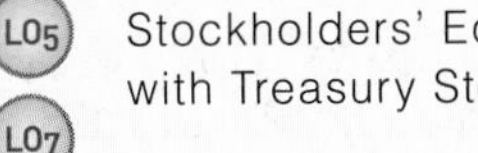

PROBLEM 11.8A
Reporting Stockholders' Equity with Treasury Stock

LO4 LO5 LO7 LO9

Early in 2005, Feller Corporation was formed with authorization to issue 50,000 shares of $1 par value common stock. All shares were issued at a price of $8 per share. The corporation reported net income of $82,000 in 2005, $25,000 in 2006, and $78,000 in 2007. No dividends were declared in any of these three years.

In 2006, the company purchased $35,000 of its own shares for $35,000 in the open market. In 2007, it reissued all of its treasury stock for $40,000.

Instructions

a. Prepare the stockholders' equity section of the balance sheet at December 31, 2007. Include a supporting schedule showing your computation of retained earnings at the balance sheet date. (Hint: Income increases retained earnings.)

b. As of December 31, compute the company's book value per share of common stock.

c. Explain how the treasury stock transactions in 2006 and 2007 were reported in the company's statement of cash flows.

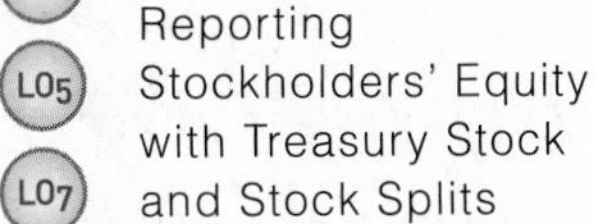

PROBLEM 11.9A
Reporting Stockholders' Equity with Treasury Stock and Stock Splits

LO4 LO5 LO7 through LO9

Early in 2003, Herndon Industries was formed with authorization to issue 200,000 shares of $10 par value common stock and 30,000 shares of $100 par value cumulative preferred stock. During 2003, all the preferred stock was issued at par, and 120,000 shares of common stock were sold for $16 per share. The preferred stock is entitled to a dividend equal to 10 percent of its par value before any dividends are paid on the common stock.

During its first five years of business (2003 through 2007), the company earned income totaling $3,700,000 and paid dividends of 50 cents per share each year on the common stock outstanding.

On January 2, 2005, the company purchased 20,000 shares of its own common stock in the open market for $400,000. On January 2, 2007, it reissued 10,000 shares of this treasury stock for $250,000. The remaining 10,000 were still held in treasury at December 31, 2007.

Instructions

a. Prepare the stockholders' equity section of the balance sheet for Herndon Industries at December 31, 2007. Include supporting schedules showing (1) your computation of any paid-in capital on treasury stock and (2) retained earnings at the balance sheet date. (Hint: Income increases retained earnings, whereas dividends reduce retained earnings. Dividends are not paid on shares of stock held in treasury.)

b. As of December 31, compute Herndon's book value per share of common stock. (Hint: Book value per share is computed only on the shares of stock outstanding.)

c. At December 31, 2007, shares of the company's common stock were trading at $30. Explain what would have happened to the market price per share had the company split its stock 3-for-1 at this date. Also explain what would have happened to the par value of the common stock and to the number of common shares outstanding.

Problem Set B

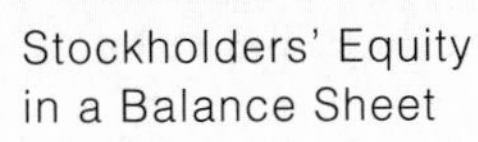

PROBLEM 11.1B
Stockholders' Equity in a Balance Sheet

LO4 through LO6

Early in 2004, Septa, Inc., was organized with authorization to issue 1,000 shares of $100 par value preferred stock and 200,000 shares of $1 par value common stock. Five hundred shares of the preferred stock were issued at par, and 80,000 shares of common stock were sold at $15 per share. The preferred stock pays a 10 percent cumulative dividend.

During the first four years of operations (2004 through 2007), the corporation earned a total of $1,800,000 and paid dividends of 40 cents per share in each year on its outstanding common stock.

Instructions

a. Prepare the stockholders' equity section of the balance sheet at December 31, 2007. Include a supporting schedule showing your computation of the amount of retained earnings reported. (Hint: Income increases retained earnings, whereas dividends decrease retained earnings.)

b. Are there any dividends in arrears on the company's preferred stock at December 31, 2007? Explain your answer.

c. Assume that interest rates increase steadily from 2004 through 2007. Would you expect the market price of the company's preferred stock to be higher or lower than its call price of $110 at December 21, 2007? (The call price is the amount the company must pay to repurchase the shares from the stockholders.)

LO4 through LO6

PROBLEM 11.2B
Stockholders' Equity Section

Banner Publications was organized early in 2002 with authorization to issue 10,000 shares of $100 par value preferred stock and 1 million shares of $1 par value common stock. All of the preferred stock was issued at par, and 400,000 shares of common stock were sold for $15 per share. The preferred stock pays a 10 percent cumulative dividend.

During the first five years of operations (2002 through 2006) the corporation earned a total of $4,100,000 and paid dividends of $.80 per share each year on the common stock. In 2007, however, the corporation reported a net loss of $1,100,000 and paid no dividends.

Instructions

a. Prepare the stockholders' equity section of the balance sheet at December 31, 2007. Include a supporting schedule showing your computation of retained earnings at the balance sheet date. (Hint: Income increases retained earnings, whereas dividends and net losses decrease retained earnings.)

b. Draft a note to accompany the financial statements disclosing any dividends in arrears at the end of 2007.

c. Do the dividends in arrears appear as a liability of the corporation as of the end of 2007? Explain.

LO4 through LO6

PROBLEM 11.3B
Stockholders' Equity in a Balance Sheet

Joy Sun organized Ray Beam, Inc., in January 2004. The corporation immediately issued at $15 per share one-half of its 260,000 authorized shares of $1 par value common stock. On January 2, 2005, the corporation sold at par value the entire 10,000 authorized shares of 10 percent, $100 par value cumulative preferred stock. On January 2, 2006, the company again needed money and issued 5,000 shares of an authorized 8,000 shares of no-par cumulative preferred stock for a total of $320,000. The no-par shares have a stated dividend of $6 per share.

The company declared no dividends in 2004 and 2005. At the end of 2005, its retained earnings were $530,000. During 2006 and 2007 combined, the company earned a total of $1,400,000. Dividends of 90 cents per share in 2006 and $2 per share in 2007 were paid on the common stock.

Instructions

a. Prepare the stockholders' equity section of the balance sheet at December 31, 2007. Include a supporting schedule showing your computation of retained earnings at the balance sheet date. (Hint: Income increases retained earnings, whereas dividends and net losses decrease retained earnings.)

b. Assume that on January 2, 2005, the corporation could have borrowed $1,000,000 at 10 percent interest on a long-term basis instead of issuing the 10,000 shares of the $100 par value cumulative preferred stock. Identify two reasons a corporation may choose to issue cumulative preferred stock rather than finance operations with long-term debt.

LO4 LO5

PROBLEM 11.4B
Stockholders' Equity: A Short Comprehensive Problem

Early in the year Debra Deal and several friends organized a corporation called Markup, Inc. The corporation was authorized to issue 100,000 shares of $100 par value, 5 percent cumulative preferred stock and 100,000 shares of $1 par value common stock. The following transactions (among others) occurred during the year:

Jan. 7 Issued for cash 30,000 shares of common stock at $10 per share. The shares were issued to Deal and four other investors.

Jan. 12 Issued an additional 1,000 shares of common stock to Deal in exchange for her services in organizing the corporation. The stockholders agreed that these services were worth $12,000.

Jan. 18 Issued 4,000 shares of preferred stock for cash of $400,000.

July 5 Acquired land as a building site in exchange for 10,000 shares of common stock. In view of the appraised value of the land and the progress of the company, the directors agreed that the common stock was to be valued for purposes of this transaction at $12 per share.

Nov. 25 The first annual dividend of $5 per share was declared on the preferred stock to be paid December 11.

Dec. 11 Paid the cash dividend declared on November 25.

Dec. 31 After the revenue and expenses were closed into the Income Summary account, that amount indicated a net income of $810,000.

Instructions

a. Prepare journal entries in general journal form to record the above transactions. Include entries at December 31 to close the Income Summary account and the Dividends account.

b. Prepare the stockholders' equity section of the Markup, Inc., balance sheet at December 31.

PROBLEM 11.5B
Analysis of an Equity Section of a Balance Sheet

The year-end balance sheet of Manor, Inc., includes the following stockholders' equity section (with certain details omitted):

Stockholders' equity:	
10% cumulative preferred stock, $100 par value, authorized 100,000 shares	$ 4,400,000
Common stock, $2 par value, authorized 2,000,000 shares	3,400,000
Additional paid-in capital: common stock	6,800,000
Donated capital	400,000
Retained earnings	3,160,000
Total stockholders' equity	$18,160,000

Instructions

From this information, compute answers to the following questions:

a. How many shares of preferred stock have been issued?

b. What is the total amount of the annual dividends paid to preferred stockholders?

c. How many shares of common stock are outstanding?

d. What was the average issuance price per share of common stock?

e. What is the amount of legal capital?

f. What is the total amount of paid-in capital?

g. What is the book value per share of common stock? (There are no dividends in arrears.)

h. Assume that retained earnings at the beginning of the year amounted to $1,200,000 and the net income for the year was $4,800,000. What was the dividend declared during the year on *each share* of common stock? (Hint: Net income increases retained earnings, whereas dividends decrease retained earnings.)

PROBLEM 11.6B
Analysis of an Equity Section—More Comprehensive

Toasty Corporation is a publicly owned company. The following information is taken from a recent balance sheet. Dollar amounts (except for per-share amounts) are stated in thousands.

Stockholders' equity:	
Convertible $10 preferred stock, no par value, 1,000,000 shares authorized, 250,000 shares issued and outstanding, $200 per share liquidation preference	$ 50,000
Common stock, $3 par value, 40,000,000 shares authorized	9,600
Additional paid-in capital	76,800
Retained earnings	50,600
Total stockholders' equity	$187,000

Instructions

From this information, compute answers to the following questions:

a. How many shares of common stock have been issued?

b. What is the total amount of the annual dividends paid to preferred stockholders?

c. What is the total amount of paid-in capital?

d. What is the book value per share of common stock?

e. Briefly explain the advantages and disadvantages to Toasty of being publicly owned rather than operating as a closely held corporation.

f. What is meant by the term *convertible* used in the caption of the preferred stock? Is there any more information that investors need to know to evaluate this conversion feature?

g. Assume that the preferred stock currently is selling at *$190* per share. Does this provide a higher or lower dividend yield than a 6 percent, $50 par value preferred with a market price of $52 per share? Show computations. Explain why one preferred stock might yield less than another.

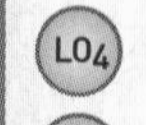

PROBLEM 11.7B
Par, Book, and Market Values

Brain Corporation is the producer of popular video games. Recently, an investment service published the following per-share amounts relating to the company's only class of stock:

Par value	$ 0.05
Book value (estimated)	10.00
Market value	96.00

Instructions

a. Without reference to dollar amounts, explain the nature and significance of *par value, book value*, and *market value*.

b. Comment on the *relationships*, if any, among the per-share accounts shown for the company. What do these amounts imply about Brain and its operations? Comment on what these amounts imply about the security of *creditors'* claims against the company.

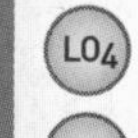

PROBLEM 11.8B
Reporting Stockholders' Equity with Treasury Stock

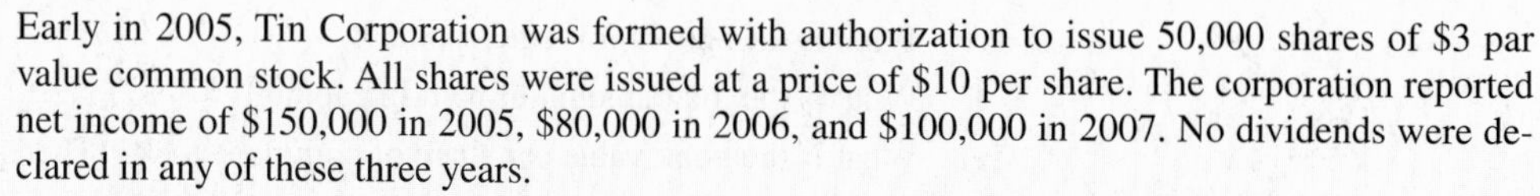

Early in 2005, Tin Corporation was formed with authorization to issue 50,000 shares of $3 par value common stock. All shares were issued at a price of $10 per share. The corporation reported net income of $150,000 in 2005, $80,000 in 2006, and $100,000 in 2007. No dividends were declared in any of these three years.

In 2006, the company purchased its own shares for $30,000 in the open market. In 2007, it reissued all of its treasury stock for $40,000.

Instructions

a. Prepare the stockholders' equity section of the balance sheet at December 31, 2007. Include a supporting schedule showing your computation of retained earnings at the balance sheet date. (Hint: Income increases retained earnings.)

b. As of December 31, compute the company's book value per share of common stock.

c. Explain how the treasury stock transactions in 2006 and 2007 were reported in the company's statement of cash flows.

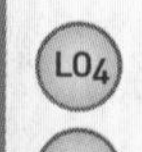

PROBLEM 11.9B
Reporting Stockholders' Equity with Treasury Stock and Stock Splits

through

Early in 2003, Parker Industries was formed with authorization to issue 100,000 shares of $20 par value common stock and 10,000 shares of $100 par value cumulative preferred stock. During 2003, all the preferred stock was issued at par, and 80,000 shares of common stock were sold for $35 per share. The preferred stock is entitled to a dividend equal to 6 percent of its par value before any dividends are paid on the common stock.

During its first five years of business (2003 through 2007), the company earned income totaling $3,800,000 and paid dividends of 60 cents per share each year on the common stock outstanding.

On January 2, 2005, the company purchased 1,000 shares of its own common stock in the open market for $40,000. On January 2, 2007, it reissued 600 shares of this treasury stock for $30,000. The remaining 400 shares were still held in treasury at December 31, 2007.

Instructions

a. Prepare the stockholders' equity section of the balance sheet at December 31, 2007. Include a supporting schedule showing (1) your computation of any paid-in capital on treasury stock and (2) retained earnings at the balance sheet date. (Hint: Income increases retained earnings, whereas dividends reduce retained earnings. Dividends are not paid on shares of stock held in treasury.)

b. As of December 31, 2007 compute the company's book value per share of common stock. (Hint: Book value per share is computed only on the shares of stock outstanding.)

c. At December 31, 2007, shares of the company's common stock were trading at $56. Explain what would have happened to the market price per share had the company split its stock 2-for-1 at this date. Also explain what would have happened to the par value of the common stock and to the number of common shares outstanding.

Critical Thinking Cases

CASE 11.1
Factors Affecting the Market Prices of Preferred and Common Stocks

ADM Labs is a publicly owned company with several issues of capital stock outstanding. Over the past decade, the company has consistently earned modest profits and has increased its common stock dividend annually by 5 or 10 cents per share. Recently the company introduced several new products that you believe will cause future sales and profits to increase dramatically. You also expect a gradual increase in long-term interest rates from their present level of about 11 percent to, perhaps, 12 percent to 12 ¼ percent.

Instructions

Based on these forecasts, explain whether you would expect to see the market prices of the following issues of ADM capital stock increase or decrease. Explain your reasoning in each answer.

a. 10 percent, $100 par value preferred stock (currently selling at $90 per share).

b. $5 par value common stock (currently paying an annual dividend of $2.50 and selling at $40 per share).

c. 7 percent, $100 par value convertible preferred stock (currently selling at $125 per share).

CASE 11.2
Factors Affecting the Market Prices of Common Stocks

Each of the following situations describes an event that affected the stock market price of a particular company.

a. The price of a common share of **McDonnell Douglas, Inc.**, increased by 5 ⅛ dollars per share in the several days after it was announced that Saudia Airlines would order $6 billion of commercial airliners from **Boeing** and **McDonnell Douglas**.

b. **Citicorp**'s common stock price fell 3 ⅝ per share shortly after the Federal Reserve Board increased the discount rate by ¼ percent. The discount rate is the rate charged to banks for short-term loans they need to meet their reserve requirements.

c. The price of a common share of **Ventitex, Inc.**, a manufacturer of medical devices, fell 10 ¼ (27.7 percent) after it was announced that representatives of the Federal Drug Administration paid a visit to the company.

Instructions

For each of the independent situations described, explain the likely underlying rationale for the change in market price of the stock.

through

CASE 11.3
Selecting a Form of Business Organization

Interview the owners of two local small businesses. One business should be organized as a corporation and the other as either a sole proprietorship or a partnership. Inquire as to:

- *Why* this form of entity was selected.
- Have there been any unforeseen complications with this form of entity?
- Is the form of entity likely to be changed in the foreseeable future? And if so, why?

through

CASE 11.4
SEC Enforcement Division

The Enforcement Division of the Securities and Exchange Commission (SEC) is an important aspect of the corporate governance structure in the United States that is intended to protect investors. Locate the home page of the SEC by doing a general search on the title, "Securities and Exchange Commission," and answer the following.

Instructions

a. Identify the four divisions of the SEC.

b. Access the category "Enforcement Division," and write a one-sentence description of the purpose of this division.

c. Access the subcategory "Investor Alerts," and locate the SEC publication that deals with pump-and-dump schemes on the Internet.

d. Write a concise description of a pump-and-dump scheme, and list the suggestions of the SEC to investors to avoid these schemes.

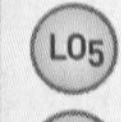

BUSINESSWEEK CASE 11.5
GM Acquisition and Preferred Stock

In "GM May Have Landed a Dandy Daewoo Deal," in the October 8, 2001, *BusinessWeek* issue, Moon Ihlwan and David Welch explained details of the purchase agreement between **General Motors Corp.** and Korea's **Daewoo Motor Co. GM** and its partners were to put $400 million into a joint venture that took control of the **Daewoo** assets. **Daewoo**'s creditors were to receive $1.2 billion in preferred stock, paying 3.5 percent, in the new company. Reports by those familiar with the deal say that **GM** had the option of buying back those preferred shares sometime after 2001. In addition, the agreement called for assuming just $830 million of **Daewoo**'s $17 billion debt.

Instructions

a. Define a preferred stock and identify the typical characteristics of preferred stock.

b. What are the advantages to **General Motors Corporation** of using preferred stock (rather than cash) in its acquisition of **Daewoo**? Why would the creditors of **Daewoo** desire preferred stock rather than common stock?

INTERNET CASE 11.6
Stockholders' Equity Items

Visit the home page of **Staples, Inc.**, at the following Internet address:

www.staples.com

Locate the company's most current balance sheet by selecting "Investor Information."

Instructions

Answer the following questions:

a. Does the company report preferred stock in its balance sheet? If so, how many shares are currently outstanding?

b. How much common stock does the company report in its most recent balance sheet? What is the par value of each share?

c. Does the company report any treasury stock? Has this amount changed since the previous year?

Internet sites are time and date sensitive. It is the purpose of these exercises to have you explore the Internet. You may need to use the Yahoo! search engine **http://www.yahoo.com** *(or another favorite search engine) to find a company's current Web address.*

Answers to Self-Test Questions

1. c **2.** d **3.** c **4.** c **5.** c, d **6.** b [(2,000 × $60) − (500 × $70)]

COMPREHENSIVE PROBLEM 3

McMinn Retail, Inc.

McMinn Retail, Inc., is a retailer that has engaged you to assist in the preparation of its financial statements at December 31, 2007. Following are the correct adjusted account balances, in alphabetical order, as of that date. Each balance is the "normal" balance for that account. (Hint: The "normal" balance is the same as the debit or credit side that increases the account.)

Accounts payable	$ 12,750
Accounts receivable	2,600
Accumulated depreciation: office equipment	12,000
Additional paid-in capital (common stock)	7,000
Bonds payable (due December 31, 2012)	22,500
Cash	15,200
Common stock (1,800 shares, $10 par value)	18,000
Cost of goods sold	100,575
Deferred income taxes	5,750
Depreciation expense: office equipment	2,750
Dividends declared	5,000
Income tax expense	8,190
Insurance expense	900
Land	37,500
Merchandise inventory	17,500
Notes payable (due December 31, 2008)	2,500
Office equipment	41,000
Office supplies	900
Office supplies expense	520
Preferred stock (250 shares, $20 par value)	5,000
Premium on bonds payable	1,750
Prepaid rent	1,800
Rent expense	6,100
Retained earnings (January 2007)	21,050
Salaries expense	88,095
Sales	226,000
Sales returns and allowances	2,500
Sales taxes payable	3,200
Treasury stock (200 common shares at cost)	2,250
Utilities expense	4,120

Instructions

a. Prepare an income statement for the year ended December 31, 2007, which includes amounts for gross profit, income before income taxes, and net income. List expenses (other than cost of goods sold and income tax expense) in order, from the largest to the smallest dollar balance. You may ignore earnings per share.

b. Prepare a statement of retained earnings for the year ending December 31, 2007.

c. Prepare a statement of financial position (balance sheet) as of December 31, 2007, following these guidelines:

- Include separate asset and liability categories for those assets which are "current."
- Include and label amounts for total assets, total liabilities, total stockholders' equity, and total liabilities and stockholders' equity.
- Present deferred income taxes as a noncurrent liability.
- To the extent information is available that should be disclosed, include that information in your statement.

Income and Changes in Retained Earnings

Learning Objectives

AFTER STUDYING THIS CHAPTER, YOU SHOULD BE ABLE TO:

LO1 Describe how irregular income items, such as discontinued operations and extraordinary items, are presented in the income statement.

LO2 Compute earnings per share.

LO3 Distinguish between basic and diluted earnings per share.

LO4 Account for cash dividends and stock dividends, and explain the effects of these transactions on a company's financial statements.

LO5 Describe and prepare a statement of retained earnings.

LO6 Define *prior period adjustments*, and explain how they are presented in financial statements.

LO7 Define *comprehensive income*, and explain how it differs from net income.

LO8 Describe and prepare a statement of stockholders' equity and the stockholders' equity section of the balance sheet.

LO9 Illustrate steps management might take to improve the appearance of the company's net income.

PROCTER & GAMBLE COMPANY

A company's pattern of sales and net income are important factors in evaluating its financial success. Consider **Procter & Gamble Company**, for example. Two billion times a day, **P&G** products are sold around the world. The company has one of the largest and strongest portfolios of recognizable brands, including Pampers, Tide, Ariel, Always, Whisper, Pantene, Bounty, Pringles, Folgers, Charmin, Downy, Lenor, Iams, Crest, Clairol, Actonel, Dawn, and Olay. Ninety-eight thousand people work for **P&G** in almost 80 countries worldwide.

One of the attributes of financially successful companies like **P&G** is their consistent growth over time in terms of primary measures of financial performance, such as net sales and net earnings. Net sales, measuring the value of merchandise sold less returns, increased from $43,377 million in 2003 to $51,407 million in 2004 and to $56,741 million in 2005. This represents an approximate 18.5 percent increase in 2004 and approximately 10.3 percent in 2005 or a combined increase for the two years of an impressive 28.8 percent. Net income, which starts with sales and is reduced by various expenses required to generate those sales, increased from $5,186 million in 2003 to $6,481 million in 2004 (an approximate 25 percent increase) and to $7,257 million in 2005 (an approximate 12 percent increase) or a combined increase for the two years of approximately 37 percent. These figures represent impressive financial performance in terms of the company's ability to provide goods to its customers and to operate in a manner that results in a profit that benefits the company's stockholders.

For investors seeking companies in which to place their funds, a pattern of increases in key performance figures such as sales and net income is very attractive. In this chapter, we look more closely at the income statement and learn about the useful information available in that financial statement for making important investment and credit decisions. In addition to learning more about how an income statement is prepared, you will learn about earnings per share, dividends, and other key factors that indicate the financial success of a company.

Reporting the Results of Operations

The most important aspect of corporate financial reporting, in the view of many investors, is periodic income. Both the market price of common stock and the amount of cash dividends per share depend on the current and future earnings of the corporation.

DEVELOPING PREDICTIVE INFORMATION

Revenue is a measure of the value of products and services that have been sold to customers. Revenue represents the increases in the company's assets that result from its profit-directed activities. Generally, revenue increases cash either at the time it is included in the income statement or at an earlier or later date. Expenses, on the other hand, are measures of the cost of producing and providing the products and services that are sold to customers. They represent decreases in the company's assets that result from its profit-directed activities. Expenses decrease cash at the time they are incurred, or at an earlier or later date. An income statement presents a company's revenue and expenses for a stated period of time, such as a quarter or year.

As this brief description of revenue and expenses indicates, the income statement provides important information for investors and creditors as they attempt to make estimates of future cash flows. Because of the importance of income reporting in making assessments about the future, events and transactions that are irregular require careful attention in the preparation and interpretation of an income statement.

For information about financial performance to be of maximum usefulness to investors, creditors, and other financial statement users, the results of items that are unusual and not likely to recur should be presented separately from the results of the company's normal, recurring activities. Two categories of unusual, nonrecurring events that require special treatment are (1) the results of *discontinued operations* and (2) the impact of *extraordinary items*. One of the challenges that has faced the accounting profession is to define these terms with sufficient clarity that users of financial statements can reliably compare the information provided by different companies.

REPORTING IRREGULAR ITEMS: AN ILLUSTRATION

To illustrate the presentation of irregular items in an income statement, assume that Farmer Corporation operates both a small chain of retail stores and two motels. Near the end of the current year, the company sells both motels to a national hotel chain. In addition, Farmer Corporation reports two "extraordinary items." An income statement illustrating the correct format for reporting these events appears in Exhibit 12–1.

CONTINUING OPERATIONS

The first section of the Farmer Corporation income statement contains only the results of *continuing business activities*—that is, the retail stores. Notice that the income tax expense shown in this section ($300,000) relates *only to continuing operations*. The income taxes relating to the irregular items are shown separately in the income statement as adjustments to the amounts of these items.

Income from Continuing Operations The subtotal *income from continuing operations* measures the profitability of the ongoing operations. This subtotal should be helpful in making predictions of the company's future earnings. For example, if we predict no significant

Exhibit 12–1

INCOME STATEMENT WITH NONRECURRING ITEMS

FARMER CORPORATION Income Statement For the Year Ended December 31, 2007		
Net sales		$8,000,000
Cost and expenses:		
Cost of goods sold	$4,500,000	
Selling expenses	1,500,000	
General and administrative expenses	920,000	
Loss on settlement of lawsuit	80,000	
Income tax (on continuing operations)	300,000	7,300,000
Income from continuing operations		$ 700,000
Discontinued operations:		
Operating loss on motels (net of $90,000 income tax benefit)	$ (210,000)	
Gain on sale of motels (net of $195,000 income tax)	455,000	245,000
Income before extraordinary items and cumulative effect of accounting change		$ 945,000
Extraordinary items:		
Gain on condemnation of land by State Highway Department (net of $45,000 income tax)	$ 105,000	
Loss from earthquake damage to Los Angeles store (net of $75,000 income tax benefit)	(175,000)	(70,000)
Net income		$ 875,000

Notice the order in which the irregular items are reported

change in the profitability of its retail stores, we would expect Farmer Corporation to earn a net income of approximately $700,000 next year.

DISCONTINUED OPERATIONS

Describe how irregular income items, such as discontinued operations and extraordinary items, are presented in the income statement.

When management enters into a formal plan to sell or discontinue a **segment of the business**, the results of that segment's operations are shown separately in the income statement. This enables users of the financial statements to better evaluate the performance of the company's ongoing (continuing) operations.

Two items are included in the **discontinued operations** section of the income statement: (1) the income or loss from *operating* the segment prior to its disposal and (2) the gain or loss on *disposal* of the segment. Notice also that the income taxes relating to the discontinued operations are *shown separately* from the income tax expense relating to continuing business operations.

EXTRAORDINARY ITEMS

The second category of irregular events requiring disclosure in a separate section of the income statement is extraordinary items. An **extraordinary item** is a gain or loss that is (1) *unusual in nature* and (2) *not expected to recur in the foreseeable future.* By definition, extraordinary items are rare and do not appear often in the same company's income statements. An example of an extraordinary item is the loss of a company's plant due to an earthquake in a geographic location where earthquakes rarely occur.

When a gain or loss qualifies as an extraordinary item, it appears after the section on discontinued operations (if any), following the subtotal *income before extraordinary items.* This subtotal is necessary to show investors what the net income *would have been* if the extraordinary gain or loss *had not occurred.* Extraordinary items are shown net of any related income tax effects.

Other Unusual Gains and Losses Some transactions are not typical of normal operations but also do not meet the criteria for separate presentation as extraordinary items. Among such events are losses incurred because of labor strikes and the gains or losses resulting from sales of plant assets. Such items, if material, should be individually listed as items of revenue or expense, rather than being combined with other items in broad categories such as sales revenue or general and administrative expenses.

In the income statement of Farmer Corporation (Exhibit 12–1), the $80,000 loss resulting from the settlement of a lawsuit was listed separately in the income statement but was *not* shown as an extraordinary item. This loss was important enough to bring to the attention of readers of the income statement by presenting it as a separate item, but it was not considered unusual or infrequent enough to be an extraordinary item.

Restructuring Charges One important type of unusual loss relates to the restructuring of operations. The restructuring of operations has become a common aspect of the American economy. In fact, the 1990s were sometimes called the decade of corporate downsizing. As companies struggle to meet the competitive challenges of a global economy, they incur significant costs to close plants, reduce workforces, and consolidate operating facilities.

Restructuring charges consist of items such as losses from write-downs or sales of plant assets, severance pay for terminated workers, and expenses related to the relocation of operations and remaining personnel. In determining operating income, they are presented in the company's income statement as a single item like the loss incurred in the settlement of a lawsuit in the Farmer Corporation income statement in Exhibit 12–1. If the restructuring involves discontinuing a segment of the business, the expenses related to that aspect of the restructuring are presented as discontinued operations.

Distinguishing between the Unusual and the Extraordinary In the past, some corporate managements had a tendency to classify many *losses* as extraordinary, while classifying many *gains* as a part of normal, recurring operations. This resulted in reporting higher income before extraordinary items, but the final net income figure was not affected. To counter this potentially misleading practice, the accounting profession now defines extraordinary items very carefully and intends for them to be quite rare. There is no comprehensive list of extraordinary items. Thus the classification of a specific event is a matter of *judgment.*

You as an Investor

One of the most important determinants of a company's stock price is expected future earnings. Assume that you are considering investing in Worsham Corporation and are evaluating the company's profitability in the current year. The net income of the corporation, which amounted to $4,000,000, includes the following items:

Loss on a discontinued segment of the business (net of income tax benefit)	$750,000
Extraordinary gain (net of income tax paid)	300,000

Adjust net income to develop a number that represents a good starting point for predicting the future net income of Worsham Corporation. Explain the reason for each of the adjustments. Explain how this adjusted number may help you predict future earnings for the company.

(See our comments on the Online Learning Center Web site.)

EARNINGS PER SHARE (EPS)

Compute earnings per share. LO2

One of the most widely used accounting statistics is **earnings per share** of common stock. Investors who buy or sell stock in a corporation need to know the annual earnings per share. Stock market prices are quoted on a per-share basis. If you are considering investing in a company's stock at a price of $50 per share, you need to know the earnings per share and the annual dividend per share to decide whether this price is reasonable.

To compute earnings per share, the common stockholders' share of the company's net income is divided by the average number of common shares outstanding. The concept of earnings per share applies only to *common stock*; preferred stockholders have no claim to earnings beyond the stipulated preferred stock dividends.

Computing earnings per share is easiest when the corporation has issued only common stock and the number of outstanding shares has not changed during the year. In this case, earnings per share is equal to net income divided by the number of shares outstanding.

In many companies, the number of shares of stock outstanding changes during the year. If additional shares are sold, or if shares of common stock are retired (repurchased from the shareholders), the computation of earnings per share is based on the *weighted-average* number of shares outstanding.[1]

The weighted-average number of shares for the year is determined by multiplying the number of shares outstanding by the fraction of the year that number of shares outstanding remained unchanged. For example, assume that 80,000 shares of common stock were outstanding during the first nine months of 2007 and 140,000 shares were outstanding during the last three months. The increase in shares outstanding resulted from the sale of 60,000 shares for cash. The weighted-average number of shares outstanding during 2007 is *95,000*, determined as follows:

80,000 shares × 9/12 of a year	60,000
140,000 shares × 3/12 of a year	35,000
Weighted-average number of common shares outstanding	95,000

By using the weighted-average number of shares, we recognize that the cash received from the sale of the 60,000 additional shares was available to generate earnings only during the last three months of the year.

Preferred Dividends and Earnings per Share

When a company has preferred stock outstanding, the preferred stockholders participate in net income only to the extent of the preferred stock dividends. To determine the earnings *applicable to the common stock*, we first deduct from net income the amount of current year preferred dividends. The annual dividend on *cumulative* preferred stock is *always* deducted, even if not declared by the board of directors for the current year. When there are preferred dividends in arrears, only the *current year's* cumulative preferred stock dividend is deducted in the earnings per share computation. Noncumulative preferred dividends are deducted only if declared.

To illustrate, let us assume that Perry Corporation has 200,000 shares of common stock and 12,000 shares of $6 cumulative preferred stock outstanding throughout the year. Net income

[1] When the number of shares outstanding changes as a result of a stock split or a stock dividend (discussed later in this chapter), the computation of the weighted-average number of shares outstanding should be adjusted *retroactively* rather than weighted for the period the new shares were outstanding. This makes earnings per share data for prior years consistent in terms of the current capital structure.

for the year totals $595,000. Earnings per share of common stock would be computed as follows:

Net income	$595,000
Less: Dividends on preferred stock (12,000 shares × $6)	72,000
Earnings applicable to common stock	$523,000
Weighted-average number of common shares outstanding	200,000
Earnings per share of common stock ($523,000 ÷ 200,000 shares)	$2.62

Earnings per share figures are required in the income statements of publicly owned companies

Presentation of Earnings per Share in the Income Statement All publicly owned corporations are *required* to present earnings per share figures in their income statements.[2] If an income statement includes subtotals for income from continuing operations, or for income before extraordinary items, per-share figures are shown for these amounts as well as for net income. These additional per-share amounts are computed by substituting the amount of the appropriate subtotal for the net income figure in the preceding calculation.

To illustrate all of the potential per-share computations, we will expand our Perry Corporation example to include income from continuing operations and income before extraordinary items. We should point out, however, that all of these figures seldom appear in the same income statement. The condensed income statement shown in Exhibit 12–2 is intended to illustrate the proper format for presenting earnings per share figures and to provide a review of the calculations.

Exhibit 12–2

EARNINGS PER SHARE PRESENTATION

PERRY CORPORATION
Condensed Income Statement
For the Year Ended December 31, 2007

Net sales	$9,115,000
Costs and expenses (including tax on continuing operations)	8,310,000
Income from continuing operations	$ 805,000
Loss from discontinued operations (net of income tax benefits)	(90,000)
Income before extraordinary items	$ 715,000
Extraordinary loss (net of income tax benefit)	$ (120,000)
Net income	$ 595,000
Earnings per share of common stock:	
Earnings from continuing operations	$3.67[a]
Loss from discontinued operations	(.45)
Earnings before extraordinary items	$3.22[b]
Extraordinary loss	(.60)
Net earnings	$2.62[c]

[a]($805,000 − $72,000 preferred dividends) ÷ 200,000 shares
[b]($715,000 − $72,000) ÷ 200,000 shares
[c]($595,000 − $72,000) ÷ 200,000 shares

Interpreting the Different per-Share Amounts To informed users of financial statements, each of these figures has a different significance. Earnings per share from continuing operations represents the results of continuing and ordinary business activity. This figure is the most useful one for predicting future operating results. *Net earnings* per share, on the other hand, shows the overall operating results of the current year, including any discontinued operations and extraordinary items.

[2] The FASB has exempted closely held corporations (those not publicly owned) from the requirement of computing and reporting earnings per share.

Financial Analysis and Decision Making

The relationship between earnings per share and stock price is expressed by the **price-earnings (p/e) ratio**. This ratio is simply the current stock price divided by the earnings per share for the year (last four quarters). (A p/e ratio is *not* computed if the company has sustained a net *loss* for this period.) Price-earnings ratios are of such interest to investors that they are published daily in the financial pages of major newspapers. Price-earnings ratios and other measures useful for evaluating financial performance are covered in Chapter 14.

Stock prices actually reflect investors' expectations of *future* earnings. The p/e ratio, however, is based on the earnings over the *past* year. Thus, if investors expect earnings to *increase* substantially from current levels, the p/e ratio will be quite high—perhaps 20, 30, or even more. But if investors expect earnings to *decline* from current levels, the p/e ratio will be quite low, say, 8 or less. A mature company with very stable earnings usually sells between 10 and 12 times earnings. Thus the p/e ratio reflects *investors' expectations* of the company's future prospects.[3]

Unfortunately, the term *earnings per share* often is used without qualification in referring to various types of per-share data. When using per-share information, it is important to know exactly *which* per-share statistic is being presented. For example, the price-earnings ratios (market price divided by earnings per share) for common stocks listed on major stock exchanges are reported daily in *The Wall Street Journal* and many other newspapers. Which earnings per share figures are used in computing these ratios? If a company reports an extraordinary gain or loss, the price-earnings ratio is computed using the per-share *earnings before the extraordinary item.* Otherwise, the ratio is based on *net earnings*.

CASE IN POINT

Valuation multiples such as price-earnings ratios are often used to estimate a firm's value. The use of price multiples to compare firms from different countries is challenging for many reasons. One important reason is that national differences in accounting principles are a source of cross-country differences. For example, research has shown that such differences in accounting principles cause p/e ratios in Japan to be generally lower than in the United States for comparable companies with similar financial results.

YOUR TURN You as a Financial Analyst

You are working for a stock market research firm and your boss tells you that she is interested in buying growth stocks that trade at reasonable valuations. She is looking for stocks that are expected to grow at a compound rate of 15 percent or more over the next five years and whose p/e ratio is not more than 25 percent greater than the company's projected growth rate (referred to as the PEG ratio—the p/e ratio divided by the company's projected growth rate). She is also willing to consider companies that are growing at 25 percent or more and where the PEG ratio is not more than 1.5 (the p/e ratio is not more than 50 percent greater than the company's projected growth rate).

Based on some preliminary analysis she has already performed, your boss has limited the stocks she is considering to **Home Depot**, **Intel**, **Coca-Cola**, **Genentech**, **eBay**, and **Amazon**. She provides you with the following information and asks you to recommend which stocks are consistent with her investment criteria.

Ryan McVay/Getty Images/DIL

[3] A word of caution—if current earnings are *very low*, the p/e ratio tends to be quite high *regardless* of whether future earnings are expected to rise or fall. In such situations, the p/e ratio is not a meaningful measurement.

(*continued*)

Company	Stock Price	Earnings per Share	PEG Ratio
Home Depot	$ 36.49	$1.880	1.21
Intel	27.53	0.973	1.53
Coca-Cola	51.05	2.437	2.40
Genentech	118.22	1.193	2.99
eBay	82.14	0.818	2.01
Amazon	46.29	0.361	1.47

(See our comments on the Online Learning Center Web site.)

Basic and Diluted Earnings per Share

LO3 Distinguish between basic and diluted earnings per share.

Let us assume that a company has an outstanding issue of preferred stock that is convertible into shares of common stock at a rate of two shares of common stock for each share of preferred stock. The conversion of this preferred stock would increase the number of common shares outstanding and might *dilute* (reduce) earnings per share. Any common stockholder interested in the trend of earnings per share needs to know what effect the conversion of the preferred stock would have on earnings per share of common stock. Keep in mind that the decision to convert the preferred shares into common shares is made by the stockholders, not the corporation.

To inform investors of the potential dilution that might occur, two figures are presented for each income number from the income statement. The first figure, called **basic earnings per share**, is based on the weighted-average number of common shares *actually outstanding* during the year. This figure excludes the potential dilution represented by the convertible preferred stock. The second figure, called **diluted earnings per share**, incorporates the *impact that conversion* of the preferred stock would have on basic earnings per share.

Basic earnings per share is computed in the same manner as illustrated in our preceding example of Perry Corporation. Diluted earnings per share, on the other hand, is computed on the assumption that all the preferred stock *has been converted into common stock as of the beginning of the current year.*[4] (The mechanics of computing diluted earnings per share are covered in more advanced accounting courses.)

The purpose of showing diluted earnings per share is to alert common stockholders to what *could* have happened. When the difference between basic and diluted earnings per share is significant, investors should recognize the *risk* that future earnings per share may be reduced by conversions of other securities into additional shares of common stock. When a company reports both basic and diluted earnings per share, the price-earnings ratio shown in newspapers is based on the *basic figure.*

Convertible preferred stock is not the only potential for dilution in earnings per share. Convertible debt instruments (e.g., convertible bonds) are another type of financial instrument that may reduce earnings per share if the holders choose to redeem them. Similarly, stock options may reduce earnings per share if the holders choose to exercise them and purchase additional shares of stock.

[4] If the preferred stock had been issued during the current year, we would assume that it was converted into common stock on the date it was issued.

Other Transactions Affecting Retained Earnings

CASH DIVIDENDS

Account for cash dividends and stock dividends, and explain the effects of these transactions on a company's financial statements.

Investors buy stock in a corporation with the expectation of getting their original investment back as well as a reasonable return on that investment. The return on a stock investment is a combination of two forms: (1) the increase in value of the stock (stock appreciation) and (2) **cash dividends**.

Some profitable corporations do not pay dividends. Generally, these corporations are in an early stage of development and must conserve cash for the purchase of plant and equipment or for other needs of the company. These so-called growth companies cannot obtain sufficient financing at reasonable interest rates to finance their operations, so they must rely on their earnings. Often only after a significant number of years of profitable operations does the board of directors decide that paying cash dividends is appropriate.

The preceding discussion suggests three requirements for the payment of a cash dividend. These are:

1. *Retained earnings.* Since dividends represent a distribution of earnings to stockholders, the theoretical maximum for dividends is the total undistributed net income of the company, represented by the credit balance of the Retained Earnings account. As a practical matter, many corporations limit dividends to amounts significantly less than annual net income, in the belief that a major portion of the net income must be retained in the business if the company is to grow and keep pace with its competitors.
2. *An adequate cash position.* The fact that the company reports earnings does not necessarily mean that it has a large amount of cash on hand. Cash generated from earnings may have been invested in new plant and equipment, or it may have already been used to pay off debts or to acquire a larger inventory. There is no necessary relationship between the balance in the Retained Earnings account and the balance in the Cash account. The common expression of "paying dividends out of retained earnings" is misleading. Cash dividends can be paid only out of cash.
3. *Dividend action by the board of directors.* Even though a company's net income is substantial and its cash position seemingly satisfactory, dividends are not paid automatically. A formal action by the board of directors is necessary to declare a dividend.

DIVIDEND DATES

Four significant dates are involved in the distribution of a dividend. These are:

1. *Date of declaration.* On the day on which the dividend is declared by the board of directors, a liability to make the payment comes into existence.
2. *Ex-dividend date.* The **ex-dividend date** is significant for investors in companies whose stocks trade on stock exchanges. To permit the compilation of the list of stockholders as of the record date, it is customary for the stock to go *ex-dividend* three business days before the date of record (see following discussion). A person who buys the stock before the ex-dividend date is entitled to receive the dividend that has already been declared; conversely, a stockholder who sells shares before the ex-dividend date does not receive the dividend. A stock is said to be selling ex-dividend on the day that it *loses* the right to receive the latest declared dividend.
3. *Date of record.* The **date of record** follows the date of declaration, usually by two or three weeks, and is always stated in the dividend declaration. To be eligible to receive the dividend, a person must be listed in the corporation's records as the owner of the stock on this date.
4. *Date of payment.* The declaration of a dividend always includes announcement of the date of payment as well as the date of record. Usually the date of payment comes two to four weeks after the date of record.

Journal entries are required only on the dates of declaration and of payment, as these are the only transactions affecting the corporation declaring the dividend. These entries are illustrated below:

Dec. 15	Dividends	125,000	
	Dividends Payable		125,000
	To record declaration of a cash dividend of $1 per share on the 125,000 shares of common stock outstanding. Payable Jan. 25 to stockholders of record on Jan. 10.		

Entries made on declaration date and . . .

Jan. 25	Dividends Payable	125,000	
	Cash		125,000
	To record payment of $1 per share dividend declared Dec. 15 to stockholders of record on Jan. 10.		

on payment date

No entries are made on either the ex-dividend date or the date of record. These dates are of importance only in determining *to whom* the dividend checks should be sent. From the stockholders' point of view, it is the *ex-dividend date* that determines who receives the dividend. The date of record is of significance primarily to the stock transfer agent and the stock registrar.

At the end of the accounting period, a closing entry is required to transfer the debit balance of the Dividends account into the Retained Earnings account. (Some companies follow the alternative practice of debiting Retained Earnings when the dividend is declared instead of using a Dividends account. Under either method, the balance of the Retained Earnings account ultimately is reduced by all dividends declared during the period.)

LIQUIDATING DIVIDENDS

A *liquidating dividend* occurs when a corporation pays a dividend that *exceeds the balance in the Retained Earnings account.* Thus the dividend returns to stockholders all or part of their paid-in capital investment. Liquidating dividends usually are paid only when a corporation is going out of existence or is making a permanent reduction in the size of its operations. Stockholders may assume that a dividend represents a distribution of profits unless they are notified by the corporation that the dividend is a return of invested capital.

STOCK DIVIDENDS

Stock dividend is a term used to describe a distribution of *additional shares of stock* to a company's stockholders in proportion to their present holdings. In other words, the dividend is payable in additional shares of stock rather than in cash. Most stock dividends consist of additional shares of common stock distributed to holders of common stock. Therefore, our discussion focuses on this type of stock dividend.

An important distinction exists between a cash dividend and a stock dividend. A *cash dividend* is a distribution of cash by a corporation to its stockholders. A cash dividend reduces both assets and stockholders' equity. In a *stock dividend,* however, *no assets are distributed.* Thus a stock dividend causes *no change* in assets or in total stockholders' equity. Each stockholder receives additional shares, but his or her percentage ownership in the corporation is *no larger than before.*

To illustrate this point, assume that a corporation with 2,000 shares of stock is owned equally by James Davis and Susan Miller, each owning 1,000 shares of stock. The corporation declares a stock dividend of 10 percent and distributes 200 additional shares (10 percent of 2,000 shares), with 100 shares going to each of the two stockholders. Davis and Miller now hold 1,100 shares apiece, but each *still owns one-half of the business.* Furthermore, the corporation has not changed in size; its assets and liabilities and its total stockholders' equity are exactly the same as before the dividend.

Now let us consider the logical effect of this stock dividend on the *market price* of the company's stock. Assume that, before the stock dividend, the outstanding 2,000 shares in our example had a market price of $110 per share. This price indicates a total market value for the corporation of $220,000 (2,000 shares × $110 per share). As the stock dividend does not change total assets or total stockholders' equity, the total market value of the corporation *should remain $220,000* after the stock dividend. As 2,200 shares are now outstanding, the market price of each share *should fall* to $100 ($220,000 ÷ 2,200 shares). In other words, the market value of the stock *should fall in proportion* to the number of new shares issued. Whether the market price per share *will* fall in proportion to a small increase in the number of outstanding shares is another matter.

Entries to Record a Stock Dividend

In accounting for relatively *small* stock dividends (say, less than 20 percent), the *market value* of the new shares is transferred from the Retained Earnings account to the paid-in capital accounts. This process sometimes is called *capitalizing* retained earnings. The overall effect is the same as if the dividend had been paid in cash, and the stockholders had immediately reinvested the cash in the business in exchange for additional shares of stock. Of course, no cash actually changes hands—the new shares of stock are sent directly to the stockholders.

To illustrate, assume that on June 1, Aspen Corporation has outstanding 100,000 shares of $5 par value common stock with a market value of $25 per share. On this date, the company declares a 10 percent stock dividend, distributable on July 15 to stockholders of record on June 20. The entry at June 1 to record the *declaration* of this dividend is:

Retained Earnings	250,000	
Stock Dividend to Be Distributed		50,000
Additional Paid-in Capital: Stock Dividends		200,000
Declared a 10% stock dividend consisting of 10,000 shares (100,000 shares × 10%) of $5 par value common stock, market price $25 per share. Distributable July 15 to stockholders of record on June 20.		

Stock dividend declared; use market price of stock

The Stock Dividend to Be Distributed account is *not a liability* because there is no obligation to distribute cash or any other asset. If a balance sheet is prepared between the date of declaration of a stock dividend and the date of distribution of the shares, this account, as well as the Additional Paid-in Capital: Stock Dividends account, should be presented in the stockholders' equity section of the balance sheet.

Notice that the Retained Earnings account was reduced by the *market value* of the shares to be issued (10,000 shares × $25 per share = $250,000). Notice also that *no change* occurs in the total amount of stockholders' equity. The amount removed from the Retained Earnings account was simply transferred into two other stockholders' equity accounts.

On July 15, the entry to record the *distribution* of the dividend shares is:

Stock Dividend to Be Distributed	50,000	
Common Stock		50,000
Distributed 10,000-share stock dividend declared June 1.		

Stock dividend distributed

Reasons for Stock Dividends Although stock dividends cause *no change* in total assets, liabilities, or stockholders' equity, they are popular both with management and with stockholders. Management often finds stock dividends appealing because they allow management to distribute something of perceived value to stockholders while conserving cash which may be needed for other purposes like expanding facilities and introducing new product lines.

Stockholders like stock dividends because they receive more shares, often the stock price does *not* fall proportionately, and the dividend is not subject to income taxes (until the shares received are sold). Also, *large* stock dividends tend to keep the stock price down in a trading range that appeals to most investors.

CASE IN POINT

An investor who purchased 100 shares of **Home Depot, Inc.**, early in 1985 would have paid about $1,700. By 2000, 15 years later, that stock was worth about $273,000!

Does this mean that each share increased in value from $17 to more than $2,730? No—in fact, this probably couldn't happen. Investors like to buy stock in lots of 100 shares. At $2,730 per share, who could afford 100 shares? Certainly not the average small investor.

Home Depot's board of directors *wanted* to attract small investors. These investors help create more demand for the company's stock—and in many cases, they also become loyal customers.

So as the price of **Home Depot**'s stock rose, the board declared numerous stock splits and stock dividends. By 2000, an investor who had purchased 100 shares in 1985 owned over *3,900* shares without ever having had to purchase additional shares. Each share had a market value of up to $70. But, most important, each of these shares was trading at a price affordable to the average investor.

Distinction between Stock Splits and Stock Dividends What is the difference between a stock dividend and a stock split (discussed in Chapter 11)? In some respects the two are similar. Both involve the distribution of shares of a company's own stock to its present stockholders without payment by those stockholders to the company. Both stock dividends and stock splits increase the number of outstanding shares of stock in the company's stockholders' equity. The difference between a stock dividend and a stock split lies in the intent of management and the related issue of the size of the distribution. A stock dividend usually is intended to substitute for a cash dividend and is small enough that the market price of the stock is relatively unaffected. Stock dividends typically increase the number of outstanding shares by 5 percent, 10 percent, or even 20 percent. Stock splits, on the other hand, have the intent of reducing the market price of the stock to bring it down to a desired trading range. Stock splits typically represent much greater increases in the number of outstanding shares, such as 100 percent (2:1 split) or 200 percent (3:1 split).

The previous discussion focuses on the purposes and management intent of stock dividends and stock splits. Accounting for the two also varies. Stock dividends do not result in a change in the par value of the stock, and usually an amount equal to the market value of the shares issued is transferred from retained earnings to the par value and additional paid-in capital accounts. Stock splits, on the other hand, result in a pro rata reduction in the par value of the stock and no change in the actual dollar balances of the stockholders' equity accounts. Both stock dividends and stock splits are integral parts of management strategy with regard to the company's ownership, and the accounting differences parallel these differences in management intent.

STATEMENT OF RETAINED EARNINGS

LO5 Describe and prepare a statement of retained earnings.

The term *retained earnings* refers to the portion of stockholders' equity derived from profitable operations. Retained earnings is increased by earning net income and is reduced by incurring net losses and by the declaration of dividends.

In addition to a balance sheet, an income statement, and a statement of cash flows, some companies present a **statement of retained earnings**, as in Exhibit 12–3.

Exhibit 12–3

STATEMENT OF RETAINED EARNINGS FOR SALT LAKE CORPORATION

SALT LAKE CORPORATION Statement of Retained Earnings For the Year Ended December 31, 2007		
Retained earnings, Dec. 31, 2006		$ 750,000
Net income for 2007		280,000
Subtotal		$1,030,000
Less dividends:		
Cash dividends on preferred stock ($5 per share)	$ 15,000	
Cash dividends on common stock ($2 per share)	59,600	
10% stock dividend	140,000	214,600
Retained earnings, Dec. 31, 2007		$ 815,400

Notice that the 2007 net income is added to the beginning balance of retained earnings. Earlier in this text when we studied the accounting cycle, we learned that, as part of the end-of-period process of closing the books and preparing financial statements, the revenue and expense accounts are brought to a zero balance, and the net amount of these items (either net income or net loss) is added to or subtracted from owners' equity. For a corporation, net income or loss is added to or subtracted from retained earnings. The addition of net income in the statement of retained earnings is a reflection of this closing process. Notice, also, that in the statement of retained earnings the balance is reduced by the amounts of cash dividends declared during the year, as well as the amount of the stock dividend that was declared.

PRIOR PERIOD ADJUSTMENTS

On occasion, a company may discover that a *material error* was made in the measurement of net income in a prior year. Because net income is closed into the Retained Earnings account, an error in reported net income will cause an error in the amount of retained earnings shown in all subsequent balance sheets. When such errors are discovered, they should be corrected. The correction, called a **prior period adjustment**, is shown in the *statement of retained earnings* as an adjustment to the balance of retained earnings at the beginning of the current year. The amount of the adjustment is shown net of any related income tax effects.

Define *prior period adjustments*, and explain how they are presented in financial statements.

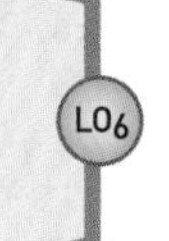

To illustrate, assume that late in 2007 Salt Lake Corporation discovers that it failed to record depreciation on certain assets in 2006. After considering the income tax effects of this error, the company finds that the net income reported in 2006 was overstated by $35,000. Thus the beginning 2007 balance of the Retained Earnings account ($750,000 at December 31, 2006) also is *overstated by $35,000*. The statement of retained earnings in *2007* must include a *correction* of the retained earnings at the beginning of the year. (See the illustration in Exhibit 12–4.)

Exhibit 12–4
STATEMENT OF RETAINED EARNINGS WITH PRIOR PERIOD ADJUSTMENT

SALT LAKE CORPORATION
Statement of Retained Earnings
For the Year Ended December 31, 2007

Retained earnings, Dec. 31, 2006		
As originally reported		$750,000
Less: Prior period adjustment for error in recording 2006 depreciation expense (net of $15,000 income taxes)		35,000
As restated		$715,000
Net income for 2007		280,000
Subtotal		$995,000
Less dividends:		
Cash dividends on preferred stock ($5 per share)	$ 15,000	
Cash dividends on common stock ($2 per share)	59,600	
10% stock dividend	140,000	214,600
Retained earnings, Dec. 31, 2007		$780,400

Adjust beginning retained earnings for correction

Prior period adjustments rarely appear in the financial statements of large, publicly owned corporations. The financial statements of these corporations are audited annually by certified public accountants and are not likely to contain material errors that subsequently will require correction by prior period adjustments. Such adjustments are much more likely to appear in the financial statements of closely held corporations that are not audited on an annual basis.

Restrictions of Retained Earnings

Some portion of retained earnings may be restricted because of various contractual agreements. A restriction of retained earnings prevents a company from declaring a dividend that would cause retained earnings to fall below a designated level. Most companies disclose restrictions of retained earnings in notes accompanying the financial statements. For example, a company with total retained earnings of $10 million might include the following note in its financial statements:

> **Note 7: Restriction of retained earnings**
> As of December 31, 2007, certain long-term debt agreements prohibited the declaration of cash dividends that would reduce the amount of retained earnings below $5,200,000. Retained earnings in excess of this restriction total $4,800,000.

Note disclosure of restrictions placed on retained earnings

COMPREHENSIVE INCOME

The Financial Accounting Standards Board (FASB) has identified certain changes in financial position that should be recorded but should not enter into the determination of net income. One way to describe these events is that they are *recognized* (that is, recorded and incorporated in the financial statements) but not *realized* (that is, not included in the determination

Define *comprehensive income*, and explain how it differs from net income. LO7

of the company's net income). We have studied one of these items earlier in this text—the change in market value of available-for-sale debt and equity investments.

Recall from Chapter 7 the way changes in value for various types of investments are recorded. Those investments identified as available for sale are revalued to their current market value at the end of each accounting period. These changes in value are accumulated and reported in a separate stockholders' equity account. The change in value does *not* enter into the determination of net income as it would had investments been sold. The change in market value of available-for-sale investments adds to the amount of stockholders' equity if the value has gone up; it reduces the amount of stockholders' equity if the value has gone down. This adjustment is described as an element of *other comprehensive income.*

Comprehensive income is a term that identifies the total of net income plus or minus the elements of other comprehensive income. Comprehensive income may be displayed to users of financial statements in any of the following ways:

- *As a second income statement.* One income statement displays the components of net income and the other displays the components of comprehensive income, one element of which is net income.
- *As a single income statement* that includes both the components of net income and the components of other comprehensive income.
- *As an element in the changes in stockholders' equity* displayed as a column in the statement of stockholders' equity (discussed later in this chapter).

In addition to the presentation of each year's changes in the elements of other comprehensive income, the accumulated amount of these changes is an element in the stockholders' equity section of the balance sheet. The components of comprehensive income are presented net of income tax, much like an extraordinary item.

Home Depot, Inc., whose 2005 financial statements are included in Appendix A of this text, follows the third of these alternatives and presents comprehensive income as a column in its Consolidated Statement of Stockholders' Equity and Comprehensive Income. For each of the three years presented, the only adjustments to "Accumulated Other Comprehensive Income (Loss)" are gains from translation adjustments related to the company's foreign operations. These are considered part of the company's overall income history, but are not part of its net income that is presented in the income statement. Although some companies choose to present these types of gains and losses in another manner, such as in a multiple-stage income statement or in two separate income statements, in all cases elements of other comprehensive income are carefully labeled to differentiate them from elements of net income. The majority of publicly held companies present the elements of other comprehensive income in a manner similar to **Home Depot, Inc.**

STATEMENT OF STOCKHOLDERS' EQUITY

LO8 **Describe and prepare a statement of stockholders' equity and the stockholders' equity section of the balance sheet.**

Many corporations expand their statement of retained earnings to show the changes during the year in *all* of the stockholders' equity accounts. This expanded statement, called a **statement of stockholders' equity**, is illustrated in Exhibit 12–5 for Salt Lake Corporation.

The top line of the statement includes the beginning balance of each major category of stockholders' equity. Notice that the fourth column, Retained Earnings, includes the same information as the statement of retained earnings for Salt Lake Corporation that was presented in Exhibit 12–4. We have added several other stock transactions to illustrate the full range of information you will typically find in a statement of stockholders' equity:

- Issuance of common stock for $260,000 (resulting in an increase in both common stock and additional paid-in capital).
- Conversion of shares of preferred stock into common stock at $100,000, resulting in a decrease in 5 percent convertible preferred stock and an increase in common stock and additional paid-in capital.
- Purchase of $47,000 of treasury stock, increasing the amount of treasury stock and decreasing the total of stockholders' equity (as discussed in Chapter 11).

Exhibit 12–5 **STATEMENT OF STOCKHOLDERS' EQUITY**

SALT LAKE CORPORATION
Statement of Stockholders' Equity
For the Year Ended December 31, 2007

	5% Convertible Preferred Stock ($100 par value)	Common Stock ($10 par value)	Additional Paid-in Capital	Retained Earnings	Treasury Stock	Total Stockholders' Equity
Balances, Dec. 31, 2006	$400,000	$200,000	$300,000	$750,000	$ -0-	$1,650,000
Prior period adjustment (net of $15,000 taxes)				(35,000)		(35,000)
Issued 5,000 common shares @ $52		50,000	210,000			260,000
Conversion of 1,000 preferred into 3,000 common shares	(100,000)	30,000	70,000			
Distributed 10% stock dividend (2,800 shares at $50; market price)		28,000	112,000	(140,000)		
Purchased 1,000 shares of common stock held in treasury at $47 a share					(47,000)	(47,000)
Net income				280,000		280,000
Cash dividends:						
Preferred ($5 a share)				(15,000)		(15,000)
Common ($2 a share)				(59,600)		(59,600)
Balances, Dec. 31, 2007	$300,000	$308,000	$692,000	$780,400	$(47,000)	$2,033,400

Note: The numbers that are not bracketed represent positive stockholders' equity amounts. The bracketed numbers represent negative stockholders' equity amounts.

STOCKHOLDERS' EQUITY SECTION OF THE BALANCE SHEET

The stockholders' equity section of Salt Lake Corporation's balance sheet for the year ended December 31, 2007, is shown in Exhibit 12–6. Note that these figures are taken directly from the last line of the statement of stockholders' equity as illustrated in Exhibit 12–5. You should be able to explain the nature and origin of each account and disclosure printed in red as a result of having studied this chapter.

The published financial statements of leading corporations indicate that there is no one standard arrangement for the various items making up the stockholders' equity section. Variations occur in the selection of titles, in the sequence of items, and in the extent of detailed classification. Many companies, in an effort to avoid excessive detail in the balance sheet, combine several related ledger accounts into a single balance sheet item.

Exhibit 12–6

STOCKHOLDERS' EQUITY SECTION OF BALANCE SHEET

Stockholders' Equity

Capital stock:		
5% convertible preferred, $100 par value, 3,000 shares authorized and issued		$ 300,000
Common stock, $10 par value, 100,000 shares authorized, issued 30,800 (of which 1,000 are held in treasury)		308,000
Additional paid-in capital:		
From issuance of common stock	$580,000	
From stock dividends	112,000	692,000
Total paid-in capital		$1,300,000
Retained earnings		780,400
Subtotal		$2,080,400
Less: Treasury stock (1,000 shares at $47 per share)		47,000
Total stockholders' equity		$2,033,400

Ethics, Fraud & Corporate Governance

As discussed in this chapter, the most important aspect of periodic reporting for many investors is the reporting of net income. Investors often are attracted to companies that report increasing income each year. As a result, overstating net income is the most common objective for engaging in inappropriate financial reporting.

LO9 **Illustrate steps management might take to improve the appearance of the company's net income.**

In 2003 and 2004, the Securities and Exchange Commission (SEC) brought a series of enforcement actions against Just for Feet, Inc., its former employees, and employees of former vendors related to the overstatement of Just for Feet's reported income. Although Just for Feet overstated its income through a number of different techniques, two prominent techniques used to overstate income related to fictitious co-op revenue and fictitious "booth" income.

Just for Feet was a national retailer of athletic and outdoor footwear and apparel. Just for Feet filed for bankruptcy protection in November 1999, and it began the process of liquidating its assets and settling its liabilities in 2000.

Just for Feet incurred large amounts of advertising expenses. A vendor (e.g., Adidas, Fila, Nike) would often reduce the amount that Just for Feet owed for merchandise purchases if a particular advertisement featured the vendor's products. These reductions in amounts owed were referred to as "advertising co-op" or "vendor allowances." These vendor allowances were unwritten and not guaranteed. Just for Feet sent vendors copies of advertisements placed, and the vendor determined whether to grant an advertising allowance.

During Just for Feet's 1998 fiscal year, it recorded $19.4 million in co-op receivables (and recognized revenue as a result of recording the receivables) that was not earned. The fictitious revenue of over $19 million was a substantial percentage of Just for Feet's reported income in 1998 of $43 million.

A marketing strategy employed by Just for Feet was the concept of a "store within the store." A particular vendor would install a "booth" in a Just for Feet store that sold its products. For example, if a customer entered a Just for Feet store and was interested in a Nike product, the customer could go to the Nike booth where only Nike products were displayed. When this marketing strategy was introduced, the vendor absorbed the cost of purchasing and installing the booth. By 1998, Just for Feet was ostensibly buying the booths from vendors and receiving back from vendors reductions in the amounts owed for merchandise purchases (merchandise credits). The net effect of these transactions—which the SEC describes as "round-trip" transactions—was that merchandise purchases would be reduced because of the credits issued by vendors, and fixed assets, the booths, were increased by a like amount. This had the effect of overstating current period income.

In addition, by 1998, Just for Feet was reducing advertising expenses (this is how the booth income was recognized) and reducing accounts payable based on projected purchases of booths during the year. Vendors did not bill Just for Feet for the booths it ostensibly purchased, so Just for Feet had no support for the $9 million in booth income recognized as a reduction of advertising expenses. Just for Feet's auditor confirmed with vendors the dollar amounts owed due to purchases of booths (a confirmation of accounts payable). In a number of instances, Just for Feet's management was able to persuade representatives of the vendor to return false confirmations.

One important facet of the Just for Feet fraud is that the SEC has brought enforcement actions against a number of vendor representatives for providing false confirmations to Just for Feet's auditor. When fraud exists, management at the company committing the fraud often tries to convince customers to falsely confirm to the auditors that they owe amounts that are in fact not owed. Such behavior has always represented a crime. It is worth noting that the criminal penalties for lying to external auditors have been substantially increased under the Sarbanes-Oxley Act, and that the SEC and the U.S. Justice Department are more likely to prosecute individuals for this type of behavior than has been the case in the past. Individuals in sales and marketing positions are often targets for requests to falsely confirm facts to external auditors (i.e., to lie)—please be aware of the substantial civil and criminal penalties that can result from lying to auditors.

© Dwayne Newton/PhotoEdit

Concluding Remarks

We discussed various aspects of stockholders' equity, focusing first on paid-in capital in Chapter 11 and then on earned capital in Chapter 12. These discussions complete our detailed coverage of assets, liabilities, and stockholders' equity, which began in Chapter 7 and included financial assets, inventories, plant and intangible assets, liabilities, and, finally, stockholders' equity. While these chapters generally follow a balance sheet organization, in Chapter 12 we also covered the income statement, including the presentation of irregular income items and earnings per share.

In the next chapter, we turn our attention to the statement of cash flows. Recall that companies present three primary financial statements to their stockholders, creditors, and other interested parties—a balance sheet, an income statement, and a statement of cash flows. We leave the detailed coverage of the statement of cash flows to the end because of the importance of the material we have now covered, particularly in Chapters 7 to 12, for a full understanding of that financial statement.

END-OF-CHAPTER REVIEW

SUMMARY OF LEARNING OBJECTIVES

LO1 **Describe how irregular income items, such as discontinued operations and extraordinary items, are presented in the income statement.** Each of these irregular items is shown in a separate section of the income statement, following income or loss from ordinary and continuing operations. Each special item is shown net of any related income tax effects.

LO2 **Compute earnings per share.** Earnings per share is computed by dividing the income applicable to the common stock by the weighted-average number of common shares outstanding. If the income statement includes subtotals for income from continuing operations, or for income before extraordinary items, per-share figures are shown for these amounts, as well as for net income.

LO3 **Distinguish between basic and diluted earnings per share.** Diluted earnings per share is computed for companies that have outstanding securities convertible into shares of common stock. In such situations, the computation of basic earnings per share is based on the number of common shares actually outstanding during the year. The computation of diluted earnings per share, however, is based on the potential number of common shares outstanding if the various securities were converted into common shares. The purpose of showing diluted earnings is to alert investors to the extent to which conversions of securities could reduce basic earnings per share.

LO4 **Account for cash dividends and stock dividends, and explain the effects of these transactions on a company's financial statements.** Cash dividends reduce retained earnings at the time the company's board of directors declares the dividends. At that time, the dividends become a liability for the company. Stock dividends generally are recorded by transferring the market value of the additional shares to be issued from retained earnings to the appropriate paid-in capital accounts. Stock dividends increase the number of shares outstanding but do not change total stockholders' equity, nor do they change the relative amount of the company owned by each individual stockholder.

LO5 **Describe and prepare a statement of retained earnings.** A statement of retained earnings shows the changes in the balance of the Retained Earnings account during the period. In its simplest form, this financial statement shows the beginning balance of retained earnings, adds the net income for the period, subtracts any dividends declared, and thus computes the ending balance of retained earnings.

LO6 **Define *prior period adjustments*, and explain how they are presented in financial statements.** A prior period adjustment corrects errors in the amount of net income reported in a *prior* year. Because the income of the prior year has already been closed into retained earnings, the error is corrected by increasing or decreasing the Retained Earnings account. Prior period adjustments appear in the statement of retained earnings as adjustments to beginning retained earnings. They are *not* reported in the income statement for the current period.

LO7 **Define *comprehensive income*, and explain how it differs from net income.** Net income is a component of comprehensive income. Comprehensive income is broad and includes the effect of certain transactions that are recognized in the financial statements but that are not included in net income because they have not yet been realized. An example is the change in market value of available-for-sale investments. Net income is presented in the income statement. Comprehensive income may be presented in a combined statement with net income, in a separate statement of comprehensive income, or as a part of the statement of stockholders' equity.

LO8 **Describe and prepare a statement of stockholders' equity and the stockholders' equity section of the balance sheet.** This expanded version of the statement of retained earnings explains the changes during the year in each stockholders' equity account. It is not a required financial statement but is often prepared instead of a statement of retained earnings. The statement lists the beginning balance in each stockholders' equity account, explains the nature and the amount of each change, and computes the ending balance in each equity account.

LO9 **Illustrate steps management might take to improve the appearance of the company's net income.** Companies may take certain steps that are intended to improve the appearance of the company's financial performance in its financial statements. The Securities and Exchange Commission brought a series of enforcement actions against Just for Feet for taking steps to artificially enhance the appearance of the company's performance.

Key Terms Introduced or Emphasized in Chapter 12

basic earnings per share (p. 536) Net income applicable to the common stock divided by the weighted-average number of common shares outstanding during the year.

cash dividend (p. 536) A distribution of cash by a corporation to its stockholders.

comprehensive income (p. 542) Net income plus or minus certain changes in financial position that are recorded as direct adjustments to stockholders' equity (for example, changes in the value of available-for-sale investments) rather than as elements in the determination of net income.

date of record (p. 537) The date on which a person must be listed as a shareholder to be eligible to receive a dividend. Follows the date of declaration of a dividend by two or three weeks.

diluted earnings per share (p. 536) Earnings per share computed under the assumption that all convertible securities were converted into additional common shares at the beginning of the current year. The purpose of this pro forma computation is to alert common stockholders to the risk that future earnings per share might be reduced by the conversion of other securities into common stock.

discontinued operations (p. 531) The net operating results (revenue and expenses) of a segment of a company that has been or is being sold, as well as the gain or loss on disposal.

earnings per share (p. 533) Net income applicable to the common stock divided by the weighted-average number of common shares outstanding during the year.

ex-dividend date (p. 537) A date three days prior to the date of record specified in a dividend declaration. A person buying a stock prior to the ex-dividend date also acquires the right to receive the dividend. The three-day interval permits the compilation of a list of stockholders as of the date of record.

extraordinary items (p. 531) Transactions and events that are unusual in nature and occur infrequently—for example, most large earthquake losses. Such items are shown separately in the income statement after the determination of income before extraordinary items.

price-earnings (p/e) ratio (p. 535) Market price of a share of common stock divided by annual earnings per share.

prior period adjustment (p. 541) A correction of a material error in the earnings reported in the financial statements of a prior year. Prior period adjustments are recorded directly in the Retained Earnings account and are not included in the income statement of the current period.

restructuring charges (p. 532) Costs related to reorganizing and downsizing the company to make the company more efficient. These costs are presented in the income statement as a single line item in determining operating income.

segment of the business (p. 531) Those elements of a business that represent a separate and distinct line of business activity or that service a distinct category of customers.

statement of retained earnings (p. 540) A financial statement explaining the change during the year in the amount of retained earnings. May be expanded into a statement of stockholders' equity.

statement of stockholders' equity (p. 542) An expanded version of a statement of retained earnings. Summarizes the changes during the year in all stockholders' equity accounts. Not a required financial statement, but widely used as a substitute for the statement of retained earnings.

stock dividend (p. 538) A distribution of additional shares to common stockholders in proportion to their holdings.

Demonstration Problem

The stockholders' equity of Embassy Corporation at December 31, 2006, is shown below.

Stockholders' equity:	
Common stock, $10 par, 100,000 shares authorized, 40,000 shares issued and outstanding	$ 400,000
Additional paid-in capital: common stock	200,000
Total paid-in capital	$ 600,000
Retained earnings	1,700,000
Total stockholders' equity	$2,300,000

Transactions affecting stockholders' equity during 2007 are as follows:

Mar. 31 A 5-for-4 stock split proposed by the board of directors was approved by vote of the stockholders. The 10,000 new shares were distributed to stockholders.

Apr. 1 The company purchased 2,000 shares of its common stock on the open market at $37 per share.

July 1 The company reissued 1,000 shares of treasury stock at $48 per share.

July 1 The company issued for cash 20,000 shares of previously unissued $8 par value common stock at a price of $47 per share.

Dec. 1 A cash dividend of $1 per share was declared, payable on December 30, to stockholders of record at December 14.

Dec. 22 A 10 percent stock dividend was declared; the dividend shares are to be distributed on January 15 of the following year. The market price of the stock on December 22 was $48 per share.

The net income for the year ended December 31, 2007, amounted to $173,000, after an extraordinary loss of $47,400 (net of related income tax benefits).

Instructions

a. Prepare journal entries (in general journal form) to record the transactions affecting stockholders' equity that took place during the year.

b. Prepare the lower section of the income statement for 2007, beginning with *income before extraordinary items* and showing the extraordinary loss and the net income. Also illustrate the presentation of earnings per share in the income statement, assuming that earnings per share is determined on the basis of the *weighted-average* number of shares outstanding during the year.

c. Prepare a statement of retained earnings for the year ending December 31, 2007.

Solution to the Demonstration Problem

a.

GENERAL JOURNAL — Page 1

Date		Account Titles and Explanations	Debit	Credit
Mar.	31	Memorandum: A 5-for-4 stock split increased the number of shares of common stock outstanding from 40,000 to 50,000 and reduced the par value from $10 to $8 per share. The 10,000 new shares were distributed.		
Apr.	1	Treasury Stock	74,000	
		Cash		74,000
		Acquired 2,000 shares of treasury stock at $37.		
July	1	Cash	48,000	
		Treasury Stock		37,000
		Additional Paid-in Capital: Treasury Stock Transactions		11,000
		Sold 1,000 shares of treasury stock at $48 per share.		
July	1	Cash	940,000	
		Common Stock, $8 par		160,000
		Additional Paid-in Capital: Common Stock		780,000
		Issued 20,000 shares at $47.		
Dec.	1	Dividends	69,000	
		Dividends Payable		69,000
		To record declaration of cash dividend of $1 per share on 69,000 shares of common stock outstanding (1,000 shares in treasury are not entitled to receive dividends).		
		Note: Entry to record the payment of the cash dividend is not shown here because the action does not affect the stockholders' equity.		
Dec.	22	Retained Earnings	331,200	
		Stock Dividends to Be Distributed		55,200
		Additional Paid-in Capital: Stock Dividends		276,000
		To record declaration of 10% stock dividend consisting of 6,900 shares of $8 par value common stock to be distributed on Jan. 15 of next year. Market price $48.		
Dec.	31	Income Summary	173,000	
		Retained Earnings		173,000
		To close Income Summary account.		
Dec.	31	Retained Earnings	69,000	
		Dividends		69,000
		To close Dividends account.		

b.

EMBASSY CORPORATION
Partial Income Statement
For the Year Ended December 31, 2007

Income before extraordinary items	$220,400
Extraordinary loss (net of income tax benefit)	(47,400)
Net income	$173,000
Earnings per share:*	
Income before extraordinary items	$3.73
Extraordinary loss	(0.80)
Net income	$2.93

*The 59,000 weighted-average number of shares of common stock outstanding during 2007 determined as follows:

Jan. 1–Mar. 31: (40,000 + 10,000 shares issued pursuant to a 5-for-4 split) × ¼ of year	12,500
Apr. 1–June 30: (50,000 − 2,000 shares of treasury stock) × ¼ of year	12,000
July 1–Dec. 31: (50,000 + 20,000 shares of new stock − 1,000 shares of treasury stock) × ½ of year	34,500
Weighted-average number of shares outstanding	59,000

c.

EMBASSY CORPORATION
Statement of Retained Earnings
For the Year Ended December 31, 2007

Retained earnings, Dec. 31, 2006		$1,700,000
Net income for 2007		173,000
Subtotal		$1,873,000
Less: Cash dividends ($1 per share)	$ 69,000	
10% stock dividend	331,200	400,200
Retained earnings, Dec. 31, 2007		$1,472,800

Self-Test Questions

The answers to these questions appear on page 569.

1. The primary purpose of showing special types of events separately in the income statement is to:
   - **a.** Increase earnings per share.
   - **b.** Assist users of the income statement in evaluating the profitability of normal, ongoing operations.
   - **c.** Minimize the income taxes paid on the results of ongoing operations.
   - **d.** Prevent unusual losses from recurring.
2. Which of the following situations would *not* be presented in a separate section of the current year's income statement of Hamilton Corporation? During the current year:
   - **a.** Hamilton's Los Angeles headquarters are destroyed by a tornado.
   - **b.** Hamilton sells its entire juvenile furniture operations and concentrates on its remaining children's clothing segment.
   - **c.** Hamilton's accountant discovers that the entire price paid several years ago to purchase company offices in Texas had been charged to a Land account; consequently, no depreciation has ever been taken on these buildings.
   - **d.** As a result of labor union contract changes, Hamilton paid increased compensation expense during the year.
3. When a corporation has outstanding both common and preferred stock:
   - **a.** Basic and diluted earnings per share are reported only if the preferred stock is cumulative.
   - **b.** Earnings per share is reported for each type of stock outstanding.
   - **c.** Earnings per share is computed without regard to the amount of the annual preferred dividends.
   - **d.** Earnings per share is computed without regard to the amount of dividends declared on common stock.

4. Which of the following is (are) *not* true about a stock dividend?
   a. Total stockholders' equity does not change when a stock dividend is declared but does change when it is distributed.
   b. Between the time a stock dividend is declared and when it is distributed, the company's commitment is presented in the balance sheet as a current liability.
   c. Stock dividends do not change the relative portion of the company owned by individual stockholders.
   d. Stock dividends have no impact on the amount of the company's assets.

5. The statement of retained earnings:
   a. Includes prior period adjustments, cash dividends, and stock dividends.
   b. Indicates the amount of cash available for the payment of dividends.
   c. Need not be prepared if a separate statement of stockholders' equity accompanies the financial statements.
   d. Shows revenue, expenses, and dividends for the accounting period.

ASSIGNMENT MATERIAL Discussion Questions

1. What is the purpose of arranging an income statement to show subtotals for *income from continuing operations* and *income before extraordinary items*?
2. Frank's Fun Company owns 30 pizza parlors and a minor league baseball team. During the current year, the company sold three of its pizza parlors and closed another when the lease on the building expired. Should any of these events be classified as discontinued operations in the company's income statement? Explain.
3. Define *extraordinary items*. How are extraordinary items distinguished from items that are presented as separate line items in an income statement, but are not extraordinary?
4. In an effort to make the company more competitive, Fast-Guard, Inc., incurred significant expenses related to a reduction in the number of employees, consolidation of offices and facilities, and disposition of assets that are no longer productive. Explain how these costs should be presented in the financial statements of the company, and describe how an investor should view these costs in predicting future earnings of the company.
5. A *prior period adjustment* relates to the income of past accounting periods. Explain how such an item is shown in the financial statements.
6. In evaluating the potential future profitability of a company, how would you consider irregular income items, such as extraordinary items, discontinued operations, and prior period adjustments?
7. *Earnings per share* and *book value per share* are statistics that relate to common stock. When both preferred and common stock are outstanding, explain the computation involved in determining the following:
   a. Earnings allocable to the common stockholders.
   b. Aggregate book value allocable to the common stockholders.
8. Assume a corporation has only common stock outstanding. Is the number of common shares used in the computation of earnings per share *always* the same as the number of common shares used in computing book value per share for this corporation? Is the number of common shares used in computing these two statistics *ever* the same? Explain.
9. Explain how each of the following is computed:
   a. Price-earnings ratio.
   b. Basic earnings per share.
   c. Diluted earnings per share.
10. Throughout the year, Baker Construction Company had 3 million shares of common stock and 150,000 shares of convertible preferred stock outstanding. Each share of preferred is convertible into two shares of common. What number of shares should be used in the computation of (**a**) basic earnings per share and (**b**) diluted earnings per share?
11. A financial analyst notes that Collier Corporation's earnings per share have been rising steadily for the past five years. The analyst expects the company's net income to continue to increase at the same rate as in the past. In forecasting future basic earnings per share, what special risk should the analyst consider if Collier's basic earnings are significantly larger than its diluted earnings?
12. Explain the significance of the following dates relating to cash dividends: date of declaration, date of record, date of payment, ex-dividend date.
13. What is the purpose of a *stock dividend*?
14. Distinguish between a *stock split* and a *stock dividend*. Is there any reason for the difference in accounting treatment of these two events?
15. What are *restructuring charges*? How are they presented in financial statements?
16. Identify three items that may appear in a statement of retained earnings as changes in the amount of retained earnings.
17. If a company's total stockholders' equity is unchanged by the distribution of a stock dividend, how is it possible for a stockholder who received shares in the distribution of the dividend to benefit?
18. What is a liquidating dividend, and how does it relate to a regular (nonliquidating) dividend?
19. In discussing stock dividends and stock splits in an investments class you are taking, one of the students says, "Stock splits and stock dividends are exactly the same—both are distributions of a company's stock to existing owners without payment to the company." Do you agree? Why or why not?
20. A *statement of stockholders' equity* sometimes is described as an "expanded" statement of retained earnings. Why?

Brief Exercises

BRIEF EXERCISE 12.1
Extraordinary Loss

Fellups, Inc., had net income for the year just ended of $75,000, without considering the following item or its tax effects. During the year, a tornado damaged one of the company's warehouses and its contents. Tornado damage is quite rare in Fellups's location. The estimated amount of the loss from the tornado is $100,000 and the related tax effect is 40 percent. Prepare the final section of Fellups's income statement, beginning with income before extraordinary items.

BRIEF EXERCISE 12.2
Extraordinary Gain

Walker Company had total revenue and expense numbers of $1,500,000 and $1,200,000, respectively, in the current year. In addition, the company had a gain of $230,000 that resulted from the passage of new legislation, which is considered unusual and infrequent for financial reporting purposes. The gain is expected to be subject to a 35 percent income tax rate. Prepare an abbreviated income statement for Walker for the year.

BRIEF EXERCISE 12.3
Discontinued Operations

Wabash, Inc., had revenue and expenses from ongoing business operations for the current year of $480,000 and $430,000, respectively. During the year, the company sold a division which had revenue and expenses (not included in the previous figures) of $100,000 and $75,000, respectively. The division was sold at a loss of $55,000. All items are subject to an income tax rate of 40 percent. Prepare an abbreviated income statement for Wabash for the year.

BRIEF EXERCISE 12.4
Cash and Stock Dividends

Gannon, Inc., had 100,000 shares of common stock outstanding. During the current year, the company distributed a 10 percent stock dividend and subsequently paid a $.50 per share cash dividend. Calculate the number of shares outstanding at the time of the cash dividend and the amount of cash required to fund the cash dividend.

BRIEF EXERCISE 12.5
Statement of Retained Earnings

Messer Company had retained earnings at the beginning of the current year of $590,000. During the year, the following activities occurred:

- Net income of $88,000 was earned.
- A cash dividend of $1.20 per share was declared and distributed on the 50,000 shares of common stock outstanding.

Prepare a statement of retained earnings for the year.

BRIEF EXERCISE 12.6
Statement of Retained Earnings

Salt & Pepper, Inc., had retained earnings at the beginning of the current year of $460,000. During the year the company earned net income of $250,000 and declared dividends as follows:

- $1 per share for the current-year dividend on the 10,000 shares of preferred stock outstanding.
- $1 per share for the dividend in arrears for one year on the 10,000 shares of preferred stock outstanding.
- $.50 per share for the current-year dividend on the 200,000 shares of common stock outstanding.

In addition, the company discovered an overstatement in the prior year's net income of $65,000 and corrected that error in the current year. Prepare a statement of retained earnings for the year.

BRIEF EXERCISE 12.7
Cash Dividend Journal Entries

Gammon, Inc., declared dividends during the current year as follows:

- The current year's cash dividend on the 6 percent, $100 par value preferred stock. 100,000 shares were outstanding at the time of the declaration.
- A cash dividend of $.75 per share on the $10 par value common stock. 750,000 shares were outstanding at the time of the declaration.

Prepare the general journal entries to record the declaration and payment of these dividends, assuming the declaration is recorded directly to retained earnings.

BRIEF EXERCISE 12.8
Stock Dividend Journal Entries

WOW! Inc. declared a 5 percent stock dividend on its 500,000 shares of common stock. The $10 par value common stock was originally sold for $12 and was selling at $15 at the time the stock dividend was declared. Prepare the general journal entries to record and distribute the stock dividend.

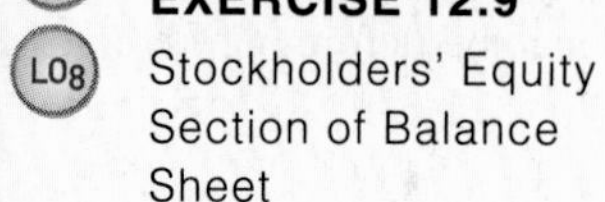

BRIEF EXERCISE 12.9
Stockholders' Equity Section of Balance Sheet

Alexander, Inc., declared and distributed a 10 percent stock dividend on its 700,000 shares of outstanding $5 par value common stock when the stock was selling for $12 per share. The outstanding shares had originally been sold at $8 per share. The balance in retained earnings before the declaration of the stock dividend, but after the addition of the current year's net income, was $995,000. Prepare the stockholders' section of Alexander's balance sheet to reflect these facts.

BRIEF EXERCISE 12.10
Comprehensive Income

Crasher Company had net income in the current year of $500,000. In addition, the company had an unrealized gain on its portfolio of available-for-sale investments of $20,000, net of related income taxes. Assuming the company uses the two-income statement approach for presenting elements of other comprehensive income to its investors and creditors, prepare the statement of comprehensive income for the current year.

Exercises

EXERCISE 12.1
Stock Dividends and Stock Splits

Assume that when you were in high school you saved $1,000 to invest for your college education. You purchased 200 shares of Smiley Incorporated, a small but profitable company. Over the three years that you have owned the stock, the corporation's board of directors have taken the following actions:

1. Declared a 2-for-1 stock split.
2. Declared a 20 percent stock dividend.
3. Declared a 3-for-1 stock split.

The current price of the stock is $12 per share.

a. Calculate the current number of shares and the market value of your investment.
b. Explain the likely reason the board of directors of the company has not declared a cash dividend.
c. State your opinion as to whether or not you would have been better off if the board of directors had declared a cash dividend instead of the stock dividend and stock splits.

LO1 through

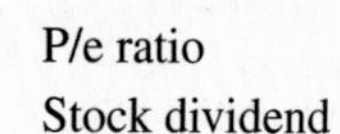

EXERCISE 12.2
Accounting Terminology

The following are 10 technical accounting terms introduced or emphasized in Chapters 11 and 12:

P/e ratio	Treasury stock	Discontinued operations
Stock dividend	Extraordinary item	Prior period adjustment
Basic earnings per share	Additional paid-in capital	Diluted earnings per share
Comprehensive income		

Each of the following statements may (or may not) describe one of these technical terms. For each statement, indicate the term described, or answer "None" if the statement does not correctly describe any of the terms.

a. A gain or loss that is unusual in nature and not expected to recur in the foreseeable future.
b. The asset represented by shares of capital stock that have not yet been issued.
c. A distribution of additional shares of stock that reduces retained earnings but causes no change in total stockholders' equity.
d. The amount received when stock is sold in excess of par value.
e. An adjustment to the beginning balance of retained earnings to correct an error previously made in the measurement of net income.
f. A statistic expressing a relationship between the current market value of a share of common stock and the underlying earnings per share.
g. A separate section sometimes included in an income statement as a way to help investors evaluate the profitability of ongoing business activities.

h. A pro forma figure indicating what earnings per share would have been if all securities convertible into common stock had been converted at the beginning of the current year.

i. A broadly defined measure of financial performance that includes, but is not limited to, net income.

LO1 LO2

EXERCISE 12.3
Discontinued Operations

During the current year, Sports +, Inc., operated two business segments: a chain of surf and dive shops and a small chain of tennis shops. The tennis shops were not profitable and were sold near year-end to another corporation. Sports + operations for the current year are summarized below. The first two captions, "Net sales" and "Costs and expenses," relate only to the company's continuing operations.

Net sales	$12,500,000
Costs and expenses (including applicable income tax)	8,600,000
Operating loss from tennis shops (net of income tax benefit)	192,000
Loss on sale of tennis shops (net of income tax benefit)	348,000

The company had 182,000 shares of a single class of capital stock outstanding throughout the year.

a. Prepare a condensed income statement for the year. At the bottom of the statement, show any appropriate earnings per share figures. (A condensed income statement is illustrated in Exhibit 12–2.)

b. Which earnings per share figure in part **a** do you consider most useful in predicting future operating results for Sports +, Inc.? Why?

LO2

EXERCISE 12.4
Reporting an Extraordinary Item

For the year ended December 31, Global Exports had net sales of $7,750,000, costs and other expenses (including income tax) of $6,200,000, and an extraordinary gain (net of income tax) of $420,000.

a. Prepare a condensed income statement (including earnings per share), assuming that 910,000 shares of common stock were outstanding throughout the year. (A condensed income statement is illustrated in Exhibit 12–2.)

b. Which earnings per share figure is used in computing the price-earnings ratio for Global Exports reported in financial publications such as *The Wall Street Journal*? Explain briefly.

EXERCISE 12.5
Computing Earnings per Share: Effect of Preferred Stock

The net income of Foster Furniture, Inc., amounted to $1,920,000 for the current year.

a. Compute the amount of earnings per share assuming that the shares of capital stock outstanding throughout the year consisted of:

1. 400,000 shares of $1 par value common stock and no preferred stock.
2. 100,000 shares of 8 percent, $100 par value preferred stock and 300,000 shares of $5 par value common stock.

b. Is the earnings per share figure computed in part **a(2)** considered to be basic or diluted? Explain.

LO4

EXERCISE 12.6
Restating Earnings per Share after a Stock Dividend

The 2006 annual report of Software City, Inc., included the following comparative summary of earnings per share over the last three years:

	2006	2005	2004
Earnings per share	$3.15	$2.40	$1.64

In 2007, Software City, Inc., declared and distributed a 100 percent stock dividend. Following this stock dividend, the company reported earnings per share of $1.88 for 2007.

a. Prepare a three-year schedule similar to the one above, but compare earnings per share during the years 2007, 2006, and 2005. (Hint: All per-share amounts in your schedule should be based on the number of shares outstanding *after* the stock dividend.)

b. In preparing your schedule, which figure (or figures) did you have to restate? Why? Explain the logic behind your computation.

EXERCISE 12.7
Cash Dividends, Stock Dividends, and Stock Splits

HiTech Manufacturing Company has 1,000,000 shares of $1 par value capital stock outstanding on January 1. The following equity transactions occurred during the current year:

Apr. 30 Distributed additional shares of capital stock in a 2-for-1 stock split. Market price of stock was $35 per share.

June 1 Declared a cash dividend of 60 cents per share.

July 1 Paid the 60-cent cash dividend to stockholders.

Aug. 1 Declared a 5 percent stock dividend. Market price of stock was $19 per share.

Sept. 10 Issued shares resulting from the 5 percent stock dividend declared on August 1.

a. Prepare journal entries to record the above transactions.

b. Compute the number of shares of capital stock outstanding at year-end.

c. What is the par value per share of HiTech Manufacturing stock at the end of the year?

d. Determine the effect of each of the following on *total* stockholders' equity: stock split, declaration and payment of a cash dividend, declaration and distribution of a stock dividend. (Your answers should be either *increase, decrease,* or *no effect.*)

EXERCISE 12.8
Effect of Stock Dividends on Stock Price

Express, Inc., has a total of 80,000 shares of common stock outstanding and no preferred stock. Total stockholders' equity at the end of the current year amounts to $5 million and the market value of the stock is $66 per share. At year-end, the company declares a 10 percent stock dividend—one share for each 10 shares held. If all parties concerned clearly recognize the nature of the stock dividend, what should you expect the market price per share of the common stock to be on the ex-dividend date?

EXERCISE 12.9
Reporting the Effects of Transactions

Five events pertaining to Lubbock Manufacturing Co. are described below.

a. Declared and paid a cash dividend.

b. Issued a 10 percent stock dividend.

c. Issued a 2-for-1 stock split.

d. Purchased treasury stock.

e. Reissued the treasury stock at a price greater than the purchase price.

Indicate the immediate effects of the events on the financial measurements in the four columnar headings listed below. Use the code letters **I** for increase, **D** for decrease, and **NE** for no effect.

Event	Current Assets	Stockholders' Equity	Net Income	Net Cash Flow (from any source)

EXERCISE 12.10
Effects of Various Transactions on Earnings per Share

Explain the immediate effects, if any, of each of the following transactions on a company's earnings per share:

a. Split the common stock 3-for-1.

b. Realized a gain from the sale of a discontinued operation.

c. Declared and paid a cash dividend on common stock.

d. Declared and distributed a stock dividend on common stock.

e. Acquired several thousand shares of treasury stock.

LO8

EXERCISE 12.11
Where to Find Financial Information

You have now learned about the following financial statements issued by corporations: balance sheet, income statement, statement of retained earnings, statement of stockholders' equity, and statement of cash flows. Listed below are various items frequently of interest to a corporation's owners, potential investors, and creditors, among others. You are to specify which of the above corporate financial statements, if any, reports the desired information. If the listed item is not reported in any formal financial statement issued by a corporation, indicate an appropriate source for the desired information.

a. Number of shares of stock outstanding as of year-end.

b. Total dollar amount of cash dividends declared during the current year.

c. Market value per share at balance sheet date.

d. Cumulative dollar effect of an accounting error made in a previous year.

e. Detailed disclosure of why the number of shares of stock outstanding at the end of the current year is greater than the number of shares of stock outstanding at the end of the prior year.

f. Earnings per share of common stock.

g. Book value per share.

h. Price-earnings (p/e) ratio.

i. The total amount the corporation paid to buy back shares of its own stock, which it now holds.

EXERCISE 12.12
Comprehensive Income

Minor, Inc., had revenue of $572,000 and expenses (other than income taxes) of $282,000 for the current year. The company is subject to a 35 percent income tax rate. In addition, available-for-sale investments, which were purchased for $17,500 early in the year, had a market value at the end of the year of $19,200.

a. Determine the amount of Minor's net income for the year.

b. Determine the amount of Minor's comprehensive income for the year.

c. How would your answers to parts **a** and **b** differ if the market value of Minor's investments at the end of the year had been $14,200?

EXERCISE 12.13
Cash and Stock Dividends

Kosmier Company has outstanding 500,000 shares of $50 par value common stock that originally sold for $60 per share. During the three most recent years, the company carried out the following activities in the order presented: declared and distributed a 10 percent stock dividend, declared and paid a cash dividend of $1 per share, declared and distributed a 2-for-1 stock split, and declared and paid a $.60 per share cash dividend.

a. Determine the number of shares of stock outstanding after the four transactions described above.

b. Determine the amount of cash that the company paid in the four transactions described above.

c. If you were a stockholder who held 100 shares of stock that you purchased four years ago when the market value of the shares was $65, how many shares would you own after the four transactions described above? If the market value of the stock was $40 after the four transactions, would you be better or worse off than before the four transactions?

EXERCISE 12.14
EPS and Dividends Using **Home Depot, Inc.**, Financial Statements

Home Depot, Inc.'s income statements for 2003, 2004, and 2005 show basic earnings per share of $1.88, $2.27, and $2.73, respectively. Diluted earnings per share figures are slightly lower than these numbers, indicating the impact of potential capital stock activity that could reduce earnings per share for current stockholders.

The company paid cash dividends of $.26, $.325, and $.40 per share in 2003, 2004, and 2005, respectively.

a. Why do you think **Home Depot** is paying out only about 14 percent to 15 percent of its net income to stockholders in the form of cash dividends?

b. If you were an investor in **Home Depot**'s stock, would you be unhappy because your dividends represented such a small percentage of the company's net income?

EXERCISE 12.15
Analysis of Stock Information using **Home Depot, Inc.**, Financial Statements

Use the financial statements of **Home Depot, Inc.**, in Appendix A of this text to answer these questions:

a. Study the income statements of **Home Depot, Inc.**, for the three years ending on or about February 1, 2006, 2005, and 2004. Do these statements include any irregular items that might affect your use of the information to project future earnings?

b. Review the stockholders' equity section of the company's balance sheet at January 29, 2006. What type of capital stock is in the capital structure, and how many shares are authorized, issued, and outstanding, and held in treasury on that date?

c. Locate the statement of stockholders' equity and comprehensive income. What treasury stock transactions has **Home Depot** engaged in during the three-year period presented? Has any additional stock (other than treasury stock) been issued during the period reported? If so, what were the circumstances in which that stock was issued?

Problem Set A

PROBLEM 12.1A
Reporting Unusual Events; Using Predictive Subtotals

Atlantic Airlines operated both an airline and several motels located near airports. During the year just ended, all motel operations were discontinued and the following operating results were reported:

Continuing operations (airline):	
Net sales	$55,120,000
Costs and expenses (including income taxes on continuing operations)	43,320,000
Other data:	
Operating income from motels (net of income tax)	864,000
Gain on sale of motels (net of income tax)	4,956,000
Extraordinary loss (net of income tax benefit)	3,360,000

The extraordinary loss resulted from the destruction of an airliner by an earthquake. Atlantic Airlines had 1,000,000 shares of capital stock outstanding throughout the year.

Instructions

a. Prepare a condensed income statement, including proper presentation of the discontinued motel operations and the extraordinary loss. Include all appropriate earnings per share figures.

b. Assume that you expect the profitability of Atlantic Airlines operations to *decline by 5 percent* next year, and the profitability of the motels to decline by 10 percent. What is your estimate of the company's net earnings per share next year?

PROBLEM 12.2A
Format of an Income Statement and a Statement of Retained Earnings

The following data relate to the operations of Slick Software, Inc., during 2007.

Continuing operations:	
Net sales	$19,850,000
Costs and expenses (including applicable income tax)	16,900,000
Other data:	
Operating income during 2007 on segment of the business discontinued near year-end (net of income tax)	140,000
Loss on disposal of discontinued segment (net of income tax benefit)	550,000
Extraordinary loss (net of income tax benefit)	900,000
Prior period adjustment (increase in 2006 depreciation expense, net of income tax benefit)	350,000
Cash dividends declared	950,000

Instructions

a. Prepare a condensed income statement for 2007, including earnings per share figures. Slick Software, Inc., had 200,000 shares of $1 par value common stock and 80,000 shares of $6.25, $100 par value preferred stock outstanding throughout the year.

b. Prepare a statement of retained earnings for the year ended December 31, 2007. As originally reported, retained earnings at December 31, 2006, amounted to $7,285,000.

c. Compute the amount of cash dividend *per share of common stock* declared by the board of directors for 2007. Assume no dividends in arrears on the preferred stock.

d. Assume that 2008 earnings per share is a single figure and amounts to $8.00. Assume also that there are no changes in outstanding common or preferred stock in 2008. Do you consider the $8.00 earnings per share figure in 2008 to be a favorable or unfavorable statistic in comparison with 2007 performance? Explain.

LO2
LO5

PROBLEM 12.3A
Reporting Unusual Events: A Comprehensive Problem

The income statement below was prepared by a new and inexperienced employee in the accounting department of Phoenix, Inc., a business organized as a corporation.

PHOENIX, INC.
Income Statement
For the Year Ended December 31, 2007

Net sales		$10,800,000
Gain on sale of treasury stock		62,000
Excess of issuance price over par value of capital stock		510,000
Prior period adjustment (net of income tax)		60,000
Extraordinary gain (net of income tax)		36,000
Total revenue		$11,468,000
Less:		
Cost of goods sold	$6,000,000	
Selling expenses	1,104,000	
General and administrative expenses	1,896,000	
Loss from settlement of litigation	24,000	
Income tax on continuing operations	720,000	
Operating loss on discontinued operations (net of income tax benefit)	252,000	
Loss on disposal of discontinued operations (net of income tax benefit)	420,000	
Dividends declared on common stock	350,000	
Total costs and expenses		10,766,000
Net income		$ 702,000

Instructions

a. Prepare a corrected income statement for the year ended December 31, 2007, using the format illustrated in Exhibit 12–2. Include at the bottom of your income statement all appropriate earnings-per-share figures. Assume that throughout the year the company had outstanding a weighted average of 180,000 shares of a single class of capital stock.

b. Prepare a statement of retained earnings for 2007. (As originally reported, retained earnings at December 31, 2006, amounted to $2,175,000.)

c. What does the $62,000 "gain on sale of treasury stock" represent? How would you report this item in Phoenix's financial statements at December 31, 2007?

PROBLEM 12.4A
Effects of Stock Dividends, Stock Splits, and Treasury Stock Transactions

At the beginning of the year, Albers, Inc., has total stockholders' equity of $840,000 and 40,000 outstanding shares of a single class of capital stock. During the year, the corporation completes the following transactions affecting its stockholders' equity accounts:

Jan. 10 A 5 percent stock dividend is declared and distributed. (Market price, $20 per share.)

Mar. 15 The corporation acquires 2,000 shares of its own capital stock at a cost of $21.00 per share.

May 30 All 2,000 shares of the treasury stock are reissued at a price of $31.50 per share.

July 31 The capital stock is split 2-for-1.

Dec. 15 The board of directors declares a cash dividend of $1.10 per share, payable on January 15.

Dec. 31 Net income of $525,000 is reported for the year ended December 31.

Instructions

Compute the amount of total stockholders' equity, the number of shares of capital stock outstanding, and the book value per share following each successive transaction. Organize your solution as a three-column schedule with these separate column headings: (1) Total Stockholders' Equity, (2) Number of Shares Outstanding, and (3) Book Value per Share.

PROBLEM 12.5A
Preparing a Statement of Stockholders' Equity

A summary of the transactions affecting the stockholders' equity of Strait Corporation during the current year follows:

Prior period adjustment (net of income tax benefit)	$ (80,000)
Issuance of common stock: 10,000 shares of $10 par value capital stock at $34 per share	340,000
Declaration and distribution of 5% stock dividend (6,000 shares, market price $36 per share)	(216,000)
Purchased 1,000 shares of treasury stock at $35	(35,000)
Reissued 500 shares of treasury stock at a price of $36 per share	18,000
Net income	845,000
Cash dividends declared	(142,700)

Note: Parentheses ( ) indicate a reduction in stockholders' equity.

Instructions

a. Prepare a statement of stockholders' equity for the year. Use these column headings and beginning balances. (Notice that all additional paid-in capital accounts are combined into a single column.)

	Capital Stock ($10 par value)	Additional Paid-in Capital	Retained Earnings	Treasury Stock	Total Stock-holders' Equity
Balances, Jan. 1	$1,100,000	$1,765,000	$950,000	$ -0-	$3,815,000

b. What was the overall effect on total stockholders' equity of the 5 percent stock dividend of 6,000 shares? What was the overall effect on total stockholders' equity of the cash dividends declared? Do these two events have the same impact on stockholders' equity? Why or why not?

PROBLEM 12.6A
Recording Stock Dividends and Treasury Stock Transactions

At the beginning of 2007, Thompson Service, Inc., showed the following amounts in the stockholders' equity section of its balance sheet:

Stockholders' equity:	
Capital stock, $1 par value, 500,000 shares authorized, 382,000 issued and outstanding	$ 382,000
Additional paid-in capital: capital stock	4,202,000
Total paid-in capital	$4,584,000
Retained earnings	2,704,600
Total stockholders' equity	$7,288,600

The transactions relating to stockholders' equity during the year are as follows:

Jan. 3 Declared a dividend of $1 per share to stockholders of record on January 31, payable on February 15.

Feb. 15 Paid the cash dividend declared on January 3.

Apr. 12 The corporation purchased 6,000 shares of its own capital stock at a price of $40 per share.

May 9 Reissued 4,000 shares of the treasury stock at a price of $44 per share.

June 1 Declared a 5 percent stock dividend to stockholders of record at June 15, to be distributed on June 30. The market price of the stock at June 1 was $42 per share. (The 2,000 shares remaining in the treasury do not participate in the stock dividend.)

June 30 Distributed the stock dividend declared on June 1.

Aug. 4 Reissued 600 of the 2,000 remaining shares of treasury stock at a price of $37 per share.

Dec. 31 The Income Summary account, showing net income for the year of $1,928,000, was closed into the Retained Earnings account.

Dec. 31 The $382,000 balance in the Dividends account was closed into the Retained Earnings account.

Instructions

a. Prepare in general journal form the entries to record the above transactions.

b. Prepare the stockholders' equity section of the balance sheet at December 31, 2007. Use the format illustrated in Exhibit 12–6. Include a supporting schedule showing your computation of retained earnings at that date.

c. Compute the maximum cash dividend per share that legally could be declared at December 31, 2007, without impairing the paid-in capital of Thompson Service. (Hint: The availability of retained earnings for dividends is restricted by the cost of treasury stock owned.)

PROBLEM 12.7A
Effects of Transactions

Tech Process, Inc., manufactures a variety of computer peripherals, such as tape drives and printers. Listed below are five events that occurred during the current year.

1. Declared a $1.00 per share cash dividend.
2. Paid the cash dividend.
3. Purchased 1,000 shares of treasury stock for $20.00 per share.
4. Reissued 500 shares of the treasury stock at a price of $18.00 per share.
5. Declared a 15 percent stock dividend.

Instructions

a. Indicate the effects of each of these events on the financial measurements listed in the four columnar headings listed below. Use the following code letters: **I** for increase, **D** for decrease, and **NE** for no effect.

Event	Current Assets	Stockholders' Equity	Net Income	Net Cash Flow (from any source)

b. For each event, *explain* the reasoning behind your answers. Be prepared to explain this reasoning in class.

PROBLEM 12.8A
Preparing the Stockholders' Equity Section: A Challenging Case

The Mandella family decided early in 2006 to incorporate their family-owned vineyards under the name Mandella Corporation. The corporation was authorized to issue 500,000 shares of a single class of $10 par value capital stock. Presented below is the information necessary to prepare the stockholders' equity section of the company's balance sheet at the end of 2006 and at the end of 2007.

2006. In January the corporation issued to members of the Mandella family 150,000 shares of capital stock in exchange for cash and other assets used in the operation of the vineyards. The fair market value of these assets indicated an issue price of $30 per share. In December, Joe Mandella died, and the corporation purchased 10,000 shares of its own capital stock from his estate at $34 per share. Because of the large cash outlay to acquire this treasury stock, the directors decided not to declare cash dividends in 2006 and instead declared a 10 percent stock dividend to be distributed in January 2007. The stock price at the declaration date was $35 per share. (The treasury shares do not participate in the stock dividend.) Net income for 2006 was $940,000.

2007. In January the corporation distributed the stock dividend declared in 2006, and in February, the 10,000 treasury shares were sold to Maria Mandella at $39 per share. In June, the capital stock was split 2-for-1. (Approval was obtained to increase the authorized number of shares to 1 million.) On December 15, the directors declared a cash dividend of $2 per share, payable in January 2008. Net income for 2007 was $1,080,000.

Instructions

Using the format illustrated in Exhibit 12–6, prepare the stockholders' equity section of the balance sheet at:

a. December 31, 2006.

b. December 31, 2007.

Show any necessary computations in supporting schedules.

PROBLEM 12.9A
Format of an Income Statement; EPS

The following information is excerpted from the financial statements in a recent annual report of Esper Corporation. (Dollar figures and shares of stock are in thousands.)

Extraordinary loss on extinguishment of debt	$ (8,490)
Loss from continuing operations	$(16,026)
Income from discontinued operations	$ 6,215
Preferred stock dividend requirements	$ (2,778)
Weighted-average number of shares of common stock outstanding	39,739

Instructions

a. Rearrange the items to present in good form the last portion of the income statement for Esper Corporation, beginning with "Loss from continuing operations."

b. Calculate the amount of *net loss* per share for the period. (Do *not* calculate per-share amounts for subtotals, such as income from continuing operations, loss before extraordinary items, etc. You are required to compute only a single earnings per share amount.)

Problem Set B

PROBLEM 12.1B
Reporting Unusual Events: Using Predictive Subtotals

Pacific Airlines operated both an airline and several rental car operations located near airports. During the year just ended, all rental car operations were discontinued and the following operating results were reported:

Continuing operations (airline):	
Net sales	$61,440,000
Costs and expenses (including income taxes on continuing operations)	53,980,000
Other data:	
Operating income from car rentals (net of income tax)	670,000
Gain on sale of rental car business (net of income tax)	4,330,000
Extraordinary loss (net of income tax benefit)	3,120,000

The extraordinary loss resulted from the destruction of an airliner by terrorists. Pacific Airlines had 4,000,000 shares of capital stock outstanding throughout the year.

Instructions

a. Prepare a condensed income statement, including proper presentation of the discontinued rental car operations and the extraordinary loss. Include all appropriate earnings per share figures.

b. Assume that you expect the profitability of Pacific's airline operations to *decline by 10 percent* next year and the profitability of the rental car operation to decline by 10 percent. What is your estimate of the company's net earnings per share next year?

PROBLEM 12.2B
Format of an Income Statement and a Statement of Retained Earnings

Shown below are data relating to the operations of Beach, Inc., during 2007.

Continuing operations:	
Net sales	$37,400,000
Costs and expenses (including applicable income taxes)	21,500,000
Other data:	
Operating income during 2007 on segment of the business discontinued near year-end (net of income taxes)	205,000
Loss on disposal of discontinued segment (net of income tax benefit)	510,000
Extraordinary loss (net of income tax benefit)	930,000
Prior period adjustment (increase in 2006 amortization expense, net of income tax benefit)	310,000
Cash dividends declared	2,000,000

Instructions

a. Prepare a condensed income statement for 2007, including earnings per share statistics. Beach, Inc., had 200,000 shares of $1 par value common stock and 100,000 shares of $6, $100 par value preferred stock outstanding throughout the year.

b. Prepare a statement of retained earnings for the year ended December 31, 2007. As originally reported, retained earnings at December 31, 2006, amounted to $10,700,000.

c. Compute the amount of cash dividend *per share of common stock* declared by the board of directors for 2007. Assume no dividends in arrears on the preferred stock.

d. Assume that 2008 earnings per share is a single figure and amounts to $75. Assume also that there are no changes in outstanding common or preferred stock in 2008. Do you consider the $75 earnings per share figure in 2008 to be a favorable or unfavorable statistic in comparison with 2007 performance? Explain.

LO1 LO2 LO5 

PROBLEM 12.3B
Reporting Unusual Events: A Comprehensive Problem

The income statement below was prepared by a new and inexperienced employee in the accounting department of Dexter, Inc., a business organized as a corporation:

DEXTER, INC.
Income Statement
For the Year Ended December 31, 2007

Net sales		$10,200,000
Gain on sale of treasury stock		56,000
Excess of issuance price over par value of capital stock		710,000
Prior period adjustment (net of income tax)		80,000
Extraordinary gain (net of income tax)		110,000
Total revenue		$11,156,000
Less:		
Cost of goods sold	$4,000,000	
Selling expenses	1,050,000	
General and administrative expenses	840,000	
Loss from settlement of litigation	10,000	
Income tax on continuing operations	612,000	
Operating loss on discontinued operations (net of income tax benefit)	180,000	
Loss on disposal of discontinued operations (net of income tax benefit)	240,000	
Dividends declared on common stock	300,000	
Total costs and expenses		7,232,000
Net income		$ 3,924,000

Instructions

a. Prepare a corrected income statement for the year ended December 31, 2007, using the format illustrated in Exhibit 12–2. Include at the bottom of your income statement all appropriate earnings per share figures. Assume that throughout the year the company had outstanding a weighted average of 500,000 shares of a single class of capital stock.

b. Prepare a statement of retained earnings for 2007. (As originally reported, retained earnings at December 31, 2006, amount to $3,200,000.)

c. What does the $56,000 "Gain on sale of treasury stock" represent? How would you report this item in Dexter's financial statements at December 31, 2007?

PROBLEM 12.4B
Effects of Stock Dividends, Stock Splits, and Treasury Stock Transactions

At the beginning of the year, Jessel, Inc., has total stockholders' equity of $600,000 and 20,000 outstanding shares of a single class of capital stock. During the year, the corporation completes the following transactions affecting its stockholders' equity accounts:

Jan. 16	A 5 percent stock dividend is declared and distributed. (Market price, $50 per share.)
Feb. 9	The corporation acquires 300 shares of its own capital stock at a cost of $55 per share.
Mar. 3	All 300 shares of the treasury stock are reissued at a price of $65 per share.
Jul. 5	The capital stock is split 2-for-1.
Nov. 22	The board of directors declares a cash dividend of $6 per share, payable on January 22.
Dec. 31	Net income of $87,000 is reported for the year ended December 31.

Instructions

Compute the amount of total stockholders' equity, the number of shares of capital stock outstanding, and the book value per share following each successive transaction. Organize your solution as a three-column schedule with these separate column headings: (1) "Total Stockholders' Equity," (2) "Number of Shares Outstanding," and (3) "Book Value per Share."

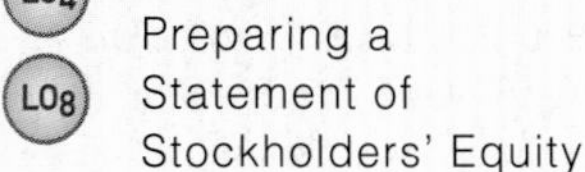

PROBLEM 12.5B
Preparing a Statement of Stockholders' Equity

The following is a summary of the transactions affecting the stockholders' equity of Dry Wall, Inc., during the current year:

Prior period adjustment (net of income tax benefit)	$ (47,000)
Issuance of common stock: 20,000 shares of $1 par value capital stock at $15 per share	300,000
Declaration and distribution of 10% stock dividend (15,000 shares, market price $17 per share)	255,000*
Purchased 3,000 shares of treasury stock at $16	(48,000)
Reissued 1,000 shares of treasury stock at a price of $18 per share	18,000
Net income	1,200,000
Cash dividends declared ($1 per share)	(163,000)

Note: Parentheses ( ) indicate a reduction in stockholders' equity. Asterisk * indicates no change in total shareholders' equity.

Instructions

a. Prepare a statement of stockholders' equity for the year. Use the column headings and beginning balances shown below. (Notice that all additional paid-in capital accounts are combined into a single column.)

	Capital Stock ($1 par value)	Additional Paid-in Capital	Retained Earnings	Treasury Stock	Total Stockholders' Equity
Balances, Jan. 1	$130,000	$1,170,000	$1,400,000	–0–	$2,700,000

b. What was the overall effect on total stockholders' equity of the 10 percent stock dividend of 15,000 shares? What was the overall effect on total stockholders' equity of the cash dividends declared? Do these two events have the same impact on stockholders' equity? Why or why not?

PROBLEM 12.6B
Recording Stock Dividends and Treasury Stock Transactions

At the beginning of 2007, Greene, Inc., showed the following amounts in the stockholders' equity section of its balance sheet:

Stockholders' equity:	
Capital stock, $1 par value, 1,000,000 shares authorized, 560,000 issued and outstanding	$ 560,000
Additional paid-in capital: capital stock	4,480,000
Total paid-in capital	5,040,000
Retained earnings	3,000,000
Total stockholders' equity	$8,040,000

The transactions relating to stockholders' equity during the year are as follows:

Jan. 5 Declared a dividend of $1 per share to stockholders of record on January 31, payable on February 18.

Feb. 18 Paid the cash dividend declared on January 5.

Apr. 20 The corporation purchased 1,000 shares of its own capital stock at a price of $10 per share.

May 25 Reissued 500 shares of the treasury stock at a price of $12 per share.

June 15 Declared a 5 percent stock dividend to stockholders of record at June 22, to be distributed on June 30. The market price of the stock at June 15 was $11 per share. (The 500 shares remaining in the treasury do not participate in the stock dividend.)

June 30 Distributed the stock dividend declared on June 15.

Aug. 12 Reissued 300 of the 500 remaining shares of treasury stock at a price of $9.75 per share.

Dec. 31 The Income Summary account, showing net income for the year of $1,750,000, was closed into the Retained Earnings account.

Dec. 31 The $560,000 balance in the Dividends account was closed into the Retained Earnings account.

Instructions

a. Prepare in general journal form the entries to record the above transactions.

b. Prepare the stockholders' equity section of the balance sheet at December 31, 2007. Use the format illustrated in Exhibit 12–6. Include a supporting schedule showing your computation of retained earnings at that date.

c. Compute the maximum cash dividend per share that legally could be declared at December 31, 2007, without impairing the paid-in capital of Greene, Inc. (Hint: The availability of retained earnings for dividends is restricted by the cost of treasury stock owned.)

PROBLEM 12.7B
Effects of Transactions

Hot Water, Inc., manufactures a variety of dry cleaning equipment. Listed below are five events that occurred during the current year:

1. Declared a $5 per share cash dividend.
2. Paid the cash dividend.
3. Purchased 1,000 shares of treasury stock for $37 per share.
4. Reissued 600 shares of the treasury stock at a price of $36 per share.
5. Declared a 5 percent stock dividend.

Instructions

a. Indicate the effects of each of these events on the financial measurements listed in the four column headings listed below. Use the following code letters: **I** for increase, **D** for decrease, and **NE** for no effect.

Event	Current Assets	Stockholders' Equity	Net Income	Net Cash Flow (from any source)

b. For each event, *explain* the reasoning behind your answers. Be prepared to explain this reasoning in class.

PROBLEM 12.8B
Preparing the Stockholders' Equity Section: A Challenging Case

The Adams family decided early in 2006 to incorporate their family-owned farm under the name Adams Corporation. The corporation was authorized to issue 100,000 shares of a single class of $1 par value capital stock. Presented below is the information necessary to prepare the stockholders' equity section of the company's balance sheet at the end of 2006 and at the end of 2007.

2006. In January the corporation issued to members of the Adams family 20,000 shares of capital stock in exchange for cash and other assets used in the operation of the farm. The fair market value of these assets indicated an issue price of $25 per share. In December, George Adams died and the corporation purchased 4,000 shares of its own capital stock from his estate at $30 per share. Because of the large cash outlay to acquire this treasury stock, the directors decided not to declare cash dividends in 2006 and instead declared a 10 percent stock dividend to be distributed in January 2007. The stock price at the declaration date was $31 per share. (The treasury shares do not participate in the stock dividend.) Net income for 2006 was $850,000.

2007. In January the corporation distributed the stock dividend declared in 2006, and in February, the 4,000 treasury shares were sold to Joan Adams at $35 per share. In June, the capital stock was split 2-for-1. (Approval was obtained to increase the authorized number of shares to 200,000.) On December 11, the directors declared a cash dividend of $1 per share, payable in January 2008. Net income for 2007 was $810,000.

Instructions

Using the format illustrated in Exhibit 12–6, prepare the stockholders' equity section of the balance sheet at:

a. December 31, 2006.

b. December 31, 2007.

Show any necessary computations in supporting schedules.

PROBLEM 12.9B
Format of an Income Statement EPS

The following information is excerpted from the financial statements in a recent annual report of Blue Jay Manufacturing Corporation. (Dollar figures and shares of stock are in thousands.)

Extraordinary loss on extinguishment of debt	$ (8,750)
Loss from continuing operations	(19,470)
Income from discontinued operations	12,000
Preferred stock dividend requirements	(3,100)
Weighted-average number of shares of common stock outstanding	10,000

Instructions

a. Rearrange the items to present in good form the last portion of the income statement for Blue Jay Manufacturing Corporation, beginning with "Loss from continuing operations."

b. Calculate the amount of *net loss* per share for the period. (Do *not* calculate per-share amounts for subtotals, such as income from continuing operations, loss before extraordinary items, and so forth. You are required to compute only a single earnings per share amount.)

Critical Thinking Cases

CASE 12.1
What's This?

The following events were reported in the financial statements of large, publicly owned corporations:

a. **Atlantic Richfield Company (ARCO)** sold or abandoned the entire noncoal minerals segment of its operations. In the year of disposal, this segment had an operating loss. **ARCO** also incurred a loss of $514 million on disposal of its noncoal minerals segment of the business.

b. **American Airlines** increased the estimated useful life used in computing depreciation on its aircraft. If the new estimated life had always been in use, the net income reported in prior years would have been substantially higher.

c. **Union Carbide Corp.** sustained a large loss as a result of the explosion of a chemical plant.

d. **Georgia-Pacific Corporation** realized a $10 million gain as a result of condemnation proceedings in which a governmental agency purchased assets from the company in a "forced sale."

Instructions

Indicate whether each event should be classified as a discontinued operation, or an extraordinary item, or included among the revenue and expenses of normal and recurring business operations. Briefly explain your reasons for each answer.

CASE 12.2
Is There Life without Baseball?

Jackson Publishing, Inc. (JPI), publishes two newspapers and, until recently, owned a professional baseball team. The baseball team had been losing money for several years and was sold at the end of 2007 to a group of investors who plan to move it to a larger city. Also in 2007, JPI suffered an extraordinary loss when its Raytown printing plant was damaged by a tornado. The damage has since been repaired. A condensed income statement follows:

JACKSON PUBLISHING, INC.
Income Statement
For the Year Ended December 31, 2007

Net revenue		$41,000,000
Costs and expenses		36,500,000
Income from continuing operations		$ 4,500,000
Discontinued operations:		
Operating loss on baseball team	$(1,300,000)	
Gain on sale of baseball team	4,700,000	3,400,000
Income before extraordinary items		$ 7,900,000
Extraordinary loss:		
Tornado damage to Raytown printing plant		(600,000)
Net income		$ 7,300,000

Instructions

On the basis of this information, answer the following questions. Show any necessary computations and explain your reasoning.

a. What would JPI's net income have been for 2007 if it *had not* sold the baseball team?

b. Assume that for 2008 you expect a 7 percent increase in the profitability of JPI's newspaper business but had projected a $2,000,000 operating loss for the baseball team if JPI had continued to operate the team in 2008. What amount would you forecast as JPI's 2008 net income *if the company had continued to own and operate the baseball team*?

c. Given your assumptions in part **b**, but given that JPI *did* sell the baseball team in 2007, what would you forecast as the company's estimated net income for 2008?

d. Assume that the expenses of operating the baseball team in 2007 amounted to $32,200,000, net of any related income tax effects. What was the team's *net revenue* for the year?

through
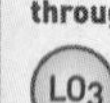

CASE 12.3
Using Earnings per Share Statistics

For many years New York Studios has produced television shows and operated several FM radio stations. Late in the current year, the radio stations were sold to Times Publishing, Inc. Also during the current year, New York Studios sustained an extraordinary loss when one of its camera trucks caused an accident in an international grand prix auto race. Throughout the current year, the company had 3 million shares of common stock and a large quantity of convertible preferred stock outstanding. Earnings per share reported for the current year were as follows:

	Basic	Diluted
Earnings from continuing operations	$8.20	$6.80
Earnings before extraordinary items	$6.90	$5.50
Net earnings	$3.60	$2.20

Instructions

a. Briefly explain why New York Studios reports diluted earnings per share amounts as well as basic earnings per share. What is the purpose of showing investors the diluted figures?

b. What was the total dollar amount of the extraordinary loss sustained by New York Studios during the current year?

c. Assume that the price-earnings ratio shown in the morning newspaper for New York Studios's common stock indicates that the stock is selling at a price equal to 10 times the reported earnings per share. What is the approximate market price of the stock?

d. Assume that you expect both the revenue and expenses involved in producing television shows to increase by 10 percent during the coming year. What would you forecast as the company's basic earnings per share for the coming year under each of the following independent assumptions? (Show your computations and explain your reasoning.)

1. *None* of the convertible preferred stock is converted into common stock during the coming year.
2. *All* of the convertible preferred stock is converted into common stock at the beginning of the coming year.

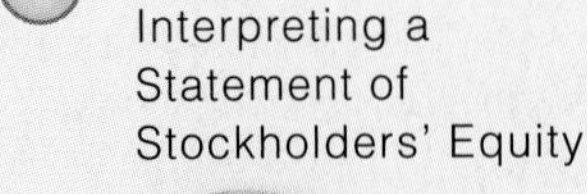

LO8

CASE 12.4
Interpreting a Statement of Stockholders' Equity

The following information has been excerpted from the statement of stockholders' equity included in a recent annual report of Thompson Supply Company. (Dollar figures are in millions.)

	Common Stock		Additional Paid-in Capital	Retained Earnings	Treasury Stock	
	Shares	Amount			Shares	Amount
Balances, beginning of year	82,550,000	$425.0	$29.5	$ 950.2	4,562,500	$(135.9)
Net income				200.0		
Cash dividends declared on common stock				(95.7)		
Common stock issued for stock option plans			(1.4)		(601,300)	16.7
Repurchases of common stock					1,235,700	(78.6)
Balances, year-end	82,550,000	$425.0	$28.1	$1,054.5	5,196,900	$(197.8)

Instructions

Use the information about Thompson Supply to answer the following questions.

a. How many shares of common stock are outstanding at the *beginning* of the year? At the *end* of the year?

b. What was the total common stock dividend declared during the presented year? Thompson's annual report disclosed that the common stock dividend during that year was $1.23 per share. Approximately how many shares of common stock were entitled to the $1.23 per share dividend during the year? Is this answer compatible with your answers in part **a**?

c. The statement presented indicates that common stock was both issued and repurchased during the year, yet the number of common shares shown and the common stock amount (first and second columns) did not change from the beginning to the end of the year. Explain.

d. What was the average price per share Thompson paid to acquire the treasury shares held at the *beginning* of the year?

e. Was the aggregate issue price of the 601,300 treasury shares issued during the year for stock option plans higher or lower than the cost Thompson paid to acquire those treasury shares? (Hint: Analyze the impact on Additional Paid-in Capital.)

f. What was the average purchase price per share paid by Thompson to acquire treasury shares *during the current year*?

g. In its annual report, Thompson disclosed that the (weighted) average number of common shares outstanding during the year was 77,500,000. In part **a** above, you determined the number of common shares outstanding as of the end of the year. Which figure is used in computing *earnings per share*? Which is used in computing *book value per share*?

CASE 12.5
Classification of Unusual Items—and the Potential Financial Impact

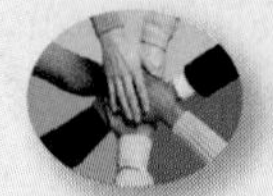

Elliot-Cole is a publicly owned international corporation, with operations in over 90 countries. Net income has been growing at approximately 15 percent per year, and the stock consistently trades at about 20 times earnings.

To attract and retain key management leadership, the company has developed a compensation plan in which managers receive earnings in the form of bonuses as well as opportunities to purchase shares of the company's stock at a reduced price. In general, the higher the company's net income each year, the greater the benefit to management in terms of their personal compensation.

During the current year, political unrest and economic upheaval threatened Elliot-Cole's business operations in three foreign countries. At year-end, the company's auditors insisted that management write off the company's assets in these countries, stating that these assets were "severely impaired." Said one corporate official, "We can't argue with that. Each of these countries is a real trouble spot. We might be pulling out of these places at any time, and any assets probably would just be left behind."

Management agreed that the carrying value of Elliot-Cole's assets in these three countries should be reduced to "scrap value"—which was nothing. These write-downs amounted to approximately 18 percent of the company's income *prior* to recognition of these losses. (These write-offs are for financial reporting purposes only; they have *no effect* on the company's income tax obligations.)

At the meeting with the auditors, one of Elliot-Cole's officers states, "There's no doubt we should write these assets off. But of course, this is an extraordinary loss. A loss of this size can't be considered a routine matter."

Instructions

a. Explain the logic behind writing down the book values of assets that are still in operation.

b. Evaluate the officer's statement concerning the classification of these losses. Do you agree that they should be classified as an extraordinary item? Explain.

c. Explain the effect that the classification of these losses—that is, as ordinary or extraordinary—will have in the current period on Elliot-Cole's:

1. Net income.
2. Income before extraordinary items.
3. Income from continuing operations.
4. Net cash flow from operating activities.

d. Explain how the classification of these losses will affect the p/e ratio reported in newspapers such as *The Wall Street Journal.*

e. Does management appear to have any self-interest in the classification of these losses? Explain.

f. Explain how (if at all) these write-offs are likely to affect the earnings of *future* periods.

g. What "ethical dilemma" confronts management in this case?

CASE 12.6
Managing Profitability

You are a staff accountant for Pearce, Pearce, and Smith, CPAs, and have worked for several years on the audit of a major client of the firm, Flexcom, Inc. Flexcom sells its products in a highly competitive market and relies heavily on the careful management of inventory because of the unique nature of the products sold and the importance of minimizing the company's investment in inventory. Flexcom sells cellular phones, personal handheld computers, and other communications devices that are particularly sensitive to changes in consumer demands and changes in technology, which are both frequent and significant in terms of their impact on the attractiveness of Flexcom's products to buyers.

In the course of your work, you have noticed several trends related to inventory that interest you and that have caused you to explore further the underlying details. Specifically, you have determined the following:

- Despite sluggish sales volume, the company's net income has steadily increased for each of the last three years.
- Inventory has been increasing at a higher-than-normal rate.
- The allowance to reduce inventory for obsolescence has dramatically declined during the last three years, going from nearly 10 percent of inventory three years ago to approximately 2 percent at the end of the most recent year.

You are aware that, within Flexcom, profitability is a major factor in the evaluation of management and has been cited in at least two recent situations as the basis for replacing individuals in leadership positions.

Instructions

Prepare a brief report to your supervisor explaining why you are bothered by these trends and offer one or more explanations that may underlie what is actually going on within Flexcom.

BUSINESSWEEK CASE 12.7

Extraordinary Items and Judgment

BusinessWeek

David Henry, in a March 2003 *BusinessWeek* article entitled, "Ouch! Real Numbers," indicates that new accounting rules will deflate earnings hype and, perhaps, stocks. He describes tighter accounting rules that will reveal a lower level of normal earnings.

Henry goes on to say that extraordinary items were once just that—extraordinary. In recent years, however, they have become much too common, with large adjustments taken for certain "special one-time items," such as layoffs, inventory write-downs, acquisitions (of other companies), and so on.

Instructions

Why do you think there has been an increase in the frequency of "special items" in the income statements of major U.S. corporations? Is it important for different companies to treat these special items in the same way? Why or why not?

INTERNET CASE 12.8

Comparing Price-Earnings Ratios

The normal price-earnings ratio of a company varies depending on expected future earnings of the company and the general price level of the stock market. On average, mature companies have lower price-earnings ratios, usually less than 20, than do emerging companies, which may have p/e ratios over 100. This is because of the steep growth in earnings that is characteristic of an emerging company.

Instructions

a. Visit *Fortune* magazine's Internet site and select a Fortune 500 corporation. The site's address is

www.fortune.com

b. Visit NASDAQ's home page at

www.nasdaq.com

Click on "Quotes+" at the top of the screen, then click "FlashQuotes" for NASDAQ-100 and select a small corporation.

c. Get "Detail Quotes" for the companies from PCQUOTE's Internet site at

www.pcquote.com

Indicate the current price of each corporation's stock, including its high and low price for the day. (If either of the companies has a net loss for the most recent period, go back and replace it with a profitable company.)

d. Compare the price-earnings ratios (as shown on the Detailed Quote Snapshot screen) of the two companies. Speculate as to why one company has a higher price-earnings ratio than the other.

Internet sites are time and date sensitive. It is the purpose of these exercises to have you explore the Internet. You may need to use the Yahoo! search engine **http://www.yahoo.com** *(or another favorite search engine) to find a company's current Web address.*

Answers to Self-Test Questions

1. b **2.** c, d **3.** d **4.** a, b **5.** a, c

13

Statement of Cash Flows

Learning Objectives

AFTER STUDYING THIS CHAPTER, YOU SHOULD BE ABLE TO:

- LO1 Explain the purposes and uses of a statement of cash flows.
- LO2 Describe how cash transactions are classified in a statement of cash flows.
- LO3 Compute the major cash flows relating to operating activities.
- LO4 Compute the cash flows relating to investing and financing activities.
- LO5 Distinguish between the direct and indirect methods of reporting operating cash flows.
- LO6 Explain why net income differs from net cash flows from operating activities.
- LO7 Compute net cash flows from operating activities using the *indirect* method.
- LO8 Discuss the likely effects of various business strategies on cash flows.
- LO9 Explain how a worksheet may be helpful in preparing a statement of cash flows.

Getty Images

KRAFT FOODS INC.

Kraft Foods Inc. states its mission "to be the undisputed global food leader." The company attempts to achieve this mission through the development and sale of many of the popular food brands on the shelves of grocery stores today, including Oreo (cookies), Miracle Whip (salad dressing), Ritz (crackers), Post (cereal), Oscar Mayer (prepared meat), and others.

Cash flow is an important consideration for all companies, but particularly for a giant company like Kraft Foods Inc. as it continuously expands its global reach. Kraft Foods Inc.'s 2005 annual report includes its statement of cash flows. This statement is one of the major financial statements required for companies to provide information to investors, creditors, and others that is in compliance with generally accepted accounting principles. This statement displays cash flows in three major categories: operating activities, investing activities, and financing activities. In the case of Kraft Foods Inc. for 2005, cash provided by operating activities was approximately $3.5 billion. This cash was used to support major capital expenditures and to retire debt. Efficiently managing cash flows of this magnitude is an important responsibility of the company's top leadership and is critical for the company's continued success.

Cash flow information about a company is helpful to investors and creditors in judging future cash flows. If the company itself does not have strong cash flow, it is unlikely that the company will be in a cash position to provide strong cash flows to its investors and creditors. We introduced in Chapter 2 the idea of a financial statement that describes cash flows, and in Chapter 13 we go into greater depth regarding this important financial statement. **Kraft Foods Inc.** had $282 million in cash at the beginning of 2005 and $316 million at the end of that year. Does that mean that the company's cash simply increased $34 million during the year? Actually, cash went up by $3,464 million from its operating activities, but went down $3,430 million from a combination of its financing, investing, and other activities. In other words, the $34 million increase represents a net amount of significantly larger positive and negative amounts. The statement of cash flows shows the details underlying these changes and explains how the company managed its cash during the year.

Statement of Cash Flows

PURPOSES OF THE STATEMENT

LO1 Explain the purposes and uses of a statement of cash flows.

The objective of a statement of cash flows is to provide information about the *cash receipts* and *cash payments* of a business entity during the accounting period. The term **cash flows** includes both cash receipts and payments. In a statement of cash flows, information about cash receipts and cash payments is classified in terms of the company's operating activities, investing activities, and financing activities. The statement of cash flows assists investors, creditors, and others in assessing such factors as:

- The company's ability to generate positive cash flows in future periods.
- The company's ability to meet its obligations and to pay dividends.
- The company's need for external financing.
- Reasons for differences between the amount of net income and the related net cash flows from operating activities.
- Both the cash and noncash aspects of the company's investment and financing transactions for the period.
- Causes of the change in the amount of cash and cash equivalents between the beginning and the end of the accounting period.

Stated simply, a statement of cash flows helps users of financial statements evaluate a company's ability to have sufficient cash—both on a short-run and on a long-run basis. For this reason, the statement of cash flows is useful to virtually everyone interested in the company's financial health: short- and long-term creditors, investors, management—and both current and prospective competitors.

EXAMPLE OF A STATEMENT OF CASH FLOWS

An example of a statement of cash flows appears in Exhibit 13–1. Cash outflows are shown in parentheses.[1]

CLASSIFICATION OF CASH FLOWS

LO2 Describe how cash transactions are classified in a statement of cash flows.

The cash flows shown in the statement are presented in three major categories: (1) **operating activities**, (2) **investing activities**, and (3) **financing activities**.[2] We will now look briefly at the way cash flows are classified among these three categories.

Operating Activities

The operating activities section shows the *cash effects* of revenue and expense transactions. Stated another way, the operating activities section of the statement of

[1] In this illustration, net cash flows from operating activities are determined by the *direct method*. An alternative approach, called the *indirect method*, is illustrated later in this chapter.

[2] To reconcile to the ending cash balance, "effects of changes in exchange rates on cash" is used in the cash flow statements of companies with foreign currency holdings. This classification, as well as other complexities, is discussed in more advanced accounting courses.

Exhibit 13–1

ALLISON CORPORATION STATEMENT OF CASH FLOWS

ALLISON CORPORATION Statement of Cash Flows For the Year Ended December 31, 2007		
Cash flows from operating activities:		
Cash received from customers	$ 870,000	
Interest and dividends received	10,000	
Cash provided by operating activities		$880,000
Cash paid to suppliers and employees	$(764,000)	
Interest paid	(28,000)	
Income taxes paid	(38,000)	
Cash disbursed for operating activities		(830,000)
Net cash flows from operating activities		$ 50,000
Cash flows from investing activities:		
Purchases of marketable securities	$ (65,000)	
Proceeds from sales of marketable securities	40,000	
Loans made to borrowers	(17,000)	
Collections on loans	12,000	
Purchases of plant assets	(160,000)	
Proceeds from sales of plant assets	75,000	
Net cash flows from investing activities		(115,000)
Cash flows from financing activities:		
Proceeds from short-term borrowing	$ 45,000	
Payments to settle short-term debts	(55,000)	
Proceeds from issuing bonds payable	100,000	
Proceeds from issuing capital stock	50,000	
Dividends paid	(40,000)	
Net cash flows from financing activities		100,000
Net increase (decrease) in cash		$ 35,000
Cash and cash equivalents, Jan. 1		20,000
Cash and cash equivalents, Dec. 31		$ 55,000

cash flows includes the cash effects of those transactions reported in the continuing operations section of the income statement. To illustrate this concept, consider the effects of credit sales. Credit sales are reported in the income statement in the period when the sales occur. But the cash effects occur later—when the receivables are collected in cash. If these events occur in different accounting periods, the income statement and the operating activities section of the statement of cash flows will differ. Similar differences may exist between the recognition of an expense and the related cash payment. Consider, for example, the expense of postretirement benefits earned by employees during the current period. If this expense is not funded with a trustee, the cash payments may not occur for many years—after today's employees have retired.

Cash flows from operating activities include:

Cash Receipts	Cash Payments
Collections from customers for sales of goods and services	Payments to suppliers of merchandise and services, including payments to employees
Interest and dividends received	Payments of interest
Other receipts from operations; for example, proceeds from settlement of litigation	Payments of income taxes
	Other expenditures relating to operations; for example, payments in settlement of litigation

Notice that receipts of *interest and dividends* and payments of *interest* are classified as operating activities, not as investing or financing activities.

Investing Activities Cash flows relating to investing activities present the cash effects of transactions involving plant assets, intangible assets, and investments. They include:

Cash Receipts	Cash Payments
Cash proceeds from selling investments and plant and intangible assets	Payments to acquire investments and plant and intangible assets
Cash proceeds from collecting principal amounts on loans	Amounts advanced to borrowers

Financing Activities Cash flows classified as financing activities include the following items that result from debt and equity financing transactions:

Cash Receipts	Cash Payments
Proceeds from both short-term and long-term borrowing	Repayment of amounts borrowed (excluding interest payments)
Cash received from owners (for example, from issuing stock)	Payments to owners, such as cash dividends

Repayment of amounts borrowed refers to repayment of *loans*, not to payments made on accounts payable or accrued liabilities. Payments of accounts payable and of accrued liabilities are payments to suppliers of merchandise and services related to revenues and expenses and are classified as cash outflows from operating activities. Also, remember that all interest payments are classified as operating activities.

Why Are Receipts and Payments of Interest Classified as Operating Activities? The case can be made that interest and dividend receipts are related to investing activities, and that interest payments are related to financing activities. The Financial Accounting Standards Board (FASB) considered this point of view but decided instead to classify interest and dividend receipts and interest payments as operating activities. The FASB wanted net cash flows from operating activities to reflect the cash effects of the revenue and expense transactions entering into the determination of net income. Because dividend and interest revenue and interest expense enter into the determination of net income, the FASB decided to classify the related cash flows as operating activities. Payments of dividends, however, *do not* enter into the determination of net income. Therefore, dividend payments are classified as financing activities.

Cash and Cash Equivalents For purposes of preparing a statement of cash flows, cash is defined as including *both cash and cash equivalents.* **Cash equivalents** are short-term, highly liquid investments, such as money market funds, commercial paper, and Treasury bills that will mature within ninety days from the acquisition date.

If an item is determined to not be a cash equivalent, its cash flows is presented in the investing activities section of the statement of cash flows. The amount shown as *cash and cash equivalents* in the balance sheet must be the same as the amount shown on the statement of cash flows. Transfers of money between a company's bank accounts and these cash equivalents are *not viewed as cash receipts or cash payments*. Money is considered cash regardless of whether it is held in currency, in a bank account, or in the form of cash equivalents. Interest received from owning cash equivalents is included in cash receipts from operating activities.

Marketable securities, such as investments in the stocks and bonds of other companies, *do not qualify as cash equivalents*. Therefore, purchases and sales of marketable securities *do* result in cash flows that are reported in the statement of cash flows as investing activities.

In the long run, a company must have a strategy that generates positive net cash flows from its operating activities if it is to survive. A business with negative cash flows from operations will not be able to raise cash from other sources indefinitely. In fact, the ability of a business to raise cash through financing activities is highly dependent on its ability to generate cash from its normal business operations. Creditors and stockholders are reluctant to invest in a company that does not generate enough cash from operating activities to ensure prompt payment of maturing liabilities, interest, and dividends.

Similarly, companies cannot expect to survive indefinitely on cash provided by investing activities. At some point, plant assets, investments, and other assets available for sale will be depleted.

CASE IN POINT

Both the FASB and the IASB require the cash flow statement to be organized into three categories: operating activities, investing activities, and financing activities. However, the United Kingdom's financial reporting standards for the cash flow statement require many more categories, including dividends from joint ventures and associates; return on investment and servicing of finance, taxation, capital expenditure, and financial investments; acquisitions and disposals; equity dividend paid; and management of liquid resources. United Kingdom standard setters believe more disclosure in the cash flow statement allows investors to understand the amount of cash companies have available to grow their operations.

Cash versus Accrual Information The items listed in an income statement and a balance sheet represent the balances of specific general ledger accounts. Notice, however, that the captions used in the statement of cash flows *do not* correspond to specific ledger accounts. A statement of cash flows summarizes *cash transactions* during the accounting period. The general ledger, however, is maintained on the **accrual basis** of accounting, not the cash basis. Thus an amount such as "Cash received from customers . . . $870,000" does not appear as the balance in a specific ledger account, but it is derived from one or more such accounts.

In a small business, it may be practical to prepare a statement of cash flows directly from the special journals for cash receipts and cash payments. For most businesses, however, it is easier to prepare the statement of cash flows by examining the income statement and the *changes* during the period in all of the balance sheet accounts *except for* Cash. This approach is based on the double-entry system of accounting; any transaction affecting cash must also affect some other asset, liability, or owners' equity account.[3] The change in these *other accounts* determines the nature of the cash transaction, as we see in the example that follows.

Preparing a Statement of Cash Flows

Earlier in this chapter we illustrated the statement of cash flows of Allison Corporation. We will now show how this statement was developed from the company's accrual-basis accounting records.

Basically, a statement of cash flows can be prepared from the information contained in an income statement and *comparative* balance sheets at the beginning and end of the period. It is also necessary, however, to have some detailed information about the *changes* occurring during the period in certain balance sheet accounts. Shown in Exhibit 13–2 is Allison's income statement, and in Exhibit 13–3 the firm's comparative balance sheets for the current year are presented.

Additional Information An analysis of changes in the balance sheet accounts of Allison Corporation provides the following information about the company's activities in the current year. To assist in the preparation of a statement of cash flows, we have classified this information into the categories of operating activities, investing activities, and financing activities.

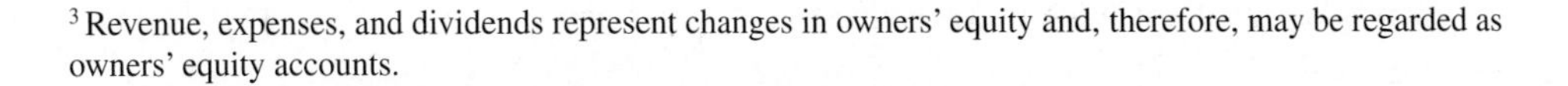

[3] Revenue, expenses, and dividends represent changes in owners' equity and, therefore, may be regarded as owners' equity accounts.

Exhibit 13–2

ALLISON CORPORATION INCOME STATEMENT

ALLISON CORPORATION
Income Statement
For the Year Ended December 31, 2007

Revenue and gains:		
Net sales		$900,000
Dividend revenue		3,000
Interest revenue		6,000
Gain on sales of plant assets		31,000
Total revenue and gains		$940,000
Costs, expenses, and losses:		
Cost of goods sold	$500,000	
Operating expenses (including depreciation of $40,000)	300,000	
Interest expense	35,000	
Income tax expense	36,000	
Loss on sales of marketable securities	4,000	
Total costs, expenses, and losses		875,000
Net income		$ 65,000

OPERATING ACTIVITIES

1. Accounts receivable increased by $30,000 during the year.
2. Dividend revenue is recognized on the cash basis, but interest revenue is recognized on the accrual basis. Accrued interest receivable decreased by $1,000 during the year.
3. Inventory increased by $10,000 and accounts payable increased by $15,000 during the year.
4. During the year, short-term prepaid expenses increased by $3,000 and accrued expenses payable (other than for interest or income taxes) decreased by $6,000. Depreciation for the year amounted to $40,000.
5. The accrued liability for interest payable increased by $7,000 during the year.
6. The accrued liability for income taxes payable decreased by $2,000 during the year.

INVESTING ACTIVITIES

7. Analysis of the Marketable Securities account shows debit entries of $65,000, representing the cost of securities purchased, and credit entries of $44,000, representing the cost of securities sold. (No marketable securities are classified as cash equivalents.)
8. Analysis of the Notes Receivable account shows $17,000 in debit entries, representing cash loaned by Allison Corporation to borrowers during the year, and $12,000 in credit entries, representing collections of notes receivable. (Collections of interest were recorded in the Interest Revenue account and are considered cash flows from operating activities.)
9. Allison's plant asset accounts increased by $116,000 during the year. An analysis of the underlying transactions indicates the following:

	Effect on Plant Asset Accounts
Purchased $200,000 in plant assets, paying $160,000 cash and issuing a long-term note payable for the $40,000 balance	$200,000
Sold for $75,000 cash plant assets with a book value of $44,000	(44,000)
Recorded depreciation expense for the period	(40,000)
Net change in plant asset controlling accounts	$116,000

Exhibit 13–3

ALLISON CORPORATION BALANCE SHEETS

ALLISON CORPORATION
Comparative Balance Sheets
December 31, 2007 and 2006

	2007	2006
Assets		
Current assets:		
Cash and Cash Equivalents	$ 55,000	$ 20,000
Marketable Securities	85,000	64,000
Notes Receivable	17,000	12,000
Accounts Receivable	110,000	80,000
Accrued Interest Receivable	2,000	3,000
Inventory	100,000	90,000
Prepaid Expenses	4,000	1,000
Total current assets	$373,000	$270,000
Plant and Equipment (net of accumulated depreciation)	616,000	500,000
Total assets	$989,000	$770,000
Liabilities & Stockholders' Equity		
Current liabilities:		
Notes Payable (short-term)	$ 45,000	$ 55,000
Accounts Payable	76,000	61,000
Interest Payable	22,000	15,000
Income Taxes Payable	8,000	10,000
Other Accrued Expenses Payable	3,000	9,000
Total current liabilities	$154,000	$150,000
Long-term liabilities:		
Notes Payable (long-term)	40,000	-0-
Bonds Payable	400,000	300,000
Total liabilities	$594,000	$450,000
Stockholders' equity:		
Capital Stock	$ 60,000	$ 50,000
Additional Paid-in Capital	140,000	100,000
Retained Earnings	195,000	170,000
Total stockholders' equity	$395,000	$320,000
Total liabilities & stockholders' equity	$989,000	$770,000

FINANCING ACTIVITIES

10. During the year, Allison Corporation borrowed $45,000 cash by issuing short-term notes payable to banks. Also, the company repaid $55,000 in principal amounts due on these loans and other notes payable. (Interest payments are classified as operating activities.)
11. The company issued bonds payable for $100,000 cash.
12. The company issued 1,000 shares of $10 par value capital stock for cash at a price of $50 per share.
13. Cash dividends declared and paid to stockholders amounted to $40,000 during the year.

CASH AND CASH EQUIVALENTS

14. Cash and cash equivalents as shown in Allison Corporation's balance sheets amounted to $20,000 at the beginning of the year and $55,000 at year-end—a net increase of $35,000.

Using this information, we will now illustrate the steps in preparing Allison Corporation's statement of cash flows and a supporting schedule disclosing the noncash investing and financing activities. In our discussion, we will often refer to these items of additional information by citing the paragraph numbers shown in the list just described.

The distinction between accrual-basis measurements and cash flows is of fundamental importance in understanding financial statements and other accounting reports. To assist in making this distinction, we use two colors in our illustrated computations. We show in **blue** the accrual-based data from Allison Corporation's income statement and the preceding numbered paragraphs. The cash flows that we compute from these data are shown in **red**.

CASH FLOWS FROM OPERATING ACTIVITIES

LO3 **Compute the major cash flows relating to operating activities.**

As shown in our statement of cash flows in Exhibit 13–1, the net cash flows from operating activities are determined by combining certain cash inflows and subtracting certain cash outflows. The inflows are cash received from customers and interest and dividends received; the outflows are cash paid to suppliers and employees, interest paid, and income taxes paid.

In computing each of these cash flows, our starting point is an income statement amount, such as net sales, cost of goods sold, or interest expense. As you study each computation, be sure that you *understand why* the income statement amount must be increased or decreased to determine the related cash flows. You will find that an understanding of these computations will do more than show you how to compute cash flows; it will also strengthen your understanding of the income statement and the balance sheet.

Cash Received from Customers

To the extent that sales are made for cash, there is no difference between the amount of cash received from customers and the amount recorded as sales revenue. Differences arise, however, when sales are made on account. If accounts receivable increase during the year, credit sales will have exceeded collections of accounts receivable. Therefore, we *deduct the increase* in accounts receivable from net sales to determine the amount of cash received during the year. If accounts receivable decrease, collections of these accounts will have exceeded credit sales. Therefore, we *add the decrease* in accounts receivable to net sales to determine the amount of cash received during the year. The relationship between cash received from customers and net sales is summarized below:

$$\text{Cash Received from Customers} = \text{Net Sales} \begin{Bmatrix} + \text{Decrease in Accounts Receivable} \\ \text{or} \\ - \text{Increase in Accounts Receivable} \end{Bmatrix}$$

In our Allison Corporation example, paragraph **1** of the additional information tells us that accounts receivable *increased* by $30,000 during the year. The income statement shows net sales for the year of $900,000. Therefore, the amount of cash received from customers is computed as follows:

Net sales (accrual basis)	$900,000
Less: Increase in accounts receivable	30,000
Cash received from customers	$870,000

Interest and Dividends Received

Our next objective is to determine the amounts of cash received during the year from dividends and interest on the company's investments. As explained in paragraph **2** of the additional information, dividend revenue is recorded on the cash basis. Therefore, the $3,000 shown in the income statement also represents the amount of cash received as dividends.

Interest revenue, on the other hand, is recognized on the accrual basis. We have already shown how to convert one type of revenue, net sales, from the accrual basis to the cash basis. We use the same approach to convert interest revenue from the accrual basis to the **cash basis**.

Our formula for converting net sales to the cash basis may be modified to convert interest revenue to the cash basis as follows:

$$\text{Interest Received} = \text{Interest Revenue} \begin{Bmatrix} + \text{ Decrease in Interest Receivable} \\ \text{or} \\ - \text{ Increase in Interest Receivable} \end{Bmatrix}$$

The income statement for Allison Corporation shows interest revenue of $6,000, and paragraph **2** states that the amount of accrued interest receivable *decreased* by $1,000 during the year. Thus the amount of cash received as interest may be computed as follows:

Interest revenue (accrual basis)	$6,000
Add: Decrease in accrued interest receivable	1,000
Interest received (cash basis)	$7,000

The amounts of interest and dividends received in cash are combined for presentation in the statement of cash flows:

Interest received (cash basis)	$ 7,000
Dividends received (cash basis)	3,000
Interest and dividends received	$10,000

CASH PAYMENTS FOR MERCHANDISE AND FOR EXPENSES

The next item in the statement of cash flows, "Cash paid to suppliers and employees," includes all cash payments for purchases of merchandise and for operating expenses (excluding interest and income taxes). Payments of interest and income taxes are listed as separate items in the statement. The amounts of cash paid for purchases of merchandise and for operating expenses are computed separately.

Cash Paid for Purchases of Merchandise

An accrual basis income statement reflects the *cost of goods sold* during the year, regardless of whether the merchandise was acquired or paid for in that period. The statement of cash flows, on the other hand, reports the *cash paid* for merchandise during the year, even if the merchandise was acquired in a previous period or remains unsold at year-end. The relationship between cash payments for merchandise and the cost of goods sold depends on the changes during the period in *two* related balance sheet accounts: inventory and accounts payable to suppliers of merchandise. This relationship may be stated as follows:

$$\text{Cash Payments for Purchases} = \text{Cost of Goods Sold} \begin{Bmatrix} + \text{ Increase in Inventory} \\ \text{or} \\ - \text{ Decrease in Inventory} \end{Bmatrix} \text{ and } \begin{Bmatrix} + \text{ Decrease in Accounts Payable} \\ \text{or} \\ - \text{ Increase in Accounts Payable} \end{Bmatrix}$$

Using information from the Allison Corporation income statement and paragraph **3**, the cash payments for purchases may be computed as follows:

Cost of goods sold	$500,000
Add: Increase in inventory	10,000
Net purchases (accrual basis)	$510,000
Less: Increase in accounts payable to suppliers	15,000
Cash payments for purchases of merchandise	$495,000

Here is the logic behind this computation: If a company is increasing its inventory, it is *buying more merchandise than it sells* during the period. If the company is increasing its accounts payable to merchandise creditors, it is *not paying cash* for all of these purchases.

Cash Payments for Expenses Expenses, as shown in the income statement, represent the cost of goods and services used up during the period. However, the amounts shown as expenses may differ from the cash payments made during the period. Consider, for example, depreciation expense. Recording depreciation expense *requires no cash payment*, but it does increase total expenses measured on the accrual basis. Thus, in converting accrual-basis expenses to the cash basis, we must deduct depreciation expense and any other noncash expenses from our accrual-basis operating expenses. Other noncash expenses—expenses not requiring cash outlays—include amortization of intangible assets, any unfunded portion of postretirement benefits expense, and amortization of bond discount.

A second type of difference arises from short-term *timing differences* between the recognition of expenses and the actual cash payments. Expenses are recorded in accounting records when the related goods or services are used. However, the cash payments for these expenses might occur (1) in an earlier period, (2) in the same period, or (3) in a later period. Let us briefly consider each case.

1. If payment is made in advance, the payment creates an asset, termed a prepaid expense, or, in our formula, a "prepayment." Thus, to the extent that prepaid expenses increase over the year, cash payments *exceed* the amount recognized as expense.
2. If payment is made in the same period, the cash payment is equal to the amount of expense.
3. If payment is made in a later period, the payment reduces a liability for an accrued expense payable. Thus, to the extent that accrued expenses payable decrease over the year, cash payments exceed the amount recognized as expense.

The relationship between cash payments for expenses and accrual-basis expenses is summarized below:

$$\begin{array}{c}\textbf{Cash Payments}\\ \textbf{for Expenses}\end{array} = \textbf{Expenses} \left\{ - \begin{array}{l}\textbf{Depreciation}\\ \textbf{and Other}\\ \textbf{Noncash}\\ \textbf{Expenses}\end{array} \right\} \textbf{ and } \left\{ \begin{array}{l} \textbf{Increase in}\\ +\ \textbf{Related}\\ \textbf{Prepayments}\\ \quad\textbf{or}\\ \textbf{Decrease in}\\ -\ \textbf{Related}\\ \textbf{Prepayments}\end{array}\right\} \textbf{ and } \left\{ \begin{array}{l} \textbf{Decrease in}\\ +\ \textbf{Related Accrued}\\ \textbf{Liabilities}\\ \quad\textbf{or}\\ \textbf{Increase in}\\ -\ \textbf{Related Accrued}\\ \textbf{Liabilities}\end{array}\right\}$$

In a statement of cash flows, cash payments for interest and for income taxes are shown separately from cash payments for operating expenses. Using information from Allison Corporation's income statement and from paragraph **4**, we may compute the company's cash payments for operating expenses as follows:

Operating expenses (including depreciation)		$300,000
Less: Noncash expenses (depreciation)		40,000
Subtotal		$260,000
Add: Increase in short-term prepayments	$3,000	
Decrease in accrued liabilities	6,000	9,000
Cash payments for operating expenses		$269,000

Cash Paid to Suppliers and Employees The caption used in our cash flow statement, "Cash paid to suppliers and employees," includes cash payments for both purchases of merchandise and for operating expenses. This cash outflow may now be computed by combining the two previous calculations:

Cash payments for purchases of merchandise	$495,000
Cash payments for operating expenses	269,000
Cash payments to suppliers and employees	$764,000

Cash Payments for Interest and Taxes Interest expense and income taxes expense may be converted to cash payments with the same formula we used to convert operating expenses. Allison Corporation's income statement shows interest expense of $35,000, and paragraph **5** states that the liability for interest payable increased by $7,000 during the year. The fact that the liability for unpaid interest *increased* over the year means that *not all of the interest expense shown in the income statement was paid in cash* in the current year. To determine the amount of interest actually paid, we *subtract* from total interest expense the portion that has been financed through an increase in the liability for interest payable. The computation is as follows:

Interest expense	$35,000
Less: Increase in related accrued liability	7,000
Interest paid	$28,000

Similar reasoning is used to determine the amount of income tax paid by Allison Corporation during the year. The accrual-based income tax expense reported in the income statement amounts to $36,000. However, paragraph **6** states that the company has reduced its liability for income taxes payable by $2,000 over the year. Incurring income tax expense increases the tax liability; making cash payments to tax authorities reduces it. Thus, if the liability *decreased* over the year, cash payments to tax authorities *must have been greater* than the income tax expense for the current year. The amount of the cash payments is determined as follows:

Income tax expense	$36,000
Add: Decrease in related accrued liability	2,000
Income tax paid	$38,000

A Quick Review We have now shown the computation of each cash flow relating to Allison Corporation's operating activities. In Exhibit 13–1 we illustrated a complete statement of cash flows for the company. For your convenience, we again show the operating activities section of that statement, illustrating the information developed in the preceding paragraphs.

Cash flows from operating activities:		
Cash received from customers	$ 870,000	
Interest and dividends received	10,000	
Cash provided by operating activities		$ 880,000
Cash paid to suppliers and employees	$(764,000)	
Interest paid	(28,000)	
Income taxes paid	(38,000)	
Cash disbursed for operating activities		(830,000)
Net cash flows from operating activities		$ 50,000

CASH FLOWS FROM INVESTING ACTIVITIES

Paragraphs **7** through **9** in the additional information for our Allison Corporation example provide most of the information necessary to determine the cash flows from investing activities. In the following discussion, we illustrate the presentation of these cash flows and explain the sources of the information contained in the numbered paragraphs.

Compute the cash flows relating to investing and financing activities.

Much information about investing activities can be obtained simply by looking at the changes in the related asset accounts during the year. Debit entries in these accounts represent purchases of the assets, or cash outlays. Credit entries represent sales of the assets, or cash receipts. However, credit entries in asset accounts represent only the *cost* (or *book value*) of the assets sold. To determine the cash proceeds from these sales transactions, we must adjust the amount of the credit entries for any gains or losses recognized on the sales.

Purchases and Sales of Securities To illustrate, consider paragraph **7**, which summarizes the debit and credit entries to the Marketable Securities account. As explained earlier in this chapter, the $65,000 in debit entries represents purchases of marketable securities. The $44,000 in credit entries represents the *cost* of marketable securities sold during the period. However, the income statement shows that these securities were sold at a *$4,000 loss*. Thus the cash proceeds from these sales amounted to only *$40,000* ($44,000 cost, minus $4,000 loss on sale). In the statement of cash flows, these investing activities are summarized as follows:

Purchases of marketable securities	$(65,000)
Proceeds from sales of marketable securities	40,000

Loans Made and Collected Paragraph **8** provides all the information necessary to summarize the cash flows from making and collecting loans:

Loans made to borrowers	$(17,000)
Collections on loans	12,000

This information comes directly from the Notes Receivable account. Debit entries in the account represent new loans made during the year; credit entries indicate collections of the *principal* amount on outstanding notes (loans). (Interest received is credited to the Interest Revenue account and is included among the cash receipts from operating activities.)

YOUR TURN **You as a Sales Manager**

Assume you are a regional sales manager for Wiggins Foods, Inc., a distributor of bulk food products to schools, nursing homes, hospitals, prisons, and other institutions. Recently, the purchasing agent for Baggins Preschools, Inc., tells you the company will likely have to forgo its normal monthly order because of cash flow problems. The purchasing agent tells you other companies are helping it through the cash flow squeeze and asks if your company could loan the payment to Baggins. The purchasing agent suggests you could record the sale as revenue and increase notes receivable (rather than accounts receivable) by the same amount. Baggins is one of your largest customers. Without its order, you will not meet your sales goals for the month—so you are tempted to say yes. However, on reflection you wonder if it might be unethical for the company to lend its customer money to finance purchases. What should you do?

(See our comments on the Online Learning Center Web site.)

Cash Paid to Acquire Plant Assets Paragraph **9** states that Allison Corporation purchased plant assets during the year for $200,000, paying $160,000 in cash and issuing a long-term note payable for the $40,000 balance. Notice that *only the $160,000 cash payment* appears in the statement of cash flows. However, one objective of this financial statement is to show all of the company's *investing and financing activities* during the year. Therefore, the *noncash aspects* of these transactions are shown in a supplementary schedule, as follows:

Supplementary Schedule of Noncash Investing and Financing Activities	
Purchases of plant assets	$200,000
Less: Portion financed through issuance of long-term debt	40,000
Cash paid to acquire plant assets	$160,000

This supplementary schedule accompanies the statement of cash flows.

Proceeds from Sales of Plant Assets Assume that an analysis of the plant asset accounts shows net credit entries totaling $44,000 in the year. ("Net credit entries" means all credit entries, net of related debits to accumulated depreciation when assets were sold.) These net credit entries represent the *book value* of plant assets sold during the year. However, the income statement shows that these assets were sold at a *gain of $31,000*. Therefore, the *cash proceeds* from sales of plant assets amounted to $75,000, as follows:

Book value of plant assets sold	$44,000
Add: Gain on sales of plant assets	31,000
Proceeds from sales of plant assets	$75,000

The amount credited to the Accumulated Depreciation account during the year is not a cash flow and is not included in the statement of cash flows.

A Quick Review We have now shown the computation of each cash flow related to Allison Corporation's investing activities. In Exhibit 13–1 we illustrated a complete statement of cash flows for the company. For your convenience, we again show the investing activities section of that statement, illustrating the information developed in the preceding paragraphs.

Cash flows from investing activities:		
Purchases of marketable securities	$ (65,000)	
Proceeds from sales of marketable securities	40,000	
Loans made to borrowers	(17,000)	
Collections on loans	12,000	
Purchases of plant assets	(160,000)	
Proceeds from sales of plant assets	75,000	
Net cash flows from investing activities		$(115,000)

An important feature of the investing activities section of a statement of cash flows is that increases and decreases in cash from similar transactions are presented separately rather than being combined and netted against each other. For example, in this illustration the negative cash flow from purchasing marketable securities ($65,000) is shown separately from the positive cash flow from the sales of marketable securities ($40,000) rather than netting the two to a negative figure of $25,000 ($65,000 − $40,000).

CASH FLOWS FROM FINANCING ACTIVITIES

Cash flows from financing activities are determined by analyzing the debit and credit changes recorded during the period in the related liability and stockholders' equity accounts. Cash flows from financing activities are more easily determined than those relating to investing activities, because financing activities seldom involve gains or losses.[4] Thus the debit or credit changes in the balance sheet accounts usually are equal to the amounts of the related cash flows.

Credit changes in such accounts as Notes Payable and the accounts for long-term debt and paid-in capital usually indicate cash receipts; debit changes indicate cash payments.

Short-Term Borrowing Transactions To illustrate, consider paragraph **10**, which provides the information supporting the following cash flows:

Proceeds from short-term borrowing	$45,000
Payments to settle short-term debts	(55,000)

[4] An early retirement of debt is an example of a financing transaction that may result in a gain or a loss.

Both the proceeds from short-term borrowing of $45,000 (a positive cash flow) and the payments to settle short-term debts of $55,000 (a negative cash flow) are presented in the statement of cash flows. Presenting both directions of the changes in cash, rather than combining the two and presenting a net amount of $10,000 ($55,000 − $45,000), is an important feature of the statement of cash flows. Presenting both positive and negative cash flows is referred to as presenting *gross* cash flows rather than presenting *net* cash flows.

Is it possible to determine the proceeds of short-term borrowing transactions throughout the year without carefully reviewing each cash receipt? The answer is yes—the proceeds from short-term borrowing are equal to the *sum of the credit entries* in the short-term *Notes Payable* account. Payments to settle short-term debts are equal to the *sum of the debit entries* in this account.

Proceeds from Issuing Bonds Payable and Capital Stock Paragraph **11** states that Allison Corporation received cash of $100,000 by issuing bonds payable. This amount was determined by summing the credit entries in the Bonds Payable account. The Bonds Payable account included no debit entries during the year; thus no bonds were retired.

Paragraph **12** states that during the year Allison Corporation issued capital stock for $50,000. The proceeds from issuing stock are equal to the sum of the credit entries made in the Capital Stock and Additional Paid-in Capital accounts ($10,000 + $40,000).

Cash Dividends Paid to Stockholders Paragraph **13** states that Allison Corporation declared and paid cash dividends of $40,000 during the year. If dividends are both declared and paid during the same year, the cash payments are equal to the related debit entries in the Retained Earnings account.

If the balance sheet includes a liability for dividends payable, the amounts debited to Retained Earnings represent dividends *declared* during the period, which may differ from the amount of dividends *paid*. To determine cash dividends paid, we must adjust the amount of dividends declared by adding any decrease (or subtracting any increase) in the Dividends Payable account over the period.

A Quick Review We have now shown the computation of each cash flow related to Allison Corporation's financing activities. In Exhibit 13–1 we illustrated a complete statement of cash flows for the company. For your convenience, we again show the financing activities section of that statement, illustrating the information developed in the preceding paragraphs.

Cash flows from financing activities:		
Proceeds from short-term borrowing	$ 45,000	
Payments to settle short-term debts	(55,000)	
Proceeds from issuing bonds payable	100,000	
Proceeds from issuing capital stock	50,000	
Dividends paid	(40,000)	
Net cash flows from financing activities		$100,000

RELATIONSHIP BETWEEN THE STATEMENT OF CASH FLOWS AND THE BALANCE SHEET

The first asset appearing in the balance sheet is Cash and Cash Equivalents. The statement of cash flows explains in some detail the change in this asset from one balance sheet date to the next. The last three lines in the statement of cash flows illustrate this relationship, as shown in our Allison Corporation example:

Net increase (decrease) in cash and cash equivalents	$35,000
Cash and cash equivalents, beginning of year	20,000
Cash and cash equivalents, end of year	$55,000

This is often referred to as a reconciliation of the beginning and ending cash balances.

CASE IN POINT

In the year ending June 30, 2003, **Microsoft Corporation** reported a *decrease* in cash in excess of $9,446,000,000. Does this mean that the company was experiencing extreme financial stress? Not necessarily. That year, operations provided over $16 billion and investing activities provided over $15 billion of cash. The overall decline was due to approximately $41 billion being used in financing activities, primarily for paying cash dividends to stockholders. In fact, that year the company did very well, with a net income of more than $12 billion. By comparison, the two following years resulted in cash *increases* of $8,920 million (year ended June 30, 2004, which resulted in net income of $8,168 million) and $3,079 million (year ended June 30, 2005, which resulted in net income of $7,531 million).

Lessons to be learned from this example are twofold. First, a decrease in cash does not necessarily signal financial problems, and second, a company's cash position may change in ways very different from its net income.

© Microsoft Corporation

REPORTING OPERATING CASH FLOWS BY THE INDIRECT METHOD

In determining cash flows from operating activities for Allison Corporation, we have followed what is commonly referred to as the direct method. To this point in our study of the statement of cash flows, we have emphasized the direct method because we consider it to be the more informative and more readily understood approach. The direct method is recommended by the FASB, although companies are permitted to use either the direct or the indirect method and the majority of companies use the indirect method. When presenting cash flows from operating activities by the direct method, companies are required to disclose information that is consistent with the indirect method. Before completing our Allison Corporation illustration of preparing a statement of cash flows, we first look more carefully at the indirect method.

Exhibit 13–4 includes a comparison of the direct and indirect methods of determining net cash provided by operating activities for Allison Corporation. The direct method is the same as discussed earlier in this chapter. The indirect method is discussed below. The two methods are more similar than it may appear at first glance. Both methods are based on the same underlying information and they result in the same net cash flow amount—in Allison Corporation's case, $50,000. Both methods convert information originally prepared on the accrual basis to information prepared on the cash basis. In Exhibit 13–4, accrual-based data appear in **blue**; cash flows are shown in **red**.

To illustrate the similarity in the computations, look briefly at the formulas for computing the cash inflows and outflows shown under the direct method (pages 578–581). Each formula begins with an income statement amount and then adds or subtracts the change during the period in related balance sheet accounts. Now look at our illustration of the indirect method in Exhibit 13–4. Notice that this computation also focuses on the net changes during the period in balance sheet accounts.

The difference between the two methods lies only in approach. However, the two approaches provide readers of the statement of cash flows with different types of information. The direct method informs these readers of the nature and dollar amounts of the *specific cash inflows and outflows* comprising the operating activities of the business. The indirect method, in contrast, *explains why* the net cash flows from operating activities differ from another measurement of performance—net income.

Exhibit 13–4

COMPARISON OF DIRECT AND INDIRECT METHODS

Direct Method

Cash flows from operating activities:		
Cash received from customers	$ 870,000	
Interest and dividends received	10,000	
Cash provided by operating activities		$880,000
Cash paid to suppliers and employees	$(764,000)	
Interest paid	(28,000)	
Income taxes paid	(38,000)	
Cash disbursed for operating activities		(830,000)
Net cash provided by operating activities		$ 50,000

Distinguish between the direct and indirect methods of reporting operating cash flows. (LO5)

Indirect Method

Net income		$ 65,000
Add: Depreciation expense		40,000
Decrease in accrued interest receivable		1,000
Increase in accounts payable		15,000
Increase in accrued interest liabilities		7,000
Nonoperating loss on sales of marketable securities		4,000
Subtotal		$132,000
Less: Increase in accounts receivable	$30,000	
Increase in inventory	10,000	
Increase in prepaid expenses	3,000	
Decrease in accrued operating expenses payable	6,000	
Decrease in accrued income taxes payable	2,000	
Nonoperating gain on sales of plant assets	31,000	82,000
Net cash provided by operating activities		$ 50,000

RECONCILING NET INCOME WITH NET CASH FLOWS

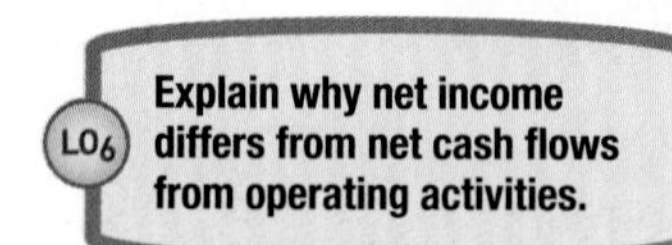

To further develop your understanding of the indirect method, we now discuss common adjustments required to reconcile net income with net cash flows from operating activities. The nature and dollar amounts of these adjustments are determined by an accountant using a worksheet or a computer program; they are *not* entered in the company's accounting records.

1. *Adjusting for Noncash Expenses*
   Depreciation is an example of a noncash expense—that is, depreciation expense reduces net income but does not require any cash outlay during the period. (The cash outflow related to depreciation resulted when the asset was purchased and was presented as an investing activity at that time—before any depreciation was ever recognized.) Depreciation causes expenses on the accrual basis to exceed cash payments, and net income for the period is less than net cash flows. To reconcile net income with net cash flows, we add back to net income the amount of depreciation and any other noncash expenses. (Other noncash expenses included unfunded pension expense, amortization of intangible assets, depletion of natural resources, and amortization of bond discount.)
2. *Adjusting for Timing Differences*
   Timing differences between elements of net income and net cash flows arise whenever revenue or expenses are recognized by debiting or crediting an account *other than* Cash. Changes over the period in the balances of these asset and liability accounts represent differences between the amount of revenue or expenses recognized in the income statement and the net cash flows from operating activities. The balance sheet accounts that give rise to these timing differences include Accounts Receivable, Inventories, Prepaid Expenses, Accounts Payable, and Accrued Expenses Payable.
3. *Adjusting for Nonoperating Gains and Losses*
   Nonoperating gains and losses include gains and losses from sales of investments, plant assets, and discontinued operations (which relate to investing activities); and gains and losses on early retirement of debt (which relate to financing activities).

In a statement of cash flows, cash flows are classified as operating activities, investing activities, or financing activities. Nonoperating gains and losses, by definition, do not affect *operating activities*. However, these gains and losses do enter into the determination of net income. Therefore, in converting net income to net cash flows from operating activities, we *add back any nonoperating losses* and *deduct any nonoperating gains* included in net income. The full cash effect of the transaction is then presented as an investing activity (for example, sale of a building) or as a financing activity (for example, retirement of debt) in the statement of cash flows.

THE INDIRECT METHOD: A SUMMARY

The adjustments to net income explained in our preceding discussion are summarized as follows:

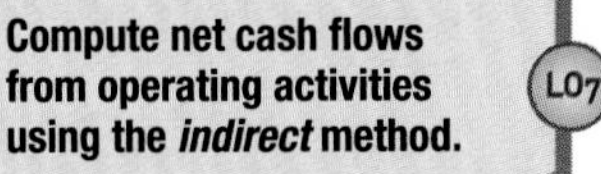

Net income	
Add:	Depreciation
	Decrease in accounts receivable
	Decrease in inventories
	Decrease in prepaid expenses
	Increase in accounts payable
	Increase in accrued expenses payable
	Increase in deferred income taxes payable
	Nonoperating losses deducted in computing net income
Deduct:	Increase in accounts receivable
	Increase in inventories
	Increase in prepaid expenses
	Decrease in accounts payable
	Decrease in accrued expenses payable
	Decrease in deferred income taxes payable
	Nonoperating gains added in computing net income
Net cash provided by (used in) operating activities	

INDIRECT METHOD MAY BE REQUIRED IN A SUPPLEMENTARY SCHEDULE

The FASB recommends use of the *direct method* in presenting net cash flows from operating activities. The majority of companies, however, elect to use the indirect method. One reason is that the FASB requires companies opting for the direct method to meet an additional reporting requirement.

Companies using the direct method are required to provide a *supplementary schedule* showing the computation of net cash flows from operating activities by the indirect method. However, no supplementary computations are required of companies that present the indirect method computations in their cash flow statements because this same information is already presented in the body of the statement under the indirect method. In the opinion of these authors, this reporting requirement undermines the FASB's efforts to encourage use of the direct method.

THE STATEMENT OF CASH FLOWS: A SECOND LOOK

We have now completed our explanation of Allison Corporation's statement of cash flows. We have analyzed each type of cash flow by reconciling amounts included in the other two financial statements—the income statement and the balance sheet—to determine the amounts of individual operating, investing, and financing cash flows. In computing cash flows from operating activities, we began by using the direct method, in which major categories of both positive and negative cash flows were determined and presented.

We also illustrated the indirect method to determine the amount of operating cash flows. Rather than adjusting each individual operating cash flow category for changes in balance sheet accounts, these same adjustments were made to net income.

Exhibit 13–5 includes an expanded statement of cash flows for Allison Corporation. This statement uses the direct method for operating activities and includes two supplementary schedules.

Exhibit 13-5

ALLISON CORPORATION (EXPANDED) STATEMENT OF CASH FLOWS

ALLISON CORPORATION
Statement of Cash Flows
For the Year Ended December 31, 2007

Cash flows from operating activities:		
Net cash provided by operating activities (see Supplementary Schedule A)		$ 50,000
Cash flows from investing activities:		
Purchases of marketable securities	$ (65,000)	
Proceeds from sales of marketable securities	40,000	
Loans made to borrowers	(17,000)	
Collections on loans	12,000	
Cash paid to acquire plant assets (see Supplementary Schedule B)	(160,000)	
Proceeds from sales of plant assets	75,000	
Net cash used in investing activities		(115,000)
Cash flows from financing activities:		
Proceeds from short-term borrowing	$ 45,000	
Payments to settle short-term debts	(55,000)	
Proceeds from issuing bonds payable	100,000	
Proceeds from issuing capital stock	50,000	
Dividends paid	(40,000)	
Net cash provided by financing activities		100,000
Net increase (decrease) in cash		$ 35,000
Cash and cash equivalents, Jan. 1		20,000
Cash and cash equivalents, Dec. 31		$ 55,000

Supplementary Schedule A: Net Cash Provided by Operating Activities

Net income		$ 65,000
Add: Depreciation expense		40,000
Decrease in accrued interest receivable		1,000
Increase in accounts payable		15,000
Increase in accrued liabilities		7,000
Nonoperating loss on sales of marketable securities		4,000
Subtotal		$ 132,000
Less: Increase in accounts receivable	$ 30,000	
Increase in inventory	10,000	
Increase in prepaid expenses	3,000	
Decrease in accrued liabilities	8,000	
Nonoperating gain on sales of plant assets	31,000	82,000
Net cash provided by operating activities		$ 50,000

Supplementary Schedule B: Noncash Investing and Financing Activities

Purchases of plant assets	$ 200,000
Less: Portion financed through issuance of long-term debt	40,000
Cash paid to acquire plant assets	$ 160,000

Notice this supplementary schedule illustrates the indirect method of determining cash flows from operations

Supplementary Schedule A in Exhibit 13–5 illustrates the determination of net cash flows from operating activities by the *indirect method. Supplementary Schedule B* in Exhibit 13–5 discloses any noncash aspects of the company's investing and financing activities. This type of supplementary schedule is required whenever some aspects of the company's investing and financing activities do not coincide with cash flows occurring within the current period.

How would the statement of cash flows in Exhibit 13–5 differ if the indirect method were used? The information included in Supplementary Schedule A would be moved up into the "Cash flows from operating activities" section of the financial statement and would no longer be required as a supplemental disclosure. In fact, this is one reason for the popularity of the indirect method. Because it is required to be disclosed if the direct method is used, many companies simply prefer to include the reconciliation of net income to net cash from operating activities in the body of the statement of cash flows and avoid the need for the supplemental disclosure of that same information.

Financial Analysis and Decision Making

The users of a statement of cash flows usually are particularly interested in the *net cash flows from operating activities*. Is the amount large enough to provide for necessary replacements of plant assets and maturing liabilities? And if so, is there enough left for the current dividend to look secure—or even be increased?

Consider two competitors in the import craft supplies business, Gonzalez, Inc., and Alvarez Company. These companies have approximately the same size assets, liabilities, and sales. Selected information from their most recent statements of cash flows follows:

	Beginning Cash Balance	Net Cash Flow from (in thousands) Operating Activities	Investing Activities	Financing Activities	Ending Cash Balance
Gonzalez	$150	$600	$(500)	$400	$650
Alvarez	150	50	500	(50)	650

Which company is in the stronger cash flow position? Although both have the same beginning and ending cash balances ($150,000 and $650,000, respectively), Gonzalez is in the stronger position because of its strong operating cash flows of $600,000. Gonzalez has been able to invest $500,000 in operating assets, while financing only $400,000, and still has a $650,000 ending cash balance. Alvarez, on the other hand, has generated only a small amount of cash from operations ($50,000) and has sold assets to generate cash ($500,000) to support its ending cash balance. Also, Alvarez has not been able to finance its assets acquisitions and even has had to reduce its financing, possibly due to its weak operating cash flows.

Assume further that each company has current liabilities at the end of the year totaling $500,000. While both are in an equally good cash position with regard to paying these liabilities, Gonzalez followed a much more positive path to get in this position than did Alvarez. Whether Alvarez will be able to sustain its cash position over time, and therefore be able to meet its recurring obligations in the future, is questionable.

Even more important than net cash flows from operating activities in any one year is the *trend* in cash flows over a period of years—and the *consistency* of that trend from year to year. From everyone's perspective, the best results are net cash flows from operating activities that increase each year by a substantial—but also predictable—percentage.[5]

Free Cash Flow Many analysts put a company's cash flows into perspective by computing an amount called **free cash flow**. Free cash flow is intended to represent the cash flow available to management for discretionary purposes, *after* the company has met all of its basic obligations relating to business operations.

The term *free cash flow* is widely cited within the business community. Different analysts compute this measure in different ways because there is no widespread agreement as to the basic obligations relating to business operations. For example, are all expenditures for plant assets "basic obligations," or only those expenditures made to maintain the current level of productive capacity?

One common method of computing free cash flow is to deduct from the net cash flows from operating activities any net cash used for investments in plant assets and any dividends paid. This computation follows, using information from the Allison Corporation statement of cash flows shown earlier.

Net cash flows from operating activities		$ 50,000
Less: Net cash used for acquiring plant assets ($160,000 − $75,000 proceeds)	$85,000	
Dividends paid	40,000	125,000
Free cash flow		$(75,000)

What's left for discretionary purposes?

[5] Percentage change is the dollar amount of change from one year to the next, expressed as a percentage of (divided by) the amount from the *earlier* of the two years. For example, if net cash provided by operating activities was $100,000 in the first year and $120,000 in the second year, the percentage increase is 20 percent, computed as follows: ($120,000 − $100,000) ÷ $100,000.

(continued)

This computation suggests that Allison Corporation *did not* generate enough cash from operations to meet its basic obligations. Thus management had to raise cash from other sources. But, of course, an analyst always should look behind the numbers. For example, was Allison's purchase of plant assets during the year a basic obligation, or did it represent a discretionary expansion of the business?

As we have stated throughout this text, no single ratio or financial measurement ever tells the whole story.

YOUR TURN **You as a Financial Analyst**

You are working for the same stock market research firm as in Chapter 12, but unlike your previous boss (who tended to focus on growth and relative value, both based on reported earnings), your new boss focuses primarily on free cash flow and dividends in choosing stocks.

Your new boss is interested in stocks where free cash flow equals at least 50 percent of cash flow from operations. He also wants dividends to be 25 percent or more of cash flow from operations. You are considering the same stocks as before: **Home Depot**, **Intel**, **Coca-Cola**, **Genentech**, **eBay**, and **Amazon**. Your new boss provides you with the following information and asks you to recommend which stocks are consistent with his investment criteria.

	In Millions		
Company	**Cash Flow from Operations (CFO)**	**Net Capital Expenditures**	**Dividends**
Home Depot	$6,545	$3,243	$ 595
Intel	9,129	4,703	533
Coca-Cola	5,456	725	2,166
Genentech	1,237	322	—
eBay	252	54	—
Amazon	392	46	—

He also tells you that a potential new client is going to be calling you this afternoon. This potential client is an elderly widow who is quite wealthy, and she is curious as to why the relative levels of free cash flow and dividends are important metrics. She also doesn't understand why all firms don't pay dividends. Your boss tells you to answer this prospective client's questions.

(See our comments on the Online Learning Center Web site.)

Managing Cash Flows

Management can do much to influence the cash flows of a particular period. In fact, it has a responsibility to manage cash flows. No business can afford to run out of cash and default on its obligations. Even being a few days late in meeting payrolls, or paying suppliers or creditors, can severely damage important business relationships. Thus one of management's most basic responsibilities is to ensure that the business has enough cash to meet its obligations as they come due.

BUDGETING: THE PRIMARY CASH MANAGEMENT TOOL

The primary tool used by management to anticipate and shape future cash flows is a *cash budget*. A **cash budget** is a *forecast* of future cash receipts and payments. This budget is *not* a financial statement and is not widely distributed to people outside of the organization. To managers, however, it is among the most useful of all accounting reports.

In many ways, a cash budget is similar to a statement of cash flows. However, the budget shows the results *expected in future periods*, rather than those achieved in the past. Also, the cash budget is more *detailed*, usually showing expected cash flows month-by-month and separately for every department within the organization.

Cash budgets serve many purposes. Among the most important are:

- Encouraging managers to plan and coordinate the activities of their departments in advance.
- Providing managers with advance notice of the resources at their disposal and the results they are expected to achieve.
- Providing targets useful in evaluating departmental performance.
- Providing advance warnings of potential cash shortages.

WHAT PRIORITY SHOULD MANAGERS GIVE TO INCREASING NET CASH FLOWS?

Creditors and investors look to a company's cash flows to protect their investment and provide future returns. Trends in key cash flows (such as from operations and free cash flow) affect a company's credit rating, stock price, and access to additional investment capital. For these reasons, management is under constant pressure to improve the key measures of cash flow. Unfortunately, the pressure to report higher cash flows in the current period may *conflict* with managers' long-run responsibilities.

Discuss the likely effects of various business strategies on cash flows. LO8

Short-Term Results versus Long-Term Growth

Often, short-term operating results can be improved at the expense of long-term growth. For example, reducing expenditures for developing new products will increase earnings and net cash flows in the current period. But over time, this strategy may lessen the company's competitiveness and long-term profitability.

In contrast, the strategies most likely to promote long-term growth may *reduce* earnings and cash flows in the near term—often by large amounts.

One-Time Boosts to Cash Flows

Some strategies can increase the net cash flows of the current period, but *without having much effect* on future cash flows. Such strategies include collecting receivables more quickly and reducing the size of inventory.

Assume, for example, that a company offers 60-day terms to its credit customers. Thus credit sales made in January are collected in March, and credit sales made in February are collected in April. Notice that in each month, the company is collecting about *one month's amount* of credit sales.

Now assume that on March 1 the company changes its policies to allow only *30-day* credit terms. In April, the company will collect *two months* of credit sales—those made in February (under the former 60-day terms) *and* those made in March (under the new 30-day terms).

This significantly increases the cash received from customers for the month of April. But it does not signal higher cash flows for the months ahead. In May, the company will collect only those credit sales made in April. Thus it quickly returns to the pattern of collecting about *one month's* credit sales in the current month. Shortening the collection period provided only a one-time boost in cash receipts.

A similar one-time boost may be achieved by reducing the size of inventory. This reduces the need for purchasing merchandise, *but only while inventory levels are falling*. Once the company stabilizes the size of its inventory at the new and lower level, its monthly purchases must return to approximately the quantity of goods sold during the period.

SOME STRATEGIES FOR PERMANENT IMPROVEMENTS IN CASH FLOW

Several strategies may improve cash flows in *both* the short and long term. These are *deferring income taxes, peak pricing*, and developing an *effective product mix*.

Deferring Income Taxes

Deferring income taxes means using accounting methods for income tax purposes that legally postpone the payment of income taxes. An example is using an *accelerated depreciation method* for income tax purposes.

Deferring taxes may benefit a growing business *every year*. Thus it is an effective and popular cash management strategy.[6]

Peak Pricing

Some businesses have more customers than they can handle—at least at certain times of the day or year. Examples of such businesses include popular restaurants, resort hotels, telephone companies, and providers of electricity.

Peak pricing is a strategy of using sales prices both to increase revenue and to ration goods and services when total demand exceeds supply (or capacity). A higher price is charged during the peak periods of customer demand and a lower price during off-peak periods. Peak pricing has two related goals. First, it *increases the seller's revenue* during the periods of greatest demand. Second, it *shifts* some of the demand to off-peak periods, when the business is better able to service additional customers.

CASE IN POINT

Beach House is a popular seafood restaurant in Cardiff-by-the-Sea. A lobster dinner regularly costs $16.95. But from *4:30 to 6:00 p.m.*, it's only *$9.95.* Why? Because prior to 6:00 p.m. Beach House has lots of empty tables. Later, the restaurant becomes so crowded that it often has to turn customers away.

In many situations, peak pricing benefits the business *and the public*. Off-peak prices generally are *lower* than if peak pricing were not employed. Thus peak pricing may make goods and services available to customers who otherwise could not afford them. Also, peak pricing may prevent systems, such as cellular telephones, from becoming so overloaded that they simply cannot function.

It is important to recognize, however, that peak pricing is *not always appropriate*. For example, we would not expect hospitals or physicians to raise their prices during epidemics or natural disasters. The alternative to peak pricing is a single price all the time. In a single-price situation, demand in excess of capacity normally is handled on the basis of first-come, first-served.

[6] The Modified Accelerated Cost Recovery System (MACRS) is an accelerated method widely used for income tax purposes. Deferred income taxes were discussed further in Chapter 10. The reason a growing business can benefit from deferred taxes *every year* is that each year it defers a *greater amount* than comes due from the past.

© Royalty-Free/Corbis

Develop an Effective Product Mix Another tool for increasing revenue and cash receipts is the mix of products offered for sale. The dual purposes of an effective **product mix** are to (1) increase total sales and (2) increase gross margins (that is, the excess of the selling price over the cost of the product).

Some products complement one another, meaning the customer who buys one product often may purchase the other. Common examples of **complementary products** include french fries at a hamburger stand, snacks at a movie theater, and a car wash connected to a gas station.

Some complementary products are *essential* to satisfying the customer. (Would you be happy at a sports stadium that didn't sell food?) Others increase sales by *attracting customers* who also purchase other types of merchandise.

Some complementary products appear to be only incidental to the company's main product lines. But, in reality, these incidental items may *be* the company's most important products.

CASE IN POINT

Remco Business Products, Inc., sells a variety of office products, including copy machines. Like most businesses that sell major appliances, it also sells long-term service contracts to provide maintenance and repairs at a fixed annual fee. These service contracts actually are Remco's most profitable product. In fact, if you purchase a service contract, you won't need to buy a copier. Remco will lend you one for the life of the service contract at no additional charge.

Ethics, Fraud & Corporate Governance

As discussed in this chapter, cash flow from operations is the subtotal on the statement of cash flows that is most closely scrutinized by financial statement readers. A large and growing cash flow from operations is viewed positively for at least three reasons. First, companies pay bills with cash, not with earnings. A company with significant cash flows from operations is likely to be able to pay its currently maturing bills, and also is likely to be able to take on additional debt, if needed, to finance future expansion plans. Second, a company with significant cash flows from operations is better positioned to fund future growth (e.g., capital expenditures) with its own cash flows rather than having to borrow additional monies or issue more stock. Third, the quality of a company's earnings is viewed as better if cash flow from operations closely matches reported net income. When earnings are misstated, they are typically misstated because the accrual process is abused (e.g., accounts receivable is debited and revenues are credited even though revenue has not been earned). Financial statement readers believe that it is more difficult to manipulate reported cash flows than it is to manipulate reported income. For all of the above reasons, management has an incentive to report positive and growing cash flows from operations, and sometimes that incentive can lead to inappropriate, and even illegal, behavior.

Although it may be difficult to manipulate cash flows from operations, it is certainly not impossible, as the recent Securities and Exchange Commission (SEC) enforcement action involving Dynergy, Inc., illustrates. Dynergy produces and delivers energy, including natural gas, electricity, and coal, to customers throughout North America and Europe, and its shares are traded on the New York Stock Exchange. Dynergy entered into a structured transaction

(continued)

(hereafter referred to as Project Alpha) that resulted in Dynergy reporting $300 million in cash flow from operations that should have been reported as cash flow from financing activities. A primary motivation for Dynergy's involvement with Project Alpha was to bring cash flow from operations closer to reported net income. Dynergy's overstatement of cash flow from operations equaled approximately 36 percent of operating cash flow.

Project Alpha had a five-year term and worked as follows. Dynergy sponsored a special-purpose entity, ABG Supply, to sell Dynergy natural gas. In the first year of the five-year term of Project Alpha, ABG Supply sold Dynergy gas at below-market prices. Dynergy then sold this gas at a $300 million profit and reported the resulting cash flow in the operating activities portion of the statement of cash flows. In the remaining four years of Project Alpha's life, Dynergy was obligated to buy gas from ABG Supply at above-market prices. These purchases at above-market prices would be sufficient to pay back the $300 million, plus interest. In substance, the original sale of gas to Dynergy in year 1 at $300 million below market prices represented a loan, and transactions in years 2 to 5 would result in the loan being repaid with interest. As such, the $300 million cash flow in Year 1 should have been reported in the financing activities portion of the statement of cash flows—not in the operating activities portion of the statement.

Project Alpha transactions would only have qualified as operating activities if Dynergy and ABG Supply were exposed to fluctuations in the market price of natural gas in the purchases scheduled for years 2 to 5. Dynergy and ABG Supply would have been exposed to this risk if future purchases were at a fixed price, and if any derivative contracts used to hedge risks were not tied to the gas contract. Notwithstanding this fact, Dynergy employees linked derivative transactions to the gas contract. As a result, neither Dynergy nor ABG Supply was exposed to fluctuations in the price of natural gas, and the $300 million cash flow in Year 1, which would be repaid with interest in years 2 to 5, was improperly classified as a cash flow from operating activities, whereas it should have been classified as a cash flow from financing activities.

Three midlevel Dynergy tax executives were largely responsible for Project Alpha's structure, and they participated in an active scheme to hide the details of the structure from Dynergy's outside auditors. Two of these executives pled guilty to federal *criminal* charges and testified against the third executive. The third executive, Jamie Olis, was convicted of criminal charges and was sentenced to over 20 years in federal prison. This case clearly illustrates the personal risk of violating securities laws, particularly when there is an active scheme to hide the true nature of transactions from auditors, investors, and other outside parties.

A Worksheet for Preparing a Statement of Cash Flows

LO9 Explain how a worksheet may be helpful in preparing a statement of cash flows.

A statement of cash flows is developed by *systematically analyzing changes in the noncash balance sheet accounts.* This process can be formalized and documented through the preparation of a specially designed worksheet. The worksheet also provides the accountant with visual assurance that the changes in balance sheet accounts have been fully explained.

DATA FOR AN ILLUSTRATION

We will illustrate the worksheet approach using the 2007 financial data of Auto Supply Co.[7] Shown in Exhibit 13–6 are the balances in Auto's balance sheet accounts at the beginning and end of 2007. (Please notice in this illustration that the account balances at the end of the current year appear in the *right-hand* column. This format also is used in the worksheet.)

Additional Information The following information also is used in the preparation of the worksheet. (Accrual-based measurements appear in blue, cash flows in red.)

1. Net income for the year amounted to *$250,000*. Cash dividends of *$140,000* were declared and paid.
2. Auto's only noncash expense was depreciation, which totaled *$60,000*.

[7] Our example involving Allison Corporation was quite comprehensive. Therefore, a worksheet for Allison Corporation would be too long and detailed for use as an introductory illustration of a worksheet for the statement of cash flows.

AUTO SUPPLY CO.
Comparative Balance Sheets

	December 31, 2006	December 31, 2007
Assets		
Cash	$ 50,000	$ 45,000
Marketable Securities	40,000	25,000
Accounts Receivable	320,000	330,000
Inventory	240,000	235,000
Plant and Equipment (net of accumulated depreciation)	600,000	640,000
Totals	$1,250,000	$1,275,000
Liabilities & Stockholders' Equity		
Accounts Payable	$ 150,000	$ 160,000
Accrued Expenses Payable	60,000	45,000
Mortgage Note Payable (long-term)	-0-	70,000
Bonds Payable (due in 2020)	500,000	350,000
Capital Stock (no par value)	160,000	160,000
Retained Earnings	380,000	490,000
Totals	$1,250,000	$1,275,000

Exhibit 13–6

AUTO SUPPLY CO. BALANCE SHEETS

Changes in the noncash accounts are the key to identifying cash flows

3. Marketable securities costing *$15,000* were sold for *$35,000* cash, resulting in a *$20,000* nonoperating gain.
4. The company purchased plant assets for *$100,000*, making a *$30,000* cash down payment and issuing a *$70,000* mortgage note payable for the balance of the purchase price.

THE WORKSHEET

Auto Supply Co. reports cash flows from operating activities by the *indirect method.*[8] A worksheet for preparing a statement of cash flows appears in Exhibit 13–7.

To set up the worksheet, the company's balance sheet accounts are listed in the top portion of the worksheet, with the beginning balances in the first column and the year-end balances in the last (right-hand) column. (For purposes of illustration, we have shown these accounts and account balances in **black**.)

The two middle columns are used to (1) explain the changes in each balance sheet account over the year and (2) indicate how each change affected cash.

Entries in the Two Middle Columns

The entries in the *top portion of the worksheet* summarize the transactions recorded in the account over the year. (Because these entries summarize transactions recorded on the accrual basis, they are shown in **blue**.)

For each summary entry in the top portion of the worksheet, we make an offsetting entry (in the opposite column) in the *bottom portion* of the worksheet indicating the *cash effects* of the transactions. These cash effects are classified as operating, investing, or financing activities and are explained with a descriptive caption. (Entries representing the *cash effects* of transactions and the related descriptive captions appear in **red**.)

Entries in the two middle columns may be made in any sequence, but we recommend the following approach:

1. Explain the change in the Retained Earnings account.
2. Account for depreciation expense (and any other noncash expenses).
3. Account for timing differences between net income and cash flows from operating activities.

[8] If the worksheet utilizes the direct method, numerous subclassifications are required within the operating activities section. Such worksheets are illustrated in more advanced accounting courses.

Exhibit 13–7

WORKSHEET FOR A STATEMENT OF CASH FLOWS

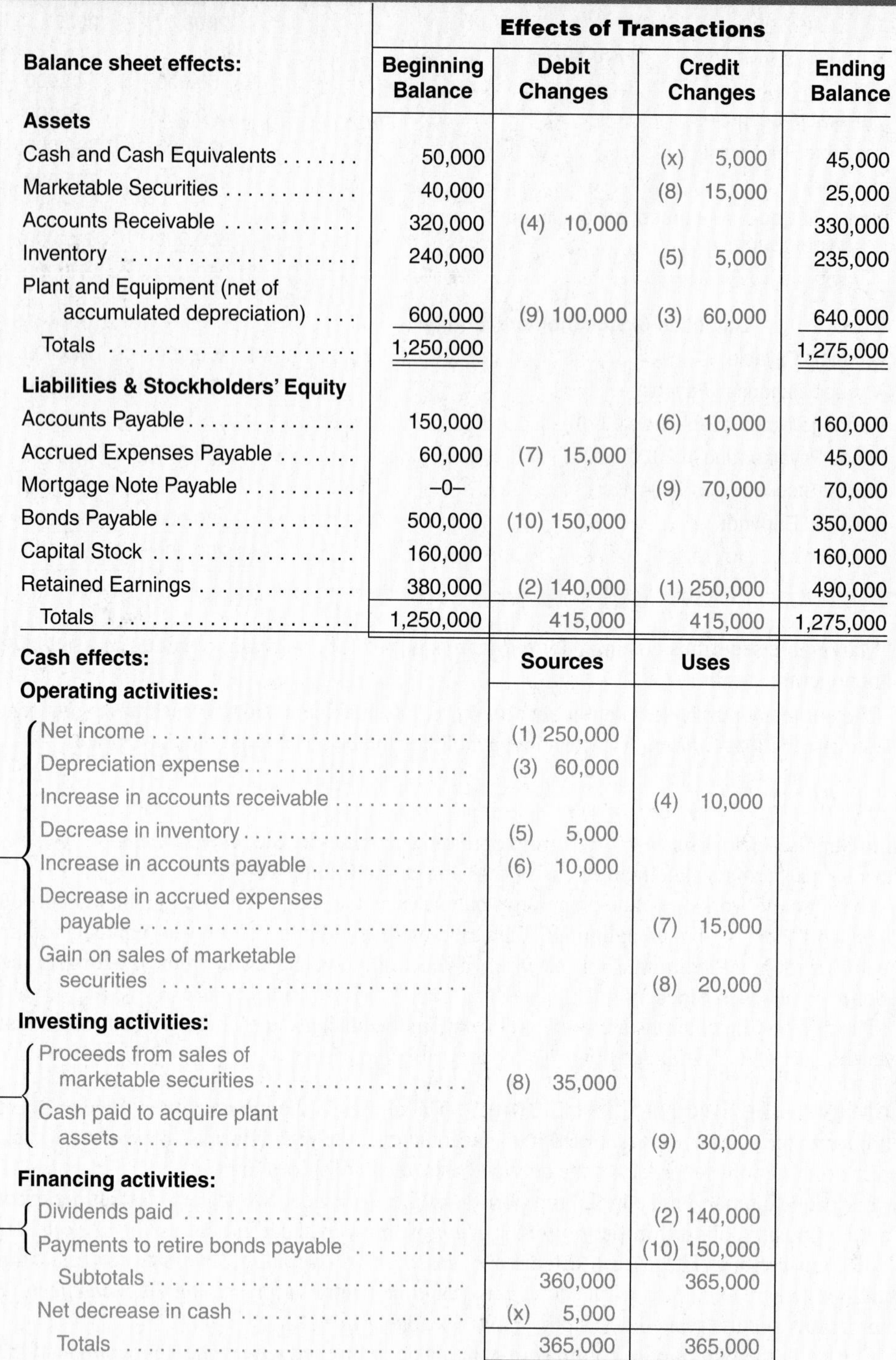

		Effects of Transactions		
Balance sheet effects:	**Beginning Balance**	**Debit Changes**	**Credit Changes**	**Ending Balance**
Assets				
Cash and Cash Equivalents	50,000		(x) 5,000	45,000
Marketable Securities	40,000		(8) 15,000	25,000
Accounts Receivable	320,000	(4) 10,000		330,000
Inventory	240,000		(5) 5,000	235,000
Plant and Equipment (net of accumulated depreciation)	600,000	(9) 100,000	(3) 60,000	640,000
Totals	1,250,000			1,275,000
Liabilities & Stockholders' Equity				
Accounts Payable	150,000		(6) 10,000	160,000
Accrued Expenses Payable	60,000	(7) 15,000		45,000
Mortgage Note Payable	–0–		(9) 70,000	70,000
Bonds Payable	500,000	(10) 150,000		350,000
Capital Stock	160,000			160,000
Retained Earnings	380,000	(2) 140,000	(1) 250,000	490,000
Totals	1,250,000	415,000	415,000	1,275,000
Cash effects:		**Sources**	**Uses**	
Operating activities:				
Net income		(1) 250,000		
Depreciation expense		(3) 60,000		
Increase in accounts receivable			(4) 10,000	
Decrease in inventory		(5) 5,000		
Increase in accounts payable		(6) 10,000		
Decrease in accrued expenses payable			(7) 15,000	
Gain on sales of marketable securities			(8) 20,000	
Investing activities:				
Proceeds from sales of marketable securities		(8) 35,000		
Cash paid to acquire plant assets			(9) 30,000	
Financing activities:				
Dividends paid			(2) 140,000	
Payments to retire bonds payable			(10) 150,000	
Subtotals		360,000	365,000	
Net decrease in cash		(x) 5,000		
Totals		365,000	365,000	

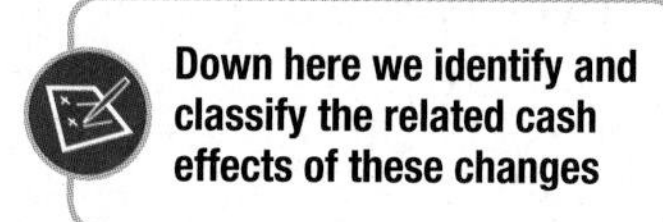

Cash provided by operations—$280,000

Cash provided by investing activities—$5,000

Cash used in financing activities—$290,000

4. Explain any remaining changes in balance sheet accounts *other than Cash.* (Hint: Changes in asset accounts represent investing activities; changes in liability and equity accounts represent financing activities.)
5. Compute and record the net increase or decrease in cash.

Using this approach, the entries in our illustrated worksheet are explained next.

ENTRY

1. Auto's net income explains a $250,000 *credit* to the Retained Earnings account. In the bottom portion of the working paper, an offsetting entry is made in the *Sources* column and is classified as an operating activity.[9]
2. Cash dividends of $140,000 caused a *debit* to the Retained Earnings account during 2007. The offsetting entry falls into the *Uses* column; payments of dividends are classified as a financing activity.

Step 1: Explain the changes in retained earnings

With these first two entries, we have explained how Auto's Retained Earnings account increased during 2007 from $380,000 to $490,000.

3. Auto's only noncash expense was depreciation. In the top portion of the worksheet, depreciation explains a $60,000 credit (decrease) in Plant and Equipment (which includes the Accumulated Depreciation accounts). The offsetting entry in the bottom of the worksheet is placed in the Sources column. We have explained that depreciation is not really a source of cash, but that it *is added back* to net income as a step in computing the cash flows from operating activities.

Step 2: Account for noncash expenses

4–7. Fluctuations in current assets and current liabilities create *timing differences* between net income and the net cash flows from operating activities. In the top portion of the worksheet, entries (4) through (7) summarize the changes in these current asset and current liability accounts. In the bottom portion, they show how these changes affect the computation of cash flows from operating activities.

Step 3: Account for timing differences

8. In 2007, Auto sold marketable securities with a cost of $15,000 for $35,000 cash, resulting in a $20,000 nonoperating gain. In the top portion of the worksheet, the entry explains the $15,000 credit change in the Marketable Securities account. In the bottom portion, it reports cash proceeds of $35,000. The difference? The $20,000 nonoperating gain, which is *removed from the Operating Activities section* of the worksheet and included instead within the amount reported as "Proceeds from sales of marketable securities" in the Investing Activities category.

Step 4: Explain any remaining changes in noncash accounts

9. Auto purchased $100,000 in plant assets, paying $30,000 cash and issuing a $70,000 note payable. These events explain a $100,000 debit in Plant and Equipment and the $70,000 credit change in Mortgage Note Payable; they involved a cash outlay of $30,000, which is classified as an investing activity. (The $70,000 financed by issuance of a note payable is a *noncash* investing and financing activity.)
10. The $150,000 debit change in Auto's Bonds Payable account indicates that this amount of the liability has been repaid—that is, $150,000 in bonds has been retired. This is included in the financing activities category.

At this point, we should check to determine that our entries in the two middle columns *fully explain* the differences between the beginning and ending balance of each noncash balance sheet account. If the top portion of the worksheet explains the changes in every noncash account, the bottom section should include all of the cash flows for the year.

(x) We now total the Sources (cash increases) and Uses (cash decreases) columns in the bottom portion of the worksheet. The difference between these column subtotals represents the *net increase or decrease* in cash. In our example, the Sources column totals $360,000, while the Uses column totals $365,000, indicating a *$5,000 decrease* in cash over the period. Notice that this is exactly the amount by which Cash decreased during 2007: $50,000 − $45,000 = $5,000. Our last entry, labeled *(x)*, explains the credit change in the Cash account at the top of the worksheet and brings the bottom of the worksheet into balance.

Step 5: Compute and record the net change in cash

The formal statement of cash flows, reporting the cash flows from operating activities by the indirect method, can be prepared directly from the bottom portion of this worksheet. In

[9] When the *indirect method* is used, net income serves as the *starting point* for computing net cash flows from operating activities.

Exhibit 13–8, amounts appearing in accrual-based accounting records are shown in blue; cash flows appear in red.

Exhibit 13–8

AUTO SUPPLY CO. STATEMENT OF CASH FLOWS

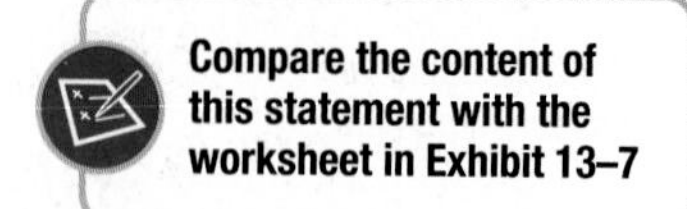

AUTO SUPPLY CO. Statement of Cash Flows For the Year Ended December 31, 2007		
Cash flows from operating activities:		
Net income		$ 250,000
Add: Depreciation expense		60,000
Decrease in inventory		5,000
Increase in accounts payable		10,000
Subtotal		$ 325,000
Less: Increase in accounts receivable	$ 10,000	
Decrease in accrued expenses payable	15,000	
Gain on sales of marketable securities	20,000	45,000
Net cash provided by operating activities		$ 280,000
Cash flows from investing activities:		
Proceeds from sales of marketable securities	$ 35,000	
Cash paid to acquire plant assets (see supplementary schedule below)	(30,000)	
Net cash provided by investing activities		5,000
Cash flows from financing activities:		
Dividends paid	$ (140,000)	
Payments to retire bonds payable	(150,000)	
Net cash used for financing activities		(290,000)
Net decrease in cash		$ (5,000)
Cash and cash equivalents, Dec. 31, 2006		50,000
Cash and cash equivalents, Dec. 31, 2007		$ 45,000
Supplementary Schedule: Noncash Investing and Financing Activities		
Purchases of plant assets		$ 100,000
Less: Portion financed through issuance of long-term debt		70,000
Cash paid to acquire plant assets		$ 30,000

Concluding Remarks

In this chapter, we have discussed the importance of cash flow information for investors and creditors and how that information is arranged and presented in the statement of cash flows. We delayed in-depth coverage of this important topic to this point because of the importance of understanding accounting for assets, liabilities, and stockholders' equity as a forerunner to understanding how cash flow information differs from accrual accounting information.

As stated earlier, companies have an option of presenting cash flow from operations information by either the direct or the indirect method. Although we have presented both in this chapter, our emphasis has been on the direct method despite the fact that most companies employ the indirect method in their financial reporting. We have done this for two reasons. First, we believe the direct method is more readily understood by students and others who are learning for the first time how cash-based and accrual-based information relate. Second, and perhaps more important, investors appear to generally favor the direct method, as evidenced by the following quote from the chief accountant of the Securities and Exchange Commission, speaking to a group of certified public accountants:

> I've heard many investors express a strong preference for use of the direct method of preparing the statement of cash flows. It's widely understood and believed by many to be a more informative presentation. We are not requiring a change, but it is an action you could consider to promote transparency given the importance to investors of cash flow information.[10]

In the next chapter, we take a broader look at financial statement analysis, including how information about cash flows is combined with information from the other financial statements, to better understand a company's financial activities. Managers and investors alike must look beyond short-term changes in earnings and cash flows from one period to the next. They must consider factors that cause these changes and how they may affect future operations. Throughout this text, we have introduced simple financial analysis techniques that are useful in analyzing a company. In Chapter 14, we bring those techniques together into a comprehensive model for analyzing financial statements in a way that assists informed decision makers in understanding a company's business activities and in anticipating the long-term effects of business strategies.

[10] Donald T. Nicolaisen in a speech entitled, "Remarks before the 2003 Thirty-First AICPA National Conference on Current SEC Developments," December 11, 2003.

END-OF-CHAPTER REVIEW

SUMMARY OF LEARNING OBJECTIVES

LO1 **Explain the purposes and uses of a statement of cash flows.** The primary purpose of a statement of cash flows is to provide information about the cash receipts and cash payments of the entity and how they relate to the entity's operating, investing, and financing activities. Readers of financial statements use this information to assess the liquidity of a business and to evaluate its ability to generate positive cash flows in future periods, pay dividends, and finance growth.

LO2 **Describe how cash transactions are classified in a statement of cash flows.** Cash flows are classified as (1) operating activities, (2) investing activities, or (3) financing activities. Receipts and payments of interest are classified as operating activities.

LO3 **Compute the major cash flows relating to operating activities.** The major operating cash flows are (1) cash received from customers, (2) cash paid to suppliers and employees, (3) interest and dividends received, (4) interest paid, and (5) income taxes paid. These cash flows are computed by converting the income statement amounts for revenue, cost of goods sold, and expenses from the accrual basis to the cash basis. This is done by adjusting the income statement amounts for changes occurring over the period in related balance sheet accounts.

LO4 **Compute the cash flows relating to investing and financing activities.** Cash flows from investing and financing activities are determined by examining the entries in the related asset and liability accounts, along with any related gains or losses shown in the income statement. Debit entries in asset accounts represent purchases of assets (an investing activity). Credit entries in asset accounts represent the cost of assets sold. The amount of these credit entries must be adjusted by any gains or losses recognized on these sales transactions.

Debit entries to liability accounts represent repayment of debt, while credit entries represent borrowing. Both types of transactions are classified as financing activities. Other financing activities include the issuance of stock (indicated by credits to the paid-in capital accounts) and payment of dividends (indicated by a debit change in the Retained Earnings account).

LO5 **Distinguish between the direct and indirect methods of reporting operating cash flows.** The direct and indirect methods are alternative formats for reporting net cash flows from operating activities. The *direct* method shows the specific cash inflows and outflows comprising the operating activities of the business. By the *indirect* method, the computation begins with accrual-based net income and then makes adjustments necessary to arrive at net cash flows from operating activities. Both methods result in the same dollar amount of net cash flows from operating activities. When the direct method is used, the indirect method must also be disclosed.

LO6 **Explain why net income differs from net cash flows from operating activities.** Net income differs from net operating cash flows for several reasons. One reason is noncash expenses, such as depreciation and the amortization of intangible assets. These expenses, which require no cash outlays when they are recognized, reduce net income but do not require cash payments. Another reason is the many timing differences existing between the recognition of revenue and expense and the occurrence of the underlying cash flows. Finally, nonoperating gains and losses enter into the determination of net income, but the related cash flows are classified as investing or financing activities, not operating activities.

LO7 **Compute net cash flows from operating activities using the *indirect* method.** The indirect method uses net income (as reported in the income statement) as the starting point in the computation of net cash flows from operating activities. Adjustments to net income necessary to arrive at net cash flows from operating activities are described in three categories: noncash expenses, timing differences, and nonoperating gains and losses. Adjustments reconcile net income (accrual basis) to net cash flows from operating activities. Specific adjustments from each category are illustrated in the summary analysis of the indirect method on page 587.

LO8 **Discuss the likely effects of various business strategies on cash flows.** It is difficult to predict the *extent* to which a business strategy will affect cash flows. However, an informed decision maker should understand the *direction* in which a strategy is likely to affect cash flows—both in the short term and over a longer term.

LO9 **Explain how a worksheet may be helpful in preparing a statement of cash flows.** A worksheet can be used to analyze the changes in balance sheet accounts other than Cash and, thereby, determine the related cash flows. In the top portion of the worksheet, entries are made summarizing the changes in each noncash account. In the bottom half, offsetting entries are made to represent the cash effects of the transactions summarized in the top portion. The entries in the bottom half of the worksheet are classified into the same categories as in a statement of cash flows—operating, investing, and financing. The statement of cash flows then is prepared from the data in the bottom portion of the worksheet.

Key Terms Introduced or Emphasized in Chapter 13

accrual basis (p. 575) A method of summarizing operating results in terms of revenue earned and expenses incurred, rather than cash receipts or cash payments.

cash basis (p. 578) The practice of summarizing operating results in terms of cash receipts and cash payments, rather than revenue earned or expenses incurred.

cash budget (p. 591) A detailed forecast of expected future cash receipts, usually organized department by department and month by month for the coming year.

cash equivalents (p. 574) Highly liquid short-term investments, such as Treasury bills, money market funds, and commercial paper. For purposes of preparing a statement of cash flows, money held in cash equivalents is considered the same as cash. Thus transfers between a bank account and cash equivalents are not considered receipts or disbursements of cash.

cash flows (p. 572) A term describing both cash receipts (inflows) and cash payments (outflows).

complementary products (p. 593) Products that "fit together" —that tie in with a company's other products. As a result, customers attracted to one product may also purchase others.

financing activities (p. 572) Transactions such as borrowing, repaying borrowed amounts, raising equity capital, or making distributions to owners. The cash effects of these transactions are reported in the financing activities section of the statement of cash flows. Noncash aspects of these transactions are disclosed in a supplementary schedule.

free cash flow (p. 589) The portion of the annual net cash flows from operating activities that remains available for discretionary purposes after the basic obligations of the business have been met. Can be computed in several different ways.

investing activities (p. 572) Transactions involving acquisitions or sales of investments or plant assets and making or collecting loans. The cash aspects of these transactions are shown in the investing activities section of the statement of cash flows. Noncash aspects of these transactions are disclosed in a supplementary schedule to this financial statement.

operating activities (p. 572) Transactions entering into the determination of net income, with the exception of gains and losses relating to financing or investing activities. The category includes such transactions as selling goods or services, earning investment income, and incurring costs and expenses, such as payments to suppliers and employees, interest, and income taxes. The cash effects of these transactions are reflected in the operating activities section of the statement of cash flows.

peak pricing (p. 592) The strategy of charging a higher price during periods of high demand, and a lower price during periods of slack demand. Intended to both maximize revenue and shift excess demand to periods in which it can be more easily accommodated.

product mix (p. 593) The variety and relative quantities of goods and services that a company offers for sale.

Demonstration Problem

You are the chief accountant for Electro Products, Inc. Your assistant has prepared an income statement for the current year and has developed the following additional information by analyzing changes in the company's balance sheet accounts.

ELECTRO PRODUCTS, INC.
Income Statement
For the Year Ended December 31, 2007

Revenue:		
Net sales		$9,500,000
Interest income		320,000
Gain on sales of marketable securities		70,000
Total revenue and gains		$9,890,000
Costs and expenses:		
Cost of goods sold	$4,860,000	
Operating expenses (including depreciation of $700,000)	3,740,000	
Interest expense	270,000	
Income tax expense	300,000	
Loss on sales of plant assets	90,000	
Total costs, expenses, and losses		9,260,000
Net income		$ 630,000

Changes in the company's balance sheet accounts over the year are summarized as follows:

1. Accounts Receivable decreased by $85,000.
2. Accrued Interest Receivable increased by $15,000.
3. Inventory decreased by $280,000, and Accounts Payable to suppliers of merchandise decreased by $240,000.
4. Short-term prepayments of operating expenses decreased by $18,000, and accrued liabilities for operating expenses increased by $35,000.
5. The liability for Accrued Interest Payable decreased by $16,000 during the year.
6. The liability for Accrued Income Taxes Payable increased by $25,000 during the year.
7. The following schedule summarizes the total debit and credit entries during the year in other balance sheet accounts:

	Debit Entries	Credit Entries
Marketable Securities	$ 120,000	$ 210,000
Notes Receivable (cash loans made to others)	250,000	190,000
Plant Assets (see paragraph **8**)	3,800,000	360,000
Notes Payable (short-term borrowing)	620,000	740,000
Bonds Payable		1,100,000
Capital Stock		50,000
Additional Paid-in Capital (from issuance of stock)		840,000
Retained Earnings (see paragraph **9**)	320,000	630,000

8. The $360,000 in credit entries to the Plant Assets account is net of any debits to accumulated depreciation when plant assets were retired. Thus the $360,000 in credit entries represents the *book value* of all plant assets sold or retired during the year.
9. The $320,000 debit to Retained Earnings represents dividends declared and paid during the year. The $630,000 credit entry represents the net income for the year.
10. All investing and financing activities were cash transactions.
11. Cash and cash equivalents amounted to $448,000 at the beginning of the year and to $330,000 at year-end.

Instructions

You are to prepare a statement of cash flows for the current year, following the format illustrated in Exhibit 13–1. Cash flows from operating activities are to be determined by the *direct method.* Place brackets around dollar amounts representing cash outlays. Show separately your computations of the following amounts:

a. Cash received from customers.
b. Interest received.
c. Cash paid to suppliers and employees.
d. Interest paid.
e. Income taxes paid.
f. Proceeds from sales of marketable securities.
g. Proceeds from sales of plant assets.
h. Proceeds from issuing capital stock.

Solution to the Demonstration Problem

ELECTRO PRODUCTS, INC.
Statement of Cash Flows
For the Year Ended December 31, 2007

Cash flows from operating activities:		
Cash received from customers **(a)**	$ 9,585,000	
Interest received **(b)**	305,000	
Cash provided by operating activities		$9,890,000
Cash paid to suppliers and employees **(c)**	$(7,807,000)	
Interest paid **(d)**	(286,000)	
Income taxes paid **(e)**	(275,000)	
Cash disbursed for operating activities		(8,368,000)
Net cash provided by operating activities		$1,522,000
Cash flows from investing activities:		
Purchases of marketable securities	$ (120,000)	
Proceeds from sales of marketable securities **(f)**	280,000	
Loans made to borrowers	(250,000)	
Collections on loans	190,000	
Cash paid to acquire plant assets	(3,800,000)	
Proceeds from sales of plant assets **(g)**	270,000	
Net cash used for investing activities		(3,430,000)
Cash flows from financing activities:		
Proceeds from short-term borrowing	$ 740,000	
Payments to settle short-term debts	(620,000)	
Proceeds from issuing bonds payable	1,100,000	
Proceeds from issuing capital stock **(h)**	890,000	
Dividends paid	(320,000)	
Net cash provided by financing activities		1,790,000
Net increase (decrease) in cash		$ (118,000)
Cash and cash equivalents, Jan. 1		448,000
Cash and cash equivalents, Dec. 31		$ 330,000

Supporting computations:

a. Cash received from customers:	
Net sales	$9,500,000
Add: Decrease in accounts receivable	85,000
Cash received from customers	$9,585,000
b. Interest received:	
Interest income	$ 320,000
Less: Increase in accrued interest receivable	15,000
Interest received	$ 305,000
c. Cash paid to suppliers and employees:	
Cash paid for purchases of merchandise:	
Cost of goods sold	$4,860,000
Less: Decrease in inventory	280,000
Net purchases	$4,580,000
Add: Decrease in accounts payable to suppliers	240,000
Cash paid for purchases of merchandise	$4,820,000

ELECTRO PRODUCTS, INC. (continued)
Statement of Cash Flows
For the Year Ended December 31, 2007

Cash paid for operating expenses:		
Operating expenses		$3,740,000
Less: Depreciation (a "noncash" expense)	$700,000	
Decrease in prepayments	18,000	
Increase in accrued liabilities for operating expenses	35,000	753,000
Cash paid for operating expenses		$2,987,000
Cash paid to suppliers and employees ($4,820,000 + $2,987,000)		$7,807,000
d. Interest paid:		
Interest expense		$ 270,000
Add: Decrease in accrued interest payable		16,000
Interest paid		$ 286,000
e. Income taxes paid:		
Income tax expense		$ 300,000
Less: Increase in accrued income taxes payable		25,000
Income taxes paid		$ 275,000
f. Proceeds from sales of marketable securities:		
Cost of marketable securities sold (credit entries to the Marketable Securities account)		$ 210,000
Add: Gain reported on sales of marketable securities		70,000
Proceeds from sales of marketable securities		$ 280,000
g. Proceeds from sales of plant assets:		
Book value of plant assets sold (paragraph **8**)		$ 360,000
Less: Loss reported on sales of plant assets		90,000
Proceeds from sales of plant assets		$ 270,000
h. Proceeds from issuing capital stock:		
Amounts credited to the Capital Stock account		$ 50,000
Add: Amounts credited to Additional Paid-in Capital account		840,000
Proceeds from issuing capital stock		$ 890,000

Self-Test Questions

The answers to these questions appear on page 629.

1. The statement of cash flows is designed to assist users in assessing each of the following, *except*:
   a. The ability of a company to remain liquid.
   b. The major sources of cash receipts during the period.
   c. The company's profitability.
   d. The reasons why net cash flows from operating activities differ from net income.

2. Which of the following is *not* included in the statement of cash flows, or in a supplementary schedule accompanying the statement of cash flows?
   a. Disclosure of investing or financing activities that did not involve cash.
   b. A reconciliation of net income to net cash flows from operating activities.
   c. Disclosure of the amount of cash invested in money market funds during the accounting period.
   d. The amount of cash and cash equivalents owned by the business at the end of the accounting period.

3. Cash flows are grouped in the statement of cash flows into the following major categories:
   a. Operating activities, investing activities, and financing activities.
   b. Cash receipts, cash disbursements, and noncash activities.
   c. Direct cash flows and indirect cash flows.
   d. Operating activities, investing activities, and collecting activities.

4. The following is a list of various cash payments and cash receipts:

Cash paid to suppliers and employees	$420,000
Dividends paid	18,000
Interest paid	12,000
Purchases of plant assets	45,000
Interest and dividends received	17,000
Payments to settle short-term bank loans	29,000
Income taxes paid	23,000
Cash received from customers	601,000

Based only on the above items, net cash flows from operating activities are:

a. $138,000
b. $91,000
c. $120,000
d. $163,000

5. During the current year, two transactions were recorded in the Land account of Duke Industries. One involved a debit of $320,000 to the Land account; the second was a $210,000 credit to the Land account. Duke's income statement for the year reported a loss on sale of land in the amount of $25,000. All transactions involving the Land account were cash transactions. These transactions would be shown in the statement of cash flows as:

a. $320,000 cash provided by investing activities, and $210,000 cash disbursed for investing activities.
b. $185,000 cash provided by investing activities, and $320,000 cash disbursed for investing activities.
c. $235,000 cash provided by investing activities, and $320,000 cash disbursed for investing activities.
d. $210,000 cash provided by investing activities, and $320,000 cash disbursed for investing activities.

6. Which of the following business strategies is *most likely* to increase the net cash flows of a software developer in the short run but *reduce* them over a longer term?

a. Develop software that is more costly to create but easier to update and improve.
b. Lower the price of existing versions of products as customer demand begins to fall.
c. Reduce expenditures for the purpose of developing new products.
d. Purchase the building in which the business operates (assume the company currently rents this location).

ASSIGNMENT MATERIAL Discussion Questions

1. Briefly state the purposes of a statement of cash flows.
2. Does a statement of cash flows or an income statement best measure the profitability of a financially sound business? Explain.
3. Two supplementary schedules frequently accompany a statement of cash flows prepared by the direct method. Briefly explain the content of these schedules.
4. Give two examples of cash receipts and two examples of cash payments that fit into each of the following classifications:
   a. Operating activities.
   b. Investing activities.
   c. Financing activities.
5. Why are payments and receipts of interest classified as operating activities rather than as financing or investing activities?
6. Define *cash equivalents* and list three examples.
7. During the current year, Nolan Corporation transferred $268,000 from its bank account into a money market fund. Will this transaction appear in a statement of cash flows? If so, in which section? Explain.
8. In the long run, is it more important for a business to have positive cash flows from its operating activities, investing activities, or financing activities? Why?
9. Of the three types of business activities summarized in a statement of cash flows, which type is *least* likely to show positive net cash flows in a successful, growing business? Explain your reasoning.
10. The items and amounts listed in a balance sheet and an income statement correspond to specific accounts in a company's ledger. Is the same true about the items and amounts in a statement of cash flows? Explain.
11. Clark, Inc., had net sales for the year of $925,000. Accounts receivable increased from $80,000 at the beginning of the year to $162,000 at year-end. Compute the amount of cash collected during the year from customers.
12. Describe the types of cash payments summarized by the caption "Cash paid to suppliers and employees."
13. Identify three factors that may cause net income to differ from net cash flows from operating activities.
14. Briefly explain the difference between the *direct* and *indirect methods* of computing net cash flows from operating activities. Which method results in higher net cash flows?
15. Are cash payments of accounts payable viewed as operating activities or financing activities? Referring to the statement of cash flows illustrated in Exhibit 13–1, state the caption that includes amounts paid on accounts payable.
16. Moss, Inc., acquired land by issuing $665,000 of capital stock. No cash changed hands in this transaction. Will the transaction be disclosed in the company's statement of cash flows? Explain.
17. The only transaction recorded in the plant assets account of Pompei Company in the current year was a $220,000 credit to the Land account. Assuming that this credit resulted from a cash transaction, does this entry indicate a cash receipt or a

cash payment? Should this $220,000 appear in the statement of cash flows, or is some adjustment necessary?

18. During the current year, the following credit entries were posted to the paid-in capital accounts of Crawford Shipyards:

Capital Stock	$12,000,000
Additional Paid-in Capital	43,500,000

Explain the type of cash transaction that probably caused these credit changes, and illustrate the presentation of this transaction in a statement of cash flows.

19. At the beginning of the current year, Callifax Corporation had dividends payable of $1,500,000. During the current year, the company declared cash dividends of $4,300,000, of which $900,000 appeared as a liability at year-end. Determine the amount of cash dividends *paid* during this year.

20. Define the term *free cash flow*. Explain the significance of this measurement to (1) short-term creditors, (2) long-term creditors, (3) stockholders, and (4) management.

21. Describe a *cash budget* and explain its usefulness to management.

22. Explain the concept of *peak pricing* and provide an example from your own experience.

23. From management's perspective, identify some of the characteristics of an effective product mix.

24. Explain why speeding up the collection of accounts receivable provides only a one-time increase in cash receipts.

Brief Exercises

BRIEF EXERCISE 13.1

Cash Flows from Operations (Direct)

Olympic, Inc., had the following positive and negative cash flows during the current year:

Positive cash flows:	
Received from customers	$240,000
Interest and dividends	50,000
Sale of plant assets	330,000
Negative cash flows:	
Paid to suppliers and employees	$127,000
Purchase of investments	45,000
Purchase of treasury stock	36,000

Determine the amount of cash provided by or used for operating activities by the direct method.

BRIEF EXERCISE 13.2

Cash Flows from Operations (Indirect)

Garagiola Company had net income in the current year of $430,000. Depreciation expense for the year totaled $67,000. During the year the company experienced an increase in accounts receivable (all from sales to customers) of $35,000 and an increase in accounts payable (all to suppliers) of $56,000. Compute the amount of cash provided by or used for operating activities by the indirect method.

BRIEF EXERCISE 13.3

Cash Flows from Operations (Direct)

Georgia Products Co. had the following positive cash flows during the current year: received cash from customers of $750,000; received bank loans of $35,000; and received cash from the sale of common stock of $145,000. During the same year, cash was paid out to purchase inventory for $335,000, to employees for $230,000, and for the purchase of plant assets of $190,000. Calculate the amount of cash provided by or used for operating activities by the direct method.

BRIEF EXERCISE 13.4

Cash Flows from Operations (Indirect)

Patterson Company reported net income for the current year of $666,000. During the year the company's accounts receivable increased by $50,000, inventory decreased by $23,000, accounts payable decreased by $55,000, and accrued expenses payable increased by $14,000. Determine the amount of cash provided by or used for operating activities by the indirect method.

BRIEF EXERCISE 13.5

Cash Flows from Investing Activities

Old Alabama Company purchased investments for $45,000 and plant assets for $127,000 during the current year, during which it also sold plant assets for $66,000, at a gain of $6,000. The company also purchased treasury stock for $78,000 and sold a new issue of common stock for $523,000. Determine the amount of cash provided by or used for investing activities for the year.

BRIEF EXERCISE 13.6

Cash Flows from Financing Activities

Texas, Inc., sold common stock for $560,000 and preferred stock for $36,000 during the current year. In addition, the company purchased treasury stock for $35,000 and paid dividends on common and preferred stock for $24,000. Determine the amount of cash provided by or used for financing activities during the year.

BRIEF EXERCISE 13.7

Cash Payment for Merchandise

Dane, Inc., reported cost of goods sold of $100,100 during the current year. Following are the beginning and ending balances of merchandise inventory and accounts payable for the year:

	Beginning	Ending
Merchandise inventory	$35,000	$43,000
Accounts payable	23,000	30,000

Determine the amount of cash payments for purchases during the year.

BRIEF EXERCISE 13.8

Determining Beginning Cash Balance

Tyler, Inc.'s cash balance at December 31, 2007, the end of its financial reporting year, was $155,000. During 2007, cash provided by operations was $145,000, cash used in investing activities was $67,000, and cash provided by financing activities was $10,000. Calculate the amount of Tyler's beginning cash balance at January 1, 2007.

BRIEF EXERCISE 13.9

Reconciling Net Income to Cash from Operations

Zephre Company reported net income for the year of $56,000. Depreciation expense for the year was $12,000. During the year, accounts receivable increased by $4,000, inventory decreased by $6,000, accounts payable increased by $3,000, and accrued expenses payable decreased by $2,000. Reconcile the amount of net income to the amount of cash provided by or used for operating activities.

BRIEF EXERCISE 13.10

Preparing Statement of Cash Flows

Watson, Inc., had a cash balance at the beginning of the year of $89,000. During the year, the following cash flows occurred:

From operating activities	$136,000
From investing activities	(56,000)
From financing activities	(34,000)

Prepare an abbreviated statement of cash flows, including a reconciliation of the beginning and ending cash balances for the year.

Exercises

EXERCISE 13.1

Using a Statement of Cash Flows

Wallace Company's statement of cash flows for the current year is summarized as follows:

Cash provided by operating activities	$200,000
Cash used in investing activities	(120,000)
Cash provided by financing activities	88,000
Increase in cash during the year	$168,000
Cash balance, beginning of the year	75,000
Cash balance, end of the year	$243,000

a. Briefly explain what is included in each of the first three categories listed (i.e., the cash from operating, investing, and financing activities categories).

b. Based on the limited information presented above, describe the company's change in cash position during the year and your interpretation of the strength of the company's current (end-of-year) cash position.

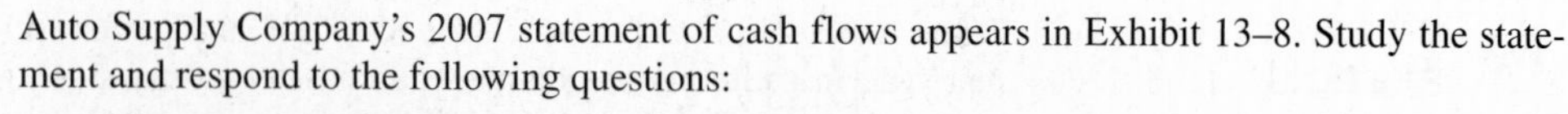

LO6

EXERCISE 13.2
Using a Statement of Cash Flows

Auto Supply Company's 2007 statement of cash flows appears in Exhibit 13–8. Study the statement and respond to the following questions:

a. What was the company's free cash flow in 2007?

b. What were the major sources and uses of cash from financing activities during 2007? Did the net effect of financing activities result in an increase or a decrease in cash during the year?

c. What happened to the total amount of cash and cash equivalents during the year? Assuming 2007 was a typical year, is the firm in a position to continue its dividend payments in the future? Explain.

d. Look at the reconciliation of net income to net cash provided by operating activities, and explain the following:

1. Net loss (gain) from the sale of marketable securities.

2. Increase in accounts receivable.

EXERCISE 13.3
Computing Cash Flows

An analysis of the Marketable Securities control account of Prosper Products, Inc., shows the following entries during the year:

Balance, Jan. 1	$ 290,000
Debit entries	125,000
Credit entries	(140,000)
Balance, Dec. 31	$ 275,000

In addition, the company's income statement includes a $35,000 loss on sales of marketable securities. None of the company's marketable securities is considered a cash equivalent.

Compute the amounts that should appear in the statement of cash flows as:

a. Purchases of marketable securities.

b. Proceeds from sales of marketable securities.

EXERCISE 13.4
Comparing Net Sales and Cash Receipts

During the current year, Technic, Inc., made cash sales of $285,000 and credit sales of $460,000. During the year, accounts receivable decreased by $32,000.

a. Compute for the current year the amounts of:

1. Net sales reported as revenue in the income statement.

2. Cash received from collecting accounts receivable.

3. Cash received from customers.

b. Write a brief statement explaining *why* cash received from customers differs from the amount of net sales.

EXERCISE 13.5
Computing Cash Paid for Purchases of Merchandise

The general ledger of MPX, Inc., provides the following information relating to purchases of merchandise:

	End of Year	Beginning of Year
Inventory	$820,000	$780,000
Accounts payable to merchandise suppliers	430,000	500,000

The company's cost of goods sold during the year was $2,975,000. Compute the amount of cash payments made during the year to suppliers of merchandise.

EXERCISE 13.6
Reporting Lending Activities and Interest Revenue

During the current year, Maine Savings and Loan Association made new loans of $15 million. In addition, the company collected $36 million from borrowers, of which $30 million was interest revenue. Explain how these cash flows will appear in the company's statement of cash flows, indicating the classification and the dollar amount of each cash flow.

EXERCISE 13.7
Format of a Statement of Cash Flows

The accounting staff of Wyoming Outfitters, Inc., has assembled the following information for the year ended December 31, 2007:

Cash and cash equivalents, Jan. 1	$ 35,800
Cash and cash equivalents, Dec. 31	74,800
Cash paid to acquire plant assets	21,000
Proceeds from short-term borrowing	10,000
Loans made to borrowers	5,000
Collections on loans (excluding interest)	4,000
Interest and dividends received	27,000
Cash received from customers	795,000
Proceeds from sales of plant assets	9,000
Dividends paid	55,000
Cash paid to suppliers and employees	635,000
Interest paid	19,000
Income taxes paid	71,000

Using this information, prepare a statement of cash flows. Include a proper heading for the financial statement, and classify the given information into the categories of operating activities, investing activities, and financing activities. Determine net cash flows from operating activities by the direct method. Place brackets around the dollar amounts of all cash disbursements.

EXERCISE 13.8
Effects of Business Strategies

Indicate how you would expect the following strategies to affect the company's net cash flows from *operating activities* (1) in the near future and (2) in later periods (after the strategy's long-term effects have "taken hold"). *Fully explain your reasoning.*

a. A successful pharmaceutical company substantially reduces its expenditures for research and development.

b. A restaurant that previously sold only for cash adopts a policy of accepting bank credit cards, such as Visa and MasterCard.

c. A manufacturing company reduces by 50 percent the size of its inventories of raw materials (assume no change in inventory storage costs).

d. Through tax planning, a rapidly growing real estate developer is able to defer significant amounts of income taxes.

e. A rapidly growing software company announces that it will stop paying cash dividends for the foreseeable future and will instead distribute stock dividends.

LO7

EXERCISE 13.9
An Analysis of Possible Reconciling Items

An analysis of the annual financial statements of Conner Corporation reveals the following:

a. The company had a $5 million extraordinary loss from insurance proceeds received due to a tornado that destroyed a factory building.

b. Depreciation for the year amounted to $8 million.

c. During the year, $2 million in cash was transferred from the company's checking account into a money market fund.

d. Accounts receivable from customers increased by $4 million over the year.

e. Cash received from customers during the year amounted to $167 million.

f. Prepaid expenses decreased by $1 million over the year.

g. Dividends declared during the year amounted to $7 million; dividends paid during the year amounted to $6 million.

h. Accounts payable (to suppliers of merchandise) increased by $2.5 million during the year.

i. The liability for accrued income taxes payable amounted to $5 million at the beginning of the year and $3 million at year-end.

In the computation of net cash flows from operating activities by the *indirect method*, explain whether each of the above items should be *added to net income, deducted from net income*, or *omitted from the computation*. Briefly explain your reasons for each answer.

EXERCISE 13.10
Computation of Net Cash Flows from Operating Activities—Indirect Method

The following data are taken from the income statement and balance sheet of Keaner Machinery, Inc.:

	Dec. 31, 2007	Jan. 1, 2007
Income statement:		
Net Income	$385,000	
Depreciation Expense	125,000	
Amortization of Intangible Assets	40,000	
Gain on Sale of Plant Assets	90,000	
Loss on Sale of Investments	35,000	
Balance sheet:		
Accounts Receivable	$335,000	$380,000
Inventory	503,000	575,000
Prepaid Expenses	22,000	10,000
Accounts Payable (to merchandise suppliers)	379,000	410,000
Accrued Expenses Payable	180,000	155,000

Using this information, prepare a partial statement of cash flows for the year ended December 31, 2007, showing the computation of net cash flows from operating activities by the *indirect* method.

EXERCISE 13.11
Classifying Cash Flows

Among the transactions of Beeler, Inc., were the following:

a. Made payments on accounts payable to merchandise suppliers.
b. Paid the principal amount of a note payable to First Bank.
c. Paid interest charges relating to a note payable to First Bank.
d. Issued bonds payable for cash; management plans to use this cash in the near future to expand manufacturing and warehouse capabilities.
e. Paid salaries to employees in the finance department.
f. Collected an account receivable from a customer.
g. Transferred cash from the general bank account into a money market fund.
h. Used the cash received in **d**, above, to purchase land and a building suitable for a manufacturing facility.
i. Made a year-end adjusting entry to recognize depreciation expense.
j. At year-end, purchased for cash an insurance policy covering the next 12 months.
k. Paid the quarterly dividend on preferred stock.
l. Paid the semiannual interest on bonds payable.
m. Received a quarterly dividend from an investment in the preferred stock of another corporation.
n. Sold for cash an investment in the preferred stock of another corporation.
o. Received cash upon the maturity of an investment in cash equivalents. (Ignore interest.)

Instructions

Most of the preceding transactions should be included among the activities summarized in a statement of cash flows. For each transaction that should be included in this statement, indicate whether the transaction should be classified as an operating activity, an investing activity, or a financing activity. If the transaction *should not be included* in the current year's statement of cash flows, briefly explain why not. (Assume that net cash flows from operating activities are determined by the *direct method.*)

EXERCISE 13.12
Classifying Cash Flows

Among the transactions of Marvel Manufacturing were the following:

1. Made payments on accounts payable to office suppliers.
2. Paid the principal amount of a mortgage to Seventh Bank.
3. Paid interest charges relating to a mortgage to Seventh Bank.
4. Issued preferred stock for cash; management plans to use this cash in the near future to purchase another company.

5. Paid salaries to employees in the finance department.
6. Collected an account receivable from a customer.
7. Transferred cash from the general bank account into a money market fund.
8. Used the cash received in **4**, above, to purchase Moran Manufacturing Co.
9. Made a year-end adjusting entry to recognize amortization expense.
10. At year-end, purchased for cash an advertising spot on a local radio station for the next eight months.
11. Paid the annual dividend on preferred stock.
12. Paid the semiannual interest on bonds payable.
13. Received a semiannual dividend from an investment in the common stock of another corporation.
14. Sold for cash an investment in the common stock of another corporation.
15. Received cash upon the maturity of an investment in cash equivalents. (Ignore interest.)

Instructions

Most of the preceding transactions should be included among the activities summarized in a statement of cash flows. For each transaction that should be included in this statement, indicate whether the transaction should be classified as an operating activity, an investing activity, or a financing activity. If the transaction *should not be included* in the current year's statement of cash flows, briefly explain why not. (Assume that net cash flows from operating activities are determined by the *direct method*.)

LO4

EXERCISE 13.13

Cash Flows from Investing Activities

Wofford Company provides the following information related to its investing and financing activities for the current year:

Cash receipts:	
Sale of common stock	$250,000
Sale of equipment (at $34,000 loss)	156,000
Sale of land (at $50,000 gain)	160,000
Cash payments:	
Purchase of equipment	$178,000
Purchase of treasury stock	45,000
Retirement of debt	36,500
Dividends on preferred and common stock	75,000

a. Calculate the net amount of cash provided by or used for investing activities for the year.

b. What impact, if any, do the following facts have on your calculation? (**1**) Equipment was sold at a loss, and (**2**) land was sold at a gain.

c. Briefly explain your decision to exclude any of the items listed above if they were not included in your calculation in part **a**.

EXERCISE 13.14

Cash Flows from Financing Activities

Shepherd Industries had the following cash flows by major categories during the current year:

Cash provided by:	
Receipts from customers	$560,000
Sale of bonds	400,000
Sale of treasury stock	34,000
Interest and dividends received	56,000
Sale of equipment (at a $56,000 loss)	236,000
Cash used for:	
Payments to employees	$135,000
Payments to purchase inventory	190,000
Dividends on common stock	60,000
Purchase of treasury stock	20,000
Interest expense	78,000

a. Calculate the net amount of cash provided by or used for financing activities for the year.
b. Briefly justify why you excluded any of the above items in your calculation in part **a**.
c. Briefly explain your treatment of interest expense in your calculation in part **a**.

LO1 LO2 LO4

EXERCISE 13.15
Home Depot, Inc.
Using a Statement of Cash Flows

Statements of cash flow for **Home Depot, Inc.**, for 2005, 2004, and 2003 are included in Appendix A of this text.

a. Focus on the information for 2005 (year ending January 29, 2006). How does net earnings compare with net cash provided by or used in operations, and what accounts for the primary difference between the two amounts?
b. What are the major uses of cash, other than operations, and how have these varied over the three-year period presented?
c. Cash flows from both investing and financing activities have been negative for all three years presented. Considering **Home Depot**'s overall cash flows, including its cash flows from operations, would you say that this leads to a negative interpretation of **Home Depot**'s cash position at January 29, 2006? Why or why not?
d. Calculate the amount of free cash flow for each of 2003, 2004, and 2005, and comment briefly on your conclusion concerning this information.

Problem Set A

LO2 through LO4

PROBLEM 13.1A
Format of a Statement of Cash Flows

The accounting staff of Harris Company has assembled the following information for the year ended December 31, 2007:

Cash sales	$ 800,000
Credit sales	2,500,000
Collections on accounts receivable	2,200,000
Cash transferred from the money market fund to the general bank account	250,000
Interest and dividends received	100,000
Purchases (all on account)	1,800,000
Payments on accounts payable to merchandise suppliers	1,500,000
Cash payments for operating expenses	1,050,000
Interest paid	180,000
Income taxes paid	95,000
Loans made to borrowers	500,000
Collections on loans (excluding receipts of interest)	260,000
Cash paid to acquire plant assets	3,100,000
Book value of plant assets sold	660,000
Loss on sales of plant assets	80,000
Proceeds from issuing bonds payable	2,500,000
Dividends paid	120,000
Cash and cash equivalents, Jan. 1	489,000

Instructions

Prepare a statement of cash flows in the format illustrated in Exhibit 13–1. Place brackets around amounts representing cash outflows. Use the *direct method* of reporting cash flows from operating activities.

Some of the items above will be listed in your statement without change. However, you will have to combine certain given information to compute the amounts of (1) collections from customers, (2) cash paid to suppliers and employees, and (3) proceeds from sales of plant assets. (Hint: Not every item listed is used in preparing a statement of cash flows.)

LO4

PROBLEM 13.2A
Reporting Investing Activities

An analysis of the income statement and the balance sheet accounts of Headrick, Inc., at December 31, 2007, provides the following information:

Income statement items:	
Gain on Sale of Marketable Securities	$ 42,000
Loss on Sales of Plant Assets	33,000
Analysis of balance sheet accounts:	
Marketable Securities account:	
Debit entries	$ 75,000
Credit entries	90,000
Notes Receivable account:	
Debit entries	210,000
Credit entries	162,000
Plant and Equipment accounts:	
Debit entries to plant asset accounts	196,000
Credit entries to plant asset accounts	120,000
Debit entries to accumulated depreciation accounts	75,000

Additional Information

1. Except as noted in **4** below, payments and proceeds relating to investing transactions were made in cash.
2. The marketable securities are not cash equivalents.
3. All notes receivable relate to cash loans made to borrowers, not to receivables from customers.
4. Purchases of new equipment during the year ($196,000) were financed by paying $60,000 in cash and issuing a long-term note payable for $136,000.
5. Debits to the accumulated depreciation accounts are made whenever depreciable plant assets are retired. Thus the book value of plant assets retired during the year was $45,000 ($120,000 − $75,000).

Instructions

a. Prepare the investing activities section of a statement of cash flows. Show supporting computations for the amounts of (1) proceeds from sales of marketable securities and (2) proceeds from sales of plant assets. Place brackets around numbers representing cash outflows.

b. Prepare the supporting schedule that should accompany the statement of cash flows in order to disclose the noncash aspects of the company's investing and financing activities.

c. Assume that Headrick's management expects approximately the same amount of cash to be used for investing activities next year. In general terms, explain how the company might generate cash for this purpose.

LO4

PROBLEM 13.3A
Reporting Investing Activities

An analysis of the income statement and the balance sheet accounts of Hayes Export Co. at December 31, 2007, provides the following information:

Income statement items:	
Gain on Sale of Plant Assets	$ 12,000
Loss on Sales of Marketable Securities	16,000
Analysis of balance sheet accounts:	
Marketable Securities account:	
Debit entries	$ 78,000
Credit entries	62,000
Notes Receivable account:	
Debit entries	55,000
Credit entries	60,000
Plant and Equipment accounts:	
Debit entries to plant asset accounts	150,000
Credit entries to plant asset accounts	140,000
Debit entries to accumulated depreciation accounts	100,000

Additional Information

1. Except as noted in **4** below, payments and proceeds relating to investing transactions were made in cash.
2. The marketable securities are not cash equivalents.
3. All notes receivable relate to cash loans made to borrowers, not to receivables from customers.
4. Purchases of new equipment during the year ($150,000) were financed by paying $50,000 in cash and issuing a long-term note payable for $100,000.
5. Debits to the accumulated depreciation accounts are made whenever depreciable plant assets are sold or retired. Thus the book value of plant assets sold or retired during the year was $40,000 ($140,000 − $100,000).

Instructions

a. Prepare the investing activities section of a statement of cash flows. Show supporting computations for the amounts of (1) proceeds from sales of marketable securities and (2) proceeds from sales of plant assets. Place brackets around amounts representing cash outflows.

b. Prepare the supplementary schedule that should accompany the statement of cash flows in order to disclose the noncash aspects of the company's investing and financing activities.

c. Does management have *more* control or *less* control over the timing and amount of cash outlays for investing activities than for operating activities? Explain.

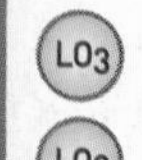

PROBLEM 13.4A
Reporting Operating Cash Flows by the Direct Method

The following income statement and selected balance sheet account data are available for Treece, Inc., at December 31, 2007:

TREECE, INC.
Income Statement
For the Year Ended December 31, 2007

Revenue:		
Net sales		$2,850,000
Dividend income		104,000
Interest income		70,000
Gain on sales of marketable securities		4,000
Total revenue and gains		$3,028,000
Costs and expenses:		
Cost of goods sold	$1,550,000	
Operating expenses	980,000	
Interest expense	185,000	
Income tax expense	90,000	
Total costs and expenses		2,805,000
Net income		$ 223,000

	End of Year	Beginning of Year
Selected account balances:		
Accounts receivable	$ 650,000	$ 720,000
Accrued interest receivable	9,000	6,000
Inventories	800,000	765,000
Short-term prepayments	20,000	15,000
Accounts payable (merchandise suppliers)	570,000	562,000
Accrued operating expenses payable	65,000	94,000
Accrued interest payable	21,000	12,000
Accrued income taxes payable	22,000	35,000

Additional Information

1. Dividend revenue is recognized on the cash basis. All other income statement amounts are recognized on the accrual basis.
2. Operating expenses include depreciation expense of $115,000.

Instructions

a. Prepare a partial statement of cash flows, including only the *operating activities* section of the statement and using the *direct method*. Place brackets around numbers representing cash payments. Show supporting computations for the following:
   1. Cash received from customers
   2. Interest and dividends received
   3. Cash paid to suppliers and employees
   4. Interest paid
   5. Income taxes paid

b. Management of Treece, Inc., is exploring ways to increase the cash flows from operations. One way that cash flows could be increased is through more aggressive collection of receivables. Assuming that management has already taken all the steps possible to increase revenue and reduce expenses, describe two other ways that cash flows from operations could be increased.

PROBLEM 13.5A
Reporting Operating Cash Flows by the Indirect Method

Using the information presented in Problem **13.4A**, prepare a partial statement of cash flows for the current year, showing the computation of net cash flows from operating activities by the *indirect method.* Explain why the decline in accounts receivable over the year was *added* to net income in computing the cash flows from operating activities.

PROBLEM 13.6A
Preparing a Statement of Cash Flows: A Comprehensive Problem without a Worksheet

You are the controller for 21st Century Technologies. Your staff has prepared an income statement for the current year and has developed the following additional information by analyzing changes in the company's balance sheet accounts.

21st CENTURY TECHNOLOGIES
Income Statement
For the Year Ended December 31, 2007

Revenue:		
Net sales		$3,200,000
Interest revenue		40,000
Gain on sales of marketable securities		34,000
Total revenue and gains		$3,274,000
Costs and expenses:		
Cost of goods sold	$1,620,000	
Operating expenses (including depreciation of $150,000)	1,240,000	
Interest expense	42,000	
Income tax expense	100,000	
Loss on sales of plant assets	12,000	
Total costs, expenses, and losses		3,014,000
Net income		$ 260,000

Additional Information

1. Accounts receivable increased by $60,000.
2. Accrued interest receivable decreased by $2,000.

3. Inventory decreased by $60,000, and accounts payable to suppliers of merchandise decreased by $16,000.
4. Short-term prepayments of operating expenses increased by $6,000, and accrued liabilities for operating expenses decreased by $8,000.
5. The liability for accrued interest payable increased by $4,000 during the year.
6. The liability for accrued income taxes payable decreased by $14,000 during the year.
7. The following schedule summarizes the total debit and credit entries during the year in other balance sheet accounts:

	Debit Entries	Credit Entries
Marketable Securities	$ 60,000	$ 38,000
Notes Receivable (cash loans made to borrowers)	44,000	28,000
Plant Assets (see paragraph **8**)	500,000	36,000
Notes Payable (short-term borrowing)	92,000	82,000
Capital Stock		20,000
Additional Paid-in Capital—Capital Stock		160,000
Retained Earnings (see paragraph **9**)	120,000	260,000

8. The $36,000 in credit entries to the Plant Assets account is net of any debits to Accumulated Depreciation when plant assets were retired. Thus the $36,000 in credit entries represents the book value of all plant assets sold or retired during the year.
9. The $120,000 debit to Retained Earnings represents dividends declared and paid during the year. The $260,000 credit entry represents the net income shown in the income statement.
10. All investing and financing activities were cash transactions.
11. Cash and cash equivalents amounted to $244,000 at the beginning of the year and to $164,000 at year-end.

Instructions

a. Prepare a statement of cash flows for the current year. Use the *direct method* of reporting cash flows from operating activities. Place brackets around dollar amounts representing cash outflows. Show separately your computations of the following amounts:
   1. Cash received from customers
   2. Interest received
   3. Cash paid to suppliers and employees
   4. Interest paid
   5. Income taxes paid
   6. Proceeds from sales of marketable securities
   7. Proceeds from sales of plant assets
   8. Proceeds from issuing capital stock

b. Explain the *primary reason* why:
   1. The amount of cash provided by operating activities was substantially greater than the company's net income.
   2. There was a net decrease in cash over the year, despite the substantial amount of cash provided by operating activities.

c. As 21st Century's controller, you think that through more efficient cash management, the company could have held the increase in accounts receivable for the year to $10,000, without affecting net income. Explain how holding down the growth in receivables affects cash. Compute the effect that limiting the growth in receivables to $10,000 would have had on the company's net increase or decrease in cash (and cash equivalents) for the year.

PROBLEM 13.7A
Prepare and Analyze a Statement of Cash Flows with a Worksheet

LO1 through LO9

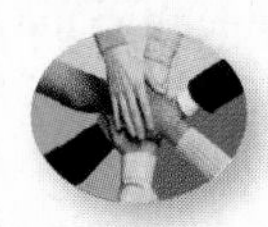

Satellite 2010 was founded in 2006 to apply a new technology for efficiently transmitting closed-circuit (cable) television signals without the need for an in-ground cable. The company earned a profit of $115,000 in 2006, its first year of operations, even though it was serving only a small test market. In 2007, the company began dramatically expanding its customer base. Management expects both sales and net income to more than triple in each of the next five years.

Comparative balance sheets at the end of 2006 and 2007, the company's first two years of operations, follow. (Notice that the balances at the end of the current year appear in the right-hand column.)

Additional Information

The following information regarding the company's operations in 2007 is available in either the company's income statement or its accounting records:

1. Net income for the year was $440,000. The company has never paid a dividend.
2. Depreciation for the year amounted to $147,000.
3. During the year the company purchased plant assets costing $2,200,000, for which it paid $1,850,000 in cash and financed $350,000 by issuing a long-term note payable. (Much of the cash used in these purchases was provided by short-term borrowing, as described below.)
4. In 2007, Satellite 2010 borrowed $1,450,000 against a $6 million line of credit with a local bank. In its balance sheet, the resulting obligations are reported as notes payable (short-term).
5. Additional shares of capital stock (no par value) were issued to investors for $500,000 cash.

SATELLITE 2010
Comparative Balance Sheets

	December 31, 2006	2007
Assets		
Cash and cash equivalents	$ 80,000	$ 37,000
Accounts receivable	100,000	850,000
Plant and equipment (net of accumulated depreciation)	600,000	2,653,000
Totals	$780,000	$3,540,000
Liabilities & Stockholders' Equity		
Notes payable (short-term)	$ -0-	$1,450,000
Accounts payable	30,000	63,000
Accrued expenses payable	45,000	32,000
Notes payable (long-term)	390,000	740,000
Capital stock (no par value)	200,000	700,000
Retained earnings	115,000	555,000
Totals	$780,000	$3,540,000

Instructions

a. Prepare a worksheet for a statement of cash flows, following the general format illustrated in Exhibit 13–7. (***Note***: If this problem is completed as a group assignment, each member of the group should be prepared to explain in class all entries in the worksheet, as well as the group's conclusions in parts **c** and **d**.)

b. Prepare a formal statement of cash flows for 2007, including a supplementary schedule of noncash investing and financing activities. (Follow the format illustrated in Exhibit 13–8. Cash provided by operating activities is to be presented by the *indirect method*.)

c. Briefly explain how operating activities can be a net *use* of cash when the company is operating so profitably.

d. Because of the expected rapid growth, management forecasts that operating activities will be an even greater use of cash in the year 2008 than in 2007. If this forecast is correct, does Satellite 2010 appear to be heading toward illiquidity? Explain.

PROBLEM 13.8A
Prepare and Analyze a Statement of Cash Flows; Involves Preparation of a Worksheet

LO1 through LO9

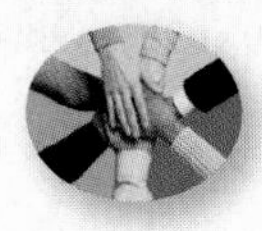

Miracle Tool, Inc., sells a single product (a combination screwdriver, pliers, hammer, and crescent wrench) exclusively through television advertising. The comparative income statements and balance sheets are for the past two years.

Additional Information

The following information regarding the company's operations in 2007 is available from the company's accounting records:

1. Early in the year the company declared and paid a $4,000 cash dividend.
2. During the year marketable securities costing $15,000 were sold for $14,000 cash, resulting in a $1,000 nonoperating loss.
3. The company purchased plant assets for $20,000, paying $2,000 in cash and issuing a note payable for the $18,000 balance.
4. During the year the company repaid a $10,000 note payable, but incurred an additional $18,000 in long-term debt as described in **3**.
5. The owners invested $15,000 cash in the business as a condition of the new loans described in paragraph **4**.

MIRACLE TOOL, INC.
Comparative Income Statement
For the Years Ended December 31, 2006 and 2007

	2006	2007
Sales	$500,000	$350,000
Less: Cost of goods sold	200,000	140,000
Gross profit on sales	$300,000	$210,000
Less: Operating expenses (including depreciation of $34,000 in 2006 and $35,000 in 2007)	260,000	243,000
Loss on sale of marketable securities	–0–	1,000
Net income (loss)	$ 40,000	($ 34,000)

MIRACLE TOOL, INC.
Comparative Balance Sheets

	December 31, 2006	2007
Assets		
Cash and cash equivalents	$ 10,000	$ 60,000
Marketable securities	20,000	5,000
Accounts receivable	40,000	23,000
Inventory	120,000	122,000
Plant and equipment (net of accumulated depreciation)	300,000	285,000
Totals	$490,000	$495,000
Liabilities & Stockholders' Equity		
Accounts payable	$ 50,000	$ 73,000
Accrued expenses payable	17,000	14,000
Note payable	245,000	253,000
Capital stock (no par value)	120,000	135,000
Retained earnings	58,000	20,000
Totals	$490,000	$495,000

Instructions

a. Prepare a worksheet for a statement of cash flows, following the general format illustrated in Exhibit 13–7. (***Note***: If this problem is completed as a group assignment, each member of the group should be prepared to explain in class all entries in the worksheet, as well as the group's conclusions in parts **c**, **d**, and **e**.)

b. Prepare a formal statement of cash flows for 2007, including a supplementary schedule of noncash investing and financing activities. (Use the format illustrated in Exhibit 13–8. Cash provided by operating activities is to be presented by the *indirect method*.)

c. Explain how Miracle Tool, Inc., achieved positive cash flows from operating activities, despite incurring a net loss for the year.

d. Does the company's financial position appear to be improving or deteriorating? Explain.

e. Does Miracle Tool, Inc., appear to be a company whose operations are growing or contracting? Explain.

f. Assume that management *agrees* with your conclusions in parts **c**, **d**, and **e**. What decisions should be made and what actions (if any) should be taken? Explain.

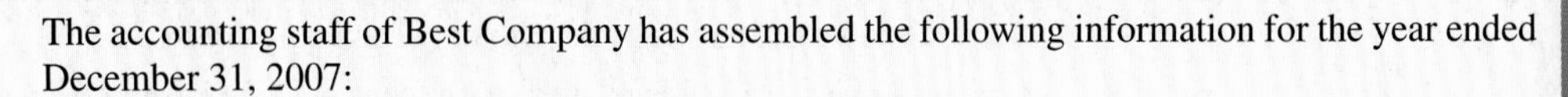

Problem Set B

LO2 through LO4

PROBLEM 13.1B
Format of a Statement of Cash Flows

The accounting staff of Best Company has assembled the following information for the year ended December 31, 2007:

Cash sales	$ 230,000
Credit sales	3,450,000
Collections on accounts receivable	2,810,000
Cash transferred from the money market fund to the general bank account	200,000
Interest and dividends received	40,000
Purchases (all on account)	1,822,000
Payments on accounts payable to merchandise suppliers	1,220,000
Cash payments for operating expenses	930,000
Interest paid	130,000
Income taxes paid	65,000
Loans made to borrowers	690,000
Collections on loans (excluding receipts of interest)	300,000
Cash paid to acquire plant assets	1,700,000
Book value of plant assets sold	520,000
Loss on sales of plant assets	30,000
Proceeds from issuing bonds payable	2,000,000
Dividends paid	250,000
Cash and cash equivalents, Jan. 1	115,000

Instructions

Prepare a statement of cash flows in the format illustrated in Exhibit 13–1. Place brackets around amounts representing cash outflows. Use the *direct method* of reporting cash flows from operating activities.

Some of the items above will be listed in your statement without change. However, you will have to combine certain given information to compute the amounts of (1) collections from customers, (2) cash paid to suppliers and employees, and (3) proceeds from sales of plant assets. (Hint: Not every item listed above is used in preparing a statement of cash flows.)

LO4

PROBLEM 13.2B
Reporting Investing Activities

An analysis of the income statement and the balance sheet accounts of Schmatah Fashions at December 31, 2007, provides the following information:

Income statement items:	
Gain on Sales of Marketable Securities	$ 15,000
Loss on Sales of Plant Assets	10,000
Analysis of balance sheet accounts:	
Marketable Securities account:	
Debit entries	65,000
Credit entries	74,000
Notes Receivable account:	
Debit entries	175,000
Credit entries	50,000
Plant and Equipment accounts:	
Debit entries to plant asset accounts	220,000
Credit entries to plant asset accounts	150,000
Debit entries to accumulated depreciation accounts	60,000

Additional Information

1. Except as noted in **4**, payments and proceeds relating to investing transactions were made in cash.
2. The marketable securities are not cash equivalents.
3. All notes receivable relate to cash loans made to borrowers, not to receivables from customers.
4. Purchases of new equipment during the year ($220,000) were financed by paying $70,000 in cash and issuing a long-term note payable for $150,000.
5. Debits to the accumulated depreciation accounts are made whenever depreciable plant assets are retired. Thus the book value of plant assets retired during the year was $90,000 ($150,000 – $60,000).

Instructions

a. Prepare the investing activities section of a statement of cash flows. Show supporting computations for the amounts of (1) proceeds from sales and marketable securities and (2) proceeds from sales from plant assets. Place brackets around numbers representing cash outflows.

b. Prepare the supporting schedule that should accompany the statement of cash flows in order to disclose the noncash aspects of the company's investing and financing activities.

c. Assume that Schmatah Fashions's management expects approximately the same amount of cash to be used for investing activities next year. In general terms, explain how the company might generate cash for this purpose.

PROBLEM 13.3B LO4
Reporting Investing Activities

An analysis of the income statement and the balance sheet accounts of RPZ Imports at December 31, 2007, provides the following information:

Income statement items:	
Gain on Sales of Plant Assets	$ 6,000
Gain on Sales of Marketable Securities	8,000
Analysis of balance sheet accounts:	
Marketable Securities account:	
Debit entries	59,000
Credit entries	60,000
Notes Receivable account:	
Debit entries	40,000
Credit entries	31,000
Plant and Equipment accounts:	
Debit entries to plant asset accounts	140,000
Credit entries to plant asset accounts	100,000
Debit entries to accumulated depreciation accounts	75,000

Additional Information

1. Except as noted in **4**, payments and proceeds relating to investing transactions were made in cash.
2. The marketable securities are not cash equivalents.
3. All notes receivable relate to cash loans made to borrowers, not to receivables from customers.
4. Purchases of new equipment during the year ($140,000) were financed by paying $50,000 in cash and issuing a long-term note payable for $90,000.
5. Debits to the accumulated depreciation accounts are made whenever depreciable plant assets are retired. Thus the book value of plant assets sold or retired during the year was $25,000 ($100,000 − $75,000).

Instructions

a. Prepare the investing activities section of a statement of cash flows. Show supporting computations for the amounts of (1) proceeds from sales and marketable securities and (2) proceeds from sales from plant assets. Place brackets around numbers representing cash outflows.

b. Prepare the supplementary schedule that should accompany the statement of cash flows in order to disclose the noncash aspects of the company's investing and financing activities.

c. Does management have *more* control or *less* control over the timing and amount of cash outlays for investing activities than for operating activities? Explain.

PROBLEM 13.4B
Reporting Operating Cash Flows by the Direct Method

The following income statement and selected balance sheet account data are available for Royce Interiors, Inc., at December 31, 2007:

ROYCE INTERIORS, INC.
Income Statement
For the Year Ended December 31, 2007

Revenue:		
Net sales		$2,600,000
Dividend income		55,000
Interest income		40,000
Gain on sales of marketable securities		3,000
Total revenue and gains		$2,698,000
Costs and expenses:		
Cost of goods sold	$1,300,000	
Operating expenses	300,000	
Interest expense	60,000	
Income tax expense	110,000	
Total costs and expenses		$1,770,000
Net income		$ 928,000

	End of Year	Beginning of Year
Selected account balances:		
Accounts receivable	$ 450,000	$ 440,000
Accrued interest receivable	7,000	3,000
Inventories	575,000	550,000
Short-term prepayments	9,000	8,000
Accounts payable (merchandise suppliers)	415,000	410,000
Accrued operating expenses payable	86,000	90,000
Accrued interest payable	10,000	8,000
Accrued income taxes payable	20,000	22,000

Additional Information

1. Dividend revenue is recognized on the cash basis. All other income statement amounts are recognized on the accrual basis.
2. Operating expenses include depreciation expense of $49,000.

Instructions

a. Prepare a partial statement of cash flows, including only the *operating activities* section of the statement and using the *direct method.* Place brackets around numbers representing cash payments. Show supporting computations for the following:
   1. Cash received from customers
   2. Interest and dividends received
   3. Cash paid to suppliers and employees
   4. Interest paid
   5. Income taxes paid

b. Management of Royce Interiors, Inc., is exploring ways to increase the cash flows from operations. One way that cash flows could be increased is through more aggressive collection of receivables. Assuming that management has already taken all the steps possible to increase revenue and reduce expenses, describe two other ways that cash flows from operations could be increased.

PROBLEM 13.5B
Reporting Operating Cash Flows by the Indirect Method

Using the information presented in Problem **13.4B**, prepare a partial statement of cash flows for the current year, showing the computation of net cash flows from operating activities using the *indirect method.* Explain why the increase in accounts receivable over the year was *subtracted* from net income in computing the cash flows from operating activities.

PROBLEM 13.6B
Preparing a Statement of Cash Flows: A Comprehensive Problem without a Worksheet

You are the controller for Foxboro Technologies. Your staff has prepared an income statement for the current year and has developed the following additional information by analyzing changes in the company's balance sheet accounts.

FOXBORO TECHNOLOGIES
Income Statement
For the Year Ended December 31, 2007

Revenue:		
Net sales		$3,400,000
Interest income		60,000
Gain on sales of marketable securities		25,000
Total revenue and gains		$3,485,000
Costs and expenses:		
Cost of goods sold	$1,500,000	
Operating expenses (including depreciation of $75,000)	900,000	
Interest expense	27,000	
Income tax expense	115,000	
Loss on sales of plant assets	8,000	
Total costs, expenses, and losses		2,550,000
Net income		$ 935,000

Additional Information

1. Accounts receivable increased by $60,000.
2. Accrued interest receivable decreased by $5,000.
3. Inventory decreased by $30,000, and accounts payable to suppliers of merchandise decreased by $22,000.
4. Short-term prepayments of operating expenses increased by $8,000, and accrued liabilities for operating expenses decreased by $9,000.
5. The liability for accrued interest payable increased by $4,000 during the year.
6. The liability for accrued income taxes payable decreased by $10,000 during the year.
7. The following schedule summarizes the total debit and credit entries during the year in other balance sheet accounts:

	Debit Entries	Credit Entries
Marketable Securities	$ 50,000	$ 40,000
Notes Receivable (cash loans made to borrowers)	30,000	27,000
Plant Assets (see paragraph **8**)	350,000	30,000
Notes Payable (short-term borrowing)	70,000	56,000
Capital Stock		60,000
Additional Paid-in Capital—Capital Stock		100,000
Retained Earnings (see paragraph **9**)	300,000	935,000

8. The $30,000 in credit entries to the Plant Assets account is net of any debits to Accumulated Depreciation when plant assets were retired. Thus the $30,000 in credit entries represents the book value of all plant assets sold or retired during the year.
9. The $300,000 debit to Retained Earnings represents dividends declared and paid during the year. The $935,000 credit entry represents the net income shown in the income statement.
10. All investing and financing activities were cash transactions.
11. Cash and cash equivalents amount to $20,000 at the beginning of the year and to $473,000 at year-end.

Instructions

a. Prepare a statement of cash flows for the current year. Use the *direct method* of reporting cash flows from operating activities. Place brackets around dollar amounts representing cash outflows. Show separately your computations of the following amounts:
   1. Cash received from customers
   2. Interest received
   3. Cash paid to suppliers and employees
   4. Interest paid
   5. Income taxes paid
   6. Proceeds from sales of marketable securities
   7. Proceeds from sales of plant assets
   8. Proceeds from issuing capital stock

b. Explain why cash paid to suppliers is so much higher than cost of goods sold.

c. Does the fact that Foxboro's cash flows from both investing and financing activities are negative indicate that the company is in a weak cash position?

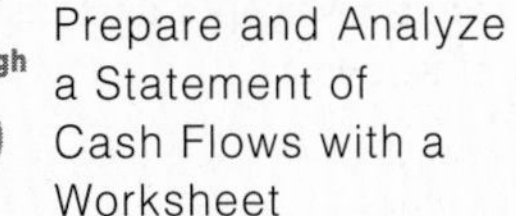

LGIN was founded in 2006 to apply a new technology for the Internet. The company earned a profit of $190,000 in 2006, its first year of operations. Management expects both sales and net income to more than double in each of the next four years.

Comparative balance sheets at the end of 2006 and 2007, the company's first two years of operations, appear below. (Notice that the balances at the end of the current year appear in the right-hand column.)

LGIN
Comparative Balance Sheets

	December 31, 2006	December 31, 2007
Assets		
Cash and cash equivalents	$ 45,000	$ 42,000
Accounts receivable	15,000	880,000
Plant and equipment (net of accumulated depreciation)	680,000	3,140,000
Totals	$740,000	$4,062,000
Liabilities and Stockholders' Equity		
Notes payable (short-term)	$ 0	$1,490,000
Accounts payable	45,000	82,000
Accrued expenses payable	55,000	38,000
Notes payable (long-term)	200,000	785,000
Capital stock (no par value)	250,000	915,000
Retained earnings	190,000	752,000
Totals	$740,000	$4,062,000

Additional Information

The following information regarding the company's operations in 2007 is available in either the company's income statement or its accounting records:

1. Net income for the year was $562,000. The company has never paid a dividend.
2. Depreciation for the year amounted to $125,000.
3. During the year the company purchased plant assets costing $2,585,000, for which it paid $2,000,000 in cash and financed $585,000 by issuing a long-term note payable. (Much of the cash used in these purchases was provided by short-term borrowing, as described below.)
4. In 2007, LGIN borrowed $1,490,000 against a $5 million line of credit with a local bank. In its balance sheet, the resulting obligations are reported as notes payable (short-term).
5. Additional shares of capital stock (no par value) were issued to investors for $665,000 cash.

Instructions

a. Prepare a formal statement of cash flows for 2007, including a supplementary schedule of noncash investing and financing activities. (Follow the format illustrated in Exhibit 13–8. Cash provided by operating activities is to be presented by the *indirect method.*)

b. Briefly explain how operating activities can be a net *use* of cash when the company is operating so profitably.

c. Because of the expected rapid growth, management forecasts that operating activities will include an even greater use of cash in the year 2008 than in 2007. If this forecast is correct, does LGIN appear to be heading toward insolvency? Explain.

PROBLEM 13.8B
LO1 through LO9
Prepare and Analyze a Statement of Cash Flows; Involves Preparation of a Worksheet

Extra-Ordinaire, Inc., sells a single product (Pulsa) exclusively through newspaper advertising. The comparative income statements and balance sheets are for the past two years.

EXTRA-ORDINAIRE, INC.
Comparative Income Statement
For the Years Ended December 31, 2006 and 2007

	2006	2007
Sales	$640,000	$ 410,000
Less: Cost of goods sold	310,000	190,000
Gross profit on sales	330,000	220,000
Less: Operating expenses (including depreciation of $28,000 in 2006 and $29,000 in 2007)	260,000	250,000
Loss on sale of marketable securities	0	4,000
Net income (loss)	$ 70,000	$ (34,000)

EXTRA-ORDINAIRE, INC.
Comparative Balance Sheets

	December 31, 2006	2007
Assets		
Cash and cash equivalents	$ 22,000	$ 60,000
Marketable securities	27,000	12,000
Accounts receivable	40,000	35,000
Inventory	120,000	128,000
Plant and equipment (net of accumulated depreciation)	250,000	241,000
Totals	$459,000	$476,000
Liabilities & Stockholders' Equity		
Accounts payable	50,000	70,000
Accrued expenses payable	16,000	14,000
Notes payable	235,000	237,000
Capital stock (no par value)	108,000	143,000
Retained earnings	50,000	12,000
Totals	$459,000	$476,000

Additional Information

The following information regarding the company's operations in 2007 is available from the company's accounting records:

1. Early in the year the company declared and paid a $4,000 cash dividend.
2. During the year marketable securities costing $15,000 were sold for $11,000 cash, resulting in a $4,000 nonoperating loss.
3. The company purchased plant assets for $20,000, paying $8,000 in cash and issuing a note payable for the $12,000 balance.
4. During the year the company repaid a $10,000 note payable, but incurred an additional $12,000 in long-term debt as described in **3**, above.
5. The owners invested $35,000 cash in the business as a condition of the new loans described in paragraphs **3** and **4**, above.

Instructions

a. Prepare a worksheet for a statement of cash flows, following the example shown in Exhibit 13–7.

b. Prepare a formal statement of cash flows for 2007, including a supplementary schedule of noncash investing and financing activities. (Use the format illustrated in Exhibit 13–8. Cash provided by operating activities is to be presented by the *indirect method.*)

c. Explain how Extra-Ordinaire, Inc., achieved positive cash flows from operating activities, despite incurring a net loss for the year.

d. Does the company's financial position appear to be improving or deteriorating? Explain.

e. Does Extra-Ordinaire, Inc., appear to be a company whose operations are growing or contracting? Explain.

f. Assume that management *agrees* with your conclusions in parts **c**, **d**, and **e**. What decisions should be made and what actions (if any) should be taken? Explain.

Critical Thinking Cases

CASE 13.1

Another Look at Allison Corporation

This case is based on the statement of cash flows for Allison Corporation, illustrated in Exhibit 13–1. Use this statement to evaluate the company's ability to continue paying the current level of dividends—$40,000 per year. The following information also is available:

1. The net cash flows from operating activities shown in the statement are relatively normal for Allison Corporation. Net cash flows from operating activities have not varied by more than a few thousand dollars in any of the past three years.
2. The net outflow for investing activities was unusually high, because the company modernized its production facilities during the year. The normal investing cash outflow is about $45,000 per year, the amount required to replace existing plant assets as they are retired. Over the long run, marketable securities transactions and lending transactions have a very small impact on Allison's net cash flows from investing activities.
3. The net cash flows from financing activities were unusually large in the current year because of the issuance of bonds payable and capital stock. These securities were issued to finance the modernization of the production facilities. In a typical year, financing activities include only short-term borrowing transactions and payments of dividends.

Instructions

a. Based solely on the company's past performance, do you believe that the $40,000 annual dividend payments are secure? That is, does the company appear able to pay this amount in dividends every year without straining its cash position? Do you think it more likely that Allison Corporation will increase or decrease the amount of dividends that it pays? Explain fully.

b. Should any of the unusual events appearing in the statement of cash flows for the current year affect your analysis of the company's ability to pay future dividends? Explain.

LO8

CASE 13.2

Cash Budgeting for You as a Student

Individuals generally do not prepare statements of cash flows concerning their personal activities. But they do engage in cash budgeting—if not on paper, then at least in their heads.

Assume, for example, it is December 29—a Monday. In two days your rent for January, $200, will be due. You now have $140 in the bank; every Friday you receive a paycheck for $100. You probably see the problem. And it probably doesn't look too serious; you can find a way to deal with it. That's what *budgeting* is all about.

Let's take this example a step further. In addition to the facts given above, your weekly cash payments include meals, $30; entertainment, $20; and gasoline, $10.

Instructions

a. Using the following cash budget, compute your cash balance at the end of weeks 2, 3, and 4.

	Week			
	1	2	3	4
Beginning cash balance	$ 140	$(20)	$?	$?
Expected cash receipts	100	100	100	100
Less: Expected cash outlays:				
Monthly rent	(200)			
Meals	(30)			
Entertainment	(20)			
Gasoline	(10)			
Ending cash balance	$ (20)	$?	$?	$?

b. Evaluate your financial situation.

CASE 13.3
Lookin' Good?

It is late summer and General Wheels, Inc., an auto manufacturer, is facing a financial crisis. A large issue of bonds payable will mature next March, and the company must issue stock or new bonds to raise the money to retire this debt. Unfortunately, profits and cash flows have been declining over recent years. Management fears that if cash flows and profits do not improve in the current year, the company will not be able to raise the capital needed to replace the maturing bonds. Therefore, members of management have made the following proposals to improve the cash flows and profitability that will be reported in the financial statements dated this coming December 31.

1. Switch from the LIFO method to the FIFO method of valuing inventories. Management estimates that the FIFO method will result in a lower cost of goods sold but in higher income taxes for the current year. However, the additional income taxes will not actually be paid until early next year.
2. Switch from the 150 percent declining-balance method of depreciation to the straight-line method and lengthen the useful lives over which assets are depreciated. (These changes would be made only for financial reporting purposes, not for income tax purposes.)
3. Pressure dealers to increase their inventories—in short, to buy more cars. (The dealerships are independently owned; thus dealers are the customers to whom General Wheels sells automobiles.) Management estimates that this strategy could increase sales for the current year by 5 percent. However, any additional sales in the current year would be almost entirely offset by fewer sales in the following year.
4. Require dealers to pay for purchases more quickly. Currently, dealers must pay for purchases of autos within 60 days. Management is considering reducing this period to 30 days.
5. Pass up cash discounts offered for prompt payment (that is, 2/10, n/30), and do not pay any bills until the final due date.
6. Borrow at current short-term interest rates (about 10 percent) and use the proceeds to pay off long-term debt bearing an interest rate of 13 percent.
7. Substitute stock dividends for the cash dividends currently paid on capital stock.

Instructions

a. Prepare a schedule with four columns. The first column is to be headed "Proposals" and is to contain the paragraph numbers of the seven proposals listed above. The next three columns are to be headed with the following financial statement captions: (1) "Net Income," (2) "Net Cash Flows from Operating Activities," and (3) "Cash."

   For each of the seven proposals in the left-hand column, indicate whether you expect the proposal to "Increase," "Decrease," or have "No Effect" in the current year on each of the financial statement captions listed in the next three columns. (***Note***: Only a few months remain in the current year. Therefore, you are to determine the *short-term* effects of these proposals.)

b. For each of the seven proposals, write a short paragraph explaining the reasoning behind your answers to part **a**.

CASE 13.4
Peak Pricing

"Peak pricing is unfair. It makes goods and services available only to the wealthy and prices the average person out of the market."

Instructions

a. Comment on the extent to which you agree or disagree with the preceding statement.
b. What is the alternative to peak pricing?
c. Explain how peak pricing might be applied by:
   1. A hotel in Palm Springs, California. (Palm Springs is a winter resort in southern California with wonderful golf facilities. In the summer months, however, temperatures are well over 100 degrees and the tourist business slows dramatically.)
   2. Movie theaters.
d. Both in general terms and using specific examples, describe the conditions (if any) under which you might regard peak pricing as *unethical*.

CASE 13.5
Improving the Statement of Cash Flows

The Securities and Exchange Commission (SEC) is an important governmental organization that exists primarily for the protection of the interests of investors in the U.S. securities markets. The SEC provides a wealth of information through its Web site, www.sec.gov.

Instructions

a. Access the SEC's Web site at the above address. Generally review the site to become familiar with the types of information provided.

b. Enter the section of the Web site identified as "About the SEC," then proceed to the section on "Commissioners." Within that section, maneuver around until you are able to access speeches made by the SEC and its staff.

c. Locate the following speech given by Scott A. Taub, Deputy Chief Accountant, Office of the Chief Accountant of the SEC, in 2004: "Remarks at the University of Southern California, Leventhal School of Accounting, SEC and Financial Reporting Conference."

d. Peruse that entire speech, and then read carefully Mr. Taub's conclusion. Write a paragraph that captures what Mr. Taub had to say about how financial reporting could be improved in general, and how he specifically believes the statement of cash flows could be improved.

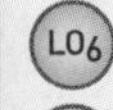

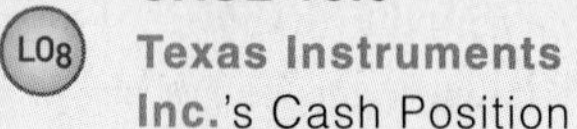

***BUSINESSWEEK* CASE 13.6**
Texas Instruments Inc.'s Cash Position

Texas Instruments Inc. (TI) didn't get to be 71 years old without knowing how to ride out hard times. In "Up a Creek—with Lots of Cash," from the November 12, 2001, edition of *BusinessWeek*, Peter Coy reports about the impact of the tech-led downturn on Texas Instruments. TI's net sales fell more than 40 percent in the third quarter of 2001 as compared to a year earlier, and it lost nearly $120 million in the third quarter compared to profits of $680 million the previous year.

TI is hardly up against the wall, however. With a stockpile of $3 billion in cash and marketable securities, TI continued payment of $150 million in dividends per year and TI continued to buy back its own shares to cover exercise of employee stock options. Peter Coy comments:

> As always in an economic slump, cash is once again king, and companies are going all out to make sure they have enough of it. . . . Businesses are taking steps to keep cash from going out the door, and they are bringing in fresh money. . . .

Instructions

a. Explain how it is possible to have cash increasing and net income decreasing.

b. Name at least three strategies that TI's management might undertake to "keep cash from going out the door."

c. Name at least three strategies that TI's management might undertake to "bring in fresh money."

INTERNET CASE 13.7
Comparing Cash Flow Information from Two Companies

In the long run, a company must generate positive net cash flows from operating activities to survive. A business that has negative cash flows from operations will not be able to raise cash indefinitely from other sources and will eventually cease existing. Many creditors and stockholders are reluctant to invest in companies that do not generate positive cash flows from operations. However, some investors will invest in companies with negative cash flows from operations due to an optimistic future outlook for the company. Thus, investors have invested millions of dollars in Internet companies that have negative cash flows from operations.

Instructions

a. Visit Coca-Cola's Internet site (www.coke.com) and select "Investors." Under "Financial Information," select the most recent annual report. In the annual report, view the Consolidated Statements of Cash Flows.

b. Visit Amazon.com's Internet site (www.amazon.com) and select "Investor Relations" at the bottom of the page, then click "SEC Filings." Select the most recent 10-K filing and view the Cash Flow Statement.

c. Compare the Net Cash Provided by Operating Activities for each company. Which company has higher Net Cash Provided by Operating Activities? Speculate why one company has much higher Net Cash Provided by Operating Activities than the other.

d. What type of company may have Negative Net Cash Provided by Operating Activities?

e. What type of company may have large Positive Net Cash Provided by Operating Activities?

Internet sites are time and date sensitive. It is the purpose of these exercises to have you explore the Internet. You may need to use the Yahoo! search engine **http://www.yahoo.com** *(or another favorite search engine) to find a company's current Web address.*

Answers to Self-Test Questions

1. c **2.** c **3.** a **4.** d ($601,000 − $420,000 − $12,000 + $17,000 − $23,000)
5. b **6.** c

14

Financial Statement Analysis

Learning Objectives

AFTER STUDYING THIS CHAPTER, YOU SHOULD BE ABLE TO:

- LO1 Explain the uses of dollar and percentage changes, trend percentages, component percentages, and ratios.
- LO2 Discuss the quality of a company's earnings, assets, and working capital.
- LO3 Explain the nature and purpose of classifications in financial statements.
- LO4 Prepare a classified balance sheet and compute widely used measures of liquidity and credit risk.
- LO5 Prepare a multiple-step and a single-step income statement and compute widely used measures of profitability.
- LO6 Put a company's net income into perspective by relating it to sales, assets, and stockholders' equity.
- LO7 Compute the ratios widely used in financial statement analysis and explain the significance of each.
- LO8 Analyze financial statements from the viewpoints of common stockholders, creditors, and others.

JOHNSON & JOHNSON

Johnson & Johnson is the world's most comprehensive and broadly based manufacturer of health care products and related services. In 2005 it had over $50 billion in sales. Other measures of **Johnson & Johnson**'s size include the facts that it employs over 115,000 people, has operating companies in 57 countries, and conducts business in virtually all countries of the world.

How does one get a handle on the financial performance of a huge company such as **Johnson & Johnson**? Financial statements, including the balance sheet, income statement, and statement of cash flows, provide a wealth of information that is helpful in performing this significant task. Financial statement analysis involves taking key items from these financial statements and gleaning as much useful information as possible from them. For example, we can determine that the amount of **Johnson & Johnson**'s 2005 net income ($10,411 million) represented a return of almost 18 percent on the total assets used to generate that income ($58,025 million). Is a return on assets of 18 percent satisfactory or unsatisfactory? This is a difficult question to answer. To make this judgment we would need more information than we have at this point. For example, we would like to know the trend in various financial measures for **Johnson & Johnson** for several years. We would also like to know information about other companies with similar operating characteristics (i.e., in the same industry). We will study all of this and more in this chapter as we look at the interesting and challenging subject of financial statement analysis.

Financial measures are used often to evaluate corporate performance. As a result, the Securities and Exchange Commission, the Financial Accounting Standards Board, the financial press, and the accounting profession are committed to high-quality financial reporting. Throughout this text, we have emphasized the importance of integrity in financial reporting as a means of protecting the interests of investors and creditors. This chapter explores financial statement analysis in depth, building on the introductory sections of this important subject in preceding chapters.

Our discussion of financial statement analysis is divided into three sections. First, we consider general tools of analysis that emphasize comparing information about enterprises with relevant benchmarks. Second, we consider measures of liquidity and credit risk, followed by a consideration of profitability. Third, we present and discuss a comprehensive illustration in which we analyze a company's financial statements from the perspective of three important users of information—common stockholders, long-term creditors, and short-term creditors. Throughout this chapter, we draw on information that was covered in earlier chapters and we use new information that is presented here for the first time.

FINANCIAL STATEMENTS ARE DESIGNED FOR ANALYSIS

In today's global economy, investment capital is always on the move. Through organized capital markets such as the New York Stock Exchange, investors each day shift billions of investment dollars among different companies, industries, and nations. Capital flows to those areas in which investors expect to earn the greatest returns with the least risk. How do investors forecast risk and potential returns? One of the most important ways is by analyzing accounting information for a specific company in the context of its unique industry setting.

The goal of accounting information is to provide economic decision makers with useful information. The financial statements generated through the accounting process are designed to assist users in identifying key relationships and trends. The financial statements of most publicly owned companies are classified and are presented in comparative form. Often, the word *consolidated* appears in the headings of the statements. Users of financial statements should have a clear understanding of these terms.

Most business organizations prepare **classified financial statements**, meaning that items with certain characteristics are placed together in a group, or classification. The purpose of these classifications is to *develop useful subtotals* that will assist users of the statements in their analyses. These classifications and subtotals are standardized throughout most of American business, a practice that assists decision makers in comparing the financial statements of different companies. An example of a classified financial statement is a balance sheet that separates assets and liabilities into current and noncurrent categories.

In **comparative financial statements**, the financial statement amounts *for several time periods* appear side by side in vertical columns. This assists investors in identifying and evaluating significant changes and trends.

Most large corporations own other companies through which they conduct some of their business activities. A corporation that owns other businesses is the **parent company**, and the owned companies are called divisions or **subsidiaries**. For example, PepsiCo, which makes Pepsi-Cola, also owns and operates the companies that make Frito-Lay and Quaker Foods products. In essence, these subsidiaries are part of the organization generally known as PepsiCo. **Consolidated financial statements** present the financial position and operating results of the parent company and its subsidiaries *as if they were a single business organization.*

For Example... At this point, take a brief look at the financial statements of Home Depot, Inc., which appear in Appendix A at the end of the text. These financial statements illustrate all of the concepts discussed; they are classified and presented in comparative form, and they describe a consolidated business entity. These financial statements also have been *audited* by KPMG LLP, an international public accounting firm.

Tools of Analysis

Significant changes in financial data are easier to see when financial statement amounts for two or more years are placed side by side in adjacent columns. Such a statement is called a *comparative financial statement*. The amounts for the most recent year are usually placed in the left-hand money column, closest to the words that describe the item. The balance sheet, income statement, and statement of cash flows are often prepared in the form of comparative statements. A highly condensed comparative income statement covering three years is shown in Exhibit 14–1.

Exhibit 14–1

COMPARATIVE INCOME STATEMENT

BENSON CORPORATION
Comparative Income Statement
For the Years Ended December 31, 2007, 2006, 2005
(in thousands of dollars)

	2007	2006	2005
Net sales	$600	$500	$400
Cost of goods sold	370	300	235
Gross profit	$230	$200	$165
Expenses	194	160	115
Net income	$ 36	$ 40	$ 50

Comparative statements place important financial information in a context that is useful for gaining better understanding. For example, knowing that Benson Corporation had sales of $600,000 in 2007 after years in which sales were $500,000 (2006) and $400,000 (2005) is helpful in understanding Benson's sales trend.

Few figures in a financial statement are highly significant in and of themselves. It is their relationship to other quantities or the amount and direction of change that is important. Analysis is largely a matter of establishing significant relationships and identifying changes and trends. Four widely used analytical techniques are (1) dollar and percentage changes, (2) trend percentages, (3) component percentages, and (4) ratios.

DOLLAR AND PERCENTAGE CHANGES

Explain the uses of dollar and percentage changes, trend percentages, component percentages, and ratios. LO1

The dollar amount of change from year to year is significant, and expressing the change in percentage terms adds perspective. For example, if sales this year have increased by $100,000, the fact that this is an increase of 10 percent over last year's sales of $1 million puts it in a different perspective than if it represented a 1 percent increase over sales of $10 million for the prior year.

The dollar amount of any change is the difference between the amount for a *comparison* year and the amount for a *base* year. The percentage change is computed by dividing the amount of the dollar change between years by the amount for the base year. This is illustrated in the following tabulation, using data from the comparative income statement shown in Exhibit 14–1.

Dollar and percentage changes

	In Thousands			Increase or (Decrease)			
				2007 over 2006		2006 over 2005	
	Year 2007	Year 2006	Year 2005	Amount	%	Amount	%
Net sales	$600	$500	$400	$100	20%	$100	25%
Net income	36	40	50	(4)	(10)	(10)	(20)

Although net sales increased $100,000 in both 2006 and 2007, the percentage change differs because of the change in the base from 2005 to 2006. These calculations present no problems when the figures for the base year are positive amounts. If a negative amount or a zero amount appears in the base year, however, a percentage change cannot be computed. Thus if Benson Corporation had incurred a net loss in 2006, the percentage change in net income from 2006 to 2007 could not have been calculated.

Evaluating Percentage Changes in Sales and Earnings

Computing the percentage changes in sales, gross profit, and net income from one year to the next gives insight into a company's rate of growth. If a company is experiencing growth in its economic activities, sales and earnings should increase at *more than the rate of inflation*. Assume, for example, that a company's sales increase by 6 percent while the general price level rises by 10 percent. The entire increase in the dollar amount of sales may be explained by inflation, rather than by an increase in sales volume (the number of units sold). In fact, the company may well have sold *fewer* goods than in the preceding year.

In measuring the dollar or percentage change in *quarterly* sales or earnings, it is customary to compare the results of the current quarter with those of the *same quarter in the preceding year*. Use of the same quarter of the preceding year as the base period prevents our analysis from being distorted by seasonal fluctuations in business activity.

Percentages Become Misleading When the Base Is Small

Percentage changes may create a misleading impression when the dollar amount used as a base is unusually small. Occasionally we hear a television newscaster say that a company's profits have increased by a very large percentage, such as 900 percent. The initial impression created by such a statement is that the company's profits must now be excessively large. But assume, for example, that a company had net income of $100,000 in its first year, that in the second year net income drops to $10,000, and that in the third year net income returns to the $100,000 level. In this third year, net income has increased by $90,000, representing a 900 percent increase over the profits of the second year. What needs to be added to the news commentary is that this 900 percent increase in profits in the third year follows a very small profit in the second year and *exactly offsets* the 90 percent decline in profits in the second year.

TREND PERCENTAGES

The changes in financial statement items from a base year to following years are often expressed as *trend percentages* to show the extent and direction of change. Two steps are necessary to compute trend percentages. First, a base year is selected and each item in the financial statements for the base year is given a weight of 100 percent. The second step is to express each item in the financial statements for following years as a percentage of its base-year amount. This computation consists of dividing an item such as sales in the years after the base year by the amount of sales in the base year.

For example, assume that 2002 is selected as the base year and that sales in the base year amounted to $300,000, as shown in the following table. The trend percentages for sales are computed by dividing the sales amount of each following year by $300,000. Also shown in the illustration are the yearly amounts of net income. The trend percentages for net income are computed by dividing the net income amount for each following year by the base-year amount of $15,000.

Dollar Amounts	**2007**	**2006**	**2005**	**2004**	**2003**	**2002**
Sales.	$450,000	$360,000	$330,000	$321,000	$312,000	$300,000
Net income	22,950	14,550	21,450	19,200	15,600	15,000
Trend Percentages	**2007**	**2006**	**2005**	**2004**	**2003**	**2002**
Sales.	150%	120%	110%	107%	104%	100%
Net income	153	97	143	128	104	100

These trend percentages indicate a modest growth in sales in the early years and accelerated growth in 2006 and 2007. Net income also shows an increasing growth trend with the exception of the year 2006, when net income declined despite a solid increase in sales. The problem was overcome in 2007 with a sharp rise in net income. Overall the trend percentages give a picture of a profitable, growing enterprise.

COMPONENT PERCENTAGES

Component percentages indicate the *relative size* of each item included in a total. For example, each item in a balance sheet could be expressed as a percentage of total assets. This shows quickly the relative importance of each type of asset as well as the relative amount of financing obtained from current creditors, long-term creditors, and stockholders. By computing component percentages for several successive balance sheets, we can see which items are increasing in importance and which are becoming less significant.

Another application of component percentages is to express all items in an income statement as a percentage of net sales. Such a statement is called a *common size income statement.* See the condensed income statement in dollars and in common size form in Exhibit 14–2.

Income Statement

	Dollars		Component Percentages	
	2007	2006	2007	2006
Net sales	$1,000,000	$600,000	100.0%	100.0%
Cost of goods sold	700,000	360,000	70.0	60.0
Expenses (including income taxes)	250,000	180,000	25.0	30.0
Net income	$ 50,000	$ 60,000	5.0%	10.0%

Exhibit 14–2
COMPONENT PERCENTAGES

Are the year-to-date changes favorable?

Looking only at the component percentages, we see that the increase in cost of goods sold (60 percent to 70 percent) was only partially offset by the decrease in expenses as a percentage of net sales, causing net income to decrease from 10 percent to 5 percent of net sales.

RATIOS

A ratio is a simple mathematical expression of the relationship of one item to another. Every percentage may be viewed as a ratio—that is, one number expressed as a percentage of another.

Ratios may be stated in several ways. To illustrate, let us consider the current ratio, which expresses the relationship between a company's most liquid assets (current) and its liabilities that require payment soon (current). If current assets are $240,000 and current liabilities are $80,000, we may say either that the current ratio is 3 to 1 (which is written as 3:1) or that current assets are 300 percent of current liabilities. Either statement correctly summarizes the relationship—that is, that current assets are three times as large as current liabilities.

Ratios are particularly important in understanding financial statements because they permit us to compare information from one financial statement with information from another financial statement. For example, we might compare net income (taken from the income statement) with total assets (taken from the balance sheet) to see how effectively management is using available resources to earn a profit. For a ratio to be useful, however, the two amounts being compared must be logically related. In subsequent sections of this chapter, we will make extensive use of ratios to better demonstrate important dimensions of an enterprise's financial activities.

STANDARDS OF COMPARISON

In using dollar and percentage changes, trend percentages, component percentages, and ratios, financial analysts constantly search for some standard of comparison against which to judge whether the relationships they have found are favorable or unfavorable. Two such standards are (1) the past performance of the company and (2) the performance of other companies in the same industry. For internal management purposes, another important comparison is with expected or budgeted numbers.

Past Performance of the Company Comparing financial information for a current period with similar information for prior years affords some basis for judging whether the condition of the business is improving or worsening. This comparison of data over time is sometimes called *horizontal analysis*, to express the idea of reviewing data for a number of consecutive periods. It is distinguished from *vertical*, or *static*, analysis, which refers to the review of the financial information within a single accounting period.

In addition to determining whether the situation is improving or becoming worse, horizontal analysis may aid in making estimates of future prospects. Because changes may reverse their direction at any time, however, projecting past trends into the future always involves risk.

A weakness of horizontal analysis is that comparison with the past does not afford any basis for evaluation in absolute terms. The fact that net income was 2 percent of sales last year and is 3 percent of sales this year indicates improvement, but if there is evidence that net income *should be* 7 percent of sales, the record for both years is unfavorable.

Industry Standards The limitations of horizontal analysis may be overcome to some extent by finding appropriate benchmarks against which to measure a particular company's performance. The benchmarks used by most analysts are the performance of comparable companies and the average performance of several companies in the same industry.[1]

Assume, for example, that the revenue of Alpha Airlines drops by 8 percent during the current year. If the revenue for the airlines industry had dropped an average of 15 percent during this year, Alpha's 8 percent decline might be viewed as a *favorable* performance. As another example, assume that Omega Co. earns a net income equal to 3 percent of net sales. This would be substandard if Omega were a pharmaceutical company, but it would be satisfactory performance if it were a retail grocery chain because of the difference in earnings expected in the two industries.

When we compare a given company with its competitors or with industry averages, our conclusions are valid only if the companies in question are reasonably comparable. Because of the large number of diversified companies formed in recent years, the term *industry* is difficult to define, and even companies that fall roughly within the same industry may not be comparable in many respects. For example, one company may engage only in the marketing of oil products; another may be a fully integrated producer from the well to the gas pump; yet both are said to be in the oil industry.

QUALITY OF EARNINGS

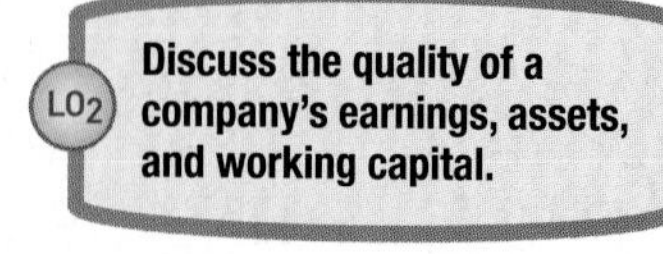

Profits are the lifeblood of a business entity. No entity can survive for long and accomplish its other goals unless it is profitable. Continuous losses drain assets from the business, consume owners' equity, and leave the company at the mercy of creditors. In assessing the prospects of a company, we are interested not only in the total *amount* of earnings but also in the *rate* of earnings on sales, on total assets, and on owners' equity. In addition, we must look at the *stability* and *source* of earnings. An erratic earnings performance over a period of years, for example, is less desirable than a steady level of earnings. A history of increasing earnings is preferable to a flat earnings record.

A breakdown of sales and earnings by *major product lines* may be useful in evaluating the future performance of a company. Publicly owned companies include with their financial statements supplementary schedules showing sales and profits by product line and by geographical area. These schedules assist financial analysts in forecasting the effect on the company of changes in consumer demand for particular types of products.

[1] Industry data are available from a number of sources. For example, Robert Morris Associates publishes *Annual Statement Studies*, which includes data from many thousands of annual reports, grouped into several hundred industry classifications. Industry classifications are subdivided further by company size. Dun & Bradstreet, Inc., annually publishes *Key Business Ratios* for more than 800 lines of business.

Financial analysts often express the opinion that the earnings of one company are of higher quality than the earnings of other similar companies. This concept of *quality of earnings* arises because each company's management can choose from a variety of accounting principles and methods, all of which are considered generally acceptable. A company's management often is under heavy pressure to report rising earnings, and accounting policies may be tailored toward this objective. We have already pointed out the impact on current reported earnings of the choice between the LIFO and FIFO methods of inventory valuation and the choice of depreciation policies. In judging the quality of earnings, the financial analyst should consider whether the accounting principles and methods selected by management lead to a conservative measurement of earnings (high quality) or tend to inflate reported earnings (low quality).

QUALITY OF ASSETS AND THE RELATIVE AMOUNT OF DEBT

Although a satisfactory level of earnings may be a good indication of the company's long-run ability to pay its debts and dividends, we must also look at the composition of assets, their condition and liquidity, the timing of repayment of liabilities, and the total amount of debt outstanding. A company may be profitable and yet be unable to pay its liabilities on time; sales and earnings may appear satisfactory, but plant and equipment may be deteriorating because of poor maintenance policies; valuable patents may be expiring; substantial losses may be imminent due to slow-moving inventories and past-due receivables. Companies with large amounts of debt often are vulnerable to increases in interest rates and are particularly vulnerable to declines in profitability and operating cash flows.

Measures of Liquidity and Credit Risk

Liquidity refers to a company's ability to meet its continuing obligations as they arise. For example, a company that has borrowed money must make interest and principal payments to a financial institution. A company that has purchased its inventory and other necessities on credit may be required to pay the seller within 30 days of the purchase date. Transactions like these require a company to maintain a close watch on its liquidity.

We emphasize throughout this text the importance to investors, creditors, and other users of financial statements of information that permits them to assess the amount, timing, and uncertainty of future cash flows from the enterprise to them. As a result, analyzing an enterprise's liquidity and its credit risk is very important and is a natural place for us to start our study of analyzing financial statements.

In this section we learn about ways to assess liquidity, starting with the classified balance sheet and then looking at a number of ratios commonly used to glean information about liquidity from the financial statements.

A CLASSIFIED BALANCE SHEET

Explain the nature and purpose of classifications in financial statements. LO3

In a classified balance sheet, assets usually are presented in three groups: (1) current assets, (2) plant and equipment, and (3) other assets. Liabilities are classified into two categories: (1) current liabilities and (2) long-term or noncurrent liabilities. A classified balance sheet for Computer City appears in Exhibit 14–3.

The classifications *current assets* and *current liabilities* are especially useful in evaluating a company's liquidity.

Current Assets

Current assets represent relatively liquid resources. This category includes cash, investments in marketable securities, receivables, inventories, and prepaid expenses. To qualify as a current asset, an asset must already be cash or must be capable of *being converted into cash* or used up within a relatively short period of time, without interfering with normal business operations.

Current assets are tied to an enterprise's **operating cycle**. Most companies have several operating cycles within a year. This means that they take cash and purchase inventory, sell the inventory, and collect the receivable in cash several times within a year. For these companies, the time period used to identify current assets is one year, so any asset that is expected to be

Exhibit 14–3

COMPUTER CITY CLASSIFIED BALANCE SHEET

COMPUTER CITY
Balance Sheet
December 31, 2007

Assets			
Current assets:			
Cash			$ 30,000
Marketable Securities			11,000
Notes Receivable			5,000
Accounts Receivable			60,000
Inventory			70,000
Prepaid Expenses			4,000
Total current assets			$180,000
Plant and equipment:			
Land		$151,000	
Building	$120,000		
Less: Accumulated Depreciation	9,000	111,000	
Sales Fixtures and Equipment	$ 45,000		
Less: Accumulated Depreciation	27,000	18,000	
Total plant and equipment			280,000
Other assets:			
Land Held as a Future Building Site			170,000
Total assets			$630,000
Liabilities & Stockholders' Equity			
Current liabilities:			
Notes Payable (due in 6 months)			$ 10,000
Accounts Payable			62,000
Income Taxes Payable			13,000
Sales Taxes Payable			3,000
Accrued Expenses Payable			8,000
Unearned Revenue and Customer Deposits			4,000
Total current liabilities			$100,000
Long-term liabilities:			
Mortgage Payable (due in 10 years)			110,000
Total liabilities			$210,000
Stockholders' equity:			
Capital Stock (15,000 shares issued and outstanding)		$150,000	
Retained Earnings		270,000	
Total stockholders' equity			420,000
Total liabilities & stockholders' equity			$630,000

LO4 **Prepare a classified balance sheet and compute widely used measures of liquidity and credit risk.**

converted into cash within one year is classified as a current asset in the enterprise's balance sheet. Some enterprises, however, have relatively long operating cycles. For example, a company that constructs very large items (for example, airplanes or ships) may have a production period that extends well beyond one year. In these cases, the length of the company's operating cycle is used to define those assets that are classified as current. While most current assets are expected to be converted into cash, we also include as current assets those that will be used up or consumed during the year or operating cycle, if longer. For example, prepaid expenses are classified as current assets on the basis that their having been paid in advance preserves cash that otherwise would have to be paid in the current period. Combining these ideas, current assets can be defined as assets that are already cash, or are expected to be converted into cash or used up within the next year or operating cycle, whichever is longer.

In a balance sheet, current assets are listed in order of liquidity. (The closer an asset is to becoming cash, the greater its liquidity.) Thus cash always is listed first among the current assets, usually followed by investments in marketable securities, receivables, inventory, and prepaid expenses, in that order.

Current Liabilities **Current liabilities** are *existing debts* that are expected to be paid by using the enterprise's current assets. Among the most common current liabilities are notes payable (due within one year), accounts payable, unearned revenue, and accrued expenses, such as income taxes payable, salaries payable, or interest payable. In the balance sheet, notes payable usually are listed first, followed by accounts payable; other types of current liabilities may be listed in any sequence.

The *relationship* between current assets and current liabilities is as important as the total dollar amount in either category. Current liabilities must be paid in the near future, and the cash to pay these liabilities is expected to come from current assets. Thus decision makers evaluating the liquidity of a business often compare the relative amounts of current assets and current liabilities, whereas an evaluation of *long-term* credit risk requires a comparison of total assets to total liabilities.

We will now use Computer City's classified balance sheet to examine some widely applied measures of short-term liquidity and long-term credit risk.

WORKING CAPITAL

Working capital is a measurement sometimes used to express the relationship between current assets and current liabilities. **Working capital** is the *excess* of current assets over current liabilities. Computer City's working capital is *$80,000*, computed as follows:

Current assets	$180,000
Less: Current liabilities	100,000
Working capital	$ 80,000

Working capital varies by industry and company size

Recall that current assets are expected to convert into cash (or be used up) within a relatively short period of time, and that current liabilities require a prompt cash payment. Thus working capital measures a company's potential excess *sources* of cash over its upcoming *uses* of cash.

The amount of working capital that a company needs to satisfy its liabilities as they come due varies with the size of the organization and the nature of its business activities. An analyst familiar with the nature of a company's operations usually can determine from the amount of working capital whether the company is in a sound financial position or is heading for financial difficulties.

CURRENT RATIO

A widely used measure of short-term debt-paying ability is the **current ratio**. This ratio is computed by *dividing* total current assets by total current liabilities.

In the illustrated balance sheet of Computer City, current assets amount to $180,000 and current liabilities total $100,000. Therefore, Computer City's current ratio is *1.8 to 1*, computed as follows:

Current assets	$180,000
Current liabilities	$100,000
Current ratio ($180,000 ÷ $100,000)	1.8 to 1

A widely used measure of liquidity

A current ratio of 1.8 to 1 means that the company's current assets are 1.8 times as large as its current liabilities.

The *higher* the current ratio, the more liquid the company appears to be. Historically, some bankers and other short-term creditors have believed that a company should have a current ratio of 2 to 1 or higher to qualify as a good credit risk. Such rules of thumb should be used carefully, however, because many successful businesses have current ratios of less than 2 to 1 because their receivables and inventory convert into cash quickly relative to the amount and timing of their payables. Likewise, it is possible for financially weak businesses to have high current ratios as a result of slow turnover in receivables and inventory. In other words, care must be taken in interpreting all ratios, including the current ratio, to ensure that inappropriate conclusions are not reached as a result of superficial analysis. Confirming the information communicated via one ratio by looking at other financial measures is often a good way to help ensure a valid interpretation.

QUICK RATIO

Inventory and prepaid expenses are the *least liquid* of the current assets. In a business with a long operating cycle, it may take several months to convert inventory into cash. Therefore, some short-term creditors prefer the **quick ratio** (sometimes called the acid-test ratio) to the current ratio as a measure of short-term liquidity.

The quick ratio compares only the *most liquid* current assets—called **quick assets**—with current liabilities. Quick assets include cash, marketable securities, and receivables—the current assets that can be converted most quickly into cash. Computer City's quick ratio is *1.06 to 1*, computed as follows:

Quick assets (cash, marketable securities, and receivables)	$106,000
Current liabilities	$100,000
Quick ratio ($106,000 ÷ $100,000)	1.06 to 1

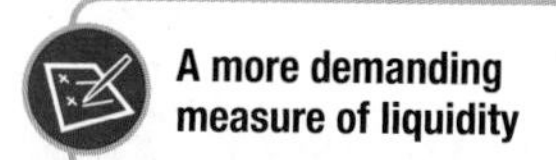
A more demanding measure of liquidity

Quick ratios are especially useful in evaluating the liquidity of companies that have inventories of slow-moving merchandise (such as real estate) or inventories that have become excessive in size.

DEBT RATIO

If a business fails and must be liquidated, the claims of creditors take priority over those of the owners. But if the business has a great deal of debt, there may not be enough assets even to make full payment to all creditors.

A basic measure of the safety of creditors' claims is the **debt ratio**, which states total liabilities as a *percentage* of total assets. A company's debt ratio is computed by dividing total liabilities by total assets, as shown below for Computer City:

Total liabilities	$210,000
Total assets	$630,000
Debt ratio ($210,000 ÷ $630,000)	33⅓%

The debt ratio is not a measure of short-term liquidity. Rather, it is a measure of creditors' *long-term* risk. The smaller the portion of total assets financed by creditors, the smaller the risk that the business may become unable to pay its debts. From the creditors' point of view, the *lower* the debt ratio, the *safer* their position.

Many financially sound American companies traditionally have maintained debt ratios under 50 percent. But again, the financial analyst must be familiar with industry characteristics. Banks, for example, may have very high debt ratios—often over 90 percent.

EVALUATING FINANCIAL RATIOS

We caution users of financial statements *against* placing much confidence in rules of thumb, such as *a current ratio should be at least 2 to 1, a quick ratio should be at least 1 to 1*, or *a debt ratio should be under 50 percent*. To interpret any financial ratio properly, the decision maker must first understand the characteristics of the company and the industry in which it operates.

Retailers, for example, tend to have higher current ratios than do wholesalers or manufacturing companies. Service-type businesses—which have no inventory—generally have lower current ratios than merchandising or manufacturing companies. Large businesses with good credit ratings and reliable sources of cash receipts are able to operate with lower current ratios than are small companies whose continuous inflow of cash may be less predictable.

Although a high current ratio is one indication of strong debt-paying ability, an extremely high ratio—say, 4 or 5 to 1—may indicate that *too much* of the company's resources are tied up in current assets. In maintaining such a highly liquid position, the company may be using its financial resources inefficiently and not earning the return that could be earned if the assets were invested in a more productive way.

Standards for Comparison Financial analysts generally use two criteria in evaluating the reasonableness of a financial ratio. One criterion is the *trend* in the ratio over a period of years. By reviewing this trend, analysts are able to determine whether a company's performance or financial position is improving or deteriorating. Second, analysts often compare a company's financial ratios with those of *similar companies* and with *industrywide averages*. These comparisons assist analysts in evaluating a particular ratio in light of the company's current business environment.

Annual Reports Publicly owned corporations issue **annual reports** that provide a great deal of information about the company. For example, annual reports include comparative financial statements that have been audited by a firm of independent public accountants. They also include 5- or 10-year *summaries* of key financial data and **management's discussion and analysis** of the company's operating results, liquidity, and financial position. This is where management identifies and discusses favorable and unfavorable trends and events that may affect the company in the future.

Bob Pardue

Annual reports are mailed directly to all stockholders of the corporation. They are also available to the public either through the Internet, in libraries, or by writing or calling the stockholder relations department of the corporation.

Industry Information Financial information about *entire industries* is available through financial publications (such as Dun & Bradstreet, Inc.) and through online databases (such as Media General Financial Services). Such information allows investors and creditors to compare the financial health of an individual company with the industry in which that company operates.

Usefulness and Limitations of Financial Ratios A financial ratio expresses the relationship of one amount to another. Most users of financial statements find that certain ratios assist them in quickly evaluating the financial position, profitability, and future prospects of a business. A comparison of key ratios for several successive years usually indicates whether the business is becoming stronger or weaker. Ratios also provide a way to compare quickly the financial strength and profitability of different companies.

Users of financial statements should recognize, however, that ratios have several limitations. For example, management may enter into year-end transactions that temporarily improve key ratios—a process called **window dressing**.

CASE IN POINT

Two issues confront accountants analyzing international companies. First, there is great variation in accounting measurement, disclosure, and audit quality across countries. Second, obtaining the information necessary to conduct cross-border accounting analyses is frequently difficult and sometimes not possible. Financial reporting in China is a case in point. Until recent years China did not have active stock markets requiring financial reporting. In addition, there was no external auditing in forms that would be familiar to Westerners.

To illustrate, the balance sheet of Computer City (Exhibit 14–3) includes current assets of $180,000 and current liabilities of $100,000, indicating a current ratio of *1.8 to 1*. What would happen if, shortly before year-end, management used $20,000 of the company's cash to pay accounts payable that are not due until January 2008? This transaction would reduce current assets to $160,000 ($180,000 − $20,000) and current liabilities to $80,000 ($100,000 − $20,000), resulting in an increase in the current ratio to a more impressive 2 to 1 ($160,000 ÷ $80,000). Is the company really better off as a result of having simply paid $20,000 of liabilities a few days early? The answer is probably no, although looking only at the current ratio one might think it is stronger after paying the $20,000 than before. Such steps to improve the company's appearance in its financial statements are common and, within reason, are a natural part of financial reporting. The astute reader of financial statements needs to be aware of this, however, and should look for instances where there is evidence that steps have been taken to artificially improve a company's appearance. Usually this can be done by looking at multiple financial measures rather than focusing on a single financial measure.

Financial statement ratios contain the same limitations as do the dollar amounts used in financial statements. For example, many assets are reported at historical cost rather than current market value. Also, financial statement ratios express only *financial* relationships. They give no indication of a company's progress in achieving nonfinancial goals, such as improving customer satisfaction or worker productivity. A thorough analysis of investment opportunities involves more than merely computing and comparing financial ratios.

LIQUIDITY, CREDIT RISK, AND THE LAW

Accountants view a business entity as separate from the other economic activities of its owners, regardless of how the business is organized. The law, however, draws an important distinction between *corporations* and *unincorporated* business organizations. Users of financial statements should understand this legal distinction, as it may affect both creditors and owners.

Under the law, the owners of unincorporated businesses (sole proprietorships and partnerships) are *personally liable* for any and all debts of the business organization. Therefore, creditors of unincorporated businesses often base their lending decisions on the financial position of the *owners*, rather than the financial strength of the business entity.[2]

If a business is organized as a corporation, however, the owners (stockholders) are *not* personally responsible for the liabilities of the business. Creditors may look *only to the business entity* in seeking payment of their claims. Therefore, the liquidity of the business entity becomes much more important if the business is organized as a corporation.

Small Corporations and Loan Guarantees Small corporations often do not have sufficient financial resources to qualify for the credit they need. In such cases, creditors may require that one or more of the company's stockholders personally guarantee (or co-sign) specific debts of the business entity. By co-signing debts of the corporation, the individual stockholders *do* become personally liable for the debt if the corporation fails to make payment.

Measures of Profitability

Measures of a company's *profitability* are of interest to equity investors and management and are drawn primarily from the income statement. The measures that we discuss in this chapter include percentage changes in key measurements, gross profit rates, operating income, net income as a percentage of sales, earnings per share, return on assets, and return on equity.

[2] In a *limited* partnership, only the *general partners* are personally responsible for the debts of the business. Every limited partnership must have one or more general partners.

Public opinion polls show that many people believe that most businesses earn a profit equal to 30 percent or more of the sales price of their merchandise. Actually, this is far from true. Most successful companies earn a net income that is between 5 percent and, perhaps, 15 percent of sales revenue.

CLASSIFICATIONS IN THE INCOME STATEMENT

An income statement may be prepared in either the *multiple-step* or the *single-step* format. The multiple-step income statement is more useful in illustrating accounting concepts because it provides more detailed information than the single-step format. A multiple-step income statement for Computer City is shown in Exhibit 14–4.

Exhibit 14–4

COMPUTER CITY INCOME STATEMENT (MULTIPLE-STEP)

COMPUTER CITY Income Statement For the Year Ended December 31, 2007			
Net sales			$900,000
Less: Cost of goods sold (including transportation-in)			540,000
Gross profit			$360,000
Less: Operating expenses:			
Selling expenses:			
Sales salaries and commissions	$64,800		
Advertising	42,000		
Delivery service	14,200		
Depreciation: store equipment	9,000		
Other selling expenses	6,000		
Total selling expenses		$136,000	
General and administrative expenses:			
Administrative and office salaries	$93,000		
Utilities	3,100		
Depreciation: building	3,000		
Other general and administrative expenses	4,900		
Total general and administrative expenses		104,000	
Total operating expenses			240,000
Operating income			$120,000
Less (add): Nonoperating items:			
Interest expense	$12,000		
Purchase discounts lost	1,200		
Interest revenue	(3,200)		10,000
Income before income taxes			$110,000
Income tax expense			38,000
Net income			$ 72,000
Earnings per share			$4.80

A knowledge of accounting does not enable you to say what the level of corporate earnings *should be*; however, it does enable you to read audited financial statements that show what corporate earnings *actually are*. Moreover, you are aware that the information in published financial statements of corporations has been audited by CPA firms and has been periodically reviewed in detail by government agencies, such as the Securities and Exchange Commission (SEC). Consequently, you know that the profits reported in these published financial statements are reasonably reliable; they have been determined in accordance with generally accepted accounting principles and verified by independent experts.

YOUR TURN **You as a Member of the House of Representatives**

Assume you are a member of the U.S. House of Representatives. Because of the financial frauds at **Enron**, **WorldCom**, and other public companies, the Congress passed, and President Bush signed, the Sarbanes-Oxley Act of 2002. The Sarbanes-Oxley Act significantly expands the compliance burden, particularly related to financial reporting, on public companies. Certain of your business constituents argue that the compliance burden is now excessive and that smaller public companies will go private, and that private businesses that need capital to expand will not go public because of the increased compliance burden. Your constituents also argue that the economy will grow more slowly, creating fewer jobs for your constituents, if companies are excluded from the capital markets because of the compliance burden imposed by the Sarbanes-Oxley Act. How would you respond?

(See our comments on the Online Learning Center Web site.)

MULTIPLE-STEP INCOME STATEMENTS

LO5 **Prepare a multiple-step and a single-step income statement and compute widely used measures of profitability.**

A multiple-step income statement draws its name from the *series of steps* in which costs and expenses are deducted from revenue. As a first step, the cost of goods sold is deducted from net sales to determine the subtotal *gross profit*. As a second step, operating expenses are deducted to obtain a subtotal called **operating income** (or income from operations). As a final step, income tax expense and other nonoperating items are taken into consideration to arrive at *net income*.

Notice that the income statement is divided into four major sections: (1) revenue, (2) cost of goods sold, (3) operating expenses, and (4) nonoperating items. Multiple-step income statements are noted for their numerous sections and the development of significant subtotals.

The Revenue Section In a merchandising company, the revenue section of the income statement usually contains only one line, entitled *net sales*. (Other types of revenue, if any, appear in the final section of the statement.)

Investors and managers are vitally interested in the *trend* in net sales. As one means of evaluating this trend, they often compute the percentage change in net sales from year to year. As discussed earlier in this chapter, a **percentage change** is the dollar amount of the *change* in a financial measurement, expressed as a percentage. It is computed by dividing the dollar amount of increase or decrease by the dollar amount of the measurement *before* the change occurred. (Dollar changes *cannot* be expressed as percentages if the financial statement amount in the earlier period is zero or has changed from a negative amount to a positive amount.)

In our economy, most prices increase over time. The average increase in prices during the year is called the *rate of inflation*. Because of inflation, a company's net sales may increase slightly from year to year even if the company is not selling greater amounts of merchandise. If a company's physical sales volume is increasing, net sales usually will grow faster than the rate of inflation.

If a company's sales grow faster than the *industry average*, the company increases its **market share**—that is, its share of total industry sales.

Publicly owned corporations include in their annual reports schedules summarizing operating data—such as net sales—for a period of 5 or 10 years. This information is also readily available through several online databases.

The Cost of Goods Sold Section The second section of a merchandising company's income statement shows cost of goods sold for the period. Cost of goods sold usually appears as a single dollar amount, which includes such incidental items as freight costs and normal shrinkage losses.

Gross Profit: A Key Subtotal In a multiple-step income statement, gross profit appears as a subtotal. This makes it easy for users of the income statement to compute the company's *gross profit rate* (or profit margin).

The gross profit rate is gross profit expressed as a *percentage of net sales*. In 2007, Computer City earned an average gross profit rate of *40 percent*, computed as follows:

Dollar amount of gross profit	$360,000
Net sales	$900,000
Gross profit rate ($360,000 ÷ $900,000)	40%

In evaluating the gross profit rate of a particular company, the analyst should consider the rates earned in prior periods, as well as the rates earned by *other companies* in the same industry. For most merchandising companies, gross profit rates usually lie between 20 percent and 50 percent, depending on the types of products they sell. These rates usually are lowest on fast-moving merchandise, such as groceries, and highest on specialty and novelty products.

Under normal circumstances, a company's gross profit rate tends to remain *reasonably stable* from one period to the next. Significant changes in this rate may provide investors with an early indication of changing consumer demand for the company's products.

The Operating Expenses Section Operating expenses are incurred for the purpose of *producing revenue*. These expenses often are subdivided into the classifications of *selling expenses* and *general and administrative expenses*. Subdividing operating expenses into functional classifications aids management and other users of the statements in separately evaluating different aspects of the company's operations. For example, selling expenses often rise and fall in concert with changes in net sales. Administrative expenses, on the other hand, usually remain more constant from one period to the next.

Operating Income: Another Key Subtotal Some of the revenue and expenses of a business result from activities other than the company's basic business operations. Common examples include interest earned on investments and income tax expense.

Operating income (or income from operations) shows the relationship between revenue earned from customers and expenses incurred in producing this revenue. In effect, operating income measures the profitability of a company's *basic or core business operations* and leaves out other types of revenue and expenses.

Nonoperating Items Revenue and expenses that are not directly related to the company's primary business activities are listed in a final section of the income statement following operating income.

Two significant nonoperating items are interest expense and income tax expense. Interest expense results from the manner in which assets are *financed*, not the manner in which these assets are used in business operations. Income tax expense is not included among the operating expenses because paying income taxes *does not help to produce revenue*. Nonoperating revenues, such as interest and dividends earned on investments, also are listed in this section of the income statement.

Net Income Many equity investors consider net income (or net loss) to be the most important figure in a company's financial statements. This amount usually represents the overall increase (or decrease) in owners' equity resulting from all profit-directed activities during the period.

Financial analysts often compute net income as a *percentage of net sales* (net income divided by net sales). This measurement provides an indication of management's *ability to control expenses* and to retain a reasonable portion of its revenue as profit.

The normal ratio of net income to net sales varies greatly by industry. In some industries, companies may be successful by earning a net income equal to only 2 percent or 3 percent of net sales. In other industries, net income may be much higher. In 2007, Computer City's net income amounts to *8 percent* of net sales, which is very good for a computer retailer.

LO6 Put a company's net income into perspective by relating it to sales, assets, and stockholders' equity.

Net income	$ 72,000
Net sales	$900,000
Net income as a percentage of net sales ($72,000 ÷ $900,000)	8%

EARNINGS PER SHARE

Ownership of a corporation is evidenced by *shares* of capital stock. What does the net income of a corporation mean to someone who owns, say, 100 shares of a corporation's capital stock? To assist individual stockholders in relating the corporation's net income to *their ownership shares*, public companies compute **earnings per share** and show these amounts at the bottom of their income statements.[3]

In the simplest case, earnings per share is net income, expressed on a per-share basis. For example, the balance sheet in Exhibit 14–3 indicates that Computer City has 15,000 shares of capital stock outstanding.[4] Assuming these shares had been outstanding all year, earnings per share amounts to *$4.80*:

Net income	$72,000
Shares of capital stock outstanding	15,000
Earnings per share ($72,000 ÷ 15,000 shares)	$4.80

Earnings per share is one of the most widely used of all accounting ratios. The *trend* in earnings per share and the expected earnings in future periods are *major factors* affecting the market value of a company's shares.

PRICE-EARNINGS RATIO

LO7 Compute the ratios widely used in financial statement analysis and explain the significance of each.

Financial analysts express the relationship between the market price of a company's stock and the underlying earnings per share as a **price-earnings (p/e) ratio**. This ratio is computed by dividing the current market price per share of the company's stock by annual earnings per share. (A p/e ratio cannot be computed for a period in which the company incurs a net loss.)

To illustrate, assume that, at the end of 2007, Computer City's capital stock is trading among investors at a market price of *$96* per share. The p/e ratio of the company's stock is computed as follows:

Current market price per share of stock	$96
Earnings per share (for the last 12 months)	$4.80
Price-earnings ratio ($96 ÷ $4.80)	20

Technically, this ratio is 20 to 1. But it is common practice to omit the "to 1" and merely describe a p/e ratio by the first number. The p/e ratios of many publicly owned corporations are quoted daily in the financial pages of many newspapers.

The p/e ratio reflects *investors' expectations* concerning the company's *future performance*. The more optimistic these expectations, the higher the p/e ratio is likely to be.

A p/e ratio of 10 or less often indicates that investors expect earnings to *decline* from the current level. It could also mean, however, that the stock is *undervalued*. Likewise, a stock with a p/e ratio of 30 or more usually means that investors expect earnings to *increase* from the current level. However, it may also signal that the stock is *overvalued*.

One word of caution. If earnings decline to *very low levels*, the price of the stock usually does not follow the earnings all the way down. Therefore, a company with *very low earnings* is likely to have a *high p/e ratio* even if investors are not optimistic about future earnings.

[3] Only publicly held corporations are *required* to report earnings on a per-share basis. For small businesses such as Computer City, the reporting of earnings per share is optional.

[4] Assume that all 15,000 shares have been outstanding throughout the year. Computation of earnings per share in more complex situations is addressed in Chapter 12.

SINGLE-STEP INCOME STATEMENTS

In their annual reports, many publicly owned corporations present their financial statements in a highly condensed format. For this reason, the *single-step* income statement is widely used in annual reports. The 2007 income statement of Computer City appears in Exhibit 14–5 in a single-step format.

Exhibit 14–5

COMPUTER CITY INCOME STATEMENT (SINGLE-STEP)

COMPUTER CITY Income Statement For the Year Ended December 31, 2007		
Revenue:		
Net sales		$900,000
Interest earned		3,200
Total revenue		$903,200
Less: Costs and expenses:		
Cost of goods sold	$540,000	
Selling expenses	136,000	
General and administrative expenses	104,000	
Interest expense	12,000	
Purchase discounts lost	1,200	
Income tax expense	38,000	
Total costs and expenses		831,200
Net income		$ 72,000
Earnings per share		$4.80

The single-step form of income statement takes its name from the fact that all costs and expenses are deducted from total revenue in a single step. No subtotals are shown for gross profit or for operating income, although the statement provides investors with enough information to compute these subtotals on their own.

EVALUATING THE ADEQUACY OF NET INCOME

How much net income must a business earn to be considered successful? Obviously, the dollar amount of net income that investors consider adequate depends on the *size of the business*. An annual net income of $1 million might seem impressive for an automobile dealership but would represent very poor performance for a company the size of General Motors, Ford, or DaimlerChrysler.

Stone/Getty Images

Investors usually consider two factors in evaluating a company's profitability: (1) the trend in earnings and (2) the amount of current earnings in relation to the amount of the resources needed to produce the earnings.

Some investors regard the *trend* in earnings from year to year as more important than the amount of net income in the current period. Equity investors stand to benefit from the company's performance over the long run. Years of steadily increasing earnings may increase the value of the stockholders' investment manyfold.

In evaluating the current level of earnings, many investors use *return on investment* analysis.

RETURN ON INVESTMENT (ROI)

We have emphasized throughout this text that a basic purpose of accounting is to assist decision makers in efficiently allocating and using economic resources. In deciding where to invest their money, equity investors want to know how efficiently companies utilize resources. A common method of evaluating the efficiency with which financial resources are employed is to compute the rate of return earned on these resources. This rate of return is called the *return on investment*, or *ROI*, and is sometimes referred to as return on assets.

Mathematically, computing return on investment is simple: the annual return (or profit) generated by the investment is stated as a *percentage* of the average amount invested throughout the year. The basic idea is illustrated by the following formula:

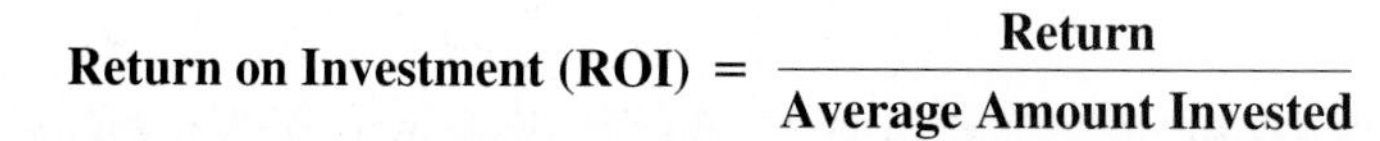

$$\textbf{Return on Investment (ROI)} = \frac{\textbf{Return}}{\textbf{Average Amount Invested}}$$

The return is earned throughout the period. Therefore, it is logical to express this return as a percentage of the *average* amount invested during the period, rather than the investment at year-end. The average amount invested usually is computed by adding the amounts invested as of the beginning and end of the year, and dividing this total by 2.

The concept of ROI is applied in many different situations, such as evaluating the profitability of a business, a branch location, or a specific investment opportunity. As a result, a number of variations in the basic ROI ratio have been developed, each suited to a particular type of analysis. These ratios differ in the manner in which return and average amount invested are defined. We will discuss two common applications of the ROI concept: *return on assets* and *return on equity*.

RETURN ON ASSETS (ROA)

This ratio is used in evaluating whether management has earned a reasonable return with the assets under its control. In this computation, return usually is defined as *operating income*, since interest expense and income taxes are determined by factors other than the manner in which assets are used. The **return on assets** is computed as follows:

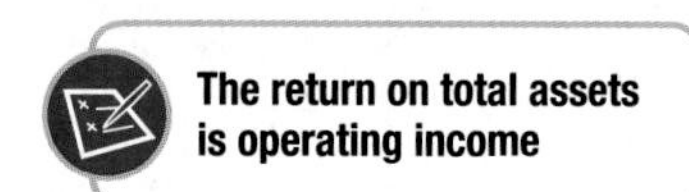

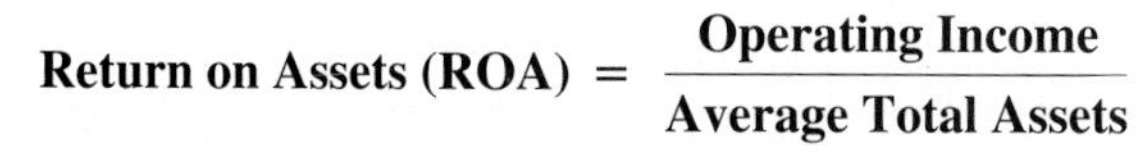

$$\textbf{Return on Assets (ROA)} = \frac{\textbf{Operating Income}}{\textbf{Average Total Assets}}$$

Let us now determine the return on assets earned by the management of Computer City in 2007. Operating income, as shown in the income statement in Exhibit 14–4, amounts to *$120,000*. Assume that Computer City's assets at the beginning of 2007 totaled $570,000. The illustrated balance sheet in Exhibit 14–3 shows total assets of $630,000 at year-end. Therefore, the company's *average* total assets during the year amounted to *$600,000* [($570,000 + $630,000) ÷ 2]. The return on assets in 2007 is *20 percent*, determined as follows:

$$\frac{\textbf{Operating Income}}{\textbf{Average Total Assets}} = \frac{\textbf{\$120,000}}{\textbf{\$600,000}} = \textbf{20\%}$$

Most successful businesses earn a return on average total assets of, perhaps, 15 percent or more. At this writing, businesses must pay interest rates of between 3 percent and 8 percent to borrow money. However, interest rates are at historic lows in the United States and are likely to rise in the future. If a business is well managed and has good future prospects, management should be able to earn a return on assets that is higher than the company's cost of borrowing.

RETURN ON EQUITY (ROE)

The return on assets that we calculated above measures the efficiency with which management has utilized the assets under its control, regardless of whether these assets were financed with debt or equity capital. The **return on equity** ratio, in contrast, looks only at the return earned by management on the stockholders' investment—that is, on *owners' equity*.

The return to stockholders is *net income*, which represents the return from all sources, both operating and nonoperating. Thus return on equity is computed as follows:

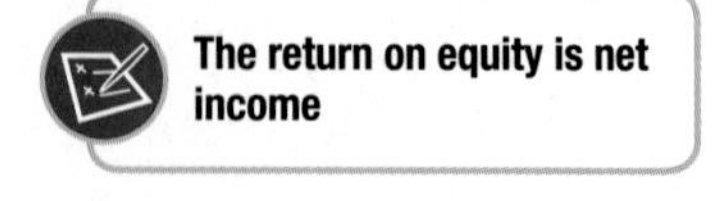

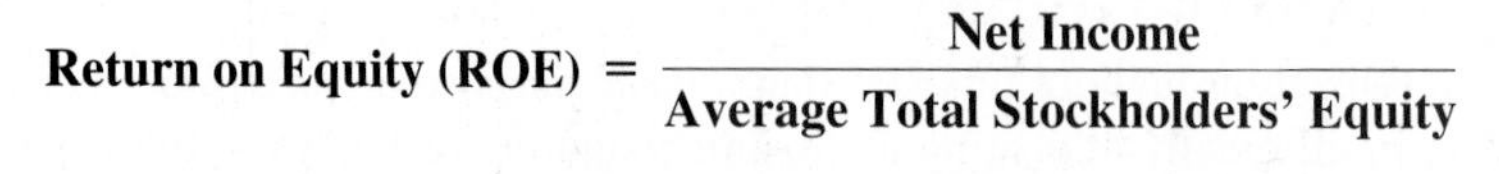

$$\textbf{Return on Equity (ROE)} = \frac{\textbf{Net Income}}{\textbf{Average Total Stockholders' Equity}}$$

To illustrate, let us again turn to the 2007 financial statements of Computer City. The company earned net income of *$72,000*. The year-end balance sheet (Exhibit 14–3) shows total stockholders' equity of $420,000. To enable us to complete our computation, we will assume that the stockholders' equity at the *beginning* of the year amounted to $380,000. Therefore, the *average* stockholders' equity for the year amounts to *$400,000* [($380,000 + $420,000) ÷ 2]. The return on stockholders' equity in 2007 is *18 percent*, computed as follows:

$$\frac{\textbf{Net Income}}{\textbf{Average Total Stockholders' Equity}} = \frac{\$72{,}000}{\$400{,}000} = 18\%$$

Traditionally, stockholders have expected to earn an average annual return of 12 percent or more from equity investments in large, financially strong companies. Annual returns on equity of 30 percent or more are not uncommon, especially in rapidly growing companies with new or highly successful products.

The return on equity may be higher or lower than the overall return on assets, depending on how the company has financed its assets and on the amounts of its nonoperating revenue and expenses. A company that suffers a net loss provides its stockholders with a *negative* return on stockholders' equity.

Comprehensive Illustration: Seacliff Company

Now that we have presented techniques that are useful in better understanding an enterprise's financial statements, we will show the comprehensive analysis of a company. This illustration draws from material presented in this chapter as well as from information presented earlier in the text. We take a comprehensive look at the analysis of financial statements from the perspectives of three important groups: common stockholders, long-term creditors, and short-term creditors.

The basic information for our analysis is contained in a set of condensed two-year comparative financial statements for Seacliff Company shown in Exhibits 14–6 through 14–10. Summarized statement data, together with computations of dollar increases and decreases, and component percentages where applicable, have been compiled. For convenience in this illustration, relatively small dollar amounts have been used in the Seacliff Company financial statements.

© Royalty-Free/Corbis

Exhibit 14–6 SEACLIFF INCOME STATEMENTS

SEACLIFF COMPANY
Comparative Income Statement
For the Years Ended December 31, 2007, and December 31, 2006

			Increase or (Decrease)		Percentage of Net Sales	
	2007	2006	Dollars	%	2007	2006
Net sales	$900,000	$750,000	$150,000	20.0	100.0	100.0
Cost of goods sold	530,000	420,000	110,000	26.2	58.9	56.0
Gross profit on sales	$370,000	$330,000	$ 40,000	12.1	41.1	44.0
Operating expenses:						
Selling expenses	$117,000	$ 75,000	$ 42,000	56.0	13.0	10.0
General and administrative expenses	126,000	95,000	31,000	32.6	14.0	12.7
Total operating expenses	$243,000	$170,000	$ 73,000	42.9	27.0	22.7
Operating income	$127,000	$160,000	$ (33,000)	(20.6)	14.1	21.3
Interest expense	24,000	30,000	(6,000)	(20.0)	2.7	4.0
Income before income tax	$103,000	$130,000	$ (27,000)	(20.8)	11.4	17.3
Income tax expense	28,000	40,000	(12,000)	(30.0)	3.1	5.3
Net income	$ 75,000	$ 90,000	$ (15,000)	(16.7)	8.3	12.0
Earnings per share of common stock	$ 13.20	$ 20.25	$ (7.05)	(34.8)		

Exhibit 14–7 SEACLIFF STATEMENTS OF RETAINED EARNINGS

SEACLIFF COMPANY
Statement of Retained Earnings
For the Years Ended December 31, 2007, and December 31, 2006

			Increase or (Decrease)	
	2007	2006	Dollars	%
Retained earnings, beginning of year	$176,000	$115,000	$ 61,000	53.0
Net income	75,000	90,000	(15,000)	(16.7)
	$251,000	$205,000	$ 46,000	22.4
Less: Dividends on common stock ($5.00 per share in 2006, $4.80 per share in 2007)	$ 24,000	$ 20,000	$ 4,000	20.0
Dividends on preferred stock ($9 per share)	9,000	9,000		
	$ 33,000	$ 29,000	$ 4,000	13.8
Retained earnings, end of year	$218,000	$176,000	$ 42,000	23.9

Exhibit 14–8 SEACLIFF BALANCE SHEETS

SEACLIFF COMPANY
Condensed Comparative Balance Sheet*
December 31, 2007, and December 31, 2006

			Increase or (Decrease)		Percentage of Total Assets	
Assets	2007	2006	Dollars	%	2007	2006
Current assets	$390,000	$288,000	$102,000	35.4	41.1	33.5
Plant and equipment (net)	500,000	467,000	33,000	7.1	52.6	54.3
Other assets (loans to officers)	60,000	105,000	(45,000)	(42.9)	6.3	12.2
Total assets	$950,000	$860,000	$ 90,000	10.5	100.0	100.0
Liabilities & Stockholders' Equity						
Liabilities:						
Current liabilities	$112,000	$ 94,000	$ 18,000	19.1	11.8	10.9
12% long-term note payable (due in 7 years)	200,000	250,000	(50,000)	(20.0)	21.1	29.1
Total liabilities	$312,000	$344,000	$ (32,000)	(9.3)	32.9	40.0
Stockholders' equity:						
9% preferred stock, $100 par	$100,000	$100,000	—	—	10.5	11.6
Common stock, $50 par	250,000	200,000	$ 50,000	25.0	26.3	23.2
Additional paid-in capital	70,000	40,000	30,000	75.0	7.4	4.7
Retained earnings	218,000	176,000	42,000	23.9	22.9	20.5
Total stockholders' equity	$638,000	$516,000	$122,000	23.6	67.1	60.0
Total liabilities & stockholders' equity	$950,000	$860,000	$ 90,000	10.5	100.0	100.0

*In order to focus attention on important subtotals, this statement is highly condensed and does not show individual asset and liability items. These details will be introduced as needed in the text discussion. For example, a list of Seacliff Company's current assets and current liabilities appears in Exhibit 14–18.

Exhibit 14–9 SEACLIFF STATEMENT OF CASH FLOWS

SEACLIFF COMPANY
Condensed Comparative Statement of Cash Flows
For the Years Ended December 31, 2007, and December 31, 2006

			Increase or (Decrease)	
	2007	**2006**	**Dollars**	**%**
Cash flows from operating activities:				
Net cash flows from operating activities	$ 19,000	$ 95,000	$(76,000)	(80.0)
Cash flows from investing activities:				
Purchases of plant assets	(63,000)	(28,000)	(35,000)	125.0
Collections of loans from officers	45,000	(35,000)	80,000	N/A*
Net cash used by investing activities	$(18,000)	$(63,000)	$ 45,000	(71.4)
Cash flows from financing activities:				
Dividends paid	$(33,000)	$(29,000)	$ (4,000)	13.8
Repayment of long-term debt	(50,000)	–0–	(50,000)	N/A*
Proceeds from issuing capital stock	80,000	–0–	80,000	N/A*
Net cash used by financing activities	$ (3,000)	$(29,000)	$ 26,000	(89.7)
Net increase (decrease) in cash and cash equivalents	$ (2,000)	$ 3,000	$ (5,000)	N/A*
Cash and cash equivalents, beginning of the year	40,000	37,000	3,000	8.1
Cash and cash equivalents, end of the year	$ 38,000	$ 40,000	$ (2,000)	(5.0)

*N/A indicates that computation of the percentage change is not appropriate. Percentage changes cannot be determined if the base year is zero or if a negative amount (cash outflow) changes to a positive amount (cash inflow).

Exhibit 14–10 SEACLIFF NOTES TO FINANCIAL STATEMENTS

SEACLIFF COMPANY
Notes to Financial Statements
For the Years Ended December 31, 2007, and December 31, 2006

Note 1—Accounting Policies

Inventories Inventories are determined by the LIFO method.

Depreciation Depreciation is computed by the straight-line method. Buildings are depreciated over 40 years, and equipment and fixtures over periods of 5 or 10 years.

Note 2—Unused Lines of Credit

The company has a confirmed line of credit in the amount of $35,000. None was in use at December 31, 2007.

Note 3—Contingencies and Commitments

As of December 31, 2007, the company has no material commitments or noncancellable obligations. There currently are no loss contingencies known to management.

Note 4—Current Values of Financial Instruments

All financial instruments appear in the financial statements at dollar amounts that closely approximate their current values.

Note 5—Concentrations of Credit Risk

The company engages in retail sales to the general public from a single location in Seattle, Washington. No individual customer accounts for more than 2% of the company's total sales or accounts receivable. Accounts receivable are unsecured.

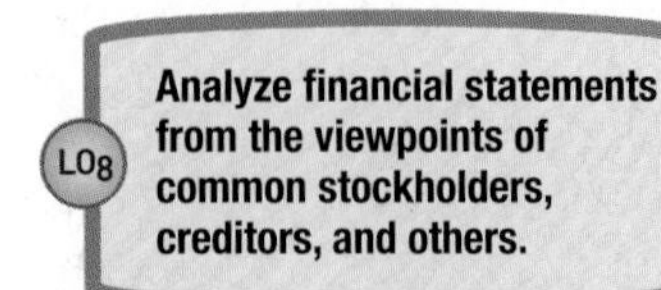

ANALYSIS BY COMMON STOCKHOLDERS

Common stockholders and potential investors in common stock look first at a company's earnings record. Their investment is in shares of stock, so *earnings per share* and *dividends per share* are of particular interest.

Earnings per Share of Common Stock As indicated in Chapter 12, earnings per share of common stock are computed by dividing the income applicable to the common stock by the weighted-average number of shares of common stock outstanding during the year. Any preferred dividend requirements must be subtracted from net income to determine income applicable to common stock, as shown in the computations for Seacliff Company in Exhibit 14–11.

Exhibit 14–11
EARNINGS PER SHARE OF COMMON STOCK

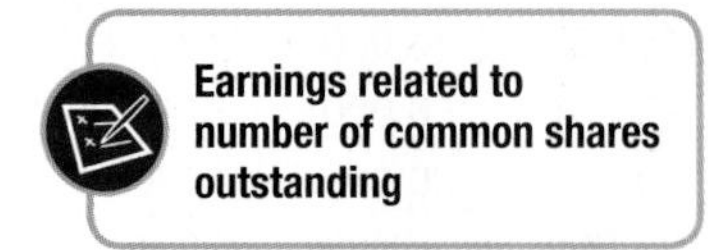

	2007	2006
Net income	$75,000	$90,000
Less: Preferred dividend requirements	9,000	9,000
Income applicable to common stock	(a) $66,000	$81,000
Shares of common stock outstanding, during the year	(b) 5,000	4,000
Earnings per share of common stock (a ÷ b)	$ 13.20	$ 20.25

Notice that earnings per share have decreased by *$7.05* in 2007, representing a decline of nearly *35 percent* from their level in 2006 ($7.05 ÷ $20.25 = 34.8%). Common stockholders consider a decline in earnings per share to be an unfavorable development. A decline in earnings per share generally represents a decline in the profitability of the company and creates uncertainty as to the company's prospects for future growth.

With such a significant decline in earnings per share, we should expect to see a decline in the market value of Seacliff's common stock during 2007. [For purposes of our illustration, we assume the common stock had a market value of *$160* at December 31, 2006, and of *$132* at the end of 2007. This drop of $28 per share represents a *17½ percent* decline in the market value of every common stockholder's investment ($28 decline ÷ $160 = 17.5%).]

Price-Earnings Ratio As we mentioned earlier in this chapter, the relationship between the market price of common stock and earnings per share is widely recognized and is expressed as a ratio, called the *price-earnings ratio* (or *p/e ratio*). The p/e ratio is determined by dividing the market price per share by the annual earnings per share.

The outlook for future earnings is the major factor influencing a company's p/e ratio. Companies with track records of rapid growth may sell at p/e ratios of perhaps 30 to 1, or even higher. Companies with "flat" earnings or earnings expected to decline in future years often sell at price-earnings ratios below 10 to 1.

At the end of 2006, Seacliff's p/e ratio was approximately *8 to 1* ($160 ÷ $20.25 = 7.9), suggesting that investors *were expecting* earnings to decline in 2007. At December 31, 2007, the price-earnings ratio was *10 to 1* ($132 ÷ $13.20 = 10.0). A p/e ratio in this range suggests that investors expect future earnings to stabilize around the current level.

Dividend Yield Dividends are of prime importance to some stockholders, but a secondary factor to others. Some stockholders invest primarily to receive regular cash income, while others invest in stocks principally with the expectation of rising market prices. If a corporation is profitable and retains its earnings for expansion of the business, the expanded operations should produce an increase in the net income of the company and thus tend to make each share of stock more valuable.

In comparing the merits of alternative investment opportunities, we should relate earnings and dividends per share to the *market value* of the stock at a particular date. Dividends per share divided by market price per share determine the *yield* rate of a company's stock. Dividend yield is especially important to those investors whose objective is to maximize the dividend revenue from their investments. For Seacliff, the dividend yield on its common stock was 3.1 percent in 2006 ($5/$160) and 3.6 percent in 2007 ($4.80/$132).

Summary of Earnings and Dividend Data for Seacliff The relationships of Seacliff's per-share earnings and dividends to its year-end stock prices are summarized in Exhibit 14–12.

Date	Market Value per Share	Earnings per Share	Price-Earnings Ratio	Dividends per Share	Dividend Yield, %
Dec. 31, 2006	$160	$20.25	8	$5.00	3.1
Dec. 31, 2007	132	13.20	10	4.80	3.6

Exhibit 14–12
EARNINGS AND DIVIDENDS PER SHARE OF COMMON STOCK

The decline in market value during 2007 presumably reflects the decreases in both earnings and dividends per share. Investors appraising this stock at December 31, 2007, should consider whether a price-earnings ratio of 10 and a dividend yield of 3.6 percent meet their expectations in light of alternative investment opportunities. These investors will also place considerable weight on estimates of the company's prospective future earnings and the probable effect of such estimated earnings on the market price of the stock and on dividend payments.

Earnings and dividends related to market price of common stock

Revenue and Expense Analysis The trend of earnings of Seacliff Company is unfavorable, and stockholders will want to know the reasons for the decline in net income. The comparative income statements in Exhibit 14–6 show that despite a 20 percent increase in net sales, net income fell from $90,000 in 2006 to $75,000 in 2007, a decline of 16.7 percent. As a percentage of net sales, net income fell from 12 percent to only 8.3 percent. The primary causes of this decline were the increases in selling expenses (56.0 percent), general and administrative expenses (32.6 percent), and the cost of goods sold (26.2 percent), all of which exceeded the 20 percent increase in net sales.

Let us assume that further investigation reveals Seacliff Company decided in 2007 to reduce its sales prices in an effort to generate greater sales volume. This would explain the decrease in the gross profit rate from 44 percent to 41.1 percent of net sales. Since the dollar amount of gross profit increased $40,000 in 2007, the strategy of reducing sales prices to increase volume would have been successful if there had been little or no increase in operating expenses. However, operating expenses rose by $73,000, resulting in a $33,000 decrease in operating income.

The next step is to find which expenses increased and why. An investor may be limited here, because detailed operating expenses are not usually shown in published financial statements. Some conclusions, however, can be reached on the basis of even the condensed information available in the comparative income statements for Seacliff Company shown in Exhibit 14–6.

The substantial increase in selling expenses presumably reflects greater selling effort during 2007 in an attempt to improve sales volume. However, the fact that selling expenses increased $42,000 while gross profit increased only $40,000 indicates that the cost of this increased sales effort was not justified in terms of results. Even more bothersome is the increase in general and administrative expenses. Some growth in administrative expenses might be expected to accompany increased sales volume, but because some of the expenses are fixed, the growth generally should be *less than proportional* to any increase in sales. The increase in general and administrative expenses from 12.7 percent to 14 percent of sales should be of concern to informed investors.

Management generally has greater control over operating expenses than over revenue. The *operating expense ratio* is often used as a measure of management's ability to control its operating expenses. We show the unfavorable trend in this ratio for Seacliff Company in Exhibit 14–13.

	2007	2006
Operating expenses	(a) $243,000	$170,000
Net sales	(b) $900,000	$750,000
Operating expense ratio (a ÷ b)	27.0%	22.7%

Exhibit 14–13
OPERATING EXPENSE RATIO

Does a higher operating expense ratio indicate higher net income?

If management were able to increase the sales volume while at the same time increasing the gross profit rate and decreasing the operating expense ratio, the effect on net income could be dramatic. For example, if in the year 2008 Seacliff Company can increase its sales by approximately 11 percent, to $1,000,000, increase its gross profit rate from 41.1 to 44 percent, and reduce the operating expense ratio from 27 to 24 percent, its operating income will increase from $127,000 to $200,000 ($1,000,000 − $560,000 − $240,000), an increase of over 57 percent.

RETURN ON INVESTMENT (ROI)

The rate of return on investment (often called ROI) is a measure of management's efficiency in using available resources. Regardless of the size of the organization, capital is a scarce resource and must be used efficiently. In judging the performance of branch managers or of companywide management, it is reasonable to raise the question: What rate of return have you earned on the resources under your control?

Return on Assets An important test of management's ability to earn a return on funds supplied from all sources is the rate of return on total assets.

As noted previously, the income figure used in computing this ratio should be *operating income*, since interest expense and income taxes are determined by factors other than the efficient use of resources. Operating income is earned throughout the year and therefore should be related to the *average* investment in assets during the year. In Exhibit 14–14, the computation of this ratio of Seacliff Company assumes total assets at the beginning of 2006 were $820,000.

Exhibit 14–14

PERCENTAGE RETURN ON ASSETS

Earnings related to investment in assets

	2007	2006
Operating income	(a) $127,000	$160,000
Total assets, beginning of year	(b) $860,000	$820,000
Total assets, end of year	(c) $950,000	$860,000
Average investment in assets [(b + c) ÷ 2]	(d) $905,000	$840,000
Return on assets (a ÷ d)	14%	19%

This ratio shows that the rate of return earned on the company's assets fell in 2007. Before drawing conclusions as to the effectiveness of Seacliff's management, however, we should consider the trend in the return on assets earned by other companies of similar kind and size.

Return on Common Stockholders' Equity We introduced the concept of return on equity using a company that had only one class of capital stock. Therefore, the return on equity was simply net income divided by average stockholders' equity. But Seacliff has issued both preferred stock *and* common stock. The preferred stock does not participate fully in the company's earnings; rather, the return to preferred stockholders is limited to their dividend. Thus, we must adjust the return on equity computation to reflect the return on *common* stockholders' equity.

The return to common stockholders is equal to net income *less* any preferred dividends. Thus the return on common stockholders' equity, assuming common stockholders' equity at the beginning of 2006 was $355,000, is computed in Exhibit 14–15.

Exhibit 14–15

RETURN ON COMMON STOCKHOLDERS' EQUITY

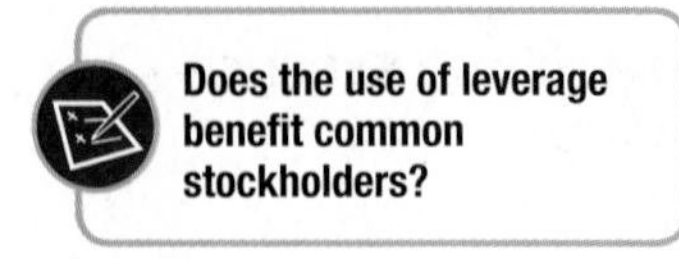
Does the use of leverage benefit common stockholders?

	2007	2006
Net income	$ 75,000	$ 90,000
Less: Preferred dividend requirements	9,000	9,000
Net income applicable to common stock	(a) $ 66,000	$ 81,000
Common stockholders' equity, beginning of year	(b) $416,000	$355,000
Common stockholders' equity, end of year	(c) $538,000	$416,000
Average common stockholders' equity [(b + c) ÷ 2]	(d) $477,000	$385,500
Return on common stockholders' equity (a ÷ d)	13.8%	21.0%

In both years, the rate of return on common stockholders' equity was higher than the 12 percent rate of interest paid to long-term creditors or the 9 percent dividend rate paid to preferred stockholders. This result was achieved through the favorable use of leverage.

LEVERAGE

Applying leverage means using borrowed money to earn a return *greater* than the cost of borrowing, increasing net income and the return on common stockholders' equity. In other words, if you can borrow money at 12 percent and use it to earn 20 percent, you will benefit by doing so. However, leverage can act as a double-edged sword; the effects may be favorable or unfavorable to the holders of common stock.

If the rate of return on total assets should fall *below* the average rate of interest on borrowed capital, leverage will *reduce* the return on common stockholders' equity. In this situation, paying off the loans that carry high interest rates would appear to be a logical move. However, many companies do not have enough cash to retire long-term debt on short notice. Therefore, the common stockholders may become locked in to the unfavorable effects of leverage.

In deciding how much leverage is appropriate, the common stockholders should consider the *stability* of the company's return on assets as well as the relationship of this return to the average cost of borrowed capital. If a business incurs so much debt that it becomes unable to meet the required interest and principal payments, the creditors may force liquidation or reorganization of the business.

Debt Ratio One indicator of the amount of leverage used by a business is the debt ratio. This ratio measures the proportion of the total assets financed by creditors, as distinguished from stockholders. It is computed by dividing total liabilities by total assets. A *high* debt ratio indicates an extensive use of leverage, that is, a large proportion of financing provided by creditors. A low debt ratio, on the other hand, indicates that the business is making little use of leverage.

The debt ratio at year-end for Seacliff is determined as shown in Exhibit 14–16.

	2007	2006
Total liabilities	(a) $312,000	$344,000
Total assets (or total liabilities & stockholders' equity)	(b) $950,000	$860,000
Debt ratio (a ÷ b)	32.8%	40.0%

Exhibit 14–16
DEBT RATIO

Proportion of assets financed by creditors

Seacliff Company has a lower debt ratio in 2007 than in 2006. Is this favorable or unfavorable?

From the viewpoint of the common stockholder, a high debt ratio produces maximum benefits if management is able to earn a rate of return on assets greater than the rate of interest paid to creditors. However, a high debt ratio can be *unfavorable* if the return on assets falls *below* the rate of interest paid to creditors. Since the return on total assets earned by Seacliff Company has declined from 19 percent in 2006 to a relatively low 14 percent in 2007, the common stockholders probably would *not* want to risk a high debt ratio. The action by management in 2007 of retiring $50,000 in long-term liabilities will help to protect the common stockholders from the unfavorable effects of leverage if the rate of return on assets continues to decline.

CASE IN POINT

Dell Inc. provides an interesting case study in how financial leverage can be used to greatly increase the returns earned by common stockholders without appreciably increasing the company's risk profile. **Dell**'s 2004 return on assets is an impressive 20 percent, but its return on common equity is an eye-popping 47 percent. Clearly **Dell** has benefited from favorable financial leverage.

Moreover, **Dell** has benefited from favorable financial leverage without increasing its risk profile. That is, most of **Dell**'s leverage is in the form of *non-interest*-bearing liabilities. Although liabilities comprise 67.5 percent of **Dell**'s assets, *interest-bearing* liabilities represent only 2.6 percent of assets. Approximately 84 percent of **Dell**'s liabilities are current, representing either trade credit (accounts payable) or accrued liabilities (e.g., unpaid salaries and benefits). In essence, much of **Dell**'s financing is provided by its creditors and employees, which are essentially free sources of financing.

ANALYSIS BY LONG-TERM CREDITORS

Bondholders and other long-term creditors are primarily interested in three factors: (1) the rate of return on their investment, (2) the firm's ability to meet its interest requirements, and (3) the firm's ability to repay the principal of the debt when it falls due.

Yield Rate on Bonds

The yield rate on bonds or other long-term indebtedness cannot be computed in the same manner as the yield rate on shares of stock, because bonds, unlike stocks, have a definite maturity date and amount. The ownership of a 12 percent, 10-year, $1,000 bond represents the right to receive $120 each year for 10 years plus the right to receive $1,000 at the end of 10 years. If the market price of this bond is $950, the yield rate on an investment in the bond is the rate of interest that will make the *present value* of these two contractual rights equal to the $950 market price.

When bonds sell at maturity value, the yield rate is equal to the bond interest rate. *The yield rate varies inversely with changes in the market price of the bond.* If interest rates rise, the market price of existing bonds will fall; if interest rates decline, the price of bonds will rise. If the price of a bond is above maturity value, the yield rate is less than the bond interest rate; if the price of a bond is below maturity value, the yield rate is higher than the bond interest rate.

Interest Coverage Ratio

Bondholders feel that their investments are relatively safe if the issuing company earns enough income to cover its annual interest obligations by a comfortable margin.

A common measure of creditors' safety is the ratio of operating income available for the payment of interest to the annual interest expense, called the *interest coverage ratio* or *times interest earned.* See this computation for Seacliff Company in Exhibit 14–17.

Exhibit 14–17
INTEREST COVERAGE RATIO

	2007	2006
Operating income (before interest and income taxes)	(a) $127,000	$160,000
Annual interest expense	(b) $ 24,000	$ 30,000
Interest coverage (a ÷ b)	5.3 times	5.3 times

The ratio remained unchanged at a satisfactory level during 2007. Generally an interest coverage ratio above 2.0 is considered strong.

Debt Ratio

Long-term creditors are interested in the percentage of total assets financed by debt, as distinguished from the percentage financed by stockholders. The percentage of total assets financed by debt is measured by the debt ratio, which was computed in Exhibit 14–16.

From a creditor's viewpoint, the lower the debt ratio, the better, since this means that stockholders have contributed a higher percentage of the funds to the business, and therefore the margin of protection to creditors against a shrinkage of the assets is high.

As shown in Exhibit 14–16, the debt ratio, or the percentage of assets financed by debt, decreased from 2006 to 2007 from 40 percent to 32.8 percent. This would generally be considered by long-term creditors to be a favorable change because the debt burden, including required interest payments, is less in 2007 than in 2006, thereby making the claim of each creditor more secure.

Secured Claims

Sometimes the claims of long-term creditors are secured with specific collateral, such as the land and buildings owned by the borrower. In these situations, the secured creditors may look primarily to the *value of the collateral* in assessing the safety of their claims.

Assets pledged as collateral to secure specific liabilities are disclosed in notes to the financial statements. As Seacliff makes no such disclosures, we may assume that none of its assets have been pledged as collateral to secure specific liabilities.

ANALYSIS BY SHORT-TERM CREDITORS

Bankers and other short-term creditors share the interest of stockholders and bondholders in the profitability and long-run stability of a business. Their primary interest, however, is in the current position of the company—its ability to generate sufficient funds (working capital) to meet current operating needs and to pay current debts promptly. Thus the analysis of financial statements by a banker considering a short-term loan, or by a trade creditor investigating the credit status of a customer, is likely to center on the working capital position of the prospective debtor.

Amount of Working Capital Working capital is the excess of current assets over current liabilities. It represents the cash and near-cash assets that provide a "cushion" of liquidity over the amount expected to be needed in the near future to satisfy maturing obligations. The details of the working capital of Seacliff Company are shown in Exhibit 14–18.

Exhibit 14–18 SEACLIFF SCHEDULE OF WORKING CAPITAL

SEACLIFF COMPANY
Comparative Schedule of Working Capital
As of December 31, 2007, and December 31, 2006

			Increase or (Decrease)		Percentage of Total Current Items	
	2007	2006	Dollars	%	2007	2006
Current assets:						
Cash	$ 38,000	$ 40,000	$ (2,000)	(5.0)	9.7	13.9
Receivables (net)	117,000	86,000	31,000	36.0	30.0	29.9
Inventories	180,000	120,000	60,000	50.0	46.2	41.6*
Prepaid expenses	55,000	42,000	13,000	31.0	14.1	14.6
Total current assets	$390,000	$288,000	$102,000	35.4	100.0	100.0
Current liabilities:						
Notes payable to creditors	$ 14,600	$ 10,000	$ 4,600	46.0	13.1*	10.7*
Accounts payable	66,000	30,000	36,000	120.0	58.9	31.9
Accrued liabilities	31,400	54,000	(22,600)	(41.9)	28.0	57.4
Total current liabilities	$112,000	$ 94,000	$ 18,000	19.1	100.0	100.0
Working capital	$278,000	$194,000	$ 84,000	43.3		

*Amounts adjusted so that totals equal 100.0.

This schedule shows that current assets increased $102,000, while current liabilities rose by only $18,000. As a result, working capital increased $84,000.

Quality of Working Capital In evaluating the debt-paying ability of a business, short-term creditors should consider the quality of working capital as well as the total dollar amount. The principal factors affecting the quality of working capital are (1) the nature of the current assets and (2) the length of time required to convert those assets into cash.

The schedule in Exhibit 14–18 shows an unfavorable shift in the composition of Seacliff Company's working capital during 2007: cash decreased from 13.9 percent to 9.7 percent of current assets, while inventory rose from 41.6 percent to 46.2 percent. Inventory is a less liquid resource than cash. Therefore, the quality of working capital is not as liquid as in 2006. *Turnover rates* (or *ratios*) may be used to assist short-term creditors in estimating the time required to turn assets such as receivables and inventory into cash.

Accounts Receivable Turnover Rate As explained in Chapter 7, the accounts receivable turnover rate indicates how quickly a company converts its accounts receivable into cash. The accounts receivable turnover *rate* is determined by dividing net sales by the average balance of accounts receivable.[5] The number of *days* required (on average) to collect accounts receivable then may be determined by dividing the number of days in a year (365) by the turnover rate. The computations in Exhibit 14–19 use the data in our Seacliff example, assuming accounts receivable at the beginning of 2006 were $80,000.

Exhibit 14–19
ACCOUNTS RECEIVABLE TURNOVER

Are customers paying promptly?

	2007	2006
Net sales	(a) $900,000	$750,000
Receivables, beginning of year	$ 86,000	$ 80,000
Receivables, end of year	$117,000	$ 86,000
Average receivables	(b) $101,500	$ 83,000
Receivable turnover per year (a ÷ b)	8.9 times	9.0 times
Average number of days to collect receivables (divide 365 days by receivable turnover)	41 days	41 days

There has been no change in the average time required to collect receivables. The interpretation of the average age of receivables depends upon the company's credit terms and the seasonal activity immediately before year-end. For example, if the company grants 30-day credit terms to its customers, the analysis in Exhibit 14–19 indicates that accounts receivable collections are lagging. If the terms are for 60 days, however, collections are being made ahead of schedule.

Inventory Turnover Rate The inventory turnover rate indicates how many times during the year the company is able to sell a quantity of goods equal to its average inventory. Mechanically, this rate is determined by dividing the cost of goods sold for the year by the average amount of inventory on hand during the year. The number of days required to sell this amount of inventory may be determined by dividing 365 days by the turnover rate. These computations were explained in Chapter 8 and are demonstrated in Exhibit 14–20 using the data of Seacliff Company, assuming inventory at the beginning of 2006 was $100,000. The trend indicated by this analysis is unfavorable, since the length of time required for Seacliff to turn over (sell) its inventory is increasing.

Exhibit 14–20
INVENTORY TURNOVER

	2007	2006
Cost of goods sold	(a) $530,000	$420,000
Inventory, beginning of year	$120,000	$100,000
Inventory, end of year	$180,000	$120,000
Average inventory	(b) $150,000	$110,000
Average inventory turnover per year (a ÷ b)	3.5 times	3.8 times
Average number of days to sell inventory (divide 365 days by inventory turnover)	104 days	96 days

Companies that have low gross profit rates often need high inventory turnover rates in order to operate profitably. This is another way of saying that if the gross profit rate is low, a high volume of transactions is necessary to produce a satisfactory amount of profits. Companies that sell high markup items, such as jewelry stores and art galleries, can operate successfully with much lower inventory turnover rates.

Operating Cycle The inventory turnover rate indicates how quickly inventory *sells*, but not how quickly this asset converts into *cash*. Short-term creditors, of course, are interested primarily in the company's ability to generate cash.

The period of time required for a merchandising company to convert its inventory into cash is called the *operating cycle*. The illustration appeared in Chapter 6 and is repeated in Exhibit 14–21 for your convenience.

[5] Ideally, the accounts receivable turnover is computed by dividing net *credit* sales by the *monthly* average of receivables. Such detailed information, however, generally is not provided in annual financial statements.

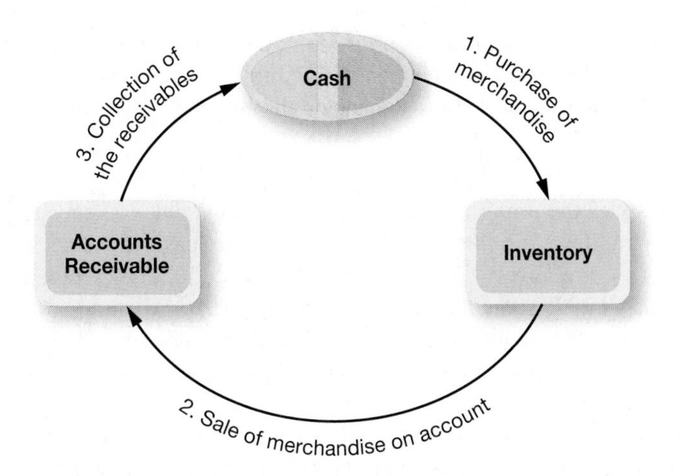

Exhibit 14–21
OPERATING CYCLE

The operating cycle repeats continuously

Seacliff's operating cycle in 2007 was approximately 145 days, computed by adding the 104 days required to turn over inventory and the average 41 days required to collect receivables. This compares to an operating cycle of only 137 days in 2006, computed as 96 days to dispose of the inventory plus 41 days to collect the resulting receivables. From the viewpoint of short-term creditors, the *shorter* the operating cycle, the *higher the quality* of the borrower's working capital. Therefore, these creditors would regard the lengthening of Seacliff Company's operating cycle as an unfavorable trend.

Current Ratio The current ratio expresses the relationship between current assets and current liabilities. A strong current ratio provides considerable evidence that a company will be able to meet its obligations coming due in the near future. The current ratio for Seacliff Company is computed in Exhibit 14–22.

	2007	2006
Total current assets	(a) $390,000	$288,000
Total current liabilities	(b) $112,000	$ 94,000
Current ratio (a ÷ b)	3.5	3.1

Exhibit 14–22
CURRENT RATIO

Does this indicate satisfactory debt-paying ability?

Quick Ratio Because inventories and prepaid expenses are further removed from conversion into cash than other current assets, the *quick ratio* is sometimes computed as a supplement to the current ratio. The quick ratio compares the most liquid current assets (cash, marketable securities, and receivables) with current liabilities. Seacliff Company has no marketable securities; its quick ratio is computed in Exhibit 14–23.

	2007	2006
Quick assets (cash and receivables)	(a) $155,000	$126,000
Current liabilities	(b) $112,000	$ 94,000
Quick ratio (a ÷ b)	1.4	1.3

Exhibit 14–23
QUICK RATIO

A measure of liquidity

Here again the analysis reveals a favorable trend and a strong position. If the credit periods extended to customers and granted by creditors are roughly equal, a quick ratio of 1.0 or better is considered satisfactory.

Unused Lines of Credit From the viewpoint of a short-term creditor, a company's unused lines of credit represent a resource almost as liquid as cash. An unused line of credit means that a bank has agreed in advance to lend the company any amount, up to the specified limit. As long as this line of credit remains available, creditors know that the business can borrow cash quickly and easily for any purpose, including payments of creditors' claims.

Existing unused lines of credit are *disclosed* in notes accompanying the financial statements. See Note 2 to the financial statements in Exhibit 14–10. Short-term creditors would view Seacliff's $35,000 line of credit as enhancing the company's liquidity.

CASH FLOW ANALYSIS

We often have stressed the importance of a company's being able to generate sufficient cash flows from its operations. In 2006, Seacliff generated net cash flows of $95,000 from its operating activities—a relatively "normal" amount, considering that net income for the year was $90,000. This $95,000 remained *after* payment of interest to creditors and amounted to more than three times the dividends paid to stockholders. Thus in 2006 the net cash flows from operating activities appeared quite sufficient to ensure that Seacliff could pay its interest obligations and also pay dividends.

In 2007, however, net cash flows from operating activities declined to $19,000, an amount far below the company's $75,000 net income and only approximately 58 percent of the amount of dividends paid. Stockholders and creditors would view this dramatic decline in cash flows as a negative and potentially dangerous development.

A reconciliation of Seacliff's net income in 2007 with its net cash flows from operating activities is shown in Exhibit 14–24. For purposes of this analysis, we assume that the notes payable to creditors resulted from purchases from suppliers rather than loans from a financial institution. Therefore, the increase in notes payable is treated in the same way as the increase in accounts payable as part of the reconciliation of net income to net cash from operating activities. Had the notes payable resulted from borrowing activities, the change would be classified as a financing activity and not as an adjustment to net income in determining net cash from operating activities.

Exhibit 14–24

SEACLIFF RECONCILIATION OF NET INCOME TO NET CASH FROM OPERATING ACTIVITIES

Net income		$ 75,000
Add:		
Depreciation expense	$30,000	
Increase in notes payable to creditors	4,600	
Increase in accounts payable	36,000	70,600
		$145,600
Less:		
Increase in accounts receivable	$31,000	
Increase in inventories	60,000	
Increase in prepaid expenses	13,000	
Decrease in accrued liabilities	22,600	126,600
Net cash flows from operating activities		$ 19,000

As explained in Chapter 13, the FASB requires companies to provide this reconciliation either in the body of the statement of cash flows or in a supplemental schedule.

The primary reasons for Seacliff's low net operating cash flows appear to be the growth in uncollected accounts receivable and inventories, combined with the substantial reduction in accrued liabilities. Given the significant increase in sales during 2007, the increase in accounts receivable is to be expected. The large reduction in accrued liabilities may be a one-time event that will not necessarily recur next year. The large increase in inventory, however, may have reduced Seacliff's liquidity unnecessarily.

Seacliff's financial position, particularly its short-term liquidity, would appear considerably stronger if its increased sales volume were supported by a higher *inventory turnover rate*, instead of a larger inventory.

Cash Flows from Operations to Current Liabilities

An additional measure of liquidity that is sometimes computed, based in part on information from the statement of cash flows, is the ratio of cash flows from operations to current liabilities. This measure provides evidence of the company's ability to cover its currently maturing liabilities from normal operations. For 2006 and 2007, the ratio is computed for Seacliff Corporation in Exhibit 14–25.

Exhibit 14–25
CASH FLOWS FROM OPERATIONS TO CURRENT LIABILITIES

	2007	2006
Cash flows from operations	(a) $ 19,000	$95,000
Current liabilities	(b) $112,000	$94,000
Cash flows from operations to current liabilities (a ÷ b)	.17	1.01

As you can see from this measure, Seacliff was much stronger in 2006 than in 2007. In 2006, operating cash flows were slightly more than current liabilities at year-end, indicating an ability to cover current obligations from normal operations without regard to the amount of existing current assets. In 2007, however, operations provided only 17 percent as much cash as needed to meet current obligations, implying a need to rely more heavily on existing current assets than in 2006. Generally a ratio of cash flows from operations to current liabilities of .40 or higher is considered strong.

USEFULNESS OF NOTES TO FINANCIAL STATEMENTS

A set of financial statements normally is accompanied by several *notes*, disclosing information useful in *interpreting* the statements. Users should view these notes as an *integral part* of the financial statements.

In preceding chapters we have identified many items that are disclosed in notes accompanying the financial statements. Among the most useful are the following:

- Accounting policies and methods
- Unused lines of credit
- Significant commitments and loss contingencies
- Current values of financial instruments (if different from the carrying values shown in the statements)
- Dividends in arrears
- Concentrations of credit risk
- Assets pledged to secure specific liabilities

In Exhibit 14–10 the notes accompanying Seacliff's financial statements are quite clean—that is, they contain no surprises or cause for concern. Of course, the unused line of credit disclosed in Note 2 would be of interest to anyone evaluating the company's short-term debt-paying ability.

YOUR TURN **You as a Financial Analyst**

Assume that you are a financial analyst and that two of your clients are requesting your advice on certain companies as potential investments. Both clients are interested in purchasing common stock. One is primarily interested in the dividends to be received from the investment. The second is primarily interested in the growth of the market value of the stock. What information would you advise your clients to focus on in their respective analyses?

(See our comments on the Online Learning Center Web site.)

SUMMARY OF ANALYTICAL MEASUREMENTS

The financial ratios and other measurements introduced in this textbook thus far, including this chapter—and their significance—are summarized in Exhibit 14–26.

Exhibit 14–26 SUMMARY OF ANALYTICAL MEASURES

Ratios or Other Measurements	Method of Computation	Significance
Measures of short-term liquidity		
Current ratio	$\frac{\text{Current Assets}}{\text{Current Liabilities}}$	A measure of short-term debt-paying ability
Quick ratio	$\frac{\text{Quick Assets}}{\text{Current Liabilities}}$	A measure of short-term debt-paying ability
Working capital	Current Assets − Current Liabilities	A measure of short-term debt-paying ability
Net cash provided by operating activities	Appears in the statement of cash flows	Indicates the cash generated by operations after allowing for cash payment of expenses and operating liabilities
Cash flow from operations to current liabilities	$\frac{\text{Cash Flows from Operating Activities}}{\text{Current Liabilities}}$	Indicates ability to cover currently maturing obligations from recurring operations
Receivables turnover rate	$\frac{\text{Net Sales}}{\text{Average Accounts Receivable}}$	Indicates how quickly receivables are collected
Days to collect average accounts receivable	$\frac{\text{365 Days}}{\text{Receivables Turnover Rate}}$	Indicates in days how quickly receivables are collected
Inventory turnover rate	$\frac{\text{Cost of Goods Sold}}{\text{Average Inventory}}$	Indicates how quickly inventory sells
Days to sell the average inventory	$\frac{\text{365 Days}}{\text{Inventory Turnover Rate}}$	Indicates in days how quickly inventory sells
Operating cycle	Days to Sell Inventory + Days to Collect Receivables	Indicates in days how quickly cash invested in inventory converts back into cash
Free cash flow	Net Cash from Operating Activities − Cash Used for Investing Activities and Dividends	Excess of operating cash flow over basic needs
Measures of long-term credit risk		
Debt ratio	$\frac{\text{Total Liabilities}}{\text{Total Assets}}$	Percentage of assets financed by creditors; indicates relative size of the equity position
Trend in net cash provided by operating activities	Appears in comparative statements of cash flows	Indicator of a company's ability to generate the cash necessary to meet its obligations
Interest coverage ratio	$\frac{\text{Income before Interest and Taxes}}{\text{Annual Interest Expense}}$	Indicator of a company's ability to meet its interest payment obligations
Measures of profitability		
Percentage changes; that is, in net sales and net income	$\frac{\text{Dollar Amount of Change}}{\text{Financial Statement Amount in the Earlier Year}}$	The rate at which a key measure is increasing or decreasing; the "growth rate"
Gross profit rate	$\frac{\text{Gross Profit}}{\text{Net Sales}}$	A measure of the profitability of the company's products
Operating expense ratio	$\frac{\text{Operating Expenses}}{\text{Net Sales}}$	A measure of management's ability to control expenses
Operating income	Gross Profit − Operating Expenses	The profitability of a company's basic business activities
Net income as a percentage of net sales	$\frac{\text{Net Income}}{\text{Net Sales}}$	An indicator of management's ability to control costs
Earnings per share	$\frac{\text{Net Income − Preferred Dividends}}{\text{Average Number of Common Shares Outstanding}}$	Net income applicable to each share of common stock

(continued on next page)

Ratios or Other Measurements	Method of Computation	Significance
Return on assets	Operating Income / Average Total Assets	A measure of the productivity of assets, regardless of how the assets are financed
Return on equity	Net Income / Average Total Equity	The rate of return earned on the stockholders' equity in the business
Return on common stockholders' equity	Net Income − Preferred Dividends / Average Common Stockholders' Equity	The rate of return earned on the common stockholders' equity; appropriate when company has both common and preferred stock
Measures for evaluating the current market price of common stock		
Market value of financial instruments	Quoted in financial press or disclosed in financial statements	Reflects both investors' expectations and current market conditions
Price-earnings ratio	Current Stock Price / Earnings per Share	A measure of investors' expectations about the company's future prospects
Dividend yield	Annual Dividend / Current Stock Price	Dividends expressed as a rate of return on the market price of the stock
Book value per share	Common Stockholders' Equity / Shares of Common Stock Outstanding	The recorded value of net assets underlying each share of common stock

Ethics, Fraud & Corporate Governance

As discussed in this chapter, investors and creditors analyze financial statements to help them decide whether to invest in the equity securities of a company and whether to loan a company funds. The tools discussed in this chapter involve using financial statement numbers to help make investment and credit decisions. Given the high-profile accounting frauds of the early 2000s and the resulting focus on corporate governance, a new type of tool has arisen to help investors and creditors make investment decisions. This new tool involves ratings of the quality of a company's corporate governance. Many investors and creditors believe that better-governed firms are better managed, and that these firms will either offer superior performance (returns) over time and/or will offer returns comparable to less well governed firms but with less risk. Although the research literature is mixed as to whether better-governed firms produce superior returns, the literature generally finds that firms with weak governance suggest greater risk, particularly the risk associated with fraudulent financial reporting.

A number of organizations provide ratings of corporate governance quality for public companies. Two of the most prominent of these organizations are **Institutional Shareholder Services (ISS)** and **The Corporate Library**.

ISS (Rockville, Maryland) describes itself as the "world's leading provider of proxy voting and corporate governance services." **ISS** has more than 1,600 institutional and corporate clients. These clients hire **ISS** to analyze corporate proxy statements and to make recommendations on the manner in which these institutional and corporate clients should vote on matters subject to shareholder ratification. For example, shareholders typically must approve mergers and acquisitions. A few years ago **Hewlett-Packard (HP)** was interested in buying **Compaq**. A descendant of the founders—an influential shareholder at **HP**—opposed the **Compaq** acquisition and actively campaigned to convince other **HP** shareholders to oppose the transaction. On the other side of the debate, **HP**'s management, led by its CEO—Carly Fiorina—was actively campaigning for the acquisition of **Compaq**. There was substantial uncertainty as to whether **HP**'s shareholders would approve the **Compaq** acquisition, and both sides tried to convince **ISS** to support their position. **ISS** ultimately supported the acquisition, which was approved by **HP**'s shareholders, and was credited by many in the business press with turning the outcome in favor of **HP**'s management.

ISS rates the quality of a company's corporate governance by computing a Corporate Governance Quotient (CGQ). The CGQ is designed to assess the quality of a company's board of

(continued)

directors and to assess the likely impact of a company's governance practices on performance. ISS computes CGQs for more than 7,500 companies worldwide. A company's CGQ is based on its ratings in these eight core categories: (1) board of directors, (2) audit, (3) charter and bylaw provisions, (4) anti-takeover provisions, (5) executive and director compensation, (6) qualitative factors, (7) ownership, and (8) director education. ISS gathers data for 63 items in these eight categories in computing a company's CGQ. A listing of the 63 data items considered by ISS is reproduced below.

U.S. CGQ Rating Criteria

Note that some of the ratings factors are also looked at in combination under the premise that corporate governance is enhanced when selected combinations of these criteria are adopted.

Board

1	Board Composition
2	Nominating Committee
3	Compensation Committee
4	Governance Committee
5	Board Structure
6	Board Size
7	Changes In Board Size
8	Cumulative Voting
9	Boards Served On—CEO
10	Boards Served On—Other Than CEO
11	Former CEO's
12	Chairman/CEO Separation
13	Governance Guidelines
14	Response To Shareholder Proposals
15	Board Attendance
16	Board Vacancies
17	Related Party Transactions—CEO
18	Related Party Transactions—Other than CEO

Audit

19	Audit Committee
20	Audit Committee—Financial Experts
21	Audit Fees
22	Auditor Ratification

Charter / Bylaws

23	Poison Pill Adoption
24–28	Features of Poison Pills
29	Vote Requirements—Charter/Bylaw amendments
30	Vote Requirements—Approval of Mergers
31	Written Consent
32	Special Meetings
33	Board Amendments
34	Capital Structure—Dual Class
35	Capital Structure—Blank Check Preferred

State of Incorporation

36–42	State Anti-takeover Provisions

Executive and Director Compensation

43	Cost of Option Plans
44	Option Re-pricing Permitted in Plan?
45	Shareholder Approval of Option Plans
46	Compensation Committee Interlocks
47	Director Compensation
48	Option Expensing
49	Option Burn Rate
50	Performance Based Compensation

Qualitative Factors

51	Board Performance Reviews
52	Individual Director Performance Reviews
53	Meetings of Outside Directors
54	CEO Succession Plan
55	Directors Resign Upon Job Change
56	Outside Advisors Available to Board

Ownership

57	Director Ownership
58	Executive Stock Ownership Guidelines
59	Director Stock Ownership Guidelines
60	Officer and Director Stock Ownership
61	Mandatory Holding Period for Options
62	Mandatory Holding Period for Restricted Stock

Director Education

63	Director Education

CGQ is a registered trademark of Institutional Shareholder Services Inc.

The Corporate Library (TCL) (Portland, Maine) is a more recent entrant into the market for rating governance effectiveness. TCL was founded in 1999 by Nell Minow and Robert A. G. Monks, arguably the two pioneers in the corporate governance movement in the United States. To paraphrase the noted country singer Barbara Mandrell—Minow and Monks were governance when governance wasn't cool.

Unlike ISS, TCL claims that its "proprietary dynamic indicators go beyond conventional benchmarks for good corporate governance." Many rating systems are based on a company's compliance with governance practices perceived as "best practices"; TCL attempts to differentiate its rating system by focusing only on those board characteristics that its proprietary research has found to be associated with preserving and enhancing shareholder wealth. TCL considers a company's governance in these seven key areas: (1) board composition, (2) CEO compensation, (3) shareholder responsiveness, (4) accounting, (5) strategic decision making, (6) litigation and regulatory problems, and (7) takeover defenses.

An interesting feature of TCL's Web site is its listing of the 10 worst large U.S. corporate boards.

Concluding Remarks

For the most part, our discussion in this chapter has been limited to the kinds of analysis that can be performed by external users who do not have access to the company's accounting records. Investors and creditors must rely to a considerable extent on the financial statements published in annual and quarterly reports. In the case of publicly owned corporations, additional information is filed with the Securities and Exchange Commission (SEC) and is available to the public in hard copy, as well as on the Internet. In fact, the Internet is the fastest growing source of *free* information available to decision makers in this information age.

Many financial analysts who evaluate the financial statements and future prospects of publicly owned companies sell their conclusions and investment recommendations for a fee. For example, detailed financial analyses of most large companies are available from **Standard & Poor's**, **Moody's Investors Service**, and **The Value Line Investment Survey**. Anyone may subscribe to these investment services.

Bankers and major creditors usually are able to obtain detailed financial information from borrowers simply by requesting it as a condition for granting a loan. Suppliers and other trade creditors may obtain some financial information about almost any business from credit-rating agencies, such as **Dun & Bradstreet**.

Stock prices, like p/e ratios, are a *measure of investors' expectations*. A company may be highly profitable and growing fast. But if investors had expected even better performance, the market price of its stock may decline. Similarly, if a troubled company's losses are smaller than expected, the price of its stock may rise.

In financial circles, evaluating stock price by looking at the underlying profitability of the company is termed **fundamental analysis**. This approach to investing works better in the long run than in the short run. In the short run, stock prices can be significantly affected by many factors, including short-term interest rates, current events, political events, fads, and rumors. But in the long run, good companies increase in value.

END-OF-CHAPTER REVIEW

SUMMARY OF LEARNING OBJECTIVES

LO1 Explain the uses of dollar and percentage changes, trend percentages, component percentages, and ratios. An important aspect of financial statement analysis is determining relevant relationships among specific items of information. Companies typically present financial information for more than one time period, which permits users of the information to make comparisons that help them understand changes over time. Dollar and percentage changes and trend percentages are tools for comparing information from successive time periods. Component percentages and ratios, on the other hand, are tools for establishing relationships and making comparisons within an accounting period. Both types of comparisons are important in understanding an enterprise's financial position, results of operations, and cash flows.

LO2 Discuss the quality of a company's earnings, assets, and working capital. Assessing the quality of information is an important aspect of financial statement analysis. Enterprises have significant latitude in the selection of financial reporting methods within generally accepted accounting principles. Assessing the quality of a company's earnings, assets, and working capital is done by evaluating the accounting methods selected for use in preparing financial statements. Management's choice of accounting principles and methods that are in the best long-term interests of the company, even though they may currently result in lower net income, reported total assets, or working capital, leads to a conclusion of high quality in reported accounting information.

LO3 Explain the nature and purpose of classifications in financial statements. In classified financial statements, items with certain common characteristics are placed together in a group, or classification. The purpose of these classifications is to develop subtotals that will assist users in analyzing the financial statements.

LO4 Prepare a classified balance sheet and compute widely used measures of liquidity and credit risk. In a classified balance sheet, assets are subdivided into the categories of current assets, plant and equipment, and other assets. Liabilities are classified either as current or long-term.

The liquidity measures derived from the balance sheet are as follows:

Working capital. Current assets minus current liabilities.

Current ratio. Current assets divided by current liabilities.

Quick ratio. Quick assets divided by current liabilities.

A measure of long-term credit risk is the debt ratio, which is total liabilities expressed as a percentage of (divided by) total assets.

LO5 Prepare a multiple-step and a single-step income statement and compute widely used measures of profitability. In a multiple-step income statement, the cost of goods sold is deducted from net sales to provide the subtotal, gross profit. Operating expenses then are deducted to arrive at income from operations. As a final step, nonoperating items are added together and subtracted from income from operations to arrive at net income. In a single-step income statement, all revenue items are listed first, and then all expenses are combined and deducted from total revenue.

The profitability measures discussed in this chapter are as follows:

Percentage change. The dollar amount of change in a financial statement item from one period to the next, expressed as a percentage of (divided by) the item value in the earlier of the two periods being compared.

Gross profit rate. Dollar amount of gross profit divided by net sales. A measure of the profitability of a company's products.

Net income as a percentage of sales. Net income divided by net sales. A measure of management's ability to control expenses.

Earnings per share. In the simplest case, net income divided by shares of capital stock outstanding. Indicates the earnings applicable to each share of stock.

Price-earnings ratio. Market price of the stock divided by earnings per share. A measure of investors' expectations regarding future profitability.

Return on assets. Operating income divided by average total assets. Measures the return generated by assets, regardless of how the assets are financed.

Return on equity. Net income divided by average total equity. Indicates the rate of return earned on owners' equity.

LO6 Put a company's net income into perspective by relating it to sales, assets, and stockholders' equity. Financial accounting information is most useful if viewed in comparison with other relevant information. Net income is an important measure of the financial success of an enterprise. To make the amount of net income even more useful than if it were viewed simply in isolation, it is often compared with the sales from which net income results, the assets used to generate the income, and the amount of stockholders' equity invested by owners to earn the net income.

LO7 Compute the ratios widely used in financial statement analysis and explain the significance of each. Ratios are mathematical calculations that compare one financial statement item with another financial statement item. The two items may come from the same financial statement, such as the current ratio, which compares the amount of current assets with the amount of current liabilities, both of which appear in the statement of financial position (balance sheet). On the other hand, the items may come from two different financial statements, such as the return on stockholders' equity, which compares net income from the income statement with the amount of stockholders' equity from the statement of financial position (balance sheet). Accountants and financial analysts have developed many ratios that place information from a company's financial statements in a context to permit better understanding to support decision making.

LO8 **Analyze financial statements from the viewpoints of common stockholders, creditors, and others.** Different groups of users of financial statements are interested in different aspects of a company's financial activities. Short-term creditors are interested primarily in the company's ability to make cash payments in the short term; they focus their attention on operating cash flows and current assets and liabilities. Long-term creditors, on the other hand, are more interested in the company's long-term ability to pay interest and principal and would not limit their analysis to the company's ability to make cash payments in the immediate future. The focus of common stockholders can vary from one investor to another, but generally stockholders are interested in the company's ability to pay dividends and increase the market value of the stock of the company. Each group may focus on different information in the financial statements to meet its unique objectives.

Key Terms Introduced or Emphasized In Chapter 14

annual report (p. 641) A document issued annually by publicly owned companies to their stockholders. Includes audited comparative financial statements, management's discussion and analysis of performance and liquidity, and other information about the company.

classified financial statements (p. 632) Financial statements in which similar items are arranged in groups, and subtotals are shown to assist users in analyzing the statements.

comparative financial statements (p. 632) Financial statements of one company for two or more years presented in a side-by-side format to facilitate comparison.

consolidated financial statements (p. 632) Financial statements that show the combined activities of a parent company and its subsidiaries.

current assets (p. 637) Cash and other assets that can be converted into cash or used up within one year or the operating cycle (whichever is longer) without interfering with normal business operations.

current liabilities (p. 639) Existing liabilities that are expected to be satisfied by using the enterprise's current assets.

current ratio (p. 639) Current assets divided by current liabilities. A measure of short-term debt-paying ability.

debt ratio (p. 640) Total liabilities divided by total assets. Represents the portion of total assets financed by debt, rather than by equity capital.

earnings per share (p. 646) Net income expressed on a per-share basis.

fundamental analysis (p. 665) Evaluating the reasonableness of a company's stock price by evaluating the performance and financial strength of the company.

management's discussion and analysis (p. 641) A discussion by management of the company's performance during the current year and its financial position at year-end. These discussions are included in the annual reports of publicly owned companies.

market share (p. 644) A company's percentage share of total dollar sales within its industry.

operating cycle (p. 637) The time required to invest cash in inventory, sell the inventory, and collect the receivable, resulting in an increase in cash.

operating income (p. 644) A subtotal in a multiple-step income statement representing the income resulting from the company's principal business activities.

parent company (p. 632) A corporation that does portions of its business through other companies that it owns (termed *subsidiaries*).

percentage change (p. 644) The change in a dollar amount between two accounting periods, expressed as a percentage of the amount in an earlier period. Used in evaluating rates of growth (or decline).

price-earnings (p/e) ratio (p. 646) The current market price of a company's capital stock, expressed as a multiple of earnings per share. Reflects investors' expectations regarding future earnings.

quick assets (p. 640) The most liquid current assets, which include only cash, marketable securities, and receivables.

quick ratio (p. 640) Quick assets (cash, marketable securities, and receivables) divided by current liabilities. A measure of short-term debt-paying ability. (Sometimes referred to as the acid-test ratio.)

return on assets (p. 648) Operating income expressed as a percentage of average total assets. A measure of the efficiency with which management utilizes the assets of a business.

return on equity (p. 648) Net income expressed as a percentage of average total stockholders' equity. A measure of the rate of return earned on the stockholders' equity in the business.

subsidiary (p. 632) A company that is owned and operated by a parent company. In essence, the subsidiary is a part of the parent organization.

window dressing (p. 641) Measures taken by management to make a business look as strong as possible at the balance sheet date.

working capital (p. 639) Current assets less current liabilities. A measure of short-term debt-paying ability.

Demonstration Problem

The following data are adapted from a recent annual report of Walgreen Drug Stores (dollar amounts are stated in millions):

	2005	2004
Balance sheet data:		
Quick assets	$ 2,467.9	$ 2,864.6
Current assets	8,316.5	7,764.4
Current liabilities	4,481.0	4,077.9
Stockholders' equity	8,889.7	8,139.7
Total assets	14,608.8	13,342.1
Income statement data:		
Net sales	$42,201.6	$37,508.2
Gross profit	11,787.8	10,197.8
Operating income	2,424.0	2,142.4
Net income	1,559.5	1,349.8

Instructions

a. Compute the following for 2005 and 2004. (Round to one decimal place.)
  1. Working capital
  2. Current ratio
  3. Quick ratio

b. Comment on the trends in the liquidity measures and state whether Walgreen appears to be able to satisfy its liabilities at the end of 2005.

c. Compute the percentage changes for 2005 in the amounts of net sales and net income. (Round to one-tenth of 1 percent.)

d. Compute the following for 2005 and 2004. (Round to one-tenth of 1 percent. For items **3** and **4**, use the year-end amounts stated above as substitutes for average assets and average stockholders' equity.)
  1. Gross profit rate
  2. Net income as a percentage of sales
  3. Return on assets
  4. Return on stockholders' equity

e. Comment on the trends in the profitability measures computed in parts **c** and **d**.

Solution to the Demonstration Problem

a.

		2004	2005
1.	**Working capital:**		
	$7,764.4 − $4,077.9	$3,686.5	
	$8,316.5 − $4,481.0		$3,835.5
2.	**Current ratio:**		
	$7,764.4 ÷ $4,077.9	1.90 to 1	
	$8,316.5 ÷ $4,481.0		1.86 to 1
3.	**Quick ratio:**		
	$2,864.6 ÷ $4,077.9	.70 to 1	
	$2,467.9 ÷ $4,481.0		.55 to 1

b. Working capital at the end of 2005 increased by $149 million, from $3,686.5 to $3,835.5. Both the current and quick ratios, on the other hand, declined. The current ratio declined from 1.90 to 1.86 and the quick ratio declined from .70 to .55. The relatively low quick ratio of .55 may be of some concern in terms of the company's ability to satisfy its future obligations.

c. Percentage change from 2004:

	2005
Net sales: [($42,201.6 − $37,508.2) ÷ $37,508.2]	+12.5%
Net income: [($1,559.5 − $1,349.8) ÷ $1,349.8]	+15.5%

d.

		2004	2005
1.	**Gross profit rate:**		
	$10,197.8 ÷ $37,508.2	27.2%	
	$11,787.8 ÷ $42,201.6		27.9%
2.	**Net income as a percentage of sales:**		
	$1,349.8 ÷ $37,508.2	3.6%	
	$1,559.5 ÷ $42,201.6		3.7%
3.	**Return on assets:**		
	$2,142.4 ÷ $13,342.1	16.1%	
	$2,424.0 ÷ $14,608.8		16.6%
4.	**Return on equity:**		
	$1,349.8 ÷ $8,139.7	16.6%	
	$1,559.5 ÷ $8,889.7		17.5%

e. All of the profitability ratios are positive. Both net sales (+12.5%) and net income (+15.5%) increased. The gross profit rate increased by .7% (27.9% − 27.2%), the ratio of net income as a percentage of sales increased by .1% (3.7% − 3.6%), return on assets increased by .5% (16.6% − 16.1%), and return on equity increased by .9% (17.5% − 16.6%). All of these are positive indicators regarding the company's profitability.

Self-Test Questions

The answers to these questions appear on page 689.

1. Which of the following usually is *least* important as a measure of short-term liquidity?
   - **a.** Quick ratio.
   - **b.** Debt ratio.
   - **c.** Current ratio.
   - **d.** Cash flows from operating activities.
2. In each of the past five years, the net sales of Plaza Co. have increased at about half the rate of inflation, but net income has increased at approximately *twice* the rate of inflation. During this period, the company's total assets, liabilities, and equity have remained almost unchanged; dividends are approximately equal to net income. These relationships suggest (indicate all correct answers):
   - **a.** Management is successfully controlling costs and expenses.
   - **b.** The company is selling more merchandise every year.
   - **c.** The annual return on assets has been increasing.
   - **d.** Financing activities are likely to result in a net use of cash.
3. From the viewpoint of a stockholder, which of the following relationships do you consider of *least* significance?
   - **a.** The return on assets consistently is higher than the industry average.

b. The return on equity has increased in each of the past five years.

c. Net income is greater than the amount of working capital.

d. The return on assets is greater than the rate of interest being paid to creditors.

4. The following data are available from the annual report of Frixell, Inc.:

Current assets	$ 480,000	Current liabilities	$300,000
Average total assets	2,000,000	Operating income	240,000
Average total equity	800,000	Net income	80,000

Which of the following statements are correct? (More than one statement may be correct.)

a. The return on equity exceeds the return on assets.

b. The current ratio is .625 to 1.

c. Working capital is $1,200,000.

d. None of the above answers is correct.

5. Hart Corporation's net income was $400,000 in 2006 and $160,000 in 2007. What percentage increase in net income must Hart achieve in 2008 to offset the decline in profits in 2007?

a. 60%.

b. 150%.

c. 600%.

d. 67%.

6. If a company's current ratio declined in a year during which its quick ratio improved, which of the following is the most likely explanation?

a. Inventory is increasing.

b. Inventory is declining.

c. Receivables are being collected more rapidly than in the past.

d. Receivables are being collected more slowly than in the past.

7. In financial statement analysis, the most difficult of the following items to predict is whether:

a. The company will be liquid in six months.

b. The company's market share is increasing or declining.

c. Profits have increased since the previous year.

d. The market price of capital stock will rise or fall over the next two months.

ASSIGNMENT MATERIAL Discussion Questions

1. In financial statement analysis, what is the basic objective of observing trends in data and ratios? Suggest some other standards of comparison.
2. In financial statement analysis, what information is produced by computing a ratio that is not available in a simple observation of the underlying data?
3. Distinguish between *trend percentages* and *component percentages*. Which would be better suited for analyzing the change in sales over a term of several years?
4. Differentiate between *horizontal* and *vertical* analysis.
5. Fowler Corporation is engaged in the manufacture and distribution of a variety of chemicals. In analyzing the financial statements of this corporation, why would you want to refer to the ratios and other measurements of companies in the chemical industry? In comparing the financial results of Fowler with another chemical company, why would you be interested in the accounting principles used by the two companies?
6. What is the basic purpose of *classifications* in financial statements? Identify the classifications widely used in a balance sheet, a multiple-step income statement, and a statement of cash flows.
7. Distinguish between the terms *classified, comparative*, and *consolidated* as they apply to financial statements. May a given set of financial statements have more than one of these characteristics?
8. What is the characteristic common to all *current assets*? Many retail stores regularly sell merchandise on installment plans, calling for payments over a period of 24 or 36 months. Do such receivables qualify as current assets? Explain.
9. What is the *quick ratio*? Under what circumstances are short-term creditors most likely to regard a company's quick ratio as more meaningful than its current ratio?
10. Distinguish between a multiple-step and a single-step income statement. Which format results in the higher amount of net income?
11. Identify four ratios or other analytical tools used to evaluate profitability. Explain briefly how each is computed.
12. Distinguish between *operating income* and *net income*.
13. Net sales of the Oneida General Store have been increasing at a reasonable rate, but net income has been declining steadily as a percentage of these sales. What appears to be the problem?
14. Why might earnings per share be more significant to a stockholder in a large corporation than the total amount of net income?
15. Assume that Congress announces its intention to limit the prices and profits of pharmaceutical companies as part of an effort to control health care costs. What effect would you expect this announcement to have on the p/e ratios and stock prices of pharmaceutical companies such as **Merck** and **Bristol-Myers Squibb**? Explain.

16. Under what circumstances might a company have a high p/e ratio even when investors are *not* optimistic about the company's future prospects?

17. Spencer Company earned a 16 percent return on its total assets. Current liabilities are 10 percent of total assets. Long-term bonds carrying an 11 percent coupon rate are equal to 30 percent of total assets. There is no preferred stock. Is this application of leverage favorable or unfavorable from the viewpoint of Spencer's stockholders?

18. Ahi Co. has a current ratio of 3 to 1. Ono Corp. has a current ratio of 2 to 1. Does this mean that Ahi's operating cycle is longer than Ono's? Why?

19. An investor states, "I bought this stock for $50 several years ago and it now sells for $100. It paid $5 per share in dividends last year so I'm earning 10 percent on my investment." Evaluate this statement.

20. Felker, Inc., experiences a considerable seasonal variation in its business. The high point in the year's activity comes in November, the low point in July. During which month would you expect the company's current ratio to be higher? If the company were choosing a fiscal year for accounting purposes, what advice would you give?

Brief Exercises

BRIEF EXERCISE 14.1

Dollar and Percentage Change

Wofford Company had net sales of $150,000 in its first year and $187,500 in its second year. Calculate the amount of change in terms of both dollars and percentage.

BRIEF EXERCISE 14.2

Trend Percentages

White, Inc., had depreciation expenses on its plant assets as follows for 2005, 2006, and 2007, respectively: $267,000, $289,000, and $357,000. Compute the trend percentages for these years, assuming 2005 is the base year.

BRIEF EXERCISE 14.3

Component Percentages

Yankee Doodle, Inc., had the following income statement figures:

Sales	$560,000
Cost of sales	(340,000)
Gross margin	$220,000
Operating expenses	(150,000)
Net income	$ 70,000

Calculate component percentages for this information.

BRIEF EXERCISE 14.4

Working Capital and Current Ratio

Harrisonburg Company had current and total assets of $450,000 and $1,000,000, respectively. The company's current and total liabilities were $267,000 and $600,000, respectively. Calculate the amount of working capital and the current ratio using this information.

BRIEF EXERCISE 14.5

Current and Quick Ratio

Garrett Company had current assets and current liabilities as follows:

Current assets:	
Cash	$ 50,000
Accounts receivable	75,000
Inventory	125,000
Current liabilities:	
Accrued expenses	$ 25,000
Accounts payable	110,000
Current portion of long-term debt	45,000

Calculate the current and quick ratios using the information provided.

LO4 **BRIEF EXERCISE 14.6**
Debt Ratio

Maxey Company had current and noncurrent liabilities of $50,000 and $150,000, respectively. The company's current assets were $76,000, out of a total asset figure of $424,000. Calculate the company's debt ratio.

LO6 **BRIEF EXERCISE 14.7**
Net Income as Percentage of Sales

Lone Star, Inc., reported sales of $560,000, cost of sales of $240,000, and operating expenses of $130,000 for the current year. Using this information, calculate the amount of net income and net income as a percentage of sales.

LO6 **BRIEF EXERCISE 14.8**
Earnings Per Share

Multi-Star, Inc., had sales of $890,000, cost of sales and operating expenses of $450,000 and $200,000, respectively, and 10,000 shares of common stock outstanding. Calculate the amount of earnings per share.

LO7 **BRIEF EXERCISE 14.9**
Return on Assets

Walland Company's operating income for the current year was $450,000. The company's average total assets for the same period were $3,500,000, and its total liabilities were $1,000,000. Calculate the company's return on assets.

LO7 **BRIEF EXERCISE 14.10**
Return on Equity

Fillips Company had net income of $36,700 in a year when its stockholders' equity averaged $450,000 and its total assets averaged $2,500,000. Calculate the company's return on equity for the period.

Exercises

LO1 **EXERCISE 14.1**
Percentage Changes

Selected information taken from the financial statements of Maxum Company for two successive years follows. You are to compute the percentage change from 2006 to 2007 whenever possible. Round all calculations to the nearest whole percentage.

	2007	2006
a. Accounts receivable	$126,000	$160,000
b. Marketable securities	–0–	250,000
c. Retained earnings	80,000	(80,000)
d. Notes receivable	120,000	–0–
e. Notes payable	870,000	800,000
f. Cash	84,000	80,000
g. Sales	970,000	910,000

LO1 **EXERCISE 14.2**
Trend Percentages

Compute *trend percentages* for the following items taken from the financial statements of Lopez Plumbing over a five-year period. Treat 2003 as the base year. State whether the trends are favorable or unfavorable. (Dollar amounts are stated in thousands.)

	2007	2006	2005	2004	2003
Sales	$81,400	$74,000	$61,500	$59,000	$50,000
Cost of goods sold	58,500	48,000	40,500	37,000	30,000

LO1 **EXERCISE 14.3**
Common Size Income Statements

Prepare *common size* income statements for Pellum Company, a sole proprietorship, for the two years shown below by converting the dollar amounts into percentages. For each year, sales will appear as 100 percent and other items will be expressed as a percentage of sales. (Income taxes are not involved as the business is not incorporated.) Comment on whether the changes from 2006 to 2007 are favorable or unfavorable.

	2007	2006
Sales	$500,000	$400,000
Cost of goods sold	330,000	268,000
Gross profit	$170,000	$132,000
Operating expenses	130,000	116,000
Net income	$ 40,000	$ 16,000

LO3 LO4

EXERCISE 14.4
Measures of Liquidity

Roy's Toys is a manufacturer of toys and children's products. The following are selected items appearing in a recent balance sheet (dollar amounts are in millions):

Cash and short-term investments	$ 47.3
Receivables	159.7
Inventories	72.3
Prepaid expenses and other current assets	32.0
Total current liabilities	130.1
Total liabilities	279.4
Total stockholders' equity	344.0

a. Using the information above, compute the amounts of Roy's Toys (**1**) quick assets and (**2**) total current assets.

b. Compute for Roy's Toys the (**1**) quick ratio, (**2**) current ratio, and (**3**) dollar amount of working capital. (Round ratios to one decimal place.)

c. Discuss whether Roy's Toys appears liquid from the viewpoint of a short-term creditor.

EXERCISE 14.5
Multiple-Step Income Statements

LINK, INC.
Statement of Earnings
For the Year Ended December 31, 2007

Net sales	$4,395,253
Costs and expenses:	
Cost of goods sold	(2,821,455)
Operating expenses	(1,004,396)
Interest revenue	15,797
Earnings before income tax	$ 585,199
Income tax expense	(204,820)
Net earnings	$ 380,379
Earnings per share	$1.70

Comparative balance sheets report average total assets for the year of *$2,450,000* and average total equity of *$1,825,000* (dollar amounts in thousands, except earnings per share).

a. Prepare an income statement for the year in a multiple-step format.

b. Compute the (**1**) gross profit rate, (**2**) net income as a percentage of net sales, (**3**) return on assets, and (**4**) return on equity for the year. (Round computations to the nearest one-tenth of 1 percent.)

c. Explain why interest revenue is not included in the company's gross profit computation.

EXERCISE 14.6
ROI

Shown below are selected data from a recent annual report of **Sprint Corporation**, a large telecommunications provider. (Dollar amounts are in millions.)

	Beginning of the Year	End of the Year
Total assets	$45,293	$42,850
Total stockholders' equity	12,294	13,224
Operating income		861
Net income		1,215

a. Compute for the year **Sprint**'s return on average total assets. (Round computations to the nearest two-tenths of 1 percent.)

b. Compute for the year **Sprint**'s return on average total stockholders' equity. (Round computations to the nearest two-tenths of 1 percent.)

c. Could the increase in **Sprint**'s total stockholders' equity for the year be the result of an increase in the *market value* of the company's stock? Explain.

EXERCISE 14.7
Computing and Interpreting Rates of Change

Selected information from the financial statements of Rochet, Inc., includes the following:

	2007	2006
Net sales	$2,200,000	$2,000,000
Total expenses	1,998,000	1,800,000

a. Compute the percentage change in 2007 for the amounts of (**1**) net sales and (**2**) total expenses.

b. Using the information developed in part **a**, express your opinion as to whether the company's *net income* for 2007:

1. Increased at a greater or lower percentage rate than did net sales.
2. Represented a larger or smaller percentage of net sales revenue than in 2006. For each answer, explain your reasoning *without* making any computations or references to dollar amounts.

EXERCISE 14.8
Research Problem

Obtain from your library (or other source) the most recent annual report of a publicly owned company.

a. Using the annual report data, compute the basic measures of liquidity, long-term credit risk, and profitability summarized in Exhibit 14–26. Compare these measures to the appropriate industry norms available in your library. Briefly comment on your findings.

b. Using the financial pages of a daily newspaper (such as *The Wall Street Journal*), determine (**1**) the current market price of your company's common stock, (**2**) its 52-week high and low market prices, and (**3**) its p/e ratio. Briefly comment on your findings.

c. Based on your analysis in parts **a** and **b**, make a recommendation as to whether investors should buy shares of the stock, hold the shares they currently own, or sell the shares they currently own. Defend your position.

EXERCISE 14.9
Home Depot, Inc., Management's Discussion and Analysis

The financial statements of large public companies are often accompanied by a multiple-year summary of key financial and other information that is helpful in understanding the company. Appendix A of this text includes the financial statements of **Home Depot, Inc.**, and selected other information from the company's annual report. Included is a ten-year Summary of Financial and Operating Results for the period 1996–2005. Locate this summary in Appendix A and respond to the following.

a. Considering the "store data" section of the ten-year summary, what conclusions can you draw about the change in size of **Home Depot, Inc.**, during the ten-year period?

b. Comment on the ten-year trend in net earnings as a percentage of sales and what this trend means to you as an investor in the company.

c. Has the company's liquidity improved or diminished over the ten-year period? Justify your answer.

EXERCISE 14.10
Evaluating Employment Opportunities

Assume that you will soon graduate from college and that you have job offers with two pharmaceutical firms. The first offer is with Alpha Research, a relatively new and aggressive company. The second is with Omega Scientific, a very well established and conservative company.

Financial information pertaining to each firm, and to the pharmaceutical industry as a whole, is as follows:

Financial Measure	Alpha	Omega	Industry Average
Current ratio	2.2 to 1	4.5 to 1	2.5 to 1
Quick ratio	1.2 to 1	2.8 to 1	1.5 to 1
Return on assets	17%	8%	10%
Return on equity	28%	14%	16%
P/e ratio	20 to 1	10 to 1	12 to 1

The Omega offer is for \$36,000 per year. The Alpha offer is for \$32,000. However, unlike Omega, Alpha awards its employees a stock option bonus based on profitability for the year. Each option enables the employee to purchase shares of Alpha's common stock at a significantly reduced price. The more profitable this company is, the more stock each employee can buy at a discount.

Show how the above information may help you justify accepting the Alpha Research offer, even though the starting salary is \$4,000 lower than the Omega Scientific offer.

EXERCISE 14.11
Ratios for a Retail Store

Selected financial data for SellFast, Inc., a retail store, appear as follows:

	2007	2006
Sales (all on account)	\$750,000	\$610,000
Cost of goods sold	495,000	408,000
Average inventory during the year	110,000	102,000
Average receivables during the year	150,000	100,000

a. Compute the following for both years:
 1. Gross profit percentage
 2. Inventory turnover
 3. Accounts receivable turnover

b. Comment on favorable and unfavorable trends.

EXERCISE 14.12
Computing Ratios

A condensed balance sheet for Bradford Corporation prepared at the end of the year appears as follows:

Assets		Liabilities & Stockholders' Equity	
Cash	\$ 95,000	Notes payable (due in 6 months)	\$ 40,000
Accounts receivable	155,000	Accounts payable	110,000
Inventory	270,000	Long-term liabilities	360,000
Prepaid expenses	60,000	Capital stock, \$5 par	300,000
Plant & equipment (net)	570,000	Retained earnings	430,000
Other assets	90,000	Total	\$1,240,000
Total	\$1,240,000		

During the year the company earned a gross profit of \$1,116,000 on sales of \$2,950,000. Accounts receivable, inventory, and plant assets remained almost constant in amount throughout the year.

Compute the following:

a. Current ratio.

b. Quick ratio.

c. Working capital.

d. Debt ratio.

e. Accounts receivable turnover (all sales were on credit).

f. Inventory turnover.

g. Book value per share of capital stock.

EXERCISE 14.13
Current Ratio, Debt Ratio, and Earnings per Share

Selected items from successive annual reports of Carey, Inc., appear as follows:

	2007	2006
Total assets (40% of which are current)	$400,000	$325,000
Current liabilities	$ 80,000	$100,000
Bonds payable, 12%	100,000	50,000
Capital stock, $5 par value	100,000	100,000
Retained earnings	120,000	75,000
Total liabilities & stockholders' equity	$400,000	$325,000

Dividends of $16,000 were declared and paid in 2007.

Compute the following:

a. Current ratio for 2007 and 2006.

b. Debt ratio for 2007 and 2006.

c. Earnings per share for 2007.

EXERCISE 14.14
Ratio Analysis for Two Similar Companies

Selected data from the financial statements of Italian Marble Co. and Brazil Stone Products for the year just ended follow. Assume that for both companies dividends declared were equal in amount to net earnings during the year and therefore stockholders' equity did not change. The two companies are in the same line of business.

	Italian Marble Co.	Brazil Stone Products
Total liabilities	$ 200,000	$ 100,000
Total assets	800,000	400,000
Sales (all on credit)	1,800,000	1,200,000
Average inventory	240,000	140,000
Average receivables	200,000	100,000
Gross profit as a percentage of sales	40%	30%
Operating expenses as a percentage of sales	36%	25%
Net income as a percentage of sales	3%	5%

Compute the following for each company and state a brief conclusion about which company is in the stronger financial position.

a. Net income.

b. Net income as a percentage of stockholders' equity.

c. Accounts receivable turnover.

d. Inventory turnover.

EXERCISE 14.15
Ratio Analysis for Feature Company

Johnson & Johnson's 2005 financial statements include the following items (all dollars in millions):

	2005	2004
Balance sheet		
Current assets	$31,394	$27,320
Current liabilities	12,635	13,927
Total assets	58,025	53,317
Income statement		
Sales	$50,514	$47,348
Gross profit	36,560	33,926
Net income	10,411	8,509

Compute the following ratios and comment on the trend you can observe from the limited two years of data you have available.

a. Gross profit rate
b. Net income as a percentage of sales
c. Current ratio

Problem Set A

PROBLEM 14.1A
Comparing Operating Results with Average Performance in the Industry

Campers, Inc., manufactures camping equipment. Shown below for the current year are the income statement for the company and a common size summary for the industry in which the company operates. (Notice that the percentages in the right-hand column are *not* for Campers, Inc., but are average percentages for the industry.)

	Campers, Inc.	Industry Average
Sales (net)	$20,000,000	100%
Cost of goods sold	9,800,000	57
Gross profit on sales	$10,200,000	43%
Operating expenses:		
Selling	$ 4,200,000	16%
General and administrative	3,400,000	20
Total operating expenses	$ 7,600,000	36%
Operating income	$ 2,600,000	7%
Income tax expense	1,200,000	3
Net income	$ 1,400,000	4%
Return on assets	23%	14%

Instructions

a. Prepare a two-column common size income statement. The first column should show for Campers, Inc., all items expressed as a percentage of net sales. The second column should show the equivalent industry average for the data given in the problem. The purpose of this common size statement is to compare the operating results of Campers, Inc., with the average for the industry.

b. Comment specifically on differences between Campers, Inc., and the industry average with respect to gross profit on sales, selling expenses, general and administrative expenses, operating income, net income, and return on assets. Suggest possible reasons for the more important disparities.

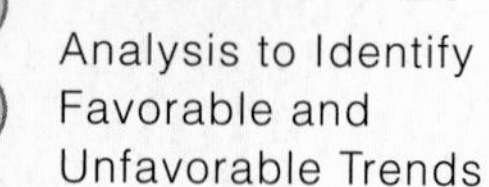

PROBLEM 14.2A
Analysis to Identify Favorable and Unfavorable Trends

LO3 LO5

The following information was developed from the financial statements of Darwin, Inc. At the beginning of 2007, the company's former supplier went bankrupt, and the company began buying merchandise from another supplier.

	2007	2006
Gross profit on sales	$1,008,000	$1,134,000
Income before income tax	230,400	252,000
Net income	172,800	189,000
Net income as a percentage of net sales	6.0%	7.5%

Instructions

a. Compute the net sales for each year.

b. Compute the cost of goods sold in dollars and as a percentage of net sales for each year.

c. Compute operating expenses in dollars and as a percentage of net sales for each year. (Income taxes expense is not an operating expense.)

d. Prepare a condensed comparative income statement for 2006 and 2007. Include the following items: net sales, cost of goods sold, gross profit, operating expenses, income before income tax, income taxes expense, and net income. Omit earnings per share statistics.

e. Identify the significant favorable and unfavorable trends in the performance of Darwin, Inc. Comment on any unusual changes.

PROBLEM 14.3A
Measures of Liquidity

LO3 LO4

Some of the accounts appearing in the year-end financial statements of Roger Grocery, Inc., appear below. This list includes all of the company's current assets and current liabilities.

Sales	$1,880,000
Accumulated depreciation: equipment	370,000
Notes payable (due in 90 days)	70,000
Retained earnings	241,320
Cash	67,600
Capital stock	150,000
Marketable securities	175,040
Accounts payable	127,500
Mortgage payable (due in 15 years)	320,000
Salaries payable	7,570
Dividends	25,000
Income taxes payable	14,600
Accounts receivable	230,540
Inventory	179,600
Unearned revenue	10,000
Unexpired insurance	4,500

Instructions

a. Prepare a schedule of the company's current assets and current liabilities. Select the appropriate items from the preceding list.

b. Compute the current ratio and the amount of working capital. Explain how each of these measurements is computed. State, with reasons, whether you consider the company to be in a strong or weak current position.

PROBLEM 14.4A
Liquidity of **Safeway**

Safeway, Inc., is one of the world's largest supermarket chains. These selected items were adapted from a recent Safeway balance sheet. (Dollar amounts are in millions.)

Cash	$ 174.8
Receivables	383.2
Merchandise inventories	2,642.2
Prepaid expenses	307.5
Fixtures and equipment	5,539.8
Retained earnings	4,117.8
Total current liabilities	3,464.3

Instructions

a. Using the information above, compute the amounts of Safeway's total current assets and total quick assets.

b. Compute the company's (**1**) current ratio, (**2**) quick ratio, and (**3**) working capital. (Round to one decimal place.)

c. From these computations, are you able to conclude whether Safeway is a good credit risk for short-term creditors or on the brink of bankruptcy? Explain.

d. Is there anything unusual about the operating cycle of supermarkets that would make you think that they normally would have lower current ratios than, say, large department stores?

e. What *other types of information* could you utilize in performing a more complete analysis of Safeway's liquidity?

PROBLEM 14.5A
Balance Sheet Measures of Liquidity and Credit Risk

A recent balance sheet of Sweet Tooth, Inc., included the following items, among others. (Dollar amounts are stated in thousands.)

Cash	$ 49,625
Marketable securities (short-term)	55,926
Accounts receivable	23,553
Inventories	32,210
Prepaid expenses	5,736
Retained earnings	121,477
Notes payable to banks (due within one year)	20,000
Accounts payable	5,912
Dividends payable	1,424
Accrued liabilities (short-term)	21,532
Income taxes payable	6,438

The company also reported total assets of $353,816 thousand, total liabilities of $81,630 thousand, and a return on total assets of *18.1 percent.*

Instructions

a. Compute Sweet Tooth's (**1**) quick assets, (**2**) current assets, and (**3**) current liabilities.

b. Compute Sweet Tooth's (**1**) quick ratio, (**2**) current ratio, (**3**) working capital, and (**4**) debt ratio. (Round to one decimal place.)

c. Discuss the company's liquidity from the viewpoints of (1) short-term creditors, (2) long-term creditors, and (3) stockholders.

PROBLEM 14.6A
Financial Statement Analysis

Shown below are selected data from the financial statements of Rentsch, Inc., a retail furniture store.

From the balance sheet:		
Cash		$ 30,000
Accounts receivable		150,000
Inventory		200,000
Plant assets (net of accumulated depreciation)		500,000
Current liabilities		150,000
Total stockholders' equity		300,000
Total assets		1,000,000
From the income statement:		
Net sales		$1,500,000
Cost of goods sold		1,080,000
Operating expenses		315,000
Interest expense		84,000
Income tax expense		6,000
Net income		15,000
From the statement of cash flows:		
Net cash provided by operating activities (including interest paid of $79,000)		$ 40,000
Net cash used in investing activities		(46,000)
Financing activities:		
Amounts borrowed	$ 50,000	
Repayment of amounts borrowed	(14,000)	
Dividends paid	(20,000)	
Net cash provided by financing activities		16,000
Net increase in cash during the year		$ 10,000

Instructions

a. Explain how the interest expense shown in the income statement could be $84,000, when the interest payment appearing in the statement of cash flows is only $79,000.

b. Compute the following (round to one decimal place):

1. Current ratio
2. Quick ratio
3. Working capital
4. Debt ratio

c. Comment on these measurements and evaluate Rentsch, Inc.'s short-term debt-paying ability.

d. Compute the following ratios (assume that the year-end amounts of total assets and total stockholders' equity also represent the average amounts throughout the year):

1. Return on assets
2. Return on equity

e. Comment on the company's performance under these measurements. Explain *why* the return on assets and return on equity are so different.

f. Discuss (1) the apparent safety of long-term creditors' claims and (2) the prospects for Rentsch, Inc., continuing its dividend payments at the present level.

LO4 LO5 LO7

PROBLEM 14.7A
Basic Ratio Analysis

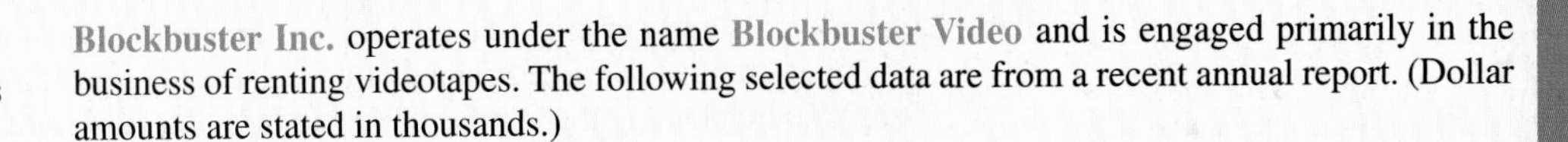

Blockbuster Inc. operates under the name Blockbuster Video and is engaged primarily in the business of renting videotapes. The following selected data are from a recent annual report. (Dollar amounts are stated in thousands.)

	Beginning of the Year	End of the Year
Total current assets	$ 958,900	$ 960,300
Total current liabilities	1,477,600	1,327,800
Total assets	6,243,800	4,854,900
Total stockholders' equity	4,167,000	3,249,300
Operating income		(845,200)
Net income		(983,900)

The company has long-term liabilities that bear interest at annual rates ranging from 6 percent to 8 percent.

Instructions

a. Compute the company's current ratio at (**1**) the *beginning* of the year and (**2**) the *end* of the year. (Carry to two decimal places.)

b. Compute the company's working capital at (**1**) the beginning of the year and (**2**) the end of the year. (Express dollar amounts in thousands.)

c. Is the company's short-term debt-paying ability improving or deteriorating?

d. Compute the company's (**1**) return on average total assets and (**2**) return on average stockholders' equity. (Round average assets and average equity to the nearest dollar and final computations to the nearest 1 percent.)

e. As an equity investor, do you think that Blockbuster's management is utilizing the company's resources in a reasonably efficient manner? Explain.

LO5 LO7

PROBLEM 14.8A
Ratios; Consider Advisability of Incurring Long-Term Debt

At the end of the year, the following information was obtained from the accounting records of Zachery, Inc.

Sales (all on credit)	$2,750,000
Cost of goods sold	1,755,000
Average inventory	375,000
Average accounts receivable	290,000
Interest expense	45,000
Income tax expense	84,000
Net income	159,000
Average investment in assets	1,800,000
Average stockholders' equity	895,000

Instructions

a. From the information given, compute the following:

1. Inventory turnover.
2. Accounts receivable turnover.
3. Total operating expenses.
4. Gross profit percentage.
5. Return on average stockholders' equity.
6. Return on average assets.

b. Zachery has an opportunity to obtain a long-term loan at an annual interest rate of 12 percent and could use this additional capital at the same rate of profitability as indicated by the given data. Would obtaining the loan be desirable from the viewpoint of the stockholders? Explain.

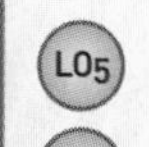

PROBLEM 14.9A
Ratios: Evaluation of Two Companies

LO5 LO7 LO8

Shown below are selected financial data for Another World and Imports, Inc., at the end of the current year:

	Another World	Imports, Inc.
Net credit sales	$675,000	$560,000
Cost of goods sold	504,000	480,000
Cash	51,000	20,000
Accounts receivable (net)	75,000	70,000
Inventory	84,000	160,000
Current liabilities	105,000	100,000

Assume that the year-end balances shown for accounts receivable and for inventory approximate the average balances of these items throughout the year.

Instructions

a. For each of the two companies, compute the following:
   1. Working capital.
   2. Current ratio.
   3. Quick ratio.
   4. Number of times inventory turned over during the year and the average number of days required to turn over inventory (round computation to the nearest day).
   5. Number of times accounts receivable turned over during the year and the average number of days required to collect accounts receivable (round computation to the nearest day).
   6. Operating cycle.

b. From the viewpoint of a short-term creditor, comment on the *quality* of each company's working capital. To which company would you prefer to sell $20,000 in merchandise on a 30-day open account?

Problem Set B

PROBLEM 14.1B
Comparing Operating Results with Average Performance in the Industry

LO1 LO5

Bathrooms, Inc., manufactures bathroom equipment. Shown below for the current year are the income statements for the company and a common size summary for the industry in which the company operates. (Notice that the percentages in the right-hand column are *not* for Bathrooms, Inc., but are average percentages for the industry.)

	Bathrooms, Inc.	Industry Average
Sales (net)	$12,000,000	100%
Cost of goods sold	7,320,000	70
Gross profit on sales	$ 4,680,000	30%
Operating expenses:		
Selling	$ 1,800,000	10%
General and administrative	720,000	14
Total operating expenses	$ 2,520,000	24%
Operating income	$ 2,160,000	6%
Income tax expense	120,000	2
Net income	$ 2,040,000	4%
Return on assets	20%	12%

Instructions

a. Prepare a two-column common size income statement. The first column should show for Bathrooms, Inc., all items expressed as a percentage of net sales. The second column should show the equivalent industry average for the data given in the problem. The purpose of this common size statement is to compare the operating results of Bathrooms, Inc., with the average for the industry. (Round to the nearest percent.)

b. Comment specifically on differences between Bathrooms, Inc., and the industry average with respect to gross profit on sales, selling expenses, general and administrative expenses, operating income, net income, and return on assets. Suggest possible reasons for the more important disparities.

PROBLEM 14.2B

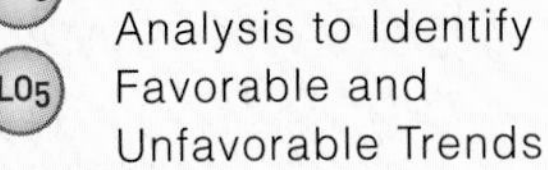

Analysis to Identify Favorable and Unfavorable Trends

The following information was developed from the financial statements of Slow Time, Inc. At the beginning of 2007, the company's former supplier went bankrupt, and the company began buying merchandise from another supplier.

	2007	2006
Gross profit on sales	$720,000	$800,000
Income before income tax	200,000	220,000
Net income	150,000	170,000
Net income as a percentage of net sales	8%	10%

Instructions

a. Compute the net sales for each year.

b. Compute the cost of goods sold in dollars and as a percentage of net sales for each year.

c. Compute operating expenses in dollars and as a percentage of net sales for each year. (Income taxes expense is not an operating expense.)

d. Prepare a condensed comparative income statement for 2006 and 2007. Include the following items: net sales, cost of goods sold, gross profit, operating expenses, income before income tax, income tax expense, and net income. Omit earnings per share statistics.

e. Identify the significant favorable and unfavorable trends in the performance of Slow Time, Inc. Comment on any unusual changes.

PROBLEM 14.3B

Measures of Liquidity

Some of the accounts appearing in the year-end financial statements of Gino, Inc., appear below. This list includes all of the company's current assets and current liabilities.

Sales	$2,500,000
Accumulated depreciation: equipment	180,000
Notes payable (due in 120 days)	85,000
Retained earnings	240,000
Cash	61,000
Capital stock	250,000
Marketable securities	160,000
Accounts payable	105,000
Mortgage payable (due in 20 years)	650,000
Salaries payable	5,800
Dividends	20,000
Income taxes payable	14,400
Accounts receivable	217,000
Inventory	195,000
Unearned revenue	15,000
Unexpired insurance	8,000

Instructions

a. Prepare a schedule of the company's current assets and current liabilities. Select the appropriate items from the above list.

b. Compute the current ratio and the amount of working capital. Explain how each of these measurements is computed. State, with reasons, whether you consider the company to be in a strong or weak current position.

PROBLEM 14.4B
Liquidity of Cheese, Inc.

Cheese, Inc., is one of the world's largest cheese store chains. Shown below are selected items adapted from a recent Cheese, Inc., balance sheet. (Dollar amounts are in the millions.)

Cash	$ 72.4
Receivables	150.4
Merchandise inventories	1,400.0
Prepaid expenses	91.0
Fixtures and equipment	3,150.0
Retained earnings	295.0
Total current liabilities	2,500.0

Instructions

a. Using the information above, compute the amounts of Cheese's total current assets and total quick assets.

b. Compute the company's (**1**) current ratio, (**2**) quick ratio, and (**3**) working capital. (Round to two decimal places.)

c. From these computations, are you able to conclude whether Cheese is a good credit risk for short-term creditors or on the brink of bankruptcy? Explain.

d. Is there anything unusual about the operating cycle of cheese stores that would make you think that they normally would have lower current ratios than, say, large department stores?

e. What *other types of information* could you utilize in performing a more complete analysis of Cheese's liquidity?

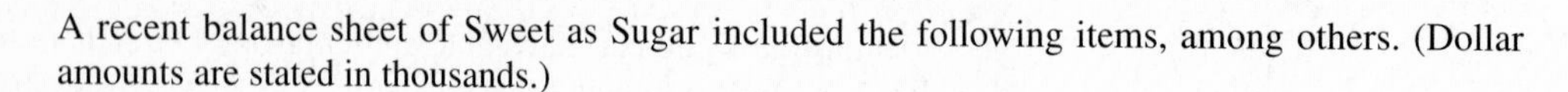

PROBLEM 14.5B
Balance Sheet Measures of Liquidity and Credit Risk

A recent balance sheet of Sweet as Sugar included the following items, among others. (Dollar amounts are stated in thousands.)

Cash	$ 49,630
Marketable securities (short-term)	65,910
Accounts receivable	25,330
Inventories	44,000
Prepaid expenses	5,850
Retained earnings	350,000
Notes payable to banks (due within one year)	28,000
Accounts payable	4,900
Dividends payable	1,800
Accrued liabilities (short-term)	21,500
Income taxes payable	8,500

The company also reported total assets of $600,000, total liabilities of $90,000, and a return on total assets of 20 percent.

Instructions

a. Compute Sweet as Sugar's: (**1**) quick assets, (**2**) current assets, and (**3**) current liabilities.

b. Compute Sweet as Sugar's: (**1**) quick ratio, (**2**) current ratio, (**3**) working capital, and (**4**) debt ratio. (Round to one decimal place.)

c. Discuss the company's liquidity from the viewpoints of (**1**) short-term creditors, (**2**) long-term creditors, and (**3**) stockholders.

PROBLEM 14.6B
Financial Statement Analysis

LO4 LO5 LO7

Shown below are selected data from the financial statements of Hamilton Stores, a retail lighting store.

From the balance sheet:		
Cash		$ 35,000
Accounts receivable		175,000
Inventory		225,000
Plant assets (net of accumulated depreciation)		550,000
Current liabilities		190,000
Total stockholders' equity		500,000
Total assets		1,300,000
From the income statement:		
Net sales		$2,400,000
Cost of goods sold		1,800,000
Operating expenses		495,000
Interest expense		80,000
Income tax expense		4,000
Net income		21,000
From the statement of cash flows:		
Net cash provided by operating activities (including interest paid of $72,000)		$ 50,000
Net cash used in investing activities		(54,000)
Financing activities:		
Amounts borrowed	$ 56,000	
Repayment of amounts borrowed	(25,000)	
Dividends paid	(24,000)	
Net cash provided by financing activities		7,000
Net increase in cash during the year		$ 3,000

Instructions

a. Explain how the interest expense shown in the income statement could be $80,000, when the interest payment appearing in the statement of cash flows is only $72,000.

b. Compute the following (round to one decimal place):

1. Current ratio **3.** Working capital

2. Quick ratio **4.** Debt ratio

c. Comment on these measurements and evaluate Hamilton's short-term debt-paying ability.

d. Compute the following ratios (assume that the year-end amounts of total assets and total stockholders' equity also represent the average amounts throughout the year):

1. Return on assets

2. Return on equity

e. Comment on the company's performance under these measurements. Explain *why* the return on assets and return on equity are so different.

f. Discuss (**1**) the apparent safety of long-term creditors' claims and (**2**) the prospects for Hamilton Stores continuing its dividend payments at the present level.

PROBLEM 14.7B
Basic Ratio Analysis

LO4 LO5 LO7

Balsum Corporation is engaged primarily in the business of manufacturing raincoats. Shown below are selected data from a recent annual report. (Dollar amounts are stated in thousands.)

	Beginning of the Year	End of the Year
Total current assets	$ 43,000	$ 82,000
Total current liabilities	54,000	75,000
Total assets	230,000	390,000
Total stockholders' equity	120,000	205,000
Operating income		74,000
Net income		51,000

The company has long-term liabilities that bear interest at annual rates ranging from 8 percent to 12 percent.

Instructions

a. Compute the company's current ratio at (1) the beginning of the year and (2) the end of the year. (Carry to two decimal places.)

b. Compute the company's working capital at (1) the beginning of the year and (2) the end of the year. (Express dollar amounts in thousands.)

c. Is the company's short-term debt-paying ability improving or deteriorating?

d. Compute the company's (1) return on average total assets and (2) return on average stockholders' equity. (Round average assets and average equity to the nearest dollar and final computations to the nearest 1 percent.)

e. As an equity investor, do you think that Balsum's management is utilizing the company's resources in a reasonably efficient manner? Explain.

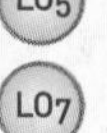

PROBLEM 14.8B

Ratios: Consider Advisability of Incurring Long-Term Debt

At the end of the year, the following information was obtained from the accounting records of Clips Systems, Inc.:

Sales (all on credit)	$4,800,000
Cost of goods sold	3,000,000
Average inventory	420,000
Average accounts receivable	380,000
Interest expense	50,000
Income tax expense	80,000
Net income	280,000
Average investment in assets	2,600,000
Average stockholders' equity	1,000,000

Instructions

a. From the information given, compute the following:
   1. Inventory turnover.
   2. Accounts receivable turnover.
   3. Total operating expenses.
   4. Gross profit percentage.
   5. Return on average stockholders' equity.
   6. Return on average assets.

b. Clips Systems has an opportunity to obtain a long-term loan at an annual interest rate of 8 percent and could use this additional capital at the same rate of profitability as indicated by the given data. Would obtaining the loan be desirable from the viewpoint of the stockholders? Explain.

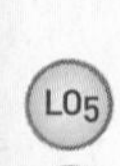

PROBLEM 14.9B

Ratios: Evaluation of Two Companies

Shown below are selected financial data for THIS Star, Inc., and THAT Star, Inc., at the end of the current year:

	THIS Star, Inc.	THAT Star, Inc.
Net credit sales	$900,000	$840,000
Cost of goods sold	700,000	640,000
Cash	90,000	40,000
Accounts receivable (net)	100,000	90,000
Inventory	50,000	160,000
Current liabilities	120,000	110,000

Assume that the year-end balances shown for accounts receivable and for inventory also represent the average balances of these items throughout the year.

Instructions

a. For each of the two companies, compute the following:
   1. Working capital.
   2. Current ratio.

3. Quick ratio.
4. Number of times inventory turned over during the year and the average number of days required to turn over inventory (round computation to the nearest day).
5. Number of times accounts receivable turned over during the year and the average number of days required to collect accounts receivable (round computation to the nearest day).
6. Operating cycle.

b. From the viewpoint of a short-term creditor, comment on the *quality* of each company's working capital. To which company would you prefer to sell $50,000 in merchandise on a 30-day open account?

Critical Thinking Cases

CASE 14.1
Season's Greetings

Holiday Greeting Cards is a local company organized late in July of 2006. The company's net income for each of its first six calendar quarters of operations is summarized below. (Amounts are stated in thousands of dollars.)

	2007	2006
First quarter (Jan. through Mar.)	$ 253	–0–
Second quarter (Apr. through June)	308	–0–
Third quarter (July through Sept.)	100	$ 50
Fourth quarter (Oct. through Dec.)	450	500
Total for the calendar year	$1,111	$550

Glen Wallace reports the business and economic news for a local radio station. On the day that Holiday Greeting Cards released the above financial information, you heard Wallace make the following statement during his broadcast: "Holiday Greeting Cards enjoyed a 350 percent increase in its profits for the fourth quarter, and profits for the entire year were up by over 100 percent."

Instructions

a. Show the computations that Wallace probably made in arriving at his statistics. (Hint: Wallace did not make his computations in the manner recommended in this chapter. His figures, however, can be developed from these financial data.)

b. Do you believe that Wallace's percentage changes present a realistic impression of Holiday Greeting Cards's rate of growth in 2007? Explain.

c. What figure would you use to express the percentage change in Holiday's fourth-quarter profits in 2007? Explain why you would compute the change in this manner.

LO3 through LO5

CASE 14.2
Evaluating Debt-Paying Ability

You are a loan officer with Third Texas Bank. Dan Scott owns two successful restaurants, each of which has applied to your bank for a $250,000 one-year loan for the purpose of opening a second location. Condensed balance sheets for the two business entities are shown below.

TEXAS STEAK RANCH
Balance Sheet
December 31, 2007

Assets		Liabilities & Stockholders' Equity	
Current assets	$ 75,000	Current liabilities	$ 30,000
Plant and equipment	300,000	Long-term liabilities	200,000
		Capital stock	100,000
		Retained earnings	45,000
Total assets	$375,000	Total liabilities & stockholders' equity	$375,000

THE STOCKYARDS
Balance Sheet
December 31, 2007

Assets		Liabilities & Owners' Equity	
Current assets	$ 24,000	Current liabilities	$ 30,000
Plant and equipment	301,000	Long-term liabilities	200,000
		Capital, Dan Scott	95,000
Total assets	$325,000	Total liabilities & owners' equity	$325,000

Both restaurants are popular and have been successful over the past several years. Texas Steak Ranch has been slightly more profitable, but the operating results for the two businesses have been quite similar. You think that either restaurant's second location should be successful. On the other hand, you know that restaurants are a very "faddish" type of business and that their popularity and profitability can change very quickly.

Dan Scott is one of the wealthiest people in Texas. He made a fortune—estimated at more than $2 billion—as the founder of Micro Time, a highly successful manufacturer of computer software. Scott now is retired and spends most of his time at Second Life, his 50,000-acre cattle ranch. Both of his restaurants are run by experienced professional managers.

Instructions

a. Compute the current ratio and working capital of each business entity.

b. Based on the information provided in this case, which of these businesses do you consider to be the better credit risk? Explain fully.

c. What simple measure might you insist upon that would make the other business as good a credit risk as the one you identified in part **b**? Explain.

CASE 14.3

Strategies to Improve the Current Ratio

Nashville Do-It-Yourself owns a chain of nine retail stores that sell building materials, hardware, and garden supplies. In early October, the company's current ratio is 1.7 to 1. This is about normal for the company, but it is lower than the current ratios of several large competitors. Management feels that, to qualify for the best credit terms from its suppliers, the company's year-end balance sheet should indicate a current ratio of at least 2 to 1.

Instructions

a. Indicate whether taking each of the following actions would increase or decrease the company's current ratio. Explain your reasoning.

1. Pay some of the company's current liabilities.
2. Purchase large amounts of inventory on account.
3. Offer credit customers a special discount if they pay their account balance prior to year-end.

b. Propose several other ethical steps that management might take to increase the company's current ratio prior to year-end.

CASE 14.4

Evaluating Corporate Governance Quality

Assume that you are an intern working for the **California Public Employees Retirement System (CALPERS)** in its investments office and you have been asked to evaluate a number of companies for possible investment by **CALPERS**. You prepare an analysis of each company's prospects using the tools of financial statement analysis (e.g., trend analysis, common size statements, ratio analysis). Thinking you are done, you present your analysis to your boss. She tells you that, although your analysis of each company's financial information is fine, she is also interested in the quality of each company's corporate governance. Pick two public companies, download their most recent proxy statement in support of the annual meeting of shareholders, and evaluate the quality of each company's board of directors (use the criteria developed by **Institutional Shareholder Services** in assessing board quality presented in the chapter).

BUSINESSWEEK CASE 14.5

Financial Analysis and the Quality of Earnings at **Amazon.com**

BusinessWeek

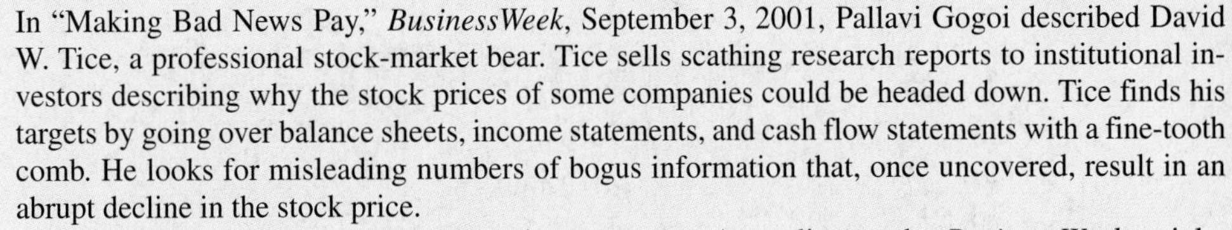

In "Making Bad News Pay," *BusinessWeek*, September 3, 2001, Pallavi Gogoi described David W. Tice, a professional stock-market bear. Tice sells scathing research reports to institutional investors describing why the stock prices of some companies could be headed down. Tice finds his targets by going over balance sheets, income statements, and cash flow statements with a fine-tooth comb. He looks for misleading numbers of bogus information that, once uncovered, result in an abrupt decline in the stock price.

For example, Tice has focused on **Amazon.com**. According to the *BusinessWeek* article, Tice is convinced that **Amazon**'s business is flawed because of the difficulty of translating rising sales into profits. Tice also suggests that **Amazon**'s growth in its core business of books, music, and videos has slowed to a crawl, and that it now emphasizes its faster-growing consumer electronics business. He calls it a classic case of "Don't look over here, look over there."

Instructions

a. Identify and describe at least four tools of analysis that Tice is likely to use when evaluating companies to include in his research reports.

b. Describe how the tools you identified in part **a** would help Tice come to the conclusions discussed in the *BusinessWeek* article about **Amazon.com**.

INTERNET CASE 14.6

Evaluating Liquidity and Profitability

Use the Internet search engine of your choice and do a general search on the name of a company of interest to you (e.g., **General Motors**, **Johnson & Johnson**, **Coke**, etc.). Explore the Web site of the company you choose and locate that company's most recent financial statements. You may need to look under a category that provides general information about the company and/or investor information.

Instructions

a. Find and read the description of the company, including the type of business it is in. Why is gaining an understanding of the industry and type of business an important starting point for financial statement analysis?

b. Locate the company's primary financial statements. Find the summary table of ratios in this chapter in Exhibit 14–26. Calculate three of the listed ratios under each of the following categories: "Measures of short-term liquidity" and "Measures of profitability." Show your work in calculating these ratios. Write a brief statement describing what you have learned about your company's liquidity and profitability.

c. Why do you think the Internet has become such a widely used source of financial information by investors and creditors?

Internet sites are time and date sensitive. It is the purpose of these exercises to have you explore the Internet. You may need to use the Yahoo! search engine **http://www.yahoo.com** *(or another favorite search engine) to find a company's current Web address.*

Answers to Self-Test Questions

1. b **2.** a, c, d **3.** c **4.** d (see below) **5.** b (see below) **6.** b **7.** d

Why answers a, b, and c in question **4** are incorrect:

a. The return on assets, 12 percent ($240,000 ÷ $2,000,000), exceeds the return on equity, which is 10 percent ($80,000 ÷ $800,000).

b. The current ratio is 1.6 to 1 ($480,000 ÷ $300,000).

c. Working capital amounts to $180,000 ($480,000 − $300,000).

Increase in net income required in question **5**: ($400,000 − $160,000) ÷ $160,000 = 150%

COMPREHENSIVE PROBLEM 4

Home Depot, Inc.

ANALYSIS OF THE FINANCIAL STATEMENTS OF A PUBLICLY OWNED CORPORATION

This Comprehensive Problem is to acquaint you with the content of the 2005 financial statements of **Home Depot, Inc.**, reproduced in Appendix A of this textbook. (The 2005 financial statements are for the fiscal year ended January 29, 2006.) The problem contains three major parts, which are independent of one another: *Part I* is designed to familiarize you with the general contents of a company's financial statements; *Part II* involves analysis of the company's liquidity; and *Part III* analyzes the trend in its profitability.

If you work this problem as a group assignment, each group member should be prepared to discuss the group's findings and conclusions in class.

A good starting point for understanding the financial statements of a company such as **Home Depot, Inc.**, is to understand the accounting policies used in preparing those statements. The first note accompanying the financial statements provides a brief description of the major accounting policies the company used. Most of the areas discussed in this note have been covered in this text.

Part I Annual reports include not only comparative financial statements but also other sources of information, such as:

- A multiyear summary of financial highlights, a summary of key statistics for the past 5 or 10 years.
- Several pages of *Notes* that accompany the financial statements.
- Reports by management and by the independent auditors in which they express their respective responsibilities for the financial statements.

Instructions

Answer each of the following questions and briefly explain *where* in the statements, notes, or other sections of the annual report you located the information used in your answer.

a. How many years are covered in each of the primary comparative financial statements? Were all of these statements audited? Name the auditors. What were the auditors' conclusions concerning these statements?

b. **Home Depot, Inc.**, combines its statement of retained earnings with another financial statement. Where are details about changes in the amount of retained earnings found?

c. Over the three years presented, have the company's annual net cash flows been positive or negative from (**1**) operating activities, (**2**) investing activities, and (**3**) financing activities? Has the company's cash balance increased or decreased during each of these three years?

Part II Assume that you are the credit manager of a medium-size supplier of building supplies. **Home Depot** wants to make credit purchases from your company, with payment due in 60 days.

Instructions

a. As general background, read the first note to the financial statements, "Summary of Significant Accounting Policies." Next compute the following for the fiscal years ending January 29, 2006, and January 30, 2005 (round percentages to the nearest tenth of 1 percent, and other computations to one decimal place):

1. Current ratio.
2. Quick ratio.

3. Amount of working capital.
4. Percentage change in working capital from the prior year.
5. Percentage change in cash and cash equivalents from the prior year.

b. Based upon your analysis in part **a**, does the company's liquidity appear to have *increased* or *decreased* during the most recent fiscal year? Explain.

c. Other than the ability of **Home Depot** to pay for its purchases, do you see any major considerations that should enter into your company's decision? Explain.

d. Your company assigns each customer one of the four credit ratings listed below. Assign a credit rating to **Home Depot, Inc.**, and write a memorandum explaining your decision. (In your memorandum, you may refer to any of your computations or observations in parts **a** through **c**, and to any information contained in the annual report.)

Possible Credit Ratings

A Outstanding Little or no risk of inability to pay. For customers in this category, we fill any reasonable order without imposing a credit limit. The customer's credit is reevaluated annually.

B Good Customer has good debt-paying ability but is assigned a credit limit that is reviewed every 90 days. Orders above the credit limit are accepted only on a cash basis.

C Marginal Customer appears sound, but credit should be extended only on a 30-day basis and with a relatively low credit limit. Creditworthiness and credit limit are reevaluated every 90 days.

D Unacceptable Customer does not qualify for credit.

Part III As general background, study the "10-Year Summary of Financial and Operating Results."

Instructions

a. Compute the following for the fiscal years ending January 29, 2006, and January 30, 2005 (round percentages to the nearest tenth of 1 percent):

1. Percentage change in net sales (relative to the prior year).
2. Percentage change in net earnings.
3. Gross profit rate.
4. Net income as a percentage of sales.
5. Return on average total assets.
6. Return on average total equity.

b. Write a statement that describes your conclusion(s) concerning trends in **Home Depot**'s profitability during the period covered in your analysis in part **a** above. Justify your conclusion(s).

APPENDIX A

Home Depot 2005 Financial Statements

Home Depot 2005 Financial Statements Contents

Item 8. Financial Statements and Supplementary Data.

Management's Responsibility for Financial Statements

The financial statements presented in this Annual Report have been prepared with integrity and objectivity and are the responsibility of the management of The Home Depot, Inc. These financial statements have been prepared in conformity with U.S. generally accepted accounting principles and properly reflect certain estimates and judgments based upon the best available information.

The financial statements of the Company have been audited by KPMG LLP, an independent registered public accounting firm. Their accompanying report is based upon an audit conducted in accordance with the standards of the Public Company Accounting Oversight Board (United States).

The Audit Committee of the Board of Directors, consisting solely of outside directors, meets five times a year with the independent registered public accounting firm, the internal auditors and representatives of management to discuss auditing and financial reporting matters. In addition, a telephonic meeting is held prior to each quarterly earnings release. The Audit Committee retains the independent registered public accounting firm and regularly reviews the internal accounting controls, the activities of the independent registered public accounting firm and internal auditors and the financial condition of the Company. Both the Company's independent registered pubic accounting firm and the internal auditors have free access to the Audit Committee.

Management's Report on Internal Control over Financial Reporting

Our management is responsible for establishing and maintaining adequate internal control over financial reporting, as such term is defined in Rule 13a-15(f) promulgated under the Securities Exchange Act of 1934, as amended. Under the supervision and with the participation of our management, including our principal executive officer and principal financial officer, we conducted an evaluation of the effectiveness of our internal control over financial reporting based on the framework in *Internal Control – Integrated Framework* issued by the Committee of Sponsoring Organizations of the Treadway Commission (COSO). Based on our evaluation, our management concluded that our internal control over financial reporting was effective as of January 29, 2006. Our management's assessment of the effectiveness of our internal control over financial reporting as of January 29, 2006 has been audited by KPMG LLP, an independent registered public accounting firm, as stated in its report which is included herein.

/s/ ROBERT L. NARDELLI	**/s/ CAROL B. TOMÉ**
Robert L. Nardelli **Chairman, President &** **Chief Executive Officer**	**Carol B. Tomé** **Executive Vice President &** **Chief Financial Officer**

Report of Independent Registered Public Accounting Firm

The Board of Directors and Stockholders
The Home Depot, Inc.:

We have audited the accompanying Consolidated Balance Sheets of The Home Depot, Inc. and subsidiaries as of January 29, 2006 and January 30, 2005, and the related Consolidated Statements of Earnings, Stockholders' Equity and Comprehensive Income, and Cash Flows for each of the fiscal years in the three-year period ended January 29, 2006. These Consolidated Financial Statements are the responsibility of the Company's management. Our responsibility is to express an opinion on these Consolidated Financial Statements based on our audits.

We conducted our audits in accordance with the standards of the Public Company Accounting Oversight Board (United States). Those standards require that we plan and perform the audit to obtain reasonable assurance about whether the financial statements are free of material misstatement. An audit includes examining, on a test basis, evidence supporting the amounts and disclosures in the financial statements. An audit also includes assessing the accounting principles used and significant estimates made by management, as well as evaluating the overall financial statement presentation. We believe that our audits provide a reasonable basis for our opinion.

In our opinion, the Consolidated Financial Statements referred to above present fairly, in all material respects, the financial position of The Home Depot, Inc. and subsidiaries as of January 29, 2006 and January 30, 2005, and the results of their operations and their cash flows for each of the fiscal years in the three-year period ended January 29, 2006, in conformity with U.S. generally accepted accounting principles.

As discussed in Note 1 to the Consolidated Financial Statements, effective February 3, 2003, the Company changed its method of accounting for cash consideration received from a vendor to conform to Emerging Issues Task Force No. 02-16 and adopted the fair value method of recording stock-based compensation expense in accordance with Statement of Financial Accounting Standards No. 123.

We also have audited, in accordance with the standards of the Public Company Accounting Oversight Board (United States), the effectiveness of The Home Depot, Inc. and subsidiaries' internal control over financial reporting as of January 29, 2006, based on criteria established in *Internal Control – Integrated Framework* issued by the Committee of Sponsoring Organizations of the Treadway Commission (COSO), and our report dated March 22, 2006 expressed an unqualified opinion on management's assessment of, and the effective operation of, internal control over financial reporting.

/s/ KPMG LLP

Atlanta, Georgia
March 22, 2006, except as to note 12
which is as of March 24, 2006

THE HOME DEPOT, INC. AND SUBSIDIARIES

CONSOLIDATED STATEMENTS OF EARNINGS

	Fiscal Year Ended (1)		
amounts in millions, except per share data	January 29, 2006	January 30, 2005	February 1, 2004
NET SALES	$ **81,511**	$ 73,094	$ 64,816
Cost of Sales	**54,191**	48,664	44,236
GROSS PROFIT	**27,320**	24,430	20,580
Operating Expenses:			
Selling, General and Administrative	**16,485**	15,256	12,713
Depreciation and Amortization	**1,472**	1,248	1,021
Total Operating Expenses	**17,957**	16,504	13,734
OPERATING INCOME	**9,363**	7,926	6,846
Interest Income (Expense):			
Interest and Investment Income	**62**	56	59
Interest Expense	**(143)**	(70)	(62)
Interest, net	**(81)**	(14)	(3)
EARNINGS BEFORE PROVISION FOR INCOME TAXES	**9,282**	7,912	6,843
Provision for Income Taxes	**3,444**	2,911	2,539
NET EARNINGS	$ **5,838**	$ 5,001	$ 4,304
Weighted Average Common Shares	**2,138**	2,207	2,283
BASIC EARNINGS PER SHARE	$ **2.73**	$ 2.27	$ 1.88
Diluted Weighted Average Common Shares	**2,147**	2,216	2,289
DILUTED EARNINGS PER SHARE	$ **2.72**	$ 2.26	$ 1.88

(1) *Fiscal years ended January 29, 2006, January 30, 2005 and February 1, 2004 include 52 weeks.*

See accompanying Notes to Consolidated Financial Statements.

THE HOME DEPOT, INC. AND SUBSIDIARIES

CONSOLIDATED BALANCE SHEETS

amounts in millions, except per share data	January 29, 2006	January 30, 2005
ASSETS		
Current Assets:		
Cash and Cash Equivalents	**$ 793**	$ 506
Short-Term Investments	**14**	1,659
Receivables, net	**2,396**	1,499
Merchandise Inventories	**11,401**	10,076
Other Current Assets	**742**	533
Total Current Assets	**15,346**	14,273
Property and Equipment, at cost:		
Land	**7,924**	6,932
Buildings	**14,056**	12,325
Furniture, Fixtures and Equipment	**7,073**	6,195
Leasehold Improvements	**1,207**	1,191
Construction in Progress	**843**	1,404
Capital Leases	**427**	390
	31,530	28,437
Less Accumulated Depreciation and Amortization	**6,629**	5,711
Net Property and Equipment	**24,901**	22,726
Notes Receivable	**348**	369
Cost in Excess of the Fair Value of Net Assets Acquired	**3,286**	1,394
Other Assets	**601**	258
Total Assets	**$ 44,482**	$ 39,020
LIABILITIES AND STOCKHOLDERS' EQUITY		
Current Liabilities:		
Short-Term Debt	**$ 900**	$ —
Accounts Payable	**6,032**	5,766
Accrued Salaries and Related Expenses	**1,176**	1,055
Sales Taxes Payable	**488**	412
Deferred Revenue	**1,757**	1,546
Income Taxes Payable	**388**	161
Current Installments of Long-Term Debt	**513**	11
Other Accrued Expenses	**1,647**	1,504
Total Current Liabilities	**12,901**	10,455
Long-Term Debt, excluding current installments	**2,672**	2,148
Other Long-Term Liabilities	**977**	871
Deferred Income Taxes	**1,023**	1,388
STOCKHOLDERS' EQUITY		
Common Stock, par value $0.05; authorized: 10,000 shares; issued 2,401 shares at January 29, 2006 and 2,385 shares at January 30, 2005; outstanding 2,124 shares at January 29, 2006 and 2,185 shares at January 30, 2005	**120**	119
Paid-In Capital	**7,287**	6,650
Retained Earnings	**28,943**	23,962
Accumulated Other Comprehensive Income	**409**	227
Unearned Compensation	**(138)**	(108)
Treasury Stock, at cost, 277 shares at January 29, 2006 and 200 shares at January 30, 2005	**(9,712)**	(6,692)
Total Stockholders' Equity	**26,909**	24,158
Total Liabilities and Stockholders' Equity	**$ 44,482**	$ 39,020

See accompanying Notes to Consolidated Financial Statements.

THE HOME DEPOT, INC. AND SUBSIDIARIES

CONSOLIDATED STATEMENTS OF STOCKHOLDERS' EQUITY AND COMPREHENSIVE INCOME

amounts in millions, except per share data	Common Stock Shares	Common Stock Amount	Paid-In Capital	Retained Earnings	Accumulated Other Comprehensive Income (Loss) [1]	Unearned Compensation	Treasury Stock Shares	Treasury Stock Amount	Total Stockholders' Equity	Comprehensive Income [2]
BALANCE, FEBRUARY 2, 2003	**2,362**	**$ 118**	**$ 5,858**	**$ 15,971**	**$ (82)**	**$ (63)**	**(69)**	**$ (2,000)**	**$ 19,802**	
Net Earnings	—	—	—	4,304	—	—	—	—	4,304	$ 4,304
Shares Issued Under Employee Stock Plans	11	1	249	—	—	(26)	—	—	224	
Tax Effect of Sale of Option Shares by Employees	—	—	24	—	—	—	—	—	24	
Translation Adjustments	—	—	—	—	172	—	—	—	172	172
Stock Options, Awards and Amortization of Restricted Stock	—	—	53	—	—	13	—	—	66	
Repurchase of Common Stock	—	—	—	—	—	—	(47)	(1,590)	(1,590)	
Cash Dividends ($0.26 per share)	—	—	—	(595)	—	—	—	—	(595)	
Comprehensive Income										$ 4,476
BALANCE, FEBRUARY 1, 2004	**2,373**	**$ 119**	**$ 6,184**	**$ 19,680**	**$ 90**	**$ (76)**	**(116)**	**$ (3,590)**	**$ 22,407**	
Net Earnings	—	—	—	5,001	—	—	—	—	5,001	$ 5,001
Shares Issued Under Employee Stock Plans	12	—	340	—	—	(54)	—	—	286	
Tax Effect of Sale of Option Shares by Employees	—	—	26	—	—	—	—	—	26	
Translation Adjustments	—	—	—	—	137	—	—	—	137	137
Stock Options, Awards and Amortization of Restricted Stock	—	—	100	—	—	22	—	—	122	
Repurchase of Common Stock	—	—	—	—	—	—	(84)	(3,102)	(3,102)	
Cash Dividends ($0.325 per share)	—	—	—	(719)	—	—	—	—	(719)	
Comprehensive Income										$ 5,138
BALANCE, JANUARY 30, 2005	**2,385**	**$ 119**	**$ 6,650**	**$ 23,962**	**$ 227**	**$ (108)**	**(200)**	**$ (6,692)**	**$ 24,158**	
Net Earnings	—	—	—	5,838	—	—	—	—	5,838	$ 5,838
Shares Issued Under Employee Stock Plans	16	1	472	—	—	(63)	—	—	410	
Tax Effect of Sale of Option Shares by Employees	—	—	24	—	—	—	—	—	24	
Translation Adjustments	—	—	—	—	182	—	—	—	182	182
Stock Options, Awards and Amortization of Restricted Stock	—	—	141	—	—	33	—	—	174	
Repurchase of Common Stock	—	—	—	—	—	—	(77)	(3,020)	(3,020)	
Cash Dividends ($0.40 per share)	—	—	—	(857)	—	—	—	—	(857)	
Comprehensive Income										$ 6,020
BALANCE, JANUARY 29, 2006	**2,401**	**$ 120**	**$ 7,287**	**$ 28,943**	**$ 409**	**$ (138)**	**(277)**	**$ (9,712)**	**$ 26,909**	

(1) Balance at January 29, 2006 consists primarily of foreign currency translation adjustments.

(2) Components of Comprehensive Income are reported net of related income taxes.

See accompanying Notes to Consolidated Financial Statements.

THE HOME DEPOT, INC. AND SUBSIDIARIES

CONSOLIDATED STATEMENTS OF CASH FLOWS

amounts in millions	Fiscal Year Ended (1) January 29, 2006	January 30, 2005	February 1, 2004
CASH FLOWS FROM OPERATING ACTIVITIES:			
Net Earnings	**$ 5,838**	$ 5,001	$ 4,304
Reconciliation of Net Earnings to Net Cash Provided by Operating Activities:			
Depreciation and Amortization	**1,579**	1,319	1,076
Impairment Related to Disposition of EXPO Real Estate	**78**	—	—
Stock-Based Compensation Expense	**175**	125	67
Changes in Assets and Liabilities, net of the effects of acquisitions:			
(Increase) Decrease in Receivables, net	**(358)**	(266)	25
Increase in Merchandise Inventories	**(971)**	(849)	(693)
Decrease (Increase) in Other Current Assets	**16**	29	(49)
Increase in Accounts Payable and Accrued Liabilities	**12**	917	790
Increase in Deferred Revenue	**209**	263	279
Increase (Decrease) in Income Taxes Payable	**175**	2	(27)
(Decrease) Increase in Deferred Income Taxes	**(609)**	319	605
Increase in Other Long-Term Liabilities	**151**	119	33
Other	**189**	(75)	135
Net Cash Provided by Operating Activities	**6,484**	6,904	6,545
CASH FLOWS FROM INVESTING ACTIVITIES:			
Capital Expenditures, net of $51, $38 and $47 of non-cash capital expenditures in fiscal 2005, 2004 and 2003, respectively	**(3,881)**	(3,948)	(3,508)
Purchase of Assets from Off-Balance Sheet Financing Arrangement	**—**	—	(598)
Payments for Businesses Acquired, net	**(2,546)**	(727)	(215)
Proceeds from Sales of Property and Equipment	**164**	96	265
Purchases of Investments	**(18,230)**	(25,890)	(38,649)
Proceeds from Sales and Maturities of Investments	**19,907**	25,990	38,534
Net Cash Used in Investing Activities	**(4,586)**	(4,479)	(4,171)
CASH FLOWS FROM FINANCING ACTIVITIES:			
Proceeds from Short-Term Borrowings, net	**900**	—	—
Proceeds from Long-Term Borrowings, net of discount	**995**	995	—
Repayments of Long-Term Debt	**(24)**	(510)	(9)
Repurchase of Common Stock	**(3,040)**	(3,106)	(1,554)
Proceeds from Sale of Common Stock, net	**414**	285	227
Cash Dividends Paid to Stockholders	**(857)**	(719)	(595)
Net Cash Used in Financing Activities	**(1,612)**	(3,055)	(1,931)
Increase (Decrease) in Cash and Cash Equivalents	**286**	(630)	443
Effect of Exchange Rate Changes on Cash and Cash Equivalents	**1**	33	20
Cash and Cash Equivalents at Beginning of Year	**506**	1,103	640
Cash and Cash Equivalents at End of Year	**$ 793**	$ 506	$ 1,103
SUPPLEMENTAL DISCLOSURE OF CASH PAYMENTS MADE FOR:			
Interest, net of interest capitalized	**$ 114**	$ 78	$ 70
Income Taxes	**$ 3,860**	$ 2,793	$ 2,037

(1) *Fiscal years ended January 29, 2006, January 30, 2005 and February 1, 2004 include 52 weeks.*

See accompanying Notes to Consolidated Financial Statements.

NOTES TO CONSOLIDATED FINANCIAL STATEMENTS

1. SUMMARY OF SIGNIFICANT ACCOUNTING POLICIES

Business, Consolidation and Presentation

The Home Depot, Inc. and subsidiaries (the "Company") operate The Home Depot stores, which are full-service, warehouse-style stores averaging approximately 105,000 square feet in size. The stores stock approximately 35,000 to 45,000 different kinds of building materials, home improvement supplies and lawn and garden products that are sold to do-it-yourself customers, do-it-for-me customers, home improvement contractors, tradespeople and building maintenance professionals. In addition, the Company operates EXPO Design Center stores ("EXPO"), which offer products and services primarily related to design and renovation projects, The Home Depot Landscape Supply stores, which service landscape professionals and garden enthusiasts with lawn, landscape and garden products and Home Depot Supply stores and Contractors' Warehouse stores serving primarily professional customers. The Company also operates The Home Depot Floor Stores, which offer primarily flooring products and installation services. At the end of fiscal 2005, the Company was operating 2,042 stores in total, which included 1,793 The Home Depot stores, 34 EXPO Design Center stores, 11 The Home Depot Landscape Supply stores, eight Contractors' Warehouse stores, three Home Depot Supply stores and two The Home Depot Floor Stores in the United States, including the territories of Puerto Rico and the Virgin Islands ("U.S."); 137 The Home Depot stores in Canada and 54 The Home Depot stores in Mexico.

Additionally, Home Depot Supply, through the Company's wholly-owned subsidiaries, distributes products and sells installation services primarily to professional business contractors, businesses and municipalities and operates in three primary areas. Maintenance, Repair and Operations ("MRO") supplies maintenance, repair and operating products primarily to multi-family housing, hospitality and lodging facilities. The second area, Builder, provides products and arranges installation services for production home builders. Professional Supply, the third area, distributes specialty hardware, tools and materials to construction contractors. The Consolidated Financial Statements include the accounts of the Company and its wholly-owned subsidiaries. All significant intercompany transactions have been eliminated in consolidation.

Fiscal Year

The Company's fiscal year is a 52 or 53-week period ending on the Sunday nearest to January 31. Fiscal years ended January 29, 2006 ("fiscal 2005"), January 30, 2005 ("fiscal 2004") and February 1, 2004 ("fiscal 2003") include 52 weeks.

Use of Estimates

Management of the Company has made a number of estimates and assumptions relating to the reporting of assets and liabilities, the disclosure of contingent assets and liabilities, and reported amounts of revenues and expenses in preparing these financial statements in conformity with generally accepted accounting principles. Actual results could differ from these estimates.

Fair Value of Financial Instruments

The carrying amounts of Cash and Cash Equivalents, Receivables, Short-Term Debt and Accounts Payable approximate fair value due to the short-term maturities of these financial instruments. The fair value of the Company's investments is discussed under the caption "Short-Term Investments" in this Note 1. The fair value of the Company's Long-Term Debt is discussed in Note 3.

Cash Equivalents

The Company considers all highly liquid investments purchased with maturities of three months or less to be cash equivalents. The Company's Cash and Cash Equivalents are carried at fair market value and consist primarily of high-grade commercial paper, money market funds, U.S. government agency securities and tax-exempt notes and bonds.

Short-Term Investments

Short-Term Investments at the end of fiscal 2004 are primarily auction rate securities. The interest rates on these securities are typically reset to market prevailing rates every 35 days or less, and in all cases every 90 days or less, but have longer stated maturities. Short-Term Investments are recorded at fair value based on current market rates and are classified as available-for-sale. Changes in the fair value are included in Accumulated Other Comprehensive Income (Loss), net of applicable taxes in the accompanying Consolidated Financial Statements.

Accounts Receivable

The Company has an agreement with a third-party service provider who manages the Company's private label credit card program and directly extends credit to customers. In addition, certain subsidiaries of the Company extend credit directly to customers in the ordinary course of business. The receivables due from customers were $865 million and $321 million as of January 29, 2006 and January 30, 2005, respectively. The Company's valuation reserve related to accounts receivable was not material as of January 29, 2006 and January 30, 2005.

Merchandise Inventories

The majority of the Company's Merchandise Inventories are stated at the lower of cost (first-in, first-out) or market, as determined by the retail inventory method. As the inventory retail value is adjusted regularly to reflect market conditions, the inventory valued using the retail method approximates the lower of cost or market. Certain subsidiaries and distribution centers record Merchandise Inventories at the lower of cost (first-in, first-out) or market, as determined by the cost method. These Merchandise Inventories represent approximately 14% of the total Merchandise Inventories balance. The Company evaluates the inventory valued using the cost method at the end of each quarter to ensure that it is carried at the lower of cost or market. The valuation allowance for Merchandise Inventories valued under the cost method was not material to the Company as of the end of fiscal 2005 and fiscal 2004.

Independent physical inventory counts or cycle counts are taken on a regular basis in each store, distribution center and Home Depot Supply location to ensure that amounts reflected in the accompanying Consolidated Financial Statements for Merchandise Inventories are properly stated. During the period between physical inventory counts in stores, the Company accrues for estimated losses related to shrink on a store-by-store basis based on historical shrink results and current trends in the business. Shrink (or in the case of excess inventory, "swell") is the difference between the recorded amount of inventory and the physical inventory. Shrink may occur due to theft, loss, inaccurate records for the receipt of inventory or deterioration of goods, among other things.

Income Taxes

The Company provides for federal, state and foreign income taxes currently payable, as well as for those deferred due to timing differences between reporting income and expenses for financial statement purposes versus tax purposes. Federal, state and foreign tax benefits are recorded as a reduction of income taxes. Deferred tax assets and liabilities are recognized for the future tax consequences attributable to temporary differences between the financial statement carrying amounts of existing assets and liabilities and their respective tax bases.

(continued on the next page)

Deferred tax assets and liabilities are measured using enacted income tax rates expected to apply to taxable income in the years in which those temporary differences are expected to be recovered or settled. The effect of a change in income tax rates is recognized as income or expense in the period that includes the enactment date.

The Company and its eligible subsidiaries file a consolidated U.S. federal income tax return. Non-U.S. subsidiaries and certain U.S. subsidiaries, which are consolidated for financial reporting purposes, are not eligible to be included in the Company's consolidated U.S. federal income tax return. Separate provisions for income taxes have been determined for these entities. The Company intends to reinvest the unremitted earnings of its non-U.S. subsidiaries and postpone their remittance indefinitely. Accordingly, no provision for U.S. income taxes for non-U.S. subsidiaries was recorded in the accompanying Consolidated Statements of Earnings.

The American Jobs Creation Act of 2004 ("AJC Act") provides a one-time 85% dividends-received deduction that applies to qualified cash dividends received from controlled foreign corporations if the funds are reinvested in the United States. The deduction can result in an effective income tax rate of 5.25% on the repatriation of foreign earnings, a rate much lower than the normal statutory tax rate of 35%. The Company has determined that it will not repatriate earnings of foreign subsidiaries under the AJC Act.

The AJC Act also provides a new deduction for qualified domestic production activities. When fully phased-in, the deduction will be up to 9% of the lesser of qualified production activities income or taxable income. Because this provision is targeted toward manufacturing activities, the Company does not expect to recognize a material benefit in the current or future tax years.

Depreciation and Amortization

The Company's Buildings, Furniture, Fixtures and Equipment are depreciated using the straight-line method over the estimated useful lives of the assets. Leasehold Improvements are amortized using the straight-line method over the original term of the lease or the useful life of the improvement, whichever is shorter. The Company's Property and Equipment is depreciated using the following estimated useful lives:

	Life
Buildings	10-45 years
Furniture, Fixtures and Equipment	3-20 years
Leasehold Improvements	5-30 years

Capitalized Software Costs

The Company capitalizes certain costs related to the acquisition and development of software and amortizes these costs using the straight-line method over the estimated useful life of the software, which is three to six years. These costs are included in Furniture, Fixtures and Equipment in the accompanying Consolidated Balance Sheets. Certain development costs not meeting the criteria for capitalization are expensed as incurred.

Revenues

The Company recognizes revenue, net of estimated returns, at the time the customer takes possession of merchandise or receives services. The liability for sales returns is estimated based on historical return levels. When the Company receives payment from customers before the customer has taken possession of the merchandise or the service has been performed, the amount received is recorded as Deferred Revenue in the accompanying Consolidated Balance Sheets until the sale or service is complete. The Company also records Deferred Revenue for the sale of gift cards and recognizes this revenue upon the redemption of gift cards in Net Sales. Gift card breakage income is recognized based

(continued on the next page)

upon historical redemption patterns and represents the balance of gift cards for which the Company believes the likelihood of redemption by the customer is remote. During fiscal 2005, the Company recognized $52 million of gift card breakage income. Fiscal 2005 was the first year in which the Company recognized gift card breakage income, and therefore, the amount recognized includes the gift card breakage income related to gift cards sold since the inception of the gift card program. This income is recorded as other income and is included in the Consolidated Statement of Earnings as a reduction in Selling, General and Administrative Expenses ("SG&A").

Services Revenue

Net Sales include services revenue generated through a variety of installation and home maintenance programs. In these programs, the customer selects and purchases material for a project and the Company provides or arranges professional installation. These programs are offered through the Company's stores and focus primarily on providing products and services to do-it-for-me customers. The Company also arranges for the provision of flooring, countertop, cabinet and window covering installation services to production home builders through its Creative Touch Interiors brand. Under certain programs, when the Company provides or arranges the installation of a project and the subcontractor provides material as part of the installation, both the material and labor are included in services revenue. The Company recognizes this revenue when the service for the customer is complete.

All payments received prior to the completion of services are recorded in Deferred Revenue in the accompanying Consolidated Balance Sheets. Services revenue, including the impact of deferred revenue, was $4.3 billion, $3.6 billion and $2.8 billion for fiscal 2005, 2004 and 2003, respectively.

Self-Insurance

The Company is self-insured for certain losses related to general liability, product liability, automobile, workers' compensation and medical claims. The expected ultimate cost for claims incurred as of the balance sheet date is not discounted and is recognized as a liability. The expected ultimate cost of claims is estimated based upon analysis of historical data and actuarial estimates.

Prepaid Advertising

Television and radio advertising production costs along with media placement costs are expensed when the advertisement first appears. Included in Other Current Assets in the accompanying Consolidated Balance Sheets are $42 million and $33 million, respectively, at the end of fiscal 2005 and 2004 relating to prepayments of production costs for print and broadcast advertising.

Vendor Allowances

The Company currently receives two types of vendor allowances: volume rebates that are earned as a result of attaining certain purchase levels and advertising co-op allowances for the promotion of vendors' products that are typically based on guaranteed minimum amounts with additional amounts being earned for attaining certain purchase levels. All vendor allowances are accrued as earned, and those allowances received as a result of attaining certain purchase levels are accrued over the incentive period based on estimates of purchases.

In fiscal 2003, the Company adopted Emerging Issues Task Force No. 02-16, "Accounting by a Customer (Including a Reseller) for Certain Consideration Received from a Vendor" ("EITF 02-16"), which states that cash consideration received from a vendor is presumed to be a reduction of the prices of the vendor's products or services and should, therefore, be characterized as a reduction of Cost of Sales when recognized in the Company's Consolidated Statements of Earnings. That presumption is overcome when the consideration is either a reimbursement of specific, incremental and identifiable costs incurred to sell the vendor's product or a payment for assets or services

(continued on the next page)

delivered to the vendor. The Company receives consideration in the form of advertising co-op allowances from its vendors pursuant to annual agreements, which are generally on a calendar year basis. As permitted by EITF 02-16, the Company elected to apply the provisions of EITF 02-16 prospectively to all agreements entered into or modified after December 31, 2002.

There was no material impact to the Company's Consolidated Statements of Earnings or Consolidated Balance Sheets for fiscal 2005. The impact of EITF 02-16 in fiscal 2004 and fiscal 2003 resulted in a reduction of Cost of Sales of $891 million and $40 million, an increase to SG&A of $1.0 billion and $47 million and a reduction to Earnings before Provision for Income Taxes of $158 million and $7 million, respectively. The impact on the Company's Diluted Earnings per Share was a reduction of $0.04 in fiscal 2004. There was no material impact on the Company's Diluted Earnings per Share in fiscal 2003.

Volume rebates and advertising co-op allowances earned are initially recorded as a reduction in Merchandise Inventories and a subsequent reduction in Cost of Sales when the related product is sold. Prior to the adoption of EITF 02-16 in January 2004, advertising co-op allowances earned had been offset against advertising expense to the extent of advertising costs incurred, with the excess treated as a reduction of Cost of Sales.

The Company continues to earn certain advertising co-op allowances that are recorded as an offset against advertising expense as they are reimbursements of specific, incremental and identifiable costs incurred to promote vendors' products. In fiscal 2005, 2004 and 2003, net advertising expense was $1.1 billion, $1.0 billion and $58 million, respectively, which was recorded in SG&A.

Cost of Sales

Cost of Sales includes the actual cost of merchandise sold and services performed, the cost of transportation of merchandise from vendors to the Company's stores, locations or customers, the operating cost of the Company's distribution centers and the cost of deferred interest programs offered through the Company's private label credit card program.

The cost of handling and shipping merchandise from the Company's stores, locations or distribution centers to the customer is classified as SG&A. The cost of shipping and handling, including internal costs and payments to third parties, classified as SG&A was $563 million, $499 million and $387 million in fiscal 2005, 2004 and 2003, respectively.

Cost in Excess of the Fair Value of Net Assets Acquired and Other Intangible Assets

Goodwill represents the excess of purchase price over fair value of net assets acquired. The Company does not amortize goodwill, but does assess the recoverability of goodwill in the third quarter of each year by determining whether the fair value of each reporting unit supports its carrying value. The fair values of the Company's identified reporting units were estimated using the expected present value of discounted cash flows. The Company recorded no impairment charges for fiscal 2005, 2004 or 2003.

The Company amortizes the cost of other intangible assets over their estimated useful lives, which range from 1 to 12 years, unless such lives are deemed indefinite. Intangible assets with indefinite lives are tested in the third quarter of each year for impairment and written down to fair value as required. The Company recorded no impairment charges for fiscal 2005, 2004 or 2003.

Impairment of Long-Lived Assets

The Company evaluates the carrying value of long-lived assets when management makes the decision to relocate or close a store, or when circumstances indicate the carrying amount of an asset may not be recoverable. Losses related to the impairment of long-lived assets are recognized to the extent the sum of undiscounted estimated future cash flows expected to result from the use of the asset are less than

(continued on the next page)

the asset's carrying value. If the carrying value is greater than the future cash flows, a provision is made to write down the related assets to the estimated net recoverable value. Impairment losses were recorded as a component of SG&A in the accompanying Consolidated Statements of Earnings. When a location closes, the Company also recognizes in SG&A the net present value of future lease obligations, less estimated sublease income.

In fiscal 2005, the Company closed 20 of its EXPO stores, four of which are being converted to The Home Depot store format. In fiscal 2005, the Company charged $91 million to SG&A related to the dispositions, of which $78 million was for asset impairment charges and $13 million was for lease obligations. The Company remains contingently liable for future minimum lease payments related to the affected stores, for which the amounts are not material. Additionally, the Company incurred $29 million of expense in Cost of Sales in fiscal 2005 related to inventory markdowns in these stores. Affected customers are being served by existing The Home Depot and EXPO stores. In fiscal 2005, the Company also closed two Home Depot Supply stores which did not have a material impact to the Company's financial results.

Stock-Based Compensation

Effective February 3, 2003, the Company adopted the fair value method of recording stock-based compensation expense in accordance with SFAS No. 123, "Accounting for Stock-Based Compensation" ("SFAS 123"). The Company selected the prospective method of adoption as described in SFAS No. 148, "Accounting for Stock-Based Compensation – Transition and Disclosure" and accordingly, stock-based compensation expense was recognized related to stock options granted, modified or settled and expense related to the Employee Stock Purchase Plan ("ESPP") after the beginning of fiscal 2003. The fair value of stock options and ESPP as determined on the date of grant using the Black-Scholes option-pricing model is being expensed over the vesting period of the related stock options and ESPP. Prior to February 3, 2003, the Company elected to account for its stock-based compensation plans under Accounting Principles Board Opinion No. 25, "Accounting for Stock Issued to Employees" ("APB 25"), which requires the recording of stock-based compensation expense for some, but not all, stock-based compensation.

The per share weighted average fair value of stock options granted during fiscal 2005, 2004 and 2003 was $12.83, $13.57 and $9.79, respectively. The fair value of these options was determined at the date of grant using the Black-Scholes option-pricing model with the following assumptions:

	Fiscal Year Ended		
	January 29, 2006	**January 30, 2005**	**February 1, 2004**
Risk-free interest rate	**4.3%**	2.6%	3.0%
Assumed volatility	**33.7%**	41.3%	44.6%
Assumed dividend yield	**1.1%**	0.8%	1.0%
Assumed lives of option	**5 years**	5 years	5 years

The following table illustrates the effect on Net Earnings and Earnings per Share as if the Company had applied the fair value recognition provisions of SFAS 123 to all stock-based compensation in each period (amounts in millions, except per share data):

	Fiscal Year Ended		
	January 29, 2006	January 30, 2005	February 1, 2004
Net Earnings, as reported	**$ 5,838**	$ 5,001	$ 4,304
Add: Stock-based compensation expense included in reported Net Earnings, net of related tax effects	**110**	79	42
Deduct: Total stock-based compensation expense determined under fair value based method for all awards, net of related tax effects	**(197)**	(237)	(279)
Pro forma net earnings	**$ 5,751**	$ 4,843	$ 4,067
Earnings per Share:			
Basic – as reported	**$ 2.73**	$ 2.27	$ 1.88
Basic – pro forma	**$ 2.69**	$ 2.19	$ 1.78
Diluted – as reported	**$ 2.72**	$ 2.26	$ 1.88
Diluted – pro forma	**$ 2.68**	$ 2.19	$ 1.78

In April 2005, the Securities and Exchange Commission issued guidance delaying the effective date of SFAS No. 123 (revised 2004), "Share-Based Payment" ("SFAS 123(R)"), therefore it will now be effective for The Home Depot in the first quarter of fiscal 2006. The Company intends to adopt SFAS 123(R) using the modified-prospective method, therefore, in addition to continuing to recognize stock-based compensation expense for all share-based payments awarded since the adoption of SFAS 123 in fiscal 2003, the Company will also begin expensing unvested options granted prior to 2003 upon the adoption of SFAS 123(R). The Company currently estimates the impact of adopting SFAS 123(R) will be a reduction of Earnings before Provision for Income Taxes of approximately $40 million for fiscal 2006.

Derivatives

The Company measures its derivatives at fair value and recognizes these assets or liabilities on the Consolidated Balance Sheets. The Company's primary objective for entering into derivative instruments is to manage its exposure to interest rate fluctuations, as well as to maintain an appropriate mix of fixed and variable rate debt. At January 29, 2006, the Company had several outstanding interest rate swaps, accounted for as fair value hedges, with a notional amount of $475 million that swap fixed rate interest on the Company's $500 million 5 3/8 % Senior Notes for variable interest rates equal to LIBOR plus 30 to 245 basis points and expire on April 1, 2006. At January 29, 2006, the fair market value of these agreements was a liability of $1 million, which is the estimated amount that the Company would have paid to settle similar interest rate swap agreements at current interest rates.

Comprehensive Income

Comprehensive Income includes Net Earnings adjusted for certain revenues, expenses, gains and losses that are excluded from Net Earnings under generally accepted accounting principles. Adjustments to Net Earnings are primarily for foreign currency translation adjustments.

Foreign Currency Translation

Assets and Liabilities denominated in a foreign currency are translated into U.S. dollars at the current rate of exchange on the last day of the reporting period. Revenues and Expenses are generally translated at a daily exchange rate and equity transactions are translated using the actual rate on the day of the transaction.

Segment Information

The Company operates within a single operating segment within North America. Net Sales for Canada and Mexico were $5.3 billion, $4.2 billion and $3.4 billion during fiscal 2005, 2004 and 2003, respectively. Long-lived assets in Canada and Mexico totaled $2.2 billion and $1.7 billion as of January 29, 2006 and January 30, 2005, respectively.

Reclassifications

Certain amounts in prior fiscal years have been reclassified to conform with the presentation adopted in the current fiscal year.

10-Year Summary of Financial and Operating Results
The Home Depot, Inc. and Subsidiaries

amounts in millions, except where noted	10-Year Compound Annual Growth Rate	2005	2004
STATEMENT OF EARNINGS DATA			
Net sales	18.1%	$ 81,511	$ 73,094
Net sales increase (%)	—	11.5	12.8
Earnings before provision for income taxes	22.8	9,282	7,912
Net earnings	23.1	5,838	5,001
Net earnings increase (%)	—	16.7	16.2
Diluted earnings per share ($) (2)	23.1	2.72	2.26
Diluted earnings per share increase (%)	—	20.4	20.2
Diluted weighted average number of common shares	—	2,147	2,216
Gross margin – % of sales	—	33.5	33.4
Total operating expenses – % of sales	—	22.0	22.6
Net interest income (expense) – % of sales	—	(0.1)	—
Earnings before provision for income taxes – % of sales	—	11.4	10.8
Net earnings – % of sales	—	7.2	6.8
BALANCE SHEET DATA AND FINANCIAL RATIOS			
Total assets	19.7%	$ 44,482	$ 39,020
Working capital	6.9	2,445	3,818
Merchandise inventories	18.0	11,401	10,076
Net property and equipment	18.8	24,901	22,726
Long-term debt	14.0	2,672	2,148
Stockholders' equity	18.4	26,909	24,158
Book value per share ($)	18.5	12.67	11.06
Long-term debt-to-equity (%)	—	9.9	8.9
Total debt-to-equity (%)	—	15.2	8.9
Current ratio	—	1.19:1	1.37:1
Inventory turnover	—	4.8x	4.9x
Return on invested capital (%)	—	22.4	21.5
STATEMENT OF CASH FLOWS DATA			
Depreciation and amortization	24.2%	$ 1,579	$ 1,319
Capital expenditures (3)	11.5	3,881	3,948
Cash dividends per share ($)	25.3	0.400	0.325
STORE DATA (4)			
Number of stores	17.1%	2,042	1,890
Square footage at fiscal year-end	17.2	215	201
Increase in square footage (%)	—	7.0	9.8
Average square footage per store (in thousands)	—	105	106
STORE SALES AND OTHER DATA			
Comparable store sales increase (%) (5)(6)(7)	—	3.8	5.4
Weighted average weekly sales per operating store (in thousands)	(0.3)%	$ 763	$ 766
Weighted average sales per square foot ($) (4)(5)	(0.3)	377	375
Number of customer transactions (4)	13.6	1,330	1,295
Average ticket ($) (4)	3.3	57.98	54.89
Number of associates at fiscal year-end	15.6	344,810	323,149

(1) Fiscal years 2001 and 1996 include 53 weeks; all other fiscal years reported include 52 weeks.
(2) Diluted earnings per share for fiscal 1997, excluding a $104 million non-recurring charge, were $0.55.
(3) Excludes payments for businesses acquired (net, in millions) for fiscal years 2005 ($2,546), 2004 ($727), 2003 ($215), 2002 ($235), 2001 ($190), 2000 ($26), 1999 ($101), 1998 ($6) and 1997 ($61).
(4) Excludes all non-store locations since their inclusion may cause distortion of the data presented due to operational differences from our retail stores. The total number of the excluded locations and their total square footage are immaterial to our total number of locations and total square footage.
(5) Adjusted to reflect the first 52 weeks of the 53-week fiscal years in 2001 and 1996.

	2003	2002	2001 [1]	2000	1999	1998	1997	1996 [1]
STATEMENT OF EARNINGS DATA								
Net sales	$ 64,816	$ 58,247	$ 53,553	$ 45,738	$ 38,434	$ 30,219	$ 24,156	$ 19,535
Net sales increase (%)	11.3	8.8	17.1	19.0	27.2	25.1	23.7	26.3
Earnings before provision for income taxes	6,843	5,872	4,957	4,217	3,804	2,654	1,898	1,535
Net earnings	4,304	3,664	3,044	2,581	2,320	1,614	1,160	938
Net earnings increase (%)	17.5	20.4	17.9	11.3	43.7	31.9	23.7	28.2
Diluted earnings per share ($) [2]	1.88	1.56	1.29	1.10	1.00	0.71	0.52	0.43
Diluted earnings per share increase (%)	20.5	20.9	17.3	10.0	40.8	29.1	20.9	26.5
Diluted weighted average number of common shares	2,289	2,344	2,353	2,352	2,342	2,320	2,287	2,195
Gross margin – % of sales	31.8	31.1	30.2	29.9	29.7	28.5	28.1	27.8
Total operating expenses – % of sales	21.2	21.1	20.9	20.7	19.8	19.7	19.8	20.0
Net interest income (expense) – % of sales	—	0.1	—	—	—	—	—	0.1
Earnings before provision for income taxes – % of sales	10.6	10.1	9.3	9.2	9.9	8.8	7.9	7.9
Net earnings – % of sales	6.6	6.3	5.7	5.6	6.0	5.3	4.8	4.8
BALANCE SHEET DATA AND FINANCIAL RATIOS								
Total assets	$ 34,437	$ 30,011	$ 26,394	$ 21,385	$ 17,081	$ 13,465	$ 11,229	$ 9,342
Working capital	3,774	3,882	3,860	3,392	2,734	2,076	2,004	1,867
Merchandise inventories	9,076	8,338	6,725	6,556	5,489	4,293	3,602	2,708
Net property and equipment	20,063	17,168	15,375	13,068	10,227	8,160	6,509	5,437
Long-term debt	856	1,321	1,250	1,545	750	1,566	1,303	1,247
Stockholders' equity	22,407	19,802	18,082	15,004	12,341	8,740	7,098	5,955
Book value per share ($)	9.93	8.38	7.71	6.46	5.36	3.95	3.23	2.75
Long-term debt-to-equity (%)	3.8	6.7	6.9	10.3	6.1	17.9	18.4	20.9
Total debt-to-equity (%)	6.1	6.7	6.9	10.3	6.1	17.9	18.4	20.9
Current ratio	1.40:1	1.48:1	1.59:1	1.77:1	1.75:1	1.73:1	1.82:1	2.01:1
Inventory turnover	5.0x	5.3x	5.4x	5.1x	5.4x	5.4x	5.4x	5.6x
Return on invested capital (%)	20.4	18.8	18.3	19.6	22.5	19.3	16.1	16.3
STATEMENT OF CASH FLOWS DATA								
Depreciation and amortization	$ 1,076	$ 903	$ 764	$ 601	$ 463	$ 373	$ 283	$ 232
Capital expenditures [3]	3,508	2,749	3,393	3,574	2,618	2,094	1,464	1,248
Cash dividends per share ($)	0.26	0.21	0.17	0.16	0.11	0.08	0.06	0.05
STORE DATA [4]								
Number of stores	1,707	1,532	1,333	1,134	930	761	624	512
Square footage at fiscal year-end	183	166	146	123	100	81	66	54
Increase in square footage (%)	10.2	14.1	18.5	22.6	23.5	22.8	23.1	21.6
Average square footage per store (in thousands)	107	108	109	108	108	107	106	105
STORE SALES AND OTHER DATA								
Comparable store sales increase (%) [5][6][7]	3.8	—	—	4	10	7	7	7
Weighted average weekly sales per operating store (in thousands)	$ 763	$ 772	$ 812	$ 864	$ 876	$ 844	$ 829	$ 803
Weighted average sales per square foot ($) [4][5]	371	370	388	415	423	410	406	398
Number of customer transactions [4]	1,246	1,161	1,091	937	797	665	550	464
Average ticket ($) [4]	51.15	49.43	48.64	48.65	47.87	45.05	43.63	42.09
Number of associates at fiscal year-end	298,800	280,900	256,300	227,300	201,400	156,700	124,400	98,100

(6) *Includes Net Sales at locations open greater than 12 months, including relocated and remodeled stores, and Net Sales of all the subsidiaries of The Home Depot, Inc. Stores and subsidiaries became comparable on the Monday following their 365 th day of operation and include certain locations acquired in the current year by existing subsidiaries. Comparable store sales is intended only as supplemental information and is not a substitute for Net Sales or Net Earnings presented in accordance with generally accepted accounting principles.*

(7) *Beginning in fiscal 2003, comparable store sales increases were reported to the nearest one-tenth of a percentage. Comparable store sales increases in fiscal years prior to 2003 were not adjusted to reflect this change.*

APPENDIX B

The Time Value of Money

Future Amounts and Present Values

Learning Objectives

AFTER STUDYING THIS APPENDIX, YOU SHOULD BE ABLE TO:

- LO1 Explain what is meant by the phrase *time value of money.*
- LO2 Describe the relationships between *present values* and *future amounts.*
- LO3 Explain three basic ways in which decision makers apply the time value of money.
- LO4 Compute future amounts and the investments necessary to accumulate future amounts.
- LO5 Compute the present values of future cash flows.
- LO6 Discuss accounting applications of the concept of present value.

The Concept

Explain what is meant by the phrase *time value of money*. LO1

One of the most basic—and important—concepts of investing is the *time value of money*. This concept is based on the idea that an amount of money available today can be safely invested to accumulate to a larger amount in the future. As a result, an amount of money available today is considered to be equivalent in value to a *larger sum* available at a future date.

Describe the relationships between *present values* and *future amounts*. LO2

In our discussion, we will refer to an amount of money available today as a *present value*. In contrast, an amount receivable or payable at a future date will be described as a *future amount*.

To illustrate, assume that you place $500 in a savings account that earns interest at the rate of 8 percent per year. The balance of your account at the end of each of the next four years is illustrated in Exhibit B–1.

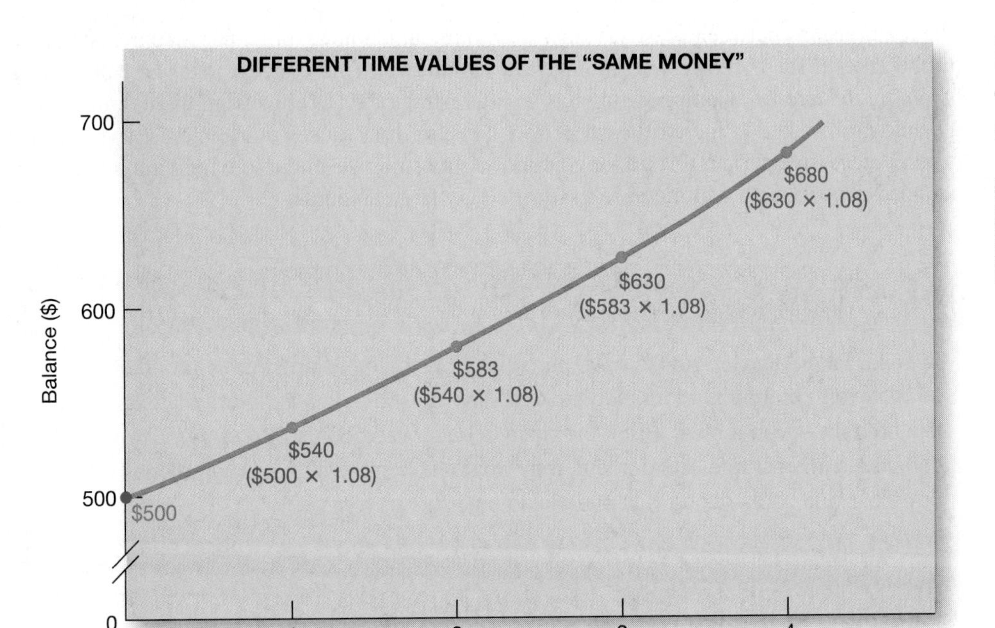

Exhibit B–1

THE VALUES OF MONEY OVER TIME

Future values are bigger, but are they worth more? This is the real issue.

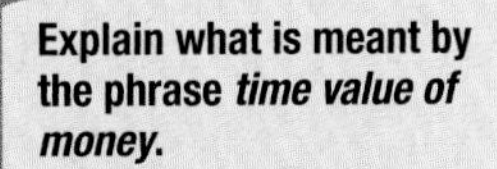

These balances represent different time values of your $500 investment. When you first open the account, your investment has a *present value* of only $500. As time passes, the value of your investment increases to the *future amounts* illustrated in the graph. (Throughout this appendix, present values will be illustrated in red, and future amounts will be shown in **blue**.)

RELATIONSHIPS BETWEEN PRESENT VALUES AND FUTURE AMOUNTS

The difference between a present value and any future amount is the *interest* that is included in the future amount. We have seen that interest accrues over time. Therefore, the difference between the present value and a future amount depends on *two factors*: (1) the *rate of interest* at which the present value increases and (2) the *length of time* over which interest accumulates. (Notice in our graph, the farther away the future date, the larger the future amount.)

Present Values Change over Time

The present value of an investment gradually increases toward the future amount. In fact, when a future date *arrives*, what once was a future amount becomes the present value of the investment. For example, at the end of the first year, $540 will no longer be a future amount—it will be the present value of your savings account.

The Basic Concept (Stated Several Different Ways)

Notice that the present value of our savings account is *always less than its future amounts*. This is the basic idea underlying the time value of money. But this idea often is expressed in different ways, including the following:

- A present value is always *less than* a future amount.
- A future amount is always *greater than* a present value.
- A dollar available today is always worth *more* than a dollar that does not become available until a future date.
- A dollar available at a future date is always worth *less* than a dollar that is available today.

Read these statements carefully. All four reflect the idea that a present value is the "equivalent" of a larger number of dollars at a future date. This is what is meant by the time value of money.

COMPOUND INTEREST

The relationships between present values and future amounts assume that the interest earned on the investment is *reinvested*, rather than withdrawn. This concept often is called *compounding the interest*. Compounding has an interesting effect. Reinvesting the interest causes the amount invested to increase each period. This, in turn, causes more interest to be earned in each successive period. Over a long period of time, an investment in which interest is compounded continuously will increase to surprisingly large amounts.

CASE IN POINT

In 1626, Peter Minuit is said to have purchased Manhattan Island from a group of Indians for $24 worth of "beads, cloth, and trinkets." This episode often is portrayed as an incredible bargain—even a steal. But if the Indians had invested this $24 to earn interest at a compound interest rate of 8 percent, they would have more than enough money today to buy the island back—along with everything on it.

APPLICATIONS OF THE TIME VALUE OF MONEY CONCEPT

LO3 Explain three basic ways in which decision makers apply the time value of money.

Investors, accountants, and other decision makers apply the time value of money in three basic ways. These applications are summarized below, along with a typical example.

1. To determine the amount to which an investment will accumulate over time. *Example*: If we invest $5,000 each year and earn an annual rate of return of 10 percent, how much will be accumulated after 10 years?
2. To determine the amount that must be invested every period to accumulate a required future amount. *Example*: We must accumulate a $200 million bond sinking fund over the next 20 years. How much must we deposit into this fund each year, assuming that the fund's assets will be invested to earn an annual rate of return of 8 percent?
3. To determine the present value of cash flows expected to occur in the future. *Example*: Assuming that we require a 15 percent return on our investments, how much can we afford to pay today for new machinery that is expected to reduce production costs by $20,000 per year for the next 10 years?

We will now introduce a framework for answering such questions.

Future Amounts

A future amount is simply the dollar amount to which a present value *will accumulate* over time. As we have stated, the difference between a present value and a related future amount depends on (1) the interest rate and (2) the period of time over which the present value accumulates.

Starting with the present value, we may compute future amounts through a series of multiplications, as illustrated in our graph in Exhibit B–1. But there are faster and easier ways. For example, many financial calculators are programmed to compute future amounts; you merely enter the present value, the interest rate, and the number of periods. Or you may use a *table of future amounts*, such as **Table FA–1** in Exhibit B–2.

Table FA–1
Future Value of $1 after *n* Periods

Number of Periods (*n*)	Interest Rate								
	1%	1½%	5%	6%	8%	10%	12%	15%	20%
1	1.010	1.015	1.050	1.060	1.080	1.100	1.120	1.150	1.200
2	1.020	1.030	1.103	1.124	1.166	1.210	1.254	1.323	1.440
3	1.030	1.046	1.158	1.191	1.260	1.331	1.405	1.521	1.728
4	1.041	1.061	1.216	1.262	1.360	1.464	1.574	1.749	2.074
5	1.051	1.077	1.276	1.338	1.469	1.611	1.762	2.011	2.488
6	1.062	1.093	1.340	1.419	1.587	1.772	1.974	2.313	2.986
7	1.072	1.110	1.407	1.504	1.714	1.949	2.211	2.660	3.583
8	1.083	1.126	1.477	1.594	1.851	2.144	2.476	3.059	4.300
9	1.094	1.143	1.551	1.689	1.999	2.358	2.773	3.518	5.160
10	1.105	1.161	1.629	1.791	2.159	2.594	3.106	4.046	6.192
20	1.220	1.347	2.653	3.207	4.661	6.727	9.646	16.367	38.338
24	1.270	1.430	3.225	4.049	6.341	9.850	15.179	28.625	79.497
36	1.431	1.709	5.792	8.147	15.968	30.913	59.136	153.152	708.802

Exhibit B–2
THE FUTURE VALUE OF $1

Approach to computing future amount

THE TABLES APPROACH

Compute future amounts and the investments necessary to accumulate future amounts. LO4

A table of future amounts shows the future amount to which *$1* will accumulate over a given number of periods, assuming that it has been invested to earn any of the illustrated interest rates. We will refer to the amounts shown in the body of this table as *factors*, rather than as dollar amounts.

To find the future amount of a present value *greater* than $1, simply multiply the present value by the factor obtained from the table. The formula for using the table in this manner is:

Future Amount = Present Value × Factor (from Table FA–1)

Using the table to compute the amounts in our graph

Let us demonstrate this approach using the data for our savings account, illustrated in Exhibit B–1. The account started with a present value of $500, invested at an annual interest rate of 8 percent. Thus the future values of the account in each of the next four years can be computed as follows (rounded to the nearest dollar):

Year	Future Amount	Computation (Using Table FA–1)
1	$540	$500 × 1.080 = $540
2	$583	$500 × 1.166 = $583
3	$630	$500 × 1.260 = $630
4	$680	$500 × 1.360 = $680

Computing a future amount is relatively easy. The more interesting question is: How much must we *invest today* to accumulate a required future amount?

Computing the Required Investment At the end of 2007, Metro Recycling agrees to create a fully funded pension plan for its employees by December 31, 2012 (in five years). It is estimated that $5 million will be required to fully fund the pension plan at December 31, 2012. How much must Metro invest in this plan *today* (December 31, 2007) to accumulate the promised $5 million by the end of 2012, assuming that payments to the fund will be invested to earn an annual return of 8 percent?

Let us repeat our original formula for computing future amounts using Table FA–1:

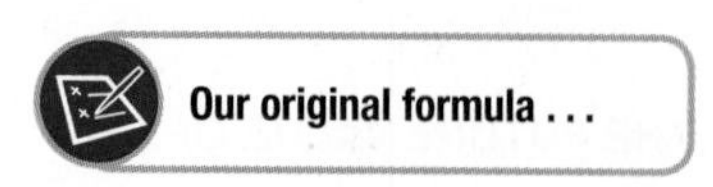

Future Amount = Present Value × Factor (from Table FA–1)

In this situation, we *know* the future amount—$5 million. We are looking for the *present value* which, when invested at an interest rate of 8 percent, will accumulate to $5 million in five years. To determine the *present value*, the formula shown above may be restated as follows:

restated to find the present value

$$\text{Present Value} = \frac{\text{Future Amount}}{\text{Factor (from Table FA–1)}}$$

Referring to Table FA–1, we get a factor of 1.469 at the intersection of five periods and 8 percent interest. Thus, the amount of the required investment at the end of 2005 is $3,403,676 ($5 million ÷ 1.469). Invested at 8 percent, this amount will accumulate to the required $5 million at the end of five years as illustrated in Exhibit B–3.

Exhibit B–3

THE FUTURE AMOUNT OF A SINGLE INVESTMENT

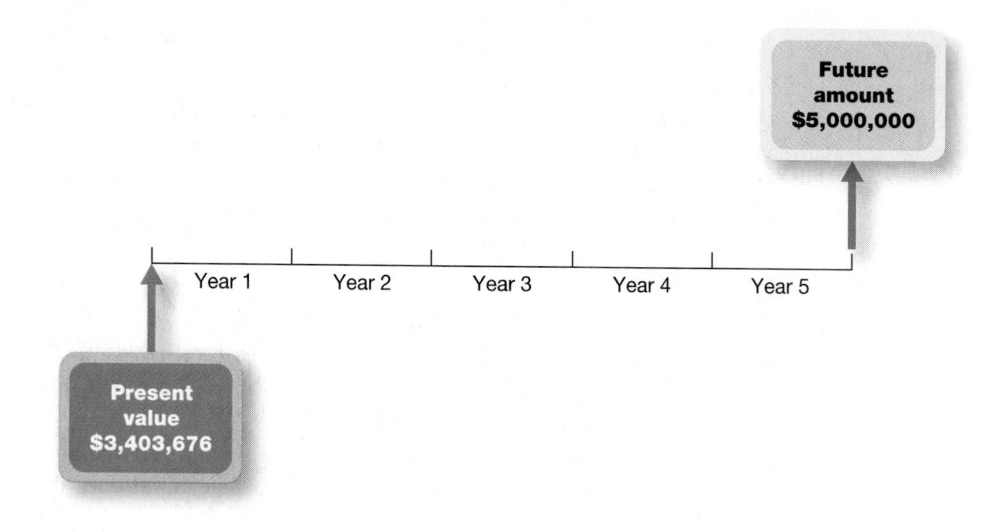

THE FUTURE AMOUNT OF AN ANNUITY

In many situations, an investor will make a *series* of investment payments rather than a single payment. As an example, assume that you plan to deposit $500 into your savings account at the end of each of the next five years. If the account pays annual interest of 8 percent, what will be the balance in your savings account at the end of the fifth year? Tables, such as Table FA–2 in Exhibit B–4, may be used to answer this question. Table FA–2 presents the future amount of an *ordinary annuity of $1*, which is a series of payments of $1 made at the *end* of each of a specified number of periods.

To find the future amount of an ordinary annuity of payments greater than $1, we simply multiply the amount of the periodic payment by the factor appearing in the table, as shown here:

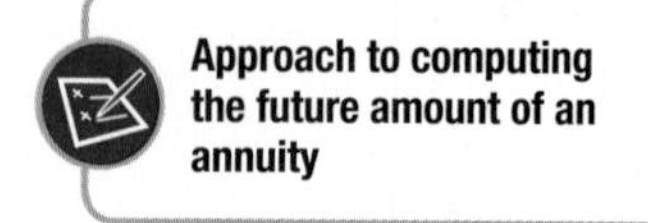

$$\text{Future Amount of an Annuity} = \text{Periodic Payment} \times \text{Factor (from Table FA–2)}$$

In our example, a factor of 5.867 is obtained from the table at the intersection of five periods and 8 percent interest. If this factor is multiplied by the periodic payment of $500, we find that your savings account will accumulate to a balance of $2,934 ($500 × 5.867) at the end of

Exhibit B–4

FUTURE VALUE OF AN ORDINARY ANNUITY

Table FA–2
Future Amount of $1 Paid Periodically for *n* Periods

Number of Periods (*n*)	Interest Rate 1%	1½%	5%	6%	8%	10%	12%	15%	20%
1	1.000	1.000	1.000	1.000	1.000	1.000	1.000	1.000	1.000
2	2.010	2.015	2.050	2.060	2.080	2.100	2.120	2.150	2.200
3	3.030	3.045	3.153	3.184	3.246	3.310	3.374	3.473	3.640
4	4.060	4.091	4.310	4.375	4.506	4.641	4.779	4.993	5.368
5	5.101	5.152	5.526	5.637	5.867	6.105	6.353	6.742	7.442
6	6.152	6.230	6.802	6.975	7.336	7.716	8.115	8.754	9.930
7	7.214	7.323	8.142	8.394	8.923	9.487	10.089	11.067	12.916
8	8.286	8.433	9.549	9.897	10.637	11.436	12.300	13.727	16.499
9	9.369	9.559	11.027	11.491	12.488	13.579	14.776	16.786	20.799
10	10.462	10.703	12.578	13.181	14.487	15.937	17.549	20.304	25.959
20	22.019	23.124	33.066	36.786	45.762	57.275	72.052	102.444	186.688
24	26.974	28.634	44.502	50.816	66.765	88.497	118.155	184.168	392.484
36	43.077	47.276	95.836	119.121	187.102	299.127	484.463	1014.346	3539.009

five years. Therefore, if you invest $500 at the end of each of the next five years in the savings account, you will accumulate $2,934 at the end of the five-year period.

While computing the future amount of an investment is sometimes necessary, many business and accounting problems require us to determine the *amount of the periodic payments* that must be made to accumulate the required future amount.

Computing the Required Periodic Payments Assume that Ultra Tech Company is required to accumulate $10 million in a *bond sinking fund* to retire bonds payable five years from now. The *bond indenture* requires Ultra Tech to make equal payments to the fund at the end of each of the next five years. What is the amount of the required periodic payment, assuming that the fund will earn 10 percent annual interest? To answer this question, we simply rearrange the following formula for computing the future amount of an annuity:

$$\text{Future Amount of an Annuity} = \text{Periodic Payment} \times \text{Factor (from Table FA–2)}$$

Our original formula . . .

In our example, we know that Ultra Tech is required to accumulate a future amount of $10 million. However, we need to know the amount of the periodic payments that, when invested at 10 percent annual interest, will accumulate to that future amount. To make this calculation, the formula may be restated as follows:

$$\text{Periodic Payment} = \frac{\text{Future Amount of an Annuity}}{\text{Factor (from Table FA–2)}}$$

restated to find the amount of the periodic payments

The amount of each required payment, therefore, is $1,638,000 ($10 million ÷ 6.105). If payments of $1,638,000 are made at the end of each of the next five years to a bond sinking fund that earns 10 percent annual interest, the fund will accumulate to $10 million, as shown in Exhibit B–5.

INTEREST PERIODS OF LESS THAN ONE YEAR

In our computations of future amounts, we have assumed that interest is paid (compounded) or payments are made annually. Therefore, in using the tables, we used *annual* periods and an *annual* interest rate. Investment payments or interest payments may be made on a more

Exhibit B–5 FUTURE AMOUNT OF A SERIES OF INVESTMENTS

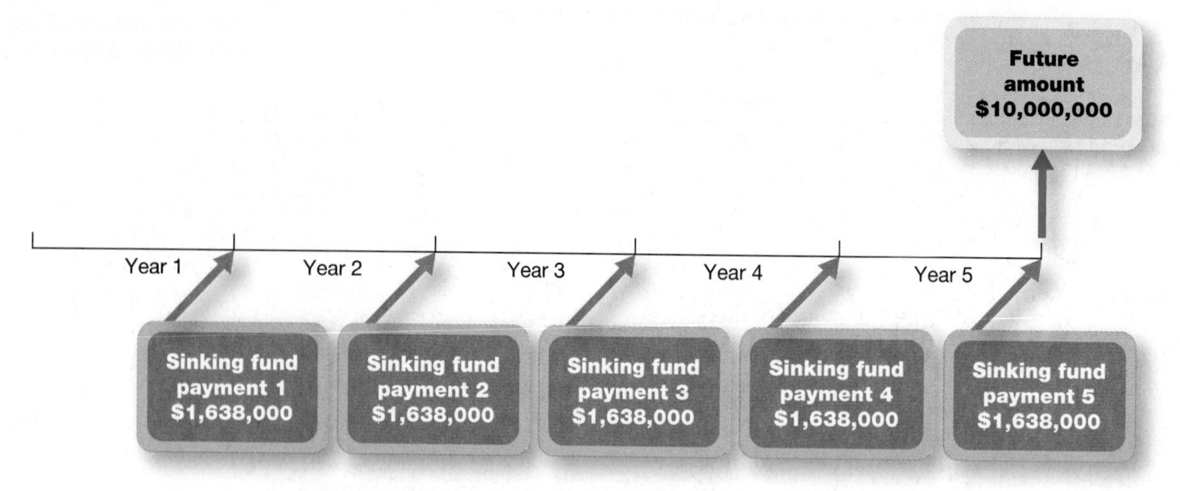

frequent basis, such as monthly, quarterly, or semiannually. **Tables FA–1 and FA–2** may be used with any of these payment periods, *but the rate of interest must represent the interest rate for that period.*

As an example, assume that 24 monthly payments are to be made to an investment fund that pays a 12 percent annual interest rate. To determine the future amount of this investment, we would multiply the amount of the monthly payments by the factor from **Table FA–2** for 24 periods, using a *monthly* interest rate of 1 percent—the 12 percent annual rate divided by 12 months.

Present Values

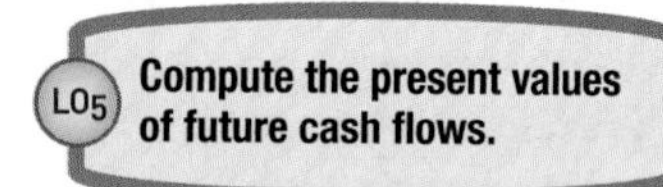

As indicated previously, the present value is *today's* value of funds to be received in the future. While present value has many applications in business and accounting, it is most easily explained in the context of evaluating investment opportunities. In this context, the present value is the amount that a knowledgeable investor would pay *today* for the right to receive an expected future amount of cash. The present value is always *less* than the future amount, because the investor will expect to earn a return on the investment. The amount by which the future cash receipt exceeds its present value represents the investor's profit.

The amount of the profit on a particular investment depends on two factors: (1) the rate of return (called the *discount rate*) required by the investor and (2) the length of time until the future amount will be received. The process of determining the present value of a future cash receipt is called *discounting* the future amount.

To illustrate the computation of present value, assume that an investment is expected to result in a $1,000 cash receipt at the end of one year and that an investor requires a 10 percent return on this investment. We know from our discussion of present and future values that the difference between a present value and a future amount is the return (interest) on the investment. In our example, the future amount would be equal to 110 percent of the original investment, because the investor expects 100 percent of the investment back plus a 10 percent return on the investment. Thus the investor would be willing to pay *$909* ($1,000 ÷ 1.10) for this investment. This computation may be verified as follows (amounts rounded to the nearest dollar):

Amount to be invested (present value)	$ 909
Required return on investment ($909 × 10%)	91
Amount to be received in one year (future value)	$1,000

As illustrated in Exhibit B–6, if the $1,000 is to be received *two years* in the future, the investor would pay only *$826* for the investment today [($1,000 ÷ 1.10) ÷ 1.10]. This computation may be verified as follows (amounts rounded to the nearest dollar):

Amount to be invested (present value)	$ 826
Required return on investment in first year ($826 × 10%)	83
Amount invested after one year	$ 909
Required return on investment in second year ($909 × 10%)	91
Amount to be received in two years (future value)	$1,000

The amount that our investor would pay today, $826, is the present value of $1,000 to be received two years from now, discounted at an annual rate of 10 percent. The $174 difference between the $826 present value and the $1,000 future amount is the return (interest revenue) to be earned by the investor over the two-year period.

Exhibit B–6

PRESENT VALUE OF $1,000 TO BE RECEIVED IN A SINGLE SUM IN TWO YEARS

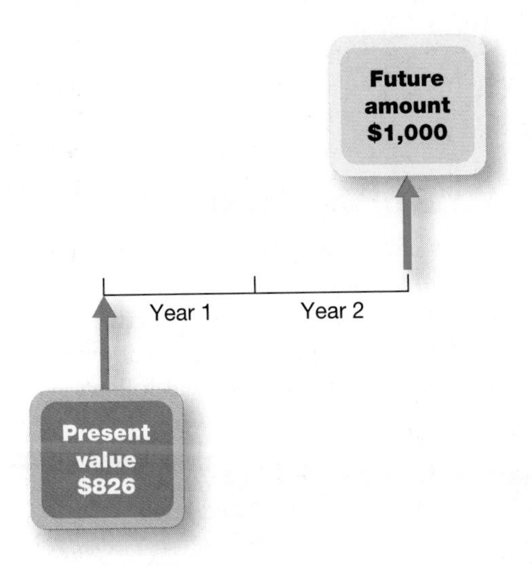

USING PRESENT VALUE TABLES

Although we can compute the present value of future amounts by a series of divisions, tables are available that simplify the calculations. We can use a table of present values to find the present value of $1 at a specified discount rate and then multiply that value by the future amount as illustrated in the following formula:

Formula for finding present value

Present Value = Future Amount × Factor (from Table PV–1)

Referring to Table PV–1 in Exhibit B–7, we find a factor of .826 at the intersection of two periods and 10 percent interest. If we multiply this factor by the expected future cash receipt of $1,000, we get a present value of *$826* ($1,000 × .826), the same amount computed previously.

WHAT IS THE APPROPRIATE DISCOUNT RATE?

As explained earlier, the *discount rate* may be viewed as the investor's required rate of return. All investments involve some degree of risk that actual future cash flows may turn out to be less than expected. Investors will require a rate of return that justifies taking this risk. In today's market conditions, investors require annual returns of between 2 percent and 6 percent on low-risk investments, such as government bonds and certificates of deposit. For relatively high-risk investments, such as the introduction of a new product line, investors may expect to earn an annual return of perhaps 15 percent or more. When a higher discount rate is used, the present value of the investment will be lower. In other words, as the risk of an investment increases, its value to investors decreases.

Exhibit B–7

PRESENT VALUE OF $1

Table PV–1
Present Values of $1 Due in *n* Periods

Number of Periods (*n*)	Discount Rate								
	1%	1½%	5%	6%	8%	10%	12%	15%	20%
1	.990	.985	.952	.943	.926	.909	.893	.870	.833
2	.980	.971	.907	.890	.857	.826	.797	.756	.694
3	.971	.956	.864	.840	.794	.751	.712	.658	.579
4	.961	.942	.823	.792	.735	.683	.636	.572	.482
5	.951	.928	.784	.747	.681	.621	.567	.497	.402
6	.942	.915	.746	.705	.630	.564	.507	.432	.335
7	.933	.901	.711	.665	.583	.513	.452	.376	.279
8	.923	.888	.677	.627	.540	.467	.404	.327	.233
9	.914	.875	.645	.592	.500	.424	.361	.284	.194
10	.905	.862	.614	.558	.463	.386	.322	.247	.162
20	.820	.742	.377	.312	.215	.149	.104	.061	.026
24	.788	.700	.310	.247	.158	.102	.066	.035	.013
36	.699	.585	.173	.123	.063	.032	.017	.007	.001

THE PRESENT VALUE OF AN ANNUITY

Many investment opportunities are expected to produce annual cash flows for a number of years, instead of one single future cash flow. Let us assume that Camino Company is evaluating an investment that is expected to produce *annual net cash flows of* $10,000 in *each of the next three years.*[1] If Camino Company expects a 12 percent return on this type of investment, it may compute the present value of these cash flows as follows:

Year	Expected New Cash Flows	×	Present Value of $1 Discounted at 12%	=	Present Value of Net Cash Flows
1	$10,000		.893		$ 8,930
2	10,000		.797		7,970
3	10,000		.712		7,120
Total present value of the investment					$24,020

This analysis indicates that the present value of the expected net cash flows from the investment, discounted at an annual rate of 12 percent, amounts to $24,020. This is the maximum amount that Camino Company could afford to pay for this investment and still expect to earn the 12 percent required rate of return, as shown in Exhibit B–8.

In the preceding analysis, we computed the present value of the investment by separately discounting each period's cash flows, using the appropriate factors from Table PV–1. Separately discounting each period's cash flows is necessary only when the cash flows vary in amount from period to period. Since the annual cash flows in our example are *uniform in amount*, there are easier ways to compute the total present value.

Many financial calculators are programmed to compute the present value of an investment after the interest rate, the future cash flows, and the number of periods have been entered.

[1] "Annual net cash flows" normally are the net result of a series of cash receipts and cash payments occurring throughout the year. For convenience, we follow the common practice of assuming that the entire net cash flows for each year occur at *year-end*. This assumption causes relatively little distortion and greatly simplifies computations.

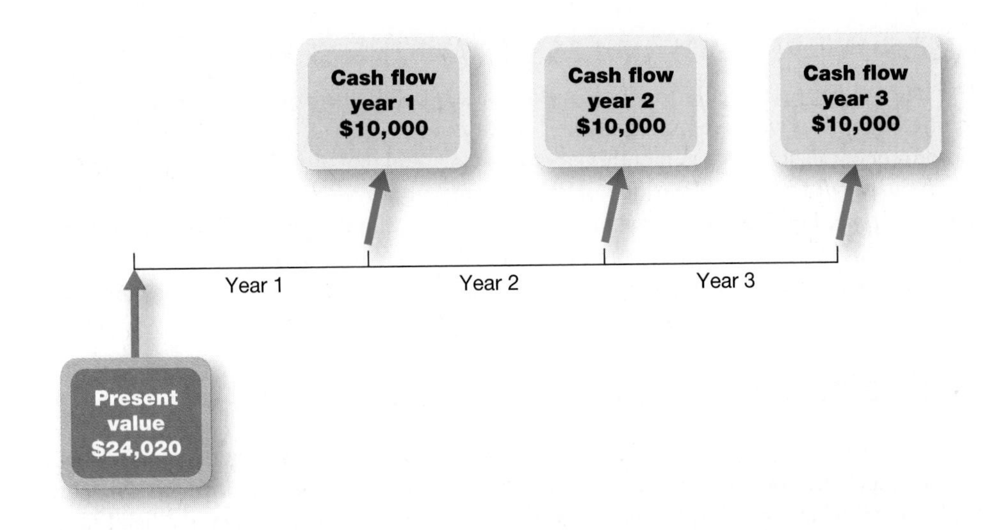

Exhibit B–8

PRESENT VALUE OF THREE $10,000 CASH FLOWS DISCOUNTED AT 12%

Another approach is to refer to a *present value annuity table*, which shows the present value of *$1 to be received each period for a specified number of periods*. An annuity table labeled Table PV–2 appears in Exhibit B–9.[2]

To illustrate the use of Table PV–2, let's return to the example of the investment by Camino Company. That investment was expected to return $10,000 per year for the next three years, and the company's required rate of return was 12 percent per year. Using Table PV–2, we can compute the present value of the investment with the following formula:

Present Value of an Annuity = Periodic Cash Flows × Factor (from Table PV–2)

Formula to find the present value of a series of cash flows

As illustrated in Table PV–2, the present value of $1 to be received at the end of the next three years, discounted at an annual rate of 12 percent, is 2.402. If we multiply 2.402 by the expected future annual cash receipt of $10,000, we get a present value of $24,020, which is the same amount produced by the series of calculations made earlier.

Exhibit B–9

PRESENT VALUE OF AN ORDINARY ANNUITY

Table PV–2
Present Values of $1 to Be Received Periodically for *n* Periods

Number of Periods (*n*)	Discount Rate								
	1%	1½%	5%	6%	8%	10%	12%	15%	20%
1	0.990	0.985	0.952	0.943	0.926	0.909	0.893	0.870	0.833
2	1.970	1.956	1.859	1.833	1.783	1.736	1.690	1.626	1.528
3	2.941	2.912	2.723	2.673	2.577	2.487	2.402	2.283	2.106
4	3.902	3.854	3.546	3.465	3.312	3.170	3.037	2.855	2.589
5	4.853	4.783	4.329	4.212	3.993	3.791	3.605	3.352	2.991
6	5.795	5.697	5.076	4.917	4.623	4.355	4.111	3.784	3.326
7	6.728	6.598	5.786	5.582	5.206	4.868	4.564	4.160	3.605
8	7.652	7.486	6.463	6.210	5.747	5.335	4.968	4.487	3.837
9	8.566	8.361	7.108	6.802	6.247	5.759	5.328	4.772	4.031
10	9.471	9.222	7.722	7.360	6.710	6.145	5.650	5.019	4.192
20	18.046	17.169	12.462	11.470	9.818	8.514	7.469	6.259	4.870
24	21.243	20.030	13.799	12.550	10.529	8.985	7.784	6.434	4.937
36	30.108	27.661	16.547	14.621	11.717	9.677	8.192	6.623	4.993

[2] This table is for an *ordinary* annuity, which assumes that the periodic cash flows occur at the *end* of each period.

DISCOUNT PERIODS OF LESS THAN ONE YEAR

The interval between regular periodic cash flows is called the *discount period.* In our preceding examples, we have assumed cash flows once a year. Often cash flows occur on a more frequent basis, such as monthly, quarterly, or semiannually. The present value tables can be used with discount periods of any length, *but the discount rate must be for that length of time*. For example, if we use Table PV–2 to find the present value of a series of *quarterly* cash payments, the discount rate must be the *quarterly* rate.

There are many applications of the present value concept in accounting. In the next several pages, we will discuss some of the most important of these applications.

Valuation of Financial Instruments

LO6 Discuss accounting applications of the concept of present value.

Accountants use the phrase *financial instruments* to describe cash, equity investments in another business, and any contracts that call for receipts or payments of cash. (Notice that this phrase applies to all financial assets, as well as most liabilities. In fact, the only common liabilities *not* considered financial instruments are unearned revenue and deferred income taxes.)

Whenever the present value of a financial instrument *differs significantly* from the sum of the expected future cash flows, the instrument is recorded in the accounting records at its *present value*—not at the expected amount of the future cash receipts or payments.

Let us illustrate with a few common examples. Cash appears in the balance sheet at its face amount. This face value *is* a present value—that is, the value of the cash today.

Marketable securities appear in the balance sheet at their *current market values*. These too are present values—representing the amount of cash into which the security can be converted *today*.

Accounts receivable and accounts payable normally appear in the balance sheet at the amounts expected to be collected or paid in the near future. Technically, these are *future amounts*, not present values. But they usually are received or paid within 30 or 60 days. Considering the short periods of time involved, the differences between these future amounts and their present values simply are *not material*.

INTEREST-BEARING RECEIVABLES AND PAYABLES

When a financial instrument calls for the receipt or payment of interest, the difference between the present value and the future amounts *does* become material. Thus interest-bearing receivables and payables initially are recorded in accounting records at the *present value* of the future cash flows—also called the "principal amount" of the obligation. This present value often is *substantially less* than the sum of the expected future amounts.

Consider, for example, $100 million in 30-year, 9 percent bonds payable issued at par. At the issuance date, the present value of this bond issue is $100 million—the amount of cash received. But the future payments to bondholders are expected to total *$370* million, computed as follows:

Future interest payments ($100 million × 9% × 30 years)	$ 270,000,000
Maturity value of the bonds (due in 30 years)	100,000,000
Sum of the future cash payments	$370,000,000

Thus the $100 million issuance price represents the present value of $370 million in future cash payments to be made over a period of 30 years.

In essence, interest-bearing financial instruments are "automatically" recorded at their present values simply because we do not include future interest charges in the original valuation of the receivable or the liability.

"NON-INTEREST-BEARING" NOTES

On occasion, companies may issue or accept notes that make no mention of interest, or in which the stated interest rates are unreasonably low. If the difference between the present value of such a note and its face amount is *material*, the note initially is recorded at its present value.

To illustrate, assume that on January 1, 2007, Elron Corporation purchases land from U.S. Development Co. As full payment for this land, Elron issues a $300,000 installment note payable, due in three annual installments of $100,000, beginning on December 31, 2007. This note makes *no mention* of interest charges.

Clearly, three annual installments of $100,000 are not the equivalent of $300,000 available today. Elron should use the *present value* of this note—not the face amount—in determining the cost of the land and reporting its liability.

Assume that a realistic interest rate for financing land over a three-year period currently is 10 percent per annum. The present value of Elron's installment note, discounted at 10 percent, is *$248,700* [$100,000, 3-year annuity × 2.487 (from Table PV–2) in Exhibit B–9]. Elron should view this $248,700 as the "principal amount" of this installment note payable. The remaining $51,300 ($300,000 − $248,700) represents interest charges included in the installment payments.

Elron should record the purchase of the land and the issuance of this note as follows:[3]

Land	248,700	
Notes Payable		248,700
Purchased land, issuing a 3-year installment note payable with a present value of $248,700.		

(U.S. Development Co. should make similar computations in determining the sales price of the land and the valuation of its note receivable.)

Elron also should prepare an *amortization table* to allocate the amount of each installment payment between interest expense and reduction in the principal amount of this obligation. This table, based on an original unpaid balance of $248,700, three annual payments of $100,000, and an annual interest rate of 10 percent, is illustrated in Exhibit B–10.

Exhibit B–10

AMORTIZATION TABLE FOR A DISCOUNTED NOTE PAYABLE

AMORTIZATION TABLE
(3-Year, $300,000 Installment Note Payable, Discounted at 10% per Annum)

Interest Period	Payment Date	Annual Payment	Interest Expense (10% of the Last Unpaid Balance)	Reduction in Unpaid Balance	Unpaid Balance
Issue date	Jan. 1, 2007				$248,700
1	Dec. 31, 2007	$100,000	$24,870	$75,130	173,570
2	Dec. 31, 2008	100,000	17,357	82,643	90,927
3	Dec. 31, 2009	100,000	9,073*	90,927	–0–

*In the last period, interest expense is equal to the amount of the final payment minus the remaining unpaid balance. This compensates for the use of a present value table with factors carried to only three decimal places.

The entry at December 31, 2007, to record the first installment payment will be as follows:

Interest Expense	24,870	
Notes Payable	75,130	
Cash		100,000
Made annual payment on installment note payable to U.S. Development Co.		

[3] There is an alternative recording technique that makes use of an account entitled Discount on Notes Payable. This alternative approach produces the same results and will be explained in later accounting courses.

MARKET PRICES OF BONDS

The market price of bonds may be regarded as the *present value* to bondholders of the future principal and interest payments, discounted at the prevailing market rate of interest at the time of issuance. To illustrate, assume that Driscole Corporation issues $1,000,000 of 10-year, 10 percent bonds when the going market rate of interest is 12 percent. Because bond interest is paid semiannually, we must use 20 *semiannual* periods as the life of the bond issue and a 6 percent *semiannual* market rate of interest in our present value calculations. The discounted present value of the bond's future cash flows, discounted for 20 semiannual periods at 6 percent, is $885,500, computed as follows:

Present value of future principal payments:	
$1,000,000 due after 20 semiannual periods, discounted at 6%:	
$1,000,000 × .312 (from Table PV–1)	$312,000
Present value of future interest payments:	
$50,000 per period ($1,000,000 × 10% × ½) for 20 semiannual periods, discounted at 6%: $50,000 × 11.470 (from Table PV–2)	573,500
Expected issuance price of bond issue	$885,500

Note that, because the market rate of interest exceeds the bond's coupon rate, the bonds are issued at a $114,500 discount ($1,000,000 face value − $885,500 issue price). Thus we know that these bonds were sold to an underwriter at 88.55 (meaning 88.55 percent of their face value).

As illustrated in Chapter 10, the entire amount of the discount is debited to an account titled Discount on Bonds Payable at the time the bonds are issued. The entry to record the issuance of this bond is:

Cash	885,500	
Discount on Bonds Payable	114,500	
Bonds Payable		1,000,000
Issued 10%, 10-year bonds with $1,000,000 face value to an underwriter at a price of 88.55.		

When the bonds mature in 10 years, Driscole must pay bondholders the *full* $1 million face value of the bond issue, or $114,500 *more* than it received at the time the bonds were issued. As discussed in Chapter 10, the additional $114,500 due at maturity represents a portion of the company's total *interest expense* that must be amortized over the 10-year life of the bond. Thus, Driscole will incur interest expense of $55,725 every six months, computed as follows:

Semiannual interest *payment* (1,000,000 × 10% × ½)	$50,000
Add: Semiannual amortization of bond discount ([$114,500 ÷ 10 years] × ½)	5,725
Semiannual interest expense	$55,725

The entry to record $55,725 of semiannual interest expense is:

Bond Interest Expense	55,725	
Cash		50,000
Discount on Bonds Payable		5,725
To record semiannual interest expense and to recognize six months' amortization of the $114,500 discount on 10-year bonds payable.		

Notice that, while the amortization of the discount increases semiannual interest expense by $5,725, it does not require an immediate cash outlay. The $114,500 of additional interest expense for the *entire* 10-year period will not be paid until the bonds mature.

CAPITAL LEASES

We briefly discuss capital leases in Chapter 10, but do not illustrate the accounting for these instruments. This appendix gives us an opportunity to explore this topic in greater detail.

A capital lease is regarded as a sale of the leased asset by the lessor to the lessee. At the date of this sale, the lessor recognizes sales revenue equal to the *present value* of the future lease payments receivable, discounted at a realistic rate of interest. The lessee also uses the present value of the future payments to determine the cost of the leased asset and the valuation of the related liability.

To illustrate, assume that, on December 1, Pace Tractor uses a *capital lease* to finance the sale of a tractor to Kelly Grading Co. The tractor was carried in Pace Tractor's perpetual inventory records at a cost of $15,000. Terms of the lease call for Kelly Grading Co. to make *24* monthly payments of *$1,000* each, beginning on December 31. These lease payments include an interest charge of *1 percent* per month. At the end of the 24-month lease, title to the tractor will pass to Kelly Grading Co. at no additional cost.

Accounting by the Lessor (Pace Tractor)

Table PV–2 shows that the present value of $1 to be received monthly for 24 months, discounted at 1 percent per month, is **21.243**. Therefore, the present value of the 24 future lease payments is $1,000 × **21.243**, or *$21,243*. Pace Tractor should record this capital lease as a sale of the tractor at a price equal to the present value of the lease payments, as follows:

	Debit	Credit
Lease Payments Receivable (net)	21,243	
Sales		21,243
Financed sale of a tractor to Kelly Grading Co. using a capital lease requiring 24 monthly payments of $1,000. Payments include a 1% monthly interest charge.		
Cost of Goods Sold	15,000	
Inventory		15,000
To record cost of tractor sold under capital lease.		

Notice that the sales price of the tractor is only $21,243, even though the gross amount to be collected from Kelly Grading Co. amounts to $24,000 ($1,000 × 24 payments). The difference between these two amounts, $2,757, will be recognized by Pace Tractor as interest revenue over the term of the lease.

To illustrate the recognition of interest revenue, the entry on December 31 to record collection of the first monthly lease payment (rounded to the nearest dollar) will be:

	Debit	Credit
Cash	1,000	
Interest Revenue		212
Lease Payments Receivable (net)		788
Received first lease payment from Kelly Grading Co.: $1,000 lease payment received, less $212 interest revenue ($21,243 × 1%), equals $788 reduction in lease payments receivable.		

After this first monthly payment is collected, the present value of the lease payments receivable is reduced to $20,455 ($21,243 original balance, less $788). Therefore, the interest revenue earned during the *second* month of the lease (rounded to the nearest dollar) will be *$205* ($20,455 × 1%).[4]

[4] Both Pace Tractor and Kelly Grading Co. would prepare *amortization tables* showing the allocation of each lease payment between interest and the principal amount due.

Accounting by the Lessee (Kelly Grading Co.) Kelly Grading Co. also should use the present value of the lease payments to determine the cost of the tractor and the amount of the related liability, as follows:

Leased Equipment	21,243	
Lease Payments Obligation		21,243
To record acquisition of a tractor through a capital lease from Pace Tractor. Terms call for 24 monthly payments of $1,000, which include a 1% monthly interest charge.		

The entry on December 31 to record the first monthly lease payment (rounded to the nearest dollar) will be:

Interest Expense	212	
Lease Payments Obligation	788	
Cash		1,000
To record first monthly lease payment to Pace Tractor: $1,000 lease payment, less $212 interest expense ($21,243 × 1%), equals $788 reduction in lease payments obligation.		

OBLIGATIONS FOR POSTRETIREMENT BENEFITS

As we explain in Chapter 10, any unfunded obligation for postretirement benefits appears in the balance sheet at the *present value* of the expected future cash outlays to retired employees. The computation of this present value is so complex that it is performed by a professional actuary. But the present value of this obligation normally is far less than the expected future payments, as the cash payments will take place many years in the future.

Each year, the present value of an unfunded obligation for postretirement benefits will increase—as the future payment dates become closer. This steady growth in the present value of the unfunded obligation is recognized annually as part of the company's current postretirement benefits expense. (One might argue that the growth in this liability actually represents interest expense. Nonetheless, the present value of the liability increases as the payment dates draw closer.)

DISCLOSURE OF UP-TO-DATE PRESENT VALUE INFORMATION

Financial instruments originally are recorded in accounting records at (or near) their present values. But present values represent future cash flows discounted at *current* interest rates. Thus, as interest rates change, so do the present values of many financial instruments. (For the remainder of this discussion, we refer to present value determined under *current* market conditions as *current value*.)

Cash, investments in marketable securities, and postretirement obligations appear in the financial statements at current values. For most short-term instruments, current values remain quite close to the original carrying values. But for long-term financial instruments, such as bonds payable, current values may differ substantially from the amounts originally recorded.

The Financial Accounting Standards Board (FASB) requires companies to disclose the current values of financial instruments whenever these values *differ significantly* from the recorded amounts. These disclosures are most likely to affect long-term notes receivable and payable (including bonds payable) and long-term lease obligations.

In computing current value, current interest rates serve as the discount rate. Thus, as interest rates *rise*, current values *fall*; as interest rates *fall*, current values *rise*. The amount of change is greatest on long-term financial instruments for which the future cash flows are fixed—that is, not adjustable to reflect changes in interest rates.

The disclosure of current values can shed light on a company's past investing and financing activities. Assume, for example, that a company's long-term debt has a current value well *below* its carrying value in the company's balance sheet. This means that interest rates have *increased* since the company arranged this debt. Thus the company apparently arranged its long-term financing in a period of low interest rates—a good move.

DEFERRED INCOME TAXES

The only long-term liability *not* shown at the present value of the expected future payments is the obligation for deferred income taxes. Deferred taxes are treated differently because they do not involve a "contract" for future payments. Future payments of deferred taxes, if any, depend on the company's taxable income in future periods and also the corporate income tax laws in future years.

Many accountants believe that deferred income taxes *should* be shown at the estimated present value of the future outlays. This is not likely to happen, however, as the computations would be overwhelmingly complex.

In conclusion, the obligation for deferred income taxes is the only long-term liability that is *not* reported at its present value. Hence, one might argue that these obligations are overstated in terms of an equivalent number of today's dollars.

ASSIGNMENT MATERIAL Discussion Questions

1. Explain what is meant by the phrase *time value of money.*
2. Explain why the present value of a future amount is always *less* than the future amount.
3. Identify the two factors that determine the difference between the present value and the future amount of an investment.
4. Describe three basic investment applications of the concept of the time value of money.
5. Briefly explain the relationships between present value and (**a**) the length of time until the future cash flow occurs, and (**b**) the discount rate used in determining present value.
6. Define *financial instruments.* Explain the valuation concept used in initially recording financial instruments in financial statements.
7. Are normal accounts receivable and accounts payable financial instruments? Are these items shown in the balance sheet at their present values? Explain.
8. Identify three financial instruments shown in financial statements at present values that may *differ significantly* from the sum of the expected future payments or receipts.
9. What is the only long-term liability that is *not* recorded at its present value? What are the implications in terms of today's dollars?
10. Assuming no change in the expected amount of future cash flows, what factors may cause the present value of a financial instrument to change? Explain fully.

Problems

PROBLEM B.1
Using Future Amount Tables

Use Table FA–1 (in Exhibit B–2) and Table FA–2 (in Exhibit B–4) to determine the future amounts of the following investments:

a. $20,000 is invested for 10 years, at 6 percent interest, compounded annually.

b. $100,000 is to be received five years from today, at 10 percent annual interest.

c. $10,000 is invested in a fund at the end of each of the next 10 years, at 8 percent interest, compounded annually.

d. $50,000 is invested initially, plus $5,000 is invested annually at the end of each of the next three years, at 12 percent interest, compounded annually.

PROBLEM B.2
Bond Sinking Fund

Tilman Company is required by a bond indenture to make equal annual payments to a bond sinking fund at the end of each of the next 20 years. The sinking fund will earn 8 percent interest and must accumulate to a total of $500,000 at the end of the 20-year period.

Instructions

a. Calculate the amount of the annual payments.

b. Calculate the total amount of interest that will be earned by the fund over the 20-year period.

c. Make the general journal entry to record redemption of the bond issue at the end of the 20-year period, assuming that the sinking fund is recorded on Tilman's accounting records at $500,000 and bonds payable are recorded at the same amount.

d. What would be the effect of an increase in the rate of return on the required annual payment? Explain.

PROBLEM B.3
Using Present Value Tables

Use Table PV–1 (in Exhibit B–7) and Table PV–2 (in Exhibit B–9) to determine the present values of the following cash flows:

a. $15,000 to be paid annually for 10 years, discounted at an annual rate of 6 percent. Payments are to occur at the end of each year.

b. $9,200 to be received today, assuming that the money will be invested in a two-year certificate of deposit earning 8 percent annually.

c. $300 to be paid monthly for 36 months, with an additional "balloon payment" of $12,000 due at the end of the thirty-sixth month, discounted at a monthly interest rate of 1½ percent. The first payment is to be one month from today.

d. $25,000 to be received annually for the first three years, followed by $15,000 to be received annually for the next two years (total of five years in which collections are received), discounted at an annual rate of 8 percent. Assume collections occur at year-end.

PROBLEM B.4
Present Value and Bond Prices

On June 30 of the current year, Rural Gas & Electric Co. issued $50,000,000 face value, 9 percent, 10-year bonds payable, with interest dates of December 31 and June 30. The bonds were issued at a discount, resulting in an effective *semiannual* interest rate of 5 percent.

Instructions

a. Compute the issue price for the bond that results in an effective semiannual interest rate of 5 percent. (Hint: Discount both the interest payments and the maturity value over 20 semiannual periods.)

b. Prepare a journal entry to record the issuance of the bonds at the sales price you computed in part **a**.

c. Explain why the bonds were issued at a discount.

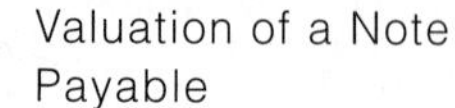

PROBLEM B.5
Valuation of a Note Payable

On December 1, Showcase Interiors purchased a shipment of furniture from Colonial House by paying $10,500 cash and issuing an installment note payable in the face amount of $28,800. The note is to be paid in 24 monthly installments of $1,200 each. Although the note makes no mention of an interest charge, the rate of interest usually charged to Showcase Interiors in such transactions is 1½ percent per month.

Instructions

a. Compute the present value of the note payable, using a discount rate of 1½ percent per month.

b. Prepare the journal entries in the accounts of Showcase Interiors on:

1. December 1, to record the purchase of the furniture (debit Inventory).
2. December 31, to record the first $1,200 monthly payment on the note and to recognize interest expense for one month by the effective interest method. (Round interest expense to the nearest dollar.)

c. Show how the liability for this note would appear in the balance sheet at December 31. (Assume that the note is classified as a current liability.)

PROBLEM B.6
Capital Leases: A Comprehensive Problem

Custom Truck Builders frequently uses long-term lease contracts to finance the sale of its trucks. On November 1, 2007, Custom Truck Builders leased to Interstate Van Lines a truck carried in the perpetual inventory records at $33,520. The terms of the lease call for Interstate Van Lines to make 36 monthly payments of $1,400 each, beginning on November 30, 2007. The present value of these payments, after considering a built-in interest charge of 1 percent per month, is equal to the regular $42,150 sales price of the truck. At the end of the 36-month lease, title to the truck will transfer to Interstate Van Lines.

Instructions

a. Prepare journal entries for 2007 in the accounts of Custom Truck Builders on:

1. November 1, to record the sale financed by the lease and the related cost of goods sold. (Debit Lease Payments Receivable for the $42,150 present value of the future lease payments.)
2. November 30, to record receipt of the first $1,400 monthly payment. (Prepare a compound journal entry that allocates the cash receipt between interest revenue and reduction of Lease Payments Receivable. The portion of each monthly payment recognized as interest revenue is equal to 1 percent of the balance of the account Lease Payments Receivable, at the beginning of that month. Round all interest computations to the nearest dollar.)
3. December 31, to record receipt of the second monthly payment.

b. Prepare journal entries for 2007 in the accounts of Interstate Van Lines on:

1. November 1, to record acquisition of the leased truck.
2. November 30, to record the first monthly lease payment. (Determine the portion of the payment representing interest expense in a manner parallel to that described in part **a.**)
3. December 31, to record the second monthly lease payment.
4. December 31, to recognize depreciation on the leased truck through year-end. Compute depreciation expense by the straight-line method, using a 10-year service life and an estimated salvage value of $6,150.

c. Compute the net carrying value of the leased truck in the balance sheet of Interstate Van Lines at December 31, 2007.

d. Compute the amount of Interstate Van Lines's lease payment obligation at December 31, 2007.

PROBLEM B.7
Valuation of a Note Receivable with an Unrealistic Interest Rate

On December 31, Richland Farms sold a tract of land, which had cost $930,000, to Skyline Developers in exchange for $150,000 cash and a five-year, 4 percent note receivable for $900,000. Interest on the note is payable annually, and the principal amount is due in five years. The accountant for Richland Farms did not notice the unrealistically low interest rate on the note and made the following entry on December 31 to record this sale.

Cash	150,000	
Notes Receivable.	900,000	
Land		930,000
Gain on Sale of Land		120,000
Sold land to Skyline Developers in exchange for cash and five-year note with interest due annually.		

Instructions

a. Compute the present value of the note receivable from Skyline Developers at the date of sale, assuming that a realistic rate of interest for this transaction is 12 percent. (Hint: Consider both the annual interest payments and the maturity value of the note.)

b. Prepare the journal entry on December 31 to record the sale of the land correctly. Show supporting computations for the gain or loss on the sale.

c. Explain what effects the error made by Richland Farms's accountant will have on (**1**) the net income in the year of the sale and (**2**) the combined net income of the next five years. Ignore income taxes.

Index

A

D

E

F

G

H

I

J

K

L

M

N

O

P